Yes

Assisted suicide, or taking one's own life with the aid of another, is an illegal practice in the United States of America. Currently, numerous Americans lie suffering tremendously in hospitals, nursing homes, or their private residences without the ability to legally end their pain. If these citizens receive assistance in painlessly ending their lives from a physician or specialist, the assisting party can be prosecuted in all states but Oregon. The laws that prevent individuals from making decisions regarding the end of their lives are flagrant violations of the intrinsic rights of human beings.

The underlying rationale for the illegality of assisted suicide is derived from religion. Nearly all major religions condemn self-imposed or assisted suicide because it violates one's natural desire to live and harms other people, and because a life given by God is only to be taken by God.[1] The idea of a natural desire to live is nearly always applicable to an individual, but in extreme instances, some people choose not to persist on this earth. As one's own life is relevant only to oneself and one's family, decisions regarding one's demise must not be subject to laws that assume a "natural desire to live." The second facet of this religious rationale asserts that ending one's life may emotionally harm others. This is true, yet the emotional distress of watching a loved one suffer is just as significantly damaging. Additionally, a patient wishing to die would rarely make a decision independent of family consulting and guidance. Finally, opponents of legalized human euthanasia proclaim that a life given by God may only be taken by God. This idea is inconsistent with the libertarian ideology of America. Not all Americans choose to follow deities or religions, and thus not all Americans should be subservient to laws that reflect such phenomena. It is clear that the motive for outlawing assisted suicide is outdated and inapplicable in the secularized society we live in.

Contemporary arguments against human euthanasia often maintain that allowing individuals to assist others in dying will open the door to numerous wrongful acts. There are fears of legalized assisted suicide opening the door to unpunished murders or even the systematic killing of patients by hospitals in order to create more space. The lack of empirical evidence showing the existence of these occurrences in the state of Oregon or countries such as Japan and the Netherlands,[2] which currently allow assisted suicide, invalidates these arguments. Assuring that an individual who wishes to die is not suffering from clinical depression, is of sound mind, and plans to have his or her death administered by a licensed physician will also eliminate any worries of foul play. With these guidelines followed, a system in which euthanasia is legal will not be corrupted by criminal acts.

Human beings are given the gift of life the minute they are born, and with this gift comes an abundance of responsibilities and rights. One of the rights intrinsically guaranteed to humans when they are born is the right to be autonomous over their own lives. This right includes the decision of when one may end one's life. There is no reason for laws to prevent those who are terminally ill and decidedly ready to die from seeking help to painlessly end their suffering and to die with dignity. The law must protect us from harm, yet it must not prevent us from helping ourselves. Assisted suicide's illegality does not benefit society in any manner, and it removes a citizen's right to control his or her own life.

A human who is of sound mind and feels that his or her life is not worth living because of intractable pain, loss of dignity, or loss of capability should be able to legally seek help in dying. The segment of society that has moral or religious objections to this idea must not extend its beliefs to the entire population. U.S. law should be based on what is in the nation's interests and the interests of its citizenry. Preventing people from choosing to die with dignity, an outcome of current U.S. state law, does not benefit the nation or its citizens; it merely appeases a certain societal element that has succeeded in maintaining a moralized law in the United States. Allowing an individual the right to die must be legalized in the United States.

Shane Singh, Michigan State University

The Right to Die — Just and Inherent

[1] www.religioustolerance.org/euth2.htm
[2] www.religioustolerance.org/euth_wld.htm

Participate and be rewarded.

WE THE PEOPLE

An Introduction to American Politics

FOURTH EDITION

WE THE PEOPLE

PEOPLE

An Introduction to American Politics

BENJAMIN GINSBERG
THE JOHNS HOPKINS UNIVERSITY

THEODORE J. LOWI
CORNELL UNIVERSITY

MARGARET WEIR
UNIVERSITY OF CALIFORNIA AT BERKELEY

FOURTH EDITION

W • W • NORTON & COMPANY • NEW YORK • LONDON

Illustration credits and copyrights are given on page A68, which constitutes an extension of this copyright page.

Editor: Stephen Dunn
Book design: Chris Welch
Figures: John McAusland
Composition: TSI Graphics
Manufacturing: Quebecor/Versailles
Cover illustration: Mick Wiggins

Library of Congress Cataloging-in-Publication Data

Ginsberg, Benjamin
   We the people: an introduction to American politics/Benjamin Ginsberg,
Theodore J. Lowi, Margaret Weir.—4th ed.
      p. cm.
Includes bibliographical references and index.

ISBN 0-393-97928-8

   1. United States—Politics and government. I. Lowi, Theodore J. II. Weir, Margaret, 1952-III.
Title.

JK276.G55 2003
320.473—dc21   2002043234

W. W. Norton & Company, Inc., 500 Fifth Avenue, New York, N.Y. 10110
                          www.wwnorton.com

W. W. Norton & Company Ltd., Castle House, 75/76 Wells Street, London W1T 3QT

1 2 3 4 5 6 7 8 9 0

TO

SANDY, CINDY, AND ALEX GINSBERG

ANGELE, ANNA, AND JASON LOWI

NICHOLAS ZIEGLER

CONTENTS

5 CIVIL RIGHTS 160

6 PUBLIC OPINION   208

Part II
POLITICS

11 GROUPS AND INTERESTS   **414**

Part III
INSTITUTIONS

12 CONGRESS 454

13 THE PRESIDENCY 506

16 GOVERNMENT AND THE ECONOMY   636

Part IV
POLICY

17 SOCIAL POLICY   684

18 FOREIGN POLICY AND DEMOCRACY   724

CONTENTS

xxii

PREFACE

This book has been and continues to be dedicated to developing a satisfactory response to the question more and more Americans are asking: Why should we be engaged with government and politics? Through the first three editions, we sought to answer this question by making the text directly relevant to the lives of the students who would be reading it. As a result, we tried to make politics interesting by demonstrating that students' interests are at stake and that they therefore need to take a personal, even selfish, interest in the outcomes of government. At the same time, we realized that students needed guidance in how to become politically engaged. Beyond providing students with a core of political knowledge, we needed to show them how they could apply that knowledge as participants in the political process. The "Get Involved: What You Can Do" conclusions to each chapter helped achieve that goal.

This Fourth Edition retains the same goals and methods as earlier editions, but goes beyond them. As events from the last months of 2001 reminded us, "what government does" can be a matter of life and death. Before September 11, most Americans had concluded that government, especially the national government, had grown too large and too expensive to operate. The solution was simply to make government smaller. But September 11 changed everything. When crises occur, Americans look to the government for solutions. After September 11, the relevance and importance of government to our lives became tragically obvious. With September 11 as its backdrop, *We the People* introduces a new theme that reinforces the book's emphasis on the relevance of government to our lives: "What Government Does and Why It Matters." This new theme is incorporated in the following ways:

- **New chapter introductions focus on "What Government Does and Why It Matters."** During the past two decades, cynicism about "big government" has dominated the political zeitgeist. But critics of government often forget that governments do a great deal for citizens. Every year, Americans are the beneficiaries of billions of dollars of goods and services from government. Government "does" a lot, and it matters a great deal to everyone, including college students. At the start of each chapter, this theme is introduced and applied to the chapter's topic. The goal is to show students that government and politics mean something to their daily lives.
- **New boxes: "What Government Does . . . After September 11"** Americans' dependence on the government is brought into particularly sharp focus during times of danger. These boxes, one per chapter, highlight the ways in which the government has taken action following September 11.

Most of these actions have positive benefits for almost all citizens, such as beefing up airport security or combating bioterrorism. Others have positive benefits for the economy, such as the financial support given to the airline industry. Some of these actions have potentially negative consequences, however, and deserve scrutiny from citizens, such as ethnic profiling by government officials or the potential infringement of civil liberties by recent government actions.

- **Analysis of "who benefits?" from what government does** Government is not a neutral force in any society. Some individuals or groups always benefit more than others from the government's actions. In addition, there are constant debates over the ends or goals of government. Who benefits most from certain government actions? What should government do? These questions, and their potential answers, are now addressed more explicitly and more extensively in every chapter.

- **Post–September 11 content**   In addition to the new chapter introductions and new boxes, there is an abundance of new material related to post– September 11 government. For example, the bureaucracy chapter includes discussions of the Office for Homeland Security, the controversy over the FBI's role in combating terrorism, the Center for Disease Control's initiatives to fight bioterrorism, the expansion of the federal workforce through the hiring of new airport security personnel, the Justice Department's encroachment on civil liberties, the debate over the effectiveness of the Immigration and Naturalization Service, the State Department's role in building the multilateral coalition that fought the Taliban in Afghanistan, the costs and benefits of privatizing security, and the broader issue of bureaucratic reform.

History, such as the tragic events of 2001, reminds us that there will always be government because there will always be a need for government. Why is government necessary? As Adam Smith wrote in 1776,

> According to the system of natural liberty, the sovereign has only three duties to attend to; three duties of great importance: first, the duty of protecting the society from the violence and invasion of other independent societies; secondly, the duty of protecting, as far as possible, every member of the society from the injustice or oppression of every other member of it [with] an exact administration of justice; and, thirdly, the duty of erecting and maintaining certain publick [sic] works and certain publick institutions, which it can never be for the interest of any individual, or smaller number of individuals, to erect and maintain; because the profit could never repay the expense....[1]

Reasonable people can disagree over questions of *what kind of government* or *how much government,* but, other than anarchy, there is no place for argument over *whether.*

In addition to our focus on "What Government Does and Why It Matters," we have also addressed the debate over what government does and who benefits from the outcomes. This is where politics comes in. Ultimately, the purpose of politics is

---

[1] Adam Smith, *An Inquiry into the Nature and Causes of the Wealth of Nations,* Vol. II (Indianapolis: Liberty Classics edition of original Oxford University Press edition, 1981), pp. 687–88.

to influence what government does. This influence can come from eloquence of rhetoric, perseverance of effort, or pure and simple nuisance value. The method can be technologically rich, employing facts, e-mail, and Web sites; or it can be simple and personal, relying on picketing, heckling, and badgering members of Congress or state and local legislatures. But, as we have emphasized in all four editions of the book, influence requires knowledge about government and politics and it requires participation in the political process.

But *We the People* doesn't rely on sentimental and moralistic appeals to encourage student-citizens to participate in politics. We would be laughed out of the classroom if we pulled out the old adages that every citizen can be president or that the views of every citizen are taken equally into account in the representative process. "The People" is a collective noun; as individuals we may have extremely limited influence, but that does not diminish the validity of the message we convey in each and every chapter. First, we demonstrate in every chapter that one and the few *can* count. Moreover, those who doubt this are engaging in a self-fulfilling prophecy; that is, to be *in*active as a result of the pessimistic view of the capacity of citizens is to confirm to the fullest that citizen action cannot count. Two sets of issues that we employ help bring this point into focus for students.

The first of these sets of issues is the question of who is and who is not part of the American political community. This question has been the source of enormous conflict for Americans. Because there have been many restrictions throughout American history on who are "we the people" and what powers and rights "we the people" should have, we hope that students don't take their own powers and rights for granted. We also hope that students recognize that some groups benefit more from "what government does" than others. If students or any citizens for that matter wish to change that fact, knowledge and participation are essential. The second set of issues concerns American political values. The American nation is defined not only by its form of government but also by a set of shared beliefs and values, the most basic of which are liberty, equality, and democracy. Although these values are the basis of the structures and rules of American government, our job as authors is to recognize the gap between ideals and realities and to treat the gap honestly. After all, what is the meaning of "government by the people" if broad popular influence over political actions is diminished? Liberty, equality, and democracy are concepts that link all the chapters of our book. They are also criteria against which to measure, judge, and even criticize "what government does." And it's our view that a good citizen is a critical citizen.

One remaining feature of our text that we hope will help students become informed and critical citizens is what we call our "Greek chorus." Each chapter includes a "Student Debate" that presents the opposing views of students on current issues. As with the chorus in Greek drama, our student chorus illustrates the range of enlightenment. We continue to hope that our book will itself be accepted as a form of enlightened political action. This Fourth Edition is another chance. It is an advancement toward our goal. We promise to keep trying.

ACKNOWLEDGMENTS

Our students at Cornell, Johns Hopkins, Harvard, and Berkeley have been an essential factor in the writings of this book. They have been our most immediate intellectual community, a hospitable one indeed. Another part of our community, perhaps a large suburb, is the discipline of political science itself. Our debt to the scholarship of our colleagues is scientifically measurable, probably to several decimal points, in the endnotes of each chapter. Despite many complaints that the field is too scientific or not scientific enough, political science is alive and well in the United States. It is an aspect of democracy itself, and it has grown and changed in response to the developments in government and politics that we have chronicled in our book. If we did a "time line" on the history of political science, it would show a close association with developments in "the American state." Sometimes the discipline has been out of phase and critical; at other times, it has been in phase and perhaps apologetic. But political science has never been at a loss for relevant literature, and without it, our job would have been impossible.

We are especially pleased to acknowledge our debt to the many colleagues who had a direct and active role in criticism and preparation of the manuscript. Our thanks go to

First Edition Reviewers
Sarah Binder, Brookings Institution
Kathleen Gille, Office of Representative David Bonior
Rodney Hero, University of Colorado at Boulder
Robert Katzmann, Brookings Institution
Kathleen Knight, University of Houston
Robin Kolodny, Temple University
Nancy Kral, Tomball College
Robert C. Lieberman, Columbia University
David A. Marcum, University of Wyoming
Laura R. Winsky Mattei, State University of New York at Buffalo
Marilyn S. Mertens, Midwestern State University
Barbara Suhay, Henry Ford Community College
Carolyn Wong, Stanford University
Julian Zelizer, State University of New York at Albany

Second Edition Reviewers
Lydia Andrade, University of North Texas
John Coleman, University of Wisconsin at Madison

Daphne Eastman, Odessa College
Otto Feinstein, Wayne State University
Elizabeth Flores, Delmar College
James Gimpel, University of Maryland at College Park
Jill Glaathar, Southwest Missouri State University
Shaun Herness, University of Florida
William Lyons, University of Tennessee at Knoxville
Andrew Polsky, Hunter College, City University of New York
Grant Reeher, Syracuse University
Richard Rich, Virginia Polytechnic
Bartholomew Sparrow, University of Texas at Austin

Third Edition Reviewers
Amy Jasperson, University of Texas at San Antonio
Loch Johnson, University of Georgia
Mark Kann, University of Southern California
Andrea Simpson, University of Washington
Brian Smentkowski, Southeast Missouri State University
Nelson Wikstrom, Virginia Commonwealth University

Fourth Edition Reviewers
M. E. Banks, Virginia Commonwealth University
Mark Cichock, University of Texas at Arlington
Del Fields, St. Petersburg College
Nancy Kinney, Washtenaw Community College
William Klein, St. Petersburg College
Christopher Muste, Louisiana State University
David Rankin, State University of New York at Fredonia
Paul Roesler, St. Charles Community College
J. Philip Rogers, San Antonio College
Greg Shaw, Illinois Wesleyan University
Tracy Skopek, Stephen F. Austin State University
Don Smith, University of North Texas
Terri Wright, Cal State, Fullerton

We also must pay thanks to the many collaborators we have had on this project: Robert J. Spitzer of the State University of New York at Cortland; Mark Kann and Marcella Marlowe of the University of Southern California; John Robertson of Texas A&M University; Paul Gronke of Reed College; Van Wigginton of San Jacinto College; and Marilyn Mertens of Midwestern State University.

We are also grateful for the talents and hard work of several research assistants, whose contributions can never be adequately compensated. In particular, Mingus Mapps, Doug Harris, and Ben Bowyer put an enormous amount of thought and time into the figures, tables, and study aids that appear in the text. Israel Waismel-Manor also kept a close eye on keeping the book as up-to-date as possible.

We would like to give special thanks to Jacqueline Pastore at Cornell University, who not only prepared portions of the manuscript but also helped to hold the entire project together. We especially thank her for her hard work and dedication.

Perhaps above all, we wish to thank those at W. W. Norton. For its four editions, our editor, Steve Dunn, has helped us shape the book in countless ways. We thank Nora Morrison, Susan Cronin, Gilbert Lee, Neil Ryder Hoos, Nathan Odell, and Penni Zivian for devoting an enormous amount of time to finding new photos and selecting pieces for the "Student Debate." For our interactive Web site for the book, Denise Shanks has been an energetic and visionary editor. Jan Hoeper edited the manuscript with Marian Johnson's superb direction, and project editors JoAnn Simony and Kim Yi kept on top of myriad details. Diane O'Connor has been dedicated in managing production. Finally, we wish to thank Roby Harrington, the head of Norton's college department.

We are more than happy, however, to absolve all these contributors from any flaws, errors, and misjudgments that will inevitably be discovered. We wish the book could be free of all production errors, grammatical errors, misspellings, misquotes, missed citations, etc. From that standpoint, a book ought to try to be perfect. But substantively we have not tried to write a flawless book; we have not tried to write a book to please everyone. We have again tried to write an effective book, a book that cannot be taken lightly. Our goal was not to make every reader a political scientist or a political activist. Our goal was to restore politics as a subject matter of vigorous and enjoyable discourse, recapturing it from the bondage of the thirty-second sound bite and the thirty-page technical briefing. Every person can be knowledgeable because everything about politics is accessible. One does not have to be a television anchorperson to profit from political events. One does not have to be a philosopher to argue about the requisites of democracy, a lawyer to dispute constitutional interpretations, an economist to debate a public policy. We would be very proud if our book contributes in a small way to the restoration of the ancient art of political controversy.

BENJAMIN GINSBERG
THEODORE J. LOWI
MARGARET WEIR

NOVEMBER 2002

WE THE PEOPLE

An Introduction to American Politics

FOURTH EDITION

Part I

FOUNDATIONS

1 AMERICAN POLITICAL CULTURE

☆ What Americans Think about Government
Why is it important that Americans think that they can influence what the government does?

☆ What Americans Know about Government
Why is political knowledge the key to effective participation in political life?

☆ Government
What are the different forms that a government can take?
How did the principle of limited government develop?
How can people participate in politics and influence what the government does?

☆ American Political Culture: Shared Values, but Disagreements over the Role of Government
What are Americans' core political values? What are the meanings of these values?
Does the political system uphold American political values?
How do American political values conflict with one another?

What Government Does and Why It Matters

MERICANS SOMETIMES APPEAR to believe that the government is an institution that does things *to* them and from which they need protection. Business owners complain that federal health and safety regulations threaten their ability to make a profit. Farmers and ranchers complain that federal and state environmental rules intrude upon their property rights. Motorists allege that municipal "red light" cameras, designed to photograph traffic violators, represent the intrusion of "Big Brother" into their lives. Civil libertarians—including groups like the American Civil Liberties Union (ACLU), organized to defend First Amendment freedoms—express concern over what they view as sometimes overly aggressive police and prosecutorial practices. Everyone complains about federal, state, and local taxes.

Yet many of the same individuals who complain about what the government does *to* them also want the government to do a great deal *for* them. Business owners receive billions of dollars in federal assistance in the form of low-interest loans, marketing services, export assistance, and government contracts. Farmers are the beneficiaries of billions in federal subsidies and research programs. Motorists would have no roads upon which to be photographed by those hated cameras if not for the tens of billions of dollars spent each year on road construction and maintenance by federal, state, and municipal authorities. Individuals accused of crimes benefit from procedural safeguards and state-funded defense attorneys. And, as to those detested taxes, without them there would be no government benefits at all.

Americans' dependence on the government is brought into particularly sharp focus during times of danger. When Pearl Harbor was bombed on December 7, 1941, Americans listened to their radios, waiting for President Franklin D. Roosevelt to tell them how he intended to defend Americans' lives and property. In a similar vein, after the September 11, 2001, terrorist attacks on the World Trade Center and the Pentagon, followed by the delivery of anthrax-contaminated letters to government officials, media corporations, and other sites, Americans demanded government action. President George W. Bush responded by mobilizing powerful military forces and organizing an international coalition for what he defined as a lengthy and worldwide campaign against terrorism. This campaign began with an extensive military operation in Afghanistan, where it appeared that the terrorists responsible for the September 11 attacks were based. Bush also created an Office of Homeland Security, naming Pennsylvania governor Tom Ridge as its first director, and instituted massive new law-enforcement measures to combat terrorism. Subsequently, the president ordered that suspected foreign terrorists could be tried before special military tribunals, bypassing the civilian courts and their numerous procedural safeguards. Federal agencies, including the Justice Department and the Transportation Department (which houses the U.S. Coast Guard) developed antiterrorism programs. The Centers for Disease Control moved to develop methods for preventing bioterrorism. The Treasury Department began tracking funds used to support terrorist activities worldwide. The State Department sought to enhance international support for American antiterrorism efforts. Congress, for its part, authorized tens of billions of dollars in new federal expenditures to combat terrorism and to repair the damage already caused by the terrorists. Congress also enacted legislation aimed at safeguarding the nation's airports. The states mobilized their own police and national guard forces for duties such as airport security, and local police and public safety departments were placed on high alert.

In the face of this national emergency, an overwhelming majority of Americans supported the federal government's actions. Nearly 90 percent of Americans consistently approved of the president's actions in both the foreign and domestic arenas, and a surprisingly high percentage also said they trusted the government to do the right thing. We will return to this finding below. In the face of danger, Americans looked to the government for action and protection and were less likely to view government as a hostile force. Former president Bill Clinton famously proclaimed that the era of "big government" was over. His proclamation, however, seems to have been premature. Apparently, like atheists, libertarians are scarce in foxholes. ■

■ **In this chapter, we will explore the relationship between the government and the people it governs. First, we will assess what Americans think about their government.** Although Americans have always been distrustful of governmental power, they rely on government for many of their needs. In recent decades, however, trust in government and the belief that individuals can influence government have both been in decline. These trends have important consequences that we need to examine.

■ **Second, we will explore the principle of democratic citizenship.** We believe that good citizenship begins with political knowledge—knowledge of government, of politics, and of democratic principles. With this knowledge, citizens can identify their interests and take advantage of their opportunities to influence politics.

■ **Next, we will look at the principles of government and politics.** The relationship between a government and its citizens is especially dependent on the form that a government takes. In order to better understand the opportunities that citizens have to influence government, we will look at the alternative forms government can take and the key differences among them. We will also examine the factors that led to the emergence of representative democracy in the United States and elsewhere around the world. In doing so, we will consider one of the most fundamental and enduring problems of democratic politics: the relationship between government and the people it governs.

■ **Finally, we will look at American political culture.** Here, we will examine the political principles that serve as the basis for American government and assess how well government upholds these ideals. We will conclude by suggesting what ordinary citizens can do to make these American political ideals more of a reality.

What Americans Think about Government

Since the United States was established as a nation, Americans have been reluctant to grant government too much power, and they have often been suspicious of politicians. But over the course of the nation's history, Americans have also turned to government for assistance in times of need and have strongly supported the government in periods of war, such as during the war against the Taliban in Afghanistan. For example, in 1933, the power of the government began to expand to meet the crises created by the stock market crash of 1929, the Great Depression, and the run on banks of 1933. Congress passed legislation that brought the government into the businesses of home mortgages, farm mortgages, credit, and relief of personal distress. Today, the national government is an enormous institution with programs and policies reaching into every corner of American life. It oversees the nation's economy; it is the nation's largest employer; it provides citizens with a host of services; it controls the world's most formidable military establishment; and it regulates a wide range of social and commercial activities in which Americans engage.

Citizens are so dependent upon government today that much of what they have come to take for granted—as, somehow, part of the natural environment—is in fact created by government. For example, a college student who drives her car to school may think that she is engaged in a purely private activity. Yet the simple act of driving an automobile is heavily dependent upon a multitude of government initiatives and is surrounded by a host of governmental rules. The roads upon which the student drives were constructed by a local government, probably with the assistance of some fraction of the more than $20 billion in federal highway funds spent each year. The roads are maintained by municipal, county, and state governments. During the winter, snow is removed from the roads by local governments. Traffic is regulated by local governments. Road signs are placed and maintained by local and state governments. The student holds a driver's license issued by her state government, which has also registered her vehicle and inspected it for safety and compliance with emissions standards. The vehicle itself has been manufactured to meet safety and emissions standards set by the federal government. The contract under which the student purchased the automobile as well as the loan she signed if she borrowed money for the purchase were both governed by commercial sales and banking regulations established by the state and federal governments. The list goes on.

It might be possible for this student to drive to school without all this government assistance and regulation. In principle, roads could be privately owned, traffic unregulated, and neither drivers nor their autos required to meet any standards. Perhaps our student could still reach her destination in such an environment. Certainly, her driving experience would be markedly different from the current one.

The example of this driver could be applied in endless other situations. Government plays a role in everyone's activities and, by the same token, regulates almost everything we do. Figure 1.1 is a diagram of some of the governmental services received by and controls exerted upon any recent college graduate. Some of these governmental activities are federal, while others are the province of state and local governments.

Perspectives on Politics

YOUNG AMERICANS' TRUST IN GOVERNMENT

"Do you think that people in the government waste money we pay in taxes?"

Waste a lot 61%
Waste some 37%
Don't waste much 2%

"How much of the time do you think you can trust the government in Washington to do what is right?"

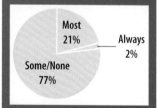

Most 21%
Always 2%
Some/None 77%

SOURCE: Diana Owen, "Mixed Signals: Generation X's Attitudes toward the Political System," in *After the Boom: The Politics of Generation X*, eds. Stephen C. Craig and Stephen Earl Bennett (Lanham, MD: Rowman and Littlefield, 1997), p. 95.

The Role of Government in Your Life

Figure 1.1

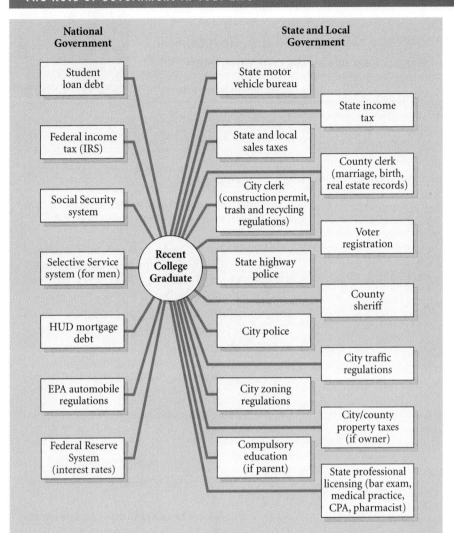

Government is a pervasive force in the lives of all Americans, especially at the state and local level. Think of the many ways in which government affects your life every day.

TRUST IN GOVERNMENT

Ironically, even as popular dependence upon it has grown, the American public's view of government has turned more sour. Public trust in government has declined, and Americans are now more likely to feel that they can do little to influence the government's actions. The decline in public trust among Americans is striking. In the early 1960s, three-quarters of Americans said they trusted government most of the time. By 1994, only one-quarter of Americans expressed trust in government; three-quarters stated that they did not trust government most of the time.[1] Different groups vary somewhat in their levels of trust: African Americans and Latinos actually express more confidence in the federal government than do whites. But even among the most supportive groups, more

What Government Does ... After September 11

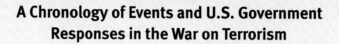

A Chronology of Events and U.S. Government Responses in the War on Terrorism

Date	Event	Government Response
September 11	Four U.S. airliners are hijacked. Two are flown into the World Trade Center in New York. One is flown into the Pentagon in northern Virginia. The fourth crashes in Pennsylvania.	Air traffic in the United States is grounded. Inbound international flights are diverted out of the country. Airports remain closed for several days. The New York Stock Exchange is closed, but the Federal Reserve and banks remain open. FEMA, the Federal Emergency Management Agency, leads recovery efforts in Washington and New York.
September: the days following the attacks	Osama bin Laden and his organization Al Qaeda are identified as prime suspects in the attacks. (9/13)	World leaders express condolences and condemn terrorist acts. President Bush begins to build international coalition to support action against terrorists, their networks, and states that harbor them. Congress passes bills providing $40 billion in relief and allowing the administration to use force to reply to the attacks. (9/14) U.S. government demands the Taliban's cooperation in apprehending bin Laden. Pakistan offers limited support. (9/16)
	Intelligence warnings of new terrorist threats.	The FBI begins to detain and arrest people potentially associated with terrorism. (9/18)
September 20–30		President Bush declares a "war on terrorism." (9/20) President Bush appoints Tom Ridge as homeland security director. (9/20) Sanctions, imposed on India and Pakistan, are lifted in anticipation of their support in the war on terrorism. (9/22) President Bush informs Congress of unspecified troop deployment and military engagement abroad. (9/24) U.S. government freezes assets of terrorists and calls on other countries to do the same. (9/24) President delivers $5 billion to aid ailing airlines. (9/25)
October	Anthrax infection occurs in Florida. Others follow, causing widespread fear. U.S. Postal Service (USPS) warns of mail contaminated with anthrax. Microsoft and NBC workers are exposed to anthrax that came in the	NATO reports that it has evidence that Al Qaeda is responsible for the September 11 attacks. (10/2) United States begins food drops in Afghanistan. (10/7) President Bush announces the first air offensive against Al Qaeda positions in Afghanistan. (10/7) USPS begins to irradiate some mail to kill anthrax. (10/24)

mail. Anthrax is found in Tom Daschle's Senate offices. The Senate's Hart Office Building is closed. (10/15)

The House of Representatives is shut down for five days to screen for anthrax. (10/17)

Two USPS workers die after exposure to anthrax. (10/22)

Congress approves antiterrorism bill that expands government's ability to search, to share information among agencies, to detain suspected terrorists, and to prevent money from reaching terrorist groups. (10/25)

Donald Rumsfeld, the U.S. secretary of defense, announces that U.S. ground forces are in Afghanistan. (10/30)

November

New warnings of terrorist threats.

Military tribunals are announced as a way of legally dealing with suspected terrorists. (11/13)

Taliban forces pull out of Kabul (11/12). Anti-Taliban forces take half of Afghanistan. (11/13)

Congress approves an aviation security bill that puts federal employees in charge of airport security and mandates many changes aimed at enhancing the safety of air travel. (11/16)

United States calls for renewed arms inspections in Iraq. (11/26)

December

Bomb-carrying passenger with ties to Al Qaeda subdued on airplane.

Taliban surrenders Kandahar in Afghanistan. Pockets of Taliban still remain, and leaders still evade anti-Taliban agents. (12/6)

United States pulls out of Anti-Ballistic Missile Treaty that had stood since 1972. The Bush administration continues to support development of missile-defense technologies. (12/13)

2002

White House concern about possible terrorist use of radiological weapons discussed in press.

Al Qaeda detainees are brought to Guantanamo Bay, Cuba. (1/14)

Philippine and U.S. troops commence antiterrorist training together in the Philippines. (1/15)

United States and other countries renew intentions to help rebuild Afghanistan, pledging billions in support in addition to the billions already spent. (1/25)

President Bush delivers his State of the Union address and emphasizes the war on terrorism. (1/29)

Taliban and Al Qaeda forces regroup.

Operation Anaconda seeks to destroy regrouped Taliban and Al Qaeda forces in Afghanistan. (early March)

President Bush announces "second stage" of war on terrorism, which involves pursuing terrorists in other parts of the world. (3/11)

President Bush proposes creation of cabinet-level Department of Homeland Security to coordinate antiterrorism efforts. (6/02)

Americans' trust in their government has fluctuated heavily over time and hit a high point in the 1960s. Hundreds of thousands of demonstrators joined the March on Washington in 1963 to demand civil rights for African Americans. These protesters sought justice from the federal government, which they saw as powerful enough to overcome racist laws in individual states. However, during the late 1960s, trust in the federal government began a precipitous decline that accelerated in the 1970s. The Watergate scandal originated with a break-in at the Democratic National Committee headquarters in Washington, D.C., and ended with the resignation of President Richard Nixon. The illegal tactics of the Nixon campaign and administration disgraced the office of the president and shook Americans' trust in government.

than half do not trust the government.[2] These developments are important because politically engaged citizens and public confidence in government are vital for the health of a democracy.

In the aftermath of the September 11 terrorist attacks, a number of studies reported a substantial increase in popular trust in government. For example, in October 2001, 60 percent of American college students surveyed said they trusted the government to "do the right thing" all or most of the time. Before September 11, only 36 percent expressed a similar view. In addition, 75 percent said they trusted the military, 69 percent expressed trust in the president, and 62 percent trusted Congress.[3] It remains to be seen whether these views, expressed during a national crisis, actually reflect a renewed *trust* in government to do the right thing or a fervent *hope* that it will.

Levels of trust in government can also differ according to the political context. In early 2002, an ABC News poll found that 68 percent of Americans trusted the government to do what is right "when it comes to handling national security and the war on terrorism," but only 38 percent had the same trust "when it comes to handling social issues like the economy, health care, Social Security, and education." And congressional investigations into the security failures of September 11 may well erode the public's currently high levels of trust on national security issues.

In 2002, following revelations of misconduct by some of America's largest corporations—including the energy giant Enron, telecommunications conglomerate Worldcom, and the accounting firm Arthur Anderson—Americans wondered if they could trust the government to regulate business and the economy. Congress quickly enacted legislation designed to curb corporate abuses and restore public confidence in business. The full extent of the damage, however, will take some time to assess.

Does it matter if Americans trust their government? For the most part, the answer is yes. As we have seen, most Americans rely on government for a wide range of

During the Reagan years, faith in government recovered somewhat. This trend coincided with Reagan's plan to scale back government. In this photo, he is signing a massive tax cut into law—apparently, his attempts to reduce the size of government improved people's perception of it (left). President Clinton waves his "veto pen" during his State of the Union address in 1994 (right). Universal health care was a central part of Clinton's platform, but his health care bill did not make it through Congress intact. This failure helped bring trust in government to a historic low.

services and laws that they simply take for granted. But long-term distrust in government can result in public refusal to pay taxes adequate to support such widely approved public activities. Low levels of confidence may also make it difficult for government to attract talented and effective workers to public service.[4] The weakening of government as a result of prolonged levels of distrust may ultimately harm our capacity to defend our national interest in the world economy and may jeopardize our national security. Likewise, a weak government can do little to assist citizens who need help in weathering periods of sharp economic or technological change.

> **Why is it important that Americans think that they can influence what the government does?**

In response to the terrorist attacks of September 11, 2001, Americans rallied around government officials and offered unprecedented support. Government employees like these firefighters became symbols of heroism and reliability. After the state of emergency abated somewhat, federal policy makers were subject to sharper scrutiny, and trust levels dropped.

political efficacy the ability to influence government and politics

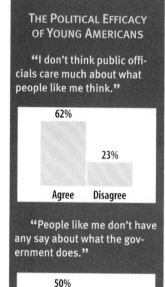

THE POLITICAL EFFICACY OF YOUNG AMERICANS

"I don't think public officials care much about what people like me think."

62% Agree
23% Disagree

"People like me don't have any say about what the government does."

50% Agree
35% Disagree

"Over the years, how much attention do you feel the government pays to what the people think when it decides what to do?"

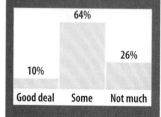

64% Some
26% Not much
10% Good deal

SOURCE: Diana Owen, "Mixed Signals: Generation X's Attitudes toward the Political System," in *After the Boom: The Politics of Generation X*, eds. Stephen C. Craig and Stephen Earl Bennett (Lanham, MD: Rowman and Littlefield, 1997), p. 98.

POLITICAL EFFICACY

Another important trend in American views about government has been a declining sense of **political efficacy,** the belief that citizens can affect what government does, that they can take action to make government listen to them. In recent decades, the public belief that government is responsive to ordinary citizens has declined. In 2000, 56 percent of Americans said that government officials don't care what people think; in 1960, only 25 percent felt so shut out of government. Accompanying this sense that ordinary people can't get heard is a growing belief—held by 61 percent of the public in 2000—that "government is run by a few big interests looking out only for themselves."[5] These views are widely shared across the age spectrum.

Many young Americans feel that government has ignored their views in particular. They feel that older officials cannot understand the challenges and problems facing the younger generation. For example, 72 percent of young people polled agreed that "our generation has an important voice but no one seems to hear it." But young Americans are not alone in feeling that government doesn't listen to them. In fact, most people of earlier generations feel even more strongly than young Americans that public officials have little interest in what they think.[6] The sense that government is out of touch and the feelings of powerlessness and lack of political efficacy that come with it seem to affect most Americans, regardless of age.

This widely felt loss of political efficacy is bad news for American democracy. The feeling that you can't affect government decisions can lead to a self-perpetuating cycle of apathy, declining political participation, and withdrawal from political life. Why bother to participate if you believe it makes no difference? Yet, the belief that you can be effective is the first step needed to influence government. Not every effort of ordinary citizens to influence government will succeed, but without any such efforts, government decisions will be made by a smaller and smaller circle of powerful people. Such loss of broad popular influence over government actions undermines the key feature of American democracy—government by the people.

What Americans Know about Government

The first prerequisite to achieving an increased sense of political efficacy is knowledge. Political indifference is often simply a habit that stems from a lack of knowledge about how your interests are affected by politics and from a sense that you can do nothing to affect politics. But political efficacy is a self-fulfilling prophecy: if you think you cannot be effective, chances are you will never try. Most research suggests that people active in politics have a high sense of their efficacy. This means they believe they can make a difference—even if they do not win all the time. Most people do not want to be politically active every day of their lives, but it is essential to our political ideals that all citizens be informed and able to act.

Sadly, the state of political knowledge in the United States today is dismal. Most Americans know little about current issues or debates. A recent survey that tested the knowledge of the institutions and processes of government in the United States found that 70 percent of the respondents answered fewer than 60 percent of the

Time of Day	Schedule
7:00 AM	Wake up. Standard time set by the national government.
7:10 AM	Shower. Water courtesy of local government, either a public entity or a regulated private company. Brush your teeth with toothpaste, with cavity-fighting claims verified by federal agency. Dry your hair with electric dryer, manufactured according to federal government agency guidelines.
7:30 AM	Have a bowl of cereal with milk for breakfast. "Nutrition Facts" on food labels are a federal requirement, pasteurization of milk required by state law, freshness dating on milk based on state and federal standards, recycling the empty cereal box and milk carton required by state or local laws.
8:30 AM	Drive or take public transportation to campus. Air bags and seat belts required by federal and state laws. Roads and bridges paid for by state and local governments, speed and traffic laws set by state and local governments, public transportation subsidized by all levels of government.
8:45 AM	Arrive on campus of large public university. Buildings are 70 percent financed by state taxpayers.
9:00 AM	First class: Chemistry 101. Tuition partially paid by a federal loan (more than half the cost of university instruction is paid for by taxpayers), chemistry lab paid for with grants from the National Science Foundation (a federal agency) and smaller grants from business corporations made possible by federal income tax deductions for charitable contributions.
Noon	Eat lunch. College cafeteria financed by state dormitory authority on land grant from federal Department of Agriculture.
2:00 PM	Second class: American Government 101 (your favorite class!). You may be taking this class because it's required by the state legislature or because it fulfills a university requirement.
4:00 PM	Third class: Computer lab. Free computers, software, and Internet access courtesy of state subsidies plus grants and discounts from IBM and Microsoft, the costs of which are deducted from their corporate income taxes; Internet built in part by federal government. Duplication of software protected by federal copyright laws.
6:00 PM	Eat dinner: hamburger and french fries. Meat inspected by federal agencies for bacteria.
7:00 PM	Work at part-time job at the campus library. Minimum wage set by federal government, books and journals in library paid for by state taxpayers.
10:00 PM	Go to local bar. Purchase and consumption of alcohol regulated by state law and enforced by city police.
11:00 PM	Go home. Street lighting paid for by county and city governments, police patrols by city government.
11:15 PM	Watch TV. Networks regulated by federal government, cable public-access channels required by city law. Weather forecast provided to broadcasters by a federal agency.
Midnight	Put out the garbage before going to bed. Garbage collected by city sanitation department, financed by "user charges."

| Table 1.1 | Who Knows What? |

QUESTION	PERCENTAGE ANSWERING CORRECTLY
What is affirmative action?	31
When was the New Deal?	29
How long is a senator's term?	25
Name two First Amendment rights.	20
What is the Food and Drug Administration?	20
Name all three branches of government.	19
What was the New Deal?	15

SOURCE: Michael X. Delli Carpini and Scott Keeter, *What Americans Know about Politics and Why It Matters* (New Haven, CT: Yale University Press, 1996), pp. 58–94.

questions correctly (see Table 1.1). In most colleges and universities, below 60 is a failing grade. But, rather than dwell on the widespread political ignorance of many Americans, we prefer to view this as an opportunity for the readers of this book. Those of you who make the effort to become among the knowledgeable few will be much better prepared to influence the political system regarding the issues and concerns that you care most about. Finally, bear in mind that no citizen has to be alone in the effort to influence government. An important aspect of political knowledge is knowing who shares your interests.

CITIZENSHIP: KNOWLEDGE AND PARTICIPATION

After September 11, many commentators noted a revival in Americans' sense of citizenship, as manifested by ubiquitous flag displays and other demonstrations of patriotic sentiment. There seems to be little doubt that millions of Americans experienced a renewed sense of identification with their nation. Citizenship, however, has a broader meaning that just patriotism.

Beginning with the ancient Greeks, citizenship has meant membership in one's community. In fact, the Greeks did not even conceive of the individual as a complete person. The complete person was the public person, the *citizen;* noncitizens and private persons were referred to as *idiotés.* Participation in public affairs was virtually the definition of citizenship. Citizenship was never defined as voting. Although voting was not excluded, the essence of citizen participation was talking. As one political philosopher put it, "What counts is argument among the citizens. . . . [T]he citizen who makes the most persuasive argument gets [his or her] way but can't use force, or pull rank, or distribute money; [the citizen] must talk about the issues at hand. . . . Citizens must come into the forum with nothing but their arguments."[7] Involvement in the public debate is the central, quintessential right of citizenship. Following the Greek ideal, the First Amendment to the U.S. Constitution makes freedom of speech the primary right of American citizenship.

Our meaning for **citizenship** derives from the Greek ideal: enlightened political engagement.[8] To be politically engaged in a meaningful way, citizens require resources, especially political knowledge and information. Democracy functions best when citizens are informed.

But to be a citizen in the full sense as understood first by the ancient Greeks requires more than an occasional visit to an election booth. A true citizen must have the knowledge needed to participate in political debate. If you want to be a citizen rather than an *idiote*, it is important that you acquire three forms of political knowledge from this course and this textbook:

1. *Knowledge of government.* Citizens must understand the "rules of the game." From the citizen's perspective, the most important rules concern one's own political rights, which can vary greatly according to the type of government under which one lives. In the United States, these rights are extensive and concrete, and they affect every citizen directly.
2. *Knowledge of politics.* We need to understand what is at stake in the political world. This understanding includes the capacity to discern our own interests in the political arena and identify the best means through which to realize them.
3. *Knowledge of democratic principles.* Although politics may divide Americans, democratic ideals hold them together. As citizens, we need to know what forms of political conduct are consistent with democratic principles. Democracy requires that both government and citizens be aware of and respect the constraints upon their political activities.

Political knowledge means more than having a few opinions to offer the pollster or to guide your decisions in a voting booth. It is important to know the rules and strategies that govern political institutions and the principles upon which they are based, but it is more important to know them in ways that relate to your own interests. Citizens need knowledge in order to assess their interests and know when to act upon them. Knowledgeable citizens are more attentive to and more engaged in politics because they understand how and why politics is relevant to their lives.

THE NECESSITY OF POLITICAL KNOWLEDGE

Political knowledge is the key to effective participation in political life. Without political knowledge, no citizen can be aware of her interests or stake in a political dispute. In the year preceding the 2000 presidential election, for example, many of the prospective Democratic and Republican candidates presented rather detailed proposals on ways of changing the current American tax system. How many voters paid enough attention to the discussion to be able to meaningfully distinguish among the various proposals and their implications? Did you attempt to ascertain whether you and your family would be better off under the tax system envisioned by Bush or Bradley, Gore or McCain? How could you participate intelligently without this knowledge? Interestingly, various public and private interest groups devote enormous time and energy to understanding alternative policy proposals and their implications so they will know whom to support. Interest groups understand something that every citizen should also understand: effective participation requires knowledge.

Citizens also need political knowledge to identify the best ways of acting upon their interests. If your road is rendered impassable by snow, what can you do? Is

citizenship informed and active membership in a political community

> **Why is political knowledge the key to effective participation in political life?**

snow removal the responsibility of the federal government? Is it a state or munici-pal responsibility? Knowing that you have a stake in a clear road does not help much if you do not know that snow removal is a city or county responsibility and cannot identify the municipal agency that deals with the problem. Americans are fond of complaining that government is not responsive to their needs, but is it not possible that many citizens simply lack the information they need to present their problems to the appropriate government officials?

Citizens need political knowledge, as well, to ascertain what they cannot or should not ask of politicians and the government. The famous Scottish economist Adam Smith once observed that in the economic realm the selfish pursuit of pri-vate interests improved the general good as if by "an invisible hand." Smith's idea is the basis for our belief in free markets today. It is not so clear, however, that Smith's logic applies as well to political life. One of the reasons that we take part in political life is that many of our most important collective goals, including defense, protec-tion of the environment, and safety from crime, are unlikely to be achieved purely by individual action. We need to cooperate in order to defend our nation, protect our environment, and keep our homes safe. Thus, political knowledge includes knowing the limits upon, as well as the possibilities for pursuing, one's own indi-vidual interests through political action. This is, perhaps, the most difficult form of political knowledge to acquire.

The rest of this chapter will look at the forms of political knowledge that we be-lieve are most critical for a citizen to possess. In the next section, we will examine the principles of government and politics. Following that, we will review the de-mocratic principles upon which the United States is based and assess how well American government fulfills these principles. Finally, we will conclude with sug-gestions of what you and other ordinary citizens can do to become more knowl-edgeable and more engaged.

Government

government institutions and pro-cedures through which a territory and its people are ruled

Government is the term generally used to describe the formal institutions through which a land and its people are ruled. To govern is to rule. A government may be as simple as a tribal council that meets occasionally to advise the chief, or as complex as the vast establishments, with their forms, rules, and bureaucracies, found in the United States. A more complex government is sometimes referred to as "the state." In the history of civilization, governments have not been difficult to establish. There have been thousands of them. The hard part is establishing a government that lasts. Even more difficult is developing a stable government that is compatible with liberty, equality, and democracy.

IS GOVERNMENT NEEDED?

Americans have always harbored some suspicion of government and have won-dered how extensive a role it should play in their lives. Thomas Jefferson famously observed that the best government was one that "governed least." Generally speak-ing, a government is needed to provide those services, sometimes called "public goods," that all citizens need but are not likely to be able to adequately provide for themselves. These might include defense against foreign aggression, maintenance of public order, enforcement of contractual obligations and property rights, and a guarantee of some measure of social justice. The precise extent to which government involvement in our society is needed has been debated throughout our history and will continue to be a central focus of political contention in America.

FORMS OF GOVERNMENT

Governments vary in their structure, in their size, and in the way they operate. Two questions are of special importance in determining how governments differ: Who governs? And how much government control is permitted?

In some nations, governing is done by a single individual—a king or dictator, for example. This state of affairs is called **autocracy.** Where a small group—perhaps landowners, military officers, or wealthy merchants—controls most of the governing decisions, that government is said to be an **oligarchy.** If more people participate and have some influence over decision making, that government is a **democracy.**

Governments also vary considerably in terms of how they govern. In the United States and a small number of other nations, governments are limited as to what they are permitted to control (substantive limits), as well as how they go about it (procedural limits). Governments that are so limited are called **constitutional governments,** or liberal governments. In other nations, including many in Europe as well as in South America, Asia, and Africa, though the law imposes few real limits, the government is nevertheless kept in check by other political and social institutions that the government is unable to control and must come to terms with—such as autonomous territories, an organized church, organized business groups, or organized labor unions. Such governments are generally called **authoritarian.** In a third group of nations, including the Soviet Union under Joseph Stalin, Nazi Germany, and perhaps prewar Japan and Italy, governments not only are free of legal limits but also seek to eliminate those organized social groups that might challenge or limit the government's authority. These governments typically attempt to dominate or control every sphere of political, economic, and social life and, as a result, are called **totalitarian.**

Americans have the good fortune to live in a nation in which limits are placed on what governments can do and how they can do it. But such constitutional democracies are relatively rare in today's world; it is estimated that only twenty or so of the world's nearly two hundred governments could be included in this category. And constitutional democracies were unheard of before the modern era. Prior to the eighteenth and nineteenth centuries, governments seldom sought—and rarely received—the support of their ordinary subjects. The available evidence strongly suggests that the ordinary people had little love for the government or for the social order. After all, they had no stake in it. They equated government with the police officer, the bailiff, and the tax collector.[9]

Beginning in the seventeenth century, in a handful of Western nations, two important changes began to take place in the character and conduct of government. First, governments began to acknowledge formal limits upon their power. Second, a small number of governments began to provide the ordinary citizen with a formal voice in public affairs—through the vote. Obviously, the desirability of limits on government and the expansion of popular influence were at the heart of the

> **What are the different forms that a government can take?**

autocracy a form of government in which a single individual—a king, queen, or dictator—rules

oligarchy a form of government in which a small group—landowners, military officers, or wealthy merchants—controls most of the governing decisions

democracy a system of rule that permits citizens to play a significant part in the governmental process, usually through the election of key public officials

constitutional government a system of rule in which formal and effective limits are placed on the powers of the government

authoritarian government a system of rule in which the government recognizes no formal limits but may nevertheless be restrained by the power of other social institutions

totalitarian government a system of rule in which the government recognizes no formal limits on its power and seeks to absorb or eliminate other social institutions that might challenge it

American Revolution in 1776. "No taxation without representation," as we shall see in Chapter 2, was hotly debated from the beginning of the Revolution through the Founding in 1789. But even before the Revolution, a tradition of limiting government and expanding participation in the political process had developed throughout western Europe. Thus, to understand how the relationship between rulers and the ruled was transformed, we must broaden our focus to take into account events in Europe as well as in America. We will have to divide the transformation into its two separate parts. The first is the effort to put limits on government. The second is the effort to expand the influence of the people through access to government and politics.

LIMITING GOVERNMENT

> **How did the principle of limited government develop?**

The key force behind the imposition of limits on government power was a new social class, the bourgeoisie. *Bourgeoisie* is a French word for freeman of the city, or *bourg.* Being part of the bourgeoisie later became associated with being "middle class" and with being in commerce or industry. In order to gain a share of control of government, joining or even displacing the kings, aristocrats, and gentry who had dominated government for centuries, the bourgeoisie sought to change existing institutions—especially parliaments—into instruments of real political participation. Parliaments had existed for centuries, but were generally aristocratic institutions. The bourgeoisie embraced parliaments as means by which they could exert the weight of their superior numbers and growing economic advantage against their aristocratic rivals. At the same time, the bourgeoisie sought to place restraints on the capacity of governments to threaten these economic and political interests by placing formal or constitutional limits on governmental power.

Although motivated primarily by the need to protect and defend their own interests, the bourgeoisie advanced many of the principles that became the central underpinnings of individual liberty for all citizens—freedom of speech, freedom of assembly, freedom of conscience, and freedom from arbitrary search and seizure. It is important to note here that the bourgeoisie generally did not favor democracy as we know it. They were advocates of electoral and representative institutions, but they favored property requirements and other restrictions so as to limit participation to the middle classes. Yet once these institutions of politics and the protection of the right to engage in politics were established, it was difficult to limit them to the bourgeoisie.

ACCESS TO GOVERNMENT: THE EXPANSION OF PARTICIPATION

The expansion of participation from the bourgeoisie to ever-larger segments of society took two paths. In some nations, popular participation was expanded by the crown or the aristocracy, which ironically saw common people as potential political allies against the bourgeoisie. Thus in nineteenth-century Prussia, for example, it was the emperor and his great minister Otto von Bismarck who expanded popular participation in order to build political support among the lower orders.

In other nations, participation expanded because competing segments of the bourgeoisie sought to gain political advantage by reaching out and mobilizing the support of working- and lower-class groups who craved the opportunity to take part in politics—"lining up the unwashed," as one American historian put it.[10] To be sure, excluded groups often agitated for greater participation. But seldom was such agitation, by itself, enough to secure the right to participate. Usually, expansion of voting rights resulted from a combination of pressure from below and help from above.

This pattern of suffrage expansion by groups hoping to derive some political advantage has been typical in American history. After the Civil War, one of the chief reasons that Republicans moved to enfranchise newly freed slaves was to use the support of the former slaves to maintain Republican control over the defeated southern states. Similarly, in the early twentieth century, upper-middle-class "Progressives" advocated women's suffrage because they believed that women were likely to support the reforms espoused by the Progressive movement.

INFLUENCING THE GOVERNMENT THROUGH PARTICIPATION: POLITICS

Expansion of participation means that more and more people have a legal right to take part in politics. Politics is an important term. In its broadest sense, "politics" refers to conflicts over the character, membership, and policies of any organization to which people belong. As Harold Lasswell, a famous political scientist, once put it, politics is the struggle over "who gets what, when, how."[11] Although politics is a phenomenon that can be found in any organization, our concern in this book is more narrow. Here, **politics** will be used to refer only to conflicts and struggles over the leadership, structure, and policies of governments. The goal of politics, as we define it, is to have a share or a say in the composition of the government's leadership, how the government is organized, or what its policies are going to be. Having a share is called **power** or influence.

Politics can take many forms, including everything from sending letters to government officials to voting, lobbying legislators on behalf of particular programs, and participating in protest marches and even violent demonstrations. A system of government that gives citizens a regular opportunity to elect the top government officials is usually called a **representative democracy** or **republic.** A system that permits citizens to vote directly on laws and policies is often called a **direct democracy.** At the national level, America is a representative democracy in which citizens select government officials but do not vote on legislation. Some states and cities, however, have provisions for direct legislation through popular referendum. For example, in 1999, Ohio University professor Scott Hooper organized students in a successful referendum campaign to overturn a city housing-code provision banning couches on porches.[12]

Groups and organized interests obviously do not vote (although their members do), but they certainly do participate in politics. Their political activities usually consist of such endeavors as providing funds for candidates, lobbying, and trying to influence public opinion. The pattern of struggles among interests is called group politics, or **pluralism.** Americans have always been ambivalent about pluralist politics. Although the right of groups to press their views is the essence of liberty, Americans often fear that organized groups may sometimes exert too much influence, advancing special interests at the expense of larger public interests. We will return to this problem in Chapter 11.

> **How can people participate in politics and influence what the government does?**

politics conflict over the leadership, structure, and policies of governments

power influence over a government's leadership, organization, or policies

representative democracy/ republic a system of government in which the populace selects representatives, who play a significant role in governmental decision making

direct democracy a system of rule that permits citizens to vote directly on laws and policies

pluralism the theory that all interests are and should be free to compete for influence in the government. The outcome of this competition is compromise and moderation

direct action politics a form of
politics, such as civil disobedience
or revolutionary action, that takes
place outside formal channels

Sometimes, of course, politics does not take place through formal channels at
all, but instead involves direct action. **Direct action politics** can include either violent politics or civil disobedience, both of which attempt to shock rulers into be-
having more responsibly. Direct action can also be a form of revolutionary politics,
which rejects the system entirely and attempts to replace it with a new ruling group
and a new set of rules. In recent years in the United States, groups ranging from
animal-rights activists to right-to-life advocates have used direct action and even
violence to underline their demands. Direct political action is protected by the U.S.
Constitution; violence is not. The country's Founders knew that the right to
protest is essential to the maintenance of political freedom, even where the ballot
box is available.

American Political Culture: Shared Values, but Disagreements over the Role of Government

Underlying and framing political life in the United States are agreements on basic
political values but disagreements over the ends or goals of government. Values
shape citizens' views of the world and define their sense of what is right and wrong,
just and unjust, possible and impossible. If Americans shared no values, they
would have difficulty communicating, much less agreeing upon a common system
of government and politics. On the other hand, sharing broad values does not
guarantee political consensus. We can agree on principles but disagree over their
application.

For example, some critics claim that measures such as affirmative action
have not promoted political inclusion and instead have condoned reverse discrimination and a segmented society. Far from fulfilling American ideals, they
argue, these policies represent a movement away from our most fundamental
values. An opposing perspective questions the progress that has been made in
promoting equality. Pointing to the disproportionately high rates of poverty
among women and minorities and continuing evidence of discrimination
against these groups, this side questions whether Americans are serious about
equality. Much of the debate over the role of government has been over what
government should do and how far it should go to reduce the inequalities
within our society and political system.

Even though Americans have disagreed over the meaning of such political
ideals as equality, they still agree on the importance of these ideals. The shared values, beliefs, and attitudes that form our **political culture** and serve to hold the
United States and its people together date back to the time of the founding of the
union.

political culture broadly shared
values, beliefs, and attitudes about
how the government should function. American political culture emphasizes the values of liberty,
equality, and democracy

The essential documents of the American Founding—the Declaration of Independence and the Constitution—enunciated a set of political principles about the
purposes of the new republic. In contrast with many other democracies, in the
United States these political ideals did not just remain words on dusty documents.
Americans actively embraced the principles of the Founders and made them central to the national identity. Let us look more closely at three of these ideals: liberty,
equality, and democracy.

LIBERTY

No ideal is more central to American values than liberty. The Declaration of Independence defined three inalienable rights: "life, liberty and the pursuit of happiness." The preamble of the Constitution likewise identified the need to secure "the blessings of liberty" as one of the key reasons for drawing up the Constitution. For Americans, **liberty** means both personal freedom and economic freedom. Both are closely linked to the idea of **limited government.**

The Constitution's first ten amendments, known collectively as the Bill of Rights, above all preserve individual personal liberties and rights. In fact, liberty has come to mean many of the freedoms guaranteed in the Bill of Rights: freedom of speech and writing, the right to assemble freely, and the right to practice religious beliefs without interference from the government. Over the course of American history, the scope of personal liberties has expanded, as laws have become more tolerant and as individuals have successfully used the courts to challenge restrictions on their individual freedoms. Far fewer restrictions exist today on the press, political speech, and individual moral behavior than in the early years of the nation. Even so, conflicts persist over how personal liberties should be extended and when personal liberties violate community norms. For example, one of the most contentious issues in the last thirty years has been that of abortion. Whereas defenders of the right to choose abortion view it is an essential personal freedom for women, opponents view it as murder—something that no society should allow.

In addition to personal freedom, the American concept of liberty means economic freedom. Since the Founding, economic freedom has been linked to capitalism, free markets, and the protection of private property. Free competition, unfettered movement of goods, and the right to enjoy the fruits of one's labor are all essential aspects of economic freedom and American capitalism.[13] In the first century of the Republic, support for capitalism often meant support for the doctrine of laissez-faire. Translated literally as "to leave alone," **laissez-faire capitalism** allowed very little room for the national government to regulate trade or restrict the use of private property, even in the public interest. Americans still strongly support capitalism and economic liberty, but they now also endorse some restrictions on economic freedoms to protect the public. Federal and state governments now deploy a wide array of regulations in the name of public protection. These include health and safety laws, environmental rules, and workplace regulations. Not surprisingly, fierce disagreements often erupt over what the proper scope of government regulation should be. What some people regard as protecting the public, others see as an infringement on their own freedom to run their businesses and use their property as they see fit.

EQUALITY

The Declaration of Independence declares as its first "self-evident" truth that "all men are created equal." As central as it is to the American political creed, however, equality has been a less well defined ideal than liberty because people interpret "equality" in different ways. Few Americans have wholeheartedly embraced full equality of results, but most Americans share the ideal of **equality of opportunity**—

> **What are Americans' core political values? What are the meanings of these values?**

liberty freedom from governmental control

limited government a principle of constitutional government; a government whose powers are defined and limited by a constitution

laissez-faire capitalism an economic system in which the means of production and distribution are privately owned and operated for profit with minimal or no government interference

equality of opportunity a widely shared American ideal that all people should have the freedom to use whatever talents and wealth they have to reach their fullest potential

Since the Founding, liberty—personal and economic freedom—has been central to the political values of Americans. Patrick Henry's famous "Give me liberty, or give me death" speech demanded freedom at any cost and has resonated with Americans throughout the nation's history.

The new country did not meet Henry's demand for freedom, at least not for all people. Samuel Jennings painted this work, Liberty Displaying the Arts and Sciences, in 1792. The books, instruments, and classical columns at the left of the painting contrast with the kneeling slaves at the right—illustrating the divide between America's rhetoric of liberty and the political and economic reality of slavery.

Americans' political devotion to freedom manifests itself in many everyday ways. For example, all U.S. coins have been inscribed with the word "liberty" since 1792.

that is, the notion that each person should be given a fair chance to go as far as his or her talents will allow. Yet it is hard for Americans to reach agreement about what constitutes equality of opportunity. Must *past* inequalities be remedied in order to ensure equal opportunity in the *present?* Should inequalities in the legal, political, and economic spheres be given the same weight? In contrast to liberty, which requires limits on the role of government, equality implies an *obligation* of the government to the people.[14]

Americans do make clear distinctions between political equality and social or economic equality. **Political equality** means that members of the American political community have the right to participate in politics on equal terms. Beginning from a very restricted definition of political community, which originally included only propertied white men, the United States has moved much closer to an ideal of political equality that can be summed up as "one person, one vote." Broad support for the ideal of political equality has helped expand the American political community and extend the right to participate to all. Although considerable conflict remains over whether the political system makes it harder for some people to participate and easier for others and about whether the role of

The issue of freedom plays out in a personal way in abortion rights. Politically, the debate hinges on the extent of government control over personal liberty.

money in politics has drowned out the public voice, Americans agree that all citizens should have an equal right to participate and that government should enforce that right.

In part because Americans believe that individuals are free to work as hard as they choose, they have always been less concerned about social or economic inequality. Many Americans regard economic differences as the consequence of individual choices, virtues, or failures. Because of this, Americans tend to be less supportive than most Europeans of government action to ensure equality. Yet when major economic forces, such as the Great Depression of the 1930s, affect many people or when systematic barriers appear to block equality of opportunity, Americans support government action to promote equality. Even then, however, Americans have endorsed only a limited government role designed to help people get back on their feet or to open up opportunity.

political equality the right to participate in politics equally, based on the principle of "one person, one vote"

Washington passed legislation to ban or limit tobacco advertising in 1997 and 1998, pitting tobacco companies and farmers against health and children's advocates. Government regulations intended to protect the public are sometimes viewed by business as infringements on economic liberty.

DEMOCRACY

popular sovereignty a principle of democracy in which political authority rests ultimately in the hands of the people

The essence of democracy is the participation of the people in choosing their rulers and the people's ability to influence what those rulers do. In a democracy, political power ultimately comes from the people. The idea of placing power in the hands of the people is known as **popular sovereignty.** In the United States, popular sovereignty and political equality make politicians accountable to the people. Ideally, democracy envisions an engaged citizenry prepared to exercise its power over rulers. As we saw earlier, the United States is a representative democracy, meaning that the people do not rule directly but instead exercise power through elected representatives. Forms of participation in a democracy vary greatly, but voting is a key element of the representative democracy that the American Founders established.

majority rule/minority rights the democratic principle that a government follows the preferences of the majority of voters but protects the interests of the minority

American democracy rests on the principle of **majority rule** with **minority rights.** Majority rule means that the wishes of the majority determine what government does. The House of Representatives—a large body elected directly by the people—was designed in particular to ensure majority rule. But the Founders feared that popular majorities could turn government into a "tyranny of the majority" in which individual liberties would be violated. Concern for individual rights has thus been a part of American democracy from the beginning. The rights enumerated in the Bill of Rights and enforced through the courts provide an important check on the power of the majority.

DOES THE SYSTEM UPHOLD AMERICAN POLITICAL VALUES?

> **Does the political system uphold American political values?**

Clearly, the ideals of liberty, equality, and democracy are open to diverse interpretations. We should note, moreover, that debates about ideals are not only discussions of abstract principles, but they also involve questions of who will benefit from the government's actions. In general, the assertion that individual liberty should be America's primary political value is an argument for limiting the government's power in America's economy and society. Frequently, though not always, this is an argument made on behalf of those who are satisfied with their place in the scheme of things and who fear that government intervention might threaten that place. In a similar vein, those who point to equality as the fundamental value also see themselves as potential beneficiaries of the powerful and activist government that would be needed to bring about a more egalitarian society. Debates over democracy, therefore, often pit forces satisfied with the current balance of power against those who would like to see new political procedures that might shake up the political establishment and bring new groups to power. Sometimes these debates are subtle. For example, some proponents of campaign finance reform—presented as a democratizing measure—see limits on campaign spending as a vehicle for protecting the status quo by preventing challengers from mounting well-financed campaigns against incumbents. Thus, debates over core values are also disputes over what the government should do and, more importantly, over who will benefit. Also, the ideals can easily conflict with one another in practice. When we examine American history, we can see that there have been large gaps between these ideals and the practice of American politics. We can also see that some ideals have been prized more than others at different historical moments. But it is also clear that as Americans have engaged in political conflict about who should participate in politics and how political institutions should be

Freedom and Democracy in the World

How common is democracy as a form of government throughout the world? How unique are the general freedoms that Americans enjoy and that underscore our rich democratic traditions? Foremost among those who specialize in monitoring the extent of democracy and freedom in the world is an organization known as Freedom House. It was founded in 1941 and remains a nonprofit, nonpartisan American organization dedicated to protecting freedom and liberty around the world. Since the 1950s, the organization has sent survey teams to various countries to analyze and compare the structure of their governments and content of their laws and has then assigned a standard score representing the degree of freedom found in that country.

For the past twenty-eight years Freedom House has presented a widely respected and utilized annual report on the degree of freedom and democracy in countries around the world. Freedom House assesses a country's freedom along two critical dimensions: political rights enjoyed by the citizenry (for example, fair, free, and competitive elections) and the extent of civil liberties extended to the population (for example, diverse opportunities for and different forms of cultural expression, such as religion). While specific scores are assigned to each country, Freedom House also organizes all countries of the world into three general categories based on the extent of their political rights and civil liberties: "free," "partly free," or "not free."

Many democracies that allow free elections and tolerate political opposition nevertheless practice various forms of human rights violations or have populations that are caught in the middle of internal wars and terrorism. Thus, in 2001, Freedom House reported that 121 countries were electoral democracies, yet only 86 of these "electoral democracies" were classified as "free." Thirty-five of these democracies were "partly free" (including Brazil, Turkey, Paraguay, Colombia, Russia, and Ukraine).

The most "free" countries were those with perfect scores on civil liberties and political rights. Twenty-nine independent countries were in this category, including some whose names are probably quite familiar to most students—the United States, Switzerland, Australia, Canada, Denmark, Finland, Luxembourg, the Netherlands, New Zealand, Ireland, Norway, and Sweden.

Also within this "elite" group are countries whose names may be less familiar to many students, including San Marino, Dominica, Barbados, Andorra, Belize, Tuvalu, the Marshall Islands, and Kiribati. Among the forty-eight countries of the world that Freedom House ranks as "not free" are Egypt, Belarus, China, Kenya, Algeria, Laos, Kazakhstan, Tajikistan, and Rwanda. Eleven countries have populations that are denied virtually any of the basic freedoms and rights found in other countries. These include Afghanistan, Burma, Cuba, Iraq, North Korea, Saudi Arabia, and Syria.

Overall, while only a minority of the world's population lives in "free" countries, Freedom House has documented a steady increase over time in the degree of freedom and the foundations for democracy across the globe. In 1988, sixty-one countries (representing 38.9 percent of the world's population) were "free," thirty-nine were "partly free" (21 percent of the world's population), and sixty-eight were "not free" (42 percent of the world's population). Today approximately 41 percent of the world's population is "free" and only 35 percent is "not free." In 1989, there were sixty-nine democracies in the world that were democratic, only about half of what exists today.

SOURCE: http://freedomhouse.org/research/freeworld/2002/essay2002.pdf (accessed 7/11/02).

organized, they have called upon these ideals to justify their actions. Now let's re-examine these ideals, noting key historical conflicts and current controversies about what they should mean in practice.

Liberty   The central historical conflict regarding liberty in the United States was the enslavement of blacks. The facts of slavery and the differential treatment of the races has cast a long shadow over all of American history. In fact, scholars today note that the American definition of freedom has been formed in relation to the concept of slavery. The right to control one's labor and the right to receive rewards for that labor have been central elements of our definition of freedom precisely because these freedoms were denied to slaves.[15]

Concerns about the meaning of liberty also arise in connection with government regulation of economic and social activity. Economic regulations imposed to ensure public health and safety are often decried by the affected businesses as infringements on their freedom. For example, in 1994, the Occupational Safety and Health Administration (OSHA) of the national government prepared to issue regulations intended to protect workers from repetitive stress injuries. Such injuries, which affect 700,000 workers a year, are caused by long hours on the assembly line or at the computer. OSHA's regulations would have required employers to provide specified work breaks and proper furniture and other equipment. Although such regulations might have been welcomed by workers, employers viewed them as intrusive and extremely costly. In the face of strong opposition from employers, OSHA backed down and decided not to issue the regulations.[16]

Social regulations prompt similar disputes. Some citizens believe that government should enforce certain standards of behavior or instill particular values in citizens. Examples of such activity abound: welfare rules that once denied benefits to women who were found with a "man in the house," the practice of saying prayers in school, laws that require parents to pay child support for their children even if those children no longer live with them, and laws that require citizens to wear seat belts are just a few examples. Deciding the proper scope of economic and social regulation is a topic of great concern and much conflict among Americans today.

More recently, concerns about liberty have arisen in relation to the government's efforts to combat terrorism. In November 2001, President Bush issued an executive order mandating that suspected foreign terrorists would be tried before special military tribunals rather than in the regular federal courts. Hypothetically, such tribunals could impose severe penalties—on the basis of evidence that might not be admitted in civilian courts. Earlier, the Justice Department had announced that federal investigators would be allowed to eavesdrop on conversations between terrorist suspects and their attorneys. In the months following September 11, hundreds of individuals—mainly of Middle Eastern origin—were arrested by federal authorities and held on immigration charges or by material witness warrants that allowed the government to incarcerate them without having to show any evidence they were linked to terrorist activities. The events of September 11 leave us with an extraordinary dilemma. On the one hand, we treasure liberty, but on the other hand, we recognize that the lives of thousands of Americans have already been lost and countless others are threatened by terrorism. Can we reconcile liberty and security? Liberty and order? In previous national emergencies, Americans accepted restrictions on liberty with the understanding that these would be temporary. For example, military tribunals were established during World War II to try German saboteurs who landed on the East Coast. President Bush, however, has said that the war against terrorism will last years and years. Clearly, the implications for American liberty will be profound.

Equality Because equality is such an elusive concept, many conflicts have arisen over what it should mean in practice. Americans have engaged in three kinds of controversies about the public role in addressing inequality. The first is determining what constitutes equality of access to public institutions. In 1896, the Supreme Court ruled in _Plessy v. Ferguson_ that "separate but equal" accommodations for blacks and whites were constitutional. In 1954, in a major legal victory for the civil rights movement, the Supreme Court overturned the separate but equal doctrine in _Brown v. Board of Education_ (see Chapter 5). Today, new questions have been raised about what constitutes equal access to public institutions. Some argue that the unequal financing of public schools in cities, suburbs, and rural districts is a violation of the right to equal education. To date, these claims have not been supported by the federal courts, which have rejected the notion that the unequal economic impacts of public policy outcomes are a constitutional matter.[17] Lawsuits arguing a right to "economic equal protection" stalled in 1973 when the Supreme Court ruled that a Texas school-financing law did not violate the Constitution even though the law affected rich and poor students differently.[18]

A second debate concerns the public role in ensuring equality of opportunity in private life. Although Americans generally agree that discrimination should not be tolerated, people disagree over what should be done to ensure equality of opportunity (see Table 1.2). Controversies about affirmative action programs reflect these disputes. Supporters of affirmative action claim that such programs are necessary to compensate for past discrimination in order to obtain true equality of opportunity today. Opponents maintain that affirmative action amounts to reverse discrimination and that a society that espouses true equality should not acknowledge gender or racial differences. The question of the public responsibility for private inequalities is

---

American Attitudes about Equality, 1996 and 1998　　　　Table 1.2

STATEMENT	PERCENTAGE WHO AGREE
Our society should do whatever is necessary to make sure that everyone has an equal opportunity to succeed.	82
We have gone too far in pushing equal rights in this country.	45*
One of the big problems in this country is that we don't give everyone an equal chance.	48
It is not really that big a problem if some people have more of a chance in life than others.	37
The country would be better off if we worried less about how equal people are.	53
If people were treated more equally in this country, we would have many fewer problems.	83*

*Indicates 1998 data.
SOURCE: Based on data from the American National Election Studies, conducted by the University of Michigan, Center for Political Studies, and provided by the Inter-University Consortium for Political and Social Research, Ann Arbor, Michigan.

Political participation was greatest during the nineteenth century. In George Caleb Bingham's Verdict of the People *(1853–54), a crowd seems half delighted with and half regretful about the outcome of the vote. But as this painting indicates, white men were virtually the only people who could vote at the time.*

central to gender issues. The traditional view, still held by many today, sees the special responsibilities of women in the family as something that falls outside the range of public concern. Indeed, from this perspective, the role of women within families is essential to the functioning of a democratic society. In the past thirty years, especially, these traditional views have come under fire, as advocates for women have argued that women occupy a subordinate place within the family and that such private inequalities *are* a topic of public concern.[19]

Voting rights expanded dramatically during the civil rights movement, which forced the government to allow people to vote regardless of their race. Here, residents of Wilcox County, Alabama, line up to vote in 1966. Prior to the passage of the Voting Rights Act of 1965, Wilcox County had no registered black voters.

Although Americans are no longer legally barred from voting on the basis of sex or race, political participation is minimal for most people. In the 2000 election, only 51 percent of eligible voters came to the polls.

A third debate about equality concerns differences in income and wealth. Unlike in other countries, income inequality has not been an enduring topic of political controversy in the United States, which currently has the largest gap in income and wealth between rich and poor citizens of any developed nation. But Americans have generally tolerated great differences among rich and poor citizens, in part because of a pervasive belief that mobility is possible and that economic success is the product of individual effort.[20] At times, however, concern about economic inequalities emerges, often around the issue of fair taxation. Some analysts today warn that the growing division between rich and poor may invigorate a politics of class and polarize political debate along income lines.[21]

Democracy Despite Americans' deep attachment to the *ideal* of democracy, many questions can be raised about our *practice* of democracy. The first is the restricted definition of the political community during much of American history. The United States was not a full democracy until the 1960s, when African Americans were at last guaranteed the right to vote. Property restrictions on the right to vote were eliminated by 1828; in 1870, the Fifteenth Amendment to the Constitution granted African Americans the vote, although later exclusionary practices denied them that right; in 1920, the Nineteenth Amendment guaranteed women the right to vote; and in 1965, the Voting Rights Act finally secured the right of African Americans to vote.

Just securing the right to vote does not end concerns about democracy, however. The organization of electoral institutions can have a significant impact on access to elections and on who

Special interests have been all too willing to influence government in the absence of popular political participation. Lobbyists not only attempt to convince politicians with their arguments; they also control large donations to political campaigns. Corporate donations support candidates, but this support has become something of a political liability after the Enron collapse.

can get elected. During the first two decades of the twentieth century, states and cities enacted many reforms that made it harder to vote, including strict registration requirements and scheduling of elections. The aim was to rid politics of corruption but the consequence was to reduce participation. Other institutional decisions affect which candidates stand the best chance of getting elected (see Chapter 10).

A further consideration about democracy concerns the relationship between economic power and political power. Money has always played an important role in elections and governing in the United States. Many argue that the pervasive influence of money in American electoral campaigns today undermines democracy. With the decline of locally based political parties that depended on party loyalists to turn out the vote, and the rise of political action committees, political consultants, and expensive media campaigns, money has become the central fact of life in American politics. Money often determines who runs for office; it can exert a heavy influence on who wins; and, some argue, money affects what politicians do once they are in office.[22]

A final consideration that must be raised about democracy is the engagement of the citizenry. Low turnout for elections and a pervasive sense of apathy and cynicism characterize American politics today. Many people say that it does not matter if they participate because their votes will not make any difference. This disillusionment and sense of ineffectiveness undermines the vitality of democracy, which in turn reduces the accountability of the rulers to the ruled.

VALUES AND THE ENDS OF GOVERNMENT

> **How do American political values conflict with one another?**

Many of the most important dilemmas of American political life involve conflicts among fundamental political values as those values are put into operation. For example, Americans strongly value both liberty and equality, but often programs designed to promote one may impose restraints upon the other. Thus, affirmative action programs or statutes designed to prevent discrimination against the handicapped, such as the Americans with Disabilities Act, may promote equality but may also infringe upon the liberty of employers to hire whomever they wish. In a similar vein, democratic political processes may sometimes produce results that can challenge both liberty and equality. After all, Adolf Hitler and the Nazis came to power in Germany in the 1930s partly through democratic means. Even in America, political extremists who oppose both liberty and equality have been elected to office. As recently as 1991, a white supremacist, David Duke, was very nearly elected governor of Louisiana.

Conversely, in the name of equality or liberty, courts often hand down verdicts that undo decisions of democratically elected legislatures and even decisions reached in popular referenda. Principles that seem incontrovertible in the abstract become more problematic in operation. In the process of resolving conflicts among core beliefs, America's political principles change and evolve. Even core values should be understood as works in progress rather than immutable facts.

WHO BENEFITS FROM GOVERNMENT?

Government is not a neutral force in any society. Some groups always benefit more than others from the government's actions. Some regimes are run by small cliques or even by families for their own benefit. Our government is dominated by shifting coalitions of electoral forces along with interest groups; local, state, and national politicians; civic leaders; labor groups; ethnic and religious groups; professional associations; and a host of others. Almost every piece of legislation or governmental regulation bears the stamp of some set of interests that pushed for its enactment because it seemed to serve their purposes. In some instances, interests have turned getting what they want into a science. For example, the Enron Corporation, a now-bankrupt Texas energy giant, developed a computer program named "Matrix" that could evaluate the net impact upon the company of any proposed federal energy regulation. This information, in turn, guided the firm's lobbying efforts and campaign contributions, which were designed to influence the government's activities.[23]

Although we know that most pieces of legislation and many regulations have particular beneficiaries, we hope that the benefits and costs of our government's policies are not narrowly defined. That is, we hope that the net benefits of government do not always flow to the same groups. James Madison, the principal author of the U.S. Constitution, argued that in a large and diverse republic there would be so many groups fighting for power that no one group or coalition of groups would always prevail. Today, we call this idea pluralism, and we fervently hope that in our society some benefits of government accrue to all citizens—or at least to all participants in the political process. We can certainly observe that even apparently powerful forces are sometimes defeated in the political arena and that for most political actors, power is short-lived. The once-mighty Enron Corporation was destroyed despite its grasp of sophisticated political techniques. Perhaps this is the best outcome for which we can hope—that political power will be dispersed and short-lived, so that government will benefit many and favor few for very long.

GET INVOLVED

What You Can Do: Test the Political Waters

You may not be interested in politics. You probably distrust politicians. You certainly have other priorities. Why bother with politics? After all, there is not much you can do about children's access to guns or mounting tensions in the Middle East.

Before you decide that public life is strictly for other people, consider several factors. First, political involvement can be fascinating. It may put you at the center of challenging issues that have important effects on many people's lives. Should Americans promote environmental safeguards that protect some people's health but cost other people jobs? Should Americans spend scarce public resources on prenatal care for poor women or build libraries that provide Internet access to all community members?

Second, political engagement can be energizing. Imagine how it feels to be the person who organizes a group that gives voice to the concerns of elderly people who had previously been ignored or neglected. Consider how exciting it would be to participate in a coalition that places a referendum to save wildlife reserves on the state ballot, to feel the tension of campaign volunteers as the first election returns trickle in.

Third, political activism can produce political efficacy—the sense that you can make a difference. If you do nothing, you cannot be part of the solution. When you get involved, you can continue the efforts of those who precede you, try innovative approaches to old problems, and create a legacy for those who will follow. You may ease existing dilemmas and contribute to their resolution. Occasionally, one determined person does make a significant difference.

Accordingly, before you say no to political participation, consider the potential fascination, energy, and accomplishments that await you. Do more than consider. Test the political waters. Here are a few easy ways to see if political involvement can be meaningful and fulfilling to you.

- **Assess your political interests.**
  Read a newspaper or a weekly news magazine. Watch national or local news on television. Listen to a political talk show. What issues catch your eye? Which ones seem important to you? How do any of them affect your life? Identify one or two issues and follow them for a week or so. You may discover that political knowledge generates interest.
- **Initiate a discussion with family members, friends, or classmates.**
  Ask a few people what they think about an issue that interests you. Do they care? Are they knowledgeable? Do they have a position on the issue? If so, how do they defend their position? Do you agree or disagree with them? The point here is to *listen* to and *learn* from other people's political viewpoints.
- **Articulate your own views on the issue.**
  Experiment with expressing your own views on the issue. Are they clear? Coherent? Cogent? Now see if you can articulate your views with enough force that other people take you seriously but also with sufficient civility to keep up the attention and interest of people who disagree with you.
- **Write a letter to the editor of a campus or community newspaper.**
  Write a letter to the editor expressing your view. Make the letter short, direct, and civil. That will increase the likelihood that it will be selected for publication. A few readers may answer your letter by submitting written responses to it.
- **Call in to a radio talk show.**
  State your point clearly and succinctly to the person who screens callers. If you get on air, state your main point, present your key arguments, and invite a response from the host or the call-in audience.

Democracy begins with discussion. Adopt an experimental attitude and join the discussion. It is not important to persuade other people that you are right. People change their minds very slowly. Instead, aim at expressing yourself clearly and knowledgeably so that your views will be communicated effectively. Often, it is as important to be taken seriously as it is to be heeded.

Summary

The citizen's role in political life begins with information and knowledge. A citizen's knowledge should include knowledge of government, of politics, and of democratic principles. Knowledgeable citizens are better able to identify and act upon their political interests. In short, knowledgeable citizens better understand how and why politics and government influence their lives.

The form that a government takes affects citizens because it determines who governs and how much governmental control is permitted. Americans live in a constitutional democracy, where limits are placed on what governments can do and how they can do it. Americans are also given access to government through legal rights to political participation. Through politics, Americans are able to struggle over the leadership, structure, and policies of governments.

Although politics may divide Americans from one another, the core values of American political culture—liberty, equality, and democracy—hold the United States and its people together. Although these values have been important since the time the United States was founded, during much of American history there have been large gaps between these ideals and the practice of American politics. Moreover, liberty, equality, and democracy often conflict with one another in American political life.

For Further Reading

Craig, Stephen C., and Stephen Earl Bennett, eds. *After the Boom: The Politics of Generation X.* Lanham, MD: Rowman and Littlefield, 1997.

Dahl, Robert. *Democracy and Its Critics.* New Haven, CT: Yale University Press, 1989.

Delli Carpini, Michael X., and Scott Keeter. *What Americans Know about Politics and Why It Matters.* New Haven, CT: Yale University Press, 1996.

Hochschild, Jennifer L. *Facing Up to the American Dream: Race, Class, and the Soul of the Nation.* Princeton, NJ: Princeton University Press, 1995.

Huntington, Samuel P. *American Politics: The Promise of Disharmony.* Cambridge, MA: Harvard University Press, 1981.

Lasswell, Harold. *Politics: Who Gets What, When, How.* New York: Meridian Books, 1958.

McClosky, Herbert, and John Zaller. *The American Ethos: Public Attitudes toward Capitalism and Democracy.* Cambridge, MA: Harvard University Press, 1984.

Nie, Norman H., Jane Junn, and Kenneth Stehlik-Barry. *Education and Democratic Citizenship in America.* Chicago: University of Chicago Press, 1996.

Nye, Joseph S., Jr., Philip D. Zelikow, and David C. King, eds. *Why People Don't Trust Government.* Cambridge, MA: Harvard University Press, 1997.

Putnam, Robert. *Making Democracy Work: Civic Traditions in Modern Italy.* Princeton, NJ: Princeton University Press, 1993.

de Tocqueville, Alexis. *Democracy in America.* Trans. Phillips Bradley. New York: Knopf, Vintage Books, 1945; orig. published 1835.

Study Outline

www.wwnorton.com/wtp4e

What Americans Think about Government

1. In recent decades, the public's trust in government has declined considerably. Some Americans believe that government has grown too large and that government programs do not benefit them. As public distrust of government has increased, so has public dissatisfaction with the government's performance.

2. Americans today are less likely to think that they can influence what the government does. This view has led to increased apathy and cynicism among the citizenry.

What Americans Know about Government

1. Informed and active membership in a political community is the basis for citizenship. Citizens require political knowledge in order to be aware of their interests in a political dispute, to identify the best ways of acting upon their interests, and to know what political action can and cannot achieve. However, today many Americans have little political knowledge.

Government

1. Governments vary in their structure, in their size, and in the way they operate.

2. Beginning in the seventeenth century, two important changes began to take place in the governance of some Western nations: governments began to acknowledge formal limits on their power, and governments began to give citizens a formal voice in politics through the vote.

3. Political participation can take many forms: the vote, group activities, and even direct action, such as violence or civil disobedience.

American Political Culture: Shared Values, but Disagreements over the Role of Government

1. Three important political values in American politics are liberty, equality, and democracy.
2. At times in American history there have been large gaps between the ideals embodied in Americans' core values and the practice of American government.
3. Many of the important dilemmas of American politics revolve around conflicts over fundamental political values. One such conflict involves the ideals of liberty and equality. Over time, efforts to promote equality may threaten liberty.

Practice Quiz

www.wwnorton.com/wtp4e

1. Political efficacy is the belief that
   a) government operates efficiently.
   b) government has grown too large.
   c) government cannot be trusted.
   d) one can influence what government does.

2. The famous political scientist Harold Lasswell defined politics as the struggle over
   a) who gets elected.
   b) who gets what, when, how.
   c) who protests.
   d) who gets to vote.

3. What is the basic difference between autocracy and oligarchy?
   a) the extent to which the average citizen has a say in government affairs
   b) the means of collecting taxes and conscripting soldiers
   c) the number of people who control governing decisions
   d) They are fundamentally the same thing.

4. According to the authors, good citizenship requires
   a) political knowledge.
   b) political engagement.
   c) a good education.
   d) both a and b

5. The principle of political equality can be best summed up as
   a) "equality of results."
   b) "equality of opportunity."

   c) "one person, one vote."
   d) "equality between the sexes."

6. Which of the following is an important principle of American democracy?
   a) popular sovereignty
   b) majority rule/minority rights
   c) limited government
   d) All of the above are important principles of American democracy.

7. Which of the following is not related to the American conception of "liberty"?
   a) freedom of speech
   b) free enterprise
   c) freedom of religion
   d) All of the above are related to liberty.

8. Which of the following is *not* part of the American political culture?
   a) belief in equality of results
   b) belief in equality of opportunity
   c) belief in individual liberty
   d) belief in free competition

9. Which of the following does *not* represent a current discrepancy between the ideal and practice of democracy in America?
   a) the use of property restrictions for voting in three remaining states
   b) the influence of money in electoral politics
   c) the low voter turnout in American elections
   d) All of the above represent discrepancies between the ideal and practice of democracy in modern America.

10. Americans' trust in their government
    a) declined steadily from the early 1960s to the mid-1990s but rose slightly since then.
    b) declined during Watergate, but rose again during the 1980s.
    c) has risen since 1990.
    d) rose during the 1970s and 1980s, but has declined since 1992.

Critical Thinking Questions

www.wwnorton.com/wtp4e

1. What type of government does the United States have? Is it the most democratic government possible? Do citizens make the decisions of government or do they merely influence them?
2. Think of some examples that demonstrate the gaps between the ideals of America's core political values and the practice of American politics. Describe how such gaps were reconciled

in the past. Identify one current gap between Americans' values and their political practices. How might this discrepancy be reconciled?

3. Combating terrorism has entailed restrictions on civil liberties. Does America believe in liberty only when it is convenient? How can we reconcile civil liberty and national security? When we, as a nation, are compelled to make choices, are we better off opting for more liberty or more security?

Key Terms

www.wwnorton.com/wtp4e

authoritarian government (p. 17)
autocracy (p. 17)
citizenship (p. 15)
constitutional government (p. 17)
democracy (p. 17)
direct action politics (p. 20)

direct democracy (p. 19)
equality of opportunity (p. 21)
government (p. 16)
laissez-faire capitalism (p. 21)
liberty (p. 21)
limited government (p. 21)
majority rule/minority rights (p. 24)
oligarchy (p. 17)
pluralism (p. 19)

political culture (p. 20)
political efficacy (p. 12)
political equality (p. 22)
politics (p. 19)
popular sovereignty (p. 24)
power (p. 19)
representative democracy (or republic)
  (p. 19)
totalitarian government (p. 17)

2 THE FOUNDING AND THE CONSTITUTION

What Government Does and Why It Matters

HE STORY OF AMERICA'S Founding and the Constitution is generally presented as something both inevitable and glorious: it was inevitable that the American colonies would break away from England to successfully establish their own country; and it was glorious in that it established the best of all possible forms of government under a new Constitution, which was easily adopted and quickly embraced, even by its critics. In reality, though, America's successful breakaway from England was by no means assured, and the Constitution that we revere today as one of the most brilliant creations of any nation was in fact highly controversial. Moreover, its ratification and durability were often in doubt. George Washington, the man revered as the father of the country and the person chosen to preside over the Constitutional Convention of 1787, thought the document produced that hot summer in Philadelphia would probably last no more than twenty years, at which time leaders would have to convene again to come up with something new.

That Washington's prediction proved wrong is, indeed, a testament to the enduring strength of the Constitution. But none of the Founders was Moses, and the Constitution was no Ten Commandments, carved by lightning in stone. The Constitution was a product of political bargaining and compromise, formed very much in the same way political decisions are made today. This fact is often overlooked because of what historian Michael Kammen has called the "cult of the Constitution"—a tendency of Americans, going back more than a century, to blindly venerate, sometimes to the point of near worship, the Founders and the document they created.[1] As this chapter will show, the Constitution reflects political self-interest, but high principle, too. It also defines the relationship between American citizens and their government.

Often, the story of the Founding and the Constitution is written to emphasize the framers' concerns regarding individual liberty and limits on government. And, of course, the framers had such concerns. It is important to note, however, that the primary goal of the framers was the creation of an *effective* government. They sought a government with the capacity to provide for the nation's safety in a sometimes hostile world: "Among the many objects to which a wise and free people find it necessary to direct their attention," wrote John Jay in *Federalist 3,* "that of providing for their safety seems to be the first." The framers endeavored to create a government with the power to maintain public order, promote prosperity, and secure the nation's independence, powers that the government under the Articles of Confederation lacked. The Constitution begins not with a statement of the limits on government, but with an affirmative statement of the ends a government is designed to achieve—to establish justice, insure domestic tranquility, and provide for the common defense and general welfare. ■

- **In this chapter, we will first assess the political backdrop of the American Revolution, which led to the Declaration of Independence and the establishment of a governmental structure under the Articles of Confederation.**

- **We will then consider the conditions that led to the Constitutional Convention of 1787 and the great issues that were debated by the framers.** To fully understand the character of the Founding and the meaning of the Constitution, it is essential to look beyond the myths and rhetoric and to explore the conflicting interests and forces at work during the period.

- **Next, we will examine the Constitution that ultimately emerged as the basis for the national government.** Although the Constitution was the product of a particular set of political forces, the principles of government it established have had long-lasting significance. The framers sought to create a powerful national government, but guarded against possible misuse of that power through the separation of powers, federalism, and the Bill of Rights.

- **We will then examine the first hurdle that the Constitution faced, the fight for ratification.** Two sides, the Federalists and the Antifederalists, vigorously debated the great political issues and principles at stake. The resolution of this debate created the framework for a national government that has lasted more than two hundred years.

■ **We will then look at how the Constitution has changed over the past two centuries.** The framers designed an amendment process so that the Constitution could change, but the process has succeeded only on rare occasions.

■ **Finally, we will ask what liberty, equality, and democracy meant to the framers of the Constitution.** Although the framers established a system of government that would eventually allow each of these political values to thrive, they championed liberty as the most important of the three.

The First Founding: Interests and Conflicts

Competing ideals and principles often reflect competing interests, and so it was in Revolutionary America. The American Revolution and the American Constitution were outgrowths and expressions of a struggle among economic and political forces within the colonies. Five sectors of society had interests that were important in colonial politics: (1) the New England merchants; (2) the southern planters; (3) the "royalists"—holders of royal lands, offices, and patents (licenses to engage in a profession or business activity); (4) shopkeepers, artisans, and laborers; and (5) small farmers. Throughout the eighteenth century, these groups were in conflict over issues of taxation, trade, and commerce. For the most part, however, the southern planters, the New England merchants, and the royal office and patent holders—groups that together made up the colonial elite—were able to maintain a political alliance that held in check the more radical forces representing shopkeepers, laborers, and small farmers. After 1750, however, by seriously threatening the interests of New England merchants and southern planters, British tax and trade policies split the colonial elite, permitting radical forces to expand their political influence, and set into motion a chain of events that culminated in the American Revolution.[2]

BRITISH TAXES AND COLONIAL INTERESTS

Beginning in the 1750s, the debts and other financial problems faced by the British government forced it to search for new revenue sources. This search rather quickly led to the Crown's North American colonies, which, on the whole, paid remarkably little in taxes to their parent country. The British government reasoned that a sizable fraction of its debt was, in fact, attributable to the expenses it had incurred in defense of the colonies during the recent French and Indian wars, as well as to the continuing protection that British forces were giving the colonists from Indian attacks and that the British navy was providing for colonial shipping. Thus, during the 1760s, England sought to impose new, though relatively modest, taxes upon the colonists.

Like most governments of the period, the British regime had limited ways in which to collect revenues. The income tax, which in the twentieth century has become the single most important source of governmental revenues, had not yet been developed. For the most part, in the mid-eighteenth century, governments relied on tariffs, duties, and other taxes on commerce, and it was to such taxes, including the Stamp Act, that the British turned during the 1760s.

The British helped radicalize colonists through bad policy decisions in the years before the Revolution. For example, Britain gave the ailing East India Company a monopoly on the tea trade in the American colonies. Colonists feared the monopoly would hurt colonial merchants' business and protested by throwing the East India Company tea into Boston Harbor. The Boston Tea Party of 1773 brought on oppressive retribution from Britain, which led to colonial resistance and, ultimately, revolution.

The Stamp Act and other taxes on commerce, such as the Sugar Act of 1764, which taxed sugar, molasses, and other commodities, most heavily affected the two groups in colonial society whose commercial interests and activities were most extensive—the New England merchants and the southern planters. Under the famous slogan "no taxation without representation," the merchants and planters together sought to organize opposition to these new taxes. In the course of the struggle against British tax measures, the planters and merchants broke with their royalist allies and turned to their former adversaries—the shopkeepers, small farmers, laborers, and artisans—for help. With the assistance of these groups, the merchants and planters organized demonstrations and a boycott of British goods that ultimately forced the Crown to rescind most of its new taxes.

From the perspective of the merchants and planters, however, the British government's decision to eliminate most of the hated taxes represented a victorious end to their struggle with the mother country. They were anxious to end the unrest they had helped to arouse, and they supported the British government's efforts to restore order. Indeed, most respectable Bostonians supported the actions of the British soldiers involved in the Boston Massacre. In their subsequent trial, the soldiers were defended by John Adams, a pillar of Boston society and a future president of the United States. Adams asserted that the soldiers' actions were entirely justified, provoked by "a motley rabble of saucy boys, Negroes and mulattos, Irish teagues and outlandish Jack tars." All but two of the soldiers were acquitted.[3]

Britain eventually sent troops to subdue the American colonists. Grant Wood's Midnight Ride of Paul Revere *(1931) depicts Revere alerting colonists to the British army's arrival. The subsequent battle between colonial and British forces at Concord and Lexington began the Revolutionary War.*

Despite the efforts of the British government and the better-to-do strata of colonial society, it proved difficult to bring an end to the political strife. The more radical forces representing shopkeepers, artisans, laborers, and small farmers, who had been mobilized and energized by the struggle over taxes, continued to agitate for political and social change within the colonies. These radicals, led by individuals like Samuel Adams, a cousin of John Adams, asserted that British power supported an unjust political and social structure within the colonies, and began to advocate an end to British rule.[4]

POLITICAL STRIFE AND THE RADICALIZING OF THE COLONISTS

The political strife within the colonies was the background for the events of 1773–74. In 1773, the British government granted the politically powerful East India Company a monopoly on the export of tea from Britain, eliminating a lucrative form of trade for colonial merchants. To add to the injury, the East India Company sought to sell the tea directly in the colonies instead of working through the colonial merchants. Tea was an extremely important commodity in the 1770s, and these British actions posed a mortal threat to the New England merchants. Together with their southern allies, the merchants once again called upon their radical adversaries for support. The most dramatic result was the Boston Tea Party of 1773, led by Samuel Adams.

This event was of decisive importance in American history. The merchants had hoped to force the British government to rescind the Tea Act, but they did not support any demands beyond this one. They certainly did not seek independence from Britain. Samuel Adams and the other radicals, however, hoped to provoke the British government to take actions that would alienate its colonial supporters and pave the way for a rebellion. This was precisely the purpose of the Boston Tea Party, and it succeeded. By dumping the East India Company's tea into Boston Harbor, Adams and his followers goaded the British into enacting a number of harsh reprisals. Within five months after the incident in Boston, the House of Commons passed a series of acts that closed the port of Boston to commerce, changed the provincial government of Massachusetts, provided for the removal of accused persons to England

This picture of a segmented snake, printed in Benjamin Franklin's newspaper, urged the colonies to unite during the French and Indian War of the 1750s. Again during the Revolutionary War, cooperation among the states was crucial to the independence movement. Thirty years before the Constitution was written, Franklin recognized the importance of national concerns as well as state ones.

> **What conflicts were apparent and what interests prevailed during the American Revolution and the drafting of the Articles of Confederation?**

The year after fighting began between American colonists and the British army, the Continental Congress voted for independence, on July 2, 1776. The Declaration of Independence famously summarized the colonists' grievances against Britain and declared the "self-evident" rights of equality, "Life, Liberty, and the pursuit of Happiness."

for trial, and most important, restricted movement to the West—further alienating the southern planters, who depended upon access to new western lands. These acts of retaliation confirmed the worst criticisms of England and helped radicalize Americans. Radicals like Samuel Adams and Christopher Gadsden of South Carolina had been agitating for more violent measures to deal with England. But ultimately they needed Britain's political repression to create widespread support for independence.

Thus, the Boston Tea Party set into motion a cycle of provocation and retaliation that in 1774 resulted in the convening of the First Continental Congress—an assembly of delegates from all parts of the country—that called for a total boycott of British goods and, under the prodding of the radicals, began to consider the possibility of independence from British rule. The eventual result was the Declaration of Independence.

THE DECLARATION OF INDEPENDENCE

In 1776, the Second Continental Congress appointed a committee consisting of Thomas Jefferson of Virginia, Benjamin Franklin of Pennsylvania, Roger Sherman of Connecticut, John Adams of Massachusetts, and Robert Livingston of New York to draft a statement of American independence from British rule. The Declaration of Independence, written by Jefferson and adopted by the Second Continental Congress, was an extraordinary document in both philosophical and political terms. Philosophically, the Declaration was remarkable for its assertion that certain rights, called "unalienable rights"—including life, liberty, and the pursuit of happiness—could not be abridged by governments. In the world of 1776, a world in which some kings still claimed to rule by divine right, this was a dramatic statement. Politically, the Declaration was remarkable because, despite the differences of interest that divided the colonists along economic, regional, and philosophical lines, the Declaration identified and focused on problems, grievances, aspirations, and principles that might unify the various colonial groups. The Declaration was an attempt to identify and articulate a history and set of principles that might help to forge national unity.[5]

THE ARTICLES OF CONFEDERATION

Articles of Confederation America's first written constitution; served as the basis for America's national government until 1789

Having declared their independence, the colonies needed to establish a governmental structure. In November of 1777, the Continental Congress adopted the **Articles of Confederation and Perpetual Union**—the United States's first written constitution. Although it was not ratified by all the states until 1781, it was the country's operative constitution for almost twelve years, until March 1789.

The Articles of Confederation was a constitution concerned primarily with limiting the powers of the central government. The central government, first of all, was based entirely in a Congress. Since it was not intended to be a powerful government, it was given no executive branch. Execution of its laws was to be left to the individual states. Second, the Congress had little power. Its members were not much more than delegates or messengers from the state legislatures. They were chosen by the state legislatures, their salaries were paid out of the state treasuries, and they were subject to immediate recall by state authorities. In addition, each state, regardless of its size, had only a single vote.

The Congress was given the power to declare war and make peace, to make treaties and alliances, to coin or borrow money, and to regulate trade with the Native

Americans. It could also appoint the senior officers of the United States army. But it could not levy taxes or regulate commerce among the states. Moreover, the army officers it appointed had no army to serve in because the nation's armed forces were composed of the state militias. Probably the most unfortunate part of the Articles of Confederation was that the central government could not prevent one state from discriminating against other states in the quest for foreign commerce.

In brief, the relationship between the Congress and the states under the Articles of Confederation was much like the contemporary relationship between the United Nations and its member states, a relationship in which virtually all governmental powers are retained by the states. It was properly called a **confederation** because, as provided under Article II, "each state retains its sovereignty, freedom, and independence, and every power, jurisdiction, and right, which is not by this Confederation expressly delegated to the United States, in Congress assembled." Not only was there no executive, there also was no judicial authority and no other means of enforcing the Congress's will. If there was to be any enforcement at all, it would be done for the Congress by the states.[6]

confederation a system of government in which states retain sovereign authority except for the powers expressly delegated to the national governments

The Second Founding: From Compromise to Constitution

The Declaration of Independence and the Articles of Confederation were not sufficient to hold the new nation together as an independent and effective nation-state. From almost the moment of armistice with the British in 1783, moves were afoot to reform and strengthen the Articles of Confederation.

> **Why were the Articles of Confederation unable to hold the nation together?**

INTERNATIONAL STANDING AND BALANCE OF POWER

There was a special concern for the country's international position. Competition among the states for foreign commerce allowed the European powers to play the states off against one another, which created confusion on both sides of the Atlantic. At one point during the winter of 1786–87, John Adams of Massachusetts, a leader in the independence struggle, was sent to negotiate a new treaty with the British, one that would cover disputes left over from the war. The British government responded that, since the United States under the Articles of Confederation was unable to enforce existing treaties, it would negotiate with each of the thirteen states separately.

At the same time, well-to-do Americans—in particular the New England merchants and southern planters—were troubled by the influence that "radical" forces exercised in the Continental Congress and in the governments of several of the states. The colonists' victory in the Revolutionary War had not only meant the end of British rule, but also significantly changed the balance of political power within the new states. As a result of the Revolution, one key segment of the colonial elite—the royal land, office, and patent holders—was stripped of its economic and political privileges. In fact, many of these individuals, along with tens of thousands of other colonists who considered themselves loyal British subjects, left for Canada after the British surrender. And while the pre-Revolutionary elite was weakened, the pre-Revolutionary radicals were now better organized than ever before and were the controlling forces in such states as Pennsylvania and Rhode Island, where they pursued economic and political policies that struck terror into the hearts of the pre-Revolutionary political establishment. In Rhode Island, for example, between 1783 and 1785, a legislature dominated by representatives of small farmers, artisans, and shopkeepers had instituted economic policies, including drastic currency inflation, that frightened business and property owners throughout the country. Of course, the central government under the Articles of Confederation was powerless to intervene.

THE ANNAPOLIS CONVENTION

The continuation of international weakness and domestic economic turmoil led many Americans to consider whether their newly adopted form of government might not already require revision. In the fall of 1786, many state leaders accepted an invitation from the Virginia legislature for a conference of representatives of all the states. Delegates from five states actually attended. This conference, held in Annapolis, Maryland, was the first step toward the second founding. The one positive thing that came out of the Annapolis Convention was a carefully worded resolution calling on the Congress to send commissioners to Philadelphia at a later time "to devise such further provisions as shall appear to them necessary to render the Constitution of the Federal Government adequate to the exigencies of the Union."[7] This resolution was drafted by Alexander Hamilton, a thirty-four-year-old New York lawyer who had played a significant role in the Revolution as George Washington's secretary and who would play a still more significant role in framing the Constitution and forming the new government in the 1790s. But the resolution did not necessarily imply any desire to do more than improve and reform the Articles of Confederation.

SHAYS'S REBELLION

It is quite possible that the Constitutional Convention of 1787 in Philadelphia would never have taken place at all except for a single event that occurred during the winter following the Annapolis Convention: Shays's Rebellion.

Daniel Shays, a former army captain, led a mob of farmers in a rebellion against the government of Massachusetts. The purpose of the rebellion was to prevent foreclosures on their debt-ridden land by keeping the county courts of western Massachusetts from sitting until after the next election. The state militia dispersed the mob, but for several days Shays and his followers terrified the state government by attempting to capture the federal arsenal at Springfield, provoking an appeal to the Congress to help restore order. Within a few days, the state government regained control and captured fourteen of the rebels (all were eventually pardoned). In 1787, a newly elected Massachusetts legislature granted some of the farmers' demands.

Although the incident ended peacefully, its effects lingered and spread. Washington summed it up: "I am mortified beyond expression that in the moment of our acknowledged independence we should by our conduct verify the predictions of our transatlantic foe, and render ourselves ridiculous and contemptible in the eyes of all Europe."[8]

The Congress under the Confederation had been unable to act decisively in a time of crisis. This provided critics of the Articles of Confederation with precisely the evidence they needed to push Hamilton's Annapolis resolution through the Congress. Thus, the states were asked to send representatives to Philadelphia to discuss constitutional revision. Delegates were eventually sent by every state except Rhode Island.

Opponents of the Articles called for a new Constitutional Convention to explore a stronger form of national government. George Washington, a hero of the Revolution, presided over the convention. In creating the Constitution, the convention faced a host of pitfalls caused by the dramatic differences between the states.

The Articles of Confederation created a weak national government at the end of the Revolutionary War. The states were largely left to make their own policy. In the winter of 1787, the Massachusetts legislature levied heavy taxes that hit the poor particularly hard. In protest, Daniel Shays led a makeshift army against the federal arsenal at Springfield. Shays's group was soon stopped, but the rebellion proved the Articles too weak to protect the fledgling nation.

THE CONSTITUTIONAL CONVENTION

Delegates selected by the state governments convened in Philadelphia in May 1787, with political strife, international embarrassment, national weakness, and local rebellion fixed in their minds. Recognizing that these issues were symptoms of fundamental flaws in the Articles of Confederation, the delegates soon abandoned the plan to revise the Articles and committed themselves to a second founding—a second, and ultimately successful, attempt to create a legitimate and effective national system of government. This effort occupied the convention for the next five months.

A Marriage of Interest and Principle   Scholars have for years disagreed about the motives of the Founders in Philadelphia. Among the most controversial views of the framers' motives is the "economic interpretation" put forward by historian Charles Beard and his disciples.[9] According to Beard's account, America's Founders were a collection of securities speculators and property owners whose only aim was personal enrichment. From this perspective, the Constitution's lofty principles were little more than sophisticated masks behind which the most venal interests sought to enrich themselves.

Contrary to Beard's approach is the view that the framers of the Constitution *were* concerned with philosophical and ethical principles. Indeed, the framers sought to devise a system of government consistent with the dominant philosophical and moral principles of the day. But, in fact, these two views belong together; the Founders' interests were reinforced by their principles. The convention that drafted the American Constitution was chiefly organized by the New England merchants and southern planters. Although the delegates representing these groups did not all hope to profit personally from an increase in the value of their securities, as Beard

> **In what ways is the United States Constitution a marriage of interest and principle?**

would have it, they did hope to benefit in the broadest political and economic sense by breaking the power of their radical foes and establishing a system of government more compatible with their long-term economic and political interests. Thus, the framers sought to create a new government capable of promoting commerce and protecting property from radical state legislatures. At the same time, they hoped to fashion a government less susceptible than the existing state and national regimes to populist forces hostile to the interests of the commercial and propertied classes.

> **How did the framers of the Constitution reconcile their competing interests and principles?**

The Great Compromise The proponents of a new government fired their opening shot on May 29, 1787, when Edmund Randolph of Virginia offered a resolution that proposed corrections and enlargements in the Articles of Confederation. The proposal, which showed the strong influence of James Madison, was not a simple motion. It provided for virtually every aspect of a new government. Randolph later admitted it was intended to be an alternative draft constitution, and it did in fact serve as the framework for what ultimately became the Constitution. (There is no verbatim record of the debates, but Madison was present during virtually all of the deliberations and kept full notes on them.)[10]

The portion of Randolph's motion that became most controversial was called the **Virginia Plan.** This plan provided for a system of representation in the national legislature based upon the population of each state or the proportion of each state's revenue contribution to the national government, or both. (Randolph also proposed a second branch of the legislature, but it was to be elected by the members of the first branch.) Since the states varied enormously in size and wealth, the Virginia Plan was thought to be heavily biased in favor of the large states.

Virginia Plan a framework for the Constitution, introduced by Edmund Randolph, which called for representation in the national legislature based upon the population of each state

A stronger national government would have to overcome deep divisions between the states and their interests. "The Looking Glass for 1787" showcases Connecticut's debate about the newly drafted Constitution. In the cartoon, Federalists stand for trade and commerce. Antifederalists say "Tax Luxary" [sic] and "Success to Shays"— showing the cartoonist's Federalist leaning while implying that Antifederalists were troublemakers.

While the convention was debating the Virginia Plan, additional delegates were arriving in Philadelphia and were beginning to mount opposition to it. Their resolution, introduced by William Paterson of New Jersey and known as the **New Jersey Plan,** did not oppose the Virginia Plan point for point. Instead, it concentrated on specific weaknesses in the Articles of Confederation, in the spirit of revision rather than radical replacement of that document. Supporters of the New Jersey Plan did not seriously question the convention's commitment to replacing the Articles. But their opposition to the Virginia Plan's scheme of representation was sufficient to send its proposals back to committee for reworking into a common document. In particular, delegates from the less-populous states, which included Delaware, New Jersey, Connecticut, and New York, asserted that the more populous states, such as Virginia, Pennsylvania, North Carolina, Massachusetts, and Georgia, would dominate the new government if representation were determined by population. The smaller states argued that each state should be equally represented in the new regime regardless of that state's population.

New Jersey Plan a framework for the Constitution, introduced by William Paterson, which called for equal state representation in the national legislature regardless of population

The issue of representation was one that threatened to wreck the entire constitutional enterprise. Delegates conferred, factions maneuvered, and tempers flared. James Wilson of Pennsylvania told the small-state delegates that if they wanted to disrupt the union they should go ahead. The separation could, he said, "never happen on better grounds." Small-state delegates were equally blunt. Gunning Bedford of Delaware declared that the small states might look elsewhere for friends if they were forced. "The large states," he said, "dare not dissolve the confederation. If they do the small ones will find some foreign ally of more honor and good faith, who will take them by the hand and do them justice." These sentiments were widely shared. The union, as Oliver Ellsworth of Connecticut put it, was "on the verge of dissolution, scarcely held together by the strength of a hair."

Great Compromise the agreement reached at the Constitutional Convention of 1787 that gave each state an equal number of senators regardless of its population, but linked representation in the House of Representatives to population

The outcome of this debate was the Connecticut Compromise, also known as the **Great Compromise.** Under the terms of this compromise, in the first branch of Congress—the House of Representatives—the representatives would be apportioned according to the number of inhabitants in each state. This, of course, was what delegates from the large states had sought. But in the second branch—the Senate—each state would have an equal vote regardless of its size; this provision addressed the concerns of the small states. This compromise was not immediately satisfactory to all the delegates. Indeed, two of the most vocal members of the small-state faction, John Lansing and Robert Yates of New York, were so incensed by the concession that their colleagues had made to the large-state forces that they stormed out of the convention. In the end, however, both sets of forces preferred compromise to the breakup of the Union, and the plan was accepted.

Although there was much acrimonious debate and necessary compromise as the new Constitution was written, this print suggests that farmers, artisans, and gentlemen alike supported it after its ratification. Liberty is enshrined above the crowd, and the Constitution seems to have been accepted by all.

The Question of Slavery: The Three-Fifths Compromise

The story so far is too neat, too easy, and too anticlimactic. If it were left here, it would only contribute to American

bicameral having a legislative assembly composed of two chambers or houses

mythology. After all, the notion of a **bicameral** (two-chambered) legislature was very much in the air in 1787. Some of the states had had bicameral legislatures for years. The Philadelphia delegates might well have gone straight to the adoption of two chambers based on two different principles of representation even without the dramatic interplay of conflict and compromise. But a far more fundamental issue had to be confronted before the Great Compromise could take place: the issue of slavery.

Many of the conflicts that emerged during the Constitutional Convention were reflections of the fundamental differences between the slave and the nonslave states—differences that pitted the southern planters and New England merchants against one another. This was the first premonition of a conflict that would almost destroy the Republic in later years. In the midst of debate over large versus small states, Madison observed,

> The great danger to our general government is the great southern and northern interests of the continent, being opposed to each other. Look to the votes in Congress, and most of them stand divided by the geography of the country, not according to the size of the states.[11]

More than 90 percent of the country's slaves resided in five states—Georgia, Maryland, North Carolina, South Carolina, and Virginia—where they accounted for 30 percent of the total population. In some places, slaves outnumbered nonslaves by as much as ten to one. If the Constitution were to embody any principle of national supremacy, some basic decisions would have to be made about the place of slavery in the general scheme. Madison hit on this point on several occasions as different aspects of the Constitution were being discussed. For example, he observed,

> It seemed now to be pretty well understood that the real difference of interests lay, not between the large and small but between the northern and southern states. The institution of slavery and its consequences formed the line of discrimination. There were five states on the South, eight on the northern side of this line. Should a proportional representation take place it was true, the northern side would still outnumber the other: but not in the same degree, at this time; and every day would tend towards an equilibrium.[12]

Three-fifths Compromise the agreement reached at the Constitutional Convention of 1787 that stipulated that for purposes of the apportionment of congressional seats, every slave would be counted as three-fifths of a person

Northerners and southerners eventually reached agreement through the **Three-fifths Compromise.** The seats in the House of Representatives would be apportioned according to a "population" in which five slaves would count as three free persons. The slaves would not be allowed to vote, of course, but the number of representatives would be apportioned accordingly.

The issue of slavery was the most difficult one faced by the framers, and it nearly destroyed the Union. Although some delegates believed slavery to be morally wrong, an evil and oppressive institution that made a mockery of the ideals and values espoused in the Constitution, morality was not the issue that caused the framers to support or oppose the Three-fifths Compromise. Whatever they thought of the institution of slavery, most delegates from the northern states opposed counting slaves in the distribution of congressional seats. Wilson of Pennsylvania, for example, argued that if slaves were citizens they should be treated and counted like other citizens. If, on the other hand, they were property, then why should not other forms of property be counted toward the apportionment of representatives? But southern

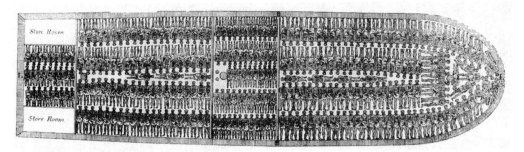

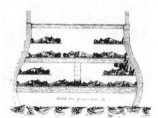 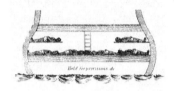

Despite its Enlightenment language, the new Constitution supported slavery. The Three-fifths Compromise made a concession to the slaveholding South by counting each slave as three-fifths of a person in apportioning seats in the House of Representatives. The Constitution explicitly prevented Congress from banning the slave trade until 1808. These cross-sectional views of a slave ship show the inhuman conditions that African slaves endured on the passage to America.

delegates made it clear that if the northerners refused to give in, they would never agree to the new government. William R. Davie of North Carolina heatedly said that it was time "to speak out." He asserted that the people of North Carolina would never enter the Union if slaves were not counted as part of the basis for representation. Without such agreement, he asserted ominously, "the business was at an end." Even southerners like Edmund Randolph of Virginia, who conceded that slavery was immoral, insisted upon including slaves in the allocation of congressional seats. This conflict between the southern and northern delegates was so divisive that many came to question the possibility of creating and maintaining a union of the two. Pierce Butler of South Carolina declared that the North and South were as different as Russia and Turkey. Eventually, the North and South compromised on the issue of slavery and representation. Indeed, northerners even agreed to permit a continuation of the odious slave trade to keep the South in the union. But, in due course, Butler proved to be correct, and a bloody war was fought when the disparate interests of the North and the South could no longer be reconciled.

The Constitution

The political significance of the Great Compromise and the Three-fifths Compromise was to reinforce the unity of the mercantile and planter forces that sought to create a new government. The Great Compromise reassured those who feared that the importance of their own local or regional influence would be reduced by the new governmental framework. The Three-fifths Compromise temporarily defused the rivalry between the merchants and planters. Their unity secured, members of the alliance supporting the establishment of a new government moved to fashion a constitutional framework consistent with their economic and political interests.

> **What principles does the Constitution embody?**

checks and balances mechanisms through which each branch of government is able to participate in and influence the activities of the other branches. Major examples include the presidential veto power over congressional legislation, the power of the Senate to approve presidential appointments, and judicial review of congressional enactments

electoral college the presidential electors from each state who meet after the popular election to cast ballots for president and vice president

Bill of Rights the first ten amendments to the U.S. Constitution, ratified in 1791; they ensure certain rights and liberties to the people

separation of powers the division of governmental power among several institutions that must cooperate in decision making

federalism a system of government in which power is divided, by a constitution, between a central government and regional governments

> ➤ **What were the intents of the framers of the Constitution regarding the legislative, executive, and judicial branches?**

In particular, the framers sought a new government that, first, would be strong enough to promote commerce and protect property from radical state legislatures such as Rhode Island's. This became the constitutional basis for national control over commerce and finance, as well as for the establishment of national judicial supremacy and the effort to construct a strong presidency. Second, the framers sought to prevent what they saw as the threat posed by the "excessive democracy" of the state and national governments under the Articles of Confederation. This led to such constitutional principles as bicameralism (division of the Congress into two chambers), **checks and balances,** staggered terms in office, and indirect election (selection of the president by an **electoral college** rather than by voters directly). Third, the framers, lacking the power to force the states or the public at large to accept the new form of government, sought to identify principles that would help to secure support. This became the basis of the constitutional provision for direct popular election of representatives and, subsequently, for the addition of the **Bill of Rights** to the Constitution. Finally, the framers wanted to be certain that the government they created did not pose even more of a threat to its citizens' liberties and property rights than did the radical state legislatures they feared and despised. To prevent the new government from abusing its power, the framers incorporated principles such as the **separation of powers** and **federalism** into the Constitution. Let us assess the major provisions of the Constitution's seven articles (listed in Box 2.1) to see how each relates to these objectives.

THE LEGISLATIVE BRANCH

The Constitution provided in Article I, Sections 1–7, for a Congress consisting of two chambers—a House of Representatives and a Senate. Members of the House of Representatives were given two-year terms in office and were to be elected directly by the people. Members of the Senate were to be appointed by the state legislatures (this was changed in 1913 by the Seventeenth Amendment, which instituted direct election of senators) for six-year terms. These terms were staggered so that the appointments of one-third of the senators would expire every two years. The Constitution assigned somewhat different tasks to the House and Senate. Though the approval of each body was required for the enactment of a law, the Senate alone was given the power to ratify treaties and approve presidential appointments. The House, on the other hand, was given the sole power to originate revenue bills.

The character of the legislative branch was directly related to the framers' major goals. The House of Representatives was designed to be directly responsible to the people in order to encourage popular consent for the new Constitution and to help enhance the power of the new government. At the same time, to guard against "excessive democracy," the power of the House of Representatives was checked by the Senate, whose members were to be appointed by the states for long terms rather than be elected directly by the people. The purpose of this provision, according to Alexander Hamilton, was to avoid "an unqualified complaisance to every sudden breeze of passion, or to every transient impulse which the people may receive."[13] Staggered terms of service in the Senate, moreover, were intended to make that body even more resistant to popular pressure. Since only one-third of the senators would be selected at any given time, the composition of the institution would be protected from changes in popular preferences transmitted by the state legislatures. This would prevent what James Madison called "mutability in the public councils arising from a rapid succession of new members."[14] Thus, the structure of the legislative branch was designed to contribute to governmental power, to promote popular consent for the new government, and at the same time to place limits on the popular political currents that many of the framers saw as a radical threat to the economic and social order.

The issues of power and consent were important throughout the Constitution. Section 8 of Article I specifically listed the powers of Congress, which include the authority to collect taxes, to borrow money, to regulate commerce, to declare war, and to maintain an army and navy. By granting Congress these powers, the framers indicated very clearly that they intended the new government to be far more influential than its predecessor. At the same time, by defining the new government's most important powers as belonging to Congress, the framers sought to promote popular acceptance of this critical change by reassuring citizens that their views would be fully represented whenever the government exercised its new powers.

As a further guarantee to the people that the new government would pose no threat to them, the Constitution implied that any powers not listed were not granted at all. This is the doctrine of **expressed power.** The Constitution grants only those powers specifically expressed in its text. But the framers intended to create an active and powerful government, and so they included the **elastic clause,** sometimes known as the necessary and proper clause, which signified that the enumerated powers were meant to be a source of strength to the national government, not a limitation on it. Each power could be used with the utmost vigor, but no new powers could be seized upon by the national government without a constitutional amendment. In the absence of such an amendment, any power not enumerated was conceived to be "reserved" to the states (or the people).

expressed powers specific powers granted to Congress under Article I, Section 8, of the Constitution

elastic clause Article I, Section 8, of the Constitution (also known as the "necessary and proper" clause), which enumerates the powers of Congress and provides Congress with the authority to make all laws "necessary and proper" to carry them out

THE EXECUTIVE BRANCH

The Constitution provided for the establishment of the presidency in Article II. As Alexander Hamilton commented, the presidential article aimed toward "energy in the Executive." It did so in an effort to overcome the natural tendency toward stalemate that was built into the bicameral legislature as well as into the separation of powers among the three branches. The Constitution afforded the president a measure of independence from the people and from the other branches of government—particularly the Congress.

In line with the framers' goal of increased power to the national government, the president was granted the unconditional power to accept ambassadors from other countries; this amounted to the power to "recognize" other countries. The president was also given the power to negotiate treaties, although their acceptance required the approval of the Senate. The president was given the unconditional right to grant reprieves and pardons, except in cases of impeachment. And the president was provided with the power to appoint major departmental personnel, to convene Congress in special session, and to veto congressional enactments. (The veto power is formidable, but it is not absolute, since Congress can override it by a two-thirds vote.)

The framers hoped to create a presidency that would make the federal government rather than the states the agency capable of timely and decisive action to

What Government Does . . . After September 11

The Constitution makes few explicit provisions dealing with national emergencies. It allows Congress to declare war and suspend the writ of *habeas corpus;* it recognizes the president as commander in chief of the armed forces. Although the Supreme Court has emphasized that the Constitution "covers . . . all classes of men, at all times, and under all circumstances,"[1] several decisions of the Court have permitted the exercise of emergency powers and wartime suppression of civil liberties. This leads some to argue that, when the union is threatened, the constitutional priorities of political institutions change to favor the needs of national security.

After September 11, the Bush administration undertook several actions with profound constitutional implications. Among these were the proposal of military tribunals, an increase in surveillance and detention authority, and the establishment of the Office of Homeland Security.

Military Tribunals

Two months after the attacks, President Bush issued an executive order allowing the use of military tribunals.[2] Citing his authority as commander in chief, the order allowed the president to use military tribunals to try individuals who had engaged in terrorism or knowingly aided terrorists.

Several months of legal debate followed Bush's proposal. The administration emphasized the need for the military venue and procedures to allow quick, effective, and secure trials.[3] Supporters looked to a World War II case that permitted, as an extension of the commander in chief's powers endorsed by congressional legislation, the creation of a military commission to try German saboteurs.[4] Critics argued that Bush's order lacked congressional support and also compromised constitutional due-process guarantees by eliminating judicial review of tribunal verdicts, establishing a lesser standard of evidence, and not providing for juries. In March 2002, the Pentagon issued rules for the tribunals that answered some of these concerns.[5]

Surveillance and Detention

Having information about terrorist connections and plans is crucial in combating terrorism. Attorney General John Ashcroft approved a Justice Department rule to allow federal agents to monitor some meetings between federal inmates and their lawyers, if he determined that the inmates might use these conversations to communicate information about terrorism. Traditionally, attorney-client conversations are confidential. The USA PATRIOT Act gave the government more latitude to conduct searches and to detain uncharged suspects longer than normally allowed, authority many critics argued challenges the right to counsel and to be free from unreasonable searches and seizures.[6]

Executive Privilege

The creation of the Office of Homeland Security triggered few constitutional problems, because Congress and the president enjoy broad discretion to delegate legislative and executive functions to administrative agencies. The reluctance of Homeland Security Director Tom Ridge to testify before congressional committees regarding appropriations requests, however, raised concerns about accountability and the use of executive privilege. The White House argued that the homeland security director is a presidential adviser, protected by executive privilege.[7] Since George Washington, presidents have asserted executive privilege as the basis for withholding information, citing both national security concerns and the need to receive candid advice from advisers. Although the Court has acknowledged the validity of the principle, the use of executive privilege is limited by the functional claims of other branches and the ability of those branches to use checks such as the budgeting and confirmation processes as means of encouraging presidential disclosure.

---

[1] *Ex Parte Milligan,* 71 U.S. 2 (1866).

[2] "Military Order of November 13, 2001: Detention, Treatment and Trial of Certain Non-Citizens in the War against Terrorism," 66 Federal Register 57833, November 14, 2001.

[3] Alberto Gonzales, "Martial Justice, Full and Fair," *New York Times,* November 30, 2001, p. A27.

[4] *Ex Parte Quirin,* 317 U.S. 1 (1942).

[5] Katherine Q. Seelye, "Government Sets Rules for Military on War Tribunals," *New York Times,* March 21, 2002, p. A1; William Safire, "Military Trials Modified," *New York Times,* March 21, 2002, p. A33.

[6] George Lardner, Jr., "US Will Monitor Calls to Lawyers," *Washington Post,* November 9, 2001, p. A1.

[7] Allison Mitchell, "Letter to Ridge Is Latest Jab in Fight over Balance of Powers," *New York Times,* March 5, 2002, p. A8.

deal with public issues and problems. This was the meaning of the "energy" that Hamilton hoped to impart to the executive branch.[15] At the same time, however, the framers sought to help the president withstand excessively democratic pressures by creating a system of indirect rather than direct election through a separate electoral college.

THE JUDICIAL BRANCH

In establishing the judicial branch in Article III, the Constitution reflected the framers' preoccupations with nationalizing governmental power and checking radical democratic impulses while guarding against potential interference with liberty and property from the new national government itself.

Under the provisions of Article III, the framers created a court that was to be literally a supreme court of the United States, and not merely the highest court of the national government. The most important expression of this intention was granting the Supreme Court the power to resolve any conflicts that might emerge between federal and state laws. In particular, the Supreme Court was given the right to determine whether a power was exclusive to the national government, concurrent with the states, or exclusive to the states. In addition, the Supreme Court was assigned jurisdiction over controversies between citizens of different states. The long-term significance of this provision was that as the country developed a national economy, it came to rely increasingly on the federal judiciary, rather than on the state courts, for the resolution of disputes.

Judges were given lifetime appointments in order to protect them from popular politics and from interference by the other branches. This, however, did not mean that the judiciary would remain totally impartial to political considerations or to the other branches, for the president was to appoint the judges, and the Senate to approve the appointments. Congress would also have the power to create inferior (lower) courts, to change the jurisdiction of the federal courts, to add or subtract federal judges, and even to change the size of the Supreme Court.

No direct mention is made in the Constitution of **judicial review**—the power of the courts to render the final decision when there is a conflict of interpretation of the Constitution or of laws between the courts and Congress, the courts and the executive branch, or the courts and the states. The Supreme Court eventually assumed the power of judicial review. Its assumption of this power, as we shall see in Chapter 15, was based not on the Constitution itself but on the politics of later decades and the membership of the Court.

judicial review the power of the courts to declare actions of the legislative and executive branches invalid or unconstitutional. The Supreme Court asserted this power in *Marbury v. Madison*

NATIONAL UNITY AND POWER

Various provisions in the Constitution addressed the framers' concern with national unity and power, including Article IV's provisions for comity (reciprocity) among states and among citizens of all states. Each state was prohibited from discriminating against the citizens of other states in favor of its own citizens, with the Supreme Court charged with deciding in each case whether a state had discriminated against goods or people from another state. The Constitution restricted the power of the states in favor of ensuring enough power to the national government to give the country a free-flowing national economy.

Box 2.1   The Seven Articles of the Constitution

1. The Legislative Branch

House: two-year terms, elected directly by the people.

Senate: six-year terms (staggered so that only one-third of the Senate changes in any given election), appointed by state legislature (changed in 1913 to direct election).

Expressed powers of the national government: collecting taxes, borrowing money, regulating commerce, declaring war, and maintaining an army and a navy; all other power belongs to the states, unless deemed otherwise by the elastic ("necessary and proper") clause.

Exclusive powers of the national government: states are expressly forbidden to issue their own paper money, tax imports and exports, regulate trade outside their own borders, and impair the obligation of contracts; these powers are the exclusive domain of the national government.

2. The Executive Branch

Presidency: four-year terms (limited in 1951 to a maximum of two terms), elected indirectly by the electoral college.

Powers: can recognize other countries, negotiate treaties, grant reprieves and pardons, convene Congress in special sessions, and veto congressional enactment.

3. The Judicial Branch

Supreme Court: lifetime terms, appointed by the president with the approval of the Senate.

Powers: include resolving conflicts between federal and state laws, determining whether power belongs to the national government or the states, and settling controversies between citizens of different states.

4. National Unity and Power

Reciprocity among states: establishes that each state must give "full faith and credit" to official acts of other states, and guarantees citizens of any state the "privileges and immunities" of every other state.

5. Amending the Constitution

Procedure: requires approval by two-thirds of Congress and adoption by three-fourths of the states.

6. National Supremacy

The Constitution and national law are the supreme law of the land and cannot be overruled by state law.

7. Ratification

The Constitution became effective when approved by nine states.

---

supremacy clause Article VI of the Constitution, which states that laws passed by the national government and all treaties are the supreme law of the land and superior to all laws adopted by any state or any subdivision

The framers' concern with national supremacy was also expressed in Article VI, in the **supremacy clause,** which provided that national laws and treaties "shall be the supreme Law of the Land." This meant that all laws made under the "Authority of the United States" would be superior to all laws adopted by any state or any other subdivision, and the states would be expected to respect all treaties made under that authority. The supremacy clause also bound the officials of all state and local as well as federal governments to take an oath of office to support the national Constitution. This meant that every action taken by the United States Congress would have to be applied within each state as though the action were in fact state law.

AMENDING THE CONSTITUTION

The Constitution established procedures for its own revision in Article V. Its provisions are so difficult that Americans have availed themselves of the amending process only seventeen times since 1791, when the first ten amendments were adopted. Many other amendments have been proposed in Congress, but fewer than forty of them have even come close to fulfilling the Constitution's requirement of a two-thirds vote in Congress, and only a fraction have gotten anywhere near adoption by three-fourths of the states. Article V also provides that the Constitution can be amended by a constitutional convention. Occasionally, proponents of particular measures, such as a balanced-budget amendment, have called for a constitutional convention to consider their proposals. Whatever the purpose for which it were called, however, such a convention would presumably have the authority to revise America's entire system of government.

RATIFYING THE CONSTITUTION

The rules for the ratification of the Constitution were set forth in Article VII. Nine of the thirteen states would have to ratify, or agree upon, the terms in order for the Constitution to pass.

CONSTITUTIONAL LIMITS ON THE NATIONAL GOVERNMENT'S POWER

As we have indicated, although the framers sought to create a powerful national government, they also wanted to guard against possible misuse of that power. To that end, the framers incorporated two key principles into the Constitution—the separation of powers and federalism. A third set of limitations, in the form of the Bill of Rights, was added to the Constitution to help secure its ratification when opponents of the document charged that it paid insufficient attention to citizens' rights.

> ➤ **What limits on the national government's power are embodied in the Constitution?**

The Separation of Powers   No principle of politics was more widely shared at the time of the 1787 founding than the principle that power must be used to balance power. The French political theorist Baron de la Brède et de Montesquieu (1689–1755) believed that this balance was an indispensable defense against tyranny, and his writings, especially his major work, *The Spirit of the Laws,* "were taken as political gospel" at the Philadelphia Convention.[16] The principle of the separation of powers is not stated explicitly in the Constitution, but it is clearly built on Articles I, II, and III, which provide for the following:

1. Three separate and distinct branches of government (see Figure 2.1);
2. Different methods of selecting the top personnel, so that each branch is responsible to a different constituency. This is supposed to produce a "mixed regime," in which the personnel of each department will develop very different

Figure 2.1   The Separation of Powers

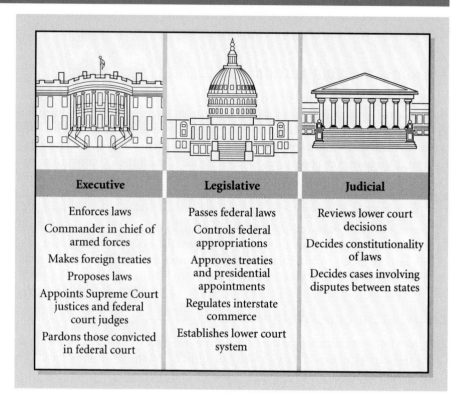

Executive	Legislative	Judicial
Enforces laws	Passes federal laws	Reviews lower court decisions
Commander in chief of armed forces	Controls federal appropriations	Decides constitutionality of laws
Makes foreign treaties	Approves treaties and presidential appointments	Decides cases involving disputes between states
Proposes laws	Regulates interstate commerce	
Appoints Supreme Court justices and federal court judges	Establishes lower court system	
Pardons those convicted in federal court		

interests and outlooks on how to govern, and different groups in society will be assured some access to governmental decision making; and

3. Checks and balances—a system under which each of the branches is given some power over the others. Familiar examples are the presidential veto power over legislation, the power of the Senate to approve presidential appointments, and judicial review of acts of Congress (see Figure 2.2).

One clever formulation of the separation of powers is that of a system not of separated powers but of "separated institutions sharing power,"[17] and thus diminishing the chance that power will be misused.

Federalism   Compared to the confederation principle of the Articles of Confederation, federalism was a step toward greater centralization of power. The delegates agreed that they needed to place more power at the national level, without completely undermining the power of the state governments. Thus, they devised a system of two sovereigns—the states and the nation—with the hope that competition between the two would be an effective limitation on the power of both.

The Bill of Rights   Late in the Philadelphia Convention, a motion was made to include a list of citizens' rights in the Constitution. After a brief debate in which hardly

Checks and Balances

Figure 2.2

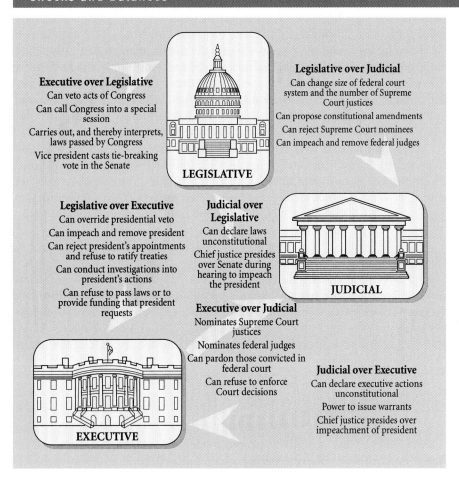

Executive over Legislative
Can veto acts of Congress
Can call Congress into a special session
Carries out, and thereby interprets, laws passed by Congress
Vice president casts tie-breaking vote in the Senate

LEGISLATIVE

Legislative over Judicial
Can change size of federal court system and the number of Supreme Court justices
Can propose constitutional amendments
Can reject Supreme Court nominees
Can impeach and remove federal judges

Legislative over Executive
Can override presidential veto
Can impeach and remove president
Can reject president's appointments and refuse to ratify treaties
Can conduct investigations into president's actions
Can refuse to pass laws or to provide funding that president requests

Judicial over Legislative
Can declare laws unconstitutional
Chief justice presides over Senate during hearing to impeach the president

JUDICIAL

Executive over Judicial
Nominates Supreme Court justices
Nominates federal judges
Can pardon those convicted in federal court
Can refuse to enforce Court decisions

Judicial over Executive
Can declare executive actions unconstitutional
Power to issue warrants
Chief justice presides over impeachment of president

EXECUTIVE

a word was said in its favor and only one speech was made against it, the motion was almost unanimously turned down. Most delegates sincerely believed that since the federal government was already limited to its expressed powers, further protection of citizens was not needed. The delegates argued that the states should adopt bills of rights because their greater powers needed greater limitations. But almost immediately after the Constitution was ratified, there was a movement to adopt a national bill of rights. This is why the Bill of Rights, adopted in 1791, comprises the first ten amendments to the Constitution rather than being part of the body of it. We will have a good deal more to say about the Bill of Rights in Chapter 4.

The Fight for Ratification

The first hurdle faced by the Constitution was ratification by state conventions of delegates elected by the people of each state. This struggle for ratification was carried out in thirteen separate campaigns. Each involved different people, moved at a

> **What sides did the Federalists and the Antifederalists represent in the fight over ratification?**

Federalists those who favored a strong national government and supported the constitution proposed at the American Constitutional Convention of 1787

Antifederalists those who favored strong state governments and a weak national government and who were opponents of the constitution proposed at the American Constitutional Convention of 1787

different pace, and was influenced by local as well as national considerations. Two sides faced off throughout the states, however, calling themselves Federalists and Antifederalists (see Table 2.1). The **Federalists** (who more accurately should have called themselves "Nationalists," but who took their name to appear to follow in the revolutionary tradition) supported the Constitution and preferred a strong national government. The **Antifederalists** opposed the Constitution and preferred a federal system of government that was decentralized; they took their name by default, in reaction to their better-organized opponents. The Federalists were united in their support of the Constitution, while the Antifederalists were divided over what they believed the alternative to the Constitution should be.

During the struggle over ratification of the Constitution, Americans argued about great political issues and principles. How much power should the national government be given? What safeguards were most likely to prevent the abuse of power? What institutional arrangements could best ensure adequate representation for all Americans? Was tyranny to be feared more from the many or from the few?

FEDERALISTS VS. ANTIFEDERALISTS

During the ratification struggle, thousands of essays, speeches, pamphlets, and letters were presented in support of and in opposition to the proposed Constitution. The best-known pieces supporting ratification of the Constitution were the eighty-five essays written, under the name of "Publius," by Alexander Hamilton, James Madison, and John Jay between the fall of 1787 and the spring of 1788. These

Table 2.1	Federalists vs. Antifederalists	
	FEDERALISTS	**ANTIFEDERALISTS**
Who were they?	Property owners, creditors, merchants	Small farmers, frontiersmen, debtors, shopkeepers
What did they believe?	Believed that elites were best fit to govern; feared "excessive democracy"	Believed that government should be closer to the people; feared concentration of power in hands of the elites
What system of government did they favor?	Favored strong national government; believed in "filtration" so that only elites would obtain governmental power	Favored retention of power by state governments and protection of individual rights
Who were their leaders?	Alexander Hamilton James Madison George Washington	Patrick Henry George Mason Elbridge Gerry George Clinton

Religious Freedom and School Prayer

The first two rights enshrined in the First Amendment bar the government from establishing a state religion and from inhibiting the free exercise of religion by individuals. Thus, the government is barred from breaching the "wall of separation" between church and state, so that religious liberty may find full expression. Yet is that wall breached if individuals wish to express their religious beliefs in schools? At first glance, the answer would appear to be yes. In the 1962 case of *Engel v. Vitale*, the Supreme Court barred government-organized and -led religious prayer. Since then, proponents of prayer in school have marshaled much support for a more flexible approach, arguing in part that courts have misunderstood the framers' intent. Proponents have also pushed for a constitutional amendment guaranteeing free religious expression in public schools.

Proponents of prayer in school argue that the Constitution's framers were pious men who were not out to drive religion from schools or other aspects of public life. Thomas Jefferson, for example, who wrote of maintaining a "wall of separation" between church and state, also wrote of the importance of religious training as an integral part of education. Every congress since the Founding has opened its daily session with a prayer. Supreme Court sessions begin with the words "God save the United States and this Honorable Court." Schoolchildren have prayed in public schools for most of the country's history. By now shunning any form of religious expression at a time when children seem increasingly in need of moral and spiritual guidance, schools are sending the wrong message to the nation's children. Moreover, the absence of school religion implicitly encourages another belief system—secularism. The elimination of all religious teachings elevates a secular ideology that, in the minds of many, amounts to little more than state-sponsored atheism. Thus, some argue, schools that ignore or deny the existence of God and religion are promoting another belief—that there is no God.

School prayer need not be led by teachers or administrators, nor need it be required. Voluntary prayer led by students would pose no threat to the First Amendment. Instead, it would reflect the proper extension of religious liberty into schools. In short, an enlightened approach to school prayer requires neither a government stamp of approval nor any form of coercion.

Opponents of school prayer argue that both the First Amendment and American respect for individual freedom require that schools avoid any role in religious teaching, instruction, or prayer. They point out the important fact that prayer is not barred from any school, as any student may pray at any time. It is organized prayer, they assert, that must be avoided. Government meddling in religion drove many European settlers to America, and the Founders understood that keeping government out of religious matters was not an expression of hostility to religion, but a simple acknowledgment that both government and religion were better off if the former let the latter alone.

Although most Americans hold some form of religious belief, the range of those beliefs is wide and growing, meaning that any form of religious teaching or prayer is bound to offend the sensibilities of some religious groups. Moreover, the rights of nonbelievers are equal to those of believers. School actions that ostracize, penalize, or stigmatize nonbelievers violate their right to equal treatment and their right not to be subjected to religious teachings in what is a public and secular institution.

The desire to teach moral values in schools is not limited to, or by, religion. Moral and ethical training does not require the infusion of religion. Moral problems related to drugs and sex, for example, already receive considerable attention in public school curricula. Finally, the teaching of religious beliefs is best left to professionals—churches and their clergy—and to families.

Should School Prayer Be Allowed?

Yes

Benjamin Franklin stated, "Freedom is not a gift bestowed upon us by other men, but a right that belongs to us by the laws of God and nature."

Recently, there have been quite a few letters and opinion pieces speaking to the issue of prayer in public schools, the First Amendment, and separation of church and state. What many fail to understand is the perspective of the founding fathers of our great nation.

What would those men think of these atheists and humanists who rail against the "religious right" and prayer in school as a violation of the separation of church and state and the First Amendment?

Certainly the founding fathers have taken quite a bit of heat in the recent past. They have been accused of being racist and bigoted slave-owning white men who cared about nothing but keeping their own property.

I bring this up because a rare few do not believe it matters what these leaders of the revolution had to think at all. I encourage those few to stop reading here, find a good history book, and educate themselves on the creation of our nation.

To those of you interested in the perspective of those respected and wise leaders of the revolution, please continue.

The founding fathers all believed in God, in one form or another. There is no disputing that. While some, such as Jefferson, had some qualms with corruption in various churches, they all believed in one God. Most would describe themselves as Christian, and all believed "that all Men are created equal, that they are endowed by their Creator with certain unalienable Rights. . . ."

As any of the founding fathers would have told you, mere governments do not grant us our human rights. Our rights are derived from the laws of nature and from nature's God. God is the foundation for liberty. Without a fundamental belief in God, government would then be the source of our rights. As the founders understood, that would be a precarious situation. As many public-funded charities understand, anything granted by the government can be taken away by the government.

Government is instituted to secure the rights people are given by their Creator, not to disperse them. This idea comes directly from the Declaration of Independence. To deny it is to deny the very basis of the Bill of Rights and the sanctity of the Constitution.

Thomas Jefferson put it well: "God who gave us life gave us liberty. And can the liberties of a nation be thought secure when we have removed their only firm basis, a conviction in the minds of the people that these liberties are the Gift of God?

Or as the fiery Patrick Henry warned, "It is when people forget God that tyrants forge their chains."

The founders believed religion was not only the foundation of a good government, but also the foundation for a good society. In the times of the revolution, a good education included a firm knowledge of the Bible. Many universities required incoming students to be well acquainted with the Bible.

Society had a vested interest in promoting a good moral code, and the founders knew the Bible was the best and most pure moral code to live by. Gouverneur Morris, member of the Constitutional Convention and a drafter of the Constitution, pointed out, "Religion is the only solid basis of good morals; therefore education should teach the precepts of religion, and the duties of man toward God.

Clearly, religion was never intended to be precluded from education by the Constitution. The First Amendment was constructed to prevent the federal government from instituting a state religion and mandating all citizens adhere to it, as had happened in England with the Church of England and the Catholic Church.

For most of the history of the United States, the courts agreed with the founding fathers. In *Holy Trinity Church v. United States,* the Supreme Court ruled the United States was a Christian nation. The United States' first Supreme Court chief justice and co-author of the Federalist Papers, John Jay, stated it was in "the duty, as well as the privilege and interest of our Christian nation to select and prefer Christians for their rulers."

If we were to believe, as some do, that separation of church and state was absolute, then we would have to rule that the Bill of Rights (including the First Amendment) and the Declaration of Independence are unconstitutional, since they derive so much from religion and God.

Should we then declare the founding of our country as unconstitutional? Should we dissolve our nation because of its wicked God-fearing origins? The idea is simply ridiculous.

As Ronald Reagan said, there are no easy answers, but there are simple answers. In the case of prayer in public schools, there is a simple answer that might not be easy. Leave the decision about whether to pray in school or not up to the parents and community.

The federal government has no constitutional role in education at all, and prayer should be no different. The Supreme Court should rule prayer constitutional again and bring the issue back to the good and decent people of America to decide whether they want their kids taught religion and whether they want prayer in the classroom.

That is what the founding fathers would have wanted.

SOURCE: Dan Nelson, "Precluding Prayer Disrespects Forefathers," *The Minnesota Daily*, May 7, 2002.

No

The First Amendment of the United States Constitution clearly states that a religion may not be established by the government under any circumstances. Our founding fathers were sensible enough to realize that the establishment of a national religion would have a detrimental effect on our nation's fledgling democracy. With this in mind, the American Civil Liberties Union filed suit on behalf of two cadets from the Virginia Military Institute in May 2001. The suit argued that the prayer recited before each dinner at the academy was a violation of the establishment clause of the First Amendment. Cadets were required to attend the prayer, which included God's name in it.

Thankfully, last Thursday a federal court judge in Lynchburg was sensible enough to recognize that this prayer was indeed a violation of separation of church and state. U.S. District Judge Norman K. Moon wrote in his ruling that "the primary effect of this practice has been to compel students to participate in a state-sponsored religious exercise." Now, here is the statement that actually gives me the chills: Moon wrote that "the result is that government has become impermissibly entangled with religion." Religion intermixing with government? What would our founding fathers say?

Well, James Madison said that he had "no doubt that every new example will succeed, as every past one has done, in showing that religion and government will both exist in greater purity the less they are mixed together." I agree with Madison and I disagree with VMI that it is a special institution that deserves special treatment because they are grooming "citizen-soldiers." Nor is the prayer any less "non-religious" in nature because it fails to mention Jesus. The prayer is a violation of the First Amendment, plain and simple. What about the cadets who do not believe in God?

They were being forced to attend a practice that clearly violated their rights. The Supreme Court of the United States made it evident in *Engel v. Vitale* (1962) that reciting a prayer in public school, even if "denominationally neutral," was prohibited. In addition, the Supreme Court ruled in *Santa Fe Independent School District v. Doe* (2000) that official prayers before public football games are unconstitutional. Neither of these rulings prohibits students from practicing their religion, or even from praying in public. Students are guaranteed these rights by the First Amendment.

The ruling simply clarifies the First Amendment and the meaning behind the establishment clause. Church and state should remain separate from one another. Mixing the two is like mixing magnesium and water. Functioning independently of one another, each is able to demonstrate its beneficial properties. However, when the two are combined, disaster is inevitable.

SOURCE: Tina Doran, "Re-emphasizing Separation," *Broadside* (George Mason University), January 28, 2002.

Federalist Papers a series of essays written by James Madison, Alexander Hamilton, and John Jay supporting the ratification of the Constitution

Federalist Papers, as they are collectively known today, defended the principles of the Constitution and sought to dispel fears of a national authority. The Antifederalists published essays of their own, arguing that the new Constitution betrayed the Revolution and was a step toward monarchy. Among the best of the Antifederalist works were the essays, usually attributed to New York Supreme Court justice Robert Yates, that were written under the name of "Brutus" and published in the *New York Journal* at the same time the Federalist Papers appeared. The Antifederalist view was also ably presented in the pamphlets and letters written by a former delegate to the Continental Congress and future U.S. senator, Richard Henry Lee of Virginia, using the pen name "The Federal Farmer." These essays highlight the major differences of opinion between Federalists and Antifederalists. Federalists appealed to basic principles of government in support of their nationalist vision. Antifederalists cited equally fundamental precepts to support their vision of a looser confederacy of small republics.

> ➤ **Over what key principles did the Federalists and the Antifederalists disagree?**

Representation   One major area of contention between the two sides was the question of representation. The Antifederalists asserted that representatives must be "a true picture of the people, . . . [possessing] the knowledge of their circumstances and their wants."[18] This could be achieved, argued the Antifederalists, only in small, relatively homogeneous republics such as the existing states. In their view, the size and extent of the entire nation precluded the construction of a truly representative form of government. As Brutus put it, "Is it practicable for a country so large and so numerous . . . to elect a representation that will speak their sentiments? . . . It certainly is not."[19]

Federalists, for their part, saw no reason that representatives should be precisely like those they represented. In the Federalist view, one of the great advantages of representative government over direct democracy was precisely the possibility that the people would choose as their representatives individuals possessing ability, experience, and talent superior to their own. In Madison's words, rather than serve as a mirror or reflection of society, representatives must be "[those] who possess [the] most wisdom to discern, and [the] most virtue to pursue, the common good of the society."[20]

Although the terms of discussion have changed, this debate over representation continues today. Some argue that representatives must be very close in life experience, race, and ethnic background to their constituents to truly understand the needs and interests of those constituents. This argument is made by contemporary proponents of giving the states more control over social programs. This argument is also made by proponents of "minority districts"—legislative districts whose boundaries are drawn so as to guarantee that minorities will be able to elect their own representative to Congress. Opponents of this practice, which we will explore further in Chapter 10, have argued in court that it is discriminatory and unnecessary; blacks, they say, can be represented by whites and vice versa. Who is correct? It would appear that this question can never be answered to everyone's complete satisfaction.

tyranny oppressive and unjust government that employs cruel and unjust use of power and authority

Tyranny of the Majority   A second important issue dividing Federalists and Antifederalists was the threat of **tyranny**—unjust rule by the group in power. Both opponents and defenders of the Constitution frequently affirmed their fear of tyrannical rule. Each side, however, had a different view of the most likely source of tyranny and, hence, of the way in which the threat was to be forestalled.

From the Antifederalist perspective, the great danger was the tendency of all governments—including republican governments—to become gradually more and more "aristocratic" in character, wherein the small number of individuals in positions of authority would use their stations to gain more and more power over the general citizenry. In essence, the few would use their power to tyrannize the many. For this reason, Antifederalists were sharply critical of those features of the Constitution that divorced governmental institutions from direct responsibility to the people—institutions such as the Senate, the executive, and the federal judiciary. The latter, appointed for life, presented a particular threat: "I wonder if the world ever saw ... a court of justice invested with such immense powers, and yet placed in a situation so little responsible," protested Brutus.[21]

The Federalists, too, recognized the threat of tyranny, but they believed that the danger particularly associated with republican governments was not aristocracy, but instead, majority tyranny. The Federalists were concerned that a popular majority, "united and actuated by some common impulse of passion, or of interest, adversed to the rights of other citizens," would endeavor to "trample on the rules of justice."[22] From the Federalist perspective, it was precisely those features of the Constitution attacked as potential sources of tyranny by the Antifederalists that actually offered the best hope of averting the threat of oppression. The size and extent of the nation, for instance, was for the Federalists a bulwark against tyranny.

Governmental Power   A third major difference between Federalists and Antifederalists was the issue of governmental power. Both the opponents and proponents of the Constitution agreed on the principle of **limited government.** They differed, however, on the fundamentally important question of how to place limits on governmental action. Antifederalists favored limiting and enumerating the powers granted to the national government in relation both to the states and to the people at large. To them, the powers given the national government ought to be "confined to certain defined national objects."[23] Otherwise, the national government would "swallow up all the power of the state governments."[24] Antifederalists bitterly attacked the supremacy clause and the elastic clause of the Constitution as unlimited and dangerous grants of power to the national government.[25] Antifederalists also demanded that a bill of rights be added to the Constitution to place limits upon the government's exercise of power over the citizenry.

Federalists favored the construction of a government with broad powers. They wanted a government that had the capacity to defend the nation against foreign foes, guard against domestic strife and insurrection, promote commerce, and expand the nation's economy. Antifederalists shared some of these goals but still feared governmental power. Hamilton pointed out, however, that these goals could not be achieved without allowing the government to exercise the necessary power. Federalists acknowledged that every power could be abused but argued that the way to prevent misuse of power was not by depriving the government of the powers needed to achieve national goals. Instead, they argued that the threat of abuse of power would be mitigated by the Constitution's internal checks and controls. As Madison put it, "the power surrendered by the people is first divided between two distinct governments, and then the portion

limited government   a government whose powers are defined and limited by a constitution

Contrasting Approaches to Constitutional Democracy

Constitutions are, in effect, the codification of the basic rules and procedures designed to regulate and control the balance between mathematical minorities and majorities within society.

There are generally three critical characteristics of the constitutional tradition of a country (whether that constitution is formally written or not). These three characteristics provide the comparative perspective by which students of constitutional theory may evaluate the constitutional tradition within the broader political culture of a country. These three characteristics are (1) the *determination* of the actual content of the constitutional rules; (2) the *distinctiveness* of the constitution's structure; and (3) the degree to which the specific rules and codes within the constitution are *entrenched* aspects of the political culture.

Being a majoritarian democracy, the British have a constitution that is characterized by *indeterminate content, indistinct structure,* and an *unentrenched constitutional process.* With respect to content, the Queen's Stationary Office published the Official Revised Edition of the statutes in force within Britain. This consists in part of 138 acts of Parliament dating from 1297 through the present, including the Parliamentary Acts of 1911 and 1949, as well as an additional 32 statutes dealing with the "rights of the subjects," including what is left of the Magna Carta.

In contrast to the British "constitution," it is hard to miss the determining content of the American constitution. Its preamble, 7 articles, and 27 amendments are written in an explicit document. Similarly, the German constitution (commonly referred to as the Basic Laws or *Grundgesetz*) is clearly and explicitly written for strict interpretation. It consists of a preamble and 141 articles. Even the content of the French Constitution (of the current Fifth Republic, formed in October 1958) is rather explicit: it consists of the famous Declaration of the Rights of Man and the Citizen drafted in 1789, specifying the general principles of human liberties, including 17 specific Rights of Man and the Citizen; the preamble to the French Fourth Republic (1946–58); and the Fifth Republic's own preamble and 93 articles.

The British constitution is also indistinct in structure: it consists, in effect, of a miscellany of statutes of Parliament (which, in English law, consists of the monarch and two chambers of the British legislature—the House of Lords and the House of Commons), a variety of "legal conventions," and a series of special laws passed by Parliament. This contrasts with the clear and sharply defined targets found in the articles of the American, French, and German constitutions. Thus, the American Supreme Court has a distinct body of articles to evaluate in the event it examines the constitutionality of an act of Congress.

Finally, the British constitutional tradition is clearly unentrenched in the political process of government because there are no formal requirements for enacting or amending the norms of the unwritten constitution. In other words, there is no special procedure to establish British constitution principles: its enactment is, in effect, ongoing and is indistinguishable from the way any ordinary statute or law is promulgated in Parliament. The unwritten British constitution, therefore, stands vulnerable to the political will of a bare majority within the House of Commons. This contrasts sharply with the American, French, and German written constitutions, each of which specify strict rules and procedures by which the constitution may be amended. Such amendments and enactments require special voting procedures (both for ratification and amendment) as well as complicated popular referendums (in the case of the French Fifth Republic).

The American, French, and German constitutions were each drafted during difficult and trying times for their respective democracies, thus reflecting the anxieties among majorities and minorities within each society (revolution in America, attempted military coup d'état in France, and the painful memories and lessons of the Third Reich, as well as the rise of the Cold War, in Germany). Britain's constitution reflects a tradition of gradual compromise and stability achieved over several centuries, thereby nurturing public tolerance for a constitution less distinct, less structured, and less entrenched than that found in the more recent American, French, and German constitutional democracies. Constitutions, while often overlooked and ignored by many modern students of political science, are invaluable windows into the political culture and formal power structure of any democracy, consensual or majoritarian.

SOURCE: S. E. Finer, Vernon Bogdanor, and Bernard Rudden, *Comparing Constitutions* (Oxford: Clarendon Press, 1995).

allotted to each subdivided among distinct and separate departments. Hence, a double security arises to the rights of the people. The different governments will control each other, at the same time that each will be controlled by itself."[26] The Federalists' concern with avoiding unwarranted limits on governmental power led them to oppose a bill of rights, which they saw as nothing more than a set of unnecessary restrictions on the government.

The Federalists acknowledged that abuse of power remained a possibility, but felt that the risk had to be taken because of the goals to be achieved. "The very idea of power included a possibility of doing harm," said the Federalist John Rutledge during the South Carolina ratification debates. "If the gentleman would show the power that could do no harm," Rutledge continued, "he would at once discover it to be a power that could do no good."[27] This aspect of the debate between the Federalists and the Antifederalists, perhaps more than any other, continues to reverberate through American politics. Should the nation limit the federal government's power to tax and spend? Should Congress limit the capacity of federal agencies to issue new regulations? Should the government endeavor to create new rights for minorities, the disabled, and others? What is the proper balance between promoting equality and protecting liberty? Though the details have changed, these are the same great questions that have been debated since the time of the Founding.

REFLECTIONS ON THE FOUNDING

The final product of the Constitutional Convention would have to be considered an extraordinary victory for the groups that had most forcefully called for the creation of a new system of government to replace the Articles of Confederation. Antifederalist criticisms forced the Constitution's proponents to accept the addition of a bill of rights designed to limit the powers of the national government. In general, however, it was the Federalist vision of America that triumphed. The Constitution adopted in 1789 created the framework for a powerful national government that for more than two hundred years has defended the nation's interests, promoted its commerce, and maintained national unity. In one notable instance, the national government fought and won a bloody war to prevent the nation from breaking apart. And despite this powerful government, the system of internal checks and balances has functioned reasonably well, as the Federalists predicted, to prevent the national government from tyrannizing its citizens.

Of course, the groups whose interests were served by the Constitution in 1789, mainly the merchants and planters, are not the same groups that benefit from the Constitution's provisions today. Once incorporated into the law, political principles often take on lives of their own and have consequences that were never anticipated by their original champions. Indeed, many of the groups that benefit from constitutional provisions today did not even exist in 1789. Who would have thought that the principle of free speech would influence the transmission of data on the Internet? Who would have predicted that commercial interests that once sought a powerful government might come, two centuries later, to denounce governmental activism as "socialistic"? Perhaps one secret of the Constitution's longevity is that it did not confer permanent advantage upon any one set of economic or social forces.

Although they were defeated in 1789, the Antifederalists present us with an important picture of a road not taken and of an America that might have been. Would the country have been worse off if it had been governed by a confederacy of small republics linked by a national administration with severely limited powers? Were the Antifederalists correct in predicting that a government given great power in the hope that it might do good would, through "insensible progress," inevitably turn to evil purposes? Two hundred years of government under the federal Constitution are not necessarily enough to definitively answer these questions. Time must tell.

The Citizen's Role and the Changing Constitution

The Constitution has endured for more than two centuries as the framework of government. But it has not endured without change. Without change, the Constitution might have become merely a sacred text, stored under glass.

AMENDMENTS: MANY ARE CALLED, FEW ARE CHOSEN

amendment a change added to a bill, law, or constitution

The need for change was recognized by the framers of the Constitution, and the provisions for **amendment** incorporated into Article V were thought to be "an easy, regular and Constitutional way" to make changes, which would occasionally be necessary because members of Congress "may abuse their power and refuse their consent on that very account . . . to admit to amendments to correct the source of the abuse."[28] Madison made a more balanced defense of the amendment procedure in Article V: "It guards equally against that extreme facility, which would render the Constitution too mutable; and that extreme difficulty, which might perpetuate its discovered faults."[29]

➤Why is the Constitution difficult to amend?

Experience since 1789 raises questions even about Madison's more modest claims. The Constitution has proven to be extremely difficult to amend. In the history of efforts to amend the Constitution, the most appropriate characterization is "many are called, few are chosen." Between 1789 and 1996, more than 11,000 amendments were formally offered in Congress. Of these, Congress officially proposed only twenty-nine, and twenty-seven of these were eventually ratified by the states. But the record is even more severe than that. Since 1791, when the first ten amendments, the Bill of Rights, were added, only seventeen amendments have been adopted. And two of them—Prohibition and its repeal—cancel each other out, so that for all practical purposes, only fifteen amendments have been added to the Constitution since 1791. Despite vast changes in American society and its economy, only twelve amendments have been adopted since the Civil War amendments in 1868.

Four methods of amendment are provided for in Article V:

1. Passage in House and Senate by two-thirds vote; then ratification by majority vote of the legislatures of three-fourths (thirty-eight) of the states.
2. Passage in House and Senate by two-thirds vote; then ratification by conventions called for the purpose in three-fourths of the states.
3. Passage in a national convention called by Congress in response to petitions by two-thirds of the states; ratification by majority vote of the legislatures of three-fourths of the states.

Four Ways the Constitution Can Be Amended

Figure 2.3

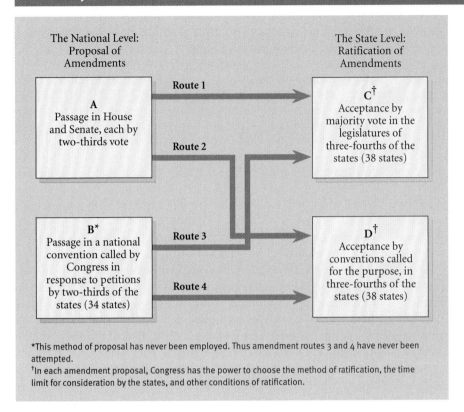

The National Level:
Proposal of
Amendments

The State Level:
Ratification of
Amendments

A
Passage in House
and Senate, each by
two-thirds vote

Route 1

Route 2

C†
Acceptance by
majority vote in the
legislatures of
three-fourths of the
states (38 states)

B*
Passage in a national
convention called by
Congress in
response to petitions
by two-thirds of the
states (34 states)

Route 3

Route 4

D†
Acceptance by
conventions called
for the purpose, in
three-fourths of the
states (38 states)

*This method of proposal has never been employed. Thus amendment routes 3 and 4 have never been attempted.
†In each amendment proposal, Congress has the power to choose the method of ratification, the time limit for consideration by the states, and other conditions of ratification.

4. Passage in a national convention, as in (3); then ratification by conventions called for the purpose in three-fourths of the states.

(Figure 2.3 illustrates each of these possible methods.) Since no amendment has ever been proposed by national convention, however, methods (3) and (4) have never been employed. And method (2) has only been employed once (the Twenty-first Amendment, which repealed the Eighteenth, or Prohibition, Amendment). Thus, method (1) has been used for all the others.

Now it should be clear why it has been so difficult to amend the Constitution. The requirement of a two-thirds vote in the House and the Senate means that any proposal for an amendment in Congress can be killed by only 34 senators or 136 members of the House. What is more, if the necessary two-thirds vote is obtained, the amendment can still be killed by the refusal or inability of only thirteen state legislatures to ratify it. Since each state has an equal vote regardless of its population, the thirteen holdout states may represent a very small fraction of the total American population.

THE CASE OF THE EQUAL RIGHTS AMENDMENT

The Equal Rights Amendment (ERA) is a case study of a proposed amendment that almost succeeded. In fact, the ERA is one of the very few proposals that got the necessary two-thirds vote in Congress yet failed to obtain the ratification of the requisite thirty-eight states.

On October 12, 1971, the U.S. House of Representatives approved the Equal Rights Amendment by the required two-thirds majority; the Senate followed suit on March 22, 1972. The amendment was simple:

Sec. 1. Equality of rights under the law shall not be denied or abridged by the United States or by any State on account of sex.

Sec. 2. The Congress shall have the power to enforce, by appropriate legislation, the provisions of this article.

Sec. 3. This amendment shall take effect two years after the date of ratification.

The congressional resolution provided for the accustomed method of ratification through the state legislatures rather than by state conventions—route (1) rather than route (2) in Figure 2.3—and that it had to be completed within seven years, by March 22, 1979.

Since the amendment was the culmination of nearly a half-century of efforts, and since the women's movement had spread its struggle for several years prior to 1971, the amendment was ratified by twenty-eight state legislatures during the very first year. But opposition forces quickly organized into the "Stop ERA" movement. By the end of 1974, five more states had ratified the amendment, but three states that had ratified it in 1973—Idaho, Nebraska, and Tennessee—had afterwards voted to rescind their ratification. This posed an unprecedented problem: whether a state legislature had the right to rescind its approval. The Supreme Court refused to deal with this question, insisting that it was a political question to be settled by Congress. If the ERA had been ratified by the thirty-eight-state minimum, Congress would have had to decide whether to respect the rescissions or to count them as ratifications.

This point was rendered moot by events. By the end of 1978, thirty-five state legislatures had ratified the ERA—counting the three rescinding legislatures as ratifiers. But even counting them, the three additional state ratifications necessary to reach thirty-eight became increasingly difficult to get. In each of the remaining fifteen states, the amendment had already been rejected at least once. The only hope of the ERA forces was that the 1978 elections would change the composition of some of those state legislatures. Pinning their hopes on that, the ERA forces turned back to Congress and succeeded in getting an extension of the ratification deadline to June 30, 1982. This was an especially significant victory, because it was the first time Congress had extended the time limit since it began placing time restrictions on ratification in 1917. But this victory in Washington failed to impress any of the fifteen holdout legislatures. June 30, 1982, came and went, and the ERA was, for the time being at least, laid to rest. It was beaten by the efforts of Stop ERA and by the emergence of conservatism generally, which had culminated in Ronald Reagan's election as president.[30]

> **What purposes do the amendments to the Constitution serve?**

WHICH WERE CHOSEN? AN ANALYSIS OF THE TWENTY-SEVEN

There is more to the amending difficulties than the politics of campaigning and voting. It would appear that only a limited number of changes needed by society can actually be made through the Constitution. Although we shall see that the ERA fits the pattern of successful amendments, most efforts to amend the Constitution have failed because they were simply attempts to use the Constitution as an alternative to legislation for dealing directly with a public problem. A review of the successful amendments will provide two insights: First, it will give us some understanding of the conditions underlying successful amendments; and second, it will reveal a great deal about what constitutionalism means.

The purpose of the ten amendments in the Bill of Rights was basically structural, to give each of the three branches clearer and more restricted boundaries. The First Amendment clarified the jurisdiction of Congress. Although the powers of Congress under Article I, Section 8, would not have justified laws regulating religion, speech, and the like, the First Amendment made this limitation explicit: "Congress shall make no law. . . ." The Second, Third, and Fourth amendments similarly spelled out specific limits on the executive branch. This was seen as a necessity given the abuses of executive power Americans had endured under British rule.

The Fifth, Sixth, Seventh, and Eighth amendments contain some of the most important safeguards for individual citizens against the arbitrary exercise of government power. These amendments sought to accomplish their goal by defining the judicial branch more concretely and clearly than had been done in Article III of the Constitution. Table 2.2 analyzes the ten amendments included in the Bill of Rights.

Five of the seventeen amendments adopted since 1791 are directly concerned with the expansion of the electorate and, thus, political equality (see

The Bill of Rights: Analysis of Its Provisions

Table 2.2

AMENDMENT	PURPOSE
I	*Limits on Congress:* Congress is not to make any law establishing a religion or abridging speech, press, assembly, or petition freedoms.
II, III, IV	*Limits on Executive:* The executive branch is not to infringe on the right of people to keep arms (II), is not to arbitrarily take houses for a militia (III), and is not to engage in the search or seizure of evidence without a court warrant swearing to belief in the probable existence of a crime (IV).
V, VI, VII, VIII	*Limits on Courts:* The courts are not to hold trials for serious offenses without provision for a grand jury (V), a petit (trial) jury (VII), a speedy trial (VI), presentation of charges (VI), confrontation of hostile witnesses (VI), immunity from testimony against oneself (V), and immunity from trial more than once for the same offense (V). Neither bail nor punishment can be excessive (VIII), and no property can be taken without just compensation (V).
IX, X	*Limits on National Government:* All rights not enumerated are reserved to the states or the people.

Table 2.3 Amending the Constitution to Expand the Electorate

AMENDMENT	PURPOSE	YEAR PROPOSED	YEAR ADOPTED
XV	Extended voting rights to all races	1869	1870
XIX	Extended voting rights to women	1919	1920
XXIII	Extended voting rights to residents of the District of Columbia	1960	1961
XXIV	Extended voting rights to all classes by abolition of poll taxes	1962	1964
XXVI	Extended voting rights to citizens aged 18 and over	1971	1971*

*The Twenty-sixth Amendment holds the record for speed of adoption. It was proposed on March 23, 1971, and adopted on July 5, 1971.

Table 2.3). The Founders were unable to establish a national electorate with uniform voting qualifications. They decided to evade it by providing in the final draft of Article I, Section 2, that eligibility to vote in a national election would be the same as "the Qualifications requisite for Electors of the most numerous Branch of the State Legislature." Article I, Section 4, added that Congress could alter state regulations as to the "Times, Places and Manner of holding Elections for Senators and Representatives." Nevertheless, this meant that any important *expansion* of the American electorate would almost certainly require a constitutional amendment.

Six more amendments are also electoral in nature, although they are not concerned directly with voting rights and the expansion of the electorate (see Table 2.4 on the following page). These six amendments are concerned with the elective offices themselves (the Twentieth, Twenty-second, and Twenty-fifth) or with the relationship between elective offices and the electorate (the Twelfth, Fourteenth, and Seventeenth). One could conclude that one effect was the enhancement of democracy.

Another five amendments serve to expand or limit the power of government (see Table 2.5 on the following page).[31] The Eleventh Amendment protected the states from suits by private individuals and took away from the federal courts any power to take suits by private individuals of one state (or a foreign country) against another state. The other three amendments in Table 2.5 are obviously designed to reduce state power (Thirteenth), to reduce state power and expand national power (Fourteenth), and to expand national power (Sixteenth). The Twenty-seventh put a limit on Congress's ability to raise its own salary.

The one missing amendment underscores the meaning of the rest: the Eighteenth, or Prohibition, Amendment. This is the only instance in which the

Amending the Constitution to Change the Relationship Between Elected Offices and the Electorate

Table 2.4

AMENDMENT	PURPOSE	YEAR PROPOSED	YEAR ADOPTED
XII	Provided separate ballot for vice president in the electoral college	1803	1804
XIV	(Part 1) Provided a national definition of citizenship*	1866	1868
XVII	Provided direct election of senators	1912	1913
XX	Eliminated "lame duck" session of Congress	1932	1933
XXII	Limited presidential term	1947	1951
XXV	Provided presidential succession in case of disability	1965	1967

*In defining *citizenship,* the Fourteenth Amendment actually provided the constitutional basis for expanding the electorate to include all races, women, and residents of the District of Columbia. Only the "eighteen-year-olds' amendment" should have been necessary, since it changed the definition of citizenship. The fact that additional amendments were required following the Fourteenth suggests that voting is not considered an inherent right of U.S. citizenship. Instead, it is viewed as a privilege.

Amending the Constitution to Expand or Limit the Power of Government

Table 2.5

AMENDMENT	PURPOSE	YEAR PROPOSED	YEAR ADOPTED
XI	Limited jurisdiction of federal courts over suits involving the states	1794	1798
XIII	Eliminated slavery and eliminated the right of states to allow property in persons	1865*	1865
XIV	(Part 2) Applied due process of Bill of Rights to the states	1866	1868
XVI	Established national power to tax incomes	1909	1913
XXVII	Limited Congress's power to raise its own salary	1789	1992

*The Thirteenth Amendment was proposed January 31, 1865, and adopted less than a year later, on December 18, 1865.

The Constitution has evolved over time through the addition of amendments; this process continues today. In the 1990s, some conservatives pushed to add an amendment preventing flag burning or desecration. In this 1990 photograph, Bob Dole calls for the Twenty-seventh Amendment, backed by Senators Alfonse D'Amato, James McClure, John McCain, and Bennett Johnston (left). The flag desecration amendment is problematic in that its enforcement depends on the intent of the alleged desecrator. Even Boy Scouts burn flags in a display of patriotism—ceremonial flag burning is the official way to dispose of old flags (right). Burning the flag is not desecration in itself; burning it as political protest, however, would be illegal under the amendment.

country tried to *legislate* by constitutional amendment. In other words, it is the only amendment that was designed to deal directly with some substantive social problem. And it was the only amendment ever to have been repealed. Two other amendments—the Thirteenth, which abolished slavery, and the Sixteenth, which established the power to levy an income tax—can be said to have had the effect of legislation. But the purpose of the Thirteenth was to restrict the power of the states by forever forbidding them to treat any human being as property. As for the Sixteenth, it is certainly true that income tax legislation followed immediately; nevertheless, the amendment concerns itself strictly with establishing the power of Congress to enact such legislation. The legislation came later; and if down the line a majority in Congress had wanted to abolish the income tax, they could also have done this by legislation rather than through the arduous path of a constitutional amendment repealing the income tax.

All of this points to the principle underlying the twenty-five existing amendments: all are concerned with the structure or composition of government. This is consistent with the dictionary, which defines *constitution* as the makeup or composition of something. And it is consistent with the concept of a constitution as "higher law," because the whole point and purpose of a higher law is to establish a framework within which government and the process of making ordinary law can take place. Even those who would have preferred more changes in the Constitution would have to agree that there is great wisdom in this principle. A constitution ought to enable legislation and public policies to take place, but it should not determine what that legislation or those public policies ought to be.

For those whose hopes for change center on the Constitution, it must be emphasized that the amendment route to social change is, and always will be, extremely limited. Through a constitution it is possible to establish a working structure of government, and through a constitution it is possible to establish basic rights of citizens by placing limitations on the powers of that government. Once these things have been accomplished, the real problem is how to extend rights to those people who do not already enjoy them. Of course, the Constitution cannot enforce itself. But it can and does have a real influence on everyday life because a right or an obligation set forth in the Constitution can become a cause of action in the hands of an otherwise powerless person.

Private property is an excellent example. Property is one of the most fundamental and well-established rights in the United States; but it is well established not because it is recognized in so many words in the Constitution, but because legislatures and courts have made it a crime for anyone, including the government, to trespass or to take away property without compensation.

A constitution is good if it produces the cause of action that leads to good legislation, good case law, and appropriate police behavior. A constitution cannot eliminate power. But its principles can be a citizen's dependable defense against the abuse of power.

Scott Tyler, an artist known as "Dread Scott," provoked the rage of Twenty-seventh Amendment supporters with his 1989 piece "What Is the Proper Way to Display a U.S. Flag?" The installation consisted of a poster with flags on it, a book on a shelf, and a flag lying on the floor below the shelf. Viewers were invited to stand on the flag. Veterans groups and a Republican state senator protested outside the School of the Art Institute of Chicago in an effort to close the show. The First Amendment clearly defends such displays as legal, but the government retaliated against the work by cutting the school's funding by almost $70,000. Supporters of the proposed Twenty-seventh Amendment pushed harder for the constitutional change after the show. The proposed amendment did not pass in Congress.

Reflections on Liberty, Equality, and Democracy

> **Did the framers value liberty, equality, and democracy? Why or why not?**

The Constitution's framers placed individual liberty ahead of all other political values. Their concern for liberty led many of the framers to distrust both democracy and equality. They feared that democracy could degenerate into a majority tyranny in which the populace, perhaps led by a rabble-rousing demagogue, would trample on liberty. As to equality, the framers were products of their time and place; our contemporary ideas of racial and gender equality would have been foreign to them. The framers were concerned primarily with another manifestation of equality: they feared that those without property or position might be driven by what some called a "leveling spirit" to infringe upon liberty in the name of greater economic or social equality. Indeed, the framers believed that this leveling spirit was most likely to produce demagoguery and majority tyranny. As a result, the basic structure of the Constitution—separated powers, internal checks and balances, and federalism—was designed to safeguard liberty, and the Bill of Rights created further safeguards for liberty. At the same time, however, many of the Constitution's other key provisions, such as indirect election of senators and the president, as well as the appointment of judges for life, were designed to limit democracy and, hence, the threat of majority tyranny.

By championing liberty, however, the framers virtually guaranteed that democracy and even a measure of equality would sooner or later evolve in the United States. For liberty inevitably leads to the growth of political activity and the expansion of political participation. In James Madison's famous phrase, "Liberty is to faction as air is to fire."[32] Where they have liberty, more and more people, groups, and interests will almost inevitably engage in politics and gradually overcome whatever restrictions might have been placed upon participation. This is precisely what happened in the early years of the American Republic. During the Jeffersonian period, political parties formed. During the Jacksonian period, many state suffrage restrictions were removed and popular participation greatly expanded. Over time, liberty is conducive to democracy.

Liberty does not guarantee that everyone will be equal. It does, however, reduce the threat of inequality in one very important way. Historically, the greatest inequalities of wealth, power, and privilege have arisen where governments have used their power to allocate status and opportunity among individuals or groups. From the aristocracies of the early modern period to the *nomenklatura* of twentieth-century despotisms, the most extreme cases of inequality are associated with the most tyrannical regimes. In the United States, however, by promoting a democratic politics, over time liberty unleashed forces that militated against inequality. As a result, over the past two hundred years, groups that have learned to use the political process have achieved important economic and social gains.

One limitation of liberty as a political principle, however, is that the idea of limits upon government action can also inhibit effective government. Take one of the basic tasks of government, the protection of citizens' lives and property. A government limited by concerns over the rights of those accused of crimes may be limited in its ability to maintain public order. Currently, the U.S. government is asserting that protecting the nation against terrorists requires law enforcement measures that seem at odds with legal and constitutional formalities. The conflict between liberty and governmental effectiveness is another tension at the heart of the American constitutional system.

What You Can Do: Become a Framer

Constitutions are "higher law." They spell out general principles and procedures for how people should interact, make decisions, and enforce them. Like the U.S. Constitution and the fifty state constitutions, they also structure politics. The U.S. Constitution outlines three major branches of government, limits their powers, and reserves authority for the states. State constitutions set up state institutions and processes, delegating some authority to regional and local governments. These constitutions declare or imply that the courts should interpret and enforce higher law to ensure that all government actions are consistent with it.

Very few people found new nations or frame constitutions; relatively few people propose and promote amendments to constitutions. However, students and citizens can and do get involved in setting forth general principles, establishing decision-making procedures, and structuring institutions on their campuses and in their communities.

For example, many college campuses have "principles of community" that are very much like constitutions. They articulate the aspirations and values that bind faculty, staff, alumni, and students into a cohesive community. Typically, principles of community highlight the educational mission of the institution and call on all members to show respect for people with diverse racial/ethnic backgrounds, religious beliefs, abilities and disabilities, and so forth. The principles may prohibit activities (such as the use of racial slurs) and outline processes for adjudicating and punishing infractions.

Organizations often frame "bylaws" that are similar to constitutions. Bylaws might include "mission statements," outline organization arrangements, detail procedures for choosing officers, specify decision-making processes, and set down the frequency and timing of meetings. Some colleges require student groups to establish bylaws in order to be eligible for funding. And many groups voluntarily frame bylaws to focus and structure their activities.

Common variations on constitutions are "charters." A state may share its power with city governments by approving city charters that authorize local officials to make some decisions without requiring explicit state approval. A local government may create an agency by issuing a charter that specifies the new agency's goals, structure, personnel, and timeline. Similarly, a college may approve the charter of a student organization to authorize it to exercise discretionary authority in distributing student-generated funds for a variety of campus activities.

Here are some possibilities for you to become a framer of "constitutions" on your campus and in your community.

- Identify a general problem on your campus. Perhaps administrators ignore student voices, tolerate long lines for financial aid, and serve poor-quality food in cafeterias. Working with a few classmates or an appropriate student organization, discuss, develop, circulate, and promote a "Student Bill of Rights" that expresses principles that protect students from abuse and promotes student voices on campus.
- If you are starting a group, such as a campus chapter of Human Rights Watch, consider drafting bylaws to focus and structure the group as well as to initiate

a conversation about its goals and strategies. When you invite other students to be group founders and bylaw framers, they are likely to develop a sense of ownership that strengthens their commitment and loyalty to the group.

- If you are a member of a group, whether it is Campus Republicans or a youth service group, consider raising "constitutional" questions. Does the group have bylaws? If not, would they be useful? If so, perhaps current bylaws should be re-examined and amended. Take the constitutional pulse of your group.
- Perhaps you are working on a student government or community political campaign. Is the campaign inefficient, disorganized, and chaotic? Do workers and volunteers grumble because little is being accomplished? Many groups hit a low point marked by morale problems. To prevent or resolve morale problems, you might suggest that members draft a "mission statement." The drafting process encourages individuals to strengthen commitment, identifies sources of cohesion, and prods folks to set aside minor complaints to achieve major goals.

By articulating shared principles, framing and rethinking bylaws, or drafting mission statements, you do not directly accomplish group goals. However, you do clarify goals, establish processes, and set up structures that empower group members to collaborate and cooperate more effectively.

Summary

Political conflicts between the colonies and Britain, and among competing groups within the colonies, led to the first founding as expressed by the Declaration of Independence. The first constitution, the Articles of Confederation, was adopted one year later (1777). Under this document, the states retained their sovereignty and the central government had few powers and no means of enforcing its will. The national government's weakness led to the Constitution of 1787, the second founding.

The Constitution's framers sought, first, to fashion a new government sufficiently powerful to promote commerce and protect property from radical state legislatures. Second, the framers sought to bring an end to the "excessive democracy" of the state and national governments under the Articles of Confederation. Third, the framers introduced mechanisms that helped secure popular consent for the new government. Finally, the framers made certain that their new government would not itself pose a threat to liberty and property.

The struggle for the ratification of the Constitution pitted the Antifederalists, who thought the proposed new government would be too powerful, against the Federalists, who supported the Constitution and were able to secure its ratification after a nationwide political debate.

This chapter also sought to convey an appreciation of constitutionalism itself. In addition to describing how the Constitution is formally amended, we analyzed the twenty-seven amendments in order to determine what they had in common, contrasting them with the hundreds of amendments that were offered but never adopted. We found that with the exception of the two Prohibition amendments, all amendments were oriented toward some change in the framework or structure of government. The Prohibition Amendment was the only adopted amendment that sought to legislate by constitutional means.

For Further Reading

Beard, Charles. *An Economic Interpretation of the Constitution of the United States.* New York: Macmillan, 1913.

Cohler, Anne M. *Montesquieu's Politics and the Spirit of American Constitutionalism.* Lawrence: University Press of Kansas, 1988.

Farrand, Max, ed. *The Records of the Federal Convention of 1787.* 4 vols. New Haven, CT: Yale University Press, 1966.

Hamilton, Alexander, James Madison, and John Jay. *The Federalist Papers.* Edited by Isaac Kramnick. New York: Viking, 1987.

Jensen, Merrill. *The Articles of Confederation.* Madison: University of Wisconsin Press, 1963.

Lipset, Seymour M. *The First New Nation: The United States in Historical and Comparative Perspective.* New York: Basic Books, 1963.

McDonald, Forrest. *The Formation of the American Republic.* New York: Penguin, 1967.

Main, Jackson Turner. *The Social Structure of Revolutionary America.* Princeton, NJ: Princeton University Press, 1965.

Rossiter, Clinton. *1787: Grand Convention.* New York: Macmillan, 1966.

Storing, Herbert, ed. *The Complete Anti-Federalist.* 7 vols. Chicago: University of Chicago Press, 1981.

Wills, Gary. *Explaining America.* New York: Penguin, 1982.

Wood, Gordon S. *The Creation of the American Republic.* New York: Norton, 1982.

Study Outline

ON THE WEB

www.wwnorton.com/wtp4e

The First Founding: Interests and Conflicts

1. In an effort to alleviate financial problems, including considerable debt, the British government sought to raise revenue by taxing its North American colonies. This energized New England merchants and southern planters, who then organized colonial resistance.

2. Colonial resistance set into motion a cycle of provocation and reaction that resulted in the First Continental Congress and eventually the Declaration of Independence.

3. The Declaration of Independence was an attempt to identify and articulate a history and set of principles that might help to forge national unity.

4. The colonies established the Articles of Confederation and Perpetual Union. Under the Articles, the central government was based entirely in Congress, yet Congress had little power.

The Second Founding: From Compromise to Constitution

1. Concern over America's precarious position in the international community coupled with domestic concern that "radical forces" had too much influence in Congress and in state governments led to the Annapolis Convention in 1786.

2. Shays's Rebellion in Massachusetts provided critics of the Articles of Confederation with the evidence they needed to push for constitutional revision.

3. Recognizing fundamental flaws in the Articles, the delegates to the Philadelphia Convention abandoned the plan to revise the Articles and committed themselves to a second founding.

4. Conflict between large and small states over the issue of representation in Congress led to the Great Compromise, which created a bicameral legislature based on two different principles of representation.

5. The Three-fifths Compromise addressed the question of slavery by apportioning the seats in the House of Representatives according to a population in which five slaves would count as three persons.

The Constitution

1. The new government was to be strong enough to defend the nation's interests internationally, promote commerce and protect property, and prevent the threat posed by "excessive democracy."

2. The House of Representatives was designed to be directly responsible to the people in order to encourage popular consent for the Constitution. The Senate was designed to guard against the potential for excessive democracy in the House.

3. The Constitution grants Congress important and influential powers, but any power not specifically enumerated in its text is reserved specifically to the states.

4. The framers hoped to create a presidency with energy—one that would be capable of timely and decisive action to deal with public issues and problems.

5. The establishment of the Supreme Court reflected the framers' preoccupations with nationalizing governmental power and checking radical democratic impulses while guarding against potential interference with liberty and property from the new national government itself.

6. Various provisions in the Constitution addressed the framers' concern with national unity and power. Such provisions included clauses promoting reciprocity among states.

7. Procedures for amending the Constitution are provided in Article V. These procedures are so difficult that amendments are quite rare in American history.
8. To guard against possible misuse of national government power, the framers incorporated the principles of the separation of powers and federalism, as well as a Bill of Rights, in the Constitution.
9. The separation of powers was based on the principle that power must be used to balance power.
10. Although the framers' move to federalism was a step toward greater centralization of national government power, they retained state power by devising a system of two sovereigns.
11. The Bill of Rights was adopted as the first ten amendments to the Constitution in 1791.

The Fight for Ratification

1. The struggle for ratification was carried out in thirteen separate campaigns—one in each state.
2. The Federalists supported the Constitution and a stronger national government. The Antifederalists, on the other hand, preferred a more decentralized system of government and fought against ratification.
3. Federalists and Antifederalists had differing views regarding issues such as representation and the prevention of tyranny.
4. Antifederalist criticisms helped to shape the Constitution and the national government, but it was the Federalist vision of America that triumphed.

The Citizen's Role and the Changing Constitution

1. Provisions for amending the Constitution, incorporated into Article V, have proven to be difficult criteria to meet. Relatively few amendments have been made to the Constitution.
2. Most of the amendments to the Constitution deal with the structure or composition of the government.

Reflections on Liberty, Equality, and Democracy

1. The Constitution's framers placed individual liberty ahead of all other political values. But by emphasizing liberty, the framers virtually guaranteed that democracy and equality would evolve in the United States.

Practice Quiz

www.wwnorton.com/wtp4e

1. In the Revolutionary struggles, which of the following groups was allied with the New England merchants?
   a) artisans
   b) southern planters
   c) western speculators
   d) laborers

2. How did the British attempt to raise revenue in the North American colonies?
   a) income tax
   b) taxes on commerce
   c) expropriation and government sale of land
   d) government asset sales

3. The first governing document in the United States was
   a) the Declaration of Independence.
   b) the Articles of Confederation and Perpetual Union.
   c) the Constitution.
   d) none of the above.

4. Which state's proposal embodied a principle of representing states in the Congress according to their size and wealth?
   a) Connecticut
   b) Maryland
   c) New Jersey
   d) Virginia

5. Where was the execution of laws conducted under the Articles of Confederation?
   a) the presidency
   b) the Congress
   c) the states
   d) the expanding federal bureaucracy

6. Which of the following was *not* a reason that the Articles of Confederation seemed too weak?
   a) the lack of a single voice in international affairs
   b) the power of radical forces in the Congress
   c) the impending "tyranny of the states"
   d) the power of radical forces in several states

7. What mechanism was instituted in the Congress to guard against "excessive democracy"?
   a) bicameralism
   b) staggered Senate terms
   c) appointment of senators for long terms
   d) all of the above

8. Which of the following best describes the Supreme Court as understood by the Founders?
   a) the highest court of the national government
   b) arbiter of disputes within the Congress
   c) a figurehead commission of elders
   d) a supreme court of the nation and its states

9. Which of the following were the Antifederalists most concerned with?
   a) interstate commerce
   b) the protection of property
   c) the distinction between principles and interests
   d) the potential for tyranny in the central government

10. The draft constitution that was introduced at the start of the Constitutional Convention was authored by
    a) Edmund Randolph.
    b) Thomas Jefferson.
    c) James Madison.
    d) George Clinton.

Critical Thinking Questions

www.wwnorton.com/wtp4e

1. In many ways, the framers of the Constitution created a central government much stronger than the government created by the Articles of Confederation. Still, the framers seem to have taken great care to limit the power of the central government in various ways. Describe the ways in which the central government under the Constitution was stronger than the central government under the Articles. Describe the ways in which the framers limited the national government's power under the Constitution. Why might the framers have placed such limits on the government they had just created?

2. Recount and explain the ideological, geographical, social, and political conflicts both at the time of the American Revolution and at the time of the writing of the United States Constitution. What experiences and interests informed the forces involved in each of these conflicts? How did the framers resolve these conflicts? Were there any conflicts left unresolved?

3. The framers of the Constitution were very concerned with creating an effective system of government. Yet whenever crises loom, critics charge that America's government is too cumbersome and too filled with checks on power to promote effective action. Does the war on terrorism reveal our constitutional government's effectiveness or lack of effectiveness? Are there ways in which we benefit from the government's occasional lack of efficiency?

Key Terms

www.wwnorton.com/wtp4e

amendment (p. 66)
Antifederalists (p. 58)
Articles of Confederation (p. 42)
bicameral (p. 48)
Bill of Rights (p. 50)
checks and balances (p. 50)

confederation (p. 43)
elastic clause (p. 51)
electoral college (p. 50)
expressed powers (p. 51)
federalism (p. 50)
Federalist Papers (p. 62)
Federalists (p. 58)
Great Compromise (p. 47)
judicial review (p. 53)

limited government (p. 63)
New Jersey Plan (p. 47)
separation of powers (p. 50)
supremacy clause (p. 54)
Three-fifths Compromise (p. 48)
tyranny (p. 62)
Virginia Plan (p. 46)

3 FEDERALISM

What Government Does and Why It Matters

I F YOU LIVE in Huntington, West Virginia, you might decide to spend a Saturday night cruising in a friend's new car; in Fargo, North Dakota, the same weekend plans would get you a ticket. And if you decide to take your car out to the highway, in Montana, during the day, you could go as fast as you like, but if you live in New York State, you would risk getting a speeding ticket if you drove over 65 miles per hour.

Driving is just one of the many areas in which where you live affects what you can do and what the government does. If you lose your job in New Hampshire, the highest level of unemployment insurance benefits you can get is $301 per week; in neighboring Massachusetts, you could receive as much as $646 per week. By giving the states power to set benefit levels on such social policies as unemployment insurance and welfare, the American system of federalism allows substantial inequalities to exist across the country. Likewise, what kinds of classes are offered in high schools, the taxes citizens pay for public schools, and the tuition you pay if you attend a state university or college are all affected by where you live. In fact, most of the rules and regulations that Americans face in their daily lives are set by state and local governments.[1]

State and local governments play such important roles in the lives of American citizens because the United States is a federal system. Throughout American history, lawmakers, politicians, and citizens have wrestled with questions about how responsibilities should be allocated across the different levels of government. Some responsibilities, such as international relations, clearly lie with the federal government. Others, such as the divorce laws, are controlled by state governments. However, the vast majority of government responsibilities are now shared in American federalism.

These include such activities as building transportation systems (roads, bridges, airports, mass transit); providing education; protecting the health and safety of citizens; providing social benefits; protecting civil liberties; and administering criminal justice. Reflecting the Founders' mistrust of centralized power and the long-standing preference of Americans for local self-government as the best form of democracy, state and local governments have retained substantial power. Yet over the course of American history, the federal government has grown far more powerful. Especially since the New Deal in the 1930s, the national government has played a much more prominent role in protecting liberty and promoting equality. It has done so through a growing body of social programs and regulations, enacted by the federal government but often implemented by the states. In the 1980s, the tide turned against the federal government, as a new generation of lawmakers sought to enhance the responsibilities of the states. Since the terrorist attacks of September 11, 2001, Washington has once again come to dominate the federal system, this time with national security as the driving objective. This shifting balance highlights an old debate in American politics; it traces back to the Founding, when the Federalists argued in favor of a stronger national government and the Antifederalists opposed them. ∎

THE debate about "who should do what" remains one of the most important discussions in American politics. Much is at stake in how authority is divided up among the different levels of government. The debate about how responsibilities should be divided is often informed by conflicting principles and differing evaluations about what each level of government is best suited to do. For example, many people believe that the United States needs national goals and standards to ensure equal opportunities for citizens across the nation; others contend that state and local governments can do a better job at most things because they are closer to the people. For this reason the states have been called "laboratories of democracy": they can experiment with different policies to find measures that best meet the needs of their citizens.

But decisions about who should do what are also highly political. Groups that want government to do more to promote equality frequently prefer a stronger national role. After all, it was the national government that first implemented the civil rights policies in the 1960s and guaranteed civil liberties in all states. Groups that want less government, on the other hand, often favor shifting power to the states or localities. Many conservatives oppose a strong national role because they believe that nationwide regulations infringe on individual liberties. Furthermore, different interest groups argue for placing policy responsibilities at the level of government that they find easiest to influence. And politicians in national, state, and local governments often have quite different views about which level of government should be expected to do what.

Thus, both political principles and interests influence decisions about how power and responsibility should be sorted out across the levels of government. At various points in history, Americans have given different answers to questions about the appropriate role of national, state, and local governments. National power increased as the national government initiated new social and regulatory policies during the New Deal of the 1930s and the Great Society of the 1960s. But in the 1970s and 1980s, states began to claim more authority over these policies. The effort to increase state responsibility and reduce the national role received a boost when the Republicans took over Congress in 1995. With the support of a growing number of Republican governors, congressional Republicans advocated a strategy of devolution, in which the national government would grant the states more authority over a range of policies. For the most part, Republicans did not deliver on their promise to devolve more responsibility to state and local governments; in some areas, they actually increased federal control.

■ **In this chapter, we will first look at how federalism was defined in the Constitution.** The framers sought to limit national power with the creation of a separate layer of government in opposition to it. For the first 150 years of American government, the states were most important in governing the lives of American citizens. Over time, however, the Supreme Court interpreted the principle of federalism in a way that gave the national government more expansive powers.

■ **We will then examine how the federal framework has changed in recent years, especially in the growth of the national government's role.** After the 1930s, the national government began to expand, yet the states maintained most of their traditional powers.

■ **We will then assess how changes in federalism reflect the changes in how Americans perceive liberty, equality, and democracy.** American federalism has always been a work in progress. As federal, state, and local governments change, questions about the relationship between American political values and federalism continue to emerge.

■ **Finally, we will discuss how political participation by citizens at the local, state, and national levels affects the federal system.**

The Federal Framework

The Constitution has had its most fundamental influence on American life through federalism. **Federalism** can be defined with misleading ease and simplicity as the division of powers and functions between the national government and the

federalism a system of government in which power is divided, by a constitution, between a central government and regional governments

unitary system a centralized government system in which lower levels of government have little power independent of the national government

federal system a system of government in which the national government shares power with lower levels of government, such as states

> **How does federalism limit the power of the national government?**

expressed powers specific powers granted to Congress under Article I, Section 8, of the Constitution

implied powers powers derived from the "necessary and proper" clause of Article I, Section 8, of the Constitution. Such powers are not specifically expressed, but are implied through the expansive interpretation of delegated powers

necessary and proper clause from Article I, Section 8, of the Constitution, it provides Congress with the authority to make all laws "necessary and proper" to carry out its expressed powers

state governments. Governments can organize power in a variety of ways. One of the most important distinctions is between unitary and federal governments. In a **unitary system,** the central government makes the important decisions, and lower levels of government have little independent power. In such systems, lower levels of government primarily serve to implement decisions taken by the central government. In France, for example, the central government was once so involved in the smallest details of local activity that the minister of education boasted that by looking at his watch he could tell what all French schoolchildren were learning at that time because the central government set the school curriculum. In a **federal system,** by contrast, the central government shares power or functions with lower levels of government, such as regions or states. Nations with diverse ethnic or language groupings, such as Switzerland and Canada, are most likely to have federal arrangements. In federal systems, lower levels of government often have significant independent power to set policy in some areas, such as education and social programs, and to impose taxes. Yet the specific ways in which power is shared vary greatly: no two federal systems are exactly the same.

FEDERALISM IN THE CONSTITUTION

The United States was the first nation to adopt federalism as its governing framework. With federalism, the framers sought to limit the national government by creating a second layer of state governments. American federalism recognized two sovereigns in the original Constitution and reinforced the principle in the Bill of Rights by granting a few **"expressed powers"** to the national government and reserving all the rest to the states.

The Powers of the National Government   As we saw in Chapter 2, the "expressed powers" granted to the national government are found in Article I, Section 8, of the Constitution. These seventeen powers include the power to collect taxes, to coin money, to declare war, and to regulate commerce (which, as we will see, became a very important power for the national government). Article I, Section 8, also contains another important source of power for the national government: the **implied powers** that enable Congress "to make all Laws which shall be necessary and proper for carrying into Execution the foregoing Powers." Not until several decades after the Founding did the Supreme Court allow Congress to exercise the power granted in this **necessary and proper clause,** but, as we shall see later in this chapter, this doctrine allowed the national government to expand considerably the scope of its authority, although the process was a slow one. In addition to these expressed and implied powers, the Constitution affirmed the power of the national government in the supremacy clause (Article VI), which made all national laws and treaties "the supreme Law of the Land."

The Powers of State Government   One way in which the framers sought to preserve a strong role for the states was through the Tenth Amendment to the Constitution. The Tenth Amendment states that the powers that the Constitution does not delegate to the national government or prohibit to the states are "reserved to the States respectively, or to the people." The Antifederalists, who feared that a strong central government would encroach on individual liberty, repeatedly pressed for such an amendment as a way of limiting national power. Federalists agreed to the amendment because they did not think it would do much harm, given the powers of the Constitution already granted to the national government. The Tenth Amendment is also called the **reserved powers** amendment because it aims to reserve powers to the states.

The most fundamental power that is retained by the states is that of coercion—the power to develop and enforce criminal codes, to administer health and safety rules, to regulate the family via marriage and divorce laws. The states have the power to regulate individuals' livelihoods; if you're a doctor or a lawyer or a plumber or a barber, you must be licensed by the state. Even more fundamentally, the states had the power to define private property—private property exists because state laws against trespass define who is and is not entitled to use a piece of property. If you own a car, your ownership isn't worth much unless the state is willing to enforce your right to possession by making it a crime for anyone else to drive your car. These are fundamental matters, and the powers of the states regarding these domestic issues are much greater than the powers of the national government, even today.

A state's authority to regulate these fundamental matters is commonly referred to as the **police power** of the state and encompasses the state's power to regulate the health, safety, welfare, and morals of its citizens. Policing is what states do—they coerce you in the name of the community in order to maintain public order. And this was exactly the type of power that the Founders intended the states to exercise.

In some areas, the states share **concurrent powers** with the national government, wherein they retain and share some power to regulate commerce and to affect the currency—for example, by being able to charter banks, grant or deny corporate charters, grant or deny licenses to engage in a business or practice a trade, and regulate the quality of products or the conditions of labor. This issue of concurrent versus exclusive power has come up from time to time in our history, but wherever there is a direct conflict of laws between the federal and the state levels, the issue will most likely be resolved in favor of national supremacy.

State Obligations to One Another The Constitution also creates obligations among the states. These obligations, spelled out in Article IV, were intended to promote national unity. By requiring the states to recognize actions and decisions taken in other states as legal and proper, the framers aimed to make the states less like independent countries and more like parts of a single nation.

Article IV, Section I, calls for "Full Faith and Credit" among states, meaning that each state is normally expected to honor the "public Acts, Records, and Judicial Proceedings" that take place in any other state. So, for example, if a couple is married in Texas—marriage being regulated by state law—Missouri must also recognize that marriage, even though they were not married under Missouri state law.

This **full faith and credit clause** has recently become embroiled in the controversy over gay and lesbian marriage. In 1993, the Hawaii Supreme Court prohibited discrimination against gay and lesbian marriage except in very limited circumstances. Many observers believed that Hawaii would eventually fully legalize gay marriage. In fact, after a long political battle, Hawaii passed a constitutional amendment in 1998 outlawing gay marriage. However, in December 1999, the Vermont Supreme Court ruled that gay and lesbian couples should have the same

reserved powers powers, derived from the Tenth Amendment to the Constitution, that are not specifically delegated to the national government or denied to the states

police power power reserved to the government to regulate the health, safety, and morals of its citizens

concurrent powers authority possessed by *both* state and national governments, such as the power to levy taxes

full faith and credit clause provision from Article IV, Section 1, of the Constitution, requiring that the states normally honor the public acts and judicial decisions that take place in another state

Different Forms of Federalism

Federalism is an institutional feature central to the logic of consensual democracy. A federal form of government is most commonly found in countries that have geographically concentrated population pockets, which exhibit distinctly different cultures (based on languages, religions, races, or ethnic features that distinguish the groups from the national majority) and which wish to preserve their distinctiveness by having some autonomy over their defined geographical region. For countries with histories of ethnic and religious conflict, federalism allows power to be shared among different major cultural groups and, in so doing, may effectively reduce tensions and animosities between different cultures within a democracy, which otherwise would find it difficult or impossible to cooperate.

Since 1800, federalism has been an institutional device associated not merely with democracy but with nationalism. Nationalism is a cultural group's awareness that it is distinct, that it deserves its own institutions to preserve its culture, and that any central or "alien" power trying to impose laws and policies will lack legitimacy because the majority power may not fully appreciate or understand the local culture. Indeed, there may be deep historical animosities and even hatred among the different cultures. In 1800, according to data collected by Ted Robert Gurr and his colleagues, there were four federal political systems in the world, one of which was the United States. There were none in Europe. By 1994, of the 151 countries for which Gurr and his associates have data, only 18 were strong federal systems (separate, sovereign regional governments, with some linguistic religious or racial/ethnic distinctiveness, and authority over local fiscal and cultural affairs). Within the Americas, the United States, Canada, Trinidad, Mexico, Venezuela, and Brazil were strong federal systems. In Europe, Germany, Belgium, Switzerland, and Russia were classified as strong federal governments, with Spain, Austria, Yugoslavia, Ukraine, Georgia, and Azerbaijan classified as intermediate, or weak, federal governments.

Despite the numerous institutional similarities in the broad structural outlines common to federal democracies as well as certain institutional features common to federal nation-states (such as a bicameral legislature—with the upper chambers usually reserved for territorial representation—and a written constitution that is determinate in content, distinct in structure, and entrenched within the political process—see Chapter 2), the specific nature and features of the federal process found within each country varies greatly among democracies.

Compared to many federal democracies, the American political system is relatively free from sharp cultural tensions that define the relationship between the national and subnational units in other federal democracies. In the case of Canada, French-speaking Quebec stands apart from the other nine provinces (all of which are predominately English-speaking) because of a belief among many in Quebec that became entrenched following a Canadian Supreme Court ruling in 1988. The ruling held that Quebec's "French-only" sign law violated Canada's Charter of Human Rights. In 1995, separatists within the province campaigned for a referendum to secede from the Canadian federal democracy, coming within an eyelash of winning.

The federal "experiment" among democracies, which began with the American constitutional system, remains a very powerful and attractive institutional device for nations that have had historically centralized governments. For instance, complicated pressures associated with the European Union—an emerging federal structure in its own right, which now competes directly with national governments for authority over the domestic laws of member countries of the Union—have prompted the British national government (a nonfederal democracy) to recently extend a form of limited autonomy to its historical subnational regions of Scotland and Wales. These two regions now have their own separately elected parliamentary bodies with a wide range of policy autonomy (excluding, of course, foreign policy and defense). This reform, however, is having an unintended consequence for Great Britain: it is causing some in England (the third major geographical region of Great Britain) to argue that the British constitution should be wholly revamped to create something akin to an American federal structure in order to allow the degree of representation of English interests to be equal to that afforded the citizens of Scotland and Wales.

SOURCES: The Council for Canadian Unity, www.ccu-cuc.ca/en/op/archives (accessed 7/11/02); *The Polity Data Archive*, http://k-gleditsch.socsci.gla.ac.uk/Polity.html (accessed 7/11/02); and Sanford Lakoff, *Democracy: History, Theory, Practice* (Boulder: Westview Press, 1996).

rights as heterosexuals. The Vermont legislature responded with a new law that allowed gays and lesbians to form "civil unions." Although not legally considered marriages, such unions allow gay and lesbian couples most of the benefits of marriage, such as eligibility for the partner's health insurance, inheritance rights, and the right to transfer property. The Vermont statute could have broad implications for other states. More than thirty states have passed "defense of marriage acts" that define marriage as a union between men and women only. Anxious to show its disapproval of gay marriage, Congress passed the Defense of Marriage Act in 1996, which declared that states will *not* have to recognize a same-sex marriage, even if it is legal in one state. The act also said that the federal government will not recognize gay marriage—even if it is legal under state law—and that gay marriage partners will not be eligible for the federal benefits, such as Medicare and Social Security, normally available to spouses.[2] For a further discussion of gay and lesbian marriage, see Chapter 5.

Because of this controversy, the extent and meaning of the full faith and credit clause is sure to be considered by the Supreme Court. In fact, it is not clear that the clause requires states to recognize gay marriage because the Court's past interpretation of the clause has provided exceptions for "public policy" reasons: if states have strong objections to a law, they do not have to honor it. In 1997 the Court took up a case involving the full faith and credit clause. The case concerned a Michigan court order that prevented a former engineer for General Motors from testifying against the company. The engineer, who left the company on bad terms, later testified in a Missouri court about a car accident in which a woman died when her Chevrolet Blazer caught fire. General Motors challenged his right to testify, arguing that Missouri should give "full faith and credit" to the Michigan ruling. The Supreme Court ruled that the engineer could testify and that the court system in one state cannot hinder other state courts in their "search for the truth."[3]

Article IV, Section 2, known as the "comity clause," also seeks to promote national unity. It provides that citizens enjoying the **"Privileges and Immunities"** of one state should be entitled to similar treatment in other states. What this has come to mean is that a state cannot discriminate against someone from another state or give special privileges to its own residents. For example, in the 1970s, when Alaska passed a law that gave residents preference over nonresidents in obtaining work on the state's oil and gas pipelines, the Supreme Court ruled the law illegal because it discriminated against citizens of other states.[4] This clause also regulates criminal justice among the states by requiring states to return fugitives to the states from which they have fled. Thus, in 1952, when an inmate escaped from an Alabama prison and sought to avoid being returned to Alabama on the grounds that he was being subjected to "cruel and unusual punishment" there, the Supreme Court ruled that he must be returned according to Article IV, Section 2.[5] This example highlights the difference between the obligations among states and those among different countries. Recently, France refused to return an American fugitive because he might be subject to the death penalty, which does not exist in France.[6] The Constitution clearly forbids states from doing something similar.

States' relationships to one another are also governed by the interstate compact clause (Article I, Section 10), which states that "No State shall, without the Consent of Congress . . . enter into any Agreement or Compact with another State." The Court has interpreted the clause to mean that states may enter into

privileges and immunities clause provision from Article IV, Section 2, of the Constitution, that a state cannot discriminate against someone from another state or give its own residents special privileges

agreements with one another, subject to congressional approval. Compacts are a way for two or more states to reach a legally binding agreement about how to solve a problem that crosses state lines. In the early years of the Republic, states turned to compacts primarily to settle border disputes. Today they are used for a wide range of issues but are especially important in regulating the distribution of river water, addressing environmental concerns, and operating transportation systems that cross state lines.[7]

Local Government and the Constitution   Local government occupies a peculiar but very important place in the American system. In fact, the status of American local government is probably unique in world experience. First, it must be pointed out that local government has no status in the American Constitution. *State* legislatures created local governments, and *state* constitutions and laws permit local governments to take on some of the responsibilities of the state governments. Most states amended their own constitutions to give their larger cities **home rule**—a guarantee of noninterference in various areas of local affairs. But local governments enjoy no such recognition in the Constitution. Local governments have always been mere conveniences of the states.[8]

Local governments became administratively important in the early years of the Republic because the states possessed little administrative capability. They relied on local governments—cities and countries—to implement the laws of the state. Local government was an alternative to a statewide bureaucracy (see Table 3.1).

RESTRAINING NATIONAL POWER WITH DUAL FEDERALISM, 1789–1937

As we have noted, the Constitution created two layers of government: the national government and the state governments. The consequences of this **dual federalism** are fundamental to the American system of government in theory and in practice; they have meant that states have done most of the fundamental

home rule power delegated by the state to a local unit of government to manage its own affairs

dual federalism the system of government that prevailed in the United States from 1789 to 1937, in which most fundamental governmental powers were shared between the federal and state governments

Table 3.1	87,504 Governments in the United States

TYPE	NUMBER
National	1
State	50
County	3,043
Municipal	19,372
Townships	16,629
School districts	13,726
Other special districts	34,683

SOURCE: *Statistical Abstract of the United States, 2001* (Washington, DC: U.S. Government Printing Office, 2001), p. 258.

The Federal System: Specialization of Governmental Functions in the Traditional System (1800–1933)

Table 3.2

NATIONAL GOVERNMENT POLICIES (DOMESTIC)	STATE GOVERNMENT POLICIES	LOCAL GOVERNMENT POLICIES
Internal improvements	Property laws (including	Adaptation of state laws
Subsidies	slavery)	to local conditions
Tariffs	Estate and inheritance	("variances")
Public lands disposal	laws	Public works
Patents	Commerce laws	Contracts for public
Currency	Banking and credit laws	works
	Corporate laws	Licensing of public
	Insurance laws	accommodations
	Family laws	Assessible improve-
	Morality laws	ments
	Public health laws	Basic public services
	Education laws	
	General penal laws	
	Eminent domain laws	
	Construction codes	
	Land-use laws	
	Water and mineral laws	
	Criminal procedure	
	laws	
	Electoral and political	
	parties laws	
	Local government laws	
	Civil service laws	
	Occupations and profes-	
	sions laws	

governing. For evidence, look at Table 3.2. It lists the major types of public policies by which Americans were governed for the first century and a half under the Constitution. We call it the "traditional system" because it prevailed for three-quarters of American history and because it closely approximates the intentions of the framers of the Constitution.

Under the traditional system, the national government was quite small by comparison both to the state governments and to the governments of other Western nations. Not only was it smaller than most governments of that time, it was actually very narrowly specialized in the functions it performed. The national government built or sponsored the construction of roads, canals, and bridges (internal improvements). It provided cash subsidies to shippers and shipbuilders and distributed free or low-priced public land to encourage western settlement and business ventures. It placed relatively heavy taxes on imported goods (tariffs), not only to raise revenues but to protect "infant industries" from competition from the more advanced European enterprises. It protected patents and provided for a common currency, also to encourage and facilitate enterprises and to expand markets.

What do these functions of the national government reveal? First, virtually all its functions were aimed at assisting commerce. It is quite appropriate to refer to the traditional American system as a "commercial republic." Second, virtually none of the national government's policies directly coerced citizens. The emphasis of governmental programs was on assistance, promotion, and encouragement—the allocation of land or capital where they were insufficiently available for economic development.

Meanwhile, state legislatures were actively involved in economic regulation during the nineteenth century. In the United States, then and now, private property exists only in state laws and state court decisions regarding property, trespass, and real estate. American capitalism took its form from state property and trespass laws, as well as from state laws and court decisions regarding contracts, markets, credit, banking, incorporation, and insurance. Laws concerning slavery were a subdivision of property law in states where slavery existed. The practice of important professions, such as law and medicine, was and is illegal, except as provided for by state law. Marriage, divorce, and the birth or adoption of a child have always been regulated by state law. To educate or not to educate a child has been a decision governed more by state laws than by parents, and not at all by national law. It is important to note also that virtually all criminal laws—regarding everything from trespass to murder—have been state laws. Most of the criminal laws adopted by Congress are concerned with the District of Columbia and other federal territories.

All this (and more, as shown in the middle column of Table 3.2) demonstrates without any question that most of the fundamental governing in the United States was done by the states. The contrast between national and state policies, as shown by Table 3.2, demonstrates the difference in the power vested in each. The list of items in the middle column could actually have been made longer. Moreover, each item on the list is a category of law that fills many volumes of statutes and court decisions.

This contrast between national and state governments is all the more impressive because it is basically what the framers of the Constitution intended. Since the 1930s, the national government has expanded into local and intrastate matters, far beyond what anyone would have foreseen in 1790, 1890, or even in the 1920s. But this significant expansion of the national government did not alter the basic framework. The national government has become much larger, but the states have continued to be central to the American system of government.

Here lies probably the most important point of all: the fundamental impact of federalism on the way the United States is governed comes not from any particular provision of the Constitution but from the framework itself, which has determined the flow of government functions and, through that, the political development of the country. By allowing state governments to do most of the fundamental governing, the Constitution saved the national government from many policy decisions that might have proven too divisive for a large and very young country. There is no doubt that if the Constitution had provided for a unitary rather than a federal system, the war over slavery would have come in 1789 or 1809 rather than in 1860; and if it had come that early, the South might very well have seceded and established a separate and permanent slaveholding nation.

> **How strong a role have the states traditionally had in the federal framework?**

In helping the national government remain small and aloof from the most divisive issues of the day, federalism contributed significantly to the political stability of the nation, even as the social, economic, and political systems of many of the states and regions of the country were undergoing tremendous, profound, and sometimes violent, change.[9] As we shall see, some important aspects of federalism have changed, but the federal framework has survived two centuries and a devastating civil war.

FEDERALISM AND THE SLOW GROWTH OF THE NATIONAL GOVERNMENT'S POWER

Having created the national government, and recognizing the potential for abuse of power, the states sought through federalism to constrain the national government. The "traditional system" of a weak national government prevailed for over a century despite economic forces favoring its expansion and despite Supreme Court cases giving a pro-national interpretation to Article I, Section 8, of the Constitution.

That article delegates to Congress the power "to regulate commerce with foreign nations, and among the several States and with the Indian tribes." This **commerce clause** was consistently interpreted *in favor* of national power by the Supreme Court for most of the nineteenth century. The first and most important case favoring national power over the economy was *McCulloch v. Maryland*.[10] This case involved the question of whether Congress had the power to charter a national bank, since such an explicit grant of power was nowhere to be found in Article I, Section 8. Chief Justice John Marshall answered that the power could be "implied" from other powers that were expressly delegated to Congress, such as the "powers to lay and collect taxes; to borrow money; to regulate commerce; and to declare and conduct a war."

By allowing Congress to use the necessary and proper clause to interpret its delegated powers expansively, the Supreme Court created the potential for an unprecedented increase in national government power. Marshall also concluded that whenever a state law conflicted with a federal law (as in the case of *McCulloch v. Maryland*), the state law would be deemed invalid since the Constitution states that "the Laws of the United States . . . shall be the supreme Law of the Land." Both parts of this great case are pro-national, yet Congress did not immediately seek to expand the policies of the national government.

Another major case, *Gibbons v. Ogden* in 1824, reinforced this nationalistic interpretation of the Constitution. The important but relatively narrow issue was whether the state of New York could grant a monopoly to Robert Fulton's steamboat company to operate an exclusive service between New York and New Jersey. Chief Justice Marshall argued that New York State did not have the power to grant this particular monopoly. In order to reach this decision, it was necessary for Marshall to define what Article I, Section 8, meant by "commerce among the several states." He insisted that the definition was "comprehensive," extending to "every species of commercial intercourse." He did say that this comprehensiveness was limited "to that commerce which concerns more states than one," giving rise to what later came to be called "interstate commerce." *Gibbons* is important because it established the supremacy of the national government in all matters

commerce clause Article I, Section 8, of the Constitution, which delegates to Congress the power "to regulate commerce with foreign nations, and among the several States and with the Indian tribes." This clause was interpreted by the Supreme Court in favor of national power over the economy affecting interstate commerce.[11] But what would remain uncertain during several decades of constitutional discourse was the precise meaning of interstate commerce.

Article I, Section 8, backed by the implied powers decision in *McCulloch* and by the broad definition of "interstate commerce" in *Gibbons,* was a source of power for the national government as long as Congress sought to facilitate commerce through subsidies, services, and land grants. But later in the nineteenth century, when the national government sought to use those powers to *regulate* the economy rather than merely to promote economic development, federalism and the concept of interstate commerce began to operate as restraints on, rather than sources of, national power. Any effort of the national government to regulate commerce in such areas as fraud, the production of impure goods, the use of child labor, or the existence of dangerous working conditions or long hours was declared unconstitutional by the Supreme Court as a violation of the concept of interstate commerce. Such legislation meant that the federal government was entering the factory and the workplace—local areas—and was attempting to regulate goods that had not passed into commerce. To enter these local workplaces was to exercise police power—the power reserved to the states for the protection of the health, safety, and morals of their citizens. No one questioned the power of the national government to regulate businesses that intrinsically involved interstate commerce, such as railroads, gas pipelines, and waterway

The role of the national government in the economy has expanded gradually since the time of the Founding. In 1815, President James Madison called for a federally funded program of "internal improvements," which was one of the few policy roles for the national government during the first half of the nineteenth century. By improving transportation through the construction of roads and canals, the government fostered the growth of the market economy and boosted federal power (left). In 1916, the national government passed the Keating-Owen Child Labor Act, which excluded from interstate commerce all goods manufactured by children under fourteen. The act was ruled unconstitutional by the Supreme Court on the grounds that the regulation of interstate commerce could not extend to the conditions of labor. Despite this attempt at federal control, the regulation of child labor remained in the hands of state governments until the 1930s (right).

During the Great Depression, the national government became more active in regulating the economy and supporting the poor. New Deal programs sought to aid those affected by the Depression, such as residents of this Hooverville outside of Seattle, which was photographed in 1933 (left). The national government funded 90 percent of the cost of building more than 42,500 miles of interstate highways during the 1950s. State governments paid for the remaining 10 percent. Since the highways would improve interstate commerce, the federal government took the lead in funding them (right).

transportation. But well into the twentieth century, the Supreme Court used the concept of interstate commerce as a barrier against most efforts by Congress to regulate local conditions.

This aspect of federalism was alive and well during an epoch of tremendous economic development, the period between the Civil War and the 1930s. It gave the American economy a freedom from federal government control that closely approximated the ideal of free enterprise. The economy was never entirely free, of course; in fact, entrepreneurs themselves did not want complete freedom from government. They needed law and order. They needed a stable currency. They needed courts and police to enforce contracts and prevent trespass. They needed roads, canals, and railroads. But federalism, as interpreted by the Supreme Court for seventy years after the Civil War, made it possible for business to have its cake and eat it, too. Entrepreneurs enjoyed the benefits of national policies facilitating commerce and were protected by the courts from policies regulating commerce.[12]

All this changed after 1937, when the Supreme Court threw out the old distinction between interstate and intrastate commerce, converting the commerce clause from a source of limitations to a source of power for the national government. The Court began to refuse to review appeals challenging acts of Congress protecting the rights of employees to organize and engage in collective bargaining, regulating the amount of farmland in cultivation, extending low-interest credit to small businesses and farmers, and restricting the activities of corporations dealing in the stock market, and many other laws that contributed to the construction of the "welfare state."[13]

THE CHANGING ROLE OF THE STATES

As we have seen, the Constitution contained the seeds of a very expansive national government—in the commerce clause. For much of the nineteenth century, federal power remained limited. The Tenth Amendment was used to bolster arguments about **states' rights,** which in their extreme version claimed that the states did not have to submit to national laws when they believed the national government had exceeded its authority. These arguments in favor of states' rights were voiced less often after the Civil War. But the Supreme Court continued to use the Tenth Amendment to strike down laws that it thought exceeded national power, including the Civil Rights Act passed in 1875.

In the early twentieth century, however, the Tenth Amendment appeared to lose its force. Reformers began to press for national regulations to limit the power of large corporations and to preserve the health and welfare of citizens. The Supreme Court approved of some of these laws but it struck others down, including a law combating child labor. The Court stated that the law violated the Tenth Amendment because only states should have the power to regulate conditions of employment. By the late 1930s, however, the Supreme Court had approved such an expansion of federal power that the Tenth Amendment appeared irrelevant. In fact, in 1941, Justice Harlan Fiske Stone declared that the Tenth Amendment was simply a "truism," that it had no real meaning.[14]

Yet the idea that some powers should be reserved to the states did not go away. Indeed, in the 1950s, southern opponents of the civil rights movement revived the idea of states' rights. In 1956, ninety-six southern members of Congress issued a "Southern Manifesto" in which they declared that southern states were not constitutionally bound by Supreme Court decisions outlawing racial segregation. They believed that states' rights should override individual rights to liberty and formal equality. With the triumph of the civil rights movement, the slogan of "states' rights" became tarnished by its association with racial inequality.

states' rights the principle that the states should oppose the increasing authority of the national government. This principle was most popular in the period before the Civil War

States' rights have been embraced by many causes in the past fifty years. Governor George Wallace of Alabama defiantly turned back U.S. Attorney General Nicholas Katzenbach, who tried to enroll two black students at the University of Alabama at Tuscaloosa in 1963. Wallace, who proclaimed "segregation now, segregation tomorrow, segregation forever," was a vocal supporter of states' rights.

Especially in the mid-1990s, Republican Party leaders have contended that the national government has grown too powerful at the expense of the states and argue that the Tenth Amendment should restrict the growth of national power.

Recent years have seen a revival of interest in the Tenth Amendment and important Supreme Court decisions limiting federal power. Much of the interest in the Tenth Amendment stems from conservatives who believe that a strong federal government encroaches on individual liberties. They believe such freedoms are better protected by returning more power to the states through the process of **devolution.** In 1996, Republican presidential candidate Bob Dole carried a copy

devolution a policy to remove a program from one level of government by delegating it or passing it down to a lower level of government, such as from the national government to the state and local governments

The conflict between state and national power has also been staged in the courts. In 2002, protesters at the Supreme Court argued over whether the states had the right to fund school-choice vouchers, or whether vouchers favor religious schools and run afoul of the Constitution.

of the Tenth Amendment in his pocket as he campaigned, pulling it out to read at rallies.[15] The Supreme Court's ruling in *United States v. Lopez* in 1995 fueled further interest in the Tenth Amendment.[16] In that case, the Court, stating that Congress had exceeded its authority under the commerce clause, struck down a federal law that barred handguns near schools. This was the first time since the New Deal that the Court had limited congressional powers in this way. In 1997, the Court again relied on the Tenth Amendment to limit federal power in *Printz v. United States.*[17] The decision declared unconstitutional a provision of the Brady Handgun Violence Prevention Act that required state and local law enforcement officials to conduct background checks on handgun purchasers. The Court declared that this provision violated state sovereignty guaranteed in the Tenth Amendment because it required state and local officials to administer a federal regulatory program. The Court also limited the power of the federal government over the states in a 1996 ruling that prevented Native Americans from the Seminole tribe from suing the state of Florida in federal court. A 1988 law had given Indian tribes the right to sue a state in federal court if the state did not negotiate in good faith over issues related to gambling casinos on tribal land. The Supreme Court's ruling appeared to signal a much broader limitation on national power by raising new questions about whether individuals can sue a state if it fails to uphold federal law.[18] The Court has reaffirmed these limits on the reach of federal power in subsequent cases. But, to date, these rulings fall far short of a major reworking of the constitutional balance between the national government and the states.

The expansion of the power of the national government has not left the states powerless. The state governments continue to make most of the fundamental laws; the national government did not expand at the expense of the states. The growth of the national government has been an addition, not a redistribution of power from the states. No better demonstration of the continuing influence of the federal framework can be offered than the fact that the middle column of Table 3.2 is still a fairly accurate characterization of state government today.

Who Does What? The Changing Federal Framework

Questions about how to divide responsibilities between the states and the national government first arose more than two hundred years ago, when the framers wrote the Constitution to create a stronger union. But they did not solve the issue of who should do what. There is no "right" answer to that question; each generation of Americans has provided its own answer. In recent years, Americans have grown distrustful of the federal government and have supported giving more responsibility to the states.[19] Even so, they still want the federal government to set standards and promote equality.

Political debates about the division of responsibility often take sides: some people argue for a strong federal role to set national standards, while others say the states should do more. These two goals are not necessarily at odds. The key is to find the right balance. During the first 150 years of American history, that balance favored state power. But the balance began to shift toward Washington in the

1930s. In this section, we will look at how the balance shifted, and then we will consider current efforts to reshape the relationship between the national government and the states.

EXPANSION OF THE NATIONAL GOVERNMENT

The New Deal of the 1930s signaled the rise of a more active national government. The door to increased federal action opened when states proved unable to cope with the demands brought on by the Great Depression. Before the Depression, states and localities took responsibility for addressing the needs of the poor, usually through private charity. But the extent of the need created by the Depression quickly exhausted local and state capacities. By 1932, 25 percent of the workforce was unemployed. The jobless lost their homes and settled into camps all over the country, called "Hoovervilles," after President Herbert Hoover. Elected in 1928, the year before the Depression hit, Hoover steadfastly maintained that there was little the federal government could do to alleviate the misery caused by the Depression. It was a matter for state and local governments, he said.

Yet demands mounted for the federal government to take action. In Congress, some Democrats proposed that the federal government finance public works to aid the economy and put people back to work. Other members of Congress introduced legislation to provide federal grants to the states to assist them in their relief efforts. None of these measures passed while Hoover remained in the White House.

When Franklin D. Roosevelt took office in 1933, he energetically threw the federal government into the business of fighting the Depression. He proposed a variety of temporary measures to provide federal relief and work programs. Most of the programs he proposed were to be financed by the federal government but administered by the states. In addition to these temporary measures, Roosevelt presided over the creation of several important federal programs designed to provide future economic security for Americans.

> **Why did the balance of responsibility shift toward the national government in the 1930s?**

FEDERAL GRANTS

For the most part, the new national programs that the Roosevelt administration developed did not directly take power away from the states. Instead, Washington typically redirected states by offering them **grants-in-aid,** whereby Congress appropriates money to state and local governments on the condition that the money be spent for a particular purpose defined by Congress.

The principle of the grant-in-aid can be traced back to the nineteenth-century land grants that the national government made to the states for the improvement of agriculture and farm-related education. Since farms were not in "interstate commerce," it was unclear whether the Constitution permitted the national government to provide direct assistance to agriculture. Grants made to the states, but designated to go to farmers, presented a way of avoiding the question of constitutionality while pursuing what was recognized in Congress as a national goal.

grants-in-aid programs through which Congress provides money to state and local governments on the condition that the funds be employed for purposes defined by the federal government

> **What means does the national government use to control the actions of the states?**

categorical grants congressional grants given to states and localities on the condition that expenditures be limited to a problem or group specified by law

project grants grant programs in which state and local governments submit proposals to federal agencies and for which funding is provided on a competitive basis

formula grants grants-in-aid in which a formula is used to determine the amount of federal funds a state or local government will receive

Franklin Roosevelt's New Deal expanded the range of grants-in-aid into social programs, providing grants to the states for financial assistance to poor children. Congress added new grants after World War II, creating new programs to help states fund activities such as providing school lunches and building highways. Sometimes the national government required state or local governments to match the national contribution dollar for dollar, but in some programs, such as the development of the interstate highway system, the congressional grants provided 90 percent of the cost of the program.

These types of federal grants-in-aid are also called **categorical grants,** because the national government determines the purposes, or categories, for which the money can be used. For the most part, the categorical grants created before the 1960s simply helped the states perform their traditional functions.[20] In the 1960s, however, the national role expanded and the number of categorical grants increased dramatically (see Figure 3.1). For example, during the Eighty-ninth Congress (1965–66) alone, the number of categorical grant-in-aid programs grew from 221 to 379.[21] The grants authorized during the 1960s announced national purposes much more strongly than did earlier grants. Central to that national purpose was the need to provide opportunities to the poor.

Many of the categorical grants enacted during the 1960s were **project grants,** which require state and local governments to submit proposals to federal agencies. In contrast to the older **formula grants,** which used a formula (composed of such elements as need and state and local capacities) to distribute funds, the new project

| Figure 3.1 | The Rise and Decline of Federal Aid, 1960–2000 |

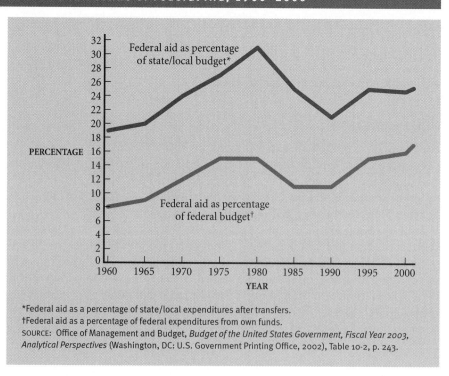

*Federal aid as a percentage of state/local expenditures after transfers.
†Federal aid as a percentage of federal expenditures from own funds.
SOURCE: Office of Management and Budget, *Budget of the United States Government, Fiscal Year 2003, Analytical Perspectives* (Washington, DC: U.S. Government Printing Office, 2002), Table 10-2, p. 243.

Evolving Federalism

Figure 3.2

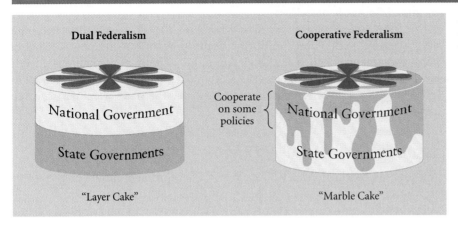

Dual Federalism

National Government

State Governments

"Layer Cake"

Cooperate on some policies

Cooperative Federalism

National Government

State Governments

"Marble Cake"

In marble-cake federalism, national policies, state policies, and local policies overlap in many areas.

grants made funding available on a competitive basis. Federal agencies would give grants to the proposals they judged to be the best. In this way, the national government acquired substantial control over which state and local governments got money, how much they got, and how they spent it.

COOPERATIVE FEDERALISM

The growth of categorical grants created a new kind of federalism. If the traditional system of two sovereigns performing highly different functions could be called dual federalism, historians of federalism suggest that the system since the New Deal could be called **cooperative federalism.** The most important student of the history of American federalism, Morton Grozdins, characterized this as a move from "layer-cake federalism" to "marble-cake federalism,"[22] in which intergovernmental cooperation and sharing have blurred a once-clear distinguishing line, making it difficult to say where the national government ends and the state and local governments begin (see Figure 3.2).

For a while in the 1960s, however, it appeared as if the state governments would become increasingly irrelevant to American federalism. Many of the new federal grants bypassed the states and instead sent money directly to local governments and even to local nonprofit organizations. The theme heard repeatedly in Washington was that the states simply could not be trusted to carry out national purposes.[23]

One of the reasons that Washington distrusted the states was because of the way African American citizens were treated in the South. The southern states' forthright defense of segregation, justified on the grounds of states' rights, helped to tarnish the image of the states as the civil rights movement took hold. The national officials who planned the War on Poverty in the 1960s pointed to the racial exclusion practiced in the southern states as a reason for bypassing state governments. Political scientist James Sundquist described how the "Alabama syndrome" affected the War on Poverty: "In the drafting of the Economic Opportunity Act, an 'Alabama syndrome' developed. Any suggestion within the

cooperative federalism a type of federalism existing since the New Deal era in which grants-in-aid have been used strategically to encourage states and localities (without commanding them) to pursue nationally defined goals. Also known as "intergovernmental cooperation"

poverty task force that the states be given a role in the administration of the act was met with the question, 'Do you want to give that kind of power to [Alabama governor] George Wallace?' "[24]

Yet, even though many national policies of the 1960s bypassed the states, other new programs, such as Medicaid—the health program for the poor—relied on state governments for their implementation. In addition, as the national government expanded existing programs run by the states, states had to take on more responsibility. These new responsibilities meant that the states were playing a very important role in the federal system.

REGULATED FEDERALISM AND NATIONAL STANDARDS

> **How has the relationship between the national government and the states evolved over the last several decades?**

The question of who decides what each level of government should do goes to the very heart of what it means to be an American citizen. How different should things be when one crosses a state line? In what policy areas is it acceptable to have state differences and in what areas should states be similar? Supreme Court decisions about the fundamental rights of American citizens provide the most important answers to these questions. Over time, the Court has pushed for greater uniformity across the states. In addition to legal decisions, the national government uses two other tools to create similarities across the states: grants-in-aid and regulations.

regulated federalism a form of federalism in which Congress imposes legislation on states and localities, requiring them to meet national standards

Grants-in-aid, as we have seen, are a little like bribes: Congress gives money to state and local governments if they agree to spend it for the purposes Congress specifies. But as Congress began to enact legislation in new areas, such as environmental policy, it also imposed additional regulations on states and localities. Some political scientists call this a move toward **regulated federalism.**[25] The national government began to set standards of conduct or required the states to set standards that met national guidelines. The effect of these national standards is that state and local policies in the areas of environmental protection, social services, and education are more uniform from coast to coast than are other nationally funded policies.

preemption the principle that allows the national government to override state or local actions in certain policy areas

Some national standards require the federal government to take over areas of regulation formerly overseen by state or local governments. Such **preemption** occurs when state and local actions are found to be inconsistent with federal requirements. If this occurs, all regulations in the preempted area must henceforth come from the national government. In many cases, the scope of the federal authority to preempt is decided by the courts. For example, in 1973 the Supreme Court struck down a local ordinance prohibiting jets from taking off from the airport in Burbank, California, between 11 P.M. and 7 A.M. It ruled that the Federal Aeronautics Act granted the Federal Aviation Administration all authority over flight patterns, takeoffs, and landings and that local governments could not impose regulations in this area. As federal regulations increased after the 1970s, Washington increasingly preempted state and local action in many different policy areas. This preemption has escalated since 1995, when Republicans gained control of Congress. Although the Republicans came to power promising to grant more responsibility to the states, they have reduced state control in many areas by preemption. For example, in 1998 Congress passed a law that prohibits states and localities from taxing Internet commerce for the next three to six years. State and local governments often contest federal preemptions. For example, in 2001, Attorney General John Ashcroft declared that Oregon's law permitting doctor-assisted suicide was illegal under federal drug regulations. Oregon took the Justice Department to federal court, which ruled in favor of the local law, stating that the federal government had overstepped its boundaries. In other recent cases, federal preemption of local laws has been more successful, as in federal efforts to nullify the medical marijuana statutes passed by several states. Although voters in three states have approved medical use of marijuana, the federal government has conducted raids on dispensers of medical marijuana, charging that they violate federal law.

The growth of national standards has created some new problems and has raised questions about how far federal standardization should go. One problem that emerged in the 1980s was the increase in **unfunded mandates**—regulations or new conditions for receiving grants that impose costs on state and local governments for which they are not reimbursed by the national government. The growth of unfunded mandates was the product of a Democratic Congress, which wanted to achieve liberal social objectives, and a Republican president, who opposed increased social spending. Between 1983 and 1991, Congress mandated standards in many policy areas, including social services and environmental regulations, without providing additional funds to meet those standards. Altogether, Congress enacted twenty-seven laws that imposed new regulations or required states to expand existing programs.[26] For example, in the late 1980s, Congress ordered the states to extend the coverage provided by Medicaid, the medical insurance program for the poor. The aim was to make the program serve more people, particularly poor children, and to expand services. But Congress did not supply additional funding to help states meet these new requirements; the states had to shoulder the increased financial burden themselves.

States and localities quickly began to protest the cost of unfunded mandates. Although it is very hard to determine the exact cost of federal regulations, the Congressional Budget Office estimated that between 1983 and 1990, new federal regulations cost states and localities between $8.9 and $12.7 billion.[27] States complained that mandates took up so much of their budgets that they were not able to set their own priorities.

These burdens became part of a rallying cry to reduce the power of the federal government—a cry that took center stage when a Republican Congress was elected in 1994. One of the first measures the new Congress passed was an act to limit the cost of unfunded mandates, the Unfunded Mandate Reform Act (UMRA). Under this law, Congress must estimate the cost of any proposal it believes will cost more than $50 million. It must then vote to approve the regulation, acknowledging the expenditure. At most, UMRA represented an effort to move the national-state relationship a bit further to the state side. But it has had no significant impact on mandates. The act does not prevent congressional members from passing unfunded mandates, but only makes them think twice before they do. Moreover, the act exempts several areas of regulation. States must still enforce antidiscrimination laws and meet other requirements to receive federal assistance.

Despite considerable talk about unfunded mandates, the federal government has not acted to help states pay for existing mandates, many of which have grown very costly over the years. For example, federal law requires states to offer education

unfunded mandates regulations or conditions for receiving grants that impose costs on state and local governments for which they are not reimbursed by the federal government

to disabled children. Despite its promises, the federal government has offered little new support for states confronting the rapidly rising costs of this responsibility. This issue became the focus of national attention in 2001 when Vermont Republican senator Jim Jeffords threatened to leave the Republican Party in part because congressional Republicans refused to provide full funding to the states for the costs of educating disabled children. In a dramatic move, Jeffords, a lifelong Republican, decided to switch his party affiliation to independent and to vote with the Democrats. His move robbed Republicans of their one-vote majority and turned control of the Senate over to Democrats.

New national problems inevitably raise the question of "who pays?" Since the terrorist attacks, state governments have grown deeply concerned about the costs of security. The National Governors' Association estimated that enhanced security for the first year alone would cost the states $4 billion. Director of Homeland Security Tom Ridge assured state leaders that the federal government would help with these new expenses but cautioned that states would also have to contribute.[28] The relationship between national security needs and state and local capabilities will remain a critical area for the future of state and federal relations.

NEW FEDERALISM AND STATE CONTROL

> **What methods have been employed to give more control back to the states?**

In 1970, the mayor of Oakland, California, told Congress that there were twenty-two separate employment and training programs in his city but that few poor residents were being trained for jobs that were available in the local labor market.[29] National programs had proliferated as Congress enacted many small grants, but little effort was made to coordinate or adapt programs to local needs. Today many governors argue for more control over such national grant programs. They complain that national grants do not allow for enough local flexibility and instead take a "one size fits all" approach.[30] These criticisms point to a fundamental problem in American federalism: how to get the best results for the money spent. Do some divisions of responsibility between states and the federal government work better than others? Since the 1970s, as states have become more capable of administering large-scale programs, the idea of devolution—transferring responsibility for policy from the federal government to the states and localities—has become popular.

block grants federal grants-in-aid that allow states considerable discretion in how the funds are spent

New Federalism attempts by Presidents Nixon and Reagan to return power to the states through block grants

general revenue sharing the process by which one unit of government yields a portion of its tax income to another unit of government, according to an established formula. Revenue sharing typically involves the national government providing money to state governments

Proponents of more state authority have looked to **block grants** as a way of reducing federal control. Block grants are federal grants that allow the states considerable leeway in spending federal money. President Nixon led the first push for block grants in the early 1970s, as part of his **New Federalism.** Nixon's block grants consolidated programs in the areas of job training, community development, and social services into three large block grants. These grants imposed some conditions on states and localities for how the money should be spent, but not the narrow regulations contained in the categorical grants. In addition, Congress provided an important new form of federal assistance to state and local governments called **general revenue sharing.** Revenue sharing provided money to local governments and counties with no strings attached; localities could spend the money as they wished. In enacting revenue sharing, Washington acknowledged both the critical role that state and local governments play in implementing national priorities and their need for increased funding and enhanced flexibility in order to carry out that role. Reagan's version of New Federalism also looked to block grants. Like Nixon, Reagan wanted to reduce the national government's control and return power to the states. In all, Congress created twelve new block grants between 1981 and 1990.[31]

Another way of letting the states do more is by having the national government do less. When Nixon implemented block grants he increased federal spending. But Reagan's block grants cut federal funding by 12 percent. His view was that the states could spend their own funds to make up the difference, if they chose to do so. Revenue sharing was also eliminated during the Reagan administration, leaving localities to fend for themselves. The Republican Congress elected in 1994 took this strategy even further, supporting block grants as well as substantial cuts in federal programs. Their biggest success was the 1996 welfare reform law, which delegated to states important new responsibilities. Most of the other major proposed block grants or spending reductions failed to pass Congress or were vetoed by President Clinton. The Republican congressional leadership had found that it was much easier to promise a "devolution revolution" than to deliver on that promise.[32]

Neither block grants nor reduced federal funding have proven to be magic solutions to the problems of federalism. For one thing, there is always a trade-off between accountability, that is, whether the states are using funds for the purposes intended, and flexibility. Accountability and proper use of funds continue to be troublesome issues. Even after block grants were created, Congress reimposed regulations in order to increase the states' accountability. If the objective is to have accountable and efficient government, it is not clear that state bureaucracies are any more efficient or more capable than national agencies. In Mississippi, for example, the state Department of Human Services spent money from the child care block grant for office furniture and designer salt and pepper shakers that cost $37.50 a pair. As one Mississippi state legislator said, "I've seen too many years of good ol' boy politics to know they shouldn't [transfer money to the states] without stricter controls and requirements."[33]

Reduced federal funding may leave states with problems that they do not have the resources to solve. During the 1980s, many states had to raise taxes in order to make up for some of the cuts in federal funding. (The impact of these cuts can be seen in Table 3.3.) And in the early 1990s and again in 2002, when recession hit, states had to cut back services because they were short of funds even after raising taxes.

Federal Aid as a Percentage of General Annual Expenditure, 1977 and 1998

Table 3.3

CITY	1977	1998	CITY	1977	1998
Chicago	20%	7%	Houston	13%	4%
Cleveland	29	9	Indianapolis	21	4
Denver	14	2	Los Angeles	22	4
Detroit	31	9	San Antonio	28	2
Honolulu	30	9	Seattle	23	3

SOURCE: Department of Commerce, *Statistical Abstract of the United States, 2001* (Washington, DC: U.S. Government Printing Office, 2001), Tables 445 and 446.

Most discussion of New Federalism has focused on increased state control over government spending programs. On balance, we have seen, states did gain more power over spending policies during the 1980s and 1990s. Yet, in other important respects, states lost power during the same time period. As discussed in the previous section, the federal government has used its power of preemption to limit state discretion. The Republican Congress was especially active in asserting federal power in the areas of criminal law, securities law, and telecommunications. The imposition of federal standards has likewise continued to grow. The first major bipartisan legislation of the George W. Bush administration was an education bill that gave schools more discretion over how they used federal dollars but, at the same time, imposed educational standards by requiring annual reading and math tests.

DEVOLUTION: FOR WHOSE BENEFIT?

Since the expansion of the national government in the 1930s, questions about "who does what" have frequently provoked conflict in American politics. Why does such an apparently simple choice set off such highly charged political debate? One reason is that many decisions about federal versus state responsibility have implications for who benefits from government action.

Let's consider the benefits of federal control versus devolution in the realm of **redistributive programs.** These are programs designed primarily for the benefit of the poor. Many political scientists and economists maintain that states and localities should not be in charge of redistributive programs. They argue that since states and local governments have to compete with one another, they do not have the incentive to spend their money on the needy people in their areas. Instead, they want to keep taxes low and spend money on things that promote economic development.[34] In this situation, states might engage in a "race to the bottom": if one state cuts assistance to the poor, neighboring states will institute similar or deeper cuts both to reduce expenditures and to discourage poorer people from moving into their states. As one New York legislator put it, "The concern we have is that unless we make our welfare system and our tax and regulatory system competitive with the states around us, we will have too many disincentives for business to move here. Welfare is a big part of that."[35]

In 1996, when Congress enacted a major welfare reform law, it followed a different logic. By changing welfare from a combined federal-state program into a block grant to the states, Congress gave the states more responsibility for programs that serve the poor. One argument in favor of this decision was that states can act as "laboratories of democracy," by experimenting with many different approaches to find ones that best meet the needs of their citizens.[36] As states have altered their welfare programs in the wake of the new law, they have indeed designed diverse approaches. For example, Minnesota has adopted an incentive-based approach that offers extra assistance to families that take low-wage jobs. Other states, such as California, have more "sticks" than "carrots" in their new welfare programs. In the years since the passage of the law, welfare rolls have declined dramatically. On average they have declined by 47 percent from their peak in 1994; in six states the decline was 70 percent or higher. Politicians have cited these statistics to claim that the poor have benefited from greater state control of

redistributive programs economic policies designed to control the economy through taxing and spending, with the goal of benefiting the poor

Perspectives on Politics

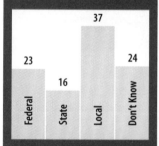

THE EFFICIENCY OF DIFFERENT LEVELS OF GOVERNMENT

Responses of eighteen- to twenty-four-year-olds to the question,
"From which level of government do you feel you get the most for your money?"

Federal	State	Local	Don't Know
23	16	37	24

SOURCE: 1993 U.S. Advisory Commission on Intergovernmental Relations survey, reported in Susan A. MacManus, *Young v. Old: Generational Combat in the 21st Century* (Boulder, CO: Westview, 1996), p. 185.

Welfare Reform

President Franklin D. Roosevelt's New Deal effort to improve America's social and economic condition established the modern social welfare state, inaugurated with the enactment of the Social Security Act of 1935. This act provided income benefits for retired workers, the disabled, and the unemployed. In the 1960s, social welfare programs were expanded to improve conditions for the nation's poor. In the 1980s, Presidents Ronald Reagan and George H. W. Bush won cuts in programs like food stamps, Aid to Families with Dependent Children (AFDC), and job programs. President Bill Clinton also seized on what is now called welfare reform, promising to reorganize and streamline these programs. Congress approved legislation to end AFDC and give the money to the states to run their own welfare programs, limit benefits eligibility to five years, and insist on work requirements for welfare recipients. Yet these and other proposed changes continue to be controversial.

Supporters of welfare reform argue that the federal welfare system has spiraled out of control. Spending on all social welfare programs topped $300 billion a year in the 1990s, at a time when government resources were shrinking. Despite the vast spending of the past decade, poverty persists. The United States today supports a self-perpetuating culture of poverty that discourages able-bodied people from working. Welfare tears the fabric of society by producing generations of young people who are ignorant of the work ethic; it encourages unwed motherhood among a rising number of teenagers (three-fourths of all teenage mothers land on welfare within five years); and it spawns rising rates of crime. Furthermore, the welfare system is expensive because it is inefficiently run. Too many able-bodied or ineligible people continue to receive government benefits.

Welfare reform seeks not only to weed out those who cheat the system, but to break the cycle of welfare dependency. Proponents of reform argue that the states are in the best position to decide how to handle poverty, since patterns vary widely from state to state. Beyond this, they assert, greater emphasis needs to be placed on the work ethic, so that those who *can* work *do*. "Deadbeat dads," men who fail to support the children they father, should be forced to support their families. The values of family life need to be emphasized to help break the cycle of unmarried teenage motherhood and dependency. Educational opportunities provide a vital route for the poor to acquire the skills they need to lead self-supporting, productive lives. Private charities and the spirit of voluntarism should replace government largesse. A good example of this is the private program Habitat for Humanity, which helps the poor build and occupy their own homes. In short, government welfare may not be ended, but the poor can be aided more cheaply and more effectively through private means.

Opponents of welfare reform argue that a governmental welfare safety net is necessary, and that welfare-related spending levels and problems have been greatly exaggerated. For example, the argument that increases in welfare benefits have encouraged unwed teenage motherhood is not borne out by most studies of the matter. The biggest cause of poverty is economic dislocation and shifts in the nature and demands of the workplace—factors over which individuals have no control. The primary "welfare" programs, including AFDC,

A New Beginning
Welfare to Work

food stamps, rent subsidies, and school lunches, comprised only about 3.5 percent of the 2001 national budget. The most expensive social programs are aimed mostly at the middle class, including Social Security and Medicare, which took up over 33 percent of the 2001 budget. Government spending for AFDC and similar programs has declined by over 40 percent, in real dollars, since the start of the 1980s.

Many of the social and behavioral problems associated with poverty arise from the fact that the government spends far less per capita on its poor than do most other industrialized nations. This keeps the poor at a subsistence level that makes it even more difficult for them to improve their situation. The culture of poverty idea is also greatly exaggerated, as six-sevenths of those who receive AFDC leave the benefits system within five years. Rather than stigmatizing and berating the poor, the government needs to emphasize constructive measures to assist those in need, so that they may get the child care, education, and other support necessary to break out of poverty. Only the federal government can ensure a consistent and fair level of support to those most in need.

Does Welfare Reform Work?

Yes

President Bush has called for an increased number of welfare recipients in the workforce, a needed step in the right direction.

"The right direction" is a complete end to welfare as we know it.

Bush's welfare proposal would escalate the 50 percent of welfare recipients who are required to work to 70 percent by 2007. His proposal would also increase the number of hours that they work a week from 30 to 40. These would be improvements on the welfare reform legislation of 1996.

There are several reasons why the welfare system needs to be changed and several reasons why it has failed.

Welfare is based on the wrong assumptions. It is based on the assumption that low family wealth is the cause of problems in social behavior. The intention is to help low-income families raise their income. Time has shown that income has not improved social and psychological conditions; instead, things have tended to become worse. Studies show that children are done more harm than good living in welfare homes. One study shows that the longer a child was raised in a welfare home the lower that child's IQ. The study shows that welfare dependence, not poverty, is the root of the lower IQ. Other studies indicate that children from welfare homes are more likely to commit crime, have children out of wedlock, and be on welfare themselves.

Welfare reform, on the other hand, tries a different approach. It, in effect, tries to reduce dependence on welfare, increasing the number of recipients in the workforce and reducing illegitimacy.

Opponents of welfare reform will contend that the suffering caused by cutting benefits to anyone is unacceptable for moral reasons and that low-income jobs are no better at lifting families out of poverty.

Yet, the long-term suffering caused by the instilled ideals of a welfare youth is far greater than the suffering that may occur when people stay on welfare. Many of these children never learn the values to support themselves responsibly.

In 1997, 41,000 families in Massachusetts were told that their welfare grants would stop at the end of the following year. Before the deadline came, 90 percent of those families were already out of the program; indicating that a move into the workforce was possible and had not been actively pursued previously.

The liberal opponents of welfare reform had said that dependence on welfare was unavoidable. They said that even strong reform would do little to improve welfare numbers.

However, since the welfare reform laws of 1996, the welfare caseload has dropped nearly 60 percent, from an all-time high in 1994.

The welfare system is a government experiment that is ineffective at improving the social conditions of lower income groups. It is a waste of taxpayer money, providing a lifestyle that has increased illegitimacy and crime and decreased scholastic achievement.

In contrast, reform programs have been shown to be effective in decreasing dependence and improving the economic condition of recipients in the program, providing incentive for maintaining marriages and workfare programs to gain experience.

Fundamentally, it is the impetus to work and the responsibility of work itself that has the desired effect on individual achievement.

It is the pressure to achieve and then the achievement itself that affects your self-esteem and therefore your outlook on life. I believe that once the pressure is applied, most individuals will continue down the path of success.

Bush's proposal will take us steps closer to removing the failed welfare system by increasing requirements that get people working and hopefully pulling individuals away from government dependence completely.

SOURCE: Ian Clift, "Welfare Reform Will Successfully Replace Old System," *The Purdue Exponent*, February 28, 2002.

No In 1995, back when there were Top 40 stars who had already gone through puberty, our country entered the era of welfare reform. In that year, Congress passed a law saying five years on welfare was all anyone could get and leaders of both major parties excitedly championed "workfare over welfare."

These politicians believed if they withheld government aid from welfare recipients, these former recipients would get out into the marketplace and find jobs out of necessity. Once they got jobs, the reasoning went, former welfare recipients would be better off than they were on welfare. By reforming welfare, our friends in Washington actually thought they were doing America's hardpressed a favor.

Now the five years have passed and the federal government is dumping people from the rolls. Some of them may be getting jobs just as predicted, but with the current economic slowdown, many are not. However, even for those lucky enough to find jobs, there is a little problem. It seems millions of people who work full time in the United States are still unable to support their families, including those who support children.

The question is this: Where does this fit into the welfare reform equation? The basic assumption behind welfare reform—that work, or full-time work in particular, ensures a modest standard of living—is fatally flawed. A report released last month by the Washington-based Economic Policy Institute, "Hardships in America: The Real Story of Working Families," is the most comprehensive study of family hardships ever published, and its findings are frightening. "Hardships in America" exposes the danger of using the federal poverty line as a threshold for a decent standard of living. The study examines the cost of living in every community nationwide and determines the "basic family budget" a family of four living in each community would need for food, housing, health care, child care, transportation, and utilities. The study determined the national median basic family budget to be $33,511 for a family of four, 91 percent greater than the federal poverty line of $17,463 for a family of that size.

Naturally, some will be suspicious of this inorganically calculated figure, but the results of the report's study on real working families are even more convincing. Researchers found nearly one-third of families with incomes below twice the poverty level faced a "critical hardship" such as going without food, getting evicted, having to "double up" in housing with another family, or not having access to medical care during a serious illness. Nearly three-quarters of families below twice the poverty line faced difficulties such as worrying about food, failing to pay rent, using the emergency room as their primary source of health care, having their phone disconnected, or having inadequate childcare.

Of course, there is a racial element to this story as well. Black and Hispanic families are about two and a half times more likely than white families to fall below basic family budget levels. All in all, "Hardships in America" tells a story of intense struggle by great numbers of families in one of the world's richest nations.

The most important lesson here is that work does not cure all. The federal minimum wage continues to stand at $5.15 per hour, while the median basic family budget requires two parents, working full-time, to each make $8.06 an hour or a single parent working full-time to make $16.11.

***

If the wages of America's lowest-paid workers are not going to raise enough to meet the needs of families, then the federal government must take more of the responsibility for these families' well-being. Welfare reform was a tricky way for the federal government to shirk its responsibility of ensuring all Americans have the basic necessities. The report shows many who have gone from welfare to work and a vast majority of low-wage workers who have never been on the welfare rolls are not making ends meet even if they are clocking in 40 or more hours a week.

SOURCE: Peter Asen, "Welfare Families Slave as Hard as the Rest of Us," *Brown Daily Herald,* September 10, 2001.

The debate over national versus state control is illustrated by the question of speed limits. The issue arose in 1973, when gas prices skyrocketed and supplies became scarce. Drivers nationwide were forced to wait in long lines at gas stations (right). The federal government responded to the gas crisis by instituting a national 55-mile-per-hour speed limit. The new limit was mandatory on all federal highways and was intended to reduce gas use (below).

welfare, yet analysts caution that we do not yet know enough about the fate of those who have left welfare to judge the effect of welfare reform. Most studies have found that the majority of those leaving welfare remain in poverty. Many analysts are also concerned that the poor who rely on support from states become particularly vulnerable during economic recessions. Because states have to balance their budgets each year, they have little cushion to fall back on during an economic downturn. As a recession began in 2001, welfare rolls began to rise once again and the fate of current and former welfare recipients remained in doubt. Sharper limits on receiving welfare benefits and weak state unemployment insurance systems threatened to leave many with no support. Critics believe that the poor would be better off with a national program that guaranteed a basic level of support for needy people. They contrast welfare to Social Security, a fully national program that has greatly reduced poverty among the elderly.

In other decisions about federalism, local concerns have been overridden in the name of the national interest. In the example of air traffic, which was cited in a previous section, local residents of Burbank, California, lost out to the national interest in having a smoothly operating air transportation system. The question of speed limits, discussed at the beginning of this chapter, raised a similar set of concerns. Speed limits had traditionally been a state and local responsibility. But in 1973, at the height of the oil shortage, Congress passed legislation to withhold federal highway funds from states that did not adopt a maximum speed limit of 55 miles per hour (mph). The lower speed limit, it was argued, would reduce energy consumption by cars. Although Congress had not formally taken over the authority to set speed limits, the power of its purse was so important that every state adopted the new speed limit. The national interest in energy conservation had outweighed local preferences for higher speed limits. As the crisis faded, concern about energy conservation diminished. The national speed limit lost much of its support, even though it was found to have reduced the number of traffic deaths. In 1995, Congress repealed the penalties for higher speed limits, and states once again became free to set their own speed limits. Many states with large rural areas raised their maximum to 75 mph; Montana set unlimited speeds in the rural areas during daylight hours. Early research indicates that numbers of highway deaths have indeed risen in the states that increased the limits.[37]

Because the division of responsibility in the federal system has important implications for who benefits, few conflicts over state versus national control will ever be settled once and for all. As new evidence becomes available about the costs and benefits of different arrangements, it provides fuel for ongoing debates about what are properly the states' responsibilities and what the federal government should do. Likewise, changes in the political control of the national government usually provoke a rethinking of responsibilities as new leaders seek to alter federal arrangements for the benefit of the groups they represent.

In 1995, Congress removed its speed limit restrictions and gave the states the right to determine their own road speeds. As a result, speed limits went up on many highways (above). Proponents of the states' right to set higher speed limits had insisted that it would not increase the number of accidents on the road. However, car accidents like this fatal crash—in which a truck carrying speed limit signs rolled over and caught fire—suggest that high speed limits may have dangerous consequences (left).

Federalism and American Political Values

> **How do changes in American federalism reflect different interpretations of liberty, equality, and democracy?**

It is often argued that liberals prefer a strong federal government because they value equality more than liberty. Conservatives are said to prefer granting more power to states and localities because they care most about liberty. Although this greatly oversimplifies liberal and conservative views about government, such arguments underscore the fact that ideas about federalism are linked to different views about the purposes of government. For what ends should government powers be used? What happens when widely shared national values conflict in practice? The connections between federalism and our fundamental national values have made federalism a focus of political contention throughout our nation's history.

The Constitution limited the power of the federal government in order to promote liberty. This decision reflected the framers' suspicions of centralized power, based on their experience with the British Crown. The American suspicion of centralized power lives on today in widespread dislike of "big government," which generally evokes a picture of a bloated federal government. But over the course of our history we have come to realize that the federal government is also an important guarantor of liberty. As we'll see in Chapter 4, it took enhanced federal power to ensure that local and state governments adhered to the fundamental constitutional freedoms in the Bill of Rights.

One of the most important continuing arguments for a strong federal government is its role in ensuring equality. A key puzzle of federalism is deciding when differences across states represent the proper democratic decisions of the states and when such differences represent inequalities that should not be tolerated. Sometimes a decision to eliminate differences is made on the grounds of equality and individual rights, as in the Civil Rights Act of 1964, which outlawed legal segregation. At other times, a stronger federal role is justified on the grounds of national interest, as in the case of the oil shortage and the institution of a 55 mph speed limit in the 1970s. Advocates of a more limited federal role often point to the value of democracy. Public actions can more easily be tailored to fit distinctive local or state desires if states and localities have more power to make policy. Viewed this way, variation across states can be an expression of democratic will.

In recent years, many Americans have grown disillusioned with the federal government and have supported efforts to give the states more responsibilities. A 1997 poll, for example, found that Americans tended to have the most confidence in governments that were closest to them. Thirty-eight percent expressed "a great deal" of confidence in local government, 32 percent in state government, and 22 percent in the federal government. Nearly two-thirds of those polled believed that shifting some responsibility to states and localities would help achieve excellence in government. After the terrorist attacks, however, support for the federal government soared. With issues of security topping the list of citizens' concerns, the federal government, which had seemed less important with the waning of the cold war, suddenly reemerged as the central actor in American politics. As one observer put it, "Federalism was a luxury of peaceful times."[38] Yet the newfound respect for the federal government is likely to be contingent on how well the government performs. If the federal government does not appear to be effective in the fight against terrorism, its stature may once again decline in the minds of many Americans.

What Government Does . . . After September 11

As a federal system, the United States government faces special challenges in protecting its citizens against terrorism. The national government does not have sufficient capability to provide domestic security by itself, since it commands no national police force. Instead, Washington must rely on some 18,000 state and local law enforcement agencies to carry out its domestic security strategy. The need for new forms of cooperation and coordination among different levels of government raised many thorny issues in the months after the terrorist attacks.

The lack of coordination among the governments in the federal system became vividly clear to New York City police commissioner Bernard B. Kerik on the very day of the attacks. As the commissioner and the mayor ran from the scene of the collapsing World Trade Center towers, Kerik realized he had no idea whom he was supposed to call to shut down the airspace around New York City and to get F-16 fighter jets to protect the city against further attacks.[1]

As state and local officials began to grapple with their new security responsibilities, information emerged as a critical concern. State and local officials expressed frustration with the Federal Bureau of Investigation and other federal agencies for not providing them with enough information to do their jobs effectively. Criticizing the FBI's "go it alone" strategy, New York senator Charles E. Schumer charged that "chronic lack of communication between federal and local authorities undermines efforts to protect the homeland."[2] Mayors complained that if they were to assist in homeland defense, they needed specific and timely information. In the months after September 11, repeated warnings from the Justice Department about the possibility of additional terrorist attacks frustrated many mayors and police chiefs. Without more specific information, they did not know what actions to take.

Mayors also found that when there were specific threats of special concern to their cities, they were not alerted. Boston mayor Thomas M. Menino assumed that he would be informed by the federal government if there were threats on gas supplies since his city is a major center for tankers carrying gas. When he did learn of a such a threat, it was not from federal officials. "'You know how I found that out?' [he] said. 'Reading the Internet. Nobody called and told me. I think the first thing that should happen is the mayor should be contacted because the mayor is on the front lines.'"[3]

State and local police officers rely on the FBI's national crime database to identify suspects in routine traffic stops. Yet the FBI's detailed information about suspects to watch after September 11 was not made available to state and local officials until a month after the attacks. Without such basic information, local law enforcement cannot play its part in domestic security. Baltimore mayor Martin O'Malley expressed his frustration with the delay: "Unless they think they all graduated from the Osama bin Laden school of perfect driving, why wouldn't they ask us to be looking for these folks on traffic stops or speeding stops? . . . It's mind-boggling to me."[4]

The costs of domestic security posed another set of challenges for the federal system. The terrorist attacks blurred the lines between national security, which the federal government pays for, and law enforcement, which is a state and local responsibility. State governments are responsible for protecting vital installations such as bridges, dams, ports, and chemical plants. States also have to pay the costs of posting the National Guard to protect these facilities. Faced with mounting costs, some states began to resist federal warnings to beef up security because they could not afford it. As Maine governor Angus King put it, "We just aren't financially geared up for this level of what is really a national defense expenditure. . . . The question for us is where do you stop with providing security?"[5]

Faced with such challenges, the first months after the attacks were a period of intense learning for political leaders and government officials. Several different efforts were launched to improve coordination across the federal system. Federal officials pledged to improve communication with state and local law enforcement agencies. Director of Homeland Security Tom Ridge promised to help states with the costs of security. Congress considered new legislation designed to remove legal barriers to sharing FBI information with state and local officials. Through such initiatives, local, state, and federal officials began to take the first steps needed to make the federal system rise to the challenge of providing greatly enhanced domestic security.

[1] Jennifer Steinhauer with David W. Chen, "Mayor Urges U.S. to Improve Its Exchange of Information," *New York Times,* October 30, 2001, p. B5.

[2] Adam Clymer, "Schumer and Mrs. Clinton Want FBI to Share Facts," *New York Times,* November 1, 2001, p. B11.

[3] Pam Belluck and Timothy Egan, "A Nation Challenged: Domestic Defense; Cities and States Say Confusion and Cost Hamper U.S. Security Drive," *New York Times,* December 10, 2001, p. B1.

[4] *Ibid.*

[5] *Ibid.*

American federalism remains a work in progress. As public problems shift and as local, state, and federal governments change, questions about the relationship between American values and federalism naturally emerge. The different views that people bring to this discussion suggest that concerns about federalism will remain a central issue in American democracy.

What You Can Do: Participate at Different Levels of the Federal System

How can citizens contribute to the ongoing design of American federalism? To be effective participants in a federal system, citizens must first understand how responsibilities are divided among the different levels of government. They also need to be aware of how decisions taken at one level of government may affect the possibilities for public action at other levels. In other words, if citizens are to be politically effective they must understand the connections among the levels of the federal system and target their activities where they will be most effective.

One of the striking features of political participation in the United States is the preference for engaging in politics at the state and local levels. One study of political participation found that 92 percent of Americans who participated beyond voting—by campaigning, contacting public officials, or sitting on a governing board, for example—engaged in an activity focused on state and local activity. Fifty-one percent of those questioned engaged only in state and local action, while 41 percent added some form of national participation to their state and local activities.[39] This pattern of participation makes sense because politics at these levels—especially the local level—is more personal and often easier to get involved in. Moreover, many of the things that people care most about are close to home. Here are two local arenas that may attract your interest.

1. *Public education.* State governments mandate the general requirements for curricula and minimal requirements for graduation, but these state mandates are administered by local school districts. In turn, local school districts are managed by superintendents who have considerable discretion in shaping elementary, middle, high school, and sometimes community college education. Most school districts and superintendents are accountable to local school boards. School board members are usually selected by voters in competitive elections in the same way that mayors or council members are chosen.
2. *Law enforcement.* Most states have several different police agencies, for example, state police or highway patrol, county sheriffs, and city or town peace officers. Other state and local officials may have police powers, too. We do not necessarily think of lifeguards or forest rangers as police personnel, but they often are.

Many police agencies practice community policing. Rather than simply react to crime, they try to prevent crime by promoting a local environment conducive to law-abiding behavior. They may sponsor after-school programs for at-risk youth; they may provide mediation services to settle domestic disputes; or they may host community forums aimed at easing racial tensions and promoting interracial cooperation.

To be broadly effective, citizens must also be able to engage in political activity at different levels of the federal system. For example, in the 1970s, community groups frustrated in their efforts to revitalize inner-city neighborhoods lobbied Congress to pass the Community Reinvestment Act, which requires banks to invest in the neighborhoods where they do business. With this federal law behind them, community organizations have been much more effective in promoting investment. But it is often not easy for groups of citizens to focus their activity at different levels of government as needed. Often they do not have the expertise or the contacts or the information to be effective in a different setting.

In recent years, as states have taken on a greater role in making public policy, it has become more important for citizens to become effective participants in state politics. Moreover, the media coverage of state politics is generally not as deep or informative as coverage of national politics. Citizens need a better knowledge of what states do today and more information about state politics simply as a first step to being effective participants in our federal system.

The federal system makes American democracy a flexible form of government for a large and diverse nation. But citizens must be knowledgeable about how public actions across the federal system are connected and they must be able to act at different levels if federalism is to be an effective and representative form of government.

Summary

In this chapter, we have examined one of the central principles of American government—federalism. The Constitution divides powers between the national government and the states, but over time national power has grown substantially. Many aspects of expanded federal power stem from struggles to realize the ideals of liberty and equality for all citizens.

The aim of federalism in the Constitution was to limit national power by creating two sovereigns—the national government and the state governments. The Founders hoped that this system of dual federalism would ensure the liberty of citizens by preventing the national government from becoming too powerful. But during the 1930s, American citizens used the democratic system to change the balance between federal and state governments. The failure of the states to provide basic economic security for citizens during the Great Depression led to an expansion of the federal government. Most Americans were supportive of this growing federal power because they believed that economic power had become too concentrated in the hands of big corporations and the common person was the loser. Thus, the ideal of equality—in this case, the belief that working people should have a fighting chance to support themselves—overrode fears that a strong federal government would abridge liberties. Expanded federal powers first took the form of grants-in-aid to states. Later, federal regulations became more common.

In recent years, many Americans have come to believe that the pendulum has swung too far in the direction of expanded federal power. A common charge is that the federal government is too big and, as a result, has encroached on fundamental liberties. State and local governments complain that they cannot govern because their powers have been preempted or because they have to use their own funds to fulfill unfunded mandates imposed by the federal government. The move to devolve more powers to the states has been called "New Federalism." Advocates of reduced federal power believe that states can protect liberty without creating unacceptable inequalities. Others continue to believe that a strong central government is essential to ensuring basic equalities. They argue that economic competition among the states means that states cannot ensure equality as well as the federal government can. Since September 11, Americans have looked to the federal government to ensure national security. Charges of "big government" have become less compelling as we face threats to domestic safety and national defense that only the federal government can address.

For Further Reading

Bensel, Richard. *Sectionalism and American Political Development: 1880–1980.* Madison: University of Wisconsin Press, 1984.

Bowman, Ann O'M., and Richard Kearny. *The Resurgence of the States.* Englewood Cliffs, NJ: Prentice-Hall, 1986.

Donahue, John D. *Disunited States.* New York: Basic Books, 1997.

Dye, Thomas R. *American Federalism: Competition among Governments.* Lexington, MA: Lexington Books, 1990.

Elazar, Daniel. *American Federalism: A View from the States,* 3rd ed. New York: Harper & Row, 1984.

Grodzins, Morton. *The American System.* Chicago: Rand McNally, 1974.

Kelley, E. Wood. *Policy and Politics in the United States: The Limits of Localism.* Philadelphia: Temple University Press, 1987.

Kettl, Donald. *The Regulation of American Federalism.* Baltimore: Johns Hopkins University Press, 1987.

Peterson, Paul E. *The Price of Federalism.* Washington, DC: Brookings, 1995.

Study Outline

www.wwnorton.com/wtp4e

The Federal Framework

1. In an effort to limit national power, the framers of the Constitution established a system of dual federalism, wherein both the national and state governments would have sovereignty.

2. The Constitution granted a few "expressed powers" to the national government and, through the Tenth Amendment, reserved all the rest to the states.

3. The Constitution also created obligations among the states in the "full faith and credit" and "privileges and immunities" clauses.

4. Federalism and a restrictive definition of "interstate commerce" limited the national government's control over the economy.

5. Federalism allows a great deal of variation between states.

6. Under the traditional system of federalism, the national government was small and very narrowly specialized in its functions compared with other Western nations. Most of its functions were aimed at promoting commerce.

7. Under the traditional system, states rather than the national government did most of the fundamental governing in the country.

8. The system of federalism limited the expansion of the national government despite economic forces and expansive interpretations of the Constitution in cases such as *McCulloch v. Maryland* and *Gibbons v. Ogden.*

9. For most of U.S. history, the concept of interstate commerce kept the national government from regulating the economy. But in 1937, the Supreme Court converted the commerce clause from a source of limitations to a source of power for the national government.

10. Recent years have seen a revival of interest in returning more power to the states through devolution.

Who Does What? The Changing Federal Framework

1. The rise of national government activity after the New Deal did not necessarily mean that states lost power directly.

Rather, the national government paid states through grants-in-aid to administer federal programs.

2. Some federal programs bypass the states by sending money directly to local governments or local organizations. The states are most important, however; they are integral to federal programs such as Medicaid.

3. The national government also imposed regulations on states and localities in areas such as environmental policy in order to guarantee national standards.

4. Under President Nixon, many categorical grants were combined into larger block grants that offered greater flexibility in the use of the money. The Nixon administration also developed revenue sharing that was not tied to any specific programs.

5. As states have become more capable of administering large-scale programs, the idea of devolution has become popular.

Federalism and American Political Values

1. Some of the sharpest tensions among liberty, equality, and democracy are visible in debates over federalism.

2. The Constitution limited the power of the national government as a safeguard for liberty, but over the course of American history, a strong national government has been an important guarantor of liberty.

3. A key puzzle of federalism is deciding when differences across states represent the proper democratic decisions of the states and when such differences represent inequalities that should not be tolerated.

Practice Quiz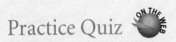

www.wwnorton.com/wtp4e

1. Which term describes the sharing of powers between the national government and the state governments?
   a) separation of powers
   b) federalism
   c) checks and balances
   d) shared powers

2. The system of federalism that allowed states to do most of the fundamental governing from 1789 to 1937 was
   a) home rule.
   b) regulated federalism.
   c) dual federalism.
   d) cooperative federalism.

3. Which of the following resulted from the federal system?
   a) It limited the power of the national government in relation to the states.
   b) It restrained the power of the national government over the economy.
   c) It allowed variation among the states.
   d) all of the above

4. The overall effect of the growth of national policies has been
   a) to weaken state government.
   b) to strengthen state government.
   c) to provide uniform laws in the nation.
   d) to make the states more diverse culturally.

5. Which amendment to the Constitution stated that the powers not delegated to the national government or prohibited to the states were "reserved to the states"?
   a) First Amendment
   b) Fifth Amendment
   c) Tenth Amendment
   d) Twenty-sixth Amendment

6. The process of returning more of the responsibilities of governing from the national level to the state level is known as
   a) dual federalism.
   b) devolution.
   c) preemption.
   d) home rule.

7. One of the most powerful tools by which the federal government has attempted to get the states to act in ways that are desired by the federal government is by
   a) providing grants-in-aid.
   b) requiring licensing.
   c) granting home rule.
   d) defending states' rights.

8. The form of regulated federalism that allows the federal government to take over areas of regulation formerly overseen by states or local governments is called
   a) categorical grants.
   b) formula grants.
   c) project grants.
   d) preemption.

9. To what does the term "New Federalism" refer?
   a) the national government's regulation of state action through grants-in-aid
   b) the type of federalism relying on categorical grants
   c) efforts to return more policy-making discretion to the states through the use of block grants
   d) the recent emergence of local governments as important political actors

10. A recent notable example of the process of giving the states more responsibility for administering government programs is
   a) campaign finance reform.
   b) prison reform.
   c) trade reform.
   d) welfare reform.

Critical Thinking Questions

www.wwnorton.com/wtp4e

1. The role of the national government has changed significantly from the Founding era to the present. In what ways and to what extent do you think the framers of the Constitution would recognize modern American federalism? Do you think they would be pleased by the current balance of power between the sovereign national government and the sovereign state governments? In what ways did the system of federalism perform its intended functions? In what ways did it not?

2. Should states be required to implement unfunded mandates? Are Americans better off or worse off as a result of devolution?

3. Decisions about how responsibilities should be allocated across levels of government are often contentious because they have implications for who benefits. Who has benefited from recent decisions to devolve more power to the states? What would be the advantages and disadvantages of a unitary system in which the federal government had all power? What would be the advantages and disadvantages of a fully decentralized system in which states had all the power?

Key Terms

www.wwnorton.com/wtp4e

block grants (p. 102)
categorical grants (p. 98)
commerce clause (p. 91)
concurrent powers (p. 85)
cooperative federalism (p. 99)
devolution (p. 95)
dual federalism (p. 88)
expressed powers (p. 84)

federal system (p. 84)
federalism (p. 83)
formula grants (p. 98)
full faith and credit clause (p. 85)
general revenue sharing (p. 102)
grants-in-aid (p. 97)
home rule (p. 88)
implied powers (p. 84)
necessary and proper clause (p. 84)
New Federalism (p. 102)
police power (p. 85)

preemption (p. 100)
privileges and immunities clause (p. 87)
project grants (p. 98)
redistributive programs (p. 104)
regulated federalism (p. 100)
reserved powers (p. 85)
states' rights (p. 94)
unfunded mandates (p. 101)
unitary system (p. 84)

4 CIVIL LIBERTIES

What Government Does and Why It Matters

HE FIRST TEN AMENDMENTS of the United States Constitution, together called the **Bill of Rights,** are the basis for the freedoms we enjoy as American citizens. The Bill of Rights might well have been entitled the "Bill of Liberties," because the provisions that were incorporated in the Bill of Rights were seen as defining a private sphere of personal liberty, free of governmental restrictions. These freedoms include the right to free speech, the right to the free exercise of religion, prohibitions against unreasonable searches and seizures, guarantees of due process of law, and the right to privacy, including a woman's right to have an abortion.

As Jefferson had put it, a bill of rights "is what people are entitled to against every government on earth. . . ." Note the emphasis—people *against* government. **Civil liberties** are *protections from* improper government action. Thus, the Bill of Rights is a series of "thou shalt nots"—restraints imposed upon government. Some of these restraints are **substantive liberties,** which put limits on *what* the government shall and shall not have power to do—such as establishing a religion, quartering troops in private homes without consent, or seizing private property without just compensation. Other restraints are **procedural liberties,** which deal with *how* the government is supposed to act. These procedural liberties are usually grouped under the general category of **due process of law,** which first appears in the Fifth Amendment provision that "no person shall be . . . deprived of life, liberty, or property, without due process of law." For example, even though the government has the substantive power to declare certain acts to be crimes and to arrest and imprison persons who violate criminal laws, it may not do so without meticulously observing procedures designed to protect the accused person. The best known procedural rule is that an accused person is

Bill of Rights the first ten amendments to the Constitution, which guarantee certain rights and liberties to the people

civil liberties areas of personal freedom with which governments are constrained from interfering

substantive liberties restraints on what the government shall and shall not have the power to do

procedural liberties restraints on how the government is supposed to act; for example, citizens are guaranteed the due process of law

due process of law the right of every citizen against arbitrary action by national or state governments

presumed innocent until proven guilty. This rule does not question the government's power to punish someone for committing a crime; it questions only the way the government determines who committed the crime. Substantive and procedural restraints together identify the realm of civil liberties.

Today, we may take the liberties contained within the Bill of Rights for granted. Few citizens of other countries can make such a claim. In fact, few people in recorded history have enjoyed such protections, including American citizens before the 1960s. For more than 170 years after its passage in 1789, the Bill of Rights meant little to most Americans. As we shall see in this chapter, guaranteeing the liberties articulated in the Bill of Rights to all Americans required a long struggle. As new challenges to the Bill of Rights arise, this struggle will likely continue.

As recently as the early 1960s many of the freedoms we enjoy today were not guaranteed. At that time, abortion was illegal everywhere in the United States, criminal suspects in state cases did not have to be informed of their rights, some states required daily Bible readings and prayers in their public schools, and some communities regularly censored reading material that they deemed to be obscene. Since the early 1960s, the Supreme Court has expanded the scope of individual freedoms considerably. But since these liberties are constantly subject to judicial interpretation, their provisions are fragile and need to be vigilantly safeguarded, especially during times of war or a threat to national security, such as in the aftermath of September 11, 2001. ■

■ **In this chapter, our first task is to define the Bill of Rights and establish its relationship to personal liberty.** As we shall see, it is through the Bill of Rights that Americans are protected from government.

■ **We then turn to the process by which the Bill of Rights was applied, not only to the national government, but also to the state governments.** This nationalizing process has been long and selective in applying only certain provisions of the Bill of Rights.

- **The bulk of this chapter is an analysis of the state of civil liberties today, beginning with the First Amendment and the freedom of religion.** Questions over the meaning of this First Amendment guarantee continue to be a focal point of judicial interpretation of the Bill of Rights.

- **We then turn to the other First Amendment rights regarding the freedoms of speech and of the press.** Although freedom of speech and freedom of the press are critical for a democracy, some forms of speech are only conditionally protected.

- **After briefly reviewing the Second Amendment right to bear arms, we move on to the rights of those accused of a crime.** These rights, contained in the Fourth, Fifth, Sixth, and Eighth Amendments, make up the due process of law, a concept that the Supreme Court continues to reinterpret.

- **We then turn to a right that has become increasingly important in recent decades, the right to privacy.** This right takes many forms and, like the freedoms found directly in the Bill of Rights, has been subject to new judicial interpretations.

- **We conclude by pondering the future of civil liberties in the United States.** As we emphasize throughout this chapter, the Bill of Rights is constantly subject to the interpretations of the Supreme Court. Will the Court try to limit the extent of civil liberties in the near future?

A Brief History of the Bill of Rights

When the first Congress under the newly ratified Constitution met in late April of 1789, the most important item of business was the consideration of a proposal to add a bill of rights to the Constitution. Such a proposal had been turned down with little debate in the waning days of the Philadelphia Constitutional Convention in 1787, not because the delegates were against rights, but because, as the Federalists, led by Alexander Hamilton, later argued, it was "not only unnecessary in the proposed Constitution but would even be dangerous."[1] First, according to Hamilton, a bill of rights would be irrelevant to a national government that was given only delegated powers in the first place. To put restraints on "powers which are not granted" could provide a pretext for governments to claim more powers than were in fact granted: "For why declare that things shall not be done which there is no power to do?"[2] Second, the Constitution was to Hamilton and the Federalists a bill of rights in itself, or contained provisions that amounted to a bill of rights without requiring additional amendments (see Table 4.1). For example, Article I, Section 9, included the right of *habeas corpus,* which prohibits the government from depriving a person of liberty without an open trial before a judge.

Despite the power of Hamilton's arguments, when the Constitution was submitted to the states for ratification, Antifederalists, most of whom had not been delegates in Philadelphia, picked up on the argument of Thomas Jefferson (who also had not been a delegate) that the omission of a bill of rights was a

habeas corpus a court order demanding that an individual in custody be brought into court and shown the cause for detention

| Table 4.1 | Rights in the Original Constitution (Not in the Bill of Rights) |

CLAUSE	RIGHT ESTABLISHED
Article I, Sec. 9	guarantee of *habeas corpus*
Article I, Sec. 9	prohibition of **bills of attainder**
Article I, Sec. 9	prohibition of **ex post facto laws**
Article I, Sec. 9	prohibition against acceptance of titles of nobility, etc., from any foreign state
Article III	guarantee of trial by jury in state where crime was committed
Article III	treason defined and limited to the life of the person convicted, not to the person's heirs

bills of attainder laws that decree a person guilty of a crime without a trial

ex post facto laws laws that declare an action to be illegal after it has been committed

major imperfection of the new Constitution. The Federalists conceded that in order to gain ratification they would have to make an "unwritten but unequivocal pledge" to add a bill of rights that would include a confirmation (in what became the Tenth Amendment) of the understanding that all powers not expressly delegated to the national government or explicitly prohibited to the states were reserved to the states.[3]

"After much discussion and manipulation . . . at the delicate prompting of Washington and under the masterful prodding of Madison," the House of Representatives adopted seventeen amendments; of these, the Senate adopted twelve. Ten of the amendments were ratified by the states on December 15, 1791; from the start these ten were called the Bill of Rights (see Box 4.1).[4]

NATIONALIZING THE BILL OF RIGHTS

> **Does the Bill of Rights put limits only on the national government or does it limit state governments as well?**

The First Amendment provides that "Congress shall make no law. . . ." But this is the only amendment in the Bill of Rights that addresses itself exclusively to the national government. For example, the Second Amendment provides that "the right of the people to keep and bear Arms, shall not be infringed." And the Fifth Amendment says, among other things, that "no person shall . . . be twice put in jeopardy of life or limb" for the same crime. Since the First Amendment is the only part of the Bill of Rights that is explicit in its intention to put limits on Congress and therefore on the national government, a fundamental question inevitably arises: do the remaining provisions of the Bill of Rights put limits only on the national government, or do they limit the state governments as well?

The Supreme Court first answered this question in 1833 by ruling that the Bill of Rights limited only the national government and not the state governments.[5] But in 1868, when the Fourteenth Amendment was added to the Constitution, the question arose once again. The Fourteenth Amendment reads as if it were meant to impose the Bill of Rights upon the states:

Amendment I: Limits on Congress

Congress cannot make any law establishing a religion or abridging freedoms of religious exercise, speech, assembly, or petition.

Amendments II, III, IV: Limits on the Executive

The executive branch cannot infringe on the right of the people to keep arms (II), cannot arbitrarily take houses for militia (III), and cannot search for or seize evidence without a court warrant swearing to the probable existence of a crime (IV).

Amendments V, VI, VII, VIII: Limits on the Judiciary

The courts cannot hold trials for serious offenses without provision for a grand jury (V), a trial jury (VII), a speedy trial (VI), presentation of charges and confrontation by the accused of hostile witnesses (VI), and immunity from testimony against oneself and immunity from trial more than once for the same offense (V). Furthermore, neither bail nor punishment can be excessive (VIII), and no property can be taken without "just compensation" (V).

Amendments IX, X: Limits on the National Government

Any rights not enumerated are reserved to the state or the people (X), but the enumeration of certain rights in the Constitution should not be interpreted to mean that those are the only rights the people have (IX).

No *State* shall make or enforce any law which shall abridge the privileges or immunities of citizens of the United States; nor shall any *State* deprive any person of life, liberty, or property, without due process of law; nor deny to any person within its jurisdiction the equal protection of the laws [emphasis added].

This language sounds like an effort to extend the Bill of Rights in its entirety to all citizens, wherever they might reside.[6] Yet this was not the Supreme Court's interpretation of the amendment for nearly a hundred years. Within five years of ratification of the Fourteenth Amendment, the Court was making decisions as though the amendment had never been adopted.[7]

The only change in civil liberties during the first sixty years following the adoption of the Fourteenth Amendment came in 1897, when the Supreme Court held that the due process clause of the Fourteenth Amendment did in fact prohibit states from taking property for a public use without just compensation.[8] However, the Supreme Court had selectively "incorporated" into the Fourteenth Amendment only the property protection provision of the Fifth Amendment and no other clause of the Fifth or any other amendment of the Bill of Rights. In other words, although according to the Fifth Amendment "due process" applied to the taking of life and liberty as well as property, only property was incorporated into the Fourteenth Amendment as a limitation on state power.

No further expansion of civil liberties via the Fourteenth Amendment occurred until 1925, when the Supreme Court held that freedom of speech is "among the fundamental personal rights and 'liberties' protected by the due process clause of the Fourteenth Amendment from impairment by the states."[9] In 1931, the Court added freedom of the press to that short list protected by the Bill of Rights from state action; in 1939, it added freedom of assembly.[10]

But that was as far as the Court was willing to go. As late as 1937, the Supreme Court was still unwilling to nationalize civil liberties beyond the First Amendment. The Constitution, as interpreted as late as 1937 by the Supreme Court in *Palko v. Connecticut*, left standing the framework in which the states had the power to determine their own law on a number of fundamental issues. *Palko* established the principle of **selective incorporation,** by which the provisions of the Bill of Rights were to be considered one-by-one and selectively applied as limits on the states through the Fourteenth Amendment.[11] In order to make clear that "selective incorporation" should be narrowly interpreted, Justice Benjamin Cardozo, writing for an 8-to-1 majority, asserted that although many rights have value and importance, not all are of the same value and importance:

> [Not all rights are of] the very essence of a scheme of ordered liberty. To abolish them is not to violate a "principle of justice so rooted in the traditions and conscience of our people as to be ranked as fundamental." . . . What is true of jury trials and indictments is true also . . . of the immunity from compulsory self-incrimination [as in *Palko*]. . . . This too might be lost, and justice still be done. . . . If the Fourteenth Amendment has absorbed them [for example, freedom of thought and speech] the process of absorption has had its source in the belief that neither liberty nor justice would exist if they were sacrificed.

Palko left states with most of the powers they had possessed even before the adoption of the Fourteenth Amendment, including the power to pass laws segregating the races—a power in fact that the thirteen former Confederate states chose to continue to exercise on into the 1960s, despite *Brown v. Board of Education* in 1954. The constitutional framework also left states with the power to engage in searches and seizures without a warrant, to indict accused persons without a grand jury, to deprive accused persons of trial by jury, to deprive persons of their right not to have to testify against themselves, to deprive accused persons of their right to confront adverse witnesses, and to prosecute accused persons more than once for the same crime.[12] Few states chose to use these kinds of powers, but some states did, and the power to do so was available for any state whose legislative majority or courts so chose.

So, until 1961, only the First Amendment and one clause of the Fifth Amendment had been clearly incorporated into the Fourteenth Amendment as binding on the states as well as on the national government.[13] After that, one by one, most of the important provisions of the Bill of Rights were incorporated into the Fourteenth Amendment and applied to the states. Table 4.2 shows the progress of this revolution in the interpretation of the Constitution.

But the controversy over incorporation lives on. Since liberty requires restraining the power of government, the general status of civil liberties can never be considered fixed and permanent. Every provision in the Bill of Rights is subject to interpretation, and in any dispute involving a clause of the Bill of Rights, interpretations will always be shaped by the interpreter's interest in the outcome. As we shall see, the Court continually reminds everyone that if it has the power to expand the Bill of Rights, it also has the power to contract it.[14]

selective incorporation the process by which different protections in the Bill of Rights were incorporated into the Fourteenth Amendment, thus guaranteeing citizens protection from state as well as national governments

➤ How and when did the Supreme Court nationalize the Bill of Rights?

Incorporation of the Bill of Rights into the Fourteenth Amendment

Table 4.2

SELECTED PROVISIONS AND AMENDMENTS	NOT "INCORPORATED" UNTIL	KEY CASE
Eminent domain (V)	1897	*Chicago, Burlington, and Quincy R.R. v. Chicago*
Freedom of speech (I)	1925	*Gitlow v. New York*
Freedom of press (I)	1931	*Near v. Minnesota*
Free exercise of religion (I)	1934	*Hamilton v. Regents of the University of California*
Freedom of assembly (I)	1939	*Hague v. CIO*
Freedom from unnecessary search and seizure (IV)	1949	*Wolf v. Colorado*
Freedom from warrantless search and seizure (IV) ("exclusionary rule")	1961	*Mapp v. Ohio*
Freedom from cruel and unusual punishment (VIII)	1962	*Robinson v. California*
Right to counsel in any criminal trial (VI)	1963	*Gideon v. Wainwright*
Right against self-incrimination and forced confessions (V)	1964	*Mallory v. Hogan* *Escobedo v. Illinois*
Right to privacy (III, IV, & V)	1965	*Griswold v. Connecticut*
Right to remain silent (V)	1966	*Miranda v. Arizona*
Right against double jeopardy (V)	1969	*Benton v. Maryland*

The best way to examine the Bill of Rights today is the simplest way—to take each of the major provisions one at a time. Some of these provisions are settled areas of law, and others are not. Any one of them can be reinterpreted by the Court at any time.

The First Amendment and Freedom of Religion

> Congress shall make no law respecting an establishment of religion, or prohibiting the free exercise thereof; or abridging the freedom of speech, or of the press; or the right of the people peaceably to assemble, and to petition the Government for a redress of grievances.

The Bill of Rights begins by guaranteeing freedom, and the First Amendment provides for that freedom in two distinct clauses: "Congress shall make no law [1] respecting an establishment of religion, or [2] prohibiting the free exercise thereof." The first clause is called the "establishment clause," and the second is called the "free exercise clause."

> **How does the First Amendment guarantee the nonestablishment and free exercise of religion?**

SEPARATION BETWEEN CHURCH AND STATE

establishment clause the First Amendment clause that says that "Congress shall make no law respecting an establishment of religion." This law means that a "wall of separation" exists between church and state

The **establishment clause** has been interpreted quite strictly to mean that a virtual "wall of separation" exists between church and state. The separation of church and state was especially important to the great numbers of American colonists who had sought refuge from persecution for having rejected membership in state-sponsored churches. The concept of a "wall of separation" was Jefferson's own formulation, and this concept has figured in all of the modern Supreme Court cases arising under the establishment clause.

Despite the absolute sound of the phrase "wall of separation," there is ample room to disagree on how high the wall is or of what materials it is composed. For example, the Court has been consistently strict in cases of school prayer, striking down such practices as Bible reading,[15] nondenominational prayer,[16] a moment of silence for meditation and pre-game prayer at public sporting events.[17] In each of these cases, the Court reasoned that school-sponsored observations, even of an apparently nondenominational character, are highly suggestive of school sponsorship and therefore violate the prohibition against establishment of religion. On the other hand, the Court has been quite permissive (and some would say inconsistent) about the public display of religious symbols, such as city-sponsored Nativity scenes in commercial or municipal areas.[18] And although the Court has consistently disapproved of government financial support for religious schools, even when the purpose has been purely educational and secular, the Court has permitted certain direct aid to students of such schools in the form of busing, for example. In 1971, after thirty years of cases involving religious schools, the Court attempted to specify some criteria to guide its decisions and those of lower courts, indicating, for example, in a decision invalidating state payments for the teaching of secular subjects in parochial schools, circumstances under which the Court might allow certain financial assistance. The case was *Lemon v. Kurtzman;* in its decision, the Supreme Court established three criteria to guide future cases, in what came to be called the ***Lemon* test.** The Court held that government aid to religious schools would be accepted as constitutional if (1) it had a secular purpose, (2) its effect was neither to advance nor to inhibit religion, and (3) it did not entangle government and religious institutions in each other's affairs.[19]

***Lemon* test** a rule articulated in *Lemon v. Kurtzman* that government action toward religion is permissible if it is secular in purpose, does not lead to "excessive entanglement" with religion, and neither promotes nor inhibits the practice of religion

Although these restrictions make the *Lemon* test a hard test to pass, imaginative authorities are finding ways to do so, and the Supreme Court has demonstrated a willingness to let them. For example, in 1995, the Court narrowly ruled that a student religious group at the University of Virginia could not be denied student activities funds merely because it was a religious group espousing a particular viewpoint about a deity. The Court called the denial "viewpoint discrimination" that violated the free speech rights of the group. Dissenting members of the Court argued that since the message was not scholarly discourse but "the evangelists' mission station and the pulpit," any state aid violated the First Amendment's prohibition against the establishment of a religion.[20] This led two years later to a new, more conservative approach to the "separation of church and state." In 1997, the Court explicitly recognized a change in its interpretation of the establishment clause, and then went on to reverse an important 1985 decision that had forbidden the practice of sending public school teachers into parochial schools to provide remedial education to disadvantaged children.[21] In the aftermath of the 1985 case, teachers from the public schools had to hold their classes in vans parked across the street from the parochial schools. This had added greatly to the cost of the remedial education and had led to a request for relief from the 1985 decision. The Court provided that relief in 1997 and went beyond that to assert that such cooperation between public school teachers and parochial schools was not an "entanglement" that amounted to public support (i.e., establishment) of a religion.

More recently, the establishment clause has been put under pressure by the school voucher and charter school movements. Vouchers financed by public revenues are supporting student tuitions at religious schools, where common prayer and religious instruction are known parts of the curriculum. In addition, many financially needy church schools are actively recruiting students with tax-supported vouchers, considering them an essential source of revenue to keep their schools operating. In both these respects, vouchers and charter schools are creating the impression that public support is aiding the establishment of religion.[22] Yet, the Supreme Court has refused to rule on the constitutionality of these programs. All of these developments represent quite a change in the prevailing view of the establishment clause.

FREE EXERCISE OF RELIGION

The **free exercise clause** protects the right to believe and to practice whatever religion one chooses; it also protects the right to be a nonbeliever. The precedent-setting case involving free exercise is *West Virginia State Board of Education v. Barnette* (1943), which involved the children of a family of Jehovah's Witnesses who refused to salute and pledge allegiance to the American flag on the grounds that their religious faith did not permit it. Three years earlier, the Court had upheld such a requirement and had permitted schools to expel students for refusing to salute the flag. But the entry of the United States into a war to defend democracy coupled with the ugly treatment to which the Jehovah's Witnesses' children had been subjected induced the Court to reverse itself and to endorse the free exercise of religion even when it may be offensive to the beliefs of the majority.[23]

Although the Supreme Court has been fairly consistent and strict in protecting the free exercise of religious belief, it has taken pains to distinguish between religious beliefs and *actions* based on those beliefs. In one case, for example, two Native Americans had been fired from their jobs for smoking peyote, an illegal drug. They claimed that they had been fired from their jobs illegally because smoking peyote was a religious sacrament protected by the free exercise clause. The Court disagreed with their claim in an important 1990 decision,[24] but Congress supported the claim and it went on to engage in an unusual controversy with the Court, involving the separation of powers as well as the proper application of the separation of church and state. Congress literally reversed the Court's 1990 decision with the enactment of the Religious Freedom Restoration Act of 1993 (RFRA), forbidding any federal agency or state government from restricting a person's free exercise of religion unless the federal agency or state government demonstrates that its action "furthers a compelling government interest" and "is the least restrictive means of furthering that compelling governmental interest."

free exercise clause the First Amendment clause that protects a citizen's right to believe and practice whatever religion he or she chooses

> **In what way has the free exercise of religion become a recent political issue?**

Despite the establishment clause, the United States still uses the motto "In God we trust" and calls itself "one nation, under God." This South Carolina license plate was introduced in 2002. But such displays of religious patriotism are not universally accepted. Michael Newdow filed suit against his daughter's school district because the Pledge of Allegiance refers to God. A California circuit court ruled that the pledge refers to religion in school and is thus illegal. The decision angered many Americans; Newdow was publicly reviled and received phone threats. Though the establishment clause explicitly bars religious references from the state, the case is still expected to be reversed on appeal; Americans are often less hostile to religion in schools than the Constitution is.

The First Amendment affects everyday life in a multitude of ways. Because of its ban on state-sanctioned religion, the Supreme Court ruled in 2000 that student-initiated public prayer at school is illegal. Pregame prayer at public schools violates the establishment clause of the First Amendment.

IN GOD WE TRUST
ABC 123
South Carolina

One of the first applications of the RFRA was to a case brought by St. Peter's Catholic Church against the city of Boerne, Texas, which had denied permission to the church to enlarge its building because the building had been declared an historic landmark. The case went to federal court on the argument that the city had violated the church's religious freedom as guaranteed by Congress in RFRA. The Supreme Court declared RFRA unconstitutional, but on grounds rarely utilized, if not unique to this case: Congress had violated the separation of powers principle, infringing on the powers of the judiciary by going so far beyond its lawmaking powers that it ended up actually expanding the scope of religious rights rather than just enforcing them. The Court thereby implied that questions requiring a balancing of religious claims against public policy claims were reserved strictly to the judiciary.[25]

The *City of Boerne* case did settle some matters of constitutional controversy over the religious exercise and the establishment clauses of the First Amendment but left a lot more unsettled. What about polygamy, a practice allowed in the Mormon faith? What about snake worship? Or the refusal of Amish parents to send

The First Amendment also refers to freedom of speech and of the press. As the Internet became a larger part of daily life, opponents of obscenity and pornography sought legislation to restrict children's access to the Internet. These demonstrators voice opinions for and against the 1996 Communications Decency Act, which made it a crime to make "indecent" or "patently offensive" works or pictures available online. The Supreme Court unanimously struck down the CDA. Citing the First Amendment, the justices refused to censor material because children might see it.

their children to school beyond eighth grade because exposing their children to "modern values" would undermine their religious commitment? In this last example, the Court decided in favor of the Amish and endorsed a very strong interpretation of the protection of free exercise.[26]

Freedom of the press remains a point of contention. In April 2001, an Atlanta judge ruled that The Wind Done Gone, *a retelling of* Gone with the Wind, *could not be published since it violated copyright and plagiarized* Gone with the Wind. *Appellate judges reversed this ruling, calling the initial injunction "unlawful prior restraint in violation of the First Amendment."*

The First Amendment and Freedom of Speech and the Press

"Congress shall make no law . . . abridging the freedom of speech, or of the press. . . ."

Because democracy depends upon an open political process and because politics is basically talk, freedom of speech and freedom of the press are considered critical. For this reason, they were given a prominence in the Bill of Rights equal to that of freedom of religion. In 1938, freedom of speech (which in all important respects includes freedom of the press) was given extraordinary constitutional status when the Supreme Court established that any legislation that attempts to restrict these fundamental freedoms "is to be subjected to a more exacting judicial scrutiny . . . than are most other types of legislation."[27]

strict scrutiny test, used by the Supreme Court in racial discrimination cases and other cases involving civil liberties and civil rights, which places the burden of proof on the government rather than on the challengers to show that the law in question is constitutional

What the Court was saying is that the democratic political process must be protected at almost any cost. This higher standard of judicial review came to be called **strict scrutiny.** Strict scrutiny implies that speech—at least some kinds of speech—will be protected almost absolutely. But as it turns out, only some types of speech are fully protected against restrictions (see Figure 4.1 on the following page). As we shall see, many forms of speech are less than absolutely protected—even though they are entitled to strict scrutiny. This section will look at these two categories of speech: (1) absolutely protected speech, and (2) conditionally protected speech.

ABSOLUTELY PROTECTED SPEECH

> **What forms of speech are protected by the First Amendment? What forms are not protected?**

There is one and only one absolute defense against efforts to place limitations on speech, oral or in print: the truth. The truth is protected even when its expression damages the person to whom it applies. And of all forms of speech, political speech is the most consistently protected.

Political Speech Political speech was the activity of greatest concern to the framers of the Constitution, even though they found it the most difficult provision to observe. Within seven years of the ratification of the Bill of Rights in 1791, Congress adopted the infamous Alien and Sedition Acts, which, among other things, made it a crime to say or publish anything that might tend to defame or bring into disrepute the government of the United States. Quite clearly, the acts' intentions were to criminalize the very conduct given absolute protection by the First Amendment (see also Chapter 9). Fifteen violators—including several newspaper editors—were indicted, and a few were actually convicted before the relevant portions of the acts were allowed to expire.

The first modern free speech case arose immediately after World War I. It involved persons who had been convicted under the federal Espionage Act of 1917 for opposing U.S. involvement in the war. The Supreme Court upheld the Espionage Act and refused to protect the speech rights of the defendants on the grounds that their activities—appeals to draftees to resist the draft—constituted a **"clear and present danger"** test test to determine whether speech is protected or unprotected, based on its capacity to present a "clear and present danger" to society

"clear and present danger" to security.[28] This is the first and most famous "test" for when government intervention or censorship could be permitted.

It was only after the 1920s that real progress toward a genuinely effective First Amendment was made. Since then, political speech has been consistently pro-

The Protection of Free Speech by the First Amendment

Figure 4.1

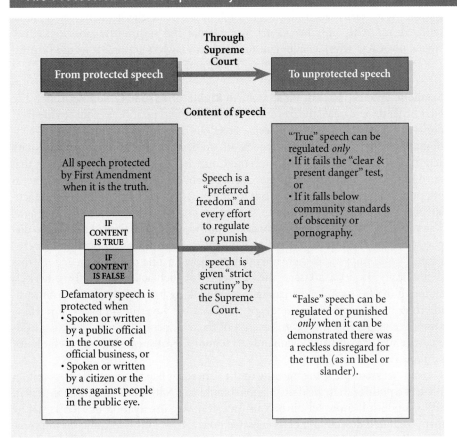

Through Supreme Court

From protected speech → To unprotected speech

Content of speech

All speech protected by First Amendment when it is the truth.

IF CONTENT IS TRUE

Speech is a "preferred freedom" and every effort to regulate or punish

IF CONTENT IS FALSE

Defamatory speech is protected when
• Spoken or written by a public official in the course of official business, or
• Spoken or written by a citizen or the press against people in the public eye.

speech is given "strict scrutiny" by the Supreme Court.

"True" speech can be regulated *only*
• If it fails the "clear & present danger" test, or
• If it falls below community standards of obscenity or pornography.

"False" speech can be regulated or punished *only* when it can be demonstrated there was a reckless disregard for the truth (as in libel or slander).

tected by the courts even when it has been deemed "insulting" or "outrageous." Here is the way the Supreme Court put it in one of its most important statements on the subject:

> The constitutional guarantees of free speech and free press do not permit a State to forbid or proscribe advocacy of the use of force or of law violation *except where such advocacy is directed to inciting or producing imminent lawless action and is likely to incite or produce such action* [emphasis added].[29]

This statement was made in the case of a Ku Klux Klan leader, Charles Brandenburg, who had been arrested and convicted of advocating "revengent" action against the president, Congress, and the Supreme Court, among others, if they continued "to suppress the white, Caucasian race...." Although Brandenburg was not carrying a weapon, some of the members of his audience were. Nevertheless, the Supreme Court reversed the state courts and freed Brandenburg while also declaring Ohio's Criminal Syndicalism Act unconstitutional because it punished persons who "advocate, or teach the duty, necessity, or propriety [of violence] as a means of accomplishing industrial or political reform . . ."; or who publish materials or "voluntarily assemble . . . to teach or advocate the doctrines of criminal syndicalism." The Supreme Court argued that the statute did not distinguish "mere advocacy" from "incitement to imminent lawless action." It would be difficult to go much further in protecting freedom of speech.

Symbolic Speech, Speech Plus, and the Rights of Assembly and Petition   The First Amendment treats the freedoms of assembly and petition as equal to the freedoms of religion and political speech. Freedom of assembly and freedom of petition are closely associated with speech but go beyond it to speech associated with action. Since at least 1931, the Supreme Court has sought to protect actions that are designed to send a political message. (Usually the purpose of a symbolic act is not only to send a direct message but to draw a crowd—to do something spectacular in order to draw spectators to the action and thus strengthen the message.) Thus the Court held unconstitutional a California statute making it a felony to display a red flag "as a sign, symbol or emblem of opposition to organized government."[30] Although today there are limits on how far one can go with actions that symbolically convey a message, the protection of such action is very broad. Thus, although the Court upheld a federal statute making it a crime to burn draft cards to protest the Vietnam War on the grounds that the government had a compelling interest in preserving draft cards as part of the conduct of the war itself, it considered the wearing of black armbands to school a protected form of assembly for symbolic action.

Another example is the burning of the American flag as a symbol of protest. In 1984, at a political rally held during the Republican National Convention in Dallas, Texas, a political protester burned an American flag in violation of a Texas statute that prohibited desecration of a venerated object. In a 5-to-4 decision, the Supreme Court declared the Texas law unconstitutional on the grounds that flag burning was expressive conduct protected by the First Amendment.[31] Congress reacted immediately with a proposal for a constitutional amendment reversing the Court's Texas decision, and when the amendment failed to receive the necessary two-thirds majority in the Senate, Congress passed the Flag Protection Act of 1989. Protesters promptly violated this act and their prosecution moved quickly into the federal district court, which declared the new law unconstitutional. The Supreme Court, in another 5-to-4 decision, affirmed the lower court decision.[32] A renewed effort began in Congress to propose a constitutional amendment that would reverse the Supreme Court and place this form of expressive conduct outside the realm of protected speech or assembly.

Closer to the original intent of the assembly and petition clause is the category of **"speech plus"**—following speech with physical activity such as picketing, distributing leaflets, and other forms of peaceful demonstration or assembly. Such assemblies are consistently protected by courts under the First Amendment; state and local laws regulating such activities are closely scrutinized and frequently overturned. But the same assembly on private property is quite another matter and can in many circumstances be regulated. For example, the directors of a shopping center can lawfully prohibit an assembly protesting a war or supporting a ban on abortion. Assemblies in public areas can also be restricted under some circumstances,

speech plus speech accompanied by conduct such as sit-ins, picketing, and demonstrations; protection of this form of speech under the First Amendment is conditional, and restrictions imposed by state or local authorities are acceptable if properly balanced by considerations of public order especially when the assembly or demonstration jeopardizes the health, safety, or rights of others. This condition was the basis of the Supreme Court's decision to uphold a lower court order that restricted the access abortion protesters had to the entrances of abortion clinics.[33]

FREEDOM OF THE PRESS

For all practical purposes, freedom of speech implies and includes freedom of the press. With the exception of the broadcast media, which are subject to federal regulation, the press is protected under the doctrine against **prior restraint.** Beginning with the landmark 1931 case of *Near v. Minnesota,* the U.S. Supreme Court has held that, except under the most extraordinary circumstances, the First Amendment of the Constitution prohibits government agencies from seeking to prevent newspapers or magazines from publishing whatever they wish.[34] Indeed, in the case of *New York Times v. U.S.,* the so-called *Pentagon Papers* case, the Supreme Court ruled that the government could not even block publication of secret Defense Department documents furnished to *The New York Times* by an opponent of the Vietnam War who had obtained the documents illegally.[35] In a 1990 case, however, the Supreme Court upheld a lower-court order restraining Cable News Network (CNN) from broadcasting tapes of conversations between former Panamanian dictator Manuel Noriega and his lawyer, supposedly recorded by the U.S. government. By a vote of 7 to 2, the Court held that CNN could be restrained from broadcasting the tapes until the trial court in the Noriega case had listened to the tapes and had decided whether their broadcast would violate Noriega's right to a fair trial.

prior restraint an effort by a governmental agency to block the publication of material it deems libelous or harmful in some other way; censorship. In the United States, the courts forbid prior restraint except under the most extraordinary circumstances

CONDITIONALLY PROTECTED SPEECH

At least four forms of speech fall outside the absolute guarantees of the First Amendment and therefore outside the realm of absolute protection. Since they do enjoy some protection, they qualify as "conditionally protected" types of speech: (1) libel and slander, (2) obscenity and pornography, (3) fighting words, and (4) commercial speech. It should be emphasized once again that these four types of speech still enjoy considerable protection by the courts.

Libel and Slander   Some speech is not protected at all. If a written statement is made in "reckless disregard of the truth" and is considered damaging to the victim because it is "malicious, scandalous, and defamatory," it can be punished as **libel.** If an oral statement of such nature is made, it can be punished as **slander.**

Today, most libel suits involve freedom of the press, and the realm of free press is enormous. Historically, newspapers were subject to the law of libel, which provided that newspapers that printed false and malicious stories could be compelled to pay damages to those they defamed. In recent years, however, American courts have greatly narrowed the meaning of libel and made it extremely difficult, particularly for politicians or other public figures, to win a libel case against a newspaper. In the important 1964 case of *New York Times v. Sullivan,* the Court held that to be deemed libelous a story about a public official not only had to be untrue, but also had to result from "actual malice" or

libel a written statement made in "reckless disregard of the truth" that is considered damaging to a victim because it is "malicious, scandalous, and defamatory"

slander an oral statement, made in "reckless disregard of the truth," which is considered damaging to the victim because it is "malicious, scandalous, and defamatory"

"reckless disregard" for the truth.[36] In other words, the newspaper had to *deliberately* print false and malicious material. In practice, it is nearly impossible to prove that a paper deliberately printed maliciously false information, and it is especially difficult for a politician or other public figure to win a libel case. Essentially, the print media have been able to publish anything they want about a public figure.

However, in at least one recent case, the Court has opened up the possibility for public officials to file libel suits against the press. In 1985, the Court held that the press was immune from libel only when the printed material was "a matter of public concern." In other words, in future cases a newspaper would have to show that the public official was engaged in activities that were indeed *public.* This new principle has made the press more vulnerable to libel suits, but it still leaves an enormous realm of freedom for the press. For example, Reverend Jerry Falwell, the leader of the Moral Majority, lost his libel suit against *Hustler* magazine even though the magazine had published a cartoon of Falwell showing him having drunken intercourse with his mother in an outhouse. A unanimous Supreme Court rejected a jury verdict in favor of damages for "emotional distress" on the grounds that parodies, no matter how outrageous, are protected because "outrageousness" is too subjective a test and thus would interfere with the free flow of ideas protected by the First Amendment.[37]

Obscenity and Pornography   If libel and slander cases can be difficult because of the problem of determining the truth of statements and whether those statements are malicious and damaging, cases involving pornography and obscenity can be even more sticky. It is easy to say that pornography and obscenity fall outside the realm of protected speech, but it is impossible to draw a clear line defining exactly where protection ends and unprotected speech begins. Not until 1957 did the Supreme Court confront this problem, and it did so with a definition of obscenity that may have caused more confusion than it cleared up. Justice William Brennan, in writing the Court's opinion, defined obscenity as speech or writing that appeals to the "prurient interest"—that is, books, magazines, films, etc. whose purpose is to excite lust as this appears "to the average person, applying contemporary community standards. . . ." Even so, Brennan added, the work should be judged obscene only when it is "utterly without redeeming social importance."[38] Brennan's definition, instead of clarifying the Court's view, actually caused more confusion. In 1964, Justice Potter Stewart confessed that, although he found pornography impossible to define, "I know it when I see it."[39]

All attempts by the courts to define pornography and obscenity have proved impractical, because each instance required courts to screen thousands of pages of print material and feet of film alleged to be pornographic. The vague and impractical standards that had been developed meant ultimately that almost nothing could be banned on the grounds that it was pornographic and obscene. An effort was made to strengthen the restrictions in 1973, when the Supreme Court expressed its willingness to define pornography as a work which (1) as a whole, is deemed prurient by the "average person" according to "community standards"; (2) depicts sexual conduct "in a patently offensive way"; and (3) lacks "serious literary, artistic, political, or scientific value." This definition meant that pornography would be determined by local rather than national standards. Thus, a local bookseller might be prosecuted for selling a volume that was a best-seller nationally but that was deemed pornographic locally.[40] This new definition of standards did not help much either, and not long after 1973 the Court began again to review all such community antipornography laws, reversing most of them.

Consequently, today there is a widespread fear that Americans are free to publish any and all variety of intellectual expression, whether there is any "redeeming social value" or not. Yet this area of free speech is far from settled.

In recent years, the battle against obscene speech has been against "cyberporn"—pornography on the Internet. Opponents of this form of expression argue that it should be banned because of the easy access children have to the Internet. The first major effort to regulate the content of the Internet occurred on February 1, 1996, when the 104th Congress passed major telecommunications legislation. Attached to the Telecommunications Act was an amendment, called the Communications Decency Act (CDA), that was designed to regulate the on-line transmission of obscene material. The constitutionality of the CDA was immediately challenged in court by a coalition of interests led by the ACLU. In the 1997 Supreme Court case of *Reno v. ACLU*, the Court struck down the CDA, ruling that it suppressed speech that "adults have a constitutional right to receive" and that governments may not limit the adult population to messages that are fit for children. Supreme Court Justice John Paul Stevens described the Internet as the "town crier" of the modern age and said that the Internet was entitled to the greatest degree of First Amendment protection possible. By contrast, radio and television are subject to more control than the Internet.[41]

In 2000, the Supreme Court also extended the highest degree of First Amendment protection to cable (not broadcast) television. In *U.S. v. Playboy Entertainment Group,* the Court struck down a portion of the Telecommunications Act of 1996 that required cable TV companies to limit the broadcast of sexually explicit programming to late night hours. In its decision, the Court noted that the law already provided parents with the means to restrict access to sexually explicit cable channels through various blocking devices. Moreover, such programming could only come into the home if parents decided to purchase such channels in the first place.

Fighting Words   Speech can also lose its protected position when it moves toward the sphere of action. "Expressive speech," for example, is protected until it moves from the symbolic realm to the realm of actual conduct—to direct incitement of damaging conduct with the use of so-called **fighting words.** In 1942, the Supreme Court upheld the arrest and conviction of a man who had violated a state law forbidding the use of offensive language in public. He had called the arresting officer a "goddamned racketeer" and "a damn Fascist." When his case reached the Supreme Court, the arrest was upheld on the grounds that the First Amendment provides no protection for such offensive language because such words "are no essential part of any exposition of ideas."[42] This case was reaffirmed in a much more famous and important case decided at the height of the cold war, when the Supreme Court held that "there is no substantial public interest in permitting certain kinds of utterances:

fighting words speech that directly incites damaging conduct

Banned Books

One of the more visible issues of free speech in recent years has been the banning of books in public schools. The following books were the most censored of 2002, with the reasons for which they were banned:

1. *Harry Potter* series, J. K. Rowling: wizardry and magic
2. *Of Mice and Men,* John Steinbeck: offensive language and unsuited to age group
3. *The Chocolate War,* Robert Cormier: offensive language and unsuited to age group
4. *I Know Why the Caged Bird Sings,* Maya Angelou: sexual content, racism, offensive language, violence, and unsuited to age group
5. *Summer of My German Soldier,* Bette Greene: racism, offensive language, and sexually explicit
6. *The Catcher in the Rye,* J. D. Salinger: offensive language and unsuited to age group
7. *Alice* series, Phyllis Reynolds Naylor: sexually explicit, offensive language, and unsuited to age group
8. *Go Ask Alice,* Anonymous: sexually explicit, offensive language, and drug use
9. *Fallen Angels,* Walter Dean Myers: offensive language and unsuited to age group
10. *Blood and Chocolate,* Annette Curtis Klause: sexually explicit and unsuited to age group

SOURCE: American Library Association

the lewd and obscene, the profane, the libelous, and the insulting or 'fighting' words—those which by their very utterance inflict injury or tend to incite an immediate breach of the peace."[43]

Since that time, however, the Supreme Court has reversed almost every conviction based on arguments that the speaker had used "fighting words." But again, that does not mean that this is an absolutely settled area. In recent years, the increased activism of minority and women's groups has prompted a movement against words that might be construed as offensive to members of a particular group. This movement has come to be called, derisively, "political correctness." In response to this movement, many organizations have attempted to impose codes of etiquette that acknowledge these enhanced sensitivities. These efforts to formalize the restraints on the use of certain words in public are causing great concern over their possible infringement of freedom of speech. But how should we determine what words are "fighting words" that fall outside the protections of the freedom of speech?

One category of conditionally protected speech is the free speech of high school students in public schools. In 1986, the Supreme Court backed away from a broad protection of student free-speech rights by upholding the punishment of a high school student for making sexually suggestive speech. The Court opinion held that such speech interfered with the school's goal of teaching students the limits of socially acceptable behavior.[44] Two years later, the Supreme Court took another conservative step and restricted student speech and press rights even further by defining them as part of the educational process not to be treated with the same standard as adult speech in a regular public forum.[45]

In addition, scores of universities have attempted to develop speech codes to suppress utterances deemed to be racial or ethnic slurs. What these universities find, however, is that the codes produce more problems than they solve. The University of Pennsylvania learned this when it first tried to apply its newly written "Harassment Code." Around midnight in January of 1993, Eden Jacobowitz and several other students trying to study yelled from their dorm windows at a noisy group of partying black sorority members: "Shut up, you water buffaloes." Other students also made rude comments, including racial and sexual slurs, but Jacobowitz was the only one who actually came forward and admitted to having yelled. Born in Israel and fluent in Hebrew, Jacobowitz explained that "water buffalo" loosely translated from Hebrew means "rude person." Nevertheless, the University of Pennsylvania brought Jacobowitz before a campus judicial inquiry board and charged him with racial harassment in violation of the new code. The black women at whom he had yelled also brought civil charges of racial harassment against Jacobowitz. Five months after the incident, all charges were dropped—both the civil charges and those brought by the university. After reviewing the matter, Penn officials confessed that the university's harassment code "contained flaws which could not withstand the stress of intense publicity and international attention."[46]

Such concerns are not limited to universities, although universities have probably moved furthest toward efforts to formalize "politically correct" speech guidelines. Similar developments have taken place in large corporations, both public and private, in which many successful complaints and lawsuits have been brought, alleging that the words of employers or their supervisors create a "hostile or abusive working environment." These cases arise out of the civil rights laws and will be addressed in more detail in Chapter 5. The Supreme Court has held that "sexual harassment" that creates a "hostile working environment" includes "unwelcome sexual advances, requests for sexual favors, and other *verbal* or physical conduct of a sexual nature" (emphasis added).[47] There is a fundamental free speech issue involved in these regulations of hostile speech. So far, the assumption favoring the regulation of hostile speech in universities and other workplaces is that "some speech must be shut down in the name of free speech because it tends to silence those disparaged by it,"[48] even though a threat of hostile action (usually embodied in "fighting words") is not present. The United States is on something of a collision course between the right to express hostile views and the protection of the sensitivities of minorities and women. The collisions will end up in the courts, but not before a lot more airing in public and balancing efforts by state legislatures and Congress.

Commercial Speech   Commercial speech, such as newspaper or television advertisements, does not have full First Amendment protection because it cannot be considered political speech. Initially considered to be entirely outside the protection of the First Amendment, commercial speech has made gains during the twentieth century. Some commercial speech is still unprotected and therefore regulated. For example, the regulation of false and misleading advertising by the Federal Trade Commission is an old and well-established power of the federal government. The Supreme Court long ago approved the constitutionality of laws prohibiting the electronic media from carrying cigarette advertising.[49] The Court has also upheld a state university ban on Tupperware parties in college dormitories.[50] It has also upheld city ordinances prohibiting the posting of all signs on public property (as long as the ban is total, so that there is no hint of censorship).[51] And the Supreme Court, in a heated 5-to-4 decision written by Chief Justice William Rehnquist, upheld Puerto Rico's statute restricting gambling advertising aimed at residents of Puerto Rico.[52]

However, the gains far outweigh the losses in the effort to expand the protection commercial speech enjoys under the First Amendment. "In part, this reflects the growing appreciation that commercial speech is part of the free flow of information necessary for informed choice and democratic participation."[53] For example, the Court in 1975 struck down a state statute making it a misdemeanor to sell or circulate newspapers encouraging abortions; the Court ruled that the statute infringed upon constitutionally protected speech and upon the right of the reader to make informed choices.[54] On a similar basis, the Court reversed its own earlier decisions upholding laws that prohibited dentists and other professionals from advertising their services. For the Court, medical service advertising was a matter of health that could be advanced by the free flow of information.[55] In a 1983 case, the Supreme Court struck down a congressional statute that prohibited the unsolicited mailing of advertisements for contraceptives. In 1996, the Supreme Court struck down Rhode Island laws and regulations banning the advertisement of liquor prices as a violation of the First Amendment.[56] And in a 2001 case, the Supreme Court ruled that a Massachusetts ban on all cigarette advertising violated the First Amendment right of the tobacco industry to advertise its products to adult consumers.[57] These instances of commercial speech are significant in themselves, but they are all the more significant because they indicate the breadth and depth of the freedom existing today to direct appeals broadly to a large public, not only to sell goods and services but also to mobilize people for political purposes.

The Second Amendment and the Right to Bear Arms

A well regulated Militia, being necessary to the security of a free State, the right of the people to keep and bear Arms, shall not be infringed.

> **Is the right to bear arms guaranteed by the Bill of Rights? How is its exercise restricted?**

The point and purpose of the Second Amendment is the provision for militias; they were to be the backing of the government for the maintenance of local public order. "Militia" was understood at the time of the Founding to be a military or police resource for state governments, and militias were specifically distinguished from armies and troops, which came within the sole constitutional jurisdiction of Congress.

Thus, the right of the people "to keep and bear Arms" is based on and associated with participation in state militias. The reference to citizens keeping arms underscored the fact that in the 1700s, state governments could not be relied on to provide firearms to militia members, so citizens eligible to serve in militias (white males between the ages of eighteen and forty-five) were expected to keep their own firearms at the ready.

Recent controversy has arisen concerning some citizens who have sought to form their own *private* militias, unconnected with the government. Yet the Supreme Court made clear that the Second Amendment does not allow citizens to

The Second Amendment arouses at least as much controversy as the First. The right to bear arms is constitutionally guaranteed, although an estimated 80 percent of Americans support some form of gun control. States are allowed to regulate the sale of weapons by requiring a waiting period or a background check on the buyer.

Since the Second Amendment entitles people to carry guns, police are used to facing gunfire. This can have tragic consequences: in 1998, New York police shot a sixteen-year-old boy seventeen times when he refused to drop his toy gun, which mimicked a semiautomatic weapon. Here, New York police sergeant Eric Adams calls for revised regulations dealing with toy guns.

President Reagan receives a lifetime membership to the National Rifle Association in this 1983 photo (left). The NRA is a well-disciplined group dedicated to preserving Americans' Second Amendment rights. The organization is so powerful a lobby that Reagan—who was himself shot in an assassination attempt in 1981—sought its support. Legal gun ownership is controversial because of its negative byproduct, gun violence. Former presidential press secretary James Brady, also shot during the attempted assassination of Reagan, never regained use of his legs. Here he speaks to the Democratic National Convention in support of a congressional bill to establish a waiting period and background checks for gun buyers (right). The Supreme Court declared part of the so-called Brady Bill to be in violation of the Second Amendment.

form their own militias free from government control. When a private militia tried to assert such a right, the Supreme Court denied it.[58]

Thus, while much public controversy over the gun control issue holds up the banner of the Second Amendment, it is mostly irrelevant to the modern gun control controversy. This point is underscored by the fact that no gun control law has ever been declared unconstitutional as a violation of the Second Amendment, including a local law that banned the possession of working handguns except for those who used handguns for their jobs, like police and security guards.[59] The gun control issue is one that will be settled through the political process, not by the courts.

Rights of the Criminally Accused

Except for the First Amendment, most of the battle to apply the Bill of Rights to the states was fought over the various protections granted to individuals who

➤ **What is due process?**

➤ **How do the Fourth, Fifth, Sixth, and Eighth Amendments provide for the due process of law?**

are accused of a crime, who are suspects in the commission of a crime, or who are brought before the court as a witness to a crime. The Fourth, Fifth, Sixth, and Eighth Amendments, taken together, are the essence of the due process of law, even though this fundamental concept does not appear until the very last words of the Fifth Amendment. In the next sections we will look at specific cases that illuminate the dynamics of this important constitutional issue. The procedural safeguards that we will discuss may seem remote to most law-abiding citizens, but they help define the limits of government action against the personal liberty of every citizen. Many Americans believe that "legal technicalities" are responsible for setting many actual criminals free. In many cases, that is absolutely true. In fact, setting defendants free is the very purpose of the requirements that constitute due process. One of America's traditional and most strongly held juridical values is that "it is far worse to convict an innocent man than to let a guilty man go free."[60] In civil suits, verdicts rest upon "the preponderance of the evidence"; in criminal cases, guilt has to be proven "beyond a reasonable doubt"—a far higher standard. The provisions for due process in the Bill of Rights were added in order to improve the probability that the standard of "reasonable doubt" will be respected.

THE FOURTH AMENDMENT AND SEARCHES AND SEIZURES

> The right of the people to be secure in their persons, houses, papers, and effects, against unreasonable searches and seizures, shall not be violated, and no Warrants shall issue, but upon probable cause, supported by Oath or affirmation, and particularly describing the place to be searched, and the persons or things to be seized.

The purpose of the Fourth Amendment is to guarantee the security of citizens against unreasonable (i.e., improper) searches and seizures. In 1990, the Supreme Court summarized its understanding of the Fourth Amendment brilliantly and succinctly: "A search compromises the individual interest in privacy; a seizure deprives the individual of dominion over his or her person or property."[61] But how are we to define what is reasonable and what is unreasonable?

The 1961 case of *Mapp v. Ohio* illustrates the beauty and the agony of one of the most important procedures that have grown out of the Fourth Amendment—the **exclusionary rule,** which prohibits evidence obtained during an illegal search from being introduced in a trial. Dollree (Dolly) Mapp was "a Cleveland woman of questionable reputation" (by some accounts), the ex-wife of one prominent boxer, and the fiancée of an even more famous one. Acting on a tip that Dolly Mapp was harboring a suspect in a bombing incident, several policemen forcibly entered Ms. Mapp's house claiming they had a warrant to look for the bombing suspect. The police did not find the bombing suspect but did find some materials connected to the local numbers racket (an illegal gambling operation) and a quantity of "obscene materials," in violation of an Ohio law banning possession of such materials. Although the warrant was never produced, the evidence that had been seized was admitted by a court, and Ms. Mapp was charged and convicted for illegal possession of obscene materials.

exclusionary rule the ability of courts to exclude evidence obtained in violation of the Fourth Amendment

By the time Ms. Mapp's appeal reached the Supreme Court, the issue of obscene materials had faded into obscurity, and the question before the Court was whether any evidence produced under the circumstances of the search of her home was admissible. The Court's opinion affirmed the exclusionary rule: under the Fourth Amendment (applied to the states through the Fourteenth Amendment), "all evidence obtained by searches and seizures in violation of the Constitution . . . is inadmissible."[62] This means that even people who are clearly guilty of the crime of which they are accused must not be convicted if the only evidence for their conviction was obtained illegally. This idea was expressed by Supreme Court Justice Benjamin Cardozo nearly a century ago when he wrote that "the criminal is to go free because the constable has blundered."

The exclusionary rule is the most severe restraint ever imposed by the Constitution and the courts on the behavior of the police. The exclusionary rule is a dramatic restriction because it rules out precisely the evidence that produces a conviction; it frees those people who are *known* to have committed the crime of which they have been accused. Because it works so dramatically in favor of persons known to have committed a crime, the Court has since softened the application of the rule. In recent years, the federal courts have relied upon a discretionary use of the exclusionary rule, whereby they make a judgment as to the "nature and quality of the intrusion." It is thus difficult to know ahead of time whether a defendant will or will not be protected from an illegal search under the Fourth Amendment.[63]

Another recent issue involving the Fourth Amendment is the controversy over mandatory drug testing. Such tests are most widely used on public employees, and in an important case the Supreme Court has upheld the U.S. Customs Service's drug-testing program for its employees.[64] The same year the Court approved drug and alcohol tests for railroad workers if they were involved in serious accidents.[65] After Court approvals of those two cases in 1989, more than forty federal agencies initiated mandatory employee drug tests. The practice of drug testing was reinforced by a presidential executive order widely touted as the "campaign for a drug-free federal workplace." These growing practices gave rise to public appeals against the general practice of "suspicionless testing" of employees. Regardless of any need to limit the spread of drug abuse, working in this manner through public employees seemed patently unconstitutional, in violation of the Fourth Amendment. A 1995 case, in which the Court upheld a public school district's policy requiring all students participating in interscholastic sports to submit to random drug tests, surely contributed to the efforts of federal, state, and local agencies to initiate random and suspicionless drug and alcohol testing.[66] The most recent cases suggest, however, that the Court is beginning to consider limits on the war against drugs. In a decisive 8-to-1 decision, the Court applied the Fourth Amendment as a shield against "state action that diminishes personal privacy" when the officials in question are not performing high-risk or safety-sensitive tasks.[67] Using random and suspicionless drug testing as a symbol to fight drug use was, in the Court's opinion, carrying the exceptions to the Fourth Amendment too far.

More recently, the Court found it unconstitutional for police to use trained dogs in roadblocks set up to look for drugs in cars. Unlike drunk-driving

The Rights of the Accused from Arrest to Trial

No improper searches and seizures (Fourth Amendment)

No arrest without probable cause (Fourth Amendment)

Right to remain silent (Fifth Amendment)

No self-incrimination during arrest or trial (Fifth Amendment)

Right to be informed of charges (Sixth Amendment)

Right to counsel (Sixth Amendment)

No excessive bail (Eighth Amendment)

Right to grand jury (Fifth Amendment)

Right to open trial before a judge (Article I, Section 9)

Right to speedy and public trial before an impartial jury (Sixth Amendment)

Evidence obtained by illegal search not admissible during trial (Fourth Amendment)

Right to confront witnesses (Sixth Amendment)

No double jeopardy (Fifth Amendment)

No cruel and unusual punishment (Eighth Amendment)

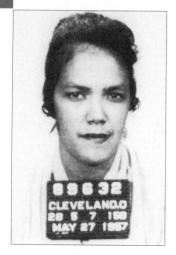

The Constitution provides several major protections for those accused of a crime. In the case of Dollree Mapp v. Ohio, the Supreme Court interpreted the Fourth Amendment to mean that if incriminating material is found through illegal search and seizure, it cannot be used as evidence in court. Mapp's case against the Cleveland Police Department resulted in the nationalization of the Fourth Amendment's exclusionary rule.

Drug testing has raised concerns about the Fourth Amendment—is a drug test an unreasonable search? Though the Supreme Court initially upheld drug and alcohol tests, the Court indicated in a 1997 case that such tests illegally invade privacy if they are conducted randomly and without suspicion of guilt. However, the Court allowed tests on those engaged in risky activities, such as driving. Here, North Carolina police conduct random alcohol tests at a roadblock.

roadblocks, where public safety is directly involved, narcotics roadblocks "cannot escape the Fourth Amendment's requirement that searches be based on suspicion of individual wrongdoing."[68] The Court also ruled that a public hospital cannot constitutionally test maternity patients for illegal drug use without their consent.[69] Finally, the Court found that the police may not use thermal imaging devices to detect suspicious patterns of heat emerging from private homes without obtaining the usual search warrant.[70]

THE FIFTH AMENDMENT

No person shall be held to answer for a capital, or otherwise infamous crime, unless on a presentment or indictment of a Grand Jury, except in cases arising in the land or naval forces, or in the Militia, when in actual service in time of War or public danger; nor shall any person be subject for the same offence to be twice put in jeopardy of life or limb; nor shall be compelled in any criminal case to be a witness against himself, nor be deprived of life, liberty, or property, without due process of law; nor shall private property be taken for public use, without just compensation.

Grand Juries The first clause of the Fifth Amendment, the right to a **grand jury** to determine whether a trial is warranted, is considered "the oldest institution known to the Constitution."[71] Grand juries play an important role in federal criminal cases. However, the provision for a grand jury is the one important civil liberties provision of the Bill of Rights that was not incorporated by the Fourteenth Amendment to apply to state criminal prosecutions. Thus, some states operate without grand juries. In such states, the prosecuting attorney simply files a "bill of information" affirming that there is sufficient evidence available to justify a trial. If the accused person is to be held in custody, the prosecutor must take the available information before a judge to determine that the evidence shows probable cause.

SPECIFIC WARNING REGARDING INTERROGATIONS

1. You have the right to remain silent.

2. Anything you say can and will be used against you in a court of law.

3. You have the right to talk to a lawyer and have him present with you while you are being questioned.

4. If you cannot afford to hire a lawyer one will be appointed to represent you before any questioning, if you wish one.

The Fifth Amendment provides additional protection from the government by barring double jeopardy and self-incrimination and by guaranteeing grand jury inquiries and eminent domain payments. The modern interpretation of the Fifth Amendment was shaped by the 1966 case Miranda v. Arizona. *In 1966, Ernesto Miranda confessed to kidnapping and rape. Since he was never told that he was not required to answer police questions, his case was appealed on the grounds that his right against self-incrimination had been violated. The trial resulted in the creation of* Miranda *rights, which must be read to those arrested to make them aware of their constitutional rights.*

Double Jeopardy "Nor shall any person be subject for the same offence to be twice put in jeopardy of life or limb" is the constitutional protection from **double jeopardy,** or being tried more than once for the same crime. The protection from double jeopardy was at the heart of the *Palko* case in 1937, which, as we saw earlier in this chapter, also established the principle of selective incorporation of the Bill of Rights. In that case, the state of Connecticut had indicted Frank Palko for first-degree murder, but a lower court had found him guilty of only second-degree murder and sentenced him to life in prison. Unhappy with the verdict, the state of Connecticut appealed the conviction to its highest court, won the appeal, got a new trial, and then succeeded in getting Palko convicted of first-degree murder. Palko appealed to the Supreme Court on what seemed an open-and-shut case of double jeopardy. Yet, although the majority of the Court agreed that this could indeed be considered a case of double jeopardy, they decided that double jeopardy was *not* one of the provisions of the Bill of Rights incorporated in the Fourteenth Amendment as a restriction on the powers of the states. It took more than thirty years for the Court to nationalize the constitutional protection against double jeopardy. Palko was eventually executed for the crime, because he lived in the state of Connecticut rather than in some state whose constitution included a guarantee against double jeopardy.

Self-Incrimination Perhaps the most significant liberty found in the Fifth Amendment, and the one most familiar to many Americans who watch television crime shows, is the guarantee that no citizen "shall be compelled in any criminal

grand jury jury that determines whether sufficient evidence is available to justify a trial; grand juries do not rule on the accused's guilt or innocence.

double jeopardy the Fifth Amendment right providing that a person cannot be tried twice for the same crime

case to be a witness against himself. . . ." The most famous case concerning self-incrimination is one of such importance that Chief Justice Earl Warren assessed its results as going "to the very root of our concepts of American criminal jurisprudence."[72] Twenty-three-year-old Ernesto Miranda was sentenced to between twenty and thirty years in prison for the kidnapping and rape of an eighteen-year-old woman. The woman had identified him in a police lineup, and, after two hours of questioning, Miranda confessed, subsequently signing a statement that his confession had been made voluntarily, without threats or promises of immunity. These confessions were admitted into evidence, served as the basis for Miranda's conviction, and also served as the basis of the appeal of his conviction all the way to the Supreme Court. In one of the most intensely and widely criticized decisions ever handed down by the Supreme Court, Ernesto Miranda's case produced the rules the police must follow before questioning an arrested criminal suspect. The reading of a person's "Miranda rights" became a standard scene in every police station and on virtually every dramatization of police action on television and in the movies. *Miranda* advanced the civil liberties of accused persons by expanding not only the scope of the Fifth Amendment clause covering coerced confessions and self-incrimination, but also by confirming the right to counsel (discussed later). The Supreme Court under Burger and Rehnquist has considerably softened the *Miranda* restrictions, making the job of the police a little easier, but the **Miranda rule** still stands as a protection against egregious police abuses of arrested persons. The Supreme Court reaffirmed *Miranda* in *Dickerson v. United States* (2000).

Eminent Domain   The other fundamental clause of the Fifth Amendment is the "takings clause," which extends to each citizen a protection against the "taking" of private property "without just compensation." Although this part of the Fifth Amendment is not specifically concerned with protecting persons accused of crimes, it is nevertheless a fundamentally important instance where the government and the citizen are adversaries. The power of any government to take private property for a public use is called **eminent domain.** This power is essential to the very concept of sovereignty. The Fifth Amendment neither invents eminent domain nor takes it away; its purpose is to put limits on that inherent power through procedures that require a showing of a public purpose and the provision of fair payment for the taking of someone's property. This provision is now universally observed in all U.S. principalities, but it has not always been meticulously observed.

Take the case of Mr. Berman, who in the 1950s owned and operated a "mom and pop" grocery store in a run-down neighborhood on the southwest side of the District of Columbia. In carrying out a vast urban redevelopment program, the city government of Washington, D.C., took Berman's property as one of a large number of privately owned lots to be cleared for new housing and business construction. Berman, and his successors after his death, took the government to court on the grounds that it was an unconstitutional use of eminent domain to take property from one private owner and eventually to turn that property back, in altered form, to another private owner. Berman and his successors lost their case. The Supreme Court's argument was a curious but very important one: the "public interest" can mean virtually anything a legislature says it means. In other words, since the overall slum clearance and redevelopment project was in the public interest, according to the legislature, the eventual transfers of property that were going to take place were justified.[73]

Miranda rule   the requirement, articulated by the Supreme Court in *Miranda v. Arizona,* that persons under arrest must be informed prior to police interrogation of their rights to remain silent and to have the benefit of legal counsel

eminent domain   the right of government to take private property for public use

What Government Does . . . After September 11

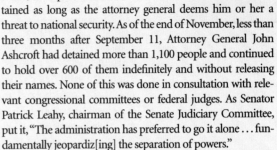

When war breaks out, there is almost always a virtual moratorium on the Bill of Rights. President Washington subjected accused spies to trial before military courts, even when capital punishment was at issue. President Lincoln abruptly and unilaterally suspended the writ of *habeas corpus* and set up military courts for those accused of being Confederate sympathizers. President Franklin Roosevelt, with only a minimal tip of the hat to Congress, arranged for the trial of accused Nazi spies in military tribunals, on the basis of which six were executed; and without consulting Congress at all he condemned over 120,000 Japanese Americans to internment camps for the duration of the war, even though they were never accused of a crime.

Six weeks to the day after September 11, the House of Representatives voted 356 to 66 and the Senate voted 98 to 1 to pass, without debate, a 342-page bill offered by the president with the imposing title "Uniting and Strengthening America by Providing Appropriate Tools Required to Intercept and Obstruct Terrorism Act"—recognized only by its acronym, the USA PATRIOT Act. There are many noncontroversial provisions in this very long statute, but the severe and controversial restrictions on civil liberties are so numerous that a selection of highlights is all that can be offered here.

Section 802 authorizes surveillance of the acts of political activists and organizations if they "*appear* to be *intended* . . . to influence the policy of a government by intimidation or coercion" [emphasis added]. Section 411 bars entry into the United States of anyone the secretary of state determines has engaged in speech that "undermines U.S. efforts to reduce or eliminate terrorist activities." Section 213 authorizes covert searches of a person's home or office without a search warrant if notification would have an adverse result on the investigation. Section 215 authorizes the FBI and other related agencies to obtain sensitive personal records by simply certifying that they are being sought for an investigation "to protect against international terrorism." Section 216 gives the government wide latitude to install its new Carnivore (DCS 1000) system which is "capable of intercepting all forms of Internet activity, including e-mail messages, etc." Section 218 (probably the most radical provision) amends existing authority to conduct secret wiretaps and personal searches without having to show "probable cause" to a judge whenever the investigator can claim it is "a significant purpose" and the content is considered "foreign intelligence." Section 203 goes still further by authorizing disclosure of intelligence information to the FBI, CIA, INS, etc., even including confidential grand jury information, if it will "assist the official . . . in . . . his official duties." Finally, Section 412 gives the attorney general power to detain immigrants on suspicion

and without any charges for up to seven days; if charged with an immigration violation, however trivial, that person can be detained as long as the attorney general deems him or her a threat to national security. As of the end of November, less than three months after September 11, Attorney General John Ashcroft had detained more than 1,100 people and continued to hold over 600 of them indefinitely and without releasing their names. None of this was done in consultation with relevant congressional committees or federal judges. As Senator Patrick Leahy, chairman of the Senate Judiciary Committee, put it, "The administration has preferred to go it alone . . . fundamentally jeopardiz[ing] the separation of powers."

For certain provisions in the USA PATRIOT Act there is a "sunset" clause providing that a particular emergency power will automatically cease in 2005. This demonstrates a certain amount of awareness that emergency powers are temporary powers. But not all of these powers will self-destruct after a prescribed period of time. For example, Carnivore, once it is installed on an Internet service provider (ISP), is not scheduled to expire, and it will be extremely difficult to keep it from devouring *all* communications on the server and not just those of interest to the FBI or other investigating agencies.

According to national polls taken during the first week of December 2001, 68 percent of the respondents reported that they generally approve of Bush's plan to deal with terrorism suspects, and 58 percent approved of the military tribunals but thought they should be public. Eighty-six percent of the respondents thought that the Bush administration had not gone too far in restricting civil liberties in its response to terrorism. *Newsweek* reported that White House officials say that every time the so-called liberal media fret about "Ashcroft's assaulting civil liberties, the president's approval ratings go up. 'Attack us some more,' quips one aide." Emergency-type infringements on civil liberties can be popular because the purpose of most of the clauses of the Bill of Rights is to protect unpopular speech and undesirable characters accused of heinous crimes. But what's the Bill of Rights worth if it only protects the popular, the harmless, and the innocent?

SOURCES: Nancy Chang, "The USA PATRIOT Act: What's So Patriotic about Trampling on the Bill of Rights?" Center for Constitutional Rights, March 1, 2002, www.ccr/ny.org (accessed 7/11/02); *Congressional Quarterly,* December 1, 2001, pp. 2820–27; *Time,* December 10, 2001, pp. 30–38; *Newsweek,* December 10, 2001, pp. 37–48; *Mother Jones,* "The World According to Ashcroft," March/April 2002, pp. 38–44.

THE SIXTH AMENDMENT AND THE RIGHT TO COUNSEL

> In all criminal prosecutions, the accused shall enjoy the right to a speedy and public trial, by an impartial jury of the State and district wherein the crime shall have been committed, which district shall have been previously ascertained by law, and to be informed of the nature and cause of the accusation; to be confronted with the witnesses against him; to have compulsory process for obtaining witnesses in his favor, and to have the Assistance of Counsel for his defence.

Like the exclusionary rule of the Fourth Amendment and the self-incrimination clause of the Fifth Amendment, the "right to counsel" provision of the Sixth Amendment is notable for freeing defendants who seem to the public to be patently guilty as charged. Other provisions of the Sixth Amendment, such as the right to a speedy trial and the right to confront witnesses before an impartial jury, are less controversial in nature.

Gideon v. Wainwright is the perfect case study because it involved a disreputable person who seemed patently guilty of the crime for which he was convicted. In and out of jails for most of his fifty-one years, Clarence Earl Gideon received a five-year sentence for breaking and entering a poolroom in Panama City, Florida. While serving time in jail, Gideon became a fairly well qualified "jailhouse lawyer," made his own appeal on a handwritten petition, and eventually won the landmark ruling on the right to counsel in all felony cases.[74]

The right to counsel has been expanded rather than contracted during the past few decades, when the courts have become more conservative. For example, although at first the right to counsel was met by judges assigning lawyers from the community as a formal public obligation, most states and cities now have created an office of public defender; these state-employed professional defense lawyers typically provide poor defendants with much better legal representation. And, although these defendants cannot choose their private defense attorney, they do have the right to appeal a conviction on the grounds that the counsel provided by the state was deficient. Moreover, the right to counsel extends beyond serious crimes to any trial, with or without jury, that holds the possibility of imprisonment.[75]

THE EIGHTH AMENDMENT AND CRUEL AND UNUSUAL PUNISHMENT

The Eighth Amendment prohibits "excessive bail," "excessive fines," and "cruel and unusual punishment." Virtually all the debate over Eighth Amendment issues focuses on the last clause of the amendment: the protection from "cruel and unusual punishment." One of the greatest challenges in interpreting this provision consistently lies in the fact that what is considered "cruel and unusual" varies from culture to culture and from generation to generation. And, unfortunately, it also varies by class and race. A sentence of ten years in prison for robbing a liquor store is not considered excessive, yet embezzlement or insider trading involving millions of dollars merits only three years of community service. Are "white-collar" crimes less serious than "working-class" crimes? Consider the 1995 action by Congress to mandate a five-year minimum sentence for offenses involving five or more grams of crack cocaine. The same five-year mandatory sentence for *powdered* cocaine, however, kicks in only when the amount involved is *five hundred* grams or more. As one black member of the House put it, "crack cocaine happens to be used by poor people, mostly black people, because it's cheap. Powdered cocaine happens to be used by wealthy white people."[76]

The Death Penalty

Since the Supreme Court gave a green light to the reenactment of death penalty laws in 1976, most states have embraced capital punishment as a "get-tough" signal to criminals. Between 1976 and 2000, states executed 683 people. Most of those executions occurred in southern states, with Texas leading the way at 239. As of 2002, thirty-eight states had adopted some form of capital punishment, a move approved of by about three-quarters of all Americans.

Despite the fact that virtually all criminal conduct is regulated by the states, Congress has also jumped on the bandwagon, imposing capital punishment for more than fifty federal crimes. Despite the seeming popularity of the death penalty, the debate has become, if anything, more intense. In 1997, for example, the American Bar Association passed a resolution calling for a halt to the death penalty until concerns about its fairness—that is, whether its application violates the principle of equality—and about ensuring due process are addressed. In 2000, the governor of Illinois imposed a moratorium on the death penalty and created a commission to review the capital punishment system. After a two-year study by the commission, Illinois adopted a number of reforms, including a ban on executions of the mentally retarded. In June 2002, the U.S. Supreme Court banned all executions of mentally retarded defendants, a decision that could move 200 or more people off death row.

Many death penalty supporters trumpet its deterrent effects on other would-be criminals. Although studies of capital crimes usually fail to demonstrate any direct deterrent effect, that may be due to the lengthy delays—typically years and even decades—between convictions and executions. A system that eliminates undue delays would surely enhance deterrence. And deterring even one murder or other heinous crime, proponents argue, is more than ample justification for such laws.

Beyond this, the death penalty is seen as a proper expression of retribution, echoed in the biblical phrase "an eye for an eye." People who commit vicious crimes deserve to forfeit their lives in exchange for the suffering they have inflicted. If the world applauded the execution of Nazis after World War II, for example, how could it deny the right of society to execute a serial killer?

Constitutional objections to the death penalty often invoke the Eighth Amendment's protection against punishments that are "cruel and unusual." Yet the death penalty can hardly be considered a violation of this protection, say supporters, since the death penalty was commonly used in the eighteenth century and was supported by most early American leaders. And while the poor, males, and blacks and Latinos are more likely to find themselves sitting on death row, this fact reflects the painful reality that these categories of individuals are more likely to commit crimes.

Death penalty opponents are quick to point out that the death penalty has not been proven to deter crime, either in the United States or abroad. In fact, America is the only Western nation that still executes criminals. The fact that American states execute criminals debases, rather than elevates, society, by extolling vengeance. If the government is to serve as an example of proper behavior, say foes, it has no business sanctioning killing when incarceration will similarly protect society.

As for the Constitution, most of the Founders surely supported the death penalty. But, foes note, they also countenanced slavery, and lived at a time when society was both less informed about, and more indifferent to, the human condition. Modern Americans' greater civility should be reflected in how it defines individual rights.

Furthermore, according to death penalty foes, execution is expensive—more expensive than life imprisonment—precisely because the government must make every effort to ensure that it is not executing an innocent person. Curtailing legal appeals would make the possibility of a mistake too great. And although most Americans do support the death penalty, people also support life without the possibility of parole as an alternative. Race also intrudes in death penalty cases: people of color (who are more likely to face economic deprivation) are disproportionately more likely to be sentenced to death, whereas whites charged with identical crimes are less likely to be given the ultimate punishment. Such disparity of treatment violates the principle of equal protection. And finally, according to opponents, a life sentence may be a worse punishment for criminals than the death penalty.

Is the Death Penalty Fair Punishment?

Yes Murder is so uniquely sinister and evil that the only equal punishment is death. Lesser punishments fall short of sufficiently condemning the gravity of the crime. A just society must declare that we so value the sanctity of human life that if you steal somebody else's, you will pay with your own.

But many good people find capital punishment abhorrent. A decent society is a compassionate one that would never stoop to the barbaric level of the murderer, they insist. Indeed, there are lots of reasons to oppose the death penalty.

Let's consider them:

1. The death penalty is barbaric state-sanctioned murder.

   First, let us differentiate between the terms "kill" and "murder." While killing is a broader term, murder is very specific. Killing can be legal and justified (self-defense) or unjustified and illegal (shooting schoolchildren). Murder is always illegal, evil, and claims the life of an innocent human victim. In fact, the Bible's Sixth Commandment actually reads, "You shall not murder." It is erroneous to translate the original Hebrew to "Thou shalt not kill."

   Moreover, the death penalty for those who commit murder is the only law God demands in each of the first five books of Moses (the Torah).

   It is barbaric to murder 168 precious people by blowing up a federal building; it is just to eliminate such monsters from our midst.

   And as William Buckley points out, if executing murderers is state-sanctioned murder, then life imprisonment is state-sanctioned kidnapping. We must discern the essential difference and not reduce ourselves to such relativist thinking.

2. The death penalty does not deter criminals from committing murder.

   How do we know? When the average murderer serves less than twelve years in prison and has only an infinitesimal risk of being executed, of course there is no deterrent value. But, as Ernest van den Haag has proposed, if those who commit murders on Mondays, Wednesdays, and Fridays are executed and those who commit murders on all other days are sentenced to life in prison, we'll soon see if it deters.

3. The death penalty is mandated in an unfair and discriminatory manner.

   It certainly is true that high-profile lawyers are better at manipulating the justice system to get wealthy guilty defendants lesser punishments. Notice this argument doesn't claim that those sentenced to death aren't guilty, rather that some guilty murderers get lighter sentences. So, wouldn't it make sense to strive for more equal justice, rather than equal injustice?

4. An innocent person may be executed.

   This is the one moral argument that must be conceded by supporters of capital punishment. No system of justice is entirely free of mistakes, but today in America the death penalty is as close as it gets. DNA evidence and numerous appeals provide the most confidence possible in accurate sentencing.

Just as supporters of the death penalty must acknowledge the miniscule possibility that an innocent could be wrongly executed, critics must acknowledge that guilty murderers often go on to slay more people. Either by parole, serving out their truncated sentences, escape, or killing fellow inmates or prison guards, there is certain bloodshed that accompanies opposition to capital punishment.

The light of clarity must illuminate the shadows of muddled thinking that equates the killing of a convicted murderer with the killing of their victims. The only commonality between murder and capital punishment is death. There is, however, a great ethical distinction to be made. Just as the only commonality between rape and lovemaking is sex, we must consider its context. We cannot be swept away by the moral relativist tsunami that has crashed onto our shores of common sense.

SOURCE: Burnie Thompson, "Death Penalty: Pro," *The Daily Titan* (California State University, Fullerton), November 10, 1999.

No

The recent case of Andrea Yates reopened an age-old debate about capital punishment. And in this case, as with all capital cases, it is fitting that the sentence of death was avoided. It is a step in the right direction.

Though her crime—drowning her own children—was horrific and upsetting, there should be no time when death is an acceptable punishment, regardless of the circumstances. For serious crimes, life in prison is an appropriate and suitably harsh punishment, and quite simply, there are no compelling reasons that the death penalty should be an option in our justice system whatsoever.

Many supporters of capital punishment, including President George W. Bush, cite the "deterrence effect" of executions as a primary justification for it. The threat of the death penalty, they believe, discourages people from committing violent crimes for fear of losing their own lives.

If this were true, it might be an interesting argument. But this is simply not the case. In a wide body of literature on this subject, there is no conclusive or convincing evidence that the presence or exercise of the death penalty has any substantial crime-deterrence effect in the United States. Short of living in a repressive police state where summary executions occur even for petty crimes, the death penalty is no more of a discouragement to would-be criminals than, say, life in prison.

Others argue that the death penalty is a cost-reducing measure because it saves the expense of housing an inmate in a prison cell for the remainder of his natural life. Again, this turns out not to be true in practice. The Bureau of Justice Statistics indicates that the average capital crime inmate spends nearly eight years on death row, usually pending automatic reviews, litigation, and numerous appeals. This high amount of legal activity all but erases any financial savings to the government. In any case, determining the fate of a life based on the savings of a few dollars is hardly the type of justice system that we should desire.

Another argument used by proponents of capital punishment is that execution of murderers is equivalent justice that provides retribution to the families of the victims. Yet this, too, is flawed logic. Victims' families grieve over the loss of a loved one, and the essence of this grief will not be mitigated by witnessing another death. In fact, many survivors—including Bud Welch, whose daughter was killed in the Oklahoma City bombing—have said that watching the execution of the murderer has reopened a wound in their lives, adding to the feeling of emptiness and diminishment. If the sentence of life in prison is not severe enough to "satisfy" the thirst for vengeance, then it is unlikely that a death sentence will be any more effective at reducing the anger and hurt felt by victims' families. This is all the better a reason not to punish one violation of life with another.

All of this has merely served to dismiss the arguments that support the death penalty: it does not substantially deter crime, it is not less expensive, and it will not itself bring peace to families.

Nothing has yet been said of the serious problems associated with the application of capital punishment. Among these, concerns for equity top the list. Is it acceptable that defendants with high-priced lawyers are less likely to be sentenced to death? Is it acceptable that racial or gender bias might enter a jury's decision, or that mental illness may be overlooked? Or, worse yet, is it acceptable that an error could occur, depriving an innocent person of life? The answer to all of these questions is a resounding no.

The gift of life is the most precious of all, and we must be willing to defend it in all circumstances. Indeed, murder is so heinous because it violates the dignity of life, and life in prison is a severe and fitting punishment. Responding to one death with another merely continues the cycle of killing that our laws are supposed to guard against.

And so, we should continue the call to abolish the death penalty in the United States, joining numerous other nations around the world that did so long ago. In doing this, we will be promoting a consistent ethic of life that upholds the sanctity of life and rejects the taking of another life in any circumstance.

In the sentence of Andrea Yates, this consistent ethic was upheld. Now, our goal must be to maintain this ethic of life in every case.

SOURCE: William Edwards, "Andrea Yates and the Case Against the Death Penalty," *Yale Daily News*, March 25, 2002.

By far the biggest issue of class and race inconsistency as constituting cruel and unusual punishment arises over the death penalty. In 1972, the Supreme Court overturned several state death penalty laws, not because they were cruel and unusual, but because they were being applied in a capricious manner—i.e., blacks were much more likely than whites to be sentenced to death, and the poor more likely than the rich, and men more likely than women.[77] Very soon after that decision, a majority of states revised their capital punishment provisions to meet the Court's standards.[78] Since 1976, the Court has consistently upheld state laws providing for capital punishment, although the Court also continues to review numerous death penalty appeals each year.

The Right to Privacy

> **What is the right to privacy? How has it been derived from the Bill of Rights? What forms does the right to privacy take today?**

Some of the people all of the time and all of the people some of the time would just like to be left alone, to have their own private domain into which no one—friends, family, government, church, or employer—has the right to enter without permission.

Many Jehovah's Witnesses felt that way in the 1930s. They risked serious punishment in 1940 by telling their children not to salute the flag or say the "Pledge of Allegiance" in school because of their understanding of the First Commandment's prohibition of the worship of "graven images." They lost their appeal, the children were expelled, and the parents were punished.[79] However, the Supreme Court concluded that the 1940 decision was "wrongly decided."[80] These two cases arose under the freedom of religion provisions of the First Amendment, but they were also the first cases to confront the possibility of another right that is not mentioned anywhere in the Constitution or the Bill of Rights: the right to be left alone. When the Court began to take a more activist role in the mid-1950s and 1960s, the idea of a **right to privacy** was revived. In 1958, the Supreme Court recognized "privacy in one's association" in its decision to prevent the state of Alabama from using the membership list of the National Association for the Advancement of Colored People in the state's investigations.[81]

right to privacy the right to be let alone, which has been interpreted by the Supreme Court to entail free access to birth control and abortions

Birth Control   The sphere of privacy was drawn in earnest in 1965, when the Court ruled that a Connecticut statute forbidding the use of contraceptives violated the right of marital privacy. Estelle Griswold, the executive director of the Planned Parenthood League of Connecticut, was arrested by the state of Connecticut for providing information, instruction, and medical advice about contraception to married couples. She and her associates were found guilty as accessories to the crime and fined $100 each. The Supreme Court reversed the lower court decisions and declared the Connecticut law unconstitutional because it violated "a right of privacy older than the Bill of Rights—older than our political parties, older than our school system."[82] Justice William O. Douglas, author of the majority decision in the *Griswold* case, argued that this right of privacy is also grounded in the Constitution, because it fits into a "zone of privacy" created by a combination of the Third, Fourth, and Fifth Amendments. A concurring opinion, written by Justice Arthur Goldberg, attempted to strengthen Douglas's argument by adding that "the concept of liberty . . . embraces the right of marital privacy though that right is not mentioned explicitly in the Constitution [and] is supported by numerous decisions of this Court . . . and *by the language and history of the Ninth Amendment*" (emphasis added).[83]

Abortion The right to privacy was confirmed and extended in 1973 in the most important of all privacy decisions, and one of the most important Supreme Court decisions in American history: *Roe v. Wade*. This decision established a woman's right to seek an abortion and prohibited states from making abortion a criminal act.[84] The Burger Court's decision in *Roe* took a revolutionary step toward establishing the right to privacy. It is important to emphasize that the preference for privacy rights and for their extension to include the rights of women to control their own bodies was not something invented by the Supreme Court in a vacuum. Most states did not regulate abortions in any fashion until the 1840s, at which time only six of the twenty-six existing states had any regulations governing abortion at all. In addition, many states had begun to ease their abortion restrictions well before the 1973 *Roe* decision, although in recent years a number of states have reinstated some restrictions on abortion.

By extending the umbrella of privacy, this sweeping ruling dramatically changed abortion practices in America. In addition, it galvanized and nationalized the abortion debate. Groups opposed to abortion, such as the National Right to Life Committee, organized to fight the new liberal standard, while abortion rights groups sought to maintain that protection. In recent years, the legal standard shifted against abortion rights supporters in two key Supreme Court cases.

In *Webster v. Reproductive Health Services* (1989), the Court narrowly upheld (by a 5-to-4 majority) the constitutionality of restrictions on the use of public medical facilities for abortion.[85] And in the 1992 case of *Planned Parenthood v. Casey*, another 5-to-4 majority of the Court upheld *Roe* but narrowed its scope, refusing to invalidate a Pennsylvania law that significantly limits freedom of choice. The Court's decision defined the right to an abortion as a "limited or qualified" right subject to regulation by the states as long as the regulation does not constitute an "undue burden."[86] More recently, the Court had another opportunity to rule on what constitutes an undue burden. In the 2000 case of *Stenberg v. Carhart*, the Court, by a vote of 5 to 4, struck down Nebraska's ban on partial-birth abortions because the law had the "effect of placing a substantial obstacle in the path of a woman seeking an abortion."[87]

Homosexuality In the last two decades, the right to be left alone began to include the privacy rights of homosexuals. One morning in Atlanta, Georgia, in the mid-1980s, Michael Hardwick was arrested by a police officer who discovered him in bed with another man. The officer had come to serve a warrant for Hardwick's arrest for failure to appear in court to answer charges of drinking in public. One of Hardwick's unknowing housemates invited the officer to look in Hardwick's room, where he found Hardwick and another man engaging in "consensual sexual behavior." He was then arrested under Georgia's laws against heterosexual and homosexual sodomy. Hardwick filed a lawsuit against the state, challenging the constitutionality of the Georgia law. Hardwick won his case in the federal court of appeals. The state of Georgia, in an unusual move, appealed the court's decision to the Supreme Court. The majority of the Court reversed the lower court decision, holding against Mr. Hardwick, on the grounds that "the federal Constitution confers [no] fundamental right upon homosexuals to engage in sodomy," and that therefore there was no basis to invalidate "the laws of the many states that still make such conduct illegal and have done so for a very long time."[88] The Court majority concluded its opinion with a warning that it ought not and would not use its power to "discover new fundamental rights embedded in the Due Process Clause." In other words, the Court under Chief Justice Rehnquist was expressing its determination to restrict quite severely the expansion of the Ninth Amendment and the development of new substantive rights. The four dissenters argued that the case was not about a fundamental right to engage in homosexual sodomy, but was in fact about "the most comprehensive of rights and the right most valued by civilized men, [namely,] the right to be let alone."[89] It is unlikely that many states will adopt new laws against consensual homosexual activity or will vigorously enforce old laws of such a nature already on their books. But it is equally clear that the current Supreme Court will refrain from reviewing such laws and will resist expanding the Ninth Amendment as a source of new substantive rights.

The Right to Die   Another area ripe for litigation and public discourse is the so-called right to die. A number of highly publicized physician-assisted suicides in the 1990s focused attention on whether people have a right to choose their own death and to receive assistance in carrying it out. Can this become part of the privacy right or is it a new substantive right? A tentative answer came in 1997, when the Court ruled that a Washington state law establishing a ban on "causing" or "aiding" a suicide did not violate the Fourteenth Amendment or any clauses of the Bill of Rights incorporated in the Fourteenth Amendment.[90] Thus, if a state can constitutionally adopt such a prohibition, there is no constitutional right to suicide or assisted suicide. However, the Court left open the narrower question of "whether a mentally competent person who is experiencing great suffering has a constitutionally cognizable interest in controlling the circumstances of his or her imminent death."[91] "Americans are engaged in an earnest and profound debate about the morality, legality, and practicality of physician-assisted suicide. Our holding permits this debate to continue, as it should in a democratic society."[92] Never before has the Supreme Court more openly invited further litigation on a point.[93]

The Future of Civil Liberties

> **What is the likelihood that the Supreme Court will try to reverse the nationalization of the Bill of Rights?**

The next and final question for this chapter is whether the current Supreme Court, with its conservative majority, will try to reverse the nationalization of the Bill of Rights after a period of more than thirty-five years. Although such a move is possible, it is not certain. First of all, the Rehnquist Court has not actually reversed important decisions made by the Warren or Burger Courts, but instead has given narrower and more restrictive interpretations of earlier Court decisions. For example, in 1997, the Court made it easier for the police to search cars for drugs or other contraband when the cars have been pulled over only for traffic violations. Activists such as Justices Rehnquist, Antonin Scalia, and Clarence Thomas, who would prefer to overturn many of the Court's decisions from the 1960s and 1970s, do not yet command a majority on the Court. The most recent sign of the times is a case regarding the constitutionality of the 1994 Drivers' Privacy Protection Act. The purpose of the act was to protect privacy rights in general and the safety of women in particular by barring states from disclosing without consent the personal information contained in motor vehicle and driving license records. By selling these lists of registrants to anyone willing to buy them, information can be gained, by stalkers as well as by telemarketers, that many people go to great lengths to keep confidential. Justice Stephen Breyer observed that if the Court overturned this statute, it could on principle overturn "the entire body of law under which the authority of Congress to regulate interstate commerce has been understood to place corresponding limits on state authority." In a unanimous decision the Court rejected the states' rights challenge to the Drivers' Privacy Protection Act. Chief Justice William Rehnquist wrote the *Reno v. Condon* (2000) decision.

Meanwhile, the resurgence of federalism will play itself out in judicial territory. One certain trend in the Court that is likely to continue is its commitment to giving more discretion to the states, returning some of the power to state legislatures that was taken away during the "nationalization" of the Bill of Rights. But what if the state legislatures begin using their regained powers in ways they had used them before the nationalization of the Bill of Rights? What would be the reaction when states pass laws imposing further criminal restrictions on abortion? Permitting more religious practices in the public schools? Spreading the application of capital punishment to new crimes? Imposing stricter sentences on white-collar crimes? Terminating the use of buses to maintain desegregated schools? A great deal will depend upon the three or even four appointments that President Bush will likely be able to make as vacancies are produced by an aging Court membership. When that occurs, what would a majority on the Court do? Would the Court be equally respectful of state-level democracy then?

Finally, there will be even stronger and more lasting suspense as to whether the war on terrorism will have a permanent effect on civil liberties. Even some conservatives who generally approve of the direction this conservative Court has been taking are expressing concern over the initiatives taken by the Bush administration in dealing with thousands of American residents of Middle Eastern origin. For example, the eminent conservative *New York Times* columnist William Safire referred to the secretive processes in military tribunals as "kangaroo courts."[94] Even though these measures were justified as military emergencies, we must never forget Justice Jackson's warning in the *Korematsu* case that an emergency measure once established as constitutional can be "a loaded weapon ready for the hand of any authority that can bring forward a plausible claim of an urgent need."

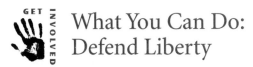

What You Can Do: Defend Liberty

The civil liberties that Americans enjoy today have been won by the struggles of ordinary citizens. The Bill of Rights offers Americans who have been denied their civil liberties a remedy through the judicial system. Individuals such as Dolly Mapp, Ernesto Miranda, and Clarence Earl Gideon fought to defend their fundamental liberties, and through their efforts all Americans now possess a more clearly defined and protected right to the due process of law. The most central aspect of a woman's right to privacy started with the difficulties of a poor high school dropout in Texas. Norma McCorvey was a twenty-one-year-old pregnant, divorced carnival worker with a five-year-old daughter. McCorvey lived regularly on the edge of poverty, and as a high school dropout, her prospects were poor, all the poorer in Texas, where the carnival had moved, because Texas had prohibited abortion unless necessary to save the mother's life. "I found one doctor who offered to abort me for $500. Only he didn't have a license, and I was scared to turn my body over to him. So there I was—pregnant, . . . alone and stuck."

The Difficult Partnership: Democracy and Civil Liberties

According to the basic principles of the Universal Declaration of Human Rights of 1948, people should be free from "fear and want." At the core of this principle are civil liberties. Yet even among democracies these liberties are often lacking. As we saw earlier in Chapter 1, of the 191 countries and sovereign territories in the world, 121 countries were classified as electoral democracies in 2001; of these, 86 were classified as "free," and 35 as "partly free."

Freedom House's classification scheme is based on the combined score of a country's *political rights* (essentially the ability of a country's citizens to participate freely in the political process via voting and other forms of political activity, and to trust that elected officials will be responsive to the public in the making of public policy) and *civil liberties* (the ability of citizens to develop independent political views, the availability of open and competitive political institutions, and a sense of personal autonomy free from the direction and interference of the state).

Scores for civil liberties across nation-states of the world as of 2001 are based on Freedom House's coding and assessment. A value of 1 is a "perfect" score, indicating the highest degree of civil liberties possible, while a value of 7 reflects the fewest possible civil liberties.

If we focus on the civil liberties of electoral democracies alone, we find that of the 121 electoral democracies in the world, as of 2001 only 29 (24 percent of the electoral democracies and less than 15 percent of all the countries and sovereign territories) had a perfect score for civil liberties. Freedom House examines four general rights to determine a country's degree of civil liberties: (1) freedom of expression and belief, (2) association and organization rights, (3) rule of law and human rights, and (4) personal autonomy and economic rights. These 29 electoral democracies possess institutions that best represent the ideals of civil liberties. This group includes, among others, the United States, Canada, Belgium, Norway, Dominica, New Zealand, Kiribati, Monaco, Marshall Islands, and Sweden.

However, 19 of the 86 electoral democracies that were classified as "free" by Freedom House had some shortcomings in all major categories of a citizen's general rights. None of these countries had *less* than a value of "3"

on civil rights. Thus, while these countries are electoral democracies with a generally higher degree of overall freedom, they have not granted their citizens the full measure of civil liberties. This group of electoral democracies includes Argentina, India, Mexico, Philippines, and Thailand.

Amnesty International, which, like Freedom House, is a widely respected nongovernmental organization that monitors the freedoms and rights of citizens around the world, has listed a number of civil liberty violations frequently seen in the world. These include the denial of rights to women and children, including forcing them to work in slave-labor conditions and often subjecting them to indignities, such as prostitution and drug trafficking; torture of suspects and prisoners; arbitrary imprisonment; denial of trial; and religious persecution.

Among those countries that are classified as electoral democracies but that exhibit sharp civil liberty violations are Turkey (rated 5—an applicant to membership in the European Union and a member of NATO) and Pakistan (rated 5—an electoral democracy until October 1999). Turkey's civil liberties violations stem largely from the Kurdish minority separatist insurgency (PKK) that plagues the southeast regions of the country. In January 1999 the government of Turkey confirmed that a government-sanctioned execution squad had killed as many as 5,000 Kurds between 1993 and 1996. Furthermore, the Turkish army, in accordance with emergency laws in effect at the time, forcibly "depopulated"—by murder and torture—thousands of villages and hamlets in the region. In Pakistan, the penal code was revised in 1979 regarding sexual offenses. According to Amnesty International, many women have been imprisoned for alleged extramarital sexual intercourse. These imprisonments are often based on false allegations by their husbands. Rape victims must meet strict legal requirements to prove the crime, or they can be charged with adultery. Even among the freest electoral democracies of the world, laws on political asylum and citizenship prevent countries such as the United Kingdom, Germany, France, and Italy from receiving perfect scores.

SOURCE: www.freedomhouse.org/research/freeworld/2002/essay2002.pdf (accessed 7/11/02).

McCorvey bore her child and gave it up immediately for adoption, but in the process she was introduced to two recent graduates of the University of Texas Law School, Sarah Weddington and Linda Coffey. These three women decided to challenge the Texas abortion statute. In order to avoid any stigma attached to such an emotionally charged case, Norma McCorvey's name was changed to Jane Roe in the court documents. Her case alleged that "she was unmarried and pregnant; that she wished to terminate her pregnancy by an abortion . . . ; [and] that she was unable to get a 'legal' abortion because her life did not appear to be threatened by the continuation of her pregnancy. . . ." The Court's ruling in *Roe v. Wade* subsequently prohibited states from making abortion illegal.[95]

In 1995, a student group at the University of Virginia scored a dramatic legal victory before the U.S. Supreme Court. The university had refused to provide support from the student activities fund for *Wide Awake,* a magazine published by a Christian student group. Although other student publications received subsidies from the activities fund, university policy prohibited grants to religious groups. Ronald Rosenberger, a Virginia undergraduate and an editor of the magazine, and his fellow editors filed suit in federal court, charging, among other things, that the university's refusal to fund their magazine because of its religious focus violated their First Amendment right to freedom of speech. A federal district court ruled in favor of the university on the grounds that funding for a religious newspaper by a state university would violate the Constitution's prohibition against government support for religion. Rosenberger and his colleagues appealed, but lost again when the district court's decision was affirmed by the Fourth Circuit Court of Appeals, which said that the Constitution mandated a strict separation of church and state. Undeterred, the student editors appealed the circuit court's decision to the Supreme Court. As we saw earlier in this chapter, the Supreme Court ruled in favor of the student group, holding that the university's policies amounted to state support for some ideas but not others. This, said the Court, represented a fundamental violation of the First Amendment.[96] The *Rosenberger* decision represents a potential loosening of the Court's long-standing opposition to any government support for religious groups or ideas, and it demonstrates how much influence can be exerted by a determined group of students.

One way to become politically involved is to seize on a civil liberties issue that stimulates your emotions and start a campus group to defend your position on the issue. Precisely because civil liberties issues generate strong feelings, there is a good chance that you can identify a small core of committed students who are willing to lend their support, commitment, and time to the group. Talk to classmates and friends. Circulate your ideas around the dormitory. Ask for a few minutes to speak to campus Democrats or Republicans or whatever groups might be sympathetic to your position. With only three or four initial members, you can launch your group.

Most college campuses have a central student board that handles funding for student groups. If so, consider applying for funding. Money widens your options for action. However, even without funding, you can go far. You might announce an organization meeting in your political science class or in the upcoming events section of the student newspaper. Contact the campus radio station (if you have one) or post flyers on campus bulletin boards. Even if just a few people show up, here are some of the kinds of activities and events you can organize.

- Hold informal gatherings where members and interested people can brainstorm possible activities around your civil liberties issue.
- Host prominent speakers who will talk about your issue and address questions from the audience.
- Plan or participate in debates with students or campus groups that have different views on the issue.
- Invite professors and students to participate in a "roundtable discussion" about your civil liberties issue.
- Set up card tables in high-traffic locations at lunch time to disseminate information or to gather signatures for a petition relevant to your issue.
- Make contact with national political groups that share your position. They may be able to provide you materials for dissemination and other resources.

Starting a campus group is a great way to get involved, encourage others to become more politically active, and at the same time focus your energy on an issue that is important to you. You may be surprised to discover that a relatively small but entrepreneurial group can make a difference on campus and beyond.

Summary

The provisions of the Bill of Rights seek to protect citizens from improper government action. Civil liberties ought to be carefully distinguished from civil rights, which did not become part of the Constitution until the Fourteenth Amendment and its provision for "equal protection of the laws."

During its first century, the Bill of Rights was applicable only to the national government and not to the state governments. The Fourteenth Amendment (1868) seemed to apply the Bill of Rights to the states, but the Supreme Court continued to apply the Bill of Rights as though the Fourteenth Amendment had never been adopted. For sixty years following the adoption of the Fourteenth Amendment, only one provision was "incorporated" into the Fourteenth Amendment and applied as a restriction on the state governments: the Fifth Amendment "eminent domain" clause, which was incorporated in 1897. Even as recently as 1961, only the eminent domain clause and the clauses of the First Amendment had been incorporated into the Fourteenth Amendment and applied to the states. After 1961, one by one, most of the provisions of the Bill of Rights were finally incorporated and applied to the states, although a conservative Supreme Court tried to reverse this trend during the 1980s and 1990s. The status of the First Amendment seems to have been least affected by this conservative trend. Protection of purely political speech remains close to absolute. The categories of conditionally protected speech include "speech plus," libel and slander, obscenity and pornography, fighting words, and commercial speech. Nevertheless, the realm of free speech in all these areas is still quite broad.

Of the other amendments and clauses in the Bill of Rights, the ones most likely to receive conservative interpretations are the religious clauses of the First Amendment, illegal search and seizure cases arising under the Fourth Amendment, and cases involving the Eighth Amendment cruel and unusual punishment clause.

For Further Reading

Abraham, Henry J. *Freedom and the Court: Civil Rights and Liberties in the United States.* 6th ed. New York: Oxford University Press, 1994.

Bryner, Gary C., and A. Don Sorensen, eds. *The Bill of Rights: A Bicentennial Assessment.* Albany: State University of New York Press, 1993.

Eisenstein, Zillah. *The Female Body and the Law.* Berkeley: University of California Press, 1988.

Friendly, Fred W. *Minnesota Rag: The Dramatic Story of the Landmark Supreme Court Case that Gave New Meaning to Freedom of the Press.* New York: Vintage, 1982.

Glendon, Mary Ann. *Rights Talk: The Impoverishment of Political Discourse.* New York: Free Press, 1991.

Hentoff, Nat. *The First Freedom: The Tumultuous History of Free Speech in America.* New York: Basic Books, 1994.

Levy, Leonard. *Legacy of Suppression: Freedom of Speech and Press in Early American History.* New York: Harper, 1963.

Lewis, Anthony. *Gideon's Trumpet.* New York: Random House, 1964.

Meyer, Michael J., and William A. Parent. *The Constitution of Rights: Human Dignity and American Values.* Ithaca, NY: Cornell University Press, 1992.

Minow, Martha. *Making All the Difference: Inclusion, Exclusion, and American Law.* Ithaca, NY: Cornell University Press, 1990.

Silverstein, Mark. *Constitutional Faiths.* Ithaca, NY: Cornell University Press, 1984.

Stone, Geoffrey R., Richard A. Epstein, and Cass R. Sunstein, eds. *The Bill of Rights in the Modern State.* Chicago: University of Chicago Press, 1992.

Study Outline

www.wwnorton.com/wtp4e

A Brief History of the Bill of Rights

1. Despite the insistence of Alexander Hamilton that a bill of rights was both unnecessary and dangerous, adding a list of explicit rights was the most important item of business for the First Congress in 1789.
2. The Bill of Rights would have been more aptly named the "Bill of Liberties," because it is made up of provisions that protect citizens from improper government action.
3. Civil rights did not become part of the Constitution until 1868 with the adoption of the Fourteenth Amendment, which sought to provide for each citizen "the equal protection of the laws."
4. In 1833, the Supreme Court found that the Bill of Rights limited only the national government and not state governments.

5. Although the language of the Fourteenth Amendment seems to indicate that the protections of the Bill of Rights apply to state governments as well as the national government, for the remainder of the nineteenth century the Supreme Court (with only one exception) made decisions as if the Fourteenth Amendment had never been adopted.
6. As of 1961, only the First Amendment and one clause of the Fifth Amendment had been "selectively incorporated" into the Fourteenth Amendment. After 1961, however, most of the provisions of the Bill of Rights were incorporated into the Fourteenth Amendment and applied to the states.

The First Amendment and Freedom of Religion

1. The "establishment clause" of the First Amendment has been interpreted to mean the strict separation of church and state.
2. The "free exercise clause" protects the right to believe and to practice whatever religion one chooses; it also involves protection of the right to be a nonbeliever.

The First Amendment and Freedom of Speech and the Press

1. Although freedom of speech and freedom of the press hold an important place in the Bill of Rights, the extent and nature of certain types of expression are subject to constitutional debate.
2. Among the forms of speech that are absolutely protected are the truth, political speech, symbolic speech, and "speech plus," which is speech plus a physical activity such as picketing. The forms of speech that are currently only conditionally protected include libel and slander; obscenity and pornography; fighting words; and commercial speech.

The Second Amendment and the Right to Bear Arms

1. Constitutionally, the Second Amendment unquestionably protects citizens' rights to bear arms, but this right can be regulated by both state and federal law.

Rights of the Criminally Accused

1. The purpose of due process is to equalize the playing field between the accused individual and the all-powerful state.
2. The Fourth Amendment protects against unreasonable searches and seizures.

3. The Fifth Amendment requires a grand jury for most crimes, protects against double jeopardy, and provides that you cannot be forced to testify against yourself.

4. The Sixth Amendment requires a speedy trial and the right to witnesses and counsel.

5. The Eighth Amendment prohibits cruel and unusual punishment.

The Right to Privacy

1. In the case of *Griswold v. Connecticut*, the Supreme Court found a right of privacy in the Constitution. This right was confirmed and extended in 1973 in the case of *Roe v. Wade*.

The Future of Civil Liberties

1. Under Chief Justice William Rehnquist, the Court has somewhat restricted civil liberties without actually overturning any of the important decisions from the 1960s and 1970s that established many of the liberties enjoyed today.

Practice Quiz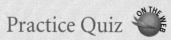

www.wwnorton.com/wtp4e

1. From 1789 until the 1960s, the Bill of Rights put limits on
   a) the national government only.
   b) the state government only.
   c) both the national and state governments.
   d) neither the national nor the state governments.

2. The amendment that provided the basis for the modern understanding of the government's obligation to protect civil rights was the
   a) First Amendment.
   b) Ninth Amendment.
   c) Fourteenth Amendment.
   d) Twenty-second Amendment.

3. The so-called *Lemon* test, derived from the Supreme Court's ruling in *Lemon v. Kurtzman,* concerns the issue of
   a) school desegregation.
   b) aid to religious schools.
   c) prayer in school.
   d) obscenity.

4. The process by which some of the liberties in the Bill of Rights were applied to the states (or nationalized) is known as
   a) selective incorporation.
   b) judicial activism.
   c) civil liberties.
   d) establishment.

5. Which of the following provided that all of the protections contained in the Bill of Rights applied to the states as well as the national government?
   a) the Fourteenth Amendment
   b) *Palko v. Connecticut*
   c) *Gitlow v. New York*
   d) none of the above

6. Which of the following protections are not contained in the First Amendment?
   a) the establishment clause
   b) the free exercise clause
   c) freedom of the press
   d) All of the above are First Amendment protections.

7. Which of the following describes a written statement made in "reckless disregard of the truth" that is considered damaging to a victim because it is "malicious, scandalous, and defamatory"?
   a) slander
   b) libel
   c) fighting words
   d) expressive speech

8. The Fourth, Fifth, Sixth, and Eighth Amendments, taken together, define:
   a) due process of law.
   b) free speech.
   c) the right to bear arms.
   d) civil rights of minorities.

9. In what case was a right to privacy first found in the Constitution?
   a) *Griswold v. Connecticut*
   b) *Roe v. Wade*
   c) *Baker v. Carr*
   d) *Planned Parenthood v. Casey*

10. Which famous case deals with Sixth Amendment issues?
    a) *Miranda v. Arizona*
    b) *Mapp v. Ohio*
    c) *Gideon v. Wainwright*
    d) *Terry v. Ohio*

Critical Thinking Questions

www.wwnorton.com/wtp4e

1. In many ways it seems that the Bill of Rights is an ambiguous document. Choose one protection offered in the Bill of Rights and explain how it has been interpreted in various ways. What does this say about the role of politics and the Constitution in defining the limits of governmental power? What does it say about the power of the Supreme Court in American politics?

2. Recount the history of the constitutional "right to privacy." How has this right affected American politics since the 1960s? How has this right interacted with the other rights in the Bill of Rights? Read the Third, Fourth, Fifth, and Ninth Amendments. In your opinion, do American citizens have a right to privacy?

3. The perennial trouble between war and civil liberties came to a head in early 1942 when hundreds of Japanese, many of them American citizens, were sent to "relocation camps" and kept there for the duration of the war. In 1944, the Supreme Court held this action to be constitutional, within "the war power of Congress and the Executive. . . ." In an eloquent dissent, Justice Jackson argued that holding it constitutional simply because it was necessary "is a far more subtle blow to liberty than the promulgation of the order itself. . . ." What does sixty years of experience since 1942 tell us about what we should do in this post–September 11 era to balance the needs of war and the protection of civil liberties?

Key Terms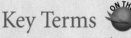

www.wwnorton.com/wtp4e

Bill of Rights (p. 119)
bills of attainder (p. 122)
civil liberties (p. 119)
"clear and present danger" test (p. 130)
double jeopardy (p. 143)
due process of law (p. 119)
eminent domain (p. 144)

establishment clause (p. 126)
ex post facto laws (p. 122)
exclusionary rule (p. 140)
fighting words (p. 135)
free exercise clause (p. 127)
grand jury (p. 142)
habeas corpus (p. 121)
Lemon test (p. 126)
libel (p. 133)

Miranda rule (p. 144)
prior restraint (p. 133)
procedural liberties (p. 119)
right to privacy (p. 150)
selective incorporation (p. 124)
slander (p. 133)
speech plus (p. 132)
strict scrutiny (p. 130)
substantive liberties (p. 119)

5 CIVIL RIGHTS

★ **The Struggle for Civil Rights**

What is the legal basis for civil rights?

How has the equal protection clause historically been enforced?

What is the critical Supreme Court ruling in the battle for equal protection?

How has Congress tried to make equal protection a reality?

In what areas did the civil rights acts seek to provide equal access and protection?

★ **The Universalization of Civil Rights**

What groups were spurred by the provision of the Civil Rights Act of 1964, outlawing discrimination in employment practices based on race, religion, and gender, to seek broader protection under the law?

What is the politics of the universalization of civil rights?

★ **Affirmative Action**

What is the basis for affirmative action? What forms does it take?

How does affirmative action contribute to the polarization of the politics of civil rights?

How does the debate about affirmative action reflect the debate over American political values?

What Government Does and Why It Matters

N 1960, FOUR BLACK STUDENTS from North Carolina A&T made history: the four freshmen sat down at Woolworth's whites-only lunch counter in Greensboro, North Carolina, challenging the policies of segregation that kept blacks and whites in separate public and private accommodations across the South. Day after day the students sat at the counter, ignoring the taunts of onlookers, determined to break the system of segregation. Their actions and those of many other students, clergy members, and ordinary citizens finally did abolish such practices as separate white and black park benches, water fountains, and waiting rooms; the end of segregation meant opening access to public and private institutions on equal terms to all. But the victories of the civil rights movement did not come cheaply: many marchers, freedom riders, and sit-in participants were beaten; some were murdered.

Today, the Greensboro lunch counter is a part of history, on display at the Smithsonian Institution in Washington, D.C. Many goals of the civil rights movement that aroused such controversy in 1960 are now widely accepted as the proper expression of the American commitment to equal rights. But the question of what is meant by "equal rights" is hardly settled. While most Americans reject the idea that government should create equal outcomes for its citizens, they do widely endorse government action to prohibit public and private discrimination and they support the idea of equality of opportunity. However, even this concept is elusive. When past denial of rights creates unequal starting points for some groups, should government take additional steps to ensure equal opportunity? What kinds of groups should be specially protected against discrimination? Should the disabled receive special protection? Should gays

civil rights legal or moral claims that citizens are entitled to make upon government

and lesbians? Finally, what kinds of steps are acceptable to remedy discrimination, and who should bear the costs? These questions are at the heart of contemporary debates over **civil rights,** the obligation imposed on government to *take positive action* to protect citizens from any illegal action of government agencies as well as of other private citizens. ■

discrimination use of any unreasonable and unjust criterion of exclusion

equal protection clause provision of the Fourteenth Amendment guaranteeing citizens "the equal protection of the laws." This clause has served as the basis for the civil rights of African Americans, women, and other groups

I N THE United States, the history of slavery and legalized racial **discrimination** against African Americans coexists uneasily with a strong tradition of individual liberty. Indeed, for much of our history Americans have struggled to reconcile such exclusionary racial practices with our notions of individual rights. With the adoption of the Fourteenth Amendment in 1868, civil rights became part of the Constitution, guaranteed to each citizen through "equal protection of the laws." This **equal protection clause** launched a century of political movements and legal efforts to press for racial equality. The African American quest for civil rights in turn inspired many other groups, including members of other racial and ethnic groups, women, the disabled, and gays and lesbians, to seek new laws and constitutional guarantees of their civil rights.

■ **First, we review the legal developments and political movements that have expanded the scope of civil rights since the Fourteenth Amendment was adopted in 1868.** In this section, we look at the establishment of legal segregation in the South and the civil rights movement that overthrew it.

■ **Second, we trace the broad impact that civil rights legislation has had on American life.** The Civil Rights Act of 1964 was especially critical in guaranteeing the "equal protection of the laws" set forth in the Fourteenth Amendment almost one hundred years earlier.

■ **We then explore how other groups, including women, Native Americans, Latinos, the disabled, and gays and lesbians, formed movements to win active protection of their rights as well.** This universalization of civil rights has become the new frontier of the civil rights struggle.

■ **Next, we turn to the development of affirmative action and the controversies surrounding it.** The debate over affirmative action has intensified in recent years, revealing the ways in which Americans differ over the meaning of equality.

■ **Finally, we review the role that citizens play in determining the meaning of civil rights.** As we see, students have often been in the forefront of the civil rights debate.

The Struggle for Civil Rights

For African Americans, the central fact of political life has been a denial of full citizenship rights for most of American history. By accepting the institution of slavery, the Founders embraced a system fundamentally at odds with the "Blessings of Liberty" promised in the Constitution. Their decision set the stage for two centuries of African American struggles to achieve full citizenship. For women as well, electoral politics was a decidedly masculine world. Until 1920, not only were women barred from voting in national politics, but electoral politics was closely tied to such male social institutions as lodges, bars, and clubs. Yet the exclusion of women from this political world did not prevent them from engaging in public life. Instead, women carved out a "separate sphere" for their public activities. Emphasizing female stewardship over the moral realm, women became important voices in social reform well before they won the right to vote.[1] For example, prior to the Civil War, women played leading roles in the abolitionist movement.

SLAVERY AND THE ABOLITIONIST MOVEMENT

No issue in the nation's history so deeply divided Americans as that of the abolition of slavery. The importation and subjugation of Africans kidnapped from their native lands was a practice virtually as old as the country itself: the first slaves brought to what became the United States arrived in 1619, a year before the Plymouth colony was established in Massachusetts. White southerners built their agricultural economy (especially cotton production) on a large slave labor force. By 1840, for example, nearly half of the populations of Alabama and Louisiana consisted of black slaves. Even so, only about a quarter of southern white families owned slaves.

The subjugation of blacks through slavery was so much a part of the southern culture that efforts to restrict or abolish slavery were met with fierce resistance. Despite the manifest cruelties of the slave system, southerners referred to the system by the quaint term "peculiar institution." The label meant little to slavery's opponents, however, and an abolitionist movement grew and spread among northerners in the 1830s (although abolitionist sentiment could be traced back to the pre-Revolutionary era). The movement was most closely identified with the writing of William Lloyd Garrison. Slavery had been all but eliminated in the North by this time, but few northerners favored outright abolition. In fact, most whites held attitudes toward blacks that would be considered racist today.

The abolitionist movement spread primarily through local organizations in the North. Antislavery groups coalesced in New York, Ohio, New Hampshire, Pennsylvania, New Jersey, and Michigan. In addition to forming antislavery societies, the movement spawned two political parties: the Liberty Party, a staunchly antislavery party, and the Free Soil Party, a larger but more moderate third party that sought primarily to restrict the spread of slavery into new western territories. Garrison noted his dismay at the Free Soil Party's more modest and pragmatic approach: "It is a party for keeping Free Soil and not for setting men free."

Some opponents of slavery took matters into their own hands, aiding in the escape of runaway slaves along the Underground Railroad. Even today, private homes and churches, scattered throughout the northeast, that were used to hide blacks on their trips to Canada, attest to the involvement of local citizenry. In the South, a similar, if contrary, fervor prompted mobs to break into post offices in order to seize and destroy antislavery literature.

The emotional power of the slavery issue was such that it precipitated the nation's most bloody conflict, the Civil War. From the ashes of the Civil War came the Thirteenth, Fourteenth, and Fifteenth Amendments, which would redefine civil rights from that day to this.

THE LINK TO THE WOMEN'S RIGHTS MOVEMENT

The quiet upstate New York town of Seneca Falls played host to what would later come to be known as the starting point of the modern women's movement. Convened in July 1848, and organized by activists Elizabeth Cady Stanton (who lived in Seneca Falls) and Lucretia Mott, the Seneca Falls Convention drew three hundred delegates to discuss and formulate plans to advance the political and social rights of women.

The centerpiece of the convention was its Declaration of Sentiments and Resolutions. Patterned after the Declaration of Independence, the Seneca Falls document declared, "We hold these truths to be self-evident: that all men and women are created equal," and "The history of mankind is a history of repeated injuries and usurpations on the part of man toward woman, having in direct object the establishment of an absolute tyranny over her." The most controversial provision of the declaration, nearly rejected as too radical, was the call for the right to vote for women. Although most of the delegates were women, about forty men participated, including the renowned abolitionist Frederick Douglass.

The link to the antislavery movement was not new. Stanton and Mott had attended the World Anti-slavery Convention in London in 1840, but had been denied delegate seats because of their sex. This rebuke helped precipitate the 1848 convention. The movements for abolition of slavery and women's rights were also closely linked with the temperance movement (because alcohol abuse was closely linked to male abuses of women). The convergence of the antislavery, temperance, and suffrage movements was reflected in the views and actions of other women's movement leaders, such as Susan B. Anthony.

The convention and its participants were subjected to widespread ridicule, but similar conventions were organized in other states, and in the same year, New York State passed the Married Women's Property Act in order to restore the right of a married woman to own property.

THE CIVIL WAR AMENDMENTS TO THE CONSTITUTION

Thirteenth Amendment one of three Civil War amendments; abolished slavery

Fourteenth Amendment one of three Civil War amendments; guaranteed equal protection and due process to all residents of the United States

Fifteenth Amendment one of three Civil War amendments; guaranteed voting rights for African American men

The hopes of African Americans for achieving full citizenship rights initially seemed fulfilled when three constitutional amendments were adopted after the Civil War: the **Thirteenth Amendment** abolished slavery; the **Fourteenth Amendment** guaranteed equal protection under the law; and the **Fifteenth Amendment** guaranteed voting rights for blacks. Protected by the presence of federal troops, African American men were able to exercise their political rights immediately after the war. During Reconstruction, blacks were elected to many political offices: two black senators were elected from Mississippi and a total of fourteen African Americans were elected to the House of Representatives between 1869 and 1877. African Americans also held many state-level political offices. As voters and public officials, black citizens found a home in the Republican Party, which had secured the ratification of the three constitutional amendments guaranteeing black rights. After the war, the Republican Party continued to reach out to black voters as a means to build party strength in the South.[2]

This political equality was short-lived, however. The national government withdrew its troops from the South and turned its back on African Americans in 1877. In the Compromise of 1877, southern Democrats agreed to allow the Republican candidate, Rutherford B. Hayes, to become president after a disputed election. In exchange, northern Republicans dropped their support for the civil liberties and political participation of African Americans. After that, southern states erected a **"Jim Crow"** system of social, political, and economic inequality that made a mockery of the promises in the Constitution.

Around the same time, some women pressed for the right to vote at the national level immediately after the Civil War, when male ex-slaves won the franchise. Politicians in both parties rejected women's suffrage as disruptive and unrealistic. Women also started to press for the vote at the state level in 1867 when a referendum to give women the vote in Kansas failed. Frustration with the general failure to win reforms in other states accelerated suffrage activism. In 1872, Susan B. Anthony and several other women were arrested in Rochester, New York, for illegally registering and voting in that year's national election. (The men who allowed the women to register and vote were also indicted; Anthony paid their expenses, and eventually won presidential pardons for them.) At her trial, Judge Ward Hunt ordered the jury to find her guilty without deliberation. Yet Anthony was allowed to address the court, saying, "Your denial of my citizen's right to vote is the denial of my right of consent as one of the governed, the denial of my right of representation as one of the taxed, the denial of my right to a trial of my peers as an offender against the law."[3] Hunt assessed Anthony a fine of $100, but did not sentence her to jail. Anthony refused to pay the fine.

> **What is the legal basis for civil rights?**

"Jim Crow" laws enacted by southern states following reconstruction that discriminated against African Americans

CIVIL RIGHTS AND THE SUPREME COURT: "SEPARATE BUT EQUAL"

Resistance to equality for African Americans in the South led Congress to adopt the Civil Rights Act of 1875, which attempted to protect blacks from discrimination by proprietors of hotels, theaters, and other public accommodations. But the Court declared the Civil Rights Act of 1875 unconstitutional on the grounds that the act sought to protect blacks against discrimination by *private* businesses, while the Fourteenth Amendment, according to the Court's interpretation, was intended to protect individuals from discrimination only against actions by *public* officials of state and local governments.

In 1896, the Court went still further, in the infamous case of *Plessy v. Ferguson*, by upholding a Louisiana statute that *required* segregation of the races on trolleys and other public carriers (and by implication in all public facilities, including schools). Plessy, a man defined as "one-eighth black," had violated a Louisiana law that provided for "equal but separate accommodations" on trains and a $25 fine for any white passenger who sat in a car reserved for blacks or any black passenger

> **How has the equal protection clause historically been enforced?**

who sat in a car reserved for whites. The Supreme Court held that the Fourteenth Amendment's "equal protection of the laws" was not violated by racial distinction as long as the facilities were equal, thus establishing the **"separate but equal" rule** that prevailed through the mid-twentieth century. People generally pretended that segregated accommodations were equal as long as some accommodation for blacks existed. The Court said that although "the object of the [Fourteenth] Amendment was undoubtedly to enforce the absolute equality of the two races before the law, . . . it could not have intended to abolish distinctions based on color, or to enforce social, as distinguished from political, equality, or a commingling of the two races upon terms unsatisfactory to either."[4] What the Court was saying in effect was that the use of race as a criterion of exclusion in public matters was not unreasonable.

"separate but equal" rule doctrine that public accommodations could be segregated by race but still be equal

ORGANIZING FOR EQUALITY

The National Association for the Advancement of Colored People (NAACP)   The creation of a "Jim Crow" system in the southern states and the lack of a legal basis for "equal protection under the laws" prompted the beginning of a long process in which African Americans built organizations and devised strategies for asserting their constitutional rights.

One such strategy sought to win political rights through political pressure and litigation. This approach was championed by the NAACP, established by a group of black and white reformers in 1909. Among the NAACP's founders was W. E. B. Du Bois, one of the most influential and creative thinkers on racial issues of the twentieth century. Because the northern black vote was so small in the early decades of the twentieth century, the organization primarily relied on the courts to press for black political rights. After the 1920s, the NAACP built a strong membership base, with some strength in the South, which would be critical when the civil rights movement gained momentum in the 1950s.

The great migration of blacks to the North beginning around World War I enlivened a protest strategy. Although protest organizations had existed in the nineteenth century, the continuing migration of blacks to the North made protest an increasingly useful tool. Black labor leader A. Philip Randolph forced the federal government to address racial discrimination in hiring practices during World War II by threatening a massive march on Washington. The federal government also grew more attentive to blacks as their voting strength increased as a result of the northward migration. By the 1940s, the black vote had swung away from Republicans, but the Democratic hold on black votes was by no means absolute.

Women's Organizations and the Right to Suffrage   Suffragists used the occasion of the Constitution's centennial in 1887 to protest the continued denial of their rights. For these women, the centennial represented "a century of injustice." The unveiling of the Statue of Liberty, depicting liberty as a woman, in New York Harbor in 1886 prompted women's rights advocates to call it " the greatest hypocrisy of the nineteenth century," in that "not one single woman throughout the length and breadth of the Land is as yet in possession of political Liberty."[5]

The climactic movement toward suffrage was formally launched in 1878 with the introduction of a proposed constitutional amendment in Congress. Parallel efforts were made in the states. Many states granted women the right to vote before the national government did; western states with less-entrenched political systems opened politics to women earliest. When Wyoming became a state in 1890, it was the first state to grant full suffrage to women. Colorado, Utah, and Idaho all followed suit in the next several years. Suffrage organizations grew—the National American Woman Suffrage Association (NAWSA), formed in 1890, claimed two million members by 1917—and staged mass meetings, parades, petitions, and protests. NAWSA organized state-by-state efforts to win the right to vote. A more militant group, the National Women's Party, staged pickets and got arrested in front of the White House to protest President Wilson's opposition to a constitutional amendment granting women the right to vote. Finally in 1920, the Nineteenth Amendment was ratified, guaranteeing women the right to vote.

LITIGATING FOR EQUALITY AFTER WORLD WAR II

The shame of discrimination against black military personnel during World War II, plus revelations of Nazi racial atrocities, moved President Harry S. Truman finally to bring the problem to the White House and national attention, with the appointment in 1946 of the President's Commission on Civil Rights. In 1948, the commission submitted its report, *To Secure These Rights,* which laid bare the extent of the problem of racial discrimination and its consequences. The report also revealed the success of experiments with racial integration in the armed forces during World War II to demonstrate to southern society that it had nothing to fear. But the committee recognized that the national government had no clear constitutional authority to pass and implement civil rights legislation. The committee proposed tying civil rights legislation to the commerce power, although it was clear that discrimination was not itself part of the flow of interstate commerce.[6] The committee even suggested using the treaty power as a source of constitutional authority for civil rights legislation.[7]

As for the Supreme Court, it had begun to change its position on racial discrimination before World War II by being stricter about the criterion of equal facilities in the "separate but equal" rule. In 1938, for example, the Court rejected Missouri's policy of paying the tuition of qualified blacks to out-of-state law schools rather than admitting them to the University of Missouri Law School.[8]

After the war, modest progress resumed. In 1950, the Court rejected Texas's claim that its new "law school for Negroes" afforded education equal to that of the all-white University of Texas Law School. Without confronting the "separate but equal" principle itself, the Court's decision anticipated its future civil rights rulings by opening the question of whether *any* segregated facilities could be truly equal.[9]

But the Supreme Court, in ordering the admission of blacks to all-white state law schools, did not directly confront the "separate but equal" rule because the Court needed only to recognize the absence of any *equal* law school for blacks. The same was true in 1944, when the Supreme Court struck down the southern practice of "white primaries," which legally excluded blacks from participation in the nominating process. Here the Court simply recognized that primaries could no longer be regarded as the private affairs of the parties but were an integral aspect of the electoral process. This made parties "an agency of the State," and therefore any practice of discrimination against blacks was "state action within the meaning of the Fifteenth Amendment."[10] The most important pre-1954 decision was probably *Shelley v. Kraemer,* in which the Court ruled against the widespread practice of "restrictive covenants," whereby the seller of a home added a clause to the sales contract requiring the buyer to agree not to sell the home later to any non-Caucasian, non-Christian, etc. The Court ruled that although private persons could sign such restrictive covenants, they could not be judicially enforced since the Fourteenth Amendment prohibits any organ of the state, including the courts, from denying equal protection of its laws.[11]

Although none of those pre-1954 cases confronted "separate but equal" and the principle of racial discrimination as such, they were extremely significant to black leaders in the 1940s and gave them encouragement enough to believe that there was at last an opportunity and enough legal precedent to change the constitutional framework itself. Much of this legal work was done by the Legal Defense and Educational Fund of the NAACP. Until the late 1940s, lawyers working for the Legal Defense Fund had concentrated on winning small victories within that framework. Then, in 1948, the Legal Defense Fund upgraded its approach by simultaneously filing suits in different federal districts and through each level of schooling from unequal provision of kindergarten for blacks to unequal sports and science facilities in all-black high schools. After nearly two years of these mostly successful equalization suits, the lawyers decided the time was ripe to confront the "separate but equal" rule head-on, but they felt they needed some heavier artillery to lead the attack. Their choice to lead this attack was African American lawyer Thurgood Marshall, who had been fighting, and often winning, equalization suits since the early 1930s. Marshall was pessimistic about the readiness of the Supreme Court for a full confrontation with segregation itself and the constitutional principle sustaining it. But the unwillingness of Congress after the 1948 election to consider fair employment legislation seems to have convinced Marshall that the courts were the only hope.

> **What is the critical Supreme Court ruling in the battle for equal protection?**

The Supreme Court must have come to the same conclusion because, during the four years following 1948, there emerged a clear impression that the Court was willing to take more civil rights cases on appeal. Yet, this was no guarantee that the Court would reverse *on principle* the separate but equal precedent of *Plessy v. Ferguson*. All through 1951 and 1952, as cases were winding slowly through the lower-court litigation maze, intense discussions and disagreements arose among NAACP lawyers as to whether a full-scale assault on *Plessy* was good strategy or whether it might not be better to continue with specific cases alleging unequal treatment and demanding relief with a Court-imposed policy of equalization.[12] But for some lawyers like Marshall, these kinds of victories could amount to a defeat. South Carolina, for example, under the leadership of Governor James F. Byrnes, a former Supreme Court justice, had undertaken a strategy of equalization of school services on a large scale in order to satisfy the *Plessy* rule and to head off or render moot litigation against the principle of separate but equal.

In the fall of 1952, the Court had on its docket cases from Kansas, South Carolina, Virginia, Delaware, and the District of Columbia challenging the constitutionality of school segregation. Of these, the case filed in Kansas became the chosen one. It seemed to be ahead of the pack in its district court, and it had the special advantage of being located in a state outside the Deep South.[13]

Oliver Brown, the father of three girls, lived "across the tracks" in a low-income, racially mixed Topeka neighborhood. Every school-day morning, Linda Brown took the school bus to the Monroe School for black children about a mile away. In September 1950, Oliver Brown took Linda to the all-white Sumner School, which was closer to home, to enter her into the third grade in defiance of state law and local segregation rules. When they were refused, Brown took his case to the NAACP, and soon thereafter *Brown v. Board of Education* was born. In mid-1953, the Court announced that the several cases on their way up would be reargued within a set of questions having to do with the intent of the Fourteenth Amendment. Almost exactly a year later, the Court responded to those questions in one of the most important decisions in its history.

In deciding the *Brown* case, the Court, to the surprise of many, basically rejected as inconclusive all the learned arguments about the intent and the history of the Fourteenth Amendment and committed itself to considering only the consequences of segregation:

> Does segregation of children in public schools solely on the basis of race, even though the physical facilities and other "tangible" factors may be equal, deprive the children of the minority group of equal educational opportunities? We believe that it does. . . . We conclude that in the field of public education the doctrine of "separate but equal" has no place. Separate educational facilities are inherently unequal.[14]

The *Brown* decision altered the constitutional framework in two fundamental respects. First, after *Brown*, the states no longer had the power to use race as a criterion of discrimination in law. Second, the national government from then on had the power (and eventually the obligation) to intervene with strict regulatory policies against the discriminatory actions of state or local governments, school boards, employers, and many others in the private sector.

CIVIL RIGHTS AFTER *BROWN V. BOARD OF EDUCATION*

Brown v. Board of Education withdrew all constitutional authority to use race as a criterion of exclusion, and it signaled more clearly the Court's determination to use the **strict scrutiny** test in cases related to racial discrimination. This meant that the burden of proof would fall on the government—not on the challengers—to show that the law in question *was* constitutional.[15] Although the use of strict scrutiny in cases relating to racial discrimination would give an advantage to those attacking racial discrimination, the historic decision in *Brown v. Board of Education* was merely a small opening move. First, most states refused to cooperate until sued, and many ingenious schemes were employed to delay obedience (such as paying the tuition for white students to attend newly created "private" academies). Second, even as southern school boards began to cooperate by eliminating their legally enforced (**de jure**) school segregation, there remained extensive actual (**de facto**) school segregation in the North as well as in the South, as a consequence of racially segregated housing that could not be reached by the 1954–55 *Brown* principles. Third, discrimination in employment, public accommodations, juries, voting, and other areas of social and economic activity were not directly touched by *Brown*.

School Desegregation, Phase One   Although the District of Columbia and some of the school districts in the border states began to respond almost immediately to court-ordered desegregation, the states of the Deep South responded with a carefully

---

Brown v. Board of Education the 1954 Supreme Court decision that struck down the "separate but equal" doctrine as fundamentally unequal. This case eliminated state power to use race as a criterion of discrimination in law and provided the national government with the power to intervene by exercising strict regulatory policies against discriminatory actions

strict scrutiny test, used by the Supreme Court in racial discrimination cases and other cases involving civil liberties and civil rights, which places the burden of proof on the government rather than on the challengers to show that the law in question is constitutional

de jure literally, "by law"; legally enforced practices, such as school segregation in the South before the 1960s

de facto literally, "by fact"; practices that occur even when there is no legal enforcement, such as school segregation in much of the United States today

The push for equality for African Americans began in the nineteenth century. African Americans won the right to vote after the Civil War with the passage of the Thirteenth, Fourteenth, and Fifteenth Amendments, and many former slaves began registering and voting in state elections as early as 1867. This political influence soon evaporated in the face of Jim Crow laws and the end of Reconstruction.

The infamous 1896 Supreme Court case of Plessy v. Ferguson *upheld legal segregation and created the "separate but equal" rule, which fostered national segregation. This 1941 photograph of a rural Georgia school for black students shows the inferior conditions that African Americans faced under the* Plessy *ruling (left). Overt discrimination in public accomodations was common (right).*

planned delaying tactic commonly called "massive resistance" by the more dema-gogic southern leaders and "nullification" and "interposition" by the centrists. Either way, southern politicians stood shoulder-to-shoulder to declare that the Supreme Court's decisions and orders were without effect. The legislatures in these states enacted statutes ordering school districts to maintain segregated schools and state superintendents to terminate state funding wherever there was racial mixing in the classroom. Some southern states violated their own long traditions of local school autonomy by centralizing public school authority under the governor or the state board of education and by giving states the power to close the schools and to provide alternative private schooling wherever local school boards might be tending to obey the Supreme Court.

Most of these plans of "massive resistance" were tested in the federal courts and were struck down as unconstitutional.[16] But southern resistance was not confined

In the 1950s, school segregation came under attack at the federal level. "Massive resistance" among white Southerners attempted to block the desegregation attempts of the national government. For example, at Little Rock Central High School in 1957, an angry mob of white students prevented black students from entering the school. As a result, the federal government sent troops to protect the black students and to uphold the desegregation plan.

to legislation. For example, in Arkansas in 1957, Governor Orval Faubus mobilized the Arkansas National Guard to intercede against enforcement of a federal court order to integrate Central High School of Little Rock, and President Eisenhower was forced to deploy U.S. troops and literally place the city under martial law. The Supreme Court considered the Little Rock confrontation so historically important

The 1964 Civil Rights Act made desegregation a legal requirement. One government remedy was court-ordered busing from black schools to white schools. Busing bitterly divided the black and white communities in Boston. In 1976, a mob of white protesters outside the Boston federal courthouse sought to impale this innocent black bystander—a lawyer on his way to his office—on a flag. In the face of institutional and white resistance, school desegregation remains incomplete fifty years after it began.

that the opinion it rendered in that case was not only agreed to unanimously but was, unprecedentedly, signed personally by each and every one of the justices.[17] The end of massive resistance, however, became simply the beginning of still another southern strategy, "pupil placement" laws, which authorized school districts to place each pupil in a school according to a whole variety of academic, personal, and psychological considerations, never mentioning race at all. This put the burden of transferring to an all-white school on the nonwhite children and their parents, making it almost impossible for a single court order to cover a whole district, let alone a whole state. This delayed desegregation a while longer.[18]

Social Protest and Congressional Action   Ten years after *Brown,* fewer than 1 percent of black school-age children in the Deep South were attending schools with whites.[19] A decade of frustration made it fairly obvious to all observers that adjudication alone would not succeed. The goal of "equal protection" required positive, or affirmative, action by Congress and by administrative agencies. And given massive southern resistance and a generally negative national public opinion toward racial integration, progress would not be made through courts, Congress, or federal agencies without intense, well-organized support. Table 5.1 shows the increase in civil rights demonstrations for voting rights and public accommodations during

Table 5.1   Peaceful Civil Rights Demonstrations, 1954–68

Year	Total	For Public Accommodations	For Voting
1954	0	0	0
1955	0	0	0
1956	18	6	0
1957	44	9	0
1958	19	8	0
1959	7	11	0
1960	173	127	0
1961	198	122	0
1962	77	44	0
1963	272	140	1
1964	271	93	12
1965	387	21	128
1966	171	15	32
1967	93	3	3
1968	97	2	0

NOTE: This table is drawn from a search of the *New York Times Index* for all references to civil rights demonstrations during the years the table covers. The table should be taken simply as indicative, for the data—news stories in a single paper—are very crude. The classification of the incident as peaceful or violent and the subject area of the demonstration are inferred from the entry in the *Index,* usually the headline from the story. The two subcategories reported here—public accommodations and voting—do not sum to the total because demonstrations dealing with a variety of other issues (e.g., education, employment, police brutality) are included in the total.
SOURCE: Jonathan D. Casper, *The Politics of Civil Liberties* (New York: Harper & Row, 1972), p. 90.

the fourteen years following *Brown*. It shows that organized civil rights demonstrations began to mount slowly but surely after *Brown v. Board of Education*. By the 1960s, the many organizations that made up the civil rights movement had accumulated experience and built networks capable of launching massive direct-action campaigns against southern segregationists. The Southern Christian Leadership Conference, the Student Nonviolent Coordinating Committee, and many other organizations had built a movement that stretched across the South. The movement used the media to attract nationwide attention and support. In the massive March on Washington in 1963, the Reverend Martin Luther King, Jr., staked out the movement's moral claims in his famous "I Have a Dream" speech. The image of protesters being beaten, attacked by police dogs, and set upon with fire hoses did much to win broad sympathy for the cause of black civil rights and to discredit state and local governments in the South. In this way, the movement created intense pressure for a reluctant federal government to take more assertive steps to defend black civil rights.

The first modern effort to legislate in the field of civil rights was made in 1957, but the law contained only a federal guarantee of voting rights, without any powers of enforcement, although it did create the Civil Rights Commission to study abuses. Much more important legislation for civil rights followed, especially the Civil Rights Act of 1964. It is important to observe here the mutual dependence of the courts and legislatures—not only do the legislatures need constitutional authority to act, but the courts need legislative and political assistance, through the power of the purse and the power to organize administrative agencies to implement court orders, and through the focusing of political support. Consequently, even as the U.S. Congress finally moved into the field of school desegregation (and other areas of "equal protection"), the courts continued to exercise their powers, not only by placing court orders against recalcitrant school districts, but also by extending and reinterpreting aspects of the "equal protection" clause to support legislative and administrative actions (see Figure 5.1).

THE CIVIL RIGHTS ACTS

The right to equal protection of the laws could be established and, to a certain extent, implemented by the courts. But after a decade of very frustrating efforts, the courts and Congress ultimately came to the conclusion that the federal courts alone were not adequate to the task of changing the social rules, and that legislation and administrative action would be needed.

Three civil rights acts were passed during the first decade after the 1954 Supreme Court decision in *Brown v. Board of Education*. But these acts were of only marginal importance. The first two, in 1957 and 1960, established that the Fourteenth Amendment of the Constitution, adopted almost a century earlier, could no longer be disregarded, particularly with regard to voting. The third, the Equal Pay Act of 1963, was more important, but it was concerned with women, did not touch the question of racial discrimination, and had no enforcement mechanisms.

By far the most important piece of legislation passed by Congress concerning equal opportunity was the Civil Rights Act of 1964. It not only put some teeth in

> **How has Congress tried to make equal protection a reality?**

Figure 5.1   **Cause and Effect in the Civil Rights Movement**

Political action and government action spurred each other to produce dramatic changes in American civil rights policies.

Judicial and Legal Action	Political Action
1954 *Brown v. Board of Education*	
1955 *Brown* II—Implementation of *Brown* I	**1955** Montgomery, Alabama, bus boycott
1956 Federal courts order school integration, especially one ordering Autherine Lucy admitted to University of Alabama, with Governor Wallace officially protesting	
1957 Civil Rights Act creating Civil Rights Commission; President Eisenhower sends paratroops to Little Rock, Arkansas, to enforce integration of Central High School	**1957** Southern Christian Leadership Conference (SCLC) formed, with Martin Luther King, Jr., as president
1960 First substantive Civil Rights Act, primarily voting rights	**1960** Student Nonviolent Coordinating Committee formed to organize protests, sit-ins, freedom rides
1961 Interstate Commerce Commission orders desegregation on all buses and trains, and in terminals	
1961 JFK favors executive action over civil rights legislation	
1963 JFK shifts, supports strong civil rights law; assassination; LBJ asserts strong support for civil rights	**1963** Nonviolent demonstrations in Birmingham, Alabama, lead to King's arrest and his "Letter from the Birmingham Jail"
	1963 March on Washington
1964 Congress passes historic Civil Rights Act covering voting, employment, public accommodations, education	
1965 Voting Rights Act	**1965** King announces drive to register 3 million blacks in the South
1966 War on Poverty in full swing	**Late 1960s** Movement dissipates: part toward litigation, part toward community action programs, part toward war protest, part toward more militant "Black Power" actions

the voting rights provisions of the 1957 and 1960 acts but also went far beyond voting to attack discrimination in public accommodations, segregation in the schools, and at long last, the discriminatory conduct of employers in hiring, promoting, and laying off their employees. Discrimination against women was also included, extending the important 1963 provisions. The 1964 act seemed bold at the time, but it was enacted ten years after the Supreme Court had declared racial discrimination "inherently unequal" under the Fifth and Fourteenth Amendments. And it was enacted long after blacks had demonstrated that discrimination was no longer acceptable. The choice in 1964 was not between congressional action or inaction but between legal action and expanded violence.

Public Accommodations   After the passage of the 1964 Civil Rights Act, public accommodations quickly removed some of the most visible forms of racial discrimination. Signs defining "colored" and "white" rest rooms, water fountains, waiting rooms, and seating arrangements were removed and a host of other practices that relegated black people to separate and inferior arrangements were ended. In addition, the federal government filed more than 400 antidiscrimination suits in federal courts against hotels, restaurants, taverns, gas stations, and other "public accommodations."

> ➤ **In what areas did the civil rights acts seek to provide equal access and protection?**

Many aspects of legalized racial segregation—such as separate Bibles in the courtroom—seem like ancient history today. But the issue of racial discrimination in public settings is by no means over. In 1993, six African American Secret Service agents filed charges against the Denny's restaurant chain for failing to serve them; white Secret Service agents at a nearby table had received prompt service. Similar charges citing discriminatory service at Denny's restaurants surfaced across the country. Faced with evidence of a pattern of systematic discrimination and numerous lawsuits, Denny's paid $45 million in damages to plaintiffs in Maryland and California in what is said to be the largest settlement ever in a public accommodation case.[20] The Denny's case shows how effective the Civil Rights Act of 1964 can be in challenging racial discrimination. In addition to the settlement, the chain vowed to expand employment and management opportunities for minorities in Denny's restaurants. Other forms of racial discrimination in public accommodations are harder to challenge, however. For example, there is considerable evidence that taxicabs often refuse to pick up black passengers.[21] Such practices may be common, but they are difficult to prove and remedy through the law.

School Desegregation, Phase Two   The 1964 Civil Rights Act also declared discrimination by private employers and state governments (school boards, etc.) illegal, then went further to provide for administrative agencies to help the courts implement these laws. Title IV of the act, for example, authorized the executive branch, through the Justice Department, to implement federal court orders to desegregate schools, and to do so without having to wait for individual parents to bring complaints. Title VI of the act vastly strengthened the role of the executive branch and the credibility of court orders by providing that federal grants-in-aid to state and local governments for education must be withheld from any school system practicing racial segregation. Title VI became the most effective weapon for desegregating schools outside the South, because the situation in northern communities was more subtle and difficult to reach. In the South, the problem was segregation by law coupled with overt resistance to the national government's efforts to change the situation. In contrast, outside the South, segregated facilities were the outcome of hundreds of thousands of housing choices made by individuals and families. Once racial residential patterns emerged, racial homogeneity, property values, and neighborhood schools and churches were defended by realtors, neighborhood organizations, and the like. Thus, in order to eliminate discrimination nationwide, the 1964 Civil Rights Act (1) gave the president through the Office for Civil Rights of the Justice Department the power to withhold federal education grants,[22] and (2) gave the attorney general of the United States the power to initiate suits (rather than having to await complaints) wherever there was a "pattern or practice" of discrimination.[23]

In the decade following the 1964 Civil Rights Act, the Justice Department brought legal action against more than five hundred school districts. During the same period, administrative agencies filed actions against six hundred school districts, threatening to suspend federal aid to education unless real desegregation steps were taken.

Busing   One step taken toward desegregation was busing children from poor urban school districts to wealthier suburban ones. In 1971, the Supreme Court held that state-imposed desegregation could be brought about by busing children across school districts, even where relatively long distances were involved:

> If school authorities fail in their affirmative obligations judicial authority may be invoked. Once a right and a violation have been shown, the scope of a district court's equitable powers to remedy past wrongs is broad.... Bus transportation [is] a normal and accepted tool of educational policy.[24]

But the decision went beyond that, adding that under certain limited circumstances even racial quotas could be used as the "starting point in shaping a remedy to correct past constitutional violations," and that pairing or grouping of schools and reorganizing school attendance zones would also be acceptable.

Three years later, however, this principle was severely restricted when the Supreme Court determined that only cities found guilty of deliberate and de jure racial segregation would have to desegregate their schools.[25] This ruling had the effect of exempting most northern states and cities from busing because school segregation in northern cities is generally de facto segregation that follows from segregated housing and from thousands of acts of private discrimination against blacks and other minorities.

Boston provides the best illustration of the agonizing problem of making further progress in civil rights in the schools under the constitutional framework established by these decisions. Boston school authorities were found guilty of deliberately building school facilities and drawing school districts "to increase racial segregation." After vain efforts by Boston school authorities to draw up an acceptable plan to remedy the segregation, federal judge W. Arthur Garrity ordered an elaborate desegregation plan of his own, involving busing between the all-black neighborhood of Roxbury and the nearby white, working-class community of South Boston. Opponents of this plan were organized and eventually took the case to the Supreme Court, where *certiorari* (the Court's device for accepting appeals; see Chapter 15) was denied; this had the effect of approving Judge Garrity's order.

The city's schools were so segregated and uncooperative that even the conservative administration of President Richard Nixon had already initiated a punitive cutoff of funds. But many liberals also criticized Judge Garrity's plan as being badly conceived, because it involved two neighboring communities with a history of tension and mutual resentment. The plan worked well at the elementary school level but proved so explosive at the high school level that it generated a continuing crisis for the city of Boston and for the whole nation over court-ordered, federally directed desegregation in the North.[26]

Additional progress in the desegregation of schools is likely to be extremely slow unless the Supreme Court decides to permit federal action against de facto segregation and against the varieties of private schools and academies that have sprung up for the purpose of avoiding integration. The prospects for further school integration diminished with a Supreme Court decision handed down on January 15, 1991. The opinion, written for the Court by Chief Justice William Rehnquist, held that lower federal courts could end supervision of local school boards if those boards could show compliance "in good faith" with court orders to desegregate and could show that "vestiges of past discrimination" had been eliminated "to the extent practicable."[27] It is not necessarily easy for a school board to prove that the new standard has been met, but this was the first time since *Brown* and the 1964 Civil Rights Act that the Court had opened the door at all to retreat.

That door of retreat was opened further by a 1995 decision in which the Court ruled that the remedies being applied in Kansas City, Missouri, were improper.[28] In accordance with a lower court ruling, the state was pouring additional funding into salaries and remedial programs for Kansas City schools, which had a history of segregation. The aim of the spending was to improve student performance and to attract white students from the suburbs into the city schools. The Supreme Court declared the interdistrict goal improper and reiterated its earlier ruling that states can free themselves of court orders by showing a good faith effort. This decision indicated the Court's new willingness to end desegregation plans even when predominantly minority schools continue to lag significantly behind white suburban schools.

Outlawing Discrimination in Employment   Despite the agonizingly slow progress of school desegregation, there was some progress made in other areas of civil rights during the 1960s and 1970s. Voting rights were established and fairly quickly began to revolutionize southern politics. Service on juries was no longer denied to minorities. But progress in the right to participate in politics and government dramatized the relative lack of progress in the economic domain, and it was in this area that battles over civil rights were increasingly fought.

The federal courts and the Justice Department entered this area through Title VII of the Civil Rights Act of 1964, which outlawed job discrimination by all private and public employers, including governmental agencies (such as fire and police departments), that employed more than fifteen workers. We have already seen (in Chapter 3) that the Supreme Court gave "interstate commerce" such a broad definition that Congress had the constitutional authority to cover discrimination by virtually any local employers.[29] Title VII makes it unlawful to discriminate in employment on the basis of color, religion, sex, or national origin, as well as race.

Title VII delegated some of the powers to enforce fair employment practices to the Justice Department's Civil Rights Division and others to a new agency created in the 1964 act, the Equal Employment Opportunity Commission (EEOC). By executive order, these agencies had the power of the national government to revoke public contracts for goods and services and to refuse to engage in contracts for goods and services with any private company that could not guarantee that its rules for hiring, promotion, and firing were nondiscriminatory. Executive orders in 1965, 1967, and 1969 by Presidents Johnson and Nixon extended and reaffirmed nondiscrimination practices in employment and promotion in the federal government service. And in 1972, President Nixon and a Democratic Congress cooperated to strengthen the EEOC by giving it authority to initiate suits rather than wait for grievances.

But one problem with Title VII was that the complaining party had to show that deliberate discrimination was the cause of the failure to get a job or a training opportunity. Rarely does an employer explicitly admit discrimination on the basis of race, sex, or any other illegal reason. Recognizing the rarity of such an admission, the courts have allowed aggrieved parties (the plaintiffs) to make their case if they can show that an employer's hiring practices had the *effect* of exclusion. A leading case in 1971 involved a "class action" by several black employees in North Carolina attempting to show with statistical evidence that blacks had been relegated to only one department in the Duke Power Company, which involved the least desirable, manual-labor jobs, and that they had been kept out of contention for the better jobs because the employer had added attainment of a high school education and the passing of specially prepared aptitude tests as qualifications for higher jobs. The Supreme Court held that although the statistical evidence did not prove intentional discrimination, and although the requirements were race-neutral in appearance, their effects were sufficient to shift the burden of justification to the employer to show that the requirements were a "business necessity" that bore "a demonstrable relationship to successful performance."[30] The ruling in this case was subsequently applied to other hiring, promotion, and training programs.[31]

Voting Rights   Although 1964 was the *most* important year for civil rights legislation, it was not the only important year. In 1965, Congress significantly strengthened legislation protecting voting rights by barring literacy and other tests as a condition for voting in six southern states,[32] by setting criminal penalties for interference with efforts to vote, and by providing for the replacement of local registrars with federally appointed registrars in counties designated by the attorney general as significantly resistant to registering eligible blacks to vote. The right to vote was further strengthened with ratification in 1964 of the Twenty-fourth Amendment, which abolished the poll tax, and in 1975 with legislation permanently outlawing literacy tests in all fifty states and mandating bilingual ballots or oral assistance for Spanish, Chinese, Japanese, Koreans, Native Americans, and Eskimos.

In the long run, the laws extending and protecting voting rights could prove to be the most effective of all the great civil rights legislation, because the progress in black political participation produced by these acts has altered the shape of American politics. In 1965, in the seven states of the Old Confederacy covered by the Vot-

**Registration by Race and State in Southern States Covered
by the Voting Rights Act**

Table 5.2

	Before the Act*			After the Act* 1971–72		
	White	**Black**	**Gap†**	**White**	**Black**	**Gap†**
Alabama	69.2%	19.3%	49.9%	80.7%	57.1%	23.6%
Georgia	62.6	27.4	35.2	70.6	67.8	2.8
Louisiana	80.5	31.6	48.9	80.0	59.1	20.9
Mississippi	69.9	6.7	63.2	71.6	62.2	9.4
North Carolina	96.8	46.8	50.0	62.2	46.3	15.9
South Carolina	75.7	37.3	38.4	51.2	48.0	3.2
Virginia	61.1	38.3	22.8	61.2	54.0	7.2
TOTAL	73.4	29.3	44.1	67.8	56.6	11.2

*Available registration data as of March 1965 and 1971–72.
†The gap is the percentage point difference between white and black registration rates.
SOURCE: U.S. Commission on Civil Rights, *Political Participation* (1968), Appendix VII: Voter Education
Project, Attachment to Press Release, October 3, 1972.

ing Rights Act, 29.3 percent of the eligible black residents were registered to vote, compared to 73.4 percent of the white residents (see Table 5.2). Mississippi was the extreme case, with 6.7 percent black and 69.9 percent white registration. In 1967, a mere two years after implementation of the voting rights laws, 52.1 percent of the eligible blacks in the seven states were registered, comparing favorably to 79.5 percent of the eligible whites, a gap of 27.4 points. By 1972, the gap between black and white registration in the seven states was only 11.2 points, and in Mississippi the gap had been reduced to 9.4 points. At one time, white leaders in Mississippi attempted to dilute the influence of this growing black vote by **gerrymandering** districts to ensure that no blacks would be elected to Congress. But the black voters changed Mississippi before Mississippi could change them. In 1988, 11 percent of all elected officials in Mississippi were black. This was up one full percentage point from 1987 and closely approximates the size of the national black electorate, which at the time was just over 11 percent of the American voting-age population. Mississippi's blacks had made significant gains (as was true in other Deep South states) as elected state and local representatives, and Mississippi was one of only eight states in the country in which a black judge presided over the highest state court. (Four of the eight were Deep South states.)[33]

The 2000 elections reminded black leaders that even basic rights, such as voting, must be monitored. The U.S. Commission on Civil Rights conducted hearings on the election in Florida, at which black voters testified about being turned away from the polls, about being wrongly purged from the voting rolls, and about the unreliable voting technology in their neighborhoods. On the basis of this testimony and after an analysis of the vote, the Commission

gerrymandering apportionment of voters in districts in such a way as to give unfair advantage to one racial or ethnic group or political party

charged that there had been extensive racial discrimination. A subsequent thorough analysis of the Florida vote by a consortium of newspapers showed that black precincts had three times the number of rejected ballots as white precincts even after the effects of income, education, and ballot design were taken into account.[34]

Housing   The Civil Rights Act of 1964 did not address housing, but in 1968, Congress passed another civil rights act specifically to outlaw housing discrimination. Called the Fair Housing Act, the law prohibited discrimination in the sale or rental of most housing—eventually covering nearly all the nation's housing. Housing was among the most controversial of discrimination issues because of deeply entrenched patterns of residential segregation across the United States. Such segregation was not simply a product of individual choice. Local housing authorities deliberately segregated public housing, and federal guidelines had sanctioned discrimination in Federal Housing Administration mortgage lending, effectively preventing blacks from joining the exodus to the suburbs in the 1950s and 1960s. Nonetheless, Congress had been reluctant to tackle housing discrimination, fearing the tremendous controversy it could arouse. But, just as the housing legislation was being considered in April 1968, civil rights leader Martin Luther King, Jr., was assassinated; this tragedy brought the measure unexpected support in Congress.

Although it pronounced sweeping goals, the Fair Housing Act had little effect on housing segregation because its enforcement mechanisms were so weak. Individuals believing they had been discriminated against had to file suit themselves. The burden was on the individual to prove that housing discrimination had occurred, even though such discrimination is often subtle and difficult to document. Although local fair-housing groups emerged to assist individuals in their court claims, the procedures for proving discrimination proved a formidable barrier to effective change. These procedures were not altered until 1988, when Congress passed the Fair Housing Amendments Act. This new law put more teeth in the enforcement procedures and allowed the Department of Housing and Urban Development (HUD) to initiate legal action in cases of discrimination. With vigorous use, these provisions may prove more successful than past efforts at combating housing discrimination.[35]

Other avenues for challenging residential segregation also had mixed success. HUD tried briefly in the early 1970s to create racially "open communities" by withholding federal funds to suburbs that refused to accept subsidized housing. Confronted with charges of "forced integration" and bitter local protests, however, the administration quickly backed down. Efforts to prohibit discrimination in lending have been somewhat more promising. Several laws passed in the 1970s required banks to report information about their mortgage lending patterns, making it more difficult for them to engage in **redlining,** the practice of refusing to lend to entire neighborhoods. The 1977 Community Reinvestment Act required banks to lend in neighborhoods in which they do business. Through vigorous use of this act, many neighborhood organizations have reached agreements with banks that, as a result, have significantly increased investment in some poor neighborhoods.

redlining a practice in which banks refuse to make loans to people living in certain geographic locations

The Universalization of Civil Rights

Even before equal employment laws began to have a positive effect on the economic situation of blacks, something far more dramatic began happening—the universalization of civil rights. The right not to be discriminated against was being successfully claimed by the other groups listed in Title VII of the 1964 Civil Rights Act—those defined by sex, religion, or national origin—and eventually by still other groups defined by age or sexual preference. This universalization of civil rights has become the new frontier of the civil rights struggle.

As gender discrimination began to be seen as an important civil rights issue, other groups arose demanding recognition and active protection of their civil rights. Under Title VII, any group or individual can try, and in fact is encouraged to try, to convert goals and grievances into questions of rights and of the deprivation of those rights. A plaintiff must establish only that his or her membership in a group is an unreasonable basis for discrimination—i.e., that it cannot be proven to be a "job-related" or otherwise clearly reasonable and relevant decision. In America today, the list of individuals and groups claiming illegal discrimination is lengthy.

WOMEN AND GENDER DISCRIMINATION

Title VII provided a valuable tool for the growing women's movement in the 1960s and 1970s. In fact, in many ways the law fostered the growth of the women's movement. The first major campaign of the National Organization for Women (NOW) involved picketing the Equal Employment Opportunity Commission for its refusal to ban sex-segregated employment advertisements. NOW also sued *The New York Times* for continuing to publish such ads after the passage of Title VII. Another organization, the Women's Equity Action League (WEAL), pursued legal action on a wide range of sex discrimination issues, filing lawsuits against law schools and medical schools for discriminatory admission policies, for example.

Building on these victories and the growth of the women's movement, feminist activists sought an "Equal Rights Amendment" (ERA) to the Constitution. The proposed amendment was short: its substantive passage stated that "equality of rights under the law shall not be denied or abridged by the United States or by any State on account of sex." The amendment's supporters believed that such a sweeping guarantee of equal rights was a necessary tool for ending all discrimination against women and for making gender roles more equal. Opponents charged that it would be socially disruptive and would introduce changes—such as coed rest rooms—that most Americans did not want. The amendment easily passed Congress in 1972 and won quick approval in many state legislatures, but it fell three states short of the thirty-eight needed to ratify the amendment by the 1982 deadline for its ratification.[36]

Despite the failure of the ERA, gender discrimination expanded dramatically as an area of civil rights law. In the 1970s, the conservative Burger Court (under Chief Justice Warren Burger) helped to establish gender discrimination as a major and highly visible civil rights issue. Although the Burger Court

> **What groups were spurred by the provision of the Civil Rights Act of 1964, outlawing discrimination in employment practices based on race, religion, and gender, to seek broader protection under the law?**

> **What is the politics of the universalization of civil rights?**

Political Rights and Enabling of Citizens within Democracies

In Chapter 4, we discussed Freedom House's civil rights ratings of countries; it also assigns a political rights score to each country based upon a specific checklist of features built mainly around free elections and the right to form political parties and organizations.

However, these criteria do not fully capture the broader meaning of rights. From a global perspective, the ability of citizens within a country to make a moral or legal claim on government requires more than political and institutional opportunities.

The United Nations' Development Program argues that rights in a global perspective should be understood within the context of human development: *the process of creating an enabling environment for citizens within a country, which permits the people to enjoy long, healthy, and creative lives.* How are people enabled? How are their broader human rights maximized and sustained? People are enabled through political participation and through the application of their talents, which both depend upon their well-being and the range of opportunities for active engagement in the politics and economy of their country.

The United Nations produces an annual assessment of the progress of human development. Their *Human Development Report* records for each country the degree of human development, the degree of gender development, and the degree of gender empowerment. The composite measure for human development (the Human Development Index, or HDI) combines scores on life expectancy within the country, adult literacy rates, educational enrollment among the population, and the per capita income for citizens within the country. The score ranges from 0 (the lowest degree of human development) to 1.000 (the highest degree). The Gender Development Index (GDI) is based on the same measures as the HDI, except that it separates each measure for men and women. The higher the score, the greater the degree of female development within the country. By comparing the GDI to the HDI, one can gauge the extent to which a country has been successful or unsuccessful in sustaining the development of its women relative to the whole population. The Gender Empowerment Measure (GEM) reflects the degree of gender inequality in key areas of political partici-

pation and decision making (for instance, the number of female legislators and heads of state, etc.). Again, the maximum score is 1.000, with 0 representing the lowest possible degree of female empowerment.

By comparing the GEM to the HDI and GDI, one can achieve yet another measure of the relative gap within a country between what is possible and what in fact may be achieved by women. In 2001, the average HDI was .716. This is lower than the development level for the thirty-one countries that comprise the most industrialized countries of the world, and lower than the level for western European nations (.902) or the eighty-five "free" electoral democracies that were also characterized as having perfect or near-perfect political rights scores (.815). The gap between overall human development and gender development is noticeably wide among those thirty-two electoral democracies that were classified by Freedom House as only "partly free" and that had more numerous political rights deficiencies (GEM = .385, HDI = .640). Based on UN data, women within electoral democracies generally enjoy more development capabilities than men, as evidenced by a GDI score (.782) larger than the HDI score (.780), though gender equality has a way to go before it matches the more general capabilities measures (GEM = .536). This trend is also shown among electoral democracies in eastern Europe (Poland, Czech Republic, Romania, etc.) and among the former republics of the Soviet Union (the CIS—Commonwealth of Independent States—such as Ukraine). Generally, broad measures of human development, including gender empowerment and development, are shown to be higher among electoral emocracies and among European and industrialized democracies (including Japan, Australia, Canada, and the United States) and lower as one moves from the highest forms of democracy and political rights. The values for HDI, GDI, and GEM for the United States are .934, .932, and .738, respectively. These scores ranked sixth, fourth, and tenth, respectively, among all countries of the world.

SOURCES: Amartya Sen, *Development As Freedom* (New York: Knopf, 1999); United Nations Development Program, *Human Development Report 2002* (New York: Oxford University Press, 2002).

refused to treat gender discrimination as the equivalent of racial discrimination,[37] it did make it easier for plaintiffs to file and win suits on the basis of gender discrimination by applying an "intermediate" level of review to these cases.[38] This **intermediate scrutiny** is midway between traditional rules of evidence, which put the burden of proof on the plaintiff, and the doctrine of strict scrutiny, which requires the defendant to show not only that a particular classification is reasonable but also that there is a need or compelling interest for it. Intermediate scrutiny shifts the burden of proof partially onto the defendant, rather than leaving it entirely on the plaintiff.

One major step was taken in 1992, when the Court decided in *Franklin v. Gwinnett County Public Schools* that violations of Title IX of the 1972 Education Act could be remedied with monetary damages.[39] Title IX forbade gender discrimination in education, but it initially sparked little litigation because of its weak enforcement provisions. The Court's 1992 ruling that monetary damages could be awarded for gender discrimination opened the door for more legal action in the area of education. The greatest impact has been in the areas of sexual harassment—the subject of the *Franklin* case—and in equal treatment of women's athletic programs. The potential for monetary damages has made universities and public schools take the problem of sexual harassment more seriously. Colleges and universities have also started to pay more attention to women's athletic programs. In the two years after the *Franklin* case, complaints to the Education Department's Office for Civil Rights about unequal treatment of women's athletic programs nearly tripled. In several high-profile legal cases, some prominent universities have been ordered to create more women's sports programs; many other colleges and universities have begun to add more women's programs in order to avoid potential litigation.[40] In 1997, the Supreme Court refused to hear a petition by Brown University challenging a lower court ruling that the university establish strict sex equity in its athletic programs. The Court's decision meant that in colleges and universities across the country, varsity athletic positions for men and women must now reflect their overall enrollment numbers.[41]

In 1996, the Supreme Court made another important decision about gender and education by putting an end to all-male schools supported by public funds. It ruled that the policy of the Virginia Military Institute not to admit women was unconstitutional.[42] Along with the Citadel, another all-male military college in South Carolina, VMI had never admitted women in its 157-year history. VMI argued that the unique educational experience it offered—including intense physical training and the harsh treatment of freshmen—would be destroyed if women students were admitted. The Court, however, ruled that the male-only policy denied "substantial equality" to women. Two days after the Court's ruling, the Citadel announced that it would accept women. VMI considered becoming a private institution in order to remain all-male, but in September 1996, the school board finally voted to admit women. The legal decisions may have removed formal barriers to entry, but the experience of the new female cadets at these schools has not been easy. The first female cadet at the Citadel, Shannon Faulkner, won admission in 1995 under a federal court order but quit after four days. Although four women were admitted to the Citadel after the Supreme Court decision, two of the four quit several months later. They charged harassment from male students, including attempts to set the female cadets on fire.[43]

intermediate scrutiny test, used by the Supreme Court in gender discrimination cases, which places the burden of proof partially on the government and partially on the challengers to show that the law in question is constitutional

Women were not originally outlawed from voting by the Constitution. Although a few women could vote in the early American republic, such as these New Jersey women who satisfied state property qualifications, laws were soon enacted to block women from the ballot box. At the beginning of the nineteenth century, no American woman could legally vote.

Courts began to find sexual harassment a form of sex discrimination during the late 1970s. Although sexual harassment law applies to education, most of the law of sexual harassment has been developed by courts through interpretation of Title VII of the Civil Rights Act of 1964. In 1986, the Supreme Court recognized two forms of sexual harassment—the quid pro quo type, which involves sexual extortion, and the hostile environment type, which involves sexual intimidation.[44] Employers and many employees have worried that hostile-environment sexual ha-

People had been agitating for women's right to vote since the 1830s, especially during the Civil War era. However, the Fourteenth Amendment explicitly referred to voters as men, squelching women's hope for the vote. Another suffragist push in the 1910s reinvigorated the fight for women's political equality with men. Here, a police officer arrests two suffragists in front of the White House. Women finally gained the constitutional right to vote in 1920.

Political equality did not end discrimination against women in the workplace or in society at large. African Americans' struggle for civil rights in the 1950s and 1960s spurred a parallel equal rights movement for women in the 1960s and 1970s. Activists sought to add the Equal Rights Amendment (ERA) to the Constitution as a way to end sex discrimination permanently. Despite Congressional and state support, it mustered approval from only thirty-five of the necessary thirty-eight state legislatures and failed to become law in 1982.

rassment is too ambiguous. When can an employee bring charges? When is the employer liable? In 1986, the Court said that sexual harassment may be legally actionable even if the employee did not suffer tangible economic or job-related losses in relation to it. In 1993, the Court said that sexual harassment may be legally actionable even if the employee did not suffer tangible psychological costs as a result of it.[45] In two 1998 cases, the Court further strengthened the law when it said that whether or not sexual harassment results in economic harm to the employee, an employer is liable for the harassment if it was committed by someone with authority over the employee—by a supervisor, for example. But the Court also said that an employer may defend itself by showing that it had a sexual harassment prevention and grievance policy in effect.[46]

The development of gender discrimination as an important part of the civil rights struggle has coincided with the rise of women's politics as a discrete movement in American politics. As with the struggle for racial equality, the relationship between changes in government policies and political action suggests that changes in government policies to a great degree produce political action. Today, the existence of a powerful women's movement derives in large measure from the enactment of Title VII of the Civil Rights Act of 1964 and from the Burger Court's vital steps in applying that law to protect women. The recognition of women's civil rights has become an issue that in many ways transcends the usual distinctions of American political debate. In the heavily partisan debate over the federal crime bill enacted in 1994, for instance, the section of the bill that enjoyed the widest support was the Violence Against Women Act, whose most important feature was that it defined gender-biased violent crimes as a matter of civil rights, and created a civil rights remedy for women who have been the victims of such crimes. But since the act was ruled unconstitutional by the Supreme Court in 2000, the struggle for women's rights will likely remain part of the political debate.

The ERA never passed, but women's struggle against gender discrimination continued. Under the Civil Rights Act of 1964 and the Education Act of 1972, women could legally demand treatment equal to men. One result of this has been that college athletics programs must be gender-balanced. Colleges and universities have added more women's sports programs to comply with government regulations.

LATINOS AND ASIAN AMERICANS

The labels "Latino"/"Hispanic" and "Asian American" encompass a wide range of groups with diverse national origins, distinctive cultural identities, and particular experiences. For example, the early political experiences of Mexican Americans were shaped by race and by region. In 1898, Mexican Americans were given formal political rights, including the right to vote. In many places, however, and especially in Texas, Mexican Americans were segregated and prevented from voting through such means as the white primary and the poll tax.[47] Region made a difference too. In contrast to the northeastern and midwestern cities to which most European ethnics immigrated, the Southwest did not have a tradition of ethnic mobilization associated with machine politics. Particularly after the political reforms enacted in the first decade of the twentieth century, city politics in the Southwest was dominated by a small group of Anglo elites. In the countryside, when Mexican Americans participated in politics, it was often as part of a political organization dominated by a large white landowner, or *patron.*

The earliest Mexican American independent political organizations, the League of United Latin American Citizens (LULAC) and the GI Forum, worked to stem discrimination against Mexican Americans in the years after World War II. By the late 1950s, the first Mexican American was elected to Congress, and four others followed in the 1960s. In the late 1960s a new kind of Mexican American political movement was born. Inspired by the black civil rights movement, Mexican American students launched boycotts of high school classes in East Los Angeles, Denver, and San Antonio. Students in colleges and universities across California joined in as well. Among their demands were bilingual education, an end to discrimination, and more cultural recognition. In Crystal City, Texas, which had been dominated by Anglo politicians despite a population that was overwhelmingly Mexican American, the newly formed La Raza Unida Party took over the city government.[48]

Since that time, Mexican American political strategy has developed along two tracks. One is a traditional ethnic-group path of voter registration and voting along ethnic lines. The second is a legal strategy using the various civil rights laws designed to ensure fair access to the political system. The Mexican American Legal Defense Fund (MALDEF) has played a key role in designing and pursuing the latter strategy.

The early Asian experience in the United States was shaped by a series of naturalization laws dating back to 1790, the first of which declared that only white aliens were eligible for citizenship. Chinese immigrants had begun arriving in California in the 1850s, drawn by the boom of the Gold Rush, but they were immediately met with hostility. The virulent antagonism toward Chinese immigrants in California led Congress to declare Chinese immigrants ineligible for citizenship in 1870. In 1882, the first Chinese Exclusion Act suspended the entry of Chinese laborers.

At the time of the Exclusion Act, the Chinese community was composed predominantly of single male laborers, with few women and children. The few Chinese children in San Francisco were initially denied entry to the public schools; only after parents of American-born Chinese children pressed legal action were the

What Government Does . . . After September 11

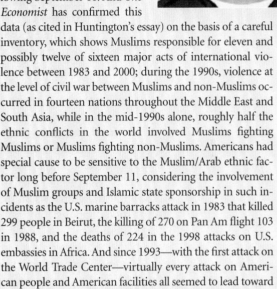

Historically, international war has been an important factor in producing domestic strife among ethnic groups in the United States. During and after World War I, Americans singled out Germans for ethnic vilification. The teaching of the German language in secondary schools disappeared. The most prominent directors of American symphony orchestras, mostly of German origin, lost their jobs. Italians in particular and Catholics in general were also singled out, not only at the hands of a resurgent Ku Klux Klan but as a matter of policy in the U.S. Department of Justice, where "criminal syndicalism," anarchism, and even treason in opposing America's role in World War I were intensely Italianized. During World War II, Congress passed a law that authorized the military to exclude from designated areas any person it deemed a threat. Under this law, more than 120,000 people of Japanese descent—two-thirds of them American citizens—were rounded up and sent to "relocation camps." There they were kept for up to three years, deprived of their property, their jobs, and their freedom.

All that serves as background to the American response after September 11. To a certain extent, like in World War I and World War II, the enemy has an ethnic face. But unlike previous wars, the adversaries this time are not the people of one or more nations; they are a vaguely defined, regionally dispersed, amorphous force known only as "terrorists." According to the best American intelligence, these adversaries are concentrated in Arab regions, and their appeals justifying the violent methods of terror are drawn largely from the Koran. Before September 11, China had already adopted a law prohibiting any national from an Arab country from entering the country. Israel, Saudi Arabia, and Egypt have adopted less severe but still quite restrictive and pejorative measures, using the same profile. The United States is also now in full-scale commitment to using ethnic profiling but is inexplicit about its guidelines and methods. Hundreds of persons of Arab descent—often identified solely by their Arabic facial features—have been detained, some for very long periods of time, and all without their names being made public. Military tribunals will be used to try those Arabic citizens, residents, and travelers for whom agents of the Department of Justice have reasons of their own to believe a trial is warranted—without having to show probable cause as in a normal judicial procedure. Even before evidence was amassed, the attorney general of the United States was referring to detainees as "terrorists" who don't deserve access to the Bill of Rights—as though he already knew they were guilty.

Some ethnic profiling is inevitable as long as the data on terrorism so overwhelmingly points toward the Middle East in general and toward Muslim nations or regions in particular. Samuel Huntington has catalogued considerable evidence from various respectable sources on the sources of civil, national, and international violence in the years, months, and days leading up to and following September 11. And *The Economist* has confirmed this data (as cited in Huntington's essay) on the basis of a careful inventory, which shows Muslims responsible for eleven and possibly twelve of sixteen major acts of international violence between 1983 and 2000; during the 1990s, violence at the level of civil war between Muslims and non-Muslims occurred in fourteen nations throughout the Middle East and South Asia, while in the mid-1990s alone, roughly half the ethnic conflicts in the world involved Muslims fighting Muslims or Muslims fighting non-Muslims. Americans had special cause to be sensitive to the Muslim/Arab ethnic factor long before September 11, considering the involvement of Muslim groups and Islamic state sponsorship in such incidents as the U.S. marine barracks attack in 1983 that killed 299 people in Beirut, the killing of 270 on Pan Am flight 103 in 1988, and the deaths of 224 in the 1998 attacks on U.S. embassies in Africa. And since 1993—with the first attack on the World Trade Center—virtually every attack on American people and American facilities all seemed to lead toward Muslims and ultimately to Osama bin Laden.

Is there an alternative to ethnic profiling? Conservative Charles Krauthammer says there isn't, and he makes a lot of sense, especially with the key issue of air travel. Calling the present alternative to ethnic profiling a "parody of civic duty," Krauthammer claims universal surveillance coupled with random searches is in large part merely a method of avoiding charges of ethnic profiling. The random searches involve head-to-toe searches of both genders and all races, even though almost no women have been identified as terrorists, and no Africans, African Americans, Asians, or Asian Americans, no individuals over the age of, say, forty-five, no disabled persons, and no blond, fair-skinned males have been identified as terrorists. The ludicrous spectacle of random individuals being thoroughly searched while types with high terrorist potential walk casually through the checkpoints leads Krauthammer to conclude that while we'd "rather not make any calculations based on ethnicity, religion, gender [etc.], . . . on airplanes our lives are at stake."

SOURCES: Samuel Huntington, *Newsweek Special Issue*, December 2001–February 2002, pp. 8–13; *Washington Post National Weekly Edition*, Robert O'Harrow, "Will Passenger Profiling Fly?" February 11–17, 2002, p. 29; Charles Krauthammer, "The Case for Profiling," *Time*, March 18, 2002, endpaper essay.

children allowed to attend public school. Even then, however, they were segregated into a separate Chinese school. American-born Chinese children could not be denied citizenship, however; this right was confirmed by the Supreme Court in 1898, when it ruled in *United States v. Wong Kim Ark* that anyone born in the United States was entitled to full citizenship.[49] Still, new Chinese immigrants were barred from the United States until 1943, after China had become a key wartime ally and Congress repealed the Chinese Exclusion Act and permitted Chinese residents to become citizens.

Immigration climbed rapidly after the 1965 Immigration Act, which lifted discriminatory quotas. In spite of this and other developments, limited English proficiency barred many Asian Americans and Latinos from full participation in American life. Two developments in the 1970s, however, established rights for language minorities. In 1974, the Supreme Court ruled in *Lau v. Nichols,* a suit filed on behalf of Chinese students in San Francisco, that school districts have to provide education for students whose English is limited.[50] It did not mandate bilingual education but it established a duty to provide instruction that the students could understand. The 1970 amendments to the Voting Rights Act permanently outlawed literacy tests in all fifty states and mandated bilingual ballots or oral assistance for those who speak Spanish, Chinese, Japanese, Korean, Native American languages, or Eskimo languages.

Asian Americans and Latinos have also been concerned about the impact of immigration laws on their civil rights. Many Asian American and Latino organizations opposed the Immigration Reform and Control Act of 1986 because it imposed sanctions on employers who hire undocumented workers. Such sanctions, they feared, would lead employers to discriminate against Latinos and Asian Americans. These suspicions were confirmed in a 1990 report by the General Accounting Office that found employer sanctions had created a "widespread pattern of discrimination" against Latinos and others who appear foreign.[51] Organizations such as MALDEF and the Asian Law Caucus monitor and challenge such discrimination. These groups have turned their attention to the rights of legal and illegal immigrants, as anti-immigrant sentiment has grown in recent years.

The Supreme Court has ruled that illegal immigrants are eligible for education and medical care but can be denied other social benefits; legal immigrants are to be treated much the same as citizens. But growing immigration—including an estimated 300,000 illegal immigrants per year—and mounting economic insecurity have undermined these practices. Groups of voters across the country now strongly support drawing a sharper line between immigrants and citizens. Not surprisingly, the movement to deny benefits to noncitizens began in California, which experienced sharp economic distress in the early 1990s and has the highest levels of immigration of any state. In 1994, Californians voted in favor of Proposition 187, denying illegal immigrants all services except emergency medical care. Supporters of the measure hoped to discourage illegal immigration and to pressure illegal immigrants already in the country to leave. Opponents contended that denying basic services to illegal immigrants risked creating a subclass of residents in the United States whose lack of education and poor health threaten all Americans. In 1994 and 1997, a federal court declared most of Proposition 187 unconstitutional, affirming previous rulings that illegal immigrants should be granted public education. A booming economy helped to reduce public concern about illegal immigration, but supporters of Proposition 187 promised to reintroduce similar measures in the future.

The question of the rights of legal immigrants poses an even tougher problem. Congress has the power to deny public benefits to this group but doing so would go against long-standing traditions in American political culture. Legal immigrants have traditionally enjoyed most of the rights and obligations (such as paying taxes) of citizens. As constitutional scholar Theodore Bikel points out, the Constitution begins with "We the People of the United States"; likewise the Bill of Rights refers to the rights of *people,* not citizens.[52]

NATIVE AMERICANS

The political status of Native Americans was left unclear in the Constitution. But by the early 1800s, the courts had defined each of the Indian tribes as a nation. As members of an Indian nation, Native Americans were declared noncitizens of the United States. The political status of Native Americans changed in 1924, when congressional legislation granted citizenship to those who had been born in the United States. A variety of changes in federal policy toward Native Americans during the 1930s paved the way for a later resurgence of their political power. Most important was the federal decision to encourage Native Americans on reservations to establish local self-government.[53]

The Native American political movement gathered force in the 1960s, as Native Americans began to use protest, litigation, and assertion of tribal rights to improve their situation. In 1968, Dennis Banks cofounded the American Indian Movement (AIM), the most prominent Native American protest organization. AIM won national attention in 1969 when two hundred of its members, representing twenty different tribes, took over the famous prison island of Alcatraz in San Francisco Bay, claiming it for Native Americans. In 1971, AIM members took over the town of Wounded Knee, South Dakota, the site of the last major battle between Native Americans and the U.S. Army, in which a Sioux village had been massacred. The federal government responded to the rise in Indian activism with the Indian Self-Determination and Education Assistance Act, which began to give Indians more control over their own land.[54]

As a language minority, Native Americans were also affected by the 1975 amendments to the Voting Rights Act and the *Lau* decision. The *Lau* decision established the right of Native Americans to be taught in their own languages. This marked quite a change from the boarding schools once run by the Bureau of Indian Affairs, at which members of Indian tribes had been forbidden to speak their own languages. In addition to these language-related issues, Native Americans have sought to expand their rights on the basis of their sovereign status. Since the 1920s and 1930s, Native American tribes have sued the federal government for illegally seizing land, seeking monetary reparations and land as damages. Both types of damages have been awarded in such suits, but only in small amounts. Native American tribes have been more successful in winning federal recognition of their sovereignty. Sovereign status has, in turn, allowed them to exercise greater self-determination. Most significant economically was a 1987 Supreme Court decision that freed Native American tribes from most state regulations prohibiting gambling. The establishment of casino gambling on Native American lands has brought a substantial flow of new income into desperately poor reservations.

DISABLED AMERICANS

The concept of rights for the disabled began to emerge in the 1970s as the civil rights model spread to other groups. The seed was planted in a little-noticed provision of the 1973 Rehabilitation Act, which outlawed discrimination against individuals on the basis of disabilities. As in many other cases, the law itself helped give rise to the movement demanding rights for the handicapped.[55] Modeling itself on the NAACP's Legal Defense Fund, the disability movement founded a Disability Rights Education and Defense Fund to press their legal claims. The movement achieved its greatest success with the passage of the Americans with Disabilities Act (ADA) of 1990, which guarantees equal employment rights and access to public businesses for the disabled. Claims of discrimination in violation of this act are considered by the Equal Employment Opportunity Commission. The impact of the law has been far-reaching, as businesses and public facilities have installed ramps, elevators, and other devices to meet the act's requirements.[56] In 1998, the Supreme Court interpreted the ADA to apply to people with HIV. Until then, ADA was interpreted as covering people with AIDS but not people with HIV. The case arose out of the refusal of a dentist to fill a cavity of a woman with HIV except in a hospital setting. The woman sued, and her complaint was that HIV had already disabled her because it was discouraging her from having children. (The Act prohibits discrimination in employment, housing, and in health care.) Although there have been widespread concerns that the ADA was being expanded too broadly and the costs were becoming too burdensome, corporate America did not seem to be disturbed by the Court's ruling. Stephen Bokat, General Counsel of the U.S. Chamber of Commerce, said businesses in general had already been accommodating people with HIV as well as with AIDS and that the case presented no serious problem.[57]

THE AGED

Age discrimination in employment is illegal. The 1967 federal Age Discrimination in Employment Act (ADEA) makes age discrimination illegal when practiced by employers with at least twenty employees. Many states have added to the federal provisions with their own age discrimination laws, and some such state laws are stronger than the federal provisions. The major lobbyist for seniors, the American Association of Retired Persons (AARP, see Chapter 11), with its claim to over thirty million members, has been active in keeping these laws on the books and making sure that they are vigorously implemented.

GAYS AND LESBIANS

In less than thirty years, the gay and lesbian movement has become one of the largest civil rights movements in contemporary America. Beginning with street protests in the 1960s, the movement has grown into a well-financed and sophisticated lobby. The Human Rights Campaign Fund is the primary national political action committee (PAC) focused on gay rights; it provides campaign financing and volunteers to work for candidates endorsed by the group. The movement has also formed legal rights organizations, including the Lambda Legal Defense and Education Fund.

Gay and lesbian rights drew national attention in 1993, when President Bill Clinton confronted the question of whether gays should be allowed to serve in the military. As a candidate, Clinton had said he favored lifting the ban on homosexuals in the military. The issue set off a huge controversy in the first months of Clinton's presidency. After nearly a year of deliberation, the administration enunciated a compromise: their "Don't ask, don't tell" policy. This policy allows gays and lesbians to serve in the military as long as they do not openly proclaim their sexual orientation or engage in homosexual activity. The administration maintained that the ruling would protect gays and lesbians against witch-hunting investigations, but many gay and lesbian advocates expressed disappointment, charging the president with reneging on his campaign promise.

But until 1996, there was no Supreme Court ruling or national legislation explicitly protecting gays and lesbians from discrimination. The first gay rights case that the Court decided, *Bowers v. Hardwick,* ruled against a right to privacy that would protect consensual homosexual activity.[58] After the *Bowers* decision, the gay and lesbian rights movement sought suitable legal cases to test the constitutionality of discrimination against gays and lesbians, much as the black civil rights movement did in the late 1940s and 1950s. As one advocate put it, "lesbians and gay men are looking for their *Brown v. Board of Education.*"[59] Among the cases tested were those stemming from local ordinances restricting gay rights (including the right to marry), job discrimination, and family law issues such as adoption and parental rights. In 1996, the Supreme Court, in *Romer v. Evans,* explicitly extended fundamental civil rights protections to gays and lesbians, by declaring unconstitutional a 1992 amendment to the Colorado state constitution that prohibited local governments from passing ordinances to protect gay rights.[60] The decision's forceful language highlighted the connection between gay rights and civil rights as it declared discrimination against gay people unconstitutional.

Whatever the future of Court rulings in this area, gay and lesbian Americans will continue to press their cases against the many laws they view as discriminatory. In response to the recent legalization of gay and lesbian marriage in Vermont, for example, they are likely to push for observance of the *full faith and credit clause,* as discussed in Chapter 3. But the Defense of Marriage Act of 1996, declaring that states do not have to recognize same-sex marriage, and the efforts of many states to adopt state laws to put same-sex marriage off limits, means that the gay and lesbian struggle against discrimination will follow that of other minorities, using the federal equal protection clause.[61]

Affirmative Action

Not only has the politics of rights spread to increasing numbers of groups in American society since the 1960s, it has also expanded its goal. The relatively narrow goal of equalizing opportunity by eliminating discriminatory barriers developed toward the far broader goal of **affirmative action**—compensatory action to overcome the consequences of past discrimination. An affirmative action policy tends to involve two novel approaches: (1) positive or benign discrimination in

affirmative action government policies or programs that seek to redress past injustices against specified groups by making special efforts to provide members of these groups with access to educational and employment opportunities

which race or some other status is actually taken into account, but for compensatory action rather than mistreatment; and (2) compensatory action to favor members of the disadvantaged group who themselves may never have been the victims of discrimination. Quotas may be but are not necessarily involved in affirmative action policies.

President Lyndon Johnson put the case emotionally in 1965: "You do not take a person who, for years, has been hobbled by chains . . . and then say you are free to compete with all the others, and still just believe that you have been completely fair."[62] Johnson attempted to inaugurate affirmative action by executive orders directing agency heads and personnel officers to pursue vigorously a policy of minority employment in the federal civil service and in companies doing business with the national government. But affirmative action did not become a prominent goal of the national government until the 1970s.

Affirmative action also took the form of efforts by the agencies in the Department of Health, Education, and Welfare to shift their focus from "desegregation" to "integration."[63] Federal agencies—sometimes with court orders and sometimes without them—required school districts to present plans for busing children across district lines, for pairing schools, for closing certain schools, and for redistributing faculties as well as students, under pain of loss of grants-in-aid from the federal government. The guidelines issued for such plans literally constituted preferential treatment to compensate for past discrimination, and without this legislatively assisted approach to integration orders, there would

Affirmative action programs seek to overcome past discrimination against a group by practicing benign discrimination—providing additional opportunities for those who face discrimination. Here, women's rights advocates call for more opportunities for women and equal pay for equal work.

certainly not have been the dramatic increase in black children attending integrated classes. The yellow school bus became a symbol of hope for many and a signal of defeat for others.

Affirmative action was also initiated in the area of employment opportunity. The Equal Employment Opportunity Commission often has required plans whereby employers must attempt to increase the number of their minority employees, and the office of Federal Contract Compliance in the Department of Labor has used the threat of contract revocation for the same purpose.

THE SUPREME COURT AND THE BURDEN OF PROOF

Efforts by the executive, legislative, and judicial branches to shape the meaning of affirmative action today tend to center on a key issue: what is the appropriate level of review in affirmative action cases—that is, on whom should the burden of proof be placed, the plaintiff or the defendant? The issue of qualification versus minority preference was addressed formally by the Supreme Court in the case of Allan Bakke. Bakke, a white male, brought suit against the University of California at Davis Medical School on the grounds that in denying him admission the school had discriminated against him on the basis of his race (that year the school had reserved 16 of 100 available slots for minority applicants). He argued that his grades and test scores had ranked him well above many students

> **What is the basis for affirmative action? What forms does it take?**

Especially in schools, affirmative action remains controversial. Many University of California students defended affirmative action programs in 1996, when Proposition 209 prohibited state and local governments from using race or gender as a basis for employment, education, or contracting (left). The proposition was phrased to outlaw discrimination or preferential treatment. In another instance, demonstrators on both sides of an affirmative action case had an altercation during a rally in Cincinnati in 2001 (right). At the time, a federal appeals court was reviewing whether the University of Michigan could use affirmative action policies in admitting its undergraduate and law students.

who had been accepted at the school and that the only possible explanation for his rejection was that those others accepted were black or Latino while he was white. In 1978, Bakke won his case before the Supreme Court and was admitted to the medical school, but he did not succeed in getting affirmative action declared unconstitutional. The Court rejected the procedures at the University of California because its medical school had used both a quota *and* a separate admissions system for minorities. The Court agreed with Bakke's argument that racial categorizations are suspect categories that place a severe burden of proof on those using them to show a "compelling public purpose." The Court went on to say that achieving "a diverse student body" was such a public purpose, but the method of a rigid quota of student slots assigned on the basis of race was incompatible with the equal protection clause. Thus, the Court permitted universities (and presumably other schools, training programs, and hiring authorities) to continue to take minority status into consideration, but limited severely the use of quotas to situations in which (1) previous discrimination had been shown, and (2) it was used more as a guideline for social diversity than as a mathematically defined ratio.[64]

For nearly a decade after *Bakke,* the Supreme Court was tentative and permissive about efforts by corporations and governments to experiment with affirmative action programs in employment.[65] But in 1989, the Court returned to the *Bakke* position that any "rigid numerical quota" is suspect. In *Wards Cove v. Atonio,* the Court backed away further from affirmative action by easing the way for employers to prefer white males, holding that the burden of proof of unlawful discrimination should be shifted from the defendant (the employer) to the plaintiff (the person claiming to be the victim of discrimination).[66] This decision virtually overruled the Court's prior holding.[67] That same year, the Court ruled that any affirmative action program already approved by federal courts could be subsequently challenged by white males who allege that the program discriminates against them.[68]

In 1991, Congress enacted a piece of legislation designed to undo the effects of the decisions limiting affirmative action. Under the terms of the Civil Rights Act of 1991, the burden of proof in employment discrimination cases was shifted back to employers. In addition, the act made it more difficult to mount later challenges to consent decrees in affirmative action cases. Despite Congress's actions, however, the federal judiciary will have the last word as cases under the new law reach the courts. In a 5-to-4 decision in 1993, the Supreme Court ruled that employees had to prove their employers intended discrimination, again placing the burden of proof on employees.[69]

In 1995, the Supreme Court's ruling in *Adarand Constructors v. Pena* further weakened affirmative action. This decision stated that race-based policies, such as preferences given by the government to minority contractors, must survive strict scrutiny, placing the burden on the government to show that such affirmative action programs serve a compelling government interest and are narrowly tailored to address identifiable past discrimination.[70] President Clinton responded to the *Adarand* decision by ordering a review of all government affirmative action policies and practices. Although many observers suspected that the president would use the review as an opportunity to back away from affirmative action, the conclusions of the task force largely defended existing policies. Reflecting the influence of the Supreme Court's decision in *Adarand,* President Clinton acknowledged that some government policies would need to change. But on the whole, the review found that most affirmative action policies were fair and did not "unduly burden nonbeneficiaries."[71]

Although Clinton sought to "mend, not end" affirmative action, developments in the courts and the states continued to restrict affirmative action in important ways. One of the most significant was the *Hopwood* case, in which white students challenged admissions practices in the University of Texas Law School, charging that the school's affirmative action program discriminated against whites. In 1996, a federal court (the U.S. Court of Appeals for the Fifth Circuit) ruling on the case stated that race could never be considered in granting admissions and scholarships at state colleges and universities.[72] This decision effectively rolled back the use of affirmative action permitted by the 1978 *Bakke* case. In *Bakke,* as discussed earlier, the Supreme Court had outlawed quotas but said that race could be used as one factor among many in admissions decisions. Many universities and colleges have since justified affirmative action as a way of promoting racial diversity among their student bodies. What was new in the *Hopwood* decision was the ruling that race could *never* be used as a factor in admissions decisions, even to promote diversity.

In 1996, the Supreme Court refused to hear a challenge to the *Hopwood* case. This meant that its ruling remains in effect in the states covered by the Fifth Circuit—Texas, Louisiana, and Mississippi—but does not apply to the rest of the country. The impact of the *Hopwood* ruling is greatest in Texas because Louisiana and Mississippi are under conflicting court orders to desegregate their universities. In Texas, in the year after the *Hopwood* case, minority applications to Texas universities declined. Concerned about the ability of Texas public universities to serve the state's minority students, the Texas legislature quickly passed a new law granting students who graduate in the top 10 percent of their classes automatic admission to the state's public universities. It is hoped that this measure will ensure a racially diverse student body.[73]

The weakening of affirmative action in the courts was underscored in a case the Supreme Court agreed to hear in 1998. A white schoolteacher in New Jersey who had lost her job had sued her school district, charging that her layoff was racially motivated: a black colleague hired on the same day was not laid off. Under President George Bush, the Justice Department had filed a brief on her behalf in 1989, but in 1994 the Clinton administration formally reversed course in a new brief supporting the school district's right to make distinctions based on race as long as it did not involve the use of quotas. Three years later, the administration, worried that the case was weak and could result in a broad decision against affirmative action, reversed course again. It filed a brief with the Court urging a narrow ruling in favor of the dismissed worker. Because the school board had justified its actions on the grounds of preserving diversity, the administration feared that a broad ruling by the Supreme Court could totally prohibit the use of race in employment decisions, even as one factor among many designed to achieve diversity. But before the Court could issue a ruling, a coalition of civil rights groups brokered and arranged to pay for a settlement. This unusual move reflected the widespread fear of a sweeping negative decision. Cases involving dismissals, as the New Jersey case did, are generally viewed as much more difficult to defend than cases that concern hiring. In addition, the particular facts of the New Jersey case—two equally qualified teachers hired on the same day—were seen as unusual and unfavorable to affirmative action.[74]

> **How does affirmative action contribute to the polarization of the politics of civil rights?**

REFERENDUMS ON AFFIRMATIVE ACTION

The courts have not been the only center of action: during the 1990s, challenges to affirmative action also emerged in state and local politics. One of the most significant state actions was the passage of the California Civil Rights Initiative, also known as Proposition 209, in 1996. Proposition 209 outlawed affirmative action programs in the state and local governments of California, thus prohibiting state and local governments from using race or gender preferences in their decisions about hiring, contracting, or university admissions. The political battle over Proposition 209 was heated, and supporters and defenders took to the streets as well as the airwaves to make their cases. When the referendum was held, the measure passed with 54 percent of the vote, including 27 percent of the black vote, 30 percent of the Latino vote, and 45 percent of the Asian American vote.[75] In 1997, the Supreme Court refused to hear a challenge to the new law.

Many observers predicted that the success of California's ban on affirmative action would provoke similar movements in states and localities across the country. But the political factors that contributed to the success of Proposition 209 in California may not exist in many other states. Because public opinion on the issue is very conflicted, the outcome of efforts to roll affirmative action back depends greatly on how the issue is posed to voters. California's Proposition 209 was framed as a civil rights initiative: "the state shall not discriminate against, or grant preferential treatment to, any individual or group on the basis of race, sex, color, ethnicity, or national origin." Different wording can produce quite different outcomes, as a 1997 vote on affirmative action in Houston revealed. There, the ballot initiative asked voters whether they wanted to ban affirmative action in city contracting and hiring, not whether they wanted to end preferential treatment. Fifty-five percent of Houston voters decided in favor of affirmative action.[76]

> **How does the debate about affirmative action reflect the debate over American political values?**

AFFIRMATIVE ACTION AND AMERICAN POLITICAL VALUES

Affirmative action efforts have contributed to the polarization of the politics of civil rights. At the risk of grievous oversimplification, we can divide the sides by two labels: liberals and conservatives.[77] The conservatives' argument against affirmative action can be reduced to two major points. The first is that rights in the American tradition are *individual* rights, and affirmative action violates this concept by concerning itself with "group rights," an idea said to be alien to the American tradition. The second point has to do with quotas. Conservatives would argue that the Constitution is "color-blind," and that any discrimination, even if it is called positive or benign discrimination, ultimately violates the equal protection clause.

The liberal side agrees that rights ultimately come down to individuals, but argues that, since the essence of discrimination is the use of unreasonable and unjust criteria of exclusion to deprive *an entire group* of access to something valuable the society has to offer, then the phenomenon of discrimination itself has to be attacked on a group basis. Liberals can also use Supreme Court history to support their side, because the first definitive interpretation of the Fourteenth Amendment by the Court in 1873 stated explicitly that

> [t]he existence of laws in the state where the newly emancipated Negroes resided, which discriminated with gross injustice and hardship against them *as a class,* was the evil to be remedied by this clause [emphasis added].[78]

Affirmative Action

The sweeping civil rights laws enacted in the 1960s officially ended state-sanctioned segregation. They did not, however, end racism, or erase stark inequities between the races in such areas as employment and education. As a consequence, affirmative action policies were enacted to ensure some equality between the races. In the 1978 case of *Regents of the University of California v. Bakke,* the Supreme Court upheld "race-conscious" policies in educational admissions—meaning that race could be used as an admissions criterion—but barred the use of specific, numerical racial quotas. In recent years, a more conservative Supreme Court has chipped away at the scope of such programs—which, incidentally, have become increasingly unpopular among Americans—suggesting that affirmative action programs might be further restricted or eliminated entirely. In 1997, for example, the Court let stand California's Proposition 209, a statewide referendum passed in 1996 that barred the consideration of race or gender in state hiring and school admissions.

Proponents of affirmative action cite the continued need for such programs, especially for African Americans, because of the nation's long history of discrimination and persecution. Racism was institutionalized throughout most of the country's history; indeed, the Constitution specifically recognized, and therefore countenanced, slavery. For example, it rewarded slaveowners with the Three-fifths Compromise, giving slaveowners extra representation in the House of Representatives, a provision excised from the Constitution only after the Civil War. Moreover, few would deny that racism still exists in America. Given these facts, it follows that equal treatment of unequals perpetuates inequality. Programs that give an extra boost to traditionally disadvantaged groups offer the only sure way to overcome structural inequality.

To take the example of university and college admissions, affirmative action opponents argue that admissions decisions should be based on merit, not race. Yet affirmative action does not disregard merit, and in any case, admissions does not operate purely based on merit, however defined, for any college or university. Institutions of higher education rely on such measures as grade point av-

erage, board scores, and letters of recommendation. But they also consider such nonmerit factors as region, urban vs. rural background, family relationship to alumni and wealthy donors, athletic ability, or other specialized factors unrelated to the usual definition of merit. The inclusion of race as one of these many admissions criteria is as defensible as any other; moreover, it helps ensure a more diverse student body, which in itself is a laudable educational goal. Moreover, such programs do not guarantee educational success, but simply assure that individuals from disadvantaged groups have a chance to succeed, an idea most Americans support. Affirmative action programs have in fact succeeded in providing opportunity to millions who would not otherwise have had the chance.

Opponents of affirmative action argue that such programs, while based on good intentions, do more harm than good. The belief that persons who gain employment or college admission from such programs did not earn their positions stigmatizes those who are supposed to benefit, creating self-doubt among the recipients and mistrust from others. In the realm of education, students admitted to colleges and universities under these special programs have lower graduation rates. Affirmative action also violates the fundamental American value of equality of opportunity. Although all may not possess the same opportunity, the effort expended to provide special advantages to some would be better directed toward making sure that the principles of equal opportunity and merit are followed.

America's history of discrimination, though reprehensible, should not be used as a basis for employment or educational decisions, because it is unreasonable to ask Americans today to pay for the mistakes of their ancestors. Moreover, the track record of affirmative action programs reveals another problem: the groups that have benefited most are middle-class African Americans and women. If anything, preferential programs should focus on *economic* disadvantage, regardless of race, and better education early in life. Good intentions notwithstanding, there are limits to what government social engineering can accomplish, and most Americans favor the abandonment of race-based preference programs.

Is Affirmative Action Fair?

Yes

Affirmative action was first conceived as a policy that could effectively combat the effects of what had been a long history of racial discrimination in the United States. Recently, however, supporters of affirmative action have begun to argue that the program's real justification lies in recognizing the value of racial diversity. Just as it is desirable for the university band to have a drum player and just as it is financially prudent for the admissions committee to admit a sizable number of legacies, it is also a good idea from an educational standpoint to build a racially diverse campus.

Stanford University president Gerhard Caper, for one, has favored this line of argument and chosen to abandon altogether the original social justice rationale. He writes, "University admissions offices are not set up to sit in judgment on what injustices society should compensate for and who should pay the price."

But why not? Society already holds all organizations, private and public, to minimal standards of social justice. Columbia, for instance, cannot deny admissions to an entire racial group, at least not legally. The reason for this is not merely that racial diversity is beneficial to the University, though surely that is true. The reason is instead that the law recognizes that it is simply unfair for a university to exclude members of a particular ethnic group, independent of whether or not it is beneficial for the university to do so.

But social justice demands something more: it demands that both private and public organizations proactively make opportunities available to underrepresented minorities.

Seen this way, affirmative action programs in college admissions are not just a matter of bringing something desirable to the university; they are, more importantly, a matter of entitlement in accordance with the dictates of social justice.

What gives rise to this entitlement is racism and its sinister effects, which are still very much a reality in America today. Take, for example, the well-documented sociological phenomenon popularly termed "white flight," which occurs after an influx of minority families moves into a predominantly white neighborhood. Once the percentage of minorities in the population reaches a certain level, white residents begin to move out, and white families looking for new homes refuse to move in.

This in turn traps the community in a downward spiral of plummeting real estate values, rising crime rates, and deteriorating public schools. Most remarkably, studies done on white flight show that it cannot simply be reduced to the socioeconomic status of the new minority residents. In other words, white flight is not just a case of rich people fleeing increasingly poor communities; it is, at bottom, a case of white people fleeing increasingly minority communities.

The underlying racism reflected in white flight requires some form of redress. And yet there are still cries of "reverse discrimination" from opponents of affirmitive action, cries that innocent whites are somehow being sacrificed in a grand plan of social engineering.

Truly unnerving and self-righteous arrogance is on display when a few people, after being denied admission to their first-choice schools, stand up and loudly proclaim from ther privileged backgrounds, "I deserved a spot at this school, and I would have gotten in if it weren't for affirmative action," as if their being admitted were a matter of divine right not to be tinkered with or stolen away, as if each of them had a spot specially reserved for them and for them only. Little do they realize that they themselves have benefited, have succeeded, directly or indirectly, because of the racism endured by others. Affirmative action does not deprive them of their rights; it strips them of an advantage to which they had no just claim in the first place.

The social justice rationale for affirmative action, though reasonable, has increasingly been seen as deeply paternalistic because of its supposed suggestion that minorities just cannot make it in the real world. Ward Connerly, an anti–affirmative action activist who happens to be half black, has been a poster child for that complaint. "Look at me." he seems to say, "I made it. I am successful in life, and I am black."

But Ward Connerly's success in his professional life does not invalidate the movement for affirmative action today any more than Thurgood Marshall's appointment to the Supreme Court invalidated the civil rights movement thirty years ago. And the fact that a few minorities reject affirmative action certainly does not reflect the vast majority of its beneficiaries who embrace it. No, to ensure equality for all individuals without regard to race is not paternalism. It is fairness, it is social justice, and most of all, it is America.

SOURCE: Tienmu Ma, "Justice and Affirmative Action," *Columbia Daily Spectator,* April 4, 2002.

No I am more than my race, class, and gender. In fact, I'd venture to say that my race, class, and gender probably play a small role in who I truly am. Yet, in the eyes of the University, I'm just another check in a box—another white, middle-class, male applicant.

But does a couple of checkmarks measure what I bring to campus? No, and to think so is to disrespect the very heart of human dignity. We are all much more than just the color of our skin. Yet according to yesterday's ruling, which upheld the Law School's use of racial preferences and the 1978 *Bakke* decision, that is all I am—a nameless, faceless, white guy.

I do not deny that America has a checkered history and I do not deny that enormous social inequality exists. I also believe that something must be done to resolve it, but I don't see how we, as a nation, can reconcile affirmative action and the ultimate goal of a color-blind society when affirmative action is a program that by definition makes judgments based solely on a person's race. How can just ends be achieved by unjust means? Especially when those means do not address the root of the problem or provide the best possible solution.

In the 1950s and 1960s, America decided that judging anyone by their race was inappropriate and, under Title VI of the Civil Rights Act, illegal. But that is exactly what the Sixth Circuit's decision allows and the University practices. Racial preferences in university admissions stand as the last government permissible measures that judge people by their race. How can this stand as a compelling government interest? The government is willing to allow unjust means to accomplish just ends. That is, the Sixth Circuit feels that patently racist admissions policies are A-OK, so long as they promote the dubious concept of academic diversity.

This is an important distinction, insofar as yesterday's decision rejects use of affirmative action to remedy past social injustices or promote social equality of any sort. Under the *Bakke* decision, Justice Powell said that racial preference may only be used as one of the many "plus" factors in admissions and only to create academic diversity.

As a result, the University claims that the necessity of a "critical mass" of minorities, which might as well be a quota system, is a compelling government interest. They contend that the presence of minorities in a law school positively benefits the entire institution. And they also hold that they must admit a "critical mass" of minorities to prevent the others from feeling isolated or lonely.

The problem is that academic diversity is a sham and only a cover for the University's hidden social justice agenda. Never once has an administrator uttered a word about affirmative action and social equality. To do so would be legal suicide, as their cover-up might be exposed and ruled unconstitutional under *Bakke*. Instead, they all toe the diversity line. It is not only disingenuous to the community and legal system, but disrespectful to the very dignity of minorities.

A Coalition to Defend Affirmative Action and Integration and Fight for Equality by Any Means Necessary member once said, "Minorities are not like trees—they can't bring us here to make campus a little prettier." But that is exactly what the administration is doing. The diversity defense does nothing but use minorities to make campus a little more colorful.

The sad fact is that for all the efforts the University has undertaken to create diversity, campus remains largely segregated. From separate but equal residence hall lounges to segregated so-called multicultural student groups, the University community has failed to foster true diversity.

This raises a much broader question: What is diversity?

According to the Law School, it is little more than an applicant's race, class, and gender, but we are much more than that. But the University largely ignores an applicant's true diversity, insofar as real diversity runs counter to the hidden agenda of admitting a large number of minorities to promote social justice. There is no other reason to explain why the University ignores so many other factors. In his dissent, Justice Boggs points out that the University completely disregards many other critical factors influencing diversity, such as religion, geographic region, or political persuasion; at the same time, Jews, Michiganders, and liberals are all overrepresented. Yesterday's ruling supporting the University's idea of diversity is insulting and degrading. It is divisive and runs counter to the very idea of equality.

SOURCE: Justin Wilson, "The Failures of Affirmative Action at the 'U'," *The Michigan Daily*, May 15, 2002.

Table 5.3	Americans' Opinions on Affirmative Action

Responses to the question "What should government's role be in improving the conditions for blacks and other minorities?"

	BLACKS	WHITES
Should government make every effort to improve conditions of blacks and minorities, or	59%	34%
Should government not make any special effort, they should help themselves	30	59

SOURCE: The Gallup Poll, "Black/White Relations in the U.S.," June 10, 1997; www.gallup.com/poll/socialaudits/sa970610.asp (accessed 7/11/02).

Liberals also have a response to the other conservative argument concerning quotas. The liberal response is that the Supreme Court has already accepted ratios—a form of quota—that are admitted as evidence to prove a "pattern or practice of discrimination" sufficient to reverse the burden of proof—to obligate the employer to show that there was *not* an intent to discriminate. Liberals can also argue that benign quotas often have been used by Americans both to compensate for some bad action in the past or to provide some desired distribution of social characteristics—sometimes called diversity. For example, a long and respected policy in the United States is that of "veteran's preference," on the basis of which the government automatically gives extra consideration in hiring to persons who have served the country in the armed forces. The justification is that ex-soldiers deserve compensation for having made sacrifices for the good of the country. And the goal of social diversity has justified "positive discrimination," especially in higher education, the very institution where conservatives have most adamantly argued against positive quotas for blacks and women. For example, all of the Ivy League schools and many other private colleges and universities regularly and consistently reserve admissions places for some students whose qualifications in a strict academic sense are below those of others who are not admitted. These schools not only recruit students from minority groups, but they set aside places for the children of loyal alumni and of their own faculty, even when, in a pure competition solely and exclusively based on test scores and high school records, many of those same children would not have been admitted. These practices are not conclusive justification in themselves, but they certainly underscore the liberal argument that affirmative or compensatory action for minorities who have been unjustly treated in the past is not alien to American experience.

If we think of the debate about affirmative action in terms of American political values, it is clear that conservatives emphasize liberty, whereas liberals stress equality. Conservatives believe that using government actively to promote equality for minorities and women infringes on the rights of white men. Lawsuits challenging affirmative action often cite this "reverse discrimination" as a justification. Liberals, on the other hand, traditionally have defended affirmative action as the best way to achieve equality. In recent years, however, the debate over affirmative action has become more complex and has created divisions among liberals. These divisions stem from growing doubts among some liberals about whether affirmative action can be defended as the best way to achieve equality and about the tensions between affirmative action and democratic values. One recent study of public opinion found that many self-identified liberals were angry about affirmative action.[79] These liberals felt that in the name of equality, affirmative action actually violates norms of fairness and equality of opportunity by giving special advantages to some. Moreover, it is argued, affirmative action is broadly unpopular and is therefore questionable in terms of democratic values. Because our nation has a history of slavery and legalized racial discrimination, and because discrimination continues to exist (although it has declined over time), the question of racial justice, more than any other issue, highlights the difficulty of reconciling our values in practice.

Although the problems of rights in America are agonizing, they can be looked at optimistically. The United States has a long way to go before it constructs a truly just, "equally protected" society. But it also has come very far in a relatively short time. Groups pressing for equality have been able to use government to change a variety of discriminatory practices. The federal government has become an active partner in ensuring civil rights and political equality. All explicit de jure barriers to minorities have been dismantled. Many de facto barriers have also been dismantled, and thousands upon thousands of new opportunities have been opened. Deep and fundamental differences have polarized many Americans (see Table 5.3), but political and governmental institutions have proven themselves capable of maintaining balances between them. This kind of balancing can be done without violence so long as everyone recognizes that policy choices, even about rights, cannot be absolute.

GET INVOLVED What You Can Do: Mobilize for Civil Rights

Citizens have played the leading role in determining the meaning of civil rights, and students have often been in the forefront of conflicts about civil rights. As we saw in the introduction to this chapter, students played a pivotal role in the Civil Rights movement in the 1960s. When the movement seemed to be at an impasse in 1960, students helped to reenergize it with their sit-in at the Woolworth's lunch counter. Sit-ins had been used by labor unions seeking recognition in the 1930s, but it was students who first applied this tactic in civil rights struggles. Likewise, "Freedom Summer," a movement launched in 1964 to register southern blacks to vote, was run by students, four of whom lost their lives registering people to vote that summer.

How have students been involved in civil rights issues in more recent years? Reflecting the conflicting views about what civil rights should mean today, students have been actively involved on both sides of the issue. Students across California were active in the debate about Proposition 209, staging protests and other efforts to persuade voters to reject or support the measure. Since the *Hopwood* decision, students in Texas have held rallies and teach-ins to inform other students about the issues involved. They hope to create a national movement to reinstate affirmative action. Students opposing affirmative action have been less visibly active, but their voices, too, have been heard. For example, the student newspaper at the University of California at Berkeley, *The Californian*, endorsed Proposition 209. Many students on both sides of the issue attended events with speakers presenting arguments for and against affirmative action. Participating in such public events and developing informed opinions is an important kind of political activity.

It is probable that struggles for civil rights are currently taking place on your college campus. Many higher education institutions have student groups organized around specific identities, for example, African American students, Jewish students, women students, gay and lesbian students, and so forth. These identity groups often seek to promote rights and opportunities for their members by appealing for student support and lobbying campus officials to prohibit some activities (such as racist speech) and promote other activities (such as Black History Month). Also, many colleges have campus affiliates of national or international civil rights organizations such as Amnesty International and Human Rights Watch. Numerous campuses have opened up administrative offices aimed at protecting and advancing the civil rights of particular student populations. For example, your school might have a Student Disabilities Office that monitors campus compliance with the Americans with Disabilities Act of 1990.

One way to get involved in the struggle for civil rights is to join a student identity group or volunteer to work in a relevant campus office. Once you have established your presence and membership, consider the range of activities that your group might organize to further the struggle for civil rights. Suppose that your group's immediate goal is to raise campus awareness of civil rights issues. Here are some activities that student groups use to achieve that goal:

- Sponsor a gay and lesbian rights parade.
- Conduct a "Take Back the Night" march opposing violence against women.
- Organize a noon rally to protest the lack of a Latino Studies department.
- Set up a photographic display of human rights violations around the world.
- Hold campus forums designed to facilitate multiracial dialogue and cooperation.

When you plan events, be clear about your goals and match them to appropriate means. Accordingly, you may want to orchestrate highly publicized events to build public support, but you may consider quiet negotiations to work out new policies with campus administration. Finally, learn from the past. Think back to the civil rights struggles of the 1950s and 1960s, study the creative strategies that were used to build a national movement, and then update those strategies and innovate on them to build a foundation for civil rights in the new millennium.

Summary

The constitutional basis of civil rights is the "equal protection" clause. This clause imposes a positive obligation on government to advance civil rights, and its original motivation seems to have been to eliminate the gross injustices suffered by "the newly emancipated Negroes . . . as a class." Civil rights call for the expansion of governmental power rather than restraints upon it. This expanded power allows the government to take an active role in promoting equality. But there was little advancement in the interpretation or application of the "equal protection" clause until after World War II. The major breakthrough came in 1954 with *Brown v. Board of Education,* and advancements came in fits and starts during the succeeding ten years.

After 1964, Congress finally supported the federal courts with effective civil rights legislation that outlawed a number of discriminatory practices in the private sector and provided for the withholding of federal grants-in-aid to any local government, school, or private employer as a sanction to help enforce the civil rights laws. From that point, civil rights developed in two ways. First, the definition of civil rights was expanded to include other, nonblack victims of discrimination. Second, the definition of civil rights became increasingly positive; affirmative action has become an official term. Judicial decisions, congressional statutes, and administrative agency actions all have moved beyond the original goal of eliminating discrimination, toward creating new opportunities for minorities and, in some areas, compensating today's minorities for the consequences of discriminatory actions not directly against them but against members of their group in the past. Because compensatory civil rights action has sometimes relied upon quotas, Americans have engaged in intense debate over the constitutionality as well as the desirability of affirmative action, part of a broader debate over American political values. Citizens' involvement in the civil rights movement played a leading role in determining the meaning of civil rights, although recent conflicts over affirmative action have raised questions about what is effective political action.

The story has not ended and is not likely to end. The politics of rights will remain an important part of American political discourse.

For Further Reading

Garrow, David J. *Bearing the Cross: Martin Luther King and the Southern Christian Leadership Conference: A Personal Portrait.* New York: Morrow, 1986.

Glendon, Mary Ann. *Rights Talk: The Impoverishment of Political Discourse.* New York: Free Press, 1991.

Greenberg, Jack. *Crusaders in the Courts: How a Dedicated Band of Lawyers Fought for the Civil Rights Revolution.* New York: Basic Books, 1994.

Kelly, Christine. *Tangled Up in Red, White, and Blue: Social Movements in America.* New York: Rowman & Littlefield, 2001.

Kinder, Donald, and Lynn Sanders. *Divided by Color: Racial Politics and Democratic Ideals.* Chicago: University of Chicago Press, 1996.

Klinkner, Philip A., and Rogers M. Smith. *The Unsteady March: The Rise and Decline of Racial Equality in America.* Chicago: University of Chicago Press, 1999.

Massey, Douglas S., and Nancy A. Denton. *American Apartheid: Segregation and the Making of the Underclass.* Cambridge, MA: Harvard University Press, 1993.

Mink, Gwendolyn. *Hostile Environment: The Political Betrayal of Sexually Harassed Women.* Ithaca, NY: Cornell University Press, 1999.

Nava, Michael. *Created Equal: Why Gay Rights Matter to America.* New York: St. Martin's, 1994.

Rosenberg, Gerald N. *The Hollow Hope: Can Courts Bring About Social Change?* Chicago: University of Chicago Press, 1991.

Study Outline

www.wwnorton.com/wtp4e

The Struggle for Civil Rights

1. From 1896 until the end of World War II, the Supreme Court held that the Fourteenth Amendment's equal protection clause was not violated by racial distinction as long as the facilities were equal.

2. After World War II, the Supreme Court began to undermine the separate but equal doctrine, eventually declaring it unconstitutional in *Brown v. Board of Education.*

3. The *Brown* decision marked the beginning of a difficult battle for equal protection in education, employment, housing, voting, and other areas of social and economic activity.

4. The first phase of school desegregation was met with such massive resistance in the South that, ten years after *Brown,* fewer than 1 percent of black children in the South were attending schools with whites.

5. In 1971, the Supreme Court held that state-imposed desegregation could be brought about by busing children across school districts.

6. Title VII of the Civil Rights Act of 1964 outlawed job discrimination by all private and public employers, including governmental agencies, that employed more than fifteen workers.

7. In 1965, Congress significantly strengthened legislation protecting voting rights by barring literacy and other tests as a condition for voting in southern states. In the long run, the laws extending and protecting voting rights could prove to be the most effective of all civil rights legislation, because increased political participation by minorities has altered the shape of American politics.

The Universalization of Civil Rights

1. The protections won by the African American civil rights movement spilled over to protect other groups as well, including women, Latinos, Asian Americans, Native Americans, disabled Americans, and gays and lesbians.

Affirmative Action

1. By seeking to provide compensatory action to overcome the consequences of past discrimination, affirmative action represents the expansion of the goals of groups championing minority rights.

2. Affirmative action has been a controversial policy. Opponents charge that affirmative action creates group rights and establishes quotas, both of which are inimical to the American tradition. Proponents of affirmative action argue that the long history of group discrimination makes affirmative action necessary and that efforts to compensate for some bad action in the past are well within the federal government's purview. Recent conflicts over affirmative action have raised questions about what is effective political action.

Practice Quiz

www.wwnorton.com/wtp4e

1. When did civil rights become part of the Constitution?
   a) in 1789 at the Founding
   b) with the adoption of the Fourteenth Amendment in 1868
   c) with the adoption of the Nineteenth Amendment in 1920
   d) in the 1954 *Brown v. Board of Education* case

2. Which civil rights case established the "separate but equal" rule?
   a) *Plessy v. Ferguson*
   b) *Brown v. Board of Education*
   c) *Bakke v. Regents of the University of California*
   d) *Adarand Constructors v. Pena*

3. "Massive resistance" refers to efforts by southern states during the late 1950s and early 1960s to
   a) build public housing for poor blacks.
   b) defy federal mandates to desegregate public schools.
   c) give women the right to have an abortion.
   d) bus black students to white schools.

4. Which of the following organizations established a Legal Defense Fund to challenge segregation?
   a) the Association of American Trial Lawyers
   b) the National Association for the Advancement of Colored People
   c) the Student Nonviolent Coordinating Committee
   d) the Southern Christian Leadership Council

5. Which of the following made discrimination by private employers and state governments illegal?
   a) the Fourteenth Amendment
   b) *Brown v. Board of Education*
   c) the 1964 Civil Rights Act
   d) *Bakke v. Board of Regents*

6. In what way does the struggle for gender equality most resemble the struggle for racial equality?
   a) There has been very little political action in realizing the goal.
   b) Changes in government policies to a great degree produced political action.
   c) The Supreme Court has not ruled on the issue.
   d) No legislation has passed adopting the aims of the movement.

7. Which of the following is *not* an example of an area in which women have made progress since the 1970s in guaranteeing certain civil rights?
   a) sexual harassment
   b) integration into all-male publicly supported universities
   c) more equal funding for college women's varsity athletic programs
   d) the passage of the Equal Rights Amendment

8. Which of the following civil rights measures dealt with access to public businesses and accommodations?
   a) the 1990 Americans with Disabilities Act
   b) the 1964 Civil Rights Act
   c) neither a nor b
   d) both a and b

9. Which of the following cases represents the *Brown v. Board of Education* case for lesbians and gay men?
   a) *Bowers v. Hardwick*
   b) *Lau v. Nichols*
   c) *Romer v. Evans*
   d) There has not been a Supreme Court ruling explicitly protecting gays and lesbians from discrimination.

10. In what case did the Supreme Court find that "rigid quotas" are incompatible with the equal protection clause of the Fourteenth Amendment?
    a) *Bakke v. Board of Regents*
    b) *Brown v. Board of Education*
    c) *United States v. Nixon*
    d) *Immigration and Naturalization Service v. Chadha*

Critical Thinking Questions

www.wwnorton.com/wtp4e

1. Supporters of affirmative action argue that it is intended not only to compensate for past discrimination, but also to level an uneven playing field in which discrimination still exists. What do you think? To what extent do we have a society free from discrimination? What is the impact of affirmative action on society today? What alternatives to affirmative action policies exist?

2. Describe the changes in American society between the *Plessy v. Ferguson* and the *Brown v. Board of Education* decisions. Using this as an example, explain how changes in society can lead to changes in civil rights policy or other types of government policy. How might changes in society have predicted the changes in civil rights policy in America since the *Brown* case? How might the changes in civil rights policy have changed American society?

3. When airline security officials depart from their policy of random passenger searches to detain persons for inspection who appear to be from the general region of the Middle East, is this a case of "ethnic profiling," in violation of civil rights laws, or is it a reasonable, legal, constitutional exception to civil rights under the equal protection clause?

Key Terms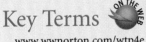

www.wwnorton.com/wtp4e

affirmative action (p. 191)
Brown v. Board of Education (p. 169)
civil rights (p. 162)
de facto (p. 169)

de jure (p. 169)
discrimination (p. 162)
equal protection clause (p. 162)
Fifteenth Amendment (p. 164)
Fourteenth Amendment (p. 164)
gerrymandering (p. 179)
intermediate scrutiny (p. 183)

Jim Crow (p. 165)
redlining (p. 180)
"separate but equal" rule (p. 166)
strict scrutiny (p. 169)
Thirteenth Amendment (p. 164)

Part II

POLITICS

6 PUBLIC OPINION

★ **Political Values**

In what ways do Americans agree on fundamental values but disagree on fundamental issues?

How are political values and beliefs formed? What influences individuals' political beliefs?

What do the differences between liberals and conservatives reveal about American political debate?

★ **How We Form Political Opinions**

What influences the way we form political opinions?

How are political issues marketed and managed by the government, private groups, and the media?

★ **Measuring Public Opinion**

How can public opinion be measured?

What problems arise from public opinion polling?

★ **Public Opinion and Democracy**

How responsive is the government to public opinion?

What Government Does and Why It Matters

OST AMERICANS BELIEVE that in a democracy it is the duty of the government to heed public opinion. This is one reason the government works hard to structure the range of opinions citizens are likely to voice. Lest this assertion appears to smack of totalitarianism and "Big Brother," consider the role of public and publicly mandated education in our society. Through the educational system, children learn about the nation's history, institutions, and political values, and they are taught ways of expressing their opinions in the political arena. It is doubtful whether any nation could survive if it failed to teach its citizens a common set of values and beliefs. Ironically, it is the government's role to teach citizens some of the ways they can influence the government. This entire process is called civic education. Traditionally, American civic education has been the domain of local public schools operating under guidelines developed by the various state governments.

In the elementary and secondary schools, through formal instruction and, more subtly, through the frequent administration of class and school elections, students are taught the importance of the electoral process. By contrast, little attention is given to lawsuits, direct action, organizing, parliamentary procedures, lobbying, or other possible modes of participation. For example, the techniques involved in organizing a sit-in or protest march are seldom part of an official school course of study.[1]

Although secondary-school students periodically elect student government representatives rather than classroom helpers and are given more sophisticated illustrations than kickball team elections, the same principle continues to be taught, in compliance with legal requirements. College students are also frequently given the opportunity to elect senators, representatives, and the like to serve on the largely ornamental representative bodies that are to be found at most institutions of higher learning. Obviously, civic education is not always completely successful. Rather than relying on the electoral process, people continue to demonstrate, sit in, and picket for various political causes. Many people also choose not to participate at all.

Civic education, of course, does not end with formal schooling. Early training is supplemented by a variety of mechanisms, ranging from the official celebration of national holidays to the activities of private patriotic and political organizations. Election campaigns themselves are occasions for the reinforcement of training to vote. Campaigns and political conventions include a good deal of oratory designed to remind citizens of the importance of voting and the democratic significance of elections. Parties and candidates, even if for selfish reasons, emphasize the value of participation, of "being counted," and the virtues of elections as instruments of popular government. Exposure to such campaign stimuli appears generally to heighten citizens' awareness of the political process. ■

DOES civic education work? In recent years, American politics seem to have some lost some of its vitality, as growing numbers of citizens have turned away from politics. Participation in most kinds of political activities—with the exception of contributing money—is declining. Instead of a distinctively American optimism, a sense of pessimism pervades our politics. Individuals express a sense of powerlessness, frustration, and disengagement from the political system. Among youth such feelings are especially strong. Many students feel that the political system is not relevant to their lives and that politics will not solve the problems in the world. Only about one in five eighteen- to twenty-year-olds vote, and political organizations that aim to represent the views of young people have a hard time staying afloat.[2] Why is this? What can be done to counteract this disturbing trend?

One solution that has been implemented in many areas of the country is "service learning." Though we generally conceive participation to connote voluntarism, in some areas of the country young people are actually being required to participate in community or civic affairs. For example, the state of Maryland now mandates fulfillment of a "student service learning" requirement as a condition for high school graduation. Students must sign up for public service jobs with charitable, civic, and public interest groups. These jobs, usually undertaken in conjunction with class work, include work with public interest groups such as the Sierra

Club, positions in hospitals and nursing homes, shopping for the elderly, caring for abandoned animals, teaching ecology lessons to small children, and demonstrating eighteenth-century farm crafts including yo-yo making.[3] Students who fail to complete the requisite number of service hours are not allowed to graduate. In 1998, thirty Maryland high school students were denied diplomas because they did not meet their obligation to provide seventy-five hours of community service over four years.[4] Other states are beginning to follow the Maryland example.

At the college level, the presidents of fifty-one American colleges and universities signed a declaration of their commitment to civic responsibility and community participation in July 1999. The declaration called upon colleges to encourage their students to learn about and engage in politics and community service. The declaration came at a conference sponsored by Campus Compact, a fifteen-year-old organization based at Brown University and composed of more than 540 college and university presidents who support the integration of public and community service into academic studies.[5] At the same time, California governor Gray Davis proposed that community service be made a mandatory requirement for graduation from California's public colleges and universities. It remains to be seen whether these efforts will change citizens' attitudes about government and politics.

Public opinion is the term used to denote the values and attitudes that people have about issues, events, and personalities. Although the terms are sometimes used interchangeably, it is useful to distinguish between values and beliefs on the one hand, and attitudes or opinions on the other. **Values (or beliefs)** are a person's basic orientations to politics. Values represent deep-rooted goals, aspirations, and ideals that shape an individual's perceptions of political issues and events. Liberty, equality, and democracy are basic political values that most Americans hold. Another useful term for understanding public opinion is *ideology*. **Political ideology** refers to a complex set of beliefs and values that, as a whole, form a general philosophy about government. As we shall see, liberalism and conservatism are important ideologies in America today.

For example, the idea that governmental solutions to problems are inherently inferior to solutions offered by the private sector is a belief held by many Americans. This general belief, in turn, may lead individuals to have negative views of specific government programs even before they know much about them. An **attitude (or opinion)** is a specific view about a particular issue, personality, or event. An individual may have an opinion about Bill Clinton or an attitude toward American policy in Bosnia. The attitude or opinion may have emerged from a broad belief about Democrats or military intervention, but an attitude itself is very specific. Some attitudes may be short-lived.

This chapter will examine the role of public opinion in American politics.

- **First, we examine the political values and beliefs that inform how Americans perceive the political process.** After reviewing the most basic American political values, we analyze how values and beliefs are formed and how certain processes and institutions influence their formation. We conclude this introductory section by looking at how a person's set of values and beliefs relates to political ideology.

- **Second, we turn to the process of how political opinions are formed.** We begin by assessing the relative importance of ideology in this process. We then look at

public opinion citizens' attitudes about political issues, leaders, institutions, and events

values (or beliefs) basic principles that shape a person's opinions about political issues and events

political ideology a cohesive set of beliefs that forms a general philosophy about the role of government

attitude (or opinion) a specific preference on a particular issue

the roles that one's knowledge of politics and influence of political leaders, private groups, and the media have on the formation of political views.

■ **Third, we view the science of gathering and measuring public opinion.** The reliability of public opinion is directly related to the way in which it is gathered. Despite the limitations of public opinion polls, they remain an important part of the American political process.

■ **Finally, we conclude with an assessment of the implications of public opinion on American democracy.** Is government responsive to public opinion? Should it be?

Political Values

When we think of opinion, we often think in terms of differences of opinion. The media are fond of reporting and analyzing political differences between blacks and whites, men and women (the so-called gender gap), the young and old, and so on. Certainly, Americans differ on many issues, and often these differences do seem to be associated with race, religion, gender, age, or other social characteristics. Today, Americans seem sharply divided on truly fundamental questions about the role of government in American society, the proper place of religious and moral values in public life, and how best to deal with racial conflicts.

FUNDAMENTAL VALUES

> **In what ways do Americans agree on fundamental values but disagree on fundamental issues?**

equality of opportunity a widely shared American ideal that all people should have the freedom to use whatever talents and wealth they have to reach their fullest potential

liberty freedom from government control

democracy a system of rule that permits citizens to play a significant part in the governmental process, usually through the election of key public officials

As we review these differences, however, it is important to remember that Americans also agree on a number of matters. Indeed, most Americans share a common set of values, including a belief in the principles—if not always the actual practice—of liberty, equality, and democracy. **Equality of opportunity** has always been an important theme in American society. Americans believe that all individuals should be allowed to seek personal and material success. Moreover, Americans generally believe that such success should be linked to personal effort and ability, rather than to family "connections" or other forms of special privilege. Similarly, Americans have always voiced strong support for the principle of individual **liberty.** They typically support the notion that governmental interference with individuals' lives and property should be kept to the minimum consistent with the general welfare (although in recent years Americans have grown accustomed to greater levels of governmental intervention than would have been deemed appropriate by the founders of liberal theory). And most Americans also believe in **democracy.** They presume that every person should have the opportunity to take part in the nation's governmental and policy-making processes and to have some "say" in determining how they are governed.[6] Figure 6.1 on the next page offers some indication of this American consensus on fundamental values: 95 percent of those polled believed in equal opportunity, 89 percent supported free speech regardless of the views being expressed, and 95 percent supported majority rule.

One indication that Americans of all political stripes share these fundamental political values is the content of the acceptance speeches delivered by Al Gore and George W. Bush upon receiving their parties' presidential nominations in 2000. Gore and Bush differed on many issues and policies. Yet the political visions they presented reveal an underlying similarity. A major emphasis of both candidates

Americans' Support for Fundamental Values

Figure 6.1

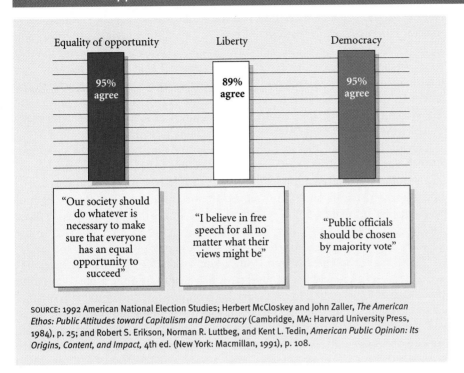

SOURCE: 1992 American National Election Studies; Herbert McCloskey and John Zaller, *The American Ethos: Public Attitudes toward Capitalism and Democracy* (Cambridge, MA: Harvard University Press, 1984), p. 25; and Robert S. Erikson, Norman R. Luttbeg, and Kent L. Tedin, *American Public Opinion: Its Origins, Content, and Impact,* 4th ed. (New York: Macmillan, 1991), p. 108.

was equality of opportunity. Gore referred frequently to opportunity in his speeches, as in this poignant story about his own parents' efforts to make better lives for themselves and their children:

> My father grew up in a small community named Possum Hollow in Middle Tennessee. When he was just eighteen he went to work as a teacher in a one-room school. . . . He entered public service to fight for the people. My mother grew up in a small farming community in northwest Tennessee. She went on to become one of the first women in history to graduate from Vanderbilt Law School. . . . Every hard-working family in America deserves to open the door to their dream.

Bush struck a similar note in his acceptance speech:

> We will seize this moment of American promise. . . . And we will extend the promise of prosperity to every forgotten corner of this country. To every man and woman, a chance to succeed. To every child, a chance to learn. To every family, a chance to live with dignity and hope.

Thus, however much the two candidates differed on means and specifics, their understandings of the fundamental goals of government were quite similar.

Agreement on fundamental political values, though certainly not absolute, is probably more widespread in the United States than anywhere else in the Western world. During the course of Western political history, competing economic, social, and political groups put forward a variety of radically divergent views, opinions, and political philosophies. America has never been socially or economically homogeneous. But two forces that were extremely powerful and important sources of ideas and beliefs elsewhere in the world were relatively weak or absent in the United States. First, the United States never had the feudal aristocracy that dominated so much of European history. Second, for reasons including America's prosperity and the early availability of political rights, no socialist movements comparable to those that developed in nineteenth-century Europe were ever able to establish themselves in the United States. As a result, during the course of American history, there existed neither an aristocracy to assert the virtues of inequality, special privilege, and a rigid class structure, nor a powerful American communist or socialist party to seriously challenge the desirability of limited government and individualism.[7]

Obviously, the principles that Americans espouse have not always been put into practice. For two hundred years, Americans were able to believe in the principles of equality of opportunity and individual liberty while denying them in practice to generations of African Americans. Yet it is important to note that the strength of the principles ultimately helped to overcome practices that deviated from those principles. Proponents of slavery and, later, of segregation, were defeated in the arena of public opinion because their practices differed so sharply from the fundamental principles accepted by most Americans. Ironically, in contemporary politics, Americans' fundamental commitment to equality of opportunity has led to divisions over racial policy. In particular, both proponents and opponents of affirmative action programs cite their belief in equality of opportunity as the justification for their position. Proponents see these programs as necessary to ensure equality of opportunity, while opponents believe that affirmative action is a form of preferential treatment that violates basic American values.[8]

FORMS OF DISAGREEMENT

Agreement on fundamentals by no means implies that Americans do not differ with one another on a wide variety of issues. American political life is characterized by vigorous debate on economic policy, foreign policy, and social policy issues; race relations; environmental affairs; and a host of other matters. At times, even in America, disagreement on issues becomes so sharp that the proponents of particular points of view have sought to stifle political debate by declaring their opponents' positions to be too repulsive to be legitimately discussed. During the 1950s, for example, some ultraconservatives sought to outlaw the expression of opinions they deemed to be "communistic." Often this label was applied as a way of discrediting what were essentially liberal views. In the 1990s, some groups sought to discredit conservatives by accusing them of racism, sexism, and homophobia when their views have not agreed with more liberal sentiments. On a number of university campuses, some African American and feminist groups have advocated the adoption of speech codes outlawing expression seen as insulting to individuals on the basis of their race or gender. In general, however, efforts to regulate the expression of opinion in this way have not been very successful in the United States. Americans believe strongly in free speech and prefer the hidden regulatory hand of the market to the heavier regulatory hand of the law. Many of the universities that initially adopted speech codes have been forced to rescind them.[9]

As we shall see later in this chapter, differences of political opinion are often associated with such variables as income, education, and occupation. Similarly, factors

Gay Marriage

The idea that all Americans are entitled to equal treatment is today a widely accepted principle. More controversial, however, is the matter of how that principle ought to apply to homosexuals. Most Americans embrace a live-and-let-live philosophy regarding homosexuality; at the same time, however, many Americans are uneasy with some highly publicized efforts to define or extend civil rights for gays. This unease is reflected in voters' rejection of some local and state resolutions barring discrimination based on sexual preference.

Central to this debate has been the question of whether states should officially sanction gay marriage. Marriage itself is a private decision, but such a union between two people must also be approved by the state through the issuance of a marriage license if the couple is to receive many of the benefits of marriage, from tax breaks to insurance protection. Complicating this debate is the "full faith and credit" clause of the Constitution (Article IV, Section 1), which says that all states must honor the public acts of any other state, including marriage licenses. Thus, if gay marriage is recognized in even one state, other states are obliged to recognize its legality, too. In 1996, Congress enacted the Defense of Marriage Act, which provided that no state was required to recognize a same-sex marriage performed in another state. Now that Vermont has legalized same-sex marriage, a constitutional test of the Defense of Marriage Act is likely to come before the Supreme Court.

Supporters of gay marriage point out that homosexuality is neither a fad nor a choice, but an involuntary condition. Given this, loving relationships are inevitable, and it is a denial of equality to discriminate against gays because they seek the same bond of marriage as heterosexuals. The objective is not to elevate gay rights above those of other persons, but to end discrimination against gays. Civil marriage for gays would amount to formal public recognition of a homosexual union, making it in principle the same as a heterosexual marriage—that is, a formal recognition of a lifelong emotional commitment of two people to each other—ending the hypocrisy of pretending that a gay union is somehow less loving or less important

than a heterosexual one. Such recognition would actually encourage traditional values of fidelity and stability among homosexuals. It would also ease financial, insurance, and other problems, because gay partners could receive health, life insurance, and pension benefits, and it would clarify such matters as inheritance, property, and adoption rights. Some localities have extended such rights through domestic-partnership laws, but these enactments are relatively uncommon and vary in their applicability. Gay marriage would not demean heterosexual marriage; rather, it would help promote the traditional virtues of marriage.

Opponents of gay marriage argue that marriage, as it is traditionally defined by law and religion, does and ought to apply only to heterosexual unions. If state governments officially sanctioned gay marriage, they would, in effect, be endorsing a lifestyle that society simply does not equate with heterosexual marriage. Law reflects society's moral values, and those values do not countenance gay unions. Furthermore, a traditional purpose of marriage is the creation of children, and that cannot occur within the confines of a gay marriage (without the intervention of a third person). Many gay couples would seek to adopt children, but not enough research exists to demonstrate whether children would be harmed by such a situation.

Opponents say that far from elevating traditional marriage values, state sanctioning of gay marriage would demean heterosexual marriage at a time when that venerable institution is being rocked by high divorce rates, spousal abuse, juvenile delinquency, and more single-parent families. The use of domestic-partnership laws can provide a remedy for problems related to insurance, inheritance, and the like, without taking the more extreme step of officially sanctioning gay marriage. Above all, marriage represents the union of a man and a woman. Efforts to redefine this relationship by incorporating gay unions violate long and deeply held societal principles of right and wrong. One can still support the right of individuals to engage in consensual behavior in private without embracing public recognition of such activity.

Should Gay Marriage Be Legal?

Yes

In the spring when the weather is inviting, it is especially difficult to sit down and concentrate on the work at hand. As a result, I found myself zoning in and out of my reading more than usual.

I was reading John Locke's "A Letter Concerning Toleration" for a politics class I'm taking. I was struggling to stay awake when a passage caught my eye: "But Idolatry (say some) is a sin, and therefore not to be tolerated. If they said it were therefore to be avoided, the Inference were good. But it does not follow, that because it is a sin it ought therefore to be punished by the Magistrate. The reason is because they are not prejudicial to other men's Rights, nor do they break the publick Peace of Societies."

After reading this, I glanced over at the newspaper. It contained two articles of interest: The first outlined the March 16 decision by the Vermont House of Representatives to approve a bill creating civil unions for gay couples. The second discussed California's controversial Proposition 22, which, in early March, revised the California Family Code to say that "Only marriage between a man and a woman is valid or recognized in California."

It's easy to convince yourself that a liberal arts education is wholly impractical—I've done it before, and I find it a tempting conclusion. But at their best, works by Locke and other long-dead writers can form attitudes. They mold our beliefs and shape the way we act.

In my case, I had been struggling with the issue of gay marriage. On the one hand, as a reader wrote to the New York Times on March 4, "Marriage is not a perfect institution, but there is no reason to redefine, confuse and compromise it by legalizing gay marriage; the well-being of our society hinges on the strength of our families."

On the other hand, it is argued, homosexuals should be treated no differently than heterosexuals and should have the option of marriage under the law. Both sides offer a reasonable view, so how do we decide where to stand? John Locke, writing on the subject of religious tolerance, hints at a solution. If we substitute the phrase "gay marriage" for "Idolatry" in the excerpt from his letter above, we find a very plausible reason to oppose Proposition 22 and applaud the bill in Vermont. Locke would urge us to ignore the question of the "sinfulness" of gay marriages (though this judgment underlies much anti-gay rhetoric) and ask whether it would affect the rights of others and whether it would disrupt the stability of society.

The first concern can be dismissed easily. Only the rights of the couples' (adopted) children would be affected by gay marriages. But this is a separate issue—even if gay marriage were legalized, the rearing of children by gay couples could still be barred.

The second concern is more valid. Isn't it possible that by allowing gay couples to get married, we are in some way compromising the respected nature of marriage? I hope the word "respected" provokes a chuckle. Nowadays, when divorce seems to be the norm, and single parents are often forced to raise their kids on meager incomes, nuclear families and "sacred" marriages are often the exception to the rule.

Furthermore, how exactly does gay marriage "devalue" the institution of marriage? It is foolish to insist that marriage has always been between a man and a woman and is therefore the best arrangement.

Why is it considered a good arrangement? Perhaps because it creates a stable, loving relationship that helps foster values and raise children. But if that's so, what precludes gay couples from achieving those same lofty goals?

Furthermore, interracial marriages, which are now widely accepted—even at Bob Jones University—were opposed for the same reasons that gay marriages are opposed now. This should make us very wary of the anti-gay marriage argument. In truth, violence on television is more of a disruption to society than gay marriage.

We are entitled to disapprove of gay marriage; we may even think it's sinful. But with a nod to Locke, we should acknowledge that there is no good reason to outlaw it. If this is a valid and well-supported conclusion, which I strongly believe it is, then we ought to be worried.

Despite the success in Vermont, more than thirty states have already passed bills that prohibit gay marriage and refuse to recognize gay marriages that were performed elsewhere. This is a troubling form of intolerance. But if there is one lesson Locke tried to teach us, it is that despite our moral objections, we must still embrace tolerance.

SOURCE: Jeff Wolf, "States Should Not Legislate Morality by Outlawing Gay Marriage," *The Daily Princetonian,* March 27, 2000.

No

In his March 27 editorial, Jeff Wolf sought to defend homosexual marriages as perfectly legitimate and thus deserving of the same legal status as heterosexual unions. To this end, he called upon our collective sense of tolerance and even summoned the ghost of John Locke to provide a sort of historical imperative on which we, as good liberals, must act. But despite a valiant attempt to seize the moral high ground on this issue, his argument does not convince me that homosexual marriages and traditional marriages should be considered equals.

Wolf suggests that tolerance toward homosexuals depends on whether or not we approve of an equal legal status for gay marriages. I would point out that one can question the legality of gay marriages while affirming that homosexuals are entitled to the same basic liberties and opportunities as everyone else. The problem comes when we play around with Wolf's idea that marriage is as fundamental a liberty as religious freedom or speech.

Marriage is not an inalienable right on the same plane with First Amendment freedoms. Rather, it is a contract that must be willingly entered into and can be legally terminated. We do not consider religious freedom or speech to be of this nature because individuals do not need permission to exercise these rights, nor can they be easily annulled. Therefore, we can challenge the idea that homosexual marriage is a right while maintaining that homosexuals themselves are deserving of the constitutional rights given to everyone.

If you are willing to agree that marriage rights are not universal but are within the domain of the legislature to determine, then you must be willing to agree that the general public has a legitimate voice in the process. As far as I can tell, the general public has definitely exercised that voice in numerous referenda on the issue of gay marriage. Now of course, ethical and religious values have played a key role in deciding the outcome of these referenda, but in any deliberation, the voter is free to use whatever criteria he or she desires to come to a conclusion.

So to me, the issue is not whether marriage is a basic right that must be protected in all circumstances, but really whether or not we like the morality of the public in legitimate decision-making processes. Wolf apparently does not like the widespread public opinion that marriage should continue to be defined as the union between a man and a woman. I think that to stand up and say that the morality of the large majority of voters is incorrect and your own morality is somehow intrinsically superior is arrogant at best and despicable at worst.

I am not convinced that homosexuals have some kind of natural right to marriage nor am I impressed by the condemnation of the religious and ethical values of the general public. We can all work toward tolerance in our society, but this means not only accepting that all individuals, regardless of sexual orientation, are guaranteed basic rights under the law, but also respecting the right of the public to express its moral values in legal referenda and through its representatives in the legislature.

SOURCE: Joel R. Wuthnow, "Gay Marriage an Issue of Moral Grounds, Not Rights," *The Daily Princetonian,* March 30, 2000.

One of the hallmarks of American democracy has been vigorous debate on important policy issues. During the 1960s and early 1970s, anti–Vietnam War protestors staged numerous demonstrations across the nation in opposition to America's foreign policies in Southeast Asia (above). Public opposition to the war and the draft played a major role in forcing President Richard Nixon to withdraw American military forces from Vietnam.

In recent years, differences of opinion on such issues as welfare policy, environmental policy, and economic policy have also sparked protests and demonstrations. For example, the environmental group Greenpeace regularly demonstrates in Washington, D.C. (top right).

With the exception of the 1999 Seattle demonstrations protesting the policies of the World Trade Organization (right), though, demonstrations have generally been peaceful.

such as race, gender, ethnicity, age, religion, and region, which not only influence individuals' interests but also shape their experiences and upbringing, have enormous influence on their beliefs and opinions. For example, individuals whose incomes differ substantially have different views on the desirability of a number of important economic and social programs. In general, the poor—who are the chief beneficiaries of these programs—support them more strongly than do those who are more wealthy, and pay more of the taxes that fund the programs. Similarly, blacks and whites have different views on questions of civil rights and civil liberties—presumably reflecting differences of interest and historical experience. In recent years, many observers have begun to take note of a number of differences between the views expressed by men and those supported by women, especially on foreign policy questions, where women appear to be much more concerned with the dangers of war, and on social welfare issues, where women show more concern than men for the problems of the poor and the unfortunate. Let us see how such differences develop.

Many of the young people who engaged in protest politics in the 1960s, such as the Reverend Jesse Jackson or National Organization for Women president Partricia Ireland, became actively engaged in electoral politics in the 1970s and later years, forming the base of the consumer, environmental, and feminist movements. Throughout the course of American political history, protest politics has generally been eventually channeled into the electoral arena, where Americans with differences of opinion have continued to work for the election of competing candidates and political parties, allowing differences of opinion to be expressed in ways that do not disrupt civic life.

HOW POLITICAL VALUES ARE FORMED

The attitudes that individuals hold about political issues and personalities tend to be shaped by their underlying political beliefs and values. For example, an individual who has basically negative feelings about government intervention into America's economy and society would probably be predisposed to oppose the development of new health care and social programs. Similarly, someone who distrusts the military would likely be suspicious of any call for the use of American troops. The processes through which these underlying political beliefs and values are formed are collectively called **political socialization.**

The process of political socialization is important. Probably no nation, and certainly no democracy, could survive if its citizens did not share some fundamental beliefs. If Americans had few common values or perspectives, it would be very difficult for them to reach agreement on particular issues. In contemporary America, some elements of the socialization process tend to produce differences in outlook, whereas others promote similarities. Four of the most important **agencies of socialization** that foster differences in political perspectives are the family, membership in social groups, education, and prevailing political conditions.

No inventory of agencies of socialization can fully explain the development of a given individual's basic political beliefs. In addition to the factors that are important for everyone, forces that are unique to each individual play a role in shaping political orientations. For one person, the character of an early encounter with a member of another racial group can have a lasting impact on that individual's view of the world. For another, a highly salient political event, such as the Vietnam War, can leave an indelible mark on that person's political consciousness. For a third person, some deepseated personality characteristic, such as paranoia, for example, may strongly influence the formation of political beliefs. Nevertheless, knowing that we cannot fully explain the development of any given individual's political outlook, let us look at some of the most important agencies of socialization that do affect one's beliefs.

> **How are political values and beliefs formed? What influences individuals' political beliefs?**

political socialization the induction of individuals into the political culture; learning the underlying beliefs and values upon which the political system is based

agencies of socialization social institutions, including families and schools, that help to shape individuals' basic political beliefs and values

INFLUENCES ON OUR POLITICAL VALUES

The Family   Most people acquire their initial orientation to politics from their families. As might be expected, differences in family background tend to produce divergent political outlooks. Although relatively few parents spend much time teaching their children about politics, political conversations occur in many households and children tend to absorb the political views of parents and other caregivers, perhaps without realizing it. Studies have suggested, for example, that party preferences are initially acquired at home. Children raised in households in which the primary caregivers are Democrats tend to become Democrats themselves, whereas children raised in homes where their caregivers are Republicans tend to favor the GOP (Grand Old Party, a traditional nickname for the Republican Party).[10] Similarly, children reared in politically liberal households are more likely than not to develop a liberal outlook, whereas children raised in politically conservative settings are prone to see the world through conservative lenses. Obviously, not all children absorb their parents' political views. Two of former conservative Republican president Ronald Reagan's three children, for instance, rejected their parents' conservative values. Moreover, even those children whose views are initially shaped by parental values may change their minds as they mature and experience political life for themselves. Nevertheless, the family is an important initial source of political orientation for everyone.

Social Groups   Another important source of divergent political orientations and values are the social groups to which individuals belong. Social groups include those to which individuals belong involuntarily—gender and racial groups, for example—as well as those to which people belong voluntarily—such as political parties, labor unions, and educational and occupational groups. Some social groups have both voluntary and involuntary attributes. For example, individuals are born with a particular social-class background, but as a result of their own efforts people may move up—or down—the class structure.

Membership in social groups can affect political values in a variety of ways. Membership in a particular group can give individuals important experiences and perspectives that shape their view of political and social life. In American society, for example, the experiences of blacks and whites can differ significantly. Blacks are a minority and have been victims of persecution and discrimination throughout American history. Blacks and whites also have different educational and occupational opportunities, often live in separate communities, and may attend separate schools. Such differences tend to produce distinctive political outlooks. For example, in 1995 blacks and whites had very different reactions to the murder trial of former football star O. J. Simpson, who was accused of killing his ex-wife and one of her friends. Seventy percent of the white Americans surveyed believed that Simpson was guilty, based on the evidence presented by the police and prosecutors. But an identical 70 percent of the black Americans surveyed immediately after the trial believed that the police had fabricated evidence and had sought to convict Simpson of a crime he had not committed; these beliefs were presumably based on blacks' experiences with and perceptions of the criminal justice system.[11]

According to other recent surveys, blacks and whites in the United States differ on a number of issues. For example, among middle-income Americans (defined as those earning between $30,000 and $75,000 per year), 65 percent of black respondents and only 35 percent of white respondents thought racism was a major problem in the United States today. Within this same group of respondents, 63 percent of blacks and only 39 percent of whites thought the federal government should provide more services even at the cost of higher taxes.[12] Other issues show a similar pattern of disagreement, reflecting the differences in experience, background, and interests between blacks and whites in America (see Figure 6.2 on the next page).

Men and women have important differences of opinion as well. Reflecting differences in social roles, political experience, and occupational patterns, women tend to be less militaristic than men on issues of war and peace, more likely than men to favor measures to protect the environment, and more supportive than men of government social and health care programs (see Table 6.1). Perhaps because of these differences on issues, women are more likely than men to vote for Democratic candidates.[13] This tendency for men's and women's opinions to differ is called the **gender gap.**

Membership in a social group can affect individuals' political orientations in another way: through the efforts of groups themselves to influence their members. Labor unions, for example, often seek to "educate" their members through meetings, rallies, and literature. These activities are designed to shape union members' understanding of politics and to make them more amenable to supporting the political positions favored by union leaders. Similarly, organization can sharpen the impact of membership in an involuntary group. Women's groups, black groups, religious groups, and the like usually endeavor to structure their members' political views through intensive educational programs. The importance of such group efforts can be seen from the impact of group membership on political opinion. Women who belong to women's organizations, for example, are likely to differ more from men in their political views than women without such group affiliation.[14] Other analysts have found that African Americans who belong to black organizations are likely to differ more from whites in their political orientations than blacks who lack such affiliations.[15]

gender gap a distinctive pattern of voting behavior reflecting the differences in views between women and men

Disagreements among Men and Women on Issues of War and Peace		Table 6.1

GOVERNMENT ACTION	PERCENTAGE APPROVING OF ACTION	
	MEN	WOMEN
Prefer cease-fire over NATO airstrikes on Yugoslavia (1999)	44	51
Favor unilateral military action against Iraq (1998)	55	35
Ending ban on homosexuals in military (1993)	34	51
Military operation against Somali warlord (1993)	72	60
Going to war against Iraq (1991)	72	53
Sending U.S. troops to Saudi Arabia in response to Iraqi invasion of Kuwait (1991)	78	54

SOURCE: Gallup Poll, 1991, 1993, 1998, 1999.

SOURCES: [1]Survey by CBS News, February 6–10, 2000. [2]Survey by the National Opinion Research Center-General Social Survey, February 1–June 25, 2000. [3]Survey by NBC News/*Wall Street Journal,* March 2–5, 2000.

Figure 6.2 **Disagreement Among Blacks and Whites**

African Americans and white Americans have strong differences of opinion on certain issues.

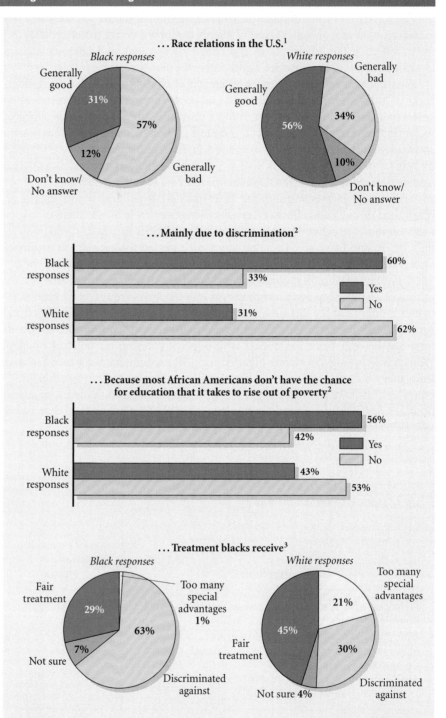

... Race relations in the U.S.[1]

Black responses

Generally good
31%
57%
Generally bad
Don't know/No answer
12%

White responses

Generally good
56%
Generally bad
34%
Don't know/No answer
10%

... Mainly due to discrimination[2]

Black responses — Yes 60% / No 33%
White responses — Yes 31% / No 62%

... Because most African Americans don't have the chance for education that it takes to rise out of poverty[2]

Black responses — Yes 56% / No 42%
White responses — Yes 43% / No 53%

... Treatment blacks receive[3]

Black responses

Fair treatment 29%
Too many special advantages 1%
Discriminated against 63%
Not sure 7%

White responses

Fair treatment 45%
Too many special advantages 21%
Discriminated against 30%
Not sure 4%

In many cases, no particular efforts are required by groups to affect their members' beliefs and opinions. Often, individuals will consciously or unconsciously adapt their views to those of the groups with which they identify. For example, an African American who is dubious about affirmative action is likely to come under considerable peer pressure and internal pressure to modify his or her views. In this and other cases, dissenters are likely gradually to shift their own views to conform to those of the group. Political psychologist Elisabeth Noelle-Neumann has called this process the "spiral of silence."[16]

A third way that membership in social groups can affect political beliefs is through what might be called objective political interests. On many economic issues, for example, the interests of the rich and poor differ significantly. Inevitably, these differences of interest will produce differences of political outlook. James Madison and other framers of the Constitution thought that the inherent gulf between the rich and the poor would always be the most important source of conflict in political life. Certainly today, struggles over tax policy, welfare policy, health care policy, and so forth are fueled by differences of interest between wealthier and poorer Americans. In a similar vein, objective differences of interest between "senior citizens" and younger Americans can lead to very different views on such diverse issues as health care policy, Social Security, and criminal justice. To take another example, in recent decades major differences of opinion and political orientation have developed between American civilians and members of the armed services. Military officers, in particular, are far more conservative in their domestic and foreign policy views than the public-at-large and are heavily Republican in their political leanings.[17] Interestingly, support for the Republicans among military officers climbed sharply during the 1980s and 1990s, decades in which the GOP championed large military budgets. Could this be another case of objective interests swaying ideology?

It is worth pointing out again that, like the other agencies of socialization, group membership can never fully explain a given individual's political views. One's unique personality and life experiences may produce political views very different from those of the group to which one might nominally belong. This is why some African Americans are conservative Republicans, or why an occasional wealthy industrialist is also a socialist. Group membership is conducive to particular outlooks, but it is not determinative.

Differences in Education   A third important source of differences in political perspectives comes from a person's education. In some respects, of course, schooling is a great equalizer. Governments use public education to try to teach all children a common set of civic values. It is mainly in school that Americans acquire their basic belief in liberty, equality, and democracy. In history classes, students are taught that the Founders fought for the principle of liberty. Through participation in class elections and student government, students are taught the virtues of democracy. In the course of studying such topics as the Constitution, the Civil War, and the civil rights movement, students are taught the importance of equality. These lessons are repeated in every grade in a variety of contexts. No wonder they are such an important element in Americans' beliefs.

At the same time, however, differences in educational attainment are strongly associated with differences in political outlook. In particular, those who attend college are often exposed to philosophies and modes of thought that will forever distinguish them from their friends and neighbors who do not pursue college diplomas. Table 6.2 outlines some general differences of opinion that are found between college graduates and other Americans.

In recent years, conservatives have charged that liberal college professors indoctrinate their students with liberal ideas. College does seem to have some "liberalizing" effect upon students, but, more significantly, college seems to convince students of the importance of political participation and of their own capacity to have an impact on politics and policy. Thus, one of the major differences between college graduates and other Americans can be seen in levels of political participation. College graduates vote, write "letters to the editor," join campaigns, take part in protests, and, generally, make their voices heard. Does this mean that college graduates are turned into dangerous radicals by liberal professors? Quite the contrary: college seems to convince individuals that it is important to involve themselves in the nation's politics. What perspective could be more conservative?

Political Conditions   A fourth set of factors that shape political orientations and values are the conditions under which individuals and groups are recruited into and involved in political life. Although political beliefs are influenced by family background and group membership, the precise content and character of these views is, to a large extent, determined by political circumstances. For example, in the nineteenth century, millions of southern Italian peasants left their homes. Some migrated to cities in northern Italy; others came to cities in the United States. Many of those who moved to northern Italy were recruited by socialist and communist parties and became mainstays of the forces of the Italian Left. At the same time, their cousins and

Table 6.2	Education and Public Opinion in 2000

The figures show the percentage of respondents in each category agreeing with the statement.

	EDUCATION			
ISSUES	**DROP-OUT**	**HIGH SCHOOL**	**SOME COLLEGE**	**COLLEGE GRAD.**
1. Women and men should have equal roles.	45%	72%	84%	85%
2. Abortion should never be allowed.	31	16	11	5
3. The government should adopt national health insurance.	50	43	38	37
4. The U.S. should not concern itself with other nations' problems.	27	34	27	12
5. Government should see to fair treatment in jobs for African Americans.	24	33	32	43
6. Government should provide fewer services to reduce government spending.	18	13	19	31

SOURCE: The American National Election Studies, 2000 data, provided by the Inter-University Consortium for Political and Social Research, University of Michigan.

neighbors who migrated to American cities were recruited by urban patronage machines and became mainstays of political conservatism. In both instances, group membership influenced political beliefs. Yet the character of those beliefs varied enormously with the political circumstances in which a given group found itself.

In a similar vein, the views held by members of a particular group can shift drastically over time, as political circumstances change. For example, American white southerners were staunch members of the Democratic Party from the Civil War through the 1960s. As members of this political group, they became key supporters of liberal New Deal and post–New Deal social programs that greatly expanded the size and power of the American national government. Since the 1960s, however, southern whites have shifted in large numbers to the Republican Party. Now they provide a major base of support for efforts to scale back social programs and to sharply reduce the size and power of the national government. The South's move from the Democratic to the Republican camp took place because of white southern opposition to the Democratic Party's racial policies and because of determined Republican efforts to win white southern support. It was not a change in the character of white southerners but a change in the political circumstances in which they found themselves that induced this major shift in political allegiances and outlooks in the South.

The moral of this story is that a group's views cannot be inferred simply from the character of the group. College students are not inherently radical or inherently conservative. Jews are not inherently liberal. Southerners are not inherently conservative. Men are not inherently supportive of the military. Any group's political outlooks and orientations are shaped by the political circumstances in which that group finds itself, and those outlooks can change as circumstances change. Quite probably, the generation of American students now coming of political age will have a very different view of the use of American military power than their parents—members of a generation that reached political consciousness during the 1960s, when opposition to the Vietnam War and military conscription were important political phenomena.

FROM POLITICAL VALUES TO IDEOLOGY

As we have seen, people's beliefs about government can vary widely. But for some individuals, this set of beliefs can fit together into a coherent philosophy about government. This set of underlying orientations, ideas, and beliefs through which we come to understand and interpret politics is called a political ideology. Ideologies take many different forms. Some people may view politics primarily in religious terms. During the course of European political history, for example, Protestantism and Catholicism were often political ideologies as much as they were religious creeds. Each set of beliefs not only included elements of religious practice but also involved ideas about secular authority and political action. Other people may see politics through racial lenses. Nazism was a political ideology that placed race at the center of political life and sought to interpret politics in terms of racial categories.

In America today, people often describe themselves as liberals or conservatives. Liberalism and conservatism are political ideologies that include beliefs about the role of the government, ideas about public policies, and notions about which groups in society should properly exercise power (see Boxes 6.1 and 6.2). These

---

Box 6.1 **Profile of a Liberal: Jesse Jackson**

Advocates increasing taxes for corporations and for the wealthy.

Advocates a "Right to Food Policy" to make available a nutritionally balanced diet for all U.S. citizens.

Advocates the establishment of a national health care program for all citizens.

Advocates higher salaries for teachers, more college grants and loans, and a doubling of the federal education budget.

Favors increasing the minimum wage.

Advocates the use of $500 billion in pension funds to finance public works programs, including the construction of a "national railroad."

Favors foreign assistance programs designed to wipe out hunger and starvation throughout the world.

Advocates dramatic expansion of federal social and urban programs.

liberal today this term refers to those who generally support social and political reform; extensive governmental intervention in the economy; the expansion of federal social services; more vigorous efforts on behalf of the poor, minorities, and women; and greater concern for consumers and the environment

ideologies can be seen as the end results of the process of political socialization that was discussed in the preceding section.

Today, the term **liberal** has come to imply support for political and social reform, extensive government intervention in the economy, the expansion of federal social services, and more vigorous efforts on behalf of the poor, minorities, and women, as well as greater concern for consumers and the environment. In social and cultural

---

Box 6.2 **Profile of a Conservative: Pat Buchanan**

Wants to trim the size of the federal government and transfer power to state and local governments. Wants to diminish government regulation of business.

Favors prayer in the public schools.

Opposes gay rights legislation.

Supports programs that would allow children and parents more flexibility in deciding what school to attend.

Supports strict regulation of pornography.

Favors making most abortions illegal.

Would eliminate some environmental regulations.

Supports harsher treatment of criminals.

Opposes affirmative action programs.

Opposes allowing women to serve in military combat units.

Opposes U.S. participation in international organizations.

Opposes the North American Free Trade Agreement (NAFTA).

areas, liberals generally support abortion rights, are concerned with the rights of persons accused of crime, and oppose state involvement with religious institutions and religious expression. In international affairs, liberal positions are usually seen as including support for arms control, opposition to the development and testing of nuclear weapons, support for aid to poor nations, opposition to the use of American troops to influence the domestic affairs of developing nations, and support for international organizations such as the United Nations. Of course, liberalism is not monolithic. For example, among individuals who view themselves as liberal, many support American military intervention when it is tied to a humanitarian purpose, as in the case of America's military action in Kosovo in 1998–99. Most liberals supported President Bush's war on terrorism, even when some of the president's actions seemed to curtail civil liberties.

By contrast, the term **conservative** today is used to describe those who generally support the social and economic status quo and are suspicious of efforts to introduce new political formulae and economic arrangements. Conservatives believe strongly that a large and powerful government poses a threat to citizens' freedom. Thus, in the domestic arena, conservatives generally oppose the expansion of governmental activity, asserting that solutions to social and economic problems can be developed in the private sector. Conservatives particularly oppose efforts to impose government regulation on business, pointing out that such regulation is frequently economically inefficient and costly and can ultimately lower the entire nation's standard of living. As to social and cultural positions, many conservatives oppose abortion, support school prayer, are more concerned for the victims than the perpetrators of crimes, oppose school busing, and support traditional family arrangements. In international affairs, conservatism has come to mean support for the maintenance of American military power. Like liberalism, conservatism is far from a monolithic ideology. Some conservatives support many government social programs. Republican George W. Bush calls himself a "compassionate conservative" to indicate that he favors programs that assist the poor and needy. Other conservatives oppose efforts to outlaw abortion, arguing that government intrusion in this area is as misguided as government intervention in the economy. Such a position is sometimes called "libertarian." In a similar vein, Pat Buchanan has angered many fellow conservatives by opposing most American military intervention in other regions. Many conservatives charge Buchanan with advocating a form of American "isolationism" that runs counter to contemporary conservative doctrine. The real political world is far too complex to be seen in terms of a simple struggle between liberals and conservatives.

To some extent, contemporary liberalism and conservatism can be seen as differences of emphasis with regard to the fundamental American political values of liberty and equality. For liberals, equality is the most important of the core values. Liberals are willing to tolerate government intervention in such areas as college admissions and business decisions when these seem to result in high levels of race, class, or gender inequality. For conservatives, on the other hand, liberty is the core value. Conservatives oppose most efforts by the government, however well intentioned, to intrude into private life or the marketplace. For example, in October and November 2001, conservatives delayed the enactment of airport safety legislation because they opposed plans for a government takeover of airline baggage inspection. Conservatives charged that private security firms could handle the job more effectively. This simple formula for distinguishing liberalism and conservatism, however, is not always accurate, because political ideologies seldom lend themselves to neat or logical characterizations. Often

conservative today this term refers to those who generally support the social and economic status quo and are suspicious of efforts to introduce new political formulae and economic arrangements. Conservatives believe that a large and powerful government poses a threat to citizens' freedom

> **What do the differences between liberals and conservatives reveal about American political debate?**

political observers search for logical connections among the various positions identified with liberalism or with conservatism, and they are disappointed or puzzled when they are unable to find a set of coherent philosophical principles that define and unite the several elements of either of these sets of beliefs. On the liberal side, for example, what is the logical connection between opposition to U.S. government intervention in the affairs of foreign nations and calls for greater intervention in America's economy and society? On the conservative side, what is the logical relationship between opposition to governmental regulation of business and support for a government ban on abortion? Indeed, the latter would seem to be just the sort of regulation of private conduct that conservatives claim to abhor.

Frequently, the relationships among the various elements of liberalism or of conservatism are political rather then logical. One underlying basis of liberal views is that all or most represent criticisms of or attacks on the foreign and domestic policies and cultural values of the business and commercial strata that have been prominent in the United States for the past century. In some measure, the tenets of contemporary conservatism represent this elite's defense of its positions against its enemies, who include organized labor, minority groups, and some intellectuals and professionals. Thus, liberals attack business and commercial elites by advocating more governmental regulation, including consumer protection and environmental regulation, opposing new military weapons programs, and supporting expensive social programs. Conservatives counterattack by asserting that governmental regulation of the economy is ruinous and that new military weapons are needed in a changing world, and they seek to stigmatize their opponents for showing no concern for the rights of "unborn" Americans.

Figure 6.3   **Americans' Shifting Ideology, 1973–2000**

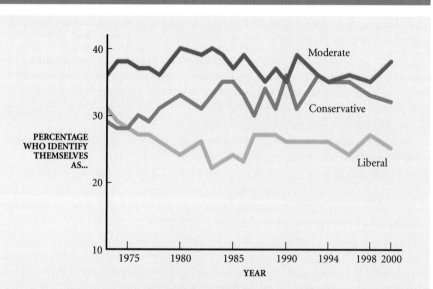

SOURCE: Harold W. Stanley and Richard G. Niemi, *Vital Statistics on American Politics 2001–2002* (Washington, DC: Congressional Quarterly Press, 2001), p. 118.

Of course, it is important to note that many people who call themselves liberals or conservatives accept only part of the liberal or conservative ideology. During the 1980s, many political commentators asserted that Americans were becoming increasingly conservative. Indeed, it was partly in response to this view that the Democrats in 1992 selected a presidential candidate, Bill Clinton, drawn from the party's moderate wing. Although it appears that Americans have adopted more conservative outlooks on some issues, their views in most areas have remained largely unchanged or even have become more liberal in recent years. Thus, many individuals who are liberal on social issues are conservative on economic issues. There is nothing illogical about these mixed positions. They simply indicate the relatively open and fluid character of American political debate. As Figure 6.3 indicates, Americans are often apt to shift their ideological preferences.

How We Form Political Opinions

An individual's opinions on particular issues, events, and personalities emerge as he or she evaluates these phenomena through the lenses of the beliefs and orientations that, taken together, comprise his or her political ideology. Thus, if a conservative is confronted with a plan to expand federal social programs, he or she is likely to express opposition to the endeavor without spending too much time pondering the specific plan. Similarly, if a liberal is asked to comment on conservative former president Ronald Reagan, he or she is not likely to hesitate long before offering a negative view. Underlying beliefs and ideologies tend to automatically color people's perceptions and opinions about politics.

Opinions on particular issues, however, are seldom fully shaped by underlying ideologies. Few individuals possess ideologies so cohesive and intensely held that they will automatically shape all their opinions. Indeed, when we occasionally encounter individuals with rigid worldviews, who see everything through a particular political lens, we tend to dismiss them as "ideologues," or lacking common sense.

Although ideologies color our political perspectives, they seldom fully determine our views. This is true for a variety of reasons. First, as noted earlier, most individuals' ideologies contain internal contradictions. Take, for example, a conservative view of the issue of abortion. Should conservatives favor outlawing abortion as an appropriate means of preserving public morality, or should they oppose restrictions on abortion because these represent government intrusions into private life? Or take the issue of America's response to terrorism. Should conservatives support President Bush's plans to try terrorists before military tribunals as a properly harsh reaction to international criminals or should they oppose the president's plans as an unwarranted expansion of the government's power? In this instance, as in many others, ideology can point in different directions.

Second, individuals may have difficulty linking particular issues or personalities to their own underlying beliefs. Some issues defy ideological characterization. Should conservatives have supported or opposed the 1999 "Patient's Bill of Rights" that made it easier for individuals to file suit against the widely unpopular health maintenance organizations (HMOs), which came to dominate American health care in the 1990s? What should liberals think about America's 1998–99 bombing campaign against Serbia, our 2001–02 war in Afghanistan, and continued conflict with Iraq? Each of these policies combines a mix of issues and is too complex to be viewed through simple ideological lenses.

Finally, most people have at least some conflicting underlying attitudes. Most conservatives support *some* federal programs—defense, or tax deductions for businesses, for example—and wish to see them, and hence the government, expanded. Many liberals favor American military intervention in other nations for what they deem to be humanitarian purposes, but generally oppose American military intervention in the affairs of other nations.

> **What influences the way we form political opinions?**

Thus, most individuals' attitudes on particular issues do not spring automatically from their ideological predispositions. It is true that most people have underlying beliefs that help to shape their opinions on particular issues, but two other factors are also important: a person's knowledge of political issues, and outside influences on that person's views.

POLITICAL KNOWLEDGE

As we have seen, general political beliefs can guide the formation of opinions on specific issues, but an individual's beliefs and opinions are not always consistent with one another. Studies of political opinion have shown that most people don't hold specific and clearly defined opinions on every political issue. As a result, they are easily influenced by others. What best explains whether citizens are generally consistent in their political views or inconsistent and open to the influence of others? The key is knowledge and information about political issues. In general, knowledgeable citizens are better able to evaluate new information and determine whether it is relevant to and consistent with their beliefs and opinions. As a result, better-informed individuals can recognize their political interests and act consistently on behalf of them.

One of the most obvious and important examples of this proposition is voting. Despite the predisposition of voters to support their own party's candidates (see Chapter 9 for a discussion of party identification), millions of voters are affected by the information they receive about candidates during a campaign. During the 2000 presidential campaign, for instance, voters weighed the arguments of Al Gore against those of George W. Bush about who was better fit to run the U.S. economy based on what they (the voters) knew about the country's economic health. Some Republican voters actually supported Gore because they approved of the economic policies followed during the Clinton years. Thus citizens can use information and judgment to overcome their predispositions. Without some political knowledge, citizens would have a difficult time making sense of the complex political world in which they live.

This point brings up two questions, however. First, how much political knowledge is necessary for one to act as an effective citizen? And second, how is political knowledge distributed throughout the population? In a recent study of political knowledge in the United States, political scientists Michael X. DelliCarpini and Scott Keeter found that the average American exhibits little knowledge of political institutions, processes, leaders, and policy debates. For example, in a 1996 poll, only about half of all Americans could correctly identify Newt Gingrich as the Speaker of the House of Representatives.[18] Does this ignorance of key political facts matter?

Another important concern is the character of those who possess and act upon the political information that they acquire. Political knowledge is not evenly distributed throughout the population. Those with higher education, income, and occupational status and who are members of social or political organizations are more likely to know about and be active in politics. An interest in politics reinforces an individual's sense of **political efficacy** and provides more incentive to acquire additional knowledge and information about politics. Those who don't think they can have an effect on government tend not to be interested in learning about or participating in politics. As a result, individuals with a disproportionate share of income and education also have a disproportionate share of knowledge and influence and are better able to get what they want from government.

THE INFLUENCE OF POLITICAL LEADERS, PRIVATE GROUPS, AND THE MEDIA

political efficacy the ability to influence government and politics

When individuals attempt to form opinions about particular political issues, events, and personalities, they seldom do so in isolation. Typically, they are confronted—sometimes bombarded—by the efforts of a host of individuals and groups seeking to persuade them to adopt a particular point of view. Someone trying to decide what to think about George W. Bush, Colin Powell, or Dick Cheney could hardly avoid an avalanche of opinions expressed through the media, in meetings, or in conversations with friends. The **marketplace of ideas** is the interplay of opinions and views that takes place as competing forces attempt to persuade as many people as possible to accept a particular position on a particular event. Given constant exposure to the ideas of others, it is virtually impossible for most individuals to resist some modification of their own beliefs. For example, as we saw earlier, African Americans and white Americans disagree on a number of matters. Yet, as political scientists Paul Sniderman and Edward Carmines have shown, considerable cross-racial agreement has evolved on fundamental issues of race and civil rights.[19]

> **How are political issues marketed and managed by the government, private groups, and the media?**

marketplace of ideas the public forum in which beliefs and ideas are exchanged and compete

The marketplace of ideas has created a common ground on which the discussion of issues is encouraged, based on common understandings. Despite the many and often sharp divisions that exist in the twentieth century—between liberals and conservatives or different income groups—most Americans see the world through similar lenses. This idea market makes it possible for ideas of all sorts to compete for attention and acceptance.

Few ideas spread spontaneously. Usually, whether they are matters of fashion, science, or politics, ideas must be vigorously promoted to become widely known and accepted. For example, the clothing, sports, and entertainment fads that occasionally seem to appear from nowhere and sweep the country before being replaced by some other new trend are almost always the product of careful marketing campaigns by some commercial interest, rather than spontaneous phenomena. Like their counterparts in fashion, successful—or at least widely held—political ideas are usually the products of carefully orchestrated campaigns by government or by organized groups and interests, rather than the results of spontaneous popular enthusiasm. In general, new ideas are presented in ways that make them seem consistent with, or even logical outgrowths of, Americans' more fundamental beliefs. For example, proponents of affirmative action generally present the policy as a necessary step toward racial equality. Or opponents of a proposed government regulation will vehemently assert that the rule is inconsistent with liberty. Both supporters and opponents of campaign finance reform seek to wrap their arguments in the cloak of democracy.[20]

Three forces that play important roles in shaping opinions are the government, private groups, and the news media.

Because of the importance of public opinion, most presidents have made major efforts both to ascertain the public's views and to promote opinions favorable to themselves and their policies. At least since Franklin D. Roosevelt, every president has made extensive use of polling to measure the public's mood and of professional public relations to attempt to convince Americans to support the administration. FDR was the first president to use professional pollsters and make systematic use of newspapers, movie newsreels, and the radio to reach out to the public and attempt to shape opinion on domestic and foreign policies. FDR's famous "fireside chats" brought him into every American home via the radio.

Government and the Shaping of Public Opinion   All governments attempt, to a greater or lesser extent, to influence, manipulate, or manage their citizens' beliefs. But the extent to which public opinion is actually affected by governmental public relations efforts is probably limited. The government—despite its size and power—is only one source of information and evaluation in the United States. Very often, governmental claims are disputed by the media, by interest groups, and at times by opposing forces within the government itself. Often, too, governmental efforts to manipulate public opinion backfire when the public is made aware of the government's tactics. Thus, in 1971, the United States government's efforts to build popular support for the Vietnam War were hurt when CBS News aired its documentary "The Selling of the Pentagon," which purported to reveal the extent and character of governmental efforts to sway popular sentiment. In this documentary, CBS demonstrated the techniques, including planted news stories and faked film footage, that the government had used to misrepresent its activities in Vietnam. These revelations, of course, undermined popular trust in all governmental claims.

A hallmark of the Clinton administration was the steady use of techniques like those used in election campaigns to bolster popular enthusiasm for White House initiatives. The president established a political "war room," similar to the one that operated in his campaign headquarters, where representatives from all departments meet daily to discuss and coordinate the president's public relations efforts. Many of the same consultants and pollsters who directed the successful Clinton campaign were also employed in the selling of the president's programs.[21]

Indeed, the Clinton White House made more sustained and systematic use of public-opinion polling than any previous administration. For example, during his presidency Bill Clinton relied heavily on the polling firm of Penn & Schoen to help him decide which issues to emphasize and what strategies to adopt. During the 1995–96 budget battle with Congress, the White House commissioned polls almost every night to chart changes in public perceptions about the struggle. Poll data suggested to Clinton that he should present himself as struggling to save Medicare from Republican cuts. Clinton responded by launching a media attack against what he claimed were GOP efforts to hurt the elderly. This proved to be a successful strategy and helped Clinton defeat the Republican budget.[22]

America's two most recent presidents, Bill Clinton and George W. Bush, established elaborate White House communications efforts to convince the American people of the wisdom of the president's policies. Clinton was often criticized for retaining a number of pollsters to chart shifts in public opinion on a daily basis (left). Bush established a communications office to deliver the president's message to the nation in an effort to stay ahead of the headlines by providing the media with stories and sound bites that would dominate coverage for days. Despite his efforts, President Bush was better able to persuade Americans of his foreign policy leadership than of his ability to manage the domestic economy (right). The nation's economic slump, coupled with corporate scandals, threatened the president's political fortunes in 2002 even though most Americans approved of Bush's foreign policy.

Of course, at the same time that the Clinton administration worked diligently to mobilize popular support, its opponents struggled equally hard to mobilize popular opinion against the White House. A host of public and private interest groups opposed to President Clinton's programs crafted public relations campaigns designed to generate opposition to the president. For example, in 1994, while Clinton campaigned to bolster popular support for his health care reform proposals, groups representing small businesses and segments of the insurance industry, among others, developed their own publicity campaigns that ultimately convinced many Americans that Clinton's initiative posed a threat to their own health care. These opposition campaigns played an important role in the eventual defeat of the president's proposal.

After he assumed office in 2001, President George W. Bush reduced the White House's use of poll data, asserting that political leaders should base their programs upon their own conception of the public interest rather than the polls. This, however, did not mean that Bush ignored public opinion. Quite the contrary. The Bush White House developed an extensive public relations program, led by former presidential aide Karen P. Hughes, to bolster popular support for the president's policies. Hughes, working with conservative TV personality Mary Matalin, coordinated White House efforts to maintain popular support for the administration's war against terrorism. These efforts included presidential speeches, media appearances by administration officials, numerous press conferences, and thousands of press releases presenting the

What Government Does . . . After September 11

Control of information is a vital component of victory in any war, and it has proved no different in the war on terrorism. Since the events of September 11, 2001, the president has used several important strategies to manage opinion.

First among these is the use of modern advertising methods. President Bush hired Charlotte Beers, a well-known advertising executive, as undersecretary of state for public diplomacy. She was charged with improving America's image in Islamic countries, through such techniques as making American officials available to the Arabic language television station Al Jazeera.[1]

Another strategy was the creation of a sophisticated media operation, directed (until her April 2002 resignation) by Karen Hughes, the president's communications director. Along with her British counterpart, Alexander Campbell, Hughes built a sophisticated twenty-four media operation to disseminate information and news on the war on terrorism. Through offices in London, Washington, and Islamabad, British and American teams were able to operate in relays and constantly inform the public of news about military operations in Afghanistan. This coordination helped rebut potentially damaging claims about U.S. operations. Prior to this coordination, potentially negative news emerged in Arabic newspapers nine hours before Washington staffers were awake and could respond to developments, meaning that America's viewpoint was stale by the time it was expressed.[2]

The president's chief strategist Karl Rove has been instrumental in placing foreign-language radio broadcasts into Afghanistan by means of the Voice of America and the new Radio Free Afghanistan. He was helpful in this by his extensive experience in Radio Free Europe, which once broadcast into the Soviet Union and communist Eastern Europe.[3]

In addition to these administrative means, an important tool for managing opinion has been the statements made by the president himself. In this respect the President's 2002 State of the Union address was a powerful medium for signaling new directions for American foreign policy. The president's description of Iran, Iraq, and North Korea as an "axis of evil" signaled an expansion of America's war on terror and sought to gain the support of the American people for his administration's policies.

Another initiative of the president's has been the creation of a homeland security advisory system. This alert system involves public announcements of security threats by means of colors with condition green indicating a low risk of terrorist threat and condition red indicating a very high risk of threat.[4] This is certainly a powerful tool for managing public opinion, although its potential for abuse must not be overlooked. Cynics might be able to imagine a situation in which an increase in the threat level to red "coincided" with a political scandal. Naturally, citizens would be more concerned about immediate threat to human life and so less attention might be focused on an otherwise embarrassing political scandal.

Similar worries of potential foul play arose with regard to the short-lived Office of Strategic Influence within the Defense Department. This was to have been a federal office charged with disseminating American views throughout the world. The office was closed after critics charged that the U.S. military might purposefully spread misinformation about American policy.[5]

The president's efforts to manage public opinion combine all the resources at his disposal and are an important tool in accomplishing his administration's policies. Indeed, one hallmark of the Bush administration has been an effort to stay ahead of the news curve. Bush's predecessor, Bill Clinton, was constantly involved in efforts to control the damage caused by embarrassing news stories. The Bush administration, on the other hand, has sought to anticipate news developments and to put its own spin on the news before its opponents are able to generate a full head of steam. One example is Bush's announcement in June 2002 of a major government reorganization designed to facilitate "homeland defense." The timing of the president's announcement was designed to coincide with the beginning of congressional hearings on intelligence lapses prior to the September 11 terrorist attacks. Bush successfully deflected attention from these hearings and preempted efforts by congressional Democrats to introduce their own reorganization plans. Bush's proposals had been developed in secret by a small group of trusted advisers to prevent leaks from reaching the press and undermining the administration's own control over the timing and impact of the news. In this way, the Bush administration was able to create news at a time of its own choosing rather than to simply respond to news events or the strategies of other political actors.

[1] New York Times, November 6, 2001.
[2] The Guardian, November 10, 2001.
[3] New York Times, November 11, 2001.
[4] Washington Post, March 12, 2002.
[5] The Guardian, February 26, 2002.

administration's views.[23] The White House also made a substantial effort to sway opinion in foreign countries, even sending officials to present the administration's views on television networks serving the Arab world.

Private Groups and the Shaping of Public Opinion   As the story of the health care debate may suggest, political issues and ideas seldom emerge spontaneously from the grass roots. We have already seen how the government tries to shape public opinion. But the ideas that become prominent in political life are also developed and spread by important economic and political groups searching for issues that will advance their causes. One example is the "right-to-life" issue that has inflamed American politics over the past twenty years.

The notion of right-to-life, whose proponents seek to outlaw abortion and overturn the Supreme Court's *Roe v. Wade* decision, was developed and heavily promoted by conservative politicians who saw the issue of abortion as a means of uniting Catholic and Protestant conservatives and linking both groups to the Republican Party. These politicians convinced Catholic and evangelical Protestant leaders that they shared similar views on the question of abortion, and they worked with religious leaders to focus public attention on the negative issues in the abortion debate. To advance their cause, leaders of the movement sponsored well-publicized Senate hearings, where testimony, photographs, and other exhibits were presented to illustrate the violent effects of abortion procedures. At the same time, publicists for the movement produced leaflets, articles, books, and films such as *The Silent Scream* to highlight the agony and pain ostensibly felt by the "unborn" when they were being aborted. All this underscored the movement's claim that abortion was nothing more or less than the murder of millions of innocent human beings. Finally, Catholic and evangelical Protestant religious leaders were organized to denounce abortion from their church pulpits and, increasingly, from their electronic pulpits on the Christian Broadcasting Network (CBN) and the various other television forums available for religious programming. Religious leaders also organized demonstrations, pickets, and disruptions at abortion clinics throughout the nation.[24] Abortion rights remain a potent issue; it even influenced the debate over health care reform.

Typically, ideas are marketed most effectively by groups with access to financial resources, public or private institutional support, and sufficient skill or education to select, develop, and draft ideas that will attract interest and support. Thus, the development and promotion of conservative themes and ideas in recent years has been greatly facilitated by the millions of dollars that conservative corporations and business organizations such as the Chamber of Commerce and the Public Affairs Council spend each year on public information and what is now called in corporate circles "issues management." In addition, conservative business leaders have contributed millions of dollars to such conservative institutions as the Heritage Foundation, the Hoover Institution, and the American Enterprise Institute.[25] Many of the ideas that helped those on the right influence political debate were first developed and articulated by scholars associated with institutions such as these.

Although they do not usually have access to financial assets that match those available to their conservative opponents, liberal intellectuals and professionals have ample organizational skills, access to the media, and practice in creating, communicating, and using ideas. During the past three decades, the chief vehicle through which liberal intellectuals and professionals have advanced their ideas has been the "public interest group," an institution that relies heavily on voluntary contributions of time, effort, and interest on the part of its members. Through groups like Common Cause, the National Organization for Women, the Sierra Club, Friends of the Earth, and Physicians for Social Responsibility, intellectuals and professionals have been able to use their organizational skills and educational resources to develop and promote ideas.[26] Often, research conducted in universities and in liberal "think tanks" such as the Brookings Institution provides the ideas on which liberal politicians rely. For example, the welfare reform plan introduced by the Clinton administration in 1994 originated with the work of former Harvard professor David Ellwood. Ellwood's academic research led him to the conclusion that the nation's welfare system would be improved if services to the poor were expanded in scope but limited in duration. His idea was adopted by the 1992 Clinton campaign, which was searching for a position on welfare that would appeal to both liberal and conservative Democrats. The Ellwood plan seemed perfect: it promised liberals an immediate expansion of welfare benefits, yet it held out to conservatives the idea that welfare recipients would receive benefits only for a limited period of time. The Clinton welfare reform plan even borrowed phrases from Ellwood's book *Poor Support*.[27]

Journalist and author Joe Queenan has correctly observed that although political ideas can erupt spontaneously, they almost never do. Instead, he says,

issues are usually manufactured by tenured professors and obscure employees of think tanks.... It is inconceivable that the American people, all by themselves, could independently arrive at the conclusion that the depletion of the ozone layer poses a dire threat to our national well-being, or that an immediate, across-the-board cut in the capital-gains tax is the only thing that stands between us and the economic abyss. The American people do not have that kind of sophistication. *They have to have help.*[28]

The Media and Public Opinion   The communications media are among the most powerful forces operating in the marketplace of ideas. As we shall see in Chapter 7, the mass media are not simply neutral messengers for ideas developed by others. Instead, the media have an enormous impact on popular attitudes and opinions. Over time, the ways in which the mass media report political events help to shape the underlying attitudes and beliefs from which opinions emerge.[29] For example, for the past thirty years, the national news media have relentlessly investigated personal and official wrongdoing on the part of politicians and public officials. This continual media presentation of corruption in government and venality in politics has undoubtedly fostered the general attitude of cynicism and distrust that exists in the general public.

At the same time, the ways in which media coverage interprets or frames specific events can have a major impact on popular responses and opinions about these events.[30] Because media framing can be important, the Bush administration sought to persuade broadcasters to follow its lead in its coverage of terrorism and America's response to terrorism in the months following the September 11 attacks. Broadcasters, who found themselves targets of anthrax-contaminated letters apparently mailed by terrorists, needed little persuasion. For the most part, the media praised the president for his leadership and presented the administration's military campaign in Afghanistan and domestic antiterrorist efforts in a positive light. Even newspapers like the *New York Times,* which had strongly opposed Bush in the 2000 election and questioned his fitness for the presidency, asserted that he had grown into the job.

Measuring Public Opinion

As recently as fifty years ago, American political leaders gauged public opinion by people's applause and by the presence of crowds at meetings. This direct exposure to the people's views did not necessarily produce accurate knowledge of public opinion. It did, however, give political leaders confidence in their public support—and therefore confidence in their ability to govern by consent.

Abraham Lincoln and Stephen Douglas debated each other seven times in the summer and autumn of 1858, two years before they became presidential nominees. Their debates took place before audiences in parched cornfields and courthouse squares. A century later, the presidential debates, although seen by millions, take place before a few reporters and technicians in television studios that might as well be on the moon. The public's response cannot be experienced directly. This distance between leaders and followers is one of the agonizing problems of modern democracy. The media send information to millions of people, but they are not yet as efficient at getting information back to leaders. Is government by consent possible where the scale of communication is so large and impersonal? In order to compensate for the decline in their ability to experience public opinion for themselves, leaders have turned to science, in particular to the science of opinion polling.

It is no secret that politicians and public officials make extensive use of **public opinion polls** to help them decide whether to run for office, what policies to support, how to vote on important legislation, and what types of appeals to make in their campaigns. President Lyndon Johnson was famous for carrying the latest Gallup and Roper poll results in his pocket, and it is widely believed that he began to withdraw from politics because the polls reported losses in public support. All recent presidents and other major political figures have worked closely with polls and pollsters.

public opinion polls scientific instruments for measuring public opinion

CONSTRUCTING PUBLIC OPINION FROM SURVEYS

The population in which pollsters are interested is usually quite large. To conduct their polls they first choose a **sample** of the total population. The selection of this sample is important. Above all, it must be representative; the views of those in the sample must accurately and proportionately reflect the views of the whole. To a large extent, the validity of the poll's results depends on the sampling procedure used (see Box 6.3 on the next page).

The degree of reliability in polling is a function of sample size. The same sample is needed to represent a small population as to represent a large population. The typical size of a sample ranges from 450 to 1,500 respondents. This number, however, reflects a trade-off between cost and degree of precision desired. The degree of accuracy that can be achieved with even a small sample can be seen from the polls' success in predicting election outcomes. The chance that the sample used does not accurately represent the population from which it is drawn is called the *sampling error* or *margin of error*. A typical survey of 1,500 respondents will have a sampling error of approximately 3 percent. When a preelection poll indicates 51 percent of voters surveyed favor the Republican candidate and 49 percent support the Democratic candidate, the outcome is too close to call because it is within the margin of error of the survey. A figure of 51 percent means that between 54 and 48 percent of voters in the population favor the Republicans, while a figure of 49 percent indicates

> **How can public opinion be measured?**

sample a small group selected by researchers to represent the most important characteristics of an entire population

Box 6.3   Methods of Measuring Public Opinion

Interpreting Mass Opinion from Mass Behavior and Mass Attributes

Consumer behavior: predicts that people tend to vote against the party in power during a downturn in the economy

Group demographics: can predict party affiliation and voting by measuring income, race, and type of community (urban or rural)

Getting Public Opinion Directly from the People

Person-to-person: form impressions based on conversations with acquaintances, aides, and associates

Selective polling: form impressions based on interviews with a few representative members of a group or groups

Bellwether districts: form impressions based on an entire community that has a reputation for being a good predictor of the entire nation's attitudes

Constructing Public Opinion from Surveys

Quota sampling: respondents are chosen because they match a general population along several significant dimensions, such as geographic region, sex, age, and race

Probability sampling: respondents are chosen without prior screening, based entirely on a lottery system

Area sampling: respondents are chosen as part of a systematic breakdown of larger homogeneous units into smaller representative areas

Haphazard sampling: respondents are chosen by pure chance with no systematic method

Systematically biased sampling: respondents are chosen with a hidden or undetected bias toward a given demographic group

that between 52 and 46 percent of all voters support the Democrats. Thus, in this example, 52-to-48 percent Democratic victory would still be consistent with polls predicting a 51-to-49 percent Republican triumph.

PROBLEMS WITH POLLING

> **What problems arise from public opinion polling?**

Table 6.3 shows how accurate two of the major national polling organizations actually have been in predicting the outcomes of presidential elections. While pollsters have been mostly correct in their predictions, the 2000 election proved to be an exception. Before the election, their results were a statistical dead heat—within the margin of error of the poll—but most predicted that Bush would get slightly more votes. This erroneous prediction most likely resulted from last-minute changes of mind among voters.

Even with reliable sampling procedures, problems can occur. Validity can be adversely affected by poor question format, faulty ordering of questions, inappropriate vocabulary, ambiguity of questions, or questions with built-in biases. Often, seemingly minor differences in the wording of a question can convey vastly different meanings to respondents and thus produce quite different response patterns (see

Table 6.3

	HARRIS	GALLUP	ACTUAL OUTCOME
2000			
Bush	47%	48%	48%
Gore	47	46	48
Nader	5	4	3
1996			
Clinton	51%	52%	49%
Dole	39	41	41
Perot	9	7	8
1992			
Clinton	44%	44%	43%
Bush	38	37	38
Perot	17	14	19
1988			
Bush	51%	53%	54%
Dukakis	47	42	46
1984			
Reagan	56%	59%	59%
Mondale	44	41	41
1980			
Reagan	48%	47%	51%
Carter	43	44	41
Anderson		8	
1976			
Carter	48%	48%	51%
Ford	45	49	48
1972			
Nixon	59%	62%	61%
McGovern	35	38	38
1968			
Nixon	40%	43%	43%
Humphrey	43	42	43
Wallace	13	15	14
1964			
Johnson	62%	64%	61%
Goldwater	33	36	39
1960			
Kennedy	49%	51%	50%
Nixon	41	49	49
1956			
Eisenhower	NA	60%	58%
Stevenson		41	42
1952			
Eisenhower	47%	51%	55%
Stevenson	42	49	44
1948			
Truman	NA	44.5%	49.6%
Dewey		49.5	45.1

All figures except those for 1948 are rounded. NA = Not asked.
SOURCE: Data from the Gallup Poll and the Harris Survey (New York: Chicago Tribune–New York News Syndicate, various press releases 1964–2000). Courtesy of the Gallup Organization and Louis Harris Associates.

Box 6.4   It Depends on How You Ask

The public's desire for tax cuts can be hard to measure. Pollsters asking what should be done with the nation's budget surplus got different results depending on the specifics of the question.

The Question

President Clinton has proposed setting aside approximately two-thirds of an expected budget surplus to fix the Social Security system. What do you think the leaders in Washington should do with the remainder of the surplus?

Variation 1

Should the money be used for a tax cut, or should it be used to fund new government programs?

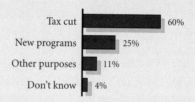

Tax cut — 60%
New programs — 25%
Other purposes — 11%
Don't know — 4%

Variation 2

Should the money be used for a tax cut, or should it be spent on programs for education, the environment, health care, crime-fighting, and military defense?

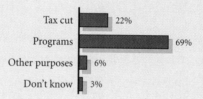

Tax cut — 22%
Programs — 69%
Other purposes — 6%
Don't know — 3%

SOURCE: Pew Research Center, reported in *The New York Times,* January 30, 2000, p. WK 3.

Box 6.4). For example, for many years the University of Chicago's National Opinion Research Center has asked respondents whether they think the federal government is spending too much, too little, or about the right amount of money on "assistance for the poor." Answering the question posed this way, about two-thirds of all respondents seem to believe that the government is spending too little. However, the same survey also asks whether the government spends too much, too little, or about the right amount for "welfare." When the word "welfare" is substituted for "assistance for the poor," about half of all respondents indicate that too much is being spent.[31]

In recent years, a new form of bias has been introduced into surveys by the use of a technique called **push polling.** This technique involves asking a respondent a loaded question about a political candidate designed to elicit the response sought by the pollster and, simultaneously, to shape the respondent's perception of the candidate in question. For example, during the 1996 New Hampshire presidential primary, push pollsters employed by the campaign of one of Lamar Alexander's rivals called thou-

push polling a polling technique in which the questions are designed to shape the respondent's opinion

sands of voters to ask, "If you knew that Lamar Alexander had raised taxes six times in Tennessee, would you be less inclined or more inclined to support him?"[32] More than one hundred consulting firms across the nation now specialize in push polling.[33] Calling push polling the "political equivalent of a drive-by shooting," Representative Joe Barton (R-Tex.) launched a congressional investigation into the practice.[34] Push polls may be one reason that Americans are becoming increasingly skeptical about the practice of polling and increasingly unwilling to answer pollsters' questions.[35]

In the early days of a political campaign when voters are asked which candidates they do, or do not, support, the answer they give often has little significance, because the choice is not yet important to them. Their preferences may change many times before the actual election. This is part of the explanation for the phenomenon of the postconvention "bounce" in the popularity of presidential candidates, which was observed after the Democratic and Republican national conventions in 1992 and 1996.[36] Respondents' preferences reflected the amount of attention a candidate had received during the conventions rather than strongly held views.

Salient interests are interests that stand out beyond others, that are of more than ordinary concern to respondents in a survey or to voters in the electorate. Politicans, social scientists, journalists, or pollsters who assume something is important to the public, when in fact it is not, are creating an **illusion of saliency.** This illusion can be created and fostered by polls despite careful controls over sampling, interviewing, and data analysis. In fact, the illusion is strengthened by the credibility that science gives survey results.

The problem of saliency has become especially acute as a result of the proliferation of media polls. The television networks and major national newspapers all make heavy use of opinion polls. Increasingly, polls are being commissioned by local television stations and local and regional newspapers as well.[37] On the positive side, polls allow journalists to make independent assessments of political realities—assessments not influenced by the partisan claims of politicians.

At the same time, however, media polls can allow journalists to make news when none really exists. Polling diminishes journalists' dependence upon news makers. A poll commissioned by a news agency can provide the basis for a good story even when candidates, politicians, and other news makers refuse to cooperate by engaging in newsworthy activities. Thus, on days when little or nothing is actually taking place in a political campaign, poll results, especially apparent changes in candidate popularity margins, can provide exciting news. Several times during the 2000 presidential campaign, for example, small changes in the relative standing of the Democratic and Republican candidates produced banner headlines around the country. Stories about what the candidates actually did or said often took second place to reporting the "horse race."

Interestingly, because rapid and dramatic shifts in candidate margins tend to take place when voters' preferences are least fully formed, horse-race news is most likely to make the headlines when it is actually least significant.[38] In other words, media interest in poll results is inversely related to the actual salience of voters' opinions and the significance of the polls' findings. However, by influencing perceptions, especially those of major contributors, media polls can influence political realities.

The most noted, but least serious, of polling problems is the **bandwagon effect,** which occurs when polling results influence people to support the candidate marked as the probable victor. Some scholars argue that this bandwagon effect can

salient interests attitudes and views that are especially important to the individual holding them

illusion of saliency the impression conveyed by polls that something is important to the public when actually it is not

bandwagon effect a shift in electoral support to the candidate that public opinion polls report as the front-runner

Though public opinion is important, it is not always easy to interpret, because very often, the pollsters ask individuals to answer questions about which they actually have no opinion. At best, the polls offer some indication of the relative name recognition of the candidates, and often, fail to accurately predict how Americans will vote. In 1948, election-night polls show Dewey defeating Truman for the presidency.

be offset by an "underdog effect" in favor of the candidate who is trailing in the polls.[39] However, a candidate who demonstrates a lead in the polls usually finds it considerably easier to raise campaign funds than a candidate whose poll standing is poor. With these additional funds, poll leaders can often afford to pay for television time and other campaign activities that will cement their advantage.

In 1998, former professional wrestler Jesse Ventura's victory in the Minnesota gubernatorial election totally confounded the pollsters and revealed another weakness of preelection polling. A poll conducted by the *Minneapolis Star Tribune* just six weeks before the election showed Ventura running a distant third to Democratic candidate Hubert Humphrey III, who seemed to have the support of 49 percent of the electorate, and the Republican Norm Coleman, whose support stood at 29 percent. Only 10 percent of those polled said they were planning to vote for Ventura. On election day, of course, Ventura out-polled both Humphrey and Coleman. Analysis of exit-poll data showed why the preelection polls had been so wrong. In an effort to be more accurate, preelection pollsters' predictions often take account of

In Minnesota's 1998 gubernatorial election, pre-election polling failed to account for Jesse Ventura's appeal among first-time voters, who, thanks to the state's same-day voter registration rule, swept Ventura into office.

In 2000, the major networks announced, on the basis of their exit polls, that Al Gore had defeated George W. Bush. Later, they were forced to retract their prediction. The pollsters' inability to accurately project the winner in Florida left the nation in suspense. Ultimately, of course, "Who won?" was not known until after a lengthy recount and a series of court cases.

the likelihood that respondents will actually vote. This is accomplished by polling only people who have voted in the past or correcting for past frequency of voting. The *Star Tribune* poll was conducted only among individuals who had voted in the previous election. Ventura, however, brought to the polls not only individuals who had not voted in the last election but many people who had never voted before in their lives. Twelve percent of Minnesota's voters in 1998 said they came to the polls only because Ventura was on the ballot. This surge in turnout was facilitated by the fact that Minnesota permits same-day voter registration (See Chapter 10 for a discussion of the consequences of registration rules). Thus, the pollsters were wrong because Ventura changed the composition of the electorate.[40]

And in 2000, network exit polls led to a major error on election night. After Florida polls closed, television networks declared Gore the winner in Florida on the basis of exit poll results. Two hours later, the networks revised their estimates on the basis of actual vote counts and declared Florida too close to call. Furious Republicans asserted that the pollsters' errors might have persuaded GOP supporters that the race was hopeless and discouraged voting on the part of Republicans in western states where polls were still open. At 2 A.M., the networks proclaimed Bush the winner in Florida and, as a result, of the national election. Within one hour, however, they withdrew their projections and announced it was again too close to call. Ultimately, of course, the Florida results were not known until after a lengthy statewide recount and litigation by both presidential hopefuls.

Public Opinion and Democracy

A major purpose of democratic government, with its participatory procedures and representative institutions, is to ensure that political leaders will heed public opinion.

> **How responsive is the government to public opinion?**

And, indeed, a good deal of evidence suggests that they do. There are many instances in which public policy and public opinion do not coincide, but in general the government's actions are consistent with citizens' preferences. One recent study, for example, found that between 1935 and 1979, in about two-thirds of all cases, significant changes in public opinion were followed within one year by changes in government policy consistent with the shift in the popular mood.[41] Other studies have come to similar conclusions about public opinion and government policy at the state level.[42] Some recent studies, however, have suggested that the responsiveness of government to public opinion has been declining, reaching an all-time low during President Clinton's first term. These findings imply that, contrary to popular beliefs, elected leaders don't always pander to the results of public opinion polls, but instead use polling to sell their policy proposals and shape the public's views.[43]

In addition, areas of disagreement always arise between opinion and policy. For example, the majority of Americans favored stricter governmental control of handguns for years before Congress finally adopted the modest restrictions on firearms purchases embodied in the Brady bill and the Violent Crime Control Act, passed in 1993 and 1994, respectively. Similarly, most Americans—blacks as well as whites—oppose school busing to achieve racial balance, yet such busing continues to be used in many parts of the nation. Most Americans are far less concerned with the rights of the accused than the federal courts seem to be. Most Americans usually oppose U.S. military intervention in other nations' affairs, yet such interventions continue to take place in such regions as Bosnia and Haiti, where American troops are currently stationed, and often win public approval after the fact. Of course, the overwhelming majority of Americans supported the Bush administration's decision to attack Afghanistan after September 11.

Several factors can contribute to a lack of consistency between opinion and governmental policy. First, the nominal majority on a particular issue may not be as intensely committed to its preference as the adherents of the minority viewpoint. An intensely committed minority may often be more willing to commit its time, energy, efforts, and resources to the affirmation of its opinions than an apathetic, even if large, majority. In the case of firearms, for example, although the proponents of gun control are by a wide margin the majority, most do not regard the issue as one of critical importance to themselves and are not willing to commit much effort to advancing their cause. The opponents of gun control, by contrast, are intensely committed, well organized, and well financed, and as a result are usually able to carry the day.

A second important reason that public policy and public opinion may not coincide has to do with the character and structure of the American system of government. The framers of the American Constitution, as we saw in Chapter 2, sought to create a system of government that was based upon popular consent but that did not invariably and automatically translate shifting popular sentiments into public policies. As a result, the American governmental process includes arrangements such as an appointed judiciary that can produce policy decisions that may run contrary to prevailing popular sentiment—at least for a time.

Perhaps the inconsistencies between opinion and policy could be resolved if we made broader use of a mechanism currently employed by a number of states—the initiative and referendum. This procedure allows propositions to be placed on the ballot and voted into law by the electorate, bypassing most of the normal machinery of representative government. In recent years, several important propositions

Opinions and the Foundations of Democracy and Markets in the "New Europe"

Since the collapse of the Soviet Union in 1991, the study of public opinion in former communist nations has exploded. For the first time in the history of the region, the people of Central and East Europe have been targets of pollsters seeking their opinions on issues similar to those of interest to their West European counterparts. Of particular concern to students of public opinion are the effects of three intense pressures that have gripped the European continent—both east and west.

First, among the more established democracies of West Europe, the public has come to feel the full force of the European Union, a new political and economic system of power that is daily reminding average citizens of just how much their lives have changed in a few years. With its own sovereign currency and a powerful complement of financial, executive, judicial, and legislative institutions, the European Union is increasingly regulating the lives of citizens in fifteen countries of West Europe. The membership of the Union will soon expand by up to thirteen additional countries, including several former communist countries of Central and East Europe. By the end of 2002 this set will probably include Poland, Hungary, the Czech Republic, Slovenia, Estonia, Latvia, Lithuania, Romania, Slovakia, Bulgaria, Turkey, Malta, and Cyprus.

Second, with the collapse of the Soviet Union and its communist form of government, the market has now entered the daily lives of virtually all citizens of Central and East Europe. The effect is to subject the average family to not only a change of lifestyle (often meaning a decline in their standard of living) but also the anxieties of uncertainty, at least in the near term, as workers and employers alike must learn to live with global economic competition and the realities of capitalism.

Third, the realities of democracy have now set in and, in many cases, only seem to compound the anxiety and fears of citizens in Central and East Europe. Any one of these changes would be a serious challenge to policy makers and citizens. Combined and compressed by the relentless pressures of globalization and financial competition, the impact of these reforms presses hard against the economic and political institutions of the region, raising the specter of instability, conflict, and social unrest. The reforms also, of course, offer the prospect of a truly revolutionary transformation of the continent—a European Union from the Atlantic to the Urals, from the Artic to the Mediterranean Sea.

A sampling of public opinion among the citizens of the major West European democracies that are the leaders of the European Union underscore (at least as of 2002) the arguments of those who have expressed warnings about lower levels of political efficacy; lower levels of satisfaction with democracy, the European Union (EU), and life in general; a decline in citizens' engagement in society's political discourse (opinion leadership); and the presence of political ideologists that still value the active role of the state in the economy and that run counter to the instincts of open, global economic competition (left ideology). This general trend is, to some degree, mirrored by the data from Central and East Europe, which reveals a general pattern of dissatisfaction with democracy, disenchantment with market capitalism, and concerns for the lack of human rights. For those countries that are indeed likely to be admitted into the European Union during the next few years, the public generally favors such a move. A minority of citizens see the United States as being the most closely tied to the future success and property of their own country.

The "New Europe" may be more free now than its immediate predecessor. It still confronts, however, the memories of its past, the uncertainties of its future, and the relentless threats and pressures of globalization and the American engine of technological innovation and entrepreneurial zeal. Americans may find it difficult to imagine why some people, even many people within the most democratic European nation-states, do not share the zest for capitalist competition and individualism that so characterizes the political culture of the United States. But the reality is that while Europe's future has the hope of a greater prosperity and deeper freedoms than ever before in its history, this region, so critical to American interests, has not yet settled its mind on how far it wishes to go, or how it wishes to get there.

SOURCES: Elizabeth Pond, *The Rebirth of Europe* (Washington, DC: Brookings Institution Press, 1999). John Newhouse, *Europe Adrift: The Conflicting Demands of Unity, Nationalism, Economic Security, Political Stability, and Military Readiness Now Facing a Europe Seeking to Redefine Itself* (New York: Pantheon, 1997).

sponsored by business and conservative groups have been enacted by voters in certain states.[44] For example, California's Proposition 209, approved by the state's voters in 1996, prohibited the state and local government agencies in California from using race or gender preferences in hiring, contracting, or university admissions decisions. Responding to conservatives' success, liberal groups launched a number of ballot initiatives in 2000. For example, in Washington state, voters were asked to consider propositions sponsored by teachers' unions that would have required annual cost-of-living raises for teachers and more than $1.8 billion in additional state spending over the next six years.[45]

Initiatives such as these seem to provide the public with an opportunity to express its will. The major problem, however, is that government by initiative offers little opportunity for reflection and compromise. Voters are presented with a proposition, usually sponsored by a special interest group, and are asked to take it or leave it. Perhaps the true will of the people, not to mention their best interest, might lie somewhere between the positions taken by various interest groups. Perhaps, for example, California voters might have wanted affirmative action programs to be modified but not scrapped altogether as Proposition 209 mandated. In a representative assembly, as opposed to a referendum campaign, a compromise position might have been achieved that was more satisfactory to all the residents of the state. This is one reason the framers of the U.S. Constitution strongly favored representative government rather than direct democracy.

When all is said and done, even without the initiative and referendum, there can be little doubt that in general the actions of the American government do not remain out of line with popular sentiment for very long. One could take these as signs of a vital and thriving democracy.

GET INVOLVED
What You Can Do: Become Politically Knowledgeable

In a democracy, one central role of the citizen is to be informed and knowledgeable. Many eighteenth- and nineteenth-century political theorists believed that popular government required an informed, aware, and involved citizenry, and wondered whether this condition could be met. The Frenchman Alexis de Tocqueville, writing in the early nineteenth century, asserted that to participate in democratic politics ordinary citizens needed to be aware of their own interests and to understand how those interests might be affected by contemporary issues. De Tocqueville and others have feared that participation by the unenlightened might be worse than no participation at all, since the ignorant could easily be swayed by demagogues to support foolish or even evil causes. Contemporary public opinion research indicates that better-informed citizens are considerably better able than their uninformed counterparts to exert influence in the political arena and to benefit from the government's actions. Knowledge, indeed, seems to be power.[46]

Fortunately, the most basic element of citizenship is also one of the simplest to achieve. Viewed correctly, reading a daily newspaper is an important political act! Watching a television news or discussion program is an important form of political participation. For some, visiting and comparing the Web sites of several candidates is a way of becoming politically involved, albeit in cyberspace.

Those who use newspapers, magazines, television, and computers to become politically knowledgeable and aware have taken a huge first step toward becoming politically influential. Those who limit their newspaper reading to the sports page and their television viewing to situation comedies are also abdicating the responsibilities and opportunities inherent in democratic citizenship. If a person opts to be indifferent or cynical about politics, his or her decision must be based on an informed indifference or cynicism to be truly meaningful.

Summary

Americans disagree on many issues, but they nevertheless share a number of important values, including liberty, equality of opportunity, and democracy. Although factors such as race, education, gender, and social class produce important differences in outlook, Americans probably agree more on fundamental values than do the citizens of most other nations.

Most people acquire their initial orientation to political life from their families. Subsequently, political views are influenced by interests, personal experiences, group memberships, and the conditions under which citizens are first mobilized into politics. Opinions on particular issues may also be influenced by political leaders and the mass media. The media help determine what Americans know about politics.

Most governments, including the U.S. government, endeavor to shape their citizens' political beliefs. In democracies, private groups compete with government to shape opinion.

Public opinion is generally measured by polling. However, polls can also distort opinion, imputing salience to issues that citizens care little about or creating the illusion that most people are moderate or centrist in their views.

Over time, the government's policies are strongly affected by public opinion, although there can be lags and divergences, especially when an intense minority confronts a more apathetic majority.

For Further Reading

Gallup, George. *The Pulse of Democracy.* New York: Simon and Schuster, 1940.

Ginsberg, Benjamin. *The Captive Public: How Mass Opinion Promotes State Power.* New York: Basic Books, 1986.

Herbst, Susan. *Numbered Voices: How Opinion Polling Has Shaped American Politics.* Chicago: University of Chicago Press, 1993.

Herbst, Susan. *Reading Public Opinion: How Political Actors View the Democratic Process.* Chicago: University of Chicago Press, 1998.

Jacobs, Lawrence R., and Robert Y. Shapiro. *Politicians Don't Pander: Political Manipulation and the Loss of Democratic Responsiveness.* Chicago: University of Chicago Press, 2000.

Key, V. O. *Public Opinion and American Democracy.* New York: Knopf, 1961.

Lippman, Walter. *Public Opinion.* New York: Harcourt, Brace, 1922.

Mayer, William G. *The Changing American Mind: How and Why American Public Opinion Changed between 1960 and 1988.* Ann Arbor: University of Michigan Press, 1992.

Mutz, Diana C. *Impersonal Influence: How Perceptions of Mass Collectives Affect Political Attitudes.* New York: Cambridge University Press, 1998.

Neuman, W. Russell. *The Paradox of Mass Politics: Knowledge and Opinion in the American Electorate.* Cambridge, MA: Harvard University Press, 1986.

Page, Benjamin I., and Robert Y. Shapiro. *The Rational Public: Fifty Years of Trends in Americans' Policy Preferences.* Chicago: University of Chicago Press, 1992.

Rinehart, Sue Tolleson. *Gender Consciousness and Politics.* New York: Routledge, 1992.

Schuman, Howard, Charlotte Steeh, and Lawrence Bobo. *Racial Attitudes in America.* Cambridge, MA: Harvard University Press, 1990.

Traugott, Michael, and Paul Lavrakas. *The Voter's Guide to Election Polls.* 2nd ed. New York: Chatham House, 2000.

Study Outline

www.wwnorton.com/wtp4e

Political Values

1. Although Americans have many political differences, they share a common set of values, including liberty, equality of opportunity, and democracy.
2. Agreement on fundamental political values is probably more widespread in the United States than anywhere else in the Western world.
3. Often for reasons associated with demographics, Americans' opinions do differ widely on a variety of issues.
4. Most people acquire their initial orientation to politics from their families.
5. Membership in both voluntary and involuntary social groups can affect an individual's political values through personal experience, the influence of group leaders, and recognition of political interests.
6. One's level of education is an important factor in shaping political beliefs.
7. Conditions under which individuals and groups are recruited into political life also shape political orientations.
8. Many Americans describe themselves as either liberal or conservative in political orientation.

How We Form Political Opinions

1. Although ideologies shape political opinions, they seldom fully determine one's views.
2. Political opinions are influenced by an individual's underlying values, knowledge of political issues, and external forces such as the government, private groups, and the media.

Measuring Public Opinion

1. In order to construct public opinion from surveys, a polling sample must be large and the views of those in the sample must accurately and proportionately reflect the views of the whole.

Public Opinion and Democracy

1. Government policies in the United States are generally consistent with popular preferences. There are, however, always some inconsistencies.
2. Disagreements between opinion and policy come about because on some issues, such as gun control, an intensely committed minority can defeat a more apathetic majority. Moreover, the American system of government is not designed to quickly transform changes in opinion into changes in government programs.

Practice Quiz

www.wwnorton.com/wtp4e

1. The term "public opinion" is used to describe
   a) the collected speeches and writings made by a president during his term in office.
   b) the analysis of events broadcast by news reporters during the evening news.
   c) the beliefs and attitudes that people have about issues.
   d) decisions of the Supreme Court.

2. Variables such as income, education, race, gender, and ethnicity
   a) often create differences of political opinion in America.
   b) have consistently been a challenge to America's core political values.
   c) have little impact on political opinions.
   d) help explain why public opinion polls are so unreliable.

3. Which of the following is an agency of socialization?
   a) the family
   b) social groups
   c) education
   d) all of the above

4. When men and women respond differently to issues of public policy, they are demonstrating an example of
   a) liberalism.
   b) educational differences.
   c) the gender gap.
   d) party politics.

5. The process by which Americans learn political beliefs and values is called
   a) brainwashing.
   b) propaganda.
   c) indoctrination.
   d) political socialization.

6. In addition to one's basic political values, what other two factors influence one's political opinions?
   a) ideology and party identification
   b) political knowledge and the influence of political leaders, private groups, and the media
   c) the gender gap and the education gap
   d) sample size and the bandwagon effect

7. Which of the following is (are) *not* an important external influence on how political opinions are formed?
   a) the government and political leaders
   b) private interest groups
   c) the media
   d) the Constitution

8. Which of the following is the term used in public opinion polling to denote the small group representing the opinions of the whole population?
   a) control group
   b) sample
   c) micropopulation
   d) respondents

9. When politicians, pollsters, journalists, or social scientists assume something is important to the public when in fact it is not, they are creating
   a) an illusion of saliency.
   b) an illusion of responsibility.
   c) a gender gap.
   d) an elitist issue.

10. A familiar polling problem is the "bandwagon effect," which occurs when
    a) the same results are used over and over again.
    b) polling results influence people to support the candidate marked as the probable victor in a campaign.
    c) polling results influence people to support the candidate who is trailing in a campaign.
    d) background noise makes it difficult for a pollster and a respondent to communicate with one another.

Critical Thinking Questions

www.wwnorton.com/wtp4e

1. In the American system of government, public opinion seems to be an important factor in political and governmental decision making. In what ways does the public, through opinion, control its political leaders? In what ways do political leaders control public opinion? What are the positive and negative consequences of governing by popular opinion?

2. Describe the differences between liberal and conservative ideologies in American politics. Using one social or demographic group as an example, describe some of the factors that may have shaped the ideological orientation of that particular group. What factors may explain inconsistencies in that group's political ideology or issue positions?

3. Former president Bill Clinton polled public opinion on an almost daily basis to try to stay in touch with shifts in popular sentiment. President George W. Bush places less emphasis on polling, apparently believing that leaders should use their own judgment rather than follow popular sentiment on every issue. Which of these views would be supported by the framers of the Constitution? Which of these views is more appropriate for a politician in a democracy?

Key Terms

www.wwnorton.com/wtp4e

agencies of socialization (p. 219)
attitude (or opinion) (p. 211)
bandwagon effect (p. 241)
conservative (p. 227)

democracy (p. 212)
equality of opportunity (p. 212)
gender gap (p. 221)
illusion of saliency (p. 241)
liberal (p. 226)
liberty (p. 212)
marketplace of ideas (p. 231)
political efficacy (p. 231)

political ideology (p. 211)
political socialization (p. 219)
public opinion (p. 211)
public opinion polls (p. 237)
push polling (p. 240)
salient interests (p. 241)
sample (p. 237)
values (or beliefs) (p. 211)

7 THE MEDIA

☆ **The Media Industry and Government**

How is the media regulated by the government? How does this regulation differ between the broadcast media and the print media?

How has the nationalization of the news media contributed to the nationalization of American politics?

☆ **News Coverage**

How are media content, news coverage, and bias affected by the producers, subjects, and consumers of the news?

☆ **Media Power in American Politics**

How do the media shape public perceptions of events, issues, and institutions?

☆ **Media Power and Democracy**

Are the media too powerful and thus in need of restriction, or are a free media necessary for democracy?

What Government Does and Why It Matters

NE AREA IN WHICH our government's role is intended to be minimal is the realm of the news media. The Constitution's First Amendment guarantees freedom of the press and most Americans believe that a free press is an essential condition for both liberty and democratic politics. Certainly, the press is usually ready to denounce any government actions that smack of censorship or news manipulation. Nevertheless, attempts to silence or discredit the opposition press have a long history in America. The infamous Alien and Sedition Acts were enacted by the Federalists in an attempt to silence the Republican press. In more recent times, during the McCarthy era of the 1950s, right-wing politicians used charges of communist infiltration to intimidate the liberal news media. During President Richard Nixon's administration, the White House attacked its critics in the media by threatening to take action to bar the television networks from owning local affiliates, as well as by illegally wiretapping the phones of government officials suspected of leaking information to the press. In the early 1980s, conservative groups financed a series of libel suits against CBS News, *Time* magazine, and other media organizations, in an attempt to discourage them from publicizing material critical of Reagan administration policies.[1] In 1998, President Clinton's political allies accused the national news media of engaging in tabloid journalism and invading the president's privacy in order to discredit him by publicizing the intimate details of Clinton's sexual relationship with former White House intern Monica Lewinsky. In all these instances, attempts to silence the press failed. ∎

■ **In this chapter, we will examine the place of the media in American politics. First, we will look at the organization and regulation of the American news media.** The media industry continues to grow larger and more centralized, resulting in little variety in what is reported about national issues. Despite the central importance of freedom of the press in the United States, the media are still subject to some regulation by the government.

■ **Second, we will discuss the factors that help to determine "what's news."** The agenda of issues and type of coverage that the media provide are affected most by those who create the news and those who consume the news.

■ **Third, we will examine the scope of media power in politics.** What the media report can have far-reaching effects on public perceptions of political events, issues, leaders, and institutions.

■ **Finally, we will address the question of responsibility: to whom, if anyone, are the media accountable for the use of their formidable power?** The answer to this question has great implications for American democracy.

The Media Industry and Government

The American news media are among the world's most vast and most free. Americans literally have thousands of available options to find political reporting. This wide variety of newspapers, newsmagazines, and broadcast media regularly present information that is at odds with the government's claims, as well as editorial opinions sharply critical of high-ranking officials. The freedom to speak one's mind is one of the most cherished of American political values—one that is jealously safeguarded by the media. Yet although thousands of media companies exist across the United States, surprisingly little variety appears in what is reported about national events and issues.

TYPES OF MEDIA

Americans get their news from three main sources: broadcast media (radio, television), print media (newspapers and magazines), and, increasingly, the Internet (see Figure 7.1 on the next page). Each of these sources has distinctive characteristics. Television news reaches more Americans than any other single news source. Tens of millions of individuals watch national and local news programs every day. Television news, however, covers relatively few topics and provides little depth of coverage. Television news is more like a series of newspaper headlines connected to pictures. It serves the extremely important function of alerting viewers to issues and events, but provides little more than a series of "sound bites," brief quotes and short characterizations of the day's events. Because they are aware of the character of television news coverage, politicians and other newsmakers often seek to manipulate the news by providing the media with sound bites that will dominate news coverage for at least a few days. George Bush's famous 1988 sound bite, "Read my lips, no new taxes," received a great deal of media coverage. Two years later he was, in effect, bitten by his own sound bite when he signed legislation that included new taxes. The twenty-four-hour news stations like Cable News Network (CNN) offer

The Use of Different Media for Political News by Age

Figure 7.1

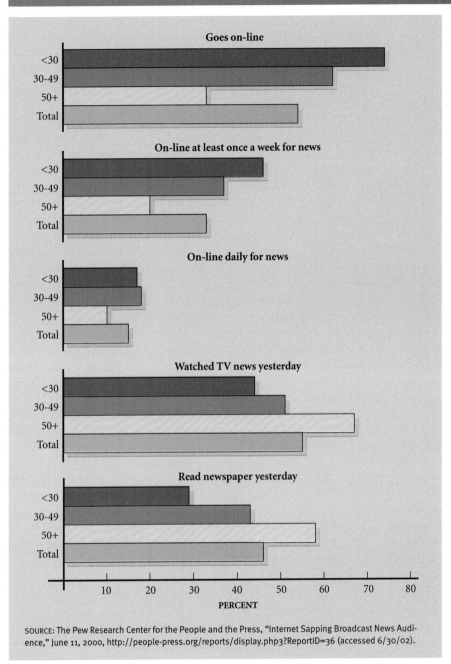

SOURCE: The Pew Research Center for the People and the Press, "Internet Sapping Broadcast News Audience," June 11, 2000, http://people-press.org/reports/display.php3?ReportID=36 (accessed 6/30/02).

more detail and commentary than the networks' half-hour evening news shows. Even CNN and the others, however, offer more headlines than analysis, especially during their prime-time broadcasts.

Politicians generally view the local broadcast news as a friendlier venue than the national news. National reporters are often inclined to criticize and question while local reporters often accept the pronouncements of national leaders at face value. For this reason, presidents often introduce new proposals in a series of short visits to a number of cities—indeed, sometimes flying from airport stop to airport stop—in addition to or instead of making a national presentation. For example, in February 2002, President Bush introduced his idea for a new national volunteer corps during his State of the Union message and then made a number of local speeches around the country promoting the same theme. While national reporters questioned the president's plans, local news coverage was overwhelmingly positive.

Radio news is also essentially a headline service, but without pictures. In the short time—usually five minutes per hour—they devote to news, radio stations announce the day's major events without providing much detail. In major cities, all-news stations provide a bit more coverage of major stories, but for the most part these stations fill the day with repetition rather than detail. All-news stations like Washington, D.C.'s WTOP or New York's WCBS assume that most listeners are in their cars and that, as a result, the people in the audience change markedly throughout the day as listeners reach their destinations. Thus, rather than use their time to flesh out a given set of stories, they repeat the same stories each hour to present them to new listeners. In recent years, radio talk shows have become important sources of commentary and opinion. A number of conservative radio hosts such as Rush Limbaugh and Dr. Laura Schlesinger have huge audiences and have helped to mobilize support for conservative political causes and candidates. Liberals have had less success in the world of talk radio.

The most important source of news is the old-fashioned newspaper. Newspapers remain critically important even though they are not the primary news source for most Americans. The print media are important for three reasons. First, as we shall see later in this chapter, the broadcast media rely upon leading newspapers such as *The New York Times* and *The Washington Post* to set their news agenda. The broadcast media engage in very little actual reporting; they primarily cover stories that have been "broken," or initially reported, by the print media. For example, sensational charges that President Bill Clinton had an affair with a White House intern were reported first by *The Washington Post* and *Newsweek* before being trumpeted around the world by the broadcast media. It is only a slight exaggeration to observe that if an event is not covered in *The New York Times,* it is not likely to appear on the *CBS Evening News*. Second, the print media provide more detailed and complete information, offering a better context for analysis. Third, the print media are important because they are the prime source of news for educated and influential individuals. The nation's economic, social, and political elites rely upon the detailed coverage provided by the print media to inform and influence their views about important public matters. The print media may have a smaller audience than their cousins in broadcasting, but they have an audience that matters.

A relatively new source of news is the Internet. Every day, several million Americans scan one of many news sites on the Internet for coverage of current events. For the most part, however, the Internet provides electronic versions of coverage offered by print sources. One great advantage of the Internet is that it allows frequent updating. It potentially can combine the depth of coverage of a newspaper with the timeliness of television and radio, and probably will become a major news source in the next decade. In 2000, many Americans relied on websites such as CNN.com for up-to-the-minute election news during the campaign and, especially, during the dramatic post-election battle in Florida. Acknowledging the growing importance of the Internet as a political communications medium, the U. S. Supreme Court posted its decisions in the Florida election cases as soon as they were issued. In 2001, millions of Americans relied on the Internet for news relating to terrorism, bioterrorism, and the military campaign in Afghanistan. Web sites providing information on anthrax and other biological threats reported hundreds of thousands of visits. As on-line access becomes simpler and faster, the Internet could give Americans access to unprecedented quantities of up-to-the-minute information. If only computers could also give Americans the ability to make good use of that information!

REGULATION OF THE BROADCAST MEDIA

In some countries, the government controls media content. In other countries, the government owns the broadcast media (e.g., the BBC in Britain) but it does not tell the media what to say. In the United States, the government neither owns nor controls the communications networks, but it does regulate the content and ownership of the broadcast media.

As we saw in Chapter 4, in the United States, the print media are essentially free from government interference. The broadcast media, on the other hand, are subject to federal regulation. American radio and television are regulated by the Federal Communications Commission (FCC), an independent regulatory agency established in 1934. Radio and TV stations must have FCC licenses that must be renewed every five years. Licensing provides a mechanism for allocating radio and TV frequencies to prevent broadcasts from interfering with and garbling one another. License renewals are almost always granted automatically by the FCC. Indeed, renewal requests are now filed by postcard.

For more than sixty years, the FCC also sought to regulate and promote competition in the broadcast industry, but in 1996 Congress passed the Telecommunications Act, a broad effort to do away with most regulations in effect since 1934. The act loosened restrictions on media ownership and allowed for telephone companies, cable television providers, and broadcasters to compete with one another for telecommunication services. Following the passage of the act, several mergers between telephone and cable companies and between different segments of the entertainment media produced an even greater concentration of media ownership.

The Telecommunications Act of 1996 also included an attempt to regulate the content of material transmitted over the Internet. This law, known as the Communications Decency Act, made it illegal to make "indecent" sexual material on the Internet accessible to those under eighteen years old. The act was immediately denounced by civil libertarians and brought to court as an infringement of free speech. The case reached the Supreme Court in 1997 and the act was ruled an unconstitutional infringement of the First Amendment's right to freedom of speech (see Chapter 4).

Although the government's ability to regulate the content of the electronic media on the Internet has been questioned, the federal government has used its licensing power to impose several regulations that can affect the political content of radio and TV broadcasts. The first of these is the **equal time rule,** under which broadcasters must provide candidates for the same political office equal opportunities to communicate their messages to the public. If, for example, a television station sells commercial time to a state's Republican gubernatorial candidate, it may not refuse to sell time to the Democratic candidate for the same position.

> ❯ **How is the media regulated by the government? How does this regulation differ between the broadcast media and the print media?**

equal time rule the requirement that broadcasters provide candidates for the same political office an equal opportunity to communicate their messages to the public.

right of rebuttal a Federal Communications Commission regulation giving individuals the right to have the opportunity to respond to personal attacks made on a radio or television broadcast.

fairness doctrine a Federal Communications Commission (FCC) requirement for broadcasters who air programs on controversial issues to provide time for opposing views. The FCC ceased enforcing this doctrine in 1985.

The second regulation affecting the content of broadcasts is the **right of rebuttal,** which requires that individuals be given the opportunity to respond to personal attacks. In the 1969 case of *Red Lion Broadcasting Company v. FCC,* for example, the U.S. Supreme Court upheld the FCC's determination that a radio station was required to provide a liberal author with an opportunity to respond to an attack from a conservative commentator that the station had aired.[2]

For many years, a third important federal regulation was the **fairness doctrine.** Under this doctrine, broadcasters who aired programs on controversial issues were required to provide time for opposing views. In 1985, however, the FCC stopped enforcing the fairness doctrine on the grounds that there were so many radio and television stations—to say nothing of newspapers and newsmagazines—that in all likelihood many different viewpoints were already being presented without having to require each station to try to present all sides of an argument. Critics of this FCC decision charge that in many media markets the number of competing viewpoints is small. Nevertheless, a congressional effort to require the FCC to enforce the fairness doctrine was blocked by the Reagan administration in 1987.

ORGANIZATION AND OWNERSHIP OF THE MEDIA

The United States boasts more than one thousand television stations, approximately eighteen hundred daily newspapers, and more than nine thousand radio stations (20 percent of which are devoted to news, talk, or public affairs).[3]

Even though the number of TV and radio stations and daily newspapers reporting news in the United States is enormous, the number of sources of national news is actually quite small—several wire services, four broadcast networks, public radio and television, two elite newspapers, three newsmagazines, and a scattering of other sources such as the national correspondents of a few large local papers and the small independent radio networks. More than three-fourths of the daily newspapers in the United States are owned by large media conglomerates such as the Hearst, Knight Ridder, or Gannett corporations; thus the diversity of coverage and editorial opinion in American newspapers is not as broad as it might seem. Much of the national news that is published by local newspapers is provided by one wire service, the Associated Press, while additional coverage is provided by services run by several major newspapers like *The New York Times* and the *Chicago Tribune.* More than five hundred of the nation's television stations are affiliated with one of the four networks and carry that network's evening news reports. Dozens of others carry PBS (Public Broadcasting System) news. Several hundred local radio stations also carry network news or National Public Radio news broadcasts. At the same time, although there are only three truly national newspapers, *The Wall Street Journal, The Christian Science Monitor,* and *USA Today,* two other papers, *The New York Times* and *The Washington Post,* are read by political leaders and other influential Americans throughout the nation. Such is the influence of these two "elite" newspapers that their news coverage sets the standard for virtually all other news outlets. Stories carried in *The New York Times* or *The Washington Post* influence the content of many other papers as well as of the network news. Note how often this text, like most others, relies upon *New York Times* and *Washington Post* stories as sources for contemporary events. National news is also carried to millions of Americans by the three major newsmagazines—*Time, Newsweek,* and *U.S. News & World Report.* Beginning in the late 1980s, CNN became

Internet Regulation: The Communications Decency Act

When Congress, with the support of President Clinton, passed the Communications Decency Act (CDA) as one part of the Telecommunications Act of 1996, it sought to bar the transmission of obscene or indecent communications to anyone under the age of eighteen. The constitutionality of the CDA was immediately challenged by Internet service providers and civil liberties groups as an improper infringement of First Amendment liberties. In a sweeping 1997 decision, the Supreme Court ruled in *Reno v. American Civil Liberties Union* that such regulations are a violation of the First Amendment. More important, the Court established that the Internet is a form of communication entitled to the maximum degree of constitutional protection, analogous to newspapers, books, and magazines (electronic media, such as television and radio, may be more strictly regulated by the government). Yet this ruling has not ended the dispute between those favoring and opposing stricter Internet controls.

Supporters of Internet regulation argue that children must be protected from the vast amount of offensive material to be found on the Internet. More than 10,000 Web sites are devoted to some form of pornography. Given the proliferation of obscene materials and sites, and given that the Internet is unregulated, government must be able to intervene to protect children. Despite the Supreme Court's ruling, the Internet is very different from newspapers and other printed media, in that there are no reporters, editors, publishers, or others who control the content of Internet communications.

Even more alarming, sexual predators have used Internet connections not only to expose children to obscene material, but to lure children to dangerous in-person meetings. For example, a California man was convicted of luring a thirteen-year-old girl from Kentucky to a meeting with him, the purpose of which was illegal sexual conduct.

From 1995 to 1997, the FBI arrested thirty-five adults seeking to solicit sex from minors via the Internet. Apart from barring children from all Internet use, parents find themselves nearly powerless to protect their children, who often possess far more knowledge of computer technologies than their parents. Some limitation on liberty is necessary to protect America's children.

Those who oppose Internet regulation argue that the total harm done by regulations like the CDA far outweighs the benefits. In constitutional terms, the Internet is a vast electronic forum for speech, expression, and education. Although some harm is likely to accompany the unfettered expression of thoughts and ideas, such expression is central to a democracy and to the fundamental liberties of its citizens. Efforts to regulate Internet content in the name of protecting children too easily restrict legitimate expression. For example, during the brief time that the

CDA was in effect, messages with the word "breast" in them were banned from the Internet by some providers. Such bans blocked not only obscene references, but also sites dealing with breast cancer, for example. Efforts to regulate indecent and obscene materials inevitably exclude useful information, and would have a chilling effect on many forms of legitimate communication, such as on-line support groups dealing with AIDS, child abuse, rape, and the like. Other information having legitimate scientific, artistic, literary, or other social value is too easily suppressed by regulations like the CDA.

Concerned parents can always monitor Internet use by their children. They can obtain software that filters out objectionable materials. Above all, parents should have primary control over what their children do and do not see.

SOURCE: Amy Harmon, "Ruling Leaves Vexing Burden for Parents," *New York Times*, June 27, 1997.

Should the Internet Be Regulated?

Yes

Helping my ten-year-old cousin with her fifth-grade final project was not the breeze I had anticipated it to be. With an ambitious assignment: to write about "The American Government," our first recourse was on-line research. My cousin insisted on typing, eager to show off her Internet proficiency to the big kid sitting next to her. As her pudgy fingers hunted and pecked for a Web site, I watched as the phrase "whitehouse.com" appeared on the screen. Then I watched as the image of a woman in a suit jacket and not much else followed, also beckoning from the screen. I quickly covered my cousin's face, muffling her questioning about the meaning of "foxy chicks" beneath my hands.

Who knew that the innocent replacement of .com for .gov would generate an NC-17 Web site? Certainly not my little cousin, who still pesters me about what "foxy chicks" means today. With new laws being passed in Virginia to ban pornography and other inappropriate content on the Web, shouts of First Amendment violations predictably blare like a foghorn. Numerous Virginia groups, like PSINet (an Internet development company in Herndon), the Comic Book Legal Defense Fund, and Lambda Rising Bookstores, the nation's largest specialty retailer of gay and lesbian materials, tout the law as an attempt to reduce cyberspace to a realm suitable only for juveniles. Civil rights advocates who are currently filing a federal suit against the Commonwealth claim that it limits the Internet as an open forum for communication and information.

To some extent, these protests are justified. A complete ban on public information undoubtedly is a violation of free speech. But one has to wonder what really is being protected in the defense of propagation of material harmful to children—the freedom of press on the Internet, or the industry that profits from it?

The argument against censorship always has been "If the government limits you in one way, who's to say it will not limit you in others?" As another generation raised on a healthy diet of rallies, marches, and sit-ins, however, we are all aware that Americans are as patient with injustice as a cranky baby is about its bottle. Limiting explicit material on the Internet will not lead to a domino effect of limitations. Groups like People for the American Way, which currently is protesting the Virginia law, and other almost militantly active freedom-of-speech groups will continue to exist. And they will continue to yelp about how the government stepped on the nation's democratic foot to protect us.

Instead of being the revolutionary turning point it is feared as, Internet censorship will be another practical exception to the First Amendment rule. No, you can't yell fire in a crowded movie theater, even if there is free speech. No, you can't print libel even if there is free press. The above are dangers, and they exceed the dangers of violating the First Amendment. For the same reason—no, you can't sell or display pornography on-line in a manner that is accessible to children.

Completely prohibiting access to explicit sites would be a blatant denial of rights. But prohibiting pornography's dissemination to minors is just another reasonable exception to the First Amendment, and not the Black Death of liberty, as civil rights activists diagnose it. In this case, those who defend free speech do it more for their own sake rather than the sake of the common good.

———

A noteworthy argument against the Virginia ban on explicit material is that, for all practical purposes, it is useless, considering how ineffective a single state law would be in curbing the entire World Wide Web. While this is true, this is also not the purpose of the law. It will not be the single finger that is wagged at explicit Web material, but a part of the larger hand that is doing the smacking. It is the Internet version of *Brown v. the Board of Education,* in that it has the potential to start a chain of events protecting innocent eyes from inappropriate material.

And that's nice to know, because when it comes down to it, who really wants to have to explain what "foxy chicks" means anyway?

SOURCE: Diya Gullapalli, "Limiting Web Makes Surfing Safer," *Cavalier Daily* (University of Virginia), October 13, 1999.

No

A trial questioning a law that would require public libraries to restrict access to pornographic Internet sites began last week in a U.S. District Court. Former president Bill Clinton signed the Children's Internet Protection Act (CIPA) in 2000. The act requires public libraries to install filtering software on their computers to protect children from objectionable material. If the libraries refuse to comply, they could lose millions of dollars in government subsidies.

The American Civil Liberties Union, along with a group of libraries, library patrons, and Web site operators, are requesting a permanent injunction against CIPA. They say CIPA violates the free speech of adults.

The requirements set forth by CIPA are inherently flawed. Few would argue that children should have access to hardcore pornography. However, filtering software is not the way to protect children. Parents should properly monitor their children instead of expecting librarians and an electronic babysitter to do it for them.

The way the software works is faulty, according to the plaintiffs. It blocks Web sites that are unobjectionable and allows access to some sites that are objectionable. The biggest problem is that the definition of "objectionable" is highly relative.

There is no such thing as a common standard of decency, so attempting to enforce decency standards at the national level can only cause problems. CIPA will restrict the First Amendment rights of adults. CIPA could also be used as a means of restricting knowledge about birth control, abortion access, homosexual rights, and other controversial subjects.

For example, Candace Morgan, associate director of the Fort Vancouver Regional Library in Washington State, was asked to examine photographs from a pornographic Web site in court. "We have sex education manuals similar to some of these," she said.

In the not so distant past, women's right to information on birth control and abortion was denied by "public decency" laws, such as the Comstock Laws of the early twentieth century. This could happen again if CIPA is upheld as it stands. Many people do not have personal access to controversial personal information at home or school—they must not be denied access in the library as well.

Although some libraries provide blocking systems on a voluntary basis, they should not be forced to do so. Morgan said her library does this, but also holds parents and guardians responsible for their children's activities.

There is no perfect way to protect children from objectionable materials. However, undermining the First Amendment rights of other patrons is inexcusable. CIPA's vagueness provides too tempting an opportunity for lawmakers to ban controversial material from public places. To be fair to all involved, the court must not uphold CIPA.

SOURCE: Jessica Crutcher, "Now Open to the Public," *The Battalion* (Texas A & M University), April 2, 2002.

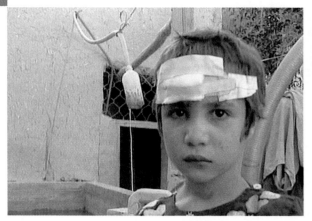 

In the wake of the September 11, 2001, terror attacks in New York and Washington, the national media generally presented a positive account of America's military campaign to eradicate terrorist bases and infrastructure in Afghanistan and to overthrow that nation's Islamic fundamentalist Taliban regime. Most commentators seemed to accept the necessity of the military effort, and, generally speaking, the media focused on issues of tactics and procedure. The media aimed for some balance, however, airing reports of civilian casualties from American bombing raids (left).

Some commentators emphasized the importance of seeking to understand why Islamic terrorists aimed their wrath at the United States. The media aired controversial tapes apparently made by terrorist mastermind Osama bin Laden and shown initially by an Arabic-language television station based in Qatar (right). In the tapes, bin Laden and his colleagues denounce the United States and its policies and promise to bring America to its knees. Critics charged that the tapes did little more than provide free publicity for America's adversaries.

another major news source for Americans. The importance of CNN increased dramatically after its spectacular coverage of the Persian Gulf War. At one point, CNN was able to provide live reports of American bombing raids on Baghdad, Iraq, after the major networks' correspondents had been forced to flee to bomb shelters. Even the availability of new electronic media on the Internet has failed to expand the number of news sources. Most national news available on the World Wide Web, for example, consists of electronic versions of the conventional print or broadcast media.

The trend toward the homogenization of national news has been hastened by dramatic changes in media ownership, which became possible in large part due to the relaxation of government regulations in the 1980s and 1990s. The enactment of the 1996 Telecommunications Act opened the way for further consolidation in the media industry, and a wave of mergers and consolidations has further reduced the field of independent media across the country. Since that time, among the major news networks, ABC was bought by the Walt Disney corporation, CBS was bought by Westinghouse Electric and later merged with Viacom, the owner of MTV and Paramount Studios, and CNN was bought by Time Warner. NBC has been owned by General Electric since 1986. Australian press baron Rupert Murdoch owns the Fox network plus a host of radio, television, and newspaper properties around the world. A small number of giant corporations now controls a wide swath of media holdings, including television networks, movie studios, record companies, cable

The news media also covered anti-American demonstrations in Europe and the Middle East as well as small antiwar demonstrations in the United States (left). Media critics accused the news media of giving the administration's opponents more weight than they deserved.

The media, however, insisted that balanced coverage was essential. The dangers of reporting on war and terrorism were brought home when Pakistani Islamic fundamentalists kidnapped and murdered Wall Street Journal *correspondent Daniel Pearl and made tapes of the crime available to the media (right). Television networks and newsmagazines presented graphic pictures of Pearl's body.*

channels and local cable providers, book publishers, magazines, and newspapers. These developments have prompted questions about whether enough competition exists among the media to produce a diverse set of views on political and corporate matters[4] or whether the U. S. has become the prisoner of media monopolies.

NATIONALIZATION OF THE NEWS

In general, the national news media cover more or less the same sets of events, present similar information, and emphasize similar issues and problems. Indeed, the national news services watch one another quite carefully. It is very likely that a major story carried by one service will quickly find its way into the pages or programming of the others. As a result, in the United States a rather centralized national news has developed, through which a relatively similar picture of events, issues, and problems is presented to the entire nation.[5] The nationalization of the news began at the turn of the century, was accelerated by the development of radio networks in the 1920s and 1930s and by the creation of the television networks after the 1950s, and has been further strengthened by the recent trends toward concentrated media ownership. This nationalization of news content has very important consequences for the American political system.

Nationalization of the news has contributed greatly to the nationalization of politics and of political perspectives in the United States. Prior to the development of the national media and the nationalization of news coverage, news traveled very slowly. Every region and city saw national issues and problems primarily through a

> **How has the nationalization of the news media contributed to the nationalization of American politics?**

local lens. Concerns and perspectives varied greatly from region to region, city to city, and village to village. Today, in large measure as a result of the nationalization of the media, residents of all parts of the country share a similar picture of the day's events.[6] They may not agree on everything, but most see the world in similar ways.

The exception to this pattern can be found with those Americans whose chief source of news is something other than the "mainstream" national media. Despite the nationalization and homogenization of the news, in some American cities, alternative news coverage is available. Such media markets are known as **news enclaves.** For example, some African Americans rely upon newspapers and radio stations that aim their coverage primarily at black audiences. This general strategy is known as "narrowcasting" (to distinguish it from broadcasting). As a result, these individuals may interpret events differently than white Americans and even other blacks do.[7] The existence of a black-focused media helps to explain why many African Americans and white Americans reacted differently to the 1995 trial of O. J. Simpson in Los Angeles. While national media outlets generally portrayed Simpson as guilty of the murder of his former wife, African American media outlets depicted Simpson as a victim of a racist criminal justice system. This latter view came to be held by a large number of African Americans.

In a similar vein, some radio stations and print media are aimed exclusively at religious and social conservatives. These individuals are also likely to develop and retain a perception of the news that is quite different from that of "mainstream" America. For example, the rural midwesterners who rely upon the ultraconservative People's Radio Network for their news coverage may become concerned about the alleged efforts of the United Nations to subordinate the United States in a world government, a viewpoint unfamiliar to most Americans.

Internet newsgroups are another form of news enclave. Newsgroups are informal and tend to develop around the discussion of a particular set of issues. Individuals post their views for others to read; comments are also posted. In some instances, posted comments are attacked by other members of the community. In general, users seem to seek out and exchange postings with those who share their opinions. Perhaps the long-term significance of the Internet is that it will increasingly allow contacts among individuals with unconventional viewpoints who are geographically dispersed and might otherwise be unaware of the existence of others who share their views. In the mid-1990s, Internet newsgroups played a role in the mobilization of "antigovernment" fringe groups.

The same principle seems to hold for another form of discussion on the Internet, known as a chat room. Chat rooms are on-line forums in which anonymous individuals form groups spontaneously and converse with one another. The topics change often as participants leave and are replaced by newcomers. Like newsgroups, chat rooms seem to function as opinion enclaves where like-minded individuals from across the nation can congregate and reinforce one another's views.

News Coverage

Because of the important role the media can play in national politics, it is vitally important to understand the factors that affect media coverage.[8] What accounts for the media's agenda of issues and topics? What explains the character of coverage—why

news enclave a group seeking specialized information not provided by the mainstream media

does a politician receive good or bad press? What factors determine the interpretation or "spin" that a particular story will receive? Although a host of minor factors plays a role, three major factors are important: (1) the journalists, or producers of the news; (2) the sources or topics of the news; and (3) the audience for the news.

JOURNALISTS

Media content and news coverage are inevitably affected by the views, ideals, and interests of those who seek out, write, and produce news and other stories. At one time, newspaper publishers exercised a great deal of influence over their papers' news content. Publishers such as William Randolph Hearst and Joseph Pulitzer became political powers through their manipulation of news coverage. Hearst, for example, almost single-handedly pushed the United States into war with Spain in 1898 through his newspapers' relentless coverage of the alleged brutality employed by Spain in its efforts to suppress a rebellion in Cuba, at that time a Spanish colony. The sinking of the American battleship *Maine* in Havana harbor under mysterious circumstances gave Hearst the ammunition he needed to force a reluctant President McKinley to lead the nation into war. Today, few publishers have that kind of power. Most publishers are concerned more with the business operations of their newspapers than with editorial content, although a few continue to impose their interests and tastes on the news.

More important than publishers, for the most part, are the reporters. Those who cover the news for the national media generally have a good deal of discretion or freedom to interpret stories and, as a result, have an opportunity to interject their views and ideals into news stories. For example, the personal friendship and respect that some reporters felt for Franklin Roosevelt or John Kennedy helped to generate more favorable news coverage for these presidents. Likewise, the dislike and distrust felt by many reporters for Richard Nixon was also communicated to the public. In the case of Ronald Reagan, the disdain that many journalists felt for the president was communicated in stories suggesting that he was often asleep or inattentive when important decisions were made.

Conservatives have long charged that the liberal biases of reporters and journalists result in distorted news coverage. A 1996 survey of Washington newspaper bureau chiefs and correspondents seems to support this charge.[9] The study, conducted by the Roper Center and the Freedom Forum, a conservative foundation, found that 61 percent of the bureau chiefs and correspondents polled called themselves "liberal" or "liberal to moderate." Only 9 percent called themselves "conservative" or "conservative to moderate." In a similar vein, 89 percent said they had voted for Democrat Bill Clinton in 1992, while only 7 percent indicated that they had voted for Republican George Bush. Fifty percent said they were Democrats, and only 4 percent claimed to be Republicans.[10] Generally speaking, reporters for major national news outlets tend to be more liberal than their local counterparts who often profess moderate or even conservative views.

The linkage between journalists and liberal ideas is by no means absolute. Most reporters, to be sure, attempt to maintain some measure of balance or objectivity whatever their personal political views. Moreover, over the past several years a conservative media complex has emerged in opposition to the liberal media. This complex includes two major newspapers, *The Wall Street Journal* and *The Washington Times,* several magazines such as the *American Spectator,* and a host of conservative

> How are media content, news coverage, and bias affected by the producers, subjects, and consumers of the news?

radio and television talk programs. Also important is media baron Rupert Murdoch, creator of Fox Network News and the financial force behind *The Weekly Standard.* Murdoch sees Fox as a conservative alternative to the more liberal networks and has staffed Fox with rather conservative broadcast personalities. The emergence of this conservative media complex has meant that liberal policies and politicians are virtually certain to come under attack even when the "liberal media" are sympathetic to them.

Probably more important than ideological bias is a selection bias in favor of news that the media view as having a great deal of audience appeal because of its dramatic or entertainment value. In practice, this bias often results in news coverage that focuses on crimes and scandals, especially those involving prominent individuals, despite the fact that the public obviously looks to the media for information about important political debates. For example, even though most journalists may be Democrats, this partisan predisposition did not prevent an enormous media frenzy in January 1998 when reports surfaced that President Clinton may have had an affair with White House intern Monica Lewinsky. Once a hint of blood appeared in the water, partisanship and ideology were swept away by the piranhalike instincts often manifested by journalists.

SUBJECTS OF THE NEWS

News coverage is also influenced by the individuals or groups who are subjects of the news or whose interests and activities are actual or potential news topics. The president, in particular, has the power to set the news agenda through his speeches and actions. All politicians, for that matter, seek to shape or manipulate their media images by cultivating good relations with reporters as well as through news leaks and staged news events. For example, during the lengthy investigation of President Clinton conducted by Special Counsel Kenneth Starr, both the Office of the Special Counsel and the White House frequently leaked information to the press designed to bolster their respective positions in the struggle. Starr admitted speaking to reporters on a not-for-attribution basis about aspects of his investigation of the president. One journalist, Steven Brill, accused a number of prominent reporters of serving as "lap dogs" for the Special Counsel by reporting as fact the information fed to them by Starr.[11] Some politicians become extremely adept image makers—or at least skilled at hiring publicists who are skillful image makers. Indeed, press releases drafted by skillful publicists often become the basis for reporters' stories. A substantial percentage of the news stories published every day are initially drafted by publicists and later rewritten only slightly, if at all, by busy reporters and editors.

Furthermore, political candidates often endeavor to tailor their images for specific audiences. For example, to cultivate a favorable image among younger voters during his 1992 campaign, Bill Clinton made several appearances on MTV, and he continued to grant interviews to MTV after his election. His MTV forays came to an end, however, when he was severely criticized for discussing his preferred type of underwear with members of an MTV audience.

President George W. Bush's administration has developed a highly sophisticated communications office under the leadership of former presidential aide Karen Hughes. Hughes, who resigned in April 2002, and her staff endeavored to craft a new media message every few days in order to continually shape the nation's press coverage. For example, Bush's reference to nations supporting terrorist groups as an "axis of evil" in February 2002 was designed to give the media a catch phrase that would dominate the headlines and provide **sound bites**—short, attention-grabbing summaries of a story—for the broadcast media for days. By the time the media tired of the "axis of evil," the White House hoped to have developed a new sound bite for the reporters.

The capacity of news subjects to influence the news is hardly unlimited. Media consultants and issues managers may shape the news for a time, but it is generally not difficult for the media to penetrate the smoke screens thrown up by news sources if they have a reason to do so.

Occasionally, however, a politician proves incredibly adept at surviving repeated media attacks. Bill Clinton, for example, was able to survive repeated revelations of sexual improprieties, financial irregularities, lying to the public, and illegal campaign fund-raising activities. Clinton and his advisers crafted what *The Washington Post* called a "toolkit" for dealing with potentially damaging media revelations. This toolkit included techniques such as chiding the press, browbeating reporters, referring inquiries quickly to lawyers who will not comment, and acting quickly to change the agenda. These techniques helped Clinton maintain a favorable public image despite the Monica Lewinsky scandal and even the humiliation of a formal impeachment and trial.

THE POWER OF CONSUMERS

The print and broadcast media are businesses that, in general, seek to show a profit. This means that like any other business, they must cater to the preferences of consumers. This has very important consequences for the content and character of the news media.

Catering to the Audience In general, and especially in the political realm, the print and broadcast media and the publishing industry are not only responsive to the interests of consumers generally, but are particularly responsive to the interests and views of the better educated and more affluent segments of their audience. The preferences of these audience segments have a profound effect on the content and orientation of the press, of radio and television programming, and of books, especially in the areas of news and public affairs.[12]

Although affluent consumers do watch television programs and read periodicals whose contents are designed simply to amuse or entertain, the one area that most directly appeals to the upscale audience is that of news and public affairs. The affluent—who are also typically well educated—are the core audience of newsmagazines, journals of opinion, books dealing with public affairs, such newspapers as *The New York Times* and *The Washington Post,* and broadcast news and weekend and evening public-affairs programs. Although other segments of the public also read newspapers and watch television news, their level of interest in world events, national political issues, and the like is closely related to their level of education. As a result, upscale Americans are overrepresented in the news and public-affairs audience. The concentration of these strata in the audience makes news, politics, and public affairs potentially very attractive topics to advertisers, publishers, radio broadcasters, and television executives. As a result, topics in which the upper-middle class is interested, such as the stock market, scientific and literary affairs, and international politics, receive extensive coverage.

At the same time, however, entire categories of events, issues, and phenomena of interest to lower-middle- and working-class Americans receive scant attention from the national print and broadcast media. For example, trade-union news and events are discussed only in the context of major strikes or revelations of corruption. No network or national periodical routinely covers labor organizations. Religious and church affairs receive little coverage. The activities of veterans', fraternal, ethnic, and patriotic organizations are also generally ignored.

The Media and Conflict   While the media respond most to the upscale audience, groups who cannot afford the services of media consultants and issues managers can publicize their views and interests through protest. Frequently, the media are accused of encouraging conflict and even violence as a result of the fact that the audience mostly watches news for the entertainment value that conflict can provide. Clearly, conflict can be an important vehicle for attracting the attention and interest of the media, and thus may provide an opportunity for media attention to groups otherwise lacking the financial or organizational resources to broadcast their views. But while conflict and protest can succeed in drawing media attention, these methods ultimately do not allow groups from the bottom of the social ladder to compete effectively in the media.

The chief problem with protest as a media technique is that, in general, the media upon which the protesters depend have considerable discretion in reporting and interpreting the events they cover. For example, should the media focus on the conflict itself, rather than the issues or concerns that created the conflict? The answer to this question is typically determined by the media, not by the protesters. This means that media interpretation of protest activities is more a reflection of the views of the groups and forces to which the media are responsive—as we have seen, usually segments of the upper-middle class—than it is a function of the wishes of the protesters themselves. It is worth noting that civil rights protesters received their most favorable media coverage when a segment of the white upper-middle class saw blacks as potential political allies in the Democratic party.

Typically, upper-middle-class protesters—student demonstrators and the like—have little difficulty securing favorable publicity for themselves and their causes. Upper-middle-class protesters are often more skilled than their lower-class counterparts in the techniques of media manipulation. That is, they typically have a better sense—often as a result of formal courses on the subject—of how to package messages for media consumption. For example, it is important to know what time of day a protest should occur if it is to be carried on the evening news. Similarly, the setting, definition of the issues, character of the rhetoric used, and so on, all help to determine whether a protest will receive favorable media coverage, unfavorable coverage, or no coverage at all. Moreover, upper-middle-class protesters can often produce their own media coverage through "underground" newspapers, college papers, student radio and television stations, and, now, over the Internet. The same resources and skills that generally allow upper-middle-class people to publicize their ideas are usually not left behind when segments of this class choose to engage in disruptive forms of political action. This helps to explain why small groups of demonstrators in Seattle, Washington, were able to garner enormous media coverage in the winter of 1999 for their protests against the World Trade Organization.

Media Power in American Politics

The content and character of news and public affairs programming—what the media choose to present and how they present it—can have far-reaching political consequences. Media disclosures can greatly enhance—or fatally damage—the careers of public officials. Media coverage can rally support for—or intensify opposition to—national policies. The media can shape and modify, if not fully form, public perceptions of events, issues, and institutions.

SHAPING EVENTS

In recent American political history, the media have played a central role in at least three major events. First, the media were a critically important factor in the civil rights movement of the 1950s and 1960s. Television photos showing peaceful civil rights marchers attacked by club-swinging police helped to generate sympathy among northern whites for the civil rights struggle and greatly increased the pressure on Congress to bring an end to segregation.[13] Second, the media were instrumental in compelling the Nixon administration to negotiate an end to American involvement in the Vietnam War. Beginning in 1967, the national media, reacting in part to a shift in elite opinion, portrayed the war as misguided and unwinnable and, as a result, helped to turn popular sentiment against continued American involvement.[14]

Finally, the media were central actors in the Watergate affair, which ultimately forced President Richard Nixon, landslide victor in the 1972 presidential election, to resign from office in disgrace. It was the relentless series of investigations launched by *The Washington Post, The New York Times,* and the television networks that led to the disclosures of the various abuses of which Nixon was guilty and ultimately forced Nixon to choose between resignation and almost certain impeachment.

> ➤ **How do the media shape public perceptions of events, issues, and institutions?**

THE SOURCES OF MEDIA POWER

Agenda Setting   The power of the media stems from several sources. The first is **agenda setting,** which means that the media help to set the agenda for political discussion. Groups and forces that wish to bring their ideas before the public in order to generate support for policy proposals or political candidacies must somehow secure media coverage. If the media are persuaded that an idea is newsworthy, then they may declare it an "issue" that must be confronted or a "problem" to be solved, thus clearing the first hurdle in the policy-making process. On the other hand, if an idea lacks or loses media appeal, its chance of resulting in new programs or policies is diminished.

agenda setting the power of the media to bring public attention to particular issues and problems

For example, in 2000, Democratic presidential candidate Bill Bradley sought to make poverty the central issue of his bid for office. Bradley appeared at numerous events to speak out against poverty and offered a plan that he said would "end child poverty as we know it." Bradley also promised to raise the minimum wage and increase tax credits for the working poor.[15] While this topic was popular among some liberal and labor groups, the national media seemed to regard it as old hat and did not make Bradley's plan a central theme in its coverage of the presidential race. Other candidates ignored the Bradley effort since the media failed to label it as a major issue in the race.

Millions of Americans depend upon newspapers, television, the radio, and, increasingly, the Internet for reporting and analysis of the major events of the day. The way in which the media portray or "frame" an event often has a major impact on popular perceptions. Media accounts critical of the Vietnam War helped to turn public opinion against the war and hastened the withdrawal of American troops. This famous photograph of the aftermath of a napalm attack was one of many media images that shaped the American public's views on the war.

On the other hand, Democrats were able to persuade the media that regulation of health maintenance organizations (HMOs) was an issue worthy of discussion. During well-publicized congressional hearings in the fall of 1999, Democrats presented many witnesses who testified that their HMOs had prevented them from receiving adequate treatment. Democrats called for a "Patient's Bill of Rights" to allow HMO physicians more autonomy and to permit unhappy patients redress in the courts. Republicans initially charged that the Democrats were simply doing the bidding of the trial lawyers, major contributors to the Democratic party, who saw HMOs as rich targets for litigation. Media coverage of the disgruntled HMO patients, however, made it impossible for Republicans to dismiss the issue from the agenda and led eventually to the enactment of legislation close to the Democratic proposal.

Civil rights protestors in the 1960s learned a variety of techniques designed to elicit favorable media coverage. Media accounts of the brutal treatment of protestors in some communities turned public opinion against the Jim Crow system of racial segregation and helped bring about the enactment of laws aimed at prohibiting racial discrimination. Television images of police brutality in Alabama led directly to the enactment of the 1965 Civil Rights Act.

During President Richard Nixon's second term in office, media accounts of the president's misdeeds, including complicity in a break-in at 1972 Democratic campaign headquarters in Washington's Watergate Hotel, led to congressional investigations that forced Nixon to resign from office. Washington Post *reporters Robert Woodward and Carl Bernstein played an important role in uncovering the Watergate conspiracy (left).*

In the late 1990s, President Bill Clinton was nearly driven from office by media revelations of his sexual misconduct with White House intern Monica Lewinsky (right). The media relentlessly pursued Clinton's evasions, lies, and indiscretions and provided fuel for a congressional effort to impeach the president.

In the fall of 2001, President Bush had little difficulty convincing the media that terrorism and his administration's campaign to combat terrorist attacks merited a dominant place on the agenda. Some stories have such overwhelming significance that political leaders' main concern is not whether the story will receive attention but whether they will figure prominently and positively in media accounts. In many instances, the media serve as conduits for agenda-setting efforts by competing groups and forces. Occasionally, however, journalists themselves play an important role in setting the agenda of political discussion. For example, whereas many of the scandals and investigations surrounding President Clinton were initiated by his political opponents, the Watergate scandal that destroyed Nixon's presidency was in some measure initiated and driven by *The Washington Post* and the national television networks.

Framing   A second source of the media's power, known as **framing,** is their power to decide how political events and results are interpreted by the American people. For example, during the 1995–96 struggle between President Clinton and congressional Republicans over the nation's budget—a struggle that led to several partial shutdowns of the federal government—the media's interpretation of events forced the Republicans to back down and agree to a budget on Clinton's terms. At the beginning of the crisis, congressional Republicans, led by then House Speaker Newt Gingrich, were confident that they could compel Clinton to accept their budget, which called for substantial cuts in domestic social programs. Republicans calculated that Clinton would fear being blamed for lengthy government shutdowns and would quickly accede to their demands, and that once Americans saw that life went on with government agencies closed, they would support the Republicans in asserting that the United States could get along with less government.

For the most part, however, the media did not cooperate with the GOP's plans. Media coverage of the several government shutdowns during this period emphasized

framing the power of the media to influence how events and issues are interpreted

Sources of Media Power

Setting the Agenda for Political Discussion

Groups wishing to generate support for policy proposals or political candidacies must secure media coverage. The media must be persuaded that an item is newsworthy.

Framing

The media's interpretation or evaluation of an event or political action can sometimes determine how people perceive the event or result.

Priming

Most citizens will never meet their political leaders, but will base opinions of these leaders on their media images. The media has a great deal of control over how a person is evaluated or whether an individual even receives public attention. The media are also able to shape how a policy issue is perceived by the public.

the hardships imposed upon federal workers who were being furloughed in the weeks before Christmas. Indeed, Newt Gingrich, who was generally portrayed as the villain who caused the crisis, came to be called the "Gin*grinch*" who stole Christmas from the children of hundreds of thousands of federal workers. Rather than suggest that the shutdown demonstrated that America could carry on with less government, media accounts focused on the difficulties encountered by Washington tourists unable to visit the capital's monuments, museums, and galleries. The woes of American travelers whose passports were delayed were given considerable attention. Thus, the "dominant frame" became the hardship and disruption caused by the Republicans. The GOP's "competing frame" was dismissed.[16] This sort of coverage eventually convinced most Americans that the government shutdown was bad for the country. In the end, Gingrich and the congressional Republicans were forced to surrender and to accept a new budget reflecting many of Clinton's priorities. The Republicans' defeat in the budget showdown contributed to the unraveling of the GOP's legislative program and, ultimately, to the Republicans' poor showing in the 1996 presidential elections and 1998 congressional races. The character of media coverage of an event thus had enormous repercussions for how Americans interpreted it.

During the 2000 Florida post-election battle, Bush and Gore fought to frame the story in very different ways. Gore forces asserted that the real story concerned a failure on the part of Florida authorities to make certain that every vote had been counted. Bush supporters, on the other hand, argued that the real story involved a Democratic effort to count the same votes again and again until Gore got the result he wanted. Thus, in their media appearances, Democrats continually reiterated the message that every vote must be counted while Republicans repeated the refrain that every vote had been counted many times. For emphasis, Republicans created placards that parodied the Democrats' Gore/Lieberman posters: in the GOP's version, the placards, frequently waved before the cameras, read Sore/Loserman.

After he assumed office in 2001, George W. Bush sought to frame media coverage by introducing a new issue—education, taxes, the budget—every week. Bush hoped to attract media attention, control the headlines, and demonstrate that his administration was vigorously undertaking the people's work. After the debut of the president's tax-cut initiative in February 2001, Bush embarked on a multi-state speaking tour in support of his program. The president hoped to dominate local news coverage in a number of key states as a way of putting pressure on members of Congress to support his proposals.

The importance of framing was underlined by the Bush administration in the fall of 2001, when presidential aides held extensive discussions with network executives and even Hollywood filmmakers about their treatment of America's war against terrorism. The White House asked the media to sound a patriotic note and frame the war as a national necessity. By all accounts, media executives responded positively, indicating that they would present the war news in a favorable light.[17]

priming process of preparing the public to take a particular view of an event or political actor

Priming A third important media power is **priming.** This occurs when media coverage affects the way the public evaluates political leaders or candidates for office. For example, nearly unanimous media praise for President Bush's speeches to the nation in the wake of the September 11 terrorist attacks prepared, or "primed," the public to view Bush's subsequent response to terrorism in an extremely positive light, even though some aspects of the administration's efforts, most notably those in the realm of bioterrorism, were quite problematic.

What Government Does . . . After September 11

Media criticism of American policy in Vietnam helped bring an end to U. S. involvement in that conflict. After Vietnam, the media were generally inclined to be critical of the use of military force as an instrument of American foreign policy. In the wake of September 11, however, media coverage of U.S. military policy has been almost uniformly positive. For example, CBS anchor Dan Rather, a critic of the Vietnam War, responded to the American bombing campaign in Afghanistan by saying, "Our thoughts and our love are with our warrior men and women. We know that some may come back in flag-draped coffins, but we . . . accept that as a reality of a war forced upon us."[1] Let us consider two perspectives on the role of the media in the post–September 11 world.

According to Susan Douglas in *The Progressive,* the media have abdicated their responsibility to present a critical view of government policy.[2] She makes several points. First, the media rely too exclusively on official sources. Immediately after the terrorist attacks, most of those people interviewed on network news were white men with military backgrounds. Few women, experts on Middle Eastern politics, or peace activists were allowed to present their interpretation of events. Second, the media do not display a healthy degree of skepticism toward the government. Why, for example, did the media not question the ("wholly unsubstantiated") claim that President Bush had initially stayed away from the capital because Air Force One was a target? Third, the media have presented a simplistic picture of the world and America's role in it; "The repeated use of pictures of Osama bin Laden to personify all terrorists has contributed to warmongering, massive oversimplification, self-delusions about American purity and innocence, and a mythologizing of one man instead of a discussion of the broader trends and global conditions that got us to this dreadful point."

According to Fred Barnes in *The Weekly Standard,* however, the press has performed admirably in its coverage and support of the war effort.[3] There are, of course, exceptions: "defeatists" who fixate on similarities between American interventions in Afghanistan and Vietnam, or who believe too quickly reports about civilian casualties from American air strikes. By and large, though, even members of the liberal media recognize that the end and the means of the war on terrorism are just. Barnes even suggests that America's war on terrorism may convince the media to turn away from its adversarial, cynical, and negative style of reporting: "Since it was the experience of covering the civil rights movement, Vietnam, and Watergate that helped create this sort of reporting, might the trauma of September 11 propel the press toward a more positive, dispassionate, and ideologically impartial style, one less confrontational toward American institutions?"

Despite the press's reaction in the immediate aftermath of the September 11 attacks, once the danger seemed to diminish, the news media began to take a more critical look at the events and America's response to them. In particular, during the months of May and June 2002, the news media gave intensive coverage to charges that America's intelligence agencies, the FBI and CIA in particular, had possessed information prior to September 11 that, if properly analyzed, might have been used to prevent the terrorists from launching their offensive. The news media gave extensive coverage to sensational charges levied by an FBI "whistle blower" who alleged that she and other agents in the Minneapolis FBI field office had made desperate attempts to convince their superiors in Washington that a terrorist attack was imminent. The media also aired charges that the CIA had failed to notify the FBI that several known terrorists had entered the United States. Administration officials reacted to these media accounts by suggesting that criticism was inappropriate in time of war because it encouraged the nation's foes to believe that America was weakened by internal division. The media, of course, responded that criticism was essential to democratic government and, indeed, to ensuring that public officials do their jobs effectively.

This debate between government officials and the news media is as old as the American republic. During the administration of President John Adams, the government responded to media criticism by enacting the Alien and Sedition Acts in an unsuccessful attempt to silence its media opponents. During every American military conflict, the government has expressed concern that media criticism might help the enemy.

How should the media behave in a democracy? Should the media support, criticize, or merely report the nation's military efforts?

---

[1] Quoted in Fred Barnes, "The Press in Time of War," *The Weekly Standard,* December 3, 2001, p. 32.
[2] Susan Douglas, "The Media Fall in Line," *The Progressive,* November 2001.
[3] Barnes, p. 31.

Political forces of every kind seek to generate favorable media coverage for themselves and their activities. American political leaders and candidates all have elaborate media strategies. Nineteen ninety-two third-party presidential candidate Ross Perot effectively used paid "infomercials" to plug his economic policies. While pundits doubted that television viewers would watch a politician present his views for half an hour, Perot's folksy style and flowcharts attracted the interest of millions of Americans.

In the case of political candidates, the media have considerable influence over whether or not a particular individual will receive public attention, whether or not a particular individual will be taken seriously as a viable contender, and whether the public will evaluate a candidate's performance favorably. Thus, if the media find a candidate interesting, they may treat him or her as a serious contender even though the facts of the matter seem to suggest otherwise. In a similar vein, the media may declare that a candidate has "momentum," a mythical property that the media confer upon candidates if they happen to exceed the media's expectations. Momentum has no substantive meaning—it is simply a media prediction that a particular candidate will do even better in the future than in the past. Such media prophecies can become self-fulfilling as contributors and supporters jump on the bandwagon of

Bill Clinton and George W. Bush made good use of appearances on entertainment programs. Clinton played his saxophone on the Arsenio Hall program and discussed his choice of underwear with a teenage interviewer on MTV (left). Bush appeared on the late-night Jay Leno program (right). Some politicians believe that entertainment and "soft interview" programs like Larry King Live *give them excellent exposure without subjecting them to the sometimes difficult questions and commentary they face in press conferences and news and interview shows.*

In 2000, many journalists developed considerable admiration for Arizona senator John McCain, who briefly ran for the Republican presidential nomination. McCain impressed reporters with his willingness to take strong stands on policy issues. The press, in turn, provided McCain with a great deal of positive coverage.

the candidate possessing this "momentum." In 1992, when Bill Clinton's poll standings surged in the wake of the Democratic National Convention, the media determined that Clinton had enormous momentum. In fact, nothing that happened during the remainder of the race led the media to change its collective judgment.

Typically, media coverage of election campaigns focuses on the "horse race" to the detriment of attention to issues and candidate records. During the 2000 presidential primaries, Senator John McCain of Arizona was able to use his Senate committee chairmanship to raise enough money to mount a challenge to Bush for the Republican nomination. In reality, McCain had little chance of defeating the front-runner. Seeing the possibility of a "horse race," however, the media gave McCain a great deal of generally positive coverage and helped him mount a noisy, if brief, challenge to Bush. McCain's hopes were dashed, though, when he was trounced by Bush in a series of primaries, including those held in South Carolina and other GOP strongholds.

The media's power to influence people's evaluation of public figures is not absolute. Throughout the last decade, politicians implemented new techniques for communicating with the public and shaping their own images. For instance, Bill Clinton pioneered the use of town meetings and television entertainment programs as means of communicating directly with voters in the 1992 election. During the 2000 presidential race between Bush and Gore, both candidates made use of town meetings, as well as talk shows and entertainment programs like *The Oprah Winfrey Show*, *The Tonight Show with Jay Leno*, and *Saturday Night Live*, to reach mass audiences. During a town meeting, talk show, or entertainment program, politicians are free to craft their own images without interference from journalists.

In 2000, George W. Bush was also able to shape his image by effectively courting the press through informal conversation and interaction. Bush's "charm offensive" was successful. Journalists concluded that Bush was a nice fellow, albeit inexperienced, and refrained from subjecting him to harsh criticism and close scrutiny. Al Gore, on the other hand, seemed to offend journalists by remaining aloof and giving an impression of disdain for the press. Journalists responded by portraying Gore as "stiff." The result was unusually positive coverage for the Republican candidate and unusually negative coverage for the Democratic candidate.

THE RISE OF ADVERSARIAL JOURNALISM

The political power of the news media vis-à-vis the government has greatly increased in recent years through the growing prominence of "adversarial journalism"—a form of reporting in which the media adopt a hostile posture toward the government and public officials.

During the nineteenth century, American newspapers were completely subordinate to the political parties. Newspapers depended upon official patronage—legal notice and party subsidies—for their financial survival and were controlled by party leaders. (A vestige of that era survived into the twentieth century in such newspaper names as the *Springfield Republican* and the *St. Louis Globe-Democrat.*) At the turn of the century, with the development of commercial advertising, newspapers became financially independent. This made possible the emergence of a formally nonpartisan press.

Presidents were the first national officials to see the opportunities in this development. By communicating directly to the electorate through newspapers and magazines, Theodore Roosevelt and Woodrow Wilson established political constituencies for themselves, independent of party organizations, and strengthened their own power relative to Congress. President Franklin Roosevelt used the radio, most notably in his famous fireside chats, to reach out to voters throughout the nation and to make himself the center of American politics. FDR was also adept at developing close personal relationships with reporters that enabled him to obtain favorable news coverage despite the fact that in his day a majority of newspaper owners and publishers were staunch conservatives. Following Roosevelt's example, subsequent presidents have all sought to use the media to enhance their popularity and power. For example, through televised news conferences, President John F. Kennedy mobilized public support for his domestic and foreign policy initiatives.

During the 1950s and early 1960s, a few members of Congress also made successful use of the media—especially television—to mobilize national support for their causes. Senator Estes Kefauver of Tennessee became a major contender for the presidency and won a place on the 1956 Democratic national ticket as a result of his dramatic televised hearings on organized crime. Senator Joseph McCarthy of Wisconsin made himself a powerful national figure through his well-publicized investigations of alleged communist infiltration of key American institutions. These senators, however, were more exceptional than typical. Through the mid-1960s, the executive branch continued to generate the bulk of news coverage, and the media served as a cornerstone of presidential power.

The Vietnam War shattered this relationship between the press and the presidency. During the early stages of U.S. involvement, American officials in Vietnam who disapproved of the way the war was being conducted leaked information critical of administrative policy to reporters. Publication of this material infuriated the White House, which pressured publishers to block its release—on one occasion, President Kennedy went so far as to ask *The New York Times* to reassign its Saigon correspondent. However, the national print and broadcast media—the network news divisions, the national newsweeklies, *The Washington Post,* and *The New York Times*—discovered that there was an audience for critical coverage and investigative reporting among segments of the public skeptical of administration policy. As the Vietnam conflict dragged on, critical media coverage fanned antiwar sentiment. Moreover, growing opposition to the war among liberals encouraged some members of Congress, most notably Senator J. William Fulbright, chair of the Senate Foreign Relations Committee, to break with the president. In turn, these shifts in popular and congressional sentiment emboldened journalists and publishers to continue to present critical news reports. Through this process, journalists developed a commitment to adversarial journalism, while a constituency emerged that would rally to the defense of the media when it came under White House attack.

This pattern, established during the Vietnam War, endured through the 1970s and into the 1980s. Political forces opposed to presidential policies, many members of Congress, and the national news media began to find that their interests often overlapped. Opponents of the Nixon, Carter, Reagan, and Bush administrations welcomed news accounts critical of the conduct of executive agencies and officials in foreign affairs and in such domestic areas as race relations, the environment, and regulatory policy. In addition, many senators and representatives found it politically advantageous to champion causes favored by the antiwar, consumer, or environmental movements because, by conducting televised hearings on such issues, they were able to mobilize national constituencies, to become national figures, and in a number of instances to become serious contenders for their party's presidential nomination.

For their part, aggressive use of the techniques of investigation, publicity, and exposure allowed the national media to enhance their autonomy and carve out a prominent place for themselves in American government and politics. The power derived by the press from adversarial journalism is one of the reasons that the media seem to relish opportunities to attack political institutions and to publish damaging information about important public officials. Increasingly, media coverage has come to influence politicians' careers, the mobilization of political constituencies, and the fate of issues and causes.

Adversarial, or "attack," journalism has become commonplace in America, and some critics have suggested that the media have contributed to popular cynicism and the low levels of citizen participation that characterize contemporary American political processes. But before we begin to think about means of compelling the media to adopt a more positive view of politicians and political issues, we should consider the possibility that media criticism is one of the major mechanisms of political accountability in the American political process. Without aggressive media coverage would we have known of Bill Clinton's misdeeds or, for that matter, those of Richard Nixon? Without aggressive media coverage would important questions be raised about the conduct of American foreign and domestic policy? It is easy to criticize the media for their aggressive tactics, but would our democracy function effectively without the critical role of the press? A vigorous and critical media are needed as the "watchdogs" of American politics. Of course, in October 2001, the adversarial relationship between the government and the media was at least temporarily transformed into a much more supportive association as the media helped rally the American people for the fight against terrorism.

Media Power and Democracy

> **Are the media too powerful and thus in need of restriction, or are a free media necessary for democracy?**

The free media are an institution absolutely essential to democratic government. Ordinary citizens depend upon the media to investigate wrongdoing, to publicize and explain governmental actions, to evaluate programs and politicians, and to bring to light matters that might otherwise be known to only a handful of governmental insiders. In short, without free and active media, popular government would be virtually impossible. Citizens would have few means through which to know or assess the government's actions—other than the claims or pronouncements of the government itself. Moreover, without active—indeed, aggressive—media, citizens would be hard-pressed to make informed choices among competing candidates at the polls. Often enough, the media reveal discrepancies between candidates' claims and their actual records, and between the images that candidates seek to project and the underlying realities. Of course, by continually emphasizing deceptions and wrongdoing on the part of political figures, the media encourage the public to become cynical and distrustful, not only of the people in office, but of the government and political process themselves. A widespread sense that all politics is corrupt or deceptive can easily lead to a sense that nothing can be done. In this way, the media's adversarial posture may contribute to the low levels of political participation seen in America today.

At the same time, the declining power of party organizations (as we will see in Chapter 9) has made politicians ever more dependent upon favorable media coverage. National political leaders and journalists have had symbiotic relationships, at least since FDR's presidency, but initially politicians were the senior partners. They benefited from media publicity, but they were not totally dependent upon it as long as they could still rely upon party organizations to mobilize votes. Journalists, on the other hand, depended upon their relationships with politicians for access to information and would hesitate to report stories that might antagonize valuable sources for fear of being excluded from the flow of information in retaliation. Thus, for example, reporters did not publicize potentially embarrassing information, widely known in Washington, about the personal lives of such figures as Franklin Roosevelt and John F. Kennedy.

With the decline of party organizations, the balance of power between politicians and journalists has been reversed. Now that politicians have become heavily dependent upon the media to reach their constituents, journalists have less fear that their access to information can be restricted in retaliation for negative coverage.

Such freedom gives the media enormous power. The media can make or break reputations, help to launch or to destroy political careers, and build support for or rally opposition to programs and institutions.[18] Wherever there is so much power, there exists at least the potential for its abuse or overly zealous use. All things considered, free media are so critically important to the maintenance of a democratic society that Americans must be prepared to take the risk that the media will occa-

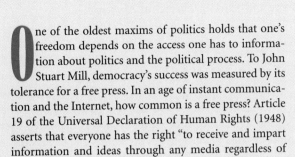

Free Press and Democracy

One of the oldest maxims of politics holds that one's freedom depends on the access one has to information about politics and the political process. To John Stuart Mill, democracy's success was measured by its tolerance for a free press. In an age of instant communication and the Internet, how common is a free press? Article 19 of the Universal Declaration of Human Rights (1948) asserts that everyone has the right "to receive and impart information and ideas through any media regardless of frontiers."

Guided by this premise, Freedom House periodically surveys the extent of free press across the globe. Its researchers survey and measure the following factors: (1) the extent of laws and administrative decisions taken by government to restrict media content; (2) political influences and controls over media content; (3) economic influences that restrict media content; and (4) acts of violence and overt physical threats against members of the media.

In 2001, one in five people on the globe lived in the seventy-five countries that Freedom House described as having a "free press." More refined measures reveal that only 8.5 percent live in what Freedom House considers "very free press" countries. This group of twenty-one countries includes the United States, Australia, Denmark, Norway, Netherlands, and Switzerland. Thirty-eight percent of the world's population (sixty-one countries) live in countries where the press is "not free." This group includes twenty-seven countries (with 20 percent of the world's population) that have virtually no semblance of a free press of any sort. These worst cases include Afghanistan, China, Myanmar (formerly Burma), Cuba, Saudi Arabia, Sudan, North Korea, and Iraq.

In general, the industrialized nations of the world enjoy a high degree of press freedom, while Arab and sub-Saharan African nations have the greatest degree of restriction on free press. Across the globe, political restrictions on content are the most pressing threat to free press, while overt acts of terrorism and threats to members of the media are relatively rare, especially among members of the broadcast media. However, even among the twenty-four industrialized electoral democracies of the world, serious restrictions on free press are common, reducing the full effects of the media as a check and balance on concentrated political power.

Perhaps the most alarming and increasingly common threat to content freedom in the media of industrialized electoral democracies is the concentration of broadcast and print media in the hands of a few large conglomerates, often headed by single individuals. In Italy, this trend is reflected in the amassed power of Silvio Berlusconi and his massive Mondadori media conglomerate. Berlusconi owns three national television networks, which control 90 percent of Italian television advertising revenue and serve 45 percent of the Italian television audience (giving his companies a decisive advantage in pricing both commercial and political advertisements in Italy). In addition, his conglomerate owns two large daily newspapers and the country's largest weekly news magazine, and it controls 30 percent of the book trade in Italy. Berlusconi is also head of Italy's largest political party (Forza Italia) and for seven months in 1994 served as prime minister of Italy, using his political power to appoint his friends and business associates to key government posts that control rules and regulations of broadcast media. Similar patterns of media concentration are found throughout the industrailized electoral democracies, for instance in Great Britain (Rupert Murdoch's News International Corporation) and in Germany (Thomas Middlehoff's Bertelsmann).

SOURCE: http://freedomhouse.org/pfs2001/pfs2001.pdf (accessed 7/11/02) "Emperor of the Air," by Alexander Stille, *The Nation*, November 29, 1999.

sionally abuse their power. The forms of governmental control that would prevent the media from misusing their power would also certainly destroy freedom. The ultimate beneficiaries of a free and active media are the American people.

What You Can Do: Analyze News Sources

In their relationship to the media, most Americans adopt a passive stance. They read, they watch, or they listen to media accounts of events. However, it is relatively easy to become an active rather than a passive media user. One way to become an active media user is through letter-writing. Every newspaper and newsmagazine, and some television programs as well, provides a forum for citizen commentary. Letter writers have an opportunity to object to editorials with which they disagree, correct errors in news coverage, and even respond to other letter writers.

On one particular day, for example, *The New York Times* published eleven letters from readers. Several objected to the paper's editorial views, two asserted that news stories published in the paper had misrepresented important facts, and others commented on issues discussed in the paper. On the same day, *The Washington Post* published three long letters objecting to facts alleged in prior *Post* stories on German politics and on global warming. Obviously, a few letters cannot completely counterbalance all the errors or biases that may affect a newspaper's coverage. But if a newspaper or magazine were truly biased, it probably would not publish letters pointing out its biases.

Most newspapers and magazines feel some obligation to publish letters critical of their published materials. Even more important, letters can make editors aware of significant errors and omissions in the paper's coverage, perhaps leading them to admonish or reassign the journalists responsible. Letters to the editor can even compel college newspapers to correct errors in news coverage. In November 1997, for example, the University of Buffalo's student newspaper published an apology and retraction after letter writers pointed out significant errors in a news story.[19] As commercial enterprises, the media are very eager to maintain a high level of customer satisfaction.

Citizens must also learn to be critical consumers of the media. It is very important to be alert to the possible biases or hidden messages in any news story. First, when watching the news or reading a story, be alert to the author or reporter's implicit assumptions. For example, the media tend to be naive about the motives of any group claiming to work on behalf of the "public interest" or "citizens" and to take the claims of such groups at face value, especially if the group is criticizing business or the government. You should think carefully about the claims and facts being presented. Second, watch for stereotypes. Many newspapers and radio and television stations make an effort to avoid the racial and gender stereotypes that were once common. However, many other stereotypes are prevalent in the news. For example, some government programs such as the space program enjoy "good press" and generally receive positive coverage despite the often dubious claims made by their backers. Other programs, such as public-assistance programs and the highway program, are treated as "wasteful" or "pork-barrel projects," despite the good they may do. Critical consumers need to make up their own minds rather than allow media stereotypes to color their judgment.

Third, take note of news sources. Very often, reporters rely upon the views of a small number of top officials or influential figures who make it their business to cultivate journalists. When Henry Kissinger was secretary of state, he was such a successful manipulator of the media that most news about American foreign policy reflected his views. Often, politicians and interest groups retain public relations firms to contact journalists and disseminate their views. Always ask yourself whose interests might be served by a particular story. Often, those interests turn out to be the source of the story.

Finally, it is important to rely upon more than one source of news. The best approach is to make use of news sources with disparate ideological perspectives. For example, residents of Washington, D.C., sometimes read both the liberal *Washington Post* and the conservative *Washington Times.* Anyone can subscribe to both a liberal magazine, such as *The Public Interest,* and a conservative one, such as the *Weekly Standard,* that often cover the same topics. The importance of using such disparate news sources is to obtain different perspectives on the same events. This, in turn, will help you see more than one possibility and, ultimately, to make up your own mind.[20]

Summary

The American news media are among the world's most free. The print and broadcast media regularly present information and opinions critical of the government, political leaders, and policies.

The media help to determine the agenda or focus of political debate in the United States, to shape popular understanding of political events and results, and to influence popular judgments of politicians and leaders.

Over the past century, the media have helped to nationalize American political perspectives. Media coverage is influenced by the perspectives of journalists, the activities of news subjects, and, most important, by the media's need to appeal to upscale audiences. The attention that the media give to conflict is also a function of audience factors.

Free media are an essential ingredient of popular government.

For Further Reading

Ansolabehere, Stephen, and Shanto Iyengar. *Going Negative: How Attack Ads Shrink and Polarize the Electorate.* New York: Free Press, 1995.

Bagdikian, Ben. *The Media Monopoly.* 5th ed. Boston: Beacon, 1997.

Cook, Timothy. *Governing with the News: The News Media as a Political Institution.* Chicago: University of Chicago Press, 1997.

Davis, Richard, and Diana Owen. *New Media and American Politics.* New York: Oxford University Press, 1998.

Graber, Doris, et al. *The Politics of News, The News of Politics.* Washington, DC: Congressional Quarterly Press, 1998.

Hallin, Daniel C. *The Uncensored War.* Berkeley and Los Angeles: University of California Press, 1986.

Hart, Roderick. *Seducing America: How Television Charms the Modern Voter.* New York: Oxford University Press, 1994.

Hess, Stephen. *Live From Capitol Hill: Studies of Congress and the Media.* Washington, DC: Brookings, 1991.

Kurtz, Howard. *Spin Cycle: Inside the Clinton Propaganda Machine.* New York: Free Press, 1998.

Sparrow, Bartholomew H. *Uncertain Guardians: The News Media as a Political Institution.* Baltimore, MD: Johns Hopkins University Press, 1998.

West, Darrell. *Air Wars: Television Advertising in Election Campaigns, 1952–1992.* Washington, DC: Congressional Quarterly Press, 1993.

Study Outline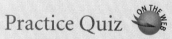

www.wwnorton.com/wtp4e

The Media Industry and Government

1. Americans obtain their news from radio, television, newspapers, magazines, and the Internet. Even though television news reaches more Americans than any other single news source, the print media are still important because they often set the agenda for the broadcast media and because they reach a more influential audience.

2. Since the passage of the Telecommunications Act of 1996, a wave of mergers and consolidations in the media industry has reduced the number of independent media in the United States.

3. The nationalization of the American news media, through which a relatively uniform picture of events, issues, and problems is presented to the entire nation, has contributed greatly to the nationalization of politics and of political perspectives in the United States.

4. Despite the widespread nationalization of news in America, news enclaves exist in which some demographic and ideological groups receive alternative news coverage.

5. Part of the Telecommunications Act of 1996, known as the Communications Decency Act, attempted to regulate the content of material transmitted over the Internet, but the law was overruled by the Supreme Court in the 1997 case *Reno v. American Civil Liberties Union*.

6. Under federal regulations, broadcasters must provide candidates seeking the same political office equal time to communicate their messages to the public.

7. Regulations also require that individuals be granted the right to rebut personal attacks.

8. Although recently diminished in importance, the fairness doctrine for many years required that broadcasters who aired programs on controversial issues provide time for opposing views.

News Coverage

1. Media content and news coverage are inevitably affected by the views, ideals, and interests of the journalists who seek out, write, and produce news stories.

2. News coverage is also influenced by the individuals or groups who are subjects of the news or whose interests and activities are actual or potential news topics.

3. Because the print and broadcast media are businesses that generally seek to show a profit, they must cater to the preferences of consumers.

4. The print and broadcast media, as well as the publishing industry, are particularly responsive to the interests and views of the upscale segments of their audiences.

5. Protest is one way that groups who cannot afford the services of media consultants and "issues managers" can publicize their views and interests.

Media Power in American Politics

1. In recent political history, the media have played a central role in the civil rights movement, the ending of American involvement in the Vietnam War, and in the Watergate investigation.

2. The power of the media stems from several sources, all of which contribute to the media's great influence in setting the political agenda, shaping electoral outcomes, and interpreting events and political results.

3. The political power of the news media has greatly increased in recent years through the growing prominence of investigative reporting.

Media Power and Democracy

1. Because the media provide the information citizens need for meaningful participation in the political process, they are essential to democratic government.

2. The decline of political parties has given the media enormous power, which creates a great potential for abuse.

Practice Quiz

www.wwnorton.com/wtp4e

1. The nationalization of the news has been influenced by which of the following trends in ownership of the media?
   a) the purchase of influential newspapers by foreign corporations
   b) the fragmentation of ownership of all media in the United States
   c) the wave of mergers and consolidations following the passage of the 1996 Telecommunications Act
   d) the purchase of the major news networks by the national government

2. Which of the following best describes national news in the United States?
   a) fragmented and localized
   b) nationalized and centralized
   c) centralized but still localized
   d) none of the above

3. Which of the following Supreme Court cases overruled the government's attempt to regulate the content of the Internet?
   a) *Near v. Minnesota*
   b) *New York Times v. United States*
   c) *Red Lion Broadcasting Company v. FCC*
   d) *Reno v. American Civil Liberties Union*

4. How do journalists compare to the general public in their political attitudes?
   a) Journalists are more conservative than the general public.
   b) The two groups' views are about the same.
   c) Journalists are more liberal than the general public.
   d) Journalists tend to be more Republican than the general public.

5. Which of the following have an impact on the nature of media coverage of politics?
   a) reporters
   b) political actors
   c) news consumers
   d) all of the above

6. Which of the following is a strategy available to poor people to increase their coverage by the news media?
   a) protest
   b) media consultants
   c) television advertising
   d) newspaper advertising "time sharing"

7. The media's powers to determine what becomes a part of the political discussion and to shape how political events are interpreted by the American people are known as
   a) issue definition and protest power.
   b) agenda setting and framing.
   c) the illusion of saliency and the bandwagon effect.
   d) the equal time rule and the right of rebuttal.

8. Which of the following can be considered an example of a news enclave?
   a) Internet chat rooms
   b) letters to the editor
   c) readers of *The New York Times*
   d) people who watch CNN

9. Which of the following exemplifies the liberal bias in the news media?
   a) talk radio programs
   b) *The Wall Street Journal*
   c) the *American Spectator*
   d) none of the above

10. The newspaper publisher William Randolph Hearst was responsible for encouraging U.S. involvement in which war?
    a) the Spanish-American War
    b) the Vietnam War
    c) the U.S. war with Mexico
    d) the Gulf War

Critical Thinking Questions

www.wwnorton.com/wtp4e

1. If the public receives most of its information about politics from the media, how accurate is its knowledge of government and politics? How does the media itself distort political reality? How do politicians use the media for their own purposes? What are the consequences for American democracy when the electorate is informed through such a filter? How might the quality of political information in America be improved?

2. There is a great deal of talk about the liberal bias of the media in American politics. To what extent is the media liberal? To what extent, do you think, is it biased? Considering the growing importance of conservative talk radio and news enclaves that support conservative causes, describe the ways in which discussions of a liberal bias in the media should be qualified. What other factors might mitigate the liberalism of the media?

3. In wartime, can media criticism of government action actually aid the nation's enemies? Should there be limits on media criticism of the government during time of war? Or does criticism actually enhance the nation's strength?

Key Terms

www.wwnorton.com/wtp4e

8 POLITICAL PARTICIPATION AND VOTING

⭐ **Political Participation**

In what different ways do Americans participate in politics? Why is voting the most important form of political participation?

⭐ **Who Participates, and How?**

What is the history of suffrage in the United States?

⭐ **Explaining Political Participation**

What explains levels of participation? Why has participation declined over time?

⭐ **Participation and American Political Values**

What roles do political institutions play in promoting participation and fulfilling American political values? Have attempts to increase participation succeeded? Why or why not? What are the implications for democracy?

O A CONSIDERABLE EXTENT, citizen participation in political life is a function of the government's policies, through which a government can make it easier or harder for citizens to participate. The most obvious example is the institution of the democratic election. When they introduce elections and grant citizens the right to vote, or *suffrage,* governments facilitate participation in politics. As we shall see, however, institutional factors such as voter registration rules strongly affect participation. Holding elections on weekends, as is the custom in much of Europe, promotes participation. The mechanical equipment used to cast and count ballots can make participation more or less effective by determining what percentage of ballots will be spoiled. In our country, voting is mainly regulated by the individual states, and their policies can have important consequences. For example, the so-called Votomatic machines used in Florida and a number of other states tended to confuse voters and result in many ballots with too many markings or no markings at all. When things like this happen, popular participation is rendered ineffective. Thus, the policies of the government play a very important role in determining the extent and effectiveness of what is, at first glance, a voluntary activity. If we want more Americans to participate effectively in politics, we should endeavor to develop policies that foster, rather than discourage, participation. ■

■ In this chapter, we shall examine the role of citizen participation in American politics. We will first examine patterns of contemporary political participation, discussing the different forms that participation can take. We will then consider the reasons for declining participation in recent decades. We will see that individual beliefs, such as a sense of efficacy, are important, but that most significant is the failure of our institutions to mobilize people into politics.

Political Participation

political participation political activities, such as voting, contacting political officials, volunteering for a campaign, or participating in a protest, whose purpose is to influence government

Political participation makes the ideals of liberty and equality come alive. But by many measures, Americans are participating less and less. For example, in the 1996 presidential election only 49 percent of eligible voters cast ballots, the lowest percentage in a presidential election in more than seventy years. In 2000, voter turnout rose only slightly to 50.7 percent. Citizens can, however, participate in ways other than voting. In this section we will examine the different ways that Americans participate in politics. We will look for changes in rates and methods of participation over time and describe the differences in participation among groups. In the second half of the chapter, we will explore the causes for the patterns we observe. Two questions in particular will concern us: Why has participation declined? Why do people with higher levels of education and wealth participate most? Finally, we will consider the role that political institutions play in promoting participation.

FORMS OF PARTICIPATION

> In what different ways do Americans participate in politics? Why is voting the most important form of political participation?

Today, voting has come to be seen as the normal or typical form of citizen political activity. Yet, ordinary people took part in politics long before the advent of the election or any other formal mechanism of popular involvement in political life. If there is any natural or spontaneous form of popular political participation, it is the riot rather than the election. The urban riot and the rural uprising were common in both Europe and America prior to the nineteenth century and not entirely uncommon even in the twentieth century. Urban riots played an important role in American politics in the 1960s and 1970s. Even as recently as 1999, riots during the Seattle, Washington, meeting of the World Trade Organization helped labor unions and other opponents of trade liberalization to slow the pace of change in the rules governing world trade.

Most Americans would not consider taking part in a riot. Yet, in recent years, growing numbers of Americans have not been exercising their right to vote. Participation in presidential elections has dropped significantly over the past forty years. In 1960, 64 percent of eligible voters cast ballots; in 2000, only about half of the electorate turned out. Voting in midterm elections is typically lower, on the order of one-third of eligible voters. It took the votes of less than a quarter of the electorate to catapult the Republicans to power in Congress in 1994 because fewer than 39 percent of eligible voters showed up at the polls. Turnout for local elections is usually even lower.[1]

Fortunately, voting and rioting are not the only forms of participation available to Americans. Citizens can contact political officials, sign petitions, attend public meetings, join organizations, give money to a politician or a political organization, volunteer in a campaign, write a letter to the editor or write an article about an issue, or participate in a protest or rally. Such activities differ from voting because they can communicate much more detailed information to public officials than voting can. Voters may support a candidate for many reasons but their actual votes do not indicate specifically what they like and don't like, nor do they tell officials how intensely voters feel about issues. A vote can convey only a general sense of approval or disapproval. By writing a letter or engaging in other kinds of political participation, people can convey much more specific information, telling public officials exactly what issues they care most about and what their views on those issues are. For that reason these other political activities are often more satisfying than voting. And citizens who engage in these other activities are more likely to try to influence state and local politics rather than national politics; in voting, people find the national scene more interesting than state and local politics.[2]

While nonelectoral political activity takes many forms, some of the most prominent in recent years include *lobbying, public relations, litigation,* and *protest.*

Lobbying is an effort by groups or individuals to take their case directly to elected or appointed officials. By voting, citizens seek to determine who will govern. By lobbying, citizens attempt to determine what those in power will do. As we shall see in Chapter 11, many interest groups employ professional lobbyists to bring their

lobbying a strategy by which organized interests seek to influence the passage of legislation by exerting direct pressure on members of the legislature

Though we often equate popular political participation with voting, Americans have expressed their views in many forums besides the polling place. Riots and demonstrations, for example, are forms of popular participation whose history in America dates back to colonial times. Both the Boston Massacre (below) and the Boston Tea Party involved acts of violence that helped bring about the American Revolution.

In the 1960s, violent protests such as the Watts riots in Los Angeles (above) signaled an ominous change of direction for African American protest. Until that time, civil rights leaders like Dr. Martin Luther King, Jr., and organizations like Dr. King's Southern Christian Leadership Conference had emphasized peaceful protest and civil disobedience. But during the mid-1960s, a new generation of black leaders like Stokeley Carmichael and new groups like the Black Panthers rejected the strategy of nonviolence and promised to respond to violence with violence. The Watts riots lasted several days and produced a number of casualties and millions of dollars in property damage. Riot leaders coined the slogan "Burn, baby burn" as whole city blocks were torched.

views to lawmakers. At the same time, however, thousands of volunteers lobby Congress and the bureaucracy each year on behalf of citizen groups like the National Organization for Women, the Sierra Club, and the Home School Legal Defense Fund.[3] The hundreds of thousands of citizens who call or write members of Congress each year, seeking to influence their votes, are also engaged in lobbying.

Public relations is an effort to sway public opinion on behalf of an issue or cause. Corporations and interest groups typically employ professional public relations firms to produce print, radio, and television advertising in support of their goals. For example, in 1999 public relations firms employed by a group of defense contractors produced a series of highly charged radio ads trumpeting the need for the construction of the F-22 fighter plane. During the same year, firms employed by competing segments of the health-care industry developed print and broadcast ads for and against different bills purporting to protect patients from abuse by health maintenance organizations (HMOs). At the same time, public relations tactics are also used by numerous citizen groups to promote issues and causes dear to them. A favorite tactic of citizen groups is the press release designed to shape news coverage. In 1999, for example, citizen groups favoring affirmative action released data purporting to show that affirmative action programs were successful. Groups opposing affirmative action released data purporting to show the opposite. The same pattern was manifest in debates about gun control, capital punishment, policy toward the homeless, and the use of school vouchers. In each of these issue areas citizen groups conducted political warfare through public relations.

public relations an attempt, usually through the use of paid consultants, to establish a favorable relationship with the public and influence its political opinions

In recent years, protestors criticizing President George W. Bush have demanded changes in American economic and foreign policy, but to little or no avail. Protest politics is most likely to be successful when protestors are able to win the sympathy of large numbers of other Americans.

Litigation is an attempt to use the courts to achieve a goal. In recent years, the federal courts have been used more and more frequently by citizen groups and even individuals to affect public policy. Using the so-called citizen-suit provisions of a number of federal statutes, citizen groups play an active role in shaping policy in such areas as air and water quality, preservation of endangered species, civil rights, and the rights of persons with disabilities. Use of the courts by citizen groups is encouraged by federal and state fee-shifting provisions that allow plaintiffs (those bringing a case in court) to recover legal fees from the government or defendant, as well as by class-action rules that allow an individual to bring suit on behalf of large groups. We will learn more about this form of participation in Chapter 15.

Though most Americans reject violent **protest** or terrorism for political ends, peaceful protest is generally recognized as a legitimate and important form of political activity and is protected by the First Amendment. During the 1960s and 1970s, hundreds of thousands of Americans took part in peaceful protests that helped bring an end to legalized racial segregation. In recent years, peaceful marches and demonstrations have been employed by a host of groups. While protests can occur anywhere, favorite spots for demonstrations include the park in front of the White House and the members' parking lot in front of the Capitol. These two areas have been the sites of demonstrations by large groups of Native Americans, by proponents and opponents of abortion rights, by veterans's groups, and by the handicapped. Occasionally, protests by unpopular groups lead to counterprotests by others. For example, in 1999, planned rallies in New York and Washington by a handful of Ku Klux Klan members led to counterdemonstrations by tens of thousands of people protesting the Klan's presence in their city. Thousands of police officers were mobilized to protect the Klan members and to safeguard their First Amendment rights.

Alternative forms of political action generally require more time, effort, or money than voting does. It is not surprising, then, that far fewer people engage in these forms of political participation than vote. A recent study of participation, for example, found that about a third of those questioned said they had contacted a public official; almost a quarter reported that they had made a campaign contribution; and fewer than 10 percent said they had been active in a political campaign (see Figure 8.1 on page 288).[4] In contrast to the sharp decline in voting, involvement in these other activities has not fallen off nearly so much and, by some measures, has actually increased. For example, Americans are more likely to contribute money to political organizations and campaigns than in the past, but they are less likely to belong to political organizations.[5]

Whether or not voting is as effective or satisfying as these other forms of political action is an open question. What is clear, however, is that for most Americans voting remains the most accessible and most important form of political activity. Moreover, precisely because of the time, energy, and money often required to lobby, litigate, and even demonstrate, these forms of political action are often, albeit not always, dominated by better educated and wealthier Americans. As we shall see, voting participation in America is also somewhat biased in favor of those with greater wealth and, especially, higher levels of education. Nevertheless, the right to vote gives ordinary Americans a more equal chance to participate in politics than almost any other form of political activity. In the remainder of this chapter, therefore, we will turn to voting in America.

litigation a lawsuit or legal proceeding; as a form of political participation, an attempt to seek relief in a court of law

protest participation that involves assembling crowds to confront a government or other official organization

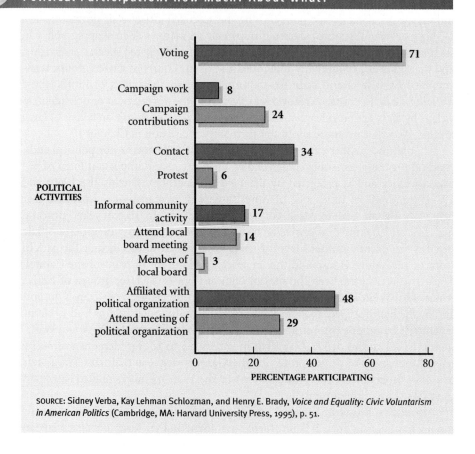

| Figure 8.1 | Political Participation: How Much? About What? |

SOURCE: Sidney Verba, Kay Lehman Schlozman, and Henry E. Brady, *Voice and Equality: Civic Voluntarism in American Politics* (Cambridge, MA: Harvard University Press, 1995), p. 51.

VOTING

Despite the availability of an array of alternatives, in practice citizen participation in American politics is generally limited to voting and a small number of other electoral activities (for example, campaigning). It is true that voter turnout in the United States is relatively low. But when, for one reason or another, Americans do seek to participate, their participation generally takes the form of voting.

The preeminent position of voting in the American political process is not surprising. The American legal and political environment is overwhelmingly weighted in favor of electoral participation. The availability of the right to vote, or **suffrage,** is, of course, a question of law. And civic eduction, also to a large extent mandated by law, encourages citizens to believe that electoral participation is the appropriate way to express opinions and grievances.

suffrage the right to vote; also called franchise

Voting Rights In principle, states determine who is eligible to vote. During the nineteenth and early twentieth centuries, voter eligibility requirements often varied greatly from state to state. Some states openly abridged the right to vote on the basis of race; others did not. Some states imposed property restrictions on voting;

others had no such restrictions. Most states mandated lengthy residency requirements, which meant that persons moving from one state to another sometimes lost their right to vote for as much as a year. In more recent years, however, constitutional amendments, federal statutes, and federal court decisions have limited states' discretion in the area of voting rights. Individual states may establish brief residency requirements, generally fifteen days, for record-keeping purposes. Beyond this, states have little or no power to regulate suffrage.

Today in the United States, all native-born or naturalized citizens over the age of eighteen, with the exception of convicted felons, have the right to vote. During the colonial and early national periods of American history, the right to vote was generally restricted to white males over the age of twenty-one. Many states also limited voting to those who owned property or paid more than a specified amount of annual tax. Property and tax requirements began to be rescinded during the 1820s, however, and had generally disappeared by the end of the Civil War.

By the time of the Civil War, blacks had won the right to vote in most northern states. In the South, black voting rights were established by the Fifteenth Amendment, ratified in 1870, which prohibited denial of the right to vote on the basis of race. Despite the Fifteenth Amendment, the voting rights of African Americans were effectively rescinded during the 1880s by the states of the former Confederacy. During this period, the southern states created what was called the "Jim Crow" system of racial segregation. As part of this system, a variety of devices, such as **poll taxes** and literacy tests, were used to prevent virtually all blacks from voting. During the 1950s and 1960s, through the civil rights movement led by Dr. Martin Luther King, Jr., and others, African Americans demanded the restoration of their voting rights. Their goal was accomplished through the enactment of the 1965 Voting Rights Act, which provided for the federal government to register voters in states that discriminated against minority citizens. The result was the reenfranchisement of southern blacks for the first time since the 1860s.

Women won the right to vote in 1920, with the adoption of the Nineteenth Amendment. This amendment resulted primarily from the activities of the women's suffrage movement, led by Elizabeth Cady Stanton, Susan B. Anthony, and Carrie Chapman Catt during the late nineteenth and early twentieth centuries. The "suffragettes," as they were called, held rallies, demonstrations, and protest marches for more than half a century before achieving their goal. The cause of women's suffrage was ultimately advanced by World War I. President Woodrow Wilson and members of Congress were convinced that women would be more likely to support the war effort if they were granted the right to vote. For this same reason, women were given the right to vote in Great Britain and Canada during World War I.

The most recent expansion of the right to vote in the United States took place in 1971, during the Vietnam War, when the Twenty-sixth Amendment was ratified, lowering the voting age from twenty-one to eighteen. Unlike black suffrage and women's suffrage, which came about in part because of the demands of groups that had been deprived of the right to vote, the Twenty-sixth Amendment was not a response to the demands of young people to be given the right to vote. Instead, many policy makers hoped that the right to vote would channel the disruptive protest activities of students involved in the anti–Vietnam War movement into peaceful participation at the ballot box.

poll tax a state-imposed tax upon voters as a prerequisite for registration. Poll taxes were rendered unconstitutional in national elections by the Twenty-fourth Amendment, and in state elections by the Supreme Court in 1966

Voting and Civic Education   Laws, of course, cannot completely explain why most people vote rather than riot or lobby. If public attitudes were completely unfavorable to elections, it is doubtful that *legal* remedies alone would have much impact.

Positive public attitudes about voting do not come into being in a completely spontaneous manner. Americans are taught to equate citizenship with electoral participation. Civic training, designed to give students an appreciation for the American system of government, is a legally required part of the curriculum in every elementary and secondary school. Although it is not as often required by law, civic education usually manages to find its way into college curricula as well.

Voter Participation   Although the United States has developed a system of civic education and a legal basis for nearly universal suffrage, America's rate of voter participation, or **turnout,** is very low. About 50 percent of those eligible participate in national presidential elections, while barely one-third of eligible voters take part in midterm congressional elections (see Figure 8.2). Turnout in state and local races that do not coincide with national contests is typically even lower. In most European countries and other Western democracies, by contrast, national voter turnout is usually between 70 and 90 percent[6] (see Figure 8.3).

turnout the percentage of eligible individuals who actually vote

---

Figure 8.2	Voter Turnout in Presidential and Midterm Elections, 1892–2002

More Americans tend to vote in presidential election years than in years when only congressional and local elections are held.

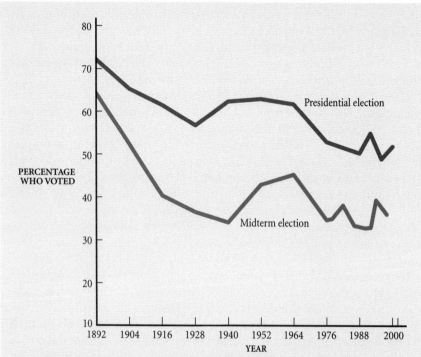

SOURCES: 1892–1958: Erik Austin and Jerome Clubb, *Political Facts of the United States since 1789* (New York: Columbia University Press, 1986), pp. 378–79; 1960–98: U.S. Bureau of the Census, *Statistical Abstract of the United States: 2001* (Washington, DC: Government Printing Office, 2001), p. 252; 2000 and 2002: Authors' tabulation.

Voter Turnout in Comparative Perspective*

Figure 8.3

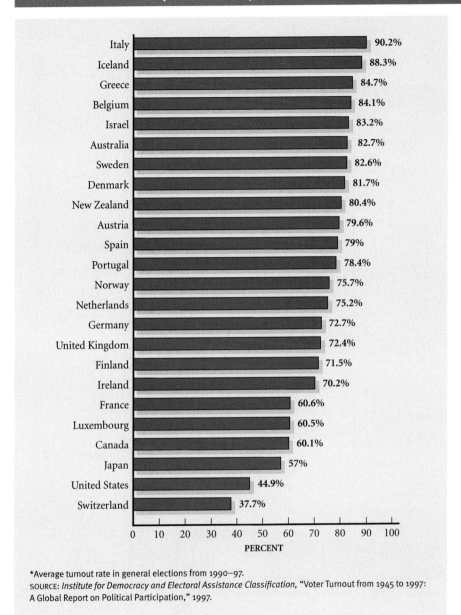

*Average turnout rate in general elections from 1990–97.
SOURCE: *Institute for Democracy and Electoral Assistance Classification,* "Voter Turnout from 1945 to 1997: A Global Report on Political Participation," 1997.

Figure 8.4 on page 292 shows the marked differences in voter turnout linked to ethnic group, education level, employment status, and age. This trend has created a political process whose class bias is so obvious and egregious that, if it continues, Americans may have to begin adding a qualifier when they describe their politics as democratic. Perhaps the terms "semidemocratic," "quasidemocratic," or "neodemocratic" are in order to describe a political process in which ordinary voters have as little influence as they do in contemporary America.

| Figure 8.4 | The Percentage of Americans Who Voted, 1976–2000 |

Whether or not Americans are likely to vote depends in part on their ethnic group, education level, employment status, and age.

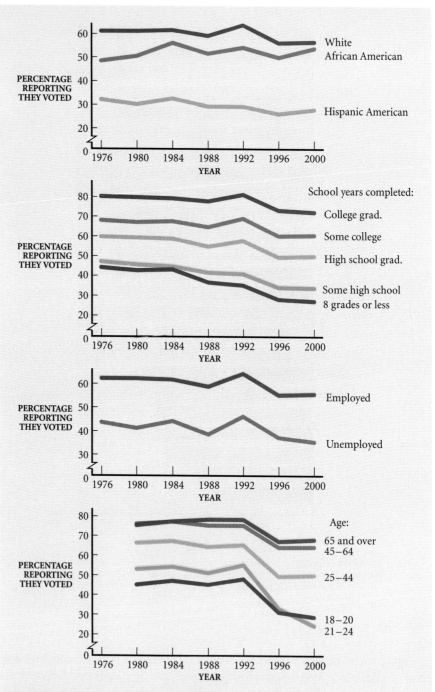

SOURCES: U.S. Bureau of the Census, *Statistical Abstract of the United States: 2001* (Washington, DC: Government Printing Office, 2001), p. 251; and www.census.gov/population/socdemo/voting/history/vot23.txt (accessed 7/11/02).

Election Turnout Rates

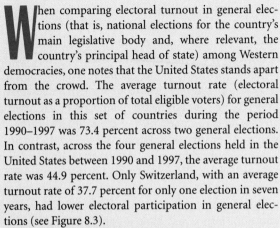

When comparing electoral turnout in general elections (that is, national elections for the country's main legislative body and, where relevant, the country's principal head of state) among Western democracies, one notes that the United States stands apart from the crowd. The average turnout rate (electoral turnout as a proportion of total eligible voters) for general elections in this set of countries during the period 1990–1997 was 73.4 percent across two general elections. In contrast, across the four general elections held in the United States between 1990 and 1997, the average turnout rate was 44.9 percent. Only Switzerland, with an average turnout rate of 37.7 percent for only one election in seven years, had lower electoral participation in general elections (see Figure 8.3).

Former communist countries of the Soviet Union and Eastern Europe (CIS-EE) recorded average turnout rates of nearly 70 percent following the collapse of European communism, while Asia and Latin America also recorded relatively high average turnout rates during the 1990s (68.5 percent and 66.3 percent, respectively). Sub-Saharan Africa and Arab nations have seen average turnout rates during the same period approaching only 50 percent, with less frequent general elections.

While observing aggregate electoral turnout patterns across countries is important in its own right, we might also inquire as to what may account for differing turnout rates among the most free and democratic countries of the world. In a recent comparative study, Mark Franklin has presented credible evidence linking four factors directly to differing turnout rates among the twenty-five or so wealthiest democracies. These are (1) the saliency of the election—are the stakes of the election high and the issues important? (2) compulsory voting—e.g., it is illegal to not vote in Australia, (3) the degree of proportionality—will voting for a loser be seen as wasting the voter's ballot because only one candidate wins and the votes for the loser are discarded? and (4) the rules of the election—do the polls remain open for more than one day (such as in India, where they are open for four days), and are the polls open on days when people have free time to vote (such as Sundays and holidays, as is customary throughout much of Europe)? Together, Franklin shows that these factors can account for nearly 80 percent of the differences in electoral turnout rates among the more advanced industrial democracies of the world.

Although a number of factors are clearly associated with global patterns of voting, a more interesting question may be why people choose not to vote when the option is available to them. In recent surveys of citizens in various democracies of Europe (and Japan), ineligibility and registration restrictions were the most common explanation offered for failing to vote. Poor knowledge of issues and candidates and a lack of interest in the election were the other reasons offered by nonvoters.

Scholars have debated the importance of voting in democracies. Certainly, large-scale apathy cannot be a healthy aspect of democracy. However, as Richard Rose, a renowned student of democracies, has noted, there is no threshold of turnout rates that one can identify as the point below which the quality of democracy declines. While a few of those who said they are not eligible to vote may be foreigners within the country, this alone cannot account for this factor being the most common reason given for not voting. Across all of the democracies of the world, with few exceptions, registration efforts have reached the voting age population. Within any democracy, a certain proportion are simply not going to vote (indeed, approximately 5 percent of those who did not vote say they never vote for reasons of conscience). Achieving turnout rates higher than three-quarters of the voting-age population may not be either possible or cost-effective. Furthermore, as most scholars have concluded with respect to Japan, Switzerland, and the United States, alternative means to voting as a vehicle of political participation and citizen involvement in civic affairs would seem to account for most nonvoting activity in countries where freedoms are the greatest and the roots of liberal democracy the deepest.

SOURCES: Richard Rose, "Evaluating Election Turnout," in *Voter Turnout from 1945–1997: A Global Report on Political Participation* (Stockholm: International Institute for Democracy and Electoral Assistance, 1997), pp. 35–47; and Mark Franklin, "Electoral Participation," in Lawrence LeDuc, Richard Niemi, and Pippa Norris, eds., *Comparing Democracies: Elections and Voting in Global Perspective* (Thousand Oaks, CA: Sage, 1996), pp. 216–35.

Who Participates, and How?

American political community
citizens who are eligible to vote
and participate in American
political life

> **What is the history of suffrage in the United States?**

The original **American political community** consisted of a rather limited group of white male property holders. Over the ensuing two centuries, "we the people" became a larger and more inclusive body as a result of such forces as the abolitionist movement, the women's suffrage movement, and the civil rights movement (see Chapter 5). This expansion of the political community was marked by enormous conflicts involving questions of race, gender, religious identity, and age. Today, these conflicts continue in the form of struggles over such issues as affirmative action, welfare reform, abortion, the gender gap, the political mobilization of religious groups, and the rise and fall of minority voting districts; the ongoing participation of groups with distinctive social and cultural identities has transformed politics, altering political coalitions and changing political debates. This section examines the experiences of different kinds of cultural and social groups in American politics: racial and ethnic, gender, religious, and age-based groups. It asks to what extent members of these particular groups have recognized common interests and have sought to act politically on those interests.

AFRICAN AMERICANS

As we saw in Chapter 5, political and legal pressure and protest all played a part in the modern civil rights movement, which took off in the 1950s. The movement drew on an organizational base and network of communication rooted in black churches, the NAACP, and black colleges.

The nonviolent protest tactics adopted by local clergy members, including Rev. Martin Luther King, Jr., eventually spread across the South and brought national attention to the movement. The clergy organized into a group called the Southern Christian Leadership Conference (SCLC). Students also played a key role. The most important student organization was the Student Nonviolent Coordinating Committee (SNCC). In 1960, four black students sat down at the lunch counter of the Greensboro, North Carolina, Woolworth's department store, which like most southern establishments did not serve African Americans. Their sit-in was the first of many. Through a combination of protest, legal action, and political pressure, the civil rights movement compelled a reluctant federal government to enforce black civil and political rights.

The victories of the civil rights movement made blacks full citizens and stimulated a tremendous growth in the number of black public officials at all levels of government, as blacks exercised their newfound political rights. Yet despite these successes, racial segregation remains a fact of life in the United States, and new problems have emerged. Most troubling is the persistence of black urban poverty, now coupled with deep social and economic isolation.[7] These conditions raise new questions about African American political participation. One question concerns black political cohesion: Will blacks continue to vote as a bloc, given the sharp economic differences that now divide a large black middle class from an equally large group of deeply impoverished African Americans? A second question concerns the benefits of participation: How can political participation improve the lives of African Americans, especially of the poor?

Public opinion and voting evidence indicate that African Americans continue to vote as a bloc despite their economic differences.[8] Surveys of black voters show that blacks across the income spectrum believe that their fates are linked because of their race. This sense of shared experience and a common fate has united blacks at the polls and in politics.[9] Since the 1960s, blacks have overwhelmingly chosen Democratic candidates and black candidates have sought election under the Democratic banner. In recent years, however, a small number of black Republicans has been elected to the House of Representatives. Evidence that affluent black Americans are less likely than poorer African Americans to support traditional policies that assist the poor suggests that this trend could continue in the future. However, Republican hostility to affirmative action and other programs of racial preference is likely to sharply check any large-scale black migration to the Republican Party.

At the same time, however, the black community and its political leadership has been considerably frustrated about the benefits of loyalty to the Democratic Party. Some analysts argue that the structure of party competition makes it difficult for African Americans to win policy benefits through political participation. Because Republicans have not sought to win the black vote and Democrats take it for granted, neither party is willing to support bold measures to address the mounting problems of poor African Americans.

LATINOS

For many years, analysts called the Latino vote "the sleeping giant" because as a group Latinos had relatively low levels of political mobilization. Two important reasons for the low mobilization levels among Latinos were the low rates of voter registration and low rates of naturalization. Among those who were eligible to vote, registration and turnout rates were relatively low.

Today, Latinos are viewed as a political group of critical importance. Rapid population growth, increased political participation, and uncertain party attachment all magnify the importance of the Latino vote in the coming decade. The Latino population grew some 60 percent between 1990 and 2000, to an estimated 35.3 million. This makes Hispanics equal in numbers to African Americans. Moreover, since 1996, Latino voters have begun to register and vote in unprecedented numbers. In 2000, Hispanics accounted for 7 percent of the total national vote, and it is estimated they will be 9 or 10 percent of the vote in 2004.[10] Latinos have traditionally voted heavily Democratic: Vice President Al Gore received two-thirds of the Hispanic vote in 2000. But Republicans also believe they can attract Hispanic voters. They see Latinos as a key "swing" vote that can tip elections toward either party. Latinos have already begun to play this role in state and local elections. In New York's 2001 mayoral election, Latino voters were credited with making the difference in electing Republican Michael Bloomberg. President Bush has actively courted Hispanic voters. Before the terrorist attacks of September 11, 2001, Bush considered enacting major substantive policy initiatives aimed at Latinos, such as amnesty for millions of undocumented Mexican workers in the United States. Although this initiative was put on hold, the power of the Latino vote means that politicians at all levels of government are now paying close attention to what Latinos want from government.

ASIAN AMERICANS

The diversity of national backgrounds among Asian Americans has impeded the development of group-based political power. No one national group dominates among the Asian American population. But in recent years there have been efforts to mobilize a more united Asian American political presence. In 1997 controversy erupted over illegal donations to President Clinton's re-election campaign by a Chinese American named John Huang. Many Asian Americans felt that the attention to this matter unfairly cast suspicion on all Asian Americans who participated in political fund-raising. This experience prompted the formation of several organizations aiming to enhance the power of the Asian vote. In Los Angeles, a group called CAUSE—Vision 21 formed in order to register Asian American voters and to highlight the importance of their vote. In addition, an effort called the 80/20 initiative was formed to persuade Asian Americans to support the candidate who promises the most to Asian voters. The goal is to have 80 percent of the Asian vote support the candidate who best addresses the interests of Asian Americans. By encouraging Asians to vote as a bloc, the organization hopes to expand group power.[11] Nonetheless, the geographic dispersion of Asian Americans and their diverse backgrounds and experiences raise questions about whether such strategies to build a common interest will succeed.

WOMEN VS. MEN

gender gap a distinctive pattern of voting behavior reflecting the differences in views between men and women

The ongoing significance of gender issues in American politics is best exemplified by the emergence of a **gender gap**—a distinctive pattern of male and female voting decisions—in electoral politics. Although proponents of women's suffrage had expected women to make a distinctive impact on politics as soon as they won the vote, not until the 1980s did voting patterns reveal a clear difference between male and female votes. In 1980, men voted heavily for Republican candidate Ronald Reagan; women divided their votes between Reagan and the incumbent Democratic president, Jimmy Carter. Since that election, gender differences have emerged in congressional and state elections, as well. Women tend to vote in higher numbers for Democratic candidates, while Republicans win more male votes. Behind these voting patterns are differing assessments of key policy issues. For one thing, more women than men take liberal positions on political issues; women are more likely than men to oppose military activities and support social spending. For example, 54 percent of women approved of the U.S. decision to send troops to Saudi Arabia in 1991, compared to 78 percent of men. The military campaign in Afghanistan was a rare exception to this pattern of gender differences: 85 percent of women and 89 percent of men expressed support for the war in Afghanistan.[12] On social spending, these trends reverse: 69 percent of women favor increased spending on Social Security, compared to 57 percent of men; 83 percent of women favor improving the nation's health care, compared to 76 percent of men; 72 percent of women advocate more spending on programs for the homeless, compared to 63 percent of men.[13] It is important to note that these differences do not mean that all women vote more liberally than all men. In fact, the voting differences between women who are homemakers and women who are in the workforce are almost as large as the differences between men and women. The sharpest differences are found between married men and single women, with single women tending to take the most liberal positions.[14]

Another key development in gender politics in recent years is the growing number of women in political office (see Figure 8.5). Journalists dubbed 1992 the "Year of the Woman" because so many women were elected to Congress: women doubled their numbers in the House and tripled them in the Senate. By 2002 women held 13.5 percent of the seats in the House of Representatives and 13 percent in the Senate; 22.6 percent of state legislators in 2002 were women.[15] Organizations supporting female candidates have worked to encourage more women to run for office and have supported them financially. In addition to the bipartisan NWPC, the Women's Campaign Fund and EMILY's List provide pro-choice Democratic women with early campaign financing, which is critical to establishing electoral momentum (the acronym of the latter group stands for Early Money Is Like Yeast). Recent research has shown that the key to increasing the numbers of women in political office is to encourage more women to run for election. Women are disadvantaged as candidates not because they are women but because male candidates are more likely to have the advantage of incumbency.[16] Although women in public office by no means take uniform positions on policy issues, surveys show that, on the whole, women legislators are more supportive of women's rights, health care spending, and children's and family issues.[17]

Increase in Number of Women in Elective Office, 1975–99   Figure 8.5

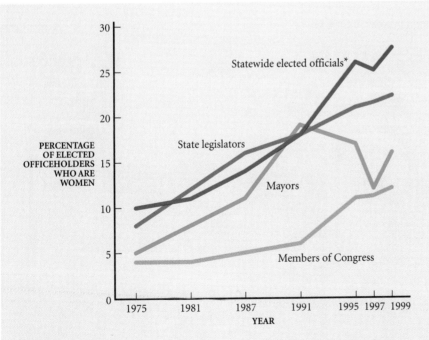

*Governors, attorneys general, etc.
SOURCE: Cynthia Costello, Shari Miles, and Anne J. Stone, eds., *The American Woman, 2001–2002* (New York: W. W. Norton, 2002), p. 328.

RELIGIOUS IDENTITY AND POLITICS

Religious identity plays an important role in American life. For some people, religious groups provide an organizational infrastructure for participating in politics around issues of special group concern. Black churches, for example, were instrumental in the civil rights movement, and black religious leaders continue to play important roles in national and local politics. Jews have also been active as a group in politics, but less through religious bodies than through a variety of social action agencies. Such agencies include the American Jewish Congress, the Anti-Defamation League, and the American Jewish Committee.

For most of American history, religious values have been woven deeply into the fabric of public life. Public school students began the day with prayers or Bible reading; city halls displayed crèches during the Christmas season. Practices that were religiously proscribed—most notably abortion—were also forbidden under law. But over the past thirty-five years, a variety of court decisions greatly reduced this kind of religious influence on public life. In 1962, the Supreme Court ruled in *Engel v. Vitale* that prayer in public schools was unconstitutional—that government should not be in the business of sponsoring official prayers. Bible reading was prohibited the following year. By 1973, with *Roe v. Wade*, the Court had made abortion legal.[18]

These decisions drew the condemnation of many Catholic and Protestant leaders. They also helped to spawn a countermovement of religious activists seeking to roll back these decisions and to find a renewed role for religion in public life. The mobilization of religious organizations and other groups that aim to reintroduce their view of morality into public life has been one of the most significant political

During the nineteenth century, universal white manhood suffrage became the rule in America, but women and most African Americans were denied voting rights. After the Civil War, the Fifteenth Amendment to the Constitution appeared to guarantee black voting rights. Blacks were elected to many political offices during Reconstruction, including a majority of seats in the South Carolina House of Representatives (right). But with the end of Reconstruction in the 1870s, African Americans were effectively deprived of the right to vote in most southern states, first by violence and intimidation and then by institutional barriers such as literacy tests. It was not until the 1965 Voting Rights Act that millions of African Americans were enfranchised.

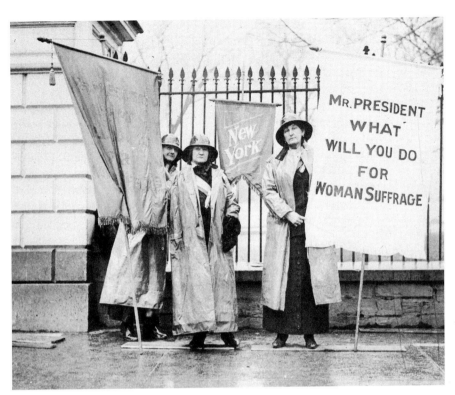

Women won the right to vote with the adoption of the Nineteenth Amendment in 1920. While suffragettes had been demanding enfranchisement for decades, it took World War I to bring women the right to vote, one reason being that many officials were convinced that women's suffrage would increase female support for the war effort.

In 1971, the Twenty-sixth Amendment lowered the voting age from 21 to 18. The impetus for the reform was antiwar protest. Public officials thought that the right to vote would encourage disgruntled students to take their concerns from the streets into the polling place. That prediction has not borne out as many young Americans have opted not to participate. As a result, voter registration drives, such as the MTV-sponsored "Choose or Lose," are frequently held on college campuses (left).

College students are not the only group to not participate in politics in great numbers. Voter turnout in general is far lower in the United States than in other western democracies. One factor is America's large population of immigrants who have not learned the ins and outs of democratic politics. The Latino community, for example, has not been fully integrated into American political processes and, consequently, shows low rates of voting participation. The size of the Latino community, however, makes it something of a "sleeping giant" in the American political system. Increasing rates of naturalization and voter registration could make the Latino vote a powerful force in American politics (right).

developments of the past two decades. Some of the most divisive conflicts in politics today, such as that over abortion, hinge on differences over religious and moral issues. These divisions have become so significant and so broad that they now constitute a major clash of cultures with repercussions throughout the political system and across many different areas of policy.

Politically, one of the most significant elements of this new politics has been the mobilization of evangelical Protestants into a cohesive and politically shrewd organization aligned with the Republican Party. The Moral Majority, the first broad political organization of evangelical Christians, showed its political muscle in the 1980 election, when it aligned with the Republican Party, eventually backing Ronald Reagan for president. Over the next few years, evangelicals strengthened their movement by registering voters and mobilizing them with sophisticated, state-of-the-art political techniques. Their success was evident in the 1984 election, when 80 percent of evangelical Christian voters cast their ballots for Reagan. The 1988 election was a turning point in the political development of the Christian Right. Televangelist Pat Robertson ran for president and, although his candidacy was unsuccessful, his effort laid the groundwork for future political strength. Robertson's supporters gained control of some state Republican parties and won positions of power in others. With this new organizational base and sharply honed political skills, Robertson formed a new organization, the Christian Coalition. This organization became one of the most important groups in American politics during the 1990s because of its ability to reach and mobilize a large grassroots base. The Christian Coalition was credited with helping to elect the Republican Congress in 1994.

President Bush has been closely aligned with religious conservatives. Many analysts viewed the president's faith-based initiative, which sought to funnel government assistance to religious groups engaged in charitable work, as a way to reward conservative Christian groups for supporting his election. In fact, conservative religious groups turned against the initiative because they feared that government control would accompany federal dollars.[19]

By the early 2000s, the political power of the religious Right had become uncertain. On the one hand, some of its strongest organizations, such as the Christian Coalition, had fallen into disarray and others had retreated from direct political engagement. On the other hand, the sympathy of President Bush for many of the goals of religious conservatives meant that their ideas were well-represented in government. As Ralph Reed, former head of the Christian Coalition and current chairman of the Georgia Republican Party, put it, "You're no longer throwing rocks at the building; you're in the building."[20]

AGE AND PARTICIPATION

One of the most significant patterns in political participation is the generational divide. Older people have much higher rates of participation than young people. This division is especially apparent in the different voting rates of the two groups. In the 2000 election, the average turnout was 54.7 percent. The elderly were significantly above the average, with 67.6 percent of people over sixty-five voting. Young people were far below the average, with only 28.4 percent of people between the ages of eighteen and twenty and 24.2 percent of those between twenty-one and twenty-four reporting that they voted.[21] Although these two groups comprise a similar portion of the population—in 2000, there were 26.8 million potential voters between the ages of eighteen and twenty-four and 32.8 million potential voters over sixty-five—the political voice of the elderly is much stronger because of their higher voting rates. When the Twenty-sixth Amendment to the Constitution granted eighteen- to twenty-year-olds the right to vote in 1971, many believed this group would be a significant new voice in politics. Instead, voting participation of the young has declined quite dramatically. Between 1980 and 2000, the percent of twenty-one- to twenty-four-year-olds who voted dropped by over 20 percent, compared with a 5 percent overall decline.

One reason that younger people vote less is that political campaigns rarely target young voters. A study of political advertising in the 2000 elections found that 64 percent of campaign television advertising was directed at people over fifty. Only 14.2 percent of advertising was aimed at eighteen- to thirty-four-year-olds.[22] This creates a vicious cycle: the less political campaigns appeal to younger voters, the less likely they are to participate, and the less they participate, the less likely they will be targeted by political campaigns. A 1998 study found that close to 70 percent of the fifteen- to twenty-four-year-olds surveyed agreed with the statement "Our generation has an important voice but no one seems to hear it."[23]

Another reason that political campaigns target older voters is that the elderly are better organized to participate than young people. The most important organization representing the elderly is the American Association of Retired Persons (AARP), which has a membership of more than 33 million. Although only a small fraction of the members are active in the organization, the AARP's ability to mobilize many thousands of individuals to weigh in on policy proposals has made the organization one of the most powerful in Washington, D.C. Young people have no comparable organization. The United States Student Association has represented college students since the 1950s, but its numbers are much smaller and it does not have the same organizational capacity to mobilize its members as the AARP. Other organizations, such as Third Millennium, have emerged to represent the voice of young people in politics. But, like most advocacy organizations, these groups do not have a membership base and have little capacity to mobilize.

The disengagement of youth from politics contrasts with their strong record in community service. More than 70 percent of young people volunteer in their own communities.[24] One recent national survey found that a majority of students believed that community service was the best way to deal with national problems. By contrast, they tended to view politics and politicians with cynicism. The declining levels of youth participation do not bode well for the future of American politics. Although participation rates increase with age, political participation is a habit that is acquired young. Low levels of youth participation today signify a more disengaged population in the future.

Explaining Political Participation

Participation is skewed toward those with more education and more money. To understand these current patterns we must go back to a basic question: Why do people participate in politics? Simple as it seems, there are different ways to answer this question.

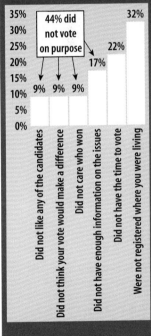

Perspectives on Politics

WHY COLLEGE STUDENTS DON'T VOTE

Responses of eighteen- to twenty-four-year-olds to the question,
  "Think about the last election you remember in which you did not vote. What was the main reason you did not vote in that election?"

44% did not vote on purpose

- Did not like any of the candidates: 9%
- Did not think your vote would make a difference: 9%
- Did not care who won: 9%
- Did not have enough information on the issues: 17%
- Did not have the time to vote: 22%
- Were not registered where you were living: 32%

SOURCE: "Youth Voices," *Who Cares*, Summer 1996, p. 17.

➤ **What explains levels of participation? Why has participation declined over time?**

SOCIOECONOMIC STATUS

socioeconomic status status in society based on level of education, income, and occupational prestige

The first explanation for participation points to the characteristics of individuals. One of the most important and consistent results of surveys about participation is that Americans with higher levels of education, more income, and higher-level occupations—what social scientists call **socioeconomic status**—participate much more in politics than do those with less education and less income. Education level alone is the strongest predictor of most kinds of participation, but income becomes important—not surprisingly—when it comes to making contributions. In addition to education and income, other individual characteristics also affect participation. For example, African Americans and Latinos are less likely to participate than are whites, although when differences in education and income are taken into account, both groups participate at the same or higher levels than do whites. Finally, young people are far less likely to participate in politics than are older people. The proportion of young people that vote has declined in almost every single election since 1972.[25]

Although they give us a picture of who participates and who does not, explanations based on individual characteristics leave many questions open. One of the biggest questions is why the relationship between education and participation—so strong in surveys—does not seem to hold true over time. As Americans have become more educated, with more people finishing high school and attending college, we would expect to see more people participating in politics. Yet participation has declined, not increased.[26] In the nineteenth century, participation in presidential elections was 20 percent higher than current levels. Moreover, politics was a much more vibrant and encompassing activity: large numbers of people joined in parades, public meetings, and electioneering.[27] This puzzle about declining participation suggests that we need to look beyond the characteristics of individuals to the larger social and political setting to understand changes in patterns of participation over time.

CIVIC ENGAGEMENT

civic engagement a sense of concern among members of the political community about public, social, and political life, expressed through participation in social and political organizations

The social setting can affect political participation in a variety of ways. One recent study argued that participation depends on three elements: resources (including time, money, and know-how), **civic engagement** (are you concerned about public issues and do you feel that you can make a difference?), and recruitment (are you asked to participate, especially by someone you know?).[28] Whether a person has resources, feels engaged, and is recruited depends very much on his or her social setting—what his parents are like, who she knows, what associations she belongs to. In the United States, churches are a particularly important social institution in helping to foster political participation. Through their church activities people learn the civic skills that prepare them to participate in the political world more broadly. It is often through church activities that people learn to run meetings, write newsletters, or give speeches and presentations. Churches are also an important setting for meeting people and creating networks for recruitment, since people are more likely to participate if asked by a friend or an acquaintance.

As this model suggests, if fewer people belong to social organizations, they may be less likely to participate in politics. The United States has often been called a nation of joiners because of our readiness to form local associations to address

Does Higher Voter Participation Really Matter?

One of the great contradictions of American politics is the fact that our elections—the hallmark of democracy—are plagued by low, and declining, voter turnout. From a high point of about 65 percent turnout in 1960 to a seven-decade low of 49 percent in the 1996 presidential election, Americans are staying away from the polls in record numbers. By comparison, voter turnout in virtually every other democratic nation of the world is significantly higher, typically in the range of 70 to 90 percent in their comparable national elections. But is this anything to worry about?

Yes, say many. Part of the problem lies in the tangle of rules that regulate voting, which are more complicated than those found in almost any other nation. Most of these rules were enacted decades ago to discourage "undesirables"—African Americans, immigrants, the poor—from voting. In many nations, voting is easier because citizens are automatically registered to vote, do not have to worry about local residency requirements, and elections are held on the weekends. A government that cares about its elections should certainly do more to make the act of voting easier. Turnout matters to campaigns, because those who run for office tailor their campaign issues and strategies to those who are likely to vote. Thus, the needs and concerns of the nonvoters—generally those with lower incomes and less education and members of disadvantaged groups—are likely to be ignored, with the result that policy fails to address the nation's most pressing needs. Three states have experimented with making voting easier. In Texas, citizens have been allowed since 1991 to vote any time during the two weeks prior to election day. In Oregon, turnout has risen since the state made balloting by mail easy, more than a decade ago. In 2000, Arizona began experimenting with voting via the Internet. These pioneering efforts demonstrate that the government could do more to make voting easier, and should

do so, many argue, because the ever-declining percentage of voting casts a shadow over the very legitimacy of the government that is elected. How can a president, or other elected leaders, claim a mandate to govern when less than a quarter of eligible voters cast ballots for the winner?

Skeptics counter these arguments by asserting that the negative consequences of nonvoting have been greatly overstated. In 1993, Congress passed the "Motor Voter" law, which allowed citizens to register to vote when they applied for a driver's license. Even though millions of new voters registered by this means, it had little or no effect on voting rates, suggesting that existing election laws may have little to do with voting rates. Further, research has demonstrated that there is often less difference between voters and nonvoters than many assume. As study of the 1988 election, for example, showed that, contrary to expectations, nonvoters would have supported the winning presidential candidate, George Bush, over challenger Michael Dukakis. This and similar research supports the idea that the interests of nonvoters are not so different from those of voters. Beyond this, nonvoting is not necessarily a sign of alienation from the political system. To some extent at least, it can be interpreted as citizen satisfaction with the overall course of the country's affairs. While indifference is a less than noble sentiment, it can at least be taken as a green light for the nation's political leaders. When crises have arisen in the past, from the Great Depression to the Gulf War, Americans have turned close attention to their political leaders. Finally, voting is only one method of political expression, and citizens with concerns ranging from race to abortion to guns increasingly express their views through means other than the ballot box, from interest group activity to the Internet. Voting is still the most frequent political activity, but citizens are free to express themselves in an ever-wider array of methods.

Does Your Vote Matter?

Yes

The right of citizens of the United States, who are 18 years of age or older, to vote, shall not be denied or abridged by the United States or any state on account of age.

Last Tuesday as I was heading off to class, I asked several friends whether they were going to vote in the special aldermanic primary in District 5. I received a variety of responses:

"How does a city council election affect me? Everything I need UW-Madison takes care of for me."

"I vote at home and I don't want to cancel my voter registration there."

"I'm too busy to walk to the polls."

"Well, I don't know the candidates."

"I don't care. It doesn't make a difference who's elected."

I became quite depressed when I went to vote at 2:30 p.m., only to find out I was the first voter in my ward, which comprises some of the Lakeshore dorms. In all, only seven students decided to vote in my ward Tuesday.

The dearth of participation last Tuesday proved yet again students are taking their 26th Amendment for granted. As students, we must remember that about three decades ago, we had no right to vote at all. Since the passage of the amendment in 1971, students have ranked last in voter turnout. Especially in Madison, where one out of every five people is a student, the 26th Amendment is wilting due to the lack of participation.

Politicians ignore students because students do not vote. Feeling ignored and not wanted, students refuse to participate in elections for these politicians. In order to break the vicious apathy cycle, students must vote. Until then, we will continue to be ignored.

As for students' excuses for not voting, they are weak and worthless under scrutiny. Understandably, students are busy and have many things to do; however, occupation or ignorance of issues is not an excuse for lack of participation. It takes no more than 10 minutes to vote on this campus.

In addition, unless you like being ignored, not caring about the candidates does not work either. Someone must be elected to a seat, and sometimes you have to choose between the lesser of two (or three, four, etc.) evils.

Don't know the candidates? In all elections in Dane County, I know the League of Women Voters surveys all candidates. In addition, general media outlets provide information about who is running and what she or he stands for.

Vote at "home"? Students spend at least nine months a year in the city of Madison. Why should students not be involved in the decisions that affect them daily? Not casting a vote in Madison is saying you do not care about local issues in your student community. Remember, the City Councils of Milwaukee or Minneapolis are not going to decide whether State Street needs to be redesigned or where a new parking ramp is going to go downtown or whether Elizabeth Link Peace Park deserves a carousel.

Furthermore, students who have more time or who care greatly about a particular issue should further enhance the 26th Amendment by serving on a city committee. City Council and the various boards and committees of the city of Madison dictate policy that affects everyone. Policy ranging from public safety to housing regulations, from affirmative action to vending machine licenses affects everyone in the city.

Remember, there are countries where people are dying (literally) to vote or to determine the livelihood of their fellow neighbors. As students in America, it is our patriotic duty to become involved in civic affairs. The 26th Amendment, in its sacredness, needs to be exercised to the fullest extent. Not choosing to do so just might lead to the roads of a dictatorship.

SOURCE: David Presberry, "We Must Exercise Our 26th Amendment Rights," *The Badger Herald* (University of Wisconsin, Madison), February 26, 2002.

No

On the first Tuesday of November every few years, good citizens doing their civic duty trudge to their district polling places to pull a lever or flip a switch, and in turn cast their vote. After performing this action, they receive a sticker from a polling worker. Then they go home. At night they flip back and forth between reruns of sitcoms and the voting results on their television. They celebrate when the person they voted for wins. They complain when the candidate they voted for loses. They turn off their television. They turn off the lights. They sleep.

The problem is that the average voting citizen does not do anything productive from the time they shut off their glowing television sets on November 6, to the day they go back to vote years later. In effect, the voter has passed the buck by voting. The self-serving notion of the average voter is that now it is the politician's responsibility and problem to fix the community and world around them. It is no longer the citizen's duty. Many seem to hold the notion that their only civic duty is voting, and once that is done, they have time to commence with their second civic duty, which seems to be complaining.

In the past the average voting citizen whines constantly at the television, to their co-workers at the water cooler, to their friends, seemingly to any creature with a pulse. Some of the voting public rage at the non-voting public, because in their ill-informed minds, they are surely the ones to blame for the problems all over the globe.

But some of the average voting public begins to feel alienated from the political sphere. They come to feel that their voice has no say in formal politics. They come to hate the party politics of Washington D.C. They wonder why there are only two main parties to represent the diverse society of America. They come to realize that the way a senator or house member votes is mainly due to how it will affect the politician's chance of re-election. They realize that special interests take precedence over public concerns. They see in the newspapers that companies receive thousands of dollars in corporate welfare from states, while the public welfare system that accounts for less than one percent of the total budget is cut. They see that about one-third of the federal budget is spent on murdering people in foreign lands through the actions of military puppets. They watch politicians on their television sets use various verbal political attacks on defenseless people, such as the homeless and those on welfare as a way of wooing citizens to their side. They realize that lobbyists are running the majority of things in Washington D.C. and in state governments. They realize that of the 100 members of the U.S. Senate that less than five represent the various ethnic backgrounds that make up this country. They realize that women, who make up about half of the total population of the United States, have less than a dozen representatives in the U.S. Senate. They realize that they are not represented. They realize that the third party candidates are nothing more than copies of major party candidates. They realize that Ralph Nader, for all of his ethical preaching, is still a wealthy businessman. They realize that polls done by various media organizations outweigh the voice of votes. The conclusion drawn is that the fickle cry of the public is what is important to decision making, over patient and rational thought. People who think this don't vote in the next election. They realize that a senior citizen will, as always, do the job for them. This is dangerous to a productive nation.

It would be counterproductive for a society if their people did not voice their views, and be represented in one fashion or another, but it is ludicrous to believe that the only way to be heard is through a vote. These alienated voters need to find other peaceful and constructive ways to voice and practice their opinions. This is not an argument for laziness. It is basically an argument for doing anything that gives decision-making power back to you.

My conclusion is this: on November 6 I am doing something that I have never done before: I am not voting. I have voted in every town, state, and national election previous to this year since I turned 18. I am now 23 years old, and in that time I have lived in other towns, states, and countries, and it is evident to me that voting is the least a person can do to make positive change in a town, in a state, in the country, or in the world. Voting is not my only civic duty. I can cause change in other peaceful and more constructive ways than voting.

SOURCE: Andrew Johnson, "As Citizens, Voting Isn't Our Only Duty," *Connecticut Daily Campus,* May 24, 2002.

common problems. As early as the 1830s, the Frenchman Alexis de Tocqueville singled out this tendency to form associations as a most distinctive American trait.[29] There is evidence, however, that Americans no longer join organizations as much as they did in the past. This declining membership raises concerns that the civic engagement that ordinary Americans once had is deteriorating. These concerns are magnified by declining levels of social trust, which further contribute to the tendency to pull back from public engagement.[30] There are many possible reasons for the decline in organizational membership and social trust, and consequently in civic engagement. Television, for example, keeps people in their houses and away from meetings or other, more civic, engagements.[31] Crime can also reduce civic engagement by reducing social trust, making people suspicious and unwilling to take part in neighborhood activities.

Another way to explain the decline in civic engagement is to look at how the experiences of different generations might make them more or less oriented toward civic engagement. The generation that came of age during the Great Depression and World War II has been called the "long civic generation" because this group tends to participate in politics and associational life much more than previous or later generations. During the 1930s, people looked to government to help them with economic hardships, and in the 1940s, the same generation fought World War II, a popular war in which the entire country pulled together.[32] Later generations have not experienced such popular common causes to bring them together in the public sphere: their wars have been less popular and their great social causes more divisive. In addition, political life has seemed much less inspiring, filled with accusations of wrongdoing and constant investigations into possible scandal. Such a generational perspective makes sense because people form habits and beliefs in their early years that are very important in how they participate later in life. A generational perspective also helps explain why participation did not decline during the twentieth century, but instead started out low in the early 1900s, rose from the 1930s through the 1960s, and then began to fall once again.

Arguments about declining public trust and generational effects don't pay enough attention to the political setting in which participation takes place. The organization of politics itself plays a key role in channeling participation in particular directions and in encouraging or discouraging people from participating. Participation depends on whether there are formal obstacles in the political system, what people think political engagement has to offer them, and most important, whether political parties and politicians try to mobilize people into politics.

FORMAL OBSTACLES

Formal obstacles can greatly decrease participation. As we saw earlier in the chapter, in the South prior to the 1960s, the widespread use of the poll tax and other measures such as the **white primary** essentially deprived black Americans (and many poor whites) of the right to vote during the first part of this century. This system of legal segregation meant that there were few avenues for black Americans in the South to participate in politics. With the removal of these legal barriers in the 1960s, black political participation shot up, with rates of turnout approaching those of southern whites, as early as 1968.[33]

Another important political factor reducing voter turnout in the United States is our nation's peculiar registration rules. In every American state but North

white primary primary election in which only white voters are eligible to participate

What Government Does . . . After September 11

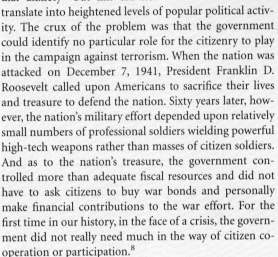

September 11, like many disasters, elicited an enormous response from the public. Although the early forms of citizen participation were largely aimed at helping the victims and the country as a whole return to normal life, later efforts have been aimed at creating a new culture of citizen action.

In the immediate aftermath of the attacks, the people of the United States responded with remarkable generosity. In the few days after September 11, blood donations increased faster than at any other time in history.[1] Cash donations to charities also surged, and had passed the $1 billion mark only five weeks after the attacks.[2] There was a parallel increase in symbolic displays of unity and patriotism, such as flying the American flag or lining the streets of lower Manhattan to cheer the rescue and salvage workers. Celebrities got into the act, too, organizing a star-studded Concert for New York in mid-October.

As these more visible forms of citizen participation began to subside, other changes emerged. One significant effect of September 11 was citizen interest in government jobs. Government institutions from the Central Intelligence Agency (CIA) to the General Accounting Office (GAO) to the Peace Corps all reported significant increases in numbers of job applicants after September 11.[3] The nonprofit sector also experienced an increase in interest from job seekers. The Red Cross reported nearly triple the usual traffic on its employment Web site in September 2001.[4]

The attacks also spurred participation from citizens critical of the government's policies. Some citizens protested the government's decision to invade Afghanistan to disrupt the Al Qaeda network. At the same time, there was a vigorous public debate surrounding President Bush's executive order of November 13,[5] which reduced the legal protections available to noncitizens suspected of supporting terrorist activity.[6] There was also public debate about the government's decision not to treat Taliban and Al Qaeda fighters captured in Afghanistan as prisoners of war, a status that confers certain legal rights and protections.

One effort to sustain the heightened citizen participation after September 11 was President Bush's creation of the USA Freedom Corps. This organization, which merged and expanded a number of existing government volunteer programs, was intended to encourage all Americans to volunteer at least 4,000 hours of community service over a lifetime. President Bush stated that the Corps was intended to bring about "a new culture of responsibility."[7]

As time went on, however, the participatory impact of the events of September 11 seemed to wane. The USA Freedom Corps remained an ill-defined initiative that inspired little popular or media interest. Terrorism continued to be a major focus of debate and discussion—to say nothing of popular anxiety—but this did not translate into heightened levels of popular political activity. The crux of the problem was that the government could identify no particular role for the citizenry to play in the campaign against terrorism. When the nation was attacked on December 7, 1941, President Franklin D. Roosevelt called upon Americans to sacrifice their lives and treasure to defend the nation. Sixty years later, however, the nation's military effort depended upon relatively small numbers of professional soldiers wielding powerful high-tech weapons rather than masses of citizen soldiers. And as to the nation's treasure, the government controlled more than adequate fiscal resources and did not have to ask citizens to buy war bonds and personally make financial contributions to the war effort. For the first time in our history, in the face of a crisis, the government did not really need much in the way of citizen cooperation or participation.[8]

[1] See: Raymond Hernandez, "Donations: Getting Too Much of a Good Thing," *New York Times*, November 12, 2001, p. G3; Newsletter of the New York Blood Center. On-line at www.nybloodcenter.org/Newsletter/lifesavers/page5.html (accessed 3/19/02).

[2] Ian Wilhelm, "September 11 Donations Hit $1 Billion," *The Chronicle of Philanthropy*, October 16, 2001. On-line at http://philanthropy.com/free/update/2001/10/2001101601.htm (accessed 7/11/02).

[3] Pamela Mendels, "A Surge of Civic Mindedness," *Business Week On-line*, November 7, 2001. On-line at www.businessweek.com/careers/content/nov2001/ca2001117_9208.htm (accessed 7/11/02).

[4] *Ibid.*

[5] "Military Order of November 13, 2001: Detention, Treatment, and Trial of Certain Non-Citizens in the War Against Terrorism," *Federal Register*, November 16, 2001 (Vol. 66, No. 222), pages 57831–36.

[6] See William Glaberson, "A Nation Challenged: The Legal Issues; Groups Gird for Long Legal Fight on New Bush Anti-Terror Powers," *New York Times*, November 30, 2001, p. A1. Elisabeth Bumiller and David Johnston, "A Nation Challenged: Immigration; Bush Sets Option of Military Trials in Terrorist Cases," *New York Times*, November 14, 2001, p. A1. Robin Toner and Janet Elder, "A Nation Challenged: Attitudes; Public Is Wary but Supportive on Rights Curbs," *New York Times*, December 12, 2001, p. A1.

[7] David S. Sanger, "Bush Rallies Volunteers for His New Corps," *New York Times*, March 13, 2002, p. A20.

[8] For a discussion of these themes see Matthew A. Crenson and Benjamin Ginsberg, *Downsizing Democracy: How America Sidelined Its Citizens and Privatized Its Public* (Baltimore: Johns Hopkins University Press, 2002).

Dakota, individuals who are eligible to vote must register with the state election board before they are actually allowed to vote. Registration requirements were introduced at the end of the nineteenth century in response to the demands of the Progressive movement. Progressives hoped to make voting more difficult both to reduce multiple voting and other forms of corruption and to discourage immigrant and working-class voters from going to the polls. When first introduced, registration was extremely difficult and, in some states, reduced voter turnout by as much as 50 percent.

Registration requirements particularly depress the participation of those with little education and low incomes because registration requires a greater degree of political involvement and interest than does the act of voting itself. To vote, a person need be concerned only with the particular election campaign at hand. Requiring individuals to register before the next election forces them to make a decision to participate on the basis of an abstract interest in the electoral process rather than a simple concern with a specific campaign. Such an abstract interest in electoral politics is largely a product of education. Those with relatively little education may become interested in political events once the issues of a particular campaign become salient, but by that time it may be too late to register. Young people tend to assign a low priority to registration even if they are well educated. As a result, personal registration requirements not only diminish the size of the electorate but also tend to create an electorate that is, on average, better educated, higher in income and social status, and composed of fewer young people, African Americans, and other minorities than the citizenry as a whole (see Figure 8.6). In Europe, there is typically no registration burden on the individual voter; voter registration is handled automatically by the government. This is one reason that voter turnout rates in Europe are higher than those in the United States.

As might be expected, in states that do not require registration (North Dakota) or that allow registration on the day of the election (Minnesota) voter turnout is not only higher than average, but younger and less affluent voters turn out in larger percentages.[34] Minnesota's same-day rule played an important role in the surprise 1998 gubernatorial victory of colorful former wrestler Jesse Ventura. Ventura won the votes of many young men who had not been registered until they came to the polls on election day. Without same-day registration, Ventura's electoral chances would have been considerably lessened.

One formal obstacle to participation that has grown more important in recent years is the restriction on the voting rights of people who have committed a felony. Forty-six states and the District of Columbia prohibit prison inmates who are serving a felony sentence from voting.[35] In thirty-two states, felons on parole are not permitted to vote, and in twenty-nine states, felons on probation are not allowed to vote. There are also numerous restrictions on the voting rights of felons who have served their sentences. Ten states permanently take away the voting rights of those with a felony conviction, and four others disfranchise some categories of offenders. Texas restricts the voting rights of ex-offenders for two years after they have served their sentence. With the sharp rise in incarceration rates in the 1980s and 1990s, these restrictions have had a significant impact on voting rights. By one estimate, 3.9 million people—one in fifty Americans—have lost their voting rights as a result of these restrictions. Black men have been disproportionately affected: 13 percent of black men have been disfranchised, a rate that is seven times higher

Differences in Voter Registration Rates by Social Group, 2000

Figure 8.6

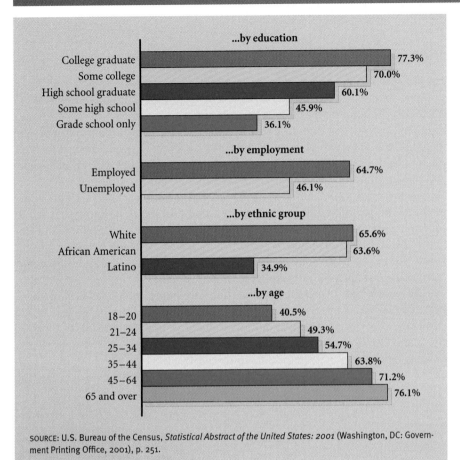

The percentage of Americans who are registered to vote varies according to education level, employment status, ethnic group, and age.

...by education

- College graduate — 77.3%
- Some college — 70.0%
- High school graduate — 60.1%
- Some high school — 45.9%
- Grade school only — 36.1%

...by employment

- Employed — 64.7%
- Unemployed — 46.1%

...by ethnic group

- White — 65.6%
- African American — 63.6%
- Latino — 34.9%

...by age

- 18–20 — 40.5%
- 21–24 — 49.3%
- 25–34 — 54.7%
- 35–44 — 63.8%
- 45–64 — 71.2%
- 65 and over — 76.1%

SOURCE: U.S. Bureau of the Census, *Statistical Abstract of the United States: 2001* (Washington, DC: Government Printing Office, 2001), p. 251.

than that of the population as a whole. In the states that deny the vote to all ex-felons, one in four black men have lost the right to vote. Concern over the impact of these voting restrictions has led to campaigns in some states—as yet unsuccessful—to restore voting rights to people who have committed a felony.

Over the years, voter registration restrictions have been modified somewhat to make registration easier. But the removal of formal obstacles is not enough to ensure that people participate, as the example of the National Voter Registration Act passed in 1993 shows. Popularly known as the Motor Voter Act, the law aimed to increase participation by making it easier to register to vote. The cumbersome process of registering (and staying registered after moving) has often been singled out as a barrier to participation. The new law aimed to remove this obstacle by allowing people to register when they apply for a driver's license and at other public facilities. Although voter registration increased, turnout did not. An estimated 3.4 million people registered to vote as a result of the Motor Voter Act, but turnout in the 1996 election—the first presidential election held after the law went into effect—actually declined by 6 percent from that in 1992.[36] The very limited success of the Motor Voter Act suggests that people need motivation to participate, not simply the removal of barriers.

POLITICAL MOBILIZATION

The political setting can play an important role in motivating people to vote. When elections are closely contested, more people tend to vote. And in political settings where they think their input will make a difference, people are more likely to participate. One study of black political participation, for example, found that blacks were more likely to vote, participate in campaigns, and contact public officials in cities run by a black mayor. Their greater attention to city politics and their belief that city government is more responsive to their concerns helps to spark participation.[37]

But the most significant factor affecting participation is whether people are mobilized by parties, candidates, interest groups, and social movements. A recent comprehensive study of the decline in participation in the United States found that fully half of the drop-off could be accounted for by reduced **mobilization** efforts.[38] People are much more likely to participate when someone—preferably someone they know—asks them to get involved.

The importance of personal contact for mobilizing voters has been demonstrated in a series of experiments recently conducted by political scientists Donald Green and Alan Gerber. Evaluating the results of several get-out-the-vote drives, Green and Gerber showed that face-to-face interaction with a canvasser greatly increased the chances that the person contacted would go to the polls. They estimated that personal contact boosted turnout from 44.5 percent to 56 percent. The

mobilization the process by which large numbers of people are organized for a political activity

During the nineteenth century, America's political parties worked hard to mobilize voters, using everything from barbecues to bribes to get out the vote. On the day of a presidential election, hundreds of thousands of party workers handed out leaflets, knocked on doors, and even provided free transportation to those unable to get to the polls on their own.

Today, political parties are weak but such institutions as ethnic organizations and labor unions endeavor to mobilize their members for electoral combat. During the 2000 presidential election, the NAACP's mobilization of African American voters in Florida nearly produced a victory for Democrat Al Gore in that state (left). In a similar vein, labor unions organized massive get-out-the-vote drives in Pennsylvania, Ohio, and Michigan to help elect Democrats (right). On the other side, the forces of business and the religious right worked to mobilize their troops on behalf of George W. Bush and the Republicans.

Young people tend not to vote in large numbers. One reason may be that civic education curricula emphasize community service, such as volunteering services to Habitat for Humanity's home-building projects, rather than voting and office-holding. High schools in many states require students to complete a certain number of hours in volunteer posts before they can graduate. While community service is a positive, it is possible that this new emphasis has inadvertently taught students that service to the local community is more important than an interest in national political affairs.

impact of direct mail was much smaller, causing only a 2.2 percent increase in voting.[39] Impersonal calls from a phone bank had no effect on voter turnout. Green and Gerber have also evaluated the impact of mobilization on young voters, studying a series of get-out-the-vote campaigns conducted near college campuses during the 2000 election. In these campaigns, phone contacts which were more chatty and informal than standard phone bank messages, increased turnout by an estimated 5 percent. Face-to-face contact again proved even more powerful, increasing turnout by 8.5 percent.[40]

In previous decades, political parties, organizations, and social movements relied on personal contact to mobilize voters. As we will see in Chapter 9, during the nineteenth century, American political party machines employed hundreds of thousands of workers to organize and mobilize voters as well as to bring them to the polls. The result was an extremely high rate of turnout, typically more than 90 percent of eligible voters.[41] But political party machines began to decline in strength in the beginning of the twentieth century and by now have, for the most part, disappeared. Without party workers to encourage them to go to the polls and even to bring them there if necessary, many eligible voters will not participate.

Rather than mobilizers of people, political parties have largely become fundraising and advertising organizations. The experience of a Connecticut woman during the 1996 election is typical. Hoping to participate in the campaign, she sent a check to the Democratic Party and asked how she could volunteer. She subsequently received many more requests to donate money but she was never informed of any other way to become involved.[42] For the most part, candidates are left on their own to mobilize voters. In the 2000 Senate race in New Jersey, Democrat Jon Corzine paid "volunteers" to help him get out the vote. In that year's presidential election, both parties did work to mobilize their supporters in a few key "battleground" states like Florida, Michigan, Wisconsin, and Pennsylvania. But not only were these efforts limited to only a handful of important swing states, they were also impersonal political advertisements disguised as "personalized" letters, phone calls, and e-mails from the candidates. For most people, politics consists of little more than irritating intrusions into their lives that become more numerous around election time.

Interest groups have also reduced their efforts at direct mobilization. Although the number of interest groups has grown dramatically in recent years, the connection that most interest-group members have to these groups often extends no further than their checkbook. Rather than being a means for contact by a friend or an acquaintance to take part in a political activity, belonging to an organization is likely to bring requests through the mail for donations. And, rather than providing a venue for meeting new people and widening your circle of engagement, organizational membership is more likely to land your name on yet another mailing list, generating still more requests for funds. In the past, social movements, such as the labor movement in the 1930s and the civil rights movement of the 1960s, played an important role in mobilizing people into politics. As such movements have ebbed, nothing has replaced their mobilizing energy. As a result, participation rates drop the most among poorer and less-educated citizens. Because of the absence of strong political parties, the American electorate is smaller and skewed more toward the middle class than the population of all those potentially eligible to vote.

Participation and American Political Values

Over the course of our history, as we have seen, the American political community has expanded to make our politics more closely match our fundamental values of liberty, equality, and democracy. But more recently, our **political institutions** have ceased to mobilize an active citizenry. Furthermore, our uneven pattern of political participation is at odds with our notions of equality and democracy. These problems highlight the tension among our basic values and raise questions about whether our institutions could help provide a better balance among them. Two questions about institutions are particularly pressing: Is "checkbook democracy" enough? Do our public institutions do enough to bring us together to engage in common problem-solving?

"Checkbook democracy" refers to the new importance of money in politics, both in electoral campaigns and in interest-group activity. Because it has been associated with declining participation and a greater inequality in participation patterns, checkbook politics has been the target of reformers who want to limit the role of money in politics. But the Supreme Court greatly limited the scope for reform in an important decision in 1976, when it ruled that individual contributions to candidates were a form of free speech and that it would be a curtailment of liberty to forbid such spending so long as it was not formally connected with a political campaign.[43] Many reformers remain dissatisfied with the Court's decision because they believe that allowing money to play such an important role in politics undermines political equality. Critics also do not think that restricting direct spending on candidates is a significant infringement of liberty.

The other charge against checkbook politics is that it saps the energy from democracy because most members have only very loose connections with the groups who receive their checks. This not only allows interest groups to lobby in Washington with little direct accountability to their membership, it also fails to mobilize people directly and thus does not build the personal connections that promote broad political engagement. Defenders of this style of politics say it does not drain democracy, it only makes it more efficient. In other words, people no longer have to go to meetings; they can simply send a check to the organizations they like and avoid the organizations they dislike.[44] These different views provoke questions about whether we need more direct participation to promote political equality and a vibrant democracy. They also cause us to ask what kinds of changes in social and political institutions would promote more direct participation.

Public institutions can play an important role in helping people understand our values in practice and find acceptable balances among them. Yet there are indications that our institutions are increasingly less able to perform this role. Some people argue that the behavior of American elites—the upper-middle class and the corporate community—has been the driving factor in the weakening of American democracy. Many American elites no longer participate in broad public institutions; instead, they send their children to private schools, obtain their medical care from generous private insurance plans, and hire private police to ensure their security. This "secession of the rich" has had damaging consequences for American democracy because these groups no longer have a stake in what happens in the public sector. Their main interest is in keeping taxes low and protecting themselves from public problems.[45] Yet clearly individuals have the right to participate as they

political institution an organization that connects people to politics, such as a political party, or a governmental organization, such as the Congress or the courts

> **What roles do political institutions play in promoting participation and fulfilling American political values? Have attempts to increase participation succeeded? Why or why not? What are the implications for democracy?**

wish and to purchase the services they think they need. But what happens when these individual choices undermine our ability to bring people together to hammer out their differences about what our values should mean in practice?

American political culture has supplied a core set of values that has helped knit together a culturally diverse nation. But the scope and meaning of these values has shifted over the course of history. In the past, these values were applied selectively, and some people were excluded from the definition of the American political community. Today, a more inclusive definition has evolved. Nonetheless, new questions about the role of our institutions in promoting political engagement and broad-based participation have emerged. We now face serious questions about what our values mean in a political system that seems irrelevant to many people and in which higher-income citizens have a disproportionately strong voice. The answers given to these questions today will shape the meaning of the American dream for future generations.

GET INVOLVED

What You Can Do: Become a Voter

In a sense, the role of the citizen in a democracy is obvious. Citizens have a right to participate. If citizens do not participate, then liberty, equality, and democracy become meaningless terms. The most common way for U.S. citizens to get involved in politics is to cast a vote in elections. Many political scientists believe that voting in competitive elections is the most important form of political participation in a democracy. It is the main means by which citizens give their consent to government, choose their governors, and hold them accountable for their actions. Furthermore, voting links people to every level of government. Citizens may be called on to cast ballots for local propositions; school board and city council members; county district attorneys and judges; state governors and treasurers; and federal officials such as the president and U.S. senators. Often, voters' choices for several levels of government are consolidated into one ballot and take place on the same day; other times, elections for different issues and levels of government are put on separate ballots and held at different times of the year.

If you are a U.S. citizen who is eighteen years old or older, you are *eligible* to vote, but you must *register* to vote with your own state government. Registration is not automatic, but it is a fairly painless process. Voter registration forms are usually available at state government offices and many other government offices, too. Post offices, motor vehicle departments, schools, and public libraries often distribute voter registration forms. You can call your local city hall to find out where you can get one. Prior to elections, you are likely to find groups on campus conducting voter registration drives. They make the forms readily accessible to you and, if you need assistance, they may help you fill out the form.

Once you have the form, completing it is fairly straightforward. You must provide general identification information such as name, address, date of birth, and so forth. The form will also ask you to declare your political party affiliation. You can list a specific political party or you can check "no party" if you do not wish to have a party affiliation. In some states, it is important to designate your party preference because that makes you eligible to vote in the primary election of your designated party. In other states, however, all registered voters are eligible to vote for all candidates running in primary elections.

When you have filled out the voter registration form, mail it to the address shown on the form or return it to the people conducting the voter registration drive. Note that different states have different deadlines regarding when you must be registered in order to be eligible to vote in an upcoming election.

After you are registered to vote, there is a strong probability that you will receive multiple campaign mailings from interest groups, political action committees, direct mail professionals, political parties, and candidates as an election approaches. These mailings may consist of a lot of junk; however, they sometimes contain useful information to help you think through your position on important issues or choose among the competing candidates. For even more information, log on to the Internet, put an issue, a political party, or a candidate's name into a search engine, and see what you can find.

Prior to an election, you should receive a sample ballot, which will lay out all of the offices and choices in the election. The sample ballot will tell you where your polling place is (where you vote on Election Day). It will also have a form on it that you can use to request an absentee ballot (if you are unable to appear at your polling place on Election Day). You may also receive information from both government sources and private sources about propositions that may appear on the ballot, the pros and cons of the propositions, and perhaps the costs (if any) to taxpayers should the propositions pass.

Assuming that you do not cast an absentee ballot, you need to go to your polling place on Election Day. Depending on where you vote, you will encounter one of the five voting systems currently used in the United States. One involves putting check marks next to your preferences on a paper ballot. A second lists all options and requires you to pull a mechanical lever next to your choices. A third system requires that you punch holes in a card to indicate your choices. A fourth system has you darken circles or rectangles beside your choices. A fifth voting method, called Direct Recording Electronic (DRE), asks you to use a touch-screen or push buttons to indicate your preferences. Regardless of the system, your polling place will be staffed by community volunteers who will answer questions about how to cast your votes.

To make democracy more vital and effective, however, citizens need to do more than vote. There are many opportunities for citizens, including college students, to become actively involved in the political process. Political parties and political campaigns are eager to sign on volunteer workers. Usually, the addresses and phone numbers of campaign offices are well publicized before elections. In addition, information about how to become involved with campaigns is available on the Internet from candidates' Web sites. Political work can be fun and rewarding. Campaign workers can make a real difference in bolstering voter turnout and even in persuading undecided voters one way or the other.

In some instances the effectiveness of citizens' political participation is easy to discern. Lobbying and demonstrations by members of the American Association for Retired Persons (AARP) has had direct and immediate effects upon legislation affecting Social Security and health care for the elderly. By writing letters and making phone calls, individuals frequently secure the assistance of members of Congress with immigration problems. Student "sit-ins" often force college administrators to revise their policies. Lobbying and demonstrating, however, are activities in which most citizens seldom, if ever, engage. Voting is the form of political participation that engages the energy of the largest number of Americans on a routine basis.

There can be little doubt that the electorate's choices can have significant implications for government and policy in the United States. When, for example, Americans elected Ronald Reagan to the presidency in 1980, they were choosing a president who promised to cut taxes, expand military spending, and limit social spending. Reagan worked successfully to implement all those promises. By the same token, when voters chose Bill Clinton in 1992, they knew they were opting for a president who would work to undo some of the consequences of Reaganism and seek to expand the role of government in the provision of social services. Clinton worked to accomplish this goal, though achieving only mixed success. In both these cases, though, citizens' participation had important implications for America's political leadership and public policies.

Summary

Political participation can take many forms, including lobbying, public relations, litigation, protest, and voting. Voting is the most common and important form of participation. At the time of America's Founding, the right to vote was generally limited to white males over the age of twenty-one. Many states also limited voting rights to those who owned property. Over the years, voting rights were expanded to give all adult Americans the right to participate in elections. Despite this, only about half of all American citizens over the age of eighteen actually vote in presidential elections.

An individual's socioeconomic status is the most important characteristic determining whether he or she participates in politics. But the efforts of political institutions to mobilize people are especially significant if we wish to understand patterns of participation over time. In recent decades political institutions, such as parties, have done less to mobilize people to participate in politics. The fact that many Americans do not participate gives the American political process a quasi-democratic character.

For Further Reading

Drew, Elizabeth. *The Corruption of American Politics: What Went Wrong and Why.* New York: Birch Lane, 1999.

Eliasoph, Nina. *Avoiding Politics: How Americans Produce Apathy in Everyday Life.* Cambridge, England: Cambridge University Press, 1998.

Frantzich, Stephen E. *Citizen Democracy: Political Activists in a Cynical Age.* New York: Rowman and Littlefield, 1999.

Miller, Warren, and J. Merrill Shanks. *The New American Voter.* Cambridge, MA: Harvard University Press, 1996.

Putnam, Robert D. *Bowling Alone: The Collapse and Revival of American Community.* New York: Simon & Schuster, 2000.

Rosenstone, Steven J, and John Mark Hansen. *Mobilization, Participation and Democracy in America.* New York: Macmillan, 1993.

Schudson, Michael. *The Good Citizen: A History of American Civic Life.* New York: Free Press, 1998.

Verba, Sidney, Kay Lehman Schlotzman, and Henry Brady. *Voice and Equality: Civic Voluntarism in American Politics.* Cambridge, MA: Harvard University Press, 1995.

Study Outline

www.wwnorton.com/wtp4e

Political Participation

1. Political participation can take many forms. The most common today are lobbying, public relations, litigation, protest, and, most important, voting.
2. Throughout American history, there has been a progressive, if uneven, expansion of suffrage to groups such as African Americans, women, and youths.
3. Americans are taught to equate citizenship with electoral participation.
4. Though the United States now has a system of universal suffrage, voter turnout continues to be low.

Explaining Political Participation

1. Several factors explain political participation. They include socioeconomic status, levels of civic engagement, formal obstacles, and efforts by political institutions to mobilize people. The most significant political factor affecting participation is whether people are mobilized by parties, candidates, interest groups, and social movements.
2. In recent decades, political institutions have ceased to mobilize an active citizenry. As a result, the ties between elected leaders and members of the upper and middle classes, who tend to vote more regularly, have been strengthened.
3. The quasidemocratic features of the American electoral system reveal its inherent inequality.

Practice Quiz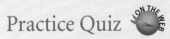

www.wwnorton.com/wtp4e

1. Which of the following is *not* a form of political participation?
   a) volunteering in a campaign
   b) attending an abortion-rights rally
   c) contributing to the Democratic Party
   d) watching the news on television

2. What is the most common form of political participation?
   a) lobbying
   b) contributing money to a campaign
   c) protesting
   d) voting

3. Which of the following best describes the electorate in the United States prior to the 1820s?
   a) landowning white males over the age of twenty-one
   b) all white males
   c) all literate males
   d) "universal suffrage"

4. Women won the right to vote in _____ with the adoption of the _____ Amendment.
   a) 1791; Fifth
   b) 1868; Fourteenth
   c) 1920; Nineteenth
   d) 1971; Twenty-sixth

5. Civic education takes place during
   a) elementary school.
   b) high school.
   c) election campaigns.
   d) all of the above

6. Which of the following negatively impacts voter turnout in the United States?
   a) registration requirements
   b) weak parties
   c) neither a nor b
   d) both a and b

7. Of all the factors explaining political participation, which is the most important?
   a) the mobilization of people by political institutions
   b) socioeconomic status
   c) civic engagement
   d) level of education

8. Which of the following are examples of obstacles to political participation for African Americans?
   a) mobilization and levels of civic engagement
   b) the Civil Rights Acts of 1957 and 1964
   c) poll taxes and white primaries
   d) churches and community centers

9. After passage of the Motor Voter Act in 1993, participation in the 1996 elections
   a) increased dramatically.
   b) increased somewhat.
   c) declined somewhat.
   d) was not affected, since few people registered to vote as a result of the act.

10. Americans who do vote tend to be _____ than the population as a whole.
   a) wealthier
   b) whiter
   c) more educated
   d) all of the above

Critical Thinking Questions

www.wwnorton.com/wtp4e

1. Describe the expansion of suffrage in the United States since the Founding. Why might the government have denied participation to so many for so long? What forces influenced the expansion of voting rights?

2. Why is voter turnout so low in the United States? What are the consequences of low levels of voter turnout? Some critics charge that the United States cannot claim to be a democracy when so few of its citizens actually vote. Is there any basis to this charge?

3. In December 1941, following the Japanese attack on American naval forces stationed at Pearl Harbor, President Franklin D. Roosevelt called upon Americans to prepare themselves for service and sacrifice. In September 2001, following terrorist attacks in New York and Washington, D.C., President George W. Bush called upon Americans to go on with their normal routines. Has popular participation become less important over the past six decades? Does the government still need the involvement of ordinary Americans to be effective?

Key Terms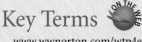

www.wwnorton.com/wtp4e

American political community (p. 294)
civic engagement (p. 302)
gender gap (p. 296)

litigation (p. 287)
lobbying (p. 285)
mobilization (p. 310)
political institution (p. 313)
political participation (p. 284)
poll tax (p. 289)

protest (p. 287)
public relations (p. 286)
socioeconomic status (p. 302)
suffrage (p. 288)
turnout (p. 290)
white primary (p. 306)

9 POLITICAL PARTIES

What Government Does and Why It Matters

OLITICAL PARTIES ARE organizations that seek to control the government. This seems to be a simple idea, but the relationship between parties and government is more complex than we sometimes think. In modern history, political parties have been the chief points of contact between governments, on the one side, and groups and forces in society, on the other. Through organized political parties, social forces can gain some control over governmental policies and personnel. Simultaneously, governments often seek to organize and influence important groups in society through political parties. All political parties have this dual character: they are instruments through which citizens and governments attempt to influence one another. In some nations, such as the People's Republic of China, the leading political party serves primarily the interests of the government. In others, such as the United States, political parties force the government to concern itself with the needs of its citizens.

The idea of political parties was not always accepted in the United States. In the early years of the Republic, parties were seen as threats to the social order. In his 1796 "Farewell Address," President George Washington warned his countrymen to shun partisan politics:

> Let me warn you in the most solemn manner against the baneful effects of the spirit of party generally. This spirit exists under different shapes in all government, more or less stifled, controlled, or repressed, but in those of the popular form it is seen in its greater rankness and is truly their worst enemy.

Often, those in power viewed the formation of political parties by their opponents as acts of treason that merited severe punishment. Thus, in 1798, the Federalist Party, which controlled the national government, in effect sought to outlaw its Jeffersonian Republican opponents through the infamous Alien and Sedition Acts, which, among other things, made it a crime to publish or say anything that might tend to defame or bring into disrepute either the president or the Congress. Under this law, fifteen individuals—including several Republican newspaper editors—were arrested and convicted.[1]

Obviously, over the past two hundred years, Americans' conception of political parties has changed considerably—from subversive organizations to bulwarks of democracy. In this chapter, we will examine the realities underlying these changing conceptions. ■

- **We begin by explaining why political parties exist.** In doing so, we will see that parties play a significant role in key aspects of the political process.

- **We then examine the history of the American two-party system.** As we will see, the history of parties has followed an interesting pattern that has had important consequences for governance.

- **In the next three sections, we look at parties as organizations, parties in the electorate, and the role of parties in the campaign process.** We will see that although party organizations remain strong, the electorate's identification with parties and the role of parties in the electoral process have been declining in recent decades.

- **We then assess the impact of parties on government and the policy-making process.** We will see that the differences between the two major parties can and do have an effect on policy.

- **Finally, we conclude with an evaluation of the importance of political parties to democracy.** Healthy political parties are extremely important for maintaining American political values.

What Are Political Parties?

political parties organized groups that attempt to influence the government by electing their members to important government offices

Political parties, like interest groups, are organizations that seek influence over government. Ordinarily, they can be distinguished from interest groups on the basis of their orientation. A party seeks to control the entire government by electing its members to office and thereby controlling the government's personnel. Interest groups usually accept government and its personnel as a given and try to influence government policies through them.

As long as political parties have existed, they have been criticized for introducing selfish, "partisan" concerns into public debate and national policy. Yet political parties are extremely important to the proper functioning of a democracy. As we shall see, parties expand popular political participation, promote more effective choice, and smooth the flow of public business in the Congress. Our problem in America today is not that political life is too partisan, but that our parties are not strong enough to function effectively. This is one reason, as we shall see, that America has such low levels of popular political involvement. Unfortunately, some reforms currently being implemented, such as restrictions on so-called soft money, might further erode party strength in America.

OUTGROWTHS OF THE ELECTORAL PROCESS

Political parties as they are known today developed along with the expansion of suffrage and can be understood only in the context of elections. The two are so intertwined that American parties actually take their structure from the electoral process. The shape of party organization in the United States has followed a simple rule: for every district where an election is held, there should be some kind of party unit. Republicans failed to maintain units in most counties of the southern states between 1900 and 1952; Democrats were similarly unsuccessful in many areas of New England. But for most of the history of the United States, two major parties have had enough of an organized presence to oppose each other in elections in most of the nation's towns, cities, and counties. This makes the American party system one of the oldest political institutions in the history of democracy.

Compared with political parties in Europe, parties in the United States have always seemed weak. They have no criteria for party membership—no cards for their members to carry, no obligatory participation in any activity. Today, they seem weaker than ever; they inspire less loyalty and are less able to control nominations. Some people are even talking about a "crisis of political parties," as though party politics were being abandoned. But there continues to be at least some substance to party organizations in the United States.

OUTGROWTHS OF THE POLICY-MAKING PROCESS

Political parties are also essential elements in the process of making policy. Within the government, parties are coalitions of individuals with shared or overlapping interests who, as a rule, will support one another's programs and initiatives. Even though there may be areas of disagreement within each party, a common party label in and of itself gives party members a reason to cooperate. Because they are permanent coalitions, parties greatly facilitate the policy-making process. If alliances had to be formed from scratch for each legislative proposal, the business of government would slow to a crawl or halt altogether. Parties create a basis for coalition and thus sharply reduce the time, energy, and effort needed to advance a legislative proposal. For example, in January 1998 when President Bill Clinton considered a series of new policy initiatives, he met first with the House and Senate leaders of the Democratic Party. Although some congressional Democrats disagreed with the president's approach to a number of issues, all felt they had a stake in cooperating with Clinton to burnish the party's image in preparation for the next round of national elections. Without the support of a party, the president would be compelled to undertake the daunting and probably impossible task of

> **How have political parties developed in the United States?**

Perspectives on Politics

STRENGTH OF PARTY IDENTIFICATION

Percentage of Americans responding yes to the question, "Do you feel a strong attachment to either the Democratic or Republican parties?"

Age group	
18–29	41%
30–50	50%
51–70	55%
70+	50%

SOURCE: Adapted from American National Election Studies data reported in Jack Dennis and Diana Owen, "The Partisanship Puzzle: Identification and Attitudes of Generation X," in *After the Boom: The Politics of Generation X*, ed. Stephen C. Craig and Stephen Earl Bennett (Lanham, MD: Rowman and Littlefield, 1997), p. 46.

forming a completely new coalition for each and every policy proposal—a virtually impossible task. As political scientist John Aldrich has noted, no group of politicians in our democracy has ever come up with a way to achieve their goals without political parties.[2]

The Two-Party System in America

two-party system a political system in which only two parties have a realistic opportunity to compete effectively for control

Although George Washington, and in fact many other leaders of his time, deplored partisan politics, the **two-party system** emerged early in the history of the new Republic. Beginning with the Federalists and the Jeffersonian Republicans in the late 1780s, two major parties would dominate national politics, although which particular two parties they were would change with the times and issues. This two-party system has culminated in today's Democrats and Republicans (see Figure 9.1).

HISTORICAL ORIGINS

> **How do parties form? What are the historical origins of today's Democratic and Republican parties?**

Historically, parties form in one of two ways. The first, which could be called "internal mobilization," occurs when political conflicts break out and government officials and competing factions seek to mobilize popular support. This is precisely what happened during the early years of the American Republic. Competition in the Congress between northeastern mercantile and southern agrarian factions led first the southerners and then the northeasterners to attempt to organize popular followings. The result was the foundation of America's first national parties—the Jeffersonians, whose primary base was in the South, and the Federalists, whose strength was greatest in the New England states.

The second common mode of party formation, which could be called "external mobilization," takes place when a group of politicians outside the established governmental framework develops and organizes popular support to win governmental power. For example, during the 1850s, a group of state politicians who opposed slavery, especially the expansion of slavery in America's territorial possessions, built what became the Republican Party by constructing party organizations and mobilizing popular support in the Northeast and West.

America's two major parties now, of course, are the Democrats and the Republicans. Each has had an important place in U.S. history.

The Democrats When the Jeffersonian Party splintered in 1824, Andrew Jackson emerged as the leader of one of its four factions. In 1830, Jackson's group became the Democratic Party. This new party had the strongest national organization of its time and presented itself as the party of the common man. Jacksonians supported reductions in the price of public lands and a policy of cheaper money and credit. Laborers, immigrants, and settlers west of the Alleghenies were quickly attracted to this new party.

From 1828, when Jackson was elected president, to 1860, the Democratic Party was the dominant force in American politics. For all but eight of those years, the Democrats held the White House. In addition, a Democratic majority controlled the Senate for twenty-six years and the House for twenty-four years during the same time period. These nineteenth-century Democrats emphasized

How the Party System Evolved

Figure 9.1

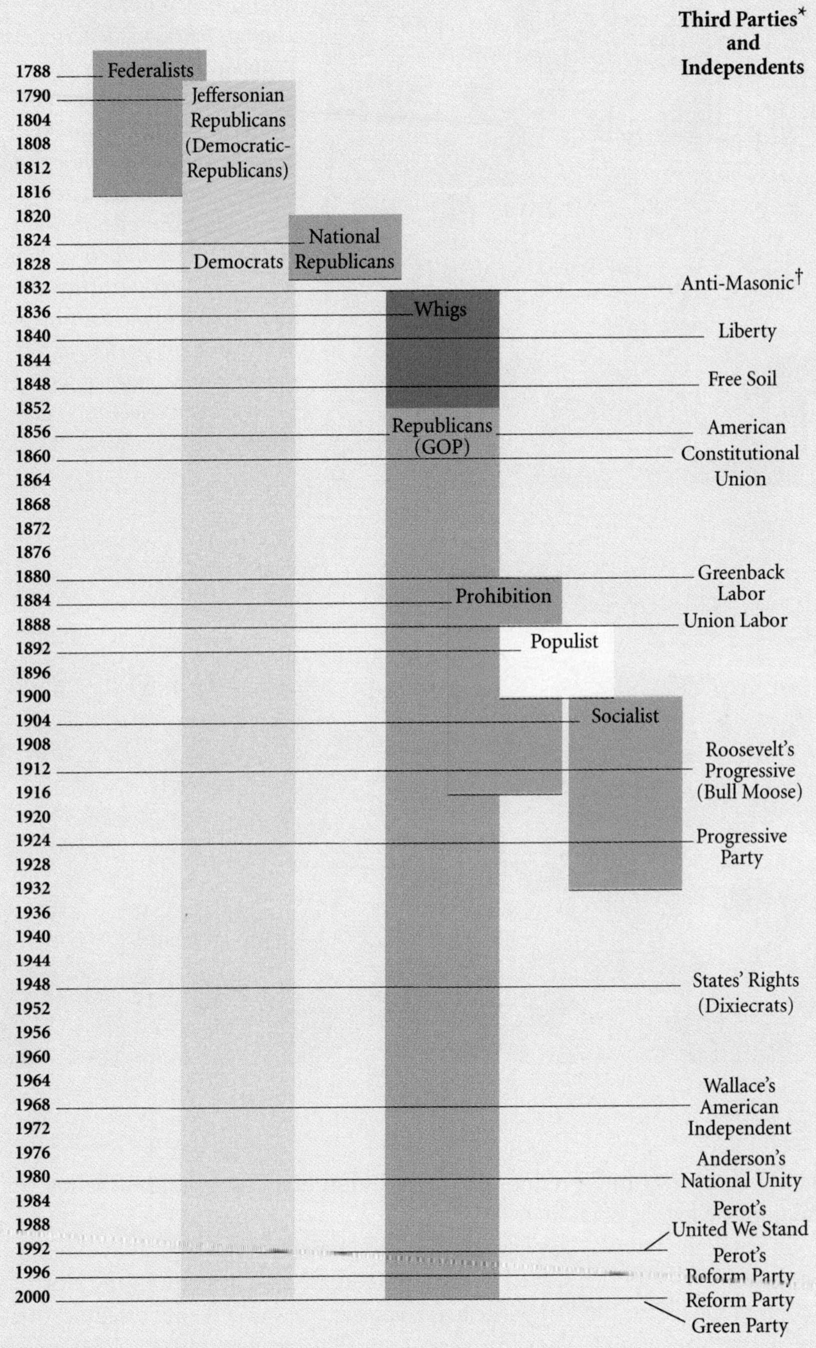

Third Parties* and **Independents**

1788	Federalists	
1790	Jeffersonian	
1804	Republicans	
1808	(Democratic-	
1812	Republicans)	
1816		
1820		
1824	National	
1828	Democrats Republicans	
1832		Anti-Masonic†
1836	Whigs	
1840		Liberty
1844		
1848		Free Soil
1852		
1856	Republicans	American
1860	(GOP)	Constitutional
1864		Union
1868		
1872		
1876		
1880		Greenback Labor
1884	Prohibition	
1888		Union Labor
1892		Populist
1896		
1900		
1904		Socialist
1908		
1912		Roosevelt's Progressive (Bull Moose)
1916		
1920		
1924		Progressive Party
1928		
1932		
1936		
1940		
1944		
1948		States' Rights (Dixiecrats)
1952		
1956		
1960		
1964		Wallace's
1968		American Independent
1972		
1976		Anderson's
1980		National Unity
1984		Perot's
1988		United We Stand
1992		Perot's Reform Party
1996		Reform Party
2000		Green Party

*Or in some cases, fourth party; most of these parties lasted through only one term.
†The Anti-Masonics had the distinction of being not only the first third party, but also the first party to hold a national nominating convention and the first to announce a party platform.

The Democratic party of the United States is the world's oldest political party. The Democrats can trace their history back to Thomas Jefferson's Jeffersonian Republicans and, later, to Andrew Jackson's Jacksonian Democrats. The Jacksonians brought patronage politics—the spoils system—and modern campaign techniques to the political arena and, in so doing, expanded voter participation and ushered in the political era of the common person, as shown in this image of Jackson's inauguration celebration on the White House lawn.

In the late nineteenth century, the Democrats organized an incongruous coalition of southerners and northern immigrant voters into powerful urban "machines," such as New York's Tammany Hall machine and Chicago's Cook County machine (run for many years by Mayor Richard J. Daley, right). These machines were capable of mobilizing hundreds of thousands of voters for the party's candidates.

the importance of interpreting the Constitution literally, upholding states' rights, and limiting federal spending.

In 1860, the issue of slavery split the Democrats along geographic lines. In the South, many Democrats served in the Confederate government. In the North, one faction of the party (the Copperheads) opposed the war and advocated negotiating a peace with the South. Thus, for years after the war, Republicans denounced the Democrats as the "party of treason."

The Democratic Party was not fully able to regain its political strength until the Great Depression. In 1933, Democrat Franklin D. Roosevelt entered the White House

Even at the height of their strength during and following the New Deal, the Democrats were never fully united. Many conservative southern Democrats opposed the party's embrace of African Americans and civil rights. After the 1948 national convention, southern segregationists broke from the party and formed the States' Rights Democratic Party, popularly known as the "Dixiecrats," and nominated Strom Thurmond (behind podium) of South Carolina for president.

By the 1960s, the Democratic Party had evolved into a liberal-labor coalition that supported minority rights and a variety of domestic social programs. The inability of this coalition to win presidential elections gave more conservative Democrats an opportunity to take the party's reins in 1992 and to nominate Bill Clinton, a leader of the party's moderate wing, for the presidency. In 2000, Clinton's vice president, Al Gore, ran a presidential campaign that sought to move the party closer to its liberal and labor roots. Some critics have charged that Gore should have remained closer to the political center.

and the Democrats won control of Congress as well. Roosevelt's New Deal coalition, composed of Catholics, Jews, blacks, farmers, intellectuals, and members of organized labor, dominated American politics until the 1970s and served as the basis for the party's expansion of federal power and efforts to remedy social problems.

The Democrats were never fully united. In Congress, southern Democrats often aligned with Republicans in the "conservative coalition" rather than with members of their own party. But the Democratic Party remained America's majority party, usually controlling both Congress and the White House, for nearly four decades after 1932. By the 1980s, the Democratic coalition faced serious problems. The once-Solid South often voted for the Republicans, along with many white, blue-collar northern voters. On the other hand, the Democrats increased their strength among African American voters and women. The Democrats maintained a strong base in the bureaucracies of the federal government and the states, in labor unions, and in the not-for-profit sector of the economy. During the 1980s and 1990s, moderate Democrats were able to take control of the party nominating process and sought to broaden middle-class support for the Democrats. This helped the Democrats elect a president in 1992. In 1994, however, growing Republican strength in the South led to the loss of the Democrats' control of both houses of Congress for the first time since 1946. Although President Clinton, a Democrat, was able to win re-election to the White House in 1996 over the weak opposition of Republican Bob Dole, Democrats were unable to recapture control of either house of Congress. Some Democrats argued that the party needed to move even further to the political right and abandon its traditional support for social programs and affirmative action. Others argued that the party should re-double its efforts to appeal to poor and working-class Americans.

Employing a strategy his aides called "triangulation," President Clinton sought to pursue a moderate course that placed him midway between the positions of conservative Republicans and liberal Democrats. This strategy helped Clinton and the Democratic Party as a whole, which gained strength and nearly regained control of the House of Representatives in the 1998 national elections. After the 1998 elections, Clinton survived an effort by Republicans to impeach him after his admission of an inappropriate sexual relationship with White House intern Monica Lewinsky. Clinton was impeached in the House on a party-line vote but acquitted in the Senate (where a two-thirds majority is needed for conviction) on another party-line vote. As the two parties licked their wounds from this bruising struggle, they began preparations for the 2000 national presidential elections. Vice President Al Gore was the obvious front-runner, but he was seriously challenged by former senator Bill Bradley. Bradley's campaign appealed to the Democratic Party's most liberal constituencies, promising them renewed efforts in the realm of social spending. Gore, like Clinton, sought to keep his campaign and the Democratic Party firmly anchored in the political center. Late in the presidential race, in which he was trailing in the polls, Gore shifted course and sought to appeal to the party's liberal, African American, and union-based wing. This strategy may have cost Gore some support among moderate Democrats. Despite the lessons of Clinton's "triangulation," the Democratic Party has not yet found a way to firmly unite its liberal and more moderate wings.

The Republicans The 1854 Kansas-Nebraska Act overturned the Missouri Compromise of 1820 and the Compromise of 1850, which had barred the expansion of slavery in the American territories. The Kansas-Nebraska Act gave each territory the right to decide whether or not to permit slavery. Opposition to this policy galvanized antislavery groups and led them to create a new party, the Republicans. It drew its membership from existing political groups—former Whigs, Know-Nothings, Free Soilers, and antislavery Democrats. In 1856, the party's first presidential candidate, John C. Fremont, won one-third of the popular vote and carried eleven states.

The early Republican platforms appealed to commercial as well as antislavery interests. The Republicans favored homesteading, internal improvements, the construction of a transcontinental railroad, and protective tariffs, as well as the containment of slavery. In 1858, the Republican Party won control of the House of Representatives; in 1860, the Republican presidential candidate, Abraham Lincoln, was victorious in a four-way race.

THE REPUBLICANS IN NOMINATING CONVENTION IN THEIR WIGWAM AT, CHICAGO, MAY, 1860.

The Republican Party was formed during the 1850s as a coalition of antislavery and other forces. The party's nomination of Abraham Lincoln for the presidency at the 1860 convention (left) sparked secession of the South and years of civil war.

Beginning in the 1940s, but especially during the 1960s and 1970s, Democratic Party support for the civil rights movement divided the party and led white southerners to the Republican camp. Starting in 1952, this bolstered the GOP's strength and gave it a decided edge in presidential elections. Between 1968 and 1988, Republicans won five of six presidential elections.

For almost seventy-five years after the North's victory in the Civil War, the Republicans were America's dominant political party, especially after 1896. Between 1860 and 1932, Republicans occupied the White House for fifty-six years, controlled the Senate for sixty years, and the House for fifty. During these years, the Republicans came to be closely associated with big business. The party of Lincoln became the party of Wall Street.

The Great Depression ended Republican hegemony, however. The voters held President Herbert Hoover responsible for the economic catastrophe, and by 1936, the party's popularity was so low that Republicans won only eighty-nine seats in the House and seventeen in the Senate. The Republican presidential candidate in 1936, Governor Alfred M. Landon of Kansas, carried only two states. The Republicans won only four presidential elections between 1932 and 1980, and they controlled Congress for only four of those years (1947–49 and 1953–55).

The Republican Party has widened its appeal over the last five decades. Groups previously associated with the Democratic Party—particularly white, blue-collar workers and white southern Democrats—have been increasingly attracted to Republican presidential candidates (for example, Dwight D. Eisenhower, Richard Nixon, Ronald Reagan, George H. W. Bush, and George W. Bush). Yet Republicans generally did not do as well at the state and local levels and, until recently, had little chance of capturing a majority in either the House or the Senate. In 1994, however, the Republican Party finally won a majority in both houses of Congress, in large part because of the party's growing strength in the South.

During the 1990s, conservative religious groups, who had been attracted to the Republican camp by its opposition to abortion and support for school prayer, made a

In 1994, Republicans took control of both houses of Congress for the first time in four decades and promised to implement a conservative agenda under the rubric of a "Contract with America." However, the GOP's ultimately unsuccessful effort to impeach Democratic president Bill Clinton diverted Republican energies from other tasks.

Republicans assert that their party is a "big tent" welcoming all groups. Its 2000 national convention attempted to portray this more inclusive image by showcasing a number of female and African American delegates and speakers. Critics charge that the GOP's positions on social programs do not serve the interests or attract the support of minority groups. While the GOP attracts few black voters, Republican efforts to court Asian and Hispanic voters have been somewhat more successful.

concerted effort to expand their influence within the party. This effort led to conflict between these members of the "religious Right" and more traditional "country-club" Republicans, whose major concerns were matters such as taxes and federal regulation of business. The coalition between these two wings won control of both houses of Congress in 1994 and was able to retain control of both houses in 1996, despite President Clinton's re-election. In 1998, however, severe strains began to show in the GOP coalition. After the GOP (which stands for "Grand Old Party") lost several House seats in the 1998 congressional elections, Speaker Newt Gingrich resigned and was eventually replaced by a relatively unknown Illinois congressman, Dennis Hastert. With their razor-thin majority and inexperienced leadership, congressional Republicans could do little more than fight the Democrats to a stalemate. In the meantime, like their Democratic rivals, Republicans prepared for the 2000 national elections. Texas governor George W. Bush, son of the former president, was the early front-runner. Bush raised an enormous amount of money and, like Bill Clinton, avoided taking positions that would upset any of his party's factions. At the same time, charging that Republicans had lost their ideological soul, commentator Pat Buchanan left the Republican Party to seek the Reform Party nomination. Republicans worried that Buchanan might draw conservative votes from the GOP ticket and help the Democrats win the election. In the end, Buchanan drew little support for his cause and was irrelevant to the outcome of the election. Bush sought to unite the party's centrist and right wings behind a program of tax cuts, education reform, military strength, and family values. Bush avoided issues that divided the GOP camp, like abortion. Most Republicans were very comfortable with Bush's message, but not with the messenger. Bush was seen, even by GOP stalwarts, as inexperienced and lacking some of the personal qualities needed for the presidency. Even so, Republicans enthusiastically supported his ticket. Bush's candidacy boded well for the future of the GOP insofar as Bush was able to find a political formula that could unite the party. Republicans hoped that future candidates might apply this formula to restore the GOP to its glory years.

ELECTORAL ALIGNMENTS AND REALIGNMENTS

American party history has followed a fascinating pattern (see Figure 9.2). Typically, the national electoral arena has been dominated by one party for a period of roughly thirty years. At the conclusion of this period, the dominant party has been supplanted by a new party in what political scientists call an **electoral realignment.** The realignment is typically followed by a long period in which the new party is the dominant political force in the United States—not necessarily winning every election but generally maintaining control of the Congress and usually of the White House as well.[3]

Although there are some disputes among scholars about the precise timing of these critical realignments, there is general agreement that at least five have occurred since the Founding. The first took place around 1800 when the Jeffersonian Republicans defeated the Federalists and became the dominant force in American politics. The second realignment occurred in about 1828, when the Jacksonian Democrats took control of the White House and the Congress. The third period of realignment centered on 1860. During this period, the newly founded Republican Party led by Abraham Lincoln won power, in the process destroying the Whig Party, which had

> **What is the history of party politics in America?**

electoral realignment the point in history when a new party supplants the ruling party, becoming in turn the dominant political force. In the United States, this has tended to occur roughly every thirty years

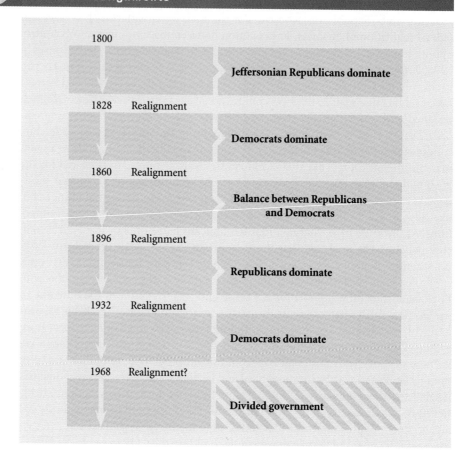

Figure 9.2 Electoral Realignments

Political scientists disagree over whether an electoral realignment occurred in 1968, because no one party clearly dominated the national government after that election.

1800

Jeffersonian Republicans dominate

1828 Realignment

Democrats dominate

1860 Realignment

Balance between Republicans and Democrats

1896 Realignment

Republicans dominate

1932 Realignment

Democrats dominate

1968 Realignment?

Divided government

been one of the nation's two major parties since the 1830s. During the fourth critical period, centered on the election of 1896, the Republicans reasserted their dominance of the national government, which had been weakening since the 1880s. The fifth realignment took place during the period 1932–36, when the Democrats, led by Franklin Delano Roosevelt, took control of the White House and Congress and, despite sporadic interruptions, maintained control of both through the 1960s. Since that time, American party politics has been characterized primarily by **divided government,** wherein the presidency is controlled by one party while the other party controls one or both houses of Congress.

Historically, realignments occur when new issues combined with economic or political crises mobilize new voters and persuade large numbers of voters to reexamine their traditional partisan loyalties and permanently shift their support from one party to another. For example, during the 1850s, diverse regional, income, and business groups supported one of the two major parties, the Democrats or the Whigs, on the basis of their positions on various economic issues, such as internal improvements, the tariff, monetary policy, and banking. This economic alignment was shattered during the 1850s. The newly formed Republican Party campaigned on the basis of oppo-

divided government the condition in American government wherein the presidency is controlled by one party while the opposing party controls one or both houses of Congress

sition to slavery and, in particular, opposition to the expansion of slavery into the territories. The issues of slavery and sectionalism produced divisions within both the Democratic and the Whig parties, ultimately leading to the dissolution of the latter, and these issues compelled voters to reexamine their partisan allegiances. Many northern voters who had supported the Whigs or the Democrats on the basis of their economic stands shifted their support to the Republicans as slavery replaced tariffs and economic concerns as the central item on the nation's political agenda. Many southern Whigs shifted their support to the Democrats. The new sectional alignment of forces that emerged was solidified by the trauma of the Civil War and persisted almost to the turn of the century.

In 1896, this sectional alignment was at least partially supplanted by an alignment of political forces based on economic and cultural factors. During the economic crises of the 1880s and 1890s, the Democrats forged a coalition consisting of economically hard-pressed midwestern and southern farmers, as well as small-town and rural economic interests. These groups tended to be native-stock, fundamentalist Protestants. The Republicans, on the other hand, put together a coalition comprising most of the business community, industrial workers, and city dwellers. In the election of 1896, Republican candidate William McKinley, emphasizing business, industry, and urban interests, defeated Democrat William Jennings Bryan, who spoke for sectional interests, farmers, and fundamentalism. Republican dominance lasted until 1932.

Such periods of party realignment in American politics have had extremely important institutional and policy results. Realignments occur when new issue concerns coupled with economic or political crises weaken the established political elite and permit new groups of politicians to create coalitions of forces capable of capturing and holding the reins of governmental power. The construction of new governing coalitions during these realigning periods has effected major changes in American governmental institutions and policies. Each period of realignment represents a turning point in American politics. The choices made by the national electorate during these periods have helped shape the course of American political history for a generation.[4]

AMERICAN THIRD PARTIES

Although the United States is said to possess a two-party system, the country has always had more than two parties. Typically, **third parties** in the United States have represented social and economic interests that, for one or another reason, were not given voice by the two major parties.[5] Such parties have had a good deal of influence on ideas and elections in the United States. The Populists, a party centered in the rural areas of the West and Midwest, and the Progressives, spokesmen for the urban middle classes in the late nineteenth and early twentieth centuries, are the most important examples in the past hundred years. More recently, Ross Perot, who ran in 1992 as an independent and in 1996 as the Reform Party's nominee, impressed voters with his folksy style; he garnered almost 19 percent of the votes cast in the 1992 presidential election. Table 9.1 on page 334 shows a listing of all the parties that offered candidates in one or more states in the presidential election of 2000, as well as independent candidates who ran. With the exception of Ralph Nader, the third-party and independent candidates together polled only 1.02 million votes. They

third parties parties that organize to compete against the two major American political parties

> **What has been the historical role of third parties in the United States?**

Table 9.1 — Parties and Candidates in 2000

In the 2000 presidential election, in addition to the Democratic and Republican nominees, at least seventeen candidates appeared on the ballot in one or more states. Ralph Nader came the closest to challenging the major-party candidates with almost 3 percent of the popular vote. The remaining sixteen candidates shared about 1 percent of the votes cast with numerous write-ins.

CANDIDATE	PARTY	VOTE TOTAL*	PERCENTAGE OF VOTE*
Al Gore	Democratic	49,307,315	48
George W. Bush	Republican	49,093,218	48
Ralph Nader	Green	2,706,947	3
Pat Buchanan	Reform	438,665	0
Harry Browne	Libertarian	375,265	0
Howard Phillips	Constitution	98,486	0
John Hagelin	Natural Law	88,088	0
James Harris	Socialist Workers	10,589	0
L. Neil Smith	Libertarian	5,195	0
Monica Moorehead	Workers World	4,372	0
David McReynolds	Socialist	3,962	0
Cathy Brown	Independent	1,636	0
Denny Lane	Grass Roots	1,052	0
Louie Youngkeit	Independent	739	0
Randall Venson	Independent	547	0
Earl Dodge	Prohibition	207	0
Jim Wright	None	23	0
Joe Schriner	None	0	0
Gloria Strickland	None	0	0
None of the above	—	3,315	0

*With 99 percent of votes tallied.

SOURCE: www.washingtonpost.com/wp-srv/onpolitics/elections/2000/results/whitehouse (accessed 6/14/02).

gained no electoral votes for president, and most of them disappeared immediately after the presidential election. The significance of Table 9.1 is that it demonstrates the large number of third parties running candidates and appealing to voters. Third-party candidacies also arise at the state and local levels. In New York, the Liberal and Conservative parties have been on the ballot for decades. In 1998, Minnesota elected a third-party governor, former professional wrestler Jesse Ventura.

Although the Republican Party was only the third American political party ever to make itself permanent (by replacing the Whigs), other third parties have enjoyed an influence far beyond their electoral size. This was because large parts of their programs were adopted by one or both of the major parties, who sought to appeal to the voters mobilized by the new party, and so to expand their own electoral strength. The Democratic Party, for example, became a great deal more liberal when it adopted most of the Progressive program early in the twentieth century. Many Socialists felt that President Roosevelt's New Deal had adopted most of their party's program, including old-age pensions, unemployment compensation, an agricultural marketing program, and laws guaranteeing workers the right to organize into unions.

This kind of influence explains the short lives of third parties. Their causes are usually eliminated by the ability of the major parties to absorb their programs and to draw their supporters into the mainstream. There are, of course, additional reasons for the short duration of most third parties. One is the usual limitation of their electoral support to one or two regions. Populist support, for example, was primarily midwestern. The 1948 Progressive Party, with Henry Wallace as its candidate, drew nearly half its votes from the state of New York. The American Independent Party polled nearly 10 million popular votes and 45 electoral votes for George Wallace in 1968—the most electoral votes ever polled by a third-party candidate. But all of Wallace's electoral votes and the majority of his popular vote came from the states of the Deep South.

Americans usually assume that only the candidates nominated by one of the two major parties have any chance of winning an election. Thus, a vote cast for a third-party or independent candidate is often seen as a vote wasted. Voters who would prefer a third-party candidate may feel compelled to vote for the major-party candidate whom they regard as the "lesser of two evils" to avoid wasting their vote in a futile gesture. Third-party candidates must struggle—usually without success—to overcome the perception that they cannot win. Thus, in 1996, many voters who favored Ross Perot gave their votes to Bob Dole or Bill Clinton on the presumption that Perot was not really electable.

During the year prior to the 2000 national elections, Perot struggled with Minnesota governor Jesse Ventura for control of the Reform Party. Perot backed Pat Buchanan as the party's presidential nominee while Ventura promoted the candidacy of real-estate tycoon Donald Trump. Buchanan ultimately won the Reform Party's nomination, but only after a bitter convention battle that prompted many delegates to storm out of the convention hall. The winner of the nomination was not only guaranteed a spot on the ticket in most states, but also received approximately $12 million in federal campaign funds. Under federal election law, any minor party receiving more than 5 percent of the national presidential vote is entitled to federal funds, though considerably less than the major parties receive. The Reform Party qualified by winning 8.2 percent in 1996. Ralph Nader, the Green Party candidate in 2000, hoped to win the 5 percent of the vote that would entitle the Green Party to federal funds. Though Nader may have drawn enough liberal votes in New Hampshire and Florida to give those states—and the national election—to the GOP, hopes of achieving the 5 percent threshold were dashed.

A PARTY OF PATCHES.
Grand Balloon Ascension—Cincinnati, May 20th, 1891.

While the Republicans and Democrats are America's dominant parties, many minor parties have presented candidates for political office throughout American history. In the nineteenth century, parties ranging from the Anti-Masons to the Vegetarians to the People's (or Populist) party competed for votes. Typically, third parties in the United States have been considered as short-lived coalitions of disgruntled outsiders, as shown in this satiric view of the People's Party as a "party of patches."

single-member district an electorate that is allowed to select only one representative from each district; the normal method of representation in the United States

As many scholars have pointed out, third-party prospects are also hampered by America's **single-member-district** plurality election system. In many other nations, several individuals can be elected to represent each legislative district. This is called a system of **multiple-member districts.** With this type of system, the candidates of weaker parties have a better chance of winning at least some seats. For their part, voters are less concerned about wasting ballots and usually more willing to support minor-party candidates.

Though few minor parties survive more than one or two campaigns, they sometimes introduce new issues into politics and affect the outcome of the race by taking votes from the major party candidates. In 1992, Ross Perot (above) created the Reform Party, emphasizing such issues as the federal budget deficit and term limits, and won nearly 19 percent of the vote. Perot made it impossible for the major parties to ignore budget issues. By 2000, the major parties had appropriated Perot's issues, and Reform Party candidate Pat Buchanan (right) won barely one-half of a percent of the popular vote.

Campaigning as the candidate of the Green Party in 2000, Ralph Nader focused on global economic issues and carried 3 percent of the vote, mainly at the expense of Democratic candidate Al Gore. Third parties seldom survive because American electoral rules are stacked against them. America's winner-take-all system encourages voters to choose between the parties that have the best chance of winning in order to avoid throwing away their votes. In Europe, most elections are based upon systems of proportional representation that can give legislative seats to second, third, and fourth place finishers.

Reinforcing the effects of the single-member district, the **plurality system** of voting (see Chapter 10) generally has the effect of setting what could be called a high threshold for victory. To win a plurality race, candidates usually must secure many more votes than they would need under most European systems of **proportional representation.** For example, to win an American plurality election in a single-member district where there are only two candidates, a politician must win more than 50 percent of the votes cast. To win a seat from a European multiple-member district under proportional rules, a candidate may need to win only 15 or 20 percent of the votes cast. This high American threshold discourages minor parties and encourages the various political factions that might otherwise form minor parties to minimize their differences and remain within the major-party coalitions.[6]

However, it would be incorrect to assert (as some scholars have) that America's single-member plurality election system is the major cause of its historical two-party pattern. All that can be said is that American election law depresses the number of parties likely to survive over long periods of time in the United States. There is nothing magical about two. Indeed, the single-member plurality system of election can also discourage second parties. After all, if one party consistently receives a large plurality of the vote, people may eventually come to see their vote *even for the second party* as a wasted effort. This happened to the Republican Party in the Deep South before World War II.

Party Organization

In the United States, **party organizations** exist at virtually every level of government (see Figure 9.3 on page 339). These organizations are usually committees made up of a number of active party members. State law and party rules prescribe how such committees are constituted. Usually, committee members are elected at local party meetings—called **caucuses**—or as part of the regular primary election. The best known examples of these committees are at the national level—the Democratic National Committee and the Republican National Committee.

NATIONAL CONVENTION

At the national level, the party's most important institution is the quadrennial **national convention.** The convention is attended by delegates from each of the states; as a group, they nominate the party's presidential and vice presidential candidates, draft the party's campaign platform for the presidential race, and approve changes in the rules and regulations governing party procedures. Before World War II, presidential nominations occupied most of the time, energy, and effort expended at the national convention. The nomination process required days of negotiation and compromise among state party leaders and often required many ballots before a nominee was selected. In recent years, however, presidential candidates have essentially nominated themselves by winning enough delegate support in primary elections to win the official nomination on the first ballot. The actual convention has played little or no role in selecting the candidates.

multiple-member district an electorate that selects all candidates at large from the whole district; each voter is given the number of votes equivalent to the number of seats to be filled

plurality system a type of electoral system in which, to win a seat in the parliament or other representative body, a candidate need only receive the most votes in the election, not necessarily a majority of votes cast

proportional representation a multiple-member district system that allows each political party representation in proportion to its percentage of the total vote

> **How are political parties organized? At what levels are they organized?**

party organization the formal structure of a political party, including its leadership, election committees, active members, and paid staff

caucus (political) a normally closed meeting of a political or legislative group to select candidates, plan strategy, or make decisions regarding legislative matters

national convention a national party political institution that serves to nominate the party's presidential and vice presidential candidates, establish party rules, and write and ratify the party's platform

Political Party Systems

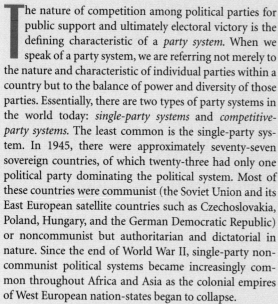

The nature of competition among political parties for public support and ultimately electoral victory is the defining characteristic of a *party system*. When we speak of a party system, we are referring not merely to the nature and characteristic of individual parties within a country but to the balance of power and diversity of those parties. Essentially, there are two types of party systems in the world today: *single-party systems* and *competitive-party systems*. The least common is the single-party system. In 1945, there were approximately seventy-seven sovereign countries, of which twenty-three had only one political party dominating the political system. Most of these countries were communist (the Soviet Union and its East European satellite countries such as Czechoslovakia, Poland, Hungary, and the German Democratic Republic) or noncommunist but authoritarian and dictatorial in nature. Since the end of World War II, single-party noncommunist political systems became increasingly common throughout Africa and Asia as the colonial empires of West European nation-states began to collapse.

By the second half of the 1990s, of the 180 or so sovereign countries of the world, roughly 39 (approximately 21 percent) were dominated by a single political party, meaning, in effect, the competition for political values and the distribution of economic and social resources in those countries were largely monopolized by one set of values: those of the dominant single party. These countries include Mexico, Cuba, Egypt, Taiwan, Madagascar, China, and Singapore.

The most common form of party system is a competitive-party system, which consists of more than a single dominant party. This second type of party system operates in approximately 58 percent of the countries in the world today. (The remaining countries have no parties at all but are governed by traditional patrons and clans, such as Saudi Arabia and other Gulf states. Others are governed by military dictatorships and allow no political parties, as in Myanmar, Nigeria, and Sudan.)

Competitive-party systems may, as in the case of the United States, have only two major political parties, or there may be two major political parties and one or two smaller parties that continually receive small but politically important electoral support. The United Kingdom, New Zealand, and Germany have this version of a *two-party system*. A two-party system is one of the institutional features of a political system associated with a

majoritarian democratic logic. In other words, one party wins a disproportionate share of resources, while the losing party awaits another electoral contest to redress the balance.

However, the very stable and distinct two-party system is not the norm among the family of industrialized democracies of North America, West Europe, and its various global "outposts," such as Australia, New Zealand, Japan, and Israel. The common pattern found among these highly developed industrialized democracies is a *multiparty system*. They are characterized by at least three political parties that are roughly proportionally balanced with respect to the percentage of votes they receive in national elections. In this group of nations, we find Norway, Sweden, Denmark, Belgium, Netherlands, Switzerland, Italy, and recently Canada. These countries usually have some form of distinctive ethnic/linguistic (Belgium, Switzerland, and Canada) or religious (Netherlands) conflict, which has historically divided the public into well-defined and unique issue-communities. This circumstance has thereby reinforced a strong bond between the competing issue-communities and various political parties. The parties have come to both protect and represent the issue-communities in a relatively balanced political struggle in society. In Italy, regional conflict (north versus south) has coincided with sharp socioeconomic distinctions among the public, which has served to undergird the multiparty system, at least until recently. Whatever the specific reasons, multiparty systems reflect a preference for more sharply defined political differences between issue-communities within society. Political parties in these systems serve to channel and mitigate conflict and thereby ensure a necessary balance of power between issue-communities that might otherwise render peaceful democratic governance impossible.

Multiparty systems are strongly associated with consensual democratic logic. The nature of historical conflict between distinct issue-communities in these countries requires political institutions, such as political parties, that can ensure the inclusion of many more interests in the policy process than is necessary within majoritarian democracies. Since the collapse of the Soviet Union and the end of the cold war, former communist countries in East and Central Europe have also adopted multiparty systems.

SOURCE: Jean Blondel, *Comparative Government: An Introduction*, 2nd ed. (Englewood Cliffs, NJ: Prentice-Hall, 1995).

How American Parties Are Organized

Figure 9.3

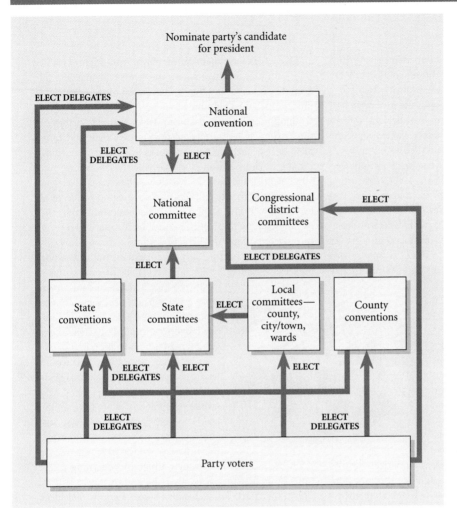

The convention's other two tasks, determining the party's rules and its platform, remain important. Party rules can determine the relative influence of competing factions within the party and can also increase or decrease the party's chances for electoral success. In 1972, for example, the Democratic National Convention adopted a new set of rules favored by the party's liberal wing. Under these rules, state delegations to the Democratic convention were required to include women and members of minority groups in rough proportion to those groups' representation among the party's membership in that state. Liberals correctly calculated that women and African Americans would generally support liberal ideas and candidates. The rules also called for the use of proportional representation—a voting system liberals thought would give them an advantage by allowing the election of more women and minority delegates. (Although Republican rules do not require proportional representation, some state legislatures have moved to compel both parties to use this system in their presidential primaries.)

Are More Parties Better Than Two Parties?

Despite occasionally strong performances by third parties, America is one of the few nations of the world that has maintained an enduring two-party political system, beginning with the Federalist and Antifederalist parties in the postcolonial period. Today's Democratic Party is the world's oldest viable party; the younger Republican Party dates from the 1850s. America's stubborn loyalty to its two parties has been complicated by persistent criticisms of those two parties, including charges that they are little different from each other and that they monopolize political power, choke off new ideas, and restrict the influx of new leaders with different ideas.

These and other criticisms have produced support for the idea of a multiparty system (any political system with three or more active parties is considered a multiparty system). American history supports the idea that third parties can help the political process. First, new parties can raise new and important issues ignored by the two major parties. In the pre–Civil War era, the Liberty and Free Soil parties advanced the cause of slavery abolition when the dominant Democratic and Whig parties were unable to come to grips with the issue. Early in the twentieth century, the Progressive Party advanced a vast array of social and political reforms eventually embraced by Democrats and Republicans. Ross Perot's Reform Party moved issues like deficit spending and budgetary responsibility to center stage in 1992. Second, as these examples suggest, a third-party option gives voters more choices among candidates and issues, addressing a persistent voter complaint. Third, most democratic nations of the world have a multiparty system, showing that the idea is not only viable, but is a routine part of the workings of democracy. Fourth, new parties might spark renewed voter interest in an electoral system that now attracts fewer than half of the eligible adult electorate to the voting booth. And fifth, states like Minnesota

and New York have maintained an active multiparty tradition (although in these states, the two major parties still dominate), suggesting that some version of the idea could indeed work on a national level.

Supporters of two-partyism argue that the virtues of the existing system are taken for granted. First and foremost, a two-party system produces automatic majorities, for the obvious reason that one will always receive over 50 percent of the vote. In a nation as large and diverse as America, governance could easily become impossible, or at least far more difficult, if multiple parties produced a bevy of candidates with no clear winner, or if American legislatures were populated with representatives from many different parties, barring any one party from organizing power. A second and related point is that the compromises that produce two candidates from two large parties also generally encourage moderation, compromise, and stability. Multiple parties might well heighten polarization and paralysis in America in a way that would make contemporary political gridlock seem tame by comparison. And while many democracies have multiparty systems, politics in those nations is often polarized and unstable. The Italian multiparty system, for example, produced over forty different governing coalitions in its first fifty years after the end of World War II. Third, the charge of exclusion of new factions and ideas by the two parties misses the fact that the two American parties are very large and diverse. In other nations, political conflict is played out between multiple parties. In America, much of that conflict occurs within the parties, especially during the nomination process. Fourth, America's enduring two-party system is a product of its political culture and historical development. The idea that a multiparty system could simply be transplanted onto the American political landscape is a leap of faith little supported by actual experience.

The convention also approves the party **platform.** Platforms are often dismissed as documents filled with platitudes that are seldom read by voters. To some extent this criticism is well founded. Not one voter in a thousand so much as glances at the party platform, and even the news media pay little attention to the documents. Furthermore, the parties' presidential candidates make little use of the platforms in their campaigns; usually they prefer to develop and promote their own themes. Nonetheless, the platform can be an important document. The platform should be understood as a contract in which the various party factions attending the convention state their terms for supporting the ticket. For one faction, welfare reform may be a key issue. For another faction, tax reduction may be more important. For a third, the critical issue might be deficit reduction. When one of these "planks" is included in the platform, its promoters are asserting that this is what they want in exchange for their support for the ticket, while other party factions are agreeing that the position seems reasonable and appropriate. Thus, party platforms should be seen more as internal party documents than as public pledges. The 2000 Democratic platform, for example, promised to protect the environment against the potentially damaging consequences of globalization. Again, this issue has little meaning to most voters but is of great concern to liberal environmentalists, an important Democratic constituency, who believe that American trade agreements should contain provisions essentially imposing U.S. environmental standards on other nations.

platform a party document, written at a national convention, that contains party philosophy, principles, and positions on issues

NATIONAL COMMITTEE

Between conventions, each national political party is technically headed by its national committee. For the Democrats and Republicans, these are called the Democratic National Committee (DNC) and the Republican National Committee (RNC), respectively. These national committees raise campaign funds, head off factional disputes within the party, and endeavor to enhance the party's media image. The actual work of each national committee is overseen by its chairperson. Governor Jim Gilmore of Virginia, chair of the Republican National Committee, is a political ally of President George W. Bush. The Democratic National Committee is chaired by real estate developer Terry McAuliffe, a close ally of former president Bill Clinton and one of the party's leading fund-raisers. Other committee members are generally major party contributors or fund-raisers and serve in a largely ceremonial capacity. In 1997, Senate hearings on campaign financing pointed to the importance of the national committees as fund-raising agencies. The DNC and RNC had each raised tens of millions of dollars for the 1996 national election campaigns.

For whichever party controls the White House, the party's national committee chair is appointed by the president. Typically, this means that that party's national committee becomes little more than an adjunct to the White House staff. For a first-term president, the committee devotes the bulk of its energy to the re-election campaign. The national committee chair of the party not in control of the White House is selected by the committee itself and usually takes a broader view of the party's needs, raising money and performing other activities on behalf of the party's members in Congress and in the state legislatures.

Are Three Parties Better Than Two?

Yes

"Meet the new boss, same as the old boss." —Pete Townshend

In the voting booth this November I'll be checking the box marked Ralph Nader (the Green Party candidate and long-time advocate for the rights of consumers). What's more, I'll be doing so with the curtain open, confident despite the chortle of Bush supporters gleefully pegging me as a "vote waster."

But contrary to the ultra-liberal zealots and Green Party pamphleteers whose ubiquitous sidewalk-chalk scrawling suggests an expedient end to America's love affair with the two-party system, I sincerely doubt the possibility of a White House represented in shades of green.

Instead, my vote for Nader will be a vote cast for a stronger two-party system and higher voter turnout.

In respect to Green Party loyalists, the list of notable third-party candidates running on the ticket has never been so vibrant as this year. Not since 1912 when Progressive Theodore Roosevelt, Socialist Eugene Debs, and Prohibitionist Eugene Chafin ran on third-party tickets has the United States witnessed such a variety of concerns. But, just as Debs and Chafin crossed the finish line long after the race had been won by Woodrow Wilson—with 6 percent and 1.4 percent of the popular vote respectively, and no electoral votes to speak of—Nader, perennial candidate Lyndon LaRouche (who likely makes millions betting against himself in Vegas), libertarian Harry Browne, and reformers Patrick Buchanan and John Hagelin will suffer the same fate. Most of them won't even be on the ballot.

Even Ross Perot, who seemingly breathed new life into the myth of an electable third-party candidate, made little, if any, difference in the predominate two-party system. Like Sasquatch, the possibility of an electable candidate outside the realm of Republicans and Democrats is little more than a figment of a vivid imagination.

None of this comes as a surprise in times like these when it's entirely possible to skip a stone across a sea of heads, each supporting a different cause and protesting a separate atrocity: this one picketing McDonald's, that one burning a flag in effigy, another protesting "Frankenfoods." Unlike unified anti-war protesters who rallied indefatigably against U.S. involvement in Vietnam, we are all too demassified, too varied for a third-party revolt to possibly occur.

Just as Senator John McCain pressed the issue of campaign finance until it became a topic discussed by presidential frontrunners as routinely as Medicare, most third-party candidates enjoy and utilize the opportunity to advance emerging trends and lesser-known sentiments of the American people. The Progressives of 1924, to give an example, nominated Robert LaFollette for president and drew support from farmers who were affected by the Great Depression far before its shock waves were felt by the masses. LaFollette only received 13 electoral votes to Calvin Coolidge's 382, but, similarly, the issue was dependent upon a third-party candidate to be raised.

And why? Because well-oiled machines such as the Republican and Democratic parties require a monotony of thought, a certain stillness, a sound and predictable platform, lest they endanger the existing unity of its base, the voting public. To be sure, William Harrison—the first presidential Whig—grasped a seat in the Oval Office after political in-fighting between Democrats whose platform was weakened by issues concerning the national treasury. Accusing his opponent, Martin Van Buren, of being indifferent to the welfare of the country—like Al Gore, only original—Harrison was thrust into office, thanks to the largest electoral vote, 234, the nation had seen.

Still, though, the most frightening shadow third-party candidates seem to cast is the one which threatens to "steal" or "waste" votes.

Contrary to popular belief, Nader's ability to "steal" votes from Gore has been exaggerated. Certainly, American Independent candidate George Wallace may have deprived Hubert Humphrey of votes and Perot may have borrowed from Bob Dole. But, generally, most third-party candidates expect little more than a vehicle for the messages they espouse—

from the Prohibitionists to Jello Biafra. Nader's intentions may run deeper, but a large chink of those who vote for him in November likely will be trolled from the ranks of non-voters—sympathetic to his decidedly different campaign.

Nader, LaRouche, hordes of future independents, and even Buchanan in his own (fascist) way can invigorate the democratic process by forcing civic discourse and giving non-voters—potentially, the most powerful voting bloc of all—a reason to participate on election day.

SOURCE: Jotham Sederstrom, "Ralph Nader: Or, How I Learned to Love Third Parties," *Columbia Chronicle*, October 2, 2000.

 I am going to vote for Al Gore come Election Day. I know, if I were really on the cutting edge of politics like some of my fellow students, I'd be for Nader and his fittingly named Green Party. However, the thought of "Mr. Smith" actually going to Washington scares the idealism out of me.

The problem I have with third parties is they haven't come close to the playing field in over a century. The idea that they matter is grossly exaggerated, along with the idea that they are needed. There may be moments in history when such wake-up calls are necessary, but I believe we're as awake as we'll ever be. We need to embrace and vote for one of the established parties—they are different, no matter what Mr. Nader will have you believe, for he is a Democrat and always was. The idea that the government should look after its people is what both Nader and the Democrats stand for. Nader has only distorted the truths and has concocted a false image in which both parties are for the same vision—when, in fact, they have never been so different.

The Democratic and Republican parties are different (pardon me for having to point this out once again, but I fear many of us get lost on the road of apathy, and then simply blame the candidates for mediocrity: the Democrats have always leaned to the left and the Republicans have always lumbered to the right. The Republicans are the party of less government for the sake of more business and profit, whereas the Democrats believe the government should have a bigger role in protecting and helping all its people. The ideologies of both parties are dissimilar; their rainbows lead to different pots of gold. These are the differences that make one proud to say they are either a Republican or a Democrat. Never believe there exists what Nader likes to call the "Republicrats."

There are those who insist that this election is about voting for the lesser of two evils—that the reason we need the third party infestation is because the candidates are too lame and similar in their views. I'll agree on one thing: I would vote for anyone but George W. Bush. How could anyone feel secure with this intellectually deprived man running the country? I feel as if all the pods have hatched and now they want one of their own to rule.

The funny thing is that I really like Al Gore. I believe he is the right person for the job at this moment. I find myself justifying to others that Al is a good guy and a smart man who will do the right things when needed. I admire his platforms and stances—plus he even has ideals, which is something rare. If you look at the only other real candidate, you will find he is still wrapping himself in the nonexistent clothes of morality, which only creates the same old problem of why we don't care anymore. Al Gore will at least bring some vision of the future for the country instead of bringing us back to where we no longer wish to go.

The election is between two candidates, like it or not—Al Gore and George W. Bush. The next President will be one of these two men. I repeat: the next President of the United States of America will be either Al Gore or George W. Bush. The two-party system is still the American political norm and to vote against it won't bring about change, but only make your vote history.

SOURCE: Amber Holst, "Two's Company, Three's a Crowd," *Columbia Chronicle*, October 16, 2000.

CONGRESSIONAL CAMPAIGN COMMITTEES

Each party also forms House and Senate campaign committees to raise funds for House and Senate election campaigns. Their efforts may or may not be coordinated with the activities of the national committees. For the party that controls the White House, the national committee and the congressional campaign committees are often rivals, since both groups are seeking donations from the same people but for different candidates: the national committee seeks funds for the presidential race while the congressional campaign committees approach the same contributors for support for the congressional contests. In recent years, the Republican Party has attempted to coordinate the fund-raising activities of all its committees. Republicans have sought to give the GOP's national institutions the capacity to invest funds in those close congressional, state, and local races where they can do the most good. The Democrats have been slower to coordinate their various committee activities, and this may have placed them at a disadvantage in recent congressional and local races.

STATE AND LOCAL PARTY ORGANIZATIONS

Each of the two major parties has a central committee in each state. The parties traditionally also have county committees and, in some instances, state senate district committees, judicial district committees, and in the case of larger cities, city-wide party committees and local assembly district "ward" committees as well. Congressional districts also may have party committees.

Some cities also have precinct committees. Precincts are not districts from which any representative is elected but instead are legally defined subdivisions of wards that are used to register voters and set up ballot boxes or voting machines. A precinct is typically composed of three hundred to six hundred voters. Well-organized political parties—especially the famous old machines of New York, Chicago, and Boston—provided for "precinct captains" and a fairly tight group of party members around them. Precinct captains were usually members of long standing in neighborhood party clubhouses, which were important social centers as well as places for distributing favors to constituents.[7]

In the nineteenth and early twentieth centuries, many cities and counties and even a few states upon occasion have had such well-organized parties that they were called **machines** and their leaders were called "bosses." Some of the great reform movements in American history were motivated by the excessive powers and abuses of these machines and their bosses. But few, if any, machines are left today. Traditional party machines depended heavily upon **patronage,** their power to control government jobs. With thousands of jobs to dispense, party bosses were able to recruit armies of political workers who, in turn, mobilized millions of voters. Today, because of civil service reform, party leaders no longer control many positions. Nevertheless, state and local party organizations are very active in recruiting candidates, conducting voter registration drives, and providing financial assistance to candidates. In many respects, federal election law has given state and local party organizations new life. Under current law, state and local party organizations can spend unlimited amounts of money on "party-building" activities such as voter registration and get-out-the-vote drives (see Chapter 10). As a result, the national party organizations, which have enormous fund-raising abilities but

machines strong party organizations in late-nineteenth- and early-twentieth-century American cities. These machines were led by "bosses" who controlled party nominations and patronage

patronage the resources available to higher officials, usually opportunities to make partisan appointments to offices and to confer grants, licenses, or special favors to supporters

are limited by law in how much they can spend on candidates, each year transfer millions of dollars to the state and local organizations. The state and local parties, in turn, spend these funds, sometimes called **"soft money,"** to promote the candidacies of national, as well as state and local, candidates. In this process, as local organizations have become linked financially to the national parties, American political parties have become somewhat more integrated and nationalized than ever before. At the same time, the state and local party organizations have come to control large financial resources and play important roles in elections despite the collapse of the old patronage machines.[8]

The McCain-Feingold campaign reform bill enacted in 2002 placed strict limits on soft money contributions. This legislation may weaken political parties and strengthen interest groups, which remain free to spend as much as they wish so long as their expenditures are not formally coordinated with a candidate's own campaign.

soft money money contributed directly to political parties for voter registration and organization

Parties and the Electorate

Party organizations are more than just organizations; they are made up of millions of rank-and-file members. Individual voters tend to develop **party identification** with one of the political parties. Although it is a psychological tie, party identification also has a rational component. Voters generally form attachments to parties that reflect their views and interests. Once those attachments are formed, however, they are likely to persist and even to be handed down to children, unless some very strong factors convince individuals that their party is no longer an appropriate object for their affections. In some sense, party identification is similar to brand loyalty in the marketplace: consumers choose a brand of automobile for its appearance or mechanical characteristics and stick with it out of loyalty, habit, and unwillingness to constantly reexamine their choices, but they may eventually change if the old brand no longer serves their interests.

Although the strength of partisan ties in the United States has declined in recent years, most Americans continue to identify with either the Republican Party or the Democratic Party (see Figure 9.4). Party identification gives citizens a stake in election outcomes that goes beyond the particular race at hand. This is why strong party identifiers are more likely than other Americans to go to the polls and, of course, are more likely than others to support the party with which they identify. **Party activists** are drawn from the ranks of the strong identifiers. Activists are those who not only vote but also contribute their time, energy, and effort to party affairs. Activists ring doorbells, stuff envelopes, attend meetings, and contribute money to the party cause. No party could succeed without the thousands of volunteers who undertake the mundane tasks needed to keep the organization going.

party identification an individual voter's psychological ties to one party or another

> **What ties do people have to political parties?**

party activists partisans who contribute time, energy, and effort to support their party and its candidates

GROUP AFFILIATIONS

The Democratic and Republican parties are America's only national parties. They are the only political organizations that draw support from most regions of the country and from Americans of every racial, economic, religious, and ethnic group. The two parties do not draw equal support from members of every social

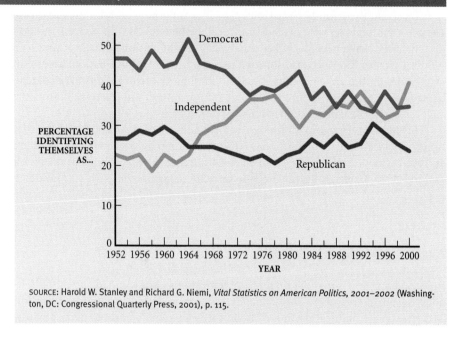

Figure 9.4 **Americans' Party Identification, 1952–2000**

SOURCE: Harold W. Stanley and Richard G. Niemi, *Vital Statistics on American Politics, 2001–2002* (Washington, DC: Congressional Quarterly Press, 2001), p. 115.

stratum, however. When we refer to the Democratic or Republican "coalition," we mean the groups that generally support one or the other party. In the United States today, a variety of group characteristics are associated with party identification. These include race and ethnicity, gender, religion, class, ideology, and region.

Race and Ethnicity Since the 1930s and Franklin Roosevelt's New Deal, African Americans have been overwhelmingly Democratic in their party identification. More than 90 percent of African Americans describe themselves as Democrats and support Democratic candidates in national, state, and local elections. Approximately 25 percent of the Democratic Party's support in presidential races comes from African American voters.

Latino voters do not form a monolithic bloc, by contrast. Cuban Americans are generally Republican in their party affiliations, whereas Mexican Americans favor the Democrats by a small margin. Other Latino voters, including those from Puerto Rico, are overwhelmingly Democratic. Asian Americans tend to be divided as well, but along class lines. The Asian American community's influential business and professional stratum identifies with the Republicans, but less-affluent Asian Americans tend to support the Democrats.

Gender Women are somewhat more likely to support Democrats, and men somewhat more likely to support Republicans, in surveys of party affiliation. This difference is known as the **gender gap.** In the 1992 presidential election, women gave Bill Clinton 47 percent of their votes, while only 41 percent of the men who voted supported Clinton. In 1996, the gender gap was even more pronounced:

gender gap a distinctive pattern of voting behavior reflecting the differences in views between men and women

women voted for Clinton 54 percent of the time, while only 43 percent of voting men did so. In the 2000 election, the gender gap closed, but only slightly.

Religion   Jews are among the Democratic Party's most loyal constituent groups and have been since the New Deal. Nearly 90 percent of all Jewish Americans describe themselves as Democrats. Catholics were also once a strongly pro-Democratic group but have been shifting toward the Republican Party since the 1970s, when the GOP began to focus on abortion and other social issues deemed to be important to Catholics. Protestants are more likely to identify with the Republicans than with the Democrats. Protestant fundamentalists, in particular, have been drawn to the GOP's conservative stands on social issues, such as school prayer and abortion. The importance of religious conservatives to the Republican Party became quite evident in 2001. After his victory in the November 2000 presidential election, George W. Bush announced that his administration would seek to award federal grants and contracts to religious groups. By using so-called faith-based groups as federal contractors, Bush was seeking to reward religious conservatives for their past loyalty to the GOP and to ensure that these groups would have a continuing stake in Republican success.

Class   Upper-income Americans are considerably more likely to affiliate with the Republicans, whereas lower-income Americans are far more likely to identify with the Democrats. This divide is reflected by the differences between the two parties on economic issues. In general, the Republicans support cutting taxes and social spending—positions that reflect the interests of the wealthy. The Democrats, however, favor increasing social spending, even if this requires increasing taxes— a position consistent with the interests of less-affluent Americans. One important exception to this principle is that relatively affluent individuals who work in the public sector or such related institutions as foundations and universities also tend to affiliate with the Democrats. Such individuals are likely to appreciate the Democratic Party's support for an expanded governmental role and high levels of public spending.

Ideology   Ideology and party identification are very closely linked. Most individuals who describe themselves as conservatives identify with the Republican Party, whereas most who call themselves liberals support the Democrats. This division has increased in recent years as the two parties have taken very different positions on social and economic issues. Before the 1970s, when party differences were more blurred, it was not uncommon to find Democratic conservatives and Republican liberals. Both of these species are rare today.

Region   Between the Civil War and the 1960s, the "Solid South" was a Democratic bastion. Today, the South is becoming solidly Republican, as is much of the West and Southwest. The area of greatest Democratic Party strength is the Northeast. The Midwest is a battleground, more or less evenly divided between the two parties.

The explanations for these regional variations are complex. Southern Republicanism has come about because conservative white southerners identify the Democratic Party with the civil rights movement and with liberal positions on abortion, school prayer, and other social issues. Republican strength in the South and in the West is also related to the weakness of organized labor in these regions, as well as to the dependence of the two regions upon military programs supported by the Republicans. Democratic strength in the Northeast is a function of the continuing influence of organized labor in the large cities of this region, as well as of the region's large population of minority and elderly voters, who benefit from Democratic social programs.

Age Age is another factor associated with partisanship. At the present time, individuals younger than fifty or older than sixty-five are fairly evenly divided between Democrats and Republicans, while those between the ages of fifty and sixty-four are much more likely to be Democrats. There is nothing about a particular numerical age that leads to a particular party loyalty. Instead, individuals from the same age cohort are likely to have experienced a similar set of events during the period when their party loyalties were formed. Thus, Americans between the ages of fifty and sixty-four came of political age during the cold-war, Vietnam, and civil-rights eras. Apparently among voters whose initial perceptions of politics were shaped during this period, more responded favorably to the role played by the Democrats than to the actions of the Republicans. Interestingly, among the youngest group of Americans, a group that came of age during an era of political scandals that tainted both parties, the majority describe themselves as Independents.

Figure 9.5 indicates the relationship between party identification and a number of social criteria. Race, religion, and income seem to have the greatest influence on Americans' party affiliations. None of these social characteristics are inevitably linked to partisan identification, however. There are black Republicans, southern white Democrats, Jewish Republicans, and even an occasional conservative Democrat. The general party identifications just discussed are broad tendencies that both reflect and reinforce the issue and policy positions the two parties take in the national and local political arenas.

Parties and Elections

> **What are the important electoral functions of parties?**

Parties play an important role in the electoral process. They provide the candidates for office, get out the vote, and facilitate mass electoral choice.

RECRUITING CANDIDATES

One of the most important but least noticed party activities is the recruitment of candidates for local, state, and national office. Each election year, candidates must be found for thousands of state and local offices as well as congressional seats. Where they do not have an incumbent running for re-election, party leaders attempt to identify strong candidates and to interest them in entering the campaign.

An ideal candidate will have an unblemished record and the capacity to raise enough money to mount a serious campaign. Party leaders are usually not willing to provide financial backing to candidates who are unable to raise substantial funds on their own. For a House seat this can mean several hundred thousand dollars; for a Senate seat a serious candidate must be able to raise several million dollars. Often, party leaders have difficulty finding attractive candidates and persuading them to

Party Identification by Social Groups, 2000

Figure 9.5

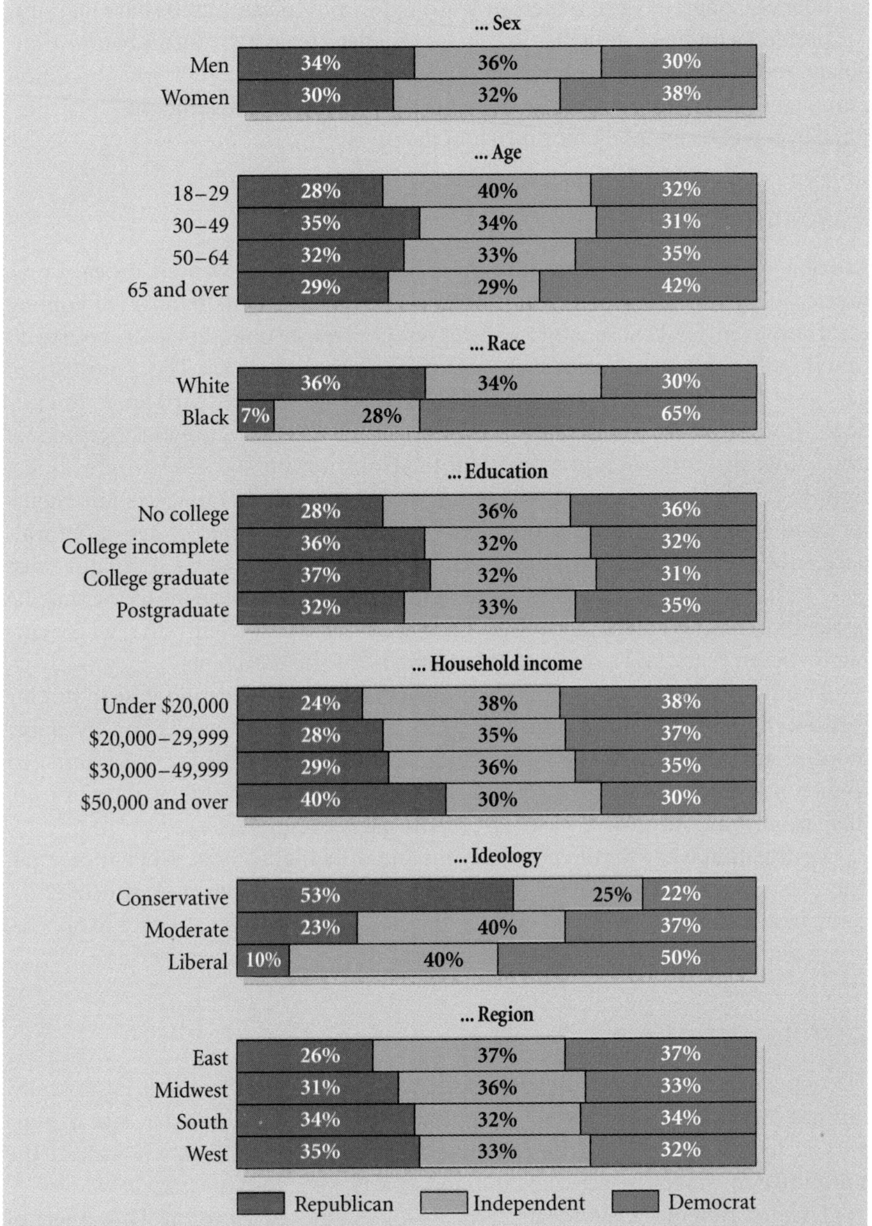

... Sex

	Republican	Independent	Democrat
Men	34%	36%	30%
Women	30%	32%	38%

... Age

	Republican	Independent	Democrat
18–29	28%	40%	32%
30–49	35%	34%	31%
50–64	32%	33%	35%
65 and over	29%	29%	42%

... Race

	Republican	Independent	Democrat
White	36%	34%	30%
Black	7%	28%	65%

... Education

	Republican	Independent	Democrat
No college	28%	36%	36%
College incomplete	36%	32%	32%
College graduate	37%	32%	31%
Postgraduate	32%	33%	35%

... Household income

	Republican	Independent	Democrat
Under $20,000	24%	38%	38%
$20,000–29,999	28%	35%	37%
$30,000–49,999	29%	36%	35%
$50,000 and over	40%	30%	30%

... Ideology

	Republican	Independent	Democrat
Conservative	53%	25%	22%
Moderate	23%	40%	37%
Liberal	10%	40%	50%

... Region

	Republican	Independent	Democrat
East	26%	37%	37%
Midwest	31%	36%	33%
South	34%	32%	34%
West	35%	33%	32%

Republican | Independent | Democrat

SOURCE: Harold W. Stanley and Richard G. Niemi, *Vital Statistics on American Politics, 2001–2002* (Washington, DC: Congressional Quarterly Press, 2001), p. 117.

run. In 1998, for example, Democratic leaders in Kansas and Washington reported difficulties in recruiting congressional candidates. A number of potential candidates reportedly were reluctant to leave their homes and families for the hectic life of a member of Congress. GOP leaders in Washington and Massachusetts have had similar problems finding candidates to oppose popular Democratic incumbents.[9] Candidate recruitment has become particularly difficult in an era when political campaigns often involve mudslinging and candidates must assume that their personal lives will be intensely scrutinized in the press.[10]

NOMINATIONS

Article I, Section 4, of the Constitution makes only a few provisions for elections. It delegates to the states the power to set the "times, places, and manner" of holding elections, even for U.S. senators and representatives. It does, however, reserve to Congress the power to make such laws if it chooses to do so. The Constitution has been amended from time to time to expand the right to participate in elections. Congress has also occasionally passed laws about elections, congressional districting, and campaign practices. But the Constitution and the laws are almost completely silent on nominations, setting only citizenship and age requirements for candidates. The president must be at least thirty-five years of age, a natural-born citizen, and a resident of the United States for fourteen years. A senator must be at least thirty, a U.S. citizen for at least nine years, and a resident of the state he or she represents. A member of the House must be at least twenty-five, a U.S. citizen for seven years, and a resident of the state he or she represents.

nomination the process through which political parties select their candidates for election to public office

Nomination is the process by which a party selects a single candidate to run for each elective office. The nominating process can precede the election by many months, as it does when the many candidates for the presidency are eliminated from consideration through a grueling series of debates and state primaries until there is only one survivor in each party—the party's nominee.

Nomination is the parties' most serious and difficult business. When more than one person aspires to an office, the choice can divide friends and associates. In comparison to such an internal dispute, the electoral campaign against the opposition is almost fun, because there the fight is against the declared adversaries.

GETTING OUT THE VOTE

The actual election period begins immediately after the nominations. Historically, this has been a time of glory for the political parties, whose popular base of support is fully displayed. All the paraphernalia of party committees and all the committee members are activated into local party work forces.

The first step in the electoral process involves voter registration. This aspect of the process takes place all year round. There was a time when party workers were responsible for virtually all of this kind of electoral activity, but they have been supplemented (and in many states virtually displaced) by civic groups such as the League of Women Voters, unions, and chambers of commerce.

Those who have registered have to decide on Election Day whether to go to the polling place, stand in line, and actually vote for the various candidates and referenda on the ballot. Political parties, candidates, and campaigning can make a big difference in convincing the voters to vote.

FACILITATING VOTER CHOICE

On any general election ballot, there are likely to be only two or three candidacies where the nature of the office and the characteristics and positions of the candidates are well known to voters. But what about the choices for judges, the state comptroller, the state attorney general, and many other elective positions? And what about referenda? This method of making policy choices is being used more and more as a means of direct democracy. A referendum may ask: Should there be a new bond issue for financing the local schools? Should there be a constitutional amendment to increase the number of county judges? In 1996, Californians approved Proposition 201, a referendum that called for an end to most statewide affirmative action programs, including those employed for college admission. Another famous proposition on the 1978 California ballot was a referendum to reduce local property taxes. It started a taxpayer revolt that spread to many other states. By the time it had spread, most voters knew where they stood on the issue. But the typical referendum question is one on which few voters have clear and knowledgeable positions. Parties and campaigns help most by giving information when voters must choose among obscure candidates and vote on unclear referenda.

Parties and Government

When the dust of the campaign has settled, does it matter which party has won? It can.

PARTIES AND POLICY

One of the most familiar observations about American politics is that the two major parties try to be all things to all people and are therefore indistinguishable from each other. Data and experience give some support to this observation. Parties in the United States are not programmatic or ideological, as they have sometimes been in Britain or other parts of Europe. But this does not mean there are no differences between them. Since the 1980s, important differences have emerged between the positions of Democratic and Republican party leaders on a number of key issues, and these differences are still apparent today. For example, the national leadership of the Republican Party supports maintaining high levels of military spending, cuts in social programs, tax relief for middle- and upper-income voters, tax incentives to businesses, and the "social agenda" backed by members of conservative religious denominations. The national Democratic leadership, on the other hand, supports expanded social welfare spending, cuts in military spending, increased regulation of business, and a variety of consumer and environmental programs.

These differences reflect differences in philosophy and differences in the core constituencies to which the parties seek to appeal. The Democratic Party at the national level seeks to unite organized labor, the poor, members of racial minorities, and liberal upper-middle-class professionals. The Republicans, by contrast, appeal to business, upper-middle- and upper-class groups in the private sector, and social conservatives. Often, party leaders will seek to develop issues they hope will add new groups to their party's constituent base. During the 1980s, for example,

> ➤ **How do the differences between Democrats and Republicans affect Congress, the president, and the policy-making process?**

under the leadership of Ronald Reagan, the Republicans devised a series of "social issues," including support for school prayer, opposition to abortion, and opposition to affirmative action, designed to cultivate the support of white southerners. This effort was extremely successful in increasing Republican strength in the once solidly Democratic South. In the 1990s, under the leadership of Bill Clinton, who called himself a "new Democrat," the Democratic Party sought to develop new social programs designed to solidify the party's base among working-class and poor voters, and new, somewhat more conservative economic programs aimed at attracting the votes of middle- and upper-middle-class voters.

As these examples suggest, parties do not always support policies just because they are already favored by their constituents. Instead, party leaders can play the role of **policy entrepreneurs,** seeking ideas and programs that will expand their party's base of support while eroding that of the opposition. It is one of the essential characteristics of party politics in America that a party's programs and policies often lead, rather than follow, public opinion. Like their counterparts in the business world, party leaders seek to identify and develop "products" (programs and policies) that will appeal to the public. The public, of course, has the ultimate voice. With its votes it decides whether or not to "buy" new policy offerings.

Thus, for example, in 1999, Democratic presidential hopefuls Al Gore and Bill Bradley both proposed new programs in the realms of health care, education, and social services, which they hoped would expand their own political bases as well as increase support for the Democratic Party. On the Republican side, Senator John McCain championed the issue of campaign finance reform, and George W. Bush pledged that he would be the "education president."

PARTIES IN CONGRESS

The ultimate test of the party system is its relationship to and influence on the institutions of government. Congress, in particular, depends more on the party system than is generally recognized. For one thing, the speakership of the House is essentially a party office. All the members of the House take part in the election of the Speaker. But the actual selection is made by the **majority party,** that is, the party that holds a majority of seats in the House. (The other party is known as the **minority party.**) When the majority party caucus presents a nominee to the entire House, its choice is then invariably ratified in a straight vote along party lines.

The committee system of both houses of Congress is also a product of the two-party system. Although the rules organizing committees and the rules defining the jurisdiction of each are adopted like ordinary legislation by the whole membership, all other features of the committees are shaped by parties. For example, each party is assigned a quota of members for each committee, depending upon the percentage of total seats held by the party. On the rare occasions when an independent or third-party candidate is elected, the leaders of the two parties must agree against whose quota this member's committee assignments will count. Presumably the member will not be able to serve on any committee until the question of quota is settled.

As we shall see in Chapter 12, the assignment of individual members to committees is a party decision. Each party has a "committee on committees" to make such decisions. Permission to transfer to another committee is also a party decision. Moreover, advancement up the committee ladder toward the chair is a

policy entrepreneur an individual who identifies a problem as a political issue and brings a policy proposal into the political agenda

majority party the party that holds the majority of legislative seats in either the House or the Senate

minority party the party that holds a minority of legislative seats in either the House or the Senate

party decision. Since the late nineteenth century, most advancements have been automatic—based upon the length of continual service on the committee. This seniority system has existed only because of the support of the two parties, however, and either party can depart from it by a simple vote. During the 1970s, both parties reinstituted the practice of reviewing each chair—voting anew every two years on whether each committee's chair would continue to be held by the same person. In their 1994 campaign document, the "Contract with America," House Republican candidates pledged to limit committee and subcommittee chairs to three two-year terms if the GOP won control of Congress. For years, Republicans had argued that entrenched Democratic committee chairs had become powerful, arrogant, and indifferent to the popular will. When Republicans took control of Congress in 1994, they reaffirmed their pledge to limit the terms of committee and subcommittee chairs. As they approached the 2000 congressional elections, however, some GOP leaders now regretted the commitment they had made six years earlier. Powerful Republican committee chairs were not very enthusiastic about the idea of surrendering their positions if the GOP maintained control of the House. Some Republican committee chairs hoped to trade positions with one another and begin new stints in charge of new panels. Younger members who had hoped to benefit from the three-term rule by claiming the vacated chairs were prepared to fight for what they now regarded as their due. Thus, a pledge made in 1994 when the GOP was out of power seemed to portend sharp conflicts among Republican members if the GOP retained power in 2000. However, in 2001, Republicans lived up to their 1995 pledge to limit House committee chairs to three terms. Existing chairmen were forced to step down but were generally replaced by the most senior Republican member of each committee.

The continuing importance of parties in Congress became especially evident after the Republicans won control of Congress in 1994. During the first few months of the 104th Congress, the Republican leadership was able to maintain nearly unanimous support among party members on vote after vote as it sought to implement the GOP's legislative agenda. Between 1995 and 1999, however, splits within the party began to surface over issues such as welfare reform and balancing the budget. This legislative struggle and its continuation after the 2000 elections will be discussed further in Chapter 12.

PRESIDENT AND PARTY

As we saw earlier, the party that wins the White House is always led, in title anyway, by the president. The president normally depends upon fellow party members in Congress to support legislative initiatives. At the same time, members of the party in Congress hope that the president's programs and personal prestige will help them raise campaign funds and secure re-election. During his two terms in office, President Bill Clinton had a mixed record as party leader. In the realm of trade policy, Clinton sometimes found more support among Republicans than among Democrats. In addition, although Clinton proved to be an extremely successful fund-raiser, congressional Democrats often complained that he failed to share his largesse with them. At the same time, however, a number of Clinton's policy initiatives seemed calculated to strengthen the Democratic Party as a whole. Clinton's early health care initiative would have linked millions of voters to the Democrats for years to come, much as FDR's Social Security program had done in a previous era. But by the middle of Clinton's second term, the president's acknowledgement of his sexual affair with a White House intern threatened his position as party leader. Initially, Democratic candidates nationwide feared that the scandal would undermine their own chances for election, and many moved to distance themselves from the president. The Democrats' surprisingly good showing in the 1998 elections, however, strengthened Clinton's position and gave him another chance to shape the Democratic agenda.

Between the 1998 and 2000 elections, however, the president's initiatives on Social Security and nuclear disarmament failed to make much headway in a Republican-controlled Congress. The GOP was not prepared to give Clinton anything for which Democrats could claim credit in the 2000 elections. Lacking strong congressional leadership, however, the GOP did agree to many of Clinton's budgetary proposals in 1999 and dropped its own plan for large-scale cuts in federal taxes.

When he assumed office in 2001, George W. Bush called for a new era of bipartisan cooperation. The new president did receive the support of some conservative Democrats. Generally, however, Bush depended upon near-unanimous backing from his own party in Congress to implement his plans, which included a substantial cut in federal income taxes. After the September 11 terrorist attacks, both parties united behind the president's military response. Even then, however, the parties were divided on a number of matters. Democrats, for example, favored the creation of a federal force of airline baggage screeners, while Republicans supported a private-sector approach to airport security. Ultimately, the Democrats prevailed, and the president signed into law a bill that federalized baggage inspection. Having given in to political necessity, the president claimed full credit for the legislation.

The Role of Parties in a Democracy

> **Do parties help or hinder democracy?**

Democracy and political parties arose together in the modern world. Without democracy, a system of competing political parties never could have emerged. At the same time, without a system of competing political parties, democracy never could have flourished. Without a strong opposition, rulers never would have surrendered power, and without well-organized parties, ordinary people never could have acquired or used the right to vote. It is because of this strong historical association between democracy and political parties that the current weakness of American political parties is a matter of concern.

Healthy political parties are extremely important for maintaining political equality, democracy, and liberty in America. First, strong parties are generally an essential ingredient for effective electoral competition by groups lacking substantial economic or institutional resources. Party building has typically been the strategy pursued by groups that must organize the collective energies of large numbers of individuals to counter their opponents' superior material means or institutional standing. Historically, disciplined and coherent party organizations were generally developed first by groups representing the political aspirations of the working classes. Parties, French political scientist Maurice Duverger notes, "are always more developed on the Left than on the Right because they are always more necessary on the Left than on the Right."[11] In the United States, the first mass party was built by the Jeffersonians as a counterweight to the superior social,

What Government Does . . . After September 11

The position of the "loyal opposition" in a democracy is difficult in a time of war. On the one hand, it is good politics—and good citizenship—to support the president and the party in power during wartime. On the other hand, the mission of the party out of power is to become, sooner rather than later, the party in power. How is it possible for the "loyal opposition" to convince the voters of this point? One strategy, illustrated by the events after September 11, is to support the president's foreign agenda and to criticize his domestic agenda.

In the months after September 11, President Bush enjoyed among the highest Gallup job-approval ratings ever recorded. Because of the near-universal horror at the terrorist attacks and the early success of the mission in Afghanistan, the president had "stratospheric numbers that have no historical parallel."[1] Republican strategists saw an opportunity to use Bush's popularity in the war to solidify Republican electoral dominance. Bush bolstered his support within a traditional Republican stronghold, supporters of a strong national defense, by proposing in the 2002 State of the Union an unprecedented $48 billion hike in defense spending. Furthermore, he hoped to bring traditionally Democratic constituencies into the Republican camp by, for example, emphasizing the women's rights component of his foreign policy. For Democrats, it was a difficult time to do anything but support the president. As Senator John Breaux said, "You can only do what you can based on the cards you have to play. We don't have many cards."[2]

In order to avoid electoral repercussions, however, the Democrats have tried to find issues to convince voters that they deserve a turn in power. One instance of this is the Enron scandal. For Democrats, the Enron scandal illustrates how the Republicans are more concerned with protecting their corporate sponsors ("Kenny Boy") than with looking out for laborers and stock holders. The Enron scandal provided a way for Democrats to talk about other issues that may benefit them, including campaign finance reform, Social Security, the economy, and the federal budget. Consider, for example, the way Senate Democratic leader Tom Daschle draws a parallel between the Enron scandal and the Republican attitude to the budget in general: "[Bush] is slowly Enronizing the economy. Enronizing the budget. We are taking the same approach Enron used in sapping retirement funds and providing them to those at the very top. That's exactly what Enron did. And I'd hate to see the U.S. do that."[3]

By the summer of 2002, some Democrats believed that they might be able to confront President Bush head-on regarding his handling of the terrorist threat. Democrats demanded congressional hearings to investigate charges that the FBI and CIA had ignored advance indications of terrorist activity that might have allowed them to intervene before the September 11 atrocities. While few Democrats were willing to suggest that the president, himself, had ignored advance warnings of the attack, a good deal of information began to surface suggesting that the nation's intelligence community had not been sufficiently alert to the threat of a major assault on the United States. Democrats calculated that, sooner or later, the public would hold intelligence lapses against the president even if they were not directly his fault. In June 2002, congressional hearings to examine intelligence failures got under way. President Bush, however, countered by announcing a massive reorganization of "homeland defense" agencies aimed at thwarting future acts of terrorism. Bush's plans distracted media attention from the hearings and seemed to show that the president was taking the appropriate actions to protect the nation. For the time being, at least, the president appeared to have blunted Democratic efforts to make use of the terrorism issue against his administration and the GOP.

Will the Democrats be able to find other issues to attain power in the 2004 elections and beyond? Perhaps. But, as Don Fierce, a GOP consultant, puts it, "When people are selling out of flags and ammunition, that's good for the Republican party."[4]

[1] GOP pollster Whit Ayres, cited in Ryan Lizza, "Divide and Conquer," *New Republic,* February 11, 2002.
[2] Cited in Michael Duffy and John F. Dickerson, "Enron Spoils the Party," *Time,* February 4, 2002.
[3] Cited in *ibid.*
[4] Cited in Ramesh Ponnuru, "Happy Days Aren't Here for Them: The Dem's Bind," *National Review,* March 11, 2002.

institutional, and economic resources that could be deployed by the incumbent Federalists. In a subsequent period of American history, the efforts of the Jacksonians to construct a coherent mass party organization were impelled by a similar set of circumstances. Only by organizing the power of numbers could the Jacksonian coalition hope to compete successfully against the superior resources that could be mobilized by its adversaries.

In the United States, the political success of party organizations forced their opponents to copy them in order to meet the challenge. It was, as Duverger points out, "contagion from the Left" that led politicians of the Center and Right to attempt to build strong party organizations.[12] These efforts were sometimes successful. In the United States during the 1830s, the Whig Party, which was led by northeastern business interests, carefully copied the effective organizational techniques devised by the Jacksonians. The Whigs won control of the national government in 1840. But even when groups nearer the top of the social scale responded in kind to organizational efforts by their inferiors, the net effect nonetheless was to give lower-class groups an opportunity to compete on a more equal footing. In the absence of coherent mass organization, middle- and upper-class factions almost inevitably have a substantial competitive edge over their lower-class rivals. When both sides organize, the net effect is to erode the relative advantage of the well-off.

Second, political parties are bulwarks of liberty. The Constitution certainly provides for freedom of speech, freedom of assembly, and freedom of the press. Maintaining these liberties, though, requires more than parchment guarantees. Of course, as long as freedom is not seriously threatened, abstract guarantees suffice to protect it. If, however, those in power actually threaten citizens' liberties, the preservation of freedom may come to depend upon the presence of a coherent and well-organized opposition. As we saw earlier in this chapter, in the first years of the Republic, it was not the Constitution or the courts that preserved free speech in the face of Federalist efforts to silence the government's critics; it was the vigorous action of the Jeffersonian-Republican opposition that saved liberty. To this day, the presence of an opposition party serves as a fundamentally important check on attempts by those in power to skirt the law and infringe upon citizens' liberties. For example, twenty-five years ago, although it was the news media that revealed President Richard Nixon's abuses of power, the concerted efforts of Nixon's Democratic opponents in Congress were required finally to drive the president from office.

Third, parties promote voter turnout. Party competition has long been known to be a key factor in stimulating voting. As political scientists Stanley Kelley, Richard Ayres, and William Bowen note, competition gives citizens an incentive to vote and politicians an incentive to get them to vote.[13] The origins of the American national electorate can be traced to the competitive organizing activities of the Jeffersonian Republicans and the Federalists. According to historian David Fischer,

> During the 1790s the Jeffersonians revolutionized electioneering. . . . Their opponents complained bitterly of endless "dinings," "drinkings," and celebrations; of handbills "industriously posted along every road"; of convoys of vehicles which brought voters to the polls by the carload; of candidates "in perpetual motion."[14]

The Federalists, although initially reluctant, soon learned the techniques of mobilizing voters: "mass meetings, barbecues, stump-speaking, festivals of many kinds, processions and parades, runners and riders, door-to-door canvassing, the distribution of tickets and ballots, . . . free transportation to the polls, outright bribery and corruption of other kinds."[15]

The result of this competition for votes was described by historian Henry Jones Ford in his classic *Rise and Growth of American Politics*.[16] Ford examined the popular clamor against John Adams and Federalist policies in the 1790s that made government a "weak, shakey affair" and appeared to contemporary observers to mark the beginnings of a popular insurrection against the government.[17] Attempts by the Federalists initially to suppress mass discontent, Ford observed, might have "caused an explosion of force which would have blown up the government."[18] What intervened to prevent rebellion was Jefferson's "great unconscious achievement," the creation of an opposition party that served to "open constitutional channels of political agitation."[19] The creation of the Jeffersonian Republican Party diverted opposition to the administration into electoral channels. Party competition gave citizens a sense that their votes were valuable and that it was thus not necessary to take to the streets to have an impact upon political affairs. Whether or not Ford was correct in crediting party competition with an ability to curb civil unrest, it is clear that competition between the parties promoted voting.

Finally, political parties make democratic government possible. We often do not appreciate that democratic government is a contradiction in terms. Government implies policies, programs, and decisive action. Democracy, on the other hand, implies an opportunity for all citizens to participate fully in the governmental process. The contradiction is that full participation by everyone is often inconsistent with getting anything done. At what point should participation stop and governance begin? How can we make certain that popular participation will result in a government capable of making decisions and developing needed policies? The problem of democratic government is especially acute in the United States because of the system of separated powers bequeathed to us by the Constitution's framers. Our system of separated powers means that it is very difficult to link popular participation and effective decision making. Often, after the citizens have spoken and the dust has settled, no single set of political forces has been able to win control of enough of the scattered levers of power to actually do anything. Instead of government, we have a continual political struggle.

Strong political parties are a partial antidote to the inherent contradiction between participation and government. Strong parties can both encourage popular involvement and convert participation into effective government. More than fifty years ago, a committee of the academic American Political Science Association (APSA) called for the development of a more "responsible" party government. By **responsible party government,** the committee meant political parties that mobilized voters and were sufficiently well organized to develop and implement coherent programs and policies after the election. Strong parties can link democratic participation and government.

Although they are significant factors in politics and government, American political parties today are not as strong as the "responsible parties" advocated by the APSA. Many politicians are able to raise funds, attract volunteers, and win office without much help from local party organizations. Once in office, these politicians have no particular reason to submit to party discipline; instead, they steer independent courses. They are often supported by voters who see independence as a virtue and party discipline as "boss rule." Sometimes analysts refer to

responsible party government a set of principles that idealizes a strong role for parties in defining their stance on issues, mobilizing voters, and fulfilling their campaign promises once in office

this pattern as a "candidate-centered" politics to distinguish it from a political process in which parties are the dominant forces. The problem with a candidate-centered politics is that it tends to be associated with low turnout, high levels of special-interest influence, and a lack of effective decision making. In short, many of the problems that have plagued American politics in recent years can be traced directly to the independence of American voters and politicians and the candidate-centered nature of American national politics.

The health of America's parties should be a source of concern to all citizens who value liberty, equality, and democracy. Can political parties be strengthened? The answer is, in principle, yes. For example, political parties could be strengthened if the rules governing campaign finance were revised to make candidates more dependent financially upon state and local party organizations rather than on personal resources or private contributors. Such a reform, to be sure, would require more strict regulation of party fund-raising practices. The potential benefit, however, of a greater party role in political finance could be substantial. If parties controlled the bulk of the campaign funds, they would become more coherent and disciplined, and might come to resemble the responsible parties envisioned by the APSA. In 2002, Congress enacted campaign finance reforms that diminished the role of the national party organizations in financing campaigns. Time will tell what consequences will be brought about by this change. Political parties have been such important features of American democratic politics that we need to think long and hard about how to preserve and strengthen them.

GET INVOLVED

What You Can Do:
Become a Party Activist

American political parties are very open to citizen involvement. Students who attend local party meetings and volunteer to assist with communication and fund-raising efforts are usually welcome. In the nineteenth century, the national parties could rely upon the efforts of tens of thousands of patronage employees who were obligated to engage in political work. Today, the parties rely upon volunteers and enthusiasts.

How do you become a party activist? First, decide which political party best represents your own values and visions. Most Americans who identify with a particular political party choose the Democratic Party or the Republican Party. If you think these parties are too close together on important issues, or if you are not particularly enamored of party politics "as usual," you may want to consider the Reform Party, the Green Party, the Natural Law Party, the Peace and Freedom Party, or other parties soliciting members and support. Determine which political party best captures your sympathies and passions.

Next, see if your campus has a student organization that is affiliated with the party that interests you. Many campuses have student chapters of the Democratic and Republican parties as well as some of the smaller parties. These campus chapters are likely to be linked to other campus chapters as well as to the local and state offices of the parties. These affiliates are always looking for new members with interest, enthusiasm, and commitment.

Alternatively, your school or political science department may have an internship program or an intern coordinating office. Local branches of political parties regularly work with internship offices to attract young people to their parties as well as to get energetic volunteers to perform innumerable labor-intensive tasks such as stuffing envelopes, manning phone banks, and knocking on doors. The advantages of taking this route to party activism are (1) program contacts should make it relatively easy for you to connect with the party of your choice and (2) you may be able to receive academic credit for your party involvement.

For some students, such volunteer work is the first step in a political career. For example, Cruz Bustamante, who in 1997 became the first Latino elected to be Speaker of the California state assembly, began his political career as a volunteer worker for local Democratic politicians in the Fresno, California, area. Interested in such issues as immigration, health care, and the status of farm workers, Bustamante saw politics as the best vehicle for doing something about these issues. In 1973, at the age of nineteen, he went to Washington as a congressional intern. He was not paid for his internship and needed support from his parents and five brothers and sisters who worked in the fields as agricultural laborers. After returning to California, Bustamante worked as a staff assistant to several Democratic legislators, and was elected to the legislature in 1993. In 1997, Bustamante replaced Assembly Speaker Willie Brown, who was unable to seek re-election because of the state's new term-limits law.[20]

Much of the work undertaken by party organizations at the local level is quite mundane. Thousands of envelopes are filled and sealed. Many meetings are held. Politics at the "grass roots" is not very glamorous. However, if politics were only glamorous it could not be democratic. Grassroots party activity helps to ensure that the more glamorous world of Washington remains tied and responsive to Bozeman, Long Beach, Raleigh, and Utica. State and even national party leaders pay close attention to the views of local party organizations and activists. They depend upon these local organizations for ideas, for campaign workers, and often, for candidates. Many prominent politicians, including former president Clinton, were themselves once young volunteers in a local party organization.

Summary

Political parties seek to control government by controlling its personnel. Elections are one means to this end. Thus, parties take shape from the electoral process.

The two-party system dominates U.S. politics. During the course of American history, the government has generally been dominated by one or the other party for long periods of time. This is generally followed by a period of realignment during which new groups attempt to seize power and the previously dominant party may be displaced by its rival. There have been five electoral realignments in American political history.

Third parties are short-lived for several reasons. They have limited electoral support, the tradition of the two-party system is strong, and a major party often adopts the platform of a third party. Single-member districts with two competing parties also discourage third parties.

Party organizations exist at every level of American government. The national party organizations are generally less important than the state and local party units. Each party's national committee and congressional campaign committees help to recruit candidates and raise money. The national conventions have, for the most part, lost their nominating functions, but still play an important role in determining party rules and party platforms.

Parties influence voting through the ties of party identification, particularly the strong ties formed with party activists. A variety of group characteristics can influence party identification, including race and ethnicity, gender, religion, class, ideology, region, and age.

Nominating and electing are the basic functions of parties. Parties are critical for getting out the vote, recruiting candidates, facilitating popular choice, and organizing the government. Strong parties are essential to the continuing vitality of American democracy.

For Further Reading

Aldrich, John H. *Why Parties? The Origin and Transformation of Political Parties in America.* Chicago: University of Chicago Press, 1995.

Andersen, Kristi. *After Suffrage: Women in Partisan and Electoral Politics before the New Deal.* Chicago: University of Chicago Press, 1996.

Carmines, Edward G., and James A. Stimson. *Issue Evolution: Race and the Transformation of American Politics.* Princeton, NJ: Princeton University Press, 1989.

Edsall, Thomas Byrne, and Mary D. Edsall. *Chain Reaction: The Impact of Race, Rights, and Taxes on American Politics.* New York: Norton, 1993.

Gerring, John. *Party Ideologies in America.* New York: Cambridge University Press, 1998.

Gilmour, John B. *Strategic Disagreement: Stalemate in American Politics.* Pittsburgh, PA: University of Pittsburgh Press, 1995.

Green, John C., and Daniel M. Shea, eds. *The State of the Parties: The Changing Role of Contemporary Parties.* 2d ed. Lanham, MD: Rowman and Littlefield, 1996.

Lawson, Kay, and Peter Merkl. *When Parties Fail: Emerging Alternative Organizations.* Princeton, NJ: Princeton University Press, 1988.

Milkis, Sidney. *The President and the Parties: The Transformation of the American Party System since the New Deal.* New York: Oxford University Press, 1993.

Shefter, Martin. *Political Parties and the State: The American Historical Experience.* Princeton, NJ: Princeton University Press, 1994.

Study Outline

www.wwnorton.com/wtp4e

1. In modern history, political parties have been the chief points of contact between governments and groups and forces in society. By organizing political parties, social forces attempt to gain some control over government policies and personnel.

What Are Political Parties?

1. Political parties as they are known today developed along with the expansion of suffrage, and actually took their shape from the electoral process.
2. Political parties, as coalitions of those with similar interests, are also important in making policy.

The Two-Party System in America

1. Historically, parties originate through either internal or external mobilization by those seeking to win governmental power.
2. The Democratic Party originated through a process of internal mobilization, as the Jeffersonian Party splintered into four factions in 1824, and Andrew Jackson emerged as the leader of one of these four groups.
3. The Republican Party grew through a process of external mobilization as antislavery groups formed a new party to oppose the 1854 Kansas-Nebraska Act.

4. The United States has experienced five realigning eras, which occur when the established political elite weakens sufficiently to permit the creation of new coalitions of forces capable of capturing and holding the reins of government.

5. American third parties have always represented social and economic protests ignored by the other parties.

Party Organization

1. Party organizations exist at virtually every level of American government—usually taking the form of committees made up of active party members.

2. Although national party conventions no longer have the power to nominate presidential candidates, they are still important in determining the party's rules and platform.

3. The national committee and the congressional campaign committees play important roles in recruiting candidates and raising money.

Parties and the Electorate

1. Individuals tend to form psychological ties with parties, called "party identification." This identification often follows demographic, ideological, and regional lines.

Parties and Elections

1. Parties are important in the electoral process for recruiting and nominating candidates for office.

2. Though not as important today as in the past, parties also can make a big difference in convincing voters to vote.

3. Parties also help voters choose among candidates.

Parties and Government

1. The differences between the two parties reflects a general difference in philosophy but also an attempt to appeal to core constituencies. These differences are often reflected in the policy agenda that party leaders adopt.

2. Political parties help to organize Congress. Congressional leadership and the committee system are both products of the two party system.

3. The president serves as an informal party head by seeking support from congressional members of the party and by supporting their bids for re-election.

The Role of Parties in a Democracy

1. Democracy depends on strong parties, which promote electoral competition and voter turnout and enable governance through their organizations in Congress.

2. The ties that parties have to the electorate are currently weak; the resulting "candidate-centered" politics has some negative consequences, including lower voter turnout, increased influence of interest groups, and a lack of effective decision making by elected leaders.

3. Parties could be strengthened by changes in campaign finance laws.

Practice Quiz

www.wwnorton.com/wtp4e

1. A political party is different from an interest group in that a political party
   a) seeks to control the entire government by electing its members to office and thereby controlling the government's personnel.
   b) seeks to control only limited, very specific, functions of government.
   c) is entirely nonprofit.
   d) has a much smaller membership.

2. The periodic episodes in American history in which an "old" dominant political party is replaced by a "new" dominant political party are called
   a) constitutional revolutions.
   b) party turnovers.
   c) presidential elections.
   d) electoral realignments.

3. Through which mechanism did Boss Tweed and other party leaders in the late nineteenth and early twentieth centuries maintain their control?
   a) civil service reform
   b) soft money contributions
   c) machine politics
   d) electoral reform

4. On what level are U.S. political parties organized?
   a) national
   b) state
   c) county
   d) all of the above

5. Contemporary national party conventions are important because they
   a) determine the party's presidential candidate.
   b) determine the party's rules and platform.
   c) Both a and b are correct.
   d) Neither a nor b is correct.

6. Which party was founded as a political expression of the antislavery movement?
   a) American Independent
   b) Prohibition
   c) Republican
   d) Democratic

7. Historically, when do realignments occur?
   a) typically, every twenty years
   b) whenever a minority party takes over Congress
   c) when large numbers of voters permanently shift their support from one party to another
   d) in odd-numbered years

8. Parties today are most important in the electoral process in
   a) recruiting and nominating candidates for office.
   b) financing all of the campaign's spending.
   c) providing millions of volunteers to mobilize voters.
   d) creating a responsible party government.

9. What role do parties play in Congress?
   a) They select leaders, e.g., Speaker of the House.
   b) They assign members to committees.
   c) Both a and b are correct.
   d) Parties play no role in Congress.

10. Parties are important to democracy because they
    a) encourage electoral competition.
    b) promote voter turnout.
    c) make governance possible by organizing elected leaders into governing coalitions.
    d) all of the above.

Critical Thinking Questions

www.wwnorton.com/wtp4e

1. Describe the factors that have contributed to the overall weakening of political parties in America. How are parties weaker? How do they remain important? What are the advantages of a political system with weak political parties? What are the disadvantages?
2. Historically, third parties have developed in American history when certain issues or constituencies have been ignored by the existing parties. Considering the similarities and differences between the Democratic and Republican parties, where might a budding third party find a constituency? What issues might it adopt? Finally, what structural and ideological obstacles might that third party face?
3. It was once said that "politics stops at the water's edge." This adage meant that parties should refrain from criticizing one another's foreign policies for fear of presenting a picture of division to foreign foes. For the most part, Democrats have supported President Bush's campaign against terrorism, but some Democrats, including Senator Hillary Rodham Clinton of New York, have criticized the president's policies. Should partisan politics stop at the "water's edge"? Is partisan politics compatible with effective governance?

Key Terms

www.wwnorton.com/wtp4e

caucus (political) (p. 337)
divided government (p. 332)
electoral realignment (p. 331)
gender gap (p. 346)
machines (p. 344)
majority party (p. 352)

minority party (p. 352)
multiple-member district (p. 336)
national convention (p. 337)
nomination (p. 350)
party activists (p. 345)
party identification (p. 345)
party organization (p. 337)
patronage (p. 344)
platform (p. 341)

plurality system (p. 337)
policy entrepreneur (p. 352)
political parties (p. 322)
proportional representation (p. 337)
responsible party government (p. 357)
single-member district (p. 336)
soft money (p. 345)
third parties (p. 333)
two-party system (p. 324)

10 CAMPAIGNS AND ELECTIONS

VER THE PAST two centuries, elections have come to play a significant role in the political processes of most nations. The forms that elections take and the purposes they serve, however, vary greatly from nation to nation. The most important difference among national electoral systems is that some provide the opportunity for opposition while others do not. Democratic electoral systems, such as those that have evolved in the United States and western Europe, allow opposing forces to compete against and even to replace current officeholders. Authoritarian electoral systems, by contrast, do not allow the defeat of those in power. In the authoritarian context, elections are used primarily to mobilize popular enthusiasm for the government, to provide an outlet for popular discontent, and to persuade foreigners that the regime is legitimate—i.e., that it has the support of the people. In the former Soviet Union, for example, citizens were required to vote even though no opposition to Communist Party candidates was allowed.

In democracies, elections can also serve as institutions of legitimation and as safety valves for social discontent. But beyond these functions, democratic elections facilitate popular influence, promote leadership accountability, and offer groups in society a measure of protection from the abuse of governmental power. Citizens exercise influence through elections by determining who should control the government. The chance to decide who will govern serves as an opportunity for ordinary citizens to make choices about the policies, programs, and directions of government action. In the United States, for example, recent Democratic and Republican candidates have differed significantly on issues of taxing, social spending, and governmental regulation. As American voters have chosen between the two parties' candidates, they have also made choices about these issues.

Elections promote leadership accountability because the threat of defeat at the polls exerts pressure on those in power to conduct themselves in a responsible manner and to take account of popular interests and wishes when they make their decisions. As James Madison observed in the Federalist Papers, elected leaders are "compelled to anticipate the moment when their power is to cease, when their exercise of it is to be reviewed, and when they must descend to the level from which they were raised, there forever to remain unless a faithful discharge of their trust shall have established their title to a renewal of it."[1] It is because of this need to anticipate the dissatisfaction of their constituents that elected officials constantly monitor public opinion polls as they decide what positions to take on policy issues.

suffrage the right to vote; also called franchise

Furthermore, the right to vote, or **suffrage,** can serve as an important source of protection for groups in American society. The passage of the 1965 Voting Rights Act, for example, enfranchised millions of African Americans in the South, paving the way for the election of thousands of new black public officials at the local, state, and national levels and ensuring that white politicians could no longer ignore the views and needs of African Americans. The Voting Rights Act was one of the chief spurs for the elimination of many overt forms of racial discrimination as well as for the diminution of racist rhetoric in American public life.

Finally, while elections allow citizens a chance to participate in politics, they also allow the government a chance to exert a good deal of control over when, where, how, and which of its citizens will participate. Electoral processes are governed by a variety of rules and procedures that allow those in power a significant opportunity to regulate the character—and perhaps also the consequences—of mass political participation. ■

■ **In this chapter, we shall examine the place of elections in American political life. We will first examine some of the formal aspects of electoral participation in the United States.** These include types of elections, the ways that election winners are determined, electoral districts, the ballot, and the electoral college. As we shall see, all of these factors affect the type and level of influence that citizens have through the electoral process.

- **In the next two sections, we will see how election campaigns are conducted in the United States.** The campaign for any political office consists of a number of steps. Election campaigns are also becoming increasingly expensive to wage.

- **We then turn to the broader issue of money and elections.** Raising campaign funds is now a crucial factor for winning. Although attempts to reform campaign finance have been made, the money keeps pouring in. As we will see, this development has important consequences for democracy.

- **Next, we assess the various factors that influence voters' decisions.** Despite the growing importance of money to elections, it is still voters who decide the outcomes.

Elections in America

In the United States, elections are held at regular intervals. National presidential elections take place every four years, on the first Tuesday in November; congressional elections are held every two years on the same Tuesday. (Congressional elections that do not coincide with a presidential election are sometimes called **midterm elections.**) Elections for state and local office also often coincide with national elections. Some states and municipalities, however, prefer to schedule their local elections for times that do not coincide with national contests to ensure that local results will not be affected by national trends.

In the American federal system, the responsibility for organizing elections rests largely with state and local governments. State laws specify how elections are to be administered, determine the boundaries of electoral districts, and specify candidate and voter qualifications. Elections are administered by state, county, and municipal election boards that are responsible for establishing and staffing polling places and verifying the eligibility of individuals who come to vote.

midterm elections congressional elections that do not coincide with a presidential election; also called off-year elections

> **What different types of elections are held in the United States? What rules determine who wins elections?**

TYPES OF ELECTIONS

Three types of elections are held in the United States: primary elections, general elections, and runoff elections. Americans occasionally also participate in a fourth voting process, the referendum, but the referendum is not actually an election.

Primary elections are used to select each party's candidates for the general election. In the case of local and statewide offices, the winners of primary elections face one another as their parties' nominees in the general election. At the presidential level, however, primary elections are indirect; they are used to select state delegates to the national nominating conventions, at which the major party presidential candidates are chosen. America is one of the only nations in the world to use primary elections. In most countries, nominations are controlled by party officials, as they once were in the United States. The primary system was introduced at the turn of the century by Progressive reformers who hoped to weaken the power of party leaders by taking candidate nominations out of their hands.

Under the laws of some states, only registered members of a political party may vote in a primary election to select that party's candidates. This is called

primary elections elections used to select a party's candidate for the general election

closed primary a primary election in which voters can participate in the nomination of candidates, but only of the party in which they are enrolled for a period of time prior to primary day

open primary a primary election in which the voter can wait until the day of the primary to choose which party to enroll in to select candidates for the general election

referendum the practice of referring a measure proposed or passed by a legislature to the vote of the electorate for approval or rejection

a **closed primary.** Other states allow all registered voters to decide on the day of the primary in which party's primary they will participate. This is called an **open primary.**

The primary is followed by the general election—the decisive electoral contest. The winner of the general election is elected to office for a specified term. In some states, however, mainly in the southeast, if no candidate wins an absolute majority in the primary, a runoff election is held before the general election. This situation is most likely to arise if there are more than two candidates, none of whom receives a majority of the votes cast. A runoff election is held between the two candidates who received the largest number of votes.

Some states also provide for referendum voting. The **referendum** process allows citizens to vote directly on proposed laws or other governmental actions. In recent years, voters in several states have voted to set limits on tax rates, to block state and local spending proposals, and to prohibit social services for illegal immigrants. Although it involves voting, a referendum is not an election. The election is an institution of representative government. Through an election, voters choose officials to act for them. The referendum, by contrast, is an institution of direct democracy; it allows voters to govern directly without intervention by government officials. The validity of referenda results, however, are subject to judicial action. If a court finds that a referendum outcome violates the state or national constitution, it can overturn the result. This happened in the case of a 1995 California referendum curtailing social services to illegal aliens.[2]

THE CRITERIA FOR WINNING

In some countries, to win a seat in the parliament or other governing body, a candidate must receive an absolute majority (50% + 1) of all the votes cast in the relevant district. This type of electoral system is called a **majority system** and, in the United States, is used in primary elections by some southern states. Majority systems usually include a provision for a runoff election between the two top candidates, because if the initial race draws several candidates, there is little chance that any one will receive a majority.

majority system a type of electoral system in which, to win a seat in the parliament or other representative body, a candidate must receive a majority of all the votes cast in the relevant district

In other nations, candidates for office need not win an absolute majority of the votes cast to win an election. Instead, victory is awarded to the candidate who receives the most votes, regardless of the actual percentage this represents. A candidate receiving 50 percent, 30 percent, or 20 percent of the vote can win if no other candidate received more votes. This type of electoral system is called a **plurality system** and is used in virtually all general elections in the United States.

plurality system a type of electoral system in which, to win a seat in the parliament or other representative body, a candidate need only receive the most votes in the election, not necessarily a majority of votes cast

Most European nations employ a third type of electoral system, called **proportional representation.** Under proportional rules, competing political parties are awarded legislative seats in rough proportion to the percentage of the popular votes cast that each party won. A party that wins 30 percent of the vote will receive roughly 30 percent of the seats in the parliament or other representative body. In the United States, proportional representation is used by many states in presidential primary elections.

proportional representation a multiple-member district system that allows each political party representation in proportion to its percentage of the total vote

In general, proportional representation works to the advantage of smaller or weaker groups in society, whereas plurality and majority rules tend to help larger and more powerful forces. Proportional representation benefits smaller or weaker groups

Electoral Systems

Because elections are the central institutional means for converting preferences into political power in free societies, students of comparative politics have focused upon the *efficiency* of elections. In other words, do the proportion of votes cast for a party's candidates match the actual number of seats awarded to that party in the national legislature?

The matter of efficiency is directly connected to the type of electoral method used. The American and British systems of elections are relatively simple and straightforward. Both countries' national elections employ a method known as "first-past-the-post," which assigns electoral victory to one political candidate per electoral district, based on a simple plurality principle. It is part of a broad family of election methods known as *single-member plurality/majority*. Among the world's 117 electoral democracies as of 1999, 42 (36 percent) rely on the single-member plurality/majority electoral method, as do approximately one in four of the world's most industrially developed democracies.

There are two basic advantages to this method. First, it affords a closer and more accountable relationship between a district and its elected representative to the national legislature. Second, the legislator knows she has the electoral support of at least a plurality of votes within the district. This offers more refined and loyal commitment of the representative to the district's interests (rather than a commitment solely to the national political party).

The disadvantage of the "first-past-the-post" system is its highly "inefficient" and disproportional nature. It "wastes" votes. How? Within any district, a party may win a plurality of votes and thereby win the district's single seat yet never come close to receiving a majority of votes cast in the district. When one adds up the total votes cast for a party across *all* the electoral districts in a country, one frequently finds the party receiving a larger proportion of seats in the legislature than the aggregate vote across the districts. For instance, in Britain following the May 1997 general elections to the House of Commons, nearly two in three of the 659 seats in the chamber were awarded to the Labour Party based on the outcome of elections, yet Labour received only 43 percent of the total votes cast.

In contrast to "first-past-the-post" is the *proportional representation* system of voting. This method is used in Japan, Hungary, Italy, Germany, Bolivia, New Zealand, and Sweden.

The advantage of multi-member proportional representation is its efficiency and minimal degree of disproportional distribution. With more than one representative per district, seats to the national legislature are not allocated for a district based on a plurality or majority of votes. Rather, each party is awarded a number of seats according to the proportion of votes received by the party in the district. Votes are more closely matched with subsequent seat allocations, thus minimizing the degree to which a democracy must violate principles of "one-person-one-vote." For instance, in Sweden's 1998 general elections, the difference between the proportion of votes received by the Social Democrats (36.4 percent) and the actual seats allocated to the party in the *Rikstag* (37.5 percent) was only 1.1 percent. But multi-member proportional representation systems bear a cost for some countries. If single-member plurality/majority systems tend to distort the representative process by disproportionately distributing seats relative to votes, proportional representation tends to complicate the process by giving political life to several relatively equal sized political parties, ensuring that often no party in the election has a strong plurality of votes, let alone majority of seats within the legislature. This compounds the difficulty of political compromise, policy cohesion, and the stability of government even within the most industrially advanced and developed democracies. For example, Italy has had fifty-eight different governments formed since 1946, a direct result of an electoral method that fragments the party system. Indeed, both Italy and Japan have chosen to move toward a mixed-member system in recent years, combining both single-member plurality/majority systems and proportional representation in order to minimize party system fragmentation, stabilize government, and enhance the public's confidence in and respect for the political system.

SOURCES: Arend Lijphart, *Patterns of Democracy: Government Forms and Performance in Thirty-Six Countries* (New Haven: Yale University Press, 1999); *Electoral Reform Society*, www.electoral-reform.org.uk/; *The Center for Voting and Democracy*, www.igc.org/cvd/.

because it usually allows a party to win legislative seats with fewer votes than would be required under a majority or plurality system. In Europe, for example, a party that wins 10 percent of the national vote might win 10 percent of the parliamentary seats. In the United States, by contrast, a party that wins 10 percent of the vote would probably win no seats in Congress. Because they give small parties little chance of success, plurality and majority systems tend to reduce the number of competitive political parties. Proportional representation, on the other hand, tends to increase the number of parties. It is in part because of its use of plurality elections that the United States has usually had only two significant political parties, while with proportional representation, many European countries have developed multiparty systems.

ELECTORAL DISTRICTS

The boundaries for congressional and state legislative districts in the United States are redrawn by the states every ten years in response to population changes determined by the decennial census. The character of district boundaries is influenced by several factors. Some of the most important influences have been federal court decisions. In the 1963 case of *Gray v. Sanders,* and in the 1964 cases of *Wesberry v. Sanders* and *Reynolds v. Sims,* the Supreme Court held that legislative districts within a state must include roughly equal populations, so as to accord with the principle of "one person, one vote."[3] During the 1980s, the Supreme Court also declared that legislative districts should, insofar as possible, be contiguous, compact, and consistent with existing political subdivisions.[4]

> **How does the government determine the boundaries of electoral districts? How is the ballot determined?**

The translation of votes into legislative seats and other political offices in the United States is shaped by the drawing of electoral districts. Districting for congressional races and state legislative contests is always a matter of controversy, with opponents accusing one another of "gerrymandering"—drawing district boundaries in such a way as to serve a particular group's interests. The original gerrymander was a districting plan attributed to Massachusetts governor Elbridge Gerry (1744–1814), who was said to have designed a district shaped like a salamander.

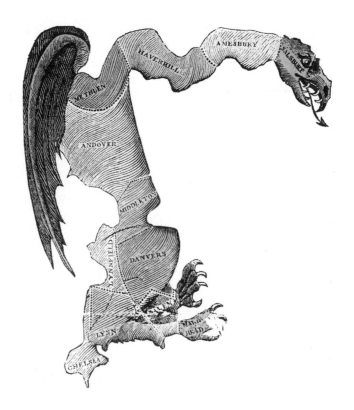

Despite judicial intervention, state legislators routinely seek to influence electoral outcomes by manipulating the organization of electoral districts. This strategy is called **gerrymandering,** in honor of a nineteenth-century Massachusetts governor, Elbridge Gerry, who was alleged to have designed a district in the shape

gerrymandering apportionment of voters in districts in such a way as to give unfair advantage to one racial or ethnic group or political party

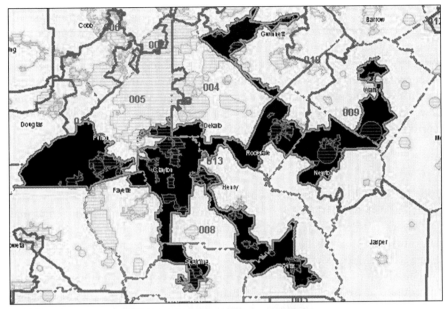

In states where a single party controls the office of the governor and a majority in both legislative houses, redistricting almost inevitably takes place at the expense of the party out of power. For example, in 2002 the Democratically controlled Georgia legislature created a "safe" district for the Democrats in the shape of a spider. In recent years, many districting plans have been challenged and the federal courts have taken the position that districts should be compact, contiguous, and respectful of established political jurisdictions such as towns and counties.

Texas' 6th District
91% White
Declared Constitutional

Georgia's 11th District
64% Black
Declared Un-Constitutional

The courts also have scrutinized districting plans for evidence of racial discrimination. In a number of recent cases, both black and white voters in the South have claimed to be the victims of racial gerrymanders. For instance, in 1995 the Supreme Court held that Cynthia McKinney's district, which was 64 percent African American, was unfairly based on race. Meanwhile, no challenge was made to Texas's 6th District, which was predominantly white. Blacks have charged old-fashioned racial discrimination, while whites have charged that they are the victims of so-called "benign gerrymandering" plans designed to help increase black representation.

of a salamander to promote his party's interests. The principle of gerrymandering is simple: different distributions of voters among districts can produce different electoral results. For example, by dispersing the members of a particular group across two or more districts, state legislators can dilute their voting power and prevent them from electing a representative in any district. Alternatively, by concentrating the members of a group or the adherents of the opposing party in as few districts as possible, state legislators can try to ensure that their opponents will elect as few representatives as possible. In recent years, the federal government has supported what is sometimes called **benign gerrymandering** through the creation of congressional districts made up primarily of minority group members. This practice was intended to increase the number of African Americans elected to public office. The Supreme Court has viewed this effort as constitutionally dubious, however. Beginning with the 1993 case of *Shaw v. Reno,* the Court has undermined efforts to create such **minority districts.**[5]

benign gerrymandering attempts to draw district boundaries so as to create districts made up primarily of disadvantaged or underrepresented minorities

minority district a gerrymandered voting district that improves the chances of minority candidates by making selected minority groups the majority within the district

THE BALLOT

Prior to the 1890s, voters cast ballots according to political parties. Each party printed its own ballots, listed only its own candidates for each office, and employed party workers to distribute its ballots at the polls. Because only one party's candidates appeared on any ballot, it was very difficult for a voter to cast anything other than a straight party vote.

The advent of a new, neutral ballot represented a significant change in electoral procedure. The new ballot was prepared and administered by the state rather than the parties. Each ballot was identical and included the names of all candidates for office. This ballot reform made it possible for voters to make their choices on the basis of the individual rather than the collective merits of a party's candidates. Because all candidates for the same office now appeared on the same ballot, voters were no longer forced to choose a straight party ticket. This gave rise to the phenomenon of split-ticket voting in American elections.

If a voter supports candidates from more than one party in the same election, he or she is said to be casting a **split-ticket vote.** Voters who support only one party's candidates are casting a **straight-ticket vote.** Straight-ticket voting occurs most often when a voter casts a ballot for a party's presidential candidate and then "automatically" votes for the rest of that party's candidates. The result of this voting pattern is known as the **coattail effect.**

split-ticket voting the practice of casting ballots for the candidates of at least two different political parties in the same election

straight-ticket voting the practice of casting ballots for candidates of only one party

coattail effect the result of voters casting their ballot for president or governor and "automatically" voting for the remainder of the party's ticket

Prior to the reform of the ballot, it was not uncommon for an entire incumbent administration to be swept from office and replaced by an entirely new set of officials. In the absence of a real possibility of split-ticket voting, any desire on the part of the electorate for change could be expressed only as a vote against all candidates of the party in power. Because of this, there always existed the possibility, particularly at the state and local levels, that an insurgent slate committed to policy change could be swept into power. The party ballot thus increased the potential impact of elections upon the government's composition. Although this potential may not always have been realized, the party ballot at least increased the chance that electoral decisions could lead to policy changes. By contrast, because it permitted choice on the basis of candidates' individual appeals, ticket splitting led to increasingly divided partisan control of government.

Electoral Redistricting and Race

The process of redrawing election districts to take account of population shifts is both necessary and controversial. America's two major political parties have always vied to obtain political advantage through redistricting in the hope that redrawn district lines will help their candidates, or hurt the opposing candidates. Yet redistricting has also been used as a weapon to minimize the electoral influence of selected groups, especially African Americans, a process many consider an undemocratic denial of equality. To remedy this problem, Congress amended the 1965 Voting Rights Act in 1982 to compel states with significant African American and Latino populations to redraw district lines in such a way as to make more likely the election of representatives from these groups. This redistricting was carried out in thirteen states after the 1990 census, and it produced the desired effect. Before the 1990 reapportionment, the House of Representatives had a record-high twenty-five African American members (5.7 percent of members). After the reapportionment, which included the creation of districts having black majorities, thirty-nine African Americans were elected (9 percent of the House); Latino representatives increased from ten to seventeen. Yet many of these race-based reapportionment schemes were challenged in court.

Supporters of race-based redistricting argue that such drastic measures are necessary to overcome traditional white dominance. Southern blacks, in particular, traditionally have been frozen out of public office, since most American elections follow the winner-take-all system, meaning that election districts with substantial nonwhite populations could always be outvoted by a white majority. Indeed, studies have shown that race matters to voters. In a study from the 1980s, more than 80 percent of white North Carolina voters reported that they would not vote for an African American candidate, even if there was no other choice on the ballot. North Carolina did not elect an African American to Congress in the twentieth century until after the 1990 reapportionment, despite the fact that between one-fifth and one-third of the state's population was black.

Although race-based redistricting has produced some odd-shaped congressional districts, it increased not only the number of nonwhite representatives in Congress, but also increased their political voice and clout. This larger number of representatives has exerted more influence over national policy making in such areas as crime and gun control. It also has increased the pool of potential office-seekers. The persistence of racism, and the resistance of institutions to change, has made such "minority" districts necessary.

Critics have argued that race-based redistricting is nothing more than racial gerrymandering, and that it perpetuates the very problem it claims to solve. While the number of minority representatives in Congress has increased, race-based reapportionment has also purged surrounding districts of nonwhite voters, transforming many of these districts from racially and politically competitive to uniformly white and Republican, a fact reflected in the shift of twelve seats to Republican candidates in the thirteen states where these changes took place (because of the shifting of Democratic-voting blacks from these formerly competitive districts). Thus, black voters have been walled off from more conservative white voters.

The shoestring shape of many of these districts—some portions of some districts are no wider than an interstate highway—reveals their blatant gerrymandering. Even though the purpose of providing more representation for African Americans and Latinos may be praiseworthy, the method violates the principle of equal protection, as the Supreme Court has noted in recent decisions. Winner-take-all elections do often disguise the preferences of minority groups, but the remedy is stronger electoral competition and greater pressure from constituent groups. Reapportionment based on race is unacceptable, regardless of which race benefits.

SOURCE: Lani Guinier, "Don't Scapegoat the Gerrymander," *New York Times Magazine,* January 8, 1995.

Is Redistricting Fair?

Yes

Gerrymandering, or the redrawing of districts to influence an election outcome, is as much a part of the American political landscape as gridlock. Districts have been redrawn by the party in power since the early 1800s to influence an election outcome.

Recent gerrymanders, such as those in North Carolina's first and 12th districts and those in Texas's 18th, 29th, and 30th districts, were drawn with an additional component in mind: race. In two 5-4 rulings, the Supreme Court invalidated the Texas districts and North Carolina's 12th on the grounds that race was used as the predominant factor in creating these minority-majority districts, thereby violating the Fourteenth Amendment rights of the districts' white voters.

The Supreme Court, however, was incorrect in its decision for two main reasons. First, race and political voting patterns are closely intertwined, making it nearly impossible to separate a legitimate political gerrymander from a race-based one. And even if race was the predominant factor in determining the districts, the states still have a "compelling interest" as required by the Court's strict scrutiny guidelines to ensure equal representation for all of its citizens.

Political interests, have long been accepted as legitimate reasons to design voting districts. Blacks, as a group, vote overwhelmingly Democratic. As a Democrat, what better way to guarantee that another Democrat will be elected than to create a black-majority district? While it would be insulting to suggest that one single characteristic will determine how a person votes, the odds that a black-majority district will elect a Democrat are too significant to ignore completely.

But politics aside, is any state justified in trying to increase the amount of minority representation in its slate of national representatives? This brings up two competing sets of rights. Everyone is guaranteed equal representation under the Fourteenth Amendment and the Voting Rights Act, but whose guarantee should weigh more when they conflict—whites or minorities?

The Fourteenth Amendment was engineered to protect the minority from the majority. Blacks in a white-majority district have more to lose than do whites in a black-majority district—after all, the interests of whites are represented by the majority of national representatives, while black interests have few voices on the federal level. It comes down to which group has more to lose by not having their voice heard; since the interests of the typical white voter are represented by the majority of Congressional representatives, it is clear that the loss of the representation of black interests is of far greater concern.

Of course, these districts should not be maintained simply so that a black person is elected—the crucial point is that the black majority in the district has a chance to elect an official to represent its interests. If the 54 percent black majority in the state's 12th district felt that a white person better represented their concerns, fine—as long as they can elect someone to represent their interests. The only way to ensure that their legitimate concerns are not muted by their minority status is to make them a majority.

The creation of race-attentive districts would not open a Pandora's Box; the combination of party interests and a generally low minority population decide where racial gerrymandering will occur. More important, without minority-majority districts, the chance for minorities to get their interests heard in Congress is greatly reduced, and their political efficacy—already low—is further diminished.

Although the 12th district was certainly unusual in shape, it should have met the Court's requirement of a solution that is "narrowly tailored" to solve the problem.

The Supreme Court—and most others—speak quixotically of a "color-blind" Constitution. But by attempting with this decision to take a step toward the goal, they ended up taking two steps back.

SOURCE: Editorial, "Redrawing, the Line," *The Chronicle* (Duke University), June 20, 1996.

No Every ten years, the nationwide census produces new changes, such as allocating more or fewer representatives in Congress depending on population shifts within the states. The redrawing of legislative districts takes place as well.

In a perfect world, the new boundaries would represent the changes in population and provide everyone with fair representation. But this world is far from perfect.

In Pennsylvania, the Republicans control the legislature and the governorship, which basically means that they can dictate how they want to redraw the borders. Last week, their proposal passed. These new districts will solidify their hold on seats in the legislature and also improve their chances to gain more seats in the 2002 elections.

One senator was quoted as saying that this was the main goal of the redistricting effort. This is a tried and true practice of both parties for generations. The majority party works to reshape the boundaries just about any way they choose because they have the necessary votes to pass their plan.

The main regulations given from the Supreme Court are that districts must be equal size or as close as possible and must be contiguous. But there is not much protection for the residents of the old districts.

Democrats are planning to file a lawsuit stating that the redistricting plan will deny voters fair representation.

Is the Republican plan 100 percent fair? Probably not, but would a Democratic one ensure complete fairness?

One state representative compared this whole process to the spoils system. In that system, the winner gets everything at the expense of somebody else. Who is the true loser: the minority party or the average citizen?

The repercussions of this year's redistricting are not merely going to affect politicians. Some districts that voted Democratic will be broken up in a way that will divide their numbers, making sure that their candidate's chances for winning are diminished. Republicans in states controlled by Democrats, such as California, will face the same dilemma.

Voting gives citizens a voice in government, but redistricting plans, which are drawn on political lines, serve more to mute the voices instead of amplifying them.

Larger issues are waiting for attention. The skyrocketing unemployment hitting the nation is a prime example. The representatives can spend more time addressing that and other issues, instead of trying to increase the power of their own party.

Rather than working to make sure that new boundaries accurately reflect the changes of the past ten years, our representatives in Harrisburg, and also in the other state capitals, are working to ensure that the majority party remains dominant. This is being done at the expense of the hard-working taxpayers of this country.

As with many of the political battles, the main casualties are the citizens.

SOURCE: Editorial Board, "Citizens Lose Out in State's Redistricting," *The Collegian* (Pennsylvania State University), January 8, 2002.

The form of the ballot can have other consequences, as well. In some instances, confusingly organized ballots can lead to voter confusion and produce results inconsistent with voters' intentions. For example, the "butterfly ballot" used in some Florida jurisdictions in 2000 did not clearly link candidates' names with the boxes voters were expected to check. This led some people to vote for the wrong candidate. Apparently, a sizable number of Jewish and African American voters who intended to vote for Al Gore wound up giving their votes to Pat Buchanan, an independent candidate whose pronouncements have not been friendly to these groups.

THE ELECTORAL COLLEGE

In the early history of popular voting, nations often made use of indirect elections. In these elections, voters would choose the members of an intermediate body. These members would, in turn, select public officials. The assumption underlying such processes was that ordinary citizens were not really qualified to choose their leaders and could not be trusted to do so directly. The last vestige of this procedure in America is the **electoral college,** the group of electors who formally select the president and vice president of the United States.

electoral college the presidential electors from each state who meet after the popular election to cast ballots for president and vice president

When Americans go to the polls on election day, they are technically not voting directly for presidential candidates. Instead, voters within each state are choosing among slates of electors selected by each state's party and pledged, if elected, to support that party's presidential candidate. In each state (except Maine and Nebraska), the slate that wins casts all the state's electoral votes for its party's candidate.[6] Each state is entitled to a number of electoral votes equal to the number of the state's senators and representatives combined, for a total of 538 electoral votes for the fifty states and the District of Columbia. Occasionally, an elector will break his or her pledge and vote for the other party's candidate. For example, in 1976, when the Republicans carried the state of Washington, one Republican elector from that state refused to vote for Gerald Ford, the Republican presidential nominee. Many states have now enacted statutes formally binding electors to their pledges, but some constitutional authorities doubt whether such statutes are enforceable.

In each state, the electors whose slate has won proceed to the state's capital on the Monday following the second Wednesday in December and formally cast their ballots. These are sent to Washington, tallied by the Congress in January, and the name of the winner is formally announced. If no candidate receives a majority of all electoral votes, the names of the top three candidates would be submitted to the House, where each state would be able to cast one vote. Whether a state's vote would be decided by a majority, plurality, or some other fraction of the state's delegates would be determined under rules established by the House.

In 1800 and 1824, the electoral college failed to produce a majority for any candidate. In the election of 1800, Thomas Jefferson, the Jeffersonian Republican Party's presidential candidate, and Aaron Burr, that party's vice presidential candidate, received an equal number of votes in the electoral college, throwing the election into the House of Representatives. (The Constitution at that time made no distinction between presidential and vice presidential candidates, specifying only that the individual receiving a majority of electoral votes would be named president.) Some members of the Federalist Party in Congress suggested that they should seize the opportunity to damage the Republican cause by supporting Burr and denying Jefferson the presidency. Federalist leader Alexander Hamilton put a stop to this mischievous notion, however, and made certain that his party supported Jefferson. Hamilton's actions enraged Burr and helped lead to the infamous duel between the two men, in which Hamilton was killed. The Twelfth Amendment, ratified in 1804, was designed to prevent a repetition of such an inconclusive election by providing for separate electoral college votes for president and vice president.

In the 1824 election, four candidates—John Quincy Adams, Andrew Jackson, Henry Clay, and William H. Crawford—divided the electoral vote; no one of them received a majority. The House of Representatives eventually chose Adams over the others, even though Jackson had won more electoral and popular votes. After 1824, the two major political parties had begun to dominate presidential politics to such an extent that by December of each election year, only two candidates remained for the electors to choose between, thus ensuring that one would receive a majority. This freed the parties and the candidates from having to plan their campaigns to culminate in Congress, and Congress very quickly ceased to dominate the presidential selection process.

On all but three occasions since 1824, the electoral vote has simply ratified the nationwide popular vote. Since electoral votes are won on a state-by-state basis, it is mathematically possible for a candidate who receives a nationwide popular plurality to fail to carry states whose electoral votes would add up to a majority. Thus, in 1876, Rutherford B. Hayes was the winner in the electoral college despite receiving fewer popular votes than his rival, Samuel Tilden. In 1888, Grover Cleveland received more popular votes than Benjamin Harrison, but received fewer electoral votes. And in 2000, Al Gore outpolled his opponent, George W. Bush, by more than 500,000 votes, but narrowly lost the electoral college by a mere four electoral votes.

The outcome of the 2000 contest, in which the electoral college produced a result that was inconsistent with the popular vote, led to many calls for the abolition of this institution and the introduction of some form of direct popular election of the president. Within days of the election, several members of Congress promised to introduce a constitutional amendment that would bring an end to the electoral college, which one congressman called an "anachronism." Efforts to introduce such a reform, however, were blocked by political forces that believe they benefit from the present system. For example, minority groups that are influential in large urban states with many electoral votes feel that their voting strength would be diminished in a direct, nationwide, popular election. At the same time, some Republicans believe that their party's usual presidential strength in the South and in parts of the Midwest and West gives them a distinct advantage in the electoral college. Some Democrats and Republicans also fear that the direct popular election of the president would give third parties more influence over the outcome. Thus, while political pressure will be great to abolish the current system, efforts toward that end will likely face the same fate as the over-700 previous attempts to reform it.

campaign an effort by political candidates and their staffs to win the backing of donors, political activists, and voters in the quest for political office

Election Campaigns

A **campaign** is an effort by political candidates and their supporters to win the backing of donors, political activists, and voters in their quest for political office. Campaigns precede every primary and general election. Because of the complexity

> **What are the steps in a successful election campaign?**

of the campaign process, and because of the amount of money that candidates must raise, presidential campaigns usually begin almost two years before the November presidential elections. The campaign for any office consists of a number of steps. Candidates must first organize groups of supporters who will help them raise funds and bring their name to the attention of the media and potential donors. This step is relatively easy for a candidate currently in the office. The current officeholder is called an **incumbent.** Incumbents usually are already well known and have little difficulty attracting supporters and contributors, unless of course they have been subject to damaging publicity while in office.

incumbent a candidate running for a position that he or she already holds

ADVISERS

The next step in a typical campaign involves recruiting advisers and creating a formal campaign organization (see Figure 10.1). Most candidates, especially for national or statewide office, will need a campaign manager, a media consultant, a pollster, a financial adviser, and a press spokesperson, as well as a staff director to

Figure 10.1 The Typical Organization of a National Political Campaign

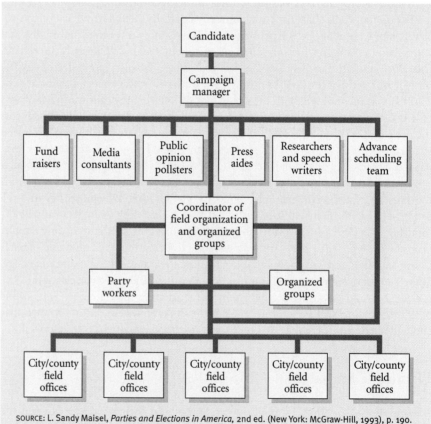

SOURCE: L. Sandy Maisel, *Parties and Elections in America*, 2nd ed. (New York: McGraw-Hill, 1993), p. 190. Copyright © 1993, McGraw-Hill. Used with permission.

coordinate the activities of volunteer and paid workers. For a local campaign, candidates generally need hundreds of workers. State-level campaigns call for thousands of workers, and presidential campaigns require tens of thousands of workers nationwide.

Professional campaign workers, including the managers, consultants, and pollsters required in a modern campaign, prefer to work for candidates who seem to have a reasonable chance of winning. For individuals like James Carville, who helped manage Bill Clinton's 1992 campaign; Dick Morris, credited as the mastermind behind Clinton's 1996 victory; or Republican strategists Roger Ailes and Bob Teeter, politics is a profession, and repeated associations with winning campaigns are the route to professional success. Candidates seen as having little chance of winning often have difficulty hiring the most experienced professional consultants. Professional political consultants have taken the place of the old-time party bosses who once controlled political campaigns. Most consultants who direct campaigns specialize in politics, although some are drawn from the ranks of corporate advertising and may work with commercial clients in addition to politicians. Campaign consultants conduct public opinion polls, produce television commercials, organize direct-mail campaigns, and develop the issues and advertising messages the candidate will use to mobilize support.

Together with their advisers, candidates must begin serious fund-raising efforts at an early stage in the campaign. To have a reasonable chance of winning a seat in the House of Representatives, a candidate may need to raise more than $500,000. To win a Senate seat, a candidate may need ten times that much. Candidates generally begin raising funds long before they face an election. For example, a year prior to the 1998 congressional elections, New York's Republican senator, Alfonse D'Amato, had already raised $9.7 million, nearly as much as he spent in his successful 1992 campaign. Throughout 1996 and 1997, D'Amato had raised money from the banking, insurance, real estate, and construction businesses that come under the jurisdiction of the Senate Banking, Housing, and Urban Affairs Committee, which he chaired. A professional staff of fund-raisers, headed by long-term D'Amato consultant Arthur Finkelstein, labored full-time on the senator's behalf. For his efforts, Finkelstein earned nearly $100,000 during the second half of 1996 alone. In many states, an incumbent able to raise as much money as D'Amato might be able to frighten away most potential challengers. In New York, however, Democratic candidates can count on the support of some of the party's wealthiest contributors; Democratic senatorial candidate and congressman Charles Schumer of Brooklyn was able to raise almost as much money as D'Amato. Schumer eventually won the election. Though partially supported by public funding, presidential candidates must raise huge amounts of money. For example, by December 1999, almost a year before the November 2000 national elections, Republican George W. Bush had already raised some $63 million to support his bid for office. We will look in more detail at political campaign fund-raising later in the chapter.

POLLING

Another important element of a campaign is public-opinion polling. To be competitive, a candidate must collect voting and poll data to assess the electorate's needs, hopes, fears, and past behavior. Polls are conducted throughout most political campaigns. Surveys of voter opinion provide the basic information that candidates and their staffs use to craft campaign strategies—i.e., to select issues, to assess their own strengths and weaknesses as well as those of the opposition, to check voter response to the campaign, and to measure the degree to which various constituent groups may be responsive to campaign appeals. The themes, issues, and messages that candidates present during a campaign are generally based upon polls and smaller face-to-face sessions with voters, called "focus groups." In the 1992 presidential campaign, Bill Clinton's emphasis on the economy, exemplified by the campaign staff's slogan "It's the economy, stupid," was based on the view that the economy was the chief concern among American voters. In preparation for the 1996 campaign, Clinton adopted a strategy of "triangulation" based upon consultant Richard Morris's interpretation of poll data. Morris advised Clinton that he would win the most votes by positioning himself between liberal Democrats and conservative Republicans, in a sense forming the apex of a triangle.[7] During the 2000 presidential race, Democratic candidate Al Gore based his decision to "distance" himself from President Clinton on poll data suggesting that the public had become weary of Clinton after years of crises and scandals, developing what some called "Clinton fatigue." First Lady Hillary Rodham Clinton, campaigning for a New York Senate seat, seemed to follow similar advice when she criticized several of her husband's policy positions. In recent years, pollsters have become central figures in most national campaigns and some have continued as advisers to their clients after they win the election.

THE PRIMARIES

For many candidates, the next step in a campaign is the primary election. In the case of all offices but the presidency, state and local primary elections determine which candidates will receive the major parties' official nominations. Of course, candidates can run for office without the Democratic or Republican nomination. In most states, however, independent and third-party candidates must obtain many thousands of petition signatures to qualify for the general election ballot. This requirement alone discourages most independent and third-party bids. More important, most Americans are reluctant to vote for candidates other than those nominated by the two major parties. Thus most of the time, a major party nomination is a necessary condition for electoral success. Some popular incumbents coast to victory without having to face a serious challenge. In most major races, however, candidates can expect to compete in a primary election.

There are essentially two types of primary contests: the personality clash and the ideological, or factional, struggle. In the first category are primaries that simply represent competing efforts by ambitious individuals to secure election to office. In 2000, for example, the major Democratic presidential aspirants, Al Gore (the eventual Democratic nominee) and Bill Bradley, were both moderate liberals who agreed on the broad outlines of most issues and policies. Whichever candidate they preferred, few Democratic loyalists considered refusing to support the other should he win the primary. Similarly, the major Republican presidential aspirants, George W. Bush (who ultimately received the Republican nomination) and John McCain, presented themselves as fiscally conservative and "pro-family" in their social views. Most Republican loyalists were willing to support a presidential bid by either individual. This type of primary can be very healthy for a political party because it can enhance interest in the campaign and can produce a nominee with the ability to win the general election.

The second type of primary—the ideological struggle—can have different consequences. Ideological struggles usually occur when one wing of a party decides that an incumbent is too willing to compromise or too moderate in his or her political views. For example, in 1992, former president George H. W. Bush was challenged for the Republican presidential nomination by conservative columnist Pat Buchanan. Buchanan charged Bush with being too willing to compromise conservative principles. Such ideological challenges not only reveal rifts within a party coalition, but the friction and resentment they cause can undermine a party's general election chances. Through his ideological crusade, Buchanan damaged President Bush's re-election chances in 1992.

Ideological struggles can also produce candidates who are too liberal or too conservative to win the general election. Primary electorates are much smaller and tend to be ideologically more extreme than the general electorate: Democratic primary voters are somewhat more liberal than the general electorate, and Republican primary voters are typically more conservative than the general electorate. Thus, the winner of an intraparty ideological struggle may prove too extreme for the general election. In 1994, for example, archconservative Oliver North won the Virginia Republican senatorial primary over a moderate opponent, but was drubbed in the general election. Many moderate Republicans, including Virginia's other senator, John Warner, refused to support North.

Presidential Elections

Although they also involve primary elections, the major party presidential nominations follow a pattern that is quite different from the nominating process employed for other political offices. In some years, particularly when an incumbent president is running for re-election, one party's nomination may not be contested. If, however, the Democratic or Republican presidential nomination is contested, candidates typically compete in primaries or presidential nominating caucuses in all fifty states, attempting to capture national convention delegates. Most states use primary elections to choose the delegates for national conventions. A few states use the **caucus,** a nominating process that begins with precinct-level meetings throughout the state. Some caucuses, called **open caucuses,** are open to anyone wishing to attend. Other states use **closed caucuses,** open only to registered party members. Citizens attending the caucuses typically elect delegates to statewide conventions at which delegates to the national party conventions are chosen.

The primaries and caucuses usually begin in February of a presidential election year and end in June (see Figure 10.2). The early ones are most important because they can help front-running candidates secure media attention and financial support. Gradually, the primary and caucus process has become "front loaded," with states vying with one another to increase their political influence by holding their nominating processes first. Traditionally, the New Hampshire primary and the

> **How is the president elected?**

caucus (political) a normally closed meeting of a political or legislative group to select candidates, plan strategy, or make decisions regarding legislative matters

open caucus a presidential nominating caucus open to anyone who wishes to attend

closed caucus a presidential nominating caucus open only to registered party members

Figure 10.2 The 2000 Presidential Election Season

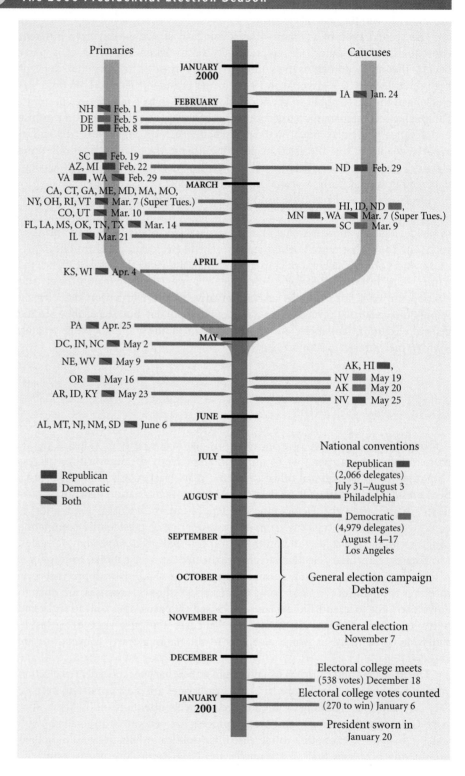

Iowa caucuses are considered the most important of the early events, and candidates spend months courting voter support in these two states. A candidate who performs well in Iowa and New Hampshire will usually be able to secure support and better media coverage for subsequent races. A candidate who fares badly in these two states may be written off as a loser.

As noted in Chapter 9, the Democratic Party requires that state presidential primaries allocate delegates on the basis of proportional representation; Democratic candidates win delegates in rough proportion to their percentage of the primary vote. The Republican Party does not require proportional representation, but most states have now written proportional representation requirements into their election laws. A few states use the **winner-take-all system,** by which the candidate with the most votes wins all the party's delegates in that state.

When the primaries and caucuses are concluded, it is usually clear which candidates have won their parties' nominations. For example, in 2000, George W. Bush arrived at the GOP national convention with the party nomination in hand; similarly, Al Gore was the Democratic winner long before the party faithful assembled in Los Angeles.

winner-take-all system a system in which all of a state's presidential nominating delegates are awarded to the candidate who wins the most votes, while runners-up receive no delegates

THE CONVENTION

The one major step that remains before a nomination is actually awarded is the national party convention. The Democratic and Republican national party conventions occur every four years to formally certify each party's presidential and vice presidential nominees. In addition, the conventions draft a statement of party principles, called a **platform,** and determine the rules that will govern party activities for the next four years.

platform a party document, written at a national convention, that contains party philosophy, principles, and positions on issues

The History of Political Conventions For more than fifty years after America's Founding, presidential nominations were controlled by each party's congressional caucus—all the party's members in the House and the Senate. Critics referred to this process as the "King Caucus" and charged that it did not take proper account of the views of party members throughout the nation. In 1824, the King Caucus method came under severe attack when the Democratic Party caucus failed to nominate Andrew Jackson, the candidate with the greatest support among both party members and activists outside the Capitol. In the 1830s, the party convention was devised as a way of allowing party leaders and activists throughout the nation an opportunity to participate in selecting presidential candidates. The first party convention was held by the Anti-Masonic Party in 1831. The Democratic Party held its first convention in 1832, when Andrew Jackson was nominated for a second term.

As it developed during the course of the next century, the convention became the decisive institution in the presidential nominating processes of the two major parties. The convention was a genuine deliberative body in which party factions argued, negotiated, and eventually reached a decision. The convention was composed of delegations from each state. The size of a state's delegation depended on the state's population, and each delegate was allowed one vote for the purpose of nominating the party's presidential and vice presidential candidates. Before 1936, victory required the support of two-thirds of the delegates. Until 1968, state

unit rule the convention voting system under which a state delegation casts all of its votes for the candidate supported by the majority of the state's delegates

delegations voted according to the **unit rule,** which meant that all the members of the state delegation would vote for the candidate favored by the majority of the state's delegates. This practice was designed to maximize a state's influence in the nominating process. The unit rule was abolished in 1968.

Between the 1830s and World War II, national convention delegates were generally selected by a state's party leaders. Usually the delegates were public officials, political activists, and party notables from all regions of the state, representing most major party factions. Some delegates would arrive at the convention having pledged in advance to give their support to a particular presidential candidate. Most delegates were uncommitted, however. This fact, coupled with the unit rule, allowed state party leaders (i.e., the delegates) to negotiate with one another and with presidential candidates for their support. State party leaders might agree to support a candidate in exchange for a promise to name them or their followers to important national positions, or in exchange for promises of federal programs and projects for their state. During the course of a convention, alliances of states would form, dissolve, and re-form in the course of tense negotiations. Typically, many votes were needed before the nomination could be decided. Often, deadlocks developed between the most powerful party factions, and state leaders would be forced to find a compromise, or "dark-horse," candidate. Among the more famous dark-horse nominees were James Polk in 1844 and Warren Harding in 1920. Although he was virtually unknown, Polk won the Democratic nomination when it became clear that none of the more established candidates could win. Similarly, Harding, another political unknown, won his nomination after the major candidates had fought one another to a standstill.

In its day, the convention was seen as a democratic reform. In later years, however, new generations of reformers came to view the convention as a symbol of rule by party leaders. The convention also strengthened the independence and power of the presidency, by taking the nominating process out of the hands of Congress.

Contemporary Party Conventions Whereas the traditional party convention was a deliberative assembly, the contemporary convention acts more to ratify than to determine the party's presidential and vice presidential nominations. Today, as we saw earlier in this chapter, the nomination is actually determined in a series of primary elections and local party caucuses held in virtually all fifty states during several months prior to the convention. These primaries and caucuses determine how each state's convention delegates will vote. Candidates now arrive at the convention knowing who has enough delegate support in hand to assure a victory in the first round of balloting. State party leaders no longer serve as power brokers, and the party's presidential and vice presidential choices are made relatively quickly.

Even though the party convention no longer controls presidential nominations, it still has a number of important tasks. The first of these is the adoption of party rules concerning such matters as convention delegate selection and future presidential primary elections. In 1972, for example, the Democratic convention accepted rules requiring convention delegates to be broadly representative of the party's membership in terms of race and gender. After those rules were passed, the convention refused to seat several state delegations that were deemed not to meet this standard.

Another important task for the convention is the drafting of a party platform—a statement of principles and pledges around which the delegates can unite. Although the two major parties' platforms tend to contain many similar principles and platitudes, differences between the two platforms can be significant. In recent years, for example, the Republican platform has advocated tax cuts and taken strong positions on such social issues as affirmative action and abortion. The Democratic platforms, on the other hand, have focused on the importance of maintaining welfare and regulatory programs. A close reading of both parties' platforms can reveal some of the ideological differences between the parties.

Convention Delegates Today, convention **delegates** are generally political activists with strong positions on social and political issues. Generally, Republican delegates tend to be more conservative than Republican voters as a whole, whereas Democratic delegates tend to be more liberal than the majority of Democratic voters. In states such as Michigan and Iowa, local party caucuses choose many of the delegates who will actually attend the national convention. In most of the remaining states, primary elections determine how a state's delegation will vote, but the actual delegates are selected by state party officials. Delegate votes won in primary elections are apportioned to candidates on the basis of proportional representation. Thus a candidate who received 30 percent of the vote in the California Democratic primary would receive roughly 30 percent of the state's delegate votes at the party's national convention.

delegates political activists selected to vote at a party's national convention

As was mentioned earlier, the Democratic Party requires that a state's convention delegation be representative of that state's Democratic electorate in terms of race, gender, and age. Republican delegates, by contrast, are more likely to be male and white. The Democrats also reserve slots for elected Democratic Party officials, called **superdelegates.** All the Democratic governors and about 80 percent of the party's members of Congress now attend the national convention as delegates.

superdelegate a convention delegate position, in Democratic conventions, reserved for party officials

Convention Procedure Each party convention lasts several days. The convention usually begins with the selection of party committees, including the credentials, rules, and platform committees, and the election of a temporary convention chairperson. This individual normally delivers a keynote address highlighting the party's appeals and concerns. After all the delegates have been seated by the credentials committee, a permanent chair is elected. This person presides over the presidential and vice presidential nominations, the adoption of a party platform, and any votes on rules that are proposed by the rules committee.

Although the actual presidential nomination is effectively decided before the convention, the names of a number of candidates are generally put in nomination and speeches made on their behalf at the convention. To be nominated is considered an honor, and ambitious politicians are eager for the media attention, however brief, that such a nomination brings.

All the nominating speeches, as well as speeches by party notables, are carefully scrutinized by the mass media, which report and analyze the major events of the convention. In the 1950s and 1960s, the television networks provided "gavel-to-gavel" coverage of the Democratic and Republican national conventions. Today, however, the major television networks carry convention highlights only. Because the parties are eager to receive as much media coverage as possible, they schedule convention events in order to reach large television audiences. The parties typically try to present the actual presidential nomination and the nominee's acceptance speech during prime viewing time, normally between 8:00 and 11:00 P.M. on a weeknight. In 1996, the major networks proclaimed that both national conventions were essentially too boring to merit detailed coverage. One important news program, ABC's *Nightline,* halted its coverage of the Republican convention earlier than had been scheduled after the program's anchor, Ted Koppel, decided that the GOP convention was little more than a staged media event.

After the nominating speeches are concluded, the voting begins. The names of the states are called alphabetically and the state delegation's vote reported by its chairperson. During this process, noisy and colorful demonstrations are staged in support of the nominees. When the nomination is formally decided, a lengthy demonstration ensues, with bands and colorful balloons celebrating the conclusion of the process. The party's vice presidential candidate is usually nominated the next day. This individual is almost always selected by the presidential nominee, and the choice is merely ratified by the convention. In 2000, George W. Bush selected Dick Cheney, who had previously served as his father's secretary of defense, while Al Gore designated Connecticut senator Joe Lieberman as his running mate. Lieberman thus became the first Jewish political candidate in U.S. history to appear on a national ticket.

Once the nominations have been settled and most other party business has been resolved, the presidential and vice presidential nominees deliver acceptance speeches. These speeches are opportunities for the nominees to begin their formal campaigns on a positive note, and they are usually meticulously crafted to make as much of an impression on the electorate as possible.

THE GENERAL ELECTION CAMPAIGN AND HIGH-TECH POLITICS

> **What factors have the greatest impact on a general election campaign?**

For those candidates lucky enough to survive the nominating process, the last hurdle is the general election. There are essentially two types of general election in the United States today. The first type is the organizationally driven, labor-intensive election. In general, local elections and many congressional races fall into this category. Candidates campaign in such elections by recruiting large numbers of volunteer workers to hand out leaflets and organize rallies. The candidates make appearances at receptions, community group meetings, and local events, and even in shopping malls and on busy street corners. Generally, local and congressional campaigns depend less upon issues and policy proposals and more upon hard work designed to make the candidate more visible than his or her opponent. Statewide campaigns, some congressional races, and, of course, the national presidential election fall into the second category: the media-driven, capital-intensive electoral campaign.

In the nineteenth and early twentieth centuries, political campaigns were waged by the parties' enormous armies of patronage workers. Throughout the year, party workers cultivated the support of voters by helping them with legal problems, helping them find jobs, and serving as liaisons with local, state, and federal agencies. On Election Day throughout the nation hundreds of thousands of party workers marched from house to house reminding their supporters to vote, helping the aged and infirm to reach the polls, and calling in the favors they had accrued during the year. Campaigns resembled the maneuvers of huge infantries vying for victory. Historians have, in fact, referred to this traditional style of party campaigning as "militarist."

Contemporary political campaigns rely less on infantries and more on "air power." That is, rather than deploy huge armies of workers, contemporary campaigns make use of a number of communications techniques to reach voters and bid for their support. Six techniques are especially important.

Polling Surveys of voter opinion provide the information that candidates and their staffs use to craft campaign strategies. Candidates employ polls to select issues, to assess their own strengths and weaknesses (as well as those of the opposition), to check voter response to the campaign, and to determine the degree to which various constituent groups are susceptible to campaign appeals. Virtually all contemporary campaigns for national and statewide office as well as many local campaigns make extensive use of opinion polling. As we saw in Chapter 6, President Clinton relied heavily on polling data both during and after the 1996 presidential election to shape his rhetoric and guide his policy initiatives.

The Broadcast Media Extensive use of the broadcast media, television in particular, has become the hallmark of the modern political campaign. Generally, media campaigns attempt to follow the guidelines indicated by a candidate's polls, emphasizing issues and personal characteristics that appear important in the poll data. The broadcast media are now so central to modern campaigns that most candidates' activities are tied to their media strategies.[8] Candidate activities are designed expressly to stimulate television news coverage. For instance, members of Congress running for re-election or for president almost always sponsor committee or subcommittee hearings to generate publicity.

Extensive use of radio and television has become the hallmark of the modern statewide or national political campaign. One commonly used broadcast technique is the fifteen-, thirty-, or sixty-second television **spot advertisement,** which permits a candidate's message to be delivered to a target audience before uninterested or hostile viewers can tune it out. Examples of effective spot ads include George Bush's 1988 "Willie Horton" ad, which implied that Bush's opponent, Michael Dukakis, coddled criminals, and Lyndon Johnson's 1964 "daisy girl" ad, which suggested that his opponent, Barry Goldwater, would lead the United States into nuclear war. Television spot ads are used to establish candidate name recognition, to create a favorable image of the candidate and a negative image of the opponent, to link the candidate with desirable groups in the community, and to communicate the candidate's stands on selected issues. Media campaigns generally follow the trail outlined by a candidate's polls, emphasizing issues and personal characteristics that appear important in the poll data.

The 1992 presidential campaign introduced three new media techniques: the talk show interview, the "electronic town hall meeting," and the "infomercial." Candidates used television and radio interview programs to reach the large audiences drawn to this newly popular entertainment program format. Some of these programs allow audience members to telephone the show with questions, which gives candidates a chance to demonstrate that they are interested in the views of ordinary people. The **town meeting** format allows candidates the opportunity to

spot advertisement a fifteen-, thirty-, or sixty-second television campaign commercial that permits a candidate's message to be delivered to a target audience

town meeting a media format in which candidates meet with ordinary citizens. Allows candidates to deliver messages without the presence of journalists or commentators

appear in an auditoriumlike setting and interact with ordinary citizens, thus underlining the candidates' concern with the views and needs of the voters. Moreover, both the talk show appearance and the town meeting allow candidates to deliver their messages to millions of Americans without the input of journalists or commentators who might criticize or question the candidates' assertions.

infomercial a lengthy campaign advertisement on television

The **infomercial** is a lengthy presentation, often lasting thirty minutes. Although infomercials are designed to have the appearance of news programs, they are actually presentations of a candidate's views. Independent candidate Ross Perot made frequent use of infomercials during the 1992 campaign.

Another use of the broadcast media in contemporary campaigns is the televised candidate debate. Televised presidential debates began with the famous 1960 Kennedy-Nixon clash. Today, both presidential and vice presidential candidates hold debates, as do candidates for statewide and even local offices. Debates allow candidates to reach voters who have not fully made up their minds about the election. Moreover, debates can increase the visibility of lesser-known candidates. In 1960, John F. Kennedy's strong performance in the presidential debate was a major factor in bringing about his victory over the much-better-known Richard Nixon.

Phone Banks   Through the broadcast media, candidates communicate with voters en masse and impersonally. Phone banks, on the other hand, allow campaign workers to make personal contact with hundreds of thousands of voters. Personal contacts of this sort are thought to be extremely effective. Again, polling data serve to identify the groups that will be targeted for phone calls. Computers select phone numbers from areas in which members of these groups are concentrated. Staffs of paid or volunteer callers, using computer-assisted dialing systems and prepared scripts, then place calls to deliver the candidate's message. The targeted groups are generally those identified by polls as either uncommitted or weakly committed, as well as strong supporters of the candidate who are contacted simply to encourage them to vote.

Direct Mail   Direct mail serves both as a vehicle for communicating with voters and as a mechanism for raising funds. The first step in a direct-mail campaign is the purchase or rental of a computerized mailing list of voters deemed to have some particular perspective or social characteristic. Often sets of magazine subscription lists or lists of donors to various causes are employed. For example, a candidate interested in reaching conservative voters might rent subscription lists from the *National Review, Human Events,* or *Conservative Digest;* a candidate interested in appealing to liberals might rent subscription lists from the *New York Review of Books* or *The New Republic.* Considerable fine-tuning is possible. After obtaining the appropriate mailing lists, candidates usually send pamphlets, letters, and brochures describing themselves and their views to voters believed to be sympathetic. Different types of mail appeals are made to different electoral subgroups. Often the letters sent to voters are personalized. The recipient is addressed by name in the text and the letter appears actually to have been signed by the candidate. Of course, these "personal" letters are written and even signed by a computer.

In addition to its use as a political advertising medium, direct mail has also become an important source of campaign funds. Computerized mailing lists permit campaign strategists to pinpoint individuals whose interests, background, and activities suggest that they may be potential donors to the campaign. Letters of solicitation are sent to these potential donors. Some of the money raised is then used to purchase additional mailing lists. Direct-mail solicitation can be enormously effective.[9]

Professional Public Relations   Modern campaigns and the complex technology upon which they rely are typically directed by professional public relations consultants. Virtually all serious contenders for national and statewide office retain the services of professional campaign consultants. Increasingly, candidates for local office, too, have come to rely upon professional campaign managers. Consultants offer candidates the expertise necessary to conduct accurate opinion polls, produce television commercials, organize direct-mail campaigns, and make use of sophisticated computer analyses.

The number of technologically oriented campaigns increased greatly after 1971. The Federal Election Campaign Act of 1971 prompted the creation of large numbers of political action committees (PACs) by a host of corporate and ideological groups. This development increased the availability of funds to political candidates—conservative candidates in particular—which meant in turn that the new technology could be used more extensively. Initially, the new techniques were employed mainly by individual candidates who often made little or no effort to coordinate their campaigns with those of other political aspirants sharing the same party label. For this reason, campaigns employing new technology sometimes came to be called "candidate-centered" efforts, as distinguished from the traditional party-coordinated campaign. Nothing about the new technology, however, precluded its use by political party leaders seeking to coordinate a number of campaigns. In recent years, party leaders have learned to make good use of modern campaign technology. The difference between the old and new political methods is not that the latter are inherently candidate-centered while the former are strictly a party tool; it is a matter of the types of political resources upon which each method depends.

The Internet   Still another new media technique was introduced in the 1996 presidential campaign. This was the use of the Internet as a political medium. The major candidates and many minor candidates created Web pages that provided biographical data, information about the candidates' positions on various issues, and even photographs of the candidates and their family members. The Web pages also provided voters with information about how to become involved in the candidates' campaign efforts. As discussed in Chapter 7, candidate Web sites are most likely to be visited by individuals who already agree with the candidate's views and hence are not likely to change many votes. Nevertheless, these sites may help reinforce the commitments of loyalists and can encourage the faithful to work on behalf of their candidate.

In addition to Web sites, candidates are beginning to use the Internet for targeted advertising campaigns. In the 2000 contest, the politician who made the most extensive use of the Internet was John McCain. McCain used his Web site to mobilize volunteers and to raise hundreds of thousands of dollars for his unsuccessful bid for the Republican presidential nomination. In the future, all politicians will use the Web to collect information about potential voters and supporters, which, in turn, will allow them to personalize mailings and calls as well as e-mail advertisements. One consultant now refers to politics on the Internet as "netwar," and asserts that "small, smart attackers" can defeat more powerful opponents in the new, information-age "battlespace."[10] Although the Internet has not yet become a dominant force in political campaigns, most politicians and consultants believe that its full potential for customizing political appeals is only now beginning to be realized.

FROM LABOR-INTENSIVE TO CAPITAL-INTENSIVE POLITICS

The displacement of organizational methods by the new political technology is, in essence, a shift from labor-intensive to capital-intensive competitive electoral practices. Campaign tasks that were once performed by masses of party workers with some cash now require fewer personnel but a great deal more money, for the new political style depends on polls, computers, and other electronic paraphernalia. Of course, even when workers and organization were the key electoral tools, money had considerable political significance. Nevertheless, during the nineteenth century, national political campaigns in the United States employed millions of people. Indeed, as many as 2.5 million individuals did political work during the 1880s.[11] The direct cost of campaigns, therefore, was relatively low. For example, in 1860, Abraham Lincoln spent only $100,000—which was approximately twice the amount spent by his chief opponent, Stephen Douglas.

Modern campaigns depend heavily on money. Each element of the new political technology is enormously expensive. A sixty-second spot announcement on prime-time network television costs hundreds of thousands of dollars each time it is aired. Opinion surveys can be quite expensive; polling costs in a statewide race can easily reach or exceed the six-figure mark. Campaign consultants can charge substantial fees. A direct-mail campaign can eventually become an important source of funds but is very expensive to initiate. The inauguration of a serious national direct-mail effort requires at least $1 million in "front-end cash" to pay for mailing lists, brochures, letters, envelopes, and postage.[12] Although the cost of televised debates is covered by the sponsoring organizations and the television stations and is therefore free to the candidates, even debate preparation requires substantial staff work, research, and, of course, money. It is the expense of the new technology that accounts for the enormous cost of recent American national elections.

Certainly "people power" is not irrelevant to modern political campaigns. Candidates continue to utilize the political services of tens of thousands of volunteer workers. Nevertheless, in the contemporary era, even the recruitment of campaign workers has become a matter of electronic technology. Employing a technique called "instant organization," paid telephone callers use phone banks to contact individuals in areas targeted by a computer (which they do when contacting potential voters, as we discussed before). Volunteer workers are recruited from among these individuals. A number of campaigns—Richard Nixon's 1968 presidential campaign was the first—have successfully used this technique.

The displacement of organizational methods by the new political technology has the most far-reaching implications for the balance of power among contending political groups. Labor-intensive organizational tactics allowed parties whose chief support came from groups nearer the bottom of the social scale to use the numerical superiority of their forces as a partial counterweight to the institutional and economic resources more readily available to the opposition. The capital-intensive technological format, by contrast, has given a major boost to the political fortunes of those forces whose sympathizers are better able to furnish the large sums now needed to compete effectively.[13] Indeed, the new technology permits financial resources to be more effectively harnessed and exploited than was ever before possible.

Dominated by the new technology, electoral politics has become a contest in which the wealthy and powerful have a decided advantage. Furthermore, both political parties are compelled to rely heavily on the support of well-funded special interests—a situation that has become clear in the fund-raising scandals that have plagued both parties in recent years. We shall return to this topic later in this chapter.

The 2000 Elections

During periods of economic prosperity, Americans generally return the party in power to office. The 2000 national elections were held during a period of peace and one of the greatest periods of economic prosperity America has ever known. To further enhance the Democrats' prospects, Democratic partisans continued to outnumber Republican identifiers in the national electorate. Thus, all things considered, it seemed more than likely that Vice President Al Gore and his running mate, Connecticut senator Joe Lieberman, would lead the Democratic Party to victory against an inexperienced and little-known Republican presidential nominee— Texas governor George W. Bush. Bush is, of course, the eldest son of former president George Bush, who had been driven from office by Bill Clinton and Al Gore in 1992. Indeed, most academic models of election outcomes predicted an easy Democratic victory, with some even forecasting a Gore landslide.

Nevertheless, when the results of the vote finally became known, George W. Bush and his running mate, former defense secretary Dick Cheney, appeared to have eked out the narrowest of electoral college victories—271 to 267—over Gore and Lieberman (see Figure 10.3 on page 392). Indeed, in terms of popular vote totals, the Gore/Lieberman ticket actually outpolled the Republicans by slightly more than 500,000 votes, or about one-half of 1 percent of the approximately 105 million votes cast across the nation.

Election night produced unusual drama and confusion when it became clear that the election's outcome would hinge on voting results in Florida, a state with twenty-five electoral votes. Initially, the television networks declared Gore the winner in Florida on the basis of exit poll results. This projection seemed to indicate that Gore would likely win the presidency. Later that night, however, as votes were counted, it became clear that the exit polls were incorrect and that the Florida results were much in doubt. In the early hours of the next morning, all of the votes were tallied and Bush seemed to have won by fewer than 2,000 votes, out of nearly six million cast across the state. Vice President Gore called Governor Bush and conceded defeat.

Within an hour, however, Gore was on the phone to Bush again—this time to withdraw his concession. Under Florida law, the narrowness of Bush's victory— less than one-tenth of 1 percent—triggered an automatic recount. Moreover,

Figure 10.3   Distribution of Electoral Votes in the 2000 Election

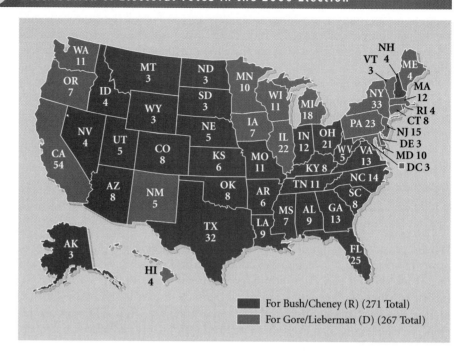

For Bush/Cheney (R) (271 Total)
For Gore/Lieberman (D) (267 Total)

reports of election irregularities had begun to surface. For example, nearly 20,000 votes in Palm Beach County had been invalidated because voters, apparently confused by the ballot, had indicated more than one presidential choice. Given the closeness of the race and the various uncertainties, Democrats decided to await the results of a statewide recount of the vote.

While the recount and the counting of overseas absentee ballots narrowed Bush's margin of victory to a mere 980 votes, it did not change the result. In the meantime, Democrats filed a series of court challenges to the outcome, calling for a hand recount in at least three counties, Miami-Dade, Broward, and Palm Beach. Although Katherine Harris, Florida's top election official, announced that she would not accept the results of these hand recounts, Florida's supreme court ruled that the recounts must be included in the state's official election results. Under disputed circumstances, Miami-Dade County decided not to recount and Palm Beach County missed the deadline for recounted ballots. Gore gained several hundred votes in Broward County but not enough to change the results. These events led to further lawsuits in the Florida courts, the U.S. Court of Appeals, and the U.S. Supreme Court, as Gore refused to concede defeat until all possible legal appeals had been made. Florida's supreme court gave Gore a last-minute reprieve by ordering the manual recounting of approximately 43,000 ballots statewide. Bush appealed this hand recount to the U.S. Supreme Court. By a narrow 5-4 margin, the Court blocked the further counting of Florida's disputed votes, effectively handing the presidency to Bush after a thirty-five-day struggle.

In Senate and House races, voting was also extremely close. Democrats gained some ground in both congressional chambers, but not enough to deprive the GOP of its control of either. Republicans held a narrow six-seat advantage in the House. The Senate was evenly divided 50-50, but with Vice President Dick Cheney casting any tie-breaking votes, the GOP held a slight advantage. Several months after the election, Republican senator Jim Jeffords of Vermont decided to leave the GOP and become an Independent. Jeffords's defection gave the Democrats a majority in the Senate and control of the upper chamber. Yet on election night, Republicans appeared to have carried the day. Given an extremely buoyant economy, a nation at peace, and an edge in partisan attachments, how could the Democrats have lost? How could the race even have been close?

One key reason Al Gore and the Democrats were unable to capitalize on what seemed to be an ideal set of conditions was the tenor of Gore's national campaign. Early in the 2000 campaign, Gore made the fateful decision to distance himself from the person and political strategy of his boss, President Bill Clinton. Gore said repeatedly to interviewers, "I am my own man." Journalists correctly interpreted this declaration to mean that Gore wanted to distance himself from the scandals of the Clinton administration. Indeed, he sought to present a picture of moral rectitude and respect for family and religion that would prevent Republicans from linking him to the moral laxity associated with Bill Clinton. Gore made much of the strength of his marriage and religious beliefs. He refused to allow Clinton to participate in his campaign. He selected as his running mate Senator Joe Lieberman, not only the first Jew nominated for national office by either major party, but a man known for his strong religious beliefs and attention to moral values. Lieberman had been one of the first Democrats to criticize Bill Clinton's conduct in the Monica Lewinsky scandal. Gore thus used Lieberman's nomination to distinguish himself from Clinton on a moral level.

Gore's assertion that he wanted to be his own man, however, had another component that many journalists overlooked. Gore sought not only to distinguish himself from Clinton's morals; he also distanced himself from his politics. In 1992 and 1996, Clinton had adopted centrist positions on most domestic and foreign policy issues. In the 1992 election, the Arkansas governor aimed to present himself as a "new Democrat," i.e., one who differed sharply from the liberalism of George McGovern and Walter Mondale, which had brought the party defeat in 1972 and 1984. He adopted moderate positions on economic policy and even seemed to question the Democratic Party's stance on civil rights. He talked about middle-class concerns like crime, welfare reform, and fiscal restraint. His strategy of moderation helped bring victory in 1992 and again in 1996. In the latter year's race, Clinton pursued a strategy of "triangulation," developed by his adviser, Dick Morris. This strategy called for the incumbent president to position himself midway between the liberalism of congressional Democrats and the conservatism of congressional Republicans. According to Morris, holding the center was the key to victory in the national election, and the strategy succeeded.

In choosing to be his own man, Gore abandoned Clinton's strategy. From his perspective, the problem with moderation and triangulation was that they failed to energize core Democratic constituencies, including liberal public interest groups, organized labor, and African Americans. Liberal groups had been furious with

Clinton over his positions on welfare reform and education. Organized labor viewed Clinton as insufficiently committed to its cause; indeed, some unions considered backing Green Party candidate Ralph Nader and his message of opposition to global capitalism. African Americans felt a real rapport with Clinton and supported him as an individual, but expected more vigorous efforts from his successor with regard to civil rights causes.

A variety of the devices used to record votes in the United States are notably prone to errors that can affect election results. For example, in 2000, in the state of Florida, the cumbersome methods used to tally votes may have affected the result of the presidential election. Some voters were confused by the "butterfly ballot" in Palm Beach County, which made it difficult to match candidates and votes and possibly led more than 3,000 people to vote for Pat Buchanan instead of the candidate they intended to vote for, Al Gore.

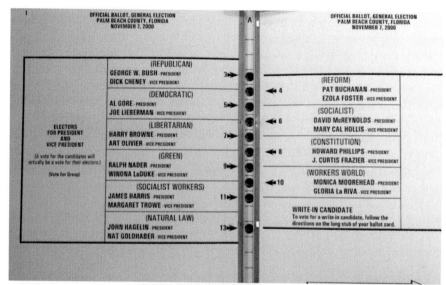

In addition, nearly 20,000 votes in Palm Beach County were invalidated because voters, apparently confused by the butterfly ballot, had indicated more than one presidential choice. Many of these votes were cast in predominantly African American districts. Some civil rights groups claimed that African American voters in other Florida counties had faced long lines and harassment by election officials.

Nationally televised recounts in several Florida counties served only to persuade Americans that the voting process in Florida was problematic. Electoral officials examined ballots to determine whether the "chads," tiny dots of paper that should have been dislodged by the voting machine to indicate a choice, were sufficiently disturbed to allow the ballot to be counted.

Confronting a restive Democratic base, Gore chose to depart from "Clintonism" and move slightly to the left. He attacked drug companies for charging too much. He promised African Americans stronger support for affirmative action. He pledged to expand Social Security and Medicare coverage for the elderly. He courted organized labor by promising to raise the minimum wage and appealed to the powerful teachers' unions by opposing school choice and voucher programs. Most importantly, Gore rejected the notion of using the projected government revenue surplus to cut federal income taxes. Thus, he promised tax cuts to selected Democratic constituencies but argued that an across-the-board cut would benefit only the wealthiest 1 percent of Americans, at the expense of everyone else. In short, Gore became his own man by abandoning triangulation in favor of a more traditional Democratic populism.

Gore's repositioning became clearly evident to the public during the first presidential debate. Bush presented himself as a centrist who would "bring the country together." He eschewed appeals based on race, class, or gender. He promised a tax cut for all Americans and embraced such middle-class issues as education reform. Gore, on the other hand, pursued the rhetoric of Democratic populism. His mantra throughout the debate was that Bush would give a tax cut to the wealthiest 1 percent while ignoring poorer Americans. Rather than wrap himself in the Clinton mantle of moderation—and unprecedented prosperity—Gore chose to appeal to the Democratic base with a message of populism and a hint of class warfare.

Because of Florida's uncertain results, a series of legal challenges and state and federal court rulings followed. A decision by the U.S. Supreme Court was required to formally settle the outcome in Bush's favor. Many Americans, however, were openly critical that our democratically elected president was decided by the unelected justices of the Supreme Court.

Soon after the first debate, Gore's standing in the polls dropped while Bush's rose. By demanding to be his own man and distancing himself from Clinton, Gore made it difficult for himself to claim credit for the prosperity of the Clinton era.

In the closing days of the campaign, Gore abandoned his populist theme and focused instead on his opponent's qualifications for the presidency—Bush was said to be inexperienced and to lack the intelligence needed for the office; also, an old drunk-driving conviction surfaced to cast doubt on his character. This change of campaign tactics helped Gore to close the gap in the final week of the campaign. On Election Day, Gore actually outpolled Bush by a relatively small margin, leading to the first instance since 1888 of the popular-vote winner losing in the electoral college. Against the backdrop of peace and unprecedented prosperity, though, the election should not even have been close. Forced to suffer the indignity of being excluded from the campaign, Bill Clinton must have secretly savored Al Gore's fumbling efforts to be his own man.

When the 2000 election finally ended, one important question remained: Could the nation be governed effectively? The House and Senate were almost evenly divided. The presidency was decided by a few hundred votes and a creaky institution last noticed in 1888. These results seemed tailor-made for a divided government and a divided nation. Consequently, the job of the next president and next Congress promised to be more difficult than at any other time in the nation's recent history.

American history is filled with surprises. As it turned out, the difficulties facing President Bush were not those he might have expected. Terrorist attacks launched against the Pentagon and World Trade Center on September 11, 2001, united the nation and the government. The divisiveness of the election was all but forgotten as Americans of all ideological and partisan stripes joined together to support the new president and his pledge to bring an end to terrorism—an even more formidable task than pacifying Democrats and Republicans.

THE 2002 ELECTIONS: A REFERENDUM ON PRESIDENTIAL LEADERSHIP

In the aftermath of the terrorist attacks of September 11, 2002, President Bush's stature rose dramatically. The president spoke eloquently about the tragedy and, more important, moved decisively to rout terrorists and their backers in Afghanistan. The success of the American military campaign coupled with the sense of determination and decisiveness projected by the White House gave Bush extraordinarily high public approval ratings. The events in Florida surrounding the 2000 elections faded into the background, with arguments about "chads" seeming unimportant relative to concerns about anthrax and nuclear terrorism.

Despite President Bush's popularity, Democrats hoped that they would be able to increase their grip on the Senate and, possibly, even take control of the House of Representatives in the November 2002 elections. Often the party controlling the White House loses congressional seats in the off year, and in this particular off-year election more Republican than Democratic Senate seats were at stake, making the GOP even more vulnerable. Beyond this, however, two other factors appeared to be working in the Democrats' favor. First, the domestic economy, which had been robust during the Clinton years, had taken a turn for the worse during Bush's first year in office. The long stock market boom had come to an end, and millions of Americans who had invested their savings and pension funds in the market found themselves forced to borrow money to pay college tuition bills and compelled to postpone retirement. Hundreds of thousands of other Americans lost their jobs as a result of business failures and corporate belt tightening. Some key sectors, including the computer and telecommunications industries, were especially hard hit. Economic hardship usually works against the party in power, and Democrats hoped that voters would blame the GOP for their problems. Generally speaking, too, since the New Deal, voters have tended to view the Democrats as the party best able to deal with the nation's economic problems. In hard times, Americans are apt to return to the party of FDR, and in the winter of 2001, when Bush took office, hardship certainly was on the rise.

A second factor leading to Democratic optimism was a series of corporate scandals that erupted in early 2002. A number of major corporations, including telecommunications giant WorldCom and energy behemoth Enron, along with their auditors and consultants, seemed to have been systematically misstating earnings and deceiving shareholders in order to inflate their stock prices. Corporate executives and insiders then sold shares at inflated values, just before share prices collapsed at the expense of hapless investors and employees whose pension funds consisted of company stock. Since voters view the GOP as the party closely associated with big business, Democrats reasoned that corporate scandals would hurt the Republicans. To remind voters of the business/GOP tie, Senate Democrats scheduled televised hearings on corporate accounting abuses and sought to link prominent Republicans, including Vice President Dick Cheney, to the scandals.

Unfortunately for Democratic hopes, however, Bush and the Republicans were able to focus public attention on an issue that has traditionally been a source of strength for the GOP, namely, foreign and defense policy. President Bush had already made the war on terrorism and homeland defense the centerpieces of his administration. In summer 2002, though, Bush increased the nation's focus on defense and foreign policy by pointing to Iraq and its dictator, Saddam Hussein, as a major threat to the United States. Bush and his advisers asserted that Saddam was developing weapons of mass destruction that might be used against the United States. The president demanded that Iraq be disarmed and Saddam ousted. Bush called for United Nations action but, asserting what came to be called the Bush doctrine, said that the United States was prepared to employ unilateral military action to preempt threats from Iraq or other sources. After first asserting that it did not need congressional authorization to use force against Iraq, the Bush administration asked for a congressional resolution supporting military action if the president deemed such action to be necessary.

Throughout the late summer and early fall 2002, the twin issues of Iraq and terrorism dominated the headlines, completely overshadowing questions about the economy and corporate greed. The central themes the Democrats hoped would carry them to victory in November had been trumped by what pundits called the Bush strategy of "Iraq around the clock." Polls showed that Iraq had become voters' chief preoccupation and that, even worse for the Democrats, most voters trusted President Bush more than his Democratic foes to lead the nation through this international crisis. In October, hoping to end the nation's focus on Iraq, Senate Democrats backed the resolution of support sought by the president and then sought to change the political subject to the economy. But with the election only weeks away, the Democrats hardly had time to regroup and launch a concerted national campaign.

In the weeks before the election, the president crisscrossed the country, raising $140 million for Republicans and staging rallies in key states and districts. During the last week of the campaign alone, Bush made seventeen campaign appearances in fifteen states. Everywhere, the president reminded loyalists of the importance of homeland defense, the war on terrorism, and Iraq. Democrats countered with the economy and corporate greed, but their message was disjointed and ineffective. Surveys indicated that voters thought both parties deserved equal blame for corporate wrongdoing and that 55 percent of the electorate trusted President Bush more than the Democrats to deal with the nation's economic problems.

By the morning after the election, it was clear that the GOP had been successful. In House races, Republicans had added four seats to increase their majority. In Senate contests, Republicans won seats in Minnesota, Missouri, and Georgia, which, after subtracting their loss in Arkansas, gave them a Senate majority for the first time in nearly two years. The Democrats took some solace from the fact that they had been successful at the gubernatorial level, including key races in Illinois, Michigan, and Pennsylvania. Voter turnout was estimated at roughly 38 percent of those eligible. Once again, most Americans had stayed home despite the heated campaign.

With their new majorities in both houses of Congress, Republicans pledged to move forward on issues that had been stalled in the Democratic Senate. These included the creation of the new Department of Homeland Security, tax cuts, energy policy, and social security. Republicans also planned to speed the confirmation of a number of Bush federal court nominees that had been held up in the Senate judiciary committee. Democrats, for their part, pledged not to "play dead" and reminded their Republican colleagues that congressional rules provided numerous opportunities for delay and obstruction by a determined minority. The day after the election, both sides resumed the real political struggle.

Money and Politics

> **How do candidates raise and spend campaign funds? How does the government regulate campaign spending?**

Modern national political campaigns are fueled by enormous amounts of money. In a national race, millions of dollars are spent on media time, as well as on public opinion polls and media consultants. In 2000, political candidates and independent groups spent a total of more than $3 billion on election campaigns. The average winning candidate in a campaign for a seat in the House of Representatives spent more than $500,000; the average winner in a senatorial campaign spent $4.5 million.[14] The 2000 Democratic and Republican presidential candidates received a total of $150 million in public funds to run their campaigns.[15] Each presidential candidate was also helped by tens of millions of dollars in so-called independent expenditures on the part of corporate and ideological "political action committees" (PACs). As long as such political expenditures are not formally coordinated with a candidate's campaign, they are considered to be constitutionally protected free speech and are not subject to legal limitation or even reporting requirements. Likewise, independent **soft money** spending by political parties is also considered to be an expression of free speech.[16]

soft money money contributed directly to political parties for voter registration and organization

SOURCES OF CAMPAIGN FUNDS

Federal Election Commission data suggest that approximately one-fourth of the private funds spent on political campaigns in the United States is raised through small, direct-mail contributions; about one-fourth is provided by large, individual gifts; and another fourth comes from contributions from PACs. The remaining fourth is drawn from the political parties and from candidates' personal or family resources.[17] Another source of campaign funds, which are not required to be reported to the Federal Election Commission, are independent expenditures by interest groups and parties.

Individual Donors   Direct mail serves both as a vehicle for communicating with voters and as a mechanism for raising funds. Direct-mail fund-raising efforts begin with the purchase or rental of computerized mailing lists of voters deemed likely to support the candidate because of their partisan ties, interests, or ideology. Candidates send out pamphlets, letters, and brochures describing their views and appealing for funds. Tens of millions of dollars are raised by national, state, and local candidates through direct mail each year, usually in $25 and $50 contributions, although in 2000, Bush and Gore collected about three-quarters of their donor contributions from individuals giving the then-$1,000 maximum amount.[18]

Political Action Committees   Political action committees (PACs) are organizations established by corporations, labor unions, or interest groups to channel the contributions of their members into political campaigns. Under the terms of the 1971 Federal Elections Campaign Act, which governs campaign finance in the United States, PACs are permitted to make larger contributions to any given candidate than individuals are allowed to make (see Box 10.1). Individuals may donate a maximum of $2,000 to any single candidate, but a PAC may donate as much as $5,000 to each candidate. Moreover, allied or related PACs often coordinate their campaign contributions, greatly increasing the amount of money a candidate actually receives from the same interest group. As a result, PACs have become central to campaign finance in the United States. Many critics assert that PACs corrupt the political process by allowing corporations and other interests to influence politicians with large contributions. It is by no means clear, however, that PACs corrupt the political process any more than large, individual contributions.

> **political action committee (PAC)**
> a private group that raises and distributes funds for use in election campaigns

In recent years, candidates have learned to use several loopholes in the law governing PACs. For example, until a potential presidential candidate has actually declared his or her candidacy, expenditures by their political action committees generally do not count toward their presidential spending limits. A number of 2000 presidential hopefuls, including Dan Quayle, Jack Kemp, and John Kasich, began early to raise funds that were not subject to the nominal federal limits. In addition, candidates have discovered that federal regulations govern federal PACs, but not state PACs. Before 2000, a number of national candidates established state PACs, which then proceeded to engage in political activities at the national level. For example, Republican presidential hopeful Lamar Alexander established a national PAC and a Tennessee PAC in preparation for the 2000 presidential race. While his national PAC was subject to federal rules, Alexander's Tennessee PAC accepted unlimited contributions. Nothing prevented the Tennessee PAC from engaging in nationally helpful activities such as polling in Iowa or sponsoring a lobster-fest in New Hampshire.

Box 10.1   Federal Campaign Finance Regulation

Campaign Contributions

No individual may contribute more than $2,000 to any one candidate in any single election. Individuals may contribute as much as $25,000 to a national party committee and up to $5,000 to a political action committee. Full disclosure is required by candidates of all contributions over $100. Candidates may not accept cash contributions over $100. Contribution limits are raised for individuals facing "millionaire" opponents.

Political Action Committees

Any corporation, labor union, trade association, or other organization may establish a political action committee (PAC). PACs must contribute to the campaigns of at least five different candidates and may contribute as much as $5,000 per candidate in any given election.

Soft Money

Contributions to state party committees are limited to $10,000 and must be used for get-out-the-vote and registration efforts. National party committees are blocked from most campaign-related expenditures.

Broadcast Advertising

Unions, corporations, and nonprofit agencies may not broadcast "issue ads" mentioning federal candidates within sixty days of a general election and thirty days of a primary election.

Presidential Elections

Candidates in presidential primaries may receive federal matching funds if they raise at least $5,000 in each of twenty states. The money raised must come in contributions of $250 or less. The amount raised by candidates in this way is matched by the federal government, dollar for dollar, up to a limit of $5 million. In the general election, major-party candidates' campaigns are fully funded by the federal government. Candidates may spend no money beyond their federal funding. Independent groups may spend money on behalf of a candidate so long as their efforts are not directly tied to the official campaign. Minor-party candidates may get partial federal funding.

Federal Election Commission (FEC)

The six-member FEC supervises federal elections, collects and publicizes campaign finance records, and investigates violations of federal campaign finance law.

The Candidates   On the basis of the Supreme Court's 1976 decision in *Buckley v. Valeo,* the right of individuals to spend their *own* money to campaign for office is a constitutionally protected matter of free speech and is not subject to limitation. Thus, extremely wealthy candidates often contribute millions of dollars to their own campaigns. Democrat Jon Corzine, for example, spent approximately $60 million of his own funds in a successful New Jersey Senate bid in 2000.

issue advocacy independent spending by individuals or interest groups on a campaign issue but not directly tied to a particular candidate

Independent Spending   As was noted above, "independent" spending is also free from regulation; private groups, political parties, and wealthy individuals, engaging in what is called **issue advocacy,** may spend as much as they wish to help elect one candidate or defeat another, as long as these expenditures are not coordinated with any political campaign. Many business and ideological groups engage in such activities. Some estimates suggest that groups and individuals spent as much as $400 million on issue advocacy—generally through television advertising—during the 2000 elections. The National Rifle Association, for example, spent $3 million reminding voters of the importance of the right to bear arms, while the National Abortion and Reproductive Rights League spent nearly $5 million to express its support for Al Gore.

Some groups are careful not to mention particular candidates in their issue ads to avoid any suggestion that they might merely be fronts for a candidate's campaign committee. Most issue ads, however, are attacks on the opposing candidate's record or character. Organized labor spent more than $35 million in 1996 to attack a number of Republican candidates for the House of Representatives. Business groups launched their own multi-million-dollar issue campaign to defend the GOP House members targeted by labor.[19] In 2000, liberal groups ran ads bashing Bush's record on capital punishment, tax reform, and Social Security. Conservative groups attacked Gore's views on gun ownership, abortion, and environmental regulation.

Parties and Soft Money   State and local party organizations use soft money for get-out-the-vote drives and voter education and registration efforts. These are the party-building activities for which soft-money contributions are nominally made. Most soft-money dollars, however, are spent to assist candidates' re-election efforts in the form of issue advocacy, campaigns on behalf of a particular candidate thinly disguised as mere advocacy of particular issues. For example, in 1996, issue advocacy commercials sponsored by state Democratic Party organizations looked just like commercials for Clinton. The issue commercials praised the president's stand on major issues and criticized the GOP's positions. The only difference was that the issue ads did not specifically call for the re-election of President Clinton. Campaign finance reforms enacted in 2002 included limits on issue ads that mentioned federal candidates by name. Such ads would be prohibited during the sixty-day period preceding a general election and in the thirty days before a primary. In 2000, the Democratic Party raised and spent $371 million in support of its national, state, and local candidates. For its part, the GOP was able to raise more than $525 million. According to the Federal Election Commission, sources of Democratic funds included lawyers and lobbyists; the finance, insurance, and real estate industries; and organized labor. The GOP benefited from contributions by agribusiness, banks and financial interests, transportation concerns, health care corporations, and small business. Critics contend that soft money is less a vehicle for building parties than it is a mechanism for circumventing federal election laws.

In 2002, federal campaign finance legislation prohibited the national parties from using soft money for most campaign purposes. State and local party units would still be permitted to accept contributions of up to $10,000 per donor and to use the money for get-out-the-vote efforts. One long-term effect of this reform will be to increase the political influence of the states vis-à-vis the federal government as each state's party leaders gain additional influence in the political process. Interest and advocacy groups engaging in independent spending will be strengthened even more.

Public Funding   The Federal Elections Campaign Act also provides for public funding of presidential campaigns. As they seek a major party presidential nomination, candidates become eligible for public funds by raising at least $5,000 in

Rules governing campaign finance have been the object of intense debate in recent years. Many Americans believe that government is for sale to the highest bidder and shudder when they watch political candidates raise millions of dollars from corporations, labor unions, lobby groups, and wealthy individuals. For example, in his last year as president, Bill Clinton attended numerous fundraisers that yielded millions of dollars in soft money for the Democratic Party.

individual contributions of $250 or less in each of twenty states. Candidates who reach this threshold may apply for federal funds to match, on a dollar-for-dollar basis, all individual contributions of $250 or less they receive. The funds are drawn from the Presidential Election Campaign Fund. Taxpayers can contribute $1 to this fund, at no additional cost to themselves, by checking a box on the first page of their federal income tax returns. Major party presidential candidates receive a lump sum (currently nearly $75 million) during the summer prior to the general election. They must meet all their general expenses from this money. Third-party candidates are eligible for public funding only if they received at least 5 percent of the vote in the previous presidential race. This stipulation effectively blocks preelection funding for third-party or independent candidates, although a third party that wins more than 5 percent of the vote can receive public funding after the election. In 1980, John Anderson convinced banks to loan him money for an independent candidacy on the strength of poll data showing that he would receive more than 5 percent of the vote and thus would obtain public funds with which to repay the loans. Under current law, no candidate is required to accept public funding for either the nominating races or general presidential election. Candidates who do not accept public funding are not affected by any expenditure limits. Thus, in 1992 Ross Perot financed his own presidential bid and was not bound by the $55 million limit to which the Democratic and Republican candidates were held that year. Perot accepted public funding in 1996. In 2000, George W. Bush refused public funding and raised enough money to finance his own primary campaign. Eventually, Bush raised and spent nearly $200 million—twice the limit to which matching funds would have subjected him. Al Gore accepted federal funding and was nominally bound by the associated spending limitations. Soft money and independent spending, however, not limited by election law at the time, allowed Gore to close the gap with his opponent.

After the 1996 and 2000 national elections, efforts were made to enact reform measures, but these failed. In 2002, however, a scandal involving contributions made by Enron, a giant Texas energy company, gave reformers the ammunition they needed to bring about a set of changes in election law. The most important of

'Of Course It's All Legal —
We Make The Laws, Don't We?'

While each major political party accuses the other of corrupt subservience to wealthy special interests, both Democratic and Republican politicians benefit from unrestricted fund raising practices and have been reluctant to significantly change the rules. One politician who has consistently championed campaign finance reform is Arizona Republican senator John McCain. In 2002, the McCain-Feingold campaign finance reform act was signed into law. This new law limited "soft money" spending by the political parties. Critics charged that the act would limit free speech and weaken political parties while merely diverting campaign funds to alternate channels.

these changes was a ban on campaign spending by the national party organizations, which had previously used hundreds of millions of dollars in so-called soft money contributions from corporations, unions, and individuals to influence electoral contests. This campaign reform may reduce the political influence of wealthy donors but, at the same time, is likely to weaken the national parties—now among the few sources of coherence in America's fragmented political process.

Another reform enacted in 2002, the limits placed upon issue advertising, serves the interests of congressional incumbents, who see advertising limits as means of warding off attack ads financed by groups tied to their opponents. It remains to be seen whether this portion of the new law, which places restraints on political expression, will survive a court test of its constitutionality.

CAMPAIGN FINANCE REFORM

The United States is one of the few advanced industrial nations that permit individual candidates to accept large private contributions from individual or corporate donors. Most mandate either public funding of campaigns or, as in the case of

Britain, require that large private donations be made to political parties rather than to individual candidates. The logic of such a requirement is that a contribution that might seem very large to an individual candidate would weigh much less heavily if made to a national party. Thus, the chance that a donor could buy influence would be reduced.

IMPLICATIONS FOR DEMOCRACY

> **How does money affect how certain social groups achieve electoral success?**

The important role played by private funds in American politics affects the balance of power among contending social groups. Politicians need large amounts of money to campaign successfully for major offices. This fact inevitably ties their interests to the interests of the groups and forces that can provide this money. In a nation as large and diverse as the United States, to be sure, campaign contributors represent many different groups and often represent clashing interests. Business groups, labor groups, environmental groups, and pro-choice and right-to-life forces all contribute millions of dollars to political campaigns. Through such PACs as EMILY's List, women's groups contribute millions of dollars to women running for political office. One set of trade associations may contribute millions to win politicians' support for telecommunications reform, while another set may contribute just as much to block the same reform efforts. Insurance companies may contribute millions of dollars to Democrats to win their support for changes in the health care system, while physicians may contribute equal amounts to prevent the same changes from becoming law.

Interests that donate large amounts of money to campaigns expect and often receive favorable treatment from the beneficiaries of their largesse. For example, in 2000 a number of major interest groups with specific policy goals made substantial donations to the Bush presidential campaign. These interests included airlines, energy producers, banks, tobacco companies, and a number of others. After Bush's election, these interests pressed the new president to promote their legislative and regulatory agendas. For example, MBNA America Bank was a major donor to the 2000 Bush campaign. The bank and its executives gave Bush $1.3 million. The bank's president helped raise millions more for Bush and personally gave an additional $100,000 to the president's inaugural committee after the election. All told, MBNA and other banking companies donated $26 million to the GOP in 2000. Within weeks of his election, President Bush signed legislation providing MBNA and the others with something they had sought for years—bankruptcy laws making it more difficult for consumers to escape credit card debts. Such laws could potentially enhance the earnings of large credit card issuers like MBNA by tens of millions of dollars every year.

In a similar vein, a coalition of manufacturers led by the U.S. Chamber of Commerce and the National Association of Manufacturers also provided considerable support for Bush's 2000 campaign. This coalition sought, among other things, the repeal of federal rules promulgated in 2000 by the federal Occupational Safety and Health Administration (OSHA), which were designed to protect workers from repetitive motion injuries. Again, within weeks of his election, the president approved a resolution rejecting the rules. In March 2001, the House and Senate both voted to kill the ergonomic regulations.

Despite the diversity of contributors, not all interests play a role in financing political campaigns. Only those interests that have a good deal of money to spend can make their interests known in this way. These interests are not monolithic, but they do not completely reflect the diversity of American society. The poor, the destitute, and the downtrodden also live in America and have an interest in the outcome of political campaigns. Who is to speak for them? Who benefits from the American system of private funding of campaigns?

THE ELECTORAL PROCESS AND AMERICAN POLITICAL VALUES

As we have seen throughout this book, Americans' most fundamental values often clash, leaving us perplexed as to the best way to proceed. In the realm of electoral politics, the question of campaign finance produces such a clash of values. On the one hand, most Americans are wary of the high cost of campaigns and the apparently sinister role of campaign contributions in the political process. Through their contributions, wealthy individuals and well-heeled interest groups seek to influence election outcomes, the behavior of elected officials and, through so-called issue advertising, even the tenor of the political debate.

The problem, however, is that we find ourselves with a case of competing political ends. While reform of spending practices might appear to advance the goal of political equality, it might do so at the expense of liberty. Don't we want to encourage vigorous and lively political debate—even though it may be expensive? Should not any group of citizens be free to promote its political ideas at its own expense? These are questions worth pondering and, as we often see in political life, dilemmas with no quick and easy solution.

How Voters Decide

Whatever the capacity of those with the money and power to influence the electoral process, it is the millions of individual decisions on Election Day that ultimately determine electoral outcomes. Sooner or later the choices of voters weigh more heavily than the schemes of campaign advisers or the leverage of interest groups.

Three factors influence voters' decisions at the polls: partisan loyalty, issue and policy concerns, and candidate characteristics.

> ➤ **What are the primary influences on voters' decisions?**

PARTISAN LOYALTY

Many studies have shown that most Americans identify more or less strongly with one or the other of the two major political parties. Partisan loyalty was considerably stronger during the 1940s and 1950s than it is today. But even now most voters feel a certain sense of identification or kinship with the Democratic or Republican party. This sense of identification is often handed down from parents to children and is reinforced by social and cultural ties. Partisan identification predisposes voters in favor of their party's candidates and against those of the opposing party (see Figure 10.4). At the level of the presidential contest, issues and candidate personalities may become very important, although even here many Americans supported George W. Bush or Al Gore in the 2000 race only because of partisan loyalty. But partisanship is more likely to assert itself in the less-visible races, where issues and

Figure 10.4   The Effect of Party Identification on the Vote, 2000

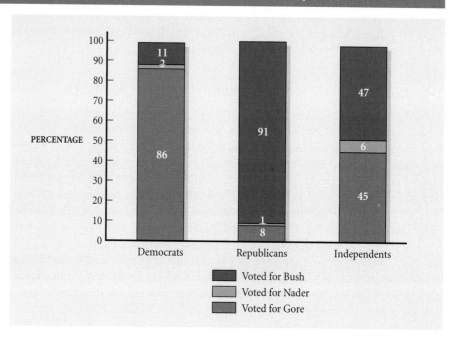

the candidates are not as well known. State legislative races, for example, are often decided by voters' party ties. Once formed, voters' partisan loyalties seldom change. Voters tend to keep their party affiliations unless some crisis causes them to reexamine the bases of their loyalties and to conclude that they have not given their support to the appropriate party. During these relatively infrequent periods of electoral change, millions of voters can change their party ties. For example, at the beginning of the New Deal era, between 1932 and 1936, millions of former Republicans transferred their allegiance to Franklin Roosevelt and the Democrats.

ISSUES

Issues and policy preferences are a second factor influencing voters' choices at the polls. Voters may cast their ballots for the candidate whose position on economic issues they believe to be closest to their own. Similarly, they may select the candidate who has what they believe to be the best record on foreign policy. Issues are more important in some races than others. If candidates actually "take issue" with one another, that is, articulate and publicize very different positions on important public questions, then voters are more likely to be able to identify and act on whatever policy preferences they may have.

The ability of voters to make choices on the basis of issue or policy preferences is diminished, however, if competing candidates do not differ substantially or do not focus their campaigns on policy matters. Very often, candidates deliberately take the safe course and emphasize topics that will not be offensive to any voters. Thus, candidates often trumpet their opposition to corruption, crime, and infla-

Elections in democratic societies offer the public an opportunity to approve or criticize the recent performance of its representatives. In elections after a recent war, for instance, one would expect democracies to throw out of office leaders who have not been militarily successful. History supports this claim. After the Korean War became stalemated, Harry Truman lost to General Dwight D. Eisenhower in the 1952 presidential election. After popular protests against American involvement in Vietnam in 1968, Lyndon Johnson's political career was effectively finished. What remains an open question, however, is whether democratic leaders actually gain much political capital from military *victories*.

There are many examples of democratic leaders who were able to translate military victory into election or re-election. George Washington was elected the first president because of his leadership during the Revolutionary War. Theodore Roosevelt became president in 1904 because of his accomplishments in the Spanish-American War. Franklin Roosevelt remained president in 1940 and 1944 because of his successful leadership during World War II. Yet there are also examples of parties and presidents who were not able to make this translation. The Democratic party suffered setbacks after both world wars. More recently, George H. W. Bush lost his re-election campaign in 1992, shortly after being one of the most successful and popular wartime leaders in American history.

What explains the inconsistent support that democratic citizens have for successful wartime leaders? One answer, according to political scientist Kurt Taylor Gaubatz, is the nature of the public.[1] On the one hand, the public can become belligerent. Especially when it has become morally outraged over an injustice, it is eager to support military campaigns to address this injustice. Sometimes, demagogues use these campaigns to reinforce their authority over the public. On the other hand, the public also has pacifistic inclinations. This position is understandable in a society in which citizens have a voice in deciding whether they or their loved ones will be potential casualties. This inconsistent support can also be explained by the presence in free societies of antiwar elites. Given the large amount of moral and material support required to sustain a war effort, it does not take much work for antiwar elites to put proponents of the war on the defensive. An example of this is the way isolationists were able to frustrate Franklin Roosevelt's efforts to enter the Second World War until the Japanese bombed Pearl Harbor. In a democratic society, leaders must be careful about being accused of warmongering. Although some politicians may hope to gain from the "rally-round-the-flag effect," most democratic politicians aim to situate themselves closer to the pacifistic sentiment of the public, especially in an election season. While President George W. Bush launched a military response to the September 11 terrorist attacks, he has, thus far, been careful not to expand military action beyond Afghanistan to the other nations, like Iraq, that he included as members of the "axis of evil."

The most accurate explanation of the democratic public, then, is that it is protean: it changes in response to the circumstances in the world. When military action seems morally justified and liable to succeed, the public is willing to back its leaders. Yet when war seems unjustified, or is no longer a pressing topic, then the public weighs its decisions on a different scale.

[1] Kurt Taylor Gaubatz, *Elections and War: The Electoral Incentive in the Democratic Politics of War and Peace* (Stanford, CA: Stanford University Press, 1999).

---

tion. Presumably, few voters favor these things. Although it may be perfectly reasonable for candidates to take the safe course and remain as inoffensive as possible, this candidate strategy makes it extremely difficult for voters to make their issue or policy preferences the basis for their choices at the polls.

Voters' issue choices usually involve a mix of their judgments about the past behavior of competing parties and candidates and their hopes and fears about candidates' future behavior. Political scientists call choices that focus on future behavior

prospective voting voting based on the imagined future performance of a candidate

retrospective voting voting based on the past performance of a candidate

prospective voting, while those based on past performance are called **retrospective voting.** To some extent, whether prospective or retrospective evaluation is more important in a particular election depends on the strategies of competing candidates. Candidates always endeavor to define the issues of an election in terms that will serve their interests. Incumbents running during a period of prosperity will seek to take credit for the economy's happy state and define the election as revolving around their record of success. This strategy encourages voters to make retrospective judgments. By contrast, an insurgent running during a period of economic uncertainty will tell voters it is time for a change and ask them to make prospective judgments. Thus, Bill Clinton focused on change in 1992 and prosperity in 1996, and through well-crafted media campaigns was able to define voters' agenda of choices.

In 2000, the key issues at the presidential level were taxes, Social Security reform, health care, and education. Bush promised an across-the-board tax cut while Gore asserted that such a move would benefit wealthy Americans, at the expense of the middle class. Both candidates proposed plans to strengthen the Social Security system, with Bush advocating partial privatization of the system; Gore, on the other hand, promised to more adequately fund the current system. In the realm of health care, both candidates promised prescription drug plans for seniors. Associated Press exit polls conducted on Election Day indicated that Bush voters saw taxes as the central issue of the campaign, while Gore voters focused on prescription drugs and Social Security.

CANDIDATE CHARACTERISTICS

Candidates' personal attributes always influence voters' decisions. Some analysts claim that voters prefer tall candidates to short ones, candidates with shorter names to candidates with longer names, and candidates with lighter hair to candidates with darker hair. Perhaps these rather frivolous criteria do play some role. But the more important candidate characteristics that affect voters' choices are race, ethnicity, religion, gender, geography, and social background. In general, voters prefer candidates who are closer to themselves in terms of these categories; voters presume that such candidates are likely to have views and perspectives close to their own. Moreover, they may be proud to see someone of their ethnic, religious, or geographic background in a position of leadership. This is why, for many years, politicians sought to "balance the ticket," making certain that their party's ticket included members of as many important groups as possible.

Just as candidates' personal characteristics may attract some voters, they may repel others. Many voters are prejudiced against candidates of certain ethnic, racial, or religious groups. And for many years voters were reluctant to support the candidacies of women, although this appears to be changing.

Voters also pay attention to candidates' personality characteristics, such as "decisiveness," "honesty," and "vigor." In recent years, integrity has become a key election issue. During the 1992 campaign, George Bush accused Bill Clinton of seeking to mislead voters about his anti–Vietnam War activities and his efforts to avoid the draft during the 1960s. This, Bush said, revealed that Clinton lacked the integrity required of a president. Clinton, in turn, accused Bush of resorting to mudslinging because of his poor standing in the polls—an indication of Bush's own character deficiencies. In the 2000 presidential race, Al Gore chose Joe Lieberman as his running mate in part because Lieberman had been sharply critical of Bill Clinton's moral lapses. The senator's presence on the Democratic ticket thus helped to defuse the GOP's efforts to link Gore to Clinton's questionable character. As the race progressed, Gore sought to portray Bush as lacking the intelligence and experience needed for the presidency. This effort met with some success, as a number of talk-show hosts began to caricature Bush as a simpleton who knew little about domestic or foreign policy. Exit polls indicated that many voters also had concerns about Bush's intelligence. For his part, Bush sought to portray Gore as dishonest and duplicitous—a man who would say anything to get elected. This effort, too, led to talk-show caricatures and raised concerns among voters. Ultimately, according to Associated Press exit polls, Bush won the votes of those who said they were concerned about "honesty," while Gore received the support of individuals who felt "experience" was an important presidential attribute.

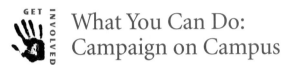

What You Can Do: Campaign on Campus

The most visible aspect of American politics may be election campaigns. Candidates do their best to get the names, images, ideas, and sound bites disseminated among potential donors and voters. They seek television and radio talk show appearances and they buy television time and radio advertisements. They hold fund-raising dinners. They often participate in mass mailings and telephone calling to targeted publics. They engineer media events to get print coverage. Generally, they seek to inundate the public with positive messages about themselves and negative messages about their opponents. Campaigning in a democracy is a high-visibility affair.

At any given moment, someone in America is considering, setting up, or actually running a campaign for elected office at the local, state, or national level. You can certainly get involved in a political campaign but your participation is likely to be highly restricted and guided. That is because today's political campaigns are increasingly orchestrated and conducted by professional political consultants who, along with the candidate, make the key decisions and then tell the amateurs what to do.

Your amateur status notwithstanding, you can participate in orchestrating and conducting a political campaign for elected office if you focus your sights on your own student government. In this area, all contenders are amateurs. Is a classmate, colleague, or friend running for the student senate or the student programming board? She will need strategists to figure out how best to get the attention and support of likely voters. She will need managers to recruit volunteers and coordinate their activities. Campaigning is hard work; it can be tiring; but it also can be exhilarating. Here are some practical suggestions for thinking through your campaign strategy.

- Gauge the preferences of the student body. Ask students what changes they think are needed or desirable. See if the concerns of residential students differ from those of commuter students or those involved in sororities and fraternities or students of particular racial, national, or religious identities. Know your electorate.

- Determine which students are most likely to vote. Student apathy on most campuses means that relatively few students will turn out for elections. Nevertheless, think strategically. What issues are likely to rouse students from apathy to action? Do students who are affiliated with particular groups have higher turnout rates than the general student population? How do you direct your appeal to likely voters?
- Develop a plan for getting your candidate known. Posters, signs, and flyers are common ways to get her name out in public. Can you get coverage in the student newspaper or on the student radio station? Can you create a catchy slogan that is likely to stick in people's minds? In an electoral campaign, gaining name recognition is half the battle.
- Figure out how to communicate your candidate's stand on key issues. Consider sponsoring or participating in candidate debates or forums, scheduling visits to student organizations and dormitories, forging alliances with student interest organizations likely to support your candidate's views, or having her spend time talking to students in a central area of campus.
- As the election approaches, devote your energy to getting out the vote among those students most likely to support your candidate. Call the leaders of allied groups and urge them to get their members to vote. Hang "get out the vote" brochures on dormitory door handles. Place posters in strategic places. On the day of the election, remind students to vote (and suggest that they vote for your wonderful candidate).
- Finally, the best strategy is useless unless you have the organization and volunteers to survey student preferences and voting patterns, gain name recognition, set up debates, visits, and alliances, and get out the vote. Accordingly, work out a strategy for recruiting, coordinating, and deploying a cadre of volunteers.

Once you get past some of the frustrations of campaigning and share in its joys, you may decide to run for student office yourself. Perhaps you can make a positive difference on your campus. Which position should you seek? Should you go after a low-profile position with limited autonomy and responsibility? Or should you run for student body president? Talk to people already involved in student government. Find out the options and the responsibilities each position entails. Then consider the time and energy involved in running for office and the likely workload if you are elected to office. If you still have an interest and think you can handle the workload, go for it.

Summary

At the time of America's Founding, the right to vote was generally limited to white males over the age of twenty-one. Many states also limited voting rights to those who owned property. Over the years, voting rights were expanded to give all adult Americans the right to participate in elections. Despite this, only about half of all American citizens over the age of eighteen actually vote in presidential elections. Turnout is limited by America's voter registration requirements and the absence of a strong party system to "get out the vote."

Three types of elections are held in the United States: general elections, primary elections, and runoff elections. In most contests, the candidate winning a plurality of the vote is the victor. In some contests, however, victory requires a majority of the votes cast, while others rely on proportional representation. State legislatures draw the boundaries of electoral districts. Often, political forces use a redistricting technique called gerrymandering to attempt to gain political advantage. Presidential elections are different from other American electoral contests. The president is elected indirectly through the electoral college.

Election campaigns are directed by candidates and their advisers. Candidates must secure endorsements, construct an organization, and raise money for both the primary and the general elections. Funds are raised from individuals and from political action committees. Presidential candidates must campaign in a series of statewide primaries and caucuses that lead up to the national party conventions, where the formal Democratic and Republican nominations take place. In addition to candidates' efforts, election outcomes are decided by partisan loyalty, voter response to issues, and voter response to candidates' personalities and qualifications.

The fact that many Americans do not vote gives the American political process a quasidemocratic character. Nonvoters tend to be drawn from low-income, low-education, and minority groups. Neither political party has shown much interest in vigorously promoting voter participation.

For Further Reading

Black, Earl, and Merle Black. *The Vital South: How Presidents Are Elected.* Cambridge, MA: Harvard University Press, 1992.

Carmines, Edward G., and James Stimson. *Issue Evolution: The Racial Transformation of American Politics.* Princeton, NJ: Princeton University Press, 1988.

Fowler, Linda, and Robert D. McClure. *Political Ambition: Who Decides to Run for Congress.* New Haven, CT: Yale University Press, 1989.

Ginsberg, Benjamin, and Martin Shefter. *Politics by Other Means: Institutional Conflict and the Declining Significance of Elections in America.* New York: Norton, 1999.

Sorauf, Frank. *Inside Campaign Finance: Myths and Realities.* New Haven, CT: Yale University Press, 1992.

Tate, Katherine. *From Protest to Politics: The New Black Voters in American Elections.* Cambridge, MA: Harvard University Press, 1994.

Wilcox, Clyde. *God's Warriors: The Christian Right in Twentieth-Century America.* Baltimore: Johns Hopkins University Press, 1991.

Witt, Linda, Karen Paget, and Glenna Matthews. *Running as a Woman: Gender and Power in American Politics.* New York: Free Press, 1994.

Study Outline

www.wwnorton.com/wtp4e

1. In democratic systems, elections can be used to replace current officeholders as well as to serve as institutions of legitimation.
2. Elections also help to promote government accountability and serve as a source of protection for groups in society.

Elections in America

1. In the American federal system, the responsibility for organizing elections rests largely with state and local governments.
2. State legislators routinely seek to influence electoral outcomes by manipulating the organization of electoral districts.
3. Prior to the 1890s, voters cast ballots according to political parties. The advent of the neutral ballot allowed voters to choose individual candidates rather than a political party as a whole.
4. Americans do not vote directly for presidential candidates. Rather, they choose electors who are pledged to support a party's presidential candidate.

Election Campaigns

1. The first step in campaigning involves the organization of supporters to help the candidate raise funds and create public name recognition.
2. The next steps of campaigning involve hiring experts—campaign managers, media consultants, pollsters, etc.—to aid in developing issues and a message and communicating them to the public.
3. Because most of the time a major-party nomination is necessary for electoral success, candidates must seek a party's nomination in primary elections.

Presidential Elections

1. Presidential candidates secure a party's nomination by running in state party primaries and caucuses.
2. Nominations of presidential candidates were first made in caucuses of a party's members of Congress. This system was replaced, in the 1830s, by nominating conventions, which were designed to be a more democratic, deliberative method of nominating candidates.
3. Contemporary conventions merely ratify a party's presidential and vice presidential nominations, although conventions still draft the party platform and adopt rules governing the party and its future conventions.
4. In recent years, the role of the parties during the general campaign has been transformed by the introduction of high-tech campaign techniques, including polls, using the broadcast media, phone banks, direct mail, and professional public relations.
5. In capital-intensive campaigns, the main technique is to use the broadcast media to present the electorate with themes and issues that will induce them to support one candidate over another.

Money and Politics

1. Campaign funds in the United States are provided by small, direct-mail contributions, large gifts, PACs, political parties, candidates' personal resources, and public funding. In 2000, some candidates also benefited from issue advocacy.
2. Campaign finance is regulated by the Federal Elections Campaign Act of 1971. Following the 1996 and 2000 elections, the role of soft money was scrutinized. The McCain-Feingold bill, a bipartisan attempt to restrict soft money contributions and issue advocacy, was passed by Congress in 2002.
3. The role played by private money in American politics affects the relative power of social groups. As a result, less affluent groups have considerably less power in the political system.

How Voters Decide

1. Three factors influence voters' decisions at the polls: partisan loyalty, issues, and candidate characteristics.
2. Partisan loyalty predisposes voters in favor of their party's candidates and against those of the opposing party.
3. The impact of issues and policy preferences on electoral choice is diminished if competing candidates do not differ substantially or do not focus their campaigns on policy matters.
4. Candidates' attributes and personality characteristics always influence voters' decisions.
5. The salience of these three bases of electoral choice varies from contest to contest and from voter to voter.

Practice Quiz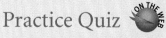

www.wwnorton.com/wtp4e

1. What is the most important difference between democratic and authoritarian electoral systems?
   a) The latter do not allow the defeat of those in power.
   b) There are no elections in authoritarian systems.
   c) Democratic systems use elections as a safety valve for social discontent.
   d) Authoritarian elections are not organized by party.

2. The neutral ballot made it possible for voters to
   a) vote the party line.
   b) split-ticket vote.
   c) send clear mandates for policy change.
   d) both a and b

3. What is the difference between an open and a closed primary?
   a) You must pay a poll tax to vote in a closed primary.
   b) Open primaries allow voters to split the ticket.
   c) In closed primaries, only registered members of a political party may vote to select that party's candidates.
   d) They are fundamentally the same thing.

4. What are the potential consequences of ideological struggles in primary contests?
   a) General election chances may be undermined.
   b) Party extremists may win the nomination.
   c) Typical party supporters may refuse to support the party's nominee.
   d) all of the above

5. What is the most fundamental change in national conventions in the twentieth century?
   a) They no longer nominate presidential candidates.
   b) Now party platforms are written at the convention.
   c) The participation of electoral officials in conventions has continued to decline.
   d) none of the above

6. Which of the following is not an example of a media technique introduced in the 1992 presidential campaign?
   a) the spot advertisement
   b) the town meeting
   c) the infomercial
   d) a, b, and c were all introduced in 1992.

7. In *Buckley v. Valeo*, the Supreme Court ruled that
   a) PAC donations to campaigns are constitutionally protected.
   b) The right of individuals to spend their own money to campaign is constitutionally protected.
   c) The political system is corrupt.
   d) The Federal Elections Campaign Act is unconstitutional.

8. Partisan loyalty
   a) is often handed down from parents to children.
   b) changes frequently.
   c) has little impact on electoral choice.
   d) is mandated in states with closed primaries.

9. Which of the following is *not* a factor that influences voters' decisions?
   a) partisanship
   b) issues
   c) candidate characteristics
   d) the electoral system used to determine the winner

10. If a state has ten members in the U.S. House of Representatives, how many electoral votes does that state have?
    a) two
    b) ten
    c) twelve
    d) can't tell from this information

Critical Thinking Questions

www.wwnorton.com/wtp4e

1. Should race be taken into account when congressional districts are redrawn after each census? If 20 percent of a state is African American, should 20 percent of the districts have an African American majority?
2. What are the sources of campaign money in American politics? Why do candidates for public office need to raise so much money? How has the government sought to balance the competing ideals of free expression and equal representation in regard to campaign financing? Is this yet another example of a conflict between liberty and democracy?
3. Campaign finance reforms enacted in 2002 banned the use of soft money in national elections. What is soft money? Who benefits and who loses from restrictions on the role of soft money?

Key Terms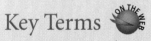

www.wwnorton.com/wtp4e

11 GROUPS AND INTERESTS

What Government Does and Why It Matters

NE OF THE GREATEST economic disasters of September 11 was the effect on America's airline industry. The tremendous losses and direct damage of the attacks coupled with the losses of revenue from the subsequent decline in passengers galvanized the airlines into action. Just ten days after September 11, the airlines were testifying before committees and lobbying in the halls of Congress as well as circulating documents and various forms of expert opinion to the effect that some major carriers would be bankrupt within days and that others might not survive even with federal help. The airlines also circulated press releases containing economic and technical data and professional and academic papers that became the basis of television reports and articles in the large metropolitan papers, news syndicates, and technical journals. Together, the airline representatives, lobbyists, documents, and press releases covered every issue that could possibly arise as members of Congress sketched out a bill to aid the airline industry. Meanwhile, two other important interest groups joined the airlines in working to influence a rescue package. Organized labor joined after receiving assurances that cost cutting would not come out of the salaries and benefits of the pilots and other airline workers. Trial lawyers also came along in support after getting the airline interests to remove from the original bill a cap on insurance claims for injuries or loss of life arising from airplane incidents.

It was late night September 21 when the Senate voted 96-1 and the House 356-54 in favor of a $15 billion rescue package. Of the $15 billion approved in that legislation, $5 billion was for direct grants to "bail out" the airlines for the losses suffered on September 11 and in its immediate aftermath. The remainder was an authorization for $10 billion in "loan guarantees," under the direction of the Office of Management and Budget and a new Air Transport Safety Board comprised of the chairman of the Federal Reserve, the Treasury Secretary, the Transportation Secretary, and the U.S. Comptroller General. These guarantees were government promises to private banks that if an airline went under or otherwise defaulted on a loan, the government would pay that loan. ■

THE case of the airlines exemplifies the power of interest groups in action. The framers of the American Constitution feared the power that could be wielded by organized interests. Yet they believed that interest groups thrived because of liberty—the freedom that all Americans enjoy to organize and express their views. If the government were given the power to regulate or in any way to forbid efforts by organized interests to interfere in the political process, the government would in effect have the power to suppress liberty. The solution to this dilemma was presented by James Madison:

> Take in a greater variety of parties and interest [and] you make it less probable that a majority of the whole will have a common motive to invade the rights of other citizens. . . . [Hence the advantage] enjoyed by a large over a small republic.[1]

According to the Madisonian theory, a good constitution encourages multitudes of interests so that no single interest, which he called a "faction," can ever tyrannize the others. The basic assumption is that competition among interests will produce balance, with all the interests regulating each other.[2] Today, this Madisonian principle of regulation is called **pluralism.** According to pluralist theory, all interests are and should be free to compete for influence in the United States. Moreover, according to a pluralist doctrine, the outcome of this competition is compromise and moderation, since no group is likely to be able to achieve any of its goals without accommodating itself to some of the views of its many competitors.[3]

pluralism the theory that all interests are and should be free to compete for influence in the government. The outcome of this competition is compromise and moderation

Tens of thousands of organized groups have formed in the United States, ranging from civic associations to huge nationwide groups like the National Rifle Association (NRA), whose chief cause is opposition to restrictions on gun ownership, or Common Cause, a public-interest group that advocates a variety of liberal political reforms. Despite the array of interest groups in American politics, however, we can be sure neither that all interests are represented equally nor that the results of this group competition are consistent with the common good. One criticism of interest-group pluralism is its class bias in favor of those with greater financial resources. As one critic put it, "The flaw in the pluralist heaven is that the heavenly chorus sings with a strong upper-class accent."[4] Another assumption of pluralism is that all groups have equal access to the political process and that achieving an outcome favorable to a particular group depends only upon that group's strength and resources, not upon biases inherent in the political system. But, as we shall see, group politics is a political format that has worked and continues to work more to the advantage of some types of interests than others.

■ **In this chapter, we will examine some of the antecedents and consequences of interest-group politics in the United States.** We will first seek to understand the character of interest groups. We will look at types of interests, the organizational components of groups, and the characteristics of members. We will also examine the important question of why people join interest groups.

■ **Second, we will assess the growth of interest-group activity in recent American political history.** The number of interest groups has proliferated in recent years and we will examine the reasons why.

■ **Third, we will review and evaluate the strategies that competing groups use in their struggles for influence.** The quest for political influence takes many forms.

■ **We conclude by evaluating some of the potential problems in trying to reduce the influence of interest groups in the political process.** Interest-group politics is biased in favor of the most wealthy and powerful, but attempts to limit this influence are limits on liberty itself.

The Character of Interest Groups

An **interest group** is a voluntary membership association organized to pursue a common interest (or interests), through political participation, toward the ultimate goal of getting favorable public policy decisions from government. Individuals form groups in order to increase the chance that their views will be heard and their interests treated favorably by the government. Interest groups are organized to influence governmental decisions.

Interest groups are sometimes referred to as "lobbies," but that is somewhat misleading; "lobbying" refers to just one strategy interest groups employ to influence policy makers (as we will see later in this chapter). Interest groups are also sometimes confused with political action committees, which are actually groups that focus on influencing elections rather than trying to influence the elected. One final distinction that we should make is that interest groups are also different from political parties: interest groups tend to concern themselves with the *policies* of government; parties tend to concern themselves with the *personnel* of government.

There are an enormous number of interest groups in the United States, and millions of Americans are members of one or more groups, at least to the extent of paying dues or attending an occasional meeting. By representing the interests of such large numbers of people and encouraging political participation, organized groups can and do enhance American democracy. Organized groups educate their members about issues that affect them. Groups lobby members of Congress and the executive, engage in litigation, and generally represent their members' interests in the political arena. Groups mobilize their members for elections and grassroots lobbying efforts, thus encouraging participation. Interest groups also monitor government programs to make certain that their members are not adversely affected.

> **Why do interest groups form?**

interest group a voluntary membership association that pursues a common cause through political participation

Interest-Group Corporatism

To those who compare and contrast different political systems around the world, the United States is a classic pluralist democracy. As with all types of electoral democracies, forging a policy agenda in the United States relies on the nature of the relationship between government and the general public. This relationship, however, is largely mediated by a diverse array of competitive, decentralized, and uncoordinated social, political, economic, and cultural groups, and is known as *interest-group pluralism*. This pattern stands in contrast to its principal alternative, *interest-group corporatism*, a pattern of interaction between interest groups (such as labor unions and business federations) and government in which interest groups are hierarchically organized; the actions of similar groups (e.g., local labor unions) across the country are closely coordinated by central and national leadership; and nationally organized "peak organizations" ensure the coordination and compliance of all affiliated groups and monopolize both the strategy and practice of negotiating directly with government, as well as implementing the outcomes of these negotiations.

Interest-group pluralism is a characteristic commonly, though not exclusively, found in *consensual democracies*. The vast diversity and decentralized and competitive nature of interest groups in this type of electoral democracy allow multiple entrance points into the political arena for organized and active citizens, increasing the likelihood that government must consider a broader but often uncoordinated front of interests when formulating public policy. Consistent with the logic of consensual democracy, interest-group pluralism expands the inclusiveness of the political system. That is, the institutions of governance in society are more exposed to multiple and largely uncoordinated pressures from groups.

Interest-group corporatism, on the other hand, is a classic feature of majoritarian democracy. The peak organizations and centrally organized nature of interest groups tend to reduce the abundant diversity of interest, funneling and screening public demands through a more restricted array of "gates" into the political arena. This allows for a more regularized and predictable flow of information and demands upon government. As the name implies, majoritarian democracies ideally prefer a design to political institutions (e.g., constitutions, legislatures, executives, courts), which tends to reward political winners with temporary disproportionate power and influence over policy. Thus, political winners enjoy most of the rewards of victory (political appointments, etc.) and share very little with the losers, who are left to await the next round of competition.

Germany is a classic interest-group corporatist democracy. Its labor unions are centrally coordinated through peak organizations. The Federation of German Labor (DGB) coordinates various labor unions, while large businesses are organized through the Federal Association of German Employers (BDA), and industrial concerns are organized through the Federation of German Industry (BDI). The BDA consists of sixty-four employer associations that represent nearly all large and medium employers in Germany, and the BDI organizes thirty-nine separate major industries. The DGB claims to represent 85 percent of the approximately ten million unionized workers in the German workforce (31 percent of German workers were unionized as of 1995). Germany's codetermination laws *(Mitbestimmung)* require all unions to be represented on the boards of large corporations. These peak business and union associations are closely aligned with the major political parties of Germany (the DGB with the left-of-center Social Democrats, and the BDA and BDI with the right-of-center Christian Democratic Union), although as in all corporatist democracies, these players maintain close working relationships with all major political parties in order to ensure continuity in policy despite shifting electoral fortunes of the political parties.

These organizations are professionally staffed and hierarchically organized within the German federal system. The corporatist logic of Germany requires the DGB to be an active player in the negotiations between government, business, and labor over wages and pension schemes, as well as an active participant in shaping federal policy in both the bureaucracy and the various committees of the national legislature.

As with any feature of democracy, no country is a perfect reflection of either interest-group pluralism or interest-group corporatism. Germany's strong federal system and constitution, as well as its complicated electoral system, all reflect features of consensual democracy. Yet, it blends these features with interest-group corporatism, a feature more common among majoritarian democracies.

SOURCES: Arend Lijphart, *Patterns of Democracy: Government Forms and Performance in Thirty-Six Countries* (New Haven: Yale University Press, 1999); Kathleen Thelen, *Union in Parts: Labor Politics in Postwar Germany* (Ithaca: Cornell University Press, 1991).

In all these ways, organized interests can be said to promote democratic politics. But because not all interests are represented equally, interest-group politics works to the advantage of some and the disadvantage of others.

WHAT INTERESTS ARE REPRESENTED?

Business and Agricultural Groups Interest groups come in as many shapes and sizes as the interests they represent. When most people think about interest groups, they immediately think of groups with a direct economic interest in governmental actions. These groups are generally supported by groups of producers or manufacturers in a particular economic sector. Examples of this type of group include the National Petroleum Refiners Association and the American Farm Bureau Federation. At the same time that broadly representative groups such as these are active in Washington, specific companies, such as Shell Oil, IBM, and General Motors, may be active on certain issues that are of particular concern to them.

Labor Groups Labor organizations are equally active lobbyists. The AFL-CIO, the United Mine Workers, and the Teamsters are all groups that lobby on behalf of organized labor. In recent years, groups have arisen to further the interests of public employees, the most significant among these being the American Federation of State, County, and Municipal Employees.

Professional Associations Professional lobbies like the American Bar Association and the American Medical Association have been particularly successful in furthering their members' interests in state and federal legislatures. Financial institutions, represented by organizations such as the American Bankers Association and the National Savings & Loan League, although often less visible than other lobbies, also play an important role in shaping legislative policy.

Public Interest Groups Recent years have witnessed the growth of a powerful "public interest" lobby, purporting to represent interests whose concerns are not addressed by traditional lobbies. These groups have been most visible in the consumer protection and environmental policy areas, although public interest groups cover a broad range of issues. The Natural Resources Defense Council, the Sierra Club, the Union of Concerned Scientists, and Common Cause are all examples of public interest groups.

Ideological Groups Closely related to and overlapping public interest groups are ideological groups, organized in support of a particular political or philosophical perspective. People for the American Way, for example, promotes liberal values, whereas the Christian Coalition focuses on conservative social goals and the National Taxpayers Union campaigns to reduce the size of the federal government.

Public-Sector Groups The perceived need for representation on Capitol Hill has generated a public-sector lobby in the past several years, including the National League of Cities and the "research" lobby. The latter group comprises think tanks and universities that have an interest in obtaining government funds for research and support, and it includes such institutions as Harvard University, the Brookings

> **What interests are represented by these groups?**

Institution, and the American Enterprise Institute. Indeed, universities have expanded their lobbying efforts even as they have reduced faculty positions and course offerings.[5]

WHAT INTERESTS ARE NOT REPRESENTED?

A similar categorization of unrepresented interests cannot be provided precisely because they are not organized and are not able to present us (or governments) their identity and their demands. David Truman tried to put a gentle turn on this phenomenon in what, after fifty years, is still the most systematic treatment of interest groups, *The Governmental Process*. He referred to these interests as "potential interest groups."[6] And he is undoubtedly correct that at any time, as long as there is freedom, any interest shared by a lot of people can develop through "voluntary association" into a genuine interest group that can demand, usually successfully, to get some representation. But the fact remains that many interests—very widely shared interests—do not get organized and recognized.

Under these special circumstances the best we can do is to provide an informed, and distinctly incomplete, inventory of unorganized and unrepresented "potential interest groups":

single mothers   adjunct college instructors
minimum-wage service workers   graduate TAs
nurses' aides   undergrads
medical interns   residents of Middle Eastern origin
the homeless   low-rent and public housing tenants
personal service labor   college athletes
midwives

ORGANIZATIONAL COMPONENTS

> **What are the organizational components of interest groups?**

Although there are many interest groups, most share certain key organizational components. These include leadership, money, an agency or office, and members.

First, every group must have a leadership and decision-making structure. For some groups, this structure is very simple. For others, it can be quite elaborate and involve hundreds of local chapters that are melded into a national apparatus. Interest-group leadership is, in some respects, analogous to business leadership. Many interest groups are initially organized by political entrepreneurs with a strong commitment to a particular set of goals. Such entrepreneurs see the formation of a group as a means both for achieving those goals and for enhancing their own influence in the political process. Just as is true in the business world, however, successful groups often become bureaucratized; the initial entrepreneurial leadership is replaced by a paid professional staff. In the 1960s, for example, Ralph Nader led a loosely organized band of consumer advocates ("Nader's Raiders") in a crusade for product safety that resulted in the enactment of a number of pieces of legislation and numerous regulations, such as the requirement that all new cars be equipped with air bags. Today, Nader remains active in the consumer movement, and his ragtag band of raiders has been transformed into a well-organized and well-financed phalanx of interlocked groups, including Public Citizen, the Center for the Study of Responsive Law, and the

Center for Science in the Public Interest. All of these groups are now led by professional staffs.

Second, every interest group must build a financial structure capable of sustaining an organization and funding the group's activities. Most interest groups rely on membership dues and voluntary contributions from sympathizers. Many also sell some ancillary services to members, such as insurance and vacation tours. Third, most groups establish an agency that actually carries out the group's tasks. This may be a research organization, a public relations office, or a lobbying office in Washington or a state capital.

Finally, all interest groups must attract and keep members. Somehow, groups must persuade individuals to invest the money, time, energy, or effort required to take part in the group's activities. Members play a larger role in some groups than in others. In **membership associations,** group members actually serve on committees and engage in projects. In the case of labor unions, members may march on picket lines, and in the case of political or ideological groups, members may participate in demonstrations and protests. In another set of groups, **staff organizations,** a professional staff conducts most of the group's activities; members are called upon only to pay dues and make other contributions. Among the well-known public interest groups, some, such as the National Organization for Women (NOW), are membership groups, whereas others, such as Defenders of Wildlife and the Children's Defense Fund, are staff organizations.

membership association an organized group in which members actually play a substantial role, sitting on committees and engaging in group projects

staff organization a type of membership group in which a professional staff conducts most of the group's activities

The "Free Rider" Problem   Whether they need individuals to volunteer or merely to write checks, both types of groups need to recruit and retain members. Yet many groups find this task difficult, even when it comes to recruiting members who agree strongly with the group's goals. Why? As economist Mancur Olson explains, the benefits of a group's success are often broadly available and cannot be denied to nonmembers.[7] Such benefits can be called **collective goods.** This term is usually associated with certain government benefits, but it can also be applied to beneficial outcomes of interest-group activity. Following Olson's own example, suppose a number of private property owners live near a mosquito-infested swamp. Each owner wants this swamp cleared. But if one or a few of the owners were to clear the swamp alone, their actions would benefit all the other owners as well, without any effort on the part of those other owners. Each of the inactive owners would be a **free rider** on the efforts of the ones who cleared the swamp. Thus, there is a disincentive for any of the owners to undertake the job alone.

collective goods benefits, sought by groups, that are broadly available and cannot be denied to nonmembers

free riders those who enjoy the benefits of collective goods but did not participate in acquiring them

Since the number of concerned owners is small in this particular case, they might eventually be able to organize themselves to share the costs as well as enjoy the benefits of clearing the swamp. But suppose the numbers of interested people are increased. Suppose the common concern is not the neighborhood swamp but polluted air or groundwater involving thousands of residents in a region, or in fact millions of residents in a whole nation. National defense is the most obvious collective good whose benefits are shared by every resident, regardless of the taxes they pay or the support they provide. As the number of involved persons increases, or as the size of the group increases, the free rider phenomenon becomes more of a problem. Individuals do not have much incentive to become active members and supporters of a group that is already working more or less on their behalf. The group would no doubt be more influential if all concerned individuals were active members—if there were no free riders. But groups will not reduce their efforts just because free riders get the same benefits as dues-paying activists. In fact, groups may try even harder precisely because there are free riders, with the hope that the free riders will be encouraged to join in.

Why Join?   Despite the free rider problem, interest groups offer numerous incentives to join. Most importantly, they make various "selective benefits" available only to group members. These benefits can be information-related, material, solidary, or purposive. Table 11.1 gives some examples of the range of benefits in each of these categories.

Informational benefits are the most widespread and important category of selective benefits offered to group members. Information is provided through conferences, training programs, and newsletters and other periodicals sent automatically to those who have paid membership dues.

Material benefits include anything that can be measured monetarily, such as special services, goods, and even money. A broad range of material benefits can be offered by groups to attract members. These benefits often include discount purchasing, shared advertising, and, perhaps most valuable of all, health and retirement insurance.

Another option identified on Table 11.1 is that of **solidary benefits.** The most notable of this class of benefits are the friendship and "networking" opportunities that membership provides. Another benefit that has become extremely important

> **What are the benefits of interest-group membership?**

informational benefits special newsletters, periodicals, training programs, conferences, and other information provided to members of groups to entice others to join

material benefits special goods, services, or money provided to members of groups to entice others to join

solidary benefits selective benefits of group membership that emphasize friendship, networking, and consciousness-raising

Table 11.1	Selective Benefits of Interest Group Membership

CATEGORY	BENEFITS
Informational benefits	Conferences
	Professional contacts
	Training programs
	Publications
	Coordination among organizations
	Research
	Legal help
	Professional codes
	Collective bargaining
Material benefits	Travel packages
	Insurance
	Discounts on consumer goods
Solidary benefits	Friendship
	Networking opportunities
Purposive benefits	Advocacy
	Representation before government
	Participation in public affairs

SOURCE: Adapted from Jack Walker, Jr., *Mobilizing Interest Groups in America: Patrons, Professions, and Social Movements* (Ann Arbor: University of Michigan Press, 1991), p. 86.

to many of the newer nonprofit and citizen groups is what has come to be called "consciousness-raising." One example of this can be seen in the claims of many women's organizations that active participation conveys to each member of the organization an enhanced sense of her own value and a stronger ability to advance individual as well as collective civil rights. A similar solidary or psychological benefit has been the mainstay of the appeal of group membership to discouraged and disillusioned African Americans since their emergence as a constitutionally free and equal people.

A fourth type of benefit involves the appeal of the purpose of an interest group. The benefits of religious interest groups provide us with the best examples of such **purposive benefits.** The Christian Right is a movement made up of a number of interest groups that offer virtually no material benefits to their members. The growth and success of these groups depends upon the religious identifications and affirmations of their members. Many such religiously based interest groups have arisen, especially at state and local levels, throughout American history. For example, both the abolition and the prohibition movements were driven by religious interest groups whose main attractions were nonmaterial benefits.

Ideology itself, or the sharing of a commonly developed ideology, is another important nonmaterial benefit. Many of the most successful interest groups of the past twenty years have been citizen groups or public interest groups, whose members are brought together largely around shared ideological goals, including government reform, election and campaign reform, civil rights, economic equality, "family values," or even opposition to government itself.

purposive benefits selective benefits of group membership that emphasize the purpose and accomplishments of the group

The AARP and the Benefits of Membership　One group that has been extremely successful in recruiting members and mobilizing them for political action is the American Association of Retired Persons (AARP). The AARP was founded in 1958 as a result of the efforts of a retired California high school principal, Ethel Percy Andrus, to find affordable health insurance for herself and for the thousands of members of the National Retired Teachers Association (NRTA). In 1955 she found an insurer who was willing to give NRTA members a low, group rate. In 1958, partly at the urging of the insurer (who found that insuring the elderly was quite profitable), Andrus founded the AARP. For the insurer it provided an expanded market; for Andrus it was a way to serve the ever-growing elderly population, whose problems and needs were expanding along with their numbers and their life expectancy.

Today, the AARP is a large and powerful organization with an annual income of $540 million. In addition, the organization receives $90 million in federal grants. Its national headquarters in Washington, D.C., staffed by 1,750 full-time employees, is so large that it has its own zip code. Its monthly periodical, *Modern Maturity,* has a circulation larger than the combined circulations of *Time, Newsweek,* and *US News & World Report.*[8]

How did this large organization overcome the free rider problem and recruit thirty-three million older people as members? First, no other organization on earth has ever provided more successfully the selective benefits necessary to overcome the free rider problem. It helps that the AARP began as an organization to provide affordable health insurance for aging members rather than as an organization to influence public policy. But that fact only strengthens the argument that members need short-term individual benefits if they are to invest effort in a longer-term and less concrete set of benefits. As the AARP evolved into a political interest group, its leadership also added more selective benefits for individual members. They provided guidance against consumer fraud, offered low-interest credit cards, evaluated and endorsed products that were deemed of best value to members, and provided auto insurance and a discounted mail-order pharmacy.

In a group as large as the AARP, members are bound to disagree on particular subjects, often creating serious factional disputes. But the resources of the AARP are so extensive that its leadership has been able to mobilize itself for each issue of importance to the group. One of its most successful methods of mobilization for political action is the "telephone tree," with which AARP leaders can quickly mobilize thousands of members for and against proposals that affect Social Security, Medicare, and other questions of security for the aging. A "telephone tree" in each state enables the state AARP chair to phone all of the AARP district directors, who then can phone the presidents of the dozens of local chapters, who can call their local officers and individual members. Within twenty-four hours, thousands of individual AARP members can be contacting local, state, and national officials to express their opposition to proposed legislation. It is no wonder that the AARP is respected and feared throughout Washington, D.C.

THE CHARACTERISTICS OF MEMBERS

> **What are the characteristics of interest-group members?**

Membership in interest groups is not randomly distributed in the population. People with higher incomes, higher levels of education, and management or professional occupations are much more likely to become members of groups than those who occupy the lower rungs on the socioeconomic ladder (see Figure 11.1).[9] Well-educated, upper-income business and professional people are more likely to have the time and the money and to have acquired through the educational process the concerns and skills needed to play a role in a group or association. Moreover, for business and professional people, group membership may provide personal contacts and access to information that can help advance their careers. At the same time, of course, corporate entities—businesses and the like—usually have ample resources to form or participate in groups that seek to advance their causes.

The result is that interest-group politics in the United States tends to have a very pronounced upper-class bias. Certainly, there are many interest groups and political associations that have a working-class or lower-class membership—labor organizations or welfare-rights organizations, for example—but the great majority of interest groups and their members are drawn from the middle and upper-middle classes. In general, the "interests" served by interest groups are the interests of society's "haves." Even when interest groups take opposing positions on issues and policies, the conflicting positions they espouse usually reflect divisions among upper-income strata rather than conflicts between the upper and lower classes.

In general, to obtain adequate political representation, forces from the bottom rungs of the socioeconomic ladder must be organized on the massive scale associated with political parties. Parties can organize and mobilize the collective energies of large numbers of people who, as individuals, may have very limited resources.

Interest Group Membership by Income Level

Figure 11.1

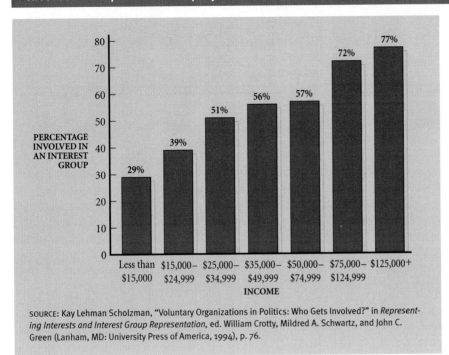

The percentage of Americans who report that they are involved in an organization that takes a stand on political issues increases with income level.

SOURCE: Kay Lehman Scholzman, "Voluntary Organizations in Politics: Who Gets Involved?" in *Representing Interests and Interest Group Representation*, ed. William Crotty, Mildred A. Schwartz, and John C. Green (Lanham, MD: University Press of America, 1994), p. 76.

Interest groups, on the other hand, generally organize smaller numbers of the better-to-do. Thus, the relative importance of political parties and interest groups in American politics has far-ranging implications for the distribution of political power in the United States. As we saw in Chapter 9, political parties have declined in influence in recent years. Interest groups, on the other hand, as we shall see in the next section, have become much more numerous, more active, and more influential in American politics.

The Proliferation of Groups

Interest groups and concerns about them are not a new phenomenon. As long as there is government, as long as government makes policies that add value or impose costs, and as long as there is liberty to organize, interest groups will abound; and if government expands so will interest groups. There was, for example, a spurt of growth in the national government during the 1880s and 1890s, arising largely from the first government efforts at economic intervention to fight large monopolies and to regulate some aspects of interstate commerce. In the latter decade, a parallel spurt of growth occurred in national interest groups, including the imposing National Association of Manufacturers (NAM) and numerous other trade associations. Many groups organized around specific agricultural commodities, as well. This period also marked the beginning of the expansion of

> **Why has the number of interest groups grown in recent years?**

As long as there is government, there will be interests trying to influence it. During the 1890s, for instance, business interests fought for protective tariffs from Congress and President McKinley. This 1897 cartoon satirizes their success in capturing Congress.

While there have always been groups trying to influence the government, since the 1960s the number of organized interests in Washington, D.C. has increased substantially. This growth includes a large number of new public interest groups representing a wide variety of issues, such as consumer protection, women's rights, and environmental protection. For instance, consumer activist Ralph Nader, shown here at a demonstration in support of mandatory airbags in cars, founded a network of consumer advocacy groups in the 1960s.

trade unions as interest groups. Later, in the 1930s, interest groups with headquarters and representation in Washington began to grow significantly, concurrent with that decade's historic and sustained expansion within the national government (see Chapter 3).

Over the past thirty years, there has been an even greater increase both in the number of interest groups seeking to play a role in the American political process and in the extent of their opportunity to influence that process. This explosion of interest-group activity has two basic origins—first, the expansion of the role of government during this period; and second, the coming of age of a new and dynamic set of political forces in the United States—a set of forces that have relied heavily on "public interest" groups to advance their causes.

THE EXPANSION OF GOVERNMENT

Modern governments' extensive economic and social programs have powerful politicizing effects, often sparking the organization of new groups and interests. The activities of organized groups are usually viewed in terms of their effects upon governmental action. But interest-group activity is often as much a consequence as an antecedent of governmental programs. Even when national policies are initially responses to the appeals of pressure groups, government involvement in any area can be a powerful stimulus for political organization and action by those whose interests are affected. For example, during the 1970s, expanded federal regulation of the automobile, oil, gas, education, and health care industries impelled each of these interests to increase substantially its efforts to influence the government's behavior. These efforts, in turn, spurred the organization of other groups to augment or counter the activities of the first.[10] Similarly, federal social programs have occasionally sparked political organization and action on the part of clientele groups seeking to influence the distribution of benefits and, in turn, the organization of groups opposed to the programs or their cost. For example, federal programs and court decisions in such

The National Organization for Women, founded in 1966 and with a current membership of 500,000, holds frequent mass marches. This rally highlighting the issue of violence against women drew 250,000 people to the Mall in Washington, D.C. (left). Similarly, the environmental group Greenpeace frequently conducts protests in front of the White House and the Capitol building (above).

areas as abortion and school prayer were the stimuli for political organization and action by fundamentalist religious groups. Thus, the expansion of government in recent decades has also stimulated increased group activity and organization.

THE NEW POLITICS MOVEMENT AND PUBLIC INTEREST GROUPS

The second factor accounting for the explosion of interest-group activity in recent years has been the emergence of a new set of forces in American politics that can collectively be called the "New Politics" movement.

The **New Politics movement** is made up of upper-middle-class professionals and intellectuals for whom the civil rights and antiwar movements were formative experiences, just as the Great Depression and World War II had been for their parents. The crusade against racial discrimination and the Vietnam War led these young men and women to see themselves as a political force in opposition to the public policies and politicians associated with the nation's postwar regime. In more recent years, the forces of New Politics have focused their attention on such issues as environmental protection, women's rights, and nuclear disarmament.

Members of the New Politics movement constructed or strengthened public interest groups such as Common Cause, the Sierra Club, the Environmental Defense Fund, Physicians for Social Responsibility, and the National Organization for Women. New Politics forces were able to influence the media, Congress, and even the judiciary and enjoyed a remarkable degree of success during the late 1960s and early 1970s in securing the enactment of policies they favored. New Politics activists played a major role in securing the enactment of environmental, consumer, and occupational health and safety legislation.

New Politics movement a political movement that began in the 1960s and 1970s, made up of professionals and intellectuals for whom the civil rights and antiwar movements were formative experiences. The New Politics movement strengthened public interest groups

public interest groups groups that claim they serve the general good rather than their own particular interest

New Politics groups seek to distinguish themselves from other interest groups—business groups, in particular—by styling themselves as **public interest groups,** terminology that suggests they serve the general good rather than their own selfish interest. These groups' claims to represent *only* the public interest should be viewed with caution, however. It is not uncommon to find decidedly private interests seeking to hide behind the term "public interest."

Strategies: The Quest for Political Power

> **What are some of the strategies interest groups use to gain influence? What are the purposes of these strategies?**

As we have seen, people form interest groups in order to improve the probability that they and their interests will be heard and treated favorably by the government. The quest for political influence or power takes many forms, but among the most frequently used strategies are lobbying, establishing access to key decision makers, using the courts, going public, and using electoral politics. These "tactics of influence" do not exhaust all the possibilities, but they paint a broad picture of groups competing for power through the maximum utilization of their resources (see Figure 11.2).

LOBBYING

lobbying a strategy by which organized interests seek to influence the passage of legislation by exerting direct pressure on members of the legislature

Lobbying is an attempt by an individual or a group to influence the passage of legislation by exerting direct pressure on members of the legislature. The person doing the lobbying is called a lobbyist. The First Amendment to the Constitution provides for the right to "petition the Government for a redress of grievances." But as early as the 1870s, "lobbying" became the common term for petitioning—and it is not an inaccurate one. Petitioning cannot take place on the floor of the House or Senate. Therefore, petitioners must confront members of Congress in the lobbies of the legislative chamber; this activity gave rise to the term "lobbying."

The 1946 Federal Regulation of Lobbying Act defines a lobbyist as "any person who shall engage himself for pay or any consideration for the purpose of attempting to influence the passage or defeat of any legislation of the Congress of the United States." The 1995 Lobbying Disclosure Act requires all organizations employing lobbyists to register with Congress and to disclose whom they represent, whom they lobby, what they are looking for, and how much they are paid. More than 7,000 organizations, collectively employing many thousands of lobbyists, are currently registered.

Lobbying involves a great deal of activity on the part of someone speaking for an interest. Lobbyists badger and buttonhole legislators, administrators, and committee staff members with facts about pertinent issues and facts or claims about public support of certain issues or facts.[11] Lobbyists can serve a useful purpose in the legislative and administrative processes by providing this kind of information. In 1978, during debate on a bill to expand the requirement for lobbying disclosures, Democratic senators Edward Kennedy of Massachusetts and Dick Clark of Iowa joined with Republican senator Robert Stafford of Vermont to issue the following statement: "Government without lobbying could not function. The flow of information to Congress and to every federal agency is a vital part of our democratic system."[12] But they also added that there is a darker side to lobbying—one that requires regulation.

How Interest Groups Influence Congress

Figure 11.2

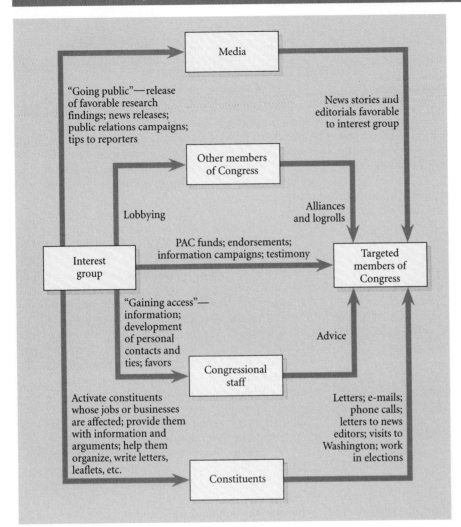

Types of Lobbyists The business of lobbying is uneven and unstable. Some groups send their own loyal members to Washington to lobby for them. These representatives usually possess a lot of knowledge about a particular issue and the group's position on it, but they have little knowledge about or experience in Washington or national politics. They tend not to remain in Washington beyond the campaign for their issue.

Other groups select lobbyists with a considerable amount of Washington experience. Many retired or defeated members of Congress join or form Washington law firms and spend all their time lobbying. An even larger number of former government officials and congressional staff members remain in Washington in order to make a living from their expertise and their connections. (Laws that limit the freedom of former government employees to take jobs in directly related private

What Government Does . . . After September 11

Congress . . . dispens[ed] last-minute legislative favors before it adjourn[ed] for the year [2001], and lobbyists for special interests . . . lined up with a long list of requests, some of which raise[d] major questions about the proper role of government in a weak economy.

Flight schools, skydiving companies, manufacturers of small aircraft, and operators of small airports [sought] a $7.5 billion package of grants and loans to compensate them for business lost since the terrorist attacks of September 11. . . .

Shipbuilders, having just won an increase in the federal subsidies that President Bush tried to abolish, are now asking Congress to defer income taxes they owe on payments for the building of Navy ships.

Not every proposal bec[a]me law, but some [were] enacted and others are well on their way.

Boeing, for example, . . . persuaded the Senate to approve a plan under which the Air Force would lease 100 new wide-body Boeing jets for use as refueling tankers, at a cost of $20 million a year for each plane—up to $20 billion over 10 years. . . .

A cellphone company, NextWave Telecom Inc., urg[ed] Congress to authorize a cash payment of $5.8 billion to the company to help settle litigation over cellular licenses that it obtained in 1996 and 1997. NextWave, which filed for bankruptcy protection in 1998, and its investors deployed a small army of lawyers and lobbyists to persuade Congress to ratify the deal. Haley Barbour, former chairman of the Republican National Committee, represent[ed] a large group of investors. . . .

The Bush administration [said] the settlement is in the public interest because it would transfer the NextWave licenses to other mobile phone companies that could use them to improve wireless services.

But Senators Ernest F. Hollings, the South Carolina Democrat who is chairman of the Committee on Commerce, Science and Transportation, and John McCain of Arizona, the senior Republican on the panel, denounced the proposal as special-interest legislation.

"This thing is an outrage," Mr. Hollings said. "They've put a gun to our heads and said, 'Do it by December 31.'" Mr. McCain said Congress was being asked to make "ransom payments" to benefit NextWave and its investors, executives and lobbyists.

Several factors help explain the large number of proposals for aid. Congress [was] in session later than it has been in years and [had] become an inviting target for lobbyists. The economy was soft before September 11, but the events of that day . . . galvanized industries into action.

The travel industry [was] one of many seeking federal aid in the aftermath of the September 11 attacks. Representative John Shadegg, a conservative Republican from Arizona, . . . push[ed] the Travel America Now Act, which would allow a $500 tax credit for personal travel expenses. Representative Patsy T. Mink, a liberal Democrat from Hawaii, . . . introduced a bill that would allow people to take tax deductions for travel to destinations at least 500 miles from home.

"People are not traveling," Ms. Mink said. "Congress needs to give the public incentives to travel."

The reparations bill . . . would provide $2.5 billion in grants and $5 billion in loan guarantees for "general aviation entities," including aircraft manufacturers, flight schools, and skydiving companies.

Lobbyists for these companies cite a $15 billion aid package for airlines, signed by Mr. Bush on September 22, as a precedent, and their message is being heard on Capitol Hill.

"Congress acted swiftly to provide the major airlines with needed relief to keep that industry going," said Representative John L. Mica (R-Fla.). . . . "Now it should do the same for general aviation."

Edward Scott, director of government relations for the United States Parachute Association, said skydive operators suffered financial losses because they were grounded for more than a week in September. "They deserve eligibility for federal financial assistance," Mr. Scott said. . . .

The new Air Force program to lease aircraft from Boeing is included in the Defense Department appropriations bill. "In this bill," Mr. McCain said, "we find a sweet deal for the Boeing Company that I'm sure is the envy of corporate lobbyists."

But Senator Patty Murray, Democrat of Washington, where Boeing has major production plants, said the arrangement was entirely defensible. She said the deal would not only help Boeing, which has laid off thousands since September 11, but also enable the Air Force to replace an aging fleet of KC-135 tanker aircraft, used heavily in the war in Afghanistan. . . .

SOURCE: Copyright 2002 The New York Times Company. Robert Pear, "Lobby Groups Find Congress in Giving Mood," *New York Times*, Dec. 18, 2001.

companies do not apply to former employees of congressional committees.) The senior partnerships of Washington's top law firms are heavily populated with these former officials and staffers, and they practice law before the very commissions and committees on which they once served. There's an old saying about members of Congress—"they never go back to Pocatello"—and it is as true today as when it was coined. During the battle over the 1996 federal budget, for example, medical specialists seeking favorable treatment under Medicare reimbursement rules retained a lobbying team that included former Minnesota Republican congressman Vin Weber, former New York Democratic congressman Tom Downey, and former Clinton chief legislative aide Patrick Griffin. Former Senate Finance Committee chair Robert Packwood was retained by lumber mills and other small businesses to secure a cut in the estate tax. Similarly, in a fight between major airlines and regional carriers over airline taxes, the major airlines hired former transportation secretary James Burnley, former deputy Federal Aviation Administration administrator Linda Daschle (whose husband, Tom, is the Senate majority leader), former Reagan chief of staff Ken Duberstein, and former RNC chair Haley Barbour. The regional carriers retained former members of Congress Tom Downey and Rod Chandler, as well as a former top Senate Finance Committee staff member, Joseph O'Neil. In this battle of the titans, the major airlines ultimately prevailed.[13]

Local observers estimate that the actual number of people engaged in significant lobbying (part-time or full-time) is close to seventeen thousand. In addition to the various unions, commodity groups, and trade associations, many important business corporations keep their own representatives in Washington.

With the growth of the lobbying industry, stricter guidelines regulating the actions of lobbyists have been adopted in the last decade. For example, as of 1993, businesses may no longer deduct lobbying costs as a business expense. Trade associations must report to members the proportion of their dues that goes to lobbying, and that proportion of the dues may not be reported as a business expense either. The most important attempt to limit the influence of lobbyists was the 1995 Lobbying Disclosure Act, which significantly broadened the definition of people and organizations that must register as lobbyists. According to the filings under the Lobbying Disclosure Act of 1995, there were almost 11,500 lobbyists working the halls of Congress.

In 1996, Congress passed legislation limiting the size of gifts to $50 and no more than $100 annually from a single source. It also banned the practice of honoraria, which had been used by special interests to supplement congressional salaries. But Congress did not limit the travel of representatives, senators, their spouses, or congressional staff members. Interest groups can pay for congressional travel as long as a trip is related to legislative business and is disclosed on congressional reports within 30 days. On these trips, meals and entertainment expenses are not limited to $50 per event and $100 annually. The rules of Congress allow its members to travel on corporate jets as long as they pay an amount equal to first-class airfare.

GAINING ACCESS

Lobbying is an effort to exert influence on Congress or government agencies by providing them with information about issues, support, and even threats of retaliation. **Access** is actual involvement in the decision-making process. It may be the outcome of long years of lobbying, but it should not be confused with

access the actual involvement of interest groups in the decision-making process

lobbying. If lobbying has to do with "influence on" a government, access has to do with "influence within" it. Many interest groups resort to lobbying because they have insufficient access or insufficient time to develop it. Access is usually a result of time and effort spent cultivating a position within the inner councils of government. This method of gaining access often requires the sacrifice of short-run influence.

Figure 11.3 illustrates one of the most important access patterns in recent American political history: that of the defense industry. Each such pattern, or **iron triangle,** is almost literally a triangular shape, with one point in an executive branch program, another point in a Senate or House legislative committee or sub-committee, and a third point in some highly stable and well-organized interest group. The points in the triangular relationship are mutually supporting; they count as access only if they last over a long period of time. For example, access to a legislative committee or subcommittee requires that at least one member of it support the interest group in question. This member also must have built up considerable seniority in Congress. An interest cannot feel comfortable about its access to Congress until it has one or more of its "own" people with ten or more years of continuous service on the relevant committee or subcommittee.

A number of important policy domains, such as the environmental and welfare arenas, are controlled, not by highly structured and unified iron triangles, but by

iron triangle the stable, cooperative relationship that often develops between a congressional committee, an administrative agency, and one or more supportive interest groups

---

Figure 11.3   **The Iron Triangle in the Defense Sector**

Defense contractors are powerful actors in shaping defense policy; they act in concert with defense committees and subcommittees in Congress and executive agencies concerned with defense.

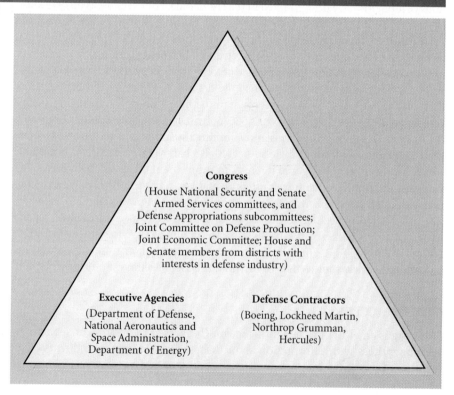

Congress
(House National Security and Senate Armed Services committees, and Defense Appropriations subcommittees; Joint Committee on Defense Production; Joint Economic Committee; House and Senate members from districts with interests in defense industry)

Executive Agencies
(Department of Defense, National Aeronautics and Space Administration, Department of Energy)

Defense Contractors
(Boeing, Lockheed Martin, Northrop Grumman, Hercules)

Lobbyists are a frequent sight in the halls of power. Frank Gladics (left) is a lobbyist for the U.S. timber industry. While the most common image is that of a lobbyist meeting with a member of Congress, lobbyists also lobby the president. Former President George H. W. Bush is seen here with lobbyists from the group Citizens for a Sound Economy (right).

rival **issue networks.** These networks consist of like-minded politicians, consultants, public officials, political activists, and interest groups who have some concern with the issue in question. Activists and interest groups recognized as being involved in the area are sometimes called "stakeholders," and are customarily invited to testify before congressional committees or give their views to government agencies considering action in their domain.

issue network a loose network of elected leaders, public officials, activists, and interest groups drawn together by a specific policy issue

Gaining Access to the Bureaucracy A bureaucratic agency is the third point in the iron triangle, and thus access to it is essential to the success of an interest group. Working to gain influence in an executive agency is what we call "corridoring"— the equivalent of lobbying in the executive branch. Even when an interest group is very successful at getting its bill passed by Congress and signed by the president, the prospect of full and faithful implementation of that law is not guaranteed. Often, a group and its allies do not pack up and go home as soon as the president turns their lobbied-for new law over to the appropriate agency. Agencies, too, can fall under the influence of or be **captured** by an interest group or a coalition of well-organized groups.[14] Granted, agencies are not passive and can do a good bit of capturing themselves. The point is that those groups that ignore the role of the agency in implementing legislation are simply not going to have any role in the outcome of agency decisions.

capture an interest's acquisition of substantial influence over the government agency charged with regulating its activities

One lawyer for an important public interest group gave an unusually frank assessment of the need of an interest group to persist in its efforts to influence the agency: "You can't be successful at a regulatory agency unless you have the financial resources to sue their asses off."[15] That may be a self-serving overstatement, but it should not be discounted. One of the most thorough studies of interest-group

Lobbyists represent not only thousands of private and public interests but also the different branches of government. For instance, President Bill Clinton employed John Hilley, pictured here, as his chief congressional lobbyist for matters concerning the federal budget.

Lobbyists are now likely to have prior professional experience in government. For example, 144 former members of Congress have stayed in Washington as registered lobbyists. Howard Metzenbaum, pictured here, is a former senator from Ohio now working as a lobbyist for the Consumer Federation of America.

In recent years, foreign interests and governments have also employed lobbyists in Washington. For example, Otilie English, a lobbyist for the Afghan Northern Alliance, is shown here shaking hands with Representative Juanita Millender-McDonald during a Congressional Women's Caucus briefing in December 2001.

activity reported that an average of 40 percent of all of the group representatives surveyed "regularly contacted" both legislative *and* executive branch organizations; while only 13 percent and 16 percent, respectively, regularly contacted only the legislature or only the executive branch.[16] Of course, few of these contacts with agencies actually involve the threat to sue. But that possibility is not something an agency can take lightly; some groups do use the lawsuit—a most formal technique of influence—to stop an agency from taking an action. Some use lawsuits to gain a more favorable interpretation of a rule. And some—most particularly women's groups, certain other civil rights groups, and a number of environmental groups—use lawsuits to get an agency to act more vigorously, as we shall see in the next section. This last category is an important aspect of the New Politics movement.

A slightly less formal method of influence occurs when an interest group participates in the regular decision-making processes of an agency. For example, many agencies hold public hearings prior to taking an action—especially if the action involves taking over property for building a road or some other public work, or intervening against a company's or community's action that would violate some environmental protection law.[17] But unfortunately, hearings involving high-stakes local decisions to be made by a federal or state administrative agency can end up in heated and often stalemated and inconclusive sessions involving individuals and interest groups pleading "NIMBY"—not in my backyard.

So broad is the discretion granted to agencies by Congress, and so eager are agencies to gain the support and cooperation of the people they are regulating or serving, that virtually all agencies join in the trumpet call to kindle the spirit of participation. Some even refer to participation in agency decisions as "participatory democracy." Moreover, the broad discretion delegated to agencies in the laws passed by Congress gives all activist interest groups the unprecedented hope that the efforts made on behalf of their members will pay off where it counts—in implementation. These conditions have produced an explosive growth not only of interest groups in general but of public interest groups in particular.

USING THE COURTS (LITIGATION)

Interest groups sometimes turn to litigation when they lack access or when they are dissatisfied with government in general or with a specific government program and feel they have insufficient influence to change the situation. Interest groups can use the courts to affect public policy in at least three ways: (1) by bringing suit directly on behalf of the group itself, (2) by financing suits brought by individuals, or (3) by filing a companion brief as *"amicus curiae"* (literally "friend of the court") to an existing court case (see Chapter 15 for a discussion of *amicus curiae* briefs).

Among the most significant modern illustrations of the use of the courts as a strategy for political influence are those that accompanied the "sexual revolution" of the 1960s and the emergence of the movement for women's rights.

The 1973 Supreme Court case of *Roe v. Wade,* which took away a state's power to ban abortions, sparked a controversy that brought conservatives to the fore on a national level.[18] These conservative groups made extensive use of the courts to whittle away the scope of the privacy doctrine. They obtained rulings, for example, that prohibit the use of federal funds to pay for voluntary abortions. And in 1989, right-to-life groups were able to use a strategy of litigation that significantly undermined the *Roe v. Wade* decision, namely in the case of *Webster v. Reproductive Health Services* (see Chapter 4), which restored the right of states to place restrictions on abortion.[19] The *Webster* case brought more than 300 interest groups on both sides of the abortion issue to the Supreme Court's door.

Another extremely significant set of contemporary illustrations of the use of the courts as a strategy for political influence are those found in the history of the NAACP. The most important of these court cases was, of course, *Brown v. Board of Education of Topeka, Kansas,* in which the U.S. Supreme Court held that legal segregation of the schools was unconstitutional.[20]

Business groups are also frequent users of the courts because of the number of government programs applied to them. Litigation involving large businesses is most mountainous in such areas as taxation, antitrust, interstate transportation, patents, and product quality and standardization. Often a business is brought to litigation against its will by virtue of initiatives taken against it by other businesses or by government agencies. But many individual businesses bring suit themselves in order to influence government policy. Major corporations and their trade associations pay tremendous amounts of money each year in fees to the most prestigious Washington law firms. Some of this money is expended in gaining access. A great proportion of it, however, is used to keep the best and most experienced lawyers prepared to represent the corporations in court or before administrative agencies when necessary.

New Politics forces made significant use of the courts during the 1970s and 1980s, and judicial decisions were instrumental in advancing their goals. Facilitated by changes in the rules governing access to the courts ("standing" is discussed in Chapter 15), the New Politics agenda was clearly visible in court decisions handed down in several key policy areas. In the environmental policy area, New Politics groups were able to force federal agencies to pay attention to environmental issues, even when the agency was not directly involved in activities related to environmental quality. For example, the Federal Trade Commission (FTC) became very responsive to the demands of New Politics activists during the 1970s and 1980s. The FTC stepped up its activities considerably, litigating a series of claims arising under regulations prohibiting deceptive advertising in cases ranging from false claims for over-the-counter drugs to inflated claims about the nutritional value of children's cereal.

Feminists and equal rights activists enjoyed enormous success in litigating discrimination claims under Title VII of the Civil Rights Act of 1964, and anti–nuclear power activists succeeded in virtually shutting down the nuclear power industry. Challenges to power plant siting and licensing regulations were instrumental in discouraging energy companies from pursuing nuclear projects over the long term.[21]

GOING PUBLIC

going public a strategy that attempts to mobilize the widest and most favorable climate of public opinion

Going public is a strategy that attempts to mobilize the widest and most favorable climate of opinion. Many groups consider it imperative to maintain this climate at all times, even when they have no issue to fight about. An increased use of this kind of strategy is usually associated with modern advertising. As early as the 1930s, political analysts were distinguishing between the "old lobby" of direct group representation before Congress and the "new lobby" of public relations professionals addressing the public at large to reach Congress.[22]

institutional advertising advertising designed to create a positive image of an organization

Institutional Advertising   One of the best known ways of going public is the use of **institutional advertising.** A casual scanning of important mass circulation magazines and newspapers will provide numerous examples of expensive and well-designed ads by the major oil companies, automobile and steel companies, other large corporations, and trade associations. The ads show how much these organizations are doing for the country, for the protection of the environment, or for the defense of the American way of life. Their purpose is to create and maintain a strongly positive association between the organization and the community at large, in the hope that these favorable feelings can be drawn on as needed for specific political campaigns later on.

Social Movements   Many groups resort to going public because they lack the resources, the contacts, or the experience to use other political strategies. The sponsorship of boycotts, sit-ins, mass rallies, and marches by Martin Luther King's Southern Christian Leadership Conference (SCLC) and related organizations in the 1950s and 1960s is one of the most significant and successful cases of going public to create a more favorable climate of opinion by calling attention to abuses. The success of these events inspired similar efforts on the part of women. Organizations such as the National Organization for Women (NOW) used public strategies in their drive for legislation and in their efforts to gain ratification of the Equal Rights Amendment. In 1993, gay rights groups organized a mass rally as part of their effort to eliminate restrictions on military service and other forms of discrimination based on individuals' sexual preferences. Gay rights leaders met with President Clinton in mid-April 1993 and were assured of his support for a demonstration in Washington to be held at the end of the month.[23] Although President Clinton had campaigned actively for gay and lesbian support during the election, he did not attend the march for fear of offending religious conservatives.

Grassroots Mobilization   Another form of going public is **grassroots mobilization.** In such a campaign, a lobby group mobilizes its members and their families throughout the country to write to their elected representatives in support of the group's position.

Among the most effective users of the grassroots effort in contemporary American politics is the religious Right. Networks of evangelical churches have the capacity to generate hundreds of thousands of letters and phone calls to Congress and the White House. For example, the religious Right was outraged when President Clinton announced soon after taking office that he planned to end the military's ban on gay and lesbian soldiers. The Reverend Jerry Falwell, an evangelical leader, called upon viewers of his television program to dial a telephone number that would add their names to a petition urging Clinton to retain the ban on gays in the military. Within a few hours, 24,000 people had called to support the petition.[24]

Grassroots campaigns have been so effective throughout the last few years that a number of Washington consulting firms have begun to specialize in this area. One example is Bonner and Associates, which was reportedly paid $3 million by a single trade association to generate a grassroots effort to defeat one bill on the Senate floor.[25] The annual tab for grassroots lobbying has been estimated at $1 billion.

Grassroots lobbying has become more prevalent in Washington over the last couple of decades. This circumstance makes all the more compelling the question of whether grassroots campaigning has reached an intolerable extreme. One case in particular may have tipped it over: in 1992, ten giant companies in the financial services, manufacturing, and technology industries began a grassroots campaign and spent untold millions of dollars over the next three years to influence a congressional decision that would limit their investors' ability to sue them for fraud. Retaining an expensive consulting firm, these corporations paid for the use of specialized computer software to persuade Congress that there was "an outpouring of popular support for the proposal." Thousands of letters from individuals flooded Capitol Hill. Many of those letters were written and sent by people who sincerely believed that investor lawsuits are often frivolous and should be curtailed. But much of the mail was phony, generated by the Washington-based campaign consultants; the letters came from people who had no strong feelings or even no opinion at all about the issue. More and more people, including leading members of Congress, are becoming quite skeptical of such methods, charging that these are not genuine grassroots campaigns but instead represent "Astroturf lobbying" (a play on the name of an artificial grass used on many sports fields). Such Astroturf campaigns have increased in frequency in recent years as members of Congress have grown more and more skeptical of Washington lobbyists and far more concerned about demonstrations of support for a particular issue by their constituents. But after the firms mentioned above spent millions of dollars and generated thousands of letters to members of Congress, they came to the somber conclusion that "it's more effective to have one hundred letters from your district where constituents took the time to write and understand the issue," because "Congress is sophisticated enough to know the difference."[26]

USING ELECTORAL POLITICS

Many interest groups decide that it is far more effective to elect the right legislators than to try to influence the incumbents through lobbying or through a changed or mobilized mass opinion. Interest groups can influence elections by two means: financial support funded through political action committees, and campaign activism.

Political Action Committees By far the most common electoral strategy employed by interest groups is that of giving financial support to the parties or to particular candidates. But such support can easily cross the threshold into outright

---

Box 11.1 **Interest Group Strategies**

Lobbying

Influencing the passage or defeat of legislation

Two types of lobbyists:

Amateur—loyal members of a group seeking passage of legislation that is currently under scrutiny

Paid—often lawyers, professionals, or former government officials without a personal interest in the legislation who are not full-time lobbyists

Access

Development of close ties to decision makers on Capitol Hill or in the executive branch

Litigation

Taking action through the courts, usually in one of three ways:

Filing suit against a specific government agency or program

Financing suits brought against the government by individuals

Filing companion briefs as *amicus curiae* (friend of the court) to existing court cases

Going Public

Especially via advertising; also through boycotts, strikes, rallies, marches, and sit-ins, generating positive news coverage

Partisan Politics

Giving financial support to a particular party or candidate

Congress passed the Federal Election Campaign Act of 1971 to try to regulate this practice by limiting the amount of funding interest groups can contribute to campaigns

bribery. Therefore, Congress has occasionally made an effort to regulate this strategy. For example, the Federal Election Campaign Act of 1971 (amended in 1974) limits campaign contributions and requires that each candidate or campaign committee itemize the full name and address, occupation, and principal business of each person who contributes more than $100. These provisions have been effective up to a point, considering the rather large number of embarrassments, indictments, resignations, and criminal convictions in the aftermath of the Watergate scandal.

The Watergate scandal was triggered by the illegal entry of Republican workers into the office of the Democratic National Committee in the Watergate apartment building. But an investigation quickly revealed numerous violations of campaign finance laws, involving millions of dollars in unregistered cash from corporate executives to President Nixon's re-election committee. Many of these revelations were made by the famous Ervin Committee, whose official name and jurisdiction was the Senate Select Committee to Investigate the 1972 Presidential Campaign Activities.

Reaction to Watergate produced further legislation on campaign finance in 1974 and 1976, but the effect was to restrict individual rather than interest-group campaign activity. Today, individuals may contribute no more than $2,000 to any candidate for federal office in any primary or general election. A **political action committee (PAC),** however, can contribute $5,000, provided it contributes to at least five different federal candidates each year. Beyond this, the laws permit corporations, unions, and other interest groups to form PACs and to pay the costs of soliciting funds from private citizens for the PACs. In other words, PACs are interest groups that choose to operate in the electoral arena, in addition to whatever they do within the interest-group system. The option to form a PAC was made available by law only in the early-1970s. Until then, it was difficult—if not downright illegal—for corporations, including unions, to get directly involved in elections by supporting parties and candidates.

Electoral spending by interest groups has been increasing steadily despite the flurry of reform following Watergate. Table 11.2 on page 440 presents a dramatic picture of the growth of PACs as the source of campaign contributions. The dollar amounts for each year reveal the growth in electoral spending. The number of PACs has also increased significantly—from 480 in 1972 to more than 4,500 in 1999 (see Figure 11.4 on page 441). Although the reform legislation of the early and mid-1970s attempted to reduce the influence that special interests have over elections, the effect has been almost the exact opposite. Opportunities for legally influencing campaigns are now widespread. The total extent of spending on national elections for 2000 was approximately $3 billion. PACs spent $579 million and contributed $260 million of this amount.

PACs and campaign contributions provide organized interests with such a useful tool for gaining access to the political process that calls to abolish PACs have been quite frequent among political reformers. Concern about PACs grew through the 1980s and 1990s, creating a constant drumbeat for reform of federal election laws. Proposals were introduced in Congress on many occasions, perhaps the most celebrated being the McCain-Feingold bill. When originally proposed in 1996, McCain-Feingold was aimed at reducing or eliminating PACs. But, in a stunning about-face, when campaign finance reform was adopted in 2002, it did not restrict PACs in any significant way. Rather, it eliminated unrestricted "soft

political action committee (PAC)
a private group that raises and distributes funds for use in election campaigns

Table 11.2   **Political Action Committee Spending, 1977–2000**

YEARS	CONTRIBUTIONS
1977–78 (est.)	$ 77,800,000
1979–80	131,153,384
1981–82	190,173,539
1983–84	266,822,476
1985–86	339,954,416
1987–88	364,201,275
1989–90	357,648,557
1991–92	394,785,896
1993–94	388,102,643
1995–96	429,887,819
1997–98	470,830,847
1999–2000	579,358,330

SOURCE: Federal Election Commission.

money" donations to the national political parties (see Chapter 10). This change probably will have the effect of strengthening PACs.

Given the enormous costs of television commercials, polls, computers, and other elements of the new political technology (see Chapter 10), most politicians are eager to receive PAC contributions and are at least willing to give a friendly hearing to the needs and interests of contributors. It is probably not the case that most politicians simply sell their services to the interests that fund their campaigns. But there is some evidence to support the contention that interest groups' campaign contributions do influence the overall pattern of political behavior in Congress and in the state legislatures.

Often, the campaign spending of activist groups is carefully kept separate from party and candidate organizations in order to avoid the restrictions of federal campaign finance laws. So long as a group's campaign expenditures are not coordinated with those of a candidate's own campaign, the group is free to spend as much money as it wishes. Such expenditures are viewed as "issue advocacy" and are protected by the First Amendment and thus not subject to statutory limitation.[27]

During the 2000 election campaign, another source of PAC money surfaced—the "stealth PAC," so-called because it "flew under the radar" of the Federal Election Commission's requirement that an independent expenditure by an individual or PAC be publicly disclosed. In that year's primaries, stealth PACs engaged in issue advocacy. However, because no reporting requirements were in place, no one knew exactly how much money they were spending, how many of them existed, where their money came from, or which candidates they supported. Nevertheless, the media and "watchdog" public interest groups were able to bring some details about them to the public's attention. For example, it was discovered that two prominent fundraisers for George W. Bush's presidential campaign spent $2.5 million on a series of "Republicans for Clean Air" ads that were critical of Senator

Growth of Political Action Committees, 1977–98

Figure 11.4

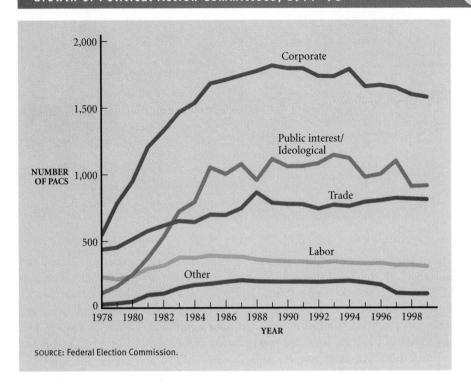

SOURCE: Federal Election Commission.

John McCain, Bush's most formidable opponent in the Republican primaries. Later in 2000, campaign finance reformers in Congress won a small victory when they passed legislation that requires stealth PACs to fully disclose the names of their contributors and to detail where their money is spent. In support of this legislation, Maine senator Olympia Snowe said, "This is a good opportunity to bring sunshine to the political process."

Campaign Activism   Financial support is not the only way that organized groups seek influence through electoral politics. Sometimes, activism can be even more important than campaign contributions. Campaign activism on the part of conservative groups played a very important role in bringing about the Republican capture of both houses of Congress in the 1994 congressional elections. For example, Christian Coalition activists played a role in many races, including ones in which Republican candidates were not overly identified with the religious Right. One postelection study suggested that more than 60 percent of the more than 600 candidates supported by the Christian Right were successful in state, local, and congressional races in 1994.[28] The efforts of conservative Republican activists to bring voters to the polls is one major reason that turnout among Republicans exceeded Democratic turnout in a midterm election for the first time since 1970. This increased turnout was especially marked in the South, where the Christian Coalition was most active. In many Congressional districts, Christian Coalition

Concern about business having too much influence in Washington dates back to the early days of the country. Here, a mid-nineteenth-century cartoon lampoons the ease with which corporate executives could bribe members of Congress (left), and an 1889 cartoon bitingly portrays the close relationship between big business and the political establishment of the time (right).

efforts on behalf of the Republicans were augmented by grassroots campaigns launched by the NRA and the National Federation of Independent Business (NFIB). The NRA had been outraged by Democratic support for gun control legislation, while the NFIB had been energized by its campaign against employer mandates in the failed Clinton health care reform initiative. Both groups are well organized at the local level and were able to mobilize their members across the country to participate in congressional races.

One remarkable fact about the political activity of interest groups is how infrequently major interest groups have tried to form their own party. The fact that they have rarely done so is to a large extent attributable to the strength of the two-party tradition in the United States. But there is also a significant negative influence: the barriers erected by state laws regarding the formation of new political parties. As a consequence, significant interests such as "the working class," women, and African Americans have not been able to find clear expression in the electoral process. Their interests are always being adulterated by other interests within their chosen party. Yet this situation has a positive side: the two-party system has—unintentionally—softened social demarcations by cutting across classes, races, and other fundamental interests that deeply divide people. These interests are adulterated and softened, subduing what might otherwise become the kind of class conflict that we see so often in European history, where class, race, and ethnic interests have become radicalized when they are not forced to reconcile themselves with other interests in a broad political party.[29]

Groups and Interests: Who Benefits?

> **What are the problems involved in curbing the influence of interest groups?**

James Madison wrote that "liberty is to faction as air is to fire."[30] By this he meant that the organization and proliferation of interests was inevitable in a free society. To seek to place limits on the organization of interests, in Madison's view, would be to limit liberty itself. Madison believed that interests should be permitted to regulate themselves by competing with one another. So long as competition among different interests was free, open, and vigorous—that is, so long as pluralism thrives—there would be some balance of power among them and no one interest would be able to dominate the political or governmental process.

There is considerable competition among organized groups in the United States. For example, prochoice and antiabortion forces continue to be locked in a bitter struggle. Nevertheless, interest-group politics is not as free of bias as Madisonian theory might suggest. Although the weak and poor do occasionally become organized to assert their rights, interest-group politics is generally a form of political competition in which the wealthy and powerful are best able to engage. In the realm of group politics, liberty seems inconsistent with equality.

Moreover, although groups sometimes organize to promote broad public concerns, interest groups more often represent relatively narrow, selfish interests. Small, self-interested groups can be organized much more easily than large and more diffuse collectives. For one thing, the members of a relatively small group—say, bankers or hunting enthusiasts—are usually able to recognize their shared interests and the need to pursue them in the political arena. Members of large and more diffuse groups—say, consumers or potential victims of firearms—often find it difficult to recognize their shared interests or the need to engage in collective action to achieve them.[31] This is why causes presented as public interests by their proponents often turn out, upon examination, to be private interests wrapped in a public mantle. Thus, group politics often appears to be inconsistent with democracy.

To make matters still more complicated, group politics seems to go hand-in-hand with government. As we saw earlier, government programs often lead to a proliferation of interest groups as competing forces mobilize to support, oppose, or take advantage of the government's actions. Often, the government explicitly encourages the formation of interest groups. From the perspective of a government agency, nothing is more useful than a well-organized constituency for its

Today, the concern about the influence of big business is greater than ever. President Clinton, shown above with Indonesian businessman John Huang, came under great scrutiny for accepting millions of dollars of donations from foreign interests. Huang himself was accused of soliciting illegal foreign donations to the Democratic National Committee. The current Bush administration, particularly Vice President Dick Cheney, has frequently been criticized for its close ties to the energy industry and its unwillingness to reveal the exact nature of those ties (left).

programs. Agencies such as the Department of Veterans Affairs, the Social Security Administration, and the Department of Agriculture devote a great deal of energy to the organization and mobilization of groups of "stakeholders" to support the agencies and their efforts. This strategy, a variant of what is sometimes called "interest-group liberalism," can be very effective. One reason that the Social Security program is considered politically invulnerable despite its fiscal shortcomings is that it is so strongly supported by a powerful group—the AARP. Significantly, the Social Security Administration played an important early role in the formation of the AARP, precisely because agency executives realized that this group could become a useful ally.

The responsiveness of government agencies to interest groups is a challenge to democracy. Groups seem to have a greater impact than voters upon the government's policies and programs. Yet, before we decide that we should do away with interest groups, we should think carefully: if there were no organized interests, would the government pay more attention to ordinary voters, or would the government simply pay no attention to anyone? In his great work *Democracy in America,* Alexis de Tocqueville argued that the proliferation of groups promoted democracy by encouraging governmental responsiveness. Does group politics foster democracy or impede democracy? It does both.

Thus, we have dilemmas for which there is no ideal answer. To regulate interest-group politics is, as Madison warned, to limit freedom and to expand governmental power. Not to regulate interest-group politics, on the other hand, may be to ignore equality and democracy. Those who believe that there are simple solutions to the issues of political life would do well to ponder this problem.

GET INVOLVED

What You Can Do:
Join an Interest Group

The dilemmas posed by group politics raise questions for citizens, as well. If you can't beat them, should you join them?

Like political parties, interest groups are always looking for volunteers and members. Given the enormous number of groups in America today, every student should be able to find several whose causes seem worthwhile.

Inventory your interests. Which issue or issues rouse your passions? What injustices do you consider intolerable? Who is not being properly represented in public life? Which class discussions have you found most provocative? What issues do you discuss with friends late into the night? What have you studied or written about that moves you? Ask yourself which issue or issue area is compelling to the point that you want to get involved in it.

For any interest that you find compelling, there are likely to be many other people who share that interest. Furthermore, there are likely to be some people who have organized a group or association aimed at promoting that interest. Consider seeking out interest groups that are already organized and active in the area that concerns you. How can you begin your search?

It is often easiest to begin on your own campus. Ask students, faculty, and staff if they know of any campus groups working on gun control, human rights, legalization of marijuana, or whatever your particular interest is. See if your college

Regulating Corporate Political Action Committees (PACs)

Corporate interest groups donate large amounts of money to campaigns and then expect, and often receive, favorable treatment from the beneficiaries of their largesse. For example, in 2000 a number of major interests with specific policy goals made substantial donations to President Bush's campaign. These interests included airlines, energy producers, banks, and tobacco companies. After Bush's election, these interests pressed the new president to promote their legislative agenda. For example, within weeks after his election, Bush signed legislation providing MBNA America Bank, which had donated $1.3 million to Bush's campaign, and other banks with stricter bankruptcy laws that made it more difficult for consumers to escape credit card debt. Following Enron's collapse at the end of 2001, the close relationship between Enron CEO Kenneth Lay and the Bush administration came to the surface. In the three-year period between 1997 and 2000, Lay had donated $326 million in soft money to the Republican Party. Enron executives contributed another $2 million. Critics argued that Enron received special legislative treatment so that its operations fell in the cracks between securities regulators and commodities regulators. These stories and others like them led many to argue that there is too much money, particularly corporate money, in politics and that the system is in need of serious reform.

Others have not asked why there is so much corporate money in politics, but rather, why is there so little? For example, the political scientist Stephen Ansolabehere, John de Figueiredo, and James M. Snyder, Jr., have argued that since business influence on government is so slight, corporations see little reason to contribute a lot to political campaigns. In an article titled "Why Is There So Little Money in U.S. Politics?," they point out that although the $3 billion spent during the 2000 elections may seem like a lot of money, it represents only 0.15 percent of government spending. It is also only one-fifth of the annual spending on tobacco advertising. More important, of this $3 billion, only about $380 million of it came from contributions by corporations, unions, and other associations. They also point out that while most of the public and the political commentators decry the influence of corporate PACs, in fact only 60 percent of Fortune 500 companies even have a PAC. Among all registered PACs, only two-thirds contributed to political candidates or parties engaged in some form of issue advocacy. Finally, the contributions made by corporate PACs to

political candidates averaged only $1,400, well below the legal limit of $10,000 and even below the average contribution of $2,200 by labor unions. Individual contributions made by the CEOs of top corporations also reflect this general trend. On average, corporate executives contributed about $7,500 of their own money to candidates, parties, and PACs, again well below the legal limit of $25,000. If corporate spending on electoral politics is so relatively small, how could corporate influence be so great?

Ansolabehere, de Figueiredo, and Snyder extend their analysis by looking at votes in Congress to see if corporate contributions have any influence on the decisions of congressional members. Their conclusion is that PAC contributions show relatively few effects. In three out of four cases, campaign contributions had no discernible effect on legislation. In the cases in which corporate PAC contributions might have an effect, the effect is quite small compared to other factors. The party, ideology, and constituency of a member of Congress together account for a much more significant proportion of a legislator's behavior.

The author's do note that, although corporate campaign spending is modest, the amount spent by businesses on lobbying is substantially greater—ten times as much in fact. For example, while the tobacco industry donated a mere $8.4 million to political candidates during the 2000 election campaign, the industry spent $61 million on lobbying and interest research in the same period. Political scientists have also pointed out that campaign contributions give interests access to government that other groups do not enjoy, thus facilitating their lobbying efforts. Keeping all of these arguments in mind, efforts to combat the influence of corporations could take one of two courses. Either the lobbying industry itself is in need of further reforms, or individuals need to contribute more to political candidates to dilute the influence of corporate contributions. Indeed, one proposal is to allow individuals to deduct a certain portion of campaign contributions from their income tax. But given that most individual campaign contributions are made by the well-to-do, this policy might just give more political influence to wealthy individuals.

SOURCES: Stephen Ansolabehere, John de Figueiredo, and James M. Snyder, Jr., "Why Is There So Little Money in U.S. Politics?" *The Journal of Economic Perspectives* (forthcoming); Alan B. Krueger, "Economic Scene," *New York Times*, September 19, 2002, p. C2.

Is There Too Much Money in Politics?

Yes

Contrary to the claims of the (supposedly liberal?) news media and Jerel Thomas [see the "No" article opposite], Enron is the biggest political-business scandal in recent decades. It is the proof in the pudding that corporate governance does not work for the people. Rather, it annihilates common folks' entire economic futures while lavishly lining the pockets of already multi-millionaire CEOs, directors, and politicians. It demonstrated the danger of the long acknowledged "revolving door" between business and government, as well as the horrific consequences of rule by economic might.

In an effort to plumb these issues . . . I'd like to correct some of the egregious errors printed in other columns.

First, the brunt of political donations are $250 or more (usually a lot more) and are usually given by wealthy individuals and corporations, not by people like us.

Second, when one speaks of "free speech" in relation to campaign donations, one is frequently speaking of a nonhuman (corporate) entity's "right" to free speech. This is true in the case of Enron. At issue here is the controversial definition of a corporation as equivalent to a human being, a decision that traces its roots back to earlier radically conservative interpretations of the Fourteenth Amendment by conservative courts.

In essence, this definition imbues with the privileges of humanity a legal entity that lasts for eternity, has the ability to amass and pass on unrestricted wealth, and can utilize the manpower of thousands of individuals. For humans, "free speech" means stating our views; for corporations, "free speech" means buying legislation that increases profits.

In the cases where this argument applies to individuals, it is the antithesis of democracy, not the bulwark of it. The problem is that some people have millions more dollars with which to exercise their right to political "free speech," making their voices louder and more listened to. If the democratic ideal is one person–one vote, the massive campaign contributions of wealthy capitalists drastically skew that ideal, creating a system of one person–300,000 votes.

Their (and their corporations') ability to spend millions on lobbyists and PR firms adds to this drastic imbalance. Average people just don't have the thousands of dollars necessary to support or influence candidates, or the millions required to buy a lobbyist on Capital Hill. Even their aggregate $10 contributions to NOW are tiny in light of corporations' and wealthy individuals' political spending.

Political Action Committees (PACs) are a good example of this. Although one would intuitively think that, in a democracy, groups with more members (e.g., unions and environmental groups) would have more influence, the inverse is true. The PACs of labor unions, for example, are outspent by corporate and probusiness PACs by a 7-to-1 ratio. The preponderance of "special interests" on Capitol Hill, including the best funded ones, represent corporations and their wealthy owners—not you or me.

Another myth is that both political parties are equally guilty in this scandal. While it is true that both parties received money from Enron and that this is indeed one reason why the Democrats are being so timid in their investigation, the distribution was far from equal. The *Nation* reported that during the 1990s Enron contributed $5.3 million to political campaigns with 73 percent of it going to Republicans. Enron and its employees have donated $735,800 to George W.'s political career alone. No Democrat comes close to that, not Al Gore, who got $13,750 for his presidential bid, and not Joe Lieberman.

As for Enron's returns on its political investments, the facts, once again, do not agree with Mr. Thomas. The House Committee on Government Reform identifies one example among many: "It is unlikely that any other corporation in America stood to gain as much from the White House [energy] plan as Enron." This is the plan that was developed in six secret meetings between Vice President Dick Cheney and Enron officials. That's just the beginning. In regards to the president and his associates' abandonment of Enron upon its collapse, this reflects political savvy and dishonesty on their parts—not proof of their innocence. Moreover, Mr. Thomas suggests that Enron appealed directly to the White House for a bailout. If that happened, it provides more incriminating evidence, not less.

SOURCE: Nate Williams, "Enron Debacle Shows Corporate Value of Profit Over People," *The Arbiter* (Boise State University), March 4, 2002.

No I just do not understand why everybody hates Ken Lay of Enron. It was Ken Lay who is credited with doing what John McCain and other suppressors of free speech could not do, and that is make campaign finance reform legislation a reality.

Congressmen Shayes, Meehan, Feingold, and McCain have been trying for months to make the public case about campaign finance reform, yet nothing could get done until Ken Lay was thrown into the public's eye....

Everybody knows that Enron gave large sums of money to both Democrats and Republicans. The failed Al Gore campaign received money from Enron as did the Bush campaign. Heck, Joe Lieberman was one of Enron's biggest beneficiaries. People read this and say, "See, this is exactly why campaign finance reform is needed!"

Why? Let's take a look at what all those millions of dollars bought for Enron.

Enron gave to the Bush campaign. When Enron asked for a bailout, the Bush administration refused. After Enron collapsed, Joe Lieberman was one of their biggest critics. The Enron executives will likely face trial. I am not seeing any benefits that Enron got by contributing millions of dollars to political actors. So far, the only thing Enron has received from their millions of dollars spent is a bankrupt company and criminal hearings. How does this give fuel to the fire for campaign finance reform? Ken Lay is probably thinking the dumbest thing he ever did was give money to any politician.

In fact, one would have a far better argument that current campaign finance laws worked exactly the way they were supposed to. Everybody knew how much money Enron contributed to each campaign. Because this information is public, the beneficiaries of Enron came out being the most critical of them. This happened because nobody wanted to be accused of being bought....

So, instead of championing the current law because it worked, these suppressors of the First Amendment are putting forth worthless unconstitutional laws that do nothing but harm the fabled "little guy" in politics.

Let's examine how politics work. We have elected officials that make laws. People give money to the political candidate who best expresses their views. In other words, the money given is the individual's way of speaking in support of their favorite candidate. To limit the amount a person may give to a political candidate is to limit the amount of political speech a person may express.

Of course, politics is not all about politicians. McCain always talks about getting the "special interests out of Washington." Does anybody know what that means? Let me explain. The National Organization of Women, labor unions, and the Rainbow Coalition are all interest groups. These groups represent millions of us "little people" and take our concerns and interests to lawmakers to make our voices heard. We all belong to interest groups. Interest groups get a large portion of their money from people donating $10–$100 to their cause. We pay this money to interest groups because most of us do not have the time to hang around Washington, D.C. to make sure our best interest is being looked out for. Our money is protected political speech because that is the means we have to make our voices heard. To get the special interests out of Washington is to silence our voices of dissent and agreement....

I'm not saying that some campaign finance reform isn't needed. However, I take a different approach. The only reform that is needed is to remove all contribution limits and require full disclosure in twenty-four hours.

Quit making politicians beg for money. More evil things happen to people who do not give politicians money than to people who do. Before being sued by the Clinton administration, Microsoft gave hardly any money to politics. They learned their lesson. Give freely to politics or get taken to court. They also learned form Enron that giving money does not buy any favors.

SOURCE: Jerel Thomas, "Enron Shows Futility of Campaign Finance Reform," *The Arbiter* (Boise State University). February 25, 2002.

publishes a directory of student organizations. Make a point of reading posted fly-ers and notifications of coming events in the campus newspaper. Observe who sets up card tables or sponsors marches to pursue their causes on campus.

Do not be discouraged if your campus search is unsuccessful. Interest groups abound in communities, at the regional and state level, and nationwide. Talk to your family and neighbors, particularly those who are politically savvy and in-volved. Try the local telephone book. It may have a section on community groups. Experiment with a search engine on the Internet. Persevere. Know that while you are looking for an interest group that fits your priorities, there are likely to be several appropriate interest groups hoping to make contact with peo-ple just like you.

Once you identify the appropriate interest group, make contact, ask questions, and discuss how you can contribute to the group's efforts. Interest groups generally carry out multiple functions. They try to enhance public awareness, raise money, build coalitions, find sympathetic candidates, and influence how public officials think and act. Working for an interest group can be one of the most effective ways of participating in politics.

While Steve Ma was growing up in suburban New Jersey, he didn't realize that his home state ranked last in the nation in industry compliance with clean water legislation. The extent of the problem and his ability to act became clear, however, when in high school he happened upon a protest over the Exxon *Valdez* oil spill. Concerned that government was taking inadequate action both in environmental legislation and in promoting citizen awareness, Ma began to search for a venue to make his voice heard. He found the place in the Student Public Interest Research Group (PIRG) of New Jersey at Rutgers University.

PIRGs exist in numerous states to promote various consumer rights, including minimizing student tuition increases, protecting the environment, and fighting homelessness. One of Ma's first activities with PIRG was to publish a guide to the goods and services available in New Brunswick, N.J., including critiques of land-lords and apartment buildings, restaurant recommendations, and ratings of book-stores that paid for returned textbooks. As the year progressed, he worked on larger projects: he and his chapter worked with local businesses to find cost-effective ways to reduce pollution emissions, saving both the environment and the money neces-sary to clean contaminated areas. He also worked as an intern at New Jersey PIRG, researching and helping to write a report on the failed implementation of the New Jersey Motor Voter Bill, which required the state's Department of Motor Vehicles to distribute voter registration information to customers.

Over the next year, New Jersey PIRG lobbied heavily for the Clean Water En-forcement Act, a bill that would make New Jersey's clean water laws the most strin-gent in the nation. "We did so much against millions of dollars of industry lobbying," says Ma. "I actually lobbied the governor himself."[32] The bill passed by a close vote. Since then, New Jersey's compliance with water regulations has in-creased from last in the nation to fifteenth.

New Jersey PIRG next worked to pass a federal bill that would give redemption value to all recycled cans and bottles. As part of the campaign, Ma led an effort to collect aluminum cans, clean them, and mail them to the White House with stick-ers stating an individual's support for the bill. "I was literally climbing in dump-sters," he says, "retrieving cans and bottles people had thrown away."[33] PIRG ultimately failed in its efforts to pass the bill, but did create enough publicity for a hearing on the matter in a congressional committee.

After graduating with a B.S. in human ecology, Ma enrolled at Indiana University for his masters in public affairs. As part of his graduate work, he helped to organize a new PIRG in Indiana. After earning his degree, he began work as a full-time grassroots organizer at the California PIRG in Sacramento. "There is really an opportunity at the state level to create the issue," says Ma. "It sounds clichéd, but states are the laboratories of democracy. We were really effective; we had our heads on straight, an eye on the future, and an incredible ability to organize. Classrooms are good, but good internships in which you can do things like lobby the governor and organize meetings are invaluable."[34]

But what about the Madisonian dilemma? Should you become involved in group politics? Would you be contributing to the solution or exacerbating the problem?

Summary

Interest groups are pervasive in America. James Madison predicted that special interest groups would proliferate in a free society, but that competition among them would lead to moderation and compromise. Today, this theory is called pluralism. Individuals join or form groups to enhance their influence. To succeed, groups need leadership, a financial base, and active members. Recruiting new members can be difficult because of the "free rider" problem. Interest groups overcome this problem by offering selective benefits to members only. These include information, material benefits, solidary benefits, or purposive benefits.

The number of interest groups in America has increased because of the expansion of the government into new areas. This increase has included not only economic interests, but also "public interest" groups whose members do not seek economic gain. Both economic and public interest groups seek influence through a variety of techniques.

Lobbying is the act of petitioning legislators. Lobbyists—individuals who receive some form of compensation for lobbying—are required to register with the House and Senate. In spite of an undeserved reputation for corruption, lobbyists serve a useful function, providing members of Congress with a vital flow of information.

Access is participation in government. Groups with access have less need for lobbying. Most groups build up access over time through great effort. They work years to get their members into positions of influence on congressional committees.

Litigation sometimes serves interest groups when other strategies fail. Groups may bring suit on their own behalf, finance suits brought by individuals, or file *amicus curiae* briefs.

Going public is an effort to mobilize the widest and most favorable climate of opinion. Advertising is a common technique in this strategy. Other techniques are boycotts, strikes, rallies, and marches.

Groups engage in electoral politics either by embracing one of the major parties, usually through financial support, or through a nonpartisan strategy. Interest groups' campaign contributions now seem to be flowing into the coffers of candidates at a faster rate than ever before.

For Further Reading

Cigler, Allan J., and Burdett A. Loomis, eds. *Interest Group Politics.* Washington, DC: Congressional Quarterly Press, 1983.

Clawson, Dan, Alan Neustadt, and Denise Scott. *Money Talks: Corporate PACs and Political Influence.* New York: Basic Books, 1992.

Costain, Anne. *Inviting Women's Rebellion: A Political Process Interpretation of the Women's Movement.* Baltimore, MD: Johns Hopkins University Press, 1992.

Day, Christine. *What Older Americans Think: Interest Groups and Aging Policy.* Princeton, NJ: Princeton University Press, 1990.

Goldfield, Michael. *The Decline of Organized Labor in the United States.* Chicago: University of Chicago Press, 1987.

Hansen, John Mark. *Gaining Access: Congress and the Farm Lobby, 1919–1981.* Chicago: University of Chicago Press, 1991.

Heinz, John P., Edward O. Laumann, Robert L. Nelson, and Robert H. Salisbury. *The Hollow Core: Private Interests in National Policy Making.* Cambridge, MA: Harvard University Press, 1993.

Lowi, Theodore J. *The End of Liberalism.* New York: Norton, 1979.

Moe, Terry M. *The Organization of Interests.* Chicago: University of Chicago Press, 1980.

Olson, Mancur, Jr. *The Logic of Collective Action: Public Goods and the Theory of Groups.* Cambridge, MA: Harvard University Press, 1971.

Olzak, Susan. *The Dynamics of Ethnic Competition and Conflict.* Stanford, CA: Stanford University Press, 1992.

Petracca, Mark, ed. *The Politics of Interests: Interest Groups Transformed.* Boulder, CO: Westview, 1992.

Pope, Jacqueline. *Biting the Hand that Feeds Them: Women on Welfare at the Grass Roots Level.* New York: Praeger, 1989.

Sanders, Elizabeth. *Roots of Reform: Farmers, Workers, and the American State, 1877–1917.* Chicago: University of Chicago Press, 1999.

Schlozman, Kay Lehman, and John T. Tierney. *Organized Interests and American Democracy.* New York: Harper & Row, 1986.

Staggenborg, Suzanne. *The Pro-Choice Movement: Organization and Activism in the Abortion Conflict.* New York: Oxford University Press, 1991.

Truman, David. *The Governmental Process: Political Interests and Public Opinion.* New York: Knopf, 1951.

Vogel, David. *Fluctuating Fortunes.* New York: Basic Books, 1989.

Study Outline

www.wwnorton.com/wtp4e

The Character of Interest Groups

1. An enormous number of diverse interest groups exist in the United States.
2. Most interest groups share key organizational components, such as mechanisms for member recruitment, financial and decision-making processes, and agencies that actually carry out group goals.
3. Interest-group politics in the United States tends to have a pronounced upper-class bias because of the characteristics of interest-group members.
4. Because of natural disincentives to join interest groups, groups offer material, solidary, and purposive benefits to entice people to join.

The Proliferation of Groups

1. The modern expansion of governmental economic and social programs has contributed to the enormous increase in the number of groups seeking to influence the American political system.
2. The second factor accounting for the explosion of interest-group activity in recent years was the emergence of a new set of forces in American politics: the New Politics movement.

Strategies: The Quest for Political Power

1. Lobbying is an effort by outsiders to influence Congress or government agencies by providing them with information about issues, giving them support, and even threatening them with retaliation.
2. Access is actual involvement and influence in the decision-making process.
3. Interest groups often turn to litigation when they lack access or feel they have insufficient influence over the formulation and implementation of public policy.
4. Going public is a strategy that attempts to mobilize the widest and most favorable climate of opinion.
5. Many groups use a nonpartisan strategy in electoral politics to avoid giving up access to one party by embracing the other.

Groups and Interests: Who Benefits?

1. The organization of private interests into groups to advance their own views is a necessary and intrinsic element of the liberty of citizens to pursue their private lives, and to express their views, individually and collectively.
2. The organization of private interests into groups is biased in favor of the wealthy and the powerful, who have superior knowledge, opportunity, and resources with which to organize.

Practice Quiz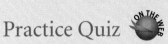

www.wwnorton.com/wtp4e

1. The theory that competition among organized interests will produce balance with all the interests regulating one another is
   a) pluralism.
   b) elite power politics.
   c) democracy.
   d) socialism.

2. To overcome the free rider problem, groups
   a) provide general benefits.
   b) litigate.
   c) go public.
   d) provide selective benefits.

3. Politically organized religious groups often make use of
   a) material benefits.
   b) solidary benefits.
   c) purposive benefits.
   d) none of the above.

4. Which of the following best describes the reputation of the AARP in the Washington community?
   a) It is respected and feared.
   b) It is supported and well liked by all political forces.
   c) It is believed to be ineffective.
   d) It wins the political battles it fights.

5. Which types of interest groups are most often associated with the New Politics movement?
   a) public interest groups
   b) professional associations
   c) government groups
   d) labor groups

6. Access politics, exemplified by defense contractors acting in concert with congressional committees and executive agencies, is an example of
   a) campaign activism.
   b) public interest politics.
   c) an iron triangle.
   d) the role of conservative interest groups.

7. "Corridoring" refers to
   a) lobbying the corridors of Congress.
   b) a litigation technique.
   c) lobbying the president and the White House staff.
   d) lobbying an executive agency.

8. In which of the following ways do interest groups use the courts to affect public policy?
   a) filing *amicus* briefs
   b) bringing lawsuits
   c) financing those bringing suit
   d) all of the above

9. According to this text, what is the limit a PAC can contribute to a primary or general election campaign?
   a) $1,000
   b) $5,000
   c) $10,000
   d) $50,000

10. Which of the following is not an activity in which interest groups frequently engage?
    a) starting their own political party
    b) litigation
    c) lobbying
    d) contributing to campaigns

Critical Thinking Questions

www.wwnorton.com/wtp4e

1. A dilemma is presented by the values of liberty and equality in regard to interest-group activity. On the one hand, individuals should have the liberty to organize themselves politically in order to express their views. On the other hand, there is a strong class bias in the politics of organized interests. How has the U.S. government sought to regulate group activity in order to balance these competing values? What else might government do to make group politics less biased? What are the potential consequences—both good and bad—of the actions you suggest?

2. Describe the different techniques of influence used by organized interests. When is one technique preferable to another?

With the rise of the New
Politics movement, different
techniques are now used
more frequently. Which
ones? Why, do you think, are
these techniques so well
suited to New Politics?

Key Terms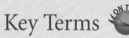

www.wwnorton.com/wtp4e

access (p. 431)
capture (p. 433)
collective goods (p. 421)
free riders (p. 421)
going public (p. 436)
grassroots mobilization (p. 437)

informational benefits (p. 422)
institutional advertising (p. 436)
interest group (p. 417)
iron triangle (p. 432)
issue network (p. 433)
lobbying (p. 428)
material benefits (p. 422)
membership association (p. 421)

New Politics movement (p. 427)
pluralism (p. 416)
political action committee (PAC)
  (p. 439)
public interest groups (p. 428)
purposive benefits (p. 423)
solidary benefits (p. 422)
staff organization (p. 421)

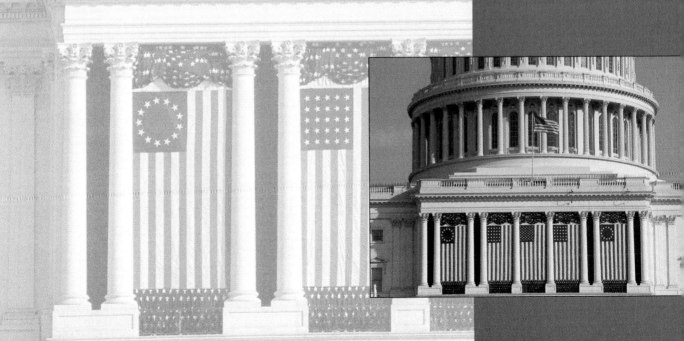

Part III

INSTITUTIONS

12 CONGRESS

★ **Congress: Representing the American People**

How does Congress represent the United States as a whole? In what ways is it not representative?

In what specific ways do members of Congress act as agents for their constituencies?

In what ways does the electoral system determine who is elected to Congress?

★ **The Organization of Congress**

What are the basic building blocks of congressional organization? What is the role of each in forming legislation?

★ **Rules of Lawmaking: How a Bill Becomes a Law**

How do the rules of congressional procedure influence the fate of legislation as well as determine the distribution of power in Congress?

★ **How Congress Decides**

What sorts of influences inside and outside of government determine how members of Congress vote on legislation? How do these influences vary according to the type of issue?

★ **Beyond Legislation: Other Congressional Powers**

Besides the power to pass legislation, what other powers allow Congress to influence the process of government?

★ **Congress and Democracy**

How do the institutional features of Congress affect meaningful representation?

What Government Does
and Why It Matters

FTER BEGINNING THE DAY with a speech to labor activists, the new junior senator from New York, Hillary Clinton, moved on to meet with a group from New York's theater district to consider how to bring Broadway back from its post–September 11 slump. During the rest of the day in her home state, Hillary Clinton participated in a panel discussion on terrorism; met with the families of victims of a downed airliner that had taken off from Kennedy airport; held a conference with the visiting president of the Philippines; and had a reunion party with her campaign staff. During the same week, Senator Clinton could be seen in Washington poring over documents as she attended a joint meeting of the House and Senate education committees. Easily the most famous member of the Senate due to her status as former first lady, Hillary Clinton began her term determined to be a Senate workhorse.[1] Her typical workweek offers a glimpse of the many different roles that members of Congress must fulfill: legislator, constituency servant, policy expert, campaigner, and "mentor-communicator" representing her New York constituency in Washington.[2]

If you want to find out what your congressional representative or senator has been doing lately, there are many ways to do so. You can watch your mailbox—most congressional offices send newsletters to constituents to report the office's activities. You can find your representative's home page on the World Wide Web at thomas.loc.gov. To get a sense of what is happening in Congress you can tune your television to C-SPAN; chances are that some congressional debate or committee hearing will be in progress. If you want to make your views known to your congressional representative, that is also pretty easy. You can

send a postcard or a letter—the address of your representative can usually be found in the blue pages of your local telephone book. You can also call or fax his or her Washington office. The number isn't hard to get; consult your local phone book or call Washington, D.C., directory information. ■

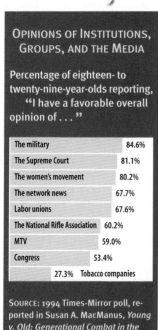

DESPITE these many different ways people can learn about Congress and contact their representatives and senators, citizens regularly complain that Congress is "out of touch." In one poll, only 12 percent of Americans said they believed that congressional representatives "pay a good deal of attention to the people who elect them when deciding what to do in Congress." Eighty percent felt that members of Congress lost touch with their constituents soon after being elected.[3] Many Americans believe there is something about politics in Washington that is corrupting. One voter described what happens to members of Congress in this way: "You find so many good people going in and the next thing you know they're corrupted."[4] Congress seems to be the least trusted of America's national institutions.

What is puzzling is that these feelings of distrust and alienation from Congress have grown stronger precisely as access to Congress and its members has increased. Most of the proceedings of Congress have been open to the public since the passage of numerous "sunshine reforms" in the 1970s; today Congress conducts very few secret hearings. Public opinion polls taken before Congress became more accessible and open showed higher levels of trust and a greater belief that citizens could influence their representatives' decisions. Why has trust in Congress dropped rather than increased as new forms of access and increased openness have been put into place?

One answer to this puzzle is the growing professionalization of Congress as an institution. Professionalization means that Congress has grown more complex as an institution, with more powerful committees, longer terms for members, larger staffs, and higher salaries.[5] In many ways, professionalization makes Congress more capable of reaching informed decisions and makes it easier for members of Congress to serve their constituents. But professionalization also has a downside. It enhances the independence of individual congressional members, often making it harder for the institution as a whole to reach decisions. Moreover, as Congress has professionalized, narrowly focused, well-funded professional interest groups have formed to influence Congress. The growth and sophistication of these groups has made many ordinary citizens feel shut out, canceling out the positive side of the new openness and professionalization of Congress in the public mind. The public feeling of distance from Congress is compounded by the decline of political parties among the electorate. A crucial link that once connected Congress with voters has been severed.

In this chapter, we will try to understand the relationship between Congress and the American people. Congress is central to American democracy because it serves as the voice of the people and because it controls a formidable battery of powers that it uses to shape policies.

Congress has vast authority over the two most important powers given to any government: the power of force (control over the nation's military forces); and the power over money. Specifically, in Article I, Section 8, Congress can "lay and collect Taxes," deal with indebtedness and bankruptcy, impose duties, borrow and coin money, and generally control the nation's purse strings. It also may "provide for the common Defense and general welfare," regulate interstate commerce, undertake public works, acquire and control federal lands, promote science and "useful Arts" (pertaining mostly to patents and copyrights), and regulate the militia.

In the realm of foreign policy, Congress has the power to declare war, deal with piracy, regulate foreign commerce, and raise and regulate the armed forces and military installations. These powers over war and the military are supreme—even the president, as commander in chief of the military, must obey the laws and orders of Congress *if* Congress chooses to assert its constitutional authority. (In the past century, Congress has usually surrendered this authority to the president.) Further, the Senate has the power to approve treaties (by a two-thirds vote) and to approve the appointment of ambassadors. Capping these powers, Congress is charged to make laws "which shall be necessary and proper for carrying into Execution the foregoing Powers, and all other Powers vested by this Constitution in the Government of the United States, or in any Department or Officer thereof."

If it seems to the reader that many of these powers belong to the president, from war power to spending power, that is because modern presidents do exercise great authority in these areas. The modern presidency is a more powerful institution than it was two hundred years ago, and much of that power has come from Congress, either because Congress has delegated the power to the president by law, or because Congress has simply allowed, or even urged, presidents to be more active in these areas. This also helps explain why the executive branch seems like a more important branch of government today than Congress. Still, the constitutional powers of Congress remain intact in the document. This takes us to Congress's pivotal role as a representative institution.

- **To understand the pivotal role that Congress plays in American democracy, we will first examine the concept of representation.** We will look closely at what it means to say that Congress represents the people. We will also look at how members of Congress act on behalf of their constituents and how the electoral process affects the relationship between Congress and the people.

- **Next, we will discuss the legislative process.** We will study the building blocks of congressional organization, including political parties, the committee system, congressional staff, and caucuses. We then turn to the rules of congressional procedure, through which laws are formulated.

- **We then look at congressional decision making, examining the influences on the legislation that Congress produces.** The complex legislative process is subject to a variety of influences from inside and outside government, including constituencies, interest groups, and party leaders.

- **We next turn to other powers that allow Congress to influence the process of government.** In addition to the power to make law, Congress has an array of instruments to use in its relationship with the president and the executive branch.

■ **We conclude by taking a closer look at Congress and democracy.** In assessing whether Congress fulfills democratic principles, we raise the question "Why do ordinary people feel so distant from Congress and how can they exercise more influence over Congress?"

Congress: Representing the American People

constituency the district comprising the area from which an official is elected

Congress is the most important representative institution in American government. Each member's primary responsibility is to the district, to his or her **constituency**, not to the congressional leadership, a party, or even Congress itself. Yet the task of representation is not a simple one. Views about what constitutes fair and effective representation differ and constituents can make very different kinds of demands on their representatives. Members of Congress must consider these diverse views and demands as they represent their districts.

HOUSE AND SENATE: DIFFERENCES IN REPRESENTATION

bicameral having a legislative assembly composed of two chambers or houses; opposite of unicameral

The framers of the Constitution provided for a **bicameral** legislature—that is, a legislative body consisting of two chambers. As we saw in Chapter 2, the framers intended each of these chambers, the House of Representatives and the Senate, to serve a different constituency. Members of the Senate, appointed by state legislatures for six-year terms, were to represent the elite members of society and to be more attuned to the interests of property than of population. Today, members of the House and Senate are elected directly by the people. The 435 members of the House are elected from districts apportioned according to population; the 100 members of the Senate are elected by state, with two senators from each. Senators continue to have much longer terms in office and usually represent much larger and more diverse constituencies than do their counterparts in the House (see Table 12.1).

Table 12.1	Differences Between the House and the Senate	
	HOUSE	**SENATE**
Minimum age of member	25 years	30 years
U.S. citizenship	at least 7 years	at least 9 years
Length of term	2 years	6 years
Number per state	Depends on population: 1 per 30,000 in 1789; now 1 per 600,000	2 per state
Constituency	Tends to be local	Both local and national

The House and Senate play different roles in the legislative process. In essence, the Senate is the more deliberative of the two bodies—the forum in which any and all ideas can receive a thorough public airing. The House is the more centralized and organized of the two bodies—better equipped to play a routine role in the governmental process. In part, this difference stems from the different rules governing the two bodies. These rules give House leaders more control over the legislative process and allow House members to specialize in certain legislative areas. The rules of the much-smaller Senate give its leadership relatively little power and discourage specialization.

Both formal and informal factors contribute to differences between the two chambers of Congress. Differences in the length of terms and requirements for holding office specified by the Constitution generate differences in how members of each body develop their constituencies and exercise their powers of office. The result is that members of the House most effectively and frequently serve as the agents of well-organized local interests with specific legislative agendas—for instance, used-car dealers seeking relief from regulation, labor unions seeking more favorable legislation, or farmers looking for higher subsidies. The small size and relative homogeneity of their constituencies and the frequency with which they must seek re-election make House members more attuned to the legislative needs of local interest groups.

Senators, on the other hand, serve larger and more heterogeneous constituencies. As a result, they are somewhat better able than members of the House to serve as the agents for groups and interests organized on a statewide or national basis. Moreover, with longer terms in office, senators have the luxury of considering "new ideas" or seeking to bring together new coalitions of interests, rather than simply serving existing ones.

SOCIOLOGICAL VS. AGENCY REPRESENTATION

We have become so accustomed to the idea of representative government that we tend to forget what a peculiar concept representation really is. A representative claims to act or speak for some other person or group. But how can one person be trusted to speak for another? How do we know that those who call themselves our representatives are actually speaking on our behalf, rather than simply pursuing their own interests?

There are two circumstances under which one person reasonably might be trusted to speak for another. The first of these occurs if the two individuals are so similar in background, character, interests, and perspectives that anything said by one would very likely reflect the views of the other as well. This principle is at the heart of what is sometimes called **sociological representation**—the sort of representation that takes place when representatives have the same racial, ethnic, religious, or educational backgrounds as their constituents. The assumption is that sociological similarity helps to promote good representation; thus, the composition of a properly constituted representative assembly should mirror the composition of society.

The second circumstance under which one person might be trusted to speak for another occurs if the two are formally bound together so that the representative is in some way accountable to those he or she purports to represent. If representatives can somehow be punished or held to account for failing to speak properly

> **How does Congress represent the United States as a whole? In what ways is it not representative?**

sociological representation a type of representation in which representatives have the same racial, ethnic, religious, or educational backgrounds as their constituents. It is based on the principle that if two individuals are similar in background, character, interests, and perspectives, then one could correctly represent the other's views

agency representation the type of representation by which representatives are held accountable to their constituency if they fail to represent that constituency properly. This is the incentive for good representation when the personal backgrounds, views, and interests of the representative differ from those of his or her constituency

For its first 128 years, Congress was a decidedly masculine world. In 1917, three years before the ratification of the Nineteenth Amendment, Jeanette Rankin (pictured back row, far right) became the first woman to serve in Congress. One of her first actions was to introduce a bill that would have allowed women citizenship independent of their husbands.

for their constituents, then we know they have an incentive to provide good representation even if their own personal backgrounds, views, and interests differ from those they represent. This principle is called **agency representation**—the sort of representation that takes place when constituents have the power to hire and fire their representatives.

Both sociological and agency representation play a role in the relationship between members of Congress and their constituencies.

The Social Composition of the U.S. Congress   The extent to which the U.S. Congress is representative of the American people in a sociological sense can be seen by examining the distribution of important social characteristics in the House and Senate today. It comes as no surprise that the religious affiliations of members of both the House and Senate are overwhelmingly Protestant—the distribution is very close to the proportion in the population at large—although the Protestant category is composed of more than fifteen denominations. Catholics are the second largest category of religious affiliation, and Jews a much smaller third category.[6] Religious affiliations directly affect congressional debate on a limited range of issues where different moral views are at stake, such as abortion.

African Americans, women, Hispanic Americans, and Asian Americans have increased their congressional representation in the past two decades (see Figure 12.1 on page 462). In 2003, fifty-nine women served in the House (up from only twenty-nine in 1990). Thirteen women now serve in the Senate. However, the

The first opportunity for African Americans to serve in Congress came during Reconstruction, when two black senators and fourteen black House representatives were elected. These numbers dropped precipitously, however, with the implementation of the Jim Crow system throughout the South. Not until the early 1970s did the number of African Americans in Congress start to increase again. In 1973, Barbara Jordan, here about to deliver the keynote speech at the 1976 Democratic National Convention, was elected as the first African American congresswoman from the South.

representation of women and minorities in Congress is still not comparable to their proportions in the general population. Since many important contemporary national issues do cut along racial and gender lines, a considerable amount of clamor for reform in the representative process is likely to continue until these groups are fully represented.

The occupational backgrounds of members of Congress have always been a matter of interest because so many issues cut along economic lines that are relevant to occupations and industries. The legal profession is the dominant career of most members of Congress prior to their election. Public service or politics is also

A key development in recent years is the growing number of women in elective office. Journalists dubbed 1992 the "Year of the Woman" because so many women were elected to Congress: women doubled their numbers in the House and tripled them in the Senate. Since 1992, policy issues of special concern to women have been put on the congressional agenda. For example, in 1997 Rosa DeLauro (D-Conn.), pictured here at a news conference with other female members of Congress, sponsored legislation providing more funding for early detection of ovarian cancer.

The increase in the number of African Americans in Congress in the last thirty years is shown by the membership of the Congressional Black Caucus. In 2002, the caucus, pictured here with former vice president Al Gore, had thirty-eight members. Since 1970, the caucus has fought for policies of special importance to African Americans, such as equal access to health care, voting rights, equal justice, and minority business development.

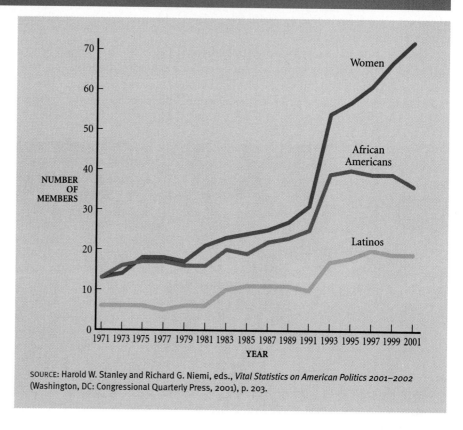

Figure 12.1 Women, African Americans, and Latinos in the U.S. Congress, 1971–2001

SOURCE: Harold W. Stanley and Richard G. Niemi, eds., *Vital Statistics on American Politics 2001–2002* (Washington, DC: Congressional Quarterly Press, 2001), p. 203.

a significant background. In addition, many members of Congress also have important ties to business and industry.[7] One composite portrait of a typical member of Congress has been that of "a middle-aged male lawyer whose father was of the professional or managerial class; a native-born 'white,' or—if he cannot avoid being an immigrant—a product of northwestern or central Europe or Canada, rather than of eastern or southern Europe, Latin America, Africa, or Asia."[8] This is not a portrait of the U.S. population. Congress is not a sociological microcosm of American society, and it probably can never become one.

Is Congress still able to legislate fairly or to take account of a diversity of views and interests if it is not a sociologically representative assembly? The task is certainly much more difficult. Yet there is reason to believe it can. Representatives, as we shall see shortly, can serve as the agents of their constituents, even if they do not precisely mirror their sociological attributes. Yet, sociological representation is a matter of some importance, even if it is not an absolute prerequisite for fair legislation on the part of members of the House and Senate. At the least, the social composition of a representative assembly is important for symbolic purposes—to demonstrate to groups in the population that they are taken seriously by the government. If Congress is not representative symbolically, then its own authority and indeed that of the entire government would be reduced.[9]

Representatives as Agents   A good deal of evidence indicates that whether or not members of Congress share their constituents' sociological characteristics, they *do* work very hard to speak for their constituents' views and serve their constituents' interests in the governmental process. The idea of representative as agent is similar to the relationship of lawyer and client. True, the relationship between the member of Congress and as many as 600,000 "clients" in the district, or the senator and millions of "clients" in the state, is very different from that of the lawyer and client. But the criteria of performance are comparable. One expects at the very least that each representative will constantly be seeking to discover the interests of the constituency and will be speaking for those interests in Congress and in other centers of government.[10]

> In what specific ways do members of Congress act as agents for their constituencies?

There is constant communication between constituents and congressional offices. For example, each year the House and Senate post offices handle nearly 100 million pieces of incoming mail, and in recent years, members of Congress have spent as much as $112 million annually to send out 458 million pieces of mail.[11]

The seriousness with which members of the House attempt to behave as representatives can be seen in the amount of time spent on behalf of their constituents. Well over a quarter of their time and nearly two-thirds of the time of their staff members is devoted to constituency service (called "case work"). This service is not merely a matter of writing and mailing letters. It includes talking to constituents, providing them with minor services, presenting special bills for them, and attempting to influence decisions by regulatory commissions on their behalf.[12]

Although no members of Congress are above constituency pressures (and they would not want to be), on many issues constituents do not have very strong views and representatives are free to act as they think best. Foreign policy issues often fall into this category. But in many districts there are two or three issues on which constituents have such pronounced opinions that representatives feel they have little freedom of choice. For example, representatives from districts that grow wheat, cotton, or tobacco probably will not want to exercise a great deal of independence on relevant agricultural legislation. In the oil-rich states (such as Oklahoma, Texas, and California), senators and members of the House are likely to be leading advocates of oil interests. For one thing, representatives are probably fearful of voting against their district interests; for another, the districts are unlikely to have elected representatives who would *want* to vote against them.

The influence of constituencies is so pervasive that both parties have strongly embraced the informal rule that nothing should be done to endanger the re-election chances of any member. Party leaders obey this rule fairly consistently by not asking any member to vote in a way that might conflict with a district interest.

THE ELECTORAL CONNECTION

The sociological composition of Congress and the activities of representatives once they are in office are very much influenced by electoral considerations. Three factors related to the U.S. electoral system affect who gets elected and what they do once in office. The first set of issues concerns who decides to run for office and which candidates have an edge over others. The second issue is that of incumbency

> In what ways does the electoral system determine who is elected to Congress?

advantage. Finally, the way congressional district lines are drawn can greatly affect the outcome of an election. Let us examine more closely the impact that these considerations have on representation.

Who Runs for Congress? Voters' choices are restricted from the start by who decides to run for office. In the past, decisions about who would run for a particular elected office were made by local party officials. A person who had a record of service to the party, or who was owed a favor, or whose "turn" had come up might be nominated by party leaders for an office. Today, few party organizations have the power to slate candidates in that way. Instead, the decision to run for Congress is a more personal choice. One of the most important factors determining who runs for office is a candidate's individual ambition.[13] A potential candidate may also assess whether he or she can attract enough money to mount a credible campaign. The ability to raise money depends on connections with other politicians, interest groups, and national party organizations. In the past, the difficulty of raising campaign funds posed a disadvantage to female candidates. Since the 1980s, however, a number of powerful **political action committees (PACs)** have emerged to recruit women and fund their campaigns. The largest of them, EMILY's List, has become one of the most powerful fund-raisers of all PACs. Recent research shows that money is no longer the barrier it once was to women running for office.[14]

Features distinctive to each congressional district also affect the field of candidates. Among them are the range of other political opportunities that may lure potential candidates away. In addition, the way the congressional district overlaps with state legislative boundaries may affect a candidate's decision to run. A state-level representative or senator who is considering running for the U.S. Congress is more likely to assess her prospects favorably if her state district coincides with the congressional district (because the voters will already know her). And for any candidate, decisions about running must be made early, because once money has been committed to already-declared candidates, it is harder for new candidates to break into a race. Thus, the outcome of a November election is partially determined many months earlier, when decisions to run are finalized.

political action committee (PAC) a private group that raises and distributes funds for use in election campaigns

incumbency holding a political office for which one is running

Incumbency Incumbency plays a very important role in the American electoral system and in the kind of representation citizens get in Washington. Once in office, members of Congress possess an array of tools that they can use to stack the deck in favor of their re-election. The most important of these is constituency service: taking care of the problems and requests of individual voters. Through such services and through regular newsletter mailings, the incumbent seeks to establish a "personal" relationship with his or her constituents. The success of this strategy is evident in the high rates of re-election for congressional incumbents: as high as 98 percent for House members and 90 percent for members of the Senate in recent years (see Figure 12.2). It is also evident in what is called "sophomore surge"—the tendency for candidates to win a higher percentage of the vote when seeking future terms in office.

As in past elections, voters returned large numbers of congressional incumbents to office in 2002—specifically, 97.4 percent to the House and 88.9 percent to the Senate.

The Power of Incumbency

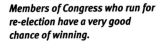

Figure 12.2

Members of Congress who run for re-election have a very good chance of winning.

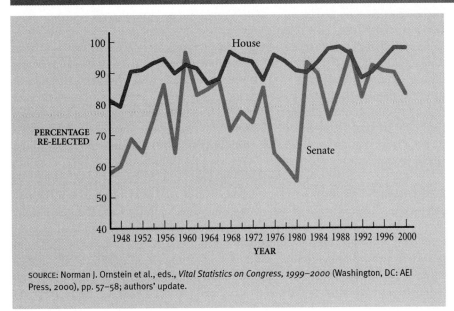

SOURCE: Norman J. Ornstein et al., eds., *Vital Statistics on Congress, 1999–2000* (Washington, DC: AEI Press, 2000), pp. 57–58; authors' update.

Incumbency can help a candidate by scaring off potential challengers. In many races, potential candidates may decide not to run because they fear that the incumbent simply has too much money or is too well liked or too well known. Potentially strong challengers may also decide that a district's partisan leanings are too unfavorable. The efforts of incumbents to raise funds to ward off potential challengers starts early. Kansas Democrat Dennis Moore, who was elected to the House in 1998, held his first fund-raiser for the 2000 campaign in December 1998—before he had even been sworn into office! Representative Thomas M. Davis III of Virginia decided to run for the House in 1994 when he saw that the incumbent had only $25,000 in her campaign warchest. As he noted, "If she had had $250,000 in the bank, I guarantee I wouldn't have run." Most incumbents are aware of the importance of fund-raising and they are able to use their connections to constituents and to other politicians to discourage opponents. The advantages of incumbents tend to grow over time. Democratic Wisconsin senator Herb Kohl first won office in 1988 by 4 percentage points; in his next race, the margin was 17 percent. As the 2000 election approached, his strength as an incumbent had discouraged potentially strong challengers from running against him.[15]

The advantage of incumbency thus tends to preserve the status quo in Congress. This fact has implications for the social composition of Congress. For example, incumbency advantage makes it harder for women to increase their numbers in Congress because most incumbents are men. Women who run for open seats (for which there are no incumbents) are just as likely to win as male candidates.[16] Supporters of **term limits** argue that such limits are the only way to get new faces into Congress. They believe that incumbency advantage and the tendency of many legislators to view politics as a career mean that very little

term limits legally prescribed limits on the number of terms an elected official can serve

turnover will occur in Congress unless limits are imposed on the number of terms a legislator can serve.

Yet the percentage of incumbents who are returned to Congress after each election also depends on how many members decide to run again. Because each year some members decide to retire, turnover in Congress is greater than the re-election rates of incumbents suggest. On average, 10 percent of the House and Senate decide to retire each election. In some years, the number of retirements is higher, as in 1992, when 20 percent of House members decided to retire; thus, the 90 percent of incumbents who were re-elected that year were a subset of all the eligible incumbents (80 percent). Opponents of term limits argue that, over time, such retirements ensure that there is sufficient turnover in Congress despite the high rates at which incumbents are re-elected.

Redistricting   The final factor that affects who wins a seat in Congress is the way congressional districts are drawn. Every ten years, state legislatures must redraw congressional districts to reflect population changes. Because the number of congressional seats has been fixed at 435 since 1929, redistricting is a zero-sum process. States with population growth gain additional seats and states with population declines lose seats. Over the past several decades, the shift of the American population to the South and the West has greatly increased the size of the congressional delegations from these regions. In the redistricting that followed the 2000 census, this trend continued: eight largely northern and midwestern states (the exceptions were Mississippi and Oklahoma) lost one representative, and two states (New York and Pennsylvania) lost two seats. By contrast, the congressional delegations from southern and western states grew. The big winners were Arizona, Texas, Florida, and Georgia, which each gained two seats.

Not surprisingly, **redistricting** is a highly political process: districts are shaped to create an advantage for the majority party in the state legislature, which controls the redistricting process. In this complex process, those charged with drawing districts use sophisticated computer technologies to come up with the most favorable district boundaries. Redistricting can create open seats and pit incumbents of the same party against one another, ensuring that one of them will lose. Redistricting can also give an advantage to one party by clustering voters with some ideological or sociological characteristics in a single district, or by separating those voters into two or more districts.

In the 2000 redistricting, the close balance of power in the House—with party control hinging on only six seats—made the process especially charged. Both Republicans and Democrats went to court to challenge remaps that they viewed as unfair.

As we saw in Chapter 10, since the passage of the 1982 amendments to the 1964 Civil Rights Act, race has become a major—and controversial—consideration in drawing voting districts. These amendments, which encouraged the creation of districts in which members of racial minorities have decisive majorities, have greatly increased the number of minority representatives in Congress. After the 1991–92 redistricting, the number of predominantly minority districts doubled, rising from twenty-six to fifty-two. Among the most fervent supporters of the new minority districts were white Republicans, who used the opportunity to create more districts dominated by white Republican voters. These developments raise

redistricting the process of redrawing election districts and redistributing legislative representatives. This happens every ten years to reflect shifts in population or in response to legal challenges to existing districts

thorny questions about representation. Some analysts argue that the system may grant minorities greater sociological representation, but it has made it more difficult for minorities to win substantive policy goals. Others dispute this argument, noting that the strong surge of Republican voters was more significant than any losses due to racial redistricting.[17]

In 1995, the Supreme Court limited racial redistricting in *Miller v. Johnson,* in which the Court stated that race could not be the predominant factor in creating electoral districts.[18] Yet concerns about redistricting and representation have not disappeared. The distinction between race being a "predominant" factor and its being one factor among many is very hazy. Because the drawing of district boundaries affects incumbents as well as the field of candidates who decide to run for office, it continues to be a key battleground on which political parties fight about the meaning of representation.

DIRECT PATRONAGE

As we saw in the preceding discussion, members of Congress often have an opportunity to provide direct benefits, or **patronage,** for their constituents. The most important of these opportunities for direct patronage is in legislation that has been described half-jokingly as the **pork barrel.** This type of legislation specifies a project to be funded or other authorizations, as well as the location of the project within a particular district. Many observers of Congress argue that pork-barrel bills are the only ones that some members are serious about moving toward actual passage, because they are seen as so important to members' re-election bids.

A common form of pork barreling is the "earmark," the practice through which members of Congress insert into otherwise pork-free bills language that provides special benefits for their own constituents. For example, the massive transportation bill enacted in 1998 contained billions of dollars in earmarks. One senator, Ted Kennedy (D-Mass.), claimed that he was able to obtain nearly $200 million in earmarks for his state. In addition to $100 million for highway construction in Boston, these included a myriad of small items such as $1.6 million for the Longfellow National Historic Site and $3.17 million for the Silvio Conte National Fish and Wildlife Refuge. The former chairman of the House Transportation and Infrastructure Committee, Bud Schuster (R-Pa.), won broad bipartisan support for expensive transportation acts by offering members special projects earmarked for their districts. He defended the practice as a routine part of the political process: "Angels in heaven don't decide where highway and transit systems are going to be built. It's a process."[19]

A limited amount of other direct patronage also exists (see Figure 12.3 on page 468). One important form of constituency service is intervention with federal administrative agencies on behalf of constituents. Members of the House and Senate and their staff members spend a great deal of time on the telephone and in administrative offices seeking to secure favorable treatment for constituents and supporters. Among the kind of services that members of Congress offer to constituents is assistance for senior citizens who are having Social Security or Medicare benefit eligibility problems. They may also assist constituents in finding federal grants for which they may be eligible to apply. As Representative Pete Stark (D-Calif.) put it on his Web site, "We cannot make the decision for a

patronage the resources available to higher officials, usually opportunities to make partisan appointments to offices and to confer grants, licenses, or special favors to supporters

pork barrel appropriations made by legislative bodies for local projects that are often not needed but that are created so that local representatives can win re-election in their home districts

Figure 12.3 — How Members of Congress Represent Their Districts

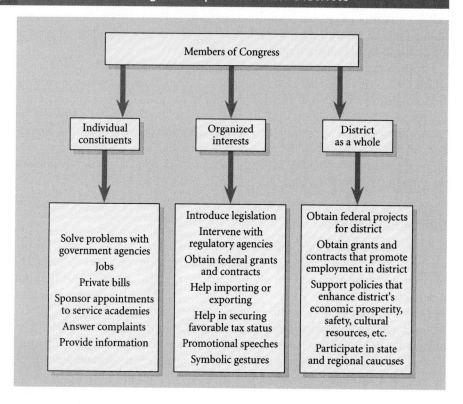

federal agency on such matters, but we can make sure that you get a fair shake."[20] A small but related form of patronage is getting an appointment to one of the military academies for the child of a constituent. Traditionally, these appointments are allocated one to a district.

A different form of patronage is the **private bill**—a proposal to grant some kind of relief, special privilege, or exemption to the person named in the bill. The private bill is a type of legislation, but it is distinguished from a public bill, which is supposed to deal with general rules and categories of behavior, people, and institutions. As many as 75 percent of all private bills introduced (and one-third of the ones that pass) are concerned with providing relief for foreign nationals who cannot get permanent visas to the United States because the immigration quota for their country is filled or because of something unusual about their particular situation.[21]

Private legislation is a congressional privilege that is often abused, but it is impossible to imagine members of Congress giving it up completely. It is one of the easiest, cheapest, and most effective forms of patronage available to each member. It can be defended as an indispensable part of the process by which members of Congress seek to fulfill their role as representatives. And obviously they like the privilege because it helps them win re-election.

private bill a proposal in Congress to provide a specific person with some kind of relief, such as a special exemption from immigration quotas

The Organization of Congress

The United States Congress is not only a representative assembly. It is also a legislative body. For Americans, representation and legislation go hand in hand. As we saw earlier, however, many parliamentary bodies are representative without the power to legislate. It is no small achievement that the U.S. Congress both represents *and* governs.

It is extraordinarily difficult for a large, representative assembly to formulate, enact, and implement laws. The internal complexities of conducting business within Congress—the legislative process—alone are daunting. In addition, there are many individuals and institutions that have the capacity to influence the legislative process. For example, legislation to raise the salaries of members of the House of Representatives received input from congressional leaders of both parties, special legislative task forces, the president, the national chairs of the two major parties, public interest lobbyists, the news media, and the mass public before it became law in 1989. Since successful legislation requires the confluence of so many distinct factors, it is little wonder that most of the thousands of bills considered by Congress each year are defeated long before they reach the president.

Before an idea or proposal can become a law, it must pass through a complex set of organizations and procedures in Congress. Collectively, these are called the policy-making process, or the legislative process. Understanding this process is central to understanding why some ideas and proposals eventually become law while most do not.

Over its more than two-hundred-year history, Congress has established procedures for creating a division of labor, setting an agenda, maintaining order through rules and procedures, and placing limits on debate and discussion. Still, congressional policy making often is an unwieldy process and the often torturous deliberation affects the kind of legislation that Congress ultimately produces. To win support for their ideas within this complex framework, sponsors of legislation must build compromises that accommodate a broad range of interests. As a consequence, it is far easier to pass bills that represent incremental change rather than comprehensive reform. In addition, legislation often resembles a Christmas tree—festooned with a variety of measures added on by individual congressional representatives. Although such measures may have little to do with the policy under consideration, they are needed to build majority support in Congress.

To exercise its power to make the law, Congress must first bring about something close to an organizational miracle. The building blocks of congressional organization include the political parties, the committee system, congressional staff, the caucuses, and the parliamentary rules of the House and Senate. Each of these factors plays a key role in the organization of Congress and in the process through which Congress formulates and enacts laws.

> **What are the basic building blocks of congressional organization? What is the role of each in forming legislation?**

PARTY LEADERSHIP IN THE HOUSE AND SENATE

Every two years, at the beginning of a new Congress, the members of each party gather to elect their House leaders. This gathering is traditionally called the **conference**

conference a gathering of House Republicans every two years to elect their House leaders. Democrats call their gathering the caucus

caucus (political) a normally closed meeting of a political or legislative group to select candidates, plan strategy, or make decisions regarding legislative matters

Speaker of the House the chief presiding officer of the House of Representatives. The Speaker is elected at the beginning of every Congress on a straight party vote. The Speaker is the most important party and House leader, and can influence the legislative agenda, the fate of individual pieces of legislation, and members' positions within the House

majority leader the elected leader of the majority party in the House of Representatives or in the Senate. In the House, the majority leader is subordinate in the party hierarchy to the Speaker of the House

minority leader the elected leader of the minority party in the House or Senate

(House Democrats call theirs the **caucus**). The elected leader of the majority party is later proposed to the whole House and is automatically elected to the position of **Speaker of the House,** with voting along straight party lines. The House majority conference or caucus then also elects a **majority leader.** The minority party goes through the same process and selects the **minority leader.** Both parties also elect whips to line up party members on important votes and to relay voting information to the leaders.

Next in line of importance for each party after the Speaker and majority or minority leader is its Committee on Committees (called the Steering and Policy Committee by the Democrats), whose tasks are to assign new legislators to committees and to deal with the requests of incumbent members for transfers from one committee to another. Currently, the Speaker serves as chair of the Republican Committee on Committees, while the minority leader chairs the Democratic Steering and Policy Committee. (The Republicans have a separate Policy Committee.) At one time, party leaders strictly controlled committee assignments, using them to enforce party discipline. Today, in principle, representatives receive the assignments they want. But assignments on the most important committees are often sought by several individuals, which gives the leadership an opportunity to cement alliances (and, perhaps, make enemies) as it resolves conflicting requests.

Generally, representatives seek assignments that will allow them to influence decisions of special importance to their districts. Representatives from farm districts, for example, may request seats on the Agriculture Committee.[22] Seats on

| Figure 12.4 | **Majority Party Structure in the House of Representatives** |

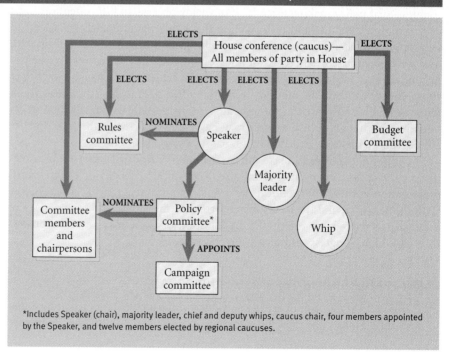

*Includes Speaker (chair), majority leader, chief and deputy whips, caucus chair, four members appointed by the Speaker, and twelve members elected by regional caucuses.

Majority Party Structure in the Senate

Figure 12.5

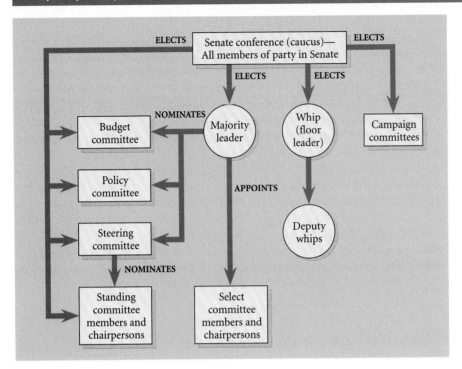

powerful committees such as Ways and Means, which is responsible for tax legislation, and Appropriations are especially popular.

Within the Senate, the president pro tempore exercises primarily ceremonial leadership. Usually, the majority party designates a member with the greatest seniority to serve in this capacity. Real power is in the hands of the majority leader and minority leader, each elected by party conference. Together they control the Senate's calendar, or agenda for legislation. In addition, the senators from each party elect a whip. Each party also elects a Policy Committee, which advises the leadership on legislative priorities.

The structure of majority party leadership in the House and the Senate is shown in Figures 12.4 and 12.5.

In addition to these tasks of organization, congressional party leaders may also seek to establish a legislative agenda. Since the New Deal, presidents have taken the lead in creating legislative agendas (this trend will be discussed in the next chapter). But in recent years congressional leaders, facing a White House controlled by the opposing party, have attempted to devise their own agendas. Democratic leaders of Congress sought to create a common Democratic perspective in 1981 when Ronald Reagan became president. The Republican Congress elected in 1994 expanded on this idea, calling its agenda the "Contract with America." In both cases, the majority party leadership sought to create a consensus among its congressional members around an overall vision to guide legislative activity and to make individual pieces of legislation part of a bigger picture that is distinct from the agenda of the president.

THE COMMITTEE SYSTEM: THE CORE OF CONGRESS

The committee system is central to the operation of Congress. At each stage of the legislative process, Congress relies on committees and subcommittees to do the hard work of sorting through alternatives and writing legislation. There are several different kinds of congressional committees; these include standing committees, select committees, joint committees, and conference committees.

Standing committees are the most important arenas of congressional policy making. These committees continue in existence from congress to congress; they have the power to propose and write legislation. The jurisdiction of each standing committee covers a particular subject matter, which in most cases parallels the major departments or agencies in the executive branch (see Table 12.2). Among the most important standing committees are those in charge of finances. The House Ways and Means Committee and the Senate Finance Committee are powerful because of their jurisdiction over taxes, trade, and expensive entitlement programs such as Social Security and Medicare. The Senate and House Appropriations committees also play important ongoing roles because they decide how much funding various programs will actually receive; they also determine exactly how the money will be spent. A seat on an appropriations committee allows a member the opportunity to direct funds to a favored program—perhaps one in his or her home district.

standing committee a permanent committee with the power to propose and write legislation that covers a particular subject, such as finance or appropriations

---

Table 12.2   **Permanent Committees of Congress**

HOUSE COMMITTEES

Agriculture	Judiciary
Appropriations	Resources
Armed Services	Rules
Budget	Science
Education and the Workforce	Select Intelligence
Energy and Commerce	Small Business
Financial Services	Standards of Official Conduct
Government Reform	Transportation and Infrastructure
House Administration	Veterans Affairs
International Relations	Ways and Means

SENATE COMMITTEES

Agriculture, Nutrition, and Forestry	Foreign Relations
Appropriations	Governmental Affairs
Armed Services	Judiciary
Banking, Housing, and Urban Affairs	Health, Education, Labor, and Pensions
Budget	Rules and Administration
Commerce, Science, and Transportation	Select Intelligence
Energy and Natural Resources	Small Business
Environment and Public Works	Veterans Affairs
Finance	

Except for the House Rules Committee, all standing committees receive proposals for legislation and process them into official bills. The House Rules Committee decides the order in which bills come up for a vote on the House floor and determines the specific rules that govern the length of debate and opportunity for amendments. The Senate, which has less formal organization and fewer rules, does not have a rules committee.

Select committees are usually not permanent and usually do not have the power to report legislation. (The House and Senate Select Intelligence committees are permanent, however, and do have the power to report legislation.) These committees may hold hearings and serve as focal points for the issues they are charged with considering. Congressional leaders form select committees when they want to take up issues that fall between the jurisdictions of existing committees, to highlight an issue, or to investigate a particular problem. Examples of select committees investigating political scandals include the Senate Watergate Committee of 1973, the committees set up in 1987 to investigate the Iran-Contra affair, and the Whitewater Committee of 1995–96. Select committees set up to highlight ongoing issues have included the House Select Committee on Hunger, established in 1984, and the House Select Narcotics Committee. A few select committees have remained in existence for many years, such as the select committees on aging; hunger; children, youth, and families; and narcotics abuse and control. In 1995, however, congressional Republicans abolished most of these select committees, both to streamline operations and to remove a forum used primarily by Democratic representatives and their allies.

Joint committees involve members from both the Senate and the House. There are four such committees: economic, taxation, library, and printing. These joint committees are permanent, but they do not have the power to report legislation. The Joint Economic Committee and the Joint Taxation Committee have often played important roles in collecting information and holding hearings on economic and financial issues.

Finally, **conference committees** are temporary committees whose members are appointed by the Speaker of the House and the presiding officer of the Senate. These committees are charged with reaching a compromise on legislation once it has been passed by the House and the Senate. Conference committees play an extremely important role in determining what laws are actually passed, because they must reconcile any differences in the legislation passed by the House and Senate.

Assignments to standing committees are made by a "committee on committees" appointed by the leadership of each party in each chamber of Congress. For the most part, these committees try to accommodate the requests of individual members for assignments. The decision about which committee seats to pursue is the most important choice an incoming member of Congress faces. Members are guided by different considerations in requesting committee assignments, but most prominent are serving constituent interests, making good public policy, and winning more influence in Congress.[23]

Within each committee, hierarchy has usually been based on seniority. **Seniority** is determined by years of continuous service on a particular committee, not years of service in the House or Senate. In general, each committee is chaired by the most senior member of the majority party. But the principle of seniority is not absolute. Both Democrats and Republicans have violated it on occasion. At the start of

select committee a (usually) temporary legislative committee set up to highlight or investigate a particular issue or address an issue not within the jurisdiction of existing committees

joint committee a legislative committee formed of members of both the House and the Senate

conference committee a joint committee created to work out a compromise on House and Senate versions of a piece of legislation

seniority priority or status ranking given to an individual on the basis of length of continuous service on a committee in Congress

the 104th Congress in 1995, House Republicans violated the principle of seniority in the selection of a number of key committee chairs, for example.

Over the years, Congress has reformed its organizational structure and operating procedures. Most changes have been made to improve efficiency, but some reforms have also represented a response to political considerations. In the 1970s, for example, a series of reforms substantially altered the organization of power in Congress. Among the most important changes put into place at that time were an increase in the number of subcommittees; greater autonomy for subcommittee chairs; the opening of most committee deliberations to the public; and a system of multiple referral of bills, which allowed several committees to consider one bill at the same time. One of the driving impulses behind these reforms was an effort to reduce the power of committee chairs. In the past, committee chairs exercised considerable power; they determined hearing schedules, selected subcommittee members, and appointed committee staff. Some chairs used their power to block consideration of bills they opposed. Because of the seniority system, many of the key committees were chaired by southern Democrats who stymied liberal legislation throughout the 1960s and early 1970s. By enhancing subcommittee power and allowing more members to chair subcommittees and appoint subcommittee staff, the reforms undercut the power of committee chairs.

Yet the reforms of the 1970s created new problems for Congress. As a consequence of the reforms, power has become more fragmented, making it harder to reach agreement on legislation. With power dissipated over a large number of committees and subcommittees, members spend more time in unproductive "turf battles." In addition, as committees expanded in size, members found they had so many committee responsibilities that they had to run from meeting to meeting. Thus their ability to specialize in a particular policy area has diminished as their responsibilities have increased.[24] The Republican leadership of the 104th Congress (1995–96) sought to reverse the fragmentation of congressional power and concentrate more authority in the party leadership. Toward this end they reduced the number of subcommittees and limited the time committee chairs could serve to three terms. They made good on this promise in 2001, when they replaced thirteen committee chairs. As a consequence of these changes, committees have not regained the central role they once held in policy making. Sharp partisan divisions among members of Congress and divisions among Republicans have made it difficult for committees to deliberate and bring bipartisan expertise to bear on policy making as in the past. With committees less able to engage in effective decision making and often unable to act, it has become more common in recent years for party-driven legislation to go directly to the floor, bypassing committees.[25]

THE STAFF SYSTEM: STAFFERS AND AGENCIES

A congressional institution second in importance only to the committee system is the staff system. Every member of Congress employs many staff members, whose tasks include handling constituency requests and, to a large and growing extent, dealing with legislative details and the activities of administrative agencies. Increasingly, staffers bear the primary responsibility for formulating and drafting proposals, organizing hearings, dealing with administrative agencies, and negotiating with lobbyists. Indeed, legislators typically deal with one another through staff, rather than through direct, personal contact. Representatives and senators together employ nearly eleven thousand staffers in their Washington and home offices. Today, staffers even develop policy ideas, draft legislation, and in some instances, have a good deal of influence over the legislative process.

In addition to the personal staffs of individual senators and representatives, Congress also employs roughly two thousand committee staffers. These individuals make up the permanent staff, who stay attached to every House and Senate committee regardless of turnover in Congress and who are responsible for organizing and administering the committee's work, including research, scheduling, organizing hearings, and drafting legislation. Committee staffers can come to play key roles in the legislative process. One example of the importance of committee staffers is the success of the House Transportation and Infrastructure Committee. In a period when many committees have become less able to deliberate or have been unable to get their expenditures approved in the budget process, the Transportation Committee has been notably successful in passing very expensive legislation. One key to the committee's success is its staff. As is common for committee staff, most of the transportation committee senior staff are trained as lawyers. The committee's chief of staff has been a committee aide for over twenty-four years and has vast knowledge of the legislative process and transportation policy in particular. The combination of legal, political, and budgetary expertise that staffers accumulate is critical to the success of the large and complex bills considered in the Transportation Committee.[26]

As Figure 12.6 shows, the number of congressional staff members grew rapidly during the 1960s and 1970s, leveled off in the 1980s, and decreased dramatically

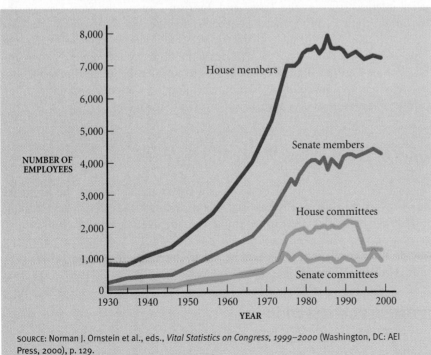

The Growth of Congressional Staffs, 1930–99

Figure 12.6

SOURCE: Norman J. Ornstein et al., eds., *Vital Statistics on Congress, 1999–2000* (Washington, DC: AEI Press, 2000), p. 129.

in 1995. This sudden drop fulfilled the Republican congressional candidates' campaign promise to reduce the size of committee staffs.

Not only does Congress employ personal and committee staff, but it has also established **staff agencies** designed to provide the legislative branch with resources and expertise independent of the executive branch. These agencies enhance Congress's capacity to oversee administrative agencies and to evaluate presidential programs and proposals. They include the Congressional Research Service, which performs research for legislators who wish to know the facts and competing arguments relevant to policy proposals or other legislative business; the General Accounting Office, through which Congress can investigate the financial and administrative affairs of any government agency or program; and the Congressional Budget Office, which assesses the economic implications and likely costs of proposed federal programs, such as health care reform proposals. A fourth agency, the Office of Technology Assessment, which provided Congress with analyses of scientific or technical issues, was abolished in 1995.

INFORMAL ORGANIZATION: THE CAUCUSES

In addition to the official organization of Congress, there also exists an unofficial organizational structure—the caucuses. **Caucuses** are groups of senators or representatives who share certain opinions, interests, or social characteristics. They include ideological caucuses such as the liberal Democratic Study Group, the conservative Democratic Forum (popularly known as the "boll weevils"), and the moderate Republican Wednesday Group. At the same time, there are a large number of caucuses composed of legislators representing particular economic or policy interests, such as the Travel and Tourism Caucus, the Steel Caucus, the Mushroom Caucus, and Concerned Senators for the Arts. Legislators who share common backgrounds or social characteristics have organized caucuses such as the Congressional Black Caucus, the Congressional Caucus for Women's Issues, and the Hispanic Caucus. All these caucuses seek to advance the interests of the groups they represent by promoting legislation, encouraging Congress to hold hearings, and pressing administrative agencies for favorable treatment.

Rules of Lawmaking: How a Bill Becomes a Law

The institutional structure of Congress is a key factor in shaping the legislative process. A second and equally important set of factors is the rules of congressional procedure. These rules govern everything from the introduction of a **bill** through its submission to the president for signing (see Figure 12.7 on the next page). Not only do these regulations influence the fate of every bill, they also help to determine the distribution of power in the Congress.

COMMITTEE DELIBERATION

Even if a member of Congress, the White House, or a federal agency has spent months developing and drafting a piece of legislation, it does not become a bill until

staff agency a legislative support agency responsible for policy analysis

caucus (congressional) an association of members of Congress based on party, interest, or social group, such as gender or race

bill a proposed law that has been sponsored by a member of Congress and submitted to the clerk of the House or Senate

How a Bill Becomes a Law

Figure 12.7

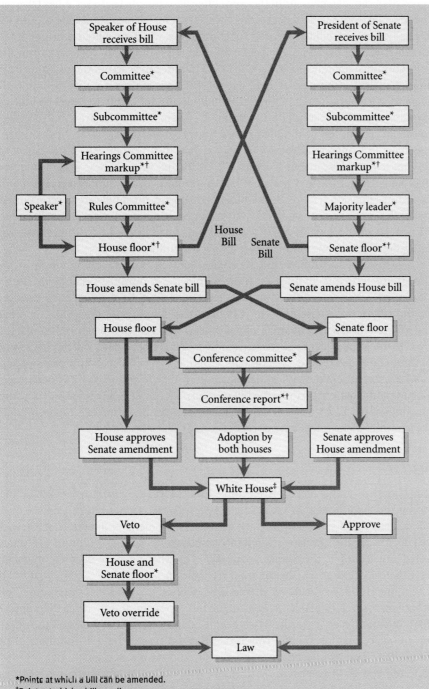

*Points at which a bill can be amended.
†Points at which a bill can die.
‡If the president neither signs nor vetoes a bill within ten days, it automatically becomes law.

> **How do the rules of congressional procedure influence the fate of legislation as well as determine the distribution of power in Congress?**

closed rule a provision by the House Rules Committee limiting or prohibiting the introduction of amendments during debate

open rule a provision by the House Rules Committee that permits floor debate and the addition of new amendments to a bill

it is submitted officially by a senator or representative to the clerk of the House or Senate and referred to the appropriate committee for deliberation. No floor action on any bill can take place until the committee with jurisdiction over it has taken all the time it needs to deliberate. During the course of its deliberations, the committee typically refers the bill to one of its subcommittees, which may hold hearings, listen to expert testimony, and amend the proposed legislation before referring it to the full committee for consideration. The full committee may accept the recommendation of the subcommittee or hold its own hearings and prepare its own amendments. Or, even more frequently, the committee and subcommittee may do little or nothing with a bill that has been submitted to them. Many bills are simply allowed to "die in committee" with little or no serious consideration given to them. Often, members of Congress introduce legislation that they neither expect nor desire to see enacted into law, merely to please a constituency group. These bills die a quick and painless death. Other pieces of legislation have ardent supporters and die in committee only after a long battle. But, in either case, most bills are never reported out of the committees to which they are assigned. In a typical congressional session, 95 percent of the roughly eight thousand bills introduced die in committee—an indication of the power of the congressional committee system.

The relative handful of bills that are reported out of committee must, in the House, pass one additional hurdle within the committee system—the Rules Committee. This powerful committee determines the rules that will govern action on the bill on the House floor. In particular, the Rules Committee allots the time for debate and decides to what extent amendments to the bill can be proposed from the floor. A bill's supporters generally prefer a **closed rule,** which puts severe limits on floor debate and amendments. Opponents of a bill usually prefer an **open rule,** which permits potentially damaging floor debate and makes it easier to add amendments that may cripple the bill or weaken its chances for passage. Thus, the outcome of the Rules Committee's deliberations can be extremely important and the committee's hearings can be an occasion for sharp conflict.

DEBATE

Party control of the agenda is reinforced by the rule giving the Speaker of the House and the president of the Senate the power of recognition during debate on a bill. Usually the chair knows the purpose for which a member intends to speak well in advance of the occasion. Spontaneous efforts to gain recognition are often foiled. For example, the Speaker may ask, "For what purpose does the member rise?" before deciding whether to grant recognition.

In the House, virtually all of the time allotted by the Rules Committee for debate on a given bill is controlled by the bill's sponsor and by its leading opponent. In almost every case, these two people are the committee chair and the ranking minority member of the committee that processed the bill—or those they designate. These two participants are, by rule and tradition, granted the power to allocate most of the debate time in small amounts to members who are seeking to speak for or against the measure. Preference in the allocation of time goes to the members of the committee whose jurisdiction covers the bill.

In the Senate, the leadership has much less control over floor debate. Indeed, the Senate is unique among the world's legislative bodies for its commitment to unlimited debate. Once given the floor, a senator may speak as long as he or she wishes. On a number of memorable occasions, senators have used this right to prevent action on legislation that they opposed. Through this tactic, called the **filibuster,** small minorities or even one individual in the Senate can force the majority to give in. During the 1950s and 1960s, for example, opponents of civil rights legislation often sought to block its passage by staging a filibuster. The votes of three-fifths of the Senate, or sixty votes, are needed to end a filibuster. This procedure is called **cloture.**

Although it is the best known, the filibuster is not the only technique used to block Senate debate. Under Senate rules, members have a virtually unlimited ability to propose amendments to a pending bill. Each amendment must be voted on before the bill can come to a final vote. The introduction of new amendments can be stopped only by unanimous consent. This, in effect, can permit a determined minority to filibuster-by-amendment, indefinitely delaying the passage of a bill. This tactic was briefly used by Republicans in 1994 to delay the Clinton administration's health care initiative. Senators can also place "holds," or stalling devices, on bills to delay debate. Senators place holds on bills when they fear that openly opposing them will be unpopular. Because holds are kept secret, the senators placing the holds do not have to take public responsibility for their actions. Such holds blocked bipartisan efforts to enact popular health insurance reforms for much of 1996. In 1997, opponents of this practice introduced an amendment that would have required publicizing the identity of the senator putting a bill on hold. But when the Senate voted on the measure, the proposal to end the practice of anonymous holds had "mysteriously disappeared."[27] Although no one took credit for killing the measure, it was evident that the majority of senators wanted to maintain the practice.

Once a bill is debated on the floor of the House and the Senate, the leaders schedule it for a vote on the floor of each chamber. By this time, congressional leaders know what the vote will be; leaders do not bring legislation to the floor unless they are fairly certain it is going to pass. As a consequence, it is unusual for the leadership to lose a bill on the floor. On rare occasions, the last moments of the floor vote can be very dramatic, as each party's leadership puts its whip organization into action to make sure that wavering members vote with the party.

CONFERENCE COMMITTEE: RECONCILING HOUSE AND SENATE VERSIONS OF LEGISLATION

Getting a bill out of committee and through one of the houses of Congress is no guarantee that a bill will be enacted into law. Frequently, bills that began with similar provisions in both chambers emerge with little resemblance to each other. Alternatively, a bill may be passed by one chamber but undergo substantial revision in the other chamber. In such cases, a conference committee composed of the senior members of the committees or subcommittees that initiated the bills may be required to iron out differences between the two pieces of legislation. Sometimes members or leaders will let objectionable provisions pass on the floor with the idea that they will get the chance to change what they want in conference. Usually, conference committees meet behind closed doors. Agreement requires a majority of each of the two delegations. Legislation that emerges successfully

filibuster a tactic used by members of the Senate to prevent action on legislation they oppose by continuously holding the floor and speaking until the majority backs down. Once given the floor, senators have unlimited time to speak, and it requires a vote of three-fifths of the Senate to end a filibuster

cloture a rule allowing a majority of two-thirds or three-fifths of the members in a legislative body to set a time limit on debate over a given bill

from a conference committee is more often a compromise than a clear victory of one set of forces over another.

When a bill comes out of conference, it faces one more hurdle. Before a bill can be sent to the president for signing, the House-Senate conference committee's version of the bill must be approved on the floor of each chamber. Usually such approval is given quickly. Occasionally, however, a bill's opponents use this round of approval as one last opportunity to defeat a piece of legislation.

PRESIDENTIAL ACTION

veto the president's constitutional power to turn down acts of Congress. A presidential veto may be overridden by a two-thirds vote of each house of Congress

pocket veto a presidential veto that is automatically triggered if the president does not act on a given piece of legislation passed during the final ten days of a legislative session

Once adopted by the House and Senate, a bill goes to the president, who may choose to sign the bill into law or **veto** it. The veto is the president's constitutional power to reject a piece of legislation. To veto a bill, the president returns it unsigned within ten days to the house of Congress in which it originated. If Congress adjourns during the ten-day period, and the president has taken no action, the bill is also considered to be vetoed. This latter method is known as the **pocket veto.** The possibility of a presidential veto affects how willing members of Congress are to push for different pieces of legislation at different times. If they think a proposal is likely to be vetoed they might shelve it for a later time.

A presidential veto may be overridden by a two-thirds vote in both the House and Senate. A veto override says much about the support that a president can expect from Congress, and it can deliver a stinging blow to the executive branch. Presidents will often back down from a veto threat if they believe that Congress will override the veto.

How Congress Decides

> **What sorts of influences inside and outside of government determine how members of Congress vote on legislation? How do these influences vary according to the type of issue?**

What determines the kinds of legislation that Congress ultimately produces? According to the most simple theories of representation, members of Congress would respond to the views of their constituents. In fact, the process of creating a legislative agenda, drawing up a list of possible measures, and deciding among them is a very complex process, in which a variety of influences from inside and outside government play important roles. External influences include a legislator's constituency and various interest groups. Influences from inside government include party leadership, congressional colleagues, and the president. Let us examine each of these influences individually and then consider how they interact to produce congressional policy decisions.

CONSTITUENCY

Because members of Congress, for the most part, want to be re-elected, we would expect the views of their constituents to be a primary influence on the decisions that legislators make. Yet constituency influence is not so straightforward. In fact, most constituents do not even know what policies their representatives support. The number of citizens who *do* pay attention to such matters—the attentive public—is usually very small. Nonetheless, members of Congress spend a lot of time worrying about what their constituents think, because these representatives realize

The typical day in the life of a member of Congress is hectic. Political scientists use the term "hill style" to refer to a member's schedule in Washington and "home style" to refer to a member's activities in her district. Committee meetings, such as this conference committee's attempt to reconcile the differences between House and Senate versions of a bill, are a major component of a member's day.

Meeting with staff, who often help in developing new policy initiatives and drafting legislation, is an important part of a member's day. Here, Representative Connie Morella meets with her staff in her Capitol Hill office.

Members also convene as a body for floor debates and votes, such as at the January 1997 opening of the 105th Congress, pictured here.

Members of Congress also spend time meeting with those trying to influence their decisions: constituents, lobbyists, and occasionally even the president. Meetings with constituents are sometimes formal presentations, such as the constituent meeting pictured here (top left) with Illinois' two senators, Dick Durbin (at the podium) and Peter Fitzgerald (greeting constituent).

More often, members meet constituents in their Capitol Hill offices. Pennsylvania representative Paul McHale (left) sets aside an "Open Till Midnight" evening every few weeks during which constituents can call him directly. Members of Congress also spend a great deal of time in their electoral districts meeting with constituents. Here, Representative Gary Ackerman, Senator Charles Schumer, and Senator Hillary Rodham Clinton present Olympic gold medalist Sarah Hughes with a large flag after a parade in her honor in her hometown of Great Neck, New York (below).

that the choices they make may be scrutinized in a future election and used as ammunition by an opposing candidate. Because of this possibility, members of Congress try to anticipate their constituents' policy views.[28] Legislators are more likely to act in accordance with those views if they think that voters will take them into account during elections. In October 1998, for example, thirty-one House Democrats broke party ranks and voted in favor of an impeachment inquiry against President Clinton because they believed a "no" vote could cost them re-election that November. In this way, constituents may affect congressional policy choices even when there is little direct evidence of their influence.

INTEREST GROUPS

Interest groups are another important external influence on the policies that Congress produces. When members of Congress are making voting decisions, those interest groups that have some connection to constituents in particular members'

districts are most likely to be influential. For this reason, interest groups with the ability to mobilize followers in many congressional districts may be especially influential in Congress. In recent years, Washington-based interest groups with little grassroots strength have recognized the importance of locally generated activity. They have, accordingly, sought to simulate grassroots pressure, using a strategy that has been nicknamed "Astroturf lobbying." Such campaigns encourage constituents to sign form letters or postcards, which are then sent to congressional representatives. Sophisticated

Before a vote, members of Congress are pressed by outside influences. Here, Congressman Tom Barrett of Michigan meets with lobbyists from the auto industry (above). Sometimes the president influences congressional decision making. President Bush meets here with members of Congress to discuss Medicare reform (right).

"grassroots" campaigns set up toll-free telephone numbers for a system in which simply reporting your name and address to the listening computer will generate a letter to your congressional representative. One Senate office estimated that such organized campaigns to demonstrate "grassroots" support account for two-thirds of the mail the office received. As such campaigns increase, however, they may become less influential, because members of Congress are aware of how rare constituent interest actually is.[29]

Interest groups also have substantial influence in setting the legislative agenda and in helping to craft specific language in legislation. Today, sophisticated lobbyists win influence by providing information about policies to busy members of Congress. As one lobbyist noted, "You can't get access without knowledge.... I can go in to see [former Energy and Commerce Committee chair] John Dingell, but if I have nothing to offer or nothing to say, he's not going to want to see me."[30] In recent years, interest groups have also begun to build broader coalitions and comprehensive campaigns around particular policy issues. These coalitions do not rise from the grass roots, but instead are put together by Washington lobbyists who launch comprehensive lobbying campaigns that combine simulated grassroots activity with information and campaign funding for members of Congress. In 1995, the Republican congressional leadership worked so closely with lobbyists that critics charged that the boundaries between lobbyists and legislators had been erased, and that lobbyists had become "adjunct staff to the Republican leadership."[31]

PARTY DISCIPLINE

In both the House and Senate, party leaders have a good deal of influence over the behavior of their party members. This influence, sometimes called "party discipline," was once so powerful that it dominated the lawmaking process. At the turn of the century, party leaders could often command the allegiance of more than 90 percent of their members. A vote on which 50 percent or more of the members of one party take one position while at least 50 percent of the members of the other party take the opposing position is called a **party vote.** At the beginning of the twentieth century, nearly half of all **roll-call votes** in the House of Representatives were party votes. Today, this type of party-line voting is rare in Congress. It is, however, fairly common to find at least a majority of the Democrats opposing a majority of the Republicans on any given issue.

Typically, party unity is greater in the House than in the Senate. House rules grant greater procedural control of business to the majority party leaders, which gives them more influence over House members. In the Senate, however, the leadership has few sanctions over its members. Senate minority leader Tom Daschle once observed that a Senate leader seeking to influence other senators has as incentives "a bushel full of carrots and a few twigs."[32]

Party unity has been on the rise in the last decade because the divisions between the parties have deepened on many high profile issues such as abortion, affirmative action, the minimum wage, and school vouchers (see Figure 12.8 on page 486). Party unity scores rise when congressional leaders try to put a partisan stamp on legislation. For example, in 1995, then-Speaker Newt Gingrich sought to enact a Republican Contract with America that few Democrats supported. The re-

party vote a roll-call vote in the House or Senate in which at least 50 percent of the members of one party take a particular position and are opposed by at least 50 percent of the members of the other party. Party votes are rare today, although they were fairly common in the nineteenth century

roll-call vote a vote in which each legislator's yes or no vote is recorded as the clerk calls the names of the members alphabetically

sult was more party unity in the House than in any year since 1954. In 1998, party unity scores rose as bitter divisions between Democrats and Republicans over impeachment reduced either party's willingness to compromise on legislation.

To some extent, party unity is based on ideology and background. Republican members of Congress are more likely than Democrats to be drawn from rural or suburban areas. Democrats are likely to be more liberal on economic and social questions than their Republican colleagues. These differences certainly help to explain roll-call divisions between the two parties. Ideology and background, however, are only part of the explanation of party unity. The other part has to do with party organization and leadership. Although party organization has weakened since the beginning of the twentieth century, today's party leaders still have some resources at their disposal: (1) committee assignments, (2) access to the floor, (3) the whip system, (4) logrolling, and (5) the presidency. These resources are regularly used and are often effective in securing the support of party members.

Leadership PACs   Leaders have increased their influence over members in recent years with aggressive use of leadership political action committees. Leadership PACs are organizations that members of Congress use to raise funds that they then distribute to other members of their party running for election. Republican congressional leaders pioneered the aggressive use of leadership PACs to win their congressional majority in 1995, and the practice has spread widely since that time. For example, House Speaker J. Dennis Hastert established a leadership PAC called Keep Our Majority PAC in preparation for the 2000 election. The influential House Whip Tom DeLay (R-Tex.) has been especially aggressive in raising funds with his PAC, Americans for a Republican Majority (ARMPAC). By 1999, there were close to one hundred such PACs, with leaders, as well as members aspiring to leadership positions, setting up their own organizations. Republicans have been in the forefront of the movement to create leadership PACs. Money from these PACs can be directed to the most vulnerable candidates or to candidates who are having trouble raising money. As such, it enhances the power of the party and creates a bond between the leaders and the members who receive their help.[33]

Committee Assignments   Leaders can create debts among members by helping them get favorable committee assignments. These assignments are made early in the congressional careers of most members and cannot be taken from them if they later balk at party discipline. Nevertheless, if the leadership goes out of its way to get the right assignment for a member, this effort is likely to create a bond of obligation that can be called upon without any other payments or favors. This is one reason the Republican leadership gave freshmen favorable assignments when the Republicans took over Congress in 1995.

Access to the Floor   The most important everyday resource available to the parties is control over access to the floor. With thousands of bills awaiting passage and most members clamoring for access in order to influence a bill or to publicize themselves, floor time is precious. In the Senate, the leadership allows ranking committee members to influence the allocation of floor time—who will speak for

Party Discipline

Party discipline is maintained through a number of sources:

Committee assignments: by giving favorable committee assignments to members, party leaders create a sense of debt.

Access to the floor: ranking committee members in the Senate, and the Speaker of the House, control the allocation of floor time, so House and Senate members want to stay on good terms with these party leaders in order that their bills get time on the floor.

Whip system: party leaders use whips to track how many votes they have for a given piece of legislation; if the vote is close, they can try to influence members to switch sides.

Logrolling: members who may have nothing in common can agree to support one another's legislation because each needs the other's vote.

Presidency: the president's legislative proposals are often the most important part of Congress's agenda. Party leaders use the president's support to rally members.

Figure 12.8

Party Unity Scores by Chamber

The party unity score is the percentage of times that members voted with the majority of their party on votes on which a majority of one party voted against the majority of the other party.

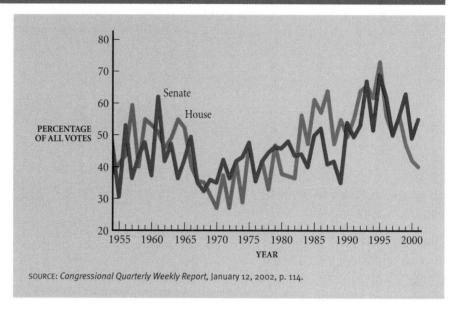

SOURCE: *Congressional Quarterly Weekly Report,* January 12, 2002, p. 114.

how long; in the House, the Speaker, as head of the majority party (in consultation with the minority leader), allocates large blocks of floor time. Thus, floor time is allocated in both houses of Congress by the majority and minority leaders. More importantly, the Speaker of the House and the majority leader in the Senate possess the power of recognition. Although this power may not appear to be substantial, it is a formidable authority and can be used to stymie a piece of legislation completely or to frustrate a member's attempts to speak on a particular issue. Because the power is significant, members of Congress usually attempt to stay on good terms with the Speaker and the majority leader in order to ensure that they will continue to be recognized.

Some House members, Republicans in particular, have also taken advantage of "special orders," under which members can address the floor after the close of business. These addresses are typically made to an empty chamber, but are usually carried live by C-SPAN, a cable television channel. As the 106th Congress ended, Speaker Dennis Hastert addressed an empty House chamber to proclaim that the Congress had "made great progress in preparing America for the next century."[34] Knowing that the press would highlight the meager accomplishments of the conflict-ridden post-impeachment Congress, Hastert was ensured that his own more positive assessment would directly reach television audiences.

The Whip System Some influence accrues to party leaders through the **whip system,** which is primarily a communications network. Between twelve and twenty assistant and regional whips are selected to operate at the direction of the majority or minority leader and the whip. They take polls of all the members in order to learn their intentions on specific bills. This enables the leaders to know if they have enough support to allow a vote as well as whether the vote is so close that they need

whip system a communications network in each house of Congress; whips take polls of the membership in order to learn their intentions on specific legislative issues and to assist the majority and minority leaders in various tasks

The Congressional Agenda: National Security or Domestic Policy?

During World War II, national security dominated the congressional agenda. With the massive mobilization of American troops and economic production geared to support the war effort, domestic policy commanded only modest attention in Congress. But in prolonged "shadow wars," such as the cold war and the current war on terrorism, the appropriate balance between national security and domestic concerns is much harder for Congress to define. In the months after the terrorist attacks, the partisan differences that had dominated Congress prior to September 11 evaporated as Democrats and Republicans united behind the president. Divisive domestic issues, such as taxes, Social Security, health care, and the environment were replaced with bipartisan cooperation around the common interest in national security. As the immediate threat of terrorism appeared to recede, President Bush and many Republicans sought to keep Congress focused on national security, the issue on which they are politically strongest. Many Democrats and some conservative Republicans, by contrast, hoped to steer the congressional agenda toward domestic policy issues.

Congress cannot afford to be distracted by partisan disputes over domestic issues when the national security is at stake, say those who believe that national security should dominate the congressional agenda. With the threat of terrorism ever present, the public expects Congress to unite behind the president rather than to quarrel over domestic issues. Partisanship dominated Congress for much of the 1990s, reducing congressional effectiveness and damaging public confidence in government. Now is the time for Congress to leave behind these divisive domestic issues and concentrate on the broader public interest in protecting the nation.

In the months after September 11, public confidence in Congress increased precisely because members put aside the narrow interests of their constituencies and parties and worked for the safety of the American people. Congress quickly passed the USA PATRIOT Act, which gave the government new powers to fight terrorism. It supported increased spending for national security and backed the war in Afghanistan. Congressional support for each of these measures was overwhelming, with very few dissenters. The passage of time since September 11 should not alter the congressional focus on national security, say supporters of this agenda. President Bush underscored the ongoing centrality of the war on terrorism in June 2002, when he asked Congress to make the Office of Homeland Security a cabinet department. The president needed congressional approval to reorganize the bureaucracy to fight a new kind of war. The complex measure involved multiple congressional committees and filled the congressional schedule well into the fall election season. By then, a new national security threat, the possibility of war with Iraq, dominated public debate.

Critics believe that security is a central issue for Congress but they contend that the public is equally concerned about such domestic issues as economic security, the future of Social Security, corporate crimes, and the cost of health care. It is possible, they argue, for Congress to support antiterrorism initiatives and to consider key domestic issues on which partisan differences are more likely to arise. The collapse of the giant energy company Enron and growing evidence about other instances of corporate misconduct require congressional attention to the problem of the accountability of America's elite business leaders. The Social Security system needs congressional action to ensure that benefits will continue for a future generation of retirees. Legitimate differences over the environment should be aired in Congress. Many supporters of this view are congressional Democrats who believe that the president has sought to sideline domestic issues because he is politically weaker in this area. Throughout the 2002 campaign season, congressional Democrats struggled with little success to draw attention to domestic issues, as the president emphasized the need for war with Iraq. The broad public interest is not served by failing to consider issues that are central to the well-being of Americans.

Some conservative Republicans agree. Anxious to push forward a socially conservative congressional agenda, they argue that by neglecting domestic issues, the president is ignoring the views of the voters that put him in office.

Should Congress Focus on Domestic Issues?

Yes

The Bush administration's proposal to use military force to overthrow Saddam Hussein has negative ramifications on the domestic front as well as the international stage. Congress and the President are pushing aside pressing national issues one month before Election Day to focus solely on the Iraq question. Party politics have no place in the debate over a war, and the government cannot afford to ignore problems at home while preparing for an attack abroad. The effects of war with Iraq would not be confined to the battlefield—they would also be felt acutely in the United States. In the second installment of a series of three editorials on the potential war in Iraq, *Spectator* examines domestic arguments for avoiding war.

War is not the only problem America faces today, and yet all other items on Congress's agenda have been put to the side while an attack is discussed. Government attention is diverted from the investigation of intelligence failures that led to September 11—and the prevention of those same mistakes—to an attack on Iraq. Congress has been reluctant to address the grave issues of corporate accountability raised by the scandals of the past year, and a war resolution provides the convenient opportunity to delay discussion of business responsibility even more.

The economy is still fragile. Unemployment remains high. In 2001, the percentage of Americans living in poverty rose for the first time in eight years, and the national median income fell. While war would provide a boost to the economy, it would be a Band-Aid and not a permanent solution. The factors that led to the recent recession—over-reliance on a volatile stock market and corporate malfeasance chief among them—would still be present. These problems need attention that they will not receive while Congress and the President prepare for war.

A host of other issues stands to lose as attention shifts to war. The millions of senior citizens who are paying exorbitant prices for their prescription drugs will have to wait even longer for relief. The massive education reforms implemented by the No Child Left Behind Act, the first results of which are starting to trickle in, will go unexamined. Social Security, a long-standing problem, spirals closer to running out of money, still without a solution in sight. Routine legislation on trade, taxes, and infrastructure will get little or no attention this fall and will languish until at least the next session of Congress. The sudden debate over war with Iraq is robbing Americans of the government's attention at a time when it is critically needed.

What should be a debate free of political pandering is instead clouded by election-year politics and animosity between Republicans and Democrats. Since the balance of power in both houses is so narrow, both parties are under pressure to deliver on Election Day. Members of Congress up for reelection fear that their statements on either side will affect the outcome of their race. In the constant tussle to be the most patriotic, Republicans are denouncing Democrats who oppose the war. Voters would benefit more from an honest debate about Iraq rather than the current political dance. Partisanship has no place in deciding whether to go to war.

Both Bush and Vice President Dick Cheney are former Texas oil moguls with ties to big business and interests in securing closer American control over the Persian Gulf's oil supply. A war in the Middle East would not only make oil more difficult to import because of chaos in the region, but it would also anger many OPEC members. The administration's concern for the accessibility and size of the oil supply is rooted in Bush's desire to keep the votes and financial backing of oil executives. Ordinary Americans should not have to pay exorbitant energy prices, but neither should they have to support a war designed to save oil for political reasons. A Hussein-free Iraq would be one less obstacle in the way of American energy companies, but the United States should not go to war because a few rich people want to get even richer. Bush's personal ties to oil should not send America to war.

The Bush administration's drive to war has shown a lack of regard for domestic concerns. America cannot afford to ignore fractures and problems in the domestic environment while pursuing patriotic triumph overseas. To maintain stability at home, the United States should not go to war abroad.

SOURCE: Managing Board, "Eye on America: The Iraq Question Detracts From Important Domestic Issues," *Columbia Daily Spectator*, October 2, 2002.

No

After more than a decade of neglect and the worst terrorist attack in U.S. history, America's national security is finally getting the attention it deserves. The Bush Administration's 2003 budget request, which was presented to Congress earlier this month, contains the largest single increase in defense spending in twenty years. To accommodate the change, all nondefense and non–homeland security discretionary spending will essentially be pegged to inflation. National security doesn't come cheap, but as the events of September 11 have shown us, it's worth every penny.

Despite its $379-billion-dollar price tag, the Department of Defense's wartime budget is only 3.3 percent of America's gross domestic product. Given that the Unites States spent closer to 5 percent of its gross domestic product on military needs during the post-Vietnam era of the late 1970s, everything included in today's budget comes at a relative bargain.

In addition to providing funding to cover the costs of the ongoing war in Afghanistan, the president's proposed budget would also fund a number of preventive operations to reduce the risk of conflict in the future. In particular, $3.5 billion would be allocated to aid countries fighting terrorism abroad. Of such funds, $121 million would be used to expand antiterrorism and security training for other countries, and $1.5 billion would be earmarked to expand efforts to reduce the proliferation of nuclear and biological weapons systems.

A portion of the 2003 budget would also be invested in the development of new technology and intelligence enhancements. Programs to further develop the kind of unmanned aerial technology that has already proven to be successful in Afghanistan would see a $146-million increase. An additional $1.2 billion would be allocated to further develop precision weapons designed to improve accuracy and minimize collateral damage on the battlefield. Further funding would go to improve the technology necessary to bring the president's proposed missile defense system online as soon as possible.

In an effort to prevent domestic terrorism on the scale that we saw on September 11, $37.7 billion would be used to shore up homeland defense. The new budget would be more than double the spending level for this year. Most of the funds would be diverted to agencies charged with securing our borders.

The Immigration and Naturalization Service, which was clearly one of the most underprepared federal agencies last September, would receive a $1.2-billion budget increase from last year. The increase will allow the agency to double the ranks of its border patrol agents and develop a new $350-million computer program to track the entry and exit of the millions of noncitizens that enter the United States each year. The lack of such technology, it is believed, was what allowed a number of the Al Qaeda terrorists to remain in the United States on expired visas prior to carrying out their mission.

The Customs Service and the U.S. Coast Guard would also be the beneficiaries of funding increases. The Customs Service would receive $619 million to increase its staff and upgrade equipment, while the Coast Guard would be directed to use its $282-million increase to develop new technology to secure our nation's harbors.

The primary function of government should always be to ensure the safety of its citizens. The Bush Administrations' 2003 budget request is evidence that it is committed to doing just that. Without security, every other function of government is irrelevant. The changes that the president has proposed will require us all to make sacrifices, but we've already seen the alternative.

SOURCE: Ben Piper, "Big Budget Pricey but Necessary," *Indiana Daily Student News*, February 18, 2002.

to put pressure on a few undecided members. Leaders also use the whip system to convey their wishes and plans to the members, but only in very close votes do they actually exert pressure on a member. In those instances, the Speaker or a lieutenant will go to a few party members who have indicated they will switch if their vote is essential. The whip system helps the leaders limit pressuring members to a few times per session.

The whip system helps maintain party unity in both houses of Congress, but it is particularly critical in the House of Representatives because of the large number of legislators whose positions and votes must be accounted for. The majority and minority whips and their assistants must be adept at inducing compromise among legislators who hold widely differing viewpoints. The whips' personal styles and their perception of their function significantly affect the development of legislative coalitions and influence the compromises that emerge.

logrolling a legislative practice wherein agreements are made between legislators in voting for or against a bill. Unlike in bargaining, logrolling parties have nothing in common but their desire to exchange support

Logrolling An agreement between two or more members of Congress who have nothing in common except the need for support is called **logrolling.** The agreement states, in effect, "You support me on bill X and I'll support you on another bill of your choice." Since party leaders are the center of the communications networks in the two chambers, they can help members create large logrolling coalitions. Hundreds of logrolling deals are made each year, and although there are no official record-keeping books, it would be a poor party leader whose whips did not know who owed what to whom. In some instances, logrolling produces strange alliances. A most unlikely alliance emerged in Congress in October 1991, which one commentator dubbed "the corn for porn plot."[35] The alliance joined Senate supporters of the National Endowment for the Arts (NEA) with senators seeking limits on the cost of grazing rights on federal lands. The NEA, which provides federal funding to the arts, had been under fire from conservative senator Jesse Helms (R-N.C.) for funding some controversial artists whose work Helms believed to be indecent. In an effort to prevent federal support for such works, Helms attached a provision to the NEA's funding that would have prohibited the agency from awarding grants to any work that in a "patently offensive way" depicted "sexual or excretory activities or organs." Supporters of the NEA condemned such restrictions as a violation of free speech and pointed out that many famous works of art could not have been funded under such restrictions. When it appeared that the amendment would pass, NEA supporters offered western senators a deal. In exchange for voting down the Helms amendment, they would eliminate a planned hike in grazing fees. Republican senators from sixteen western states switched their votes and defeated the Helms amendment. Although Helms called his defeat the product of "backroom deals and parliamentary flimflam," his amendment was simply the victim of the time-honored congressional practice of logrolling.[36]

The Presidency Of all the influences that maintain the clarity of party lines in Congress, the influence of the presidency is probably the most important. Indeed, the office is a touchstone of party discipline in Congress. Since the late 1940s, under President Harry Truman, presidents each year have identified a number of bills to be considered part of their administration's program. By the mid-1950s, both parties in Congress began to look to the president for these proposals, which became the most significant part of Congress's agenda. The president's support is a criterion for party loyalty, and party leaders are able to use it to rally some members.

WEIGHING DIVERSE INFLUENCES

Clearly, many different factors affect congressional decisions. But at various points in the decision-making process, some factors are likely to be more influential than others. For example, interest groups may be more effective at the committee stage, when their expertise is especially valued and their visibility is less obvious. Because committees play a key role in deciding what legislation actually reaches the floor of the House or Senate, interest groups can often put a halt to bills they dislike, or they can ensure that the options that do reach the floor are those that the group's members support.

Once legislation reaches the floor and members of Congress are deciding among alternatives, constituent opinion will become more important. Legislators are also influenced very much by other legislators: many of their assessments about the substance and politics of legislation come from fellow members of Congress.

The influence of the external and internal forces described in the preceding section also varies according to the kind of issue being considered. On policies of great importance to powerful interest groups—farm subsidies, for example—those groups are likely to have considerable influence. On other issues, members of Congress may be less attentive to narrow interest groups and more willing to consider what they see as the general interest.

Finally, the mix of influences varies according to the historical moment. The 1994 electoral victory of Republicans allowed their party to control both houses of Congress for the first time in forty years. That fact, combined with an unusually assertive Republican leadership, meant that party leaders became especially important in decision making. The willingness of moderate Republicans to support measures they had once opposed indicated the unusual importance of party leadership in this period.

Beyond Legislation: Other Congressional Powers

In addition to the power to make the law, Congress has at its disposal an array of other instruments through which to influence the process of government. The Constitution gives the Senate the power to approve treaties and appointments. And Congress has a number of other powers through which it can share with the other branches the capacity to administer the laws.

> **Besides the power to pass legislation, what other powers allow Congress to influence the process of government?**

OVERSIGHT

Oversight, as applied to Congress, refers not to something neglected, but to the effort to oversee or to supervise how legislation is carried out by the executive branch. Oversight is carried out by committees or subcommittees of the Senate or the House, which conduct hearings and investigations in order to analyze and

oversight the effort by Congress, through hearings, investigations, and other techniques, to exercise control over the activities of executive agencies

The Senate's approval power is significant. Occasionally, presidential appointments are given high levels of scrutiny by the Senate. For instance, when Clarence Thomas was nominated to the Supreme Court by George H.W. Bush, the Senate Judiciary Committee brought in numerous witnesses, including Anita Hill, who claimed that she had been sexually harassed by Thomas. Thomas's nomination received approval from a bare majority of both the committee and the Senate as a whole.

The appropriations process is one of Congress's essential functions. Without funding, government cannot operate. In December 1995, when Congress and the president could not agree on a budget bill, a partial shutdown of the federal government occurred.

evaluate bureaucratic agencies and the effectiveness of their programs. Their purpose may be to locate inefficiencies or abuses of power, to explore the relationship between what an agency does and what a law intended, or to change or abolish a program. Most programs and agencies are subject to some oversight every year during the course of hearings on **appropriations,** that is, the funding of agencies and government programs.

Committees or subcommittees have the power to subpoena witnesses, take oaths, cross-examine, compel testimony, and bring criminal charges for contempt (refusing to cooperate) and perjury (lying). Hearings and investigations are similar in many ways, but they differ on one fundamental point. A hearing is usually held on a specific bill, and the questions asked are usually intended to build a record with regard to that bill. In an investigation, the committee or subcommittee does not begin with a particular bill, but examines a broad area or problem and then concludes its investigation with one or more proposed bills. One example of an investigation is the congressional inquiry into the bankruptcy of the giant energy company Enron.

appropriations the amounts of money approved by Congress in statutes (bills) that each unit or agency of government can spend

executive agreement an agreement, made between the president and another country, that has the force of a treaty but does not require the Senate's "advice and consent"

ADVICE AND CONSENT: SPECIAL SENATE POWERS

The Constitution has given the Senate a special power, one that is not based on lawmaking. The president has the power to make treaties and to appoint top executive officers, ambassadors, and federal judges—but only "with the Advice

Congress, which constitutionally has the right to declare war, plays an important part in foreign policymaking. In fall 2002, President George W. Bush held several meetings with members of Congress, such as the one shown here in the White House, briefing them on U.S. intelligence on Iraq and courting their approval to go to war.

and Consent of the Senate" (Article II, Section 2). For treaties, two-thirds of those present must concur; for appointments, a simple majority is required.

The power to approve or reject presidential requests also involves the power to set conditions. The Senate only occasionally exercises its power to reject treaties and appointments. For example, only a handful of judicial nominees have been rejected by the Senate during the past century, whereas hundreds have been approved.

Most presidents make every effort to take potential Senate opposition into account in treaty negotiations and will frequently resort to **executive agreements** with foreign powers instead of treaties. The Supreme Court has held that such agreements are equivalent to treaties, but they do not need Senate approval.[37] In the past, presidents sometimes concluded secret agreements without informing Congress of the agreements' contents, or even their existence. For example, American involvement in the Vietnam War grew in part out of a series of secret arrangements made between American presidents and the South Vietnamese during the 1950s and 1960s. Congress did not even learn of the existence of these agreements until 1969. In 1972, Congress passed the Case Act, which requires that the president inform Congress of any executive agreement within sixty days of its having been reached. This provides Congress with the opportunity to cancel agreements that it opposes. In addition, Congress can limit the president's ability to conduct foreign policy through executive agreement by refusing to appropriate the funds needed to implement an agreement. In this way, for example,

The Senate also possesses the power to impeach federal officials. In American history, sixteen federal officials have been impeached, including two presidents, Andrew Johnson and Bill Clinton, who was impeached for lying under oath. During Clinton's trial in the House, House Manager Bill McCollum argued that lying under oath was sufficient grounds for Clinton's removal from office.

executive agreements to provide American economic or military assistance to foreign governments can be modified or even canceled by Congress.

IMPEACHMENT

impeachment the formal charge by the House of Representatives that a government official has committed "Treason, Bribery, or other high Crimes and Misdemeanors"

The Constitution also grants Congress the power of **impeachment** over the president, vice president, and other executive officials. Impeachment means to charge a government official (president or otherwise) with "Treason, Bribery, or other high Crimes and Misdemeanors" and bring them before Congress to determine their guilt. Impeachment is thus like a criminal indictment in which the House of Representatives acts like a grand jury, voting (by simple majority) on whether the accused ought to be impeached. If a majority of the House votes to impeach, the impeachment trial moves to the Senate, which acts like a trial jury by voting whether to convict and forcibly remove the person from office (this vote requires a two-thirds majority of the Senate).

Controversy over Congress's impeachment power has arisen over the grounds for impeachment, especially the meaning of "high Crimes and Misdemeanors." A strict reading of the Constitution suggests that the only impeachable offense is an actual crime. But a more commonly agreed upon definition is that "an impeachable offense is whatever the majority of the House of Representatives considers it to be at a given moment in history."[38] In other words, impeachment, especially impeachment of a president, is a political decision.

The political nature of impeachment was very clear in the two instances of impeachment that have occurred in American history. In the first, in 1867, President Andrew Johnson, a southern Democrat who had battled a congressional Republican majority over Reconstruction, was impeached by the House but saved from conviction by one vote in the Senate. In 1998, the House impeached President Bill Clinton on two counts, for lying under oath and obstructing justice, in the investigation into his sexual affair with White House intern Monica Lewinsky. The vote was highly partisan, with only five Democrats voting for impeachment on each charge. In the Senate, where a two-thirds majority was needed to convict the president, only forty-five senators voted to convict on the first count of lying and fifty voted to convict on the second charge of obstructing justice. As in the House, the vote for impeachment was highly partisan with all Democrats and only five Republicans supporting the president's ultimate acquittal.

The impeachment power is a considerable one; its very existence in the hands of Congress is a highly effective safeguard against the executive tyranny so greatly feared by the framers of the Constitution.

Congress and Democracy

> **How do the institutional features of Congress affect meaningful representation?**

Much of this chapter has described the major institutional components of Congress and has shown how they work as Congress makes policy. But what do these institutional features mean for how Congress represents the American public? Does the organization of Congress promote the equal representation of all Americans? Or are there institutional features of Congress that allow some interests more access and influence than others?

What Government Does . . . After September 11

Periods of war are difficult for Congress. The need for strong leadership and quick decision making inevitably bestows more power on the president. Under these circumstances, the nation pulls together and Congress willingly grants the president much greater leeway to act than in peacetime. After the September 11 terrorist attacks, Congress followed this pattern, deferring to the need for presidential leadership. Yet, as the war against terrorism progressed, Congress sought to define its role in shaping policy.

In the months after the attacks, Congress questioned the president on very few matters related to the war on terrorism. One contention raised by Congress concerned its right to be informed about the conduct of the war. Soon after September 11, President Bush sought to limit congressional access to intelligence briefings. Because of the delicate nature of the intelligence sources regarding terrorism, the need for secrecy is paramount. When a Republican senator publicly revealed information that he had received in a classified briefing, Bush issued an order limiting intelligence briefings to only eight members of Congress. Such limited information would not have allowed Congress to exercise its customary oversight authority over the executive branch. Miffed congressional leaders charged that the president had violated the 1947 National Security Act, which requires that the House and Senate Intelligence Committees be fully briefed about the executive's wartime activities. As Republican senator Chuck Hagel put it, the president had "put out a public document telling the world he doesn't trust the Congress."[1] The president quickly retracted his order.

Some members of Congress also challenged the president on his order establishing military tribunals to try suspected foreign terrorists. The tribunals placed extraordinary power in the hands of the president, who would both invoke the use of tribunals and have final say over verdicts and sentences. Members of Congress questioned the constitutionality of placing such power in the hands of the president. At a hearing of the Senate Judiciary Committee, Senator Arlen Specter (R-Pa.) declared that "the Constitution gives the authority to the Congress to establish military tribunals."[2] Committee chairman Patrick Leahy argued that there were important political reasons for the president to seek legislation authorizing the tribunals: "This war on terrorism is going to be going on long after George Bush is gone, and long after I am gone. So we want to make sure we do it right. Why not work out rules on military tribunals and get authorization from Congress before it comes back to haunt the president?"[3]

Nearly nine months after the attacks, Congress asserted its role much more strongly. In the wake of revelations that the FBI and the CIA had information before September 11 that may have prevented the terrorist attacks, the House and Senate intelligence committees launched a major investigation of the government's counterterrorism activities. The inquiry examined the response to international terrorism as far back as 1986, when President Reagan first established a counterterrorism center designed to monitor threats and to ensure information-sharing between the CIA and the FBI.

The White House initially tried to stifle congressional inquiry, fearing political damage. Indeed, as new revelations emerged in the weeks before Congress launched its inquiry, vice president Dick Cheney charged that commentary about intelligence failures was "thoroughly irresponsible and totally unworthy of national leaders in a time of war."[4] The administration quickly shifted gears, however, as evidence of missed clues related to terrorism dominated the national headlines. One year after the attacks, the president finally agreed to the creation of an independent commission to investigate intelligence failures. For the first time since September 11, congressional leaders had reasserted their role in the system of checks and balances that is challenged in periods of war.

[1] Dana Milbank, "In War, It's Power to the President," *Washington Post* (November 20, 2001), p. A1.
[2] Bob Port, "Congress Challenges W on Tribunal Rules," *Daily News* (December 5, 2001), p. 32.
[3] David E. Sanger, "There's a Small Matter of Checks and Balances," *New York Times* (January 27, 2002), Sec. 4, p. 1.
[4] Elisabeth Bumiller, "New Tone, Old Goal," *New York Times* (June 6, 2002), p. A1.

As we noted at the beginning of this chapter, Congress instituted a number of reforms in the 1970s to make itself looser and more accessible. These reforms sought to respond to public views that Congress had become a stodgy institution ruled by a powerful elite that made decisions in private. We have seen that these reforms increased the number of subcommittees, prohibited most secret hearings, and increased the staff support for Congress. These reforms spread power more evenly throughout the institution and opened new avenues for the public to contact and influence Congress.

But the opening of Congress ultimately did not benefit the broad American public, as reformers had envisioned. In fact the congressional reforms enacted in the 1970s actually made Congress less effective and, ironically, more permeable to special interests. The fragmentation of power in Congress has made it harder for members to reach decisions. "Turf battles"—struggles over who should take charge of what—often take more congressional energy than deliberations over policy. The decentralization of power in Congress has made each member more of an independent operator. Members are now less willing to compromise and more eager to take positions that benefit them individually, even if they undermine possibilities for enacting policy. These circumstances have created a Congress that sometimes seems to spend endless hours in increasingly negative debates that do not produce results. The public, therefore, has come to view Congress as a group of privileged elites concerned only about their own prerogatives. The word "gridlock" seems to sum up the state of congressional decision making.

Ironically, the measures that sought to ensure more public access to Congress have increased the access of interest groups. Open committee meetings have made it possible for sophisticated interest groups to monitor and influence every aspect of developing legislation. The narrow perspective put forth by an interest group makes it difficult for members of Congress to keep their eyes on the big picture of what they want to achieve. Hundreds of amendments can undermine the overall thrust of legislation. Open meetings also deprive members of Congress of the political "cover" often necessary to make compromises. Worried that particular actions could be used against them in a future election, members of Congress have become very risk-averse. In this sense, too much accountability can paralyze the institution.

The reforms of the 1970s, intended to distribute power more equally inside Congress in order to provide more equal representation to all constituents, instead made it more difficult for members to build coalitions and for legislators to become experts in particular policy areas. The unanticipated, negative consequences of these reforms have highlighted the trade-off between representation and effectiveness in Congress.[39] Americans are becoming increasingly aware that greater individual access to Congress and more symbolic representation do not add up to more power. The results have increased public cynicism and apathy. Rebuilding public faith in Congress may require yet another round of institutional reform, as well as efforts to organize and mobilize broad social interests to achieve meaningful representation.

For the Founders, Congress was the national institution that best embodied the ideals of representative democracy. Throughout our history, Congress has served as the symbol of the American commitment to democratic values. Members of Congress, working to represent their constituents, bring these democratic values to life. A member of Congress can interpret his job as representative in two different

Legislative "Bicameralism"

Legislative bodies among electoral democracies are of two basic types: bicameral (consisting of two separately elected chambers of representatives) and unicameral (one chamber of representatives). Approximately one in three countries in the world have, like the United States, bicameral legislatures; two of three prefer unicameral legislatures. Bicameral legislatures are most common in large countries—especially among the advanced industrial electoral democracies of Europe, North America, and Asia—where political interests among the public are exposed to degrees of sharp regional diversity.

Americans may be excused for assuming that the legislative process ought to be a tussle between two powerful and roughly equally balanced chambers of representatives. Each chamber—the Senate and the House—has various checks and balances on the other, both can veto the other chamber, both must ordinarily come to agreement and iron out their differences before legislation can become law, and both actively serve to shape the national political agenda through their legislative activities. However, this is not the case among most bicameral legislatures within the family of advanced industrial electoral democracies. Indeed, according to the classification system devised by Arend Lijphart, only three other countries within the group of democracies have "strong" national bicameral legislatures where both chambers have such power. These are Germany, Switzerland, and Australia.

What distinguishes the legislative process in these four democracies from the process in other countries within the family of advanced industrial democracies that practice bicameralism? First, strong bicameral legislatures are characterized by *political symmetry* between the two chambers of the national legislature. Symmetry implies that both chambers enjoy roughly equal constitutional powers over legislative issues, including the power to formally veto and check the power of the other chamber, and importantly, symmetrical balance assumes that both chambers have a claim to legitimate electoral support. Namely, both the upper and lower chambers are directly elected by the public. All lower chambers in the national legislatures among advanced industrial democracies are directly elected, through a variety of means. However, such is not the case for most upper chambers among this set of democracies. Many of the upper chambers have portions, or sometimes entire bodies of representatives, that are appointed by the formal sovereign to sit within the chamber, thus bypassing the electoral contest. Others are indirectly elected by special electoral bodies, which may be held accountable by the electorate, but without having their decisions sanctioned by the electorate.

The second feature of strong bicameral legislatures is the *congruence* between the two chambers. Congruence refers to the manner of selecting the membership to the upper and lower chambers in a bicameral system. Congruence is present when the two chambers are selected by electoral formulas that are basically similar and that do not allow any degree of overrepresentation among their constituent parts. For instance, the United States overrepresents small states in the U.S. Senate: Rhode Island (with roughly one million people) receives as many senators as California (with roughly thirty-four million people). When the number of representatives of a specified constituency does not vary by population, as in the case of the U.S. Senate, overrepresentation of the smallest states is maximized. However, when representation varies by population, the upper chamber achieves no such overrepresentation. This is the case, for instance, in Belgium. Overrepresentation ensures that the constituency base for the upper chamber of the national legislature differs from the lower chamber. As such, it allows the upper chamber to exercise distinctive power vis-à-vis the lower chamber of the national legislature, which accordingly enhances the degree of bicameralism within the national legislative system. When congruence is low (when there are different methods of selection or electoral algorithms for the respective chambers) and symmetry is high, the legislative process within a country is strongly bicameral. When congruence is high (similar methods and rules of selection/election) and symmetry is low (when the lower chamber dominates the legislative process) the degree of bicameralism is very weak.

SOURCE: Arend Lijphart, *Patterns of Democracy: Government Forms and Performance in Thirty-Six Countries* (New Haven, CT: Yale University Press, 1999).

delegate the role of a representative who votes according to the preferences of his or her constituency

trustee the role of a representative who votes based on what he or she thinks is best for his or her constituency

Perspectives on Politics

INTEREST-GROUP INFLUENCE IN CONGRESS

Responses of Americans to the statement,

"Congress is too heavily influenced by interest groups when making decisions."

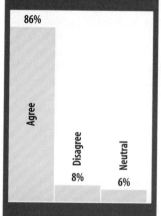

SOURCE: John R. Hibbing and Elizabeth Theiss-Morse, *Congress as Public Enemy: Public Attitudes toward American Political Institutions* (New York: Cambridge University Press, 1995), p. 64.

ways: as a delegate or as a trustee. As a **delegate,** a member of Congress acts on the express preferences of his constituents; as a **trustee,** the member is more loosely tied to constituents and makes the decisions he thinks best. The delegate role appears to be the most democratic because it forces the representative to heed the desires of his constituents. But this requires the representative to be in constant touch with constituents; it also requires constituents to follow each policy issue very closely. The problem with this form of representation is that most people do not follow every issue so carefully; instead they focus only on extremely important issues or issues of particular interest to them. Many people are too busy to get the information necessary to make informed judgments even on issues they care about. Thus, adhering to the delegate form of representation risks that the voices of only a few active and informed constituents get heard. Although it seems more democratic at first glance, the delegate form of representation may actually open Congress up even more to the influence of the voices of special interests.

If a congressional member acts as a trustee, on the other hand, there is a danger that she will not pay sufficient attention to the wishes of constituents. In this scenario, the only way the public can exercise influence is by voting every two years for representatives or every six years for senators. Yet, most members of Congress take this electoral check very seriously. They try to anticipate the wishes of their constituents even when they don't know exactly what those interests are, because they know that unpopular decisions can be used against them in the coming election.

The public understands the trade-offs entailed in these different forms of representation and is, in fact, divided on how members of Congress should represent it. In a recent poll, 69 percent of respondents agreed that when a congressional representative votes, the views of the district should be the most important; only 25 percent believed that the representative's own principles and judgment should prevail. Yet the public also recognizes that representatives are often better informed about issues than the public. On a different survey, 65 percent of respondents agreed that in making a decision members of Congress should ask themselves how the majority of the public would think if they were well informed on all sides of the issue; only 29 percent said the representative should be guided instead by what the majority actually thinks.[40]

What the public dislikes most about Congress stems from suspicions that Congress acts as neither a trustee nor a delegate of the broad public interest, but instead is swayed by narrow special interests with lots of money.[41] Indeed, there is plenty of reason for the public to worry about the power of such groups: lobbying groups have continually adjusted their tactics to increase their ability to influence Congress. As reporter Jeffrey H. Birnbaum notes, lobbyists no longer fit the old caricature of "fat, cigar-smoking men who [shoved] hundred-dollar bills into the pockets of lawmakers."[42] Their tactics have grown much more sophisticated. Interest groups have used "Astroturf" lobbying to simulate a surge of grassroots interest on the part of constituents (see Chapter 11). More recently, as Congress has come to discount such influence as not really representing its constituents, lobbyists have changed tactics: they now concentrate on "grasstops" organizing, in which they mobilize important friends or associates of the representative or senator to present information favorable to the interest group's perspective. This new strategy is more subtle and may be more effective because it relies on a previous relationship of trust.

Ideally, representative democracy grants all citizens equal opportunity to select their leaders and to communicate their preferences to these elected representatives. Yet, in reality, some citizens have more wealth, are more politically savvy, or belong to more effective organizations. Despite past efforts to reform Congress, these advantages provide special access to some interests even as they mute the voice of much of the American public. The dilemma that congressional reformers confront is how to devise safeguards that reduce the voice of special interests while allowing Congress to remain open to public influence.

GET INVOLVED

What You Can Do: Make Contact with Congress

Are ordinary citizens powerless in the face of such activity by special-interest groups? The changing tactics of interest-group politics suggest that citizens, when they are organized and active, can greatly influence representatives. After all, what the most sophisticated interest groups are doing today is trying to convince members of Congress that there is genuine widespread grassroots support for their cause. This reflects the belief—rooted in long experience—that what really sways representatives most is evidence that their constituents care about particular issues. To influence all of Congress, it is particularly important to build grassroots organization that is geographically broad. If members of Congress from many parts of the country are getting the same message from their constituents, there is a greater chance of successfully influencing policy.

The experience of some groups that have organized such broad-based grassroots activity indicates that ordinary citizens can affect what Congress does. In recent years, significant grassroots activism has emerged to influence government spending for research on diseases. The striking success of AIDS activists in dramatically increasing funding for AIDS research has inspired other groups to try similar strategies. One example is the National Breast Cancer Coalition, which represents 350 separate organizations around the country. Its aim has been to increase expenditures for federally sponsored research on breast cancer. When the coalition formed in 1991, the federal government spent $90 million a year on breast cancer research; by 1997 that amount had increased to $509 million.[43] Building on its grassroots strength and borrowing tactics from highly successful AIDS activists, the coalition sent 600,000 letters to Congress and to the White House in its first year alone. Initially told that the National Cancer Institute's priorities could not be changed so easily, they turned to the Defense Department, which had already spent some funds for breast cancer research. Today, the Defense Department is the second largest funder of breast cancer research, and citizens can monitor and affect its agenda through an independent panel overseeing the program. Both the increased expenditures and the ongoing public influence over the research agenda were a direct result of the grassroots activity of these local groups organized into a national coalition.

Organizing such grassroots groups takes time, expertise, and some resources. But the example of such groups as the Breast Cancer Coalition and AIDS activists indicates that, when organized, ordinary citizens can be effective. It is important for individuals who feel that Congress is out of touch to recognize that the path of influence may require considerable effort, but that it is

Perspectives on Politics

CONTACTING YOUR MEMBER OF CONGRESS

Percentage of Americans agreeing with the statement, **"You have called or sent a letter to your congressional representative."**

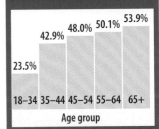

Age group	
18–34	23.5%
35–44	42.9%
45–54	48.0%
55–64	50.1%
65+	53.9%

SOURCE: 1993 Times-Mirror poll, reported in Susan A. MacManus, *Young v. Old: Generational Combat in the 21st Century* (Boulder, CO: Westview, 1996), p 141.

available. One way for you to make Congress more approachable and accessible is to make contact with its nearest embodiment, your congressional representative's local field office.

All U.S. senators and representatives have offices in Washington, D.C. But they also have one or more local field offices in their home districts. These field offices are generally run by deputies who have the job of keeping their bosses visible among voters and donors as well as keeping them informed about local events, issues, and electoral concerns. While members of Congress do not spend much time in their field offices when Congress is in session, they regularly return to them for special occasions and during congressional recesses.

Making contact with a member's local field office is fairly simple. Most telephone directories have a section near the beginning that lists government offices. Your local directory is likely to name your U.S. senators and representative, as well as provide addresses and phone numbers for their nearest field offices. Alternatively, call your local city hall and request contact information for your representatives' field offices.

Summary

The U.S. Congress plays a vital role in American democracy. It is both the key national representative body and the focal point for decision making in Washington, D.C. Throughout American history, Congress has sought to combine representation and power as it made policy. In recent years, however, many Americans have become disillusioned with the ability of Congress to represent fairly and to exercise power responsibly.

Both sociological and agency representation play a role in the relationship between members of Congress and their constituencies. However, Congress is not fully representative because it is not a sociological microcosm of the United States. Members of Congress do seek to act as agents for their constituents by representing the views and interests of those constituents in the governmental process.

The activities of members of Congress are strongly influenced by electoral considerations. Who gets elected to Congress is influenced by who runs for office, the power of incumbency, and the way congressional districts are drawn. In order to assist their chances of re-election, members of Congress provide services and patronage to their constituents.

In order to make policy, Congress depends on a complex internal organization. Six basic dimensions of Congress affect the legislative process: (1) the parties, (2) the committees, (3) the staff, (4) the caucuses, (5) the rules, and (6) the presidency.

Since the Constitution provides only for a presiding officer in each house, some method had to be devised for conducting business. Parties quickly assumed the responsibility for this. In the House, the majority party elects a leader every two years. This individual becomes Speaker. In addition, a majority leader, a minority leader, and party whips are elected. Each party has a committee whose job it is to make committee assignments. Party structure in the Senate is similar, except that the vice president of the United States is the Senate president.

The committee system surpasses the party system in its importance in Congress. In the early nineteenth century, standing committees became a fundamental aspect of Congress. They have, for the most part, evolved to correspond to executive branch departments or programs and thus reflect and maintain the separation of powers.

Congress also establishes rules of procedure to guide policy making. The Senate has a tradition of unlimited debate, on which the various cloture rules it has passed have had little effect. Filibusters still occur. The rules of the House, on the other hand, restrict talk and support committees; deliberation is recognized as committee business. The House Rules Committee has the power to control debate and floor amendments. The rules prescribe the formal procedure through which bills become law. Generally, the parties control scheduling and agenda, but the committees determine action on the floor. Committees, seniority, and rules all limit the ability of members to represent their constituents. Yet, these factors enable Congress to maintain its role as a major participant in government.

Many different factors affect how Congress ultimately decides on legislation. Among the most important influences are constituency preferences, interest group pressures, and party discipline. Typically party discipline is stronger in the House than in the Senate. Parties have several means of maintaining discipline: (1) favorable committee assignments create obligations; (2) floor time in the debate on one bill can be allocated in exchange for a specific vote on another; (3) the whip system allows party leaders to assess support for a bill and convey their wishes to members; (4) party leaders can help members create large logrolling coalitions; and (5) the president can champion certain pieces of legislation and thereby muster support along party lines. In most cases, party leaders accept constituency obligations as a valid reason for voting against the party position.

In addition to the power to make law, Congress possesses other formidable powers in its relationship with the executive branch. Among these are oversight, advice and consent on treaties and appointments, and the power to impeach executive officials. In spite of its array of powers, Congress is often accused of being ineffective and out of touch with the American people. At the heart of these criticisms lies the debate over whether members of Congress should act more as delegates or as trustees. An even more important concern facing Congress is whether it has become beholden to special interests and has, in effect, shut ordinary citizens out of the political process.

For Further Reading

Burrell, Barbara C., *A Woman's Place Is in the House: Campaigning for Congress in the Feminist Era.* Ann Arbor: University of Michigan Press, 1994.

Davidson, Roger H., ed. *The Postreform Congress.* New York: St. Martin's, 1991.

Dodd, Lawrence, and Bruce I. Oppenheimer, eds. *Congress Reconsidered.* 5th ed. Washington, DC: Congressional Quarterly Press, 1993.

Fenno, Richard F. *Congressmen in Committees.* Boston: Little, Brown, 1973.

Fenno, Richard F. *Homestyle: House Members in Their Districts.* Boston: Little, Brown, 1978.

Fiorina, Morris. *Congress: Keystone of the Washington Establishment.* 2nd ed. New Haven, CT: Yale University Press, 1989.

Fowler, Linda, and Robert McClure. *Political Ambition: Who Decides to Run for Congress?* New Haven, CT: Yale University Press, 1989.

Mayhew, David R. *Congress: The Electoral Connection.* New Haven, CT: Yale University Press, 1974.

Sinclair, Barbara. *The Transformation of the U.S. Senate.* Baltimore: Johns Hopkins University Press, 1989.

Smith, Steven S., and Christopher Deering. *Committees in Congress.* 2nd ed. Washington, DC: Congressional Quarterly Press, 1990.

Thomas, Sue. *How Women Legislate.* New York: Oxford University Press, 1994.

Study Outline

www.wwnorton.com/wtp4e

Congress: Representing the American People

1. The House and Senate play different roles in the legislative process. The Senate is more deliberative, whereas the House is characterized by greater centralization and organization.
2. House members are more attuned to localized narrow interests in society, whereas senators are more able than House members to represent statewide or national interests.
3. In recent years, the House has exhibited more partisanship and ideological division than the Senate.

4. Congress is not fully representative because it is not a sociological microcosm of American society.
5. Members of Congress frequently communicate with constituents and devote a great deal of staff time to constituency service.
6. Electoral motivations have a strong impact on both sociological and agency representation in Congress.
7. Incumbency affords members of Congress resources such as constituency service and mailing to help secure re-election.
8. In recent years, turnover rates in Congress have increased, although this is due more to incumbent retirement than to the defeat of incumbents in elections.
9. Members of Congress can supply benefits to constituents by passing pork-barrel legislation. Pork-barrel votes are exchanged by members of Congress for votes on other issues.

The Organization of Congress

1. At the beginning of each Congress, Democrats and Republicans gather to select their leaders. The leader of the majority party in the House of Representatives is elected Speaker of the House by a strict party vote.
2. In the Senate, the president pro tempore serves as the presiding officer, although the majority and minority leaders control the calendar and agenda of the Senate.

3. The committee system provides Congress with a second organizational structure that is more a division of labor than the party-based hierarchies of power.
4. With specific jurisdiction over certain policy areas and the task of processing proposals of legislation into bills for floor consideration, standing committees are the most important arenas of congressional policy making.
5. Power within committees is based on seniority, although the seniority principle is not absolute.
6. In the 1970s, reforms fragmented power in Congress—the committee system, specifically—by increasing both the number of subcommittees and the autonomy of subcommittee chairpersons.
7. Each member of Congress has a personal staff that deals with constituency requests and, increasingly, with the details of legislative and administrative oversight.

8. Groups of senators or representatives who share certain opinions, interests, or social characteristics form informal organizations called caucuses.

Rules of Lawmaking: How a Bill Becomes a Law

1. Committee deliberation is necessary before floor action on any bill.
2. Many bills receive little or no committee or subcommittee action; they are allowed to "die in committee."
3. Bills reported out of committee in the House must go through the House Rules Committee before they can be debated on the floor. The Rules Committee allots the time for floor debate on a bill and the conditions under which a bill may (or may not) be amended.
4. In the Senate, rules of debate are much less rigid. In fact, senators may delay Senate action on legislation by refusing to yield the floor; this is known as a filibuster.
5. Conference committees are often required to reconcile House and Senate versions of bills that began with similar provisions but emerged with significant differences.
6. After being adopted by the House and the Senate, a bill is sent to the president, who may choose to sign the bill or veto it. Congress can override a president's veto by a two-thirds vote in both the House and the Senate.

How Congress Decides

1. Creating a legislative agenda, drawing up a list of possible measures, and deciding among them is a complex process in which a variety of influences from inside and outside government play important roles.
2. Interest groups can influence congressional decision making by mobilizing followers in congressional districts, setting the agenda, or writing legislative language.
3. Party discipline is still an important factor in congressional voting, despite its decline throughout the twentieth century.
4. Party unity is typically greater in the House than in the Senate. Party unity on roll-call votes has increased in recent sessions of Congress.
5. Party unity is a result of a combination of the ideology and background of individual members and the resources party leaders have at their disposal.
6. The influence of the presidency is probably the most important of all the resources that maintain party discipline in Congress.

Beyond Legislation: Other Congressional Powers

1. Congress has increasingly relied on legislative oversight of administrators.
2. The Senate also has the power of approving or rejecting presidential treaties and appointments.
3. Congress has the power to impeach executive officials.

Congress and Democracy

1. Congressional reforms of the 1970s fragmented power in Congress and made it more open to special interests.
2. What the public dislikes most about Congress stems from suspicions that Congress does not act as a trustee or as a delegate of any broad interest but that it is swayed by narrow special interests with money.

Practice Quiz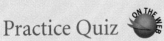

www.wwnorton.com/wtp4e

1. Members of Congress can work as agents of their constituents by
   a) providing direct patronage.
   b) taking part in a party vote.
   c) joining a caucus.
   d) supporting term limits.

2. Why has public approval of Congress as an institution declined since the 1970s?
   a) Constituents don't like their own representatives in Congress.
   b) Congress has become increasingly inaccessible to the public since the 1970s.
   c) Citizens can now see members of Congress on television every night.
   d) Congress has increasingly opened itself up to the control of special interests.

3. Because they have larger and more heterogeneous constituencies, senators
   a) are more attuned to the needs of localized interest groups.
   b) care more about re-election than House members.
   c) can better represent the national interest.
   d) face less competition in elections than House members.

4. Sociological representation is important in understanding the U.S. Congress because
   a) members often vote based on their religion.
   b) Congress is a microcosm of American society.
   c) the symbolic composition of Congress is important for the political stability of the United States.
   d) there is a distinct "congressional sociology."

5. What type of representation is described when constituents have the power to hire and fire their representative?
   a) agency representation
   b) sociological representation
   c) democratic representation
   d) trustee representation

6. Incumbency is an important factor in deciding who is elected to Congress because
   a) incumbents have tools they can use to help ensure re-election.
   b) potentially strong challengers may be dissuaded from running because of the strength of the incumbent.
   c) Both a and b are true.
   d) Neither a nor b is true.

7. Some have argued that the creation of minority congressional districts has
   a) lessened the sociological representation of minorities in Congress.
   b) made it more difficult for minorities to win substantive policy goals.
   c) been a result of the media's impact on state legislative politics.
   d) lessened the problem of "pork barrel" politics.

8. Which of the following is *not* an important influence on how members of Congress vote on legislation?
   a) the media
   b) constituency
   c) interest groups
   d) party leaders

9. Which of the following types of committees does *not* include members of both the House and the Senate?
   a) standing committee
   b) joint committee
   c) conference committee
   d) No committees include both House members and senators.

10. An agreement between members of Congress to trade support for each other's bill is known as
    a) oversight.
    b) filibuster.
    c) logrolling.
    d) patronage.

Critical Thinking Questions

www.wwnorton.com/wtp4e

1. Two of Congress's chief responsibilities are representation and lawmaking. Describe the ways in which these two responsibilities might conflict with one another. How do these responsibilities support and reinforce one another? What would Congress be like if its sole function were representative? What would it be like if it were solely legislative?

2. Describe the process by which a bill becomes a law. At the various stages of this process, assess who—both within government and outside of government—makes and influences decisions. Are there stages at which the process is more democratic than it is at others? Are there stages at which the people have less influence? In your judgment, is the overall process democratic?

3. For over a century, Congress has faced charges that it is dominated by special interests that drown out the public voice. Why is it so hard to make the voice of the public heard over the special interests in Congress? What reforms can enhance the public's influence in congressional deliberations?

Key Terms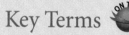

www.wwnorton.com/wtp4e

agency representation (p. 460)
appropriations (p. 492)
bicameral (p. 458)
bill (p. 476)
caucus (congressional) (p. 476)
caucus (political) (p. 470)
closed rule (p. 478)
cloture (p. 479)
conference (p. 469)
conference committee (p. 473)
constituency (p. 458)
delegate (p. 498)

executive agreement (p. 492)
filibuster (p. 479)
impeachment (p. 494)
incumbency (p. 464)
joint committee (p. 473)
logrolling (p. 490)
majority leader (p. 470)
minority leader (p. 470)
open rule (p. 478)
oversight (p. 491)
party vote (p. 484)
patronage (p. 467)
pocket veto (p. 480)
political action committee (PAC) (p. 464)

pork barrel (p. 467)
private bill (p. 468)
redistricting (p. 466)
roll-call vote (p. 484)
select committee (p. 473)
seniority (p. 473)
sociological representation (p. 459)
Speaker of the House (p. 470)
staff agency (p. 476)
standing committee (p. 472)
term limits (p. 465)
trustee (p. 498)
veto (p. 480)
whip system (p. 486)

13 THE PRESIDENCY

★ **The Constitutional Basis of the Presidency**

What were the conflicting views over presidential power of the framers of the Constitution?

What factors led to the growth of a more powerful presidency?

★ **The Constitutional Powers of the Presidency**

What powers does the Constitution provide to the president as head of state? Have presidents used these powers to make the presidency too powerful or even imperial?

What powers does the Constitution provide to the president as head of government?

★ **Institutional Resources of Presidential Power**

What institutional resources does the president use to manage the executive branch?

★ **Political Resources of Presidential Power**

What political resources can the president draw on in exercising the powers of the presidency? Which of these resources is a potential liability? Why?

★ **The Presidency and Democracy**

Did the development of a mass presidential constituency make the institution more democratic? More powerful?

LTHOUGH THE FIRST domestic impact of war is inevitably on civil liberties, war has ramifications throughout all governmental and political institutions as well as public policies. For example, President Abraham Lincoln's 1862 declaration of martial law and Congress's 1863 legislation giving the president the power to make arrests and imprisonments through military tribunals amounted to a "constitutional dictatorship," which lasted through the war and Lincoln's re-election in 1864. But these measures were viewed as emergency powers that could be taken back once the crisis of union was resolved. In less than a year after Lincoln's death, Congress had reasserted its power, leaving the presidency in many respects the same as, if not weaker than, it had been before.

War also transformed the presidency of Woodrow Wilson. In 1917, one of Congress's rare declarations of war provided America with another "constitutional dictatorship." In addition to restrictions on civil liberties, Congress gave the president a number of significant powers: to censor not only all international communications but also take over and operate the railroads and all other common carriers; to seize and operate all telephone and telegraph lines; to regulate at his discretion the manufacture and distribution of all foods and related commodities; to fix prices on all such commodities and on stock exchanges; and to take over all aspects of mines and factories. As one leading constitutional history treatise puts it, "Legislative delegation [to the president] on this scale was unprecedented and little short of revolutionary. . . . [However,] if Wilson was in any sense a dictator, it was because Congress in certain spheres came close to a virtual delegation of its entire legislative power to the president *for the duration of the war*" [emphasis added]. The setting of a precise time limit on the duration of emergency powers later came to be called a "sunset" provision. In hindsight, some of the strengthening of the presidency did last beyond Wilson and the sunset provision. Fortunately for America, civil liberties not only survived the war restrictions but First Amendment rights actually flourished afterwards.

During World War II, Franklin D. Roosevelt, like Lincoln, did not bother to wait for Congress but took executive action first and expected Congress to follow. Roosevelt brought the United States into an undeclared naval war against Germany a year before Pearl Harbor, and he ordered the unauthorized use of wiretaps and other surveillance as well as the investigation of suspicious persons for reasons not clearly specified. The most egregious (and revealing) of these was his segregation and eventual confinement of 120,000 individuals of Japanese descent, many of whom were American citizens. Even worse, the Supreme Court validated Roosevelt's treatment of the Japanese, on the flimsy grounds of military necessity. One dissenter on the Court called the president's assumption of emergency powers "a loaded weapon ready for the hand of any authority that can bring forward a plausible claim of an urgent need."

The "loaded weapon" was seized again on September 14, 2001, when Congress defined the World Trade Center and Pentagon attacks as an act of war and proceeded to adopt a joint resolution authorizing the president to use "all necessary and appropriate force against those nations, organizations or persons he determines planned, authorized, committed or aided the terrorist attacks that occurred on September 11, 2001, or harbored such organizations or persons. . . ." Congress did attach a "sunset provision" to the authorization resolution and planned for congressional oversight during the war, but it remains to be seen whether President George W. Bush's handling of the war against terrorism will lead to more power for the presidency beyond this particular war.

National emergencies provide presidents a source of power, and the way presidents exercise these powers has profound consequences for the country. As we have seen, civil liberties are particularly threatened by what presidents do during times of war. In this chapter, we will go beyond this and look at the long-term consequences of national emergencies on presidential power. What circumstances explain why some emergencies produced new and long-lasting powers for the president, while others did not? In the instances in which new powers were institutionalized, what was the long-term impact? ■

T HE task of this chapter is to explain why the American system of government could be described as presidential government and how it got to be that way. Another task is to explore how and why the president, however powerful, is also particularly vulnerable to the popular will. In other words, as the presidency became a powerful center of government, its foundation rested upon a virtually untamable mass popular democracy.

■ **Our focus in the first three parts of this chapter is to explore the resources of presidential power, which we will divide into three categories: constitutional, institutional, and political.** The Constitution provides an array of powers to the president as head of state and as head of government. Although we give these two roles separate treatment, the presidency can be understood only as a combination of the two. We will refer to this as the "dual nature" of the presidency.

■ **We turn next to the institutional resources that presidents use as tools of management.** Without these resources, such as the Cabinet, presidents would be unable to use the powers provided by the Constitution.

■ **We will then examine the political resources of presidential power.** Presidents rely on their party, interest groups, the media, and public opinion in order to build support for their programs and persuade Congress to cooperate. These resources offer great strength to the president but, as we will see, can also be a great liability.

■ **We conclude by assessing the presidency as an institution of democracy.** The presidency has developed into a democratic institution with a mass constituency so great that we now have a "presidential government." We will explain how this development occurred.

The Constitutional Basis of the Presidency

THE FRAMERS' VIEW

The separation of powers makes the presidency independent of Congress and the judiciary. But just how independent is the president supposed to be? This question has been the source of fundamental dispute since John Adams succeeded General Washington in 1797, and since scholars turned their attention to puzzling out the intent of the framers. The framers, wanting "energy in the executive," provided for

> **What were the conflicting views over presidential power of the framers of the Constitution?**

expressed powers specific powers granted to Congress under Article I, Section 8, of the Constitution

delegated powers constitutional powers that are assigned to one governmental agency but that are exercised by another agency with the express permission of the first

inherent powers powers claimed by a president that are not expressed in the Constitution, but are inferred from it

> **What factors led to the growth of a more powerful presidency?**

a single-headed office. But with no explicit powers independent of Congress, the president is constitutionally little more than a chief clerk, whose main objective is to see that the laws, as enacted by Congress, are "faithfully executed." The president would have to provide that energy and leadership by asserting powers beyond the Constitution itself and inherent in the Office of Chief Executive.

Article II of the Constitution, which establishes the presidency and defines a small number of **expressed powers** of the office, is the basis for this dispute. Although Article II has been called "the most loosely drawn chapter of the Constitution,"[1] the framers were neither indecisive nor confused. They held profoundly conflicting views of the executive branch, and Article II was probably the best compromise they could make. The formulation the framers agreed upon is magnificent in its ambiguity: "The executive Power shall be vested in a President of the United States of America" (Article II, Section 1, first sentence). The meaning of "executive power," however, is not defined except indirectly in the very last sentence of Section 3, which provides that the president "shall take Care that the Laws be faithfully executed."

One very important conclusion can be drawn from these two provisions: the office of the president was to be primarily an office of **delegated powers.** Since, as we have already seen, all of the powers of the national government are defined as powers of Congress and are incorporated into Article I, Section 8, then the "executive power" of Article II, Section 3, must be understood to be defined as the power to execute faithfully the laws *as they are adopted by Congress.* This does not doom the presidency to weakness. Presumably, Congress can pass laws delegating almost any of its powers to the president. But presidents are not free to discover sources of executive power completely independent of the laws as passed by Congress. In 1890, the Supreme Court did hold that the president could be bold and expansive in the inferences drawn from the Constitution as to "the rights, duties and obligations" of the presidency, but the **inherent powers** of the president would have to be inferred from the Constitution, not from some independent or absolute idea of executive power.[2]

CONGRESSIONAL DELEGATION OF POWER

The most important constitutional effect of Congress's actions during the New Deal was the enhancement of presidential power. Most major acts of Congress in this period involved significant exercises of control over the economy. But few programs specified the actual controls to be used. Instead, Congress authorized the president—or, in some cases, a new agency—to determine what the controls would be. Some of the new agencies were independent commissions responsible to Congress. But most of the new agencies and programs of the New Deal were placed in the executive branch directly under presidential authority.

Technically, this form of congressional act is called the "delegation of power." In theory, the delegation of power works as follows: (1) Congress recognizes a problem; (2) Congress acknowledges that it has neither the time nor the expertise to deal with the problem; and (3) Congress therefore sets the basic policies and then delegates to an agency the power to "fill in the details." But in practice, Congress was delegating not merely the power to "fill in the details," but actual and real policy-making powers, that is, real legislative powers, to the executive branch. During the 1930s, the growth of the national government through acts delegating legislative power tilted the American national structure away from a Congress-centered government toward a president-centered government.[3]

PRESIDENTIAL SELECTION

Although it would be difficult to underestimate the importance of congressional delegation of power to the president as the major contributor to the rise of president-centered government, there is still another factor that is immense in its importance. This is the process of presidential selection that was first laid out in the Constitution but then elaborated upon by informal developments as well as formal changes of party rules and legislation.

Immediately following the first sentence of Section 1, Article II of the Constitution defines the manner in which the president is to be chosen. This is a very odd sequence, but it does say something about the struggle the delegates were having over how to provide great power of action or energy to the executive and at the same time to balance that power with limitations. The struggle was between those delegates who wanted the president to be selected by, and thus responsible to, Congress and those delegates who preferred that the president be elected directly by the people. Direct popular election would create a more independent and more powerful presidency. With the adoption of a scheme of indirect election through an electoral college in which the electors would be selected by the state legislatures (and close elections would be resolved in the House of Representatives), the framers hoped to achieve a "republican" solution: a strong president responsible to state and national legislators rather than directly to the electorate. This indirect method of electing the president probably did dampen the power of most presidents in the nineteenth century.

The presidency was strengthened somewhat in the 1830s with the introduction of the national convention system of nominating presidential candidates. Until then, presidential candidates had been nominated by their party's congressional delegates. This was the **caucus** system of nominating candidates, and it was derisively called "King Caucus" because any candidate for president had to be beholden to the party's leaders in Congress in order to get the party's nomination and the support of the party's congressional delegation in the presidential election. The national nominating convention arose outside Congress in order to provide some representation for a party's voters who lived in districts where they weren't numerous enough to elect a member of Congress. The political party in each state made its own provisions for selecting delegates to attend the presidential nominating convention, and in virtually all states the selection was dominated by the party leaders (called "bosses" by the opposition party). Only in recent decades have state laws intervened to regularize the selection process and to provide (in all but a few instances) for open election of delegates. The convention system quickly became the most popular method of nominating candidates for all elective offices and remained so until well into the twentieth century, when it succumbed to the criticism that it was a nondemocratic method dominated by a few leaders in a "smoke-filled room." But in the nineteenth century, it was seen as a victory for democracy against the congressional elite. And the national convention gave the presidency a base of power independent of Congress.

caucus (political) a normally closed meeting of a political or legislative group to select candidates, plan strategy, or make decisions regarding legislative matters

This additional independence did not immediately transform the presidency into the office we recognize today, but the national convention did begin to open the presidency to larger social forces and newly organized interests in society. In other words, it gave the presidency a mass popular base that would eventually support and demand increased presidential power. Improvements in telephone, telegraph, and other forms of mass communication allowed individuals to share their complaints and allowed national leaders—especially presidents and presidential candidates—to reach out directly to people to ally themselves with, and even sometimes to create, popular groups and forces. Eventually, though more slowly, the presidential selection process began to be further democratized, with the adoption of primary elections through which millions of ordinary citizens were given an opportunity to take part in the presidential nominating process by popular selection of convention delegates.

But despite political and social conditions favoring the enhancement of the presidency, the development of presidential government as we know it today did not mature until the middle of the twentieth century. For a long period, even as the national government began to grow, Congress was careful to keep tight reins on the president's power. The real turning point in the history of American national government came during the administration of Franklin Delano Roosevelt. Since FDR, the tug of war seems to have been won for the chief executive presidency, because after FDR, as we shall see, every president has been strong whether he was committed to the strong presidency or not.

The Constitutional Powers of the Presidency

The heart of presidential power as defined by the Constitution is found in Article II, Sections 2 and 3, where the several clauses define the presidency in two dimensions: the president as head of state and the president as head of government. Although these will be given separate treatment here, the presidency can be understood only by the combination of the two.

THE PRESIDENT AS HEAD OF STATE: SOME IMPERIAL QUALITIES

> **What powers does the Constitution provide to the president as head of state? Have presidents used these powers to make the presidency too powerful or even imperial?**

The constitutional position of the president as head of state is defined by three constitutional provisions, which are the source of some of the most important powers on which presidents can draw. The areas can be classified as follows:

1. *Military.* Article II, Section 2, provides for the power as "Commander in Chief of the Army and Navy of the United States, and of the Militia of the several States, when called in to the actual Service of the United States."
2. *Judicial.* Article II, Section 2, also provides the power to "grant Reprieves and Pardons for Offences against the United States, except in Cases of Impeachment."
3. *Diplomatic.* Article II, Section 2, also provides the power "by and with the Advice and Consent of the Senate to make Treaties." Article II, Section 3, provides the power to "receive Ambassadors and other public Ministers."

Military First, the position of **commander in chief** makes the president the highest military authority in the United States, with control of the entire defense establishment. No American president, however, would dare put on a military uniform for a state function—not even a former general like Eisenhower—even though the president is the highest military officer in war and in peace. The president is also head of the secret intelligence network, which includes not only the Central Intelligence Agency (CIA) but also the National Security Council (NSC), the National Security Agency (NSA), the Federal Bureau of Investigation (FBI), and a host of less well known but very powerful international and domestic security agencies. But these impressive powers must be read in the context of Article I, wherein seven of the eighteen clauses of Section 8 provide particular military and foreign policy powers to Congress, including the power to declare wars for which presidents are responsible. Presidents have tried to evade this at their peril. In full awareness of the woe visited upon President Lyndon Johnson for evading and misleading Congress at the outset of the Vietnam War, President George Bush sought explicit congressional authorization for the Gulf War in January 1991. President George W. Bush followed in his father's footsteps by seeking congressional authorization for the war against the Taliban regime in Afghanistan; it was granted in a joint resolution adopted in the Senate by a vote of 98 to 0 and in the House by a vote of 420 to 1. In June 2002, President Bush declared that since Saddam Hussein's regime in Iraq was the biggest single threat in the war against worldwide terrorism, the United States's only recourse was to "change the regime." Later that summer, Bush

> **commander in chief** the power of the president as commander of the national military and the state national guard units (when called into service)

Even though the presidency is an office of delegated powers, for a century and a half after the Founding, many feared that the president's power could be dictatorial. This political cartoon criticized president Andrew Jackson's "usurpations" of the executive branch, in particular his attack on the Bank of the United States.

THE WORLD'S CONSTABLE.

President Theodore Roosevelt, who staked out a new role for himself and the United States as the policeman of the Western Hemisphere, claimed that the president had the power to do anything that the needs of the nation demanded.

sought a resolution from Congress authorizing him to use any means he determined appropriate, including military force. After weeks of debate in the House and Senate, Congress overwhelmingly approved, by 296 to 133 in the House and 77 to 23 in the Senate, a resolution authorizing Bush to use the armed forces "as he determines to be necessary and appropriate" and to enforce "all relevant" United Nations Security Council resolutions on Iraq. The resolution was far less broad than the initial request put forward by Bush, which would have also allowed military action outside of Iraq. It also urged Bush to work first through the United Nations before opting to invade Iraq unilaterally and required that the president report to Congress within forty-eight hours of any military action. Throughout the debate, Bush said his powers as commander in chief permitted him to act in defense of the nation. He sought congressional approval, however, so he could argue to the United Nations that the American people supported his position.

The term "the imperial presidency" was popularized in 1973 by a book of that name written during the Vietnam era. President Lyndon B. Johnson, pictured here greeting American troops in Vietnam, interpreted the Gulf of Tonkin resolution to mean that any of the nation's resources could be used to fight the war in Vietnam. His critics thought otherwise.

Given the nation's and Congress's reaction to Johnson's and Nixon's handling of Vietnam, presidents since 1973 have proceeded a little more cautiously in committing American troops to world trouble spots. Soon after the terrorist attacks of September 11, President Bush spoke before a joint session of Congress, where he presented his plan for the war on terrorism. Likewise, before taking action in Iraq, Bush sought Congress's approval.

Judicial   The presidential power to grant reprieves, pardons, and amnesties involves the power of life and death over all individuals who may be a threat to the security of the United States. Presidents may use this power on behalf of a particular individual, as did Gerald Ford when he pardoned Richard Nixon in 1974 "for all offenses against the United States which he . . . has committed or may have committed." Or they may use it on a large scale, as did President Andrew Johnson in 1868, when he gave full amnesty to all southerners who had participated in the "Late Rebellion," and President Carter in 1977, when he declared an amnesty for all the draft evaders of the Vietnam War. This power of life and death over others helped elevate the president to the level of earlier conquerors and kings by establishing him as the person before whom supplicants might come to make their pleas for mercy.

Diplomatic   The ultimate status of the president as head of state is the power to make treaties for the United States (with the advice and consent of the Senate). And when President Washington received Edmond Genêt ("Citizen Genêt") as the formal emissary of the revolutionary government of France in 1793 and had his cabinet officers and Congress back his decision, he established a greatly expanded interpretation of the power to "receive Ambassadors and other public Ministers," extending it to the power to "recognize" other countries. That power gives the president the almost unconditional authority to review the claims of any new ruling groups to determine if they indeed control the territory and population of their country, so that they can commit it to treaties and other agreements.

The Imperial Presidency?   Have presidents used these three constitutional powers—military, judicial, and diplomatic—to make the presidency too powerful, indeed "imperial?"[4] Debate over the answer to this question is no better illustrated or dramatized than by the presidential practice of using executive agreements instead of treaties to establish relations with other countries.[5] An **executive agreement** is exactly like a treaty because it is a contract between two countries, but an executive agreement does not require a two-thirds vote of approval by the Senate. Ordinarily, executive agreements are used to carry out commitments already made in treaties, or to arrange for matters well below the level of policy. But when presidents have found it expedient to use an executive agreement in place of a treaty, Congress has gone along. This verges on an imperial power.

Many recent presidents have even gone beyond formal executive agreements to engage in what amounts to unilateral action. They may seek formal congressional authorization, as in 1964 when President Lyndon Johnson convinced Congress to adopt the Gulf of Tonkin Resolution authorizing him to expand the American military presence in Vietnam. Johnson interpreted the resolution as a delegation of discretion to use any and all national resources according to his own judgment. Others may not even bother with the authorization but merely assume it, as President Nixon did when he claimed to need no congressional authorization to continue or to expand the Vietnam War.

These presidential claims and actions led to a congressional reaction, however. In 1973, Congress passed the **War Powers Resolution** over President Nixon's veto. This resolution asserted that the president could send American troops into action abroad only in the event of a declaration of war or other statutory authorization by Congress, or if American troops were attacked or directly endangered. This was an obvious effort to revive the principle that the presidency is an office of delegated powers—that is, powers granted by Congress—and that there is no blanket prerogative.

executive agreement an agreement, made between the president and another country, that has the force of a treaty but does not require the Senate's "advice and consent"

War Powers Resolution a resolution of Congress that the president can send troops into action abroad only by authorization of Congress, or if American troops are already under attack or serious threat

Iraq and Presidential Power

During the months following September 11 and the campaign against Al Qaeda and the Taliban in Afghanistan, advisors in the White House and the Pentagon convinced President Bush that Iraq was not only one of the key countries in the new "axis of evil" but was the principal one because it was the one most likely to use or provide weapons of mass destruction for world terrorism. By summer 2002, President Bush had apparently come to the conclusion that another war with Iraq was close to inevitable. These were his words during the debate in the House and Senate on the resolution authorizing the president to go to war if and when he chose:

> While there are many dangers in the world, the threat from Iraq stands alone, because it gathers the most serious dangers of our age in one place. . . . Iraq's weapons of mass destruction are controlled by a murderous tyrant who has already used chemical weapons to kill thousands of people.

This request for a congressional resolution was a curious turn of events because the president had been arguing all along that he already had constitutional power to make a unilateral, preemptive, or preventive strike without any word whatsoever from Congress or the United Nations. His argument was based on congressional approval of the Persian Gulf War against Iraq in 1991 and UN Security Council resolutions imposing severe disarmament obligations on Saddam Hussein, which Hussein wantonly and frequently violated or just plain disregarded. Nevertheless, the president sought both: the authorizing resolution from Congress and one or more resolutions from the United Nations Security Council that would reimpose new and more stringent and enforceable disarmament, supervised by a UN team without any restrictions or conditions whatsoever. If Saddam Hussein persisted, he would, in effect, be bringing more upon himself and his own people. The Bush proposal to Congress was for authorization "to use all means . . . including force . . . to enforce UN Security Council resolutions [and] to restore peace and security *in the region*." [Emphasis added.]

During the debate in Congress, Senator Robert Byrd (D-WV) argued that the president could not make war without a declaration of war and that the Constitution provided that Congress and only Congress has the power to declare war. Never mind that only five times in all of American history has Congress seen fit to declare war: the War of 1812, the Mexican War of 1846, the Spanish-American War of 1898, and the two World Wars. Senator Byrd managed to garner only 22 votes along with his own against the resolution. And, as there was no equivalent opposition leader in the House, the ultimate opposition vote was only 133, with 296 voting yea.

Meanwhile, the real debate was not over whether there was to be a resolution but over the wording of the congressional resolution. Bush asked for "all means appropriate"; the opposition emanded "all means necessary and appropriate." President Bush asked for authorization covering the entire region, which could have meant all countries in the Middle East, or all Islamic countries. Bush set no time limit on the resolution, and Congress demanded he inform them within forty-eight hours of any military action and at least every sixty days thereafter.

Bush accepted the changes demanded by the opposition, and the decisive vote followed within four days. No one claimed that the changes were in any real way a defeat for President Bush. The "means" were his to determine; the obligation to keep Congress informed was already in the law as a result of the almost forgotten War Powers Resolution of 1973. And there was absolute silence on the role of the president, the armed forces, or the money that would be required after the inevitable victory was achieved and military occupation, "regime change," and "state-building," were undertaken.

SOURCES: Hendrik Hertzberg, "Comment: Declarations," *The New Yorker,* September 30, 2002, pp. 45–48; Lawrence McQuillan and Kathy Kiely, "Bush, Key Lawmakers Settle on Iraq Resolution," *USA Today,* October 3, 2002, p. 9A; Kenneth T. Walsh, "Another Step Closer to War," *U.S. News & World Report,* October 21, 2002, pp. 30–32; and Mile Pomper, "Senate Democrats in Disarray After Gephardt's Deal on Iraq," and "Daschle's Grip on Majority Could Slip in Tussle Over Iraq, Homeland Votes," *Congressional Quarterly,* October 5, 2002, pp. 2606–10.

Nevertheless, this resolution has not prevented presidents from using force when they have deemed it necessary. For example, although President Clinton appeared at first to be reluctant to take bold international initiatives, he did not hesitate to use direct action when events seemed to threaten his own position or his view of the national interest. Clinton's series of unilateral actions in Bosnia dramatically tested his independence from Congress. First, Clinton unilaterally approved the use of American planes to bomb Serbian strategic positions in the late summer of 1995 (which pressured the Serbs to participate in peace negotiations with Croats and Bosnian Muslims). Second, to make the peace negotiations succeed, Clinton unilaterally pledged the American military to monitor the implementation of the agreement, including committing twenty thousand U.S. troops to monitor the agreement on the ground. With U.S. forces already in Bosnia, all Congress could do was pass a resolution in December 1995, after a long debate, to authorize financial support for the troops but also to disapprove of Clinton's actions and to demand further reporting to Congress in the future.

THE DOMESTIC PRESIDENCY: THE PRESIDENT AS HEAD OF GOVERNMENT

The constitutional basis of the domestic presidency also has three parts. And here again, although real power grows out of the combination of the parts, the analysis is greatly aided by examining the parts separately:

1. *Executive.* The "executive power" is vested in the president by Article II, Section 1, to see that all the laws are faithfully executed (Section 3), and to appoint, remove, and supervise all executive officers and to appoint all federal judges (Section 2).
2. *Military.* This power is derived from Article IV, Section 4, which stipulates that the president has the power to protect every state "against Invasion; and . . . against domestic Violence."
3. *Legislative.* The president is given the power under various provisions to participate effectively and authoritatively in the legislative process.

> **What powers does the Constitution provide to the president as head of government?**

Executive Power   The most important basis of the president's power as chief executive is to be found in Article II, Section 3, which stipulates that the president must see that all the laws are faithfully executed, and Section 2, which provides that the president will appoint, remove, and supervise all executive officers, and appoint all federal judges (with Senate approval). The power to appoint the principal executive officers and to require each of them to report to the president on subjects relating to the duties of their departments makes the president the true chief executive officer (CEO) of the nation. In this manner, the Constitution focuses executive power and legal responsibility upon the president. The famous sign on President Truman's desk, "The buck stops here," was not merely an assertion of Truman's personal sense of responsibility but was in fact recognition by him of the legal and constitutional responsibility of the president. The president is subject to some limitations, because the appointment of all such officers, including ambassadors, ministers, and federal judges, is subject to a majority approval by the Senate. But these appointments are at the discretion of the president, and the loyalty and the responsibility of each appointment are presumed to be directed toward the president.

Is Bush Using His Constitutional Powers Appropriately?

Yes

One hundred years ago this week, Theodore Roosevelt became the youngest man to assume the office of president of the United States. It was Roosevelt who ushered the office into the twentieth century, from a point of relative impotence to a period of popular prominence, altering the constitutional nature of the presidency to its most expanded form. A century later, confronting the most devastating terrorist attack on American soil, George W. Bush has the opportunity to usher the office into the twenty-first century by unifying the goals of the writers of the Constitution two centuries ago and the work of Theodore Roosevelt one century ago.

In actions, President Bush has used the powers of the president masterfully, but not to the point that he has abrogated the letter and spirit of the Constitution. As the commander in chief, he has mobilized the military to a state of readiness, and has made clear that he will command the military in a measured and appropriate manner. As the chief executive, he has expeditiously enacted the emergency response plans of the government and made sure that all available public services have been used to respond to the crisis. As the chief legislator, he has asked the Congress for support and funding, and has received both by almost unanimous votes in both houses. As the chief diplomat, he has received support from the member states of NATO and other world leaders. In the Roosevelt vein, he has expanded the powers of the office to their constitutional limits but has not abused them.

As the nation's leading political figure, he is also an important personal symbol of the vibrance of our national politics, a unifying figure for all the emotions that this week's tragedy has wrought. The saddened family member of a victim, the heroic fire fighter looking for his colleagues, the angry war hawks who want to bomb small and large targets alike, the peace lovers who wish not to go to war—these are all the president's constituents, and through his words, he must find a way to comfort and empower all of them. It was Theodore Roosevelt's work that lent President Bush the strength to take on this enormous task. He began the notion of a "rhetorical presidency," believing that the president had a "bully pulpit" to talk directly to the people about their needs and interests, to connect with them in a candid and forthright manner. In this time of tragedy, this is where the least has been expected of our normally less-than-eloquent president, but is the domain in which he has gone well above and beyond the call of duty.

Tuesday night, President Bush made an Oval Office address in which he used consistently harsh rhetoric about those who committed the attacks. When speaking from the heart, he quoted Psalm 23 to help Americans reconcile themselves with the tragedy, and several peers commented that it was an abhorrence to the notion of the separation of church and state. Bush's Bible usage was the "rhetorical presidency" at its best, the president sharing a personal moment with the public and using the power of his office to communicate his personal sentiments. The next day, when he wept like any other American, he again demonstrated the importance of the personal nature of the presidency.

Because he has acted appropriately according to the Constitution and spoken personally through the "bully pulpit," it is no wonder that approximately ninety percent of the public supports his actions in the wake of Tuesday's attack.

The dual relationship between the presidency and Washington's leaders and the president and the public at large is strong and vibrant, a powerful sign that the presidency works, that the government works, and that America is still open for business.

In times of crisis, the powers of the presidency do indeed expand, but the line that divides great presidents from the rest of our chief executives is how they use their mandate for change and action with relation to the rights and privileges embedded in the Constitution. President Bush must see himself as neither a war monger nor a peacemaker, but rather as his predecessor, Theodore Roosevelt, saw himself, "a steward bound actively and affirmatively to do all he could for the people."

SOURCE: Michael Ricci, "Hail to the Chief," *Columbia Spectator,* September 17, 2001.

No Consider Mr. Bush's rather open musings about possibly "consulting" Congress as to the wisdom of attacking Iraq as opposed to seeking their direct authorization, in outright defiance of Congress' unique ability to declare war upon other nations (a power given exclusively to Congress by the authors of the Constitution for very good reasons), not to mention his team of lawyers currently wrangling over legal chicanery in a weak attempt to sidestep the whole messy affair of congressional approval to begin with—all of course in the name of peace and democracy at home and abroad.

One of Mr. Bush's key defenses is in the ambiguity of the sole power of Congress to declare war. After all, this isn't the first time in history that the commander in chief has felt it necessary to go to war at the drop of a hat. Consider Lyndon B. Johnson's "Gulf of Tonkin" incident, a fabricated attack on a U.S. warship that LBJ used as a pretense to escalate U.S. involvement in Vietnam with little consultation on the part of Congress.

Such a move later spurred the War Powers Act of 1973, which specifically requires the president to consult with the leaders of Congress within forty-eight hours of committing troops into conflict as well as to receive a declaration of war from Congress (or an explicit authorization to continue action for another sixty days) or else pull troops out within sixty days—no ifs, ands, or buts.

Nowhere in the War Powers Act is the president given carte blanche simply to make war as he or she sees fit. Yet this is clearly the attitude that Mr. Bush has put forth that somehow, as the commander in chief, he is not obligated to answer to Congress (and by such, the people) or the trifling technical details of the Constitution.

Consider the tactics that Mr. Bush's legal team have already come up with: They've attempted to use the post–September 11 resolutions authorizing "the use of any and all force necessary to track down those responsible for the attacks" (despite the fact that Iraq has yet to be linked to the September 11 attacks other than by highly questionable circumstantial evidence), the 1991 authorization given three Congresses ago to his father, Bush the forty-first (which theoretically should have expired when hostilities ended, or else Japan, Germany, Italy, and England had better watch their own backs), not to mention vague allusions to the president's role as commander in chief of the armed forces.

In fact, aside from such weak arguments, it has largely been the strategy of the administration to obfuscate the legality of their proposed "one-man war" with Iraq by raising hysterics over the unspecified (and unsubstantiated) threat that Iraq poses to the United States, despite the fact that charges such as supporting terrorism largely apply to nations like Saudi Arabia and Pakistan as well.

Truly, if the case for war is so airtight, Mr. Bush would be well served to do a better job of articulating his case to the American public while having faith that Congress will do its job.

Yet even more dismaying is the lack of congressional opposition to this charade: Republicans that normally froth at the mouth about issues like "the rule of law" and the "strict text of the Constitution" (at least when it's an impeachment hearing) are now some of the most ardent hawks, while stray sheep such as Dick Armey (R-Tx.), who expressed concern over the wisdom of an unprovoked attack, are being whipped into line by the triumvirate of Vice President Dick Cheney, Defense Secretary Donald Rumsfeld, and Deputy Defense Secretary Paul Wolfowitz.

No to be out-cowed, of course, are the Democrats, who meekly sit through the circus, afraid to be called "unpatriotic" for questioning Herr Bush in a time of national emergency, especially in an election year.

Yet what the Democrats fail to realize is that beyond the threat of terror, we face an even greater crisis—the threat of a constitutional crisis brought about by an administration which is outright flouting the checks and balances set forth in the Constitution in favor of patent demagoguery and scare-mongering.

SOURCE: Steve Skutnick, "Dictating Bush Usurping Congressional Power," *Iowa State Daily*, August 28, 2002.

Military Sources of Domestic Presidential Power   Although Article IV, Section 4, provides that the "United States shall [protect] every State . . . against Invasion . . . and . . . domestic Violence," Congress has made this an explicit presidential power through statutes directing the president as commander in chief to discharge these obligations.[6] The Constitution restrains the president's use of domestic force by providing that a state legislature (or governor when the legislature is not in session) must request federal troops before the president can send them into the state to provide public order. Yet this proviso is not absolute. First, presidents are not obligated to deploy national troops merely because the state legislature or governor makes such a request. And more important, the president may deploy troops in a state or city without a specific request from the state legislature or governor if the president considers it necessary in order to maintain an essential national service during an emergency, in order to enforce a federal judicial order, or in order to protect federally guaranteed civil rights.

One historic example of the unilateral use of presidential emergency power to protect the states against domestic disorder, even when the states don't request it, was the decision by President Dwight Eisenhower in 1957 to send troops into Little Rock, Arkansas, literally against the wishes of the state of Arkansas, to enforce court orders to integrate Little Rock's Central High School. The governor of Arkansas, Orval Faubus, had actually posted the Arkansas National Guard at the entrance of Central High School to prevent the court-ordered admission of nine black students. After an effort to negotiate with Governor Faubus failed, President Eisenhower reluctantly sent a thousand paratroopers to Little Rock, who stood watch while the black students took their places in the all-white classrooms. This case makes quite clear that the president does not have to wait for a request by a state legislature or governor before acting as a domestic commander in chief.[7]

However, in most instances of domestic disorder—whether from human or from natural causes—presidents tend to exercise unilateral power by declaring a "state of emergency," thereby making available federal grants, insurance, and direct assistance. In 1992, in the aftermath of the devastating riots in Los Angeles and the hurricanes in Florida, American troops were very much in evidence, sent in by the president, but in the role more of good Samaritans than of military police.

The President's Legislative Power   The president plays a role not only in the administration of government but also in the legislative process. Two constitutional provisions are the primary sources of the president's power in the legislative arena. The first of these is the provision in Article II, Section 3, providing that the president "shall from time to time give to the Congress Information of the State of the Union, and recommend to their Consideration such Measures as he shall judge necessary and expedient." The second of the president's legislative powers is of course the veto power assigned by Article I, Section 7.[8]

Delivering a "State of the Union" address does not at first appear to be of any great import. It is a mere obligation on the part of the president to make recommendations for Congress's consideration. But as political and social conditions began to favor an increasingly prominent role for presidents, each president, especially since Franklin Delano Roosevelt, began to rely on this provision to become the primary initiator of proposals for legislative action in Congress and the principal source for public awareness of national issues, as well as the most important

The Roles of the President

Chief of State (president acting on behalf of all Americans)

Commander in Chief (president in charge of military)

Chief Jurist (president's judicial responsibilities)

Chief Diplomat (president managing our relations with other nations)

Chief Executive (president as "boss" of executive branch)

Chief Legislator (president's legislative powers)

Chief Politician (president's party leadership)

single individual participant in legislative decisions. Few today doubt that the president and the executive branch together are the primary source for many important congressional actions.[9]

The **veto** is the president's constitutional power to turn down acts of Congress (see Figure 13.1). It alone makes the president the most important single legislative leader.[10] No bill vetoed by the president can become law unless both the House and Senate override the veto by a two-thirds vote. In the case of a **pocket veto,** Congress does not even have the option of overriding the veto, but must reintroduce the bill in the next session. A pocket veto can occur when the president is presented with a bill during the last ten days of a legislative session. Usually, if a president does not sign a bill within ten days, it automatically becomes law. But this is true only while

veto the president's constitutional power to turn down acts of Congress. A presidential veto may be overridden by a two-thirds vote of each house of Congress

pocket veto a presidential veto that is automatically triggered if the president does not act on a given piece of legislation passed during the final ten days of a legislative session

The Veto Process

Figure 13.1

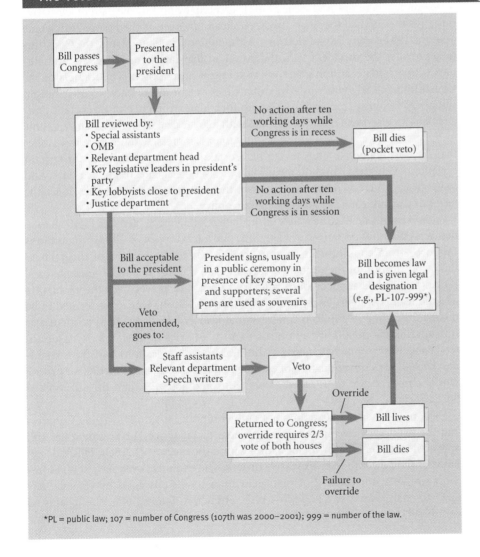

*PL = public law; 107 = number of Congress (107th was 2000–2001); 999 = number of the law.

line-item veto the power of the executive to veto specific provisions (lines) of a bill passed by the legislature

Congress is in session. If a president chooses not to sign a bill presented within the last ten days that Congress is in session, then the ten-day limit does not expire until Congress is out of session, and instead of becoming law, the bill is vetoed. In 1996 a new power was added to the president's lineup—the **line-item veto**—giving the president power to strike specific spending items from appropriations bills passed by Congress, unless reenacted by a two-thirds vote of both House and Senate. In 1997, President Clinton used this power eleven times to strike eighty-two items from the federal budget. But in 1998 the Supreme Court ruled that the Constitution does not authorize the line-item veto. Only a constitutional amendment would restore this power to the president.

Use of the veto varies according to the political situation that each president confronts. During Bill Clinton's first two years in office, when Democrats controlled both houses of Congress, he vetoed no bills. Following the congressional elections of 1994, however, Clinton confronted a Republican-controlled Congress with a definite agenda, and he began to use his veto power more vigorously.

legislative initiative the president's inherent power to bring a legislative agenda before Congress

Clinton also recaptured some of his leadership by finding the path of legislative initiative that he had lost with the Republican takeover of the House and Senate after the 1994 congressional elections. Although not explicitly stated, the Constitution provides the president with the power of **legislative initiative.** To "initiate" means to originate, and in government that can mean power. The framers of the Constitution clearly saw legislative initiative as one of the keys to executive power. Initiative obviously implies the ability to formulate proposals for important policies, and the president, as an individual with a great deal of staff assistance, is able to initiate decisive action more frequently than Congress, with its large assemblies that have to deliberate and debate before taking action. With some important exceptions, Congress banks on the president to set the agenda of public policy. And quite clearly, there is power in initiative; there is power in being able to set the terms of discourse in the making of public policy.

For example, during the weeks immediately following September 11, Bush took many presidential initiatives to Congress, and each was given almost unanimous support—from commitments to pursue al Qaeda to the removal of the Taliban, the reconstitution of the Afghanistan regime, all the way to almost unlimited approval for mobilization of both military power and power over the regulation of American civil liberties. By early 2002, however, Bush's initiatives seemed to be dissipating. Some Republican congressional leaders feared that the president was squandering his popularity by not using it to advance domestic policy issues of vital concern to Republican needs in the 2002 and 2004 elections—such as extending the 2001 tax cuts, regulation of cloning and related issues, tax credits for private school choice, aid to faith-based associations and activities, and privatization of Social Security.[11]

executive order a rule or regulation issued by the president that has the effect and formal status of legislation

The president's initiative does not end with policy making involving Congress and the making of laws in the ordinary sense of the term. The president has still another legislative role (in all but name) within the executive branch. This is designated as the power to issue **executive orders.** The executive order is first and foremost simply a normal tool of management, a power possessed by virtually any CEO to make "company policy"—rules setting procedures, etiquette, chains of command, functional responsibilities, etc. But evolving out of this normal management practice is a recognized presidential power to promulgate rules that have the effect and the formal status of legislation. Most of the executive orders of the president provide for the reorganization of structures and procedures or otherwise direct the affairs of the executive branch—either to be applied across the board to all agencies or applied in some important respect to a single agency or department. One of the most important examples is Executive Order No. 8248, September 8, 1939, establishing the divisions of the Executive Office of the President. Another one of equal importance is President Nixon's executive order establishing the Environmental Protection Agency in 1970–71, which included establishment of the Environmental Impact Statement. President Reagan's Executive Order No. 12291 of 1981 was responsible for a regulatory reform process that was responsible for more genuine deregulation in the past twenty years than was accomplished by any acts of congressional legislation. President Clinton's most important policy toward gays and gay rights in the military took the form of an executive order referred to as "Don't ask, don't tell."

This legislative or policy leadership role of the presidency is an institutionalized feature of the office that exists independent of the occupant of the office. That is to say, anyone duly elected president would possess these powers regardless of his or her individual energy or leadership characteristics.[12]

Institutional Resources of Presidential Power

Constitutional sources of power are not the only resources available to the president. Presidents possess a variety of other formal and informal resources that have important implications for their ability to govern (see Figure 13.2 on page 524). Without these other resources, presidents would lack the ability—the tools of management and public mobilization—to make much use of the power and responsibility given to them by Congress. Let us first consider the president's formal institutional resources and then, in the section following, turn to the more informal political resources that affect a president's capacity to govern, in particular the president's base of popular support.

> **> What institutional resources does the president use to manage the executive branch?**

PATRONAGE AS A TOOL OF MANAGEMENT

The first tool of management available to most presidents is a form of **patronage**—the choice of high-level political appointees. These appointments allow the president to fill top management positions with individuals who will attempt to carry out the president's agenda. But the president must appoint individuals who have experience and interest in the programs that they are to administer and who share the president's goals with respect to these programs. At the same time, presidents use the appointment process to build links to powerful political and economic constituencies by giving representation to important state political party organizations, the business community, organized labor, the scientific and university communities, organized agriculture, and certain large and well-organized religious groups.

patronage the resources available to higher officials, usually opportunities to make partisan appointments to offices and to confer grants, licenses, or special favors to supporters

Figure 13.2   The Institutional Presidency

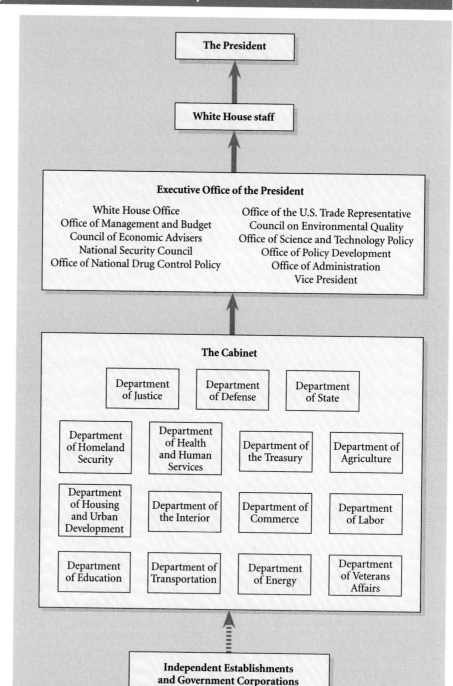

SOURCE: Office of the Federal Register, National Archives and Records Administration, *The United States Government Manual, 1995–96* (Washington, DC: Government Printing Office, 1995), p. 22.

THE CABINET

In the American system of government, the **Cabinet** is the traditional but informal designation for the heads of all the major federal government departments. The Cabinet has no constitutional status. Unlike in England and many other parliamentary countries, where the cabinet *is* the government, the American Cabinet is not a collective body. It meets but makes no decisions as a group. Each appointment must be approved by the Senate, but Cabinet members are not responsible to the Senate or to Congress at large. Cabinet appointments help build party and popular support, but the Cabinet is not a party organ. The Cabinet is made up of directors, but is not a true board of directors.

Aware of this fact, the president tends to develop a burning impatience with and a mild distrust of Cabinet members; to make the Cabinet a rubber stamp for actions already decided on; and to demand results, or the appearance of results, more immediately and more frequently than most department heads can provide. Since Cabinet appointees generally have not shared political careers with the president or with each other, and since they may meet literally for the first time after their selection, the formation of an effective governing group out of this motley collection of appointments is unlikely. Although President Clinton's insistence on a Cabinet diverse enough to resemble American society could be considered an act of political wisdom, it virtually guaranteed that few of his appointees had ever spent much time working together or even knew the policy positions or beliefs of the other appointees.[13]

Some presidents have relied more heavily on an "inner Cabinet," the **National Security Council (NSC).** The NSC, established by law in 1947, is composed of the president, the vice president, the secretaries of state, defense, and the treasury, the attorney general, and other officials invited by the president. It has its own staff of foreign-policy specialists run by the special assistant to the president for national security affairs. For these highest appointments, presidents turn to people from outside Washington, usually longtime associates. George W. Bush's "inner Cabinet" is composed largely of former and proven senior staffers and Cabinet members of former Republican administrations, most particularly Vice President Cheney, Defense Secretary Rumsfeld, and Secretary of State Powell.

A counterpart, the Homeland Security Council, was created by executive order in 2001. Led by Tom Ridge, the Homeland Security Council also comprised the attorney general; the secretaries of Defense, Treasury, Agriculture, and Health and Human Services; and the directors of the FBI and the Federal Emergency Management Agency (FEMA). Ridge's job is comparable to that of the national security adviser, a post currently occupied by the very influential Condoleezza Rice, and there is watchful waiting to see if Ridge will leverage this job into a position of influence higher than that of the relevant members of the Cabinet.[14]

Presidents have obviously been uneven and unpredictable in their reliance on the NSC and other subcabinet bodies, because executive management is inherently a personal matter. Despite all the personal variations, however, one generalization can be made: presidents have increasingly preferred the White House staff instead of the Cabinet as their means of managing the gigantic executive branch.

Cabinet the secretaries, or chief administrators, of the major departments of the federal government. Cabinet secretaries are appointed by the president with the consent of the Senate

National Security Council (NSC) a presidential foreign policy advisory council composed of the president; the vice president; the secretaries of state, defense, and the treasury; the attorney general; and other officials invited by the president

The Cabinet Departments

Department	Year Created
State	1789
Treasury	1789
Defense*	1947
Justice	1789
Interior†	1849
Agriculture	1889
Commerce	1913
Labor	1913
Health and Human Services††	1953
Housing and Urban Development	1965
Transportation	1966
Energy	1977
Education	1979
Veterans Affairs	1989
Homeland Security	2002

*Formerly the War and Navy Departments, created in 1789 and 1798, respectively.
†Created in 1862; made part of Cabinet in 1889.
††Formerly Health, Education, and Welfare; reorganized in 1979 (when separate Department of Education was created).

THE WHITE HOUSE STAFF

White House staff analysts and advisers to the president, often given the title "special assistant"

The **White House staff** is composed mainly of analysts and advisers.[15] Although many of the top White House staff members are given the title "special assistant" for a particular task or sector, the types of judgments they are expected to make and the kinds of advice they are supposed to give are a good deal broader and more generally political than those coming from the Executive Office of the President or from the Cabinet departments. The members of the White House staff also tend to be more closely associated with the president than other presidentially appointed officials.

Kitchen Cabinet an informal group of advisers to whom the president turns for counsel and guidance. Members of the official Cabinet may or may not also be members of the Kitchen Cabinet

From an informal group of fewer than a dozen people (popularly called the **Kitchen Cabinet**), and no more than four dozen at the height of the domestic Roosevelt presidency in 1937, the White House staff has grown substantially with each successive president (see Figure 13.3).[16] Richard Nixon employed 550 people in 1972. President Carter, who found so many of the requirements of presidential power distasteful, and who publicly vowed to keep his staff small and decentralized, built an even larger and more centralized staff. President Clinton reduced the White House staff by 20 percent, but a large White House staff is still essential.

Figure 13.3   **The Expanding (and Shrinking) White House Staff, 1937–2001**

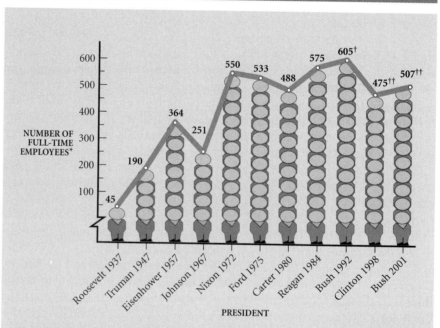

*These figures do not include the employees temporarily detailed to the White House from outside agencies (about 50–75 in 1992 and 1996).

†The vice president employs more than 20 people, and there are at least 100 people on the staff of the National Security Council. These people work in the White House and the Executive Office buildings, but are not included in these totals.

††These figures include the staffs of the Office of the President and the Executive Residence.

SOURCES: 1937–84: Thomas E. Cronin, "The Swelling of the Presidency: Can Anyone Reverse the Tide?" in *American Government: Readings and Cases,* 8th ed., ed. Peter Woll (Boston: Little, Brown, 1984), p. 347; 1992, 1998, and 2001 provided by the Office of Management and Budget and the White House.

THE EXECUTIVE OFFICE OF THE PRESIDENT

The development of the White House staff can be appreciated only in its relation to the still-larger **Executive Office of the President (EOP).** Created in 1939, the EOP is a major part of what is often called the "institutional presidency"—the permanent agencies that perform defined management tasks for the president. The most important and the largest EOP agency is the Office of Management and Budget (OMB). Its roles in preparing the national budget, designing the president's program, reporting on agency activities, and overseeing regulatory proposals make OMB personnel part of virtually every conceivable presidential responsibility. The status and power of the OMB have grown in importance with each successive president. The process of budgeting at one time was a "bottom-up" procedure, with expenditure and program requests passing from the lowest bureaus through the departments to "clearance" in OMB and hence to Congress, where each agency could be called in to reveal what its "original request" had been before OMB revised it. Now the budgeting process is a "top-down"; OMB sets the terms of discourse for agencies as well as for Congress. The director of OMB is now one of the most powerful officials in Washington.

The staff of the Council of Economic Advisers (CEA) constantly analyzes the economy and economic trends and attempts to give the president the ability to anticipate events rather than to wait and react to events. The Council on Environmental Quality was designed to do the same for environmental issues as the CEA does for economic issues. The National Security Council (NSC) is composed of designated Cabinet officials who meet regularly with the president to give advice on the large national security picture. The staff of the NSC assimilates and analyzes data from all intelligence-gathering agencies (CIA, etc.). Other EOP agencies perform more specialized tasks.

Somewhere between 1,500 and 2,000 highly specialized people work for EOP agencies.[17] The importance of each agency in the EOP varies according to the personal orientation of each president. For example, the NSC staff was of immense importance under President Nixon, especially because it served essentially as the personal staff of presidential assistant Henry Kissinger. But it was of less importance to President George H. W. Bush, who looked outside the EOP altogether for military policy matters, turning much more to the Joint Chiefs of Staff and its chair at the time, General Colin Powell.

THE VICE PRESIDENCY

The vice presidency is a constitutional anomaly even though the office was created along with the presidency by the Constitution. The vice president exists for two purposes only: to succeed the president in case of death, resignation, or incapacitation and to preside over the Senate, casting a tie-breaking vote when necessary.[18]

The main value of the vice presidency as a political resource for the president is electoral. Traditionally, a presidential candidate's most important rule for the choice of a running mate is that he or she bring the support of at least one state (preferably a large one) not otherwise likely to support the ticket. Another rule holds that the vice presidential nominee should provide some regional balance and, wherever possible, some balance among various ideological or ethnic subsections of the party. It is very doubtful that John Kennedy would have won in 1960

Executive Office of the President (EOP) the permanent agencies that perform defined management tasks for the president. Created in 1939, the EOP includes the Office of Management and Budget, the Council of Economic Advisers, the National Security Council, and other agencies

What Government Does . . . After September 11

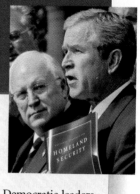

Executive privilege is the claim that confidential communications between a president and close advisors should not be revealed without the consent of the president. Presidents have made this claim ever since George Washington refused a request from the House of Representatives to deliver documents concerning negotiations of an important treaty. Washington refused (successfully) on the grounds that, first, the House was not constitutionally part of the treaty-making process and, second, that diplomatic negotiations required secrecy.

Executive privilege became a popular part of the "checks and balances" counterpoint between president and Congress, and presidents have usually had the upper hand when invoking it. The expansion of executive privilege into a claim of "uncontrolled discretion" to refuse Congress's request for information came when President Nixon was beginning to get into political trouble over the Vietnam War in 1971.[1] It was President Nixon's claim to an almost absolute immunity to congressional inquiry that led to a Supreme Court rejection of the doctrine as a constitutional feature of the presidency in *U.S. v. Nixon* (418 U.S. 683, 1974). Although the doctrine continued to be invoked by succeeding presidents, the occasions were usually when presidents had something to hide that was of questionable legality (Iran-Contra) or potentially scandalous (Clinton's various scrapes). The exercise of presidential power through the executive privilege doctrine has been all the more frequent in the past twenty years, when we have been living nearly 90 percent of the time under conditions of "divided government," where the party not in control of the White House is in control of one or both of the chambers of Congress.

After September 11, President Bush created the Office of Homeland Security, with a director of homeland security (Tom Ridge, former governor of Pennsylvania) located in the White House. Almost immediately there were tensions over the assignment of the director, and these tensions heated up during the autumn of 2001 into an open struggle early in 2002. The dispute centered on Congress's summons to Tom Ridge to testify on the substantive plans of how to coordinate security and intelligence agencies as well as on the budgetary aspects of the nation's security measures. In fact, several Republicans on the all-important Senate Appropriations Committee asserted that if the president expected to get $38 billion in 2003 appropriations for homeland security, plus another $5 billion in "supplemental" appropriations in 2002, the director had an obligation to Congress to answer questions on how the money was to be spent. Every request made by both Republican and Democratic leaders was rebuffed. The refusals were so frequent and so absolute that a bipartisan coalition in Congress began to fashion retaliatory methods to compel Ridge to testify on the Hill. One method under consideration was to refuse to cooperate with the president on a revamping of the scandalized Immigration and Naturalization Service by putting it under Ridge's control. Another possibility was to delay preparation of the 2003 appropriations bill for White House expenses until Ridge came to testify. And the ultimate threat was to issue a subpoena for Ridge's appearance, so that continued stonewalling would lead to contempt of Congress, a criminal offense. Nevertheless, the White House continued to block Ridge's public testimony, on the grounds that he is not a cabinet member but a presidential adviser, comparable to National Security Adviser Condoleezza Rice, and therefore beyond Congress's reach. The president also offered the consolation prize that Congress could summon any or all of the officials in the federal agencies. But a dramatic bipartisan response to this was that separate testimony of the very agencies whose jurisdictions and turf were rearranged would defeat the purpose of the unification and coordination that the Homeland Security Office was supposed to accomplish.

As congressional tempers flared, President Bush held to absolute executive privilege, while offering the modest compromise that he would establish a Homeland Security Advisory Council. No one doubted the president would win the battle if it came to a showdown. But the price would be high, especially in an election year and with a growing number of Republicans ready to "cross the aisle."

[1] Raoul Berger, *Executive Privilege: A Constitutional Myth* (Cambridge, MA: Harvard University Press, 1974), pp. 1–14.

SOURCES: Raoul Berger, *Executive Privilege: A Constitutional Myth* (Cambridge, MA: Harvard University Press, 1974), preface and chaps. 1–4; *Congressional Quarterly*, March 23, 2002, pp. 816–17; and Louis Fisher, *President and Congress* (New York: Free Press, 1976), pp. 77–84.

without his vice presidential candidate, Lyndon Johnson, and the contribution Johnson made to winning in Texas. George W. Bush's choice of Dick Cheney in 2000 was completely devoid of direct electoral value, since Cheney came from one of our least populous states (Wyoming, which casts only three electoral votes). But given Cheney's stalwart right-wing record both in Congress and as President Bush's secretary of defense, coupled with his even more prominently right-wing wife, Lynne Cheney, his inclusion on the Republican ticket was clearly an effort to consolidate the support of the restive right wing of his party. Al Gore's choice of Joe Lieberman was also remote from electoral consideration. Lieberman's home state, Connecticut, contributes only eight electoral votes and was already certain to go Democratic. And as the first Jewish vice presidential nominee, Lieberman could add only marginally to the national Democratic vote because 80 percent of the Jewish vote was already Democratic. However, as a devoutly religious man and the first and only Democrat in the Senate to denounce President Clinton's behavior in the Lewinsky affair—and as a conservative Democrat—Lieberman's presence was a message to the nation that Gore was not a "Clinton clone" and was solidly main-stream in all the policy initiatives he had promised to take as president.

Presidents have constantly promised to give their vice presidents more responsibility, but they almost always break their promises, indicating that they are unable to utilize the vice presidency as a management or political resource after the election. No one can explain exactly why. Perhaps it is just too much trouble to share responsibility. Perhaps the president as head of state feels unable to share any part of that status. Perhaps, like many adult Americans who do not draw up their wills, presidents may simply dread contemplating their own death. But management style is certainly a factor. George H. W. Bush, as vice president, was "kept within the loop" of decision making because President Reagan delegated so much power. A copy of virtually everything made for Reagan was made for Bush, especially during the first term, when Bush's close friend James Baker was chief of staff. Former President Bush did not take such pains to keep Dan Quayle "in the loop," but President Clinton relied greatly on his vice president, Al Gore, and Gore emerged as one of the most trusted and effective figures in the Clinton White House. Gore's most important task was to oversee the National Performance Review (NPR), an ambitious program to "reinvent" the way the federal government conducts its affairs. The presidency of George W. Bush has resulted in unprecedented power and responsibility for his vice president, Dick Cheney.

THE FIRST LADY

The president serves as both chief executive and chief of state—the equivalent of Great Britain's prime minister and king rolled into one, simultaneously leading the government and serving as a symbol of the nation at official ceremonies and functions. For their part, most first ladies (all presidents so far have been men) limit their activities to the ceremonial portion of the presidency. First ladies greet foreign dignitaries, visit other countries, attend important national ceremonies, and otherwise act as America's "queen" when the president is called upon to serve in a kingly capacity.

Because the first lady is generally associated exclusively with the head of state aspect of America's presidency, she is usually not subject to the same sort of media

Throughout history, presidential wives have played an important, even decisive role in the administrations of their spouses. The nation's first first lady, Martha Washington, called herself "the hostess of the nation." Prior to becoming first lady, Martha Washington helped feed and nurse wounded American troops during the long winter at Valley Forge.

Eleanor Roosevelt was the first first lady to hold regular press conferences; she served as the administration's spokesperson on matters pertaining to race relations and human rights.

> **What political resources can the president draw on in exercising the powers of the presidency? Which of these resources is a potential liability? Why?**

scrutiny or partisan attack as that aimed at the president. Yet this has changed in recent times as first ladies have begun to exert more influence over policy. Franklin Roosevelt's wife, Eleanor, was widely popular, but also widely criticized, for her active role in many elements of her husband's presidency. She was a tireless advocate for the poor, the working class, and African Americans. She was also the first first lady to hold a former government post—assistant director of the Office of Civil Defense. Lyndon Johnson's wife, Lady Bird, headed the national campaign to beautify America. More recently, Jimmy Carter's wife, Rosalynn, sat in on Cabinet meetings, and was considered a close adviser to her husband on policy matters. President Reagan's wife, Nancy, exercised great control over her husband's schedule and over who could and could not see him. Hillary Clinton played a major political and policy role in Bill Clinton's presidency. During the 1992 campaign, Bill Clinton often implied that she would be active in the administration by joking that voters would get "two for the price of one." After the election, Hillary took a leading role in many policy areas, most notably heading the administration's health care reform effort. Like Eleanor Roosevelt, Hillary Clinton was fiercely criticized for exercising too much influence over her husband's administration. She also became the first first lady to seek public office on her own when she ran for and won a seat in the U.S. Senate in New York in 2000.

Political Resources of Presidential Power

All presidents come to office with great strength. The Constitution and the institutional resources of presidential power that they accrue ensure this. Yet as Richard Neustadt argued in his book *Presidential Power,* a president's formal institutional resources of power are not the most important ones. Other political institutions, such as Congress, also possess formidable powers. As Neustadt put it, "Presidential power is the power to persuade."[19] But presidents have varied in their ability to "persuade" and thus vary in their real power. Their capacity to ex-

mandate a claim by a victorious candidate that the electorate has given him or her special authority to carry out promises made during the campaign

ercise that power and govern effectively is affected by a number of political re-sources that presidents have grown to rely on, foremost among them the Ameri-can people. These resources are a source of great strength but also, as we'll see, a potential source of weakness.

ELECTIONS AS A RESOURCE

Any ordinary citizen, legitimately placed in office, would be a very powerful presi-dent. Yet there is no denying that a decisive presidential election translates into a more effective presidency. Some presidents claim that a landslide election gives them a **mandate,** by which they mean that the electorate approved the programs offered in the campaign and that Congress ought therefore to go along. And Con-gress is not unmoved by such an appeal. The electoral landslides of 1964 and 1980 gave Presidents Johnson and Reagan real strength during their "honeymoon" years. In contrast, the close elections of Kennedy in 1960, Nixon in 1968, and Carter in 1976 seriously hampered those presidents' effectiveness. Although Bush was elected decisively in 1988, he had no legislative commitments that would have profited from any claim to an electoral mandate.

President Clinton, an action-oriented president, was nevertheless seriously hampered by having been elected in 1992 by a minority of the popular vote, a mere 43 percent. Clinton was re-elected in 1996 with 49 percent of the vote, a larger per-centage of the electorate, but still a minority. His appeals to bipartisanship in 1997 reflected his lack of a mandate from the electorate.

The outcome of the 2000 presidential election indicated a popular-vote dead-lock of 48 percent to 48 percent, reflecting a difference of a mere 500,000 votes out of approximately 103 million cast. Given the closeness of the election—as well as the close partisan balance in Congress—initially it mat-tered little that George W. Bush won, since any president possessing such a narrow margin of victory would have little claim to mandate. September 11, however, changed everything and gave Bush the mandate that the election failed to provide.

Hillary Rodham Clinton was active in White House policy making, most notably as head of the Task Force on National Health Care Reform, one of the policy priorities of the Clinton adminstration. Some complained about the prominent role of the first lady, and many blamed her for the failure to pass health care reform.

PARTY AS A PRESIDENTIAL RESOURCE

Although on the decline, the president's party is far from insignificant as a political resource (see also Chapter 9). Figure 13.4 dramatically demonstrates the point with a forty-four-year history of the presidential "batting aver-age" in Congress—the percentage of winning roll-call votes in Congress on bills publicly supported by the president. Bill Clinton, in his first two years in office,

Former schoolteacher Laura Bush's policy focus has been on education and literacy. She frequently visits elementary schools and also sponsors White House events focused on American literature.

enjoyed high averages of legislative success—86 percent in both 1993 and 1994—but that figure dropped dramatically to 35 percent in 1995 following the Republican takeover of Congress in the 1994 elections.

The relatively low batting averages for Republican presidents such as Nixon, Ford, Reagan, and Bush (George H. W.) are clearly attributable to the political party as a presidential resource. Democrats support Democratic presidents and Republicans support Republican presidents. Prior to 1995, during the years included in Figure 13.4, Democrats held the majority in the House of Representatives for all but the 1952–54 Congress and in the Senate except for the 1952–54 and 1980–86 Congresses; it is thus to be expected that the averages for Democratic presidents would be higher than they would be for Republican presidents. As Figure 13.4 shows clearly, the political party is the key factor.

At the same time, party has its limitations as a resource. The more unified the president's party is behind legislative requests from the White House, the more unified the opposition party is also likely to be. Unless the president's party majority is very large, appeals must also be made to the opposition to make up for the inevitable defectors within the ranks of the president's own party. Consequently, the president often poses as being above partisanship in order to win "bipartisan" support in Congress. But in pursuing a bipartisan strategy, a president cannot concentrate solely on building the party loyalty and party discipline that would maximize the value of the party's support in Congress. This is a dilemma for all presidents, particularly those faced with an opposition-controlled Congress.

Figure 13.4 **The Batting Average: Presidential Success on Congressional Votes, 1953–2000**

The presidential "batting average" is the percentage of votes on which the president took a position and that position was successful.

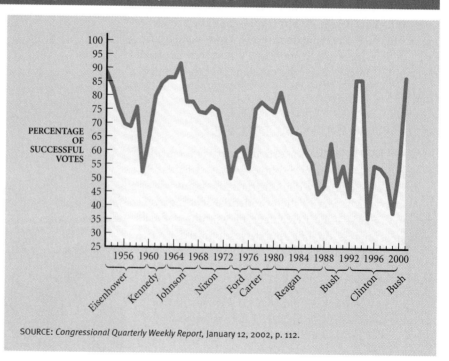

SOURCE: *Congressional Quarterly Weekly Report,* January 12, 2002, p. 112.

GROUPS AS A PRESIDENTIAL RESOURCE

The classic case in modern times of groups as a resource for the presidency was the Roosevelt or **New Deal coalition.**[20] The New Deal coalition was composed of an inconsistent, indeed contradictory, set of interests. Some of these interests were not organized interest groups, but were regional interests, such as southern whites, or residents of large cities in the industrial Northeast and Midwest, or blacks who later succeeded in organizing as an interest group. In addition to these sectional interests that were drawn to the New Deal, the coalition included several large, self-consciously organized interest groups. The most important in the New Deal coalition were organized labor, agriculture, and the financial community.[21] All of the parts were held together by a judicious use of patronage—not merely patronage in jobs but patronage in policies. Many of the groups were permitted virtually to write their own legislation. In exchange, the groups supported President Roosevelt and his successors in their battles with opposing coalitions.

New Deal coalition the coalition of northern urban liberals, southern white conservatives, organized labor, and blacks that dominated national politics until the 1960s

Republican presidents have had their group coalition base also. The most important segments of organized business have tended to support Republican presidents. They have most often been joined by upper-income groups, as well as by some ethnic groups. In recent years, Republican presidents have expanded their interest coalition base. President Reagan, for example, won the support of traditionally Democratic southern white and northern blue-collar voters as well as fundamentalist Christian conservatives.

In 2000, Al Gore's campaign strategy was to mobilize the mass base of the Democratic Party with a populist appeal to working families, African Americans, the poor, and the elderly. He was able to win the endorsement of all the major trade unions, despite some of their misgivings about his views on international trade. In a sense, Gore sought to return to the class politics of the New Deal coalition, but without the support of southern whites.

In contrast, George W. Bush attempted to rebuild the GOP base that had been shattered during the 1998 fall of former House speaker Newt Gingrich. In July 1999, at a meeting of Republican governors in St. Louis, twenty-three of twenty-nine Republican governors, along with nineteen Republican senators and 136 Republican House members, endorsed Bush for president. They did so because Bush appeared to them to be the only Republican candidate who could pull the party together and win the presidency. Consequently, Bush's strategy was not to challenge Gore head-on, but instead, to consolidate the GOP base. To do so, Bush promised a massive tax cut to appeal to upper-income groups and espoused family values to appeal to rural and small-town conservatives.

The interest bases of the two parties have remained largely unchanged since 1980, when the GOP completed its absorption of most white southerners and religious conservatives. But whether these coalitions will last remains to be seen.

PRESIDENTIAL USE OF THE MEDIA

While the media have grown increasingly important during presidential campaigns (see Chapter 10), their importance is even greater during a president's term in office. Modern presidents have sought a more direct relationship with the public and have used the media to achieve this end. Modern presidents have learned that they can use their relationship with the media to mobilize popular support for their programs and to attempt to force Congress to follow their lead.

In the media, reporting on what is new sells newspapers or attracts viewers. The president has at hand the thousands of policy proposals that come up to the White House through the administrative agencies; these can be fed to the media as newsworthy initiatives. Consequently, virtually all newspapers and television networks habitually look to the White House as the chief source of news about public policy. They tend to assign one of their most skillful reporters to the White House "beat." And since news is money, they need the president as much as the president needs them in order to meet their mutual need to make news. Members of Congress, especially senators, are also key sources of news, but the White House has more control over what and when, which is what political initiative is all about.

Different presidents use the media in quite different ways. One of the first presidents to use the media was Theodore Roosevelt, who referred to the presidency as a "bully pulpit" because its visibility allowed him to preach to the nation and bring popular pressure to bear against his opponents in Congress. But the first president to try to reach the public directly through the media was Franklin Roosevelt. During the 1930s, FDR used radio broadcasts known as "fireside chats," press conferences, speeches, and movie newsreels to rally support for his New Deal programs and, later, to build popular support for American rearmament in the face of the growing danger in Europe and the Far East. FDR also cultivated strong relationships with national news correspondents to ensure favorable publicity for his programs. FDR's efforts to reach out to the American people and mobilize their support were among the factors that made him one of the strongest presidents in American history. His appeals to the American people allowed FDR to "reach over the heads" of congressional opponents and force them to follow his lead because their constituents demanded it.

A president's personality also affects how the press conference is used. Since 1961, the presidential press conference has been a distinctive institution, available whenever the president wants to dominate the news. Between 300 and 400 certified reporters attend and file their accounts within minutes of the concluding words, "Thank you, Mr. President." But despite the importance of the press conference, its value to each president has varied. President Clinton tended to combine high-profile, elaborate press conferences and prime-time broadcasts with a more personal one-on-one approach with reporters. President Clinton also appeared on informal and basically nonpolitical talk shows, such as those of Larry King and Oprah Winfrey. Such an informal approach has its risks, however: President Clinton was widely perceived as lacking the gravity a president is expected to possess. It is hard to argue with this conclusion when one considers that he was the first president to have answered a question (on MTV) about what kind of underwear he wears. President George W. Bush had a shaky start in national politics partly because his media performances were halting and his command of the English language appeared mediocre at best. However, once in office he quickly began to show improvement, especially in impromptu situations, and he grew steadily as a media figure during the September 11 crisis and its aftermath.

Of course, in addition to the presidential press conference there are other routes from the White House to news prominence.[22] For example, President Nixon preferred direct television addresses, and President Carter tried to make initiatives more homey with a television adaptation of President Roosevelt's "fireside chats." President Reagan made unusually good use of prime-time television addresses and also instituted more informal but regular Saturday afternoon radio broadcasts, a tradition that President Clinton continued.

PUBLIC OPINION

Most Americans feel that presidents should follow public opinion. Interestingly, however, many of the most successful presidents have been public opinion leaders rather than followers.

In 1963, President John Kennedy signed a nuclear test ban treaty with the Soviet Union, even though public opinion polls seemed to show that most Americans thought the treaty was a bad idea. Kennedy believed that the treaty served the national interest and that most Americans did not know enough about the issue at stake to have fixed views on the topic. He assured his nervous advisers that, since most Americans lacked strong views on the topic, they would assume that the president's actions were correct. Kennedy was right: after he signed the treaty, polls showed that most Americans supported his decision.

Former president George Bush used the same logic during the Persian Gulf crisis that followed the Iraqi invasion of Kuwait. At the time, opinion was divided both within Congress and among the broader public. Congressional leaders tried to constrain the president's ability to use forces in combat, urging him instead to rely on diplomacy and economic sanctions to compel Iraq's withdrawal. Congressional criticism, especially televised Senate hearings, helped erode Bush's popular standing and almost undermined his power to act. In January 1991, however, Bush sought and narrowly received congressional approval to use force against Iraq. The overwhelming success of the American military effort produced a surge of popular support for Bush; his approval rating rose to over 90 percent.

Presidents also read and study polls to try to adapt their priorities to what the people want. During 1995–96, a majority of Americans indicated support for welfare reform, which included cutting social welfare spending and turning more control over to the states. After vetoing welfare reform, Clinton came to support the idea, sensing the public's support of the issue. In 1996, he signed the welfare reform bill into law, and claimed it as an achievement of his presidency.

MASS POPULARITY AS A RESOURCE (AND A LIABILITY)

In addition to utilizing the media and public opinion polls, recent presidents, particularly Bill Clinton, have reached out directly to the American public to gain its approval. President Clinton's enormously high public profile, as is indicated by the number of public appearances he made (see Figure 13.5 on page 536), is only the most recent dramatic expression of the presidency as a **"permanent campaign"** for re-election. A study by political scientist Charles O. Jones shows that President Clinton engaged in campaignlike activity throughout his presidency and was the most-traveled American president in history. In his first twenty months in office, he made 203 appearances outside of Washington, compared with 178 for George H. W. Bush and 58 for Ronald Reagan. President George W. Bush might outdo them all. During his first hundred days, Bush gave speeches and other public

permanent campaign description of presidential politics in which all presidential actions are taken with re-election in mind

Public Appearances by Presidents, 1929–95

President Bill Clinton made more public appearances in his first three years in office than any of his predecessors did in their first three years.

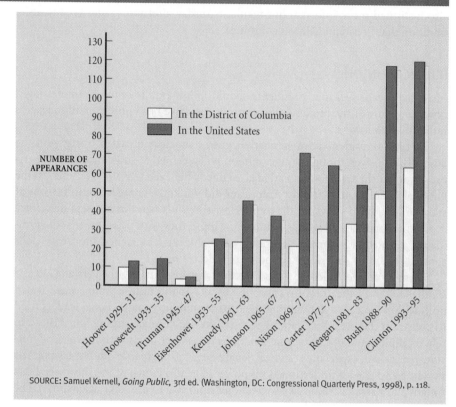

SOURCE: Samuel Kernell, *Going Public*, 3rd ed. (Washington, DC: Congressional Quarterly Press, 1998), p. 118.

appearances in twenty-six states; Clinton's and former president Bush's record during their first hundred days was fifteen states. Reagan went to a mere two states. In light of the need to mobilize the American people after September 11, 2001, it is virtually certain that the Bush record during his first twenty months in office will far exceed that of Bill Clinton.

The permanent campaign serves two major purposes related to re-election: building mass popularity and raising campaign funds. Despite the growing controversy over campaign-finance abuses in 1997 and after, President Clinton attended numerous events to raise money to pay off the $30 million of debt from his 1996 presidential campaign. In fact, even during the most intense moments of the Monica Lewinsky scandal of early 1998, Clinton continued his fund-raising for the party, and the Democratic National Committee had to add staff to answer all the telephone calls and mail that were responding positively to President Clinton's appeals.

Even with the help of all other institutional and political resources, successful presidents have to be able to mobilize mass opinion in their favor in order to keep Congress in line. But as we shall see, each president tends to *use up* mass resources. Virtually everyone is aware that presidents are constantly making appeals to the public over the heads of Congress and the Washington community. But our public is not made up of fools. The American people react to presidential actions rather than mere speeches or other image-making devices.

The public's sensitivity to presidential actions can be seen in the tendency of all presidents to lose popular support. Despite the twists and turns shown on Figure 13.6, the percentage of positive responses to "Do you approve of the way the president is handling his job?" starts out at a level significantly higher than the percentage of votes the president got in the previous national election and then declines over the next four years. Though the shape of the line differs, the destination is the same.

This downward tendency is to be expected if American voters are rational, inasmuch as almost any action taken by the president can be divisive, with some voters approving and other voters disapproving. Public disapproval of specific actions has a cumulative effect on the president's overall performance rating. Thus, all presidents are faced with the problem of boosting their approval ratings. And the public generally reacts favorably to presidential actions in foreign policy or, more precisely, to international events associated with the president. Analysts call this the **rallying effect.** Nevertheless, the rallying effect turns out to be only a momentary reversal of the more general tendency of presidents to lose popular support.

rallying effect the generally favorable reaction of the public to presidential actions taken in foreign policy, or more precisely, to decisions made during international crises

Presidential Performance Ratings from Kennedy to Clinton

Figure 13.6

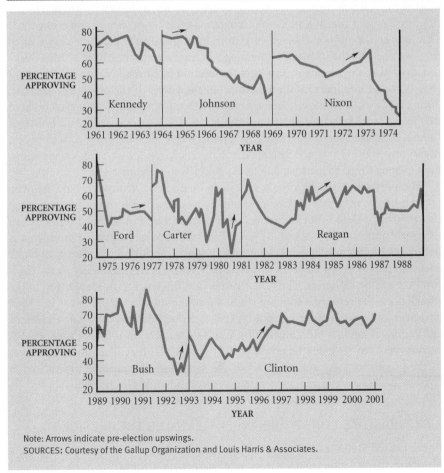

In presidential performance rating polls, respondents are asked, "Do you approve of the way the president is handling his job?" This graph shows the percentage of positive responses.

Note: Arrows indicate pre-election upswings.
SOURCES: Courtesy of the Gallup Organization and Louis Harris & Associates.

Looking again at Figure 13.6, the one notable exception to this general downward trend of presidential approval was during Clinton's second term (1997–2001). As expected, Clinton's approval rating surged before and after his re-election and then dropped over the course of 1997. But Clinton experienced two important upward blips, one early in 1998 and the other early in 1999, that were both related to the impeachment controversy, not to an international crisis. In both cases, Americans were disapproving of Clinton's behavior but they rallied behind the presidency as an institution. This rallying effect may well be what kept Clinton in office, and he was able to serve effectively during his last few years as president. President Bush's approval ratings were modest during his first eight months in office but then rose to unprecedented heights as a result of the rallying effect following September 11, 2001. Public support of the presidency is consistently high, and the public rallies around it when it is endangered by war or scandal. But that very support can work against the president, and Bush will probably follow most of his predecessors by leaving office as a disappointment—while the presidency itself remains stronger than ever.

The Presidency and Democracy

Most of the real power of the modern presidency comes from powers granted by the Constitution and the laws made by Congress delegating powers to the president.[23] Thus, any person properly elected and sworn in as president will possess almost all of the power held by the strongest of presidents in American history. Even a "lame duck" president (a sitting president who loses the election in November, but who does not leave office until January) still possesses all of the power of the office. For example, during the weeks after his electoral defeat in 1992, former president Bush committed troops to Somalia and conducted a series of air strikes against Iraq. And President Clinton completed successful trade negotiations with China and got spectacular votes of approval in the House and Senate to drop the annual review of China's trade status, thus opening China to membership in the World Trade Organization.

The presidency has become a genuinely democratic institution, and its mass popular base is respected by Congress and by all of the social forces and organized interests that seek to influence the national government. But we must recognize an extremely important fact about the presidency: the popular base of the presidency is important less because it gives the president power, and more because it gives the president *consent to use* all of the power already vested in the presidency by the Constitution and by Congress. The other formal and informal resources lodged in the presidency—the resources we have studied throughout this chapter—are just that: resources. But resources are not power; they must be converted into power. Democratization, more than the Constitution and laws, was responsible for the enormous expansion of real presidential power in the twentieth century. The formal resources of the presidency have remained about the same for 200 years. Democratization combined with these formal powers to give us presidential government.

> **Did the development of a mass presidential constituency make the institution more democratic? More powerful?**

A PRESIDENTIAL CONSTITUENCY: CITIZENS AND THE PRESIDENT

In the United States, as a general rule, democratization follows power. As already observed, many larger social forces were gathering around the presidency and

Parliamentary and Presidential Executives

Among democracies of the world, one finds two basic forms of executive leadership, the *parliamentary (cabinet) executive* and the *presidential executive*. A presidential executive is distinguished by a single person who is popularly elected by the public. This executive's term of office is fixed and is independent of the national legislature (neither the president nor the assembly can terminate the tenure of the other), and the president selects and manages a cabinet that attends to the affairs of government. At the core of a presidential system is the person of the president; personality and leadership qualities are essential features that extend and complement the formal constitutional powers of the president.

By contrast, a parliamentary executive relies on the assembly or national legislature for its ultimate legitimacy. Political parties are at the center of parliamentary executives. In a classic parliamentary executive, following national elections, key leaders of political parties from the lower chamber of the national legislature negotiate to select a coalition of parties that will subsequently appoint individual ministers to comprise the executive cabinet. Members of the cabinet remain legislators and have no independence from the tenure of the assembly. The executive cabinet is chaired by a *prime minister* who assumes the role of being the "first among equals" among her fellow ministers. The actual decisions of government remain largely collegial, forged from negotiation and discussion among the various ministers within the cabinet. The tenure of the cabinet and the prime minister can be terminated by the assembly, but the tenure of the national legislature cannot be terminated by the cabinet or the prime minister. Finally, neither the prime minister nor the other members of the executive cabinet are elected by the public—they are invested by the national legislature.

Of today's world democracies, less than a third practice the presidential form of executive leadership. Classic presidential executives are most common in North and South America, though versions of this model of executive leadership can be found around the world. Besides the United States, democracies that rely on the presidential system include Costa Rica, Bolivia, Venezuela, South Korea, Poland, Romania, Bulgaria, and Colombia. The most common means of executive leadership is some form of parliamentary executive. Most of the European democracies are parliamentary. However, there are few systems that perfectly match the ideal model of a presidential or parliamentary executive. For instance, the United States does not have a popularly elected president,

and, in Great Britian, the prime minister is far more powerful relative to the cabinet than is the typical case of prime ministers in parliamentary democracies on the European continent. Furthermore, the British prime minister can effectively dissolve the assembly (the House of Commons) by simply calling for new elections (subject to the approval of the monarch).

Among the approximately thirty-two electoral democracies where presidents are directly or indirectly elected by the public as of 2002, the powers of the American president with respect to legislation (such as initiating legislation, vetoing legislation and having those vetoes overridden by the legislature, initiating annual budget bills, and ruling by decree in emergencies) are no more than "average"; basically, the president shares power with an independent legislature (thus the concept of separate powers). The legislative powers of the Brazilian, Chilean, Colombian, Ecuadorian, Mexican, Panamanian, Paraguayan, and Uruguayan presidents are all notably greater than that of the American president. The Brazilian president, for instance, may declare an "urgent" situation and rule by decree and enjoys many more technical advantages when it comes to surviving the threats of veto overrides of legislation.

Students of comparative government cite specific advantages to the presidential type of executive. Specifically, these are accountability (one person is easier to blame and reward than a collegial body), electoral identifiableness (it is easier for the electorate to identify with the candidate of the present, rather than a collective that is selected by the political party, as in cabinet governments), mutual checks (the president stands largely apart from the legislature, fostering more active checks and balances to power), and enhanced political arbitration (because the president stands apart from direct connection to partisan political negotiations and can serve to reconcile intractable issues between political parties). These same strengths attributed to the presidential executive highlight the weaknesses of the parliamentary executive: weaker accountability, weaker identification with the electorate, concentrated powers of the executive and legislature that are not checked and balanced, and the absence of a clear separate arbitrator to political intransigence. However, for a number of students of government, these very weaknesses of the parliamentary system of government enhance its democratic quality—collegiality and collective decision making tied to the legislative body make arrogant and imbalanced executive power less likely to distort the democratic process.

looking to the presidency even before the New Deal and the rise of presidential government. But these social forces did not begin to come together as a discernible constituency or a presidential support structure until the New Deal. Relations between the presidency and this larger constituency did not become institutionalized until even later. Institutionalized relations bring close and constant communication with party, interest groups, polls, the media, and the other segments of political society that we have discussed in this and other chapters. This presidential constituency varies between Democratic and Republican administrations; it is more working-class, elderly, urban, ethnic, and intellectual during Democratic administrations and more rural, suburban, middle- and professional-class, wealthy, and "higher" in ethnic status during Republican administrations. In either case, however, it is a popular and democratized constituency. In sum, presidential power is democratized power, and democratization has made the presidency far more powerful.

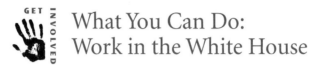

What You Can Do: Work in the White House

Johanna Atienza was a twenty-year-old junior majoring in political science at a West Coast university when she learned from other students that her school had a Washington, D.C., internship program. She was immediately interested: "What better way is there to learn about politics than from the inside?" She also felt that a semester in the nation's capital would help her to understand if the people who worked in the federal government really cared about the average citizen.

A speaker at the information session she attended spelled out the options for internships in Washington, D.C. Some were in government. Others were with the media, interest groups, and other private organizations involved in politics. Johanna's ears perked up when she learned that the White House had an intern program. The speaker suggested that she call the White House directly.

That first phone call was the beginning of her trip into what sometimes seemed like a fantasyland. After speaking directly to the White House director of the internship program, who answered her questions, Johanna received an application that asked for basic information, such as her name, address, telephone numbers, and so forth; two essays, one on why she wanted to be a White House intern and the other describing a formative experience in her life; a writing sample of approximately 500 words; and two letters of recommendation. Johanna filled out the form, devoted considerable thought and effort to the essays, and submitted the first page of a paper she had written for one of her classes as her writing sample.

Between Thanksgiving and Christmas, she received a large envelope with a return address that read, "The White House—Washington." Johanna's immediate reaction: "I was screaming!" She had been accepted into the program. Still, she needed to pass one more test. She had to fill out a form (for the FBI) that asked such questions as "Do you advocate the overthrow of the U.S. Government?" and "Have you taken illegal drugs?" The form also asked her to detail her addresses for the past seven or eight years. Johanna submitted the form. She assumed that she passed the FBI security test because she never heard anything more about it.

Several weeks later, she moved to the nation's capital. Her assignment was to work with the people who scheduled travel for the President and the First Lady.

Over the next three months, Johanna met and worked with some of the top officials in the White House. She also had the opportunity to meet President Bill Clinton and Hillary Clinton. While it was exciting to wander around the maze of offices in the White House, Johanna reports, she was often so busy that she had little time to realize that she was indeed wandering through White House corridors.

What did Johanna learn from her three-month participation in the day-to-day life of White House politics that she was unlikely to learn in a classroom? First, she was struck by the incredible complexity of the presidency and Washington politics. Procedures are detailed and time-consuming. Things moved remarkably slowly, if at all. Second, however, she gained tremendous respect for the people who work in the White House. In general, the staff believed that "you can do some good, you really can." They were dedicated people who worked long hours, often for little money. Even the older aides worked long hours and devoted themselves to public service.

Johanna went to the White House asking herself whether the staff and politicians in Washington, D.C., really care about the people back home. She returned to the West Coast with a strong sense that the people who work in the White House for the President of the United States do indeed strive to make life a little better for the rest of us.

Should other students apply for the White House intern program—even though the application process takes time and effort? Johanna answers without hesitation, "Definitely." See if your school has a Washington, D.C., program. If not, call the White House directly and ask for the intern office. At this time next year, you could be one of the bright young people wandering their way through the West Wing.

Summary

The foundations for presidential government were laid in the Constitution, which provides for a unitary executive who is head of state as well as head of government. The first section of this chapter reviewed the powers of each: the head of state with its military, judicial, and diplomatic powers; the head of government with its executive, military, and legislative powers.

The second and third sections of this chapter focused on the president's institutional and political resources. The Cabinet, the other top appointments, the White House staff, and the Executive Office of the President are some of the impressive institutional resources of presidential power. The president's political party, the supportive group coalitions, and access to the media and, through that, access to the millions of Americans who make up the general public are formidable political resources that can be used to bolster a president's power. But these resources are not cost- or risk-free. A direct relationship with the public is the president's most potent modern resource, but it is also the most problematic.

The final section of this chapter traced the rise of modern presidential government after the much longer period of congressional dominance. There is no mystery in the shift to government centered on the presidency. Congress built the modern presidency by delegating to it not only the power to implement the vast new programs of the 1930s but also by delegating its own legislative power to make the policies themselves. Presidential government is now an established fact of American politics.

For Further Reading

Barber, James David. *The Presidential Character.* Englewood Cliffs, NJ: Prentice-Hall, 1992.

Daynes, Byron W., Raymond Tatalovich, and Dennis Soden. *To Govern a Nation: Presidential Power and Politics.* New York: St. Martin's Press, 1998.

Issacharoff, Samuel, et al. *When Elections Go Bad: The Law of Democracy and the Presidential Election of 2000.* Rev. ed. New York: Foundation Press, 2001.

Jones, Charles O. *Clinton and Congress, 1993–1996: Risk, Restoration, and Re-Election.* Norman, OK: University of Oklahoma Press, 1999.

Kernell, Samuel. *Going Public: New Strategies of Presidential Leadership.* Washington, DC: Congressional Quarterly Press, 1997.

Lowi, Theodore J. *The Personal President: Power Invested, Promise Unfulfilled.* Ithaca, NY: Cornell University Press, 1985.

Milkis, Sidney M. *The President and the Parties: The Transformation of the American Party System since the New Deal.* New York: Oxford University Press, 1993.

Neustadt, Richard E. *Presidential Power: The Politics of Leadership from Roosevelt to Reagan.* Rev. ed. New York: Free Press, 1990.

Pfiffner, James P. *The Modern Presidency.* New York: St. Martin's, 2000.

Schumaker, Paul, and Burdett A. Loomis, eds. *Choosing a President: The Electoral College and Beyond.* New York: Chatham House, 2001.

Skowronek, Stephen. *The Politics Presidents Make: Leadership from John Adams to Bill Clinton.* Cambridge, MA: The Belknap Press of Harvard University Press, 1997.

Spitzer, Robert. *The Presidential Veto: Touchstone of the American Presidency.* Albany, NY: SUNY Press, 1988.

Tulis, Jeffrey. *The Rhetorical Presidency.* Princeton, NJ: Princeton University Press, 1987.

Study Outline ON THE WEB

www.wwnorton.com/wtp4e

The Constitutional Powers of the Presidency

1. The president as head of state is defined by three constitutional provisions—military, judicial, and diplomatic—that are the source of some of the most important powers on which the president can draw.
2. The position of commander in chief makes the president the highest military authority in the United States, with control of the entire military establishment.
3. The presidential power to grant reprieves, pardons, and amnesties allows the president to choose freedom or confinement, and even life or death for all individuals who have violated, or are suspected of having violated, federal laws, including people who directly threaten the security of the United States.

4. The power to receive representatives of foreign countries allows the president almost unconditional authority to determine whether a new ruling group can indeed commit its country to treaties and other agreements.
5. The president's role as head of government rests on a constitutional foundation consisting of three principal sources: executive power, domestic military authority, and legislative power.
6. The Constitution delegates to the president, as commander in chief, the obligation to protect every state against invasion and domestic violence.
7. The president's legislative power consists of the obligation to make recommendations for consideration by Congress and the ability to veto legislation.

Institutional Resources of Presidential Power

1. Presidents have at their disposal a variety of institutional resources—such as the power to fill high-level political positions—that directly affect a president's ability to govern.
2. Presidents increasingly have preferred the White House staff to the Cabinet as a tool for managing the gigantic executive branch.
3. The White House staff, which is composed primarily of analysts and advisers, has grown from an informal group of fewer than a dozen people to a new presidential bureaucracy.
4. The Executive Office of the President, often called the institutional presidency, is larger than the White House staff, and comprises the president's permanent management agencies.

Political Resources of Presidential Power

1. The president also has political resources on which to draw in exercising the powers of office.
2. Presidents often use their electoral victories to increase their power by claiming the election was a mandate for a certain course of action.
3. Although its traditional influence is on the decline, the president's party is still significant as a means of achieving legislative success.
4. Interest groups and coalitions supportive of the president's agenda are also a dependable resource for presidential government.
5. Over the past half-century, the American executive branch has harnessed mass popularity successfully as a political resource.

The Presidency and Democracy

1. The democratization of the presidency through the growth of a mass popular base has made the institution more powerful.

Practice Quiz

www.wwnorton.com/wtp4e

1. Which article of the Constitution establishes the presidency?
   a) Article I
   b) Article II
   c) Article III
   d) none of the above

2. Which of the following does not represent a classification of a constitutional provision designating the president as head of state?
   a) legislative
   b) military
   c) judicial
   d) diplomatic

3. Which of the following does not require the advice and consent of the Senate?
   a) an executive agreement
   b) a treaty
   c) Supreme Court nominations
   d) All of the above require the advice and consent of the Senate.

4. Which of the following terms has been used to describe the presidency as it has used constitutional and other powers to make itself more powerful?
   a) "the delegated presidency"
   b) "the imperial presidency"
   c) "the personal presidency"
   d) "the preemptive presidency"

5. By what process can Congress reject a presidential veto?
   a) veto override
   b) pocket veto
   c) executive delegation
   d) impeachment

6. Which of the following describes the presidential foreign policy advisory council composed of the president; the vice president; the secretaries of state, defense, and the treasury; the attorney general; and others?
   a) the "inner Cabinet"
   b) the National Security Council
   c) both a and b
   d) neither a nor b

7. The Office of Management and Budget is part of
   a) the Executive Office of the President.
   b) the White House staff.
   c) the Kitchen Cabinet.
   d) both a and b.

8. Which twentieth-century presidency transformed the American system of government from a Congress-centered to a president-centered system?
   a) Woodrow Wilson's
   b) Franklin Roosevelt's
   c) Richard Nixon's
   d) Jimmy Carter's

9. How many people work for agencies within the Executive Office of the President?
   a) 25 to 50
   b) 700 to 1,000
   c) 1,500 to 2,000
   d) 4,500 to 5,000

Critical Thinking Questions

www.wwnorton.com/wtp4e

1. At times, the Congress has been the dominant branch of government. At other times, the presidency has predominated. Describe the changes in the relationship between the presidency and the Congress throughout American history.  What factors contributed to the dominance of Congress? What factors contributed to the resurgence of the presidency? Which branch of government dominates now? Why do you think so?

2. Presidents have constitutional, institutional, and political sources of power. Which of the three do you think most accounts for the powers of the presidency? Is it, in fact, possible to discern among these the true source of presidential power? Select a president and discuss the ways in which that particular president used each source of power to succeed in the presidency.

3. President Harry Truman often said that the presidency of the United States is "the most powerful office in the history of the world." But Richard Neustadt, perhaps the leading presidential scholar and certainly the scholar who knew Harry Truman best, characterized Truman's presidential power, and that of all his successors, as "the power to persuade." Take the Israeli-Palestinian case. The efforts of President Bill Clinton and President George W. Bush to broker peace between the Israelis and Palestinians were foiled by terrorist attacks; these efforts failed even though a majority of both populations favors a peaceful solution and despite the fact that the United States has almost absolute power over both sides. Where does that particular issue place presidential power?

Key Terms

www.wwnorton.com/wtp4e

Cabinet (p. 525)
caucus (political) (p. 511)
commander in chief (p. 513)
delegated powers (p. 510)
executive agreement (p. 515)

Executive Office of the President (EOP) (p. 527)
executive order (p. 522)
expressed powers (p. 510)
inherent powers (p. 510)
Kitchen Cabinet (p. 526)
legislative initiative (p. 522)
line-item veto (p. 522)
mandate (p. 531)

National Security Council (NSC) (p.525)
New Deal coalition (p. 533)
patronage (p. 523)
permanent campaign (p. 535)
pocket veto (p. 521)
rallying effect (p. 537)
veto (p. 521)
War Powers Resolution (p. 515)
White House staff (p. 526)

14 BUREAUCRACY IN A DEMOCRACY

★ **Bureaucracy and Bureaucrats**
Why do bureaucracies exist? Why are they needed?
Has the federal bureaucracy grown too large?
What roles do government bureaucrats perform?

★ **The Organization of the Executive Branch**
What are the agencies that make up the executive branch?
How can one classify these agencies according to their missions?

★ **Can Bureaucracy Be Reinvented?**
Can government be made more responsive and efficient? Why or why not?

★ **Can the Bureaucracy Be Reduced?**
What methods have been used to reduce the size and the role of the
federal bureaucracy?

★ **Can Bureaucracy Be Controlled?**
How do the president and Congress manage and oversee the bureaucracy?

MERICANS DEPEND ON government bureaucracies to accomplish the most spectacular achievements as well as the most mundane. Yet, they often do not realize that public bureaucracies are essential for providing the services that they use every day and that they rely on in emergencies. On a typical day, a college student might check the weather forecast, drive on an interstate highway, mail the rent check, drink from a public water fountain, check the calories on the side of a yogurt container, attend a class, log on to the Internet, and meet a relative at the airport. Each of these activities is possible because of the work of a government bureaucracy: the U.S. Weather Service, the U.S. Department of Transportation, the U.S. Postal Service, the Environmental Protection Agency, the Food and Drug Administration, the student loan programs of the U.S. Department of Education, the Advanced Research Projects Agency (which developed the Internet in the 1960s), and the Federal Aviation Administration. Without the ongoing work of these agencies, many of these common activities would be impossible, unreliable, or more expensive. Even though bureaucracies provide essential services that all Americans rely on, they are often disparaged by politicians and the general public alike. Criticized as "big government," many federal bureaucracies come into public view only when they are charged with fraud, waste, and abuse.

In emergencies, the national perspective on bureaucracy and, indeed, on "big government" shifts. After the September 11 terrorist attacks, all eyes turned to Washington. The federal government responded by strengthening and reorganizing the bureaucracy to undertake a whole new set of responsibilities designed to keep America safe. The president created the new cabinet-level Office of Homeland Security, charged with coordinating all domestic antiterrorism activities. Law enforcement agencies gained new powers and resources. Reflecting the shift in priorities from crime investigation to terrorism prevention, the Federal Bureau of Investigation (FBI) received new responsibilities for domestic intelligence. Many other agencies assumed new duties associated with the antiterrorism objectives. The Treasury Department, for example, was assigned to create a financial intelligence-gathering system designed to track terrorists' financial transactions. The Centers for Disease Control (CDC) undertook a new set of activities designed to prevent bioterrorism. Congress created a new Transportation Security Agency within the Department of Transportation. Charged with making all forms of travel safe, the new agency presided over a significant expansion of the federal workforce as it hired thousands of workers to screen passengers at airports. ■

THE war on terrorism has highlighted the extensive range of the tasks shouldered by the federal bureaucracy. Both routine and exceptional tasks require the organization, specialization, and expertise found in bureaucracies. Turn to Table 14.1 on page 549, which identifies the basic characteristics of bureaucracy. To provide services, government bureaucracies employ specialists such as meteorologists, doctors, and scientists. To do their jobs effectively, these specialists require resources and tools (ranging from paper to blood samples); they have to coordinate their work with others (for example, the traffic engineers must communicate with construction engineers); and there must be effective outreach to the public (for example, private doctors must be made aware of health warnings). Bureaucracy provides a way to coordinate the many different parts that must work together in order to provide good services.

■ **We begin this chapter by clarifying what we mean by "bureaucracy."** Before we can understand the nature and character of the executive branch of the U.S. government, we must first examine why bureaucracy is necessary. From there, we then turn to the size, role, functions, and characteristics of the federal bureaucracy and bureaucrats.

■ **We next examine the organization of the executive branch as a whole, looking at the Cabinet departments, agencies, and bureaus that make up its operating parts.** Since the executive branch is vast and there are far too many agencies for us to identify here, we will instead evaluate the different broad purposes that federal agencies serve.

■ **We next turn to ways in which the size and role of the federal bureaucracy can be reduced.** Although efforts to downsize government have been popular in recent years, we question whether these attempts are effective or even address the most pressing problem regarding the control of the federal bureaucracy.

■ **We conclude this chapter by asking whether bureaucracy and democracy are contradictory.** The bureaucracy is intended to be accountable to the president and Congress and through them to the American people. We will examine the ways in which the president and Congress have tried to manage the bureaucracy and hold it accountable and whether these management techniques have been effective. We conclude by reviewing the role of the average citizen in holding bureaucracy accountable.

Bureaucracy and Bureaucrats

Bureaucracy is nothing more nor less than a form of organization, as defined by the attributes in Table 14.1. To gain some objectivity, and to appreciate the universality of bureaucracy, let us take the word and break it into its two main parts—

> ➢ Why do bureaucracies exist? Why are they needed?

The Six Primary Characteristics of Bureaucracy

Table 14.1

CHARACTERISTIC	EXPLANATION
Division of labor	Workers are specialized. Each worker develops a skill in a particular job and performs the job routinely and repetitively, thereby increasing productivity.
Allocation of functions	Each task is assigned. No one makes a whole product; each worker depends on the output of other workers.
Allocation of responsibility	Each task becomes a personal responsibility— a contractual obligation. No task can be changed without permission.
Supervision	Some workers are assigned the special task of watching over other workers rather than contributing directly to the creation of the product. Each supervisor watches over a few workers (a situation known as "span of control"), and communications between workers or between levels move in a prescribed fashion (known as "chain of command").
Purchase of full-time employment	The organization controls all the time the worker is on the job, so each worker can be assigned and held to a task. Some part-time and contracted work is tolerated, but it is held to a minimum.
Identification of career within the organization	Workers come to identify with the organization as a way of life. Seniority, pension rights, and promotions are geared to this relationship.

bureaucracy the complex structure of offices, tasks, rules, and principles of organization that are employed by all large-scale institutions to coordinate effectively the work of their personnel

bureau and *cracy. Bureau,* a French word, can mean either "office" or "desk." *Cracy* is the Greek word for "rule" or "form of rule." For example, "democracy" means rule by the people *(demos),* a form of government in which the people prevail. "Theocracy" refers to rule by clergy or churches. "Gerontocracy" would describe a system ruled by the elders of the community. Putting *bureau* and *cracy* back together produces a very interesting definition: **Bureaucracy** is a form of rule by offices and desks. Each member of an organization has an office, meaning a place as well as a set of responsibilities. That is, each "office" comprises a set of tasks that are specialized to the needs of the organization, and the person holding that office (or position) performs those specialized tasks. Specialization and repetition are essential to the efficiency of any organization. Therefore, when an organization is inefficient, it is almost certainly because it is not bureaucratized enough!

> **Has the federal bureaucracy grown too large?**

THE SIZE OF THE FEDERAL SERVICE

In his State of the Union address in 1996, President Bill Clinton declared that "the era of big government is over." Throughout the 2000 presidential election, candidate George W. Bush promised that he would curb the growth of big government. Before the federal government began to gear up for the war on terrorism, politicians of both parties were closely attuned to popular sentiments that the federal government had grown too large. Despite fears of bureaucratic growth getting out of hand, however, the federal service has hardly grown at all during the past twenty-five years; it reached its peak postwar level in 1968 with 3.0 million civilian employees plus an additional 3.6 million military personnel (a figure swollen by Vietnam). The number of civilian federal employees has since fallen to approximately 2.7 million in 1998; the number of military personnel totals only 1.4 million.[1] Both numbers are sure to rise as the government pursues the war on terrorism.

The growth of the federal service over the past fifty years is even less imposing when placed in the context of the total workforce and when compared to the size of state and local public employment. Figure 14.1 indicates that, since 1950, the ratio of federal employment to the total workforce has been steady, and in fact has *declined* slightly in the past thirty years. In 1950, there were 4.3 million state and local civil service employees (about 6.5 percent of the country's workforce). In 1998, there were almost 16.0 million (nearly 12 percent of the workforce). Federal employment, in contrast, exceeded 5 percent of the workforce only during World War II (not shown), and almost all of that momentary growth was military. After the demobilization, which continued until 1950 (as shown in Figure 14.1), the federal service has tended to grow at a rate that keeps pace with the economy and society. That is demonstrated by the lower line on Figure 14.1, which shows a constant relation between federal civilian employment and the size of the U.S. workforce. Variations in federal employment since 1946 have been in the military and are directly related to war and the cold war (as shown by the top line on Figure 14.1).

Another useful comparison is to be found in Figure 14.2, on page 552. Although the dollar increase in federal spending shown by the bars looks impressive, the trend line indicating the relation of federal spending to the Gross Domestic Product (GDP) shows that in 2001, this percentage was barely higher than in 1960.

In sum, the national government is indeed "very large," but it has not been growing any faster than the economy or the society. The same is roughly true of

Employees in the Federal Service and in the National Workforce, 1946–2000

Figure 14.1

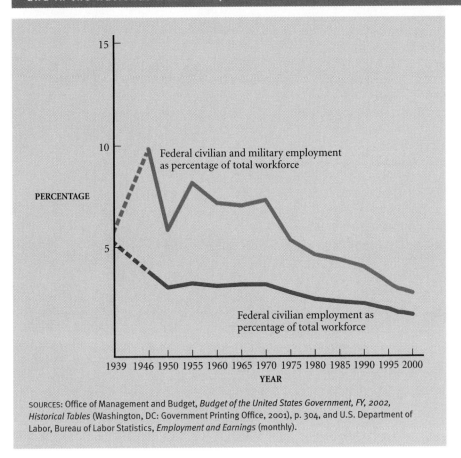

SOURCES: Office of Management and Budget, *Budget of the United States Government, FY, 2002, Historical Tables* (Washington, DC: Government Printing Office, 2001), p. 304, and U.S. Department of Labor, Bureau of Labor Statistics, *Employment and Earnings* (monthly).

the growth pattern of state and local public personnel. Bureaucracy keeps pace with society, despite people's seeming dislike for it, because the control towers, the prisons, the Social Security system, and other essential elements cannot be operated without bureaucracy. The United States certainly could not hope to protect the nation against terrorism without a large military and civilian bureaucracy.

Although the federal executive branch is large and complex, everything about it is commonplace. Bureaucracies are commonplace because they touch so many aspects of daily life. Government bureaucracies implement the decisions made by the political process. Bureaucracies are full of routine because that assures the regular delivery of services and ensures that each agency fulfills its mandate. Public bureaucracies are powerful because legislatures and chief executives, and indeed the people, delegate to them vast power to make sure a particular job is done—enabling citizens to be more free to pursue their private ends. The public sentiments that emerged after September 11 revealed this underlying appreciation of public bureaucracies. When faced with the challenge of making air travel safe again, the public strongly supported making the federal government responsible

Figure 14.2   **Annual Federal Outlays, 1960–2007**

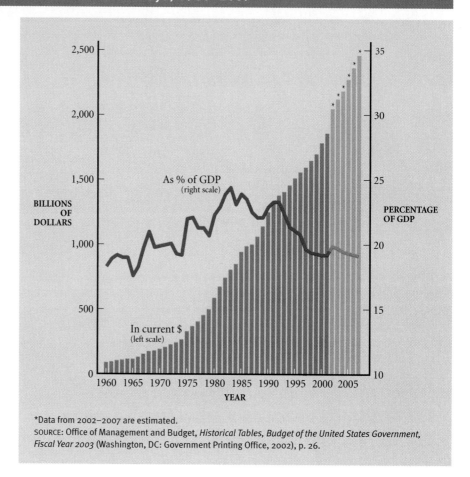

*Data from 2002–2007 are estimated.

SOURCE: Office of Management and Budget, *Historical Tables, Budget of the United States Government, Fiscal Year 2003* (Washington, DC: Government Printing Office, 2002), p. 26.

for airport security, even though this meant increasing the size of the federal bureaucracy by making the security screeners federal workers. House majority whip Tom DeLay sought to forestall this growth in the federal government, declaring that "[t]he last thing we can afford to do is erect a new bureaucracy that is unaccountable and unable to protect the American public."[2] But the antibureaucratic language that had been so effective prior to September 11 no longer resonated with a fearful public. Instead, there was a widespread belief that a public bureaucracy would provide more effective protection than the cost-conscious private security companies that had been charged with airport security in the past. Bureaucrats across the federal government felt the new appreciation for their work. As one civil servant at the Pentagon put it, "The whole mood is changed. A couple of months ago we were part of the bloated bureaucracy. Now we're Washington's equivalent of the cops and fireman in New York."[3] How long such sentiments last will depend on the effectiveness of the bureaucracy and on the public's views about whether an expanded bureaucracy is needed when (and if) the immediate threat of terrorism recedes.

BUREAUCRATS

"Government by offices and desks" conveys to most people a picture of hundreds of office workers shuffling millions of pieces of paper. There is a lot of truth in that image, but we have to look more closely at what papers are being shuffled and why. More than seventy years ago, an astute observer defined bureaucracy as "continuous routine business."[4] As we saw at the beginning of this chapter, almost any organization succeeds by reducing its work to routines, with each routine being given to a different specialist. But specialization separates people from each other; one worker's output becomes another worker's input. The timing of such relationships is essential, and this requires that these workers stay in communication with each other. Communication is the key. In fact, bureaucracy was the first information network. Routine came first; voluminous routine came as bureaucracies grew and specialized.

What Do Bureaucrats Do?   Bureaucrats, whether in public or in private organizations, communicate with each other in order to coordinate all the specializations within their organization. This coordination is necessary in order to carry out the primary task of bureaucracy, which is **implementation,** that is, implementing the objectives of the organization as laid down by its board of directors (if a private company) or by law (if a public agency). In government, the "bosses" are ultimately the legislature and the elected chief executive.

When the bosses—Congress, in particular, when it is making the law—are clear in their instructions to bureaucrats, implementation is a fairly straightforward process. Bureaucrats translate the law into specific routines for each of the employees of an agency. But what happens to routine administrative implementation when there are several bosses who disagree as to what the instructions ought to be? This requires yet another job for bureaucrats: interpretation. Interpretation is a form of implementation, in that the bureaucrats still have to carry out what they believe to be the intentions of their superiors. But when bureaucrats have to interpret a law before implementing it, they are in effect engaging in *lawmaking*. Congress often deliberately delegates to an administrative agency the responsibility of lawmaking. Members of Congress often conclude that some area of industry needs regulating or some area of the environment needs protection, but they are unwilling or unable to specify just how that should be done. In such situations, Congress delegates to the appropriate agency a broad authority within which the bureaucrats have to make law, through the procedures of **rulemaking** and **administrative adjudication.**

Rulemaking is exactly the same as legislation; in fact it is often referred to as "quasi-legislation." The rules issued by government agencies provide more detailed and specific indications of what the policy actually will mean. For example, the Occupational Safety and Health Administration is charged with ensuring that our workplaces are safe. OSHA has regulated the use of chemicals and other well known health hazards. In recent years, the widespread use of computers in the workplace has been associated with a growing number of cases of repetitive stress injury, which hurts the hands, arms, and neck. To repond to this new threat to workplace health, OSHA issued a new set of ergonomic rules in November 1999 that tell employers what they must do to prevent and address such injuries among

> **What roles do government bureaucrats perform?**

implementation the efforts of departments and agencies to translate laws into specific bureaucratic routines

rulemaking a quasi-legislative administrative process that produces regulations by government agencies

administrative adjudication applying rules and precedents to specific cases to settle disputes with regulated parties

Percentage of respondents reporting a favorable impression of certain federal departments and agencies.

Postal Service	89%
Park Service	85
Centers for Disease Control	79
Defense	76
FDA	75
NASA	73
Federal Aviation Administration	70
EPA	69
Agriculture	68
FBI	67
SSA	62
Education	61
Veterans Administration	59
Commerce	58
Justice	56
FTC	53
HUD	51
CIA	51
IRS	38

SOURCE: The Pew Research Center (1997–98), www. people-press.org/trusttab.htm (accessed 7/11/02).

their workers. Such rules only take force after a period of public comment. Reaction from the people or businesses that will be subject to the rules may cause an agency to modify the rules they first issue. The rules about ergonomic safety in the workplace, for example, were strongly contested by many businesses, which viewed them as too costly. Two months into his presidency, Bush signed a bill repealing the ergonomic regulations that had been scheduled to go into effect later in 2001. The rulemaking process is thus a highly political one. Once rules are approved, they are published in the *Federal Register* and have the force of law.

Administrative adjudication is very similar to what the judiciary ordinarily does: applying rules and precedents to specific cases in order to settle disputes. In administrative adjudication, the agency charges the person or business suspected of violating the law. The ruling in an adjudication dispute applies only to the specific case being considered. Many regulatory agencies use administrative adjudication to make decisions about specific products or practices. For example, in December 1999, the Consumer Product Safety Commission held hearings on the safety of bleachers, sparked by concern over the death of children after falls from bleachers. It will issue guidelines about bleacher construction designed to prevent falls. These guidelines have the force of law. Likewise, product recalls are often the result of adjudication.

A good case study of the role agencies can play is the story of how ordinary federal bureaucrats created the Internet. Yes, it's true: what became the Internet was developed largely by the U.S. Department of Defense, and defense considerations still shape the basic structure of the Internet. In 1957, immediately following the profound American embarrassment over the Soviet Union's launching of *Sputnik,* Congress authorized the establishment of the Advanced Research Projects Agency (ARPA) to develop, among other things, a means of maintaining communications in the event the existing telecommunications network (the telephone system) was disabled by a strategic attack. Since the telephone network was highly centralized and therefore could have been completely disabled by a single attack, ARPA developed a decentralized, highly redundant network. Redundancy in this case improved the probability of functioning after an attack. The full design, called by the pet name of ARPANET, took almost a decade to create. By 1971, around twenty universities were connected to the ARPANET. The forerunner to the Internet was born.[5]

Government bureaucrats do essentially the same things that bureaucrats in large private organizations do, and neither type deserves the disrespect embodied in the term "bureaucrat." But because of the authoritative, coercive nature of government, far more constraints are imposed on public bureaucrats than on private bureaucrats, even when their jobs are the same. During the 1970s and 1980s, the length of time required to develop an administrative rule from a proposal to actual publication in the *Federal Register* (when it takes on full legal status) grew from an average of 15 months to an average of 35 to 40 months. Inefficiency? No. Most of the increased time is attributable to new procedures requiring more public notice, more public hearings, more hearings held out in the field rather than in Washington, more cost-benefit analysis, and stronger legal obligations to prepare "environmental impact statements" demonstrating that the proposed rule or agency action will not have an unacceptably large negative impact on the human or physical environment.[6] Thus, a great deal of what is popularly paraded as the lower efficiency of public agencies can be attributed to the political, judicial, legal, and public-opinion restraints and extraordinarily high expectations imposed on public bureaucrats.

We will have more to say at the end of this chapter about bureaucratic accountability and the potential role of citizens in it. Suffice it to say here that if a private company such as Microsoft were required to open up all its decision processes and management practices to full view by the media, their competitors, and all interested citizens, Microsoft—despite its profit motive and the pressure of competition—would appear far less efficient, perhaps no more efficient than public bureaucracies.

The Merit System: How to Become a Bureaucrat   In return for all these inconveniences, public bureaucrats are rewarded in part with greater job security than employees of most private organizations enjoy. More than a century ago, the federal government attempted to imitate business by passing the Civil Service Act of 1883, which was followed by almost universal adoption of equivalent laws in state and local governments. These laws required that appointees to public office be qualified for the job to which they are appointed. This policy came to be called the **merit system;** its ideal was not merely to put an end to political appointments under the "spoils system" but also to require adequate preparation for every job by holding competitive examinations through which the very best candidates were to be hired. At the higher levels of government agencies, including such posts as cabinet secretaries and assistant secretaries, many jobs are filled with political appointees not part of the merit system.

As a further safeguard against political interference (and to compensate for the lower-than-average pay given to public employees), merit system employees—genuine civil servants—were given a form of tenure: legal protection against being fired without a show of cause. Reasonable people may disagree about the value of job tenure and how far it should extend in the civil service, but the justifiable objective of tenure—cleansing bureaucracy of political interference while upgrading performance—cannot be disputed.

merit system a product of civil service reform, in which appointees to positions in public bureaucracies must objectively be deemed qualified for the position

The Organization of the Executive Branch

Cabinet departments, agencies, and bureaus are the operating parts of the bureaucratic whole. Figure 14.3 on page 556 is an organizational chart of one of the largest and most important of the fourteen **departments,** the Department of Agriculture. At the top is the head of the department, who in the United States is called the "secretary" of the department.[7] Below the secretary and the deputy secretary is a second tier of "undersecretaries" who have management responsibilities for one or more operating agencies, shown in the smaller print directly below each undersecretary. Those operating agencies are the third tier of the department, yet they are the highest level of responsibility for the actual programs around which the entire department is organized. This third tier is generally called the "bureau level." Each bureau-level agency is usually operating under a statute, adopted by Congress, that set up the agency and gave it its authority and jurisdiction. The names of these bureau-level agencies are often quite well known to the public—the Forest Service and the Agricultural Research Service, for example. These are the so-called line agencies, or

> **What are the agencies that make up the executive branch?**

department the largest subunit of the executive branch. The secretaries of the fourteen departments form the Cabinet

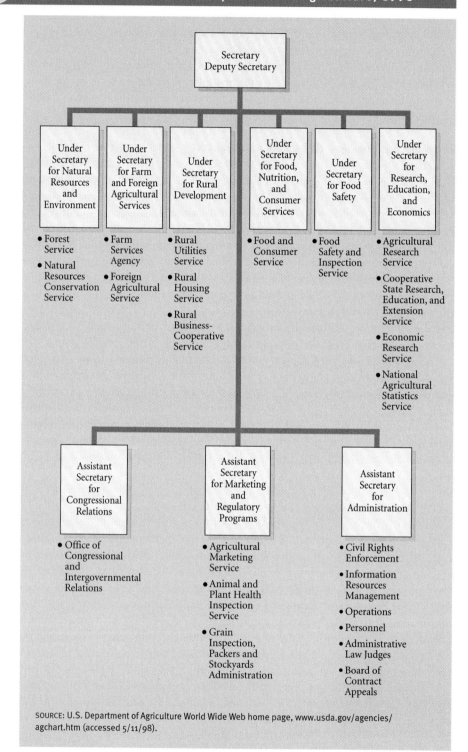

Figure 14.3 Organizational Chart of the Department of Agriculture, 1998

SOURCE: U.S. Department of Agriculture World Wide Web home page, www.usda.gov/agencies/agchart.htm (accessed 5/11/98).

agencies that deal directly with the public. Sometimes these agencies are officially called "bureaus," as in the Federal Bureau of Investigation (FBI), which is a part of the third tier of the Department of Justice. But "bureau" is also the conventional term for this level of administrative agency, even though many agencies or their supporters have preferred over the years to adopt a more palatable designation, such as "service" or "administration." Each bureau is, of course, subdivided into still other units, known as divisions, offices, or units—all are parts of the bureaucratic hierarchy.

Not all government agencies are part of Cabinet departments. Some **independent agencies** are set up by Congress outside the departmental structure altogether, even though the president appoints and directs the heads of these agencies. Independent agencies usually have broad powers to provide public services that are either too expensive or too important to be left to private initiatives. Some examples of independent agencies are the National Aeronautics and Space Administration (NASA), the Central Intelligence Agency (CIA), and the Environmental Protection Agency (EPA). **Government corporations** are a third type of government agency, but are more like private businesses performing and charging for a market service, such as delivering the mail (the United States Postal Service) or transporting railroad passengers (Amtrak).

Yet a fourth type of agency is the independent regulatory commission, given broad discretion to make rules. The first regulatory agencies established by Congress, beginning with the Interstate Commerce Commission in 1888, were set up as independent regulatory commissions because Congress recognized that regulatory agencies are "minilegislatures," whose rules are exactly the same as legislation but require the kind of expertise and full-time attention that is beyond the capacity of Congress. Until the 1960s, most of the regulatory agencies that were set up by Congress, such as the Federal Trade Commission (1914) and the Federal Communications Commission (1934), were independent regulatory commissions. But beginning in the late 1960s and the early 1970s, all new regulatory programs, with two or three exceptions (such as the Federal Election Commission), were placed within existing departments and made directly responsible to the president. Since the 1970s, no major new regulatory programs have been established, independent or otherwise.

The different agencies of the executive branch can be classified into three main groups by the services that they provide to the American public. The first category of agencies provide services and products that seek to promote the public welfare. The second group of agencies work to promote national security. The third group provides services that help to maintain a strong economy. Let us look more closely at what each set of agencies offers to the American public.

PROMOTING THE PUBLIC WELFARE

One of the most important activities of the federal bureaucracy is to promote the public welfare. Americans often think of government welfare as a single program that goes only to the very poor but a number of federal agencies provide services, build infrastructure, and enact regulations designed to enhance the well-being of the vast majority of citizens. Departments that have important responsibilities for promoting the public welfare in this sense include the Department of Housing and

independent agency an agency that is not part of a Cabinet department

government corporation a government agency that performs a service normally provided by the private sector

➤ How can one classify these agencies according to their missions?

Urban Development, the Department of Health and Human Services, the Department of Veterans Affairs, the Department of the Interior, the Department of Education, and the Department of Labor. Ensuring the public welfare is also the main activity of agencies in other departments, such as the Department of Agriculture's Food and Nutrition Service, which administers the federal school lunch program and food stamps. In addition, a variety of independent regulatory agencies enforce regulations that aim to safeguard the public health and welfare.

How Do Federal Bureaucracies Promote the Public Welfare? To get a sense of the diverse services, products, and regulations provided by public bureaucracies let us take a closer look at several of these agencies. The Department of Health and Human Services (HHS) administers the program that comes closest to the popular understanding of welfare—Temporary Assistance to Needy Families (TANF). Yet this program is one of the smallest activities of the department. HHS also oversees the National Institutes of Health, which is responsible for cutting-edge biomedical research. The National Institutes of Health (NIH) occupies a large campus-like setting with seventy-five buildings outside of Washington, D.C. In their own labs and in the grants they provide to outside researchers, the NIH's central aim is to advance knowledge about health and diseases. Five of the scientists working in NIH labs have been awarded Nobel prizes for their research. The NIH is one of the leaders in experimenting with gene therapy, which is expected to open new possibilities for curing diseases in the future. HHS is also responsible for the two major health programs provided by the federal government: Medicaid, which provides health care for low-income families and for many elderly and disabled people in nursing homes, and Medicare, which is the health insurance available to all elderly people in the United States. The Administration on Aging is another agency

The government promotes the public welfare in myriad ways. For instance, regulatory agencies have a strong presence in the lives of all Americans. One example of that presence is the subjection of the foods we eat to numerous restrictions from federal, state, and local agencies.

In emergencies, government bureaucracies are often the main source of organizational expertise to address urgent needs. For example, after September 11, the Federal Emergency Management Agency coordinated the cleanup of the sites of the terrorist attacks. Here, FEMA director Joe M. Allbaugh meets with Urban Search and Rescue teams at the Pentagon.

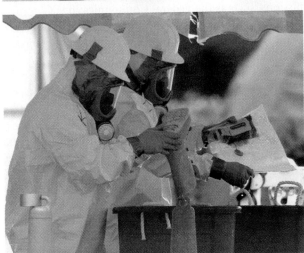

Likewise, the Centers for Disease Control and Prevention (CDC) was at the forefront of the investigation of the anthrax scare. Here, two federal workers clean up at the offices of American Media in Boca Raton, Florida, the first media company to receive an anthrax-laced letter.

The Environmental Protection Agency is another federal agency working toward the public welfare, for instance preventing the pollution of groundwater. Here, EPA project manager Bonnie Arthur stands before a plastic liner that catches acid runoff from an abandoned copper mine in Nevada.

under HHS; it provides services to the elderly such as "meals on wheels," which is designed to help keep the elderly independent. Also under HHS auspices is the Centers for Disease Control and Prevention (CDC), which is responsible for fighting bioterrorism. The CDC is charged with identifying the causes of outbreaks of sickness and assembling a national pharmaceutical stockpile to respond to major health emergencies.

A different notion of the public welfare, but one highly valued by most Americans, is provided by the National Park Service, which is under the Department of the Interior. First created in 1916, the National Park Service is responsible for the care and upkeep of national parks. The Park Service also preserves historic sites, including Civil War battlegrounds such as Gettysburg, where President Lincoln made his famous address. Over 280 million people visit national parks each year. The Department of the Interior also houses the U.S. Fish and Wildlife Service, which is one of the oldest public conservation agencies in the world. The Fish and Wildlife Service seeks to protect wildlife habitats and since 1973 has also been charged with administering the Endangered Species Act. Since the nineteenth century, Americans have seen protection of the natural environment as an important public goal and have looked to federal agencies to implement laws and administer programs that preserve natural areas and keep them open to the public.

regulatory agencies departments, bureaus, or independent agencies whose primary mission is to impose limits, restrictions, or other obligations on the conduct of individuals or companies in the private sector

The United States has no "Department of Regulation" but has many **regulatory agencies.** Some of these are bureaus within departments, such as the Food and Drug Administration (FDA) within the Department of Health and Human Services, the Occupational Safety and Health Administration (OSHA) in the Department of Labor, and the Animal and Plant Health Inspection Service in the Department of Agriculture. As we saw earlier, other regulatory agencies are independent regulatory commissions, such as the Federal Communications Commission (FCC) and the Environmental Protection Agency (EPA). But whether departmental or independent, an agency or commission is regulatory if Congress delegates to it relatively broad powers over a sector of the economy or a type of commercial activity and authorizes it to make rules restricting the conduct of people and businesses within that jurisdiction. Rules made by regulatory agencies have the force and effect of law.

The activities of these agencies seek to promote the welfare of all Americans, often working behind the scenes. The FDA, for example, works to protect public health by setting standards for food processing and inspecting plants to ensure that those standards are met. The EPA sets standards to limit polluting emissions from automobiles. The regulations required automobile manufacturers to change the way they designed cars and the result has been cleaner air in many metropolitan areas.

Bureaucracies, Clienteles, and the Public   Some of the public agencies that provide services that enhance well-being are tied to a specific group or segment of American society that is often thought of as the main clientele of that agency. For example, the Department of Agriculture was established in 1862 to promote the interests of farmers. The Departments of Commerce and Labor were founded in 1903 as a single department "to foster, promote and develop the foreign and domestic commerce, the mining, the manufacturing, the shipping, and fishing industries, and the transportation facilities of the United States."[8] They remained one department until 1913, when Congress separated them into two. Likewise, the Department of Veterans Affairs has strong links to veterans' organizations, such as the American Legion and the Veterans of Foreign Wars. The Department of Labor has a close relationship with organized labor. The Department of Education relies on teachers' organizations for support. Figure 14.4 is a representation of this type of politics. This configuration is known as an **iron triangle,** a pattern of stable relationships between an agency in the executive branch, a congressional committee or subcommittee, and one or more organized groups of agency clientele. (Iron triangles were discussed in detail in Chapter 11.)

These relationships with particular clienteles are often important in preserving agencies from political attack. During his 1980 campaign, Ronald Reagan promised to dismantle the Department of Education as part of his commitment to get government "off people's backs." After his election, President Reagan even

iron triangle the stable, cooperative relationships that often develop between a congressional committee, an administrative agency, and one or more supportive interest groups. Not all of these relationships are triangular, but the iron triangle is the most typical

Iron Triangles

Figure 14.4

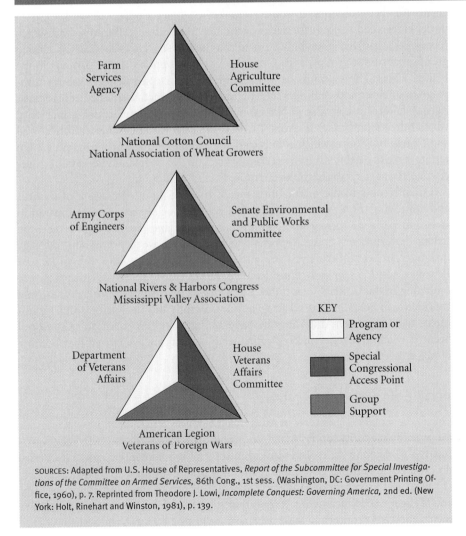

SOURCES: Adapted from U.S. House of Representatives, *Report of the Subcommittee for Special Investigations of the Committee on Armed Services*, 86th Cong., 1st sess. (Washington, DC: Government Printing Office, 1960), p. 7. Reprinted from Theodore J. Lowi, *Incomplete Conquest: Governing America*, 2nd ed. (New York: Holt, Rinehart and Winston, 1981), p. 139.

appointed a secretary of the department who was publicly committed to eliminating it. Yet, by the end of his administration, the Department of Education was still standing and barely touched. In 1995, the Republican Congress vowed to eliminate the Department of Education, along with two other departments, but it, too, failed. The educational constituency of the department mobilized to save it each time.

Such clientele groups generally have more influence over federal agencies than do people who are not part of the clientele group. But the ability of clientele groups to get their way is not automatic, as agencies have to balance limited resources, competing interests, and political pressures. For example, the Department of Veterans Affairs long resisted the efforts of Vietnam veterans to be compensated for exposure to Agent Orange, a chemical defoliant used extensively during the Vietnam War. Veterans charged that exposure to Agent Orange had left them with a variety of diseases ranging from cancer to severe birth defects in their children. Only after decades of lobbying, law suits, and federally-sponsored studies did the Department of Veterans Affairs provide assistance to affected veterans.

Moreover, federal agencies increasingly seek public support outside their direct clients for their activities. In some cases, key clientele groups will work to build more widespread support for agency activities. For example, the AFL-CIO, which represents organized labor, built a broad coalition of student organizations, church groups, consumer groups, and civil rights activists opposed to sweatshops in the United States. These groups helped to support the Department of Labor's campaign to uncover and eliminate such manufacturing practices in the United States. Agency failure to consider public opinion can result in embarrassing incidents, which bureaucrats prefer to avoid. In 1981, the Department of Agriculture's Food and Nutrition Service, which administers the federal school lunch program, had to retract its cost-cutting decision to classify ketchup as a vegetable after a public outcry that the agency was harming children.

Attentiveness to the public often means making the public aware of services and improving the way services are delivered. The Social Security Administration is an independent agency that administers old-age and disability insurance, the federal government's most important and expensive welfare program. Old-age insurance, or Social Security, is supported by the American Association of Retired Persons (AARP), generally considered to be the most powerful interest group operating in the United States today. But, worried that younger workers are losing confidence in Social Security, the agency has recently begun to issue annual statements to each worker, outlining the benefits that they can count on from Social Security when they retire and indicating what benefits are available if they become disabled before retirement.

PROVIDING NATIONAL SECURITY

One of the remarkable features of American federalism is that the most vital agencies for providing security for the American people are located in state and local governments—namely the police. But some agencies vital to maintaining national security do exist in the national government, and they can be grouped into two categories: (1) agencies for control of conduct defined as a threat to internal national security and (2) agencies for defending American security from external threats. The departments of greatest concern in these two areas are Justice, Defense, and State.

Along with state and local police, the federal government provides for domestic security, a role that changed dramatically after the September 11 attacks. The first step was the creation of the Office of Homeland Security with Tom Ridge as its head. Ridge is shown here at the Homeland Coordination Center in Washington, D.C., where security officials work together to prevent another attack.

Agencies for Internal Security The task of maintaining domestic security changed dramatically after the terrorist attacks. President Bush created a new Office of Homeland Security, intended to ensure coordination among more than fifty federal agencies. The orientation of domestic agencies shifted as well, as agencies geared up to prevent terrorism, a task that differed greatly from their former charge of investigating crime. Along with this shift in responsibility, these agencies have acquired broad new powers—many of them controversial— including the power to detain terrorist suspects and to engage in extensive domestic intelligence-gathering about possible terrorists.

Prior to September 11, most of the effort put into maintaining national security took the form of legal work related to prosecuting federal crimes. The largest and most important unit of the Justice Department is the Criminal Division. Lawyers in the Criminal Division represent the United States government when it is the plaintiff enforcing the federal criminal laws, except for those cases (about 25 percent) specifically assigned to other divisions or agencies. Criminal litigation is handled by U.S. attorneys, who are appointed by the president. There is one U.S. attorney in each of the ninety-four federal judicial districts; he or she supervises the work of a number of assistant U.S. attorneys.

The Civil Division of the Justice Department deals with litigation in which the United States is the defendant being sued for injury and damages allegedly inflicted by a government official. The missions of the other divisions of the Justice Department—Antitrust, Civil Rights, Environment and Natural Resources, and Tax—are described by their names.

The federal government has also assumed a new role in airport security. Armed forces were a common sight at airports following September 11. With the passage of the Secure Aviation and Transportation Act, the federal government also became involved with screening passengers and baggage.

The federal government's response to the terrorist attacks also led to increased responsibilities for existing agencies. For instance, the Immigration and Naturalization Service's Border Control broadened its scope to include border security.

At least one aspect of the government's efforts to provide increased domestic security was controversial. The USA PATRIOT Act gave the attorney general the power to detain foreigners suspected of being potential security threats. The subsequent detention of more than one thousand suspects led to protests, such as the one pictured here, claiming that the detainees were being denied their due process rights.

When terrorism prevention took center stage, the Justice Department reoriented its activities accordingly. It was aided in its new mission by the USA PATRIOT Act, passed soon after September 11. The act gave the Justice Department broad new powers, allowing the attorney general to detain any foreigner suspected of posing a threat to internal security. The department launched a nationwide dragnet to detain potential suspects, using minor criminal charges or immigration violations as the legal rationale. It also initiated a voluntary program to question more than 5,000 young men from the Middle East about their views on terrorist activities and radical Islamic groups. Other new measures included the suspension of confidentiality of conversations between detainees and their attorneys. Although widely popular with most Americans, these measures created concern about civil liberties. The Justice Department initially released very little information about the detainees, and it did not respond to charges that those in custody had been mistreated or denied adequate representation. Attorney General John Ashcroft alarmed many civil libertarians when he charged at a Senate Judiciary Committee hearing that questions about civil liberties "only aid terrorists, for they erode our national unity and diminish our resolve."[9]

The best-known bureau of the Justice Department is the Federal Bureau of Investigation (FBI). The FBI handles no litigation but instead serves as the principal information-gathering agency for the department and for the president. Established in 1908, the FBI expanded and advanced in stature during the 1920s and 1930s under the direction of J. Edgar Hoover.

Despite its professionalism and its fierce pride in its autonomy, the FBI has not been unresponsive to the partisan commitments of Democratic and Republican administrations. Although the FBI has always achieved its best publicity from the spectacular apprehension of famous criminals, such as John Dillinger, George "Machine Gun" Kelly, and Bonnie and Clyde,[10] it has followed the president's direction in focusing on particular crime problems. Thus it has infiltrated Nazi and Mafia organizations; it operates the vast loyalty and security investigation programs covering all federal employees since the Truman presidency; it monitored and infiltrated the Ku Klux Klan and the civil rights movement in the 1950s and 1960s; and it infiltrated radical political groups, extreme religious cults, and survivalist militias in the 1980s and 1990s.

To fight the war on terrorism, the FBI undertook a variety of new roles. It greatly beefed up its counterintelligence and counterterrorism activities. FBI agents now work closely with military intelligence to build information systems about terrorism. The agency is also increasingly involved in international activities. The FBI's international role expanded when it investigated the embassy bombings in Kenya and Tanzania during the 1990s. FBI agents played a key role in interrogating suspects in Afghanistan. This new international role has made the agency more attentive to questions of diplomacy. Once simply a law enforcement agency, in recent years the FBI "has at times resembled a spy agency, diplomatic mission, and military adviser all in one."[11]

The Immigration and Naturalization Service (INS) is another Justice Department agency whose responsibility for domestic security has expanded. The INS's Border Control has occupied a pivotal position in the war on drugs, since it is the organization charged with preventing drugs from entering the country. One of the first acts of Congress after the terrorist attacks was to allocate increased spending for border security. The INS also began to take new action to apprehend foreign nationals who remain in the United States after their visas have expired. In the past, the INS did little to go after these "absconders," focusing instead on undocumented aliens involved in criminal activity.

Agencies for External National Security Two departments occupy center stage in maintaining external national security: the departments of State and Defense.

The State Department's primary mission is diplomacy. As the United States geared up to invade Afghanistan in 2001, Secretary of State Colin Powell took the lead in building an international coalition to support U.S. actions. Although diplomacy is the primary task of the State Department, diplomatic missions are only one of its organizational dimensions. As of 2002, the State Department comprised twenty-three bureau-level units, each under the direction of an assistant secretary. Six of these are geographic or regional bureaus concerned with all problems within a defined region of the world; thirteen are "functional" bureaus, handling such things as economic and business affairs, intelligence and research, and international organizations. Four are bureaus of internal affairs, which handle such areas as security, finance and management, and legal issues.

These bureaus support the responsibilities of the elite of foreign affairs, the foreign service officers (FSOs), who staff U.S. embassies around the world and who hold almost all of the most powerful positions in the department below the rank of ambassador.[12] The ambassadorial positions, especially the plum positions

With the recognition that, for the first time in American history, internal security was a matter of vital importance, the unfamiliar words "homeland security" entered the national vocabulary. The most important bureaucratic innovation after September 11 was the creation of the Office of Homeland Security. Less than two weeks after the terrorist attacks, President Bush issued an executive order to create the new agency and appointed Pennsylvania governor Tom Ridge to be its director. The Office of Homeland Security's mission was defined mainly as one of long-term planning: to "develop and coordinate the implementation of a comprehensive national strategy to secure the United States from terrorist attacks or threats."[1] Congress and the public expressed widespread support for the new agency.

Despite such broad support, gearing up for homeland defense presented a formidable bureaucratic challenge. The new office did not have cabinet status, which meant that it had no direct operational authority. Some members of Congress argued that to be effective the agency needed to be a cabinet office with its own budget and staff. Bush administration officials dismissed this idea as unrealistic. Creating such a cabinet position, they argued, would be a massive reworking. (See Figure 14.5.) What the Bush administration wanted instead was an office that would consider how domestic security could be strengthened, make proposals about where additional spending was needed, and work with existing agencies to better coordinate their activities.

In practice, this mission presented immense difficulties. Ridge's formal power within the federal bureaucracy was virtually zero. Ridge's responsibilities were far-reaching but his power was limited to "a license to persuade."[2] If other agencies resisted his initiatives, Ridge did not have any direct power to make them comply.

Such opposition emerged as soon as Ridge floated ideas for improving coordination across agencies. One of his central targets was border security. Ridge proposed consolidating the activities of the Customs Service, the Immigration and Naturalization Service, the Border Patrol, and the Coast Guard, which were split among three different federal departments, into a single department. Arguing for a single agency, Ridge declared, "We need to change our border strategy so there is only one face greeting people, instead of the way it is now where one agency looks in the trunk and another looks in the back seat."[3] But no matter how logical such consolidation might appear on paper, in fact, it means taking power and resources from existing agencies. As one administration official put it, "If we go ahead with a new border agency, it will mean ripping big organizations out of two or three Cabinet departments, and no Cabinet secretary I have ever seen wants to give up a part of his department."[4]

In June 2002, the Bush administration abruptly reversed its position and called for the creation of a new Department of Homeland Defense. Faced with growing evidence that bureaucratic bungling in the CIA and FBI may have allowed the September 11 attacks to occur, the White House responded with a bold measure. The proposed department aimed to improve the government's capacity to fight terrorism by combining twenty-two different agencies under a single umbrella, a much more far-reaching reorganization of the federal government than Ridge had earlier recommended.

The department would have four main divisions: Border and Transportation Security; Emergency Preparedness and Response; Chemical, Biological, Radiological, and Nuclear Countermeasures; and Information Analysis and Infrastructure Protection.[5] Each of these divisions would be created by moving agencies from their previous bureaucratic homes to the new department. For example, the Border and Transportation Division would include the Immigration and Naturalization Service, Customs, the Coast Guard, the Transportation Security Administration, and the Animal and Plant Health Inspection Service.

Creation of a new cabinet department requires congressional approval. Many in Congress praised the plan, not least because cabinet status ensured congressional oversight of the new department. Nevertheless, the administration girded itself for significant opposition.

[1] Alison Mitchell, "Disputes Erupt on Ridge's Needs for His Job," *New York Times,* November 4, 2001, p. B7.
[2] Eric Pianin and Bill Miller, "For Ridge, Ambition and Realities Clash," *Washington Post,* January 23, 2002, p. A1.
[3] Joel Brinkley and Philip Shenon, "Ridge Meeting Opposition from Agencies," *New York Times,* February 7, 2002, p. A12.
[4] Pianin and Miller, "For Ridge, Ambition and Realities Clash," p. A1.
[5] There is a color-coded organizational chart of the new agency (that contrasts with the earlier chart, Figure 14.5, explaining why they couldn't create such an agency) at www.whitehouse.gov/deptofhomeland/.

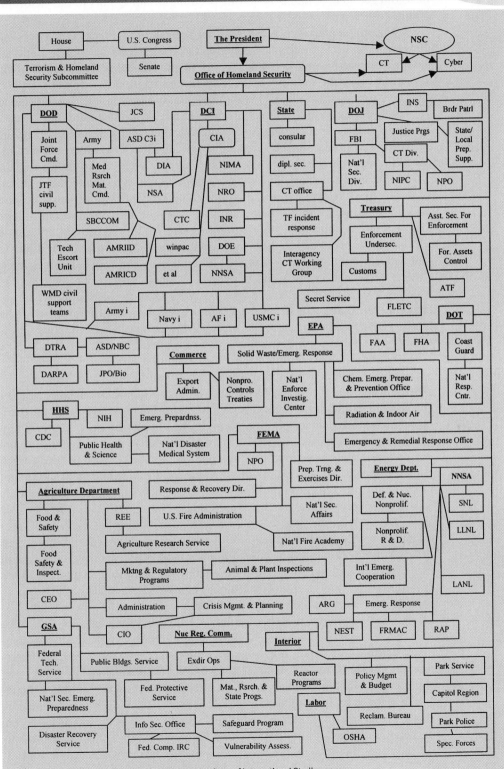

in the major capitals of the world, are filled by presidential appointees, many of whom get their positions by having been important donors to the victorious political campaign.

Despite the importance of the State Department in foreign affairs, fewer than 20 percent of all U.S. government employees working abroad are directly under its authority. By far the largest number of career government professionals working abroad are under the authority of the Defense Department.

The creation of the Department of Defense by legislation between 1947 and 1949 was an effort to unify the two historic military departments, the War Department and the Navy Department, and to integrate them with a new department, the Air Force. Real unification, however, did not occur. The Defense Department simply added more pluralism to an already pluralistic national security establishment.

The American military, following worldwide military tradition, is organized according to a "chain of command"—a tight hierarchy of clear responsibility and rank, made clearer by uniforms, special insignia, and detailed organizational charts and rules of order and etiquette. The "line agencies" in the Department of Defense are the military commands, distributed geographically by divisions and fleets to deal with current or potential enemies. The "staff agencies," such as logistics, intelligence, personnel, research and development, quartermaster, and engineering, exist to serve the "line agencies." At the top of the military chain of command are chiefs of staff (called chief of naval operations in the navy, and commandant in the marines). These chiefs of staff also constitute the membership of the Joint Chiefs of Staff—the center of military policy and management.

The Defense Department took the lead in mounting the war against the Taliban, overseeing all military operations. For the first time in our nation's history, the Defense Department also considered appointing a regional commander in chief charged with homeland defense. Creating this new position would clarify the chain of command for military operations inside the nation's borders. With military planes patrolling airspace over major cities and the National Guard defending airports, the demands of internal security drew the Defense Department deeply into domestic operations. The creation of a regional command within the United States would be an unprecedented move, breaching a long-standing line between domestic law enforcement and foreign military operations.

National Security and Democracy   Of all the agencies in the federal bureaucracy, those charged with providing national security most often come into tension with the norms and expectations of American democracy. Two issues in particular arise as these agencies work to ensure the national security: (1) the trade-offs between respecting the personal rights of individuals versus protecting the general public and (2) the need for secrecy in matters of national security versus the public's right to know what the government is doing. Standards about what is an acceptable trade-off in each area vary depending on whether the country is at war or peace. The nature of the threat facing national security also affects judgments about the appropriate trade-offs. Needless to say, Americans often disagree about such threats and therefore take different views about what activities the government should be able to pursue to defend our national security. At the outset of the war on terrorism, the nation was unusually united in its support for a wide range of government security measures that would have been highly controversial in any other circumstance.

Secrecy and Openness in the War on Terrorism

During the 1950s and 1960s, in the early decades of the cold war, the federal government argued that secrecy was essential to ensure national security. Information about a diverse range of government activities was routinely classified so that the public had no access to it. The 1973–74 Watergate scandal marked a sea change in this culture of secrecy. The Watergate hearings revealed that, under the mantle of national security, the government had initiated unlawful activities and engaged in unjustifiable invasions of individual privacy. As a consequence, new legislation opened the bureaucracy up to greater public scrutiny, and the 1974 Freedom of Information Act allowed individuals to request access to classified information. In the aftermath of the September 11 terrorist attacks, President Bush defended the need to reimpose greater secrecy in the interests of national security. His administration immediately took significant measures to limit public access to information about government activities. After September 11, the administration removed hundreds of thousands of public documents from the Internet. Some of these documents are available for consultation by special request in a government facility. Others are entirely off limits to the public. The administration also refused to reveal the identities of more than 1,100 people held in custody—but not charged—for suspected terrorism. And, in a move designed to weaken one of the most important tools promoting public disclosure, Attorney General John Ashcroft issued a directive to government agencies to use greater caution in responding to freedom of information requests.

Supporters of enhanced secrecy contend that standards of openness prevalent in peacetime must give way during a war. Although most of the war on terrorism is not visible to the public, the need for secrecy may be even greater than in other wars in which the United States has been involved. Terrorists rely on publicly available sources of information to plan their attacks. Apparently innocuous information about the location of facilities, such as nuclear power plants or water treatment facilities, provides terrorists with vulnerable targets. When such information is available on the Internet, the job of the terrorist

is even easier. Potential targets can be researched half a world away from the United States. Furthermore, counterterrorism is a delicate task. If the sources of information on which counterintelligence agencies rely become public, these sources may become unavailable in the future. For example, until 1998, the government tracked the activities of Osama bin Laden through calls he made on his satellite phone. When this knowledge became publicly available, bin Laden apparently stopped using the phone, making him much harder to track.

Critics contend that the administration has gone too far in its quest for secrecy. They agree that standards for government disclosure of information must be tightened to fight against terrorism but charge that the administration is taking advantage of the situation. The administration has claimed a right to secrecy on issues that have nothing to do with national security, as in its refusal to divulge the proceedings of its energy task force. Even in matters of national security, the administration has gone overboard, according to critics. Without access to information, Congress cannot exercise its oversight responsibilities, which are vital to democratic accountability. And, as in the past, secrecy that is officially justified by national security concerns may result in gross violations of the civil liberties of individuals who have nothing to do with terrorism. The secrecy surrounding those jailed as part of the terrorism probe distorts the American system of justice, since very few of these individuals were actually charged with a crime.

Finally, critics charge that secrecy will eventually erode public confidence in the government, thus undermining the war on terrorism. When information leaked that President Bush had been briefed in August 2001 about Al Qaeda's interest in hijacking American airplanes, the public began for the first time to question the administration's secrecy. In a public opinion poll, 68 percent of those questioned said that the administration should have revealed this information earlier. In the post-Watergate climate of Washington, it is much harder to keep secrets than it was in the cold war era. Nothing will hurt the war on terrorism more, critics charge, than a cynical public that does not believe its government.

Can the Government Withhold Information?

Yes

Americans already uneasy about the terrorist attacks on the United States should not have to worry about their government spreading misleading information.

Since September 11, rumors circulated about what was actually going on. If releasing information conflicts with maintaining national security, then don't release the information to the press. Don't spread misleading information at press conferences or through government leaks. That is irresponsible.

Explain to the press and the American public why information can't be released. No one wants to endanger American troops or the security of the nation. Media organizations will understand, even if they still ask the questions.

If the government does not act responsibly with its information, it will chip away at the public's trust at a time when it's needed most. It is unfair to lie to the public and the press.

During "Meet the Press" on September 16, Vice President Dick Cheney said he needed to be careful in answering questions about the military's actions. He said it would be inappropriate to talk about specific military operations. We agree.

But we are still left weary after conflicting reports that came forward regarding the plane that crashed in Pennsylvania. Initial reports came in that the plane crashed for unknown reasons. Then it was said to have been shot down by U.S. military forces. Now it appears that brave passengers on the plane struggled with the terrorists.

During televised press conferences before the attack on Afghanistan, U.S. Secretary of Defense Donald H. Rumsfeld didn't answer reporters' questions about where troops would be going or if they had already left. He was trying to protect the troops and the government's military strategy, and we agree with his actions. But maintaining the public's trust in the government's word is difficult to do after previous misleading information.

According to a *Washington Post* story published September 25, Pentagon officials lied about the deployment of a U.S. aircraft carrier to the Persian Gulf in 1988. This is unacceptable.

The government should not use the media to spin its tales to the American people. We want the truth, to the best of the government's ability, and we don't want to be used as pawns.

The First Amendment protects against a tyrannical government that uses the media for propaganda. We don't consider our government tyrannical, and we want to continue that tradition. We want to keep our First Amendment rights. And we agree with President George W. Bush, who was quoted about the present situation in the same *Washington Post* story, that his administration would not talk about how it gathers information and what it finds.

We understand the sensitivity of the issue. We understand that the safety of the country is in question. Yet the American citizens' questions need to be asked. They deserve to know if their sons and daughters will be called to fight—but not necessarily where they will fight.

It's a matter of balance, respect, and trust. Let the people of the United States know as much as they can without hurting the nation's security.

And above all, the government should not lie about information. Because it's the freedom of speech, the freedom of the press, and the freedom of the American people for which we're fighting this war.

SOURCE: Editorial Board, "Spinning Games," *Daily Nebraskan,* October 16, 2001.

No

Where is the line drawn between the people's right to know, and the government's duty to protect the people by keeping things from them? Thomas Jefferson argued there was no line: "Were it left for me to decide whether we should have a government without newspapers, or newspapers without a government, I should not hesitate a moment to prefer the latter." Proponents of the Intelligence Authorization Act of 2002 believe very strongly that there is a line, and they want to etch it in permanent marker to make sure no one crosses it.

The act would punish government whistle-blowers with possible jail time. So if someone leaked classified government information to journalists or to the public, he or she could go to jail. This almost happened to Daniel Ellsberg and Anthony Russo in 1971 when they gave the *New York Times* a little insight into what the United States had been doing in Southeast Asia from World War II to 1968. It was called the Pentagon Papers. The study told a story of Vietnam that the government didn't want people to know about. It revealed how the Johnson administration planned to wage war on North Vietnam a full year before telling the American public how deeply rooted the country's involvement was. The Pentagon Papers told how the government intelligence community warned that bombing North Vietnam would accomplish nothing, yet they went ahead and bombed anyway.

When the Pentagon Papers began to be published, the Justice Department asked the court to stop the *New York Times* and *Washington Post* from printing stories about the study, but they failed and the Supreme Court ruled in favor of the newspapers. All charges against Ellsberg and Russo were dropped.

Without the Pentagon Papers, the American people still wouldn't know what the United States was doing in Vietnam. It didn't hurt the country to let people know why their sons and brothers were fighting on the other side of the world. In fact, the secrecy divided the country more than when the people knew the real story. Unity and cohesiveness is what makes a country strong.

One of the biggest problems with the Intelligence Authorization Act provision is that it threatens offenders with a criminal law. The penalty is severe, which means the act could stifle speech that isn't even illegal—people won't expose government wrongdoing if they think they could go to jail for it, even if it's within legal bounds. Then we have a government free to run amuck, with no one to answer to. Is that what they want? If they aren't doing anything wrong, what is there to hide? Do they distrust the American people so much they can't tell them what they are doing? If the government is messed up and has problems, the last thing they should do is hide it.

There is information that could hurt the security of the nation, and that information should be kept safe. But there are already measures in place to not let that information leak out. Everything else should be left up to the people to decide what they should and shouldn't know. It's almost as if Thomas Jefferson were responding to this provision when he said, "Those who desire to give up freedom in order to gain security, will not have, nor do they deserve, either one."

SOURCE: Editorial, "Exchanging Freedom for Security," *Daily Illinois*, September 5, 2001.

When national security is at stake, federal agencies have taken actions that are normally considered incompatible with individual rights. For example, in World War II, thousands of American citizens of Japanese descent were interned for national security reasons. Although the Supreme Court declared this action justified, the federal government has since acknowledged that it constituted unjustified discrimination and has offered reparations to those who were interned. In the 1960s, FBI director J. Edgar Hoover authorized extensive wiretaps on civil rights leader Martin Luther King, Jr., which most people today regard as an illegal invasion of his personal privacy. With the advent of the war on terrorism, the government gained unprecedented powers to detain foreign suspects, carry out wiretaps and searches, conduct secret military tribunals, and build an integrated law enforcement and intelligence system. Congress hastily enacted many of these sweeping provisions of the USA PATRIOT Act several weeks after the terrorist attacks, with little debate. It was attentive enough to the negative impact on civil liberties, however, to stipulate that key features of the act would expire in 2005 unless it was deliberately renewed.

Protecting the national security often requires the government to conduct its activities in secret. Yet, as Americans have come to expect a more open government in the past three decades, many critics believe that federal agencies charged with national security keep too many secrets from the American public. In the words of one critic "the United States government must rest, in the words of the Declaration of Independence, on 'the consent of the governed.' And there can be no meaningful consent where those who are governed do not know to what they are consenting."[13] The effort to make information related to national security more available to the public began in 1966 with the passage of the Freedom of Information Act. Strengthened in 1974 after Watergate, the act allows any person to request classified information from any federal agency. It is estimated that the federal government spends $80 million a year responding to 600,000 requests for information.[14]

The information obtained from the Freedom of Information Act often reveals unflattering or unsuccessful aspects of national security activities. One private organization, the National Security Archive, makes extensive use of the Freedom of Information Act to obtain information about the activities of national security agencies. These include documents about a wide range of activities such as American involvement in the Cuban Bay of Pigs invasion in 1961 and human rights abuses in Latin America and the Caribbean in the past three decades. Such documents are often kept secret not because they threaten national security but rather because they are embarrassing or show that federal agencies violated accepted norms of human rights. The National Security Archive has published many of these documents on its Web site and maintains an archive in Washington, D.C., that is open to the public.

The tension between secrecy and democracy has sharpened dramatically with the war on terrorism. The Freedom of Information Act (FOIA) has been curtailed, and the range of information deemed sensitive has greatly expanded. President Bush defended the new secrecy, declaring, "We're an open society, but we're at war. Foreign terrorists and agents must never again be allowed to use our freedoms against us." While most Americans agreed that enhanced secrecy was needed to ensure domestic security, concerns about excessive secrecy mounted. Some analysts worried that secrecy would prevent Congress from carrying out its basic oversight responsibilities. As one critic of the Justice Department's dragnet of potential terrorists put it, "By considering these actions in secret before adopting them, the administration prevented any public debate about their effectiveness." Others charged that the Bush administration was reversing the trend toward a more open government on issues that had nothing to do with domestic security. Indeed, even as the war on terrorism was the central issue on the public's mind, the administration faced lawsuits from historians for blocking the release of routine documents from the Reagan administration. And in an unprecedented move, the Government Accounting Office, the investigative arm of Congress, sued the administration for failing to disclose information about Vice President Dick Cheney's task force on energy.

There are no easy answers to the questions about how the needs for national security should be reconciled with the values of a democratic society. It is clear, however, that in an era when national security is foremost in the public's mind, conflicts between democracy and secrecy are sure to increase.

MAINTAINING A STRONG ECONOMY

In our capitalist economic system, the government does not directly run the economy. Yet many federal government activities are critical to maintaining a strong economy. Foremost among these are the agencies that are responsible for fiscal and monetary policy. Other agencies, such as the Internal Revenue Service (IRS), transform private resources into use for public purposes. Tax policy may also strengthen the economy through decisions about whom to tax, how much, and when. Finally, the federal government, through such agencies as the Department of Transportation, the Commerce Department, and the Energy Department may directly provide services or goods that bolster the economy.

Fiscal and Monetary Agencies   The best term for government activity affecting or relating to money is **fiscal policy.** The *fisc* was the Roman imperial treasury; "fiscal" can refer to anything and everything having to do with public finance. However, we in the United States choose to make a further distinction, reserving "fiscal" for taxing and spending policies and using "monetary" for policies having to do with banks, credit, and currency. Yet a third term, "welfare," deserves to be treated as an equal member of this redistributive category.[15]

The administration of fiscal policy occurs primarily in the Treasury Department. In addition to collecting income, corporate, and other taxes, the Treasury is also responsible for managing the enormous national debt—$3.41 trillion in 2000. (The national debt was a mere $710 billion in 1980.)[16] Debt is not simply something the country owes; it is something a country has to manage and administer. The debt is also a fiscal instrument in the hands of the federal government that can be used—through manipulation of interest rates and through the buying and selling of government bonds—to slow down or to speed up the activity of the entire national economy, as well as to defend the value of the dollar in international trade.

The Treasury Department is also responsible for printing the U.S. currency, but currency represents only a tiny proportion of the entire money economy. Most of the trillions of dollars used in the transactions of the private and public sectors of the U.S. economy exist in computerized accounts, not in currency.

fiscal policy the use of taxing, monetary, and spending powers to manipulate the economy

Federal Reserve System a system
of twelve Federal Reserve Banks
that facilitates exchanges of cash,
checks, and credit; regulates member banks; and uses monetary policies to fight inflation and deflation

Another important fiscal agency (although for technical reasons it is called
an agency of monetary policy) is the **Federal Reserve System,** which is headed by
the Federal Reserve Board. The Federal Reserve System (called simply the Fed) has
authority over the interest rates and lending activities of the nation's most important banks. Congress established the Fed in 1913 as a clearinghouse responsible for
adjusting the supply of money and credit to the needs of commerce and industry
in different regions of the country. The Fed is also responsible for ensuring that
banks do not overextend themselves, a policy that guards against a chain of bank
failures during a sudden economic scare, such as occurred in 1929. The Federal
Reserve Board directs the operations of the twelve district Federal Reserve Banks,
which are essentially "bankers' banks," serving the monetary needs of the hundreds
of member banks in the national banking system.[17] The Fed has become one of
the most important actors in economic policy through its power to raise and lower
interest rates. Leading financial actors in the banking industry and in the stock
market anxiously anticipate quarterly meetings of the Federal Reserve Board, in
which decisions about interest rates are made.

Revenue Agencies   One of the first actions of Congress under President George
Washington was to create the Department of the Treasury, and probably its oldest
function is the collection of taxes on imports, called tariffs. Now housed in the
United States Customs Service, federal customs agents are located at every U.S. sea-
port and international airport to oversee the collection of tariffs. But far and away
the most important of the **revenue agencies** is the Internal Revenue Service (IRS).
The Customs Service and the IRS are two of at least twelve bureaus within the
Treasury Department.

revenue agencies agencies responsible for collecting taxes. Examples include the Internal
Revenue Service for income taxes,
the U.S. Customs Service for tariffs
and other taxes on imported
goods, and the Bureau of Alcohol,
Tobacco, and Firearms for collection of taxes on the sales of those
particular products

The IRS is not unresponsive to political influences, especially given the fact that
it must maintain cooperative relationships with the two oldest and most important
congressional committees, the House Ways and Means Committee and the Senate
Finance Committee. Nonetheless, as one expert put it, "probably no organization in
the country, public or private, creates as much clientele *dis*favor as the Internal Revenue Service. The very nature of its work brings it into an adversary relationship
with vast numbers of Americans every year."[18] Complaints against the IRS have cas-
caded during the past few years, particularly since 1996 presidential candidate Steve
Forbes staged his entire campaign on the need to abolish the IRS and the income tax
itself. But aside from the principle of the income tax, all the other complaints
against the IRS are against its needless complexity, its lack of sensitivity and responsiveness to individual taxpayers, and its overall lack of efficiency. As one of its critics
put it, "Imagine a company that's owed $216 billion plus interest, a company with a
22-percent error rate. A company that spent $4 billion to update a computer sys-
tem—with little success. It all describes the Internal Revenue Service."[19]

Such complaints led Congress to pass the IRS Restructuring and Reform Act of
1998, which instituted a number of new protections for taxpayers. The new laws
aim to make IRS agents more "customer-friendly" and limit the agency's ability to
collect money owed through liens on individual income or wages. Moreover, the
new law mandates the firing of IRS employees who harass taxpayers or violate their
rights. While many applaud the new law, there is also mounting concern that it has
made tax agents too timid and that revenue collection is declining as a consequence of the law.[20]

The politics of the IRS is most interesting, because, although thousands upon thousands of individual corporations and wealthy individuals have a strong and active interest in American tax policy, key taxation decisions are set by agreements between the president, the Treasury Department, and the leading members of the two tax committees in Congress. External influence is not spread throughout the fifty states, but instead is much more centralized in the majority political party, a few key figures in Congress, and a handful of professional lobbyists. Suspicions of unfair exemptions and favoritism are widespread, and they do exist, but these exemptions come largely from Congress, *not* from the IRS itself.

Economic Development Agencies Federal agencies also conduct programs designed to strengthen particular segments of the economy or to provide specific services aimed to strengthen the entire economy. Created in 1889, the Department of Agriculture is the fourth oldest cabinet department. Its initial mission, to strengthen American agriculture through research and assist farmers by providing information about effective farming practices, reflected the enormous importance of agriculture in the American economy. Through its Agricultural Extension Service, the Department of Agriculture established an important presence in rural areas throughout the country. It also built strong support for its activities among the nation's farmers and at the many land grant colleges, where agricultural research has been conducted for over one hundred years.

At first glance, the Department of Transportation, which oversees the nation's highway and air traffic systems, may seem to have little to do with economic development. But effective transportation is the backbone of a strong economy. The interstate highway system, for example, is widely acknowledged as a key factor in promoting economic growth in the decades after World War II. The Departments of Commerce and Energy also oversee programs designed to ensure a strong economy. The Small Business Administration in the Department of Commerce provides loans and technical assistance to small businesses across the country.

In recent decades dissatisfaction with government has led to calls to keep government out of the economy. Yet if the federal government were to disappear, chances are high that the economy would fall into chaos. There is widespread agreement that the federal government should set the basic rules for economic activity and intervene—through such measures as setting interest rates—to keep the economy strong. Some analysts argue that the government role should go beyond such rule setting to include more active measures such as investment in infrastructure. These advocates of government action point to the economic benefits of government investments in the interstate highway system and the government research in the 1960s that led to the creation of the Internet.

Can Bureaucracy Be Reinvented?

When citizens complain that government is too bureaucratic, what they often mean is that government bureaucracies seem inefficient and waste money. The poster child for such bureaucratic inefficiency in the late 1980s was the Department of Defense, which was revealed to have spent $640 apiece for toilet seats and $435 apiece for hammers.[21] Many citizens also had personal experience with the

> **Can government be made more responsive and efficient? Why or why not?**

federal government: a mountain of forms to fill out, lengthy waits, and unsympathetic service. Why can't government do better? many citizens asked. The application of new technologies and innovative management strategies in the private sector during the 1980s made government agencies look even more lumbering and inefficient by comparison. People were coming to expect faster service and more customer-friendly interactions in the private sector. But how can public sector bureaucracies change their ways when they are not subject to tests of efficiency and cost-effectiveness that often prompt innovation in the private sector?

In 1993, President Clinton launched the National Performance Review (NPR)—a part of his promise to "reinvent government"—to make the federal bureaucracy more efficient, accountable, and effective. Vice President Al Gore took charge of the new effort. The National Performance Review sought to prod federal agencies into adopting flexible, goal-driven practices. Clinton promised that the result would be a government that would "work better and cost less." Virtually all observers agreed that the NPR made substantial progress. Its original goal was to save more than $100 billion over five years, in large part by cutting the federal workforce by 12 percent (more than 270,000 jobs) by the end of 1999. Actually, by the end of 1999, $136 billion in savings were already assured through legislative or administrative action, and the federal workforce had been cut by 377,000.[22]

The NPR also focused on cutting red tape, streamlining procurement (how the government purchases goods and services), improving the coordination of federal management, and simplifying federal rules. For instance, the OMB abolished the notorious ten-thousand-page Federal Personnel Manual and the Standard Form 171, the government's lengthy job application form. Another example, even more revealing of the nature of the NPR's work, was the employee-designed reform of the Defense Department's method for reimbursing its employees' travel expenses: a process that used to take seventeen steps and two months was streamlined to a four-step, computer-based procedure taking less than fifteen minutes, with an anticipated savings of $1 billion over five years.

Another fact about administrative reform is that no reform movement will survive a change of president. Thus, although Republicans have an equal or better record than Democrats in the history of administrative reform, one of the first things that happened as President Bush took the oath of office in January 2001 was the termination of NPR. Nine months later, on September 11, Bush faced his own managerial crisis, when the need for coordinating the actions of the United States's many security agencies became apparent.

The new demands of domestic security have altered the thrust of bureaucratic reform. The emphasis on reducing the size of government that was so prominent during the previous two decades is gone. Instead, there is an acceptance that the federal government will grow as needed to ensure the safety of American citizens. The administration's effort to focus the entire federal bureaucracy on a single central mission will require unprecedented levels of coordination among federal agencies. Despite the strong agreement on the goal of fighting terrorism, the effort to streamline the bureaucracy around a single purpose is likely to face considerable obstacles along the way. Reform of public bureaucracies is always complex because strong constituencies may attempt to block changes that they believe will harm them. Initiatives that aim to improve coordination among agencies can easily provoke political disputes if the proposed changes threaten to alter the access of groups to the bureaucracy. And groups that oppose bureaucratic changes can appeal to Congress to intervene on their behalf. As respected reform advocate Donald Kettl said of the effort to reinvent government, "Virtually no reform that really matters can be achieved without at least implicit congressional support."[23] In wartime, many obstacles to bureaucratic reform are lifted. But the war on terrorism is an unusual war that will be fought over an extended period of time. Whether the unique features of this war improve or limit the prospects for bureaucratic reform remains to be seen.

Can the Bureaucracy Be Reduced?

Does bureaucracy serve the interests of all the American people? Or does it provide special benefits for influential interest groups, ignoring public needs? Or does bureaucracy mainly benefit government workers themselves, wasting public money by providing inefficient services? During the 1980s and 1990s, the reputation of the federal bureaucracy was at a low point. The belief that bureaucracy benefited entrenched interests and wasted taxpayer dollars was widespread. The negative image of the federal bureaucracy led to numerous efforts to reduce (or to use the popular contemporary word, "downsize") the bureaucracy. This downsizing could be achieved in at least three ways: termination, devolution, or privatization.

> **What methods have been used to reduce the size and the role of the federal bureaucracy?**

TERMINATION

The only *certain* way to reduce the size of the bureaucracy is to eliminate programs. Variations in the levels of federal personnel and expenditures (as was shown in Figures 14.1 and 14.2) demonstrate the futility of trying to make permanent cuts in existing agencies. Furthermore, most agencies have a supportive constituency that will fight to reinstate any cuts that are made. Termination is the only

In the last decade, there have been several attempts to "reinvent" government. In 1993, President Bill Clinton and Vice President Al Gore established the National Performance Review to reinvent government. Gore promoted this on David Letterman's show, where he railed against the government's procurement requirements, which even specified the number of pieces into which a government ashtray may shatter.

Gore and Clinton also succeeded in cutting back the number of rules promulgated by federal regulatory agencies and touted their success with a press conference on the south lawn of the White House, along with a forklift loaded up with the discarded regulations.

Other aspects of reinventing government have been harder to achieve, often because of the political pressures applied by those who will be affected by the change. For example, closing military bases has been difficult. Members of Congress used to try to overturn decisions to close bases in their districts. Because that is no longer possible, members of Congress such as Dianne Feinstein of California have sought to convert military bases for other government purposes. Critics say this isn't reducing bureaucracy, just shifting it around.

The latest case of reinventing government is the largest and most complex yet, the proposed creation of the Department of Homeland Security. Reorganizing the bureaucracy on this level will be a complicated procedure, as the organizational chart being held by Congresswoman Jane Harman attests.

way to ensure an agency's reduction and it is a rare occurrence, even in the Reagan administration and the first Bush administration, both of which proclaimed a strong commitment to the reduction of the national government. In fact, not a single national government agency or program was terminated during the twelve years of Reagan and Bush.

The Republican-led 104th Congress (1995–96) was even more committed to the termination of programs. Newt Gingrich, Speaker of the House, took Congress by storm with his promises of a virtual revolution in government. But when the dust had settled at the end of the first session of the first Gingrich-led Congress, no significant progress had been made toward downsizing through termination of agencies and programs.[24] The only two agencies eliminated were the Office of Technology Assessment, which provided research for Congress, and the Advisory Council on Intergovernmental Relations, which studied the relationship between the federal government and the state. Significantly, neither of these agencies had a strong constituency to defend it.

The overall lack of success in terminating bureaucracy is a reflection of Americans' love/hate relationship with the national government. As antagonistic as Americans may be toward bureaucracy in general, they benefit from the services being rendered and protections being offered by particular bureaucratic agencies; that is, they fiercely defend their favorite agencies while perceiving no inconsistency between that defense and their antagonistic attitude toward the bureaucracy in general. A good case in point is the agonizing problem of closing military bases in the wake of the cold war with the former Soviet Union, when the United States no longer needed so many bases. Since every base was in some congressional member's district, it proved impossible for Congress to decide to close any of them. Consequently, between 1988 and 1990, Congress established a Defense Base Closure and Realignment Commission to decide on base closings, taking the matter out of Congress's hands altogether.[25] And even so, the process was slow and agonizing.

Elected leaders have come to rely on a more incremental approach to downsizing the bureaucracy. Much has been done by budgetary means, reducing the budgets of all agencies across the board by small percentages, and cutting some less-supported agencies by larger amounts. Yet these changes are still incremental, leaving the existence of agencies unaddressed.

An additional approach has been taken to thwart the highly unpopular regulatory agencies, which are so small (relatively) that cutting their budgets contributes virtually nothing to reducing the deficit. This approach is called **deregulation,** simply defined as a reduction in the number of rules promulgated by regulatory agencies. President Reagan used this strategy successfully and was very proud of it. Presidents Bush, Clinton, and George W. Bush have proudly followed Reagan's lead.

deregulation a policy of reducing or eliminating regulatory restraints on the conduct of individuals or private institutions

DEVOLUTION

The next best approach to genuine reduction of the size of the bureaucracy is **devolution**—downsizing the federal bureaucracy by delegating the implementation of programs to state and local governments. Devolution often alters the pattern of who benefits most from government programs. In the early 1990s, a major devolution of transportation policy sought to open up decisions about transportation to a

devolution a policy to remove a program from one level of government by delegating it or passing it down to a lower level of government, such as from the national government to the state and local governments

new set of interests. Since the 1920s, transportation policy had been dominated by road-building interests in the federal and state governments. Many advocates for cities and many environmentalists believed that the emphasis on road building hurt cities and harmed the environment. The 1992 reform, initiated by environmentalists, put more power in the hands of metropolitan planning organizations and lifted many federal restrictions on how the money should be spent. Reformers hoped that these changes would open up the decision-making process so those advocating alternatives to road building, such as mass transit, bike paths, and walking, would have more influence over how federal transportation dollars were spent. Although the pace of change has been slow, devolution has indeed brought new voices into decisions about transportation spending, and alternatives to highways have received increasing attention.

Often the central aim of devolution is to provide more efficient and flexible government services. Yet, by its very nature, devolution entails variation across the states. In some states, government services may improve as a consequence of devolution. In other states, services may deteriorate as the states use devolution as an opportunity to cut spending and reduce services. This has been the pattern in the implementation of the welfare reform passed in 1996, the most significant devolution of federal government social programs in many decades. Some states, such as Wisconsin, have used the flexibility of the reform to design innovative programs that respond to clients' needs; other states, such as Idaho, have virtually dismantled their welfare programs. Because the legislation placed a five-year lifetime limit on receiving welfare, the states will take on an even greater role in the future as existing clients lose their eligibility for federal benefits. Welfare reform has been praised by many for reducing welfare rolls and responding to the public desire that welfare be a temporary program. At the same time, it has placed more low-income women and their children at risk for being left with no form of assistance at all, depending on the state in which they live.

This is the dilemma that devolution poses. To a point, variation can be considered one of the virtues of federalism. But there are dangers inherent in large variations in the provisions of services and benefits in a democracy.

PRIVATIZATION

Privatization seems like a synonym for termination, but that is true only at the extreme. Most of what is called "privatization" is not termination at all but the provision of government goods and services by private contractors under direct government supervision. Except for top-secret strategic materials, virtually all of the production of military hardware, from boats to bullets, is done on a privatized basis by private contractors. Billions of dollars of research services are bought under contract by governments; these private contractors are universities as well as ordinary industrial corporations and private "think tanks." **Privatization** simply means that a formerly public activity is picked up under contract by a private company or companies. But such programs are still very much government programs; they are paid for by government and supervised by government. Privatization downsizes the government only in that the workers providing the service are no longer counted as part of the government bureaucracy.

privatization removing all or part of a program from the public sector to the private sector

The central aim of privatization is to reduce the cost of government. When private contractors can perform a task as well as government but for less money, taxpayers win. Often the losers in such situations are the workers. Government workers are generally unionized and therefore receive good pay and benefits. Private sector workers are less likely to be unionized and private firms often provide lower pay and fewer benefits. For this reason, public sector unions have been one of the strongest voices arguing against privatization. Other critics of privatization observe that private firms may not be more efficient or less costly than government. This is especially likely when there is little competition among private firms and when public bureaucracies are not granted a fair chance to bid in the contracting competition. When private firms have a monopoly on service provision, they may be less efficient than government and more expensive. This problem raises important questions about how private contractors can be held accountable. As one analyst of Pentagon spending put it, "The Pentagon is supposed to be representing the taxpayer and the public interest—its national security. So it's really important to have transparency, to be able to see these competitions and hold people accountable."[26] As security has become the nation's paramount concern, new worries about privatization have surfaced. Some Pentagon officials fear that too many tasks vital to national security may have already been contracted out and that national security might best be served by limiting privatization.

Can Bureaucracy Be Controlled?

The title of this chapter, "Bureaucracy in a Democracy," is intended to convey the sense that the two are contradictory.[27] Americans cannot live with bureaucracy, but they also cannot live without it. The task is neither to retreat from bureaucracy nor to attack it, but to take advantage of its strengths while making it more accountable to the demands of democratic politics and representative government. This task will be the focus of the remainder of this chapter.

> **How do the president and Congress manage and oversee the bureaucracy?**

Two hundred years, millions of employees, and trillions of dollars after the Founding, we must return to James Madison's observation, "You must first enable the government to control the governed; and in the next place oblige it to control itself."[28] Today the problem is the same, only now the process has a name: administrative accountability. Accountability implies that there is some higher authority by which the actions of the bureaucracy will be guided and judged. The highest authority in a democracy is *demos*—the people—and the guidance for bureaucratic action is the popular will. But that ideal of accountability must be translated into practical terms by the president and Congress.

THE PRESIDENT AS CHIEF EXECUTIVE

In 1937, President Franklin Roosevelt's Committee on Administrative Management gave official sanction to an idea that had been growing increasingly urgent: "The president needs help." The national government had grown rapidly during the preceding twenty-five years, but the structures and procedures necessary to manage the burgeoning executive branch had not yet been established. The response to the call for "help" for the president initially took the

Bureaucracy, Public Trust, and Corruption

Bureaucracies are to governments as wheels are to automobiles. To validate the purchase, the car must get you to where you want to go. So with government. To legitimize the expense and the restrictions that come with government and public authority, the public must see that the policies they value are effectively implemented and managed within their society. Executives, legislatures, and judges may fashion those policies in order to keep the concentration of power in check, but bureaucracies nevertheless serve as the agents of the government and deliver the product of policy day in and day out to government's principal client—the public. Essential to the success of bureaucracies is the public trust afforded civil servants.

Cultural traditions have shaped the bureaucracies of different countries. In the United States (as well as, for example, New Zealand), a weak central state tradition has led to what students of comparative bureaucracy call a *departmental* system of administration in national government. In such a system, candidates are recruited for special departmental duties, and these civil servants do not generally move between departments. This system stands in contrast with a *unified* system of bureaucracy. Candidates in this system are recruited into the "culture" of administration, not into a specific department or agency. Bureaucrats are often seen as "generalists" in unified systems.

Some countries exhibit far more of the "generalist" administrative culture than others. For instance, the tradition of deference to authority allied with a strong sense of pragmatism within the British culture acts to place a heavy preference for the amateur bureaucrat serving the more senior minister in the British cabinet. Key cabinet ministries, such as Treasury, Foreign, and Defense, are at the core of policy making and agenda setting within Britain. The ministries rely on bureaucrats for the expertise and energy to execute the various technical and administrative duties associated with the agencies. General skills, a broad but rich university education, and judgment honed by years of experience are generally valued over specialized expertise, thus allowing the senior civil servants—the *mandarins*—and their cabinet ministers to serve as the principal sources of authority and direction of policy.

In contrast, other unified systems of bureaucracy, such as those in France, Japan, and Germany, rely heavily on technical experts—trained in areas of administrative specialization and vetted through careful systems of technical and specialized exams—who assume positions where their specialized talents will heavily influence the implementation and eventual shaping of policy. The most elite group of civil servants in France are the *Corps*—those who have graduated from the elite national schools of administration. Nothing in Britain or the United States matches the special role of the *Corps* in fashioning and manipulating policy.

Arguably, the most dangerous threat to the legitimacy and effectiveness of the bureaucracy is not the quality of the recruited candidate or the particular organizational logic of bureaucracy. Rather, it is the *perception of trust* held by the public. There is ample evidence that the citizens of major democracies are not only distrustful of their bureaucracies, but they may well in fact perceive high degrees of corruption within the broader public sector overall.

Among public servants, bribe-taking and misuse of public funds (e.g., illegal receipt of campaign contributions) are the most common forms of corruption. Recent scandals in the United States, Britain, France, Germany, Italy, Japan, and Spain feed the perception of corruption in public service and undermine the claim of the integrity of civil servants. Indeed, corruption—to the extent it exists in the bureaucracy of a society—has three general consequences, each with high costs for society.

First, it weakens the public trust, thereby weakening the capacity of government to mobilize public support for reform and policy compliance. Second, it raises the costs of public service. Knowing you will have to pay more (in the form of bribes) for public contracts ratchets the costs of public services, which are passed on to the taxpayer. Third, public corruption serves to discourage foreign investment by both public and private actors. Recent policy recommendations from the Organization for Economic Cooperation and Development (OECD) and the World Bank draw attention to the perceptions and cost of public corruption in the democracies of the world.

SOURCES: Rod Hague, Martin Harrop, and Shaun Breslin, *Political Science: A Comparative Introduction,* 2nd ed. (New York: Worth, 1998); David Martin Roodman, "Government Corruption Widespread," in Lester Brown, Michael Renner, and Brian Halweil, *Vital Signs 1999: The Environmental Trends That Are Shaping Our Future,* (Washington, DC: Worldwatch Institute, 1999); and David Kaufman, "Corruption: The Facts," *Foreign Policy* 107, (Summer 1997), pp. 114–31.

form of three management policies: (1) All communications and decisions that related to executive policy decisions must pass through the White House; (2) In order to cope with such a flow, the White House must have adequate staffs of specialists in research, analysis, legislative and legal writing, and public affairs; and (3) The White House must have additional staff to follow through on presidential decisions—to ensure that those decisions are made, communicated to Congress, and carried out by the appropriate agency.

Making the Managerial Presidency   Establishing a management capacity for the presidency began in earnest with FDR, but it did not stop there.[29] The story of the modern presidency can be told largely as a series of responses to the plea for managerial help. Indeed, each expansion of the national government into new policies and programs in the twentieth century was accompanied by a parallel expansion of the president's management authority. This pattern began even before FDR's presidency, with the policy innovations of President Woodrow Wilson between 1913 and 1920. Congress responded to Wilson's policies with the 1921 Budget and Accounting Act, which turned over the prime legislative power of budgeting to the White House. Each successive president has continued this pattern, creating what we now know as the "managerial presidency."

Presidents John Kennedy and Lyndon Johnson were committed both to government expansion and to management expansion, in the spirit of their party's hero, FDR. President Nixon also strengthened and enlarged the managerial presidency, but for somewhat different reasons. He sought the strongest possible managerial hand because he had to assume that the overwhelming majority of federal employees had sympathies with the Democratic Party, which had controlled the White House and had sponsored governmental growth for twenty-eight of the previous thirty-six years.[30]

President Jimmy Carter was probably more preoccupied with administrative reform and reorganization than any other president in the twentieth century. His reorganization of the civil service will long be recognized as one of the most significant contributions of his presidency. The Civil Service Reform Act of 1978 was the first major revamping of the federal civil service since its creation in 1883. The 1978 act abolished the century-old Civil Service Commission (CSC) and replaced it with three agencies, each designed to handle one of the CSC's functions on the theory that the competing demands of these functions had given the CSC an "identity crisis." The Merit Systems Protection Board (MSPB) was created to defend competitive merit recruitment and promotion from political encroachment. A separate Federal Labor Relations Authority (FLRA) was set up to administer collective bargaining and individual personnel grievances. The third new agency, the Office of Personnel Management (OPM), was created to manage recruiting, testing, training, and the retirement system. The Senior Executive Service was also created at this time to recognize and foster "public management" as a profession and to facilitate the movement of top, "supergrade" career officials across agencies and departments.[31]

Carter also tried to impose a stringent budgetary process on all executive agencies. Called "zero-base budgeting," it was a method of budgeting from the bottom up, wherein each agency was required to rejustify its entire mission rather than merely its next year's increase. Zero-base budgeting did not succeed, but the effort was not lost on President Reagan. Although Reagan gave the impression of being a laid-back president, he actually centralized management to an unprecedented degree. From Carter's "bottom-up" approach, Reagan went to a "top-down" approach, whereby the initial budgetary decisions would be made in the White House and the agencies would be required to fit within those decisions. This process converted the Office of Management and Budget (OMB) into an agency of policy determination and presidential management.[32] President Bush took Reagan's centralization strategy even further in using the White House staff instead of cabinet secretaries for managing the executive branch.[33]

President Clinton was often criticized for the way he managed his administration. His easygoing approach to administration led critics to liken his management style to college "bull sessions" complete with pizza and "all-nighters." Yet, as we have seen, Clinton also inaugurated one of the most systematic efforts "to change the way government does business" in his National Performance Review. Heavily influenced by the theories of management consultants who prized decentralization, customer responsiveness, and employee initiative, Clinton sought to infuse these new practices into government.[34]

George W. Bush was the first president with a degree in business. His management strategy followed a standard business school dictum: select skilled subordinates and delegate responsibility to them. Bush followed this model closely in his appointment of highly experienced officials to cabinet positions and in his selection of Dick Cheney for vice president. Indeed, at the outset of his term, Bush often appeared overshadowed by these appointees (and the vice president in particular). Many observers had the impression that Bush did not lead his own administration. The president's performance during the war in Afghanistan and the war on terrorism dispelled many doubts about his executive capabilities.

Decades of reform have increased the managerial capacity of the presidency, but such reforms themselves do not ensure democratic accountability—presidents must put their managerial powers to use. Although Ronald Reagan was an enormously popular president, he was faulted for his disengaged management style. During his administration, the National Security Council staff was not prevented from running its own policies toward Iran and Nicaragua for at least two years (1985–86) after Congress had explicitly restricted activities toward Nicaragua and the president had forbidden negotiations with Iran. The Tower Commission, appointed to investigate the Iran-Contra affair, concluded that although there was nothing fundamentally wrong with the institutions involved in foreign-policy making—the Department of State, the Department of Defense, the White House, and Congress—there had been a "flawed process," "a failure of responsibility," and a thinness of the president's personal engagement in the issues. The Tower Commission found that "at no time did [President Reagan] insist upon accountability and performance review."[35]

Presidents may also use their managerial capacities to limit democratic accountability if they believe it is a hindrance to effective government. Even in the unusual circumstances of the war on terrorism, critics began to question whether the Bush administration was too quick to assert executive privilege and shield its actions from public scrutiny. In such circumstances, the separation of powers between the branches of government may be the best way to ensure democratic accountability.

CONGRESS AND RESPONSIBLE BUREAUCRACY

Congress is constitutionally essential to responsible bureaucracy because ultimately the key to bureaucratic responsibility is legislation. When a law is passed and its intent is clear, the accountability for implementation of that law is also clear. Then the president knows what to "faithfully execute," and the responsible agency understands what is expected of it. But when Congress enacts vague legislation, agencies must resort to their own interpretations. The president and the federal courts often step in to tell agencies what the legislation intended. And so do the most intensely interested groups. Yet when everybody, from president to courts to interest groups, gets involved in the actual interpretation of legislative intent, to whom and to what is the agency accountable? Even when the agency wants to behave responsibly, how shall accountability be accomplished?

Congress's answer is **oversight.** The more power Congress has delegated to the executive, the more it has sought to reinvolve itself in directing the interpretation of laws through committee and subcommittee oversight of each agency. The standing committee system in Congress is well suited for oversight, inasmuch as most of the congressional committees and subcommittees have jurisdictions roughly parallel to one or more departments and agencies, and members of Congress who sit on these committees can develop expertise equal to that of the bureaucrats. Appropriations committees as well as authorization committees have oversight powers—as do their respective subcommittees. In addition to these, the Government Reform and Oversight Committee in the House and the Governmental Affairs Committee in the Senate have oversight powers not limited by departmental jurisdiction.

The best indication of Congress's oversight efforts is the use of public hearings, before which bureaucrats and other witnesses are summoned to discuss and defend agency budgets and past decisions. The data drawn from systematic studies of congressional committee and subcommittee hearings and meetings show quite dramatically that Congress has tried through oversight to keep pace with the expansion of the executive branch. Between 1950 and 1980, for example, the annual number of committee and subcommittee meetings in the House of Representatives rose steadily from 3,210 to 7,022; in the Senate, the number of such meetings rose from 2,607 to 4,265 (in 1975–76). Beginning in 1980 in the House and 1978 in the Senate, the number of committee and subcommittee hearings and meetings slowly began to decline, reaching 4,222 in the House and 2,597 in the Senate by the mid-1980s. New questions about the ability of Congress to exercise oversight arose when the Republicans took over Congress in 1995. Reductions in committee staffing and an emphasis on using investigative oversight to uncover scandal meant much less time spent on programmatic oversight. Moreover, congressional Republicans complained that they could not get sufficient information about programs from the White House to conduct effective oversight. Congressional records show that in 1991–92, when Democrats controlled the House, they issued reports on fifty-five federal programs, while in 1997–98, the Republican Congress issued only fourteen.[36] On issues of major national importance multiple committees may initiate oversight hearings simultaneously. No less than a dozen congressional committees (along with the Justice Department and the Securities and Exchange Commission) launched investigations into the collapse of the giant energy company Enron. Enron's close ties to the Bush administration and its campaign contributions to

oversight the effort by Congress, through hearings, investigations, and other techniques, to exercise control over the activities of executive agencies

hundreds of politicians from both parties aroused intense public interest in the hearings, many of which were televised live. The investigations covered a broad range of issues including secret partnerships, public utility laws, 401(k) retirement plans, accounting practices, and Enron's political influence.

Although congressional oversight is potent because of Congress's power to make, and therefore to change, the law, often the most effective and influential lever over bureaucratic accountability is "the power of the purse"—the ability of the House and Senate committees and subcommittees on appropriations to look at agency performance through the microscope of the annual appropriations process (see Chapter 12). This annual process makes bureaucrats attentive to Congress because they know that Congress has a chance each year to reduce their funding.[37] A more recent evaluation of the budget and appropriations process by the NPR expressed one serious concern about oversight through appropriation: pressure to cut appropriations "has put a premium on preserving particular programs, projects, and activities from Executive Branch as well as congressional action."[38] This may be another explanation for why there may be some downsizing but almost no terminations of federal agencies.

Oversight can also be carried out by individual members of Congress. Such inquiries addressed to bureaucrats are considered standard congressional "case work" and can turn up significant questions of public responsibility even when the motivation is only to meet the demand of an individual constituent. Oversight also takes place through communications between congressional staff and agency staff. The number of congressional staff has been enlarged tremendously since the Legislative Reorganization Act of 1946, and the legislative staff, especially the staff of the committees, is just as professionalized and specialized as the staff of executive agencies. In addition, Congress has created for itself three large agencies whose obligations are to engage in constant research on problems taking place in or confronted by the executive branch. These are the General Accounting Office (GAO), the Congressional Research Service (CRS), and the Congressional Budget Office (CBO). Each of these agencies is designed to give Congress information independent of the information it can get directly from the executive branch through hearings and other communications.[39] Normally a low-visibility agency, the GAO stepped into the national spotlight in 2002 when it sued the Bush administration for the release of information about its energy-policy task force. It was the first time the GAO had ever sued an administration in its eighty-year history. Another source of information for oversight is direct from citizens through the Freedom of Information Act (FOIA), which we have seen gives ordinary citizens the right to access agency files and agency data to determine whether derogatory information exists in the file about the citizens themselves and to learn about what the agency is doing in general. Nevertheless, the information gained by citizens through FOIA can be effective only through the institutionalized channels of congressional committees and, on a few occasions, through public-interest litigation in the federal courts.

As the president and Congress seek to translate the ideal of democratic accountability into practice, they struggle to find the proper balance between administrative discretion and the public's right to know. An administration whose every move is subject to intense public scrutiny may be hamstrung in its efforts to carry out the public interest. On the other hand, a bureaucracy that is shielded from the public eye may wind up pursuing its own interests rather than those of the public. The last century has seen a double movement toward strengthening the managerial capacity of the presidency and making bureaucratic decision making more transparent. The purpose of these reforms has been to create an effective, responsive bureaucracy. But reforms alone cannot guarantee democratic accountability. Presidential and congressional vigilance in defense of the public interest is essential.

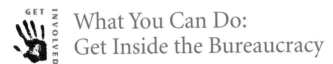

What You Can Do: Get Inside the Bureaucracy

Whether it has to do with taxes and the IRS, or passports and the State Department, or the motor vehicles agency or absentee voting or traffic cops at the state and local levels, citizens have more tools available to them than they may think. Public access to the workings of bureaucracies has been vastly facilitated in the past thirty years, in large part due to FOIA, which was enacted in 1966. Under FOIA, ordinary citizens can request documents from any government agency; even CIA and FBI files are available under certain conditions. It takes a lot of time and effort to get such files, but it can be done. The news media can (and do) also use FOIA, which is why newspapers and their reporters have so much more access to public bureaucracies than they ever had before. The public in general and interested citizens in particular gain from this access. Moreover, although general newspapers have limited space and resources for reporting on all agencies, specialized newspapers are actively involved in investigating and reporting on agency activities. This textbook regularly cites the *Congressional Quarterly,* which reports on the activities of the legislative branch but which often has information on agencies in the executive branch, as well. The *National Journal* also reports extensively on government agencies. Innumerable trade magazines, whose subscribers are largely the companies and individuals whose livings are earned in a particular trade or sector of the economy, perform superbly as critics and exposers of the agencies and decisions within their area of concern.

The activities of important "think tanks" (independently financed policy-research organizations in Washington, D.C., and elsewhere around the country) revolve around the formation and implementation of public policy. The Brookings Institution, for example, has been studying government policies and agencies for more than six decades, and, although considered more favorably disposed toward Democratic administrations, it is widely respected in all quarters. The same might be said of the best-known conservative-leaning think thank, the American Enterprise Institute, which has been a particularly important source of analysis and criticism of policies and agencies for the past twenty years.

Many of these information sources are already on the Internet. The same is true for a wide variety of government-provided publications of information on agencies and policies. Such access to information can help make bureaucracies more responsive to citizens' demands. In the first place, bureaucrats who know that their actions will be open to public scrutiny are more likely to take public wishes into account in their daily work. Second, when questionable bureaucratic practices are uncovered, citizens, through their congressional representatives, can work to change the laws and procedures that bureaucracies follow. The 1998 reform of the IRS, which, among other things, shifted the burden of proof from citizens to the government when there is a dispute, provides an example of this process. Finally, citizen dissatisfaction with bureaucracy can push politicians to institute reforms. When Clinton came to office, he wanted to take a more active governing approach than his Republican predecessors but realized that public distrust of government stood in the way. His effort to reinvent government, making bureaucracies more "customer-friendly," was a direct response to widespread public dissatisfaction.

The bad news is that, although citizen influence on bureaucracy is definitely possible, it can be expensive—in time and money. This gives it an upper-middle-class bias. The poor and uneducated lack virtually all the resources necessary to use the channels and opportunities available. But this class bias exists in all endeavors and walks of life; it is not particularly worse in the realm of bureaucracy. In fact, in many respects, now that political parties play less of a role in running the government, interaction with federal, state, and local agencies may be less daunting and discouraging than trying to influence legislatures.

Summary

Bureaucracy is a universal form of organization, found in businesses, churches, foundations, and universities, as well as in the public sphere. All essential government services and regulations are carried out by bureaucracies—specifically, by administrative agencies. Bureaucrats are appointed to their offices based on the "merit system."

The agencies of the executive branch can be grouped according to the services that they provide: (1) promoting the public welfare, (2) promoting national security, and (3) maintaining a strong economy. All of these agencies are alike in that they are all bureaucratic. These agencies differ in the way they are organized, in the way they participate in the political process, and in their levels of responsiveness to political authority. In recent years, attempts have been made to "downsize" the bureaucracy by termination, devolution, and privatization. Although these efforts are popular with the American people, they cannot reduce the size of the bureaucracy by much.

The executive and the legislative branches do the toughest job any government is called on to do: making the bureaucracy accountable to the people. Democratizing bureaucracy is the unending task of politics in a democracy.

For Further Reading

Arnold, Peri E. *Making the Managerial Presidency: Comprehensive Organization Planning.* Princeton: Princeton University Press, 1986.

Fesler, James W., and Donald F. Kettl. *The Politics of the Administrative Process.* Chatham, NJ: Chatham House, 1991.

Skowronek, Stephen. *Building a New American State: The Expansion of National Administrative Capacities, 1877–1920.* New York: Cambridge University Press, 1982.

Wildavsky, Aaron. *The New Politics of the Budget Process.* 2nd ed. New York: HarperCollins, 1992.

Wilson, James Q. *Bureaucracy: What Government Agencies Do and Why They Do It.* New York: Basic Books, 1989.

Wood, Dan B. *Bureaucratic Dynamics: The Role of Bureaucracy in a Democracy.* Boulder, CO: Westview, 1994.

Study Outline

www.wwnorton.com/wtp4e

Bureaucracy and Bureaucrats

1. Bureaucracy is simply a form of organization. Specialization and repetition are essential to the efficiency of any organization.
2. Despite fears of bureaucratic growth, the federal service has grown little during the past twenty-five years. The national government is large, but the federal service has not been growing any faster than the economy or the society.
3. The primary task of bureaucracy is to implement the laws passed by Congress.
4. Because statutes and executive orders often provide only vague instructions, one important job of the bureaucrat is to interpret the intentions of Congress and the president prior to implementation of orders.
5. The lower efficiency of public agencies can be attributed to the added constraints put on them, as compared to those put on private agencies.
6. Through civil service reform, national and state governments have attempted to reduce political interference in public bureaucracies by granting certain public bureaucrats legal protection from being fired without a show of cause.

The Organization of the Executive Branch

1. Cabinet departments, agencies, and bureaus are the operating parts of the bureaucracy. Not all government agencies are part of Cabinet departments. Independent agencies, government corporations, and independent regulatory commissions also are part of the executive branch.
2. The different agencies of the executive branch can be classified into three main groups by the services that they provide to the American public. The first category of agencies provides services and products that seek to promote the public welfare. Some of these agencies are particularly tied to a specific group or segment of American society that is often thought of as the main clientele of that agency.

3. The second category of agencies work to promote national security from internal and external threat.
4. The third group of agencies provides services that help to maintain a strong economy. Foremost among these are the agencies that are responsible for fiscal and monetary policy. In addition, the federal government may directly provide services or goods that bolster the economy.

Can Bureaucracy Be Reinvented?

1. The National Performance Review was an effort to make the bureaucracy more efficient, accountable, and effective.
2. While government bureaucracies can be made more responsive and efficient, reform is not simply a matter of management techniques but also a political matter.

Can the Bureaucracy Be Reduced?

1. The bureaucracy can be reduced in three ways: termination, devolution, and privatization.

Can Bureaucracy Be Controlled?

1. Each expansion of the national government in the twentieth century was accompanied by a parallel expansion of presidential management authority, but the expansion of presidential power cannot guarantee responsible bureaucracy.
2. Although Congress attempts to control the bureaucracy through oversight, a more effective way to ensure accountability may be to clarify legislative intent.

Practice Quiz

www.wwnorton.com/wtp4e

1. Which of the following best describes the growth of the federal service in the past twenty-five years?
   a) rampant, exponential growth
   b) little growth at all
   c) decrease in the total number of federal employees
   d) vast, compared to the growth of the economy and the society

2. What task must bureaucrats perform if Congress charges them with enforcing a law through explicit directions?
   a) implementation
   b) interpretation
   c) lawmaking
   d) quasi-judicial decision making

3. Which of the following was *not* a component of the Civil Service Act of 1883?
   a) the merit system
   b) a type of tenure system
   c) a spoils system
   d) All of the above were associated with the Civil Service Act of 1883.

4. Which of the following is a way in which the bureaucracy might be reduced?
   a) devolution
   b) termination
   c) privatization
   d) all of the above

5. Which of the following is *not* an example of a clientele agency?
   a) Department of Justice
   b) Department of Commerce
   c) Department of Agriculture
   d) Department of Housing and Urban Development

6. The concept of oversight refers to the effort made by
   a) Congress to make executive agencies accountable for their actions.
   b) the president to make Congress accountable for its actions.
   c) the courts to make executive agencies responsible for their actions.
   d) the states to make the executive branch accountable for its actions.

7. Which president instituted the bureaucratic reform of the National Performance Review?
   a) Richard Nixon
   b) Lyndon Johnson
   c) Jimmy Carter
   d) Bill Clinton

8. Which of the following are *not* part of the executive branch?
   a) cabinet departments
   b) government corporations
   c) independent regulatory commissions
   d) All of the above are parts of the executive branch.

Critical Thinking Questions

www.wwnorton.com/wtp4e

1. Often the efficiency of public bureaucracies is judged in terms of the efficiency of private business and other organizations. In many instances, government has been expected to do things that businesses in the marketplace have chosen not to do or have found unprofitable. Might the tasks that government is asked to perform be more prone to inefficiency? Think about the ways in which business might be able to perform some tasks that government currently performs. Would business necessarily perform these tasks more efficiently? Should efficiency be the only priority in the public enterprise?

2. Describe the ways in which the public controls its bureaucracy. How much and what kind of control should the public exercise? Through elected officials—i.e., the president and the Congress—the public can achieve some control over the bureaucracy. What are the relative advantages and disadvantages of presidential and congressional control of the bureaucracy?

3. Many Americans do not believe that the federal bureaucracy serves the public interest. These dissatisfied citizens have supported a range of reforms, including termination of agencies, devolution of responsibility to lower levels of government, and privatization. Are such reforms likely to make the bureaucracy more responsive to public wishes? Who benefits and loses from these reforms?

Key Terms

www.wwnorton.com/wtp4e

administrative adjudication (p. 553)
bureaucracy (p. 550)
department (p. 555)

deregulation (p. 579)
devolution (p. 579)
Federal Reserve System (p. 574)
fiscal policy (p. 573)
government corporation (p. 557)
implementation (p. 553)
independent agency (p. 557)

iron triangle (p. 561)
merit system (p. 555)
oversight (p. 585)
privatization (p. 580)
regulatory agencies (p. 560)
revenue agencies (p. 574)
rulemaking (p. 553)

15 THE FEDERAL COURTS

★ **The Legal System**
Within what broad categories of law do cases arise?
How is the U.S. court system structured?

★ **Federal Jurisdiction**
What is the importance of the federal court system?
What factors play a role in the appointment of federal judges?

★ **The Power of the Supreme Court: Judicial Review**
What is the basis for the Supreme Court's power of judicial review?
How does the power of judicial review make the Supreme Court a lawmaking body?
How does a case reach the Supreme Court? What shapes the flow of cases through the Supreme Court? Once accepted, how does a case proceed?
What factors influence the judicial philosophy of the Supreme Court?

★ **Judicial Power and Politics**
How has the power of the federal courts been limited throughout much of American history?
How have the role and power of the federal courts been transformed over the last fifty years?

EORGE W. BUSH WON the 2000 national presidential election. The final battle in the race, however, was not decided in the electoral arena and did not involve the participation of ordinary Americans. Instead, the battle was fought in the courts, in the Florida state legislature, and in the executive institutions of the Florida state government, by small groups of attorneys and political activists. During the course of the dispute, some forty lawsuits were filed in the Florida circuit and supreme courts, the U.S. District Court, the U.S. Court of Appeals, and the U.S. Supreme Court.[1] Together, the two campaigns amassed nearly $10 million in legal fees during the month of litigation. In most of the courtroom battles, the Bush campaign prevailed. Despite two setbacks before the all-Democratic Florida supreme court, Bush attorneys won most of the circuit court cases and the ultimate clash before the U.S. Supreme Court in a narrow 5-4 vote. The next day, Al Gore made a speech conceding the election, and on December 18, 2000, 271 presidential electors—the constitutionally prescribed majority—cast their votes for George W. Bush.

The court battle over Florida's twenty-five electoral votes illustrates the political power that the courts now exercise. Over the past fifty years, the prominence of the courts has been heightened by the sharp increase in the number of major policy issues that have been fought and decided in the judicial realm. But since judges are not elected and accountable to the people, what does this shift in power mean for American democracy?

Every year nearly twenty-five million cases are tried in American courts and one American in every nine is directly involved in litigation. Cases can arise from disputes between citizens, from efforts by government agencies to punish wrongdoing, or from citizens' efforts to prove that a right provided them by law has been infringed upon as a result of government action—or inaction. Many critics of the U.S. legal system assert that Americans have become much too litigious (ready to use the courts for all purposes), and perhaps that is true. But the heavy use that Americans make of the courts is also an indication of the extent of conflict in American society. And given the existence of social conflict, it is far better that Americans seek to settle their differences through the courts rather than by fighting or feuding. ■

THE framers of the American Constitution called the Supreme Court the "least dangerous branch" of American government. Today, it is not unusual to hear friends *and* foes of the Court refer to it as the "imperial judiciary."[2] Before we can understand this transformation and its consequences, however, we must look in some detail at America's judicial process.

- **In this chapter, we will first examine the legal system, including the types of cases that the federal courts consider and the types of law with which they deal.**

- **Second, we will assess the organization and structure of the federal court system as well as the flow of cases through the courts.**

- **Third, we will consider judicial review and how it makes the Supreme Court a "lawmaking body."** We will also analyze the procedures of and influences on the Supreme Court.

- **Finally, we will consider the role and power of the federal courts in the American political process, looking in particular at the growth of judicial power in the United States.** We conclude by looking at how this changing role affects liberty and democracy.

The Legal System

Originally, a "court" was the place where a sovereign ruled—where the king and his entourage governed. Settling disputes between citizens was part of governing. According to the Bible, King Solomon had to settle the dispute between two women over which of them was the mother of the child both claimed. Judging is the settling of disputes, a function that was slowly separated from the king and the king's court and made into a separate institution of government. Courts have taken over from kings the power to settle controversies by hearing the facts on both sides and deciding which side possesses the greater merit. But since judges are not kings, they must have a basis for their authority. That basis in the United

States is the Constitution and the law. Courts decide cases by hearing the facts on both sides of a dispute and applying the relevant law or principle to the facts. This is all the more sensitive a matter because courts have been given the authority to settle disputes not only between citizens but between citizens and the government itself, where the courts are obliged to maintain the same neutrality and impartiality as they do between disputes involving two citizens. This is the essence of the "rule of law," that "the state" and its officials must be judged by the same laws as the citizenry. But since judges must apply the law as well as be subject to it, they must conduct themselves as closely as possible by the principle that they are not making personal judgments but are almost mechanistically applying the Constitution and the laws to the facts. There are obviously elements of myth as well as truth in this principle. But the American judicial system, from bottom to top, must have been doing something right because, compared to the other branches, it has been amazingly free of institutional crises during its history.

CASES AND THE LAW

Court cases in the United States proceed under three broad categories of law: criminal law, civil law, and public law.

Cases of **criminal law** are those in which the government charges an individual with violating a statute that has been enacted to protect the public health, safety, morals, or welfare. In criminal cases, the government is always the **plaintiff** (the party that brings charges) and alleges that a criminal violation has been committed by a named **defendant.** Most criminal cases arise in state and municipal courts and involve matters ranging from traffic offenses to robbery and murder. A large and growing body of federal criminal law, however, deals with matters ranging from tax evasion and mail fraud to the sale of narcotics and acts of terrorism. Defendants found guilty of criminal violations may be fined or sent to prison. Recently, a number of top corporate executives were charged with criminal violations of federal securities and accounting law. Federal criminal law is becoming an increasingly important factor in American life.

Cases of **civil law** involve disputes among individuals or between individuals and the government where no criminal violation is charged. Unlike criminal cases, the losers in civil cases cannot be fined or sent to prison, although they may be required to pay monetary damages for their actions. In a civil case, the one who brings a complaint is the plaintiff and the one against whom the complaint is brought is the defendant. The two most common types of civil cases involve contracts and torts. In a typical contract case, an individual or corporation charges that it has suffered because of another's violation of a specific agreement between the two. For example, the Smith Manufacturing Corporation may charge that Jones Distributors failed to honor an agreement to deliver raw materials at a specified time, causing Smith to lose business. Smith asks the court to order Jones to compensate it for the damage allegedly suffered. In a typical tort case, one individual charges that he or she has been injured by another's negligence or malfeasance. Medical malpractice suits are one example of tort cases.

In deciding civil cases, courts apply statutes (laws) and legal **precedent** (prior decisions). State and federal statutes, for example, often govern the conditions under which contracts are and are not legally binding. Jones Distributors might

> **Within what broad categories of law do cases arise?**

criminal law the branch of law that deals with disputes or actions involving criminal penalties (as opposed to civil law); it regulates the conduct of individuals, defines crimes, and provides punishment for criminal acts

plaintiff the individual or organization who brings a complaint in court

defendant the one against whom a complaint is brought in a criminal or civil case

civil law a system of jurisprudence, including private law and governmental actions, to settle disputes that do not involve criminal penalties

precedents prior cases whose principles are used by judges as the bases for their decisions in present cases

argue that it was not obliged to fulfill its contract with the Smith Corporation because actions by Smith, such as the failure to make promised payments, constituted fraud under state law. Attorneys for a physician being sued for malpractice, on the other hand, may search for prior instances in which courts ruled that actions similar to those of their client did not constitute negligence. Such precedents are applied under the doctrine of *stare decisis,* a Latin phrase meaning "let the decision stand."

A case becomes a matter of the third category, **public law,** when a plaintiff or defendant in a civil or criminal case seeks to show that their case involves the powers of government or rights of citizens as defined under the Constitution or by statute. One major form of public law is constitutional law, under which a court will examine the government's actions to see if they conform to the Constitution as it has been interpreted by the judiciary. Thus, what began as an ordinary criminal case may enter the realm of public law if a defendant claims that his or her constitutional rights were violated by the police. Another important arena of public law is administrative law, which involves disputes over the jurisdiction, procedures, or authority of administrative agencies. Under this type of law, civil litigation between an individual and the government may become a matter of public law if the individual asserts that the government is violating a statute or abusing its power under the Constitution. For example, landowners have asserted that federal and state restrictions on land use constitute violations of the Fifth Amendment's restrictions on the government's ability to confiscate private property. Recently, the Supreme Court has been very sympathetic to such claims, which effectively transform an ordinary civil dispute into a major issue of public law.

Most of the important Supreme Court cases we will examine in this chapter involve judgments concerning the constitutional or statutory basis of the actions of government agencies. As we shall see, it is in this arena of public law that the Supreme Court's decisions can have significant consequences for American politics and society.

TYPES OF COURTS

> **How is the U.S. court system structured?**

In the United States, systems of courts have been established both by the federal government and by the governments of the individual states. Both systems have several levels, as shown in Figure 15.1. More than 99 percent of all court cases in the United States are heard in state courts. The overwhelming majority of criminal cases, for example, involve violations of state laws prohibiting such actions as murder, robbery, fraud, theft, and assault. If such a case is brought to trial, it will be heard in a state **trial court,** in front of a judge and sometimes a jury, who will determine whether the defendant violated state law. If the defendant is convicted, he or she may appeal the conviction to a higher court, such as a state **appellate court,** and from there to a state's **supreme court.** Similarly, in civil cases, most litigation is brought in the courts established by the state in which the activity in question took place. For example, a patient bringing suit against a physician for malpractice would file the suit in the appropriate court in the state where the alleged malpractice occurred. The judge hearing the case would apply state law and state precedent to the matter at hand. (It should be noted that in both criminal and civil matters, most cases are settled before trial through negotiated agreements between the parties. In criminal cases these agreements are called **plea bargains.**)

stare decisis literally, "let the decision stand." The doctrine that a previous decision by a court applies as a precedent in similar cases until that decision is overruled

public law cases in private law, civil law, or criminal law in which one party to the dispute argues that a license is unfair, a law is inequitable or unconstitutional, or an agency has acted unfairly, violated a procedure, or gone beyond its jurisdiction

trial court the first court to hear a criminal or civil case

appellate court a court that hears the appeals of trial court decisions

supreme court the highest court in a particular state or in the United States. This court primarily serves an appellate function

plea bargains negotiated agreements in criminal cases in which a defendant agrees to plead guilty in return for the state's agreement to reduce the severity of the criminal charge the defendant is facing

The U.S. Court System

Figure 15.1

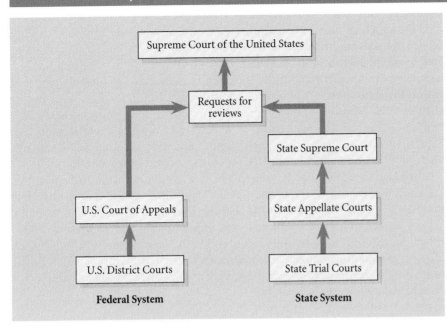

Federal System

State System

The state and federal court systems parallel each other until they reach the Supreme Court.

Although each state has its own set of laws, these laws have much in common from state to state. Murder and robbery, obviously, are illegal in all states, although the range of possible punishments for those crimes varies from state to state. Some states, for example, provide for capital punishment (the death penalty) for murder and other serious offenses; other states do not. However, some acts that are criminal offenses in one state may be legal in another state. Prostitution, for example, is legal in some Nevada counties, although it is outlawed in all other states. Considerable similarity among the states is also found in the realm of civil law. In the case of contract law, most states have adopted the **Uniform Commercial Code** in order to reduce interstate differences. In areas such as family law, however, which covers such matters as divorce and child custody arrangements, state laws vary greatly.

Cases are heard in the federal courts if they involve federal laws, treaties with other nations, or the U.S. Constitution; these areas are the official **jurisdiction** of the federal courts. In addition, any case in which the U.S. government is a party is heard in the federal courts. If, for example, an individual is charged with violating a federal criminal statute, such as evading the payment of income taxes, charges would be brought before a federal judge by a federal prosecutor. Civil cases involving the citizens of more than one state and in which more than $50,000 is at stake may be heard in either the federal or the state courts, usually depending on the preference of the plaintiff.

Federal courts serve another purpose in addition to trying cases within their jurisdiction: that of hearing appeals from state-level courts. Individuals found guilty of breaking a state criminal law, for example, can appeal their convictions to a federal court by raising a constitutional issue and asking a federal court to

Uniform Commercial Code code used in many states in the area of contract law to reduce interstate differences in judicial decisions

jurisdiction the sphere of a court's power and authority

due process of law the right of every citizen against arbitrary action by national or state governments

determine whether the state's actions were consistent with the requirements of the U.S. Constitution. An appellant might assert, for example, that the state court denied him or her the right to counsel, imposed excessive bail, or otherwise denied the appellant **due process.** Under such circumstances, an appellant can ask the federal court to overturn his or her conviction. Federal courts are not obligated to accept such appeals and will do so only if they feel that the issues raised have considerable merit and if the appellant has exhausted all possible remedies within the state courts. (This procedure is discussed in more detail later in this chapter.) The decisions of state supreme courts may also be appealed to the U.S. Supreme Court if the state court's decision has conflicted with prior U.S. Supreme Court rulings or has raised some important question of federal law. Such appeals are accepted by the U.S. Supreme Court at its discretion.

Although the federal courts hear only a small fraction of all the civil and criminal cases decided each year in the United States, their decisions are extremely important. It is in the federal courts that the Constitution and federal laws that govern all Americans are interpreted and their meaning and significance established. Moreover, it is in the federal courts that the powers and limitations of the increasingly powerful national government are tested. Finally, through their power to review the decisions of the state courts, it is ultimately the federal courts that dominate the American judicial system.

Federal Jurisdiction

Of all the cases heard in the United States in 2001, federal district courts (the lowest federal level) received 253,354. Although this number is up substantially from the 87,000 cases heard in 1961, it still constitutes about 1 percent of the judiciary's business. The federal courts of appeal listened to 56,823 cases in 2001, and the U.S. Supreme Court reviewed 7,852 in its 2000–2001 term. Only 86 cases were given full-dress Supreme Court review (the nine justices actually sitting *en banc*—in full court—and hearing the lawyers argue the case).[3]

THE LOWER FEDERAL COURTS

> **What is the importance of the federal court system?**

original jurisdiction the authority to initially consider a case. Distinguished from appellate jurisdiction, which is the authority to hear appeals from a lower court's decision

Most of the cases of original federal jurisdiction are handled by the federal district courts. Courts of **original jurisdiction** are the courts that are responsible for discovering the facts in a controversy and creating the record on which a judgment is based. Although the Constitution gives the Supreme Court original jurisdiction in several types of cases, such as those affecting ambassadors and those in which a state is one of the parties, most original jurisdiction goes to the lowest courts—the trial courts. (In courts that have appellate jurisdiction, judges receive cases after the factual record is established by the trial court. Ordinarily, new facts cannot be presented before appellate courts.)

There are eighty-nine district courts in the fifty states, plus one in the District of Columbia and one in Puerto Rico, and three territorial courts. These courts are staffed by 610 federal district judges. District judges are assigned to district courts according to the workload; the busiest of these courts may have as many as twenty-eight judges. Only one judge is assigned to each case, except where statutes provide for three-judge courts to deal with special issues. The routines and procedures of the federal district courts are essentially the same as those of the lower state courts, except that federal procedural requirements tend to be stricter. States, for example, do not have to provide a grand jury, a twelve-member trial jury, or a unanimous jury verdict. Federal courts must provide all these things.

THE APPELLATE COURTS

Roughly 10 percent of all lower court and federal agency cases are accepted for review by the federal appeals courts and by the Supreme Court in its capacity as an appellate court. The country is divided into twelve judicial circuits, each of which has a U.S. Court of Appeals. Every state, the District of Columbia, and each of the territories is assigned to the circuit in the continental United States that is closest to it.

Except for cases selected for review by the Supreme Court, decisions made by the appeals courts are final. Because of this finality, certain safeguards have been built into the system. The most important is the provision of more than one judge for every appeals case. Each court of appeals has from six to twenty-eight permanent judgeships, depending on the workload of the circuit. Although normally three judges hear appealed cases, in some instances a larger number of judges sit together *en banc*.

Another safeguard is provided by the assignment of a Supreme Court justice as the circuit justice for each of the twelve circuits. Since the creation of the appeals court in 1891, the circuit justice's primary duty has been to review appeals arising in the circuit in order to expedite Supreme Court action. The most frequent and best-known action of circuit justices is that of reviewing requests for stays of execution when the full Court is unable to do so—primarily during the summer, when the Court is in recess.

THE SUPREME COURT

The Supreme Court is America's highest court. Article III of the Constitution vests "the judicial power of the United States" in the Supreme Court, and this court is supreme in fact as well as form. The Supreme Court is made up of a chief justice and eight associate justices. The **chief justice** presides over the Court's public sessions and conferences. In the Court's actual deliberations and decisions, however, the chief justice has no more authority than his colleagues. Each justice casts one vote. To some extent, the influence of the chief justice is a function of his or her own leadership ability. Some chief justices, such as the late Earl Warren, have been able to lead the court in a new direction. In other instances, forceful associate justices, such as the late Felix Frankfurter, are the dominant figures on the Court.

The Constitution does not specify the number of justices that should sit on the Supreme Court; Congress has the authority to change the Court's size. In the early nineteenth century, there were six Supreme Court justices; later there were seven. Congress set the number of justices at nine in 1869, and the Court has remained that size ever since. In 1937, President Franklin D. Roosevelt, infuriated by several Supreme Court decisions that struck down New Deal programs, asked Congress to enlarge the Court so that he could add a few sympathetic justices to the bench.

chief justice justice on the Supreme Court who presides over the Court's public sessions

Although Congress balked at Roosevelt's "court packing" plan, the Court gave in to FDR's pressure and began to take a more favorable view of his policy initiatives. The president, in turn, dropped his efforts to enlarge the Court. The Court's surrender to FDR came to be known as "the switch in time that saved nine."

HOW JUDGES ARE APPOINTED

> **What factors play a role in the appointment of federal judges?**

Federal judges are appointed by the president and are generally selected from among the more prominent or politically active members of the legal profession. Many federal judges previously served as state court judges or state or local prosecutors. In an informal nominating process, candidates for vacancies on the U.S. District Court are generally suggested to the president by a U.S. senator from the president's own party who represents the state in which the vacancy has occurred. Senators often see such a nomination as a way to reward important allies and contributors in their states. If the state has no senator from the president's party, the governor or members of the state's House delegation may make suggestions.

Federal appeals court nominations follow much the same pattern. Since appeals court judges preside over jurisdictions that include several states, however, senators do not have as strong a role in proposing potential candidates. Instead, potential appeals court candidates are generally suggested to the president by the Justice Department or by important members of the administration. The senators from the nominee's own state are still consulted before the president will formally act.

In general, presidents endeavor to appoint judges who possess legal experience and good character and whose partisan and ideological views are similar to the president's own. During the presidencies of Ronald Reagan and George H. W. Bush, most federal judicial appointees were conservative Republicans. Bush established an advisory committee to screen judicial nominees in order to make certain that their legal and political philosophies were sufficiently conservative. Bill Clinton's appointees to the federal bench, on the other hand, tended to be liberal Democrats. Clinton also made a major effort to appoint women and African Americans to the federal courts. Nearly half of his nominees were drawn from these groups.

Once the president has formally nominated an individual, the nominee must be considered by the Senate Judiciary Committee and confirmed by a majority vote in the full Senate. Before the president makes a formal nomination, however, the senators from the candidate's own state must indicate that they support the nominee. This is an informal but seldom violated practice called **senatorial courtesy.** Because the Senate will rarely approve a nominee opposed by a senator from his or her own state, the president will usually not bother to present such a nomination to the Senate. Through this arrangement, senators are able to exercise veto power over appointments to the federal bench in their own states. In recent years, the Senate Judiciary Committee has also sought to signal the president when it has had qualms about a judicial nomination. After the Republicans won control of the Senate in 1994, for example, Judiciary Committee chair Orrin Hatch of Utah let President Clinton know that he considered two of Clinton's nominees to be too liberal. The president withdrew the nominations.

Eight of the first eleven nominations made during President George W. Bush's first two years in office were held in cold storage in the Judiciary Committee.

senatorial courtesy the practice whereby the president, before formally nominating a person for a federal judgeship, seeks the indication that senators from the candidate's own state support the nomination

As of 2002, the members of the Supreme Court are (from left to right) Antonin Scalia, Ruth Bader Ginsburg, John Paul Stevens, David Souter, Chief Justice William Rehnquist, Clarence Thomas, Sandra Day O'Connor, Stephen Breyer, and Anthony Kennedy.

While the Supreme Court presents itself to the public as a collegial body, its members are deeply divided along ideological and partisan lines. The current chief justice, William Rehnquist, was appointed to the Court by one Republican president, Richard Nixon, and elevated to chief justice by another Republican president, Ronald Reagan. This photo, from June 1986, shows Reagan announcing Rehnquist's promotion and Antonin Scalia's nomination to take Rehnquist's spot on the Court. At right is retiring chief justice Warren Burger.

Democratic senator Patrick Leahy, chairman of the Judiciary Committee, responded that those vacancies were there because of Republican intransigency against President Clinton's nominations. Even Bush's White House counsel Alberto Gonzales candidly confessed that "part of this is based on the conduct of Republican senators in the past," leaving "a lot of bitterness" among Democrats against the Republican-controlled Senate between 1994 and 2000.[4] The ultimate blow was the vote of the Senate Judiciary Committee, nine Republicans to ten Democrats, along absolutely strict party lines, to disapprove of President Bush's promotion of Mississippi federal district judge Charles W. Pickering, Sr., to the U.S. Court of Appeals, Fifth Circuit. The negative committee vote meant that the Senate would be spared a public debate and a vote, because it is accepted practice not to bring a judicial nomination up before the full Senate if the Judiciary Committee votes unfavorably. This is rare. The Congressional Research Service reports that the Committee's rejections of presidential judicial nominations have occurred only nine times since 1977. Moreover, Pickering had received the unconditional approval of the American Bar Association.

The partisan nature of the Court is also evident during confirmation hearings in the Senate. In testimony before the Senate Judiciary Committee in 1991, Anita Hill alleged that Supreme Court nominee Clarence Thomas had sexually harassed her (top). Hill's testimony brought nationwide attention to the nomination hearings. The Senate subsequently approved Thomas by the narrowest ratification margin in history, 52 to 48.

President George W. Bush, shown here in May 2001 with his first eleven candidates for federal judgeships (right), has also faced partisan opposition from the narrow Democratic majority in the Senate. While Bush has had eighty nominees approved to the federal bench, several prominent judges that he nominated were not approved.

If political factors play an important role in the selection of district and appellate court judges, they are decisive when it comes to Supreme Court appointments. Because the high court has so much influence over American law and politics, virtually all presidents have made an effort to select justices who share their own political philosophies. Presidents Ronald Reagan and George H. W. Bush, for example, appointed five justices whom they believed to have conservative perspectives: Justices Sandra Day O'Connor, Antonin Scalia, Anthony Kennedy, David Souter, and Clarence Thomas. Reagan also elevated William Rehnquist to the position of chief justice. Reagan and Bush sought appointees who believed in reducing government intervention in the economy and who supported the moral positions taken by the Republican Party in recent years, particularly opposition to abortion. However, not all the Reagan and Bush appointees have fulfilled their sponsors' expectations. Bush appointee David Souter, for example, has been attacked by conservatives as a turncoat for his decisions on school prayer and abortion rights. Nevertheless, through their appointments, Reagan and Bush were able to create a far more conservative Supreme Court. For his part, President Bill Clinton endeavored to appoint liberal justices. Clinton named Ruth Bader Ginsburg and Stephen Breyer to the Court, hoping to counteract the influence of the Reagan and Bush appointees. (Table 15.1 shows information about the current Supreme Court justices.)

In recent years, Supreme Court nominations have come to involve intense partisan struggle. Typically, after the president has named a nominee, interest groups opposed to the nomination have mobilized opposition in the media, the public, and the Senate. When President Bush proposed conservative judge Clarence Thomas for the Court, for example, liberal groups launched a campaign to discredit Thomas. After extensive research into his background, opponents of the nomination were able to produce evidence suggesting that Thomas had sexually harassed a former subordinate, Anita Hill. Thomas denied the charge. After contentious Senate Judiciary Committee hearings, highlighted by testimony from both Thomas and Hill, Thomas narrowly won confirmation.

Likewise, conservative interest groups carefully scrutinized Bill Clinton's liberal nominees, hoping to find information about them that would sabotage their appointments. During his two opportunities to name Supreme Court justices, Clinton was compelled to drop several potential appointees because of information unearthed by political opponents.

These struggles over judicial appointments indicate the growing intensity of partisan struggle in the United States today. They also indicate how much importance competing political forces attach to Supreme Court appointments. Because these contending forces see the outcome as critical, they are willing to engage in a fierce struggle when Supreme Court appointments are at stake.

Supreme Court Justices, 2002 (in Order of Seniority)

Table 15.1

Name	Year of Birth	Prior Experience	Appointed By	Year of Appointment
William H. Rehnquist* *Chief Justice*	1924	Assistant attorney general	Nixon	1972
John Paul Stevens	1920	Federal judge	Ford	1975
Sandra Day O'Connor	1930	State judge	Reagan	1981
Antonin Scalia	1936	Law professor, federal judge	Reagan	1986
Anthony Kennedy	1936	Federal judge	Reagan	1988
David Souter	1939	Federal judge	Bush	1990
Clarence Thomas	1948	Federal judge	Bush	1991
Ruth Bader Ginsburg	1933	Federal judge	Clinton	1993
Stephen Breyer	1938	Federal judge	Clinton	1994

*Appointed chief justice by Reagan in 1986.

The matter of judicial appointments became an important issue in the 2000 election. Democrats charged that, if he was elected, George W. Bush would appoint conservative judges who might, among other things, reverse the *Roe v. Wade* decision and curb abortion rights. Bush would say only that he would seek judges who would uphold the Constitution without reading their own political biases into the document.

From the liberal perspective, the danger of a conservative judiciary was underlined by the Supreme Court's decision in the Florida election case, *Bush v. Gore.* The court's conservative bloc, in recent years, has argued that the states deserve considerable deference from the federal courts. In this instance, however, the Supreme Court overturned a decision of the Florida supreme court regarding Florida election law. The Court ruled that its Florida counterpart had ignored the U.S. Constitution's equal protection doctrine when it mandated recounts in some, but not all, Florida counties. Defenders of the decision argued that it was doctrinally sound and that it averted the chaos that might have ensued if a recount gave Gore the victory and the Florida legislature carried out its threat to appoint Bush electors. Two competing slates of electors might then have sought congressional certification. Critics of the decision, however, asserted that the Court was merely searching for a rubric under which it could ensure Bush's victory. As a result of the Florida contest, there can be little doubt that the next Supreme Court vacancy will generate sharp fighting in Washington.

The Power of the Supreme Court: Judicial Review

judicial review the power of the courts to declare actions of the legislative and executive branches invalid or unconstitutional. The Supreme Court asserted this power in *Marbury v. Madison*

One of the most important powers of the Supreme Court is the power of **judicial review**—the authority and the obligation to review any lower court decision where a substantial issue of public law is involved. The disputes can be over the constitutionality of federal or state laws, over the propriety or constitutionality of the court procedures followed, or over whether public officers are exceeding their authority. The Supreme Court's power of judicial review has come to mean review not only of lower court decisions but also of state legislation and acts of Congress. For this reason, if for no other, the Supreme Court is more than a judicial agency—it is a major lawmaking body.

The Supreme Court's power of judicial review over lower court decisions has never been at issue. Nor has there been any serious quibble over the power of the federal courts to review administrative agencies in order to determine whether their actions and decisions are within the powers delegated to them by Congress. There has, however, been a great deal of controversy occasioned by the Supreme Court's efforts to review acts of Congress and the decisions of state courts and legislatures.

JUDICIAL REVIEW OF ACTS OF CONGRESS

> **What is the basis for the Supreme Court's power of judicial review?**

Since the Constitution does not give the Supreme Court the power of judicial review over congressional enactments, the Court's exercise of it is something of a usurpation. It is not known whether the framers of the Constitution opposed judicial review, but "if they intended to provide for it in the Constitution, they did so in a most obscure fashion."[5] Disputes over the intentions of the framers were settled in 1803 in the case of *Marbury v. Madison*.[6] Although Congress and the president have often been at odds with the Court, its legal power to review acts of Congress has not been seriously questioned since 1803. One reason is that judicial power has been accepted as natural, if not intended. Another reason is that the Supreme Court has rarely reviewed the constitutionality of acts of Congress, especially in the past fifty years. When such acts do come up for review, the Court makes a self-conscious effort to give them an interpretation that will make them constitutional. In some instances, however, the Court reaches the conclusion that a congressional enactment directly violates the Constitution. For example, in 1998, the Court invalidated a statute through which Congress had given the president the authority to reject specific projects contained in spending bills. The Court ruled that this "line-item veto" power violated the constitutionally mandated separation of powers.[7]

JUDICIAL REVIEW OF STATE ACTIONS

The power of the Supreme Court to review state legislation or other state action and to determine its constitutionality is neither granted by the Constitution nor inherent in the federal system. But the logic of the **supremacy clause** of Article VI of the Constitution, which declares it and laws made under its authority to be the supreme law of the land, is very strong. Furthermore, in the Judiciary Act of 1789, Congress conferred on the Supreme Court the power to reverse state constitutions and laws whenever they are clearly in conflict with the U.S. Constitution, federal laws, or treaties.[8] This power gives the Supreme Court appellate jurisdiction over all of the millions of cases handled by American courts each year.

The supremacy clause of the Constitution not only established the federal Constitution, statutes, and treaties as the "supreme Law of the Land," but also provided that "the Judges in every State shall be bound thereby, any Thing in the Constitution or Laws of the State to the Contrary notwithstanding." Under this authority, the Supreme Court has frequently overturned state constitutional provisions or statutes and state court decisions it deems to contravene rights or privileges guaranteed under the federal Constitution or federal statutes.

The civil rights area abounds with examples of state laws that were overturned because the statutes violated guarantees of due process and equal protection contained in the Fourteenth Amendment to the Constitution. For example, in the 1954 case of *Brown v. Board of Education,* the Court overturned statutes from Kansas, South Carolina, Virginia, and Delaware that either required or permitted segregated public schools, on the basis that such statutes denied black schoolchildren equal protection of the law. In 1967, in *Loving v. Virginia,* the Court invalidated a Virginia statute prohibiting interracial marriages.[9]

State statutes in other subject matter areas are equally subject to challenge. In *Griswold v. Connecticut,* the Court invalidated a Connecticut statute prohibiting the general distribution of contraceptives to married couples on the basis that the statute violated the couples' rights to marital privacy.[10] In *Brandenburg v. Ohio,* the Court overturned an Ohio statute forbidding any person from urging criminal acts as a means of inducing political reform or from joining any association that advocated such activities on the grounds that the statute punished "mere advocacy" and therefore violated the free speech provisions of the Constitution.[11]

supremacy clause Article VI of the Constitution, which states that laws passed by the national government and all treaties are the supreme law of the land and superior to all laws adopted by any state or any subdivision

American Democracy in Comparative Perspective

Judicial Review

If there is one fact of the American constitutional tradition that stands as original, it is the concept of *judicial review*. It directly influenced constitutional development in Latin and South America during the revolutionary nineteenth century and, indirectly, contributed to a recasting of philosophical interpretations of separate powers and parliamentary authority throughout continental Europe in the years following World War I. It has also served, ironically, as the model by which former British colonies (members of the British Commonwealth) constructed their constitutions during the second half of the twentieth century. Judicial review, like all major concepts undergirding the democratic process, is not uniformly applied or practiced across the democracies of the world today. Indeed, the American tradition of a strong judicial review is shared by only a few other democracies.

Two different types of judicial review systems can be distinguished among most democracies of the contemporary world. The first is the *diffused* system of judicial review. In this system, all levels of courts and judges may act as a constitutional judge. The various levels of the courts may have different degrees of jurisdiction and their scope may not be equally broad, but the concept of judicial review is such that all judges specified within the constitutional system may rule on the constitutionality of legislative acts. This underscores the preeminence of constitutional law: as all law basically derives from the written constitution, and as all judges are viewed as principal agents for adjudicating law, all judges (within the system as specified by the constitution, such as the federal court system of the United States) may judge the constitutionality of legislation. The key restriction, however, is that the legislation must be examined within a specific context and can only be initiated through a specified process. The complaints and actions of parties must be directly affected by the legislation in question, and the decision rendered by the judges must have some direct and concrete application to the incident prompting the action of the court. Finally, in these systems of judicial review, if a judge finds the legislative act unconstitutional, the law is null and void at that point.

The second variety of judicial review found among democracies is the *concentrated* form. While similar to the diffused system, there are two major differences. First, unlike the diffused system, the concentrated system restricts judicial review to only one supreme court or a single organ of the state charged explicitly with the task of reviewing the constitutionality of legislation. How the single organ—the supreme court, tribunal, or council—can actually hear the case, that is, what initiates the process, varies among the democracies that employ this type of judicial review. Yet lower courts are greatly restricted in their role with regard to judicial review. The second difference reflects a fundamental difference in logic between the diffuse and concentrated systems of judicial review. In the diffused system, there is no presumption of the constitutionality of a law simply because it has not been challenged and evaluated by a responsible court. On the other hand, in concentrated systems of judicial review, legislative law is in fact assumed to be constitutional until such time as the single supreme court has said otherwise.

The rules of governing judicial review and the degree of judicial activism within a democracy remain largely independent. Judicial activism varies greatly among democracies, and there is no clear pattern between the type of judicial review system and the degree of judicial activism shown toward legislation.

SOURCES: Arend Lijphart, *Patterns of Democracy: Government Forms and Performance in Thirty-Six Countries* (New Haven: Yale University Press, 1999); Allan R. Brewer-Carías, *Judicial Review in Comparative Law* (New York: Cambridge University Press, 1989).

JUDICIAL REVIEW AND LAWMAKING

When courts of original jurisdiction apply existing statutes or past cases directly to citizens, the effect is the same as legislation. Lawyers study judicial decisions in order to discover underlying principles, and they advise their clients accordingly. Often the process is nothing more than reasoning by analogy: the facts in a particular case are so close to those in one or more previous cases that the same decision should be handed down. Such judge-made law is called common law.

The appellate courts, however, are in another realm. Their rulings can be considered laws, but they are laws governing the behavior only of the judiciary. They influence citizens' conduct only because, in the words of Justice Oliver Wendell Holmes, who served on the Supreme Court from 1900 to 1932, lawyers make "prophecies of what the courts will do in fact."[12]

The written opinion of an appellate court is about halfway between common law and statutory law. It is judge-made and draws heavily on the precedents of previous cases. But it tries to articulate the rule of law controlling the case in question and future cases like it. In this respect, it is like a statute. But it differs from a statute in that a statute addresses itself to the future conduct of citizens, whereas a written opinion addresses itself mainly to the willingness or ability of courts in the future to take cases and render favorable opinions. Decisions by appellate courts affect citizens by giving them a cause of action or by taking it away from them. That is, they open or close access to the courts.

A specific case may help clarify the distinction. Before the Second World War, one of the most insidious forms of racial discrimination was the "restrictive covenant," a clause in a contract whereby the purchasers of a house agreed that if they later decided to sell it, they would sell only to a Caucasian. When a test case finally reached the Supreme Court in 1948, the Court ruled unanimously that citizens had a right to discriminate with restrictive covenants in their sales contracts but that the courts could not enforce these contracts. Its argument was that enforcement would constitute violation of the Fourteenth Amendment provision that no state shall "deny to any person within its jurisdiction equal protection under the law."[13] The Court was thereby predicting what it would and would not do in future cases of this sort. Most states have now enacted statutes that forbid homeowners to place such covenants in sales contracts.

The 1963 case *Gideon v. Wainwright* extends the point. When the Supreme Court ordered a new trial for Clarence Earl Gideon because he had been denied the right to legal counsel,[14] it said to all trial judges and prosecutors that henceforth they would be wasting their time if they cut corners in trials of indigent defendants. It also invited thousands of prisoners to appeal their convictions. (See Chapter 4 for a further discussion of this case.)

Many areas of civil law have been constructed in the same way—by judicial messages to other judges, some of which are codified eventually into legislative enactments. An example of great concern to employees and employers is that of liability for injuries sustained at work. Courts have sided with employees so often that it has become virtually useless for employers to fight injury cases. It has become "the law" that employers are liable for such injuries, without regard to negligence. But the law in this instance is simply a series of messages to lawyers that they should advise their corporate clients not to appeal injury decisions. In recent

> **How does the power of judicial review make the Supreme Court a lawmaking body?**

Miranda rule the requirement, articulated by the Supreme Court in *Miranda v. Arizona,* that persons under arrest must be informed prior to police interrogation of their rights to remain silent and to have the benefit of legal counsel

years, the Supreme Court has also been developing law in the realm of sexual harassment in the workplace. In one 1998 case, for example, the Court ruled that an employer can be held responsible if one of its employees is sexually harassed by a supervisor, even if the company was unaware of the supervisor's specific behavior.[15]

The appellate courts cannot decide what types of behavior will henceforth be a crime. They cannot directly prevent the police from forcing confessions from suspects or intimidating witnesses. In other words, they cannot directly change the behavior of citizens or eliminate abuses of government power. What they can do, however, is make it easier for mistreated persons to gain redress.

In redressing wrongs, the appellate courts—and even the Supreme Court itself—often call for a radical change in legal principle. Changes in race relations, for example, would probably have taken a great deal longer if the Supreme Court had not rendered the 1954 decision *Brown v. Board of Education* that redefined the rights of African Americans.

Similarly, the Supreme Court interpreted the doctrine of the separation of church and state so as to alter significantly the practice of religion in public institu-

In Marbury v. Madison *(1803), Chief Justice John Marshall established the Supreme Court's power to rule on the constitutionality of federal and state laws. This power makes the Court a lawmaking body.*

One important policy area in which the Court's decisions have the effect of law is abortion rights. For example, in 1989 the Supreme Court ruled on the constitutionality of a Missouri state law that put limitations on a woman's right to seek an abortion. Given the Court's lawmaking ability, prochoice groups such as the National Organization for Women and the National Abortion and Reproductive Rights Action League filed amicus curiae *briefs and gathered outside the Court in hopes of influencing public opinion.*

tions. For example, in a 1962 case, *Engel v. Vitale,* the Court declared that a once widely observed ritual—the recitation of a prayer by students in a public school—was unconstitutional under the establishment clause of the First Amendment. Almost all the dramatic changes in the treatment of criminals and of persons accused of crimes have been made by the appellate courts, especially the Supreme Court. The Supreme Court brought about a veritable revolution in the criminal process with three cases over less than five years: *Gideon v. Wainwright,* in 1963, was just discussed. *Escobedo v. Illinois,* in 1964, gave suspects the right to remain silent and the right to have counsel present during questioning. But the *Escobedo* decision left confusions that allowed differing decisions to be made by lower courts. In *Miranda v. Arizona,* in 1966, the Supreme Court cleared up these confusions by setting forth what is known as the **Miranda** rule: arrested people have the right to remain silent, the right to be informed that anything they say can be held against them, and the right to counsel before and during police interrogation (see Chapter 4).[16] In 2000, the Supreme Court considered overruling *Miranda* in *Dickerson v. United States,* but it decided that the wide acceptance of Miranda rights in the legal culture is "adequate reason not to overrule" it.

One of the most significant changes brought about by the Supreme Court was the revolution in legislative representation unleashed by the 1962 case of *Baker v. Carr.*[17] In this landmark case, the Supreme Court held that it could no longer avoid reviewing complaints about the apportionment of seats in state legislatures. Following that decision, the federal courts went on to force reapportionment of all state, county, and local legislatures in the country.

Another policy area in which the federal courts have assumed a dominant role has been busing. For example, federal judge W. Arthur Garrity (pictured here) ordered that Boston's schools be desegregated and created an elaborate plan for accomplishing this goal. When opponents of Garrity's plan were denied appeal by the Supreme Court, the plan effectively became law.

Due process of law is yet another area where federal courts have been critical in "making law" since the 1960s. In 2002, the issue of random drug testing of high school students who participate in extracurricular activities, a policy based on a Supreme Court decision upholding random testing of high school athletes, came before the Court. Lindsey Earls (second from right), a member of the Tecumseh, Oklahoma, high school choir and marching band, challenged the constitutionality of this policy; Sharon Smith, holding the sign, supported it. Earls's challenge was rejected, as the Court ruled that its earlier decision applied to this case as well.

> **How does a case reach the Supreme Court?**

HOW CASES REACH THE SUPREME COURT

Given the millions of disputes that arise every year, the job of the Supreme Court would be impossible if it were not able to control the flow of cases and its own caseload. The Supreme Court has original jurisdiction in a limited variety of cases defined by the Constitution. The original jurisdiction includes (1) cases between the United States and one of the fifty states, (2) cases between two or more states, (3) cases involving foreign ambassadors or other ministers, and (4) cases brought by one state against citizens of another state or against a foreign country. The most important of these cases are disputes between states over land, water, or old debts. Generally, the Supreme Court deals with these cases by appointing a "special master," usually a retired judge, to actually hear the case and present a report. The Supreme Court then allows the states involved in the dispute to present arguments for or against the master's opinion.[18]

Rules of Access   Over the years, the courts have developed specific rules that govern which cases within their jurisdiction they will and will not hear. In order to have access to the courts, cases must meet certain criteria. These rules of access can be broken down into three major categories: case or controversy, standing, and mootness.

Article III of the Constitution and Supreme Court decisions define judicial power as extending only to "cases and controversies." This means that the case before a court must be an actual controversy, not a hypothetical one, with two truly adversarial parties. The courts have interpreted this language to mean that they do not have the power to render advisory opinions to legislatures or agencies about the constitutionality of proposed laws or regulations. Furthermore, even after a law is enacted, the courts will generally refuse to consider its constitutionality until it is actually applied.

standing the right of an individual or organization to initiate a court case

Parties to a case must also have **standing,** that is, they must show that they have a substantial stake in the outcome of the case. The traditional requirement for standing has been to show injury to oneself; that injury can be personal, economic, or even aesthetic. In order for a group or class of people to have standing (as in class action suits), each member must show specific injury. This means that a general interest in the environment, for instance, does not provide a group with sufficient basis for standing.

mootness a criterion used by courts to screen cases that no longer require resolution.

The Supreme Court also uses a third criterion in determining whether it will hear a case: that of **mootness.** In theory, this requirement disqualifies cases that are brought too late—after the relevant facts have changed or the problem has been resolved by other means. The criterion of mootness, however, is subject to the discretion of the courts, which have begun to relax the rules of mootness, particularly in cases where a situation that has been resolved is likely to come up again. In the abortion case *Roe v. Wade,* for example, the Supreme Court rejected the lower court's argument that because the pregnancy had already come to term, the case was moot. The Court agreed to hear the case because no pregnancy was likely to outlast the lengthy appeals process.

Putting aside the formal criteria, the Supreme Court is most likely to accept cases that involve conflicting decisions by the federal circuit courts, cases that present important questions of civil rights or civil liberties, and cases in which the federal government is the appellant. Ultimately, however, the question of which cases to accept can come down to the preferences and priorities of the justices. If a group of justices believes that the Court should intervene in a particular area of policy or politics, they are likely to look for a case or cases that will serve as vehicles for judicial intervention. For many years, for example, the Court was not interested in considering challenges to affirmative action or other programs designed to provide particular benefits to minorities. In recent years, however, several of the Court's more conservative justices have been eager to push back the limits of affirmative action and racial preference, and have therefore accepted a number of cases that would allow them to do so. In 1995, the Court's decisions in *Adarand Constructors v. Pena, Missouri v. Jenkins,* and *Miller v. Johnson* placed new restrictions on federal affirmative action programs, school desegregation efforts, and attempts to increase minority representation in Congress through the creation of "minority districts" (see Chapter 10).[19]

Writs   Decisions handed down by lower courts can reach the Supreme Court in one of two ways: through a *writ of certiorari,* or, in the case of convicted state prisoners, through a writ of *habeas corpus.* A writ is a court document conveying an order of some sort. In recent years, an effort has been made to give the Court more discretion regarding the cases it chooses to hear. Before 1988, the Supreme Court was obligated to review cases on what was called a writ of appeal. This has since been eliminated, and the Court now has virtually complete discretion over what cases it will hear.

Most cases reach the Supreme Court through the **writ of *certiorari,*** which is granted whenever four of the nine justices agree to review a case. The Supreme Court was once so inundated with appeals that in 1925 Congress enacted laws giving it some control over its caseload with the power to issue writs of *certiorari.* Rule 10 of the Supreme Court's own rules of procedure defines *certiorari* as "not a matter of right, but of sound judicial discretion . . . granted only where there are special and important reasons therefor." The reasons provided for in Rule 10 are:

> **writ of *certiorari*** a decision of at least four of the nine Supreme Court justices to review a decision of a lower court; from the Latin "to make more certain"

1. Where a state has made a decision that conflicts with previous Supreme Court decisions;
2. Where a state court has come up with an entirely new federal question;
3. Where one court of appeals has rendered a decision in conflict with another;
4. Where there are other inconsistent rulings between two or more courts or states;
5. Where a single court of appeals has sanctioned too great a departure by a lower court from normal judicial proceedings (a reason rarely given).

The **writ of *habeas corpus*** is a fundamental safeguard of individual rights. Its historical purpose is to enable an accused person to challenge arbitrary detention and to force an open trial before a judge. But in 1867, Congress's distrust of southern courts led it to confer on federal courts the authority to issue writs of *habeas corpus* to prisoners already tried or being tried in state courts of proper jurisdiction where the constitutional rights of the prisoner were possibly being violated. This writ gives state prisoners a second channel toward Supreme Court review in case their direct appeal from the highest state court fails (see Figure 15.2 on page 612). The writ of *habeas corpus* is discretionary; that is, the Court can decide which cases to review.

> **writ of *habeas corpus*** a court order that the individual in custody be brought into court and shown the cause for detention. *Habeas corpus* is guaranteed by the Constitution and can be suspended only in cases of rebellion or invasion

Figure 15.2 **How Cases Reach the Supreme Court**

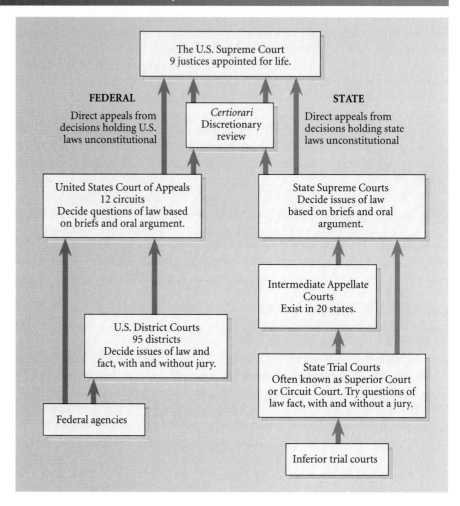

CONTROLLING THE FLOW OF CASES

> **What shapes the flow of cases through the Supreme Court?**

In addition to the judges themselves, three other agencies or groups play an important role in shaping the flow of cases through the federal courts: the solicitor general, the Federal Bureau of Investigation, and federal law clerks.

The Solicitor General If any single person has greater influence than individual judges over the federal courts, it is the **solicitor general** of the United States. The solicitor general is the third-ranking official in the Justice Department (below the attorney general and the deputy attorney general) but is the top government lawyer in virtually all cases before the Supreme Court where the government is a party. The solicitor general has the greatest control over the flow of cases; his or her actions are not reviewed by any higher authority in the executive branch. More than half the Supreme Court's total workload consists of cases under the direct charge of the solicitor general.

solicitor general the top government lawyer in all cases before the Supreme Court where the government is a party

The solicitor general exercises especially strong influence by screening cases before any agency of the federal government can appeal them to the Supreme Court; indeed, the justices rely on the solicitor general to "screen out undeserving litigation and furnish them with an agenda to government cases that deserve serious consideration."[20] Typically, more requests for appeals are rejected than are accepted by the solicitor general. Agency heads may lobby the president or otherwise try to circumvent the solicitor general, and a few of the independent agencies have a statutory right to make direct appeals, but these are almost inevitably doomed to **per curiam** rejection—rejection through a brief, unsigned opinion by the whole Court—if the solicitor general refuses to participate. Congress has given only a few agencies, including the Federal Communications Commission, the Federal Maritime Commission, and in some cases, the Department of Agriculture (even though it is not an independent agency), the right to appeal directly to the Supreme Court without going through the solicitor general.

The solicitor general can enter a case even when the federal government is not a direct litigant by writing an **amicus curiae** ("friend of the court") brief. A "friend of the court" is not a direct party to a case but has a vital interest in its outcome. Thus, when the government has such an interest, the solicitor general can file as *amicus curiae,* or a federal court can invite such a brief because it wants an opinion in writing. The solicitor general also has the power to invite others to enter cases as *amici curiae.*

In addition to exercising substantial control over the flow of cases, the solicitor general can shape the arguments used before the federal courts. Indeed, the Supreme Court tends to give special attention to the way the solicitor general characterizes the issues. The solicitor general is the person appearing most frequently before the Court and, theoretically at least, is the most disinterested. The credibility of the solicitor general is not hurt when several times each year he or she comes to the Court to withdraw a case with the admission that the government has made an error.

The solicitor general's sway over the flow of cases does not, however, entirely overshadow the influence of the other agencies and divisions in the Department of Justice. The solicitor general is counsel for the major divisions in the department, including the Antitrust, Tax, Civil Rights, and Criminal divisions. Their activities generate a great part of the solicitor general's agenda. This is particularly true of the Criminal Division, whose cases are appealed every day. These cases are generated by initiatives taken by the United States attorneys and the district judges before whom they practice.

The FBI Another important influence on the flow of cases through the federal appellate judiciary comes from the Federal Bureau of Investigation (FBI), one of the bureaus of the Department of Justice. Its work provides data for numerous government cases against businesses, individual citizens, and state and local government officials. Its data are the most vital source of material for cases in the areas of national security and organized crime.

The FBI also has the important function of linking the Justice Department very closely to cases being brought by state and local government officials. Since the FBI has a long history of cooperation with state and local police forces, the solicitor general often joins (as *amicus curiae*) appeals involving state criminal cases.

per curiam decision by an appellate court, without a written opinion, that refuses to review the decision of a lower court; amounts to a reaffirmation of the lower court's opinion

amicus curiae literally, "friend of the court"; individuals or groups who are not parties to a lawsuit but who seek to assist the Supreme Court in reaching a decision by presenting additional briefs

Law Clerks Every federal judge employs law clerks to research legal issues and assist with the preparation of opinions. Each Supreme Court justice is assigned four clerks. The clerks are almost always honors graduates of the nation's most prestigious law schools. A clerkship with a Supreme Court justice is a great honor and generally indicates that the fortunate individual is likely to reach the very top of the legal profession. The work of the Supreme Court clerks is a closely guarded secret, but it is likely that some justices rely heavily upon their clerks for advice in writing opinions and in deciding whether an individual case ought to be heard by the Court. In a recent book, a former law clerk to retired justice Harry Blackmun charged that Supreme Court justices yielded "excessive power to immature, ideologically driven clerks, who in turn use that power to manipulate their bosses."[21]

LOBBYING FOR ACCESS: INTERESTS AND THE COURT

At the same time that the Court exercises discretion over which cases it will review, groups and forces in society often seek to persuade the justices to listen to their problems. Interest groups use several different strategies to get the Court's attention. Lawyers representing these groups try to choose the proper client and the proper case, so that the issues in question are most dramatically and appropriately portrayed. They also have to pick the right district or jurisdiction in which to bring the case. Sometimes they even have to wait for an appropriate political climate.

Group litigants have to plan carefully when to use and when to avoid publicity. They must also attempt to develop a proper record at the trial court level, one that includes some constitutional arguments and even, when possible, errors on the part of the trial court. One of the most effective litigation strategies used in getting cases accepted for review by the appellate courts is bringing the same type of suit in more than one circuit (i.e., developing a "pattern of cases"), in the hope that inconsistent treatment by two different courts will improve the chance of a Supreme Court review.

Congress will sometimes provide interest groups with legislation designed to facilitate their use of litigation. One important recent example is the 1990 Americans with Disabilities Act (ADA), enacted after intense lobbying by public interest and advocacy groups. The ADA, in conjunction with the 1991 Civil Rights Act, opens the way for disabled individuals to make effective use of the courts to press their interests.

The two most notable users of the pattern of cases strategy in recent years have been the National Association for the Advancement of Colored People (NAACP) and the American Civil Liberties Union (ACLU). For many years, the NAACP (and its Defense Fund—now a separate group) has worked through local chapters and with many individuals to encourage litigation on issues of racial discrimination and segregation. Sometimes it distributes petitions to be signed by parents and filed with local school boards and courts, deliberately sowing the seeds of future litigation. The NAACP and the ACLU often encourage private parties to bring suit and then join the suit as *amici curiae.*

One illustration of an interest group employing a carefully crafted litigation strategy to pursue its goals through the judiciary was the Texas-based effort to establish a right to free public school education for children of illegal aliens. The issue arose in 1977 when the Texas state legislature, responding to a sudden public backlash against illegal immigration from Mexico, enacted a law permitting school districts to charge undocumented children hefty tuition for the privilege of attending public school. A public-interest law organization, the Mexican-American Legal Defense Fund, prepared to challenge the law in court after determining that public opposition precluded any chance of persuading the legislature to change its own law.

Part of the defense fund's litigation strategy was to bring a lawsuit in the northern section of Texas, far from the Mexican border, where illegal immigration would be at a minimum. Thus, in Tyler, Texas, where the complaint was initially filed, the trial court found only sixty undocumented alien students in a school district composed of 16,000. This strategy effectively contradicted the state's argument that the Texas law was necessary to reduce the burdens on educational resources created by masses of incoming aliens. Another useful litigation tactic was to select plaintiffs who, although illegal aliens, were nevertheless clearly planning to remain in Texas even without free public education for their children. Thus, all of the plaintiffs came from families that had already lived in Tyler for several years and included at least one child who was an American citizen by virtue of birth in the United States. By emphasizing the stability of such families, the defense fund argued convincingly that the Texas law would not motivate families to return to the poverty in Mexico from which they had fled, but would more likely result in the creation of a subclass of illiterate people who would add to the state's unemployment and crime rates. Five years after the lawsuit on behalf of the Tyler children began, the U.S. Supreme Court in the case of *Plyler v. Doe* held that the Texas law was unconstitutional under the equal protection clause of the Fourteenth Amendment.[22]

In many states, it is considered unethical and illegal for attorneys to engage in "fomenting and soliciting legal business in which they are not parties and have no pecuniary right or liability." The NAACP was sued by the state of Virginia in the late 1950s in an attempt to restrict or eliminate its efforts to influence the pattern of cases. The Supreme Court reviewed the case in 1963, recognized that the strategy was being utilized, and held that it was protected by the First and Fourteenth Amendments, just as other forms of speech and petition are protected.[23]

Thus, many pathbreaking cases are eventually granted *certiorari* because continued refusal to review one or more of them would amount to a rule of law just as much as if the courts had handed down a written opinion. In this sense, the flow of cases, especially the pattern of significant cases, influences the behavior of the appellate judiciary.

THE SUPREME COURT'S PROCEDURES

The Preparation   The Supreme Court's decision to accept a case is the beginning of what can be a lengthy and complex process (see Figure 15.3 on page 616). First, the attorneys on both sides must prepare **briefs**   written documents that may be several hundred pages long in which the attorneys explain why the Court should rule in favor of their client. Briefs are filled with referrals to precedents specifically chosen to show that other courts have frequently ruled in the same way that the Supreme Court is being asked to rule. The attorneys for both sides muster the most compelling precedents they can in support of their arguments.

> ➤ **Once accepted, how does a case proceed?**

briefs written documents in which attorneys explain, using case precedents, why the court should find in favor of their client

Figure 15.3 The Supreme Court's Decision-Making Process

In addition to the individual justices who make up the Supreme Court, various groups and factors also may influence the Court's decision on any given case.

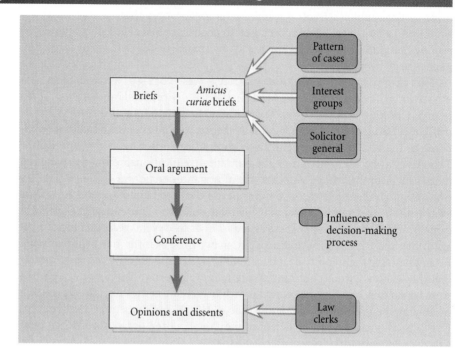

As the attorneys prepare their briefs, they often ask sympathetic interest groups for their help. Groups are asked to file *amicus curiae* briefs that support the claims of one or the other litigant. In a case involving separation of church and state, for example, liberal groups such as the ACLU and Citizens for the American Way are likely to be asked to file *amicus* briefs in support of strict separation, whereas conservative religious groups are likely to file *amicus* briefs advocating increased public support for religious ideas. Often, dozens of briefs will be filed on each side of a major case. *Amicus* filings are one of the primary methods used by interest groups to lobby the Court. By filing these briefs, groups indicate to the Court where their group stands and signal to the justices that they believe the case to be an important one.

oral argument stage in Supreme Court procedure in which attorneys for both sides appear before the Court to present their positions and answer questions posed by justices

Oral Argument The next stage of a case is **oral argument,** in which attorneys for both sides appear before the Court to present their positions and answer the justices' questions. Each attorney has only a half hour to present his or her case, and this time includes interruptions for questions. Certain members of the Court, such as Justice Antonin Scalia, are known to interrupt attorneys dozens of times. Others, such as Justice Clarence Thomas, seldom ask questions. For an attorney, the opportunity to argue a case before the Supreme Court is a singular honor and a mark of professional distinction. It can also be a harrowing experience, as justices interrupt a carefully prepared presentation. Nevertheless, oral argument can be very important to the outcome of a case. It allows justices to better understand the heart of the case and to raise questions that might not have been addressed in the opposing side's briefs. It is not uncommon for justices to go beyond the strictly legal issues and ask opposing counsel to discuss the implications of the case for the Court and the nation at large.

The Conference Following oral argument, the Court discusses the case in its Wednesday or Friday conference. The chief justice presides over the conference and speaks first; the other justices follow in order of seniority. The Court's conference is secret, and no outsiders are permitted to attend. The justices discuss the case and eventually reach a decision on the basis of a majority vote. If the Court is divided, a number of votes may be taken before a final decision is reached. As the case is discussed, justices may try to influence or change one another's opinions. At times, this may result in compromise decisions. On the current Court, for example, several justices, including Rehnquist, Scalia, and Thomas, are known to favor overturning the 1973 *Roe v. Wade* decision that prohibited the states from outlawing abortions. Other justices, including Souter, Breyer, and Ginsburg, are known to oppose such a course of action. This division has resulted in several compromise decisions, in which the Court has allowed some state restriction of abortion but has not permitted states to outlaw abortion altogether.

Opinion Writing After a decision has been reached, one of the members of the majority is assigned to write the **opinion**. This assignment is made by the chief justice, or by the most senior justice in the majority if the chief justice is on the losing side. The assignment of the opinion can make a significant difference to the interpretation of a decision. Every opinion of the Supreme Court sets a major precedent for future cases throughout the judicial system. Lawyers and judges in the lower courts will examine the opinion carefully to ascertain the Supreme Court's meaning. Differences in wording and emphasis can have important implications for future litigation. Once the majority opinion is drafted, it is circulated to the other justices. Some members of the majority may decide that they cannot accept all the language of the opinion and therefore write "concurring" opinions that support the decision but offer a somewhat different rationale or emphasis. In assigning an opinion, serious thought must be given to the impression the case will make on lawyers and on the public, as well as to the probability that one justice's opinion will be more widely accepted than another's.

opinion the written explanation of the Supreme Court's decision in a particular case

One of the more dramatic instances of this tactical consideration occurred in 1944, when Chief Justice Harlan F. Stone chose Justice Felix Frankfurter to write the opinion in the "white primary" case *Smith v. Allwright*. The chief justice believed that this sensitive case, which overturned the southern practice of prohibiting black participation in nominating primaries, required the efforts of the most brilliant and scholarly jurist on the Court. But the day after Stone made the assignment, Justice Robert H. Jackson wrote a letter to Stone urging a change of assignment. In his letter, Jackson argued that Frankfurter, a foreign-born Jew from New England, would not win the South with his opinion, regardless of its brilliance. Stone accepted the advice and substituted Justice Stanley Reed, an American-born Protestant from Kentucky and a southern Democrat in good standing.[24]

Dissent Justices who disagree with the majority decision of the Court may choose to publicize the character of their disagreement in the form of a **dissenting**

dissenting opinion a decision written by a justice in the minority in a particular case in which the justice wishes to express his or her reasoning in the case

What Government Does . . . After September 11

MILITARY COMMISSIONS
FAIR, BALANCED

Over the course of American history, war has pushed the Bill of Rights to the back burner. And the judiciary usually goes along with this by becoming something of a handmaiden to the executive and the military, by avoiding, postponing, or even declaring as constitutional executive actions that have patently violated individual civil liberties. Many of the most eloquent judicial doctrines supporting the Bill of Rights started out as dissents against a Supreme Court majority that was supporting the dubious actions of a commander in chief.[1]

As of the end of its 2002 term, the Supreme Court had not yet been confronted with a post–September 11 appeal against alleged violations of the Bill of Rights. But events and decisions were already making it clear that the federal judiciary was being diminished and virtually displaced by military tribunals for all foreigners. On November 13, 2001, President Bush issued an executive order in a press release (called a "military order") mandating that the secretary of defense "take all necessary measures" to detain any noncitizen who "there is reason to believe" is a member of Al Qaeda and has engaged in or aided and abetted acts of terrorism. Such individuals would be "tried by military commission," with punishments "including life imprisonment or death." The military commissions would be set up by the secretary of defense, with attorneys for prosecution and defendants arranged for by the secretary of defense and "subject to such . . . conditions as the secretary of defense may prescribe." A two-thirds vote of the members of the commission would be required for conviction (as distinct from the unanimity required in our judiciary). The record of the trial, the conviction and the sentence, and the review and final decision would all be reserved to the president or, if he should designate, the secretary of defense. No other remedy or review was available to these individuals in any other U.S. federal or state court, the court of any other country, or any international tribunal.

Concern about disregard of the Bill of Rights led to the White House announcement on March 21, 2002, of "new rules" softening the harshness of the original order. The new rules jacked up the jury requirement to unanimity when imposing the death penalty. Appeals of convictions were allowed, but still were limited to the military chain of command and not opened to the judiciary. Moreover, prosecutors could still use hearsay and second-hand evidence (barred even in normal military courts-martial), and the secretary of defense retained the authority to keep some prisoners in captivity indefinitely, even if acquitted in the military tribunal, in order to prevent them from allegedly engaging in terrorist activities.

We have to reach back at least to President Lincoln to find precedent for prosecution and conviction by military tribunals in secret trials without provision for judicial review. Even then, the Supreme Court ruled—albeit after the end of the war—that military tribunals for civilians could not operate as long as civilian courts were open and able to take these cases.[2] Thus, President Bush broke entirely new ground and built on it a nonjudicial process totally outside Article III of the Constitution, which provides that "the judicial Power *of the United States* shall be vested in one supreme Court, and in such inferior Courts as the Congress may from time to time ordain and establish" [emphasis added]. President Bush copied his military order in part after Lincoln but in larger part after Franklin Roosevelt's World War II order dealing with Nazi saboteurs. But even here, the differences with Roosevelt's order are greater than the similarities. First, the six Nazis were "caught in the act" on U.S. soil and had confessed. Second, Roosevelt's order was limited to a precise subgroup of persons "from any nation at war with the United States," while Bush's order covered a large population of unknowns comprised of "any individual who is not a United States citizen," including resident aliens. An order of the scale and scope of Bush's is tantamount to an amendment to the Constitution creating a new institution. But what kind of institution? Is this military tribunal system a new government for aliens? Or is it the foundation for our first national police force?

---

[1] *Schenck v. United States,* 249 U.S. 47 (1919), was followed by *Gitlow v. New York,* 268 U.S. 652 (1925), in which the First Amendment was finally "incorporated" into the due process clause of the Fourteenth Amendment. Another example is *Korematsu v. United States,* 323 U.S. 214 (1944), followed almost immediately by *Ex parte Endo,* 323 U.S. 283 (1944), and *Brown v. Board of Education,* 347 U.S. 483 (1954).

[2] *Ex parte Milligan,* 4 Wall 2 (1866).

SOURCES: Editorial, "The Politics of Judgeships," *New York Times,* February 25, 2002, p. A20; George Fletcher, "War and the Constitution," *The American Prospect,* January 1, 2002, p. 26; Ann-Marie Slaughter, "Tougher Than Terror," *The American Prospect,* January 28, 2002, p. 22; Louis Fisher, "The Nation," *Los Angeles Times,* December 2, 2001, p. 3; Katharine Q. Seelye, "Rumsfeld Backs Plan to Hold Captives Even if Acquitted," *New York Times,* March 21, 2002, p. 1; John Mintz, "U.S. Adds Legal Rights in Tribunals," *Washington Post,* March 21, 2002, p. A1.

opinion. Dissents can be used to express irritation with an outcome or to signal to defeated political forces in the nation that their position is supported by at least some members of the Court. Ironically, the most dependable way an individual justice can exercise a direct and clear influence on the Court is to write a dissent. Because there is no need to please a majority, dissenting opinions can be more eloquent and less guarded than majority opinions. Some of the greatest writing in the history of the Court is found in the dissents of Oliver Wendell Holmes, Louis D. Brandeis, and William O. Douglas, the last of whom wrote thirty-five dissents in the Court's 1952–53 term alone. By comparison, there is no great dissenter in the current Court. Justice John Paul Stevens and Justice Stephen Breyer stand out with twelve dissents each in the 2000–2001 term.

Dissent plays a special role in the work and impact of the Court because it amounts to an appeal to lawyers all over the country to keep bringing cases of the sort at issue. Therefore, an effective dissent influences the flow of cases through the Court as well as the arguments that will be used by lawyers in later cases. Even more important, dissent emphasizes the fact that, although the Court speaks with a single opinion, it is the opinion only of the majority—and one day the majority might go the other way.

EXPLAINING SUPREME COURT DECISIONS

The Supreme Court explains its decisions in terms of law and precedent. But although law and precedent do have an effect on the Court's deliberations and eventual decisions, it is the Supreme Court that decides what laws actually mean and what importance precedent will actually have. Throughout its history, the Court has shaped and reshaped the law. In the late nineteenth and early twentieth centuries, for example, the Supreme Court held that the Constitution, law, and precedent permitted racial segregation in the United States. Beginning in the late 1950s, however, the Court found that the Constitution prohibited segregation on the basis of race and indicated that the use of racial categories in legislation was always suspect. By the 1970s and 1980s, the Court once again held that the Constitution permitted the use of racial categories—when such categories were needed to help members of minority groups achieve full participation in American society. In the 1990s, the Court began to retreat from this position, too, indicating that governmental efforts to provide extra help to racial minorities could represent an unconstitutional infringement on the rights of the majority.

Although it is not the only relevant factor, the prime explanation for these movements is shifts in judicial philosophy. These shifts, in turn, result from changes in the Court's composition as justices retire and are replaced by new justices who, as we saw earlier, tend to share the philosophical outlook of the president who appointed them.

> **What factors influence the judicial philosophy of the Supreme Court?**

Activism and Restraint One element of judicial philosophy is the issue of activism versus restraint. Over the years, some justices have believed that courts should interpret the Constitution according to the stated intentions of its framers and defer to the views of Congress when interpreting federal statutes. The late justice Felix Frankfurter, for example, advocated judicial deference to legislative bodies and avoidance of the "political thicket," in which the Court would entangle itself by

judicial restraint judicial philosophy whose adherents refuse to go beyond the clear words of the Constitution in interpreting its meaning

judicial activism judicial philosophy that posits that the Court should go beyond the words of the Constitution or a statute to consider the broader societal implications of its decisions

deciding questions that were essentially political rather than legal in character. Advocates of **judicial restraint** are sometimes called "strict constructionists," because they look strictly to the words of the Constitution in interpreting its meaning.

The alternative to restraint is **judicial activism.** Activist judges such as the former chief justice Earl Warren and two of the leading members of his Court, Justices Hugo Black and William O. Douglas, believed that the Court should go beyond the words of the Constitution or a statute to consider the broader societal implications of its decisions. Activist judges sometimes strike out in new directions, promulgating new interpretations or inventing new legal and constitutional concepts when they believe these to be socially desirable. For example, Justice Harry Blackmun's decision in *Roe v. Wade* was based on a constitutional right to privacy that is not found in the words of the Constitution. Blackmun and the other members of the majority in the *Roe* case argued that the right to privacy was implied by other constitutional provisions. In this instance of judicial activism, the Court knew the result it wanted to achieve and was not afraid to make the law conform to the desired outcome.

Political Ideology   The second component of judicial philosophy is political ideology. The liberal or conservative attitudes of justices play an important role in their decisions.[25] Indeed, the philosophy of activism versus restraint is, to a large extent, a smokescreen for political ideology. For the most part, liberal judges have been activists, willing to use the law to achieve social and political change, whereas conservatives have been associated with judicial restraint. Interestingly, however, in recent years some conservative justices who have long called for restraint have actually become activists in seeking to undo some of the work of liberal jurists over the past three decades.

From the 1950s to the 1980s, the Supreme Court took an activist role in such areas as civil rights, civil liberties, abortion, voting rights, and police procedures. For example, the Supreme Court was more responsible than any other governmental institution for breaking down America's system of racial segregation. The Supreme Court virtually prohibited states from interfering with the right of a woman to seek an abortion and sharply curtailed state restrictions on voting rights. And it was the Supreme Court that placed restrictions on the behavior of local police and prosecutors in criminal cases. In a series of decisions between 1989 and 2001, however, the conservative justices appointed by presidents Ronald Reagan and George H. W. Bush were able to swing the Court to a more conservative position on civil rights, affirmative action, abortion rights, property rights, criminal procedure, voting rights, desegregation, and the power of the national government.

The importance of ideology was very clear during the Court's 2000–2001 term. In important decisions, the Court's most conservative justices—Scalia, Thomas, and Rehnquist, usually joined by Kennedy—generally voted as a bloc.[26] Indeed, Scalia and Thomas voted together in 99 percent of all cases. At the same time, the Court's most liberal justices—Breyer, Ginsburg, Souter, and Stevens—also generally formed a bloc with Ginsburg and Breyer and Ginsburg and Souter voting together 94 percent of the time.[27] Justice O'Connor, a moderate conservative, was the swing vote in many important cases. This ideological division led to a number of important 5-4 decisions. As we saw, in the main Florida election law case, *Bush v. Gore,* Justice O'Connor joined with the conservative bloc to give

Abortion and the Right to Privacy

Although the word "privacy" does not appear in the Bill of Rights, the courts have agreed that such a fundamental right exists. They disagree, however, about exactly from where the protection arises and about how far it should be applied. Nowhere is this disagreement more protracted than on the issue of abortion.

Since its 1973 landmark ruling in *Roe v. Wade*, the Supreme Court has repeatedly found that the right to privacy protects the right of a woman to end a pregnancy via abortion, subject to some court-approved restrictions. Abortion opponents, of course, have rejected the premise of *Roe* that privacy protects an act they consider murder. For example, members of Congress who oppose abortion have succeeded in restricting federal Medicaid funding for abortions. Today's more conservative Supreme Court has allowed states to impose restrictions such as parental notification for minors and twenty-four-hour waiting periods for those seeking abortions.

Supporters of privacy-based protection for abortion argue that, as a matter of law and tradition, a developing fetus cannot be accorded the same legal status as the woman carrying a fetus. If privacy means anything, it must extend to the right of a woman to decide, at least during the early months of pregnancy (when the vast majority of abortions are performed, and before the point of viability, when the fetus can live outside of the woman), whether or not to have an abortion. For the government to require women to carry most or all pregnancies to term represents extreme government intrusion into the innately personal decision over procreation. The principle of individual liberty must allow women to make such fundamental decisions themselves.

Further, the idea that all abortions are murder means that a fertilized egg does and should possess the same traits as a full-term baby, an idea that is rejected by medical science, most Americans, and many religions. For example,

when a spontaneous abortion occurs early in a pregnancy, it is called a "miscarriage," for which funeral services are not held. A late-term spontaneous abortion, called a "stillbirth," evokes a different and more complex response, reflecting the evident difference in development. Abortion laws properly reflect these differences. Finally, the Constitution speaks to the issue by noting that citizenship, and therefore the rights stemming from it, begins at birth.

Opponents of abortion argue that the relative differences observed in fetal development do not obviate the fact that, by genetic makeup, even a fertilized egg is a person. The right to privacy does not and cannot provide an excuse for murder. The absence of birth does not, in and of itself, mean that a fetus is without rights. Even if the Constitution's framers had all agreed that the Bill of Rights protected the liberty associated with privacy, there is no reason to believe that they would have countenanced its extension to abortion. Furthermore, to say that such issues are purely a matter of personal choice is to turn a blind eye to the sort of evil that government has every right to regulate or prohibit. And while pregnancy is a developmental process for the fetus, it is precisely because there is no magic, agreed-upon point at which a fetus becomes a person that the fetus must be protected as a person at all stages.

Women who become pregnant, whether by accident or intent, assume a special obligation to the innocent life they carry. Although some who oppose abortions are willing to allow exceptions for cases of rape or incest, such cases account for only a tiny percentage of all abortions. Legal abortion is harmful in other respects. It demeans respect for life by allowing, even encouraging, abortion as a means of birth control. If later-term abortions are allowed because of, say, fetal defect, it is a short step to euthanasia (so-called mercy killing) of living persons. Above all, the right of a fetus to live must supersede the privacy rights, however defined, of pregnant women.

Should Abortion Remain Legal?

Yes

For the many who bemoan the evils of abortion, including the author of a recent editorial in these pages, a common tactic to elicit sympathy for their cause is employing harrowing imagery of the abortion itself. They talk, for example, of sharp hooks ladling the fetus out of the womb. Such an image tugs on any reader's heartstrings; no one wants to see a baby impaled on a sharp hook. The problem, however, is that this picture is a gross misrepresentation of reality. The majority of abortions are performed in the first trimester with a vacuum-like device—and no hooks.

The larger error committed by nearly every anti-abortion activist is, however, that their arguments consider only the unborn fetus, without mention of the woman in whose womb it resides—as if she is no more than an incubator for this precious life. Indeed, "life" is the word used by every upstanding anti-abortion activist. But it is not life that's at stake, it is the potential for life. The law, both in word and in spirit, rightly protects life itself and not the promise of it.

What makes us human—what sets us apart from, say, dogs and chickens—is our consciousness, not the mere fact of our biological existence. A fetus in its first trimester is not a conscious being. It will never know that it might have lived. Its mother, however is conscious. The characterization of those who have abortions as cold, callous murderers is an unfair rhetorical ploy. The great majority of those who elect to have abortions do so not out of a joy of slaughtering unborn babies, but out of necessity. They inevitably agonize over the decision, both before and for many years afterwards. Yet, for many reasons, they simply cannot have a child. To bring such a child into the world—a world which, at present, cannot support it—is a far worse crime than to abort it. I invite any American who believes that abortion should be illegal to assume the burden of adopting every child that would be born if his or her wish were granted.

Many of those who have abortions are young women who either didn't have the knowledge that would have prevented contraception—a knowledge which many of us who are either more privileged or more educated take for granted—or whose contraceptive failed. Condoms break. Pills sometimes don't work. And the argument that abstinence would have prevented such tragedies is an outdated and cheaply moralizing one. Most of us live in a world in which sex has irrevocably become an integral part. Arguing that we deny the right of abortion to women who became pregnant because of neglected or failed contraception—arguing that an unwelcome child should be given the right to, more likely than not, a bad life—is akin to arguing that people who contract AIDS through intercourse should be denied treatment because, well, they deserve it.

It is all too easy for someone who has not experienced the need to have an abortion to decry its immortality; it is even easier for a man to do so, knowing that he will never be pregnant. But the protection of abortion rights is important to men as well as women—where there is a mother, there is a father. A child born into a situation in which it cannot be supported affects both.

While misuses of abortion are inevitable, it is a small price to ensure that every woman has complete authority over her body and life. The anti-abortion activists are right about one thing: the issue here is one of the right to life. But the most important life in the equation is the woman's.

To those who would still deny a woman's right to abortion, I have this, finally, to say: the decision of whether or not to have an abortion isn't yours to make. You do not—and cannot—speak for the millions who will have to make this very difficult choice. It isn't you who will carry the child in your womb for nine months; and it isn't you who will have to raise it.

SOURCE: Ian MacKenzie, "Right to Abortion Is Right to Life," *Harvard Crimson,* March 4, 2002.

No

One of the most divisive issues in public discourse is abortion. Many people have their minds made up about abortion. Some believe abortion is a choice without moral or physical consequences and others believe it is wrong because human life begins at conception and it is the taking of a human life.

At the heart of the political debate about abortion is the belief by the anti-abortion and pro-choice movements that the U.S. Supreme Court is the be-all and end-all in the decision-making process. Pro-choicers and anti-abortionists both think if conservative presidents continue to appoint strict constitutionalist judges, *Roe v. Wade* will be overturned and abortion once again will be outlawed.

I've got news for both the pro-choice advocates who believe outlawing abortion is possible with president George Bush's coming Supreme Court justice appointment and the anti-abortionists who think such appointments and overturning *Roe v. Wade* will end the debate. You're both wrong.

Politicians know the abortion issue, besides being a polarizing one, is a great way to get votes. They have many believing if you don't vote for them, abortion will increase or it will be outlawed. The truth is even if *Roe v. Wade* were overturned tomorrow, nothing would change.

Yeah, that's right. Nothing. There's the possibility of some minor change in law, but all overturning *Roe v. Wade* would do is revert the decision of the legality of abortion to the states and the odds that any state would outlaw it outright is slim to none.

The truth of the matter is abortion isn't going to be outlawed anytime soon. It can't, because as long as we have half the population believing the unborn are human beings, and the other half believing they aren't, the cultural change needed for an end to legal abortion has no chance.

Both sides will continue to fight for their ideals. But at least on the side of those who are anti-abortion, they'd be better off concentrating their efforts on public service announcement campaigns on television and radio. The law's not going to change. Legislation like the Human Life Amendment has little or no chance of passing, so why not utilize the power of television to make a reasoned, moral case to the individual hearts and minds of Americans instead of trying to change things from the top down?

In some ways the anti-abortion movement itself is its own worst enemy. With supporters that include some of the most intolerant, narrow-minded religious leaders in America, such as Pat Robertson and Jerry Falwell, it's no surprise the movement itself doesn't have larger mainstream support. Ditch the zealots and you'll be taken more seriously.

As for the pro-choice movement, supporters have a point that government shouldn't be in the business of people's personal lives. Besides, any form of prohibition doesn't work. Although I do agree abortion is morally wrong, the taking of a human life, and I would never help procure an abortion, I also think it's awfully hard to close Pandora's box once it has been opened.

The only thing to be done is to educate the minds and appeal to the hearts of all people. Couples have the choice to abort or not to abort; it seems to me it is best to let the moral responsibility concerning the abortion of their children lie squarely on their own backs.

That is not to say the argument for life and against abortion should fall by the wayside and public funding of abortion shouldn't end, but anytime government gets involved in anything, things become worse and more complicated.

However, to simply say, as pro-choice advocates do, "Well, we're not even sure when life begins, so until that's settled, go away" is an argument that lacks reason and support. It is clear a sperm and egg cell apart can't become a human being, yet together they can and do. It's as simple as that.

Legally the pro-choice movement has a point, but not morally. Their minds are made up and they don't want to be confused by the facts.

You have a choice, folks, but just remember abortion isn't cut and dried as an issue on either side. Both have points, but as it stands only you can make the decision. And that is between you, your conscience, and God.

SOURCE: Kyle Sing, "The Bottom Line on *Roe v. Wade*, Abortion, Life, and Choice," *Chicago Flame* (University of Illinois-Chicago), June 18, 2002.

Bush a 5-4 victory.[28] Indeed, more than 33 percent of all the cases heard by the Court in its 2000–2001 term were decided 5 to 4.

Yet the efforts by Reagan and Bush to reshape the federal judiciary were not fully successful. Often in American history, judges have surprised and disappointed the presidents who named them to the bench. Justice Souter, for example, has been far less conservative than President Bush and the Republicans who supported Souter's appointment thought he would be. Likewise, Justices O'Connor and Kennedy have disappointed conservatives by opposing limitations on abortion.

Nevertheless, with a combined total of twelve years in office, Reagan and Bush were also able to exercise a good deal of influence on the composition of the federal district and appellate courts. By the end of Bush's term, he and Reagan together had appointed nearly half of all federal judges. Thus, whatever impact Reagan and Bush ultimately have on the Supreme Court, their appointments will certainly influence the temperament and behavior of the district and circuit courts for years to come.

President Clinton promised to appoint more liberal jurists to the district and appellate courts, as well as to increase the number of women and minorities serving on the federal bench. During his first two years in office, Clinton held to this promise; more than 60 percent of his 128 judicial nominees were women or members of minority groups (see Figure 15.4).[29]

The political struggles of the 1980s and 1990s amply illustrate the importance of judicial ideology. Is abortion a fundamental right or a criminal activity? How much separation must there be between church and state? Does the use of the

---

Figure 15.4 — **The Diversity of Federal Court Appointees from Reagan to Clinton**

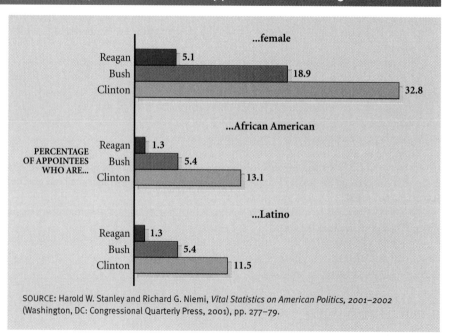

SOURCE: Harold W. Stanley and Richard G. Niemi, *Vital Statistics on American Politics, 2001–2002* (Washington, DC: Congressional Quarterly Press, 2001), pp. 277–79.

Voting Rights Act to increase minority representation constitute a violation of the rights of whites? The answers to these and many other questions cannot be found in the words of the Constitution. They must be located, instead, in the hearts of the judges who interpret that text.

Judicial Power and Politics

One of the most important institutional changes to occur in the United States during the past half-century has been the striking transformation of the role and power of the federal courts, and of the Supreme Court in particular. Understanding how this transformation came about is the key to understanding the contemporary role of the courts in America.

TRADITIONAL LIMITATIONS ON THE FEDERAL COURTS

For much of American history, the power of the federal courts was subject to five limitations.[30] First, courts were constrained by judicial rules of standing that limited access to the bench. Claimants who simply disagreed with governmental action or inaction could not obtain access. Access to the courts was limited to individuals who could show that they were particularly affected by the government's behavior in some area. This limitation on access to the courts diminished the judiciary's capacity to forge links with important political and social forces.

> ➤ How has the power of the federal courts been limited throughout much of American history?

Second, courts were traditionally limited in the character of the relief they could provide. In general, courts acted only to offer relief or assistance to individuals and not to broad social classes, again inhibiting the formation of alliances between the courts and important social forces. Third, courts lacked enforcement powers of their own and were compelled to rely on executive or state agencies to ensure compliance with their edicts. If the executive or state agencies were unwilling to assist the courts, judicial enactments could go unheeded, as when President Andrew Jackson declined to enforce Chief Justice John Marshall's 1832 order to the state of Georgia to release two missionaries it had arrested on Cherokee lands. Marshall asserted that the state had no right to enter the Cherokee lands without their assent.[31] Jackson is reputed to have said, "John Marshall has made his decision, now let him enforce it."

Fourth, federal judges are, of course, appointed by the president (with the consent of the Senate). As a result, the president and Congress can shape the composition of the federal courts and ultimately, perhaps, the character of judicial decisions. Finally, Congress has the power to change both the size and jurisdiction of the Supreme Court and other federal courts. In many areas, federal courts obtain their jurisdiction not from the Constitution but from congressional statutes. On a number of occasions, Congress has threatened to take matters out of the Court's hands when it was unhappy with the Court's policies.[32] For example, in 1996 Congress enacted several pieces of legislation designed to curb the jurisdiction of the federal courts. One of these laws was the Prison Litigation Reform Act, which limits the ability of federal judges to issue "consent decrees" under which the judges could take control of state prison systems. Another jurisdictional curb was included in the Immigration Reform Act, which prohibited the federal courts from

Class action suits have both strengthened the role of courts in the political process and increased the access that individuals seeking relief have to the political system. For example, in 1983 a group of Vietnam veterans received standing as a class to sue the manufacturers of Agent Orange. In this photo, Vietnam veteran James Burdge showed a rash on his arms that he claimed was caused by exposure to Agent Orange. The chemical companies that made the herbicide and veterans who blamed illnesses on exposure to it agreed to an out-of-court settlement of $250 million.

Likewise, in 1997 the United Farm Workers, co-founded by Dolores Huerta (above left), filed a federal class action lawsuit alleging that about five hundred workers, including Valentin Leon (above right), were forced to work without pay and consequently lost wages estimated at $750,000.

hearing class action suits against Immigration and Naturalization Service deportation orders. As to the size of the Court, on one memorable occasion, presidential and congressional threats to expand the size of the Supreme Court—Franklin Roosevelt's "court packing" plan—encouraged the justices to drop their opposition to New Deal programs. It might be argued that President Bush's 2001 directive ordering that some accused terrorists be tried in military tribunals rather than in the civil courts represents an effort by the executive branch to limit the jurisdiction of the federal courts. At the time of writing, however, it was not yet clear how military tribunals would function or what relationship they would actually have to the federal court system. The only accused terrorists actually brought to trial, as of June 2002, were brought before federal judges—not military courts.

As a result of these five limitations on judicial power, through much of their history the chief function of the federal courts was to provide judicial support for executive agencies and to legitimate acts of Congress by declaring them to be consistent with constitutional principles. Only on rare occasions have the federal courts actually dared to challenge Congress or the executive branch.[33]

TWO JUDICIAL REVOLUTIONS

Since the Second World War, however, the role of the federal judiciary has been strengthened and expanded. There have actually been two judicial revolutions in

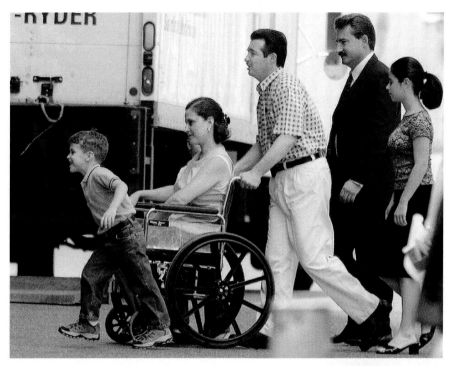

In 2001, the Bridgestone/ Firestone company was at the center of a class action suit involving people who had suffered injuries in accidents caused by faulty tires, such as the Rodriguez family of McAllen, Texas, pictured here.

In 2002, African American groups filed a federal class action suit seeking reparations from corporations that benefited from the slave trade.

the United States since World War II. The first and most visible of these was the substantive revolution in judicial policy. As we saw earlier in this chapter and in Chapters 4 and 5, in policy areas, including school desegregation, legislative apportionment, and criminal procedure, as well as obscenity, abortion, and voting rights, the Supreme Court was at the forefront of a series of sweeping changes in the role of the U.S. government, and ultimately, in the character of American society.[34]

But at the same time that the courts were introducing important policy innovations, they were also bringing about a second, less visible revolution. During the 1960s and 1970s, the Supreme Court and other federal courts instituted a series of changes in judicial procedures that fundamentally expanded the power of the courts in the United States. First, the federal courts liberalized the concept of standing to permit almost any group that seeks to challenge the actions of an administrative agency to bring its case before the federal bench. In 1971, for example, the Supreme Court ruled that public interest groups could use the National Environmental Policy Act to challenge the actions of federal agencies by claiming that the agencies' activities might have adverse environmental consequences.[35]

Congress helped to make it even easier for groups dissatisfied with government policies to bring their cases to the courts by adopting Section 1983 of the U.S. Code, which permits the practice of "fee shifting"—that is, allowing citizens

> **How have the role and power of the federal courts been transformed over the last fifty years?**

who successfully bring a suit against a public official for violating their constitutional rights to collect their attorneys' fees and costs from the government. Thus, Section 1983 encourages individuals and groups to bring their problems to the courts rather than to Congress or the executive branch. These changes have given the courts a far greater role in the administrative process than ever before. Many federal judges are concerned that federal legislation in areas such as health care reform would create new rights and entitlements that would give rise to a deluge of court cases. "Any time you create a new right, you create a host of disputes and claims," warned Barbara Rothstein, chief judge of the federal district court in Seattle, Washington.[36]

Second, the federal courts broadened the scope of relief to permit themselves to act on behalf of broad categories or classes of persons in "class action" cases, rather than just on behalf of individuals.[37] A **class action suit** is a procedural device that permits large numbers of persons with common interests to join together under a representative party to bring or defend a lawsuit. One example of a class action suit is the case of *In re Agent Orange Product Liability Litigation,* in which a federal judge in New York certified Vietnam War veterans as a class with standing to sue a manufacturer of herbicides for damages allegedly incurred from exposure to the defendant's product while in Vietnam.[38] The class potentially numbered in the tens of thousands.

Third, the federal courts began to employ so-called structural remedies, in effect retaining jurisdiction of cases until the court's mandate had actually been implemented to its satisfaction.[39] The best known of these instances was federal judge W. Arthur Garrity's effort to operate the Boston school system from his bench in order to ensure its desegregation. Between 1974 and 1985, Judge Garrity issued fourteen decisions relating to different aspects of the Boston school desegregation plan that had been developed under his authority and put into effect under his supervision.[40] In another recent case, federal judge Leonard B. Sand imposed fines that would have forced the city of Yonkers, New York, into bankruptcy if it had refused to accept his plan to build public housing in white neighborhoods. After several days of fines, the city gave in to the judge's ruling.

Through these three judicial mechanisms, the federal courts paved the way for an unprecedented expansion of national judicial power. In essence, liberalization of the rules of standing and expansion of the scope of judicial relief drew the federal courts into linkages with important social interests and classes, while the introduction of structural remedies enhanced the courts' ability to serve these constituencies. Thus, during the 1960s and 1970s, the power of the federal courts expanded in the same way the power of the executive expanded during the 1930s—through links with constituencies, such as civil rights, consumer, environmental, and feminist groups, that staunchly defended the Supreme Court in its battles with Congress, the executive, and other interest groups.

THE JUDICIARY: LIBERTY AND DEMOCRACY

In the original conception of the framers, the judiciary was to be the institution that would protect individual liberty from the government. As we saw in Chapter 2, the framers believed that in a democracy the great danger was what they termed "tyranny of the majority"—the possibility that a popular majority, "united or

class action suit a legal action by which a group or class of individuals with common interests can file a suit on behalf of everyone who shares that interest

actuated by some common impulse or passion," would "trample on the rules of justice."[41] The framers hoped that the courts would protect liberty from the potential excesses of democracy. And for most of American history, this was precisely the role played by the federal courts. The courts' most important decisions were those that protected the freedoms—to speak, worship, publish, vote, and attend school—of groups and individuals whose political views, religious beliefs, or racial or ethnic backgrounds made them unpopular.

In recent years, however, the courts have been changing their role in the political process. Rather than serving simply as a bastion of individual liberty against the excessive power of the majority, the judiciary has tried to play an active role in helping groups and forces in American society bring about social and political change in the fight for equality. In a sense, the judiciary has entered the political process and has begun to behave more like the democratic institutions whose sometimes misdirected impulses toward tyranny the courts were supposed to keep in check. This change poses a basic dilemma for students of American government. If the courts have become simply one more part of the democratic political process, then who is left to protect the liberty of individuals?

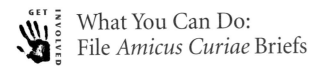

GET INVOLVED

What You Can Do:
File *Amicus Curiae* Briefs

The framers of the Constitution deliberately designed the judiciary to be independent of the ebb and flow of public sentiment. For this reason, federal judges are appointed for life. In many states, judges are appointed or elected for long terms. Citizen participation in the judicial process is, by design, limited.

One way, however, in which citizens can participate in the judicial process is by filing *amicus curiae* briefs. Although *amicus curiae* is translated as "friend of the court," it is better understood to mean an "adjunct adversary" permitted to intervene on behalf of one side or the other in which an important issue, usually constitutional in nature, is involved.

The *amicus curiae* brief has been quite effectively employed by African Americans pursuing civil rights cases. This was of particular importance in the earliest cases, beginning with *Shelley v. Kraemer* in 1948 and culminating with *Brown v. Board of Education* in 1954.[42] The NAACP and related organizations continue to maintain an interest in this method of interest group activity along with their continued efforts to influence Congress. In the past two decades, these "outside" interest groups have been joined by a very important "inside" interest group as an *amicus curiae*, the Congressional Black Caucus (CBC). This is an important caucus in the U.S. Congress, made up of the African American members of Congress (mostly from the Democratic Party). Their primary mission, of course, is to advance the interests of African Americans and other minorities in civil rights legislation. But since there has been little new legislative activity, the CBC has found itself concentrating more on the courts in order to advance its agenda of implementing existing civil rights legislation. Since the passage of the 1982 amendments to the 1964 Civil Rights Act, race has become the most important consideration in drawing voting districts following each decennial census. Drawing the district so as to guarantee that some will elect blacks to send to Congress—a form of "benign gerrymandering" (see Chapter 10)—was at first approved but then came under considerable scrutiny in the federal court system. The Justice Department under presidents Reagan and Bush opposed such districts and took their opposition to the judiciary. Former attorney general Janet Reno defended the so-called majority-minority districts. Both sides went before the Supreme Court accompanied by *amicus curiae* briefs written and promoted by the CBC. Thus, what had been a purely congressional organization became an important interest group directly representing the African American community and other minorities in court.[43]

The *amicus curiae* device is used by groups other than civil rights interests. In fact, a large number of such efforts were made in abortion litigation. Demands for the reversal of *Roe v. Wade* and *Webster v. Reproductive Health Services* included a cast of thousands. Although the Supreme Court receives thousands of letters a day from citizens, the volume increased dramatically during the litigation over *Webster;* on one day in April, the Court's mailroom received 46,000 letters on both sides of the abortion issue. Groups on both sides came forward in greater numbers than ever, and seventy-eight *amicus* briefs were filed, representing the interests of thousands of individuals and over 400 organizations. This was the largest number of *amicus* briefs ever filed on a single case.[44]

No one can say precisely when justice has been done. But we can say that when the voice of the ordinary citizen is heard—and heeded—then we have moved much closer to the ideal of justice.

Summary

Millions of cases come to trial every year in the United States. The great majority—nearly 99 percent—are tried in state and local courts. The types of law are civil law, criminal law, and public law.

Three kinds of cases fall under federal jurisdiction: (1) civil cases involving citizens from different states, (2) civil cases where a federal agency is seeking to enforce federal laws that provide for civil penalties, and (3) cases involving federal criminal statutes or where state criminal cases have been made issues of public law. Judicial power extends only to cases and controversies. Litigants must have standing to sue, and courts neither hand down opinions on hypothetical issues nor take the initiative.

Each district court is in one of the twelve appellate districts, called circuits, presided over by a court of appeals. Appellate courts admit no new evidence; their rulings are based solely on the records of the court proceedings or agency hearings that led to the original decision. Appeals court rulings are final unless the Supreme Court chooses to review them. The Supreme Court has some original jurisdiction, but its major job is to review lower court decisions involving substantial issues of public law.

Federal judges are appointed by the president, subject to confirmation by the Senate. Presidents generally attempt to select judges whose political philosophy is similar to their own. Over time, presidents have been able to exert a great deal of influence over the federal courts through their appointments.

There is no explicit constitutional authority for the Supreme Court to review acts of Congress. Nevertheless, the 1803 case of *Marbury v. Madison* established the

Court's right to review congressional acts. The supremacy clause of Article VI and the Judiciary Act of 1789 give the Court the power to review state constitutions and laws.

Both appellate and Supreme Court decisions, including the decision not to review a case, make law. The impact of such law usually favors the status quo. Yet, many revolutionary changes in the law have come about through appellate court and Supreme Court rulings—in the criminal process, in apportionment, and in civil rights. Judge-made law is like a statute in that it articulates the law as it relates to future controversies. It differs from a statute in that it is intended to guide judges rather than the citizenry in general.

Most cases reach the Supreme Court through a writ of *certiorari* or a writ of *habeas corpus*. Once the Court has accepted a case, attorneys for both sides prepare briefs and seek *amicus curiae* briefs from sympathetic groups. Cases are presented to the Court in oral argument, are discussed by the justices during the Court's conference, and are decided by a majority vote of the justices. The Court's opinion is written by a member of the majority. Members of the minority may write dissenting opinions, while other members of the majority may write concurring opinions.

The influence of any individual member of the Supreme Court is limited. Writing the majority opinion for a case is an opportunity for a justice to influence the judiciary. But the need to frame an opinion in such a way as to develop majority support on the Court may limit such opportunities. Dissenting opinions can have more impact than the majority opinion; they stimulate a continued flow of cases around an issue. The solicitor general is the most important single influence outside the Court itself because he or she controls the flow of cases brought by the Justice Department and also shapes the argument in those cases. But the flow of cases is a force in itself, which the Department of Justice cannot entirely control. Social problems give rise to similar cases that ultimately must be adjudicated and appealed. Some interest groups try to develop such case patterns as a means of gaining power through the courts.

In recent years, the importance of the federal judiciary—the Supreme Court in particular—has increased substantially as the courts have developed new tools of judicial power and forged alliances with important forces in American society.

For Further Reading

Abraham, Henry. *The Judicial Process*. 6th ed. New York: Oxford University Press, 1993.

Bryner, Gary, and Dennis L. Thompson. *The Constitution and the Regulation of Society*. Provo, UT: Brigham Young University, 1988.

Davis, Sue. *Justice Rehnquist and the Constitution*. Princeton: Princeton University Press, 1989.

Graber, Mark A. *Transforming Free Speech: The Ambiguous Legacy of Civil Libertarianism*. Berkeley: University of California Press, 1991.

Kahn, Ronald. *The Supreme Court and Constitutional Theory, 1953–1993*. Lawrence: University Press of Kansas, 1994.

McCann, Michael W. *Rights at Work*. Chicago: University of Chicago Press, 1994.

Mezey, Susan G. *No Longer Disabled: The Federal Courts and the Politics of Social Security Disability*. New York: Greenwood, 1988.

O'Brien, David M. *Storm Center: The Supreme Court in American Politics*. 5th ed. New York: Norton, 2000.

Rosenberg, Gerald. *The Hollow Hope: Can Courts Bring about Social Change?* Chicago: University of Chicago Press, 1991.

Rubin, Eva. *Abortion, Politics and the Courts*. Westport, CT: Greenwood Press, 1982.

Silverstein, Mark. *Judicious Choices: The New Politics of Supreme Court Confirmations*. New York: Norton, 1994.

Study Outline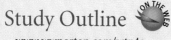

www.wwnorton.com/wtp4e

The Legal System

1. Court cases in the United States proceed under three categories of law: criminal, civil, and public.
2. In the area of criminal law, either a state government or the federal government is the plaintiff who alleges that someone has committed a crime.
3. Civil cases are those between individuals or between individuals and the government in which no criminal violation is charged. In deciding these cases, courts apply statutes and legal precedent.
4. Public law involves questions of whether the government has the constitutional or statutory authority to take action.
5. By far, most cases are heard by state courts.
6. Cases are heard in federal courts if the U.S. government is a party in the case or if the case involves federal statutes, treaties with other nations, or the U.S. Constitution.
7. Although the federal courts hear only a fraction of all the cases decided every year in the United States, federal court decisions are extremely important.

Federal Jurisdiction

1. The eighty-nine federal district courts are trial courts of original jurisdiction and their cases are, in form, indistinguishable from cases in the state trial courts.
2. The twelve U.S. courts of appeals review and render decisions in approximately 10 percent of all lower-court and agency cases.
3. Federal judges are appointed by the president and confirmed by a majority vote of the full Senate.
4. The Supreme Court is the highest court in the country and has the power and the obligation to review any lower court decision involving a substantial issue of public law, state legislation, or act of Congress.

5. The Constitution does not specify the number of justices that should sit on the Supreme Court, although since 1869 there have been nine—one chief justice and eight associate justices.
6. The solicitor general can influence the Court by screening cases before they reach the Supreme Court, submitting *amicus* briefs, and shaping the arguments used before the Court.

The Power of the Supreme Court: Judicial Review

1. The Supreme Court's power to review acts of Congress, although accepted as natural and rarely challenged, is not specifically granted by the Constitution.
2. The Supreme Court's power to review state action or legislation derives from the Constitution's supremacy clause, although it is neither granted specifically by the Constitution nor inherent in the federal system.
3. Appeals of lower court decisions can reach the Supreme Court in one of two ways: through a writ of *certiorari,* or, in the case of convicted state prisoners, through a writ of *habeas corpus.*
4. Over the years, courts have developed specific rules that govern which cases within their jurisdiction they hear. These rules of access can be broken down into three categories: case or controversy, standing, and mootness.
5. Groups and forces in society attempt to influence justices' rulings on particular issues.

6. After filing written arguments, or briefs, attorneys present oral argument to the Supreme Court. After oral argument, the justices discuss the case and vote on a final decision.
7. The Supreme Court always explains its decisions in terms of law and precedent.
8. Despite the rule of precedent, the Court often reshapes law. Such changes in the interpretation of law can be explained, in part, by changes in the judicial philosophy of activism versus restraint and by changes in political ideology.

Judicial Power and Politics

1. For much of American history, the power of the federal courts was subject to five limitations: standing, the limited relief courts could provide, the lack of enforcement powers, political appointment, and the power of Congress to change the size and jurisdiction of federal courts.
2. The role of the federal judiciary has been strengthened since World War II by two judicial revolutions. The first revolution was a substantive revolution in several policy areas. The second revolution involved changes in judicial procedures that lessened traditional limitations on the courts.

Practice Quiz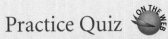

www.wwnorton.com/wtp4e

1. Which of the following is a brief submitted to the Supreme Court by someone other than one of the parties in the case?
   a) *amicus curiae*
   b) *habeas corpus*
   c) solicitor general
   d) *ex post* brief

2. By what term is the practice of the courts to uphold precedent known?
   a) *certiorari*
   b) *stare decisis*
   c) rule of four
   d) senatorial courtesy

3. Which government official is responsible for arguing the federal government's position in cases before the Supreme Court?
   a) the vice president
   b) the attorney general
   c) the U.S. district attorney
   d) the solicitor general

4. Which of the following helps to explain the expanded power of the judiciary since World War II?
   a) changes in judicial procedure
   b) changes in judicial policy areas
   c) Neither a nor b is correct.
   d) Both a and b are correct.

5. What is the name for the body of law that involves disputes between private parties?
   a) civil law
   b) privacy law
   c) household law
   d) common law

6. Under what authority is the number of Supreme Court justices decided?
   a) the president
   b) the chief justice
   c) Congress
   d) the Constitution

7. Which of the following does not influence the flow of cases heard by the Supreme Court?
   a) the Supreme Court itself
   b) the solicitor general
   c) the attorney general
   d) the FBI

8. Which of the following cases involved the "right to privacy"?
   a) *Griswold v. Connecticut*
   b) *Brown v. Board of Education*
   c) *Schneckloth v. Bustamante*
   d) *Marbury v. Madison*

9. Which of the following Supreme Court cases from the 1960s involved the rights of criminal suspects?
   a) *Gideon v. Wainwright*
   b) *Miranda v. Arizona*
   c) *Escobedo v. Illinois*
   d) all of the above

10. Where do most trials in America take place?
    a) state and local courts
    b) appellate courts
    c) federal courts
    d) the Supreme Court

Critical Thinking Questions

www.wwnorton.com/wtp4e

1. Judicial philosophies of activism and restraint are often confused with the political ideologies of liberalism and conservatism in the courts. What do you think the roots of this confusion are? To what extent is the common understanding correct? To what extent is it incorrect? Are there ways in which conservatives have been or could be activists in the courts? Are there ways in which liberals have exercised or could exercise judicial restraint?

2. In many ways, courts are expected to be apolitical institutions of government. In what ways are courts, judges, and justices shielded from politics and political pressure? In what ways are they vulnerable to political pressure? Are the courts an appropriate place for politics? What is the danger of having too much or too little political accountability in judicial decision making?

3. Are the federal courts imperial, or are they merely handmaidens to the elective branches of government? The federal judiciary has a history of approving executive and legislative restrictions on civil liberties during wars and other threats to national security. In the years following *Roe v. Wade*, which voided state laws prohibiting abortion, the Supreme Court has approved almost all efforts by states to restrict abortion to such an extent that it is tantamount to prohibition. The present Supreme Court has approved of almost all efforts by state governments to expand their power over accused persons, despite 1960s cases protecting them. In what respects does the federal judiciary still play any sort of "checks and balances" role?

Key Terms

www.wwnorton.com/wtp4e

amicus curiae (p. 613)
appellate court (p. 596)
briefs (p. 615)
chief justice (p. 599)
civil law (p. 595)
class action suit (p. 628)
criminal law (p. 595)
defendant (p. 595)
dissenting opinion (p. 617)

due process of law (p. 598)
judicial activism (p. 620)
judicial restraint (p. 620)
judicial review (p. 604)
jurisdiction (p. 597)
Miranda rule (p. 608)
mootness (p. 610)
opinion (p. 617)
oral argument (p. 616)
original jurisdiction (p. 598)
per curiam (p. 613)
plaintiff (p. 595)
plea bargains (p. 596)

precedents (p. 595)
public law (p. 596)
senatorial courtesy (p. 600)
solicitor general (p. 612)
standing (p. 610)
stare decisis (p. 596)
supremacy clause (p. 605)
supreme court (p. 596)
trial court (p. 596)
Uniform Commercial Code (p. 597)
writ of *certiorari* (p. 611)
writ of *habeas corpus* (p. 611)

Part IV

POLICY

16 GOVERNMENT AND THE ECONOMY

☆ **Why Is Government Involved in the Economy?**
What are the basic principles behind government involvement in the economy? What basic economic roles does government serve?

☆ **Should Government Be Involved in the Economy?**
What are the main arguments in the debate over the proper role of the government in the economy?

☆ **What Are the Goals of Economic Policy?**
What are government leaders trying to achieve by passing specific economic policies?

☆ **What Are the Tools of Economic Policy?**
How can we classify the broad set of tools used by the government to accomplish its economic policy goals? More specifically, what are these tools called?

☆ **The Politics of Economic Policy Making**
How do political leaders disagree about what the priorities of economic policy should be? What groups have the most influence on economic policy making?
How does the debate over economic policy reflect the broader debate over American political values?

JUST TWO WEEKS AFTER the September 11 attacks, Congress enacted a $15 billion financial package designed to prop up the airline industry. Already hurting from a weak economy, the airlines faced a grim future after September 11. With the nation's air fleet entirely grounded for three days after the attacks and predictions of sharply reduced business in the weeks and months to come, multiple bankruptcies loomed on the horizon. Congress's swift and nearly unanimous decision to provide assistance underscored the importance of the airline industry to the American economy. It also reflected the widely shared expectation that the federal government would act to address so grave an economic problem.

The airline industry bailout package and the accompanying air safety measures revealed the many purposes that drive government involvement in the economy. First and foremost is the goal of ensuring a healthy economy. As they debated the legislation, many members of Congress pointed to the strategic importance of the airlines to the entire economy. Government also routinely intervenes in the economy to protect individual welfare and promote the public good. Air safety measures, which included posting National Guardsmen in airports in the months after the attacks and the subsequent federal takeover of airport security, were the key measures designed to achieve these goals. Such government action is critical because heightened security requires expensive equipment, personnel training, and safety procedures that the airlines had avoided implementing due to cost considerations. After September 11, critics of the air security system charged that industry pressure to reduce costs had created lax security that allowed the attacks to occur in the first place.[1] A final objective of government economic policy is to regulate competition. In 1979, the government deregulated the airline industry, removing federal control over ticket prices and airline routes. The results benefited many consumers as the increased competition produced lower fares (and a less desirable outcome—more cramped seats). Even in the era of deregulation, however, the federal government continued to subsidize and regulate airline activity in order to ensure service to small or remote places. The post–September 11 airline bailout package included special provisions to ensure ongoing service to these less profitable routes.

Government involvement in the economy is now routine and widespread, touching practically every aspect of economic life. Nonetheless, specific decisions about government action in the economy often provoke heated controversy over who benefits (and who doesn't benefit) from government activity. The airline bailout package was no exception. Despite strong support for the measure, there was considerable dissatisfaction among some Democrats, who wanted the package to include specific provisions to help the thousands of laid-off airline workers. The package ensured that airline executives could continue to receive salaries up to $300,000 but did nothing to assist workers. As one frustrated Democrat shouted during the deliberations in the House of Representatives, "Why in this chamber do the big dogs always eat first?"[2] In addition to these divisions within the airline industry, representatives from other industries hard hit by the terrorist attacks, including travel agents, restaurants, hotels, and the insurance industry descended on Washington to lobby for special assistance. As Congress considered (and largely rejected) these claimants, it was effectively drawing a line between policies that would serve the larger public interest and policies that would benefit only small segments of the economy. ∎

THE job of this chapter and the succeeding two chapters is to step beyond the politics and the institutions to look at the purposes of government—the public policies. **Public policy** can be defined simply as an officially expressed purpose or goal backed by a sanction (a reward or a punishment). Public policy can be embodied in a law, a rule, a regulation, or an order. This chapter will focus on policies toward the economy. Chapter 17 will cover social and welfare policies. Chapter 18 will concentrate on foreign policy and international affairs.

public policy a law, rule, statute, or edict that expresses the government's goals and provides for rewards and punishments to promote their attainment

- **In this chapter, we will first look at the reasons why government is involved in the economy.** We will see that there are several basic economic roles that government serves, such as managing the economy, protecting the welfare and property of individuals, regulating competition, and providing public goods.

- **Next, we will examine the most influential theories in the debate over the proper role of government in the economy.** These theories include the laissez-faire, Keynesian, and monetarist approaches.

- **We then turn to the goals of economic policy.** These include promoting a strong and stable economy, encouraging business development, promoting international trade, regulating industrial relations, protecting the environment, and protecting consumers.

- **We will then classify and review the tools of economic policy.** Our discussion will focus on four major categories: monetary policies, fiscal policies, regulatory policies, and subsidies and contracting.

- **The chapter then assesses the politics of economic policy making.** We will look at the debate among political leaders over the priorities of economic policy and the role that interest groups play in that debate. We will also examine whether economic policies serve special interests or the public interest.

- **We will conclude by looking at how citizens can evaluate how economic policies affect them.**

Why Is Government Involved in the Economy?

At the most basic level, government makes it possible for the economy to function efficiently by setting the rules for economic exchange and punishing those who violate the rules. Among the most important rules for the economy are those that define property rights, contracts, and standards for goods. This kind of government rule-making allows markets to expand by making it easier for people who do not know one another to engage in economic transactions. They no longer have to rely only on personal trust to do business. Likewise, government helps markets expand by creating money and standing behind its value. Money allows diverse goods to be traded and greatly simplifies economic transactions. The importance of government to basic market transactions is evident in periods when government authority is very weak. Governments that are on the losing side of wars, for example, are often so weak that they cannot enforce the basic rules needed for markets to function. In these settings, markets often break down, money loses its value, and economies contract as the basic conditions for doing business disappear.

> **What are the basic principles behind government involvement in the economy? What basic economic roles does government serve?**

Government involvement in the economy now extends far beyond these basic market-creating functions. As we shall see in this section, government has become involved in many aspects of the economy in order to promote the public well-being. Of course, there is often vigorous disagreement about the extent to which government should intervene in the economy to promote the public welfare. In addition, beliefs about which forms of government intervention in the economy are most necessary and most effective have changed over time. Nonetheless, when government seeks to influence the economy, it does so in order to make the economy better serve the needs of society.

MANAGING THE ECONOMY

Until 1929, most Americans believed that the government had little role to play in managing the economy. The world was guided by the theory that the economy, if left to its own devices, would produce full employment and maximum production. This traditional view of the relationship between government and the economy crumbled in 1929 before the stark reality of the Great Depression of 1929–33. Some misfortune befell nearly everyone. Around 20 percent of the workforce became unemployed, and few of these individuals had any monetary resources or the old family farm to fall back upon. Banks failed, wiping out the savings of millions who had been prudent enough or fortunate enough to have any. Thousands of businesses failed, throwing middle-class Americans onto the bread lines alongside unemployed laborers and dispossessed farmers. The Great Depression had finally proven to Americans that imperfections in the economic system could exist.

Demands grew for the federal government to act. In Congress, some Democrats proposed that the federal government finance public works to aid the economy and put people back to work. Other members introduced legislation to provide federal grants to the states to assist their relief efforts.

When President Franklin D. Roosevelt took office in 1933, he energetically threw the federal government into the business of fighting the Depression. He proposed a variety of temporary measures to provide federal relief and work programs. Most of the programs he proposed were to be financed by the federal government but administered by the states. In addition to these temporary measures, Roosevelt presided over the creation of several important federal programs designed to provide future economic security for Americans. Since that time, the government has been instrumental in ensuring that the economy will never again collapse as it did during the Depression.

The experience of the 1930s transformed public expectations about federal government involvement in the economy. Since that time, the public has held the government—and the president in particular—responsible for ensuring a healthy economy. Presidents who preside over periods of economic downturn are generally punished by the electorate. In 1992, economic recession and relatively high levels of unemployment greatly improved the challenger Bill Clinton's presidential prospects, even though he was not widely known when he started campaigning. Many other potential Democratic candidates who were more well-known had decided not to run because the incumbent, President George H. W. Bush, was so popular in the wake of the 1990 Gulf War. The sagging economy, however, quickly eroded Bush's popularity. Clinton's campaign took as its central theme the slogan,

"It's the economy, stupid." This emphasis on the economy is widely credited as the strategy that got Clinton elected in 1992. The booming economy of the late 1990s also helped Clinton. Even though he lost much personal popularity after the Monica Lewinsky scandal, Americans continued to give his administration very high approval ratings because the economy was so vibrant.

PROTECTING THE WELFARE AND PROPERTY OF INDIVIDUALS

One of the central reasons for government involvement in the economy is to protect the welfare and property of individuals and businesses. Because the threats to welfare and property change as the economy grows and new technologies emerge, government actions are constantly being updated and adapted to meet new conditions.

Maintenance of law and order is one of the most important ways that government can protect welfare and property. The federal government has also passed laws designed to protect individuals and businesses in economic transactions. Federal racketeering laws, for example, aim to end criminal efforts to control businesses through such illegal means as extortion and kickbacks. Federal laws also protect consumers from fraud and deceptive advertising. The old adage *caveat emptor*—let the buyer beware—may still be good advice but government laws have helped to curb deceitful business practices and provide recourse for consumers who believe that they have been cheated.

The government's job of protecting private property has become more difficult in today's technological environment. With growth of the computer industry and the vast sums of money that have been made from software, protection of "intellectual property" has become a growing area of law in the United States. The federal government has long sought to protect property through patent law and copyrights, but new technologies have vastly increased the challenge of protecting this property. Nowhere has this been more evident than in the music industry. To record companies and musicians, copyrighted songs are property, sales of which yield handsome profits. The emergence of Napster in the mid-1990s undermined this idea by allowing users to exchange songs for free on-line. After a lengthy lawsuit, the music industry succeeded in forcing Napster to shut down in 2001. Almost immediately, however, new music exchange services, based on alternative technologies, emerged. This time not only music but films were being downloaded for free. The recording industry estimates that 3.5 billion songs are downloaded illegally each month; surveys indicate that 350,000 films are illegally downloaded each *day*. At the 2002 Grammy Awards, a record industry leader chastised those who were "stealing artists' livelihood" and called file sharing "the most insidious virus in our midst."[3] Now the motion picture industry has joined the recording industry to challenge these new services in court.

REGULATING COMPETITION

Beginning in the nineteenth century, as many sectors of the national economy flourished, certain companies began to exert monopolistic control over those sectors. Decreased competition threatened the efficiency of the market and the equitable distribution of its benefits. As a result, the national government stepped in to "level the playing field."

Another major reason why Congress began to adopt national business regulatory policies was that the regulated companies themselves felt burdened by the inconsistencies among the states. These companies often preferred a single, national regulatory authority, no matter how burdensome, because it would ensure consistency throughout the United States; the companies could thereby treat the nation as a single market.[4]

Political shifts and advances in technology make the regulation of competition a moving target. In 1913, when telephone service was becoming widely available, the federal government sanctioned AT&T's status as a publicly regulated monopoly. It

Since the 1930s, the American people have expected the government to provide emergency relief during economic downturns. During the Great Depression, the Works Progress Administration put 3.5 million unemployed people to work on a wide range of public projects, from construction to the arts.

In the summer of 2002, the stock market slide and fear of a recession led the Bush administration to pay increased attention to the economy. For example, an economic summit was held in Waco, Texas, to consider how the government could jumpstart the economy. The failure of that summit to come up with any concrete plans led to widespread criticism of President Bush, shown here speaking about the economy during a visit to the University of Alabama.

Another rationale for government involvement in economic life is its role in protecting the property of individuals and businesses. In recent years, intellectual property has been a focus of the federal government. For instance, in February 2001 a federal appeals court ruled that Napster violated copyright law by allowing Internet users to swap music files. Likewise, in the summer of 2002, the Peer-to-Peer Piracy Prevention Act was proposed in Congress, giving media companies more power to block file sharing of copyrighted materials.

The government is also involved in the provision of public goods and the regulation of economic competition. For example, during the 1930s the federal government helped bring electricity to many rural areas. Also during the 1930s, the government forced the breakup of the large interstate electric companies that controlled more than 75 percent of the country's electric generating capacity. Since the 1990s, there have been movements toward deregulating the electric industry. Shown here is the Golden Spread Electric Cooperative in Denver City, Texas, started by residents to avoid the competition among companies that could lead to higher prices for electricity.

believed that a single company—publicly regulated—could provide the best service in this industry. By the 1980s, views about the necessity and effectiveness of such monopoly control had changed, and the federal government moved to break up AT&T and open the field to new competitors. Creating competition in the telephone industry, it was hoped, would reduce prices and make the industry more responsive to consumers. And, indeed, although consumers have many complaints about telephone companies, prices dropped dramatically as competitors arose. Today, there is considerable concern about emerging monopolies in high technology. In 1999, when the federal government declared Microsoft Corporation a monopoly, it cited the negative impact of such a monopoly on future innovation as a reason to move against the software giant.

PROVIDING PUBLIC GOODS

public goods goods that are provided by the government because they either are not supplied by the market or are not supplied in sufficient quantities

Government makes the market economy possible by providing **public goods.** This term refers to facilities the state provides, because no single participant can afford to provide those facilities itself. The provision of public goods may entail supplying the physical marketplace itself—like the commons in New England towns or the provision of an interstate highway system to stimulate the trucking industry. The provision of public goods is essential to market operation, and the manner in which the government provides those goods will affect the market's character.

In the United States, public goods related to transportation have been particularly important in promoting economic development. From the first canal systems that spread commerce into the interior of the country to the contemporary public role in supporting and regulating air transportation, government has created the conditions for reliable and efficient business activity. In some cases, government will supply a public good to stimulate the economy and then allow private companies to take over. The federal government brought electricity to rural areas in the 1930s to promote economic development, but over time the provision of electricity has been taken over by private companies. Government often supplies public goods that are too big or too risky for private actors to tackle. Major dams and hydroelectric projects are an example. By bringing water and energy to new areas, such public projects transformed the American West. After September 11, government-supplied public goods sought to enhance public security through such measures as the federal takeover of airport security, the creation of a pharmaceutical stockpile to protect against bioterrorism, and the support for research to develop vaccines to counter bioterrorism agents.

Should Government Be Involved in the Economy?

> **What are the main arguments in the debate over the proper role of the government in the economy?**

Not surprisingly, there are deep differences of opinion about whether, how much, and in what ways government should be involved in the economy. Ideas about the appropriate role for government have shifted in response to unanticipated or tenacious economic problems such as recession or inflation. Beliefs about the proper government role also vary depending on the criteria that are used to judge the success or failure of government actions in the economy. For example, many economists posit that there is a trade-off between economic efficiency and economic equality: to gain more equality, an economy has to sacrifice some efficiency. If this is so, it is a political choice whether economic efficiency is emphasized or equity is promoted as a public goal. Other economic analysts maintain that there is no such stark choice. They argue that, with the proper economic and social institutions, an economy can work toward equity and efficiency at the same time. Different theories about how the economy works envision quite distinct roles for government.

LAISSEZ-FAIRE

Ideas that envision only a minimal role for government in the economy are often called **laissez-faire capitalism** (literally, "let to make") approaches. Proponents of laissez-faire argue that the economy will flourish if the government leaves it alone. The argument for laissez-faire was first elaborated in the late 1700s by the great Scottish economist Adam Smith. Smith believed that most government involvement in the economy—such as the government-authorized monopolies that dominated trade in his day—depressed economic growth. Instead, he argued that competition among free enterprises would unleash economic energy, fostering growth and innovation. In his view, the self-seeking behavior of individuals, when subject to the discipline of market competition, would create products that consumers want at the best possible price. Smith praised "the invisible hand" of the market, by which he meant that millions of individual economic transactions together create a greater good—far better than could be created by the government. Smith believed that the government role should be restricted to national defense, establishing law and order (including the protection of private property), and providing basic public goods (such as roads) that facilitate commerce.

> **laissez-faire capitalism** an economic system in which the means of production and distribution are privately owned and operated for profit with minimal or no government interference

Laissez-faire ideas were especially influential in the years before the 1930s, when the prolonged worldwide economic depression opened the door to new thinking about the role of government. After that time advocates of laissez-faire lost influence, although the hands-off approach to the economy continued to have articulate defenders. In the 1970s, University of Chicago economist Robert Lucas gave new force to laissez-faire ideas with his "rational expectations theory." Lucas argued that government intervention was bound to fail because people will anticipate government action and compensate for it. In this view, all of government's efforts would be undone as people adjust their actions.

Proponents of laissez-faire approaches are far more concerned about economic growth and efficiency than about economic inequality. They believe that government intervention to reduce inequality is misguided and often produces outcomes that leave everyone worse off. After decades of being marginal to public debate and policy, laissez-faire approaches gained new influence in the last two decades of the twentieth century.

KEYNESIANS

In the 1930s, the ideas of the British economist John Maynard Keynes laid the foundation for a revolution in thinking about the role of the government in the economy during periodic downturns. By pumping money into the economy, government can stimulate demand and create a virtuous cycle of increased production and jobs that will pull the economy out of recession. Governments can do this in several ways.

They can increase public spending through such measures as public works or public employment. Alternatively, governments can stimulate demand through temporary tax cuts. Tax cuts will allow workers to keep more of their earnings; their increased spending power will boost consumption and increase demand.[5]

Keynesian ideas provided an ongoing role for government in the economy; they also linked the economic well-being of workers to the health of the economy as a whole. To stimulate the economy, **Keynesianism** called for putting money into the hands of the working people, who would be most likely to spend it. This theory made Keynesians especially attentive to issues of economic equity. The theory did not call for eliminating inequality but it did suggest that great imbalances in income could lead to insufficient demand and harm the economy as a whole. Keynesians also placed a heavy emphasis on reducing unemployment.

After World War II, Keynesian ideas guided economic policy making across the industrialized world. By the 1960s, Keynesians believed they could ensure ongoing prosperity by "fine-tuning" the economy: policy makers could stimulate demand with spending or tax cuts when recession loomed and then cut back on spending or increase taxes when inflation threatened. Republican president Richard Nixon reflected the strong consensus behind Keynesian ideas when he remarked, "I am now a Keynesian."

Yet, by the time Keynesian ideas became the accepted wisdom, new economic conditions threatened their effectiveness. Many observers argued that increased international trade made Keynesian remedies less useful. Increased consumer spending power could "leak out" of the economy as workers bought goods manufactured abroad; in this case, their spending would not stimulate production at home. There is little consensus about how much increased international economic competition has weakened Keynesian tools. But in the past three decades, confidence that the government can fine-tune the economy has diminished and Keynesians lost the great influence they once had in economic policy.

MONETARISTS

Monetarists believe that the role of the government in managing the economy should be limited to regulating the supply of money. More active government management of the economy, monetarists argue, either has little effect or actually makes the economy worse. In contrast to Keynesians, monetarists do not believe that government can act quickly enough to fine-tune the economy. Instead, they maintain that government should promote economic stability by regulating the money supply. The most prominent monetarist in the United States, the economist Milton Friedman, recommended that the federal government let the growth in the money supply match the rate of economic growth. In this way, inflation could be kept low even as economic growth continued. This strict version of **monetarism** envisions a hands-off approach for the government; the theory calls for little exercise of discretion on the part of government officials. Instead, they must follow a simple rule about how much to increase the supply of money.

Monetarists are much more concerned about ensuring economic stability than with promoting equity. Their approach emphasizes the need to control inflation and devotes little attention to the problem of unemployment. Indeed they are often ready to accept higher levels of unemployment as the price for economic sta-

Keynesianism economic theory, based on the ideas of British economist John Maynard Keynes, that argues that the government can stimulate the economy by increasing public spending or by cutting taxes

monetarism economic theory that contends that the role of the government in the economy should be limited to regulating the supply of money

bility. Friedman, as the title of his most famous and popular book, *Free to Choose*, suggests, placed a premium on individual choice and individual liberty.[6] He believed that most government involvement in the economy restricted individual liberty and failed to produce any gains in individual economic welfare.

In the late 1970s, when high levels of inflation plagued the American economy, monetarists became especially influential in economic policy making. However, today it is impractical to implement a strict version of monetarism. Instead, economic policy makers have sought to manipulate interest rates to ensure a healthy and stable economy.

What Are the Goals of Economic Policy?

> **What are government leaders trying to achieve by passing specific economic policies?**

The goals of economic policy often shift as a new administration takes power in Washington, but such shifts are usually a matter of emphasis. Political leaders realize that the public expects the government to achieve multiple goals in its economic policy. Public expectations about what government economic policy can and should do have expanded over the course of our nation's history. This growth in public expectations has made economic policy more complex as government strives to achieve multiple goals, some of which may conflict with one another.

Three major goals have guided government involvement in the economy since the early years of our nation's history: promoting a strong and stable economy, encouraging business development, and regulating international trade. Over time, the federal government has taken on greater responsibility for meeting each of these goals. The Great Depression of the 1930s marked a decisive turning point. As Washington created new agencies and new measures to monitor the nation's economic health, it transformed public expectations about the federal role in the economy. The federal government assumed primary responsibility for achieving established goals and it faced heightened expectations about its ability to reach those goals. In addition, the federal government took on one important new goal, to regulate industrial relations. By the 1970s, two additional goals for national economic policy had emerged: protecting the environment and protecting consumers.

PROMOTE A STRONG AND STABLE ECONOMY

A strong and stable economy is the basic goal of all economic policy. What makes reaching this goal so difficult is that the key elements of a strong economy—economic growth, full employment, and low inflation—often appear to conflict with one another. Economic policy must manage the trade-offs among these goals. This is a complicated task because there is much disagreement about whether pursuing one of these economic goals really does mean sacrificing the others. Moreover, the trade-offs among these goals appear to change over time. The expansion of the American economy in the latter half of the 1990s defied all previous expectations about the relationship between growth, employment, and inflation. The fast pace of economic growth, combined with low inflation and very high employment, suggested that it was now possible to combine all three central goals of economic policy.[7] In 2001, an economic downturn reminded policymakers how difficult it is to sustain such high levels of growth.

Gross Domestic Product (GDP)
index of the total output of goods
and services produced in the
economy

Economic Growth   Since the 1930s, the federal government has carefully tracked national economic growth. Economic growth is measured in several different ways. The two most important measures are the Gross National Product (GNP), which is the market value of the goods and services produced in the economy, and the **Gross Domestic Product (GDP),** the same measure but excluding income from foreign investments. In the late 1990s, the American economy grew at a rate of over 4 percent a year, a rate considered high by modern standards (see Figure 16.1). However, growth dipped to 1.2 percent in 2001 as the economy struggled to emerge from recession.

The engine of American economic growth has shifted over the centuries. In the 1800s, our nation's rich endowment of natural resources was especially important in propelling growth. Manufacturing industries became the driving force of economic growth in the late nineteenth century as mass production made it possible to produce goods at a pace that was once unimaginable. In more recent times, the high technology boom fostered unanticipated and vigorous economic growth that made the United States the envy of the world. Despite these very different economic engines, the basic prerequisites of growth are similar in each case: strong investment, technological innovation, and a productive workforce. Throughout the nation's history the federal government has adopted policies to promote each of these conditions needed to sustain economic growth.

The most fundamental way that government affects investment is by promoting business, investor, and consumer confidence. When businesses fear political instability, unpredictable government action, or widespread disregard of the law,

Figure 16.1   **Changes in Real Gross Domestic Product, 1960–2001**

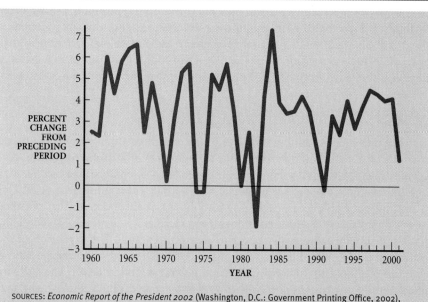

SOURCES: *Economic Report of the President 2002* (Washington, D.C.: Government Printing Office, 2002), Table B-2, p. 323; Department of Commerce, Bureau of Economic Analysis, Data from the National Income and Product Accounts, www.bea.gov/briefrm/tables/ebr1.htm#percent change (accessed June 22, 2002).

they are unlikely to invest. When consumers are insecure about the future, they are unlikely to spend. Government officials monitor surveys of business and consumer confidence as they devise economic policy. After the terrorist attacks, the federal government sought to reassure the financial markets, businesses, and consumers. Congress moved with unusual speed to enact the airline bailout discussed at the beginning of this chapter, anxious to show the world that terrorists could not stop business as usual. The Federal Reserve responded with interest-rate cuts that aimed to promote spending and investment.

Businesses also need access to new sources of capital in order to grow. The federal government promotes reliable access to new investment through its regulation of financial markets. The most important federal agency in this regard is the Securities and Exchange Commission (SEC), created after the stock market crash of 1929. The SEC requires companies to disclose information about the stocks and bonds they are selling, inform buyers of the investment risks, and protect investors against fraud. In this way, the SEC helps to maintain investor confidence and a strong supply of capital for American business. After the collapse of Enron, once the seventh largest corporation in America, many members of Congress urged greater enforcement powers for the SEC.

Public investment is another important source of growth in the American economy. Such investment may be expressly designed to promote growth in accordance with the Keynesian principles outlined earlier in this chapter. In the 1930s and again in the late 1970s, the federal government promoted public investment as a means to spark economic growth. Other kinds of public investment promote growth as a byproduct of other more central objectives. For example, after September 11, the federal government promised New York City $20 billion to clean up the site of the terrorist attack and help rebuild lower Manhattan.

The second important condition for economic growth is innovation. The federal government has sought to support innovation in a variety of ways. One of the most important is through the National Science Foundation. Created in 1950, the National Science Foundation supports basic research across a range of scientific fields. The aim is to advance fundamental knowledge that may be useful in many different applications.[8] Federal government sponsorship of health research began in the late 1800s. Today, the National Institutes of Health (NIH) conduct basic and applied research in biomedicine. The Human Genome project—the effort to map the basic genetic structure of human life—was initiated by government researchers and only later taken up by private corporations. Recently, the NIH has taken the lead in basic research to counter bioterrorism. Its efforts to understand the biology of various infectious agents and to develop vaccines are expected to produce important new knowledge about the human immune system. Research sponsored by the military has long been an important source of innovation for the American economy. Such key twentieth-century innovations as radar and nuclear power stemmed from military research. And as we saw in Chapter 14, military research also created the technology for the twenty-first century with ARPANET, the precursor of the Internet.

A third fundamental condition for economic growth is a sufficient and productive workforce. Federal immigration policy has played a key role in ensuring an adequate supply of labor throughout American history. Immigration laws routinely give special priority to workers who have skills that are in demand among

American employers. Immigrants with nursing degrees, for example, have long received special priority. In recent years, Silicon Valley employers have lobbied hard to open immigration quotas to allow more highly skilled workers in high-tech fields, such as computer programming, to work in the United States.

Today, a productive workforce is a highly educated workforce. Education, as we will see in Chapter 17, is primarily the responsibility of state and local governments. The federal government, however, supports the development of a productive workforce with a variety of programs to support higher education, such as educational grants, tax breaks, and loans. The federal government also sponsors a limited array of job-training programs that focus primarily on low-skilled workers. Some analysts argue that the federal government must do much more to support the development of a highly skilled workforce if the United States is to sustain economic growth in the future.

Full Employment   Before the 1930s, neither the federal nor the state governments sought to promote full employment. Unemployment was widely viewed as an unfortunate occurrence that government could do little to alter. The New Deal response to the prolonged and massive unemployment of the Great Depression changed that. The federal government put millions of people back to work on public projects sponsored by such programs as the Works Progress Administration (WPA). The bridges, walkways, and buildings they created can still be seen across the United States today. The federal government viewed these programs as temporary measures, however. As the buildup for World War II boosted the economy and unemployment melted away, the employment programs were dismantled.

The New Deal and government wartime spending, however, showed that government could help ensure full employment. Public expectations changed as well: Americans looked to the federal government to reduce unemployment after the war. Moreover, economic theory now supported their expectations. Keynes's theories that government could boost employment by stimulating demand had become very influential.

Federal policy placed the most emphasis on achieving full employment in the 1960s. Keynesian economists in the Council of Economic Advisers convinced President Kennedy to enact the first tax cut designed to stimulate the economy and promote full employment.[9] The policy was widely seen as a success and unemployment declined to a low of 3.4 percent in 1968.

Favorable economic conditions in the 1990s reduced unemployment to record lows once again. Many analysts characterized the transformation as the "new economy." They contended that the economy changed so much that the old trade-offs between inflation and unemployment ceased to exist. Even in these favorable conditions, many proponents of full employment argued that the government could do much more to promote employment. The official measure of unemployment counts only those people who are defined as "actively seeking work." It does not include those discouraged workers who have dropped out of the labor force. For this reason, some analysts argue that the real rate of unemployment is about 9 percentage points higher than official figures.[10]

inflation a consistent increase in the general level of prices

Low Inflation   During the 1970s and early 1980s, **inflation,** a consistent increase in the general level of prices, was one of America's most vexing problems. There was much disagreement over what to do about it—what public policies were most appropriate and effective. The first effort, beginning in 1971, was the adoption of strict controls over wages, prices, dividends, and rents—that is, authorizing an agency in the executive branch to place limits on what wage people could be paid for their work, what rent their real estate could bring, and what interest they could get on their money. After two years of effort, these particular policies were fairly well discredited, and the search resumed for one or more other policies to fight inflation. Since oil prices had become so clearly a major source of inflation in the late 1970s, President Carter experimented with the licensing of imports of oil from the Middle East, with tariffs and excise taxes on unusually large oil profits made by producers, and with sales taxes on gasoline at the pump to discourage all casual consumption of gasoline. President Carter also attempted to reduce consumer spending in general by raising income taxes, especially Social Security taxes on employees.

The continuing high rate of inflation paved the way to an entirely different approach by President Reagan in the early 1980s. In place of oil import licensing and selective tax increases, President Reagan proposed and got a general tax cut. The Reagan theory was that if tax cuts were deep enough and were guaranteed to endure, they would increase the "supply" of money, would change people's psychology from pessimism to optimism, and would thereby encourage individuals and corporations to invest enough and produce enough to get us out of inflation. At the same time, President Reagan supported the continuation of the high Social Security taxes enacted during the Carter administration, which probably went further than any other method to fight inflation by discouraging consumption. As we have said, inflation is caused by too many dollars chasing too few goods, bidding up prices. Any tax will take dollars out of consumption, but since the Social Security tax hits middle and lower-middle-income people the heaviest, and since these middle-income people are the heaviest consumers, such a tax reduces consumer dollars. Another policy supported by the Reagan administration was restraining the amount of credit in the economy by pushing up interest rates.

Inflation was finally reduced from its historic highs of nearly 20 percent down toward 2 and 3 percent each year. But no one is absolutely certain which policy, if any, contributed to this reduction. After all, the two-year recession of 1981–82 produced such significant increases in unemployment that consumption was cut, and any cut in consumption—whether from a tax policy or a loss of wages—will reduce prices. At the same time, the international price of oil dropped, independently of our policies. Consequently, we do not know exactly what policy to adopt the next time inflation becomes a problem. But no government will stand by and permit inflation or unemployment or global economic competition to become a problem without trying to do something about it.

PROMOTE BUSINESS DEVELOPMENT

During the nineteenth century, the national government was a promoter of markets. National roads and canals were built to tie states and regions together. National tariff policies promoted domestic markets by restricting imported goods; a tax on an import raised its price and weakened its ability to compete with similar domestic products. The national government also heavily subsidized the railroad system. Until the 1840s, railroads were thought to be of limited commercial value. But between 1850 and 1872, Congress granted over 100 million acres of public domain land to railroad interests, and state and local governments pitched in an estimated $280 million in cash and credit. Before the end of the century, 35,000 miles of track existed—almost half the world's total.

Railroads were not the only clients of federal support for the private markets. Many sectors of agriculture began receiving federal subsidies in the nineteenth century. Agriculture remains highly subsidized. In 2001, an environmental group caused a stir by putting the exact amounts of subsidies received by individual farmers on a widely publicized Web site (http://www.ewg.org/farm/). The top recipient of government aid in Texas, for example, received $1.3 million in 2001. President Bush continued the tradition of generous agricultural subsidies, approving a 2002 law that increased federal payments to farmers by 80 percent.

categorical grants congressional grants given to states and localities on the condition that expenditures be limited to a problem or group specified by the law

The national government also promotes business development indirectly through **categorical grants** (see Chapter 3), in which the national government offers grants to states on condition that the state (or local) government undertake a particular activity. Thus, in order to use motor transportation to improve national markets, a 900,000-mile national highway system was built during the 1930s, based on a formula whereby the national government would pay 50 percent of the cost if the state would provide the other 50 percent. Over twenty years, beginning in the late 1950s, the federal government constructed nearly 45,000 miles of interstate highways. This was brought about through a program whereby the national government agreed to pay 90 percent of the construction costs on the condition that each state provide 10 percent of the costs of any portion of a highway built within its boundaries.[11] The tremendous growth of highways was a major boon to the automobile and to the trucking industries.

The federal government supports specific business sectors with direct subsidies, loans, and tax breaks. In 1953, the Small Business Administration (SBA) was created to offer loans, loan guarantees, and disaster assistance to small businesses. Recognizing that such businesses often find it harder to obtain financing and to recover from unexpected events such as fires, the federal government has provided assistance where the market would not. Today, the SBA provides more than $45 billion in such assistance to small businesses.

Among the many contemporary examples of policies promoting private industry, Sematech may be the most instructive. Sematech is a nonprofit, research and development (R&D) consortium of major U.S. computer microchip manufacturers, set up in 1987 to work with government and academic institutions to reestablish U.S. leadership in semiconductor manufacturing. (The United States appeared to be in danger of losing out to the Japanese in this area in the 1980s.) The results of its research were distributed among the fourteen consortium members.[12] For nine years, industry and government together spent $1.7 billion to make the American microchip industry the leader in the world. The government contributed about half of the total expenditures. In 1997, federal funding was phased out. Industry leaders, convinced they no longer needed federal support, themselves initiated the break with government. At a critical moment, the federal government had stepped in to save the chip industry; it stepped out once that goal had been achieved.

Since September 11, the federal government has taken on a major role in promoting technological innovation. Even before the terrorist attacks, the CIA had set up its own venture-capital firm, In-Q-Tel (the "Q" stands for a character in James Bond movies), to invest in high-tech start-ups whose work could enhance intelligence efforts. With the surveillance and detection of potential terrorists now at the top of the national agenda, the Department of Defense is pouring money into high-tech firms to develop cutting-edge technologies for the war on terrorism. As one observer put it, "Silicon Valley is reinventing itself as the new headquarters for the military-technological complex."[13]

PROMOTE INTERNATIONAL TRADE

The promotion and advertising of American goods and services abroad is a long-standing goal of U.S. trade policy, and is one of the major obligations of the Department of Commerce. Yet modern trade policy involves a complex arrangement of treaties, tariffs, and other mechanisms of policy formation. The support for Sematech and the "infant" computer industry with an eye on foreign competition is an example of a type of national public policy—promoting the private economy—that goes all the way back to the Founding. For example, there exists the long-standing U.S. policy of granting **most favored nation status** to other countries—that is, the United States offers to another country the same tariff rate it already gives to its most favored trading partner, in return for trade (and sometimes other) concessions. In 1998, to avoid any suggestion that "most favored nation" implied some special relationship with an undemocratic country (China, for example), President Clinton changed the term from "most favored nation" to "normal trade relations."[14]

The most important international organization for promoting free trade is the **World Trade Organization (WTO),** which officially came into being in 1995. The WTO grew out of the **General Agreement on Tariffs and Trade (GATT).** Since World War II, GATT had brought together a wide range of nations for regular negotiations designed to reduce barriers to trade. Such barriers, many believed, had contributed to the breakdown of the world economy in the 1930s and had helped to cause World War II. The WTO has over 130 members worldwide; decisions about trade are made by the Ministerial Conference, which meets every two years. Similar policy goals are pursued in regional arrangements, such as the **North American Free Trade Agreement (NAFTA),** a trade treaty between the United States, Canada, and Mexico.

Working toward freer trade has been an important goal of each presidential administration since World War II. Yet as globalization has advanced, concerns about free trade and about the operation of the WTO, in particular, have grown. The WTO meetings held in Seattle in 1999 witnessed unprecedented protests by groups that included environmentalists and labor unions. Tens of thousands of protesters denounced the undemocratic decision-making process of the WTO, which, they charged, was dominated by the concerns of business. These critics believe that the WTO does not pay sufficient attention to the concerns of developing nations and to such issues as environmental degradation, human rights, and labor practices, including use of child labor in many countries. The Seattle meetings adjourned without reaching any agreement. When the WTO convened again in 2001, ongoing mobilization had produced an atmosphere more favorable to the

most favored nation status agreement to offer a trading partner the lowest tariff rate offered to other trading partners

World Trade Organization (WTO) international trade agency promoting free trade that grew out of the General Agreement on Tariffs and Trade

General Agreement on Tariffs and Trade (GATT) international trade organization, in existence from 1947 to 1995, that set many of the rules governing international trade

North American Free Trade Agreement (NAFTA) trade treaty between the United States, Canada, and Mexico to lower and eliminate tariffs between the three countries

Since the early nineteenth century, the government has been an important promoter of business development in the United States. Beginning around 1850, federal, state, and local governments gave railroad companies the land on which to lay tracks and financial aid to construct the railroads. Railroads also received additional land from the government that they could sell at low prices to attract settlers to build along their lines.

interests of developing countries in trade negotiations. In these meetings, the WTO ratified new guidelines to allow poor countries to override expensive patents that make desperately needed drugs unavailable to most of the developing world. Compared with GATT, which governed trade prior to 1995, the WTO appears to be less dominated by the "quad powers" of the United States, Europe, Japan, and Canada.[15] As the WTO writes the rules for globalization, its meetings will continue to draw business leaders and activists of all kinds who wish to stamp their vision on the rules that govern the global economy.

For over a half-century, the United States has led the world in supporting free trade as the best route to growth and prosperity. Yet the American government, too, has sought to protect domestic industry when it is politically necessary. President Bush, a vocal advocate of free trade, angered the rest of the world when he imposed protective tariffs on imported steel in 2002. Accused of hypocrisy and faced with retaliation from trading partners, the administration defended its actions by pointing to the damage that imports were doing to the domestic steel industry. At the same time, the president found himself arguing with domestic critics who sought to limit his authority to negotiate trade deals unless trade liberalization was accompanied by more assistance for workers dislocated by trade. American trade policy, once a relatively consensual area of policy in which decisions could be made behind closed doors, has moved out into the arena of public conflict, where it is likely to stay.

More recently, the federal government has played a major role in promoting technological innovation. For example, after September 11, the government formed In-Q-Tel in order to develop new technologies for national security. At the Federal Convention on Emerging Technologies, part of a forum on homeland security, In-Q-Tel chairman Gilman Louie discussed ways to avoid a future "digital Pearl Harbor."

REGULATE INDUSTRIAL RELATIONS

Stable relations between business and labor are important elements of a productive economy. In the latter half of the nineteenth century, strikes over low wages or working conditions became a standard feature of American economic life. In fact, the United States has one of the most violent histories of labor relations in the world. Yet for most of American history, the federal government did little to regulate relations between business and labor. Local governments and courts often weighed in on the side of business by prohibiting strikes and arresting strikers.

As the economic depression enveloped the United States in the 1930s, massive strikes for union recognition and plummeting wages prompted the federal government to take action. Congress passed the 1935 National Labor Relations Act, which set up a new framework for industrial relations. The new law created a permanent agency, the National Labor Relations Board (NLRB), charged with overseeing union elections and collective bargaining between labor and industry. The federal government weighed in further on the side of organized labor in 1938, when it passed the Fair Labor Standards Act, which created the minimum wage. Because it is not indexed to inflation, the value of the minimum wage declines if it is not raised periodically. Since 1938, conflicts over increasing the minimum wage have been a regular feature of American politics.

In the 1950s and 1960s, the federal government played an active role in industrial relations. The Department of Labor and, occasionally, even the president

The government not only promotes but also often protects particular sectors of the economy. The ailing steel industry recently sought and won protective tariffs on foreign imports. As part of his promotion of this policy, President Bush visited the U.S. Steel Irvin Works in Pittsburgh in 2001.

directly intervened in labor-management disputes to ensure peaceful industrial relations. Although Democrats were generally seen as more supportive to labor, both parties sought to achieve a balance between business and labor that would promote a strong stable economy.

President Reagan made a decisive break with this tradition of compromise in 1981, when he fired striking air traffic controllers and hired permanent replacements to take their jobs. Since that time, organized labor has grown weaker and the mechanisms of collective bargaining have become less effective. Politicians are much less likely to intervene in labor relations. Politicians do occasionally seek to protect workers in other ways. After the collapse of the Enron Corporation, for example, the president and several members of Congress proposed new laws to govern company retirement plans, called 401(k) accounts. Enron employees, whose accounts were heavily invested in company stocks, lost an estimated $1.2 billion in retirement funds. As it became apparent that the company was failing, employees were prohibited from selling their Enron stock, even as top executives were selling their own shares. Outrage over this unfairness and the fear it created for the 42 million Americans who have 401(k) accounts prompted congressional initiatives to protect employees.[16]

PROTECT THE ENVIRONMENT

In 1969, the Cayuhoga River in Cleveland, long a dumping ground for industrial waste, caught fire. Images of the burning river provided a vivid reminder that America's industrial prosperity had come at a cost to the natural environment and to the health of urban America. At the same time, a more affluent America, with more time for leisure, grew concerned about the quality of the environment and the need to preserve natural beauty. The first "Earth Day" in 1970 celebrated this new set of concerns that would become a major feature of American politics in the coming decades.[17]

A wave of new laws wrote environmental goals into policy. The 1969 National Environmental Policy Act (NEPA), the Clean Air Act Amendments of 1970, the 1972 Clean Water Act, and the 1974 Safe Drinking Water Act together established a new set of goals and procedures for protecting the environment. They are properly considered as part of economic policy because they regulate the activities of virtually every aspect of the economy. NEPA, for example, requires federal agencies to prepare an environmental impact statement for every major development project that they propose. In this way, environmental impacts routinely become factored into considerations about whether a particular project is feasible or desirable.

Environmental disasters have often served to draw attention to new environmental hazards and prompt greater federal regulation. For example, in the mid-1970s the residents of the Love Canal neighborhood in Buffalo, New York, discovered that their neighborhood had been built on a toxic waste dump. Many of the chemicals in the soil were suspected carcinogens. At federal and state cost, residents were moved to new homes. Partly as a result of this highly publicized incident, Congress passed legislation to facilitate cleanup of hazardous waste sites. Yet government action and corporate liability are often bitterly contested issues in this area. As the book and film *A Civil Action*—about toxic waste in a Massachusetts community—demonstrated, identifying the sources of toxic pollution and linking such pollution to health hazards can be very difficult.[18]

Protecting the environment presents policy makers with difficult trade-offs. Compliance with environmental regulations can be very costly. Moreover critics maintain that federal standards are sometimes too high. How clean should the air be? What is the difference between pure drinking water and safe drinking water? Who should bear the costs of providing environmental benefits? Not only do citizens, consumers, and businesses take different perspectives on these questions, the goals themselves often present a moving target. As new scientific evidence shows (or fails to find evidence for) new or suspected environmental hazards, conflicts over the proper government role emerge. The battle over the Bush administration's proposal to begin drilling for oil in Alaska's Arctic National Wildlife Refuge featured many competing arguments about the amount of oil available at the site, the impact on the environment, and the need for the oil in the future. In the end, the Democratic Senate's defeat of the proposal came down to a matter of values—and politics, as Democrats looked for popular issues on which they could challenge the president.

In the decades since environmental goals first became incorporated into public policy, presidents have placed more or less emphasis on these goals and federal agencies have experimented with different methods for promoting environmental objectives. But despite such shifts, there has never been any doubt that Americans now expect the federal government to play a leading role in preserving natural beauty and promoting a clean and healthful environment.

PROTECT CONSUMERS

A final goal of economic policy is to protect consumers. The idea that the federal government should protect consumers emerged in the first decade of the 1900s. Upton Sinclair's graphic exposé about the unsanitary practices of the meatpacking industry, *The Jungle*, published in 1906, galvanized public concern about unsanitary food processing. These concerns prompted the U.S. Department of Agriculture to inspect packing plants and the meat they produced, stamping approved meats with the now familiar "USDA" certification. Similar concern about food and drug safety led to the creation of the Food and Drug Administration in 1927.

The movement for consumer protection took off again in the 1960s. Consumer advocate Ralph Nader's 1965 book *Unsafe at Any Speed* helped spark new demands for federal action. Nader's book showed that design flaws in the Corvair, a popular car model, had caused deaths that could have been prevented. Nader's book not only led to the demise of the Corvair, it galvanized calls for more federal action to protect consumers. The first response was the 1966 National Traffic and Motor Vehicle Safety Act, which gave the Department of Transportation responsibility for ensuring vehicle safety. Federal responsibility for consumer safety expanded in 1972 when Congress created the Consumer Product Safety Commission. The Commission, which is an independent agency, informs consumers about hazards associated with products and works with industry to set product standards. In cases where safety concerns are severe, it will see that such products are recalled. Through the Consumer Product Safety Commission, the

Protecting consumers has been a central goal of economic policy since the early twentieth century. In 1906, Congress passed the New Meat Inspection Act, which required that all meat intended for interstate commerce meet federal health standards. This photo shows a Chicago slaughterhouse immediately following the passage of the act.

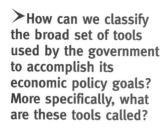

Consumer protection became an even more important focus of the federal government in the 1960s. In 1972, Congress created the Consumer Product Safety Commission. In this 1975 photo, an official from the CPSC demonstrated the potential danger of some types of baby cribs.

Department of Transportation, and the Food and Drug Administration (which regulates food, drugs, and cosmetics), the federal government continues to play an active role in protecting the public from unsafe products.

After September 11, Congress moved to enact strict legislation to protect food safety that would increase inspections of imported foods and give the government much greater authority over food manufacturers. Although food manufacturers charged that the measure would create excessive government control, Congress enacted the legislation as part of a larger bill designed to combat bioterrorism.

What Are the Tools of Economic Policy?

> **How can we classify the broad set of tools used by the government to accomplish its economic policy goals? More specifically, what are these tools called?**

The U.S. economy is no accident; it is the result of specific policies that have expanded American markets and sustained massive economic growth. The Constitution provides that Congress shall have the power

> To lay and collect Taxes, . . . to pay the Debts and provide for the common Defence and general Welfare; . . . To borrow Money; . . . To coin Money [and] regulate the Value thereof. . . .

Children's safety is one focus of the Consumer Product Safety Commission. In 2001, the government moved to force the recall of over 7 million high-velocity Daisy BB guns, alleging the air rifles can fire injury-causing pellets even when they seem to be unloaded. Becky Mahoney, whose son suffered severe brain injury when he was shot in the head with a BB gun, is shown here at a CPSC press conference.

At a Consumer Product Safety Commission press conference in 2002, the CPSC warned Americans to be careful that the use of fireworks on the Fourth of July did not result in trips to hospital emergency rooms. This photo shows the potential dangers of fireworks as the clothes of a mannequin smoke on the Washington Monument grounds during the press conference.

These clauses of Article I, Section 8, are the constitutional sources of the fiscal and monetary policies of the national government. Nothing is said, however, about *how* these powers can be used, although the way they are used shapes the economy. As it works to meet the multiple goals of economic policy outlined above, the federal government relies on a broad set of tools that has evolved over time. Let us now turn to the actual tools designed to accomplish the goals of economic policy.

MONETARY POLICIES

Monetary policies manipulate the growth of the entire economy by controlling the availability of money to banks. With a very few exceptions, banks in the United States are privately owned and locally operated. Until well into the twentieth century, banks were regulated, if at all, by state legislatures. Each bank was granted a charter, giving it permission to make loans, hold deposits, and make investments

monetary policies efforts to regulate the economy through the manipulation of the supply of money and credit. America's most powerful institution in this area of monetary policy is the Federal Reserve Board

Federal Reserve System a system of twelve Federal Reserve Banks that facilitates exchanges of cash, checks, and credit; regulates member banks; and uses monetary policies to fight inflation and deflation

within that state. Although more than 25,000 banks continue to be state-chartered banks, they are less important than they used to be in the overall financial picture, as the most important banks now are members of the federal banking system.

But banks did not become the core of American capitalism without intense political controversy. The Federalist majority in Congress, led by Alexander Hamilton, did in fact establish a Bank of the United States in 1791, but it was vigorously opposed by agrarian interests led by Thomas Jefferson, based on the fear that the interests of urban, industrial capitalism would dominate such a bank. The Bank of the United States was terminated during the administration of Andrew Jackson, but the fear of a central, public bank still existed eight decades later, when Congress in 1913 established an institution—the **Federal Reserve System**—to integrate private banks into a single national system. The Federal Reserve System did not become a central bank in the European tradition, but rather is composed of twelve Federal Reserve banks, each located in a major commercial city. The Federal Reserve banks are not ordinary banks; they are banker's banks, which make loans to other banks, clear checks, and supply the economy with currency and coins. They also play a regulatory role over the member banks. Every national bank must be a member of the Federal Reserve System; each must follow national banking rules and must purchase stock in the Federal Reserve System (which helps make the system self-financing). State banks and savings and loan associations may also join if they accept national rules. At the top of the system is the Federal Reserve Board—"the Fed"—comprising seven members appointed by the president (with Senate confirmation) for fourteen-year terms. The chairman of the Fed is selected by the president from among the seven members of the board for a four-year term. In all other concerns, however, the Fed is an independent agency (see Chapter 14) inasmuch as its members cannot be removed during their terms except "for cause," and the president's executive power does not extend to them or their policies.

The major advantage that a bank gains from being in the Federal Reserve System is that it can borrow from the system, using as collateral notes on loans that it already holds. This enables banks to expand their loan operations continually, as long as there is demand for loans in the economy. On the other hand, it is this very access of member banks to the Federal Reserve System that gives the Fed its power: the ability to expand and contract the *amount of credit* available in the United States.

The Fed can affect the total amount of credit through the interest (called the discount rate) it charges on the loans it extends to member banks. If the Fed significantly decreases the discount rate, it can give a boost to a sagging economy. During 2001, the Fed cut interest rates eleven times to combat the combined effects of recession and the terrorist attacks. If the Fed raises the discount rate, it can put a brake on the economy, because the higher discount rate also increases the general interest rates charged by leading private banks to their customers.

reserve requirement the amount of liquid assets and ready cash that banks are required to hold to meet depositors' demands for their money

A second power of the Fed is control over the **reserve requirement**—the amount of cash and negotiable securities every bank must hold readily available to cover withdrawals and checks written by their depositors. Generally the rule is that a bank must hold at least 20 percent of all of its outstanding loans as its reserve requirement. When the Fed decides to increase the reserve requirement, it can decrease significantly the amount of money banks have to lend; conversely, if the Fed lowers the reserve requirement, banks can be more liberal in extending more loans.[19]

A third power of the Fed is called **open-market operations,** whereby the Fed buys and sells government securities in order to increase or decrease the supply of money in the economy. When the Fed buys government securities in the open market, it increases the amount of money available to consumers to spend or invest; when it sells securities, it is reducing the money supply.

Finally, a fourth power is derived from one of the important services rendered by the Federal Reserve System, which is the opportunity for member banks to borrow from each other. One of the original reasons for creating a Federal Reserve System was to balance regions of the country that might be vigorously expanding with other areas that might be fairly dormant: the national system would enable the banks in a growing region, facing lots of demand for credit, to borrow money from banks in regions of the country where the demand for credit is much lower. This exchange is called the "federal funds market," and the interest rate charged by one bank to another, the **federal funds rate,** can be manipulated just like the discount rate, to expand or contract credit.[20]

The federal government also provides insurance to foster credit and encourage private capital investment. The Federal Deposit Insurance Corporation (FDIC) insures bank deposits up to $100,000. Another important promoter of investment is the federal insurance of home mortgages through the Department of Housing and Urban Development (HUD). By guaranteeing mortgages, the government can reduce the risks that banks run in making such loans, thus allowing banks to lower their interest rates and make such loans more affordable to middle- and lower-income families. Such programs have enabled millions of families who could not have otherwise afforded it to finance the purchase of a home.

open-market operations method by which the Open Market Committee of the Federal Reserve System buys and sells government securities, etc., to help finance government operations and to reduce or increase the total amount of money circulating in the economy

federal funds rate the interest rate on loans between banks that the Federal Reserve Board influences by affecting the supply of money available

FISCAL POLICIES

Fiscal policies include the government's taxing and spending powers. Personal and corporate income taxes, which raise most of the U.S. government's revenues, are the most prominent examples. While the direct purpose of an income tax is to raise revenue, each tax has a different impact on the economy, and government can plan for that impact. For example, President Clinton's commitment in his 1992 campaign to a "middle-class tax cut" was motivated by the goal of encouraging economic growth through increased consumption. Soon after the election, upon learning that the deficit would be far larger than had been earlier reported to him, he confessed he would have to break his promise of such a tax cut. Nevertheless, the idea of a middle-class tax cut is an example of a fiscal policy aimed at increased consumption, because of the theory that people in middle-income brackets tend to spend a high proportion of unexpected earnings or windfalls, rather than saving or investing them.[21]

fiscal policies the use of taxing, monetary, and spending powers to manipulate the economy

Taxation During the nineteenth century, the federal government received most of its revenue from a single tax, the **tariff.** It also relied on excise taxes, which are taxes levied on specific products, such as tobacco and alcohol. As federal activities expanded in the 1900s, the federal government added new sources of tax revenue. The most important was the income tax, proposed by Congress in 1909, ratified by the states, and added to the Constitution in 1913 as the Sixteenth Amendment. The income tax is levied on individuals as well as corporations. With the creation of the

tariff a tax on imported goods

Social Security system in 1935, social insurance taxes became an additional source of federal revenue.

Before World War II, excise taxes were by far the most important source of revenue, accounting for 49 percent of federal revenues in 1934. Relatively few Americans paid income taxes, and income taxes contributed only modestly to federal coffers. In 1934, individual income taxes accounted for only 14 percent of federal revenues.[22] The need to raise revenue for World War II made the income tax much more important. Congress expanded the base of the income tax so that most Americans paid income taxes after World War II. In addition, income tax withholding was introduced, ensuring an efficient collection system. Table 16.1 shows several notable shifts that have occurred in taxes since 1960. Social insurance taxes now comprise a much greater share of federal revenues, rising from 15.9 percent of revenues in 1960 to 33.2 percent in 2000. Receipts from corporate income taxes have declined over the same time period, dropping from 23.2 percent of receipts in 1960 to an estimated 10.4 in 2002. The share of the federal individual income tax has risen only modestly from 44 percent in 1960 to 48.8 percent in 2002.

One of the most important features of the American income tax is that it is a "progressive" or a "graduated" tax, with the heaviest burden carried by those most able to pay. A tax is called **progressive** if the rate of taxation goes up with each higher income bracket. A tax is called **regressive** if people in lower income brackets pay a higher proportion of their income toward the tax than people in higher income brackets. For example, a sales tax is deemed regressive because everybody pays at the same rate, so that the proportion of total income paid in taxes goes down as the total income goes up (assuming, as is generally the case, that as total income goes up the amount spent on sales-taxable purchases increases at a lower rate). The Social Security tax is another example of a regressive tax. In 2002, Social Security law applied a tax of 6.2 percent on the first $84,900 of income for the retirement program and an additional 1.45 percent on all income (without limit) for Medicare benefits, for a total of 7.65 percent in Social Security taxes. This means

progressive/regressive taxation taxation that hits the upper income brackets more heavily (progressive) or the lower income brackets more heavily (regressive)

Table 16.1

Federal Revenues by Type of Tax as Percentage of Total Receipts, 1960–2002

Year	Individual Income Tax	Corporation Income Tax	Social Insurance and Retirement Receipts	Excise Taxes	Other
1960	44.0	23.2	15.9	12.6	4.2
1970	46.9	17.1	23.0	8.1	4.9
1980	47.2	12.5	30.5	4.7	5.1
1990	45.2	9.1	36.8	3.4	5.4
2002 (est.)	48.8	10.4	36.4	3.4	1.1

SOURCE: Office of Management and Budget, *The Budget for Fiscal Year 2003, Historical Tables,* Table 2.2.

that a person earning an income of $84,900 pays $6,495 in Social Security taxes, a rate of 7.65 percent. But someone earning twice that income, $169,800, pays a total of $7,726 in Social Security taxes, a rate of 4.5 percent. As one's income continues to rise, the amount of Social Security taxes also rises, but the rate, or the percentage of one's income that goes to taxes, declines.

Although the primary purpose of the graduated income tax is, of course, to raise revenue, an important second objective is to collect revenue in such a way as to reduce the disparities of wealth between the lowest and the highest income brackets. We call this a policy of **redistribution.** Another policy objective of the income tax is the encouragement of the capitalist economy by rewarding investment. The tax laws allow individuals or companies to deduct from their taxable income any money they can justify as an investment or a "business expense"; this gives an incentive to individuals and companies to spend money to expand their production, their advertising, or their staff, and reduces the income taxes businesses have to pay. These kinds of deductions are called incentives or "equity" by those who support them; others call them **"loopholes."** The tax laws of the 1980s actually closed a number of important loopholes in U.S. tax laws. But others still exist—on home mortgages and on business expenses, for example—and others will return, because there is a strong consensus among members of Congress, both Democrats and Republicans, that businesses often need such incentives. The differences between the two parties focus largely on which incentives are justifiable.[23]

The tax reform laws of 1981 and 1986 significantly reduced the progressiveness of the federal income tax. Drastic rate reductions were instituted in 1986, and before Bush's 2001 reform, there were five tax brackets, ranging from a 15 percent tax on those in the lowest income bracket to 39.6 percent on those in the highest income bracket. Prior to the 1980s, the highest tax brackets sometimes were taxed at a rate of 90 percent on the last $1 million of taxable income earned in a given year. Meanwhile, Social Security taxes—the most regressive taxes of all—remain high and are likely to be increased.[24]

In every presidential election year, both Democrats and Republicans try to woo voters with pledges of tax cuts. In 2001, Bush made good on his promise to introduce major tax cuts. Although congressional Democrats believed that the administration's proposal benefited the wealthy and jeopardized the budget surplus, they eventually agreed on a compromise bill. The bill reduced taxes at all levels of income (although less than Bush had initially proposed), creating a new bottom bracket of 10 percent and reducing the tax rate in each of the other five brackets. In the highest bracket, taxes were cut from 39.6 percent to 35 percent. Most controversial was the provision to repeal the estate tax, a tax that has historically been seen as a way to prevent the emergence of a monied aristocracy in the United States. Reflecting the uneasy compromise that allowed the bill to pass, many of the provisions were slated to phase in over time. The estate tax repeal, for example, does not take effect until 2010. Moreover, all the provisions were subject to a "sunset" provision that automatically repeals the legislation in 2010 unless Congress renews it. Faced with the new budgetary demands of the war on terrorism and a budget deficit, congressional Democrats argued that the Bush tax reform had left the government with insufficient resources. Some urged that the reform be repealed, but Democratic leaders held back, fearing that they would be charged with raising taxes.

redistribution a policy whose objective is to tax or spend in such a way as to reduce the disparities of wealth between the lowest and the highest income brackets

loophole incentive to individuals and businesses to reduce their tax liabilities by investing their money in areas that the government designates

What Government Does . . . After September 11

In the weeks after September 11, there was widespread agreement in Congress and around the country that the federal government should enact a stimulus package to help the shell-shocked economy. Already teetering on the edge of recession, the economy threatened to stall out as the stock market tumbled and the hard-hit travel and tourism industries began to lay off workers. Members of Congress urged a variety of actions that included cutting taxes, extending unemployment insurance, helping laid-off workers pay their health-care premiums, providing assistance to state and local governments, and funding public construction projects that would put people back to work. Such policies would not only offer help to those facing immediate economic problems, but they would also, according to Keynesian logic, boost the entire economy by promoting spending.

The spirit of bipartisan cooperation that pervaded the Capitol quickly faded when the president unveiled his stimulus plan nearly a month after the attacks. The plan consisted almost entirely of tax cuts. Democrats recoiled, charging the president with taking "a more divisive approach to the stimulus package" than he had earlier indicated. Senator Edward M. Kennedy (D-Mass.), the venerable voice of liberal Democrats in the Senate, argued that the package should focus on the needs of workers rather than "tax breaks for wealthy corporations." Republicans defended the president, arguing that tax cuts were "the only real way to create new jobs and put our economy back on track." One Republican aide also noted a political rationale for the president's emphasis on taxes: "Bush decided to go with the people who brought him to the dance."[1]

With the reappearance of partisan differences, hopes for enacting a stimulus package dimmed. Each side dug in its heels, calling the other party obstructionist. By year's end, Democrats appeared poised to suffer the heaviest political damage for congressional inaction. A poll showed that 67 percent of those polled approved of the way Bush was handling the economy; 58 percent thought Congress had done too little to help the economy.[2]

By late February 2002, pressure to take some action mounted. Although the economy was showing signs of recovery without the stimulus package, the basic unemployment insurance benefit of twenty-six weeks was about to run out for those who had lost their jobs on September 11. If Congress did not enact an extension (as it commonly does in periods of growing unemployment), it would be open to charges of disregarding the needs of the millions of workers who remained without work. Since neither Democrats nor Republicans wanted to be identified as the party that had blocked assistance to displaced workers, party leaders finally worked out a compromise. The stimulus package they passed in early March 2002 combined a scaled-back set of tax cuts with an extension of unemployment insurance. Business-oriented tax cuts predominated; the package included no assistance for health-insurance payments or spending for job-creating construction projects.

Treasury Secretary Paul O'Neill hailed the legislation as "a great victory for American workers and their families" and predicted that the business tax provisions would help "speed Americans back to work."[3] Others were less impressed, noting that the economy had already started to pick up before the stimulus measure. For these critics, government action had come too late.

Although the stimulus package came too late to take credit for reigniting the economy, government spending—at all levels of the federal system—rose so much in the months after the attacks that some analysts argued that "aggressive government spending" had inadvertently played a key role in stimulating the economy.[4] Spending on a range of policies, including highways, school construction, medical assistance to the needy, and unemployment insurance, rose dramatically after the September 11 attacks. These increases were unplanned and uncoordinated. Yet they highlight how important government spending is to our economic prosperity. As the economy revived, pressure to enact the large stimulus bill that the president and Congress had first envisioned diminished. The package that Congress ultimately enacted included only the bare bones of a classic political compromise: unemployment assistance to workers and tax cuts for business.

[1] Mike Allen and Glenn Kessler, "Bush's Tax Cut Proposal Renews Party Differences," *Washington Post*, October 7, 2001, p. A16.
[2] Glenn Kessler and Helen Dewar, "Congress Ends Session, Buries Stimulus Bill," *Washington Post*, December 21, 2001, p. A1.
[3] Richard W. Stevenson, "Senate Approves Economic Stimulus Bill," *New York Times*, March 9, 2002, p. 13.
[4] Louis Uchitelle, "Sharp Rise in Federal Spending May Have Helped Erase Recession," *New York Times*, March 23, 2002, p. A1.

Spending and Budgeting   The federal government's power to spend is one of the most important tools of economic policy. Decisions about how much to spend affect the overall health of the economy. They also affect every aspect of American life from the distribution of income to the availability of different modes of transportation to the level of education in society. Not surprisingly, the fight for control over spending is one of the most contentious in Washington, as interest groups and politicians strive to create a healthy economy and determine the priorities and appropriate levels of spending. Decisions about spending are made as part of the annual budget process. During the 1990s, when the federal **budget deficit** became a major political issue and when parties were deeply split on spending, the budget process became the focal point of the entire policy-making process. Even though the budget deficit disappeared in the late 1990s, the budget continued to dominate the attention of policy makers. With the deficit on the rise again after September 11, budget politics are sure to remain on the national agenda.

The president and Congress have each created institutions to assert control over the budget process. The Office of Management and Budget (OMB) in the Executive Office of the President is responsible for preparing the president's budget. This budget contains the president's spending priorities and the estimated costs of the president's policy proposals. It is viewed as the starting point for the annual debate over the budget. When different parties control the presidency and Congress, the president's budget may have little influence on the budget that is ultimately adopted. Members of the president's own party also may have different priorities. In 2002, members of Congress from both parties resisted the president's efforts to cut spending for domestic programs. A key Republican staffer defended congressional prerogatives to shape the budget, declaring, "Our job is not to rubber-stamp what OMB says."[25]

Congress has its own budget institutions. Congress created the Congressional Budget Office (CBO) in 1974 so that it could have reliable information about the costs and economic impact of the policies it considers. At the same time, Congress established a budget process designed to establish spending priorities and to consider individual expenditures in light of the entire budget. A key element of the process is the annual budget resolution, which designates broad targets for spending. By estimating the costs of policy proposals, Congress hoped to control spending and to reduce deficits. When the congressional budget process proved unable to hold down deficits in the 1980s, Congress established stricter measures to control spending, including "spending caps" that limit spending on some types of programs.

A very large and growing proportion of the annual federal budget is **mandatory spending,** expenditures that are, in the words of the OMB, "relatively uncontrollable." Interest payments on the national debt, for example, are determined by the actual size of the national debt. Legislation has mandated payment rates for such programs as retirement under Social Security, retirement for federal employees, unemployment assistance, Medicare, and farm price supports (see Figure 16.2 on page 666). These payments increase with the cost of living; they increase as the average age of the population goes up; they increase as national and world agricultural surpluses go up. In 1970, 38.6 percent of the total federal budget was made up of these **uncontrollables;** in 1975, 52.5 percent fell into that category; and by 2001, around 64.7 percent was in the uncontrollable category. This means that the national government now has very

budget deficit amount by which government spending exceeds government revenue in a fiscal year

mandatory spending federal spending that is made up of "uncontrollables," budget items that cannot be controlled through the regular budget process

uncontrollables budgetary items that are beyond the control of budgetary committees and can be controlled only by substantive legislative action in Congress. Some uncontrollables are beyond the power of Congress, because the terms of payments are set in contracts, such as interest on the debt

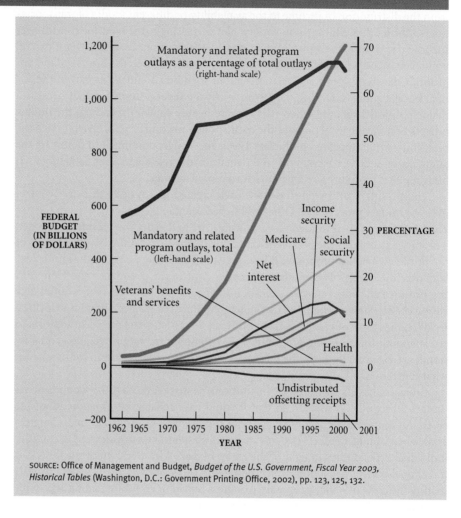

Figure 16.2

Uncontrollables as a Percentage of Total Federal Budget, 1962–2001

SOURCE: Office of Management and Budget, *Budget of the U.S. Government, Fiscal Year 2003, Historical Tables* (Washington, D.C.: Government Printing Office, 2002), pp. 123, 125, 132.

discretionary spending federal spending on programs that are controlled through the regular budget process

little **discretionary spending** to increase or decrease spending to counteract fluctuations in the business cycle.

Government spending as a fiscal policy works fairly well when deliberate deficit spending is used to stop a recession and to speed up the recovery period, but it does not work very well in fighting inflation, because elected politicians are politically unable to make the drastic expenditure cuts necessary to balance the budget, much less to produce a budgetary surplus.

REGULATION AND ANTITRUST POLICY

Americans have long been suspicious of concentrations of economic power. Federal economic regulation aims to protect the public against potential abuses by concentrated economic power in two ways. First, the federal government can establish conditions that govern the operation of big businesses to ensure fair competition. For example, it can require business to make information about its activities and account books available to the public. Second, the federal government can force large businesses to break up into smaller companies if it finds that the company has established a **monopoly.** This is called **antitrust policy.** In addition to economic regulation, the federal government engages in social regulation. Social regulation establishes conditions on businesses in order to protect workers, the environment, and consumers.

Federal regulatory policy was a reaction to public demands. As the American economy prospered throughout the nineteenth century, some companies grew so large that they were recognized as possessing "market power." This meant that they were powerful enough to eliminate competitors and to impose conditions on consumers rather than cater to consumer demand. The growth of billion-dollar corporations led to collusion among companies to control prices, much to the dismay of smaller businesses and ordinary consumers. Small businesses, laborers, farmers, and consumers all began to clamor for protective regulation. Although the states had been regulating businesses in one way or another all along, interest groups turned toward Washington as economic problems appeared to be beyond the reach of the individual state governments. If markets were national, there would have to be national regulation.[26]

The first national regulatory policy was the Interstate Commerce Act of 1887, which created the first national independent regulatory commission, the Interstate Commerce Commission (ICC), designed to control the monopolistic practices of the railroads. Two years later, the Sherman Antitrust Act extended regulatory power to cover all monopolistic practices, including "trusts" or any other agreement between companies to eliminate competition. These were strengthened in 1914 with the enactment of the Federal Trade Act (creating the Federal Trade Commission, or FTC) and the Clayton Act. The only significant addition of economic regulatory policy beyond regulation of interstate trade, however, was the establishment of the Federal Reserve System in 1913, which was given powers to regulate the banking industry along with its general monetary powers. At the same time, public demands to protect consumers led the federal government to enact a more limited number of social regulations. As we have seen, Upton Sinclair's bestseller about the meatpacking industry, *The Jungle,* led to the federal meat inspection program in 1906. Two decades later, the Food and Drug Administration was set up to test and regulate products viewed as essential to public health.

The modern epoch of comprehensive national regulation began in the 1930s. Most of the regulatory programs of the 1930s were established to regulate the conduct of companies within specifically designated sectors of American industry. For example, the jurisdiction of one agency was the securities industry; the jurisdiction of another was the radio (and eventually television) industry. Another was banking. Another was coal mining; still another was agriculture. At this time, Congress also set the basic framework of American labor regulation, including the rules for collective bargaining and the minimum wage.

When Congress turned once again toward regulatory policies in the 1970s, it became still bolder, moving beyond the effort to regulate specific sectors of industry toward regulating some aspect of the entire economy. The scope or jurisdiction of such agencies as the Occupational Safety and Health Administration (OSHA),

monopoly the existence of a single firm in a market that controls all the goods and services of that market; absence of competition

antitrust policy government regulation of large businesses that have established monopolies

Should the Government Regulate Microsoft?

When the giant computer software firm Microsoft came under government scrutiny in the late 1990s for what critics charged were anticompetitive practices, the classic debate over free enterprise versus government regulation reemerged. Throughout the nineteenth century, the prevailing government laissez-faire economic philosophy prevented interference with market forces, resulting in the exercise of unprecedented economic and political power by a handful of corporate giants in such areas as oil, steel, and railroads. The rise of the Progressive era early in the twentieth century ushered in the modern era of government regulation of market practices, as the country came to support the principle of government regulation to protect citizens and reduce market chaos. In the Microsoft case, the Justice Department and nineteen states sued in 1998, charging that the company, headed by Bill Gates, had tied its Internet browser to its Windows operating system in order to unfairly undercut its competition. Microsoft argued that the browser software was integral to Windows operation and was not a separate product. In November 1999, after almost a year and a half of testimony, a federal judge issued a finding of fact that mostly supported the government's claim of monopolistic practices, but considerable further legal wrangling lay ahead.

Throughout the dispute, Microsoft has maintained that the development of computer software differed from monopolistic practices covered by the Sherman Antitrust Act of 1890—which was used most importantly to break up Standard Oil in 1911—because the computer industry was fast-paced, fluid, and extremely competitive. Too much government interference could squelch critical product development. In addition, Microsoft's copyright on Windows could be compromised by an unfavorable antitrust ruling by forcing the company to alter its product design or reveal design secrets. Further, those whom the government has an interest in protecting—consumers—have been happy with the Microsoft system. Indeed, their interest is in having smooth and uncomplicated access to the Internet, a goal achieved by Microsoft's system. Before this development, consumers faced a chaotic and confusing series of choices that benefited neither the companies nor the consumers. Above all, Microsoft asserted that it must be free to innovate, a process that can only be hampered by government intrusion. If the courts ultimately decide to break Microsoft up into three to five separate companies, the result will be an arbitrary solution to a problem that does not exist, and it will only degrade the computer services so highly sought by industry, government, and consumers.

Government prosecutors argued that the browser software was obviously a separate product from Windows, and the fact that Microsoft gave the browser away for free when its competitors had to charge a fee to turn a profit underscored Microsoft's effort to drive its competition out of the business. While different in particulars, the Microsoft case was the same as past antitrust cases involving widely different sectors of the economy, the government argued, because the company engaged in classic monopolistic practices, including collusion, bribery, exclusionary contracts, and other predatory practices all centering on how Microsoft competed in the marketplace. And, as the federal judge noted in 1999, copyright law did not protect this, or any company, from charges of monopoly. In particular, Microsoft sought to drive its main competitor, Netscape Communications, from the marketplace by designing a product that forced users to use only the Microsoft system. Prosecutors argued that a system like Netscape's could be as technologically compatible with Windows as that of Microsoft. Beyond arguments over technology, a detailed examination of Microsoft e-mails, internal corporate documents, and eyewitness testimony generally supported prosecution claims of arm-twisting monopolistic practices.

In June 2000, Federal Judge Thomas Penfield Jackson issued his final ruling, in which he sided with the government prosecutors. He ordered the breakup of Microsoft into two companies, one for its Windows operating system, and one for other computer programs and its Internet businesses. An appeals court later overruled this remedy, although it upheld most of Judge Jackson's findings. After the election of George W. Bush, the Justice Department proposed a remedy that fell far short of a breakup. Nine states that were part of the original case rejected the settlement and continued to challenge Microsoft in court. But a 2002 ruling upheld the settlement.

the Consumer Product Safety Commission (CPSC), and the Environmental Protection Agency (EPA) is as broad and as wide as the entire economy, indeed the entire society.

The most important recent example of federal economic regulation was the government's case against Microsoft. Faced with strong competition from Netscape's Navigator browser software, Microsoft used its near-monopoly of the market for personal computer operating systems "to displace Netscape's Navigator with its own Internet Explorer browser" by requiring that computers run by Microsoft's Windows 98 operating system present users with a preloaded icon for Internet Explorer. Computer manufacturing companies would have to comply or they would "lose their Windows license and thus lose their business. . . ."[27] Such a practice—forcing a vendor to take Explorer in order to carry Windows 98—constitutes "product tying," a violation of antitrust law (the oldest of federal economic regulations).

The Justice Department's Antitrust Division went to court, and in November 1999, the federal court ruled that Microsoft had used its monopoly power to harm the consumer by reducing competition and thereby stifling innovation. The judge charged that "Microsoft has demonstrated that it will use its prodigious market power and immense profits to harm any firm that insists on pursuing initiatives that could intensify competition against one of Microsoft's core products."[28] The Justice Department initially recommended that Microsoft be split into two companies, one for the Windows operating system and another for other software applications. An appeals court later ruled against such a dramatic remedy, and after George W. Bush's election the Justice Department offered to settle the case. The settlement called for Microsoft to disclose parts of its Windows code and to allow computer manufacturers to install competing software on their machines. Critics charged that these measures would do little to change Microsoft's anticompetitive business practices in the future. Indeed, nine of the states that had joined the federal lawsuit against Microsoft were so dissatisfied with the outcome that they refused to endorse the settlement. Instead, they continued to challenge Microsoft in court, hoping to win stronger regulations. But in November 2002, U.S. District Judge Colleen Kollar-Kotelly upheld the settlement.

Despite occasional high-profile regulatory cases such as the one against Microsoft, the trend since the late 1970s has been against regulation. Businesses complained about the burden of the new regulations they confronted and many economists began to argue that excessive regulation was hurting the economy. Congress and the president responded with a wave of **deregulation.** For example, President Reagan went about the task of changing the direction of regulation by way of "presidential oversight." One of his first actions after taking office was Executive Order 12291, issued February 17, 1981, which gave the OMB the authority to review all proposals by all executive branch agencies for new regulations to be applied to companies or people within their jurisdiction. By this means, Reagan succeeded in reducing the total number of regulations issued by federal agencies to such an extent that the number of pages in the *Federal Register* dropped from 74,000 in 1980 to 49,600 in 1987.[29] Although Presidents Bush and Clinton also favored deregulation as a principle, the number of pages crept up steadily after 1987, reaching 69,680 by 1993. Although the number of regulations dropped in the early years of the Clinton administration, by 2000 the *Federal Register* had reached a record 74,258 pages.

deregulation a policy of reducing or eliminating regulatory restraints on the conduct of individuals or private institutions

Should the Government Regulate Microsoft?

Yes

For nearly fifteen years, Microsoft has led innovations in computer technology, readily supplying consumers with PC operating systems like Windows 95 and 98. These systems, highly praised for their user-friendliness, have made company chairman and CEO Bill Gates an eye-popping $75 billion fortune, and allowed his stock portfolio to go platinum. Last May, however, the Justice Department, in conjunction with twenty states, initiated an anti-trust lawsuit against his plum operation.

According to the 1890 Sherman Anti-Trust Act, on which the suit takes its basis, no corporation may monopolize any part of the trade or commerce among the several states, or with foreign nations. In other words, it's illegal for any single business to dominate the market for a particular product. In a free market economy, consumers always have the liberty to choose among several manufacturers to supply their product demands. This forces companies to price their merchandise competitively, thus contributing to a healthy economy. A monopoly occurs when a certain manufacturing body grows too large to facilitate this type of fair competition.

After assessing the current evidence, District Court Judge Thomas Penfield Jackson determined that, more likely than not, Gates's firm is guilty of just such an offense. Microsoft enjoys so much power that "it could charge a price for Windows substantially above [that elicited by the existence of] a competitive market," he said. The key to Microsoft's power, Jackson reasoned, lies in the nearly 70,000 software applications the Windows operating system supports. It seems everything finds a home (and an icon) on Gates's desktop, from the simplest card game to any number of word-processing programs, audio players, and Internet browsers. By contrast, Apple's Mac-OS can accommodate only about 12,000 applications—and this is Microsoft's biggest current competition. Something is very wrong with this picture.

Gates, of course, denies all accusations of anticompetitive conduct, maintaining his company competes legally with rival corporations. Um, right. Of course Microsoft is a monopoly. The fact that Windows boasts so many software possibilities makes it impossible for other companies to compete. In Jackson's words, it is "prohibitively costly" for companies like Apple to develop new applications to compete with Windows. As it stands, Microsoft is under no legal obligation to share its technology. This effectively stifles the industry—how many of us can name another PC or Mac operating system on par with Windows? Failing that, who can name another PC or Mac operating system, period?

A court decision against Microsoft could force the software giant to publish the intimate specifications of certain programs. Freely circulating this information would help rival companies produce similar operating systems to eclipse Gates's much-touted applications. The competition will encourage Microsoft to set fairer prices, and perhaps even develop more innovative software applications in an effort to stay one step ahead. In the end, the computing industry will advance significantly.

And why not? After all, communication facilitates both science and business. The truth is, Microsoft has had too solitary a ride on the information superhighway it helped pave. Introducing a little healthy competition to the mix only will benefit the corporation and, of course, the consumers who fuel the computing industry with their hard-earned dollars. With all the genius Bill Gates displays, he'll come up with some way to maintain himself and his company in the technological race. For now, however, he must give the little people a fair chance to succeed.

SOURCE: Kiki Petrosino, "Creating Better Computers by Ending Microsoft Monopoly," *Cavalier Daily* (University of Virginia), November 17, 1999.

No

Charles E. Wilson, Secretary of Defense during the Eisenhower Administration, is best remembered for the quote, "What's good for the country is good for General Motors, and vice versa."

Today, that quote could best be applied to the computer company Microsoft, a company that provides thousands of jobs, billions of dollars in taxes, and has revolutionized the computer industry in this country and throughout the world.

Yet despite all the good Microsoft does, it is now under attack from the Department of Justice for antitrust violations. This is not a good thing.

Microsoft is being demonized for daring to market its Internet browser, Internet Explorer, as part of its Windows 98 operating system. This is considered restraint of trade because about 90 percent of the computers on this planet run off of Windows.

Both the federal government and most of Microsoft's major competitors believe that if Microsoft is allowed to market an Internet browser with Windows, no one will have any incentive to buy a competing browser.

This is of course a baseless fear. Microsoft's main competitor in the browser industry, Netscape, already controls 40 percent of the market and its browser is available free on the Internet.

The browser industry is open to competition, which means the company that produces the best product at the cheapest price is going to win.

Microsoft is by no means all powerful. Its main strength is software for personal computers, an important market but one that is declining in importance. This means if Microsoft wants to continue the aggressive expansionist policies that have made it so successful, it is going to have to enter new markets.

Computer industry specialists believe the next major markets will be servers, information appliances, and embedded software systems. These are all markets with established companies that are more than capable of defending themselves and Microsoft has been floundering in its attempts to compete with them.

Microsoft's Windows 2000 product is already over two years behind schedule (crippling Microsoft's efforts to compete in the critical business server market), Microsoft Network only has two million customers compared to the 16 million held by America On-Line and then there is Microsoft's Web TV, the biggest commercial flop since New Coke. Microsoft is still an immensely powerful company but it faces ferocious competition in most of the markets it will need to expand in to survive.

It is appropriate to expect Microsoft to fight for its life in the marketplace, it is not appropriate to expect it to fight for its life in the courts.

Microsoft provides good products at reasonable prices and in doing so has made computers widely available across the whole country. It pumps billions of dollars into the economy every year, making the entire country richer. It helps facilitate the development of new technologies that improve the lives of everyone.

In other words, Microsoft is good for the country. Which means this antitrust suit has to be bad for the country. Microsoft has achieved its prominence by beating its competition on the open market; it should not be punished for being successful.

With the net value of Microsoft stock currently valued around 400 billion dollars, can the country afford to risk damaging a company that plays that vital of a role in the national economy? Gates is a smart man; he knows if he gets lazy and complacent he will get crushed in the marketplace, which is precisely why he has never gotten lazy and complacent.

His competitors are understandably frustrated and are trying to use the power of the federal government to beat the man they have found to be unbeatable.

Maybe they should work on improving their own products instead? Microsoft makes this country richer, stronger, and better; it should be allowed to continue to do this.

SOURCE: Brendan Guy, "Monopoly Madness," *The Battalion* (Texas A&M University), February 26, 1999.

Is deregulation good economic policy? It depends. In the late 1980s and 1990s, many states opened the electrical-power industry to competition, which resulted in lower prices. But during 2001, severe energy shortages in California caused power outages and skyrocketing prices. The energy crisis overwhelmed the state budget and threatened to push the state's utility companies into bankruptcy. California officials charged that Enron and other energy companies had used their market power to drive up the price of energy and then used their political clout to persuade federal regulators not to intervene. Enron's subsequent collapse prompted Congress to reconsider the need for stronger federal oversight of deregulated energy markets. The Enron debacle also ignited calls for federal regulation of new arenas. One of the most prominent of these arenas was accounting, since Enron's accountant, Arthur Andersen LLP, which was found guilty of obstructing justice, played a key role in hiding the firm's questionable finances and later shredded documents relevant to the case.

SUBSIDIES AND CONTRACTING

Subsidies and contracting are the carrots of economic policy. Their purpose is to encourage people to do something they might not otherwise do or to get people to do more of what they are already doing. Sometimes the purpose is merely to compensate people for something done in the past.

subsidies government grants of cash or other valuable commodities, such as land, to individuals or organizations; used to promote activities desired by the government, to reward political support, or to buy off political opposition

Subsidies Subsidies are simply government grants of cash or other valuable commodities, such as land. Although subsidies are often denounced as "giveaways," they have played a fundamental role in the history of government in the United States. Subsidies were the dominant form of public policy of the national government and the state and local governments throughout the nineteenth century. They continue to be an important category of public policy at all levels of government. The first planning document ever written for the national government, Alexander Hamilton's *Report on Manufactures,* was based almost entirely on Hamilton's assumption that American industry could be encouraged by federal subsidies and that these were not only desirable but constitutional.

The thrust of Hamilton's plan was not lost on later policy makers. Subsidies in the form of land grants were given to farmers and to railroad companies to encourage western settlement. Substantial cash subsidies have traditionally been given to shipbuilders to help build the commercial fleet and to guarantee the use of their ships as military personnel carriers in time of war. Policies using the subsidy technique continued to be plentiful in the twentieth century, even during the 1990s when there was widespread public and official hostility toward subsidies. For example, through 1994, the total annual value of subsidies to industry alone was estimated at $53 billion, based on relatively conservative Congressional Budget Office figures.[30] Crop subsidies alone, implemented by the Department of Agriculture, amount to about $6 billion annually.

Subsidies have always been a technique favored by politicians because subsidies can be treated as "benefits" that can be spread widely in response to many demands that might otherwise produce profound political conflict. Subsidies can, in other words, be used to buy off the opposition.

Another secret of the popularity of subsidies is that those who receive the benefits do not perceive the controls inherent in them. In the first place, most of the resources available for subsidies come from taxation. (In the nineteenth century, there was a lot of public land to distribute, but that is no longer the case.) Second, the effect of any subsidy has to be measured somewhat indirectly in terms of what people *would be doing* if the subsidy had not been available. For example, many thousands of people settled in lands west of the Mississippi only because land subsidies were available. Similarly, hundreds of research laboratories exist in universities and corporations only because certain types of research subsidies from the government are available.

Contracting Like any corporation, a government agency must purchase goods and services by contract. The law requires open bidding for a substantial proportion of these contracts because government contracts are extremely valuable to businesses in the private sector and because the opportunities and incentives for abuse are very great. But contracting is more than a method of buying goods and services. Contracting is also an important technique of policy because government agencies are often authorized to use their **contracting power** as a means of encouraging corporations to improve themselves, as a means of helping to build up whole sectors of the economy, and as a means of encouraging certain desirable goals or behavior, such as equal employment opportunity. For example, the infant airline industry of the 1930s was nurtured by the national government's lucrative contracts to carry airmail. A more recent example is the use of government contracting to encourage industries, universities, and other organizations to engage in research and development.

contracting power the power of government to set conditions on companies seeking to sell goods or services to government agencies

Military contracting has long been a major element in government spending. So tight was the connection between defense contractors and the federal government during the cold war that, as he was leaving office, President Eisenhower warned the nation to beware of the powerful "military-industrial complex." After the cold war, as military spending and production declined, major defense contractors began to look for alternative business activities to supplement the reduced demand for weapons. For example, Lockheed Martin, the nation's largest defense contractor, began to bid on contracts related to welfare reform. Since September 11, however, the military budget has been awash in new funds and military contractors are flooded with business. President Bush proposed to increase the Pentagon budget by $48 billion (14.3 percent), requesting so many weapons systems that one observer called the budget a "weapons smorgasbord."[31] Military contractors geared up to produce not only weapons for foreign warfare but also surveillance systems to enhance domestic security.

The Politics of Economic Policy Making

Political leaders care deeply about maintaining a healthy economy. As presidents from Herbert Hoover (who presided over the beginning of the Great Depression of the 1930s) to Jimmy Carter (who faced double-digit inflation) discovered, voters will punish politicians for poor economic performance. Yet even though all politicians want a healthy economy, they often differ in their views about how to attain it. Moreover, politicians disagree about what the priorities of economic policy should be. Democrats and Republicans alike want to promote economic growth

> **How do political leaders disagree about what the priorities of economic policy should be? What groups have the most influence on economic policy making?**

but Democrats are generally more concerned about equality and unemployment than are Republicans. Republicans stress the importance of economic freedom for maintaining a healthy economy, whereas Democrats are often more willing to support economic regulation to attain social or environmental objectives. Such differences along party lines are not hard and fast divisions, however. The politics of economic policy making are also greatly influenced by economic ideas.

As we have seen, Keynesian ideas, which used spending and tax policy to promote growth and low unemployment, dominated economic policy in the 1960s and in the first half of the 1970s. The Council of Economic Advisers (CEA) played a central role in economic policy during that time because the president relied on its advice about whether to stimulate or depress the economy. As Keynesian prescriptions became less effective, however, the CEA began to lose its central role. Since the late 1970s, when President Carter began to emphasize monetary policy, the Chairman of the Federal Reserve has occupied the pivotal position in economic policy making. The long run of economic prosperity in the 1990s made longtime Fed Chairman Alan Greenspan into something of a cult figure. Universally praised by Democrats and Republicans alike for his management of the economy, Greenspan has served four four-year terms as head of the Federal Reserve. In addition to the Federal Reserve, the Department of the Treasury plays an important role in making economic policy. Clinton's second Secretary of the Treasury, Robert Rubin, came to Washington from Wall Street and was widely regarded as essential in maintaining investor confidence in the administration. The Treasury Secretary is also an important actor in international trade policy, working to open markets around the world to American products.

The groups that influence decisions about economic policy are as wide ranging as the objectives of policy. Consumer groups, environmentalists, businesses, and labor all attempt to shape economic policy. Of these groups, organized labor and business are the most consistent actors who weigh in across the spectrum of policies. In the past, organized labor was much more important in influencing economic policy than it is today. At the height of their strength in the 1950s, unions represented some 35 percent of the labor force. Newspapers covered the "labor beat" as a critical element of economic reporting and presidents of both parties listened attentively to the views of union leaders. Today, labor unions, representing 13 percent of the labor force, are much less powerful in influencing economic policy. Newspapers no longer routinely cover their activities. Democratic presidents continue to court labor because unions control resources and votes important to Democratic politicians, but labor's overall power has waned. On particular issues, organized labor can still exercise significant influence. For example, labor played a key role in Congress's decision to increase the minimum wage in 1996. Labor has recently sought to boost its political profile and has particularly sought to influence trade policy. Labor and environmentalists, long-time antagonists, have joined to challenge free trade with countries that use unfair labor practices (such as child labor or prison labor) and that degrade their environments. Protesting at the WTO meetings in Seattle in 1999, they proclaimed the new alliance in a banner that read "Teamsters and Turtles, Together At Last!"[32] The protests in Seattle marked trade policy as an area of political contention for the future.

Business organizations are the most consistently powerful actors in economic policy. Business groups are most united around the goal of reducing government regulation. Organizations such as the U.S. Chamber of Commerce, which represents small business, and the Business Roundtable and the National Association of Manufacturers, which represent big business, actively worked to roll back government regulation in the 1970s and 1980s.

Although business groups want to reduce government regulation, they also often look to government for help. After September 11, a wave of lobbyists from industries hurt by the terrorist attacks—especially those related to travel and tourism—converged on Congress to request assistance in the form of subsidies and tax cuts. As we saw at the beginning of this chapter, the main beneficiaries of congressional assistance were the airlines.

In addition to subsidies and tax breaks, business also relies on the federal government for protection against unfair foreign competition. For example, over the past several years, the film production industry has lobbied Washington to help it compete with other countries where films can be made more cheaply. The United States loses an estimated $10 billion in annual revenues to these foreign competitors. Television shows, such as *Pasadena,* and films about Texas and other American locales are routinely filmed in Canada, where production is considerably cheaper. Industry representatives, fearing that Los Angeles could turn into a "rust belt" for film production, have sought legislation to secure wage credits.[33] The Screen Actors Guild went so far as to ask the federal government to investigate Canada for unfair trade practices.

ECONOMIC POLICY AND THE PUBLIC INTEREST

With so many groups seeking to influence economic policy, it is important to ask, does economic policy serve the public interest or does it serve special interests? Who benefits from economic policy, and how do economic policy decisions reflect our national values? The answers are not simple because many specific interests, such as business, labor, environmentalists, and consumer groups claim to act in the public interest. The old saying that "What's good for the country is good for General Motors, and what's good for General Motors is good for the country," is echoed today by consumer and environmental groups that call themselves public interest groups. Complicating matters further is the fact that the public has an interest in being protected from unregulated markets but it also has an interest in promoting a vibrant and prosperous economy. Decisions about when protection from the market is warranted and when such protection unacceptably impedes markets are at the heart of economic policy making.

Historically, Americans have been more concerned with ensuring economic liberty than with promoting economic equality. The widespread perception of openness and opportunity in American society has made Americans more tolerant of economic inequality than Europeans. American economic policy has rarely aimed to promote economic equality. Instead, economic policy has sought to ensure fairness in the marketplace and protect against the worst side effects of the free market. One of the central ways to ensure fair markets is to guard against the emergence of businesses so large that they can control markets. As we have seen, antitrust policy aims to break up such concentrations of power in the name of free and fair competition. The laws designed to strengthen labor in the 1930s likewise aimed to limit the power of big business by creating a countervailing power; they

> **How does the debate over economic policy reflect the broader debate over American political values?**

Two Visions of Western Capitalism

Among the wealthiest and most industrially developed democracies of the world, there have traditionally been two competing visions of capitalism: *Anglo-American* and *continental European*. While both visions encompass the espoused virtues of profit, property, and free enterprise, and while both grow from a core liberal philosophy that views capitalism as the base from which personal liberty and freedom arise, the two visions differ with respect to how they weight the relative values of wealth and distribution. Anglo-American capitalism traditionally values wealth over distribution, while continental European capitalism has historically been buffeted and shaped by struggles over distributional justice. Following from their respective visions of capitalism is the role of government in the market economy.

Anglo-American capitalism is built on a system of values that attributes personal liberty and political democracy to economic prosperity and opportunities for personal wealth. These goals are best achieved through self-interested activities of consumers and producers in an environment fostering maximum personal economic choice, entrepreneurial activity, free trade, and unrestricted markets. According to this liberal version of capitalism, a social harmony evolves from the unfettered competition of individuals. Consumers dictate efficient information to producers as to what to supply. In return, producers collect a profit—capital—and in turn invest the profit in even more efficient and diverse ways of producing yet more goods and services for the sovereign and rational consumer, thereby receiving yet more profit for yet more future investment. Wealth is seen as a by-product of the harmonious mechanisms of the market, all built upon the rational actions of the consumer in a free society. In contrast, government is seen as a force that distorts the efficient harmony of the marketplace. The countries most closely identified with the Anglo-American capitalism model are those countries that trace their lineage to Great Britain, especially the United States, Canada, New Zealand, Ireland, and Australia, and Britain itself.

Continental European capitalism, on the other hand, grew out of social democracy, a nineteenth-century philosophy that emphasized building a just system of economic distribution in society, not merely a wealthy society. This entailed a commitment to equalize wealth, control and ultimately diffuse capital's concentration, and empower the working class with their own political parties and labor unions. Continental European capitalism was indeed much influenced by a strong social democratic presence in such countries as Germany, France, Italy, Norway, Belgium, Sweden, Austria, and the Netherlands. By the twentieth century, though all continental European democracies were capitalist, the vestiges of social democracy remained visible on the landscape of politics as well as deeply embedded in the social fabric of several countries.

The core logic of social democracy entails a much more salient and active role of government within the market. In theory, the individual and sovereign consumer does not stand alone as in the Anglo-American version of capitalism. Rather, "workers" and individuals in general are part of a community, a society, where responsibilities are shared, risk is diffused, and the virtue of private property, while the centerpiece of all democratic capitalist systems, remains an item to be regulated through government in order to ensure a just market that does not concentrate economic power so starkly as in the Anglo-American democracies. Continental western Europe is, to be sure, capitalist, driven by private competition, individualism, and a free spirit for entrepreneurship and the advancement of private good. Nevertheless, social insurance, publicly controlled benefits, a degree of corporatism (see Chapter 9), and the protection of society from the uncertainties of capitalist competition are central tenets of the social democratic logic of capitalism. Government is seen as a necessary and legitimate partner in the economy and its market—for better or worse.

The degree of government regulation in social democratic economies has led some critics to argue that social democracy carries with it a heavy cost for its citizens. One such cost is the difficulty of reforming the economy when the world market demands cheaper and different goods than social democratic economies traditionally produce. Not only has this recently led to high unemployment challenges for governments in continental European democracies, but it has meant that many of the unemployed remain so for a much longer period of time than those in the Anglo-American countries.

SOURCES: David Landes, *The Wealth and Poverty of Nations* (New York: Norton, 1998); Adam Przeworski, *Capitalism and Social Democracy* (New York: Cambridge University Press, 1985); Robert Heilbronner, *The Nature and Logic of Capitalism* (New York: Norton, 1985).

did not attempt directly to create equality. Consumer and environmental regulations are key ways that economic policy protects against the worst side effects of the free market. Over time, as Americans have grown more concerned about the quality of life, policies in these areas have placed greater restrictions on the market. In a sense, economic prosperity and market success laid the foundation for such restrictions. As Americans felt more economically secure, they could afford to worry about how the economy affected the nonmaterial aspects of their lives, such as the environment. It is no accident that social regulation of the economy took off after the unprecedented prosperity of the 1960s.

In the 1990s, the boom in high technology made the American economy the envy of the world, and free trade created markets for American products across the globe. Yet, challenges to unrestricted markets emerged in each domain. The federal government, as we have seen, slapped the Microsoft Corporation with antitrust violations, charging that it was a market-inhibiting monopoly. Although many foes of Microsoft applauded the move, others worried that such government action would actually undermine the free market that it claims to preserve. Similar tensions characterize the free trade debate. Those proposing more restrictions on trade fear that unregulated trade will drive American labor and environmental standards down to the level of their worst competitors. Should American workers have to compete directly with child labor in China or India? they ask. Proponents of free trade argue that restrictions will hurt American workers by restricting markets. American products will not find buyers if we restrict trade, they argue. As these cases show, debates about the appropriate balance between economic liberty and protection from markets are an ongoing feature of American economic policy. Chances of addressing the public interest are greatest when all voices can participate in that debate.

GET INVOLVED

What You Can Do:
Assess the Impact of Economic Policies

Economic policy is often viewed as the domain of experts. Disputes over economic decision making can appear to be obscure debates conducted in a complicated technical language. Ordinary citizens may feel that they have no way to enter such debates and they may feel unsure about what their real interests are. Yet no area of policy is more fundamental to the lives of the majority of American citizens. Decisions about the economy affect such basic concerns as whether a student can afford to attend college and whether a family can afford to buy a home. How can citizens influence economic policy making?

Despite the often technical nature of economic policy, many major shifts in policy have occurred as a result of citizen action. The initial creation of antitrust laws at the turn of the last century was a response to a widespread public fear that business had grown too big and that its power would hurt consumers. Likewise, the social regulation of the 1960s emerged from the movement of environmental and consumer groups that pressed the government to incorporate new objectives into economic policy making. Politicians are extremely sensitive to what voters think about many aspects of the economy, in particular taxes and inflation. The "tax revolt" that started in California in the late 1970s was launched by ordinary citizens.

For the next two decades, politicians at all levels of government became very cautious about suggesting new taxes.

If citizens are to be effective actors in economic policy they must evaluate how economic policy proposals affect them. But such judgments are often not straightforward: they involve at least three different dimensions. First, and most simply, is the impact on the individual wallet: does policy hurt or help my budget? Second, citizens must ask, what is the impact of policy on the public services that I rely on? Taxpayers may dislike paying the IRS but they depend on the roads and national defense that government provides and they enjoy the national parks that their taxes support. Finally, citizens must think about how policy reflects their values and their vision about how they want the nation to develop over the long-term. The majority of Americans who earn well above the minimum wage support increases in the minimum wage because such policy is in accordance with their ideas about fairness. They believe in rewarding people who are working and trying to take responsibility for their lives. Such ideas about what is fair are one of the most important ways that public beliefs influence economic policy.

The work of politics is to translate fundamental values into policy. Even though economic policy debates are strewn with often hard-to-grasp technical decisions, citizens can exercise a powerful impact on policy when they participate. Policy makers rely on citizen participation to clarify the full range of competing objectives that economic policy must try to balance.

Summary

The study of public policy is necessary for the understanding of government in action. *Policy* is the purposive and deliberate aspect of government in action. The federal government is involved in the economy for four main reasons. First, government action seeks to manage the economy in order to prevent recessions and other major disruptions of economic life. Second, the government acts to protect the welfare and property of individuals. Third, government strives to regulate competition in order to ensure fair and free markets. Finally, the government intervenes to provide public goods, facilities—such as highways—that the state provides because no single market participant can afford to provide those facilities itself.

Views about whether government should be involved in the economy vary widely. Three main schools of economic thought have influenced the beliefs of policy makers about how and how much the federal government should become involved in the economy. The oldest school of thought, the laissez-faire approach, is associated with the Scottish economist Adam Smith. Smith argued that government should leave the economy alone. Laissez-faire ideas dominated American economic policy until the Great Depression of the 1930s. At that time, the prolonged economic slump and high rates of unemployment prompted the federal government to provide jobs for those out of work and to launch other spending programs designed to assist the needy. Rationale for such actions were found in Keynesian ideas. The British economist John Maynard Keynes argued that when the economy declined government could play a positive role by spending or taxing to stimulate the economy. By putting money in the hands of workers who would spend it on their daily needs, the economy could be revived. The third school of thought is called the monetarist school of thought. Often linked to American economist Milton Friedman, this school of thought argues that government should limit its actions to manipulating the supply of money.

Economic policy strives to achieve a variety of often conflicting goals. These include creating a strong and stable economy with high rates of growth, full employment, and low inflation. In addition, economic policy seeks to assist particular business sectors, such as housing and small business. Throughout our nation's history, promotion of international trade has been an important objective of the federal government. Economic policy is also used to achieve social goals. These include the protection of labor, the environment, and consumers. The federal government relies on a diverse assortment of tools in economic policy. Most central today in managing the overall health of the economy are monetary policies. This makes the Federal Reserve Board's decisions about whether to raise or lower interest rates the most closely watched actions in economic policy. Also of central importance are fiscal policies, which include taxing and spending. Concern about deficits during the 1990s made the federal budget the focus of all policy making in Congress. Regulation and antitrust policy implemented through the Justice Department and various independent regulatory authorities are another widely used tool of economic policy. Finally, the government provides subsidies and contracts in order to achieve economic objectives.

Economic policy making is a highly political activity. Many groups are organized to influence economic policy, including organized labor, environmentalists, and consumer advocates. Business lobbies are very influential in debates about economic policy but they are not always in agreement with one another. Big business and small business often have different priorities in economic policy. Reaching the public interest in economic policy making is not a simple matter. The public wants the prosperity that free markets can create but it also wants to be protected from the harms that unregulated markets can inflict.

For Further Reading

Bryner, Gary C. *Blue Skies, Green Politics: The Clean Air Act of 1990*, rev. ed. Washington, D.C.: Congressional Quarterly, 1995.

Friedman, Milton, and Walter Heller. *Monetary versus Fiscal Policy.* New York: Norton, 1969.

Greider, William. *Secrets of the Temple: How the Federal Reserve Runs the Country.* New York: Simon & Schuster, 1987.

Harris, Richard A., and Sidney M. Milkis. *The Politics of Regulatory Change*, 2nd ed. New York: Oxford University Press, 1996.

Kettl, Donald F. *Deficit Politics: Public Budgeting in Its Institutional and Historical Context.* New York: Macmillan, 1992.

Krugman, Paul. *Peddling Prosperity: Economic Sense and Nonsense in the Age of Diminished Expectations.* New York: Norton, 1994.

Schick, Alan. *The Federal Budget: Politics, Policy, Process.* Washington, D.C.: Brookings Institution Press, 1995.

Stein, Robert M., and Kenneth N. Bickers. *Perpetuating the Pork Barrel: Policy Subsystems and American Democracy.* New York: Cambridge University Press, 1995.

Weir, Margaret. *Politics and Jobs: The Boundaries of Employment Policy in the United States.* Princeton, N.J.: Princeton University Press, 1992.

Study Outline

www.wwnorton.com/wtp4e

1. Public policy is an officially expressed intention backed by a sanction, which can be a reward or a punishment.

Why Is Government Involved in the Economy?

1. At the most basic level, government makes it possible for markets to function efficiently by setting the rules for economic exchange and punishing those who violate the rules.
2. Since the Great Depression of the 1930s, the public has held the government responsible for maintaining a healthy economy.
3. Government protects the welfare and property of individuals by maintaining law and order, creating protection for consumers, and providing protection of private property.
4. Government helps protect markets by regulating competition.
5. Government makes the market economy possible by providing public goods.

Should Government Be Involved in the Economy?

1. There are different theories about whether, how much, and in what ways government should be involved in the economy.
2. Proponents of laissez-faire argue that the economy will flourish if the government leaves it alone.
3. Proponents of Keynesianism argue for an ongoing role for government in the economy by redistributing money and stimulating consumer demand.
4. Proponents of monetarism argue that the role of government in the economy should be limited to regulating the supply of money.

What Are the Goals of Economic Policy?

1. Government strives to achieve multiple economic goals, some of which may conflict with one another.
2. A strong and stable economy is the basic goal of all economic policy. But the key elements of a strong economy—economic growth, full employment, and low inflation—often appear to conflict with one another.
3. Government promotes business development indirectly through categorical grants and supports specific business sectors with direct subsidies, loans, and tax breaks.

4. The promotion of American goods and services abroad is a long-standing goal of U.S. policy. The most important international organization for promoting free trade today is the World Trade Organization.
5. From the 1930s to the 1980s, the government regulated industrial relations by overseeing union elections and collective bargaining between labor groups and management. But more recently, with the exception of the minimum wage, the government has significantly reduced its involvement in industrial relations.
6. Environmental protection laws are part of economic policy because they regulate the activity of virtually every aspect of the economy.
7. The federal government plays an active role in protecting consumers from unsafe products.

What Are the Tools of Economic Policy?

1. Monetary policies manipulate the growth of the entire economy by controlling the availability of money to banks through the Federal Reserve System.
2. Fiscal policies include the government's taxing and spending powers.
3. During the nineteenth century, the federal government received most of its revenue from a single tax, the tariff. Since then, the federal government added new sources of tax revenue, the most important being the income tax and social insurance taxes. One of the most important features of the American income tax is that it is a progressive tax.
4. The federal government's power to spend is one of the most important tools of economic policy because spending decisions affect every aspect of the economy. These decisions, which are typically contentious, are made as part of the annual budget process involving the president and Congress.
5. The federal government can establish conditions that govern the operation of big businesses to ensure fair competition and can force large monopolies to break up into smaller companies. In addition to economic regulation, the federal government can also impose conditions upon businesses in order to protect workers, the environment, and consumers.
6. By the late 1970s, a reaction against regulation set in. Though the deregulation movement has resulted in a reduction in the amount of regulatory laws, few regulatory programs have actually been terminated.

7. Subsidies and contracting are the carrots of economic policy. Their purpose is to encourage people to do something they might not otherwise do or to get people to do more of what they are already doing.

The Politics of Economic Policy Making

1. Politicians disagree about what the priorities of economic policy should be. While both Democrats and Republicans want to promote economic growth, Republicans stress the importance of maintaining economic freedom while Democrats are more willing to support economic regulation to attain social or environmental objectives.
2. Consumer groups, environmentalists, businesses, and labor all attempt to shape economic policy, though business groups are the most consistently influential today.
3. Historically, Americans have been more concerned about ensuring economic liberty than with promoting economic equality, though debates about the appropriate balance between the two are an ongoing feature of economic policy in the United States.

Practice Quiz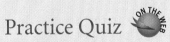

www.wwnorton.com/wtp4e

1. The argument for laissez-faire was first elaborated by
   a) James Madison.
   b) Adam Smith.
   c) Alan Greenspan.
   d) Milton Friedman.

2. Which of the following economic perspectives argues for an ongoing role for government in the economy?
   a) laissez-faire
   b) Keynesianism
   c) monetarism
   d) rational expectations

3. The theories of which economist were used to help justify the increase in government spending during the New Deal?
   a) John Maynard Keynes
   b) Milton Friedman
   c) Robert Lucas
   d) Alan Greenspan

4. Monetary policy is handled largely by
   a) Congress.
   b) the president.
   c) the Department of the Treasury.
   d) the Federal Reserve System.

5. Monetary policy seeks to influence the economy through
   a) taxing and spending.
   b) the availability of credit and money.
   c) foreign exchange of currency.
   d) administrative regulation.

6. A situation in which the government attempts to affect the economy through taxing and spending is an example of
   a) an expropriation policy.
   b) a monetary policy.
   c) a fiscal policy.
   d) eminent domain.

7. A tax that places a greater burden on those who are better able to afford it is called
   a) regressive.
   b) progressive.
   c) a flat tax.
   d) voodoo economics.

8. Which groups currently have the most political influence in economic policy making?
   a) consumer groups
   b) labor unions
   c) business groups
   d) environmental groups

9. Which of the following is *not* a reason that government forms and changes regulatory policies?
   a) public opinion
   b) politics
   c) morality
   d) budget surplus

10. Which of the following is *not* one of the reasons why government is involved in the economy?
    a) to guarantee economic equality
    b) to protect property
    c) to regulate competition
    d) to provide public goods

Critical Thinking Questions

www.wwnorton.com/wtp4e

1. Think about a specific in-stance of government in-tervention in the American economy since the New Deal. What economic pol-icy tool was used? What other tools might have been used? More generally, think about different eco-nomic perspectives about the role of government in the economy. In your opinion, when is government action in the economy necessary?

2. One of the chief functions of government is the collection of revenue. Describe the system of taxation used by the federal government. What are the multiple goals of tax policy in America? How else might some of these goals be achieved? In what ways is the tax system in the United States progressive? In what ways is it regressive? Is tax reform necessary? Why or why not?

3. Today, supporters of free trade defend it as the policy that best represents the public interest. Yet in the early years of the nation, high tariffs were widely accepted as best for the nation even though they restricted trade. What are the arguments in favor of free trade (vs. restrictions on trade)? Do the advo-cates of restrictions on trade always favor narrow special in-terests, or can they too be seen as favoring the public interest?

Key Terms

www.wwnorton.com/wtp4e

antitrust policy (p. 667)
budget deficit (p. 665)
categorical grants (p. 652)
contracting power (p. 673)
deregulation (p. 669)
discretionary spending (p. 666)
federal funds rate (p. 661)
Federal Reserve System (p. 660)
fiscal policies (p. 661)

General Agreement on Tariffs and Trade (GATT) (p. 653)
Gross Domestic Product (GDP) (p. 648)
inflation (p. 650)
Keynesianism (p. 646)
laissez-faire capitalism (p. 645)
loophole (p. 663)
mandatory spending (p. 665)
monetarism (p. 646)
monetary policies (p. 659)
monopoly (p. 667)
most favored nation status (p. 653)

North American Free Trade Agreement (NAFTA) (p. 653)
open-market operations (p. 661)
progressive/regressive taxation (p. 662)
public goods (p. 644)
public policy (p. 639)
redistribution (p. 663)
reserve requirement (p. 660)
subsidies (p. 672)
tariff (p. 661)
uncontrollables (p. 665)
World Trade Organization (WTO) (p. 653)

17 SOCIAL POLICY

☆ **The Welfare State**

What type of welfare system existed before the creation of the welfare state in the 1930s?

What are some important examples of contributory and noncontributory welfare programs?

Has welfare reform been successful? Why or why not?

How do we pay for the welfare state?

☆ **Opening Opportunity**

What policies are aimed at helping the poor find equal opportunity?

☆ **Who Gets What from Social Policy?**

Which groups receive the most benefits from social policies? Which groups receive the fewest?

How effectively does social policy reach the groups that are most likely to be poor?

☆ **The Welfare State and American Values**

How has the formation of social policy reflected the debate over liberty, equality, and democracy?

What Government Does and Why It Matters

OCIAL POLICIES PROMOTE a range of public goals. The first is to protect against the risks and insecurities that most people face over the course of their lives. These include illness, disability, temporary unemployment, and the reduced earning capability that comes with old age. Most spending on social welfare in the United States goes to programs, such as Social Security and medical insurance for the elderly, that serve these purposes. These are widely regarded as successful and popular programs. They are the least controversial areas of social spending, although the debates about funding Social Security reveal that even widely agreed upon policies can generate conflict. Such conflicts over how to achieve security against risks have prevented the United States from adopting universal health insurance. Despite the fact that most Americans support a public role in guaranteeing health coverage, disputes over how this should be done have blocked repeated efforts at health reform.

More controversial have been the other two goals of social policy: promoting **equality of opportunity** and assisting the poor. While Americans admire the ideal of equal opportunity, there is no general agreement about what government should do to address inequalities of results: groups that have suffered from past inequality generally support much more extensive government action to promote equality of opportunity than do others. Yet most Americans support some government action, especially in the area of education.

The third goal of social policy—to alleviate poverty—has long generated controversy in the United States. Americans take pride in their strong work ethic and prize the value of self-sufficiency. As a result, the majority of Americans express suspicions that the able-bodied poor will not try hard enough to support themselves if they are offered too much assistance or

equality of opportunity a widely shared American ideal that all people should have the freedom to use whatever talents and wealth they have to reach their fullest potential

if they receive the wrong kind of assistance. Yet, there is also recognition that poverty may be the product of past inequality of opportunity. Since the 1960s, a variety of educational programs and income assistance policies have sought to end poverty and promote equal opportunity. Much progress has been made toward these goals. However, the disproportionate rates of poverty among minorities suggest that our policies have not solved the problem of unequal opportunity. Likewise, the high rates of child poverty challenge us to find new ways to assist the poor.

There is no way to know precisely when the government ought to be called upon and what the government ought to do to help individuals secure the right to pursue their own happiness. Economic and social transformations pose new challenges and often alter public views about what government should do. In the 1930s, a deep and widespread economic depression created broad public support for new programs such as federal unemployment insurance. Today, the increased numbers of women in the labor force and the growth in single-parent households have prompted calls for more government assistance to help people combine work and family responsibilities more effectively. Yet there is no agreement on what government should do. Likewise, as the economy has changed, inequality among working people has grown. Should the government address such inequality? If so, with what measures? Shifting patterns of risk and opportunity provoke new demands from citizens and, in so doing, place social policy issues at the center of national politics. ■

■ **The first section of this chapter will deal with policies concerned with economic insecurity.** Most of these come under the conventional label of "social welfare policy" or "the welfare state." We will also look at how the welfare state is financed.

■ **The second section looks at policies aimed at permanently changing the status of America's poorest citizens.** Through education, job training, housing assistance, and health care, governments in America promote equality of opportunity.

■ **The third section analyzes who benefits from social policies.** In this section, we also assess how effectively welfare policies help the poor.

■ **Last, we will consider how the welfare state in America reflects (or does not reflect) the values of liberty, equality, and democracy.** Citizens have an opportunity to influence the debate over social policies, although most Americans tend to take a pragmatic perspective that strikes a balance among these core political ideals.

The Welfare State

For much of American history, local governments and private charities were in charge of caring for the poor. During the 1930s, when this largely private system of charity collapsed in the face of widespread economic destitution, the federal government created the beginnings of an American welfare state. The idea of the welfare state was new; it meant that the national government would oversee programs designed to promote economic security for all Americans—not just for the poor. The American system of social welfare comprises many different policies enacted over the years since the Great Depression. Because each program is governed by distinct rules, the kind and level of assistance available varies widely.

THE HISTORY OF THE SOCIAL WELFARE SYSTEM

There has always been a welfare system in America. But until 1935, it was almost entirely private, composed of an extensive system of voluntary philanthropy through churches and other religious groups, ethnic and fraternal societies, communities and neighborhoods, and philanthropically inclined rich individuals. Most often it was called "charity," and although it was private and voluntary, it was thought of as a public obligation.

> ➤ **What type of welfare system existed before the creation of the welfare state in the 1930s?**

There were great variations in the generosity of charity from town to town, but one thing seems to have been universal: the tradition of distinguishing between two classes of poverty—the "deserving poor" and the "undeserving poor." The deserving poor were the widows and orphans and others rendered dependent by some misfortune, such as the death or serious injury of the family's breadwinner in the course of honest labor. The undeserving poor were able-bodied persons unwilling to work, transients new to the community, and others of whom, for various reasons, the community did not approve. This private charity was a very subjective matter: the givers and their agents spent a great deal of time and resources examining the qualifications, both economic and moral, of the seekers of charity.

Much of the private charity was given in cash, called "outdoor relief." But because of fears that outdoor relief spawned poverty rather than relieving or preventing it, many communities set up settlement houses and other "indoor relief" institutions. Some of America's most dedicated and unselfish citizens worked in the settlement houses, and their efforts made a significant contribution to the development of the field of social work.

A still larger institution of indoor relief was the police station, where many of America's poor sought temporary shelter. But even in the severest weather, the homeless could not stay in police stations for many nights without being jailed as vagrants.[1] Indeed, the settlement houses and the police departments were not all that different in their approaches, since social workers in those days tended to consider "all social case work [to be] mental hygiene."[2] And even though not all social workers were budding psychiatrists, "it was true that they focused on counseling and other preventive techniques, obscuring and even ignoring larger structural problems."[3]

The severe limitations on financing faced by private charitable organizations and settlement houses slowly produced a movement by many groups toward public assumption of some of these charitable or welfare functions. Workers' compensation laws were enacted in a few states, for example, but the effect of such laws was limited because they benefited only workers injured on the job, and of them, only those who worked for certain types of companies. A more important effort, one that led more directly to the modern welfare state, was public aid to mothers with dependent children. Beginning in Illinois in 1911, the movement for mother's pensions spread to include forty states by 1926. Initially, such aid was viewed as simply an inexpensive alternative to providing "indoor relief" to mothers and their children. Moreover, applicants not only had to pass a rigorous means test, but also had to prove that they were deserving, because the laws provided that assistance would be provided only to individuals who were deemed to be "physically, mentally, and morally fit." In most states, a mother was deemed unfit if her children were illegitimate.[4]

In effect, these criteria proved to be racially discriminatory. Many African Americans in the South and ethnic immigrants in the North were denied benefits on the grounds of "moral unfitness." Furthermore, local governments were allowed to decide whether to establish such pension programs. In the South, many counties with large numbers of African American women refused to implement assistance programs.

Despite the spread of state government programs to assume some of the obligation to relieve the poor, the private sector remained dominant until the 1930s. Even as late as 1928, only 11.6 percent of all relief granted in fifteen of the largest cities came from public funds.[5] Nevertheless, the various state and local public experiences provided guidance and precedents for the national government's welfare system, once it was developed.

The traditional approach, dominated by the private sector with its severe distinction between deserving and undeserving poor, crumbled in 1929 before the stark reality of the Great Depression. During the Depression, misfortune became so widespread and private wealth shrank so drastically that private charity was out of the question and the distinction between deserving and undeserving became impossible to draw. Around 20 percent of the workforce immediately became unemployed; this figure grew as the Depression stretched into years. Moreover, few of these individuals had any monetary resources or any family farm on which to fall back. Banks failed, wiping out the savings of millions who had been prudent enough or fortunate enough to have any savings at all. Thousands of businesses failed as well, throwing middle-class Americans onto the bread lines along with unemployed laborers, dispossessed farmers, and those who had never worked in any capacity whatsoever. The Great Depression proved to Americans that poverty could be a result of imperfections in the economic system as well as of individual irresponsibility. It also forced Americans to alter drastically their standards regarding who was deserving and who was not.

Once poverty and dependency were accepted as problems inherent in the economic system, a large-scale public policy approach was not far away. By the time the Roosevelt administration took office in 1933, the question was not whether there was to be a public welfare system, but how generous or restrictive that system would be.

FOUNDATIONS OF THE WELFARE STATE

If the welfare state were truly a state, its founding would be the Social Security Act of 1935. This act created two separate categories of welfare: contributory and non-contributory. Table 17.1 lists the key programs in each of these categories, with the year of their enactment and the most recent figures on the number of Americans they benefit and their cost to the federal government.

Contributory Programs The category of welfare programs that are financed by taxation can justifiably be called "forced savings"; these programs force working

> **What are some important examples of contributory and noncontributory welfare programs?**

Public Welfare Programs

Table 17.1

Type of Program	Year Enacted	Number of Recipients in 1998 (in millions)	Federal Outlays in 1998 (in billions)
Contributory (Insurance) System			
Old Age, Survivors, and Disability Insurance	1935	44.2	$375.0
Medicare*	1965	38.4	$214.0
Unemployment Compensation*	1935	7.3	$19.7
Noncontributory (Public Assistance) System			
Medicaid*	1965	33.6	$123.6
Food Stamps	1964	19.8	$16.9
Supplemental Security Income (cash assistance for aged, blind, disabled)	1974	6.5	$29.0
Housing Assistance to low-income families**	1937	5.0†	$25.1
School Lunch Program	1946	26.6	$5.1
Temporary Assistance to Needy Families*	1996	6.8***	$16.5

*1997
**1996
***June 1999
†Number of households
SOURCES: All data (except TANF expenditure) is from U.S. Census Bureau, Statistical Abstract of the United States 1999 (Washington, D.C.: Government Printing Office, 1999). TANF expenditure is from Budget of the United States Government, Fiscal Year 1999, pp. 223–27, www.access.gpo.gov (accessed January 21, 2000).

The creation of the modern welfare state in the 1930s shifted responsibility for alleviating poverty from private charities, such as settlement houses, to the government. Chicago's Hull House was one of the most famous settlement houses in the early twentieth century. There, social workers instructed the poor in methods of hygiene and child rearing. After 1935, the federal government created new programs to help poor families. For example, the federally funded school lunch program provides nutritious meals for needy children. In many schools in poor neighborhoods, a majority of the students rely on the school lunch program.

Americans to set aside a portion of their current earnings to provide income and benefits during their retirement years. These **contributory programs** are what most people have in mind when they refer to **Social Security** or social insurance. Under the original contributory program, old-age insurance, the employer and the employee were each required to pay equal amounts, which in 1937 were set at 1 percent of the first $3,000 of wages, to be deducted from the paycheck of each employee and matched by the same amount from the employer. This percentage has increased over the years; the contribution is now 7.65 percent subdivided as follows: 6.20 percent on the first $84,900 of income for Social Security benefits, plus 1.45 percent on all earnings for Medicare.[6]

Social Security may seem to be a rather conservative approach to welfare. In effect, the Social Security tax, as a forced saving, sends a message that people cannot be trusted to save voluntarily in order to take care of their own needs. But in another sense, it is quite radical. Social Security is not real insurance; workers' contributions do not accumulate in a personal account, like they would in an annuity. Consequently, contributors do not receive benefits in proportion to their own contributions, and this means that there is a redistribution of wealth occurring. In brief, Social Security mildly redistributes wealth from higher- to lower-income people, and it quite significantly redistributes wealth from younger workers to older retirees.

Congress increased Social Security benefits every two or three years during the 1950s and 1960s. The biggest single expansion in contributory programs since 1935 was the establishment in 1965 of **Medicare,** which provides substantial med-

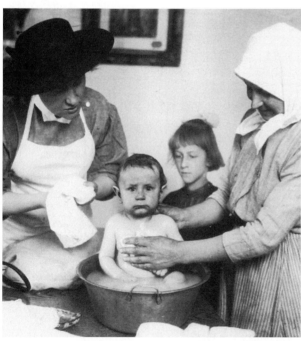

ical services to elderly persons who are already eligible to receive old-age, survivors', and disability insurance under the original Social Security system. In 1972, Congress decided to end the grind of biennial legislation to increase benefits by establishing **indexing,** whereby benefits paid out under contributory programs would be modified annually by **cost-of-living adjustments (COLAs)** designed to increase benefits to keep up with the rate of inflation. But, of course, Social Security taxes (contributions) also increased after almost every benefit increase. This made Social Security, in the words of one observer, "a politically ideal program. It bridged partisan conflict by providing liberal benefits under conservative financial auspices."[7] In other words, conservatives could more readily yield to the demands of the well-organized and ever-growing constituency of elderly voters if benefit increases were automatic; liberals could cement conservative support by agreeing to finance the increased benefits through increases in the regressive Social Security tax rather than out of the general revenues coming from the more progressive income tax. (See Chapter 16 for a discussion of regressive and progressive taxes.)

Similarly, in the early days of the Depression, much of the assistance for the destitute was provided by private groups, through projects such as this New York City soup kitchen. Just a few years later, the government became responsible for providing food to needy families, such as the efforts pictured here, where workmen for the Emergency Unemployment Relief Committee sort packages of food in New York City in 1932.

Noncontributory Programs   Programs to which beneficiaries do not have to contribute—**noncontributory programs**—are also known as "public assistance programs," or, derisively, as "welfare." Until 1996, the most important noncontributory program was **Aid to Families with Dependent Children (AFDC)**—originally called Aid to Dependent Children, or ADC—which was founded in 1935 by the original Social Security Act. In 1996, Congress abolished AFDC and replaced it with the **Temporary Assistance to Needy Families (TANF)** block grant. Eligibility for public assistance is determined by **means testing,** a procedure that requires applicants to show a financial need for assistance. Between 1935 and 1965, the government created programs to provide housing assistance, school lunches, and food stamps to other needy Americans.

As with contributory programs, the noncontributory public assistance programs also made their most significant advances in the 1960s and 1970s. The largest single category of expansion was the establishment in 1965 of **Medicaid,** a program that provides extended medical services to all low-income persons who have already established eligibility through means testing under AFDC or TANF. Noncontributory programs underwent another major transformation in the 1970s in the level of benefits they provide. Besides being means tested, noncontributory programs are federal rather than national; grants-in-aid are provided by the national government to the states as incentives to establish the programs (see Chapter 3). Thus, from the beginning there were considerable disparities in benefits from state to state. The national government sought to rectify the disparities in levels of old-age benefits in 1974 by creating the **Supplemental Security Income (SSI)** program to augment benefits for the aged, the blind, and the disabled. SSI provides uniform minimum benefits across the entire nation and includes mandatory COLAs. States are allowed to be more generous if they wish, but no state is permitted to provide benefits below the minimum level set by the national government. As a result, twenty-five states increased their own SSI benefits to the mandated level.

The new TANF program is also administered by the states and, like the old-age benefits just discussed, benefit levels vary widely from state to state (see Figure 17.1). For example, in 2000, the states' monthly TANF benefits for a family of three varied from $164 in Alabama to $923 in Alaska.[8] Even the most generous TANF payments are well below the federal poverty line. In 2000, the poverty level for a family of three included those earning less than $13,874 a year or $1,156 a month.[9]

The number of people receiving AFDC benefits expanded in the 1970s, in part because new welfare programs had been established in the mid-1960s: Medicaid (discussed earlier) and **food stamps,** which are coupons that can be exchanged for food at most grocery stores. These programs provide what are called **in-kind benefits**—noncash goods and services that would otherwise have to be paid for in cash by the beneficiary. In addition to simply adding on the cost of medical services and food to the level of benefits given to AFDC recipients, the possibility of receiving Medicaid benefits provided an incentive for poor Americans to establish their eligibility for AFDC, which would also establish their eligibility to receive Medicaid. At the same time, the government significantly expanded its publicity efforts to encourage the dependent unemployed to establish their eligibility for these various programs.

Another, more complex reason for the growth of AFDC in the 1970s was that it became more difficult for the government to terminate people's AFDC benefits for

Variations in State Spending on TANF Benefits

Figure 17.1

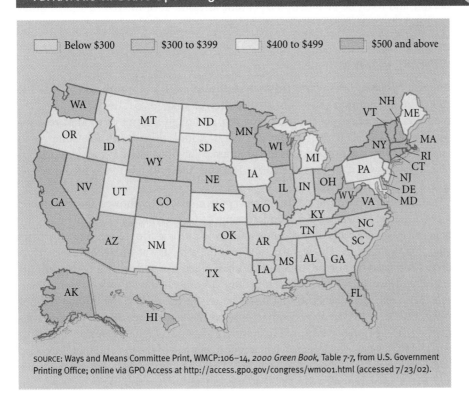

Below $300 | $300 to $399 | $400 to $499 | $500 and above

SOURCE: Ways and Means Committee Print, WMCP:106–14, *2000 Green Book*, Table 7-7, from U.S. Government Printing Office; online via GPO Access at http://access.gpo.gov/congress/wm001.html (accessed 7/23/02).

lack of eligibility. In the 1970 case of *Goldberg v. Kelly*, the Supreme Court held that the financial benefits of AFDC could not be revoked without due process—i.e., a hearing at which evidence is presented, etc.[10] This ruling inaugurated the concept of the **entitlement**, a class of government benefits with a status similar to that of property (which, according to the Fourteenth Amendment, cannot be taken from people "without due process of law"). *Goldberg v. Kelly* did not provide that the beneficiary had a "right" to government benefits; it provided that once a person's eligibility for AFDC was established, and as long as the program was still in effect, that person could not be denied benefits without due process. The decision left open the possibility that Congress could terminate the program and its benefits by passing a piece of legislation. If the welfare benefit were truly a property right, Congress would have no authority to deny it by a mere majority vote.

Thus the establishment of in-kind benefit programs and the legal obstacles involved in terminating benefits contributed to the growth of the welfare state. But it is important to note that real federal spending on AFDC itself did not rise after the mid-1970s. Unlike Social Security, AFDC was not indexed to inflation; without cost of living adjustments, the value of AFDC benefits fell by more than one-third. Moreover, the largest noncontributory welfare program, Medicaid (as shown by Table 17.1), actually devotes less than one-third of its expenditures to poor families; the rest goes to the disabled and the elderly in nursing homes.[11] Together,

Supplemental Security Income (SSI) a program providing a minimum monthly income to people who pass a "means test" and who are sixty-five or older, blind, or disabled. Financed from general revenues rather than from Social Security contributions

food stamps coupons that can be exchanged for food at most grocery stores; the largest in-kind benefits program

in-kind benefits goods and services provided to needy individuals and families by the federal government

entitlement eligibility for benefits by virtue of a category of benefits defined by legislation

these programs have significantly increased the security of the poor and the vulnerable and must be included in a genuine assessment of the redistributive influence and the cost of the welfare state today.

WELFARE REFORM

The unpopularity of welfare led to widespread calls for reform as early as the 1960s. Public opinion polls consistently showed that Americans disliked welfare more than any other government program. Although a series of modest reforms were implemented starting in the late 1960s, it took thirty years for Congress to enact a major transformation in the program. Why did welfare become so unpopular, and why was it so hard to reform? How has the 1996 law that replaced AFDC with TANF changed welfare?

From the 1960s to the 1990s, opinion polls consistently showed that the public viewed welfare beneficiaries as "undeserving."[12] Underlying that judgment was the belief that welfare recipients did not want to work. The Progressive-era reformers who first designed AFDC wanted single mothers to stay at home with their children. Motivated by horror stories of children killed in accidents while their mothers were off working or of children tied up at home all day in order to keep them safe, these reformers believed that it was better for the child if the mother did not work. By the 1960s, as more women entered the labor force and as welfare rolls rose, welfare recipients appeared in a more unfavorable light. Common criticisms charged that welfare recipients were taking advantage of the system; that they were irresponsible people who refused to work. These negative assessments were amplified by racial stereotypes. By 1973, 46 percent of welfare recipients were African American. Although the majority of recipients were white, media portrayals helped to create the widespread perception that the vast majority of welfare recipients were black. A careful study by Martin Gilens has shown how racial stereotypes of blacks as uncommitted to the work ethic reinforced public opposition to welfare.[13]

Despite public opposition, it proved difficult to reform welfare. Congress added modest work requirements in 1967 but little changed in the administration of welfare. A more significant reform in 1988 imposed stricter work requirements but also provided additional support services, such as child care and transportation assistance. This compromise legislation reflected a growing consensus that effective reform entailed a combination of sticks (work requirements) and carrots (extra services to make work possible). The 1988 reform also created a new system to identify the absent parent (usually the father) and enforce child-support payments.

These reforms were barely implemented when welfare rolls rose again with the recession of the early 1990s, reaching an all-time high in 1994. Sensing continuing public frustration with welfare, presidential candidate Bill Clinton vowed "to end welfare as we know it," an unusual promise for a Democrat. Once in office, Clinton found it difficult to design a plan that would provide an adequate safety net for recipients who were unable to find work. One possibility—to provide government jobs as a last resort—was rejected as too expensive. Clinton's major achievement in the welfare field was to increase the Earned Income Tax Credit. This credit allows working parents whose annual income falls below approximately $32,000 to file through their income tax return for an income supplement of up to $4,000, depending on their family size. It was a first step toward realizing Clinton's campaign promise to ensure that "if you work, you shouldn't be poor."

Congressional Republicans proposed a much more dramatic reform of welfare, which Clinton, faced with re-election in 1996, signed. The Personal Responsibility and Work Opportunity Reconciliation Act (PRWORA) repealed AFDC. In place of the individual entitlement to assistance, the new law created block grants to the states and allowed states much more discretion in designing their cash-assistance programs to needy families. The new law also established time limits, restricting recipients to two years of assistance and creating a lifetime limit of five years. It imposed new work requirements on those receiving welfare, and it restricted most legal immigrants from receiving benefits. The aim of the new law was to reduce welfare caseloads, promote work, and reduce out-of-wedlock births. Notably, reducing poverty was not one of its stated objectives.

After this law was enacted, the number of families receiving assistance dropped by 58 percent nationwide (see Figure 17.2). The sharp decline in the number of recipients was widely hailed as a sign that the welfare reform was working. Indeed, former welfare recipients have been more successful at finding and keeping jobs than many critics of the law predicted. The law has been less successful in other respects: researchers have found no evidence that it has helped reduce out-of-wedlock births. And critics point out that most former welfare recipients are not paid enough to pull their families out of poverty. Moreover, many families eligible for food stamps and Medicaid stopped receiving these benefits when they left the

> **Has welfare reform been successful? Why or why not?**

Welfare Caseload, 1982–1999

Figure 17.2

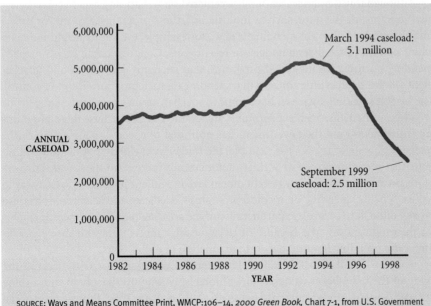

SOURCE: Ways and Means Committee Print, WMCP:106–14, *2000 Green Book,* Chart 7-1, from U.S. Government Printing Office; online via GPO Access at http://access.gpo.gov/congress/wm001.html (accessed 7/23/02).

welfare rolls. The law has helped reduce welfare caseloads, but it has done little to reduce poverty.[14]

As Congress prepared to reauthorize the welfare law in 2002, two different perspectives emerged. Democrats proposed changes that would make the welfare law "an antipoverty weapon."[15] They sought to increase spending on child care, allow more education and training, and relax time limits for those working and receiving welfare benefits. Republicans, by contrast, proposed stricter work requirements and advocated programs designed to promote marriage among welfare recipients.[16] Neither party challenged the basic features of the 1996 reform. Nonetheless, as caseloads began to rise again in 2001 due to the combined effects of the recession and the terrorist attacks, both sides were attentive to new problems. Enacted in a period of low unemployment and economic prosperity, welfare reform has yet to confront the consequences of a prolonged economic downturn.

HOW DO WE PAY FOR THE WELFARE STATE?

> **How do we pay for the welfare state?**

Since the 1930s, when the main elements of the welfare state were first created, spending on social policy has grown dramatically. Most striking has been the growth of entitlement programs, the largest of which are Social Security and Medicare. The costs of entitlement programs grew from 20 percent of the total federal budget in 1962 to nearly 59 percent by 2001. Funds to pay for these social programs have come disproportionately from increases in payroll taxes. In 1970, social insurance taxes accounted for 23 percent of all federal revenues; in 2001 they had grown to 35 percent of all federal revenues.[17] During the same time period corporate taxes fell from 17 percent to 7.6 percent of all federal revenues. Because the payroll tax is regressive, low- and middle-income families have carried the burden for funding increased social spending.

Although much public attention has centered on welfare and other social spending programs for the poor, such as food stamps, these programs account for only a small proportion of social spending. AFDC, for example, even at its height made up only 1 percent of the federal budget. In recent years, Congress has tightly controlled spending on most means-tested programs, and currently lawmakers and government officials express little concern that spending on such programs is out of control. The biggest spending increases have come in social insurance programs that provide broad-based benefits. Such expenditures are hard to control because these programs are entitlements, and the government has promised to cover all people who fit the category of beneficiary. So, for example, the burgeoning elderly population will require that spending on Social Security automatically increase in the future. Furthermore, because Social Security benefits are indexed to inflation, there is no easy way to reduce benefits. Spending on medical programs—Medicare and Medicaid—has also proven difficult to control, in part because of the growing numbers of people eligible for the programs but also because of rising health care costs. Health care expenditures have risen much more sharply than inflation in recent years.

Concern about social spending has centered on Social Security because the aging of the baby-boom generation will force spending up sharply in the coming decades. Indeed, under current law, the Social Security Trust Fund—the special government account from which Social Security payments are made—is projected to experience a shortfall beginning in 2038. Critics also contend that Americans are not getting their money's worth from Social Security and that workers would be better off if they could take at least part of the payroll tax that currently pays for Social Security and invest it in individual accounts. They highlight unfavorable rates of return in the current system, noting for example, that a single male worker born in 2000 can expect to see a return of only 0.86 percent on his Social Security contributions. This is well below what an insured bank account would pay and far below stock market returns over the past decades.[18]

President Bush came to office supporting Social Security reforms, including the creation of private retirement accounts. Soon after taking office, the president appointed a Social Security Commission whose final report prominently featured individual accounts as a reform strategy. The commission recommended three reform plans, each of which offered workers the choice of contributing a portion (ranging from 2 to 4 percent) of the payroll tax to an individual account. The worker's traditional benefits would be reduced by the amount diverted to the individual account. According to the commission, individual plans would create a better system because they would allow workers to accumulate assets and build wealth, wealth that could be passed on to their children.[19]

Supporters of the current system are deeply skeptical about the benefits of individual accounts. They charge the president's commission with presenting a rosy scenario that overestimates likely gains through the stock market. When more realistic assumptions are adopted and the costs of the private accounts are considered, they argue, individual accounts do not provide higher benefits than the current system. Moreover, these critics note that the commission also recommended technical reforms that would significantly reduce the traditional Social Security benefit. For all the changes proposed, the reforms would still not solve the budget crisis that Social Security will face.[20]

Finally, supporters of the present system emphasize that Social Security is not just a retirement account, it is a social insurance program that provides "income protection to workers and their families if the wage earner retires, becomes disabled or dies."[21] Because it provides this social insurance protection, supporters argue, Social Security's returns should not be compared to those of a private retirement account.

They contend that advocates of individual accounts have exaggerated the financial problems that the current system faces. Some opponents of individual accounts believe that the funding problems of Social Security can be addressed more simply and safely by eliminating the cap on payroll taxes. In 2002, only the first $84,900 of income was subject to the payroll tax. If this cap were lifted, these critics argue, the resulting revenues would cover more than 75 percent of the expected shortfall in the Social Security Trust Fund.

During the last half of the 1990s, the federal budget was in surplus but the costs associated with the impending retirement and medical care of aging baby boomers loomed on the horizon. After the September 11, 2001, terrorist attacks, the expenditures associated with increased domestic security created a new burden on the federal budget. These costs are not likely to decline in the future, as heightened levels of spending for domestic security are an essential part of the war on terrorism. As the costs of domestic security rise, advocates for federal programs that provide social and economic security will have to defend both kinds of security as fundamental to the promise of American life.

Does Social Security Need to Be Saved?

Since its creation in 1935, the Social Security system has provided retirement, survivor, and disability benefits to millions of Americans. Up until now, the system has run "in the black"—that is, it has collected more money than it has given out. In 1998, 44 million Americans received a total of $375 billion in Social Security benefits, given to 27 million retirees, 6 million spouses and children, 7 million survivors of deceased workers, and 5 million disabled workers. Even today, more than half of all American workers do not have a private pension plan; they will have to rely solely on Social Security for their retirement. If there were no Social Security, half of all senior citizens would be living below the poverty line. Thus, Social Security guarantees a measure of equality.

Nearly all wage earners and self-employed individuals pay into Social Security. Yet many fear that the system cannot sustain itself. When the baby boomer generation—a relatively large percentage of Americans, born between 1946 and 1964—reaches retirement age, their large numbers and longer life expectancies may place too great a demand on the system, forcing today's young people to pay ever more into a system that may be bankrupt by the time they retire.

Those who argue for a major change in Social Security point out that Social Security benefits are not drawn from an interest-bearing account; rather, they are paid for from taxes collected from current workers. Therefore, current workers carry the primary financial burden for the system. When baby boomers retire, their political and economic clout will be so great that they will be able to push aside any effort to limit benefits or relieve the financial burden on a much smaller number of younger wage earners. For Social Security to continue, it may have to borrow, or draw money from the federal Treasury, leaving younger generations with a staggering debt. If no changes are made in the current system, the Social Security Trust Fund (the account where surplus monies are held) will, according to projections, go bankrupt by 2038.

Contrary to popular impressions, Social Security benefits are not a simple repayment, plus interest, of money contributed by workers. The average retiree receives back the equivalent of all the money he or she contributed over a lifetime of work, plus interest, in the space of four to eight years. Most retirees receive far more than they put in. Why should today's student-age population provide subsidies to retirees who do not need the extra income? Several reform ideas have been suggested. One proposes an investment shift from the current low-yield, conservative, U.S. government securities to private investment in higher-yield stocks and bonds. Another proposal urges a shift to means testing, to reduce or eliminate benefits for those who already have ample income. A third proposal calls for raising the minimum retirement age. The current payroll tax for raising funds could also be altered. As of 2000, income is taxed only up to $72,600, so that a worker making a million dollars a year pays the same Social Security taxes as a worker making $73,000. If action is not taken soon, the system will likely be pushed to extinction by the burdens of the vast number of baby boomers.

Although nearly all observers favor some reform, defenders of the system argue that critics vastly overstate the problem. First, estimates of a looming Social Security crisis are based on very conservative economic projections that assume a far slower rate of growth in the nation's economy than has occurred up until now. Given the nation's history of growth, such projections are unduly pessimistic. Yet even if they are accurate, other factors will minimize the financial burden on younger workers when the baby boomers retire. In the year 2030, for example, at the height of boomer retirement, the overall workforce will be larger than during the height of the baby boom. The reasons for this surge in the twenty-first-century workforce include an increase in births and changing work patterns.

As for proposals to radically alter the distribution of benefits, system supporters point out that Social Security was created to serve several purposes. While the system provides a vital safety net to protect the elderly from poverty, it was also intended to be a universal system, entitling every worker to receive benefits from past work. It was also designed to be a progressive system by awarding greater benefits to those who earned more, and a hedge against inflation by including cost-of-living increases. Moreover, "generational sharing," whereby current workers would provide benefits for retirees, was part of the system's design. These purposes are as valid today as they were in 1935.

Opening Opportunity

The welfare state does not only supply a measure of economic security, it also provides opportunity. The American belief in equality of opportunity makes such programs particularly important. Programs that provide opportunity keep people from falling into poverty, and they offer a hand up to those who are poor. At their best, opportunity policies allow all individuals to rise as high as their talents will take them. Four types of policies are most significant in opening opportunity: education policies, employment policies, health policies, and housing policies.

> **What policies are aimed at helping the poor find equal opportunity?**

EDUCATION POLICIES

Those who understand American federalism from Chapter 3 already are aware that most of the education of the American people is provided by the public policies of state and local governments. What may be less appreciated is the fact that these education policies—especially the policy of universal compulsory public education—are the most important single force in the distribution and redistribution of opportunity in America.

Compared to state and local efforts, the role of national education policy pales in comparison. With but three exceptions, the national government did not involve itself at all in education for the first century of its existence as an independent republic (see Table 17.2 on page 702). The first two of these exceptions were actually prior to the Constitution—the Land Ordinance of 1785 and the Northwest Ordinance of 1787. These provided for a survey of all the public lands in the Northwest Territory and required that four sections of the thirty-six sections in each township be reserved for public schools and their maintenance. It was not until 1862, with adoption of the Morrill Act, that Congress took a third step, establishing the land-grant colleges and universities. Later in the nineteenth century, more federal programs were created for the education of farmers and other rural residents. But the most important national education policies have come only since World War II: the GI Bill of Rights of 1944, the National Defense Education Act (NDEA) of 1958, the Elementary and Secondary Education Act of 1965 (ESEA), and various youth and adult vocational training acts since 1958. Note, however, that since the GI Bill was aimed almost entirely at postsecondary schooling, the national government did not really enter the field of elementary education until after 1957.[22]

What finally brought the national government into elementary education was embarrassment over the fact that the Soviet Union had beaten the United States into space with the launching of Sputnik. The national policy under NDEA was aimed specifically at improving education in science and mathematics. General federal aid for education did not come until ESEA in 1965, which allocated funds to school districts with substantial numbers of children from families who were unemployed or earning less than $2,000 a year. By the early 1970s, federal expenditures for elementary and secondary education were running over $4 billion per year, and rose to a peak in 1980 at $4.8 billion.[23]

Reagan's administration signaled a new focus for federal education policy: the pursuit of higher standards. In 1983, the Department of Education issued *A Nation at Risk,* an influential report that identified low educational standards as the cause of America's declining international economic competitiveness. The report did not

Should Social Security Be Privatized?

Yes

There is much talk about reforming Social Security. As college students, we should be scared. We face the prospect of paying taxes far in excess of current levels into a system that may not exist when we retire. While that does not have to be the case, Clinton's proposal in the State of the Union address to use excess revenue to save Social Security fails to scratch the surface of the necessary changes. The only thing that can keep the system solvent is privatization.

The first thing that must be understood is that the Social Security "trust fund" cannot be shored up with excess government revenue because the trust fund does not exist. Social Security is a pay-as-you-go system. Taxes collected from workers are immediately paid out to recipients. Any money leftover is lent to the rest of the federal government, and in return, the trust fund receives IOUs from the treasury.

Unfortunately, these IOUs have absolutely no value. When payouts begin to exceed taxes in approximately 2013, the Social Security system must ask the treasury to redeem its IOUs. The treasury can get the money through tax revenues or borrowing.

In the State of the Union, Clinton proposed to use a portion of the excess revenues to pay off part of the national debt. The logic is that if the government has less outstanding debt, it will be easier to borrow from the private sector down the road.

Unfortunately, there is no reason to believe that the benefits reaped from this will be used to save Social Security. Congress could just as easily borrow money for new spending programs, there could be a war, or most likely, the extraordinarily rosy budget projections currently being used (which are the basis for Clinton's plan) will simply not hold.

The only way to make Social Security solvent over the long term is some form of privatization. What we need to do is move from a pay-as-you-go system to a wealth-based system under which individuals contribute to individual accounts under their control.

This would accomplish two important goals. First, it would increase the rate of return on each worker's contribution. Today, the average return on Social Security is 2.2 percent—in 20 years, it will be negative. Compare this to the nine percent average return historically achieved by funds investing in stocks and bonds.

Second, it would reduce payroll taxes. Given the higher rate of return on private retirement account contributions, benefits equivalent to those provided today could be financed with a payroll tax one-fifth the size of the current one.

It is time for serious reform. Although many people are concerned about the uncertainty of switching to a private system, Chile, the United Kingdom, and Sweden all have enacted similar reforms with great success. Few of us should want to be forced into a failing system—and there is no reason for that to happen. Privatization is a viable and tested alternative.

SOURCE: Ryan Sager, "Privatization Is the Only Way to Save Social Security," *The Hatchet* (George Washington University), February 11, 1999.

No Why does America need to strengthen Social Security? The answer is simple: For nearly half of Americans, Social Security is the only pension they have. The program has worked to relieve poverty among the old, disabled workers, women, and minorities. It prevents social inequality among the rich and poor. For young families, it prevents their in-laws from moving in for support.

Social Security has worked so well because all working Americans contribute to the program and all Americans receive a guaranteed benefit. Ryan Sager, president of GW Libertarians, proposed investing 2 percent of the current Social Security tax in private accounts.

What that means is the guaranteed benefits so many Americans rely on will be cut dramatically. The idea behind this scheme is that the investments will cover the difference.

This two-percent contribution from the average wage earner will only be $540 per year, which equals $21 every two weeks that a worker will contribute. For one-third of all workers, the contribution every two weeks would be $6.50. These deposits are not significant for any broker or even a mutual fund to accept. Individual accounts are too great of a risk to sacrifice over Social Security's guaranteed benefits.

The amount of risk in the stock market for an individual is so large that poor investments will leave many Americans worse off. The cost of supplying information to workers to inform them of good stocks and mutual funds will be enormous, not to mention potentially misleading.

Finally, the cost of having brokers or mutual funds conduct trades will be equal to 20 percent of the paid benefits from individual accounts, according to Professor Peter Diamond of the Massachusetts Institute of Technology. These costs are Wall Street's gain.

President Clinton's plan, on the other hand, is designed to maintain and continue the guaranteed benefits of the Social Security system. Reserving the surplus for Social Security preserves the system so that when Americans who are in their twenties retire, they not only are entitled to, but they will receive the same benefits as their parents and grandparents did.

The president's plan maintains the fairness and stability Social Security was designed to have. Many may argue that because the president has proposed investing part of the surplus in investments other than U.S. Treasury bills, politicians such as senators Lott and Daschle and representatives Gephardt and Hastert will make the Social Security investment decisions.

They are wrong.

A board of governors similar to the Federal Reserve Board will be established to pick investors. These expert investors will decide how to diversify and invest about 15 percent of the Social Security trust fund, which is equal to the assets of Fidelity or Merrill Lynch.

The final issue is how to increase the wealth and savings of all Americans. The president has proposed USA accounts to do this. Unlike individual retirement accounts, these accounts promote savings and do not replace the guaranteed benefits of Social Security. Social Security is not a retirement issue, but rather it is an issue that will affect the lives of every student at [George Washington University].

SOURCE: Adam Streisfeld, "Privatization Will Not Aid Security," *The Hatchet* (George Washington University), February 18, 1999.

Table 17.2 — Growth of the Welfare State

	WELFARE	EDUCATION	HEALTH AND HOUSING
State era (1789–1935)	Private and local charity State child labor laws State unemployment and injury compensation State mothers' pensions	Northwest Ordinance of 1787 (federal) Local academies Local public schools State compulsory education laws Federal Morrill Act of 1862 for land-grant colleges	Local public health ordinances
Federal era (1935–present)	Federal Social Security System Disability insurance VISTA, OEO* Supplemental Security Income Cost of living adjustment (indexing)	GI Bill National Defense Education Act of 1958 Elementary and Secondary Education Act of 1965 School desegregation Head Start	Public housing Hospital construction School lunch program Food stamps Medicare Medicaid

*VISTA = Volunteers in Service to America; OEO = Office of Economic Opportunity

suggest any changes in federal policy but it urged states to make excellence in education their primary goal. This theme was picked up again by President George H. W. Bush. Calling himself the "education president," Bush convened the nation's governors for a highly publicized retreat designed to promote the development of state educational standards. Because Republicans have historically opposed a strong federal role in education, the initiatives of Reagan and Bush remained primarily advisory. But they were very influential in focusing educational reform on standards and testing, now widely practiced across the states.

Both Bill Clinton and George W. Bush further energized the movement for educational achievement. The standards remained voluntary, however; the federal government restricted its role to providing grants to states that developed standards programs.[24] The federal role was substantially increased by President Bush's signature education act, the No Child Left Behind Act of 2001. This act created stronger federal requirements for testing and school accountability. It required that every child in grades 3–8 be tested yearly for proficiency in math and reading. Individual schools will be judged on the basis of how well their students perform on these tests. Parents whose child is in a failing school will have the right to transfer the child to a better school. Students in failing schools can also get access to special funds for tutoring and summer programs. Because there was strong congressional opposition to creating a national test, the states will be responsible for setting standards and devising appropriate tests.

The strong bipartisan support for No Child Left Behind reflects the broad consensus supporting higher standards and more accountability in public education. However, the act will not be easy to implement. Many states are unprepared to launch a new system of standards and testing. In addition, many education experts contend that yearly test results are too volatile to provide a good measure of school performance. Others worry that failing schools will become even weaker as students transfer out of them.[25] It will be several years before we know if federal imposition of standards and testing will improve public education.

One of the hottest areas of controversy in education is school choice. For over two hundred years, schools have been public institutions in the United States, and many name public schooling as the most important social policy in America. Today, however, there are serious challenges to the public monopoly on education. Some critics of public schools argue that government should simply provide parents with vouchers that they can use to attend the school of their choice, public or private. Supporters of vouchers claim that the public education system is too bureaucratic to provide quality education and does not allow parents enough control over their children's education. Voucher plans have so far only been implemented on a very small scale in a few places (Cleveland, Milwaukee, and Florida). In Cleveland, where most of the students using vouchers attend Catholic schools, opponents have charged that vouchers violate the constitutional separation between church and state. Uncertainty about the constitutionality of vouchers had put a damper on the movement supporting vouchers. In 2002, however, the Supreme Court ruled that the Cleveland program was constitutional because it allowed parents to exercise true choices about where their children went to school. Buoyed by the Court's decision, advocates vowed to introduce measures supporting school vouchers in state referenda and in the legislatures of the most sympathetic states. They also hoped to make vouchers a central issue in the 2004 presidential campaign.

Pressures to change the organization of schooling have led to the creation of charter schools across the country. Charter schools are publicly funded schools that are free from the bureaucratic rules and regulations of the school district in which they are located. Charter schools are free to design specialized curricula and to use resources in ways they think most effective. Since the creation of the first charter schools in Minnesota in 1990, states across the country have passed legislation to allow charter schools. The great popularity of such schools suggests that reforms allowing more flexibility and responsiveness to parents may well be possible within the existing public system.

EMPLOYMENT AND TRAINING PROGRAMS

Considering the importance that Americans attach to work and the high value they place on education, it is somewhat surprising that the United States does not have a strong system for employment and job training. Such programs have two goals. One is to prepare entry-level workers for new jobs or to retrain workers whose jobs have disappeared. A second goal is to provide public jobs during

Education policy is the most important means of providing equal opportunity for all Americans. President Bush's 2001 "No Child Left Behind" Act, an education reform bill passed by overwhelmingly bipartisan majorities in Congress, imposes stronger national requirements for school accountability and testing.

Job training is another important means of redistributing opportunity in the United States California governor Gray Davis, shown here speaking at a job training and search assistance center, has been a big supporter of job assistance groups such as Connect!, CalJOBS, Nova, and ProMatch.

Health policies can also promote equal opportunity by seeking to ensure that all classes of Americans are healthy. In 2001, Arkansas governor Mike Huckabee announced that the ARKids First Health Insurance program for children was covering 175,000 children in the state, an all-time high for the program.

economic downturns when sufficient private employment is not available. Since the 1930s, the American employment and training systems have fared poorly in terms of expenditures, stability, and results.[26]

The first public employment programs were launched during the New Deal. These programs were created to use the power of the federal government to get people back to work again. An "alphabet soup" of federal programs sought to employ those who did not have jobs: the Civilian Conservation Corps (CCC) put young men to work on environmental projects in rural areas; and the Works Progress Administration (WPA) employed many different kinds of workers, from writers and artists to manual laborers. In the despairing circumstances of the Great Depression, these public employment programs enjoyed widespread support. But by the end of the 1930s, questions about corruption and inefficiency in employment programs reduced support for them.

Not until the 1960s did the federal government try again. This time, as part of the War on Poverty, government programs were designed to train and retrain workers, primarily the poor, rather than to provide them with public employment. For the most part, the results of these programs were disappointing. It proved very difficult to design effective training policies in the federal system; lack of coordination and poor administration plagued the Great Society training programs. Concern about such administrative problems led Congress to combine funds for all the different training programs into a single block grant in 1973, via the Comprehensive Employment and Training Act (CETA). In doing this, Congress hoped that more local flexibility would create more effective programs.

CETA expanded greatly and, as unemployment rose sharply during the 1970s, became primarily a public-service employment program. The federal government

Housing policies are another means of redistributing opportunity. In this 2002 photo, New Haven mayor John DeStefano and U.S. Secretary of Housing and Urban Development Mel Martinez tour a formerly blighted area of New Haven that is being revived, thanks to funding from the federal government. The suburbanlike development is a new style of public housing.

provided state and local governments funds to create jobs for the unemployed. At its peak, CETA had a budget of more than $10 billion and provided jobs for nearly 739,000 workers—12 percent of the nation's unemployed. But complaints soon arose that CETA was providing jobs primarily to people who were the most job-ready and was doing little for the most disadvantaged. This practice of selecting the most well prepared as participants—called "creaming"—has been a persistent problem with other job-training programs as well. Critics also charged that localities were simply using CETA money to perform tasks they would have paid for out of their own funds if federal money had not been available. Congress abolished CETA in 1981, making it one of the only federal programs totally eliminated in the past twenty or so years.[27]

But job training remained a popular idea, and in 1982, Congress created a new program that supported local efforts at job training. The Job Training Partnership Act (JTPA) became the primary federal program supporting job training. In addition to retraining adult workers, JTPA provided funding for summer jobs for youth. President Clinton placed an especially high value on creating a strong system of job training. The job training law enacted during the last years of the Clinton administration, the Workforce Investment Act, sought to create a more flexible and accessible job training system. It provided for individual training accounts that allow individual workers to select their own training programs. Replacing the maze of job programs inherited from the past are "one stop centers" where workers can learn about a range of training possibilities, register for unemployment insurance, and find assistance with job placement. The act also created local "workforce investment boards" that allow employers a greater say in determining what kind of training is needed in particular areas. The aim of this provision was to make sure that job training programs fit the needs of the local labor market. The law also provides job training for at-risk youth and for the disabled. As the American economy changes and many corporations transfer operations out of the country or downsize their workforces, the need for retraining has become more pressing. Such training is particularly important for the three-quarters of American workers who have not finished four years of college. Enhancing the ability of the federal government to assist American workers, who face increasing economic insecurity, is one of the most important challenges confronting policy makers today.

HEALTH POLICIES

Until recent decades, no government in the United States—national, state, or local—concerned itself directly with individual health. But public responsibility was always accepted for *public* health. After New York City's newly created Board of Health was credited with holding down a cholera epidemic in 1867, most states followed with the creation of statewide public health agencies. Within a decade, the results were obvious. Between 1884 and 1894, for example, Massachusetts's rate of infant mortality dropped from 161.3 per 1,000 to 141.4 per 1,000.[28] Reductions in mortality rates during the late nineteenth century may be the most significant contribution ever made by government to human welfare.

The U.S. Public Health Service (USPHS) has been in existence since 1798 but was a small part of public health policy until after World War II. Established in 1937, but little noticed for twenty years, was the National Institutes of Health

(NIH), an agency within the USPHS created to do biomedical research. Between 1950 and 2002, NIH expenditures by the national government increased from $160 million to $23.3 billion. NIH research on the link between smoking and disease led to one of the most visible public-health campaigns in American history. The Centers for Disease Control and Prevention (CDC), which monitors outbreaks of disease and implements prevention measures, coordinates such public-health campaigns. Subsequently, NIH's focus turned to cancer and acquired immunodeficiency syndrome (AIDS). As with smoking, this work on AIDS resulted in massive public-health education as well as new products and regulations. Today the NIH and the CDC are on the front lines of protecting the country against the threat of bioterrorism. After the September 11 attacks, President Bush requested a 15.7 percent increase in NIH spending to support new research, including the development of a vaccine against anthrax.

Other recent commitments to the improvement of public health are the numerous laws aimed at cleaning up and defending the environment (including the creation in 1970 of the Environmental Protection Agency) and laws attempting to improve the health and safety of consumer products (regulated by the Consumer Product Safety Commission, created in 1972). Health policies aimed directly at the poor include Medicaid and nutritional programs, particularly food stamps and the school lunch program.

In the fiscal year 2002 budget, federal grants to states for Medicaid totaled $142.4 billion, up from $40 billion in 1990. Federal programs for AIDS research, treatment, prevention, and income support had a budget of $13.1 billion in 1998, a major increase from the $2.9 billion spent in 1990.[29] President Clinton also put greater emphasis on AIDS by appointing an "AIDS czar" to coordinate federal AIDS policy, and by giving this position Cabinet status. Bush continued the practice, appointing his own AIDS czar. However, the position has been a difficult balancing act between advocates, health care professionals, and the realities of government finances.

President Clinton's major attempt to reshape federal health policy, and the boldest policy initiative of his administration, was his effort to reform America's health care system. In September 1993, Clinton announced a plan with two key objectives: to limit the rising costs of the American health care system (1991 per capita health spending in America, $2,932, was 83 percent higher than in twenty-one other industrialized nations)[30] and to provide universal health insurance coverage for all Americans (almost 40 million Americans lack health insurance). Clinton's plan at first garnered enormous public support and seemed likely to win congressional approval in some form. But the plan, which entailed a major expansion of federal administration of the health care system, gradually lost momentum as resistance to it took root among those who feared changes in a system that worked well for them. Although Clinton had pledged to make health care the centerpiece of his 1994 legislative agenda, no health care bill even came up for a full congressional vote that year. Following the failure of President Clinton's health care initiative, Congress passed a much smaller program expanding health insurance coverage for low-income children not already receiving Medicaid. Called the State Children's Health Insurance Program, the law provides federal funds to states so that they can offer health insurance to more low-income children. The results have been uneven: some states have greatly expanded coverage of uninsured children

What Government Does . . . After September 11

In September 2001, bioterrorism was transformed from only a theoretical possibility into a frightening new reality for Americans. Although the anthrax letters mailed to media outlets and the Senate ultimately killed only five people, their impact was far reaching. The letters made it clear that our country was vulnerable to bioterrorism attacks whose consequences could be far more deadly. The new threat put the nation's public health system, and particularly the Centers for Disease Control and Prevention (CDC), on the front lines of domestic security.

Headquartered in Atlanta, the CDC is the federal government's "disease surveillance institution," "the first responders to an epidemic."[1] Effective response to an epidemic requires early detection, rapid dissemination of information about diagnoses and appropriate treatment, and quick access to treatment. Although the CDC has each of these capacities, during the anthrax attacks, it became apparent that the agency needed to improve its performance on each count in order to respond adequately to threat of bioterrorism.

The CDC houses the Epidemic Intelligence Service, a fifty-year-old agency of 150 highly skilled professionals who are trained to detect emerging health threats around the world. With the anthrax attacks, the agency mobilized its personnel to identify and track the cases. Its efforts received mixed reviews. On the one hand, it did learn how to treat inhalation anthrax, a disease previously thought to be fatal. On the other hand, it did not immediately recognize how deadly the anthrax was and what a significant threat it posed to postal workers, two of whom died in the attacks.[2]

In disseminating information—a key weapon in the war against bioterrorism—the CDC did even worse. During the anthrax attacks, the CDC found that its communications systems were not up to the task. Local officials complained that they could not get through to the CDC for basic information. The CDC found that it could not easily communicate with local health offices. Although the CDC operates an electronic Epidemic Information Exchange system designed to alert local officials, localities often do not receive the messages. A 1999 survey of city and county health departments found that 65 percent of the CDC's e-mails were not successfully delivered to the local departments.[3] Even before the anthrax attacks, the CDC had funds to create a National Electronic Disease Surveillance System that would link all local public health offices to the CDC, allowing for effective two-way communication. The anthrax attacks highlighted the urgent need to get such a system up and running.

Congressman Christopher Shays (R-Conn.) also urged the CDC to improve its ability to communicate with the public, noting that "The terrorists made CDC far more important than it was before Sept. 11. They're dealing with some very significant issues and I think they are not used to being in the public limelight, but they are going to have to get used to it."[4]

A final component of the war on bioterrorism is access to treatment. The CDC began to prepare for bioterrorism in 1999 when it created the National Pharmaceutical Stockpile, which stores packages of drugs in ten secret locations around the country. The purpose of the stockpile is to make sure that adequate supplies of treatment drugs are available and can be moved quickly to the site of a disease outbreak. At the time of the anthrax attacks, the government's stockpile was inadequate to respond to a major attack. Although the government claimed that drugs could be shipped to all areas of the country in twelve hours, there was much speculation that such rapid delivery would not be possible. To ensure an adequate supply of drugs and improve delivery capacities, spending on the stockpile soared after the anthrax attacks. Only $50 million a year was spent on the stockpile prior to 2001; $644 million was immediately put into improving the stockpile after the attacks.

The threat of bioterrorism poses an unprecedented challenge to the nation's public health system. Although it is a system that includes world-class scientists with long experience in disease investigation, the public health system lacked key capabilities needed to combat bioterrorism. The anthrax attacks sparked the reforms needed to facilitate rapid and effective communication across levels of government and thereby help protect against future threats. They also underscored the importance of leadership that provides the public with clear and strong advice about bioterrorism threats and treatment.

[1] M. A. J. McKenna, "Bioterrorism War Changes CDC Role," *The Atlanta Journal and Constitution*, March 23, 2002, p. A1.
[2] Sheryl Gay Stolberg and Judith Miller, "Bioterror an Uneasy Fit for the C.D.C.," *New York Times*, November 11, 2001, p. A1.
[3] *Ibid.*
[4] *Ibid.*

and have even sought to insure their parents. Other states have been far less aggressive and have not significantly increased the number of insured children. With the recession of 2002, all states had to cut back on plans for broader coverage as their budgets grew tighter.

HOUSING POLICIES

Through public housing for low-income families, which originated in 1937 with the Wagner-Steagall National Housing Act, and subsidized private housing after 1950, the percent of American families living in overcrowded conditions was reduced from 20 percent in 1940 to 9 percent in 1970. Federal policies made an even greater contribution to reducing "substandard" housing, defined by the U.S. Census Bureau as dilapidated houses without hot running water and without some other plumbing. In 1940, almost 50 percent of American households lived in substandard housing. By 1950, this had been reduced to 35 percent; by 1975, to 8 percent.[31] Urban redevelopment programs and rent-supplement programs have helped in a small way to give low-income families access to better neighborhoods and, through that, to better schools and working conditions.

The Clinton administration at first showed a strong ideological commitment to encouraging housing policies and combating homelessness. For instance, in 1994, the Department of Housing and Urban Development (HUD) launched a comprehensive plan to increase emergency shelter availability, access to transitional and rehabilitative services, and the amount of affordable permanent housing. Federal appropriations nearly doubled in 1995, to $1.7 billion. But, especially after 1994, the Clinton administration began to retreat. HUD Secretary Henry Cisneros continually had to waive, virtually to the point of abandonment, a long-standing one-for-one HUD rule, which provided that for every public housing unit destroyed, another would have to be built. And he spent most of his time consolidating programs, downsizing them, and devolving their functions to the state and local governments. In the end, HUD had taken the biggest hit of all departments from Congress. Although not able to carry out its vow to abolish HUD, Congress did cut HUD's budget by more than 10 percent for 1997—from $19.8 billion to $17.8 billion.[32]

Who Gets What from Social Policy?

The two categories of social policy—contributory and noncontributory—generally serve different groups of people. We can understand much about the development of social policy by examining which constituencies benefit from different policies.

The strongest and most generous programs are those in which the beneficiaries are widely perceived as deserving of assistance and also are politically powerful. Because Americans prize work, constituencies who have "earned" their benefits in some way or those who cannot work because of a disability are usually seen as most deserving of government assistance. Politically powerful constituencies are those who vote as a group, lobby effectively, and mobilize to protect the programs from which they benefit.

When we study social policies from a group perspective, we can see that the elderly and the middle class receive the most benefits from the government's social

> **Which groups receive the most benefits from social policies? Which groups receive the fewest?**

policies and that children and the working poor receive the fewest. (In addition, America's social policies do little to change the fact that minorities and women are more likely to be poor than white Americans and men.)

THE ELDERLY

The elderly are the beneficiaries of the two strongest and most generous social policies: old-age pensions (what we call Social Security) and Medicare (medical care for the elderly). As these programs have grown, they have provided most elderly Americans with economic security and have dramatically reduced the poverty rate among the elderly. In 1959, before very many people over the age of sixty-five received social insurance, the poverty rate for the elderly was 35 percent; by 2000, it had dropped to 10.2 percent.[33] Because of this progress, many people call Social Security the most effective antipoverty program in the United States.[34] This does not mean that the elderly are rich, however; in 2000, the median income of elderly households was $23,048, well below the national median income. The aim of these programs is to provide security and prevent poverty, rather than to assist people once they have become poor. And they succeeded in preventing poverty among most of the aged.

One reason that Social Security and Medicare are politically strong is that the elderly are widely seen as a deserving population. They are not expected to work, because of their age. Moreover, both programs are contributory, and a work history is a requirement for receiving a Social Security pension. But these programs are also strong because they serve a constituency that has become quite powerful. The elderly are a very large group: in 2000, there were 35 million Americans over the age of sixty-five. Because Social Security and Medicare are not means-tested, they are available to all former workers and their spouses over the age of sixty-five, whether they are poor or not. The size of this group is of such political importance because the elderly turn out to vote in higher numbers than the rest of the population.

In addition, the elderly have developed strong and sophisticated lobbying organizations that can influence policy making and mobilize elderly Americans to defend these programs against proposals to cut them. One important and influential organization that defends the interests of old people in Washington is the American Association of Retired Persons (AARP). The AARP had over 33 million members in 2002, amounting to one-fifth of all voters. It also has a sophisticated lobbying organization in Washington, which employs 28 lobbyists and a staff of 165 policy analysts.[35] (See Chapter 11 for more discussion of the AARP's lobbying efforts.) Although the AARP is the largest and the strongest organization of the elderly, other groups, such as the Alliance for Retired Americans, to which many retired union members belong, also lobby Congress on behalf of the elderly.

When Congress considers changes in programs that affect the elderly, these lobbying groups pay close attention. They mobilize their supporters and work with legislators to block changes they believe will hurt the elderly. Because of the tremendous political strength of the elderly, Social Security has been nicknamed the "third rail of American politics: touch it and you die."[36] The power of this lobby was apparent in 2002 as Democrats and Republicans each proposed plans to help the elderly pay for prescription drugs. Rapidly rising costs had made prescription drugs a heavy financial burden for the elderly because Medicare, the main source of health insurance for older Americans, does not cover drug costs. Even as the federal budget headed into deficit under the pressure of the recession and the costs of domestic security, politicians in both parties were anxious to show that they could address the concerns of seniors.

THE MIDDLE CLASS

Americans don't usually think of the middle class as benefiting from social policies, but government action promotes the social welfare of the middle class in a variety of ways. First, medical care and pensions for the elderly help the middle class by relieving them of the burden of caring for elderly relatives. Before these programs existed, old people were more likely to live with and depend financially on their adult children. Many middle-class families whose parents and grandparents are in nursing homes rely on Medicaid to pay nursing-home bills.

In addition, the middle class benefits from what some analysts call the **"shadow welfare state."**[37] These are the social benefits that private employers offer to their workers: medical insurance and pensions, for example. The federal government subsidizes such benefits by not taxing the payments that employers and employees make for health insurance and pensions. These **tax expenditures,** as they are called, are an important way in which the federal government helps ensure the social welfare of the middle class. (Such programs are called "tax expenditures" because the federal government helps finance them through the tax system rather than by direct spending.) Another key tax expenditure that helps the middle class is the tax exemption on mortgage interest payments: taxpayers can deduct the amount they have paid in interest on a mortgage from the income they report on their tax return. By not taxing these payments, the government makes home-ownership less expensive.

People often don't think of these tax expenditures as part of social policy because they are not as visible as the programs that provide direct payments or services to beneficiaries. But tax expenditures represent a significant federal investment: they cost the national treasury some $300 billion a year and make it easier and less expensive for working Americans to obtain health care, save for retirement, and buy homes. These programs are very popular with the middle class and Congress rarely considers reducing them. On the few occasions when public officials have tried to limit these programs—with proposals to limit the amount of mortgage interest that can be deducted, for example—they have quickly retreated. These programs are simply too popular among Americans whose power comes from their numbers at the polling booth.

THE WORKING POOR

People who are working but are poor or are just above the poverty line receive only limited assistance from government social programs. This is somewhat surprising, given that Americans value work so highly. But the working poor are typically employed in jobs that do not provide pensions or health care; often they are renters because they cannot afford to buy homes. This means they cannot benefit from the shadow welfare state that subsidizes the social benefits enjoyed by most middle-class Americans. At the same time, however, they cannot get assistance through programs such as Medicaid and TANF, which are largely restricted to the nonworking poor.

shadow welfare state social benefits that private employers offer to their workers, such as medical insurance and pensions

tax expenditures government subsidies provided to employers and employees through tax deductions for amounts spent on health insurance and other benefits; these represent one way the government helps to ensure the social welfare of the middle class

➤ **How effectively does social policy reach the groups that are most likely to be poor?**

In 1995, the Republican-led Congress proposed cuts in Medicare spending, prompting vigorous protests from senior citizens. The political influence of the elderly was evidenced by the immediate defense of Medicare spending by Democratic leaders in Congress, such as House minority leader Dick Gephardt, shown here speaking at a a senior citizens' rally in Washington, D.C. Fearing negative political repercussions in the 1996 elections, Congressional Republicans retreated from their efforts to overhaul the Medicare system.

Two government programs do assist the working poor: the Earned Income Tax Credit (EITC) and food stamps. The EITC was implemented in 1976 to provide poor workers some relief from increases in the taxes that pay for Social Security. As it has expanded, the EITC has provided a modest wage supplement for the working poor, allowing them to catch up on utility bills or pay for children's clothing. Poor workers can also receive food stamps. These two programs help supplement the income of poor workers, but they offer only modest support. Because the wages of

The poor and working poor (such as single mothers with children) have little influence on government. While organized protests representing the interests of the poor and working poor occasionally do occur, they fail to have the impact of similar protests by other groups, such as senior citizens.

less-educated workers have declined significantly over the past fifteen years and minimum wages have not kept pace with inflation, the problems of the working poor remain acute.

Even though the working poor may be seen as deserving, they are not politically powerful because they are not organized. There is no equivalent to the AARP for the poor. Nonetheless, because work is highly valued in American society, politicians find it difficult to cut the few social programs that help the working poor. In 1995, efforts to cut the EITC were defeated by coalitions of Democrats and moderate Republicans, although Congress did place new restrictions on food stamps and also reduced the level of spending on this type of aid.

THE NONWORKING POOR

The only nonworking, able-bodied poor people who receive federal cash assistance are parents who are caring for children. The primary source of cash assistance for these families was AFDC and now is the state-run TANF program, but they also rely on food stamps and Medicaid. Able-bodied adults who are not caring for children are not eligible for federal assistance other than food stamps. Many states provide small amounts of cash assistance to such individuals through programs called "general assistance," but in the past decade, many states have abolished or greatly reduced their general assistance programs in an effort to encourage these adults to work. Thus, the primary reason the federal government provides any assistance to able-bodied adults is because they are caring for children. Although Americans don't like to subsidize adults who are not working, they do not want to harm children.

AFDC was the most unpopular social spending program, and as a result, spending on it declined after 1980. Under TANF, states receive a fixed amount of federal funds, whether the welfare rolls rise or fall. Because the numbers of people on welfare have declined so dramatically since 1994—by over 50 percent—states have had generous levels of federal resources for the remaining welfare recipients. Many states, however, have used the windfall of federal dollars to cut taxes and indirectly support programs that benefit the middle class, not the poor.[38] Welfare recipients have little political power to resist cuts in their benefits. In the late 1960s and early 1970s, the short-lived National Welfare Rights Organization sought to represent the interests of welfare recipients. But it proved difficult to keep the organization operating because its members and its constituents had few resources and were difficult to organize.[39] Because welfare recipients are widely viewed as undeserving, and because they are not politically organized, they have played little part in recent debates about welfare.

MINORITIES, WOMEN, AND CHILDREN

Minorities, women, and children are disproportionately poor. Much of this poverty is the result of disadvantages that stem from the position of these groups in the labor market. African Americans and Latinos tend to be economically less well off than the rest of the American population. In 2000, the poverty rate for African Americans was 22.1 percent, and for Latinos it was 21.2 percent. Both rates are triple the poverty rate for non-Hispanic whites, which was 7.5 percent.[40] The median income for black households in 2000 was $30,439, for Hispanics it was $33,447, whereas for non-Hispanic white households the median household income was $45,904.[41] Much of this economic inequality stems from the fact that minority workers tend to have low-wage jobs. Minorities are also more likely to become unemployed and to remain unemployed for longer periods of time than are white Americans. African Americans, for example, typically have experienced twice as much unemployment than other Americans have. The combination of low-wage jobs and unemployment often means that minorities are less likely to have jobs that give them access to the shadow welfare state. They are more likely to fall into the precarious categories of the working poor or the nonworking poor.

In the past several decades, policy analysts have begun to talk about the "feminization of poverty," or the fact that women are more likely to be poor than men are. This problem is particularly acute for single mothers, who are more than twice as likely to fall below the poverty line than the average American (see Figure 17.3 on the next page). When the Social Security Act was passed in 1935, the main programs for poor women were Aid to Dependent Children (ADC) and survivors' insurance for widows. The framers of the act believed that ADC would gradually disappear as more women became eligible for survivors' insurance. The social model behind the Social Security Act was that of a male breadwinner with a wife and children. Women were not expected to work, and if a woman's husband died, ADC or survivors' insurance would help her stay at home and raise her children. The framers of Social Security did not envision today's large number of single women heading families. At the same time, they did not envision that so many women with children would also be working. This combination of changes helped make AFDC (the successor program to ADC) more controversial. Many people asked, Why shouldn't welfare recipients work, if the majority of women who are not on welfare work? Such questions led to the wel-

Poverty Level in the United States, 1960–2000

Figure 17.3

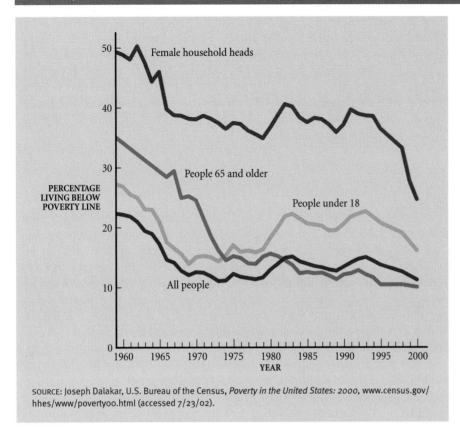

SOURCE: Joseph Dalakar, U.S. Bureau of the Census, *Poverty in the United States: 2000*, www.census.gov/hhes/www/povertyoo.html (accessed 7/23/02).

fare reform of 1996, which created TANF, specifically meant as a means of temporary assistance to families.

The need to combine work and childcare is a problem for most single parents. This problem is more acute for single mothers than for single fathers, because on average, women still earn less than men, and because working creates new expenses such as child care and transportation costs. Many women working in low-wage jobs do not receive health insurance as a benefit of their jobs; they must pay the cost of such insurance themselves. As a result, many poor women found that once they were working, the expenses of child care, transportation, insurance, etc., left them with less cash per month than they would have received if they had not worked and had instead collected AFDC and Medicaid benefits. These women concluded that it was not "worth it" for them to leave AFDC and work. Some states are now experimenting with programs to encourage women to work by allowing them to keep some of their welfare benefits even when they are working. Although Americans want individuals to be self-sufficient, research suggests that single mothers with low-wage jobs are likely to need continuing assistance to make ends meet.[42]

One of the most troubling issues related to American social policy is the number of American children who live in poverty. The rate of child poverty in 2000 was

16.2 percent—4.9 percent higher than that of the population as a whole. These high rates of poverty stem in part from the design of American social policies. Because these policies do not generously assist able-bodied adults who aren't working, and because these policies offer little help to the working poor, the children of these adults are likely to be poor as well.

As child poverty has grown, several lobbying groups have emerged to represent children's interests; the most well known of these is the Children's Defense Fund. But even with a sophisticated lobbying operation, poor children do not have much political power. Although their numbers are large, children do not vote and therefore cannot wield much political power.[43]

The Welfare State and American Values

> **How has the formation of social policy reflected the debate over liberty, equality, and democracy?**

The development of social policy in the United States reflects shifts in our views about how government can best help accomplish fundamental national goals. Until the 1930s, the federal government did very little in the domain of social policy. The country's major social policy was free public education, which was established by the states and administered locally. Americans placed especially strong emphasis on education because an educated citizenry was seen as an essential component of a strong democracy.[44] Given the strength of these beliefs, it is not surprising that free public education was available in the United States well before European nations established public education systems.

Other public social policies, established from the 1930s on, have stirred up much more controversy. Liberals often argue that more generous social policies are needed if America is to truly ensure equality of opportunity. Some liberals have argued that the government needs to go beyond simply providing opportunity and should ensure more equal conditions, especially where children are concerned. Conservative critics, on the other hand, often argue that social policies that offer income support take the ideal of equality too far and, in the process, do for individuals what they should be doing for themselves. From this perspective, social policies make the government too big, and big government is seen as a fundamental threat to Americans' liberties.

Yet conservatives do not agree about how best to achieve a balance between the ideals of liberty, equality, and democracy. Two different conservative perspectives can be distinguished. The **libertarian** view holds that government social policy interferes with society too much and, in the process, has created more problems than it has solved.[45] Many libertarians believe that the mere existence of social policies is an infringement on individual liberties: the government forces some citizens to pay taxes for the benefit of other citizens. The most extreme policy prescription that emerges from this perspective advocates the elimination of all social policies. For example, political scientist Charles Murray has proposed eliminating all social programs except temporary unemployment insurance. In his view, such a move would both enhance the freedom of all Americans and improve society, because individuals would recover their individual initiative if they had to take care of themselves.[46] A less sweeping approach would reduce social programs to a bare minimum or make them temporary.

Other conservatives see things differently. They want to use the power of the government to enforce certain standards of behavior among beneficiaries of gov-

libertarian the political philosophy that is skeptical of any government intervention as a potential threat against individual liberty; libertarians believe that government has caused more problems than it has solved

ernment social programs. Many people with these views call themselves "new paternalists."[47] They believe that government social programs have not forced recipients to behave responsibly. They reject the idea that social programs should simply be abandoned, because they fear the consequences for our democracy. New paternalists do not believe that individuals will behave more responsibly if government programs are withdrawn; instead they fear that social disorder will simply continue. In their view, such disorder will inevitably undermine a healthy democracy, and the primary role of government social policy should be to restore the social order.

Some of the measures supported by new paternalists are also backed by many liberals. These include requiring work in exchange for welfare benefits and compelling absent parents (usually fathers) to make child support payments to the families they have abandoned. Many people from varying political perspectives applauded in 1995 when the federal government tracked down and arrested a prominent investment banker who had fled from state to state in order to avoid paying child support.[48] Other measures are more controversial. For example, some states have enacted reforms denying additional welfare benefits to women who bear a child while on welfare. Liberals charge that such measures violate a most basic individual liberty: the right to have children.[49] New paternalists argue that infringement of individual liberties is simply the price that beneficiaries of government programs have to pay in return for receiving public support.

Conservatives share the view that the primary problems that many social policies address are not economic in origin but instead stem from individual deficiencies. If people behaved more responsibly—if they saved for their retirement, if they did not have children they can't afford to support—there would be little need for government social policy. Liberals, in contrast, believe that the root of many social problems is economic. They believe that opportunities for economic success are not equally available to all Americans and that it is the government's responsibility to open opportunities for all. Thus, liberals are far more likely than conservatives to believe that the ideal of equality compels the state to provide social programs. But, like conservatives, liberals do not all agree: some liberals place a greater emphasis on achieving equality as a *result;* others believe that government should do all it can to provide opportunity but that it should not go beyond providing opportunity.

Some liberals who believe that the government should do more to promote equal outcomes have argued that social benefits should be provided as a right of citizenship and that all Americans should be entitled to a basic standard of living. At particular historical moments, there have been social movements arguing in favor of such approaches to social policy in the United States, but views arguing in favor of equality of result have always been disadvantaged in the American political system. The idea of "social rights," prevalent in many European nations, has no counterpart in American politics. Moreover, the Supreme Court repeatedly refused to acknowledge social or economic rights in the 1960s and 1970s, even as it was making strong efforts to ensure political and civil rights.[50]

Most liberals, then, argue that the aim of social policy should be to provide equality of opportunity. They believe that it is particularly important to ensure that all children have an equal chance to succeed. The sharpest liberal criticism of current social policy has been directed at its failure to address the growth of child poverty. This criticism stems from the belief that poor children have far less opportunity to succeed than the children of the well-off and that such inequalities are

Government, Wealth, and Distribution in Western Democracies

As with the role of government in the economy, so goes its commitment to social policies. Anglo-American democracies (see Chapter 16) are generally characterized by a greater degree of skepticism toward an active role of government in shaping social policy, while continental European social democracies have historically shown a more active commitment to various contributory and public assistance programs. These respective attitudes in many instances result in distinctly different patterns of public expenditures devoted to various social policies across the two groups of democracies. They have also served to set the United States apart not only from democracies identified with the continental European pattern but frequently from the pattern common to that of the Anglo-American democracies, as well.

By comparing public opinion polls, we can see that on average, while nearly a third of respondents in Anglo-American democracies *strongly* favored cuts in government spending in the mid-1990s, over 40 percent of Americans are in favor of such cuts, a proportion closer to that of the continental European democracies. Cuts in spending seem to elicit a different response from respondents than questions dealing directly with taxes. If respondents are asked to choose between reduced taxes (even if this means cuts in social spending) or increased social spending, typically over half the respondents in the Anglo-American countries would prefer to reduce taxes. Ironically, respondents in the United States are less strident in their support of reduced taxes at the expense of social spending (40 percent). Perhaps this is because they already pay among the lowest taxes among industrial democracies. Indeed, the public within the continental European democracies, already paying much higher tax rates than their Anglo-American counterparts, are even more supportive of reduced taxes (57 percent).

When asked, however, whether it is the responsibility of government to provide for the health care of the sick, as well as a decent standard of living for the old, the difference between the citizens within the two traditions of capitalism diverge sharply. On average, nearly two-thirds of the respondents across the sample of twelve democracies in 1996 confirmed that it was *definitely* the responsibility of the government to provide health care for the sick, while another six in ten expressed the same attitude with respect to providing a decent standard of living for the old. These percentages were slightly higher for the continental European social democracies (71 percent and 68 percent, respectively), while they were sharply lower for the Anglo-American democracies (62 percent and 55 percent, respectively). For citizens in the United States, the respective proportions were significantly smaller. Less than 40 percent of the respondents in the United States expressed such a definite affirmative attitude toward government's obligation to provide health care for the sick or a decent standard of living for the old.

Finally, with respect to the government's role in shaping various social policies, there is virtually no difference between the degree of commitment to education and health care across the two capitalist traditions. On average, governments of both capitalist traditions spend the equivalent of 6 to 7 percent of their Gross Domestic Product on general health care and education (these are figures for all levels of government—local, regional, and national). However, social security transfers are another matter. These are primarily public assistance program expenditures that serve to redistribute income within society. These consist of benefits for sickness, old age, family allowances, social assistance grants, and welfare provisions spent by all levels of government. Such expenditures amount to 19 percent of the GDP for continental European social democracies, while only 14 percent for Anglo-American democracies (13 percent for the United States) as of the mid-1990s.

SOURCES: World Bank, *Entering the 21st Century: World Development Report, 1999/2000* (New York: Oxford University Press, 1999); United Nations Development Programme, *Human Development Report 1999* (New York: Oxford University Press, 1999); Nancy Birdsall, "Life Is Unfair: Inequality in the World," *Foreign Policy* 111 (Summer 1998), pp. 76–93.

incompatible with fundamental American ideals. Liberals also believe that the government has an important role in creating opportunities for adults.

Where do average Americans fit in all these debates? Americans are often said to be philosophical conservatives and operational liberals.[51] When asked about government social policy in the abstract, they say they disapprove of activist government—a decidedly conservative view. But when they must evaluate particular programs, Americans generally express support—a more liberal perspective. Some programs, of course, are preferred over others. Policies in which the recipients are regarded as deserving, such as programs for the elderly, receive more support than those that assist working-age people. Programs that have a reputation for effectiveness and programs that require people to help themselves through work are also viewed favorably.[52]

In sum, most Americans take a pragmatic approach to social welfare policies: they favor programs that work, and they want to reform those that seem not to work. By rejecting the policy extremes, Americans signal their awareness of the tensions that social policies generate among their most deeply held values of liberty, equality, and democracy. Political debates about social policy connect most closely with the public when they consider which mix of policies represents the appropriate balance among these three ideals, rather than when they ask the public to choose among them.

GET INVOLVED

What You Can Do: Question Social Policy

Social policy directly and indirectly touches the lives of all Americans. Most working Americans pay the payroll taxes that finance Social Security and Medicare. All Americans over the age of sixty-five are covered by Medicare and most also receive Social Security. But even people who are not directly receiving benefits are affected by the federal social role: many more people would be supporting their parents or grandparents if federal social policy did not exist. In addition, many working-age Americans would be much less secure without the protections provided by unemployment insurance, workers' compensation, food stamps, and TANF. Their quality of life would decline without the mortgage deduction and other tax expenditures that assist employers in providing benefits. Citizens thus have a direct stake in the future of social policy—both on the benefit side and on the payment side.

Because social policy is woven into the fabric of daily life for most people, it is not surprising that citizens have often played an active role in debates about social policy. This is particularly evident with regard to Social Security because it is such a big program and so many people rely on its benefits. Active citizen mobilization during the Great Depression was central to establishing Social Security in the first place. The Townsend movement of the 1930s, named after Dr. Francis Townsend, the man who led it, spurred widespread interest and built an active political movement of more than 10 million supporters pressing for public pensions for the elderly. As we saw earlier in this chapter, citizen involvement continued as Social Security grew and the AARP emerged in the 1950s as a powerful lobby to defend Social Security. With a membership of over 33 million, the AARP is one of the largest and most powerful lobbies in Washington.

In recent years, citizen interest in Social Security has begun to extend beyond the elderly. Groups such as X-PAC and the 2030 Center have emerged to represent the voices of youth in this debate. Yet it is often hard to tell what is a genuine citizen voice: groups on all sides of the reform issue receive money and support from interests that stand to benefit from one policy direction or another. As reform of Social Security has become a hot issue, efforts have been made to broaden and deepen the debate. For example in 1998, the Pew Charitable Trusts, a private philanthropic foundation, launched a project called "Americans Discuss Social Security," in which it set up citizen meetings across the country, video teleconferences, and other forums through which citizens could learn about and discuss future options for Social Security. The organizers were particularly interested in finding ways to engage college students in that debate, going so far as to sponsor a college outreach program with a $100,000 reward for the best proposal on how to encourage students to participate.[53]

Many social policies involve highly technical issues: actuaries devise complicated formulas to estimate future Social Security expenditures; health care experts propose intricate reforms designed to reduce costs. Yet social policy is far more than a technical issue—it fundamentally engages our national values. What do we owe each other as members of society? What should government do for its people and what should be expected of them in return? Only an engaged and informed citizenry can provide the best answers to these questions. They are too important to be left to the experts.

Summary

The capitalist system is the most productive type of economy on earth, but it is not perfect. Most people face some insecurity over the course of their lives; poverty amidst plenty continues. Many policies have emerged to deal with these imperfections. This chapter discussed the welfare state and gave an account of how Americans came to recognize extremes of poverty and dependency and how Congress then attempted to reduce these extremes with policies that moderately redistribute opportunity.

The first section of this chapter examined the development of social policies. These policies—and the political conflicts surrounding them—underscore the fact that Americans hold multiple ideals. Americans are truly committed to individual liberty, but they also support equality of opportunity.

Welfare state policies are subdivided into several categories. First, there are the contributory programs. Virtually all employed persons are required to contribute a portion of their wages into welfare trust funds, and later on, when they retire or are disabled, they have a right, or entitlement, to draw on those contributions. Another category of welfare is composed of noncontributory programs, also called "public assistance." These programs provide benefits for people who can demonstrate need by passing a "means test." Assistance from contributory and noncontributory programs can involve either cash benefits or in-kind benefits.

Contributory and noncontributory programs generally serve different groups of people. The elderly, who are widely viewed as deserving of benefits, receive the most comprehensive and generous social programs. The middle class benefits from the "shadow welfare state," which consists of benefits offered through their jobs but supported by federal tax breaks. There are few social programs to support the working poor because many noncontributory social programs, such as Medicaid and the Temporary Assistance to Needy Families block grant, are reserved for the nonworking poor.

The last section of the chapter considered the tensions between the welfare state and American values. Social policies represent a balance among the ideals of liberty, democracy, and equality. Although political debates often frame the issues surrounding social policies in terms that emphasize one value over others, most Americans tend to take a pragmatic perspective that strikes a balance among these core political ideals.

For Further Reading

Katz, Michael. *In the Shadow of the Poorhouse: A Social History of Welfare in America.* New York: Basic Books, 1986.

Katznelson, Ira, and Margaret Weir. *Schooling for All: Race, Class, and the Democratic Ideal.* New York: Basic Books, 1985.

Light, Paul. *Artful Work: The Politics of Social Security Reform.* New York: Random House, 1985.

Marmor, Theodore R., Jerry L. Mashaw, and Phillip L. Harvey. *America's Misunderstood Welfare State.* New York: Basic Books, 1990.

Murray, Charles. *Losing Ground: American Social Policy, 1950–1980.* New York: Basic Books, 1984.

Orfield, Gary, and Carole Ashkinaze. *The Closing Door: Conservative Policy and Black Opportunity.* Chicago: University of Chicago Press, 1991.

Patterson, James T. *America's Struggle against Poverty, 1900–1994.* Cambridge, MA: Harvard University Press, 1994.

Skocpol, Theda. *The Missing Middle: Working Families and the Future of American Social Policy.* New York: Norton, 2000.

Weir, Margaret, Ann Orloff, and Theda Skocpol. *The Politics of Social Policy in the United States.* Princeton, NJ: Princeton University Press, 1988.

Weir, Margaret, ed. *The Social Divide: Political Parties and the Future of Activist Government.* Washington, D.C.: Brookings Institution Press, 1998.

Study Outline

www.wwnorton.com/wtp4e

1. Equality of opportunity, a widely shared American ideal, was enshrined by Thomas Jefferson in the Declaration of Independence. But there remain problems associated with this ideal.

2. The lowest income brackets are disproportionately composed of members of groups who have been deprived of opportunities.

The Welfare State

1. Prior to 1935, the welfare system in America was composed of private groups rather than government. State governments gradually assumed some of the obligation to relieve the poor.

2. The founding of the welfare state can be dated to the Social Security Act of 1935; this act provided for both contributory and noncontributory welfare programs.

3. Contributory programs—such as Social Security and unemployment compensation—provide "forced savings" for individuals who, as a consequence of making a contribution, can receive program benefits at a later time.

4. Noncontributory programs—such as food stamps and Temporary Assistance to Needy Families (TANF)—provide assistance to people based on demonstrated need rather than any contribution they may have made.

5. Spending on social policies, especially Social Security and Medicare, has increased dramatically in recent decades, raising concerns about how entitlement programs will be paid for in future decades.

Opening Opportunity

1. Education, employment, health, and housing policies are four ways to break the cycle of poverty and redistribute opportunities.

2. The education policies of state and local governments are the most important single force in the distribution and redistribution of opportunity in America.

3. Employment and job training programs have not been a consistent goal of the modern welfare state.

4. Although states also took the early lead in the arena of public health policy, the federal government began to adopt policies in the early 1900s to protect citizens from the effects of pollution and other health hazards.

5. Federal housing policy consists of many pork-barrel programs, but it also represents a commitment to improving the conditions and opportunities of the poor.

Who Gets What from Social Policy?

1. The elderly are the beneficiaries of generous social policies in part because they are perceived as being a deserving population and because they have become a strong interest group.

2. The middle class benefits from social policies in many ways; one way is through the use of tax expenditures, which provide that certain payments made by employers and employees are not taxed by the government.

3. People who are working but are still poor receive limited assistance from government social programs. Although they may be seen as deserving, they receive only limited assistance because they lack organization and political power.

4. Medicaid and TANF are programs aimed at the able-bodied, nonworking poor, but they only receive assistance if they are parents caring for children. The unpopularity of such programs has prompted efforts to decrease spending in recent years.

The Welfare State and American Values

1. The development of social policy in the United States reflects the tensions between the values of liberty, equality, and democracy. Various conservative and liberal perspectives attempt to reconcile these tensions with differing views on social policy. Each of these approaches seems out of step, however, with the more pragmatic view held by most Americans.

Practice Quiz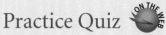

www.wwnorton.com/wtp4e

1. Which of the following is *not* an example of a contributory program?
   a) Social Security
   b) Medicare
   c) food stamps
   d) All of the above are examples of contributory programs.

2. Prior to 1935, the private welfare system in the United States made a distinction between
   a) contributory and noncontributory programs.
   b) citizens and recent immigrants.
   c) the deserving poor and the undeserving poor.
   d) religious and secular assistance.

3. America's welfare state was constructed initially in response to
   a) World War II.
   b) political reforms of the Progressive era.
   c) the Great Depression.
   d) the growth of the military-industrial complex.

4. Which of the following are examples of in-kind benefits?
   a) Medicaid and food stamps
   b) Social Security payments and cost-of-living adjustments
   c) Medicare and unemployment compensation
   d) none of the above

5. Means testing requires that applicants for welfare benefits show
   a) that they are capable of getting to and from their workplace.
   b) that they have the ability to store and prepare food.
   c) some definite need for assistance plus an inability to provide for it.
   d) that they have the time and resources to fully take advantage of federal educational opportunities.

6. In 1996, as part of welfare reform, Aid to Families with Dependent Children was abolished and replaced by
   a) the Earned Income Tax Credit.
   b) Aid to Dependent Children.
   c) Supplemental Security Income.
   d) Temporary Assistance to Needy Families.

7. In terms of receiving benefits of social policies, what distinguishes the elderly from the working poor?
   a) The elderly are perceived as deserving, whereas the working poor are not.
   b) There is no significant difference between these two groups.
   c) The elderly are more organized and more politically powerful than are the working poor.
   d) The elderly are less organized and less politically powerful than are the working poor.

8. Who are the chief beneficiaries of the "shadow welfare state"?
   a) the rich
   b) the nonworking poor
   c) the working poor
   d) the middle class

9. Which of the following is *not* aimed at breaking the cycle of poverty?
   a) drug policies
   b) education policies
   c) employment training programs
   d) health policies

Critical Thinking Questions

www.wwnorton.com/wtp4e

1. Two factors that seem to influence a particular group's ability to get what it wants from social policy are a) the perception that the group is deserving, and b) the political organization and power of the group. In some ways, it is easy to take each of these factors as an independent ingredient of social policy success. But each factor could be seen as having an impact on the other. Select a group and discuss its relative success or failure in social policy. How might the perception of a group as deserving of assistance (and the assistance it receives) help that group become organized and politically powerful? How might organization and political power help shape public opinion favorably toward the group you selected?

2. Describe the changes over time in the welfare state in the United States. What factors led to the expansion of governmental power (both state and national) over social policy? What factors might lead to a decrease of governmental activity in social policy? How do you think social policy in the United States will change in the future? Which of today's political forces and debates will be important in shaping the social policies of the future?

3. The American welfare state is very generous to some groups and much less generous to others. For example, the elderly receive many benefits from the welfare state, while young people receive relatively few benefits other than education. Likewise, the middle class enjoys many secure benefits, while the poor's access to benefits is much less certain. How did these patterns of social welfare policy become established over time? In what way do these benefit patterns reflect American values? Do you think these patterns should be changed?

Key Terms

www.wwnorton.com/wtp4e

Aid to Families with Dependent Children (AFDC) (p. 692)
contributory programs (p. 690)
cost-of-living adjustments (COLAs) (p. 691)

entitlement (p. 693)
equality of opportunity (p. 685)
food stamps (p. 692)
indexing (p. 691)
in-kind benefits (p. 692)
libertarian (p. 716)
means testing (p. 692)
Medicaid (p. 692)
Medicare (p. 690)

noncontributory programs (p. 692)
shadow welfare state (p. 711)
Social Security (p. 690)
Supplemental Security Income (SSI) (p. 693)
tax expenditures (p. 711)
Temporary Assistance to Needy Families (TANF) (p. 692)

18 FOREIGN POLICY AND DEMOCRACY

★ **The Players: The Makers and Shapers of Foreign Policy**

What institutions make up the foreign policy establishment?
What groups help shape foreign policy? Among these players, which are
  most influential?

★ **The Values in American Foreign Policy**

What are the legacies of the traditional system of foreign policy?
What new values guided U.S. foreign policy after World War II?

★ **The Instruments of Modern American Foreign Policy**

What are the six primary instruments of modern American foreign policy?
How does each instrument reflect a balance between the values of the traditional system of foreign policy and the values of cold war politics?

★ **Roles Nations Play**

What four traditional foreign policy roles has the United States adopted
  throughout its history?
Since the end of World War II, how has the role of the United States in
  world affairs evolved?

What Government Does and Why It Matters

EPTEMBER 11 MADE THE U.S. government's conduct of foreign policy far more complicated, but not fundamentally different. Historically, the United States had a fairly simple foreign policy apparatus: the State Department conducted diplomacy and depended on its embassies to provide all the intelligence the government needed. The War Department and the Navy Department presided over the armed forces and depended upon America's distance from the rest of the world to buy us time for mobilization. After World War II, the military was consolidated into a Department of Defense, in which the armed forces were subordinated to civilian political authority. The new department stressed preparedness, having learned from the attack on Pearl Harbor that there no longer lay such a big advantage in being situated between the Atlantic and the Pacific oceans. To aid in this new commitment to preparedness, the government added a vast, mysterious "intelligence community," in which the focus on secrecy was so pervasive that even its annual budget was a secret. After September 11, these agencies for foreign intelligence struggled to find ways and means of collaborating with the FBI and other agencies of domestic intelligence in order to defend the country.

Collaboration and cooperation—with the aim of coordination—for internal defense and security became a commitment to a new form of "what government does." One of President Bush's first decisions after September 11 was the creation, by executive order, of a White House Office of Homeland Security; the office would not only advise the president but would also be responsible for locating and coordinating over fifty national government agencies, plus thousands of local and state governmental bodies for intelligence, surveillance, and action against terrorism. President Bush appointed an able former Pennsylvania governor, Tom Ridge, but gave him little genuine authority to carry out the requested coordination. As Ridge soon discovered, coordinating government activities on such a scale is like herding cats. For example, six months to the day after September 11, a flying school in Florida received word from the Immigration and Naturalization Service that it had issued visas allowing Mohamed Atta and Marwan Al-Shehhi, who had been identified as the pilots of the two airliners that hit the World Trade Center, to enroll as students. The embarrassment was so extensive that it led to two very serious retaliatory proposals. The first suggestion was to abolish the Immigration and Naturalization Service, breaking it into two parts—one for immigrant services and the other for border security. The other proposal was to fuse the INS with three other agencies concerned with border security—the Customs Service, the Border Patrol, and the Coast Guard. But Ridge lacked the power to order government agencies to do anything. While his responsibilities were far-reaching, his power was limited to a license to persuade. If agencies resisted his initiatives—as the INS, Customs Service, Border Patrol, and Coast Guard did in this case—Ridge did not have the direct power to make them comply.

As a result, President Bush called for the creation of a Department of Homeland Security. The new department aimed to improve the government's capacity to fight terrorism by combining twenty-two different agencies under a single umbrella, a much more far-reaching organization than the earlier Office of Homeland Security.

This story is indicative of the difficulty of adjusting to a new era of foreign policy. It is also a demonstration that the new era does not require a governmental revolution but rather a new and better use of the apparatus that is already available. Foreign policy must be conducted by government agencies and government representatives who all pursue virtually the same national interest, national objectives, and national goals. Strategies and tactics will differ in every situation, but the institutions and instruments of what government does in international relations remain about the same. As Professor Joseph Nye put it, "Suppressing terrorism will take years of patient, unspectacular civilian cooperation with other countries. . . . Although the United States does well on the traditional measures, there is increasingly more going on in the world that those measures fail to capture."[1] ■

THIS chapter offers no solutions, but it does provide a meaningful context—through review of the history and the principles of American foreign policy—for the key contemporary problems with which our government must deal. Such an analysis must treat at least four dimensions of foreign policy, which will make up the four main sections of this chapter.

■ **First, who makes and shapes foreign policy in the United States?** Among these players, we will see that the president is most influential.

■ **Second, what values guide American foreign policy?** We will look at the history of American foreign policy and see that, while the United States adopted some new values as it emerged as a world power, some legacies of the traditional system remain.

■ **Third, what tools are available for the conduct of foreign policy?** We will examine the institutions and programs that serve to enable government to pursue America's national interests.

■ **Fourth, how does the United States conduct its foreign policy in the post–cold war world?** We will assess the roles for America today and how well those roles uphold American political values.

The Players: The Makers and Shapers of Foreign Policy

Although the power of the American people over foreign policy is impossible to overestimate, "the people" should not be given all the credit or all the blame for actual policies and their outcomes. As in domestic policy, foreign policy making is a highly pluralistic arena. First there are the official players, those who comprise the "foreign policy establishment"; these players and the agencies they head can be called the actual "makers" of foreign policy. But there are other major players, less official but still influential. We call these the "shapers."

WHO MAKES FOREIGN POLICY?

The President   Most American presidents have been domestic politicians who set out to make their place in history through achievements in domestic policy. This is consistent with the traditional place of foreign policy, which has been treated as virtually an extension of domestic policies. The standard joke during Clinton's

> ➢ **What institutions make up the foreign policy establishment?**

1992 campaign, extending well into his first year, was that he had learned his foreign policy at the International House of Pancakes! Thus, it was not shockingly unusual that President George W. Bush had virtually no foreign policy preparation. He had traveled very little outside the United States, and he had had virtually no foreign experience as governor of Texas, even though that state has the largest international border of any state in the United States. But, like his immediate predecessor, Bush displayed very soon after his inauguration that he was a quick learner. He stacked his cabinet and subcabinet with foreign and defense policy experts of extraordinary training, experience, and knowledge.

His first major foreign policy action was to bomb Iraq—a safe and inexpensive way to convey the impression that he was determined to be an effective commander in chief. And, whether right or wrong, he was decisive in the initiatives he took to define America's national interest for his administration. Examples include revival of the controversial nuclear missile shield ("Star Wars"); his readiness to abandon the ABM treaty, which meant a serious and ugly confrontation with the Russians; changes in policy priorities away from humanitarian and environmental goals with a far stronger emphasis on goals more directly within the realm of national security; and turning America's concerns (by degree or emphasis) away from Europe toward an "Asia-first" policy. His first real test of leadership—the imbroglio with China over the emergency landing of a U.S. spy plane—was almost universally praised for patience and finesse. His calm and patient approach to the unbelievably intense crisis following the September 11, 2001, terrorist attacks also revealed his leadership abilities. During the weeks following the crisis, public approval of his job as president remained extremely high, as was approval of his handling of the war itself.

September 11 and its aftermath immensely accentuated the president's role and place in foreign policy. By 2002, foreign policy was the centerpiece of the Bush administration's agenda. In a June 1 speech at West Point, the "Bush Doctrine" of preemptive war was announced. Bush argued that "Our security will require all Americans . . . to be ready for preemptive action when necessary to defend our liberty and to defend our lives." Bush's statement was clearly intended to justify his administration's plans to invade Iraq, but it had much wider implications for international relations (as we shall explore at the end of the chapter), including the central role of the American president in guiding foreign policy.

The Bureaucracy The major foreign policy players in the bureaucracy are the secretaries of the departments of State, Defense, and the Treasury; the Joint Chiefs of Staff (JCOS), especially the chair of the JCOS; and the director of the Central Intelligence Agency (CIA). A separate unit in the bureaucracy comprising these people and a few others is the National Security Council (NSC), whose main purpose is to iron out the differences among the key players and to integrate their positions in order to confirm or reinforce a decision the president wants to make in foreign policy or military policy. During the Clinton administration, the secretary of the Department of Commerce also became an increasingly important foreign policy maker, with the rise and spread of economic globalization. To this group another has been added: the Department of Homeland Security, headed by former Pennsylvania governor Tom Ridge. The department has four main divisions: Border and Transportation Security; Emergency

Preparedness and Response; Chemical, Biological, Radiological, and Nuclear Countermeasures; and Information Analysis and Infrastructure Protection. Although each of the twenty-two agencies within the four main divisions has an expertise in homeland security, their missions are more far-ranging, such as providing relief to victims of natural disasters and stopping counterfeiters.

Coordinating the diverse missions of a single agency is a challenge; coordinating the efforts of multiple agencies is especially problematic. American foreign policy is replete with instances of the CIA heading in one direction while the Department of State or Defense or the Joint Chiefs of Staff head in another. The National Security Council and now the Department of Homeland Security attempt to keep the various players on the same page. But will these agencies—each with their own authority, interests, and priorities—follow the same protocol?

In addition to these top cabinet-level officials, key lower-level staff members have policy-making influence as strong as that of the cabinet secretaries—some may occasionally exceed cabinet influence. These include the two or three specialized national security advisers in the White House, the staff of the NSC (headed by the national security adviser), and a few other career bureaucrats in the departments of State and Defense whose influence varies according to their specialty and to the foreign policy issue at hand.

Many intelligence agencies have come in for heavy criticism since September 11. Top among these is the Central Intelligence Agency, set up in 1947 to be the supervisor, coordinator, assimilator, and final integrator of all the other agencies in the intelligence community, including the National Security Agency (NSA), which breaks codes and performs electronic eavesdropping; the National Reconnaissance Office (NRO), which coordinates satellite R&D; the Central Imaging Office (CIO), which supervises photographic surveillance; the Defense Intelligence Agency (DIA, in the Defense Department), which performs military intelligence analysis; and the intelligence services of each of the armed services divisions within the Defense Department. There are also a few civilian intelligence agencies, the most important of which are the Federal Bureau of Investigation (FBI), the Immigration and Naturalization Service (INS), and the Internal Revenue Service (IRS). Though the names of these agencies are familiar to the public, in many respects they are "secret agencies," even down to their actual budgets, not to mention their espionage and sabotage operations.[2] Following World War II, the CIA began to keep strictly to activities outside the United States, and the FBI (in particular) limited itself to the domestic United States. That separation of jurisdiction no longer makes sense in our globalized world. One of the consequences of the creation of the Office (and then Department) of Homeland Security is that central coordination might make these agencies a bit more transparent.

Congress   While the Constitution gives Congress the power to declare war, Congress has exercised this power on only five occasions: the War of 1812, the Mexican War (1846), the Spanish-American War (1898), World War I, and World War II. For the first 150 years of American history, Congress's role was limited because, as we will see, the U.S.'s role in world affairs was limited. During this time, the Senate was the most important congressional foreign policy player because of its constitutional role in reviewing and approving treaties. The treaty power is still the primary entrée of the Senate into foreign policy making. But since World War II and the continual involvement of the United States in international security and foreign aid, Congress as a whole has become a major foreign policy maker because most modern foreign policies require financing, which requires the approval of both the House of Representatives and the Senate. For example, Congress's first action after September 11 was to authorize the president to use "all necessary and appropriate force," coupled with a $40 billion emergency appropriations bill for homeland defense. And while Bush believed he possessed the constitutional authority to invade Iraq, he still first sought congressional approval, which he received in October 2002. Congress has also become increasingly involved in foreign policy making because of the increasing use by the president of **executive agreements** to conduct foreign policy. Executive agreements have the force of treaties but do not require prior approval by the Senate. But, according to political scientist Loch Johnson, around 95 percent of executive agreements are made prior to or pursuant to congressional authorization. For example, many executive agreements are made to pursue, fulfill, or clear up

Besides the president, the Pentagon, the world's largest office building and home to the Department of Defense, is the most visible part of the foreign policy establishment. In September 2002, Secretary of Defense Donald Rumsfeld, shown standing with Vice Chairman of the Joint Chiefs of Staff General Peter Pace, made the case to invade Iraq by arguing that waiting for Iraq to first use chemical, biological, or nuclear weapons would be a mistake. This preemptive strategy is at the heart of the "Bush Doctrine."

Congress has the constitutional authority to declare war. Though it has rarely exercised that authority, Congress still plays an important part in foreign policymaking. After September 11, for example, Congress authorized the president's use of force and congressional leaders regularly conferred with Bush on the war on terrorism. This photo from October 2001 shows Bush meeting with (from lower left) then-Senate Minority Leader Trent Lott, House Speaker Dennis Hastert, then-Senate Majority Leader Tom Daschle, and then-House Minority Leader Richard Gephardt.

details of treaties already adopted. Others are carried out under a prior legislative act or are covered by later legislation. This gives both the House and the Senate a genuine institutional role in foreign policy.[3] Another opening for congressional involvement in foreign policy is the fact that, although executive agreements have the force of treaties and do not require prior approval by the Senate, they can in fact be revoked by action of both chambers of Congress. Such action is by "joint resolution," a form of legislative disapproval that the president cannot veto.

executive agreement an agreement, made between the president and another country, that has the force of a treaty but does not require the Senate's "advice and consent"

Another congressional player is the foreign policy and military policy committees: in the Senate these are the Foreign Relations Committee and the Armed Services Committee; in the House, the International Affairs Committee and the Armed Services Committee. Usually, a few members of these committees who have spent years specializing in foreign affairs become trusted members of the foreign policy establishment and are actually makers rather than mere shapers of foreign policy. In

Among the nonofficial, informal shapers of foreign policy, interest groups are the most influential. For example, pro-Israel Jewish groups are quite strong in the United States. At left, we see pro-Israeli demonstrators in front of a United Nations building in April 2002. Demonstrations by environmental groups, while not as influential on the president or Congress, are also a frequent sight. For instance, the February 2002 photo below shows Greenpeace members protesting U.S. energy policy with mock oil derricks in the Reflecting Pool in front of the Capitol.

fact, several members of Congress have left to become key foreign affairs cabinet members.[4] As we saw in chapter 12, after September 11 congressional committees conducted hearings on the failure of the intelligence agencies, but most members of Congress were reluctant to take on these agencies or a popular president.

WHO SHAPES FOREIGN POLICY?

> **What groups help shape foreign policy? Among these players, which are most influential?**

The shapers of foreign policy are the nonofficial, informal players, but they are typically people or groups that have great influence in the making of foreign policy. Of course, the influence of any given group varies according to the party and the ideology that is dominant at a given moment.

Interest Groups   Far and away the most important category of nonofficial players is the interest group—that is, the interest groups to whom one or more foreign policy issues are of long-standing and vital relevance. The type of interest group with the reputation for the most influence is the economic interest group. Yet the myths about their influence far outnumber and outweigh the realities. The actual influence of organized economic interest groups in foreign policy varies enormously from issue to issue and year to year. Most of these groups are "single-issue" groups and are therefore most active when their particular issue is on the agenda. On many of the broader and more sustained policy issues, such as the **North American Free Trade Agreement** (**NAFTA**) or the general question of American involvement in international trade, the larger interest groups, sometimes called "peak associations," find it difficult to maintain tight enough control of their many members to speak with a single voice. The most systematic study of international trade policies and their interest groups concluded that the leaders of these large, economic interest groups spend more time maintaining consensus among their members than they do actually lobbying Congress or pressuring major players in the executive branch.[5] The more successful economic interest groups, in terms of influencing foreign policy, are the narrower, single-issue groups, such as the tobacco industry, which over the years has successfully kept American foreign policy from putting heavy restrictions on international trade in and advertising of tobacco products, and the computer hardware and software industries, which have successfully hardened the American attitude toward Chinese piracy of intellectual property rights.

North American Free Trade Agreement (NAFTA) trade treaty between the United States, Canada, and Mexico to lower and eliminate tariffs between the three countries

Another type of interest group with a well-founded reputation for influence in foreign policy is made up of people with strong attachments and identifications to their country of national origin. The ethnic interest group with the reputation for greatest influence is the American Jewish community, whose family and emotional ties to Israel, coupled with their shared memory of the Holocaust, make them one of the most alert and active interest groups in American foreign policy. In recent years, most of the public activity of this interest group has been through AIPAC, the American Israel Public Affairs Committee, which *Fortune* magazine ranks as one of the top lobbying groups in the country. It averages between $1 million and $2 million per year in lobbying expenditures, with amounts varying according to the electoral cycle and the congressional calendar. But that public expenditure is more than outweighed by the $4 million to $5 million per year in individual contributions of AIPAC board members, committee members, and other sympathizers, over two-thirds of which goes to Democratic candidates. The leverage of Jewish political interests has been strengthened since September 11 by the support of Israel by the Christian Right and the substantial numbers of a more mainstream Republican Party right wing. In contrast, the pro-Arab community is not only less visible but also far less effective politically. Arab and Muslim political money has been increasing in recent years, but it is still comparatively small, with total Arab-American and Muslim PAC contributions rising from $31,000 in 1992 to between $110,000 and $120,000 in 2000.[6]

A third type of interest group, one with a reputation that has been growing in the past two decades, is the human rights interest group. Such groups are made up of people who, instead of having self-serving economic or ethnic interests in foreign policy, are genuinely concerned for the welfare and treatment of people throughout the world—particularly those who suffer under harsh political regimes. A relatively small but often quite influential example is Amnesty International, whose exposés of human rights abuses have altered the practices of many regimes around the world. In recent years, the Christian Right has also been a vocal advocate for the human rights of Christians who are persecuted in other parts of the world, most notably in China, for their religious beliefs. For example, the Christian Coalition joined groups like Amnesty International in lobbying Congress to cut trade with countries that permit attacks against religious believers.

A related type of group with a fast-growing influence is the ecological or environmental group, sometimes called the "greens." Groups of this nature, such as Greenpeace, often depend more on demonstrations than on the usual forms and strategies of influence in Washington—lobbying and using electoral politics, for example. Demonstrations in strategically located areas can have significant influence on American foreign policy. The most recent examples are the 1999 protests in Seattle and the 2001 protest in Genoa, Italy, against the World Trade Organization (WTO) and its authority to impose limits and restrictions on sovereign nations (even the United States).

The Media Here again, myth may outweigh truth about media influence in foreign policy. The most important element of the policy influence of the media is the speed and scale with which the media can spread political communications. In that factor alone, the media's influence is growing—more news reaches more people faster, and people's reaction times are therefore shorter. When we combine this ability to communicate faster with the "feedback" medium of public opinion polling, it becomes clear how the media have become so influential—they enable the American people to reach the president and the other official makers of foreign policy.[7]

There is one other aspect of media influence to consider. Using survey evidence, Michael Robinson demonstrated that reliance on television as a source of news gave people negative attitudes toward public policies and especially toward government and public officials.[8] Robinson called this attitude "videomalaise." A later study found, in addition, that "television news in particular has an inherent bias toward reporting negative and critical information. In other words, 'videomalaise' [is] as much a product of the medium as of the message."[9] One probable influence of the media on foreign as well as domestic policy has been to make the

American people far more cynical and skeptical than they would otherwise have been. Beyond that, however, the influence of any medium of communication or any one influential journalist or news program varies from case to case.

PUTTING IT TOGETHER

What can we say about who really makes American foreign policy? First, except for the president, the influence of players and shapers varies from case to case—this is a good reason to look with some care at each example of foreign policy in this chapter. Second, since the one constant influence is the centrality of the president in foreign policy making, it is best to evaluate other actors and factors as they interact with the president.[10] Third, the reason influence varies from case to case is that each case arises under different conditions and with vastly different time constraints: for issues that arise and are resolved quickly, the opportunity for influence is limited. Fourth, foreign policy experts will usually disagree about the level of influence any player or type of player has on policy making.

But just to get started, let's make a few tentative generalizations and then put them to the test with the substance and experience reported in the remainder of this chapter. First, when an important foreign policy decision has to be made under conditions of crisis—where "time is of the essence"—the influence of the presidency is at its strongest. Second, under those time constraints, access to the decision is limited almost exclusively to the narrowest definition of the "foreign policy establishment." The arena for participation is tiny; any discussion at all is limited to the officially and constitutionally designated players. To put this another way, in a crisis, the foreign policy establishment works as it is supposed to.[11] As time becomes less restricted, even when the decision to be made is of great importance, the arena of participation expands to include more government players and more nonofficial, informal players—the most concerned interest groups and the most important journalists. In other words, the arena becomes more pluralistic, and therefore less distinguishable from the politics of domestic policy making. Third, because there are so many other countries with power and interests on any given issue, there are severe limits on the choices the United States can make. As one author concludes, in foreign affairs, "policy takes precedence over politics."[12] Thus, even though foreign policy making in noncrisis situations may more closely resemble the pluralistic politics of domestic policy making, foreign policy making is still a narrower arena with fewer participants.

The Values in American Foreign Policy

When President Washington was preparing to leave office in 1796, he crafted with great care, and with the help of Alexander Hamilton and James Madison, a farewell address that is one of the most memorable documents in American history. We have already had occasion to look at a portion of Washington's farewell address, because in it he gave some stern warnings against political parties (see Chapter 9). But Washington's greater concern was to warn the nation against foreign influence:

History and experience prove that foreign influence is one of the most baneful foes of republican government. . . . The great rule of conduct for us in regard to foreign nations is, in extending our commercial relations to have with them as little *political* connection as possible. So far as we have already formed engagements let them be fulfilled with perfect good faith. Here let us stop. . . . There can be no greater error than to expect or calculate upon real favors from nation to nation. . . . Trust to temporary alliances for extraordinary emergencies, [but in all other instances] steer clear of permanent alliances with any portion of the foreign world. . . . Such an attachment of a small or weak toward a great and powerful nation dooms the former to be the satellite of the latter [emphasis in original].[13]

With the exception of a few leaders such as Thomas Jefferson and Thomas Paine, who were eager to take sides with the French against all others, Washington was probably expressing sentiments shared by most Americans. In fact, during most of the nineteenth century, American foreign policy was to a large extent no foreign policy. But Americans were never isolationist, if isolationism means the refusal to have any associations with the outside world. Americans were eager for trade and for treaties and contracts facilitating trade. Americans were also expansionists, but their vision of expansionism was limited to filling up the North American continent only (see Figure 18.1).

LEGACIES OF THE TRADITIONAL SYSTEM

Two legacies flowed from the long tradition based on Washington's farewell address. One is the intermingling of domestic and foreign policy institutions. The

> **What are the legacies of the traditional system of foreign policy?**

Territorial Expansion by the United States, 1803–53

Figure 18.1

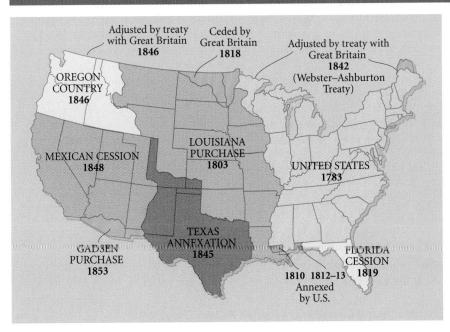

America's foreign policy during the nineteenth century was primarily focused on territorial expansion, as the nation sought to fuel its growing economy with land and natural resources.

Once the September 11 attack on the World Trade Center and the Pentagon was defined as an "act of war," a series of policy decisions were made to implement the initial strategic objective of conducting the war, first against the Taliban regime in Afghanistan and then against the Saddam Hussein regime in Iraq. War policies are pursued along not one but three tracks: (1) mobilization of all domestic militarily-related resources; (2) mobilization of the homeland, i.e., American society; and (3) logistics, assembly of forces to travel to the site or sites of conflict.

Mobilization of America for war began moments after the terrorist attacks of September 11 and continued throughout the campaign against the Taliban regime and its extension to war against the Saddam Hussein regime in Iraq. An enormous supplement to the 2002 defense budget of $14 billion was authorized in Congress during the weeks following the terrorist attacks. The current defense budget for 2003 was set in October 2002 at $379.3 billion and was likely to be significantly supplemented by additional congressional action as President Bush escalated America's determination to disarm Iraq.

In many respects, military mobilization of America is the easy part, because it has to be accompanied by policies aimed at the mobilization of the society. Part of this came into focus around homeland defense, to mobilize all of the governmental agencies and authority to strengthen our physical defense against direct terrorist attack and, still further, to mobilize the necessary disciplines on Americans to facilitate search and arrest of terrorist cells and plans and to prepare for other measures when and if detection and prevention fail. This included the far-reaching USA PATRIOT ACT (signed into law October 26, 2001) and related congressional and administration decisions to facilitate the work of the FBI and all other police agencies and prosecutors to expose and destroy clandestine terror-related activities. The Department of Homeland Security was designed to integrate 22 agencies and 170,000 government employees under one authority to make governmentally imposed disciplines more effective. Probably the most ambitious plan was construction by the Pentagon of a computer system that would create a vast electronic dragnet, containing enough relevant information on all Americans to make the hunt for terrorists more effective. This involves also the erasing of a century-old rule that international intelligence operations and related police functions should be kept entirely separate from domestic law enforcement. All these are simply current examples of conventional war mobilization.

The third track, logistics, involves all governmental actions up to the point where the first shot is fired. Military headquarters and the command center for the entire Persian Gulf region was moved from Tampa, Florida (from which the Afghan war was directed), to Qatar, with a staff of some 600 officers, who would most likely remain in that location during the war itself and afterward for the "regime change." The announcement of this move was made just a few days prior to President Bush's September 12, 2002, speech to the United Nations announcing preparations for a unilateral preemptive strike against the Iraqi regime. Finally, the logistical plan called for 200,000 to 250,000 troops from the Army, Navy, and Air Force. Accompanying these troops slated for the Persian Gulf region was a policy decision to mobilize the National Guard and Reserves with a number of troops equal to or larger than the 265,000 that had been called to active duty in Desert Storm of 1991. These troops would be assigned largely to take over functions at home usually filled by the regular military forces and also to enter into military-related situations that are novel for the kind of war being conducted. Part of this logistical operation was a plan to inoculate as many as 500,000 troops against smallpox. All of this would have to be done by early 2003 if hostilities were to begin far enough in advance of the extremely hot and forbidding summer temperatures in Iraq and the region.

other is unilateralism—America's willingness to go it alone. Each reveals much about the values behind today's conduct of foreign policy.

Intermingling of Domestic and Foreign Policy   Because the major European powers once policed the world, American political leaders could treat foreign policy as a mere extension of domestic policy. The tariff is the best example. A tax on one category of imported goods as a favor to interests in one section of the country would directly cause friction elsewhere in the country. But the demands of those adversely affected could be met without directly compromising the original tariff, by adding a tariff to still other goods that would placate those who were complaining about the original tariff. In this manner, Congress was continually adding and adjusting tariffs on more and more classes of commodities.

Unilateralism   Unilateralism, not isolationism, was the American posture toward the world until the middle of the twentieth century. Isolationism means trying to cut off contacts with the outside, to be a self-sufficient fortress. America was never isolationist; it preferred **unilateralism,** or "going it alone." Americans have always been more likely to rally around the president in support of direct action rather than for a sustained, diplomatic involvement.

THE GREAT LEAP TO WORLD POWER

The traditional era of U.S. foreign policy came to an end with World War I for two important reasons. First, the "balance of power" system[14] that had kept the major European powers from world war for a hundred years had collapsed.[15] In fact, the great powers themselves had collapsed internally. The most devastating of all wars up to that time had ruined their economies, their empires, and, in most cases, their political systems. Second, the United States was suddenly one of the great powers. Yet there was no discernible change in America's approach to foreign policy in the period between World War I and World War II. After World War I, as one foreign policy analyst put it, "the United States withdrew once more into its insularity. Since America was unwilling to use its power, that power, for purposes of foreign policy, did not really exist."[16]

The Great Leap in foreign policy was finally made thirty years after conditions demanded it and only then after another world war. Following World War II, pressure for a new tradition came into direct conflict with the old. The new tradition required foreign entanglements; the old tradition feared them deeply. The new tradition required diplomacy; the old distrusted it. The new tradition required acceptance of antagonistic political systems; the old embraced democracy and was aloof from all else.

The values of the new tradition were all apparent during the **cold war.** Instead of unilateralism, the United States pursued **multilateralism,** entering into treaties with other nations to achieve its foreign policy goals (see Figure 18.2 on page 738). The most notable of these treaties is that which formed the **North Atlantic Treaty Organization (NATO)** in 1948, which allied the United States, Canada, and most of Western Europe. With its NATO allies, the United States practiced a two-pronged policy in dealing with its cold war rival, the Soviet Union: **containment** and **deterrence.** Fearing that the Soviet Union was bent on world domination, the United States fought wars in Korea and Vietnam to "contain" Soviet power. And in order to deter a direct attack against itself or its NATO allies, the United States developed a multi-billion-dollar nuclear arsenal capable of destroying the Soviet Union many times over. An arms race between the United States and the Soviet Union was extremely difficult if not impossible to resist because there was no way

unilateralism a foreign policy that seeks to avoid international alliances, entanglements, and permanent commitments in favor of independence, neutrality, and freedom of action

cold war the period of struggle between the United States and the former Soviet Union between the late 1940s and about 1990

multilateralism a foreign policy that seeks to encourage the involvement of several nation-states in coordinated action, usually in relation to a common adversary, with terms and conditions usually specified in a multicountry treaty

North Atlantic Treaty Organization (NATO) a treaty organization, comprising the United States, Canada, and most of Western Europe, formed in 1948 to counter the perceived threat from the Soviet Union

containment the policy used by the United States during the cold war to restrict the expansion of communism and limit the influence of the Soviet Union

deterrence the development and maintenance of military strength as a means of discouraging attack

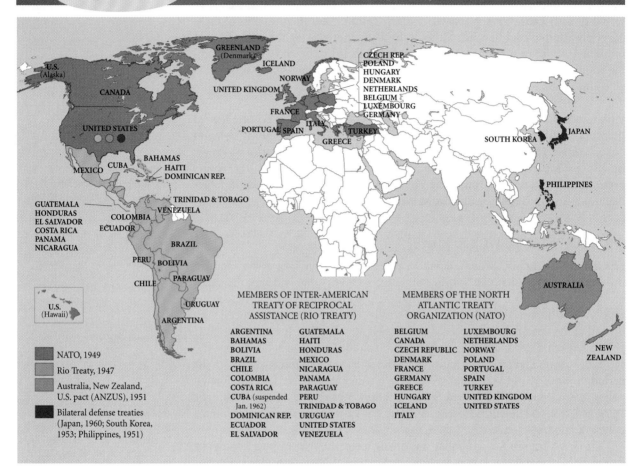

Figure 18.2   Collective Defense Treaties Signed by the United States

MEMBERS OF INTER-AMERICAN
TREATY OF RECIPROCAL
ASSISTANCE (RIO TREATY)

ARGENTINA	GUATEMALA
BAHAMAS	HAITI
BOLIVIA	HONDURAS
BRAZIL	MEXICO
CHILE	NICARAGUA
COLOMBIA	PANAMA
COSTA RICA	PARAGUAY
CUBA (suspended	PERU
Jan. 1962)	TRINIDAD & TOBAGO
DOMINICAN REP.	URUGUAY
ECUADOR	UNITED STATES
EL SALVADOR	VENEZUELA

MEMBERS OF THE NORTH
ATLANTIC TREATY
ORGANIZATION (NATO)

BELGIUM	LUXEMBOURG
CANADA	NETHERLANDS
CZECH REPUBLIC	NORWAY
DENMARK	POLAND
FRANCE	PORTUGAL
GERMANY	SPAIN
GREECE	TURKEY
HUNGARY	UNITED KINGDOM
ICELAND	UNITED STATES
ITALY	

- NATO, 1949
- Rio Treaty, 1947
- Australia, New Zealand, U.S. pact (ANZUS), 1951
- Bilateral defense treaties (Japan, 1960; South Korea, 1953; Philippines, 1951)

> **What new values guided U.S. foreign policy after World War II?**

for either side to know when they had enough deterrent to continue preventing aggression by the other side. The cold war ended abruptly in 1989, after the Soviet Union had spent itself into oblivion and allowed its empire to collapse. Many observers called the end of the cold war a victory for democracy. But more importantly, it was a victory for capitalism over communism, a vindication of the free market as the best way to produce the greatest wealth of nations. Furthering capitalism has long been one of the values guiding American foreign policy and this might be more true now than at any time before.

The Instruments of Modern American Foreign Policy

nation-state a political entity consisting of a people with some common cultural experience (nation) who also share a common political authority (state), recognized by other sovereignties (nation-states)

Any **nation-state** has at hand certain instruments, or tools, to use in implementing its foreign policy. An instrument is neutral, capable of serving many goals. There have been many instruments of American foreign policy, and we can deal here only with those instruments we deem to be most important in the modern epoch: diplomacy, the United Nations, the international monetary structure, economic aid, collective security, and military deterrence. Each of these instruments will be evaluated in this section for its utility in the conduct of American foreign policy, and each will be assessed in light of the history and development of American values.

DIPLOMACY

We begin this treatment of instruments with diplomacy because it is the instrument to which all other instruments should be subordinated, although they seldom are. **Diplomacy** is the representation of a government to other foreign governments. Its purpose is to promote national values or interests by peaceful means. According to Hans Morgenthau, "a diplomacy that ends in war has failed in its primary objective."[17]

The first effort to create a modern diplomatic service in the United States was made through the Rogers Act of 1924, which established the initial framework for a professional foreign service staff. But it took World War II and the Foreign Service Act of 1946 to forge the foreign service into a fully professional diplomatic corps.

Diplomacy, by its very nature, is overshadowed by spectacular international events, dramatic initiatives, and meetings among heads of state or their direct personal representatives. The traditional American distrust of diplomacy continues today, albeit in weaker form. Impatience with or downright distrust of diplomacy has been built not only into all the other instruments of foreign policy but also into the modern presidential system itself.[18] So much personal responsibility has been heaped upon the presidency that it is difficult for presidents to entrust any of their authority or responsibility in foreign policy to professional diplomats in the State Department and other bureaucracies.

Distrust of diplomacy has also produced a tendency among all recent presidents to turn frequently to military and civilian personnel outside the State Department to take on a special diplomatic role as direct personal representatives of the president. As discouraging as it is to those who have dedicated their careers to foreign service to have personal appointees chosen over their heads, it is probably even more discouraging when they are displaced from a foreign policy issue as soon as relations with the country they are posted in begin to heat up. When a special personal representative is sent abroad to represent the president, that envoy holds a status higher than that of the local ambassador, and the embassy becomes the envoy's temporary residence and base of operation. Despite the impressive professionalization of the American foreign service—with advanced training, competitive exams, language requirements, and career commitment—this practice of displacing career ambassadors with political appointees and with special personal presidential representatives continues. For instance, when President Clinton in 1998, sought to boost the peace process in Northern Ireland, he called upon former senator George Mitchell. Mitchell received almost unanimous praise for his skill and patience in chairing the Northern Ireland peace talks. The caliber of his work in Northern Ireland led to Senator Mitchell's becoming involved in another of the world's apparently unsolvable conflicts, that between the Israelis and the Palestinians.

Despite the United States's track record of distrust of diplomacy, immediately following the terrorist attacks of September 11, 2001, questions arose about how we could go after terrorist networks without the active cooperation of dozens of

> **What are the six primary instruments of modern American foreign policy?**

> **How does each instrument reflect a balance between the values of the traditional system of foreign policy and the values of cold war politics?**

diplomacy the representation of a government to other foreign governments

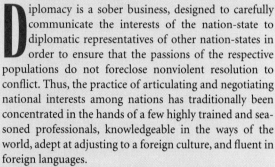

Foreign Policy, NGOs, and the Internet Revolution

Diplomacy is a sober business, designed to carefully communicate the interests of the nation-state to diplomatic representatives of other nation-states in order to ensure that the passions of the respective populations do not foreclose nonviolent resolution to conflict. Thus, the practice of articulating and negotiating national interests among nations has traditionally been concentrated in the hands of a few highly trained and seasoned professionals, knowledgeable in the ways of the world, adept at adjusting to a foreign culture, and fluent in foreign languages.

That, at least, is the ideal that most people have in mind when they think of foreign policy—specialists representing the political leaders of a nation-state working patiently to craft the policies of one nation-state toward another. The practice in today's world is somewhat different. To be sure, diplomacy still dominates formal relations between nation-states. However, eating away at the flesh of this system is the process of globalization. More specifically, what has changed is the ease by which actors who are not diplomats and therefore not attached to the government of the nation-state shape its foreign policy. These are not interest groups based solely in a nation-state that work simply to influence the preferences of their national leaders. Rather, these are transnational groups and coalitions that reach across borders and act to influence nation-states on a global basis. These nonformal, voluntary actors can rely on new forms of information technology to mobilize the interests of people through the articulation of common values and goals that affect populations within and across several nation-states. They have no interests per se in the power and sovereignty of the nation-state. Rather, they are far more likely to identify an issue that affects the security, health, and well being of people in general and to direct their efforts to influence the diplomacy of a nation to address those transnational concerns.

These new actors are known as *nongovernmental organizations,* or NGOs. An NGO is typically a private, voluntary, nonprofit organization. They are one of two major new actors on the international scene that influence the foreign policy environment of the nation-state; the other is the formal intergovernmental body (World Bank, International Monetary Fund, or the World Trade Organization). Intergovernmental bodies act as agents for the nation-states. In effect, they represent the nation-state and its foreign policy bureaucracy. The lines of control are more direct and formal. Nation-states dominate intergovernmental organizations.

Not so with NGOs, which are independent of the nation-state and its foreign policy bureaucracy and, as such, are much less constrained by the formalities of diplomacy and nation-state policies. NGOs are often associated with environmental groups, such as Greenpeace or Friends of the Earth. However, these groups encompass the full spectrum of policy interests of the nation-state and its population: education, research, business, law, philanthropic foundations, social services, culture, sports, human rights, health care, and, increasingly and importantly, labor.

What makes NGOs so powerful as a tool of foreign policy is the ease by which information technology allows nation-based NGOs to mobilize across international boundaries and form global coalitions, concentrating and coordinating their efforts to influence the domestic and foreign policies of nation-states. Fundamental to the success of NGOs is the cheap and easily accessed Internet. The Association for Progressive Communications provides 50,000 NGOs in 133 countries access to millions of Internet users around the world at the cost of a local telephone call.

While the power of the United States and the influence of its foreign policy bureaucracy may not be as vulnerable to NGO pressure as other wealthy democracies, in an age of globalization and information connectivity, the foreign policy of the United States will nonetheless be impacted by the effect of these NGOs acting through America's most powerful trading allies. Globalization has in effect shrunk the distances between countries, and NGOs have opened the doors of the foreign policy structure to pressures previously excluded from the diplomatic activities of nation-states.

SOURCES: Jessica T. Mathews, "Power Shift," *Foreign Affairs,* January/February 1997, pp. 50–66; Curtis Runyan, "Action on the Front Lines," *World Watch,* November/December 1999, pp. 12–21; and Jayne Rodgers, "NGO Use of Computer-Mediated Communications: Opening New Spaces of Political Representation," paper presented at the 1998 International Studies Association meetings, available from *Columbia International Affairs Online,* at http://www.ciaonet.org/ (accessed 9/30/02).

governments. Getting access to terrorists in various countries, plus putting together and keeping together the worldwide alliance of governments to fight terrorism, was a diplomatic, not a military, chore. In calls to more than eighty nations, Secretary of State Colin Powell helped to extract dozens of pledges that would have been more difficult to get months later, when sympathy for America began to wane. In short, global unity and success in fighting terrorism required constant diplomatic efforts, not only on the part of Powell, but also Secretary of Defense Donald Rumsfeld, National Security Adviser Condoleezza Rice, and even President Bush himself.

The administration's commitment to diplomacy as a tool of foreign policy was less clear by the following summer. The Bush Doctrine's basis of preemptive attack is a clear rejection of achieving national interests through diplomacy's peaceful means. It reveals a preference of the Bush administration that it can achieve its goals better through its military superiority, even if the United States has to go it alone, than through its diplomatic skills. Regarding Iraq, while hawks such as Rumsfeld and Vice President Dick Cheney favored toppling Saddam Hussein by military force, Powell pushed for a diplomatic approach that used the United Nations inspections program to make sure Iraq wasn't developing weapons of mass destruction. Powell's approach ultimately prevailed, though all through the debate the United States maintained that it would be forced to resort to military measures if diplomatic efforts failed. Many saw the demand for inspections as merely a pretext, assuming that Hussein would reject those demands, for military action.

The significance of diplomacy and its vulnerability to politics may be better appreciated as we proceed to the other instruments. Diplomacy was an instrument more or less imposed on Americans as the prevailing method of dealing among nation-states in the nineteenth century. The other instruments to be identified and assessed below are instruments that Americans self-consciously crafted for themselves to take care of their own chosen place in the world affairs of the second half of the twentieth century and beyond. They are, therefore, more reflective of American culture and values than is diplomacy.

THE UNITED NATIONS

The utility of the **United Nations (UN)** to the United States as an instrument of foreign policy can be too easily underestimated, because the United Nations is a very large and unwieldy institution with few powers and no armed forces to implement its rules and resolutions. Its supreme body is the UN General Assembly, comprised of one representative of each of the 191 member states, and each member representative has one vote, regardless of the size of the country. Important issues require a two-thirds majority vote, and the annual session of the General Assembly runs only from September to December (although it can call extra sessions). It has little organization that can make it an effective decision-making body, with only six standing committees, few tight rules of procedure, and no political parties to provide priorities and discipline. Its defenders are quick to add that, although it lacks armed forces, it relies on the power of world opinion; and this is not to be taken lightly. The powers of the United Nations devolve mainly to its "executive committee," the UN Security Council, which alone has the real power to make decisions and rulings that member states are obligated by the UN Charter to implement. The

United Nations (UN) an organization of nations founded in 1945 to serve as a channel for negotiation and a means of settling international disputes peaceably. The UN has had frequent successes in providing a forum for negotiation and on some occasions a means of preventing international conflicts from spreading. On a number of occasions, the UN has been a convenient cover for U.S. foreign policy goals

Security Council may be called into session at any time, and each member (or a designated alternate) must be present at UN Headquarters in New York at all times. It is composed of fifteen members: five are permanent, and ten are elected by the General Assembly for two-year, nonrepeatable terms. The five permanent members are China, France, Russia, the United Kingdom, and the United States. Each of the fifteen members has only one vote, and a nine-vote majority of the fifteen is required on all substantive matters. But each of the five permanent members also has a negative vote, a "veto," and one veto is sufficient to reject any substantive proposal.

During the first decade or more after its founding in 1945, the United Nations was a fairly consistent servant of American interests. The most spectacular example of its use as an instrument of American foreign policy was the official UN authorization and sponsorship of intervention in Korea with an international "peacekeeping force" in 1950. The Soviet Union was boycotting the United Nations at that time, and that deprived it of its ability to use its veto in the Security Council. Consequently, the United States was able to get its legitimizing resolution from the Security Council and to conduct the Korean War under the auspices of the United Nations.

The United States provided 40 percent of the UN budget in 1946 (its first full year of operation) and about 25 percent of the 2.4 billion UN budget in 2001–2.[19] Many Americans feel that the United Nations does not give good value for the investment. But any evaluation of the United Nations must take into account the purpose for which the United States sought to create it: to achieve power without diplomacy. After World War II, when the United States could no longer remain aloof from foreign policy, the nation's leaders sought to use our power to create an international structure that could be run with a minimum of regular diplomatic involvement—so that Americans could return to their normal domestic pursuits.

The United Nations gained a new lease on life in the post–cold war era, especially with its performance in the Gulf War. Although President George H.W. Bush's immediate reaction to Iraq's invasion of Kuwait was unilateral, he quickly turned to the United Nations for sponsorship. The General Assembly initially adopted resolutions in the autumn of 1990 condemning the invasion and approving the full blockade of Iraq. But once the blockade was seen as having failed to achieve the unconditional withdrawal demanded by the resolutions, further resolutions were adopted authorizing the twenty-nine-nation coalition to use force if, by January 15, 1991, the resolutions were not observed. As foreign policy expert Richard Haass put it, "The UN Security Council's authorization enhanced the undertaking's political and legal appeal, making it easier for the governments [of the twenty-nine-nation alliance] to join the common effort."[20] The Gulf War was a victory for the United Nations just as much as it was a victory for the United States and the twenty-nine-nation alliance. The cost of the operation was estimated at the time at $61.1 billion. First authorized by the U.S. Congress, actual U.S. outlays were offset by pledges from the other participants—the largest shares coming from Saudi Arabia ($15.6 billion), Kuwait ($16 billion), Japan ($10 billion), and Germany ($6.5 billion). The final U.S. costs were estimated at a maximum of $8 billion.[21]

Of course not all UN-sponsored actions are clear-cut victories. When Yugoslavia's communist regime collapsed in the early 1990s, the country broke apart into war among the ethnically distinct regions. The war concentrated in Bosnia where fierce fighting broke out between Muslims, Croatians, and Serbians, each fearing they would lose their identity if one of the others dominated Bosnia. The United States and its NATO allies pushed toward peace by creating "safe havens" in several cities and towns. But the United States and its NATO allies turned the maintenance of those "safe havens" over to United Nations troops. President Clinton criticized President Bush for not doing more, but Clinton turned out to be politically unable to muster any more support for the failing UN mission. After this failure of the international community to prevent Serbs from waging a war of aggression, which they themselves called "ethnic cleansing," UN peacekeepers and aid workers were again given the same thankless task in Kosovo immediately following the pullout of hostile Serbian troops in 1999. Despite the difficulty of restoring peace, the United Nations and its peacekeeping troops did an extraordinary job in the former Yugoslavia, dealing both with the intransigence of the warring parties and with the disagreement among the European powers about how to deal with a vicious and destructive civil war.

September 11, 2001, also implicated the United Nations. Less than three weeks afterwards, the UN Security Council unanimously (15 to 0) approved a U.S.-sponsored resolution requiring all countries to deny safe haven to anyone financing or committing a terrorist act. The resolution actually criminalized the financing of terrorist activity and extended its coverage beyond countries to individuals and "entities" within countries. The United Nations also created a committee of the Security Council members to monitor the implementation of the resolution, which included the freezing of all monetary assets available to terrorists and the passing of tougher laws to detain suspected terrorists as well as to share intelligence regarding terrorism. Moreover, although this resolution stresses economic rather than military means, it does not prohibit the "use of force," which the UN charter allows, as long as force is used for self-defense and not for "armed reprisals" after the fact.

The UN Security Council was also central in the debate over the United States's potential invasion of Iraq during the fall of 2002. At first, President Bush was reluctant to seek UN approval because he believed that he already had enough UN authority based on past Security Council resolutions that Saddam Hussein had so egregiously disregarded. But growing opposition to unilateral U.S. action against Iraq on the part of several Security Council members produced second thoughts and led Bush to appear at the United Nations and request a renewed and more authoritative, unconditional resolution. In response to this renewed U.S. cooperativeness, the Security Council unanimously adopted a resolution, calling on Iraq's president Saddam Hussein to disarm and to allow weapons inspectors into Iraq. While it was unceratin whether Iraq would fully comply with this new resolution, the fact remains that the United Nations played an essential role in this extremely important moment in world affairs. Peacekeeping and diplomacy may be the preferred UN *modus operandi*, but the organization has shown that it is willing even to support war, as long as prescribed procedures are followed and appropriate international support is evident.

These recent UN interventions show the promise and the limits of the United Nations in the post–cold war era. Although the United States can no longer control UN decisions, as it could in the United Nations's early days, the UN continues to function as a useful instrument of American foreign policy.[22]

THE INTERNATIONAL MONETARY STRUCTURE

Fear of a repeat of the economic devastation that followed World War I brought the United States together with its allies (except the USSR) to Bretton Woods, New Hampshire, in 1944 to create a new international economic structure for the post-war world. The result was two institutions: the International Bank for Reconstruction and Development (commonly called the World Bank) and the International Monetary Fund.

The World Bank was set up to finance long-term capital. Leading nations took on the obligation of contributing funds to enable the World Bank to make loans to capital-hungry countries. (The U.S. quota has been about one-third of the total.)

The **International Monetary Fund (IMF)** was set up to provide for the short-term flow of money. After the war, the dollar, instead of gold, was the chief means by which the currencies of one country would be "changed into" currencies of another country for purposes of making international transactions. To permit debtor countries with no international balances to make purchases and investments, the IMF was set up to lend dollars or other appropriate currencies to needy member countries to help them overcome temporary trade deficits. For many years after World War II, the IMF, along with U.S. foreign aid, in effect constituted the only international medium of exchange.

During the 1990s, the IMF returned to a position of enhanced importance through its efforts to reform some of the largest debtor nations and formerly communist countries, to bring them more fully into the global capitalist economy. For example, in the early 1990s, Russia and thirteen other former Soviet republics were invited to join the IMF and the World Bank with the expectation of receiving $10.5 billion from these two agencies, primarily for a currency-stabilization fund. Each republic was to get a permanent IMF representative, and the IMF increased its staff by at least 10 percent to provide the expertise necessary to cope with the problems of these emerging capitalist economies.[23]

The IMF, with $93 billion, has more money to lend poor countries than the United States, Europe, or Japan (the three leading IMF shareholders) do individually and it makes its policy decisions in ways that are generally consonant with the interests of the leading shareholders.[24] Two weeks after September 11, 2001, the IMF had approved a $135 million loan to economically troubled Pakistan, a key player in the war against the Taliban government of Afghanistan because of its strategic location. Turkey, with its strategic location in the Middle East, was also put back in the IMF pipeline.[25]

These activities of the IMF indicate just how effectively it is committed to the extension of capitalist victory. The reforms imposed on poorer countries—imposed as conditions to be met before receiving IMF loans—are reforms that commit a troubled country to joining or maintaining membership in the system of global capital exchange that allows investment institutions to seek the highest profits, without restraint. This goal can ignite a boom—as it did in South Korea, Indonesia, Singapore, and Thailand—but that boom can terminate just as abruptly, leaving the economy in question defenseless.

The future of the IMF, the World Bank, and all other private sources of international investment will depend in part on extension of more credit to the Third World and other developing countries, because credit means investment and pro-

International Monetary Fund (IMF) an institution established in 1944, which provides loans and facilitates international monetary exchange

ductivity. But the future may depend even more upon reducing the debt that is already there from previous extensions of credit. "Debt relief" is becoming a more acceptable foreign policy option. The most spectacular (and some say the most effective) champion and lobbyist for debt relief is Bono, one of the world's most prominent rock stars. In May 2002, in what may turn out to have been a culmination of his efforts, Bono made a two-week tour of equatorial Africa with Paul O'Neill, the U.S. secretary of treasury, to address investment needs as well as poverty and the AIDS epidemic. Debt relief, however, seemed highest on the agenda of this "odd couple," who seemed to view it as a kind of prerequisite for the advancement of other social and cultural goals.[26]

ECONOMIC AID

Commitment to rebuilding war-torn countries came as early as commitment to the basic postwar international monetary structure. This is the way President Franklin Roosevelt put the case in a press conference in November 1942, less than one year after the United States entered World War II:

> Sure, we are going to rehabilitate [other nations after the war]. Why? . . . Not only from the humanitarian point of view . . . but from the viewpoint of our own pocketbooks, and our safety from future war.[27]

The particular form and timing for enacting American foreign aid was heavily influenced by Great Britain's sudden decision in 1947 that it would no longer be able to maintain its commitments to Greece and Turkey. Within three weeks of that announcement, President Truman recommended a $400 million direct aid program for Greece and Turkey, and by mid-May of 1947, Congress approved it. Since President Truman had placed the Greece-Turkey action within the larger context of a commitment to help rebuild and defend all countries the world over, wherever the leadership wished to develop democratic systems or to ward off communism, the Greek-Turkish aid was followed quickly by the historically unprecedented program that came to be known as the Marshall Plan, named in honor of Secretary of State (and former five-star general) George C. Marshall.[28]

The **Marshall Plan**—officially known as the European Recovery Program (ERP)—was essential for the rebuilding of war-torn Europe. By 1952, the United States had spent over $34 billion for the relief, reconstruction, and economic recovery of Western Europe. The emphasis was shifted in 1951, with passage of the Mutual Security Act, to building up European military capacity. Of the $48 billion appropriated between 1952 and 1961, over half went for military assistance, the rest for continuing economic aid. Over those years, the geographic emphasis of U.S. aid also shifted, toward South Korea, Taiwan, the Philippines, Vietnam, Iran, Greece, and Turkey—that is, toward the rim of communism. In the 1960s, the emphasis shifted once again, toward what became known as the Third World. From 1962 to 1975, over $100 billion was sent, mainly to Latin America for economic assistance. Other countries of Africa and Asia were also brought in.[29]

Marshall Plan the U.S. European Recovery Plan, in which over $34 billion was spent for the relief, reconstruction, and economic recovery of Western Europe after World War II

Many critics have argued that foreign aid is really aid for political and economic elites, not for the people. Although this is to a large extent true, it needs to be understood in a broader context. If a country's leaders oppose distributing food or any other form of assistance to its people, there is little the United States, or any aid organization, can do, short of terminating the assistance. Goods have to be exchanged across national borders before they can reach the people who need them. Needy people would probably be worse off if the United States cut off aid altogether. The lines of international communication must be kept open. That is why diplomacy exists, and foreign aid can facilitate diplomacy, just as diplomacy is necessary to help get foreign aid where it is most needed.

Another important criticism of U.S. foreign aid policy is that it has not been tied closely enough to U.S. diplomacy. The original Marshall Plan was set up as an independent program outside the State Department and had its own separate mis-

Diplomacy is the charge of the Department of State. Current secretary of state Colin Powell's constant diplomatic effort was central to the United States's success both in building a multilateral coalition to fight the Taliban and in securing the United Nations Security Council's support of the U.S. position against Iraq. In fall 2002, for example, Powell was on the phone to his French counterpart just hours before walking his daughter down the aisle on her wedding day. Here, Powell is shown meeting with Afghan president Hamid Karzai and other Afghani officials in January 2002. A diplomat's job is never done.

The United Nations is not always but can be an important instrument of American foreign policy. In trying to build international support for the U.S. case against Iraq, President Bush went before the General Assembly and urged the United Nations to compel Iraq to disarm, backing his appeal with a hefty document accusing Iraqi president Saddam Hussein of a decade of deception and defiance of sixteen UN resolutions. Two months later, the UN Security Council gave its qualified support to Bush's position.

Loans and other forms of economic aid have helped the United States make friends around the world. Debt relief has emerged as an important tool of American foreign policy. In 2002, Secretary of the Treasury Paul O'Neill and rock star Bono toured parts of Africa to study and discuss the potential benefits of debt relief and economic aid to poor African nations. Here, the two are pictured with elementary schoolchildren in Uganda.

sions in each participating country. Essentially, "ERP became a Second State Department."[30] This did not change until the program was reorganized as the Agency for International Development (AID) in the early 1960s. Meanwhile, the Defense Department has always had principal jurisdiction over that substantial proportion of economic aid that goes to military assistance. The Department of Agriculture administers the commodity aid programs, such as Food for Peace. Each department has in effect been able to conduct its own foreign policy, leaving many foreign diplomats to ask, "Who's in charge here?"

That brings us back to the history of U.S. efforts to balance traditional values with the modern needs of world leadership. Economic assistance is an instrument of American foreign policy, but it has been less effective than it might have been because of the inability of American politics to overcome its traditional opposition to foreign entanglements and build a unified foreign policy—something that the older nation-states would call a foreign ministry. We have undoubtedly made progress, but foreigners still often wonder who is in charge.

American commitment to rebuilding war-torn countries has been essential to their recoveries. For instance, the United States has promised $4.5 billion for rebuilding Afghanistan. To help Afghanistan's immediate needs, thousands of tons of food were airlifted in to the 7.5 million Afghanis in need of it.

COLLECTIVE SECURITY

In 1947, most Americans hoped that the United States could meet its world obligations through the United Nations and economic structures alone. But most foreign policy makers recognized that it was a vain hope even as they were permitting and encouraging Americans to believe it. They had anticipated the need for military entanglements at the time of drafting the original UN Charter by insisting upon language that recognized the right of all nations to provide for their mutual defense independently of the United Nations. And almost immediately after enactment of the Marshall Plan, the White House and a parade of State and Defense Department officials followed up with an urgent request to the Senate to ratify and to Congress to finance mutual defense alliances.

At first quite reluctant to approve treaties providing for national security alliances, the Senate ultimately agreed with the executive branch. The first collective security agreement was the Rio Treaty (ratified by the Senate in September 1947), which created the Organization of American States (OAS). This was the model treaty, anticipating all succeeding collective security treaties by providing that an armed attack against any of its members "shall be considered as an attack against all the American States," including the United States. A more significant break with U.S. tradition against peacetime entanglements came with the North Atlantic Treaty (signed in April 1949), which created the North Atlantic Treaty Organization (NATO). ANZUS, a treaty tying Australia and New Zealand to the United States, was signed in September 1951. Three years later, the Southeast Asia Treaty created the Southeast Asia Treaty Organization (SEATO).

In addition to these multilateral treaties, the United States entered into a number of **bilateral treaties**—treaties between two countries. As one author has observed, the United States has been a *producer* of security while most of its allies have been *consumers* of security.[31] Figure 18.3 demonstrates that the United States has consistently devoted a greater percentage of its gross domestic product (GDP) to defense than have its NATO allies and Japan.

This pattern has continued in the post–cold war era, and its best illustration is in the Persian Gulf War, where the United States provided the initiative, the leadership, and most of the armed forces, even though its allies were obliged to reimburse over 90 percent of the cost.

It is difficult to evaluate collective security and its treaties, because the purpose of collective security as an instrument of foreign policy is prevention, and success of this kind has to be measured according to what did *not* happen. The critics have argued that U.S. collective security treaties posed a threat of encirclement to the Soviet Union, forcing it to produce its own collective security, particularly the Warsaw Pact.[32] Nevertheless, no one can deny the counterargument that the world has enjoyed more than fifty years without world war.

In 1998, the expansion of NATO took its first steps toward former Warsaw Pact members, extending membership to Poland, Hungary, and the Czech Republic. Most of Washington embraced this expansion as the true and fitting end of the cold war, and the U.S. Senate echoed this with a resounding 80-to-19 vote to induct these three former Soviet satellites into NATO. The expansion was also welcomed among European member nations, who quickly approved the move, which was hailed as the final closing of the book on Yalta, the 1945 treaty that divided Europe into Western and Soviet spheres of influence after the defeat of Germany. Expanded membership seems to have made NATO less threatening and more acceptable to Russia. Russia became a partner when the NATO-Russia Council was formed in 2002. Finally, although the expanded NATO membership (now nineteen countries) reduces the threat to Russia, it also reduces the utility of NATO as a military alliance. The September 11 attack on the United States was the first time in its fifty-plus year his-

bilateral treaties treaties made between two nations

Defense Spending as a Percentage of Gross Domestic Product, 1961–95

Figure 18.3

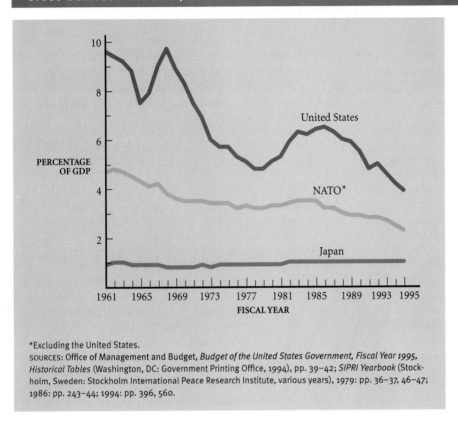

*Excluding the United States.

SOURCES: Office of Management and Budget, *Budget of the United States Government, Fiscal Year 1995, Historical Tables* (Washington, DC: Government Printing Office, 1994), pp. 39–42; *SIPRI Yearbook* (Stockholm, Sweden: Stockholm International Peace Research Institute, various years), 1979: pp. 36–37, 46–47; 1986: pp. 243–44; 1994: pp. 396, 560.

tory that Article 5 of the North Atlantic Treaty had to be invoked; it provides that an attack on one country is an attack on all the member countries. And that produced impressive results, diplomatically and militarily, even though the United States eventually preferred to wage war in Afghanistan primarily on its own.

MILITARY DETERRENCE

For the first century and a half of its existence as an independent republic, the United States held strongly to a "Minuteman" theory of defense: maintain a small corps of professional officers, a few flagships, and a small contingent of marines; leave the rest of defense to the state militias. In case of war, mobilize as quickly as possible, taking advantage of the country's immense size and its separation from Europe to gain time to mobilize.

The United States applied this policy as recently as the post–World War I years and was beginning to apply it after World War II, until the new policy of preparedness won out. The cycle of demobilization-remobilization was broken, and in its place the United States adopted a new policy of constant mobilization and preparedness: deterrence, or the development and maintenance of military strength as

Multilateralism versus Unilateralism

After the sudden end of the Cold War, with the collapse of the Soviet Union and bipolar nuclear stalemate, everyone knew international relations would never be the same, but no one could guess how they would be different. The first intimation came with the first genuine post-Cold War war, on August 2, 1990 when Iraq invaded Kuwait and occupied a substantial amount of Kuwait territory. President George H. W. Bush signaled what might become a new post-Cold War foreign policy with an immediate declaration that the Iraq occupation of Kuwait territory "will not stand." Bush then used diplomatic means behind the scenes to recruit a number of nations to join in an alliance against Iraq. The first step was the United Nations, securing a resolution condemning the invasion and authorizing a blockade of Iraq. This was followed by a UN demand for unconditional withdrawal from Kuwait, followed by a UN authorization of a 29-nation use of force if the UN resolutions were not observed by January 15, 1991. But it was not the United Nations that put the 29-nation alliance together. It was President Bush and his diplomats.

Ten years later, President George W. Bush's foreign policy behavior was quickly defined as a classic go-it-alone, cowboy presidency. With regard to the NATO alliance, built and maintained by ten Bush presidential predecessors over 52 years, he mostly acted unilaterally. He denounced arms control, rejected the Kyoto protocol on global warming, and was opposed to treaties or international agreements in principle. He and his advisors saw multilateralism not as a beneficial alliance, but as a "straightjacket."

But a revolution in American foreign policy came about immediately after September 11. When the United States demanded that Pakistan reverse its unstinting support for the Taliban, the Bush administration discovered an alliance waiting to happen. Pakistan quickly changed its position, at great political risk to its shaky military regime; Russia cooperated with the West; and other nations joined when it was clear that the United States was ready to go to war against world terrorism. Although President Bush sounded quite unilateral when he warned that those nations who weren't with us were against us, most of his actions were multilateral. Russian president Putin dropped all Russian objections to the deployment of American and NATO counterterrorism forces in the former Soviet republic key states on the long border between Russia and the Middle East. The possibility was even emerging that Russia would seek and might gain admission to NATO. President Bush also reversed other facets of his earlier unilateralism, including paying all back dues to the United Nations and making Secretary of State Colin Powell, who earlier had been losing out to the go-it-alone phalanx of the administration, a prominent player in building this alliance.

But there's a price for multilateralism. One lesson to be learned from the 1991 Gulf War alliance is that a genuine alliance is a restraint on the "hegemon." Cold War alliances (on both sides) were not genuine, because most of the member states were *satellite states*—lacking the power and autonomy to have any foreign policy of their own—or *client states*—dependent on the hegemon but enjoying some conditional freedom of action on limited "national interests" occasions. But in 1991, the influence of many of the 29-nation Desert Storm members shaped the decision to interrupt the advance to Baghdad and the eradication of the entire Saddam Hussein regime. So while multilateralism worked in Afghanistan, would it work again in Iraq in 2002? Bush's own advisors were themselves split. For example, a substantial number of top officials made no secret of their commitment to an all-out war on Iraq as the key element in what the unilateral Bush called the "axis of evil." Their purpose in invading Iraq is not only to take away any remaining nuclear, chemical, or biological threat Iraq may possess but also to fulfill their faith that a friendly, democratic regime could actually replace Saddam Hussein. Other staffers cringed at the very thought.

Obviously the way out is to balance these contending forces at home and the contradictory pulls of the large and unwieldy coalition called an alliance. This cannot be done by a series of compromises the way party leaders in Congress can work out compromises on legislation. It is going to take tremendous leadership and inspirational ideas from Bush to make certain that the contending factions at home and around the world are in support. In October 2002, Bush went to the United Nations with a different attitude from his unilateral position and agreed to abide by a stern UN Security Council resolution that Iraq disarm and subject itself to unconditional weapons inspection, with serious consequences if it did not cooperate within one month's time. But Bush balked at the provision for a second UN Security Council resolution if Iraq did not cooperate and asserted his conviction that the United States would proceed if there was not satisfaction that complete disarmament was taking place. While the UN resolution had put the United States on course to form another multilateral alliance, the Bush administration reserved the option of going it alone if necessary.

a means of discouraging attack. After World War II, military deterrence against the Soviet Union became the fundamental American foreign policy objective, requiring a vast commitment of national resources. With preparedness as the goal, peacetime defense expenditures grew steadily over the course of the cold war.

The end of the cold war raised public expectations for a "peace dividend"—surplus federal money resulting from reductions in the defense budget—after nearly a decade of the largest peacetime defense budget increases in U.S. history. Many defense experts, liberal and conservative, feared what they called a budget "free-fall," not only because deterrence was still needed but also because severe and abrupt cuts could endanger private industry in many friendly foreign countries as well as in the United States.

The Persian Gulf War brought both points dramatically into focus. First, the Iraqi invasion of Kuwait revealed the size, strength, and advanced modern technological base not only of the Iraqi armed forces but of other countries, Arab and non-Arab, including the capability, then or soon, to make atomic weapons and other weapons of massive destructive power. Moreover, the demand for advanced weaponry was intensifying. The decisive victory of the United States and its allies in the Gulf War, far from discouraging the international arms trade, gave it fresh impetus. Following the Gulf War victory, *Newsweek* reported that "industry reps quickly realized that foreign customers would now be beating a path to their doors, seeking to buy the winning weaponry." The Soviet Union at one time led the list of major world arms sellers, and Russia and several other republics of the former Soviet Union have continued to make international arms sales, particularly since now there are "no ideological limitations" in the competition for customers.[33] The United States now leads the list of military weapons exporters, followed by Great Britain, France, and Russia. Thus, some shrinkage of defense expenditure has been desirable, but Democrats and Republicans alike agree that this reduction must be guided by the continuing need to maintain U.S. and allied credibility as a deterrent to post–cold war arms races.

As to the second point, domestic pressures join international demands to fuel post–cold war defense spending. Each cut in military production and each closing of a military base or plant translates into a significant loss of jobs. Moreover, the conversion of defense industries to domestic uses is not a problem faced by the United States alone. Figure 18.4 on page 754 conveys a dramatic picture of the "international relations" of the production of one single weapons system, the F-16 fighter airplane.

Support for policies of deterrence was significantly strengthened, and doubts about the applicability of cold war theories of deterrence totally dispelled, by the sudden (because undetected by our intelligence system) entry of two new members into the nuclear club: India and Pakistan successfully tested nuclear devices in May and June of 1998. The profound conflicts between these two countries over religion, ethnic rights, and territories make resort to atomic weapons a distinct possibility. And this possibility moved more toward probability during May and June of 2002, when war threatened to break out between these two traditionally hostile countries over control of Kashmir. But of still greater import is the potential for deliberate or accidental proliferation by lesser powers and organizations. During the same trying weeks of the India/Pakistan confrontation, revelation of the sale of missile and satellite materials and technology to China by American

Should the United States Go It Alone Against Iraq?

Yes

Outside of the daunting task of building a coalition, what has multilateralism taught us? In just the past ten years, there are quite a few examples of how multilateralism has run amok. The favorite baby of the leftists is, why didn't America get rid of Saddam Hussein back in 1991? Despite the leftist opposition to the Gulf War, the answer is simply because of multilateralism. The United Nations and its multilateral coalition deemed ejecting Iraqi forces out of Kuwait the end of its mission. If we hadn't abided by the United Nations mandate, it would have been a unilateral decision.

The Clinton administration attempted multilateralism on a grand scale, downplaying America's superpower status in deference to the Europeans, the Chinese and the Islamic world. It was worth a shot. Maybe modern man could overcome his own evil tendencies through consensus and coalitions. Unfortunately, the experiment failed.

Through European and Arab pressure, a multilateral approach, we elevated the status of the Islamic world in its age-old struggle against the only democratically elected government in the Middle East, Israel. In a foolhardy attempt to "balance" our traditionally pro-Israeli foreign policy, the Clinton administration, while in bed with the Saudis and the PLO, leaned heavily on Israel with a "land for peace deal." What did it get us? The Intifada with murderous Palestinians blowing up innocent people in Israel and cheering as Saudis flew planes into the World Trade Center and Pentagon, then feigning victimhood when Israel retaliates.

How many times do you have to get knocked in the head to know that a different approach is necessary? The only requisite outcome is absolute defeat of the purveyors of terror. Then and only then is peace possible. On the other hand, where has unilateralism worked? Twenty years ago, Moammar Ghadafy of Libya was a large sponsor of the terrorism that was breaking out across Europe. Bang! One American unilateral gift landed beside his tent, and he has been quiet ever since. All was done without fly-over rights from France.

Having problems in Kosovo? Europeans balked in the Balkans, but America, under Bill Clinton, didn't, stopping genocide against a Muslim minority, no less. Noriega in Panama—good-bye. The collapse of the Soviet Union, our greatest nemesis to date, good-bye, was achieved by the unilateral resolve of America via an unprecedented defense build-up in the 1980s. The Europeans wanted nothing to do with it; yet, they benefited the most, a unified Germany, the expansion of NATO eastward, and scaled-back defense budgets. Can anyone honestly say that we shouldn't have done any of those things?

Today, we are faced with a dilemma. Do we go into Iraq? Do we go into it alone? Will the Arabs and Muslims like us? No, they won't. But that is already true. I would much rather bring the fight to their soil than watch it occur here while we sit hoping the world will like us for being so magnanimous as to allow ourselves to be bloodied with impunity. Is it too much of a leap to presume that Iraq and Saddam Hussein had an invisible hand in September 11? Do the leftist-defeatists remember the concept of "plausible deniability"? Personally, I don't need a smoking gun to know that Saddam had motive, and one doesn't have to be a rocket scientist to know that Middle Eastern governments support terrorist groups through third parties in order to deny involvement.

No one wants war. It is horrific and sad. But the stark reality is that a price greater than the fall of the Taliban has to be paid, and parts of the Muslim world need to pay for it, for they are the supporters of our enemies. Iraq should be the first domino in the democratization and liberation of the Middle East with or without the Europeans' help. An Arab leader must fall, and Saddam Hussein has won the lottery.

The simple fact remains: our citizens at home are the target of extreme Islam, the predominantly Islamic nations financially support the terrorists, and no country on the face of the planet, except the United States, has the power to do anything about it.

The Europeans have nothing to offer militarily anyway, and maybe that is why they are wary of involvement. So, we go it alone if need be.

Multilateralism is a panacea for doing nothing, which is what Europe is good at. It historically does not work. Besides, what has any country done for us lately, let alone ever, to be held in such high regard as to defer our defense to them?

SOURCE: Chris Knez, "Making the Necessary Case for Action Against Iraq," *The University Times* (UNC—Charlotte), October 2, 2002.

No

President Bush has submitted a resolution to Congress asking for the power to use the United States military to invade Iraq. Such an attack would be wrong and should not occur. In attacking Iraq without provocation, the United States would not only reverse its traditional policy against striking first, but it would also ostracize itself in the international community as a meddling aggressor nation. Particularly in a time of such global instability, the United States must retain allies and not act rashly. Saddam Hussein is an acknowledged tyrant who has invaded other countries, used biological weapons against the Kurds, and has a clandestine program for the development of other dangerous weapons, possibly including an atomic bomb, but there is no evidence to suggest that he is planning an imminent attack against the United States or American interests elsewhere in the world. He is a threat, to be sure, but not one that requires an immediate, dangerous, politically and diplomatically questionable military invasion. War should not be taken lightly, especially when nuclear weapons may be involved, but President Bush's eager resolve to attack Iraq suggests that he and his advisers have not carefully thought through the ramifications of their proposals.

The Bush administration's recent rhetoric promoting an immediate unilateral American strike on Iraq is a complete reversal of the longstanding policy against first strikes. Such a dramatic change in United States foreign policy demands careful attention, and the rashness with which the administration is pushing for the use of military force is anything but cautious. To strike preemptively in Iraq would set a dangerous precedent that would be hard to defend, and the president has not shown compelling evidence to back this proposed shift in American policy.

An American invasion of Iraq would be just that—an American invasion. The lack of international military and diplomatic support should make war an unappealing prospect. America's allies, including the United Nations and many European countries, are opposed to an attack on Iraq. Tony Blair, the British Prime Minister, is the notable, vocal exception, while German Chancellor Gerhard Schroeder won reelection last week in part because he denounced an American invasion of Iraq. War with Iraq would also jeopardize America's fragile alliances in the Middle East. Although the United Nations is negotiating to send weapons inspectors into Iraq, it will not support a war. The United States would not be able to rely on the assistance of its allies as it did in Afghanistan and the Persian Gulf War. In addition, America would lose international support in other endeavors. The Bush administration should reexamine the costs of such an unpopular action.

President Bush's call for war hinges on two claims: that Saddam Hussein has weapons of mass destruction, and that he has ties to Osama bin Laden and Al Qaeda. Intelligence reports show that Hussein has dangerous weapons, but since he has not allowed weapons inspectors into Iraq, no one is sure of the number or type of weapons in the country. In 1991, the world saw that Saddam Hussein was not reluctant to launch scud missiles against Israel. In the eleven years since the Gulf War, it is likely that his cache of weapons has grown larger, which is exactly why the United States should not attack Iraq. An attack would only provoke Hussein to use his weapons against American soldiers and America's allies.

Saddam Hussein's alleged links with the September 11 terrorists have not been proven. It is unlikely that Hussein, a secular dictator, shares the fundamentalist values of Osama bin Laden and Al Qaeda. Bin Laden has called Hussein an "infidel," and reports that the masterminds of the terrorist attacks met with Hussein are unconfirmed. To go to war on such shaky grounds is unwise and shows a careless desire to rouse American patriotism by linking all the world's evils to September 11. The government should not use such a cheap excuse to go to war, and the American public should not accept this reasoning either.

The Bush administration's proposed war with Iraq is ill-conceived. It is grounded in tenuous assumptions, shallow rhetoric, and a reckless desire for glory. A war with no international support will diminish America's global standing, and striking first would set a dangerous precedent for aggressive American overthrow of any disagreeable government. President Bush's plan is a mistake. The United States should not go to war with Iraq.

SOURCE: Managing Board, "A World Against War," *Columbia Spectator*, October 1, 2002.

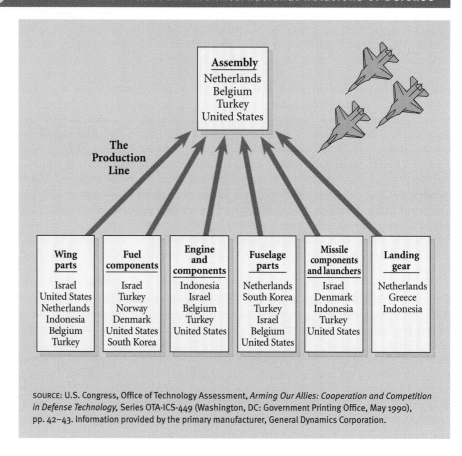

Figure 18.4 **How the F-16 Is Produced: The International Relations of Defense**

This is a summary of an elaborate diagram of at least seventy-five separate parts that go into the F-16.

SOURCE: U.S. Congress, Office of Technology Assessment, *Arming Our Allies: Cooperation and Competition in Defense Technology*, Series OTA-ICS-449 (Washington, DC: Government Printing Office, May 1990), pp. 42–43. Information provided by the primary manufacturer, General Dynamics Corporation.

corporations with U.S. government approval raised still more troubling questions, despite former president Clinton's reassurances that such sales were part of the economic engagement that would help democratize China. After September 11, there was increased awareness that several countries had at least some capability to develop "weapons of mass destruction" and those same countries were known to be supportive, to varying degrees, of people and organizations that were supportive of or associated with Al Qaeda. This was no longer a threat of a conventional arms race toward some kind of balance—as was the case during the cold war when it was called Mutual Assured Destruction (MAD). One small nuclear, biological, or chemical device delivered in a suitcase, a shipping carton, or a suicide's waistband might be sufficient to bring a powerful nation-state to its knees. Here is deterrence put to its ultimate test. President Bush warned in the hours following September 11 that any country so much as harboring terrorists is itself a terrorist. And to the best of the abilities of CIA and other international intelligence agencies, several such countries have been named, including Iran, Iraq, North Korea, Syria, and Libya. What will the sanctions be, and how, in what sequence, and with what force will these sanctions be delivered? In the event of a future terrorist attack, will we wait to determine the specific country from which the attack came, or will all six of these (and possibly others) be punished together? Are our weapons of deterrence appropriate for a terrorist war? There is an old warning in deterrence theory about appropriateness: a machine gun is a poor instrument of deterrence against an attack by a swarm of bees. This warning may become more important in the post–September 11 era.

Roles Nations Play

Although each president has hundreds of small foreign fires to fight and can choose whichever instruments of policy best fit each particular situation, the primary foreign policy problem any president faces is choosing an overall role for the country in foreign affairs. Roles help us to define a situation in order to control the element of surprise in international relations. Surprise is in fact the most dangerous aspect of international relations, especially in a world made smaller and more fragile by advances in and the proliferation of military technology.

CHOOSING A ROLE

The problem of choosing a role can be understood by identifying a limited number of roles played by nation-states in the past. Four such roles will be drawn from history—the Napoleonic, the Holy Alliance, the balance-of-power, and the economic expansionist roles. Although the definitions given here will be exaggerations of the real world, they do capture in broad outline the basic choices available.

> **What four traditional foreign policy roles has the United States adopted throughout its history?**

The Napoleonic Role The **Napoleonic role** takes its name from the role played by postrevolutionary France under Napoleon. The French at that time felt not only that their new democratic system of government was the best on earth but also that France would not be safe until democracy was adopted universally. If this meant intervention into the internal affairs of France's neighbors, and if that meant warlike reactions, then so be it. President Woodrow Wilson expressed a similar viewpoint when he supported the U.S. declaration of war in 1917 with his argument that "the world must be made safe for democracy." Obviously such a position can be adopted by any powerful nation as a rationalization for intervening at its convenience in the internal affairs of another country. But it can also be sincerely espoused, and in the United States it has from time to time enjoyed broad popular consensus. We played the Napoleonic role most recently in ousting Philippine dictator Ferdinand Marcos (February 1986), Panamanian leader Manuel Noriega (December 1989), the Sandinista government of Nicaragua (February 1990), and the military rulers of Haiti (September 1994).

Napoleonic role a strategy pursued by a powerful nation to prevent aggressive actions against themselves by improving the internal state of affairs of a particular country, even if this means encouraging revolution in that country

The Holy Alliance Role The concept of the **Holy Alliance role** emerged out of the defeat of Napoleon and the agreement by the leaders of Great Britain, Russia, Austria, and Prussia to preserve the social order against *all* revolution, including democratic revolution, at whatever cost. (Post-Napoleonic France also joined it.) The Holy Alliance made use of every kind of political instrument available—including political suppression, espionage, sabotage, and outright military intervention—to

Holy Alliance role a strategy pursued by a superpower to prevent any change in the existing distribution of power among nation-states, even if this requires intervention into the internal affairs of another country in order to keep a ruler from being overturned

keep existing governments in power. The Holy Alliance role is comparable to the Napoleonic role in that each operates on the assumption that intervention into the internal affairs of other countries is justified for the maintenance of peace. But Napoleonic intervention is motivated by fear of dictatorship, and it can accept and even encourage revolution. In contrast, Holy Alliance intervention is antagonistic to any form of political change, even when this means supporting an existing dictatorship.[34]

The Balance-of-Power Role The **balance-of-power role** is basically an effort by the major powers to play off against each other so that no great power or combination of great and lesser powers can impose conditions on others. The most relevant example of the use of this strategy is found in the nineteenth century, especially the latter half. The feature of the balance-of-power role that is most distinct from the two previously identified roles is that this role accepts the political system of each country, asking no questions except whether the country will join an alliance and will use its resources to ensure that each country will respect the borders and interests of all the others.[35]

> **balance-of-power role** the strategy whereby many countries form alliances with one or more other countries in order to counterbalance the behavior of other, usually more powerful, nation-states

The Economic Expansionist Role The **economic expansionist role,** also called the capitalist role, shares with the balance-of-power role the attitude that the political system or ideology of a country is irrelevant; the only question is whether a country has anything to buy or sell and whether its entrepreneurs, corporations, and government agencies will honor their contracts. Governments and their armies are occasionally drawn into economic expansionist relationships in order to establish, reopen, or expand trade relationships, and to keep the lines of commerce open. But the role is political, too. The point can be made that the economic expansionist role was the role consistently played by the United States in Latin and Central America, until the cold war (perhaps in the 1960s and beyond) pushed us toward the Holy Alliance role with most of those countries.

Like arms control, however, economic expansion does not happen spontaneously. In the past, economic expansion owed a great deal to military backing, because contracts do not enforce themselves, trade deficits are not paid automatically, and new regimes do not always honor the commitments made by regimes they replace. The only way to expand economic relationships is through diplomacy.

> **economic expansionist role** the strategy often pursued by capitalist countries to adopt foreign policies that will maximize the success of domestic corporations in their dealings with other countries

FOREIGN POLICY VALUES FOR AMERICA TODAY

Although "making the world safe for democracy" was used to justify the U.S. entry into World War I, it was taken more seriously after World War II, when at last the United States was willing to play a more sustained part in world affairs. The Napoleonic role was most suited to America's view of the immediate postwar world. To create the world's ruling regimes in the American image would indeed give Americans the opportunity to return to their private pursuits, for if all or even most of the world's countries were governed by democratic constitutions, there would be no more war, since no democracy would ever attack another democracy—or so it has been assumed.[36]

> ➤ Since the end of World War II, how has the role of the United States in world affairs evolved?

The Cold War and the Holy Alliance Role   The emergence of the Soviet Union as a superpower had an overwhelming influence on American foreign policy thinking in the post–World War II era. The distribution of power in the world was "bipolar," and Americans saw the world separated in two, with an "iron curtain" dividing the communist world from the free world. Immediately after the war, America's foreign policy goal had been "prodemocracy," a Napoleonic role dominated by the Marshall Plan and the genuine hope for a democratic world. This quickly shifted toward a Holy Alliance role, with "containment" as the primary foreign policy criterion.[37] Containment was fundamentally a Holy Alliance concept. According to foreign-policy expert Richard Barnet, during the 1950s and 1960s, "the United States used its military or paramilitary power on an average of once every eighteen months either to prevent a government deemed undesirable from coming to power or to overthrow a revolutionary or reformist government considered inimical to America's interests."[38] Although Barnet did not refer to a Holy Alliance, his description fits the model perfectly.

During the 1970s, the United States played the Holy Alliance role less frequently, not so much because of the outcome of the Vietnam War as because of the emergence of a multipolar world. In 1972, the United States accepted (and later recognized) the communist government of the People's Republic of China and broke forever its pure bipolar, cold war view of world power distribution. Other powers became politically important as well, including Japan, the European Economic Community (now the European Union), India, and, depending on their own resolve, the countries making up the Organization of Petroleum Exporting Countries (OPEC). The United States experimented with all four of the previously identified roles, depending on which was appropriate to a specific region of the world. In the Middle East, America tended to play an almost classic balance-of-power role, by appearing sometimes cool in its relations with Israel and by playing off one Arab country against another. The United States has been able to do this despite the fact that every country in the Middle East recognizes that for cultural, domestic, and geostrategic reasons, the United States has always considered Israel as its most durable and important ally in the region and has unwaveringly committed itself to Israel's survival in a very hostile environment. President Nixon introduced balance-of-power considerations in the Far East by "playing the China card." In other parts of the world, particularly in Latin America, we tended to hold to the Holy Alliance and Napoleonic roles.

This multipolar phase ended after 1989, with the collapse of the Soviet Union and the end of the cold war. Soon thereafter the Warsaw Pact collapsed too, ending armed confrontation in Europe. With almost equal suddenness, the popular demand for "self-determination" produced several new nation-states and the demand for still more. On the one hand, it was indeed good to witness the reemergence of some twenty-five major nationalities after anywhere from forty-five to seventy-five years of suppression. On the other hand, policy makers with a sense of history are aware that this new world order bears a strong resemblance to the world of 1914. Then, the trend was known as "Balkanization." Balkanization meant nationhood and self-determination, but it also meant war. The Soviet Union after World War I and Yugoslavia after World War II kept more than twenty nationalities from making war against each other for several decades. In 1989 and the years that followed, the world was caught unprepared for the dangers of a new disorder that the reemergence of these nationalities produced.

The Post–Cold War Era and Global Capitalism   The abrupt end of the cold war unleashed another dynamic factor, the globalization of markets; one could call it the globalization of capitalism. This is good news, but it has its problematic side because the free market can disrupt nationhood. Although the globalization of markets is enormously productive, countries like to enjoy its benefits while attempting at the same time to prevent international economic influences from affecting local jobs, local families, and established class and tribal relationships.

This struggle between capitalism and nationhood produces a new kind of bipolarity in the world. The old world order was shaped by *external bipolarity*—of West versus East. This seems to have been replaced by *internal bipolarity,* wherein each country is struggling to make its own hard policy choices to preserve its cultural uniqueness while competing effectively in the global marketplace.

Approval of the North American Free Trade Agreement (NAFTA) serves as the best example of this struggle within the United States. NAFTA was supported by a majority of Democrats and Republicans on the grounds that a freer, global market was in America's national interest. But even as NAFTA was being embraced by large bipartisan majorities in Congress, three important factions were rising to

Between 1948 and 1951, the European Recovery Program, popularly known as the Marshall Plan, spent billions of dollars rebuilding Western Europe. This Berlin site was reconstructed as an office building and shopping center. The success of the Marshall Plan in re-creating successful economies in Europe made the United States popular there. But the globalization of the economy has resulted in discontents who blame the United States and its policies for the world's economic woes. For instance, the International Monetary Fund, a global public institution, has been accused by its critics of putting the private interests of the financial community ahead of those of the developing countries the IMF is supposed to be aiding. This protest in front of IMF headquarters in Washington, D.C., accused the IMF of helping multinational tobacco companies at the expense of public health in countries around the world.

fight it. Former presidential candidate Pat Buchanan led a large segment of conservative Americans to fight NAFTA because, he argued, communities and families would be threatened by job losses and by competition from legal and illegal immigrant workers. Another large faction, led by Ross Perot, opposed NAFTA largely on the theory that American companies would move their operations to Mexico, where labor costs are lower. Organized labor also joined the fight against NAFTA.

Another form of internal bipolarity became evident in 1999 over the World Trade Organization (WTO) and its authority to impose limits and restrictions on sovereign nations, even the United States. The WTO had been around since 1994, when it was set up by the major trading nations to facilitate implementation of treaties made under the General Agreement on Tariffs and Trade (GATT). But protesters in Seattle saw the WTO as a threat to local ways of life and a contributor to job loss, environmental degradation, and violation of human rights.

These battles are examples of the "internal bipolarity" that is coming to the fore around the world. As *New York Times* foreign affairs columnist Thomas Friedman put it, ". . . now that the free market is triumphing on a global basis, the most interesting conflicts are between the winners and losers within countries. It is these internal battles that will increasingly shape international affairs."[39]

The global market is here to stay and American values have changed enough to incorporate it, despite the toll it may take on community and family tradition. Meanwhile, many of the elements of foreign policy created during the cold war still exist because they turned out to be good adjustments to the modern era. The Marshall Plan and the various forms of international economic aid that succeeded it continue to this day. Although appropriations for foreign aid have been shrinking, only a small minority of members of the Senate and the House favor the outright abolition of foreign aid programs. NATO and other collective security arrangements continue, as do some aspects of containment, even though there is no longer

Another controversial aspect of the United States's international economic policy has been its trade relations with China. In February 2002, President and First Lady Bush visited China, promoting increased trade between the two countries. At home, however, normalizing trade relations with China has been the subject of frequent criticism and protests from those who argue that it threatens the welfare of American workers and ignores human rights violations committed by the Chinese government.

a Soviet Union, because collective security arrangements have, as we shall see, proven useful in dealing with new democracies and other nations seeking to join the global market. Even though the former Soviet Union is now more often an ally than an adversary, the United States still quite frequently uses unilateral and multilateral means of keeping civil wars contained within their own borders, so that conflict does not spread into neighboring states. America is practicing a new form of containment, but one that is based on the values and institutions of cold war containment.

The quest for a global market is more than a search for world prosperity. Economic globalization carries with it the hope that economic competition will displace armed conflict, perhaps even reducing if not eliminating the need for traditional diplomacy. But since there are too many instances in world history when economic competition actually led to war rather than avoided it, the United States has added democratization to the recipe of globalization because of the fairly well-supported hypothesis that democracies never go to war against each other. Thus democratization is a genuine and strongly committed goal of U.S. foreign policy, even if it is secondary to economic expansion. Meanwhile, we play the economic card in hopes that capitalism will contribute not only to world prosperity but also to the expansion of democratization.

One of the first indications of the post–cold war American foreign policy was former President Bush's conciliatory approach to the dictatorial regime of the People's Republic of China after its brutal military suppression of the democratic student movement in Tienanmen Square in June 1989. Subsequently, President Clinton also maintained friendly relations with the dictatorial regime, and both presidents continued to grant the Chinese "normal trade relations" status. Their policy was to separate China's trade status from its human rights record, arguing that economic growth provided the only effective means to bring about political reform in a country as large and as powerful as China.

The Holy Alliance or the Napoleonic Role in the Post–Cold War Era?   During the cold war era, the purpose of the Holy Alliance role was to keep regimes in power as long as they did not espouse Soviet foreign policy goals. In the post–cold war world, the purpose of the Holy Alliance role is still to keep regimes in power, but only as long as they maintain general stability, keep their nationalities contained within their own borders, and encourage their economies to attain some level of participation in the global market. If countries fail to satisfy these conditions, the United States has shown signs of reverting back to its Napoleonic role. The United States has also continued to confront unfriendly dictators by adopting a Napoleonic strategy of intervention.

One case of the Holy Alliance role in the post–cold war era is Iraq's invasion of Kuwait and our Desert Storm response to it. Iraq's invasion of Kuwait occurred in July 1990, and Desert Storm was not undertaken until January 1991. In the interim, President Bush was mobilizing Congress and the American people, not only in case the United States had to intervene militarily, but also in hopes that the possibility of such action might convince Saddam Hussein to withdraw voluntarily. President Bush was also putting together a worldwide alliance of twenty-nine nations—he had no intention of leading the United States into Desert Storm without this alliance, even though most of its members did not send troops but instead sent political approval plus what amounted to a monetary subscription. Bush had initially taken a Napoleonic position, urging the people of Iraq to "take matters into their own hands" and to force Hussein to "step aside." But after America withdrew its troops, and uprisings inside Iraq began to emerge, President Bush backed away, thus revealing his real intent of leaving the existing dictatorship in power, with or without Hussein. It was enough that the Iraqis stayed within their borders although regular overflights and occasional shootings by American pilots in the northern and southern "no-fly" zones of Iraq later appeared to be Napoleonic departures from the Holy Alliance role.

Regarding Bosnia, at first, the United States refused to exert leadership, and it deferred to the European nations when civil war erupted after Croatia and Bosnia-Herzegovina declared independence from Yugoslavia. When Europe failed to address the problem adequately, the United States and the United Kingdom stepped in, again to no avail. Although our surprise bombing in 1995 to drive the warring factions to the negotiating table in Dayton, Ohio, was virtually unilateral, what emerged was a new alliance of twenty-five nations acting "in concert" to separate the warring factions from one another. And, although one-third of the sixty thousand occupying troops and virtually all the navy and air force units were American, twenty-four other nations established and maintained a physical presence in the field, all in order to maintain the status quo, including leaving Yugoslav president Slobodan Milosevic in power. Almost everything about the Bosnian operation was an acting out of the traditional Holy Alliance role.

Kosovo (part of Yugoslavia) in 1999 was perhaps the most spectacular case of post–cold war Holy Alliance policy—although history may prove that the United States and virtually the entire Western world stumbled into this war.[40] Throughout 1998 and early 1999, ethnic cleansing was proceeding in Kosovo, but the United States would not go it alone, and the NATO nations (except for Great Britain) were not willing to intervene in Kosovo. As late as January 1999, the CIA reported to President Clinton that "[Yugoslav President Milosevic] doesn't believe NATO is going to bomb."[41] It is clear that these delays were due less to American indecision and more to America's or President Clinton's inability to forge a European, multi-country alliance. Prospects of embarrassment at the upcoming fiftieth anniversary of NATO may have forced some European leaders to reconsider an alliance—but even so, only if the United States took the lead, and then only if it promised to limit the assault to an air war only, which guaranteed a minimum of casualties, especially on the allied side.

So the United States got its alliance—and, for NATO, a precedent-setting one—but without any ground troops. President Clinton deserves some blame for the delays and for the artificial restrictions that allowed Milosevic to make the eventual intervention by the alliance all more dangerous for the Kosovars, whom the United States wanted to defend and protect. The charge that Clinton's impeachment could not be "compartmentalized" seems to have had some basis to it.[42] But there are inherent limits to multinational coalitions, which President Clinton had to confront no matter what his domestic political distractions were at the time. NATO is simply a more formalized version of any multicountry alliance with the same fundamental problem of any such alliance: *The power of decision tends toward the weakest member.* Opposition within the NATO alliance to intervene in Kosovo came mostly from the weaker and more internally divided Italy and Greece rather than from

Britain, France, or Germany. And while the NATO alliance defeated Milosevic's troops, it did not remove him from his leadership role. Milosevic's downfall was at the hands of a democratically elected opponent the following year.

The Kosovo campaign validates what we have been observing throughout this chapter: Holy Alliance politics is the prevailing American role in the world today, and the United States draws virtually all its allies and potential allies into that role at one point or another. As *The Washington Post* put it in 1999:

> . . . Whatever the shortcomings, fighting in coalition arrangements appears to be an unavoidable fact of post–cold war life. . . . "We need partners both for political legitimacy and for risk-sharing," says . . . a senior Pentagon planner earlier in the Clinton administration.[43]

The magazine *The Economist* goes even further:

> The one-superpower world will not last. [China, Russia, and the Muslim world will all become geopolitical competitors.] . . . This is why the alliance of the democracies needs not only new members but also a new purpose. The alliance can no longer be just a protective American arm around Europe's shoulder; it also has to be a way for Europe and America to work together in other parts of the world. . . . This must be done—if it can be done at all—in partnership with America. . . .[44]

Since the end of the Cold War, a multilateral approach to tackling the world's troublespots has guided American foreign policy. For instance, in defending Kuwait against an Iraqi invasion in 1991, the United States built a 29-country alliance. One aspect of this cooperative effort was the training of Kuwaiti soldiers by U.S. troops in Saudi Arabia.

Efforts to keep the peace in Bosnia involved a NATO peace force working with the Russian military. This photo shows a live artillery exercise from 1997, the first time since World War II that U.S. and Russian troops fired live ammunition together.

The War on Terror: Holy Alliance or Napoleonic Unilateralism? A new alliance with a new purpose was struck in response to the terrorist attacks of September 11, 2001. Such a great-power alliance for international order has not been seen since the mid-nineteenth century, when the threat came from middle-class revolutionaries rather than religious fanatics. But even though the enemies are different, the goals and strategies are about the same. All countries in the West are vulnerable because Al Qaeda and its associated groups are anti-West. All capitalist and developing countries are susceptible because terrorism is intensely anti-capitalist. And all moderate Arab regimes are vulnerable because they are seen by Al Qaeda as traitors and collaborators with the West. All of these vulnerable nation-states need each other in order to deprive terrorists of the turf they need for safe havens, headquarters, training and communication, not to mention financing. Even though the war against the Taliban regime was almost entirely conducted by the United States, there was no hope for a sustained campaign without the substantial cooperation and participation of many other countries. Pakistan was most vital, and its participation came at the risk of undermining its own regime. Russia and several other former Soviet republics on the northern border of Afghanistan were vital as well.

The NATO nations were contractually an important part of the alliance, if only because the NATO charter was built on a solemn promise that an attack on any member was tantamount to an attack on all the members.

Yet once the Afghan phase of the war on world terrorism began quieting down, the United States confronted a new challenge: the resurgence of Iraq and the possibility that the weapons of mass destruction Saddam Hussein possessed would be used against the United States or one of its allies. President Bush's response, called the "Bush Doctrine," was a significant departure

The war on terrorism also relied upon a multilateral alliance. This photo shows aircraft carriers from the United States, Italy, France, and Britain stationed in the Arabian Sea.

In preparing for a potential war against Iraq, the United States fell back on more of a unilateral approach. While President Bush went before the United Nations and ultimately received the approval of its Security Council, among the world's leaders only Britain's prime minister Tony Blair explicitly endorsed the United States's pre-emptive intervention in Iraq. If troops are called for in a ground invasion of Iraq, it is unclear how many nations will provide them.

from the Holy Alliance model and movement toward a Napoleonic role. The tenets of the doctrine allowed the United States (1) to take preemptive action against a hostile state without waiting for an attack on us; (2) to eliminate permanently the threat of weapons of mass destruction; (3) to eliminate the regime itself; and (4) to remain as an occupying power in Iraq long enough to rebuild the country into a modern democratic state.

Although the Holy Alliance role continues to be the principal role among the four historically and conventionally defined roles, it is not the only role America plays, and, more to the point, it is never played exactly the same in all cases. Even in Afghanistan, the alliance to defeat the Taliban and contain terrorism was accompanied by a genuine, albeit secondary, version of the Napoleonic role. The Bush administration seemed determined not to "hit and run" as the United States had done when it fought *with* the Taliban against the Russians in the early 1980s. American policy is strongly committed both to rebuilding the Afghan economy along capitalist lines and to moving the Afghan regime toward some form of democratization. But in the short run at least, the United States quickly settled for an imposed national leader presiding over a domestic coalition of mutually distrustful warlords, with only the barest hint of any kind of democratic process. That is the underlying Holy Alliance at work. Moreover, the Bush administration is just as committed as its predecessors to a balance-of-power role in the perennial Middle East hot spot, the Israeli-Palestine conflict. The United States has succeeded in keeping the neighboring Arab countries from forming their own anti-Israel (therefore anti-U.S.) alliance. (Keeping antagonistic alliances from forming is an essential feature of the balance-of-power role—like spokes on a wheel, keeping each country dependent upon the United States at the hub while keeping each country apart from one another.) But the use of terror by the Palestinians has prevented the United States from playing the balance-of-power role of "honest broker."

No foreign policy role—however the roles are categorized—can ever relieve the United States of the need for sustained diplomacy. In fact, diplomacy has become all the more important because despotic regimes eventually fail and in their failure create instability. Since September 11, it is also more clear that failing regimes can become the breeding grounds for world terrorism. This is not to argue that war is never justifiable or that peace can always be achieved through discussions among professional diplomats. It is only to argue that there are limits to any role a country chooses to play and that failure will come faster and will be more serious if the choice of role is not made with patience, deliberation, rationality, and, most importantly, a sense of history.

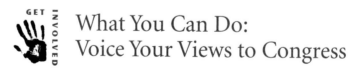

What You Can Do:
Voice Your Views to Congress

The American people are too large and diffuse a nation to participate in making foreign policy in any truly democratic way. A people, even a free and mature people, can at best set limits, or broadly defined national interests within which policy makers and policy shapers can operate. A people can constrain power but cannot guide or direct the powerful.

If the whole American people is too broad to conduct foreign policy, the American presidency is too narrow. We need a "vital middle" player to form foreign policy in our democracy. This "vital middle" is in fact provided by the Constitution. Foreign policy was always supposed to involve the president and Congress, and, now that the cold war has ended, no time is more appropriate to revive that principle. During the cold war, a genuine foreign policy debate was carried out in Congress about once every decade. Each time it happened, it was a great moment of renewal of the Constitution and redirection and revitalization of public policy. The "Cooper/Church" debate in 1970 over the continuation of military activity in Cambodia did very little to alter the course of the Vietnam War, but in focusing on the constitutionality of the war and the legality of the U.S. incursion into Cambodia, the debate revived the strength of constitutionalism in the United States and brought America to its senses about the difference between democracy and tyranny. Almost exactly twenty years later, the Persian Gulf War did the same thing. Anticipating opposition in Congress, President Bush sought and got UN support and multilateral cooperation. When he took the issue to Congress in January 1991, he was supported by a narrow margin, but he got from the debate an enlightened and guided support that no opinion poll could have provided. Success in the Gulf War brought Bush a 90 percent popular approval rating. But that was not the true measure of his political base; Congress was.

The end of the cold war has opened Congress to opportunities in foreign-policy debates that it has not had since before the Great Depression. During the cold war, following as it did a world war and a long domestic economic crisis, Congress developed what one expert has called "a culture of deference"—a bipartisan culture of defeat that can be summed up by a maxim shared by most influential members of the House and Senate: "We shouldn't make foreign policy."[45] But this doesn't make sense anymore. Foreign policy making in the United States will remain the president's domain. But public deliberation and debate, in an ongoing search for the national interest, is the domain of Congress. Congress is the vital middle between a hopeless isolationist rejection of foreign policy altogether and an equally hopeless delegation of total power to the chief executive.

How can you voice your views on a foreign policy issue? One voice is likely to have little impact. But several hundred or several thousand voices can make an impression. You and your supporters will add your voices to the chorus of citizens who have expressed similar views to Congress. The louder the chorus, the more powerful the message, and the greater the likelihood that decision makers will take notice.

Summary

Although we cannot provide solutions to the foreign policy issues that the United States faces, we can provide a well-balanced analysis of the problems of foreign policy. This analysis is based on the five basic dimensions of foreign policy: the players, the setting, the values, the instruments, and the roles.

The first section of this chapter looked at the players in foreign policy: the makers and the shapers. The influence of institutions and groups varies from case to case, with the important exception of the president. Since the president is central to all foreign policy, it is best to assess how other actors interact with the president. In most instances, this interaction involves only the narrowest element of the foreign policy establishment. The American people have an opportunity to influence foreign policy, but primarily through Congress or interest groups.

The next section, on values, traced the history of American values that had a particular relevance to American perspectives on the outside world. We found that the American fear of a big government applied to foreign as well as domestic governmental powers. The Founders and the active public of the Founding period all recognized that foreign policy was special, that the national government had special powers in its dealings with foreigners, and that presidential supremacy was justified in the conduct of foreign affairs. The only way to avoid the big national government and presidential supremacy was to avoid the foreign entanglements that made foreign policy, diplomacy, secrecy, and presidential discretion necessary. Americans held on to their "small government" tradition until World War II, long after world conditions cried out for American involvement. And even as we became involved in world affairs, we held on tightly to the legacies of 150 years of tradition: the intermingling of domestic and foreign policy institutions, and unilateralism, the tendency to "go it alone" when confronted with foreign conflicts.

We then looked at the instruments—that is, the tools—of American foreign policy. These are the basic statutes and the institutions by which foreign policy has been conducted since World War II: diplomacy, the United Nations, the international monetary structure, economic aid, collective security, and military deterrence. Although Republicans and Democrats look at the world somewhat differently, and although each president has tried to impose a distinctive flavor on foreign policy, they have all made use of these basic instruments, and that has given foreign policies a certain continuity. When Congress created these instruments after World War II, the old tradition was still so strong that it moved Congress to try to create instruments that would do their international work with a minimum of diplomacy—a minimum of human involvement.

The next section concentrated on the role or roles the president and Congress have sought to play in the world. To help simplify the tremendous variety of tactics and strategies that foreign policy leaders can select, we narrowed the field down to four categories of roles nations play, suggesting that there is a certain amount of consistency and stability in the conduct of a nation-state in its dealings with other nation-states. These were labeled according to actual roles that diplomatic historians have identified in the history of major Western nation-states: the Napoleonic, Holy Alliance, balance-of-power, and economic expansionist roles. We also attempted to identify and assess the role of the United States in the post–cold war era, essentially a Holy Alliance role. But whatever its advantages may be, the Holy Alliance approach will never allow the United States to conduct foreign policy without diplomacy. America is tied inextricably to the perils and ambiguities of international relationships, and diplomacy is still the best of all available instruments of foreign policy.

We concluded by asking: In a democracy like the United States, who should make foreign policy? The chapter provided numerous case studies to seek an answer to this question. We believe that between the extremes of isolationism and total power resting with the president resides a middle ground where the American people can express their will through the members of Congress. The national interest can be defined only through debate and deliberation, which we hope will serve as the foundations for the formation of foreign policy in the American democracy.

For Further Reading

Doremus, Paul N., William W. Keller, Louis Pauly, and Simon Reich. *The Myth of the Global Corporation.* Princeton, NJ: Princeton University Press, 1998.

Gilpin, Robert. *The Political Economy of International Relations.* Princeton, NJ: Princeton University Press, 1987.

Graubard, Stephen, ed. "The Exit from Communism." *Daedalus* 121, no. 2 (Spring 1992).

Greenfield, Liah. *Nationalism: Five Roads to Modernity.* Cambridge, MA: Harvard University Press, 1993.

Keller, William W. *Arm in Arm: The Political Economy of the Global Arms Race.* New York: Basic Books, 1995.

Kennan, George F. *Around the Cragged Hill: A Personal and Political Philosophy.* New York: Norton, 1993.

Kennedy, Paul M. *The Rise and Fall of the Great Powers: Economic Change and Military Conflict from 1500 to 2000.* New York: Random House, 1987.

LaFeber, Walter. *The American Age: United States Foreign Policy at Home and Abroad since 1750.* New York: Norton, 1989.

———. *The Clash: U.S.-Japanese Relations Throughout History.* New York: Norton, 1997.

Nye, Joseph S., Jr. *The Paradox of American Power: Why the World's Only Superpower Can't Go It Alone.* New York: Oxford University Press, 2002.

Stiglitz, Joseph E. *Globalization and Its Discontents.* New York: Norton, 2002.

Wirls, Daniel. Buildup: *The Politics of Defense in the Reagan Era.* Ithaca, NY: Cornell University Press, 1992.

Study Outline

www.wwnorton.com/wtp4e

The Players: The Makers and Shapers of Foreign Policy

1. All foreign policy decisions must be made and implemented in the name of the president.
2. The key players in foreign policy in the bureaucracy are the secretaries of State, Defense, Homeland Security, and Treasury; the Joint Chiefs of Staff (especially the chair); and the Director of the Central Intelligence Agency.
3. Although the Senate traditionally has more foreign policy power than the House, since World War II, the House and the Senate have both been important players in foreign policy.
4. Many types of interest groups help shape American foreign policy. These groups include economic interest groups, ethnic or national interest groups, and human rights and environmental interest groups.

5. The media serve to communicate issues and policies to the American people, and to communicate the public's opinions back to the president. One definite influence of television on foreign policy has been to make the American people more cynical and skeptical than they otherwise would have been.
6. Individual or group influence in foreign policy varies from case to case and from situation to situation.

The Values in American Foreign Policy

1. The intermingling of domestic and foreign policy institutions and unilateralism are the two identifiable legacies of our traditional system of maintaining sovereignty.
2. The intermingling of domestic and foreign policy institutions was originally possible because the major European powers policed the world.
3. Traditionally, unilateralism, the desire to go it alone, was the American posture toward the world.
4. Although the traditional era of American foreign policy came to an end with World War I, there was no discernible change in approach to such policy until after World War II.

The Instruments of Modern American Foreign Policy

1. Diplomacy is the representation of a government to other foreign governments, and it is the foreign policy instrument to which all other instruments must be subordinated.
2. The United Nations is an instrument whose usefulness to American foreign policy can too easily be underestimated.
3. The international monetary structure, which consists of the World Bank and the International Monetary Fund, was created to avoid the economic devastation that followed World War I.
4. Economic aid has been important as an instrument of American foreign policy, but it was put together as a balance between traditional values and the modern needs of a great, imperial power.
5. After World War II, the United States recognized the importance of collective security, and subsequently entered into multilateral collective security treaties and other bilateral treaties.
6. World War II broke the American cycle of demobilization-remobilization and led to a new policy of military preparedness.

Roles Nations Play

1. There are four roles available to a nation in the conduct of its foreign policy: the Napoleonic role, the Holy Alliance role, the balance-of-power role, and the economic expansionist role.

2. Although the United States played the Napoleonic role during the postwar era and then switched to the Holy Alliance role, the United States is now beginning to adopt all four roles, playing whichever one is appropriate to a particular region and set of circumstances.

Practice Quiz

www.wwnorton.com/wtp4e

1. The making of American foreign policy is
   a) dominated entirely by the president.
   b) dominated entirely by Congress.
   c) dominated entirely by interest groups.
   d) highly pluralistic, involving a large mix of both official and unofficial players.

2. The term "unilateralism" describes
   a) an approach to foreign policy that involves complex and time-consuming negotiations between multiple powers.
   b) a "go-it-alone" approach to foreign policy.
   c) episodes in American foreign policy during which the president dominates Congress.
   d) instances when the U.S. Supreme Court refuses to approve a treaty negotiated by the president.

3. The "cold war" refers to the
   a) competition between the United States and Canada over Alaska.
   b) the years between World War I and World War II when the United States and Germany were hostile to one another.
   c) the period of struggle between the United States and the Soviet Union between the late 1940s and the late 1980s.
   d) the economic competition between the United States and Japan today.

4. The North Atlantic Treaty Organization was formed in 1948 by the United States,
   a) Canada, and most of Eastern Europe.
   b) Canada, and Mexico.
   c) Canada, and most of Western Europe.
   d) Canada, and the United Kingdom.

5. Which of the following terms best describes the American posture toward the world prior to the middle of the twentieth century?
   a) interventionist
   b) isolationist
   c) unilateralist
   d) none of the above

6. Which of the following are important international economic institutions created after World War II?
   a) the Federal Reserve
   b) the World Bank
   c) the International Monetary Fund
   d) Both b and c are correct.

7. Which of the following terms describes the idea that the development and maintenance of military strength discourages attack?
   a) deterrence
   b) containment
   c) "minuteman" theory of defense
   d) detente

8. Which of the following was dedicated to the relief, reconstruction, and economic recovery of Western Europe?
   a) the Marshall Plan
   b) the Lend-Lease Act
   c) the General Agreement on Tariffs and Trade
   d) the North American Free Trade Agreement

Critical Thinking Questions

www.wwnorton.com/wtp4e

1. In previous chapters, we have learned about the political nature of most of the key players in American foreign policy. How might politics (in addition to democracy) impede the effectiveness of the United States in the international arena? Can you think of an instance in which the United States was hampered by domestic politics?

2. What is the proper balance between governmental effectiveness in international politics and the public's "right to know"? Surely, for tactical reasons the government should be able to keep some activities secret. But given the potential for abuse of governmental secrecy, how might the public hold the government accountable while preserving for the United States the tactical advantage of secrecy?

Key Terms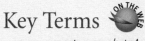

www.wwnorton.com/wtp4e

balance-of-power role (p. 756)
bilateral treaties (p. 748)
cold war (p. 737)
containment (p. 737)
deterrence (p. 737)

diplomacy (p. 739)
economic expansionist role (p. 756)
executive agreement (p. 731)
Holy Alliance role (p. 755)
International Monetary Fund (IMF)
   (p. 744)
Marshall Plan (p. 745)
multilateralism (p. 737)

Napoleonic role (p. 755)
nation-state (p. 738)
North American Free Trade Agreement
   (NAFTA) (p. 732)
North Atlantic Treaty Organization
   (NATO) (p. 737)
unilateralism (p. 737)
United Nations (UN) (p. 741)

APPENDIX

THE DECLARATION OF INDEPENDENCE

In Congress, July 4, 1776

The unanimous Declaration of the thirteen united States of America,

When in the Course of human events, it becomes necessary for one people to dissolve the political bands which have connected them with another, and to assume among the powers of the earth, the separate and equal station to which the Laws of Nature and of Nature's God entitle them, a decent respect to the opinions of mankind requires that they should declare the causes which impel them to the separation.

We hold these truths to be self-evident, that all men are created equal, that they are endowed by their Creator with certain unalienable Rights, that among these are Life, Liberty and the pursuit of Happiness.—That to secure these rights, Governments are instituted among Men, deriving their just powers from the consent of the governed. —That whenever any Form of Government becomes destructive of these ends, it is the Right of the People to alter or to abolish it, and to institute new Government, laying its foundation on such principles and organizing its powers in such form, as to them shall seem most likely to effect their Safety and Happiness. Prudence, indeed, will dictate that Governments long established should not be changed for light and transient causes; and accordingly all experience hath shewn, that mankind are more disposed to suffer, while evils are sufferable, than to right themselves by abolishing the forms to which they are accustomed. But when a long train of abuses and usurpations, pursuing invariably the same Object evinces a design to reduce them under absolute Despotism, it is their right, it is their duty, to throw off such Government, and to provide new Guards for their future security.—Such has been the patient sufferance of these Colonies; and such is now the necessity which constrains them to alter their former Systems of Government. The history of the present King of Great Britain is a history of repeated injuries and usurpations, all having in direct object the establishment of an absolute Tyranny over these States. To prove this, let Facts be submitted to a candid world.

He has refused his Assent to Laws, the most wholesome and necessary for the public good.

He has forbidden his Governors to pass Laws of immediate and pressing importance, unless suspended in their operation till his Assent should be obtained; and when so suspended, he has utterly neglected to attend to them.

He has refused to pass other Laws for the accommodation of large districts of people, unless those people would relinquish the right of Representation in the Legislature, a right inestimable to them and formidable to tyrants only.

He has called together legislative bodies at places unusual, uncomfortable, and distant from the depository of their public Records, for the sole purpose of fatiguing them into compliance with his measures.

He has dissolved Representative Houses repeatedly, for opposing with manly firmness his invasions on the rights of the people.

He has refused for a long time, after such dissolutions, to cause others to be elected; whereby the Legislative powers, incapable of Annihilation, have returned to the People at large for their exercise; the State remaining in the mean time exposed to all the dangers of invasion from without, and convulsions within.

He has endeavoured to prevent the population of these States; for that purpose obstructing the Laws for Naturalization of Foreigners; refusing to pass others to encourage their migrations hither, and raising the conditions of new Appropriations of Lands.

He has obstructed the Administration of Justice, by refusing his Assent to Laws for establishing Judiciary powers.

He has made Judges dependent on his Will alone, for the tenure of their offices, and the amount and payment of their salaries.

He has erected a multitude of New Offices, and sent hither swarms of Officers to harrass our people, and eat out their substance.

He has kept among us, in times of peace, Standing Armies without the Consent of our legislatures.

He has affected to render the Military independent of and superior to the Civil power.

He has combined with others to subject us to a jurisdiction foreign to our constitution, and unacknowledged by our laws; giving his Assent to their Acts of pretended Legislation:

For Quartering large bodies of armed troops among us:

For protecting them, by a mock Trial, from punishment for any Murders which they should commit on the Inhabitants of these States:

For cutting off our Trade with all parts of the world:

For imposing Taxes on us without our Consent:

For depriving us in many cases, of the benefits of Trial by Jury:

For transporting us beyond Seas to be tried for pretended offences:

For abolishing the free System of English Laws in a neighboring Province, establishing therein an Arbitrary government, and enlarging its Boundaries so as to render it at once an example and fit instrument for introducing the same absolute rule into these Colonies:

For taking away our Charters, abolishing our most valuable Laws, and altering fundamentally the Forms of our Governments:

For suspending our own Legislatures, and declaring themselves invested with power to legislate for us in all cases whatsoever.

He has abdicated Government here, by declaring us out of his Protection and waging War against us.

He has plundered our seas, ravaged our Coasts, burnt our towns, and destroyed the lives of our people.

He is at this time transporting large Armies of foreign Mercenaries to compleat the works of death, desolation and tyranny, already begun with circumstances of Cruelty & perfidy scarcely paralleled in the most barbarous ages, and totally unworthy the Head of a civilized nation.

He has constrained our fellow Citizens taken Captive on the high Seas to bear Arms against their Country, to become the executioners of their friends and Brethren, or to fall themselves by their Hands.

He has excited domestic insurrections amongst us, and has endeavoured to bring on the inhabitants of our frontiers, the merciless Indian Savages, whose known rule of warfare, is an undistinguished destruction of all ages, sexes and conditions.

In every stage of these Oppressions We have Petitioned for Redress in the most humble terms: Our repeated Petitions have been answered only by repeated injury. A Prince whose character is thus marked by every act which may define a Tyrant, is unfit to be the ruler of a free people.

Nor have We been wanting in attentions to our Brittish brethren. We have warned them from time to time of attempts by their legislature to extend an unwarrantable jurisdiction over us. We have reminded them of the circumstances of our emigration and settlement here. We have appealed to their native justice and magnanimity, and we have conjured them by the ties of our common kindred to disavow these usurpations, which, would inevitably interrupt our connections and correspondence. They too have been deaf to the voice of justice and of consanguinity. We must, therefore, acquiesce in the necessity, which denounces our Separation, and hold them, as we hold the rest of mankind, Enemies in War, in Peace Friends.

We, Therefore, the Representatives of the United States of America, in General Congress, Assembled, appealing to the Supreme Judge of the world for the rectitude of our intentions, do, in the Name, and by Authority of the good People of these Colonies, solemnly publish and declare, That these United Colonies are, and of Right ought to be Free and Independent States; that they are Absolved from all Allegiance to the British Crown, and that all political connection between them and the State of Great Britain, is and ought to be totally dissolved; and that as Free and Independent States, they have full Power to levy War, conclude Peace, contract Alliances, establish Commerce, and to do all other Acts and Things which Independent States may of right do. And for the support of this Declaration, with a firm reliance on the protection of divine Providence, we mutually pledge to each other our Lives, our Fortunes and our sacred Honor.

The foregoing Declaration was, by order of Congress, engrossed, and signed by the following members:

John Hancock

NEW HAMPSHIRE
Josiah Bartlett
William Whipple
Matthew Thornton

MASSACHUSETTS BAY
Samuel Adams
John Adams
Robert Treat Paine
Elbridge Gerry

RHODE ISLAND
Stephen Hopkins
William Ellery

CONNECTICUT
Roger Sherman
Samuel Huntington
William Williams
Oliver Wolcott

NEW YORK
William Floyd
Philip Livingston
Francis Lewis
Lewis Morris

NEW JERSEY
Richard Stockton
John Witherspoon
Francis Hopkinson
John Hart
Abraham Clark

PENNSYLVANIA
Robert Morris
Benjamin Rush
Benjamin Franklin
John Morton
George Clymer
James Smith

George Taylor
James Wilson
George Ross

DELAWARE
Caesar Rodney
George Read
Thomas M'Kean

MARYLAND
Samuel Chase
William Paca
Thomas Stone
Charles Carroll,
  of Carrollton

VIRGINIA
George Wythe
Richard Henry Lee
Thomas Jefferson

Benjamin Harrison
Thomas Nelson, Jr.
Francis Lightfoot Lee
Carter Braxton

NORTH CAROLINA
William Hooper
Joseph Hewes
John Penn

SOUTH CAROLINA
Edward Rutledge
Thomas Heyward, Jr.
Thomas Lynch, Jr.
Arthur Middleton

GEORGIA
Button Gwinnett
Lyman Hall
George Walton

Resolved, That copies of the Declaration be sent to the several assemblies, conventions, and committees, or councils of safety, and to the several commanding officers of the continental troops; that it be proclaimed in each of the United States, at the head of the army.

THE ARTICLES OF CONFEDERATION

Agreed to by Congress November 15, 1777;
ratified and in force March 1, 1781

To all whom these Presents shall come, we the under-signed Delegates of the States affixed to our Names, send greeting. Whereas the Delegates of the United States of America, in Congress assembled, did, on the fifteenth day of November, in the Year of Our Lord One thousand Seven Hundred and Seventy seven, and in the Second Year of the Independence of America, agree to certain articles of Confederation and perpetual Union between the States of New-hampshire, Massachusetts-bay, Rhodeisland and Providence Plantations, Connecticut, New-York, New-Jersey, Pennsylvania, Delaware, Maryland, Virginia, North-Carolina, South-Carolina and Georgia in the words following, viz. "Articles of Confederation and perpetual Union between the states of Newhampshire, Massachusettsbay, Rhodeisland and Providence Plantations, Connecticut, New-York, New-Jersey, Pennsylvania, Delaware, Maryland, Virginia, North-Carolina, South-Carolina and Georgia.

Art. I. The Stile of this confederacy shall be "The United States of America."

Art. II. Each state retains its sovereignty, freedom and independence, and every Power, Jurisdiction and right, which is not by this confederation expressly delegated to the United States, in Congress assembled.

Art. III. The said states hereby severally enter into a firm league of friendship with each other, for their common defence, the security of their Liberties, and their mutual and general welfare, binding themselves to assist each other, against all force offered to, or attacks made upon them, or any of them, on account of religion, sovereignty, trade, or any other pretence whatever.

Art. IV. The better to secure and perpetuate mutual friendship and intercourse among the people of the different states in this union, the free inhabitants of each of these states, paupers, vagabonds and fugitives from Justice excepted, shall be entitled to all privileges and immunities of free citizens in the several states; and the people of each state shall have free ingress and regress to and from any other state, and shall enjoy therein all the privileges of trade and commerce, subject to the same duties, impositions and restrictions as the inhabitants thereof respectively, provided that such restriction shall not extend so far as to prevent the removal of property imported into any state, to any other state, of which the Owner is an inhabitant; provided also that no imposition, duties or restriction shall be laid by any state, on the property of the united states, or either of them.

If any Person guilty of, or charged with treason, felony, or other high misdemeanor in any state, shall flee from Justice, and be found in any of the united states, he shall, upon demand of the Governor or executive power, of the state from which he fled, be delivered up and removed to the state having jurisdiction of his offence.

Full faith and credit shall be given in each of these states to the records, acts and judicial proceedings of the courts and magistrates of every other state.

Art. V. For the more convenient management of the general interests of the united states, delegates shall be annually appointed in such manner as the legislature of each state shall direct, to meet in Congress on the first Monday in November, in every year, with a power reserved to each state, to recall its delegates, or any of them, at any time within the year, and to send others in their stead, for the remainder of the Year.

No state shall be represented in Congress by less than two, nor by more than seven Members; and no person shall be capable of being a delegate for more than three years in any term of six years; nor shall any person, being a delegate, be capable of holding any office under the united states, for which he, or another for his benefit receives any salary, fees or emolument of any kind.

Each state shall maintain its own delegates in a meeting of the states, and while they act as members of the committee of the states.

In determining questions in the united states, in Congress assembled, each state shall have one vote.

Freedom of speech and debate in Congress shall not be impeached or questioned in any Court, or place out of Congress, and the members of congress shall be protected in their persons from arrests and imprisonments, during the time of their going to and from, and attendance on congress, except for treason, felony, or breach of the peace.

Art. VI. No state without the Consent of the united states in congress assembled, shall send any embassy to, or receive any embassy from, or enter into any conference, agreement, or alliance or treaty with any King, prince or state; nor shall any person holding any office or profit or trust under the united states, or any of them, accept of any present, emolument, office or title of any kind whatever from any king, prince or foreign state; nor shall the united states in congress assembled, or any of them, grant any title of nobility.

No two or more states shall enter into any treaty, confederation or alliance whatever between them, without the consent of the united states in congress assembled, specifying accurately the purposes for which the same is to be entered into, and how long it shall continue.

No state shall lay any imposts or duties, which may interfere with any stipulations in treaties, entered into by the united states in congress assembled, with any king, prince or state, in pursuance of any treaties already proposed by congress, to the courts of France and Spain.

No vessels of war shall be kept up in time of peace by any state, except such number only, as shall be deemed necessary by the united states in congress assembled, for the defence of such state, or its trade; nor shall any body of forces be kept up by any state, in time of peace, except such number only, as in the judgment of the united states, in congress assembled, shall be deemed requisite to garrison the forts necessary for the defence of such state; but every state shall always keep up a well regulated and disciplined militia, sufficiently armed and accoutred, and shall provide and constantly have ready for use, in public stores, a due number of field pieces and tents, and a proper quantity of arms, ammunition and camp equipage.

No state shall engage in any war without the consent of the united states in congress assembled, unless such state be actually invaded by enemies, or shall have received certain advice of a resolution being formed by some nation of Indians to invade such state, and the danger is so imminent as not to admit of a delay, till the united states in congress asssembled can be consulted; nor shall any state grant commissions to any ships or vessels of war, nor letters of marque or reprisal, except it be after a declaration of war by the united states in congress assembled, and then only against the kingdom or state and the subjects thereof, against which war has been so declared, and under such regulations as shall be established by the united states in congress assembled, unless such state be infested by pirates; in which case vessels of war may be fitted out for that occasion, and kept so long as the danger shall continue, or until the united states in congress assembled shall determine otherwise.

Art. VII. When land-forces are raised by any state for the common defence, all officers of or under the rank of colonel, shall be appointed by the legislature of each state respectively, by whom such forces shall be raised, or in such manner as such state shall direct, and all vacancies shall be filled up by the state which first made the appointment.

Art. VIII. All charges of war, and all other expences that shall be incurred for the common defence or general welfare, and allowed by the united states in congress assembled, shall be defrayed out of a common treasury, which shall be supplied by the several states in proportion to the value of all land within each state, granted to or surveyed for any Person, as such land and the buildings and improvements thereon shall be estimated according to such mode as the united states in congress assembled, shall from time to time direct and appoint.

The taxes for paying that proportion shall be laid and levied by the authority and direction of the legislatures of the several states within the time agreed upon by the united states in congress assembled.

Art. IX. The united states in congress assembled, shall have the sole and exclusive right and power of determining on peace and war, except in the cases mentioned in the sixth article—of sending and receiving ambassadors—entering into treaties and alliances, provided that no treaty of commerce shall be made whereby the legislative power of the respective states shall be restrained from imposing such imposts and duties on foreigners, as their own people are subjected to, or from prohibiting the exportation of any species of goods or commodities whatsoever—of establishing rules for deciding in all cases, what captures on land or water shall be legal, and in what manner prizes taken by land or naval forces in the service of the united states shall be divided or appropriated—of granting letters of marque and reprisal in times of peace—appointing courts for the trial of piracies and felonies committed on the high seas and establishing courts for receiving and determining finally appeals in all cases of captures, provided that no member of congress shall be appointed a judge of any of the said courts.

The united states in congress assembled shall also be the last resort on appeal in all disputes and differences now subsisting or that hereafter may arise between two or more states concerning boundary, jurisdiction or any other cause whatever; which authority shall always be exercised in the manner following. Whenever the legislative or executive authority or lawful agent of any state in controversy with another shall present a petition to congress stating the matter in question and praying for a hearing, notice thereof shall be given by order of congress to the legislative or executive authority of the other state in controversy, and a day assigned for the appearance of the parties by their lawful agents, who shall then be directed to appoint by joint consent, commissioners or judges to constitute a court for hearing and determining the matter in question: but if they cannot agree, congress shall name three persons out of each of the united states, and from the list of such persons each party shall alternately strike out one, the petitioners beginning, until the number shall be reduced to thirteen; and from that number not less than seven, nor more than nine names as congress shall direct, shall in the presence of congress be drawn out by lot, and the persons whose names shall be so drawn or any five of them, shall be commissioners or judges, to hear and finally determine the controversy, so always as a major part of the judges who shall hear the cause shall agree in the determination: and if either party shall neglect to attend at the day appointed, without shewing reasons, which congress shall judge sufficient, or being present shall refuse to strike, the congress shall proceed to nominate three persons out of each state, and the secretary of congress shall strike in behalf of such party absent or refusing; and the judgment and sentence of the court to be appointed, in the manner before prescribed, shall be final and conclusive; and if any of the parties shall refuse to submit to the authority of such court, or to appear to defend their claim or cause, the court shall nevertheless proceed to pronounce sentence, or judgment, which shall in like manner be final and decisive, the judgment or sentence and other proceedings being in either case transmitted to congress, and lodged among the acts of congress for the security of the parties concerned: provided that every commissioner, before he sits in judgment, shall take an oath to be administered by one of the judges of the supreme or superior court of the state, where the cause shall be tried, "well and truly to hear and determine the matter in question, according to the best of his judgment, without favour, affection or hope of reward:" provided also, that no state shall be deprived of territory for the benefit of the united states.

All controversies concerning the private right of soil claimed under different grants of two or more states, whose jurisdictions as they may respect such lands, and the states which passed such grants are adjusted, the said grants or either of them being at the same time claimed to have originated antecedent to such settlement of jurisdiction, shall on the petition of either party to the congress of the united states, be finally determined as near as may be in the same manner as is before prescribed for deciding disputes respecting territorial jurisdiction between different states.

The united states in congress assembled shall also have the sole and exclusive right and power of regulating the alloy and value of coin struck by their own authority, or by that of the respective states—fixing the standard of weights and measures throughout the united states—regulating the trade and managing all affairs with the Indians, not members of any of the states, provided that the legislative right of any state within its own limits be not infringed or violated—establishing and regulating post-offices from one state to another, throughout all the united states, and exacting such postage on the papers passing thro' the same as may be requisite to defray the expences of the said office—appointing all officers of the land forces, in the service of the united states, excepting regimental officers—appointing all the officers of the naval forces, and commissioning all officers whatever in the service of the united states—making rules for the government and regulation of the said land and naval forces, and directing their operations.

The united states in congress assembled shall have authority to appoint a committee, to sit in the recess of congress, to be denominated "A Committee of the States," and to consist of one delegate from each state; and to appoint such other committees and civil officers as may be necessary for managing the general affairs of the united states under their direction—to appoint one of their number to preside, provided that no person be allowed to serve in the office of president more than one year in any term of three years; to ascertain the necessary sums of Money to be raised for the service of the united states, and to appropriate and apply the same for defraying the public expenses—to borrow money, or emit bills on the credit of the united states, transmitting every half year to the respective states an account of the sums of money so borrowed or emitted,—to build and equip a navy—to agree upon the number of land forces, and to make requisitions from each state for its quota, in proportion to the number of white inhabitants in such state; which requisition shall be binding, and thereupon the legislature of each state shall appoint the regimental officers, raise the men and cloath, arm and equip then in a soldier like manner, at the expense of the united states; and the officers and men so cloathed, armed and equipped shall march to the place appointed, and within the time agreed on by the united states in congress assembled: But if the united states in congress assembled shall, on consideration of circumstances judge proper that any state should not raise men, or should raise a smaller number than its quota, and that any other state should raise a greater number of men than the quota thereof, such extra number shall be raised, officered, cloathed, armed and equipped in the same manner as the quota of such state, unless the legislature of such state shall judge that such extra number cannot be safely spared out of the same, in which case they shall raise officer, cloath, arm and equip as many of such extra number as they judge can be safely spared. And the officers and men so cloathed, armed and equipped, shall march to the place appointed, and within the time agreed on by the united states in congress assembled.

The united states in congress assembled shall never engage in a war, nor grant letters of marque and reprisal in time of peace, nor enter into any treaties or alliances, nor coin money, nor regulate the value thereof, nor ascertain the sums and expenses necessary for the defence and welfare of the united states, or any of them, nor emit bills, nor borrow money on the credit of the united states, nor appropriate money, nor agree upon the number of vessels of war, to be built or purchased, or the number of land or sea forces to be raised, nor appoint a commander in chief of the army or navy, unless nine states assent to the same: nor shall a question on any other point, except for adjourning from day to day be determined, unless by the votes of a majority of the united states in congress assembled.

The congress of the united states shall have power to adjourn to any time within the year, and to any place within the united states, so that no period of adjournment be for a longer duration than the space of six Months, and shall publish the

Journal of their proceedings monthly, except such parts thereof relating to treaties, alliances or military operations, as in their judgment require secrecy; and the yeas and nays of the delegates of each state on any question shall be entered on the Journal, when it is desired by any delegate; and the delegates of a state, or any of them, at his or their request shall be furnished with a transcript of the said Journal, except such parts as are above excepted, to lay before the legislatures of the several states.

Art. X. The committee of the states, or any nine of them, shall be authorised to execute, in the recess of congress, such of the powers of congress as the united states in congress assembled, by the consent of nine states, shall from time to time think expedient to vest them with; provided that no power be delegated to the said committee, for the exercise of which, by the articles of confederation, the voice of nine states in the congress of the united states assembled is requisite.

Art. XI. Canada acceding to this confederation, and joining in the measures of the united states, shall be admitted into, and entitled to all the advantages of this union: but no other colony shall be admitted into the same, unless such admission be agreed to by nine states.

Art. XII. All bills of credit emitted, monies borrowed and debts contracted by, or under the authority of congress, before the assembling of the united states, in pursuance of the present confederation, shall be deemed and considered as a charge against the united states, for payment and satisfaction whereof the said united states and the public faith are hereby solemnly pledged.

Art. XIII. Every state shall abide by the determinations of the united states in congress assembled, on all questions which by this confederation are submitted to them. And the Articles of this confederation shall be inviolably observed by every state, and the union shall be perpetual; nor shall any alteration at any time hereafter be made in any of them; unless such alteration be agreed to in a congress of the united states, and be afterwards confirmed by the legislatures of every state.

And Whereas it hath pleased the Great Governor of the World to incline the hearts of the legislatures we respectively represent in congress, to approve of, and to authorize us to ratify the said articles of confederation and perpetual union. Know Ye that we the undersigned delegates, by virtue of the power and authority to us given for that purpose, do by these presents, in the name and in behalf of our respective constituents, fully and entirely ratify and confirm each and every of the said articles of confederation and perpetual union, and all and singular the matters and things therein contained: And we do further solemnly plight and engage the faith of our respective constituents, that they shall abide by the determinations of the united states in congress assembled, on all questions, which by the said confederation are submitted to them. And that the articles thereof shall be inviolably observed by the states we respectively represent, and that the union shall be perpetual. In Witness whereof we have hereunto set our hands in Congress. Done at Philadelphia in the state of Pennsylvania the ninth day of July, in the Year of our Lord one Thousand seven Hundred and Seventy-eight, and in the third year of the independence of America.

THE CONSTITUTION OF THE UNITED STATES OF AMERICA

[PREAMBLE]

We the People of the United States, in Order to form a more perfect Union, establish Justice, insure domestic Tranquility, provide for the common defence, promote the general Welfare, and secure the Blessings of Liberty to ourselves and our Posterity, do ordain and establish this Constitution for the United States of America.

Article I

Section 1

[LEGISLATIVE POWERS]

All legislative Powers herein granted shall be vested in a Congress of the United States, which shall consist of a Senate and House of Representatives.

Section 2

[HOUSE OF REPRESENTATIVES, HOW CONSTITUTED, POWER OF IMPEACHMENT]

The House of Representatives shall be composed of Members chosen every second Year by the People of the several States, and the Electors in each State shall have the Qualifications requisite for Electors of the most numerous Branch of the State Legislature.

No Person shall be a Representative who shall not have attained to the Age of twenty five Years, and been seven Years a Citizen of the United States, and who shall not, when elected, be an Inhabitant of that State in which he shall be chosen.

Representatives and *direct Taxes*[1] shall be apportioned among the several States which may be included within this Union, according to their respective Numbers, *which shall be determined by adding to the whole Number of free Persons, including those bound to Service for a Term of Years, and excluding Indians not taxed, three fifths of all other Persons.*[2] The actual Enumeration shall be made within three Years after the first Meeting of the Congress of the United States, and within every subsequent Term of ten Years, in such Manner as they shall by Law direct. The Number of Representatives shall not exceed one for every thirty Thousand, but each State shall have at Least one Representative; *and until such enumeration shall be made, the State of New Hampshire shall be entitled to chuse three, Massachusetts eight, Rhode-Island and Providence Plantations one, Connecticut five, New-York six, New Jersey four, Pennsylvania eight, Delaware one, Maryland six, Virginia ten, North Carolina five, South Carolina five, and Georgia three.*[3]

When vacancies happen in the Representation from any State, the Executive Authority thereof shall issue Writs of Election to fill such Vacancies.

The House of Representatives shall chuse their Speaker and other Officers; and shall have the sole Power of Impeachment.

Section 3

[THE SENATE, HOW CONSTITUTED, IMPEACHMENT TRIALS]

The Senate of the United States shall be composed of two Senators from each State, *chosen by the Legislature thereof,*[4] for six Years; and each Senator shall have one Vote.

Immediately after they shall be assembled in Consequence of the first Election, they shall be divided as equally as may be into three Classes. The Seats of the Senators of the first Class shall be vacated at the Expiration of the second Year, of the second Class at the Expiration of the fourth Year, and of the third Class at the Expiration of the sixth Year, so that one third may be chosen every second Year; *and if Vacancies happen by Resignation, or otherwise, during the Recess of the Legislature of any State, the Executive thereof may make temporary Appointments until the next Meeting of the Legislature, which shall then fill such Vacancies.*[5]

No Person shall be a Senator who shall not have attained to the Age of thirty Years, and been nine Years a Citizen of the United States, and who shall not, when elected, be an Inhabitant of that State for which he shall be chosen.

The Vice President of the United States shall be President of the Senate, but shall have no Vote, unless they be equally divided.

---

[1]Modified by Sixteenth Amendment.

[2]Modified by Fourteenth Amendment.

[3]Temporary provision.

[4]Modified by Seventeenth Amendment.

[5]Modified by Seventeenth Amendment.

The Senate shall chuse their other Officers, and also a President pro tempore, in the Absence of the Vice President, or when he shall exercise the Office of President of the United States.

The Senate shall have the sole Power to try all Impeachments. When sitting for that Purpose, they shall be on Oath or Affirmation. When the President of the United States is tried, the Chief Justice shall preside: And no Person shall be convicted without the Concurrence of two thirds of the Members present.

Judgment in Cases of Impeachment shall not extend further than to removal from Office, and disqualification to hold and enjoy any Office of honor, Trust or Profit under the United States: but the Party convicted shall nevertheless be liable and subject to Indictment, Trial, Judgment and Punishment, according to Law.

Section 4
[ELECTION OF SENATORS AND REPRESENTATIVES]

The Times, Places and Manner of holding Elections for Senators and Representatives, shall be prescribed in each State by the Legislature thereof; but the Congress may at any time by Law make or alter such Regulations, except as to the Places of chusing Senators.

The Congress shall assemble at least once in every Year, and such Meeting shall be on the first Monday in December, unless they shall by Law appoint a different Day.[6]

Section 5
[QUORUM, JOURNALS, MEETINGS, ADJOURNMENTS]

Each House shall be the Judge of the Elections, Returns and Qualifications of its own Members, and a Majority of each shall constitute a Quorum to do Business; but a smaller Number may adjourn from day to day, and may be authorized to compel the Attendance of absent Members, in such Manner, and under such Penalties as each House may provide.

Each House may determine the Rules of its Proceedings, punish its Members for disorderly Behaviour, and, with the Concurrence of two thirds, expel a Member.

Each House shall keep a Journal of its Proceedings, and from time to time publish the same, excepting such Parts as may in their Judgment require Secrecy; and the Yeas and Nays of the Members of either House on any questions shall, at the Desire of one fifth of those Present, be entered on the Journal.

Neither House, during the Session of Congress, shall, without the Consent of the other, adjourn for more than three days, nor to any other Place than that in which the two Houses shall be sitting.

[6]Modified by Twentieth Amendment.

Section 6
[COMPENSATION, PRIVILEGES, DISABILITIES]

The Senators and Representatives shall receive a Compensation for their Services, to be ascertained by Law, and paid out of the Treasury of the United States. They shall in all Cases, except Treason, Felony and Breach of the Peace, be privileged from Arrest during their Attendance at the Session of their respective Houses, and in going to and returning from the same; and for any Speech or Debate in either House, they shall not be questioned in any other Place.

No Senator or Representative shall, during the Time for which he was elected, be appointed to any civil Office under the Authority of the United States, which shall have been created, or the Emoluments whereof shall have been encreased during such time; and no Person holding any Office under the United States, shall be a Member of either House during his Continuance in Office.

Section 7
[PROCEDURE IN PASSING BILLS AND RESOLUTIONS]

All Bills for raising Revenue shall originate in the House of Representatives; but the Senate may propose or concur with Amendments as on other Bills.

Every Bill which shall have passed the House of Representatives and the Senate, shall, before it become a Law, be presented to the President of the United States: If he approve he shall sign it, but if not he shall return it, with his Objections to that House in which it shall have originated, who shall enter the Objections at large on their Journal, and proceed to reconsider it. If after such Reconsideration two thirds of that House shall agree to pass the Bill, it shall be sent, together with the Objections, to the other House, by which it shall likewise be reconsidered, and if approved by two thirds of that House, it shall become a Law. But in all such Cases the Votes of both Houses shall be determined by yeas and Nays, and the Names of the Persons voting for and against the Bill shall be entered on the Journal of each House respectively. If any Bill shall not be returned by the President within ten Days (Sundays excepted) after it shall have been presented to him, the Same shall be a Law, in like Manner as if he had signed it, unless the Congress by their Adjournment prevent its Return, in which Case it shall not be a Law.

Every Order, Resolution, or Vote to which the Concurrence of the Senate and House of Representatives may be necessary (except on a question of Adjournment) shall be presented to the President of the United States; and before the Same shall take Effect, shall be approved by him, or being disapproved by him, shall be repassed by two thirds of the Senate and House of Representatives, according to the Rules and Limitations prescribed in the Case of a Bill.

Section 8

[POWERS OF CONGRESS]

The Congress shall have Power

To lay and collect Taxes, Duties, Imposts and Excises, to pay the Debts and provide for the common Defence and general Welfare of the United States; but all Duties, Imposts and Excises shall be uniform throughout the United States;

To borrow Money on the credit of the United States;

To regulate Commerce with foreign Nations, and among the several States, and with the Indian Tribes;

To establish an uniform Rule of Naturalization, and uniform Laws on the subject of Bankruptcies throughout the United States;

To coin Money, regulate the Value thereof, and of foreign Coin, and fix the Standard of Weights and Measures;

To provide for the Punishment of counterfeiting the Securities and current Coin of the United States;

To establish Post Offices and post Roads;

To promote the Progress of Science and useful Arts, by securing for limited Times to Authors and Inventors the exclusive Right to their respective Writings and Discoveries;

To constitute Tribunals inferior to the supreme Court;

To define and punish Piracies and Felonies committed on the high Seas, and Offences against the Law of Nations;

To declare War, grant Letters of Marque and Reprisal, and make Rules concerning Captures on Land and Water;

To raise and support Armies, but no Appropriation of Money to that Use shall be for a longer Term than two Years;

To provide and maintain a Navy;

To make Rules for the Government and Regulation of the land and naval Forces;

To provide for calling forth the Militia to execute the Laws of the Union, suppress Insurrections and repel Invasions;

To provide for organizing, arming, and disciplining, the Militia, and for governing such Part of them as may be employed in the Service of the United States, reserving to the States respectively, the Appointment of the Officers, and the Authority of training the Militia according to the discipline prescribed by Congress;

To exercise exclusive Legislation in all Cases whatsoever, over such District (not exceeding ten Miles square) as may, by Cession of particular States, and the Acceptance of Congress, become the Seat of the Government of the United States, and to exercise like Authority over all Places purchased by the Consent of the Legislature of the State in which the Same shall be, for the Erection of Forts, Magazines, Arsenals, dock-Yards, and other needful Buildings;—And

To make all Laws which shall be necessary and proper for carrying into Execution the foregoing Powers, and all other Powers vested by this Constitution in the Government of the United States, or in any Department or Officer thereof.

Section 9

[SOME RESTRICTIONS ON FEDERAL POWER]

The Migration or Importation of such Persons as any of the States now existing shall think proper to admit, shall not be prohibited by the Congress prior to the Year one thousand eight hundred and eight, but a Tax or duty may be imposed on such Importation, not exceeding ten dollars for each Person.[7]

The Privilege of the Writ of Habeas Corpus shall not be suspended, unless when in Cases of Rebellion or Invasion the public Safety may require it.

No Bill of Attainder or ex post facto Law shall be passed.

No Capitation, or other direct, Tax shall be laid, unless in Proportion to the Census or Enumeration herein before directed to be taken.[8]

No Tax or Duty shall be laid on Articles exported from any State.

No Preference shall be given by any Regulation of Commerce or Revenue to the Ports of one State over those of another; nor shall Vessels bound to, or from, one State, be obliged to enter, clear, or pay Duties in another.

No Money shall be drawn from the Treasury, but in Consequence of Appropriations made by Law; and a regular Statement and Account of the Receipts and Expenditures of all public Money shall be published from time to time.

No Title of Nobility shall be granted by the United States: And no Person holding any Office of Profit or Trust under them, shall, without the Consent of the Congress, accept of any present, Emolument, Office, or Title, of any kind whatever, from any King, Prince, or foreign State.

Section 10

[RESTRICTIONS UPON POWERS OF STATES]

No State shall enter into any Treaty, Alliance, or Confederation; grant Letters of Marque and Reprisal; coin Money; emit Bills of Credit; make any Thing but gold and silver Coin a Tender in Payment of Debts; pass any Bill of Attainder, ex post facto Law, or Law impairing the Obligation of Contracts, or grant any Title of Nobility.

No State shall, without the Consent of the Congress, lay any Imposts or Duties on Imports or Exports, except what may be absolutely necessary for executing it's inspection Laws: and the net Produce of all Duties and Imposts, laid by any State on Imports or Exports, shall be for the Use of the Treasury of the United States; and all such Laws shall be subject to the Revision and Controul of the Congress.

No State shall, without the Consent of Congress, lay any Duty of Tonnage, keep Troops, or Ships of War in time of

---

[7]Temporary provision.

[8]Modified by Sixteenth Amendment.

Peace, enter into any Agreement or Compact with another State, or with a foreign Power, or engage in War, unless actually invaded, or in such imminent Danger as will not admit of delay.

Article II

Section 1

[EXECUTIVE POWER, ELECTION, QUALIFICATIONS OF THE PRESIDENT]

The executive Power shall be vested in a President of the United States of America. *He shall hold his Office during the Term of four Years, and, together with the Vice President, chosen for the same Term, be elected, as follows*[9]

Each State shall appoint, in such Manner as the Legislature thereof may direct, a Number of Electors, equal to the whole Number of Senators and Representatives to which the State may be entitled in the Congress: but no Senator or Representative, or Person holding an Office of Trust or Profit under the United States, shall be appointed an Elector.

The electors shall meet in their respective States, and vote by ballot for two Persons, of whom one at least shall not be an Inhabitant of the same State with themselves. And they shall make a List of all the Persons voted for, and of the Number of Votes for each; which List they shall sign and certify, and transmit sealed to the Seat of the Government of the United States, directed to the President of the Senate. The President of the Senate shall, in the Presence of the Senate and House of Representatives, open all the Certificates, and the Votes shall then be counted. The Person having the greatest Number of Votes shall be the President, if such Number be a Majority of the whole Number of Electors appointed; and if there be more than one who have such Majority, and have an equal Number of Votes, then the House of Representatives shall immediately chuse by Ballot one of them for President; and if no Person have a Majority, then from the five highest on the List the said House shall in like Manner chuse the President. But in chusing the President, the Votes shall be taken by States, the Representation from each State having one Vote; A quorum for this Purpose shall consist of a Member or Members from two thirds of the States, and a Majority of all the States shall be necessary to a Choice. In every Case, after the Choice of the President, the person having the greatest Number of Votes of the Electors shall be the Vice President. But if there should remain two or more who have equal Votes, the Senate shall chuse from them by Ballot the Vice President.[10]

The Congress may determine the Time of chusing the Electors, and the Day on which they shall give their Votes; which Day shall be the same throughout the United States.

[9]Number of terms limited to two by Twenty-second Amendment.

[10]Modified by Twelfth and Twentieth Amendments.

No Person except a natural born Citizen, or a Citizen of the United States, at the time of the Adoption of this Constitution, shall be eligible to the Office of President; neither shall any Person be eligible to that Office who shall not have attained to the Age of thirty five Years, and been fourteen Years a Resident within the United States.

In Case of the Removal of the President from Office, or his Death, Resignation, or Inability to discharge the Powers and Duties of the said Office, the Same shall devolve on the Vice President, and the Congress may by Law provide for the Case of Removal, Death, Resignation or Inability, both of the President and Vice President, declaring what Officer shall then act as President, and such Officer shall act accordingly, until the Disability be removed, or a President shall be elected.

The President shall, at stated Times, receive for his Services, a Compensation, which shall neither be increased nor diminished during the Period for which he shall have been elected, and he shall not receive within that Period any other Emolument from the United States, or any of them.

Before he enter on the Execution of his Office, he shall take the following Oath or Affirmation:—"I do solemnly swear (or affirm) that I will faithfully execute the Office of President of the United States, and will to the best of my Ability, preserve, protect and defend the Constitution of the United States."

Section 2

[POWERS OF THE PRESIDENT]

The President shall be Commander in Chief of the Army and Navy of the United States, and of the Militia of the several States, when called into the actual Service of the United States; he may require the Opinion, in writing, of the principal Officer in each of the executive Departments, upon any Subject relating to the Duties of their respective Offices, and he shall have Power to grant Reprieves and Pardons for Offences against the United States, except in Cases of Impeachment.

He shall have Power, by and with the Advice and Consent of the Senate, to make Treaties, provided two thirds of the Senators present concur; and he shall nominate, and by and with the Advice and Consent of the Senate, shall appoint Ambassadors, other public Ministers and Consuls, Judges of the supreme Court, and all other Officers of the United States, whose Appointments are not herein otherwise provided for, and which shall be established by Law: but the Congress may by Law vest the Appointment of such inferior Officers, as they think proper, in the President alone, in the Courts of Law, or in the Heads of Departments.

The President shall have Power to fill up all Vacancies that may happen during the Recess of the Senate, by granting Commissions which shall expire at the End of their next Session.

Section 3

[POWERS AND DUTIES OF THE PRESIDENT]

He shall from time to time give to the Congress Information of the State of the Union, and recommend to their Consideration such Measures as he shall judge necessary and expedient; he may, on extraordinary Occasions, convene both Houses, or either of them, and in Case of Disagreement between them, with Respect to the Time of Adjournment, he may adjourn them to such Time as he shall think proper; he shall receive Ambassadors and other public Ministers; he shall take Care that the Laws be faithfully executed, and shall Commission all the Officers of the United States.

Section 4

[IMPEACHMENT]

The President, Vice President and all civil Officers of the United States, shall be removed from Office on Impeachment for, and Conviction of, Treason, Bribery, or other high Crimes and Misdemeanors.

Article III

Section 1

[JUDICIAL POWER, TENURE OF OFFICE]

The judicial Power of the United States, shall be vested in one supreme Court, and in such inferior Courts as the Congress may from time to time ordain and establish. The Judges, both of the supreme and inferior Courts, shall hold their Offices during good Behaviour, and shall, at stated Times, receive for their Services, a Compensation, which shall not be diminished during their Continuance in Office.

Section 2

[JURISDICTION]

The judicial Power shall extend to all Cases, in Law and Equity, arising under this Constitution, the Laws of the United States, and Treaties made, or which shall be made, under their Authority;—to all Cases affecting Ambassadors, other public Ministers and Consuls;—to all Cases of admiralty and maritime Jurisdiction;—to Controversies to which the United States shall be a Party;—to Controversies between two or more States;—*between a State and Citizens of another State;—*between Citizens of different States,—between Citizens of the same State claiming Lands under Grants of different States, *and between a State,* or the Citizens thereof, *and foreign States, Citizens or Subjects.*[11]

In all Cases affecting Ambassadors, other public Ministers and Consuls, and those in which a State shall be Party, the supreme Court shall have original Jurisdiction. In all the other Cases before mentioned, the supreme Court shall have appellate Jurisdiction, both as to Law and Fact, with

such Exceptions, and under such Regulations as the Congress shall make.

The Trial of all Crimes, except in Cases of Impeachment, shall be by Jury; and such Trial shall be held in the State where the said Crimes shall have been committed; but when not committed within any State, the Trial shall be at such Place or Places as the Congress may by Law have directed.

Section 3

[TREASON, PROOF, AND PUNISHMENT]

Treason against the United States, shall consist only in levying War against them, or in adhering to their Enemies, giving them Aid and Comfort. No Person shall be convicted of Treason unless on the Testimony of two Witnesses to the same overt Act, or on Confession in open Court.

The Congress shall have Power to declare the Punishment of Treason, but no Attainder of Treason shall work Corruption of Blood, or Forfeiture except during the Life of the Person attainted.

Article IV

Section 1

[FAITH AND CREDIT AMONG STATES]

Full Faith and Credit shall be given in each State to the public Acts, Records, and judicial Proceedings of every other State. And the Congress may by general Laws prescribe the Manner in which such Acts, Records and Proceedings shall be proved, and the Effect thereof.

Section 2

[PRIVILEGES AND IMMUNITIES, FUGITIVES]

The Citizens of each State shall be entitled to all Privileges and Immunities of Citizens in the several States.

A Person charged in any State with Treason, Felony or other Crime, who shall flee from Justice, and be found in another State, shall on Demand of the executive Authority of the State from which he fled, be delivered up, to be removed to the State having Jurisdiction of the Crime.

No person held to Service or Labour in one State, under the Laws thereof, escaping into another, shall, in Consequence of any Law or Regulation therein, be discharged from such Service or Labour, but shall be delivered up on Claim of the Party to whom such Service or Labour may be due.[12]

Section 3

[ADMISSION OF NEW STATES]

New States may be admitted by the Congress into this Union; but no new State shall be formed or erected within the Jurisdiction of any other State; nor any State be formed by the Junction of two or more States, or Parts of States, without

---

[11]Modified by Eleventh Amendment.

[12]Repealed by the Thirteenth Amendment.

the Consent of the Legislatures of the States concerned as well as of the Congress.

The Congress shall have Power to dispose of and make all needful Rules and Regulations respecting the Territory or other Property belonging to the United States; and nothing in this Constitution shall be so construed as to Prejudice any Claims of the United States, or of any particular State.

Section 4
[GUARANTEE OF REPUBLICAN GOVERNMENT]

The United States shall guarantee to every State in this Union a Republican Form of Government, and shall protect each of them against Invasion; and on Application of the Legislature, or of the Executive (when the Legislature cannot be convened), against domestic Violence.

Article V
[AMENDMENT OF THE CONSTITUTION]

The Congress, whenever two thirds of both Houses shall deem it necessary, shall propose Amendments to this Constitution, or, on the Application of the Legislatures of two thirds of the several States, shall call a Convention for proposing Amendments, which, in either Case, shall be valid to all Intents and Purposes, as Part of this Constitution, when ratified by the Legislatures of three fourths of the several States, or by Conventions in three fourths thereof, as the one or the other Mode of Ratification may be proposed by the Congress; *Provided that no Amendment which may be made prior to the Year One thousand eight hundred and eight shall in any Manner affect the first and fourth Clauses in the Ninth Section of the first Article;*[13] and that no State, without its Consent, shall be deprived of its equal Suffrage in the Senate.

[13]Temporary provision.

Article VI
[DEBTS, SUPREMACY, OATH]

All Debts contracted and Engagements entered into, before the Adoption of this Constitution, shall be as valid against the United States under this Constitution, as under the Confederation.

This Constitution, and the Laws of the United States which shall be made in Pursuance thereof; and all Treaties made, or which shall be made, under the Authority of the United States, shall be the supreme Law of the Land; and the Judges in every State shall be bound thereby, any Thing in the Constitution or Laws of any State to the Contrary notwithstanding.

The Senators and Representatives before mentioned, and the Members of the several State Legislatures, and all executive and judicial Officers, both of the United States and of the several States, shall be bound by Oath or Affirmation, to support this Constitution; but no religious Test shall be required as a Qualification to any Office or public Trust under the United States.

Article VII
[RATIFICATION AND ESTABLISHMENT]

The Ratification of the Conventions of nine States, shall be sufficient for the Establishment of this Constitution between the States so ratifying the Same.[14]

Done in Convention by the Unanimous Consent of the States present the Seventeenth Day of September in the Year of our Lord one thousand seven hundred and Eighty seven and of the Independence of the United States of America the Twelfth. *In Witness* whereof We have hereunto subscribed our Names,

[14]The Constitution was submitted on September 17, 1787, by the Constitutional Convention, was ratified by the conventions of several states at various dates up to May 29, 1790, and became effective on March 4, 1789.

G:[0] WASHINGTON—
Presidt. and deputy from Virginia

NEW HAMPSHIRE	*David Brearley*	DELAWARE	NORTH CAROLINA
John Langdon	*Wm. Paterson*	*Geo: Read*	*Wm. Blount*
Nicholas Gilman	*Jona: Dayton*	*Gunning Bedford jun*	*Richd. Dobbs Spaight*
MASSACHUSETTS	PENNSYLVANIA	*John Dickinson*	*Hu Williamson*
Nathaniel Gorham	*B Franklin*	*Richard Bassett*	SOUTH CAROLINA
Rufus King	*Thomas Mifflin*	*Jaco: Broom*	*J. Rutledge*
CONNECTICUT	*Robt. Morris*	MARYLAND	*Charles Cotesworth*
Wm. Saml. Johnson	*Geo. Clymer*	*James McHenry*	*Pinckney*
Roger Sherman	*Thos. FitzSimons*	*Dan of St Thos. Jenifer*	*Charles Pinckney*
NEW YORK	*Jared Ingersoll*	*Danl. Carroll*	*Pierce Butler*
Alexander Hamilton	*James Wilson*	VIRGINIA	GEORGIA
NEW JERSEY	*Gouv Morris*	*John Blair—*	*William Few*
Wil: Livingston		*James Madison Jr.*	*Abr Baldwin*

AMENDMENTS TO THE CONSTITUTION

Proposed by Congress and Ratified by the Legislatures of the Several States,
Pursuant to Article V of the Original Constitution.

Amendments I–X, known as the Bill of Rights, were proposed by Congress on September 25, 1789, and ratified on December 15, 1791.

Amendment I

[FREEDOM OF RELIGION, OF SPEECH, AND OF THE PRESS]

Congress shall make no law respecting an establishment of religion, or prohibiting the free exercise thereof; or abridging the freedom of speech, or of the press; or the right of the people peaceably to assemble, and to petition the Government for a redress of grievances.

Amendment II

[RIGHT TO KEEP AND BEAR ARMS]

A well regulated Militia, being necessary to the security of a free State, the right of the people to keep and bear Arms, shall not be infringed.

Amendment III

[QUARTERING OF SOLDIERS]

No Soldier shall, in time of peace be quartered in any house, without the consent of the Owner, nor in time of war, but in a manner to be prescribed by law.

Amendment IV

[SECURITY FROM UNWARRANTABLE SEARCH AND SEIZURE]

The right of the people to be secure in their persons, houses, papers, and effects, against unreasonable searches and seizures, shall not be violated, and no Warrants shall issue, but upon probable cause, supported by Oath or affirmation, and particularly describing the place to be searched, and the persons or things to be seized.

Amendment V

[RIGHTS OF ACCUSED PERSONS IN CRIMINAL PROCEEDINGS]

No person shall be held to answer for a capital, or otherwise infamous crime, unless on a presentment or indictment of a Grand Jury, except in cases arising in the land or naval forces, or in the Militia, when in actual service in time of War or in public danger; nor shall any person be subject for the same offence to be twice put in jeopardy of life or limb; nor shall be compelled in any criminal case to be a witness against himself, nor be deprived of life, liberty, or property, without due process of law; nor shall private property be taken for public use, without just compensation.

Amendment VI

[RIGHT TO SPEEDY TRIAL, WITNESSES, ETC.]

In all criminal prosecutions, the accused shall enjoy the right to a speedy and public trial, by an impartial jury of the State and district wherein the crime shall have been committed, which district shall have been previously ascertained by law, and to be informed of the nature and cause of the accusation; to be confronted with the witnesses against him; to have compulsory process for obtaining witnesses in his favor, and to have the Assistance of Counsel for his defence.

Amendment VII

[TRIAL BY JURY IN CIVIL CASES]

In suits at common law, where the value in controversy shall exceed twenty dollars, the right of trial by jury shall be preserved, and no fact tried by a jury, shall be otherwise reexamined in any Court of the United States, than according to the rules of the common law.

Amendment VIII

[BAILS, FINES, PUNISHMENTS]

Excessive bail shall not be required, nor excessive fines imposed, nor cruel and unusual punishments inflicted.

Amendment IX

[RESERVATION OF RIGHTS OF PEOPLE]

The enumeration in the Constitution, of certain rights, shall not be construed to deny or disparage others retained by the people.

Amendment X

[POWERS RESERVED TO STATES OR PEOPLE]

The powers not delegated to the United States by the Constitution, nor prohibited by it to the States, are reserved to the States respectively, or to the people.

Amendment XI

[Proposed by Congress on March 4, 1794; declared ratified on January 8, 1798.]

[RESTRICTION OF JUDICIAL POWER]

The Judicial power of the United States shall not be construed to extend to any suit in law or equity, commenced or prosecuted against one of the United States by Citizens of another State, or by Citizens or Subjects of any Foreign State.

Amendment XII

[Proposed by Congress on December 9, 1803; declared ratified on September 25, 1804.]

[ELECTION OF PRESIDENT AND VICE PRESIDENT]

The Electors shall meet in their respective states and vote by ballot for President and Vice-President, one of whom, at least, shall not be an inhabitant of the same state with themselves; they shall name in their ballots the person voted for as President, and in distinct ballots the person voted for as Vice-President, and they shall make distinct lists of all persons voted for as President, and of all persons voted for as Vice-President, and of the number of votes for each, which lists they shall sign and certify, and transmit sealed to the seat of the government of the United States, directed to the President of the Senate;—the President of the Senate shall, in presence of the Senate and House of Representatives, open all the certificates and the votes shall then be counted;—The person having the greatest number of votes for President, shall be the President, if such number be a majority of the whole number of Electors appointed; and if no person have such majority, then from the persons having the highest numbers not exceeding three on the list of those voted for as President, the House of Representatives shall choose immediately, by ballot, the President. But in choosing the President, the votes shall be taken by states, the representation from each state having one vote; a quorum for this purpose shall consist of a member or members from two-thirds of the states, and a majority of all the states shall be necessary to a choice. And if the House of Representatives shall not choose a President whenever the right of choice shall devolve upon them, before the fourth day of March next following, then the Vice-President shall act as President, as in the case of the death or other constitutional disability of the President.—The person having the greatest number of votes as Vice-President, shall be the Vice-President, if such number be a majority of the whole number of Electors appointed, and if no person have a majority, then from the two highest numbers on the list, the Senate shall choose the Vice-President; a quorum for the purpose shall consist of two-thirds of the whole number of Senators, and a majority of the whole number shall be necessary to a choice. But no person constitutionally ineligible to the office of President shall be eligible to that of Vice-President of the United States.

Amendment XIII

[Proposed by Congress on January 31, 1865; declared ratified on December 18, 1865.]

Section 1

[ABOLITION OF SLAVERY]

Neither slavery nor involuntary servitude, except as a punishment for crime whereof the party shall have been duly convicted, shall exist within the United States, or any place subject to their jurisdiction.

Section 2

[POWER TO ENFORCE THIS ARTICLE]

Congress shall have power to enforce this article by appropriate legislation.

Amendment XIV

[Proposed by Congress on June 13, 1866; declared ratified on July 28, 1868.]

Section 1

[CITIZENSHIP RIGHTS NOT TO BE ABRIDGED BY STATES]

All persons born or naturalized in the United States, and subject to the jurisdiction thereof, are citizens of the United States and of the State wherein they reside. No State shall make or enforce any law which shall abridge the privileges or immunities of citizens of the United States; nor shall any State deprive any person of life, liberty, or property, without due process of law; nor deny to any person within its jurisdiction the equal protection of the laws.

Section 2

[APPORTIONMENT OF REPRESENTATIVES IN CONGRESS]

Representatives shall be apportioned among the several States according to their respective numbers, counting the whole number of persons in each State, excluding Indians not taxed. But when the right to vote at any election for the choice of electors for President and Vice-President of the United States, Representatives in Congress, the Executive and Judicial officers of a State, or the members of the Legislature thereof, is denied to any of the male inhabitants of such State, being twenty-one years of age, and citizens of the United States, or in any way abridged, except for participation in rebellion, or other crime, the basis of representation therein shall be reduced in the proportion which the number of such male citizens shall bear to the whole number of male citizens twenty-one years of age in such State.

Section 3

[PERSONS DISQUALIFIED FROM HOLDING OFFICE]

No person shall be a Senator or Representative in Congress, or elector of President and Vice-President, or hold any office, civil or military, under the United States, or under any State, who, having previously taken an oath, as a member of Congress, or as an officer of the United States, or as a member of any State legislature, or as an executive or judicial officer of any State, to support the Constitution of the United States, shall have engaged in insurrection or rebellion against the same, or given aid or comfort to the enemies thereof. But Congress may by a vote of two-thirds of each House, remove such disability.

Section 4
[WHAT PUBLIC DEBTS ARE VALID]

The validity of the public debt of the United States, authorized by law, including debts incurred for payment of pensions and bounties for services in suppressing insurrection or rebellion, shall not be questioned. But neither the United States nor any State shall assume or pay any debt or obligation incurred in aid of insurrection or rebellion against the United States, or any claim for the loss or emancipation of any slave; but all such debts, obligations and claims shall be held illegal and void.

Section 5
[POWER TO ENFORCE THIS ARTICLE]

The Congress shall have power to enforce, by appropriate legislation, the provisions of this article.

Amendment XV
[Proposed by Congress on February 26, 1869; declared ratified on March 30, 1870.]

Section 1
[NEGRO SUFFRAGE]

The right of citizens of the United States to vote shall not be denied or abridged by the United States or by any State on account of race, color, or previous condition of servitude.

Section 2
[POWER TO ENFORCE THIS ARTICLE]

The Congress shall have power to enforce this article by appropriate legislation.

Amendment XVI
[Proposed by Congress on July 2, 1909; declared ratified on February 25, 1913.]
[AUTHORIZING INCOME TAXES]

The Congress shall have power to lay and collect taxes on incomes, from whatever source derived, without apportionment among the several States, and without regard to any census or enumeration.

Amendment XVII
[Proposed by Congress on May 13, 1912; declared ratified on May 31, 1913.]
[POPULAR ELECTION OF SENATORS]

The Senate of the United States shall be composed of two Senators from each State, elected by the people thereof, for six years; and each Senator shall have one vote. The electors in each State shall have the qualifications requisite for electors of the most numerous branch of the State legislatures.

When vacancies happen in the representation of any State in the Senate, the executive authority of such State shall issue writs of election to fill such vacancies: *Provided,* That the legislature of any State may empower the executive thereof to make temporary appointments until the people fill the vacancies by election as the legislature may direct.

This amendment shall not be so construed as to affect the election or term of any Senator chosen before it becomes valid as part of the Constitution.

Amendment XVIII
[Proposed by Congress December 18, 1917; declared ratified on January 29, 1919.]

Section 1
[NATIONAL LIQUOR PROHIBITION]

After one year from the ratification of this article the manufacture, sale, or transportation of intoxicating liquors within, the importation thereof into, or the exportation thereof from the United States and all territory subject to the jurisdiction thereof for beverage purposes is hereby prohibited.

Section 2
[POWER TO ENFORCE THIS ARTICLE]

The Congress and the several States shall have concurrent power to enforce this article by appropriate legislation.

Section 3
[RATIFICATION WITHIN SEVEN YEARS]

This article shall be inoperative unless it shall have been ratified as an amendment to the Constitution by the legislatures of the several States, as provided in the Constitution, within seven years from the date of the submission hereof to the States by the Congress.[1]

Amendment XIX
[Proposed by Congress on June 4, 1919; declared ratified on August 26, 1920.]
[WOMAN SUFFRAGE]

The right of citizens of the United States to vote shall not be denied or abridged by the United States or by any State on account of sex.

Congress shall have power to enforce this article by appropriate legislation.

Amendment XX
[Proposed by Congress on March 2, 1932; declared ratified on February 6, 1933.]

Section 1
[TERMS OF OFFICE]

The terms of the President and Vice President shall end at noon on the 20th day of January, and the terms of Senators and Representatives at noon on the 3d day of January, of the years

---

[1]Repealed by the Twenty-first Amendment.

in which such terms would have ended if this article had not been ratified; and the terms of their successors shall then begin.

Section 2
[TIME OF CONVENING CONGRESS]

The Congress shall assemble at least once in every year, and such meeting shall begin at noon on the 3d day of January, unless they shall by law appoint a different day.

Section 3
[DEATH OF PRESIDENT-ELECT]

If, at the time fixed for the beginning of the term of the President, the President elect shall have died, the Vice President elect shall become President. If a President shall not have been chosen before the time fixed for the beginning of his term, or if the President elect shall have failed to qualify, then the Vice President elect shall act as President until a President shall have qualified; and the Congress may by law provide for the case wherein neither a President elect nor a Vice President elect shall have qualified, declaring who shall then act as President, or the manner in which one who is to act shall be selected, and such person shall act accordingly until a President or Vice President shall have qualified.

Section 4
[ELECTION OF THE PRESIDENT]

The Congress may by law provide for the case of the death of any of the persons from whom the House of Representatives may choose a President whenever the right of choice shall have devolved upon them, and for the case of the death of any of the persons from whom the Senate may choose a Vice President whenever the right of choice shall have devolved upon them.

Section 5
[AMENDMENT TAKES EFFECT]

Sections 1 and 2 shall take effect on the 15th day of October following the ratification of this article.

Section 6
[RATIFICATION WITHIN SEVEN YEARS]

This article shall be inoperative unless it shall have been ratified as an amendment to the Constitution by the legislatures of three-fourths of the several States within seven years from the date of its submission.

Amendment XXI

[Proposed by Congress on February 20, 1933; declared ratified on December 5, 1933.]

Section 1
[NATIONAL LIQUOR PROHIBITION REPEALED]

The eighteenth article of amendment to the Constitution of the United States is hereby repealed.

Section 2
[TRANSPORTATION OF LIQUOR INTO "DRY" STATES]

The transportation or importation into any State, Territory, or Possession of the United States for delivery or use therein of intoxicating liquors, in violation of the laws thereof, is hereby prohibited.

Section 3
[RATIFICATION WITHIN SEVEN YEARS]

This article shall be inoperative unless it shall have been ratified as an amendment to the Constitution by conventions in the several States, as provided in the Constitution, within seven years from the date of the submission hereof to the States by the Congress.

Amendment XXII

[Proposed by Congress on March 21, 1947; declared ratified on February 27, 1951.]

Section 1
[TENURE OF PRESIDENT LIMITED]

No person shall be elected to the office of President more than twice, and no person who has held the office of President or acted as President, for more than two years of a term to which some other person was elected President shall be elected to the office of the President more than once. But this Article shall not apply to any person holding the office of President when this Article was proposed by the Congress, and shall not prevent any person who may be holding the office of President, or acting as President, during the term within which this Article becomes operative from holding the office of President or acting as President during the remainder of such term.

Section 2
[RATIFICATION WITHIN SEVEN YEARS]

This article shall be inoperative unless it shall have been ratified as an amendment to the Constitution by the legislatures of three-fourths of the several States within seven years from the date of its submission to the States by the Congress.

Amendment XXIII

[Proposed by Congress on June 16, 1960; declared ratified on March 29, 1961.]

Section 1
[ELECTORAL COLLEGE VOTES FOR THE DISTRICT OF COLUMBIA]

The District constituting the seat of Government of the United States shall appoint in such manner as the Congress may direct:

A number of electors of President and Vice President equal to the whole number of Senators and Representatives in Congress to which the District would be entitled if it were a State, but in no event more than the least populous State; they shall be in addition to those appointed by the States, but they shall be considered, for the purposes of the election of President and Vice President, to be electors appointed by a State; and they shall meet in the District and perform such duties as provided by the twelfth article of amendment.

Section 2
[POWER TO ENFORCE THIS ARTICLE]

The Congress shall have power to enforce this article by appropriate legislation.

Amendment XXIV

[Proposed by Congress on August 27, 1962; declared ratified on January 23, 1964.]

Section 1
[ANTI-POLL TAX]

The right of citizens of the United States to vote in any primary or other election for President or Vice President, for electors for President or Vice President, or for Senator or Representative of Congress, shall not be denied or abridged by the United States or any State by reason of failure to pay any poll tax or other tax.

Section 2
[POWER TO ENFORCE THIS ARTICLE]

The Congress shall have power to enforce this article by appropriate legislation.

Amendment XXV

[Proposed by Congress on July 6, 1965; declared ratified on February 10, 1967.]

Section 1
[VICE PRESIDENT TO BECOME PRESIDENT]

In case of the removal of the President from office or his death or resignation, the Vice President shall become President.

Section 2
[CHOICE OF A NEW VICE PRESIDENT]

Whenever there is a vacancy in the office of the Vice President, the President shall nominate a Vice President who shall take the office upon confirmation by a majority vote of both houses of Congress.

Section 3
[PRESIDENT MAY DECLARE OWN DISABILITY]

Whenever the President transmits to the President pro tempore of the Senate and the Speaker of the House of Representatives his written declaration that he is unable to discharge the powers and duties of his office, and until he transmits to them a written declaration to the contrary, such powers and duties shall be discharged by the Vice President as Acting President.

Section 4
[ALTERNATE PROCEDURES TO DECLARE AND TO END PRESIDENTIAL DISABILITY]

Whenever the Vice President and a majority of either the principal officers of the executive departments, or of such other body as Congress may by law provide, transmit to the President pro tempore of the Senate and the Speaker of the House of Representatives their written declaration that the President is unable to discharge the powers and duties of his office, the Vice President shall immediately assume the powers and duties of the office as Acting President.

Thereafter, when the President transmits to the President pro tempore of the Senate and the Speaker of the House of Representatives his written declaration that no inability exists, he shall resume the powers and duties of his office unless the Vice President and a majority of either the principal officers of the executive department, or of such other body as Congress may by law provide, transmit within four days to the President pro tempore of the Senate and the Speaker of the House of Representatives their written declaration that the President is unable to discharge the powers and duties of his office. Thereupon Congress shall decide the issue, assembling within forty eight hours for that purpose if not in session. If the Congress, within twenty one days after receipt of the latter written declaration, or, if Congress is not in session, within twenty one days after Congress is required to assemble, determines by two-thirds vote of both Houses that the President is unable to discharge the powers and duties of his office, the Vice President shall continue to discharge the same as Acting President; otherwise, the President shall resume the powers and duties of his office.

Amendment XXVI

[Proposed by Congress on March 23, 1971; declared ratified on July 1, 1971.]

Section 1
[EIGHTEEN-YEAR-OLD VOTE]

The right of citizens of the United States, who are eighteen years of age or older, to vote shall not be denied or abridged by the United States or by any State on account of age.

Section 2
[POWER TO ENFORCE THIS ARTICLE]

The Congress shall have power to enforce this article by appropriate legislation.

Amendment XXVII

[Proposed by Congress on September 25, 1789; declared ratified on May 8, 1992.]

[CONGRESS CANNOT RAISE ITS OWN PAY]

No law varying the compensation for the services of the Senators and Representatives, shall take effect, until an election of representatives shall have intervened.

THE FEDERALIST PAPERS

No. 10: Madison

Among the numerous advantages promised by a well constructed Union, none deserves to be more accurately developed than its tendency to break and control the violence of faction. The friend of popular governments never finds himself so much alarmed for their character and fate, as when he contemplates their propensity to this dangerous vice. He will not fail therefore to set a due value on any plan which, without violating the principles to which he is attached, provides a proper cure for it. The instability, injustice, and confusion introduced into the public councils have, in truth, been the mortal diseases under which popular governments have everywhere perished, as they continue to be the favorite and fruitful topics from which the adversaries to liberty derive their most specious declamations. The valuable improvements made by the American constitutions on the popular models, both ancient and modern, cannot certainly be too much admired; but it would be an unwarrantable partiality to contend that they have as effectually obviated the danger on this side, as was wished and expected. Complaints are everywhere heard from our most considerate and virtuous citizens, equally the friends of public and private faith and of public and personal liberty, that our governments are too unstable, that the public good is disregarded in the conflicts of rival parties, and that measures are too often decided, not according to the rules of justice and the rights of the minor party, but by the superior force of an interested and overbearing majority. However anxiously we may wish that these complaints had no foundation, the evidence of known facts will not permit us to deny that they are in some degree true. It will be found, indeed, on a candid review of our situation, that some of the distresses under which we labor have been erroneously charged on the operation of our governments; but it will be found, at the same time, that other causes will not alone account for many of our heaviest misfortunes; and, particularly, for that prevailing and increasing distrust of public engagements and alarm for private rights which are echoed from one end of the continent to the other. These must be chiefly, if not wholly, effects of the unsteadiness and injustice with which a factious spirit has tainted our public administration.

By a faction I understand a number of citizens, whether amounting to a majority or minority of the whole, who are united and actuated by some common impulse of passion, or of interest, adverse to the rights of other citizens, or to the permanent and aggregate interests of the community.

There are two methods of curing the mischiefs of faction: the one, by removing its causes; the other, by controlling its effects.

There are again two methods of removing the causes of faction: the one, by destroying the liberty which is essential to its existence; the other, by giving to every citizen the same opinions, the same passions, and the same interests.

It could never be more truly said than of the first remedy, that it is worse than the disease. Liberty is to faction what air is to fire, an aliment without which it instantly expires. But it could not be a less folly to abolish liberty, which is essential to political life, because it nourishes faction, than it would be to wish the annihilation of air, which is essential to animal life, because it imparts to fire its destructive agency.

The second expedient is as impracticable, as the first would be unwise. As long as the reason of man continues fallible, and he is at liberty to exercise it, different opinions will be formed. As long as the connection subsists between his reason and his self-love, his opinions and his passions will have a reciprocal influence on each other; and the former will be objects to which the latter will attach themselves. The diversity in the faculties of men, from which the rights of property originate, is not less an insuperable obstacle to a uniformity of interests. The protection of these faculties is the first object of Government. From the protection of different and unequal faculties of acquiring property, the possession of different degrees and kinds of property immediately results; and from the influence of these on the sentiments and views of the respective proprietors, ensues a division of the society into different interests and parties.

The latent causes of faction are thus sown in the nature of man; and we see them everywhere brought into different degrees of activity, according to the different circumstances of civil society. A zeal for different opinions concerning religion, concerning Government, and many other points, as well of speculation as of practice; an attachment to different leaders ambitiously contending for pre-eminence and power; or to persons of other descriptions whose fortunes have been interesting to the human passions, have in turn divided mankind into parties, inflamed them with mutual animosity, and rendered them much more disposed to vex and oppress each other, than to co-operate for their common good. So strong is this propensity of mankind to fall into mutual animosities, that where no substantial occasion presents itself, the most frivolous and fanciful distinctions have been sufficient to kindle their unfriendly passions, and excite their most violent conflicts. But the most common and durable source of factions has been the various and unequal distribution of property. Those who hold and those who are without property have ever formed distinct interests in society. Those who are creditors, and those who are debtors, fall under a like discrimination. A landed interest, a manufacturing interest, a mercantile interest, a moneyed interest, with many lesser interests, grow up of necessity in civilized nations, and divide them into different classes, actuated by different sentiments and views. The regulation of these various and interfering interests forms the principal task of modern Legislation, and involves the spirit of party and faction in the necessary and ordinary operations of Government.

No man is allowed to be judge in his own cause, because his interest would certainly bias his judgment and, not improbably, corrupt his integrity. With equal, nay with greater reason, a body of men are unfit to be both judges and parties at the same time; yet what are many of the most important acts of legislation but so many judicial determinations, not indeed concerning the rights of single persons, but concerning the rights of large bodies of citizens; and what are the different classes of legislators but advocates and parties to the causes which they determine? Is a law proposed concerning private debts? It is a question to which the creditors are parties on one side and the debtors on the other. Justice ought to hold the balance between them. Yet the parties are, and must be, themselves the judges; and the most numerous party, or in other words, the most powerful faction must be expected to prevail. Shall domestic manufacturers be encouraged, and in what degree, by restrictions on foreign manufacturers? are questions which would be differently decided by the landed and the manufacturing classes, and probably by neither with a sole regard to justice and the public good. The apportionment of taxes on the various descriptions of property is an act which seems to require the most exact impartiality; yet there is, perhaps, no legislative act in which greater opportunity and temptation are given to a predominant party to trample on the rules of justice. Every shilling with which they overburden the inferior number is a shilling saved to their own pockets.

It is in vain to say that enlightened statesmen will be able to adjust these clashing interests and render them all subservient to the public good. Enlightened statesmen will not always be at the helm. Nor, in many cases, can such an adjustment be made at all without taking into view indirect and remote considerations, which will rarely prevail over the immediate interest which one party may find in disregarding the rights of another or the good of the whole.

The inference to which we are brought is that the *causes* of faction cannot be removed and that relief is only to be sought in the means of controlling its *effects*.

If a faction consists of less than a majority, relief is supplied by the republican principle, which enables the majority to defeat its sinister views by regular vote. It may clog the administration, it may convulse the society; but it will be unable to execute and mask its violence under the forms of the Constitution. When a majority is included in a faction, the form of popular government, on the other hand, enables it to sacrifice to its ruling passion or interest both the public good and the rights of other citizens. To secure the public good and private rights against the danger of such a faction, and at the same time to preserve the spirit and the form of popular government, is then the great object to which our enquiries are directed. Let me add that it is the great desideratum by which alone this form of government can be rescued from the opprobrium under which it has so long labored and be recommended to the esteem and adoption of mankind.

By what means is this object attainable? Evidently by one of two only. Either the existence of the same passion or interest in a majority at the same time must be prevented, or the majority, having such co-existent passion or interest, must be rendered, by their number and local situation, unable to concert and carry into effect schemes of oppression. If the impulse and the opportunity be suffered to coincide, we well know that neither moral nor religious motives can be relied on as an adequate control. They are not found to be such on the injustice and violence of individuals, and lose their efficacy in proportion to the number combined together, that is, in proportion as their efficacy becomes needful.

From this view of the subject it may be concluded that a pure Democracy, by which I mean a Society consisting of a small number of citizens, who assemble and administer the Government in person, can admit of no cure for the mischiefs of faction. A common passion or interest will, in almost every case, be felt by a majority of the whole; a communication and concert results from the form of Government itself; and there is nothing to check the inducements to sacrifice the weaker party or an obnoxious individual. Hence it is that such Democracies have ever been spectacles of turbulence and contention; have ever been found incompatible with personal security or the rights of property; and have in general been as short in their lives as they have been violent in their deaths. Theoretic politicians, who have patronized this species of Government, have erroneously supposed that by reducing mankind to a perfect equality in their political rights, they would at the same time be perfectly equalized and assimilated in their possessions, their opinions, and their passions.

A Republic, by which I mean a Government in which the scheme of representation takes place, opens a different prospect and promises the cure for which we are seeking. Let us examine the points in which it varies from pure Democracy, and we shall comprehend both the nature of the cure and the efficacy which it must derive from the Union.

The two great points of difference between a Democracy and a Republic are: first, the delegation of the Government, in the latter, to a small number of citizens elected by the rest; secondly, the greater number of citizens and greater sphere of country over which the latter may be extended.

The effect of the first difference is, on the one hand, to refine and enlarge the public views by passing them through the medium of a chosen body of citizens, whose wisdom may best discern the true interest of their country and whose patriotism and love of justice will be least likely to sacrifice it to temporary or partial considerations. Under such a regulation it may well happen that the public voice, pronounced by the representatives of the people, will be more consonant to the public good than if pronounced by the people themselves, convened for the purpose. On the other hand, the effect may be inverted. Men of factious tempers, of local prejudices, or of sinister designs, may, by intrigue, by corruption, or by other means, first obtain the suffrages, and then betray the interests of the people. The question resulting is, whether small or extensive Republics are most favorable to the election of proper guardians of the public weal; and it is clearly decided in favor of the latter by two obvious considerations.

In the first place it is to be remarked that however small the Republic may be, the Representatives must be raised to a certain number in order to guard against the cabals of a few; and that however large it may be they must be limited to a certain number in order to guard against the confusion of a multitude. Hence, the number of Representatives in the two cases not being in proportion to that of the Constituents, and being proportionally greatest in the small Republic, it follows that if the proportion of fit characters be not less in the large than in the small Republic, the former will present a greater option, and consequently a greater probability of a fit choice.

In the next place, as each Representative will be chosen by a greater number of citizens in the large than in the small Republic, it will be more difficult for unworthy candidates to practise with success the vicious arts by which elections are too often carried; and the suffrages of the people being more free, will be more likely to centre on men who possess the most attractive merit and the most diffusive and established characters.

It must be confessed that in this, as in most other cases, there is a mean, on both sides of which inconveniencies will be found to lie. By enlarging too much the number of electors, you render the representative too little acquainted with all their local circumstances and lesser interests; as by reducing it too much, you render him unduly attached to these, and too little fit to comprehend and pursue great and national objects. The Federal Constitution forms a happy combination in this respect; the great and aggregate interests being referred to the national, the local and particular to the State legislatures.

The other point of difference is the greater number of citizens and extent of territory which may be brought within the compass of Republican than of Democratic Government; and it is this circumstance principally which renders factious combinations less to be dreaded in the former than in the latter. The smaller the society, the fewer probably will be the distinct parties and interests composing it; the fewer the distinct parties and interests, the more frequently will a majority be found of the same party; and the smaller the number of individuals composing a majority, and the smaller the compass within which they are placed, the more easily will they concert and execute their plans of oppression. Extend the sphere and you take in a greater variety of parties and interests; you make it less probable that a majority of the whole will have a common motive to invade the rights of other citizens; or if such a common motive exists, it will be more difficult for all who feel it to discover their own strength and to act in unison with each other. Besides other impediments, it may be remarked, that where there is a consciousness of unjust or dishonorable purposes, communication is always checked by distrust in proportion to the number whose concurrence is necessary.

Hence, it clearly appears that the same advantage which a Republic has over a Democracy in controlling the effects of faction is enjoyed by a large over a small republic—is enjoyed by the Union over the States composing it. Does this advantage consist in the substitution of representatives whose enlightened views and virtuous sentiments render them superior to local prejudices and to schemes of injustice? It will not be denied that the representation of the Union will be most likely to possess these requisite endowments. Does it consist in the greater security afforded by a greater variety of parties, against the event of any one party being able to outnumber and oppress the rest? In an equal degree does the increased variety of parties comprised within the Union increase this security? Does it, in fine, consist in the greater obstacles opposed to the concert and accomplishment of the secret wishes of an unjust and interested majority? Here again the extent of the Union gives it the most palpable advantage.

The influence of factious leaders may kindle a flame within their particular States but will be unable to spread a general conflagration through the other States: a religious sect may degenerate into a political faction in a part of the Confederacy; but the variety of sects dispersed over the entire face of it must secure the national Councils against any danger from that source: a rage for paper money, for an abolition of debts, for an equal division of property, or for any other improper or wicked project, will be less apt to pervade the whole body of the Union than a particular member of it; in the same proportion as such a malady is more likely to taint a particular county or district than an entire State.

In the extent and proper structure of the Union, therefore, we behold a republican remedy for the diseases most incident to Republican Government. And according to the degree of pleasure and pride we feel in being republicans ought to be our zeal in cherishing the spirit and supporting the character of federalist.

PUBLIUS

NO. 51: MADISON

To what expedient, then, shall we finally resort, for maintaining in practice the necessary partition of power among the several departments as laid down in the constitution? The only answer that can be given is that as all these exterior provisions are found to be inadequate the defect must be supplied, by so contriving the interior structure of the government as that its several constituent parts may, by their mutual relations, be the means of keeping each other in their proper places. Without presuming to undertake a full development of this important idea I will hazard a few general observations which may perhaps place it in a clearer light, and enable us to form a more correct judgment of the principles and structure of the government planned by the convention.

In order to lay a due foundation for that separate and distinct exercise of the different powers of government, which to a certain extent is admitted on all hands to be essential to the preservation of liberty, it is evident that each department should have a will of its own; and consequently should be so constituted that the members of each should have as little agency as possible in the appointment of the members of the others. Were this principle rigorously adhered to, it would require that all the appointments for the supreme executive, legislative, and judiciary magistracies should be drawn from the same fountain of authority, the people, through channels having no communication whatever with one another. Perhaps such a plan of constructing the several departments would be less difficult in practice than it may in contemplation appear. Some difficulties, however, and some additional expense would attend the execution of it. Some deviations, therefore, from the principle must be admitted. In the constitution of the judiciary department in particular, it might be inexpedient to insist rigorously on the principle: first, because peculiar qualifications being essential in the members, the primary consideration ought to be to select that mode of choice which best secures these qualifications; second, because the permanent tenure by which the appointments are held in that department must soon destroy all sense of dependence on the authority conferring them.

It is equally evident that the members of each department should be as little dependent as possible on those of the others for the emoluments annexed to their offices. Were the executive magistrate, or the judges, not independent of the legislature in this particular, their independence in every other would be merely nominal.

But the great security against a gradual concentration of the several powers in the same department consists in giving to those who administer each department the necessary constitutional means and personal motives to resist encroachments of the others. The provision for defence must in this, as in all other cases, be made commensurate to the danger of attack. Ambition must be made to counteract ambition. The interest of the man must be connected with the constitutional rights of the place. It may be a reflection on human nature that such devices should be necessary to control the abuses of government. But what is government itself but the greatest of all reflections on human nature? If men were angels, no government would be necessary. If angels were to govern men, neither external nor internal controls on government would be necessary. In framing a government which is to be administered by men over men, the great difficulty lies in this: You must first enable the government to control the governed; and in the next place oblige it to control itself. A dependence on the people is, no doubt, the primary control on the government; but experience has taught mankind the necessity of auxiliary precautions.

This policy of supplying, by opposite and rival interests, the defect of better motives, might be traced through the whole system of human affairs, private as well as public. We see it particularly displayed in all the subordinate distributions of power, where the constant aim is to divide and arrange the several offices in such a manner as that each may be a check on the other; that the private interest of every individual may be a sentinel over the public rights. These inventions of prudence cannot be less requisite in the distribution of the supreme powers of the State.

But it is not possible to give to each department an equal power of self-defense. In republican government, the legislative authority necessarily predominates. The remedy for this inconveniency is to divide the legislature into different branches; and to render them, by different modes of election and different principles of action, as little connected with each other as the nature of their common functions and their common dependence on the society will admit. It may even be necessary to guard against dangerous encroachments by still further precautions. As the weight of the legislative authority requires that it should be thus divided, the weakness of the executive may require, on the other hand, that it should be fortified. An absolute negative on the legislature appears, at first view, to be the natural defense with which the executive magistrate should be armed. But perhaps it would be neither altogether safe nor alone sufficient. On ordinary occasions it might not be exerted with the requisite firmness, and on extraordinary occasions it might be perfidiously abused. May not this defect of an absolute negative be supplied by some qualified connection between this weaker branch of the stronger department, by which the latter may be led to support the constitutional rights of the former, without being too much detached from the rights of its own department?

If the principles on which these observations are founded be just, as I persuade myself they are, and they be applied as a criterion to the several State constitutions, and to the federal Constitution, it will be found that if the latter does not perfectly correspond with them, the former are infinitely less able to bear such a test.

There are, moreover, two considerations particularly applicable to the federal system of America, which place that system in a very interesting point of view.

First. In a single republic, all the power surrendered by the people is submitted to the administration of a single government; and usurpations are guarded against by a division of the government into distinct and separate departments. In the compound republic of America, the power surrendered by the people is first divided between two distinct governments, and then the portion allotted to each subdivided among distinct and separate departments. Hence a double security arises to the rights of the people. The different governments will control each other, at the same time that each will be controlled by itself.

Second. It is of great importance in a republic not only to guard the society against the oppression of its rulers, but to guard one part of the society against the injustice of the other part. Different interests necessarily exist in different classes of citizens. If a majority be united by a common interest, the rights of the minority will be insecure. There are but two methods of providing against this evil: The one by creating a will in the community independent of the majority—that is, of the society itself; the other, by comprehending in the society so many separate descriptions of citizens as will render an unjust combination of a majority of the whole very improbable, if not impracticable. The first method prevails in all governments possessing an hereditary or self-appointed authority. This, at best, is but a precarious security; because a power independent of the society may as well espouse the unjust views of the major as the rightful interests of the minor party, and may possibly be turned against both parties. The second method will be exemplified in the federal republic of the United States. Whilst all authority in it will be derived from and dependent on the society, the society itself will be broken into so many parts, interests and classes of citizens, that the rights of individuals, or of the minority, will be in little danger from interested combinations of the majority. In a free gov-

ernment the security for civil rights must be the same as that for religious rights. It consists in the one case in the multiplicity of interests, and in the other in the multiplicity of sects. The degree of security in both cases will depend on the number of interests and sects; and this may be presumed to depend on the extent of country and number of people comprehended under the same government. This view of the subject must particularly recommend a proper federal system to all the sincere and considerate friends of republican government: Since it shows that in exact proportion as the territory of the Union may be formed into more circumscribed Confederacies, or States, oppressive combinations of a majority will be facilitated; the best security, under the republican form, for the rights of every class of citizens, will be diminished; and consequently the stability and independence of some member of the government, the only other security, must be proportionally increased. Justice is the end of government. It is the end of civil society. It ever has been and ever will be pursued until it be obtained, or until liberty be lost in the pursuit. In a society under the forms of which the stronger faction can readily unite and oppress the weaker, anarchy may as truly be said to reign as in a state of nature, where the weaker individual is not secured against the violence of the stronger: And as, in the latter state, even the stronger individuals are prompted, by the uncertainty of their condition, to submit to a government which may protect the weak as well as themselves: So, in the former state, will the more powerful factions or parties be gradually induced, by a like motive, to wish for a government which will protect all parties, the weaker as well as the more powerful. It can be little doubted that if the State of Rhode Island was separated from the Confederacy and left to itself, the insecurity of rights under the popular form of government within such narrow limits would be displayed by such reiterated oppressions of factious majorities that some power altogether independent of the people would soon be called for by the voice of the very factions whose misrule had proved the necessity of it. In the extended republic of the United States, and among the great variety of interests, parties, and sects which it embraces, a coalition of a majority of the whole society could seldom take place on any other principles than those of justice and the general good; and there being thus less danger to a minor from the will of the major party, there must be less pretext, also, to provide for the security of the former, by introducing into the government a will not dependent on the latter, or, in other words, a will independent of the society itself. It is no less certain than it is important, notwithstanding the contrary opinions which have been entertained, that the larger the society, provided it lie within a practicable sphere, the more duly capable it will be of self-government. And happily for the *republican cause,* the practicable sphere may be carried to a very great extent by a judicious modification and mixture of the *federal principle.*

PUBLIUS

PRESIDENTS AND VICE PRESIDENTS

President	Vice President	President	Vice President
1 George Washington (Federalist 1789)	John Adams (Federalist 1789)	16 Abraham Lincoln (Republican 1861)	Hannibal Hamlin (Republican 1861) Andrew Johnson (Unionist 1865)
2 John Adams (Federalist 1797)	Thomas Jefferson (Dem.-Rep. 1797)	17 Andrew Johnson (Unionist 1865)	
3 Thomas Jefferson (Dem.-Rep. 1801)	Aaron Burr (Dem.-Rep. 1801) George Clinton (Dem.-Rep. 1805)	18 Ulysses S. Grant (Republican 1869)	Schuyler Colfax (Republican 1869) Henry Wilson (Republican 1873)
4 James Madison (Dem.-Rep. 1809)	George Clinton (Dem.-Rep. 1809) Elbridge Gerry (Dem.-Rep. 1813)	19 Rutherford B. Hayes (Republican 1877)	William A. Wheeler (Republican 1877)
5 James Monroe (Dem.-Rep. 1817)	Daniel D. Tompkins (Dem.-Rep. 1817)	20 James A. Garfield (Republican 1881)	Chester A. Arthur (Republican 1881)
6 John Quincy Adams (Dem.-Rep. 1825)	John C. Calhoun (Dem.-Rep. 1825)	21 Chester A. Arthur (Republican 1881)	
7 Andrew Jackson (Democratic 1829)	John C. Calhoun (Democratic 1829) Martin Van Buren (Democratic 1833)	22 Grover Cleveland (Democratic 1885)	Thomas A. Hendricks (Democratic 1885)
8 Martin Van Buren (Democratic 1837)	Richard M. Johnson (Democratic 1837)	23 Benjamin Harrison (Republican 1889)	Levi P. Morton (Republican 1889)
9 William H. Harrison (Whig 1841)	John Tyler (Whig 1841)	24 Grover Cleveland (Democratic 1893)	Adlai E. Stevenson (Democratic 1893)
10 John Tyler (Whig and Democratic 1841)		25 William McKinley (Republican 1897)	Garret A. Hobart (Republican 1897) Theodore Roosevelt (Republican 1901)
11 James K. Polk (Democratic 1845)	George M. Dallas (Democratic 1845)	26 Theodore Roosevelt (Republican 1901)	Charles W. Fairbanks (Republican 1905)
12 Zachary Taylor (Whig 1849)	Millard Fillmore (Whig 1849)	27 William H. Taft (Republican 1909)	James S. Sherman (Republican 1909)
13 Millard Fillmore (Whig 1850)		28 Woodrow Wilson (Democratic 1913)	Thomas R. Marshall (Democratic 1913)
14 Franklin Pierce (Democratic 1853)	William R. D. King (Democratic 1853)	29 Warren G. Harding (Republican 1921)	Calvin Coolidge (Republican 1921)
15 James Buchanan (Democratic 1857)	John C. Breckinridge (Democratic 1857)	30 Calvin Coolidge (Republican 1923)	Charles G. Dawes (Republican 1925)

	President	Vice President		President	Vice President
31	Herbert Hoover (Republican 1929)	Charles Curtis (Republican 1929)	37	Richard M. Nixon (Republican 1969)	Spiro T. Agnew (Republican 1969) Gerald R. Ford (Republican 1973)
32	Franklin D. Roosevelt (Democratic 1933)	John Nance Garner (Democratic 1933) Henry A. Wallace (Democratic 1941) Harry S. Truman (Democratic 1945)	38	Gerald R. Ford (Republican 1974)	Nelson Rockefeller (Republican 1974)
			39	James E. Carter (Democratic 1977)	Walter Mondale (Democratic 1977)
33	Harry S. Truman (Democratic 1945)	Alben W. Barkley (Democratic 1949)	40	Ronald Reagan (Republican 1981)	George H. W. Bush (Republican 1981)
34	Dwight D. Eisenhower (Republican 1953)	Richard M. Nixon (Republican 1953)	41	George H. W. Bush (Republican 1989)	J. Danforth Quayle (Republican 1989)
35	John F. Kennedy (Democratic 1961)	Lyndon B. Johnson (Democratic 1961)	42	William J. Clinton (Democrat 1993)	Albert Gore, Jr. (Democrat 1993)
36	Lyndon B. Johnson (Democratic 1963)	Hubert H. Humphrey (Democratic 1965)	43	George W. Bush (Republican 2001)	Richard Cheney (Republican 2001)

GLOSSARY

access the actual involvement of interest groups in the decision-making process

administrative adjudication applying rules and precedents to specific cases to settle disputes with regulated parties

administrative regulation rules made by regulatory agencies and commissions

affirmative action government policies or programs that seek to address past injustices against specified groups by making special efforts to provide members of these groups with access to educational and employment opportunities

agencies of socialization social institutions, including families and schools, that help to shape individuals' basic political beliefs and values

agency representation the type of representation by which representatives are held accountable to their constituency if they fail to represent that constituency properly. This is the incentive for good representation when the personal backgrounds, views, and interests of the representative differ from those of his or her constituency

agenda setting the power of the media to bring public attention to particular issues and problems

Aid to Families with Dependent Children (AFDC) federal funds, administered by the states, for children living with parents or relatives who fall below state standards of need. Replaced in 1996 by TANF

amendment a change added to a bill, law, or constitution

American political community citizens who are eligible to vote and participate in American political life

amicus curiae literally, "friend of the court"; individuals or groups who are not parties to a lawsuit but who seek to assist the Supreme Court in reaching a decision by presenting additional briefs

Antifederalists those who favored strong state governments and a weak national government and who were opponents of the constitution proposed at the American Constitutional Convention of 1787

antitrust policy government regulation of large businesses that have established monopolies

appellate court a court that hears the appeals of trial court decisions

appropriations the amounts of money approved by Congress in statutes (bills) that each unit or agency of government can spend

Articles of Confederation America's first written constitution; served as the basis for America's national government until 1789

attitude (or opinion) a specific preference on a particular issue

authoritarian government a system of rule in which the government recognizes no formal limits but may nevertheless be restrained by the power of other social institutions

autocracy a form of government in which a single individual—a king, queen, or dictator—rules

balance-of-power role the strategy whereby many countries from alliances with one or more other countries in order to counterbalance the behavior of other, usually more powerful, nation-states

bandwagon effect a shift in electoral support to the candidate that public opinion polls report as the front-runner

benign gerrymandering attempts to draw district boundaries so as to create districts made up primarily of disadvantaged or underrepresented minorities

bicameral having a legislative assembly composed of two chambers or houses; opposite of unicameral

bilateral treaties treaties made between two nations

bill a proposed law that has been sponsored by a member of Congress and submitted to the clerk of the House or Senate

Bill of Rights the first ten amendments to the Constitution, which guarantee certain rights and liberties to the people

bills of attainder laws that decree a person guilty of a crime without a trial

block grants federal grants-in-aid that allow states considerable discretion in how the funds should be spent

briefs written documents in which attorneys explain, using case precedents, why the court should find in favor of their client

Brown v. Board of Education the 1954 Supreme Court decision that struck down the "separate but equal" doctrine as fundamentally unequal. This case eliminated state power to use race as a criterion of discrimination in law and provided the national government with the power to intervene by exercising strict regulatory policies against discriminatory actions

budget deficit   amount by which government spending exceeds government revenue in a fiscal year

bureaucracy   the complex structure of offices, tasks, rules, and principles of organization that are employed by all large-scale institutions to coordinate effectively the work of their personnel

Cabinet   the secretaries, or chief administrators, of the major departments of the federal government. Cabinet secretaries are appointed by the president with the consent of the Senate

campaign   an effort by political candidates and their staffs to win the backing of donors, political activists, and voters in the quest for political office

capture   an interest's acquisition of substantial influence over the government agency charged with regulating its activities

categorical grants   congressional grants given to states and localities on the condition that expenditures be limited to a problem or group specified by the law

caucus (congressional)   an association of members of Congress based on party, interest, or social group such as gender or race

caucus (political)   a normally closed meeting of a political or legislative group to select candidates, plan strategy, or make decisions regarding legislative matters

checks and balances   mechanisms through which each branch of government is able to participate in and influence the activities of the other branches. Major examples include the presidential veto power over congressional legislation, the power of the Senate to approve presidential appointments, and judicial review of congressional enactments

chief justice   justice on the Supreme Court who presides over the Court's public sessions

citizenship   informed and active membership in a political community

civic engagement   a sense of concern among members of the political community about public social and political life, expressed through participation in social and political organizations

civil law   a system of jurisprudence, including private law and governmental actions, to settle disputes that do not involve criminal penalties

civil liberties   areas of personal freedom with which governments are constrained from interfering

civil penalties   regulatory techniques in which fines or another form of material restitution is imposed for violating civil laws or common law principles, for example through negligence

civil rights   legal or moral claims that citizens are entitled to make upon government

class action suit   a legal action by which a group or class of individuals with common interests can file a suit on behalf of everyone who shares that interest

"clear and present danger" test   test to determine whether speech is protected or unprotected, based on its capacity to present a "clear and present danger" to society

closed caucus   a presidential nominating caucus open only to registered party members

closed primary   a primary election in which voters can participate in the nomination of candidates, but only of the party in which they are enrolled for a period of time prior to primary day

closed rule   a provision by the House Rules Committee limiting or prohibiting the introduction of amendments during debate

cloture   a rule allowing a majority of two-thirds or three-fifths of the members in a legislative body to set a time limit on debate over a given bill

coalition   a group in interests that join together for the purpose of influencing government

coattail effect   the result of voters casting their ballot for president or governor and "automatically" voting for the remainder of the party's ticket

cold war   the period of struggle between the United States and the former Soviet Union between the late 1940s and about 1990

collective goods   benefits, sought by groups, that are broadly available and cannot be denied to nonmembers

commander in chief   the power of the president as commander of the national military and the state national guard units (when called into service)

commerce clause   Article I, Section 8, of the Constitution, which delegates to Congress the power "to regulate commerce with foreign nations, and among the several States and with the Indian tribes." This clause was interpreted by the Supreme Court in favor of national power over the economy

concurrent powers   authority possessed by both state and national governments, such as the power to levy taxes

confederation   a system of government in which states retain sovereign authority except for the powers expressly delegated to the national government

conference   a gathering of House Republicans every two years to elect their House leaders. Democrats call their gathering the caucus

conference committee   a joint committee created to work out a compromise on House and Senate versions of a piece of legislation

conservative   today this term refers to those who generally support the social and economic status quo and are suspicious of efforts to introduce new political formulae and economic arrangements. Conservatives believe that a large and powerful government poses a threat to citizens' freedom

constituency   the district comprising the area from which an official is elected

constitutional government   a system of rule in which formal and effective limits are placed on the powers of the government

containment   the policy used by the United States during the cold war to restrict the expansion of communism and limit the influence of the Soviet Union

contracting power   the power of government to set conditions on companies seeking to sell goods or services to government agencies

contributory programs   social programs financed in whole or in part by taxation or other mandatory contributions by their present or future recipients. The most important example is Social Security, which is financed by a payroll tax

cooperative federalism   a type of federalism existing since the New Deal era in which grants-in-aid have been used strategically to encourage states and localities (without commanding them) to pursue nationally defined goals. Also known as intergovernmental cooperation

cost of living adjustments (COLAs) changes made to the level of benefits of a government program based on the rate of inflation

criminal law   the branch of law that deals with disputes or actions involving criminal penalties (as opposed to civil law); it regulates the conduct of individuals, defines crimes, and provides punishment for criminal acts

criminal penalties   regulatory techniques in which imprisonment or heavy fines and the loss of certain civil rights and liberties are imposed

de facto   literally, "by fact"; practices that occur even when there is no legal enforcement, such as school segregation in much of the United States today

de jure   literally, "by law"; legally enforced practices, such as school segregation in the South before the 1960s

defendant   the one against whom a complaint is brought in a criminal or civil case

delegate   the role of a representative who votes according to the preferences of his or her constituency

delegated powers   constitutional powers that are assigned to one governmental agency but that are exercised by another agency with the express permission of the first

delegates   political activists selected to vote at a party's national convention

democracy   a system of rule that permits citizens to play a significant part in the governmental process, usually through the election of key public officials

department   the largest subunit of the executive branch. The secretaries of the fourteen departments form the Cabinet

deregulation   a policy of reducing or eliminating regulatory restraints on the conduct of individuals or private institutions

deterrence   the development and maintenance of military strength as a means of discouraging attack

devolution   a policy to remove a program from one level of government by delegating it or passing it down to a lower level of government, such as from the national government to the state and local governments

diplomacy   the representation of a government to other foreign governments

direct action politics   a form of politics, such as civil disobedience or revolutionary action, that takes place outside formal channels

direct democracy   a system of rule that permits citizens to vote directly on laws and policies

discount rate   the interest rate charged by the Federal Reserve System when commercial banks borrow in order to expand their lending operations; an effective tool of monetary policy

discretionary spending   federal spending on programs that are controlled through the regular budget process

discrimination   use of any unreasonable and unjust criterion of exclusion

dissenting opinion   a decision written by a justice in the minority in a particular case in which the justice wishes to express his or her reasoning in the case

divided government   the condition in American government wherein the presidency is controlled by one party while the opposing party controls one or both houses of Congress

double jeopardy   the Fifth Amendment right providing that a person cannot be tried twice for the same crime

dual federalism   the system of government that prevailed in the United States from 1789 to 1937, in which most fundamental governmental powers were shared between the federal and state governments

due process of law   the right of every citizen against arbitrary action by national or state governments

economic expansionist role   the strategy often pursued by capitalist countries to adopt foreign policies that will maximize the success of domestic corporations in their dealings with other countries

elastic clause   Article I, Section 8, of the Constitution (also known as the necessary and proper clause), which enumerates the powers of Congress and provides Congress with the authority to make all laws "necessary and proper" to carry them out

electoral college the presidential electors from each state who meet after the popular election to cast ballots for president and vice president

electoral realignment the point in history when a new party supplants the ruling party, becoming in turn the dominant political force. In the United States, this has tended to occur roughly every thirty years

eminent domain the right of government to take private property for public use

entitlement eligibility for benefits by virtue of a category of benefits defined by legislation

equal protection clause provision of the Fourteenth Amendment guaranteeing citizens "the equal protection of the laws." This clause has served as the basis for the civil rights of African Americans, women, and other groups

equal time rule the requirement that broadcasters provide candidates for the same political office an equal opportunity to communicate their messages to the public

equality of opportunity a widely shared American ideal that all people should have the freedom to use whatever talents and wealth they have to reach their fullest potential

establishment clause the First Amendment clause that says that "Congress shall make no law respecting an establishment of religion." This law means that a "wall of separation" exists between church and state

ex post facto laws laws that declare an action to be illegal after it has been committed

exclusionary rule the ability of courts to exclude evidence obtained in violation of the Fourth Amendment

executive agreement an agreement, made between the president and another country, that has the force of a treaty but does not require the Senate's "advice and consent"

Executive Office of the President the permanent agencies that perform defined management tasks for the president. Created in 1939, the EOP includes the Office of Management and Budget, the Council of Economic Advisers, the National Security Council, and other agencies

executive order a rule or regulation issued by the president that has the effect and formal status of legislation

executive privilege the claim that confidential communications deemed vital to the national interest between the president and close advisers should not be revealed without the consent of the president

expressed powers specific powers granted to Congress under Article I, Section 8, of the Constitution

expropriation confiscation of property with or without compensation

fairness doctrine a Federal Communications Commission (FCC) requirement for broadcasters who air programs on controversial issues to provide time for opposing views. The FCC ceased enforcing this doctrine in 1985

federal funds rate the interest rate on loans between banks that the Federal Reserve Board influences by affecting the supply of money available

Federal Reserve Board (Fed) the governing board of the Federal Reserve System, comprising a chair and six other members, all appointed by the president with the consent of the Senate

Federal Reserve System a system of twelve Federal Reserve Banks that facilitates exchanges of cash, checks, and credit; regulates member banks; and uses monetary policies to fight inflation and deflation

federal system a system of government in which the national government shares power with lower levels of government, such as states

federalism a system of government in which power is divided, by a constitution, between a central government and regional governments

Federalist Papers a series of essays written by James Madison, Alexander Hamilton, and John Jay supporting the ratification of the Constitution

Federalists those who favored a strong national government and supported the constitution proposed at the American Constitutional Convention of 1787

Fifteenth Amendment one of three Civil War amendments; guaranteed voting rights for African American men

fighting words speech that directly incites damaging conduct

filibuster a tactic used by members of the Senate to prevent action on legislation they oppose by continuously holding the floor and speaking until the majority backs down. Once given the floor, senators have unlimited time to speak, and it requires a vote of three-fifths of the Senate to end a filibuster

fiscal policy the use of taxing, monetary, and spending powers to manipulate the economy

food stamps coupons that can be exchanged for food at most grocery stores; the largest in-kind benefits program

formula grants grants-in-aid in which a formula is used to determine the amount of federal funds a state or local government will receive

Fourteenth Amendment one of three Civil War amendments; guaranteed equal protection and due process to all residents of the United States

framing the power of the media to influence how events and issues are interpreted

free exercise clause the First Amendment clause that protects a citizen's right to believe and practice whatever religion he or she chooses

free riders those who enjoy the benefits of collective goods but did not participate in acquiring them

full faith and credit clause provision from Article IV, Section 1 of the Constitution, requiring that the states normally honor the public acts and judicial decisions that take place in another state

gender gap a distinctive pattern of voting behavior reflecting the differences in views between men and women

General Agreement on Tariffs and Trade (GATT) international trade organization, in existence from 1947 to 1995, that set many of the rules governing international trade

general revenue sharing the process by which one unit of government yields a portion of its tax income to another unit of government, according to an established formula. Revenue sharing typically involves the national government providing money to state governments

gerrymandering apportionment of voters in districts in such a way as to give unfair advantage to one racial or ethnic group or political party

going public a strategy that attempts to mobilize the widest and most favorable climate of public opinion

government institutions and procedures through which a territory and its people are ruled

government corporation a government agency that performs a service normally provided by the private sector

grand jury jury that determines whether sufficient evidence is available to justify a trial; grand juries do not rule on the accused's guilt or innocence

grants-in-aid programs through which Congress provides money to state and local governments on the condition that the funds be employed for purposes defined by the federal government

grassroots mobilization a lobbying campaign in which a group mobilizes its membership to contact government officials in support of the group's position

Great Compromise the agreement reached at the Constitutional Convention of 1787 that gave each state an equal number of senators regardless of its population, but linked representation in the House of Representatives to population

Gross Domestic Product (GDP) index of the total output of goods and services produced in the economy

habeas corpus a court order demanding that an individual in custody be brought into court and shown the cause for detention

Holy Alliance role a strategy pursued by a superpower to prevent any change in the existing distribution of power among nation-states, even if this requires intervention into the international affairs of another country in order to keep a ruler from being overturned

home rule power delegated by the state to a local unit of government to manage its own affairs

"horse race" coverage news coverage emphasizing changes in the candidates' poll standings rather than the issues or positions they espouse

illusion of saliency the impression conveyed by polls that something is important to the public when actually it is not

impeachment the formal charge by the House of Representatives that a government official has committed "Treason, Bribery, or other high Crimes and Misdemeanors"

implementation the efforts of departments and agencies to translate laws into specific bureaucratic routines

implied powers powers derived from the "necessary and proper" clause of Article I, Section 8, of the Constitution. Such powers are not specifically expressed, but are implied through the expansive interpretation of delegated powers

in-kind benefits goods and services provided to needy individuals and families by the federal government

incumbency holding a political office for which one is running

incumbent a candidate running for a position that he or she already holds

independent agency an agency that is not part of a Cabinet department

independent counsel an official appointed to investigate criminal misconduct by members of the executive branch

indexing periodic process of adjusting social benefits or wages to account for increases in the cost of living

inflation a consistent increase in the general level of prices

infomercial a lengthy campaign advertisement on television

informational benefits special newsletters, periodicals, training programs, conferences, and other information provided to members of groups to entice others to join

inherent powers powers claimed by a president that are not expressed in the Constitution, but are inferred from it

institutional advertising advertising designed to create a positive image of an organization

interest group a voluntary membership association that pursues a common cause through political participation

intermediate scrutiny test, used by the Supreme Court in gender discrimination cases, which places the burden of proof partially on the government and partially on the challengers to show that the law in question is constitutional

International Monetary Fund (IMF) an institution established in 1944 at Bretton Woods, New Hampshire, which provides loans and facilitates international monetary exchange

investigative journalism news coverage aimed at ferreting out the facts beneath the claims of public officials and politicians

iron triangle the stable, cooperative relationships that often develop between a congressional committee, an administrative agency, and one or more supportive interest groups. Not all of these relationships are triangular, but the iron triangle is the most typical

issue network a loose network of elected leaders, public officials, activists, and interest groups drawn together by a specific policy issue

issue advocacy independent spending by individuals or interest groups on a campaign issue but not directly tied to a particular candidate

Jim Crow laws enacted by southern states following reconstruction that discriminated against African Americans

joint committee a legislative committee formed of members of both the House and the Senate

judicial activism judicial philosophy that posits that the Court should go beyond the words of the Constitution or a statute to consider the broader societal implications of its decisions

judicial restraint judicial philosophy whose adherents refuse to go beyond the clear words of the Constitution in interpreting its meaning

judicial review the power of the courts to declare actions of the legislative and executive branches invalid or unconstitutional. The Supreme Court asserted this power in *Marbury v. Madison*

jurisdiction the sphere of a court's power and authority

Keynesianism economic theory, based on the ideas of British economist John Maynard Keynes, that argues that the government can stimulate the economy by increasing public spending or by cutting taxes

Kitchen Cabinet an informal group of advisers to whom the president turns for counsel and guidance. Members of the official Cabinet may or may not also be members of the Kitchen Cabinet

laissez-faire capitalism an economic system in which the means of production and distribution are privately owned and operated for profit with minimal or no government interference

legislative initiative the president's inherent power to bring a legislative agenda before Congress

Lemon test a rule articulated in *Lemon v. Kurtzman* that government action toward religion is permissible if it is secular in purpose, does not lead to "excessive entanglement" with religion, and neither promotes nor inhibits the practice of religion

libel a written statement made in "reckless disregard of the truth" that is considered damaging to a victim because it is "malicious, scandalous, and defamatory"

liberal a liberal today generally supports political and social reform; extensive governmental intervention in the economy; the expansion of federal social services; more vigorous efforts on behalf of the poor, minorities, and women; and greater concern for consumers and the environment

libertarian the political philosophy that is skeptical of any government intervention as a potential threat against individual liberty; libertarians believe that government has caused more problems than it has solved

liberty freedom from government control

license permission to engage in some activity that is otherwise illegal, such as hunting or practicing medicine

limited government a government whose powers are defined and limited by a constitution

line-item veto the power of the executive to veto specific provisions (lines) of a bill passed by the legislature

litigation a lawsuit or legal proceeding; as a form of political participation, an attempt to seek relief in a court of law

lobbying a strategy by which organized interests seek to influence the passage of legislation by exerting direct pressure on members of the legislature

logrolling a legislative practice wherein agreements are made between legislators in voting for or against a bill. Unlike bargaining, parties to logrolling have nothing in common but their desire to exchange support

loophole incentive to individuals and businesses to reduce their tax liabilities by investing their money in areas that the government designates

machines strong party organizations in late-nineteenth- and early-twentieth-century American cities. These machines were led by "bosses" who controlled party nominations and patronage

majority leader the elected leader of the majority party in the House of Representatives or in the Senate. In the House, the majority leader is subordinate in the party hierarchy to the Speaker of the House

majority party the party that holds the majority of legislative seats in either the House or the Senate

majority rule/minority rights the democratic principle that a government follows the preferences of the majority of voters but protects the interests of the minority

majority system a type of electoral system in which, to win a seat in the parliament or other representative body, a candidate must receive a majority of all the votes cast in the relevant district

mandate a claim by a victorious candidate that the electorate has given him or her special authority to carry out promises made during the campaign

mandatory spending federal spending that is made up of "uncontrollables," budget items that cannot be controlled through the regular budget process

marketplace of ideas the public forum in which beliefs and ideas are exchanged and compete

Marshall Plan the U.S. European Recovery Plan, in which over $34 billion was spent for the relief, reconstruction, and economic recovery of Western Europe after World War II

material benefits special goods, services, or money provided to members of groups to entice others to join

means testing a procedure by which potential beneficiaries of a public assistance program establish their eligibility by demonstrating a genuine need for the assistance

media momentum news coverage suggesting that a candidate is rapidly gaining public support

media monopoly control of multiple sources of news and information by a small number of news agencies

Medicaid a federally financed, state-operated program providing medical services to low-income people

Medicare a form of national health insurance for the elderly and the disabled

membership association an organized group in which members actually play a substantial role, sitting on committees and engaging in group projects

merit system a product of civil service reform, in which appointees to positions in public bureaucracies must objectively be deemed qualified for the position

midterm elections congressional elections that do not coincide with a presidential election; also called off-year elections

minority district a gerrymandered voting district that improves the chances of minority candidates by making selected minority groups the majority within the district

minority leader the elected leader of the minority party in the House or Senate

minority party the party that holds a minority of legislative seats in either the House or the Senate

***Miranda* rule** the requirement, articulated by the Supreme Court in *Miranda v. Arizona,* that persons under arrest must be informed prior to police interrogation of their rights to remain silent and to have the benefit of legal counsel

mobilization the process by which large numbers of people are organized for a political activity

monetarism economic theory that contends that the role of the government in the economy should be limited to regulating the supply of money

monetary policies efforts to regulate the economy through manipulation of the supply of money and credit. America's most powerful institution in the area of monetary policy is the Federal Reserve Board

monopoly the existence of a single firm in a market that controls all the goods and services of that market; absence of competition

mootness a criterion used by courts to screen cases that no longer require resolution

most favored nation status agreement to offer a trading partner the lowest tariff rate offered to other trading partners

multilateralism a foreign policy that seeks to encourage the involvement of several nation-states in coordinated action, usually in relation to a common adversary, with terms and conditions usually specified in a multi-country treaty

multiple-member district an electorate that selects all candidates at large from the whole district; each voter is given the number of votes equivalent to the number of seats to be filled

Napoleonic role a strategy pursued by a powerful nation to prevent aggressive actions against themselves by improving the internal state of affairs of a particular country, even if this means encouraging revolution in that country

nation-state a political entity consisting of a people with some common cultural experience (nation) who also share a common political authority (state), recognized by other sovereignties (nation-states)

national convention a national party political institution that serves to nominate the party's presidential and vice presidential candidates, establish party rules, and write and ratify the party's platform

National Security Council (NSC) a presidential foreign-policy advisory council composed of the president; the vice president; the secretaries of state, defense, and the treasury; the attorney general; and other officials invited by the president

necessary and proper clause from Article I, Section 8 of the Constitution, it provides Congress with the authority to make all laws "necessary and proper" to carry out its expressed powers

New Deal coalition the coalition of northern urban liberals, southern white conservatives, organized labor, and blacks that dominated national politics until the 1960s

New Federalism attempts by Presidents Nixon and Reagan to return power to the states through block grants

New Jersey Plan a framework for the Constitution, introduced by William Paterson, which called for equal state representation in the national legislature regardless of population

New Politics movement a political movement that began in the 1960s and 1970s, made up of professionals and intellectuals for whom the civil rights and antiwar movements were formative experiences. The New Politics movement strengthened public-interest groups

news enclave a group seeking specialized information not provided by the mainstream media

nomination the process through which political parties select their candidates for election to public office

noncontributory programs social programs that provide assistance to people based on demonstrated need rather than any contribution they have made

North American Free Trade Agreement (NAFTA) trade treaty between the United States, Canada, and Mexico to lower and eliminate tariffs between the three countries

North Atlantic Treaty Organization (NATO) a treaty organization, comprising the United States, Canada, and most of western Europe, formed in 1948 to counter the perceived threat from the Soviet Union

oligarchy a form of government in which a small group—landowners, military officers, or wealthy merchants—controls most of the governing decisions

open caucus a presidential nominating caucus open to anyone who wishes to attend

open market operations method by which the Open Market Committee of the Federal Reserve System buys and sells government securities, etc., to help finance government operations and to loosen or tighten the total amount of money circulating in the economy

open primary a primary election in which the voter can wait until the day of the primary to choose which party to enroll in to select candidates for the general election

open rule a provision by the House Rules Committee that permits floor debate and the addition of new amendments to a bill

opinion the written explanation of the Supreme Court's decision in a particular case

oral argument stage in Supreme Court procedure in which attorneys for both sides appear before the Court to present their positions and answer questions posed by justices

original jurisdiction the authority to initially consider a case. Distinguished from appellate jurisdiction, which is the authority to hear appeals from a lower court's decision

oversight the effort by Congress, through hearings, investigations, and other techniques, to exercise control over the activities of executive agencies

party activists partisans who contribute time, energy, and effort to support their party and its candidates

party identification an individual voter's psychological ties to one party or another

party organization the formal structure of a political party, including its leadership, election committees, active members, and paid staff

party vote a roll-call vote in the House or Senate in which at least 50 percent of the members of one party take a particular position and are opposed by at least 50 percent of the members of the other party. Party votes are rare today, although they were fairly common in the nineteenth century

patronage the resources available to higher officials, usually opportunities to make partisan appointments to offices and to confer grants, licenses, or special favors to supporters

per curiam decision by an appellate court, without a written opinion, that refuses to review the decision of a lower court; amounts to a reaffirmation of the lower court's opinion

permanent campaign description of presidential politics in which all presidential actions are taken with reelection in mind

plaintiff the individual or organization who brings a complaint in court

platform a party document, written at a national convention, that contains party philosophy, principles, and positions on issues

plea bargains negotiated agreements in criminal cases in which a defendant agrees to plead guilty in return for the state's agreement to reduce the severity of the criminal charge the defendant is facing

pluralism the theory that all interests are and should be free to compete for influence in the government. The outcome of this competition is compromise and moderation

plurality system a type of electoral system in which, to win a seat in the parliament or other representative body, a candidate need only receive the most votes in the election, not necessarily a majority of the votes cast

pocket veto a presidential veto that is automatically triggered if the president does not act on a given piece of legislation passed during the final ten days of a legislative session

police power power reserved to the government to regulate the health, safety, and morals of its citizens

policy entrepreneur an individual who identifies a problem as a political issue and brings a policy proposal into the political agenda

policy of redistribution a policy whose objective is to tax or spend in such a way as to reduce the disparities of wealth between the lowest and the highest income brackets

political action committee (**PAC**) a private group that raises and distributes funds for use in election campaigns

political culture broadly shared values, beliefs, and attitudes about how the government should function. American political culture emphasizes the values of liberty, equality, and democracy

political efficacy the ability to influence government and politics

political equality the right to participate in politics equally, based on the principle of "one person, one vote"

political ideology a cohesive set of beliefs that form a general philosophy about the role of government

political institution an organization that connects people to politics, such as a political party, or a governmental organization, such as the Congress or the courts

political machines local party organizations that controlled local politics in the late nineteenth and early twentieth centuries through patronage and control of nominations

political participation political activities, such as voting, contacting political officials, volunteering for a campaign, or participating in a protest, whose purpose is to influence government

political parties organized groups that attempt to influence the government by electing their members to important government offices

political socialization the induction of individuals into the political culture; learning the underlying beliefs and values that the political system is based on

politics conflict over the leadership, structure, and policies of governments

poll tax a state-imposed tax upon voters as a prerequisite for registration. Poll taxes were rendered unconstitutional in national elections by the Twenty-fourth Amendment, and in state elections by the Supreme Court in 1966

popular sovereignty   a principle of democracy in which political authority rests ultimately in the hands of the people

pork barrel   appropriations made by legislative bodies for local projects that are often not needed but that are created so that local representatives can win re-election in their home districts

power   influence over a government's leadership, organization, or policies

precedents   prior cases whose principles are used by judges as the bases for their decisions in present cases

preemption   the principle that allows the national government to override state or local actions in certain policy areas

priming   process of preparing the public to take a particular view of an event or political actor

primary elections   elections used to select a party's candidate for the general election

prior restraint   an effort by a governmental agency to block the publication of material it deems libelous or harmful in some other way; censorship. In the United States, the courts forbid prior restraint except under the most extraordinary circumstances

private bill   a proposal in Congress to provide a specific person with some kind of relief, such as a special exemption from immigration quotas

privatization   removing all or part of a program from the public sector to the private sector

privileges and immunities clause   provision from Article IV, Section 2 of the Constitution, that a state cannot discriminate against someone from another state or give its own residents special privileges

procedural liberties   restraints on how the government is supposed to act; for example, citizens are guaranteed the due process of law

progressive/regressive taxation   taxation that hits the upper income brackets more heavily (progressive) or the lower income brackets more heavily (regressive)

project grants   grant programs in which state and local governments submit proposals to federal agencies and for which funding is provided on a competitive basis

proportional representation   a multiple-member district system that allows each political party representation in proportion to its percentage of the total vote

prospective voting   voting based on the imagined future performance of a candidate

protest   participation that involves assembling crowds to confront a government or other official organization

public goods   goods that are provided by the government because they either are not supplied by the market or are not supplied in sufficient quantities

public interest groups   groups that claim they serve the general good rather than their own particular interest

public law   cases in private law, civil law, or criminal law in which one party to the dispute argues that a license is unfair, a law is inequitable or unconstitutional, or an agency has acted unfairly, violated a procedure, or gone beyond its jurisdiction

public opinion   citizens' attitudes about political issues, leaders, institutions, and events

public opinion polls   scientific instruments for measuring public opinion

public policy   a law, rule, statute, or edict that expresses the government's goals and provides for rewards and punishments to promote their attainment

public relations   an attempt, usually through the use of paid consultants, to establish a favorable relationship with the public and influence its political opinions

purposive benefits   selective benefits of group membership that emphasize the purpose and accomplishments of the group

push polling   a polling technique in which the questions are designed to shape the respondent's opinion

rallying effect   the generally favorable reaction of the public to presidential actions taken in foreign policy, or more precisely, to decisions made during international crises

redistributive programs   economic policies designed to control the economy through taxing and spending, with the goal of benefiting the poor

redistricting   the process of redrawing election districts and redistributing legislative representatives. This happens every ten years to reflect shifts in population or in response to legal challenges to existing districts

redlining   a practice in which banks refuse to make loans to people living in certain geographic locations

referendum   the practice of referring a measure proposed or passed by a legislature to the vote of the electorate for approval or rejection

regulated federalism   a form of federalism in which Congress imposes legislation on states and localities, requiring them to meet national standards

regulation   a technique of control in which the government adopts rules imposing restrictions on the conduct of private citizens

regulatory agencies   departments, bureaus, or independent agencies whose primary mission is to impose limits, restrictions, or other obligations on the conduct of individuals or companies in the private sector

regulatory tax   a tax whose primary purpose is not to raise revenue but to influence conduct: e.g. a heavy tax on gasoline to discourage recreational driving

representative democracy (or republic) a system of government in which the populace selects representatives, who play a significant role in governmental decision making

reserve requirement the amount of liquid assets and ready cash that banks are required to hold to meet depositors' demands for their money

reserved powers powers, derived from the Tenth Amendment to the Constitution, that are not specifically delegated to the national government or denied to the states

responsible party government a set of principles that idealizes a strong role for parties in defining their stance on issues, mobilizing voters, and fulfilling their campaign promises once in office

retrospective voting voting based on the past performance of a candidate

revenue agencies agencies responsible for collecting taxes. Examples include the Internal Revenue Service for income taxes, the U.S. Customs Service for tariffs and other taxes on imported goods, and the Bureau of Alcohol, Tobacco, and Firearms for collection of taxes on the sales of those particular products

right of rebuttal a Federal Communications Commission regulation giving individuals the right to have the opportunity to respond to personal attacks made on a radio or television broadcast

right to privacy the right to be let alone, which has been interpreted by the Supreme Court to entail free access to birth control and abortions

roll-call vote a vote in which each legislator's yes or no vote is recorded as the clerk calls the names of the members alphabetically

rulemaking a quasi-legislative administrative process that produces regulations by government agencies

salient interests attitudes and views that are especially important to the individual holding them

sample a small group selected by researchers to represent the most important characteristics of an entire population

select committee a (usually) temporary legislative committee set up to highlight or investigate a particular issue or address an issue not within the jurisdiction of existing committees

selective incorporation the process by which different protections in the Bill of Rights were incorporated into the Fourteenth Amendment, thus guaranteeing citizens protection from state as well as national government

senatorial courtesy the practice whereby the president, before formally nominating a person for a federal judgeship, seeks the indication that senators from the candidate's own state support the nomination

seniority priority or status ranking given to an individual on the basis of length of continuous service on a committee in Congress

"separate but equal" rule doctrine that public accommodations could be segregated by race but still be equal

separation of powers the division of governmental power among several institutions that must cooperate in decision making

shadow welfare state social benefits that private employers offer to their workers, such as medical insurance and pensions

single-member district an electorate that is allowed to select only one representative from each district; the normal method of representation in the United States

slander an oral statement, made in "reckless disregard of the truth," which is considered damaging to the victim because it is "malicious, scandalous, and defamatory"

Social Security a contributory welfare program into which working Americans contribute a percentage of their wages, and from which they receive cash benefits after retirement

socioeconomic status status in society based on level of education, income, and occupational prestige

sociological representation a type of representation in which representatives have the same racial, ethnic, religious, or educational backgrounds as their constituents. It is based on the principle that if two individuals are similar in background, character, interests, and perspectives, then one could correctly represent the other's views

soft money money contributed directly to political parties for voter registration and organization

solicitor general the top government lawyer in all cases before the Supreme Court where the government is a party

solidary benefits selective benefits of a group membership that emphasize friendship, networking, and consciousness-raising

sound bites short snippets of information aimed at dramatizing a story rather than explaining its substantive meaning

Speaker of the House the chief presiding officer of the House of Representatives. The Speaker is elected at the beginning of every Congress on a straight party vote. The Speaker is the most important party and House leader, and can influence the legislative agenda, the fate of individual pieces of legislation, and members' positions within the House

speech plus speech accompanied by conduct such as sit-ins, picketing, and demonstrations; protection of this form of speech under the First Amendment is conditional, and restrictions imposed by state or local authorities are acceptable if properly balanced by considerations of public order

split-ticket voting the practice of casting ballots for the candidates of at least two different political parties in the same election

spot advertisement a fifteen-, thirty-, or sixty-second television campaign commercial that permits a candidate's message to be delivered to a target audience

staff agency a legislative support agency responsible for policy analysis

staff organization a type of membership group in which a professional staff conducts most of the group's activities

standing the right of an individual or organization to initiate a court case

standing committee a permanent committee with the power to propose and write legislation that covers a particular subject, such as finance or appropriations

stare decisis literally, "let the decision stand." The doctrine that a previous decision by a court applies as a precedent in similar cases until that decision is overruled

states' rights the principle that the states should oppose the increasing authority of the national government. This principle was most popular in the period before the Civil War

straight-ticket voting the practice of casting ballots for candidates of only one party

strict scrutiny test, used by the Supreme Court in racial discrimination cases and other cases involving civil liberties and civil rights, which places the burden of proof on the government rather than on the challengers to show that the law in question is constitutional

subsidies government grants of cash or other valuable commodities such as land to individuals or organizations; used to promote activities desired by the government, to reward political support, or to buy off political opposition

substantive liberties restraints on what the government shall and shall not have the power to do

suffrage the right to vote; also called franchise

superdelegate a convention delegate position, in Democratic conventions, reserved for party officials

Supplemental Security Income (SSI) a program providing a minimum monthly income to people who pass a "means test" and who are sixty-five or older, blind, or disabled. Financed from general revenues rather than from Social Security contributions

supremacy clause Article VI of the Constitution, which states that laws passed by the national government and all treaties are the supreme law of the land and superior to all laws adopted by any state or any subdivision

supreme court the highest court in a particular state or in the United States. This court primarily serves an appellate function

tariff a tax on imported goods

tax expenditures government subsidies provided to employers and employees through tax deductions for amounts spent on health insurance and other benefits; these represent one way the government helps to ensure the social welfare of the middle class

Temporary Assistance to Needy Families (TANF) a federal block grant that replaced the AFDC program in 1996

term limits legally prescribed limits on the number of terms an elected official can serve

third parties parties that organize to compete against the two major American political parties

Thirteenth Amendment one of three Civil War amendments; abolished slavery

Three-fifths Compromise the agreement reached at the Constitutional Convention of 1787 that stipulated that for purposes of the apportionment of congressional seats, every slave would be counted as three-fifths of a person

totalitarian government a system of rule in which the government recognizes no formal limits on its power and seeks to absorb or eliminate other social institutions that might challenge it

town meeting a media format in which candidates meet with ordinary citizens. Allows candidates to deliver messages without the presence of journalists or commentators

trial court the first court to hear a criminal or civil case

trustee the role of a representative who votes based on what he or she thinks is best for his or her constituency

turnout the percentage of eligible individuals who actually vote

two-party system a political system in which only two parties have a realistic opportunity to compete effectively for control

tyranny oppressive and unjust government that employs cruel and unjust use of power and authority

uncontrollables budgetary items that are beyond the control of budgetary committees and can be controlled only by substantive legislative action in Congress. Some uncontrollables are beyond the power of Congress, because the terms of payments are set in contracts, such as interest on the debt

unfunded mandates regulations or conditions for receiving grants that impose costs on state and local governments for which they are not reimbursed by the federal government

Uniform Commercial Code code used in many states in the area of contract law to reduce interstate differences in judicial decisions

unilateralism a foreign policy that seeks to avoid international alliances, entanglements, and permanent commitments in favor of independence, neutrality, and freedom of action

unit rule the convention voting system under which a state delegation casts all of its votes for the candidate supported by the majority of the state's delegates

unitary system a centralized government system in which lower levels of government have little power independent of the national government

United Nations an organization of nations founded in 1945 to serve as a channel for negotiation and a means of settling international disputes peaceably. The UN has had frequent successes in providing a forum for negotiation and on some occasions a means of preventing international conflicts from spreading. On a number of occasions, the UN has been a convenient cover for U.S. foreign policy goals

values (or beliefs) basic principles that shape a person's opinions about political issues and events

veto the president's constitutional power to turn down acts of Congress. A presidential veto may be overridden by a two-thirds vote of each house of Congress

Virginia Plan a framework for the Constitution, introduced by Edmund Randolph, which called for representation in the national legislature based upon the population of each state

War Powers Resolution a resolution of Congress that the president can send troops into action abroad only by authorization of Congress, or if American troops are already under attack or serious threat

whip system a communications network in each house of Congress; whips take polls of the membership in order to learn their intentions on specific legislative issues and to assist the majority and minority leaders in various tasks

white ethnics white immigrants to the United States whose culture differs from that of WASPs

White House staff analysts and advisers to the president, often given the title "special assistant"

white primary primary election in which only white voters are eligible to participate

winner-take-all system a system in which all of a state's presidential nominating delegates are awarded to the candidate who wins the most votes, while runners-up receive no delegates

World Trade Organization (WTO) international trade agency promoting free trade that grew out of the General Agreement on Tariffs and Trade

writ of *certiorari* a decision of at least four of the nine Supreme Court justices to review a decision of a lower court; from the Latin "to make more certain"

writ of *habeas corpus* a court order that the individual in custody be brought into court and shown the cause for detention. *Habeas corpus* is guaranteed by the Constitution and can be suspended only in cases of rebellion or invasion

yellow journalism sensational coverage emphasizing scandals and misdeeds, often with little regard to evidence or analysis

ENDNOTES

Chapter 1

1. Gary Orren, "Fall from Grace: The Public's Loss of Trust in Government," in *Why People Don't Trust Government*, ed. Joseph S. Nye, Jr., Philip D. Zelikow, and David C. King (Cambridge, MA: Harvard University Press, 1997), pp. 80–81.

2. Robert J. Blendon et al., "Changing Attitudes in America," in *Why People Don't Trust Government*, ed. Nye, Zelikow, and King, pp. 207–8.

3. Michael A. Fletcher, "Trust and Interest in Government Soar on College Campuses," *Washington Post*, November 23, 2001, p. A3.

4. Joseph S. Nye, Jr., "Introduction: The Decline of Confidence in Government," in *Why People Don't Trust Government*, ed. Nye, Zelikow, and King, p. 4.

5. Orren, "Fall from Grace," p. 81.

6. Owen, "Mixed Signals," p. 98.

7. Michael Walzer, *Spheres of Justice* (New York: Basic Books, 1983), p. 304.

8. This definition is taken from Norman H. Nie, Jane Junn, and Kenneth Stehlik-Barry, *Education and Democratic Citizenship in America* (Chicago: University of Chicago Press, 1996).

9. See Eugen Weber, *Peasants into Frenchmen: The Modernization of Rural France, 1870–1914* (Stanford, CA: Stanford University Press, 1976), chap. 5.

10. See V. O. Key, *Politics, Parties, and Pressure Groups* (New York: Crowell, 1964), p. 201.

11. Harold Lasswell, *Politics: Who Gets What, When, How* (New York: Meridian Books, 1958).

12. Mary Lane, "Ohio University Professor Fans Flames of Student Activism," *Columbus Dispatch*, June 10, 2001, p. 5B.

13. Herbert McClosky and John Zaller, *The American Ethos: Public Attitudes toward Capitalism and Democracy* (Cambridge, MA: Harvard University Press, 1984), p. 19.

14. J. R. Pole, *The Pursuit of Equality in American History* (Berkeley: University of California Press, 1978), p. 3.

15. See Judith N. Shklar, *American Citizenship: The Quest for Inclusion* (Cambridge, MA: Harvard University Press, 1991).

16. Cindy Skrzycki, "OSHA Abandons Rules Effort on Repetitive Injury," *Washington Post*, June 13, 1995, p. D1.

17. See Rogers M. Smith, *Liberalism and American Constitutional Law* (Cambridge, MA: Harvard University Press, 1985), chap. 6.

18. The case was *San Antonio Independent School District v. Rodriguez*, 411 U.S. 1 (1973). See the discussion in Smith, *Liberalism and American Constitutional Law*, pp. 163–64.

19. See the discussion in Eileen McDonagh, "Gender Political Change," in *New Perspectives on American Politics*, ed. Lawrence C. Dodd and Calvin Jillson (Washington, DC: Congressional Quarterly Press, 1994), pp. 58–73. The argument for moving women's issues into the public sphere is made by Jean Bethke Elshtain, *Public Man, Private Woman* (Princeton, NJ: Princeton University Press, 1981).

20. On current differences in wealth, see Keith Bradsher, "Gap in Wealth in U.S. Called Widest in West," *New York Times*, April 17, 1995, p. A1; on income inequality, see Gary Burtless and Timothy Smeeding, "America's Tide Lifting the Yachts, Swamping the Rowboats," *Washington Post*, June 25, 1995, p. C3.

21. Kevin Phillips, *The Politics of Rich and Poor: Wealth and the American Electorate in the Reagan Aftermath* (New York: Random House, 1994); and Thomas Byrne Edsall, *The New Politics of Inequality* (New York: Norton, 1984).

22. Kevin Phillips, *Arrogant Capital: Washington, Wall Street, and the Frustration of American Politics* (Boston: Little, Brown, 1994).

23. Joe Stephens, "Hard Money, Strong Arms and 'Matrix,'" *Washington Post*, February 10, 2002, p. 1.

Chapter 2

1. Michael Kammen, *A Machine That Would Go of Itself* (New York: Vintage, 1986), p. 22.

2. The social makeup of colonial America and some of the social conflicts that divided colonial society are discussed in Jackson Turner Main, *The Social Structure of Revolutionary America* (Princeton, NJ: Princeton University Press, 1965).

3. George B. Tindall and David E. Shi, *America: A Narrative History*, 3rd ed. (New York: Norton, 1992), p. 194.

4. For a discussion of events leading up to the Revolution, see Charles M. Andrews, *The Colonial Background of the American Revolution* (New Haven, CT: Yale University Press, 1924).

5. See Carl Becker, *The Declaration of Independence* (New York: Knopf, 1942).

6. See Merrill Jensen, *The Articles of Confederation* (Madison: University of Wisconsin Press, 1970).

7. Reported in Samuel E. Morrison, Henry Steele Commager, and William Leuchtenberg, *The Growth of the American Republic*, vol. 1 (New York: Oxford University Press, 1969), p. 244.

8. Quoted in Morrison et al., *The Growth of the American Republic*, vol. 1, p. 242.

9. Charles A. Beard, *An Economic Interpretation of the Constitution of the United States* (New York: Macmillan, 1913).

10. Madison's notes along with the somewhat less complete records kept by several other participants in the convention are available in a four-volume set. See Max Farrand, ed., *The Records of the Federal Convention of 1787*, 4 vols., rev. ed. (New Haven, CT: Yale University Press, 1966).

11. Farrand, ed., *The Records of the Federal Convention of 1787*, vol. 1, p. 476.

12. Farrand, ed., *The Records of the Federal Convention of 1787*, vol. 2, p. 10.

13. E. M. Earle, ed., *The Federalist* (New York: Modern Library, 1937), No. 71.

14. Earle, ed., *The Federalist*, No. 62.

15. Earle, ed., *The Federalist*, No. 70.

16. Max Farrand, *The Framing of the Constitution of the United States* (New Haven, CT: Yale University Press, 1962), p. 49.

17. Richard E. Neustadt, *Presidential Power* (New York: Wiley, 1960), p. 33.

18. Melancton Smith, quoted in Storing, *What the Anti-Federalists Were For*, p. 17.

19. "Essays of Brutus," No. 1, in Herbert Storing, ed., *The Complete Anti-Federalist* (Chicago: University of Chicago Press, 1981).

20. Earle, ed., *The Federalist*, No. 57.

21. "Essays of Brutus," No. 15, in Storing, ed., *The Complete Anti-Federalist*.

22. Earle, ed., *The Federalist*, No. 10

23. "Essays of Brutus," No. 7, in Storing, ed., *The Complete Anti-Federalist*.

24. "Essays of Brutus," No. 6, in Storing, ed., *The Complete Anti-Federalist*.

25. Storing, *What the Anti-Federalists Were For*, p. 28.

26. Earle, ed., *The Federalist*, No. 51.

27. Quoted in Storing, *What the Anti-Federalists Were For*, p. 30.

28. Observation by Colonel George Mason, delegate from Virginia, early during the convention period. Quoted in Farrand, ed., *The Records of the Federal Convention of 1787*, vol. 1, pp. 202–3.

29. Clinton Rossiter, ed., *The Federalist Papers* (New York: New American Library, 1961), No. 43, p. 278.

30. See Marcia Lee, "The Equal Rights Amendment: Public Policy by Means of a Constitutional Amendment," in *The Politics of Policy-Making in America*, ed. David Caputo (San Francisco: Freeman, 1977); Jane Mansbridge, *Why We Lost the ERA* (Chicago: University of Chicago Press, 1986); and Donald Mathews and Jane Sherron DeHart, *Sex, Gender, and the Politics of the ERA* (New York: Oxford University Press, 1990).

31. The Fourteenth Amendment is included in this table as well as in Table 2.4 because it seeks not only to define citizenship but *seems* to intend also that this definition of citizenship included, along with the right to vote, all the rights of the Bill of Rights, regardless of the state in which the citizen resided. A great deal more will be said about this in Chapter 4.

32. Earle, ed., *The Federalist*, No. 10.

Chapter 3

1. Andre Henderson, "Cruise Control," *Governing*, February 1995, p. 39. Unemployment benefit figures are from U.S. House of Representatives, Committee on Ways and Means, *1998 Green Book* (Washington, DC: U.S. Government Printing Office, 1998), p. 340.

2. Ken I. Kersch, "Full Faith and Credit for Same-Sex Marriages?" *Political Science Quarterly*, 112 (Spring 1997), pp. 117–36; Joan Biskupic, "Once Unthinkable, Now Under Debate," *Washington Post*, September 3, 1996, p. A1.

3. Linda Greenhouse, "Supreme Court Weaves Legal Principles from a Tangle of Legislation," *New York Times*, June 30, 1988, p. A20.

4. *Hicklin v. Orbeck*, 437 U.S. 518 (1978).

5. *Sweeny v. Woodall*, 344 U.S. 86 (1953).

6. Marlise Simons, "France Won't Extradite American Convicted of Murder," *New York Times*, December 5, 1997, p. A9.

7. Patricia S. Florestano, "Past and Present Utilization of Interstate Compacts in the United States," *Publius* 24 (Fall 1994), pp. 13–26.

8. A good discussion of the constitutional position of local governments is in York Willbern, *The Withering Away of the City* (Bloomington: Indiana University Press, 1971). For more on the structure and theory of federalism, see Thomas R. Dye, *American Federalism: Competition among Governments* (Lexington, MA: Lexington Books, 1990), chap. 1; and Martha Derthick, "Up-to-Date in Kansas City: Reflections on American Federalism" (the 1992 John Gaus Lecture), *PS: Political Science & Politics* 25 (December 1992), pp. 671–75.

9. For a good treatment of the contrast between national political stability and social instability, see Samuel P. Huntington, *Political Order in Changing Societies* (New Haven, CT: Yale University Press, 1968), chap. 2.

10. *McCulloch v. Maryland*, 4 Wheaton 316 (1819).

11. *Gibbons v. Ogden*, 9 Wheaton 1 (1824).

12. The Sherman Antitrust Act, adopted in 1890, for example, was enacted not to restrict commerce, but rather to protect it from monopolies, or trusts, so as to prevent unfair trade practices, and to enable the market again to become self-regulating. Moreover, the Supreme Court sought to uphold liberty of contract to protect businesses. For example, in *Lochner v. New York*, 198 U.S. 45 (1905), the Court invalidated a New York law regulating the sanitary conditions and hours of labor of bakers on the grounds that the law interfered with liberty of contract.

13. The key case in this process of expanding the power of the national government is generally considered to be *NLRB v. Jones & Laughlin Steel Corporation*, 301 U.S. 1 (1937), in which the Supreme Court approved federal regulation of the workplace and thereby virtually eliminated interstate commerce as a limit on the national government's power.

14. *U.S. v. Darby Lumber Co.*, 312 U.S. 100 (1941).

15. W. John Moore, "Pleading the 10th," *National Journal*, July 29, 1995, p. 1940.

16. *United States v. Lopez*, 115 S.Ct. 1624 (1995).

17. *Printz v. United States*, 117 S.Ct. 2365 (1997).

18. *Seminole Indian Tribe v. Florida*, 116 S.Ct. 1114 (1996).

19. See the poll reported in Guy Gugliotta, "Scaling Down the American Dream," *Washington Post*, April 19, 1995, p. A21.

20. Kenneth T. Palmer, "The Evolution of Grant Policies," in *The Changing Politics of Federal Grants,* by Lawrence D. Brown, James W. Fossett, and Kenneth T. Palmer (Washington, DC: Brookings, 1984), p. 15.

21. Palmer, "The Evolution of Grant Policies," p. 6.

22. Morton Grozdins, *The American System,* ed. Daniel J. Elazar (Chicago: Rand McNally, 1966).

23. See Terry Sanford, *Storm Over the States* (New York: McGraw-Hill, 1967).

24. James L. Sundquist with David W. Davis, *Making Federalism Work* (Washington, DC: Brookings, 1969), p. 271. George Wallace was mistrusted by the architects of the War on Poverty because he was a strong proponent of racial segregation. He believed in "states' rights," which meant that states, not the federal government, should decide what liberty and equality meant.

25. See Don Kettl, *The Regulation of American Federalism* (Baton Rouge: Louisiana State University Press, 1983).

26. See Advisory Commission on Intergovernmental Relations, *Federal Regulation of State and Local Governments: The Mixed Record of the 1980s* (Washington, DC: Advisory Commission on Intergovernmental Relations, July 1993).

27. Advisory Commission on Intergovernmental Relations, *Federal Regulation of State and Local Governments,* p. iii.

28. Alison Mitchell, "A Nation Challenged: The Domestic Front," *New York Times,* December 7, 2001, p. B7.

29. Quoted in Timothy Conlon, *New Federalism: Intergovernmental Reform from Nixon to Reagan* (Washington, DC: Brookings, 1988), p. 25.

30. For the emergence of complaints about federal categorical grants, see Palmer, "The Evolution of Grant Policies," pp. 17–18. On the governors' efforts to gain more control over federal grants after the 1994 congressional elections, see Dan Balz, "GOP Governors Eager to Do Things Their Way," *Washington Post,* November 22, 1994, p. A4.

31. Advisory Commission on Intergovernmental Relations, *Federal Regulation of State and Local Governments,* p. 51.

32. For an assessment of the achievements of the 104th and 105th Congresses, see Timothy Conlan, *From New Federalism to Devolution: Twenty-Five Years of Intergovernmental Reform* (Washington, D.C.: Brookings Institution Press, 1998).

33. Robert Frank, "Proposed Block Grants Seen Unlikely to Cure Management Problems," *Wall Street Journal,* May 1, 1995, p. 1.

34. U.S. Committee on Federalism and National Purpose, *To Form a More Perfect Union* (Washington, DC: National Conference on Social Welfare, 1985). See also the discussion in Paul E. Peterson, *The Price of Federalism* (Washington, DC: Brookings, 1995), esp. chap. 8.

35. Malcolm Gladwell, "In States' Experiments, a Cutting Contest," *New York Times,* March 10, 1995, p. 6.

36. The phrase "laboratories of democracy" was coined by Supreme Court justice Louis Brandeis in his dissenting opinion in *New State Ice Co. v. Liebman,* 285 U.S. 262 (1932).

37. "Motor Vehicle Fatalities in 1996 were 12 Percent Higher on Interstates, Freeways in 12 States that Raised Speed Limits," Press Release of the Insurance Institute for Highway Safety, October 10, 1997.

38. This was a comment from Walter E. Dellinger, President Clinton's acting solicitor general. Linda Greenhouse, "Will the Court Reassert National Authority?" *New York Times,* September 30, 2001, sect. 4, p. 14.

39. Sidney Verba, Kay Lehman Schlozman, and Henry E. Brady, *Voice and Equality: Civic Voluntarism in American Politics* (Cambridge, MA: Harvard University Press, 1995), pp. 66–67.

Chapter 4

1. Clinton Rossiter, ed., *The Federalist Papers* (New York: New American Library, 1961), No. 84, p. 513.

2. Rossiter, ed., *The Federalist Papers,* No. 84, p. 513.

3. Clinton Rossiter, *1787: The Grand Convention* (New York: Norton, 1987), p. 302.

4. Rossiter, *1787,* p. 303. Rossiter also reports that "in 1941 the States of Connecticut, Massachusetts and Georgia celebrated the sesquicentennial of the Bill of Rights by giving their hitherto withheld and unneeded assent."

5. *Barron v. Baltimore,* 7 Peters 243, 246 (1833).

6. The Fourteenth Amendment also seems designed to introduce civil rights. The final clause of the all-important Section 1 provides that no state can "deny to any person within its jurisdiction the equal protection of the laws." It is not unreasonable to conclude that the purpose of this provision was to obligate the state governments as well as the national government to take *positive* actions to protect citizens from arbitrary and discriminatory actions, at least those based on race. This will be explored in Chapter 5.

7. For example, *The Slaughterhouse Cases,* 16 Wallace 36 (1883).

8. *Chicago, Burlington and Quincy Railroad Company v. Chicago,* 166 U.S. 226 (1897).

9. *Gitlow v. New York,* 268 U.S. 652 (1925).

10. *Near v. Minnesota,* 283 U.S. 697 (1931); *Hague v. C.I.O.,* 307 U.S. 496 (1939).

11. *Palko v. Connecticut,* 302 U.S. 319 (1937).

12. All of these were implicitly included in the *Palko* case as "not incorporated" into the Fourteenth Amendment as limitations on the powers of the states.

13. There is one interesting exception, which involves the Sixth Amendment right to public trial. In the 1948 case *In re Oliver,* 33 U.S. 257, the right to the public trial was, in effect, incorporated as part of the Fourteenth Amendment. However, the issue in that case was put more generally as "due process," and public trial itself was not actually mentioned in so many words. Later opinions, such as *Duncan v. Louisiana,* 391 U.S. 145 (1968), cited the *Oliver* case as the precedent for more explicit incorporation of public trials as part of the Fourteenth Amendment.

14. For a lively and readable treatment of the possibilities of restricting provisions of the Bill of Rights, without actually reversing prior decisions, see David G. Savage, *Turning Right: The Making of the Rehnquist Supreme Court* (New York: Wiley, 1992). For an indication that the Supreme Court may in fact be moving toward more restrictions on the Bill of Rights, see Richard Lacayo, "The Soul of a New Majority," *Time,* July 10, 1995, pp. 46–48.

15. *Abington School District v. Schempp*, 374 U.S. 203 (1963).

16. *Engel v. Vitale*, 370 U.S. 421 (1962).

17. *Wallace v. Jaffree*, 472 U.S. 38 (1985).

18. *Lynch v. Donnelly*, 465 U.S. 668 (1984).

19. *Lemon v. Kurtzman*, 403 U.S. 602 (1971). The *Lemon* test is still good law, but as recently as the 1994 Court term, four justices have urged that the *Lemon* test be abandoned. Here is a settled area of law that may soon become unsettled.

20. *Rosenberger v. Rector and Visitors of the University of Virginia*, 115 S.Ct. 2510 (1995).

21. *Agostini v. Felton*, 117 S.Ct. 1997 (1997). The case being overruled was *Aguilar v. Felton*, 473 U.S. 402 (1985).

22. For good coverage of voucher and charter school experiments, see Peter Schrag, "The Voucher Seduction," *American Prospect*, November 23, 1999, pp. 46–52.

23. *West Virginia State Board of Education v. Barnette*, 319 U.S. 624 (1943). The case it reversed was *Minersville School District v. Gobitus*, 310 U.S. 586 (1940).

24. *Employment Division, Department of Human Resources of Oregon v. Smith*, 494 U.S. 872 (1990).

25. *City of Boerne v. Flores*, 117 S.Ct. 293 (1996).

26. *Wisconsin v. Yoder*, 406 U.S. 205 (1972).

27. *U.S. v. Carolene Products Company*, 304 U.S. 144 (1938), note 4. This footnote is one of the Court's most important doctrines. See Alfred H. Kelly, Winfred A. Harbison, and Herman Belz, *The American Constitution: Its Origins and Development*, 7th ed. (New York: Norton, 1991), Vol. 2, pp. 519–23.

28. *Schenk v. U.S.*, 249 U.S. 47 (1919).

29. *Brandenburg v. Ohio*, 395 U.S. 444 (1969).

30. *Stromberg v. California*, 283 U.S. 359 (1931).

31. *Texas v. Johnson*, 488 U.S. 884 (1989).

32. *United States v. Eichman*, 496 U.S. 310 (1990).

33. For a good general discussion of "speech plus," see Louis Fisher, *American Constitutional Law* (New York: McGraw-Hill, 1990), pp. 544–46. The case upholding the buffer zone against the abortion protesters is *Madsen v. Women's Health Center*, 114 S.Ct. 2516 (1994).

34. *Near v. Minnesota*, 283 U.S. 697 (1931).

35. *New York Times v. U.S.*, 403 U.S. 731 (1971).

36. *New York Times v. Sullivan*, 376 U.S. 254 (1964).

37. *Hustler Magazine v. Falwell*, 108 S.Ct. 876 (1988).

38. *Roth v. U.S.*, 354 U.S. 476 (1957).

39. Concurring opinion in *Jacobellis v. Ohio*, 378 U.S. 184 (1964).

40. *Miller v. California*, 413 U.S. 15 (1973).

41. *Reno v. American Civil Liberties Union*, 117 S.Ct. 2329 (1997).

42. *Chaplinsky v. State of New Hampshire*, 315 U.S. 568 (1942).

43. *Dennis v. United States*, 341 U.S. 494 (1951), which upheld the infamous Smith Act of 1940, which provided criminal penalties for those who "willfully and knowingly conspire to teach and advocate the forceful and violent overthrow and destruction of the government."

44. *Bethel School District No. 403 v. Fraser*, 478 U.S. 675 (1986).

45. *Hazelwood School District v. Kuhlmeier*, 108 S.Ct. 562 (1988).

46. "The Penn File: An Update," *Wall Street Journal*, April 11, 1994, p. A14.

47. *Meritor Savings Bank, FBD v. Vinson*, 477 U.S. 57 (1986).

48. Charles Fried, "The New First Amendment Jurisprudence: A Threat to Liberty," in *The Bill of Rights and the Modern State*, ed. Stone, Epstein, and Sunstein, p. 249.

49. *Broadcasting Company v. Acting Attorney General*, 405 U.S. 1000 (1972).

50. *Board of Trustees of the State University of New York v. Fox*, 109 S.Ct. 3028 (1989).

51. *City Council v. Taxpayers for Vincent*, 466 U.S. 789 (1984).

52. *Posadas de Puerto Rico Associates v. Tourism Company of Puerto Rico*, 479 U.S. 328 (1986).

53. Fisher, *American Constitutional Law*, p. 546.

54. *Bigelow v. Virginia*, 421 U.S. 809 (1975).

55. *Virginia State Board of Pharmacy v. Virginia Citizens Consumer Council*, 425 U.S. 748 (1976). Later cases restored the rights of lawyers to advertise their services.

56. *44 Liquormart, Inc. and Peoples Super Liquor Stores Inc., Petitioners v. Rhode Island and Rhode Island Liquor Stores Association*, 116 S.Ct. 1495 (1996).

57. *Lorillard Tobacco v. Reilly*, 121 S.Ct. 2404 (2001)

58. *Presser v. Illinois*, 116 U.S. 252 (1886).

59. *Quilici v. Village of Morton Grove*, 695 F.2d 261 (7th Cir. 1982); cert denied, 464 U.S. 863 (1983).

60. *In re Winship*, 397 U.S. 361 (1970). An outstanding treatment of due process in issues involving the Fourth through Seventh Amendments will be found in Fisher, *American Constitutional Law*, chap. 13.

61. *Horton v. California*, 496 U.S. 128 (1990).

62. *Mapp v. Ohio*, 367 U.S. 643 (1961). Although Ms. Mapp went free in this case, she was later convicted in New York on narcotics trafficking charges and served nine years of a twenty-year sentence.

63. For a good discussion of the issue, see Fisher, *American Constitutional Law*, pp. 884–89.

64. *National Treasury Employees Union v. Von Raab*, 39 U.S. 656 (1989).

65. *Skinner v. Railroad Labor Executives Association*, 489 U.S. 602 (1989).

66. *Vernonia School District 47J v. Acton*, 115 S.Ct. 2386 (1985).

67. *Chandler et al. v. Miller, Governor of Georgia et al.*, 117 S.Ct. 1295 (1997).

68. *Indianapolis v. Edmund*, 531 U.S. 32 (2000), 121 S.Ct. 447 (2000).

69. *Ferguson v. Charleston*, 121 S.Ct. 1281 (2001).

70. *Kyllo v. U.S.*, 121 S.Ct. 2038 (2001).

71. Corwin and Peltason, *Understanding the Constitution*, p. 286.

72. *Miranda v. Arizona*, 348 U.S. 436 (1966).

73. *Berman v. Parker*, 348 U.S. 26 (1954). For a thorough analysis of the case see Benjamin Ginsberg, "*Berman v. Parker*: Congress, the Court, and the Public Purpose," *Polity* 4 (1971), pp. 48–75. For a later application of the case that suggests that "just compensation"—defined as something approximating market value—is about all a property owner can hope for protection against a public taking of property, see Theodore Lowi et al., *Poliscide; Big Government, Big Science, Lilliputian Politics*, 2nd ed. (Lanham, MD: University Press of America, 1990), pp. 267–70.

74. *Gideon v. Wainwright*, 372 U.S. 335 (1963). For a full account of the story of the trial and release of Clarence Earl Gideon, see Anthony Lewis, *Gideon's Trumpet* (New York: Random House, 1964). See also David O'Brien, *Storm Center*, 2nd ed. (New York: Norton, 1990).

75. For further discussion of these issues, see Corwin and Peltason, *Understanding the Constitution*, pp. 319–23.

76. *Congressional Quarterly Weekly Report*, October 21, 1995, p. 3212.

77. *Furman v. Georgia*, 408 U.S. 238 (1972).

78. *Gregg v. Georgia*, 428 U.S. 153 (1976).

79. *Minerville School District v. Gobitis*, 310 U.S. 586 (1940).

80. *West Virginia State Board of Education v. Barnette*, 319 U.S. 624 (1943)

81. *NAACP v. Alabama ex rel. Patterson*, 357 U.S. 449 (1958).

82. *Griswold v. Connecticut*, 381 U.S. 479 (1965).

83. *Griswold v. Connecticut*, concurring opinion. In 1972, the Court extended the privacy right to unmarried women: *Eisenstadt v. Baird*, 405 U.S. 438 (1972).

84. *Roe v. Wade*, 410 U.S. 113 (1973).

85. *Webster v. Reproductive Health Services*, 109 S.Ct. 3040 (1989), which upheld a Missouri law that restricted the use of public medical facilities for abortion. The decision opened the way for other states to limit the availability of abortion.

86. *Planned Parenthood of Southeastern Pennsylvania v. Casey*, 112 S.Ct. 2791 (1992).

87. *Stenberg v. Carhart*, 120 S.Ct. 2597 (2000).

88. *Bowers v. Hardwick*, 478 U.S. 186 (1986).

89. The dissenters were quoting an earlier case, *Olmstead v. United States*, 27 U.S. 438 (1928), to emphasize the nature of their disagreement with the majority in the *Bowers* case.

90. *Washington v. Glucksberg*, 117 S.Ct. 2258 (1997).

91. *Washington v. Glucksberg*.

92. *Washington v. Glucksberg*.

93. For an excellent discussion, see David M. O'Brien, *Supreme Court Watch* 1997 (New York: Norton, 1998), pp. 117–30.

94. William Safire, "Kangaroo Courts," *New York Times*, September 26, 2001, p. A17.

95. *Roe v. Wade*.

96. *Rosenberger v. University of Virginia*.

Chapter 5

1. Paula Baker, "The Domestication of Politics: Women and American Political Society, 1780–1920," *American Historical Review* 89 (June 1984), pp. 620–47.

2. August Meier and Elliot Rudwick, *From Plantation to Ghetto* (New York: Hill and Wang, 1976), pp. 184–88.

3. Jill Dupont, "Susan B. Anthony," New York Notes (Albany, NY: New York State Commission on the Bicentennial of the U.S. Constitution, 1988), p. 3.

4. *Plessy v. Ferguson*, 163 U.S. 537 (1896).

5. Dupont, "Susan B. Anthony," p. 4.

6. The prospect of a Fair Employment Practices law tied to the commerce power produced the Dixiecrat break with the Democratic Party in 1948. The Democratic Party organization of the States of the Old Confederacy seceded from the national party and nominated its own candidate, the then-Democratic governor of South Carolina, Strom Thurmond, who is now a Republican senator. This almost cost President Truman the election.

7. This was based on the provision in Article VI of the Constitution that "all treaties made, . . . under the Authority of the United States," shall be the "supreme Law of the Land." The committee recognized that if the U.S. Senate ratified the Human Rights Covenant of the United Nations—a treaty—then that power could be used as the constitutional umbrella for effective civil rights legislation. The Supreme Court had recognized in *Missouri v. Holland*, 252 U.S. 416 (1920), that a treaty could enlarge federal power at the expense of the states.

8. *Missouri ex rel. Gaines v. Canada*, 305 U.S. 337 (1938).

9. *Sweatt v. Painter*, 339 U.S. 629 (1950).

10. *Smith v. Allwright*, 321 U.S. 649 (1944).

11. *Shelley v. Kraemer*, 334 U.S. 1 (1948).

12. Kermit L. Hall, *The Magic Mirror: Law in American History* (New York: Oxford University Press, 1989), pp. 322–24. See also Richard Kluger, *Simple Justice* (New York: Random House, Vintage Edition, 1977), pp. 530–37.

13. The District of Columbia case came up too, but since the District of Columbia is not a state, this case did not directly involve the Fourteenth Amendment and its "equal protection" clause. It confronted the Court on the same grounds, however—that segregation is inherently unequal. Its victory in effect was "incorporation in reverse," with equal protection moving from the Fourteenth Amendment to become part of the Bill of Rights. See *Bolling v. Sharpe*, 347 U.S. 497 (1954).

14. *Brown v. Board of Education of Topeka, Kansas*, 347 U.S. 483 (1954).

15. The Supreme Court first declared that race was a suspect classification requiring strict scrutiny in the decision *Korematsu v. United States*, 323 U.S. 214 (1944). In this case, the Court upheld President Roosevelt's executive order of 1941 allowing the military to exclude persons of Japanese ancestry from the West Coast and to place them in internment camps. It is one of the few cases in which classification based on race survived strict scrutiny.

16. The two most important cases were *Cooper v. Aaron*, 358 U.S. 1 (1958), which required Little Rock, Arkansas, to desegregate; and *Griffin v. Prince Edward County School Board*, 377 U.S. 218 (1964), which forced all the schools of that Virginia county to reopen after five years of closing to avoid desegregation.

17. In *Cooper v. Aaron*, the Supreme Court ordered immediate compliance with the lower court's desegregation order and went beyond that with a stern warning that it is "emphatically the province and duty of the judicial department to say what the law is."

18. *Shuttlesworth v. Birmingham Board of Education*, 358 U.S. 101 (1958), upheld a "pupil placement" plan purporting to assign pupils on various bases, with no mention of race. This case interpreted *Brown* to mean that school districts must stop explicit racial discrimination but were under no obligation to take positive steps to desegregate. For a while black parents were doomed to case-by-case approaches.

19. For good treatments of this long stretch of the struggle of the federal courts to integrate the schools, see Paul Brest and Sanford Levinson, *Processes of Constitutional Decision-Making: Cases and Materials*, 2nd ed. (Boston: Little, Brown, 1983), pp. 471–80; and Alfred Kelly et al., *The American Constitution: Its Origins and Development*, 6th ed. (New York: Norton, 1983), pp. 610–16.

20. Pierre Thomas, "Denny's to Settle Bias Cases," *Washington Post*, May 24, 1994, p. A1.

21. See Hamil Harris, "For Blacks, Cabs Can Be Hard to Get," *Washington Post,* July 21, 1994, p. J1.

22. For a thorough analysis of the Office for Civil Rights, see Jeremy Rabkin, "Office for Civil Rights," in *The Politics of Regulation,* ed. James Q. Wilson (New York: Basic Books, 1980).

23. This was an accepted way of using quotas or ratios to determine statistically that blacks or other minorities were being excluded from schools or jobs, and then on the basis of that statistical evidence to authorize the Justice Department to bring suits in individual cases and in "class action" suits as well. In most segregated situations outside the South, it is virtually impossible to identify and document an intent to discriminate.

24. *Swann v. Charlotte-Mecklenburg Board of Education,* 402 U.S. 1 (1971).

25. *Milliken v. Bradley,* 418 U.S. 717 (1974).

26. For a good evaluation of the Boston effort, see Gary Orfield, *Must We Bus? Segregated Schools and National Policy* (Washington: Brookings Institution, 1978), pp. 144–46. See also Bob Woodward and Scott Armstrong, *The Brethren: Inside the Supreme Court* (New York: Simon and Schuster, 1979), pp. 426–27; and J. Anthony Lukas, *Common Ground* (New York: Random House, 1986).

27. *Board of Education v. Dowell,* 498 U.S. 237 (1991).

28. *Missouri v. Jenkins,* 115 S.Ct. 2038 (1995).

29. See especially *Katzenbach v. McClung,* 379 U.S. 294 (1964). Almost immediately after passage of the Civil Rights Act of 1964, a case was brought challenging the validity of Title II, which covered discrimination in public accommodations. Ollie's Barbecue was a neighborhood restaurant in Birmingham, Alabama. It was located eleven blocks away from an interstate highway and even farther from railroad and bus stations. Its table service was for whites only; there was only a take-out service for blacks. The Supreme Court agreed that Ollie's was strictly an intrastate restaurant, but since a substantial proportion of its food and other supplies were bought from companies outside the state of Alabama, there was a sufficient connection to interstate commerce; therefore, racial discrimination at such restaurants would "impose commercial burdens of national magnitude upon interstate commerce." Although this case involved Title II, it had direct bearing on the constitutionality of Title VII.

30. *Griggs v. Duke Power Company,* 401 U.S. 24 (1971). See also Allan Sindler, *Bakke, DeFunis, and Minority Admissions* (New York: Longman, 1978), pp. 180–89.

31. For a good treatment of these issues, see Charles O. Gregory and Harold A. Katz, *Labor and the Law* (New York: Norton, 1979), chap. 17.

32. In 1970, this act was amended to outlaw for five years literacy tests as a condition for voting in all states.

33. Joint Center for Political Studies, *Black Elected Officials: A National Roster—1988* (Washington, DC: Joint Center for Political Studies Press, 1988), pp. 9–10. For a comprehensive analysis and evaluation of the Voting Rights Act, see Bernard Grofman and Chandler Davidson, eds., *Controversies in Minority Voting: The Voting Rights Act in Perspective* (Washington, DC: Brookings, 1992).

34. Ford Fessenden, "Ballots Cast by Blacks and Older Voters Were Tossed in Far Greater Numbers," *New York Times,* November 12, 2001, p. A17.

35. See Douglas S. Massey and Nancy A. Denton, *American Apartheid: Segregation and the Making of the Underclass* (Cambridge, MA: Harvard University Press, 1993), chap. 7.

36. See Jane J. Mansbridge, *Why We Lost the ERA* (Chicago: University of Chicago Press, 1986); and Gilbert Steiner, *Constitutional Inequality* (Washington, DC: Brookings, 1985).

37. *See Frontiero v. Richardson,* 411 U.S. 677 (1973).

38. See *Craig v. Boren,* 423 U.S. 1047 (1976).

39. *Franklin v. Gwinnett County Public Schools,* 503 U.S. 60 (1992).

40. Jennifer Halperin, "Women Step Up to Bat," *Illinois Issues* 21 (September 1995), pp. 11–14.

41. Joan Biskupic and David Nakamura, "Court Won't Review Sports Equity Ruling," *Washington Post,* April 22, 1997, p. A1.

42. *U.S. v. Virginia,* 116 S.Ct. 2264 (1996).

43. Judith Havemann, "Two Women Quit Citadel over Alleged Harassment," *Washington Post,* January 13, 1997, p. A1.

44. *Meritor Savings Bank v. Vinson,* 477 U.S. 57 (1986).

45. *Harris v. Forklift Systems, Inc.,* 510 U.S. 17 (1993).

46. *Burlington Industries v. Ellerth,* 118 S.Ct. 2257 (1998); *Faragher v. City of Boca Raton,* 118 S.Ct. 2275 (1998).

47. New Mexico had a different history because not many Anglos settled there initially. ("Anglo" is the term for a non-Hispanic white generally of European background.) Mexican Americans had considerable power in territorial legislatures between 1865 and 1912. See Lawrence H. Fuchs, *The American Kaleidoscope* (Hanover, NH: University Press of New England, 1990), pp. 239–40.

48. On La Raza Unida Party, see "La Raza Unida Party and the Chicano Student Movement in California," in *Latinos in the American Political System,* ed. F. Chris Garcia (Notre Dame, IN: University of Notre Dame Press, 1988), pp. 213–35.

49. *United States v. Wong Kim Ark,* 169 U.S. 649 (1898).

50. *Lau v. Nichols,* 414 U.S. 563 (1974).

51. Dick Kirschten, "Not Black and White," *National Journal,* March 2, 1991, p. 497.

52. See Robert Pear, "Deciding Who Gets What in America," *New York Times,* November 27, 1994, sec. 4, p. 5.

53. Not all Indian tribes agreed with this, including the Navajos. See Ronald Takaki, *A Different Mirror: A History of Multicultural America* (Boston: Little, Brown: 1993), pp. 238–45.

54. On the resurgence of Indian political activity, see Stephen Cornell, *The Return of the Native: American Indian Political Resurgence* (New York: Oxford University Press, 1990); and Dee Brown, *Bury My Heart at Wounded Knee* (New York: Holt, 1971).

55. See the discussion in Robert A. Katzmann, *Institutional Disability: The Saga of Transportation Policy for the Disabled* (Washington, DC: Brookings, 1986).

56. For example, after pressure from the Justice Department, one of the nation's largest rental-car companies agreed to make special hand-controls available to any customer requesting them. See "Avis Agrees to Equip Cars for Disabled," *Los Angeles Times,* September 2, 1994, p. D1.

57. The case and the interview with Stephen Bokat was reported in Margaret Warner, "Expanding Coverage," *The News-Hour with Jim Lehrer Transcript,* July 1, 1998, on-line News-Hour, http://webcro5.pbs.org.

58. *Bowers v. Hardwick,* 478 U.S. 186 (1986).

59. Quoted in Joan Biskupic, "Gay Rights Activists Seek a Supreme Court Test Case," *Washington Post,* December 19, 1993, p. A1.

60. *Romer v. Evans,* 116 S.Ct. 1620 (1996).

61. For excellent coverage of the political and constitutional issues surrounding the actions of states on same-sex marriage, see Kenneth

Kersch, "Full Faith and Credit for Same-Sex Marriages?" *Political Science Quarterly,* 112 (Spring 1997), 117–36.

62. From Lyndon B. Johnson, *The Vantage Point* (New York: Holt, Rinehart, and Winston, 1971), p. 166.

63. The Department of Health, Education, and Welfare (HEW) was the cabinet department charged with administering most federal social programs. In 1980, when education programs were transferred to the newly created Department of Education, HEW was renamed the Department of Health and Human Services.

64. *Regents of the University of California v. Bakke,* 438 U.S. 265 (1978).

65. See, for example, *United Steelworkers v. Weber,* 443 U.S. 193 (1979); and *Fullilove v. Klutznick,* 100 S.Ct. 2758 (1980).

66. *Ward's Cove v. Atonio,* 109 S.Ct. 2115 (1989).

67. *Griggs v. Duke Power Company,* 401 U.S. 24 (1971).

68. *Martin v. Wilks,* 109 S.Ct. 2180 (1989). In this case, some white firefighters in Birmingham challenged a consent decree mandating goals for hiring and promoting blacks. This was an affirmative action plan that had been worked out between the employer and aggrieved black employees and had been accepted by a federal court. Such agreements become "consent decrees" and are subject to enforcement. Chief Justice Rehnquist held that the white firefighters could challenge the legality of such programs, even though they had not been parties to the original litigation.

69. *St. Mary's Honor Center v. Hicks,* 113 S.Ct. 2742 (1993).

70. *Adarand Constructors v. Pena,* 115 S.Ct. 2097 (1995).

71. Ann Devroy, "Clinton Study Backs Affirmative Action," *Washington Post,* July 19, 1995, p. A1.

72. *Hopwood v. State of Texas,* 78 F3d 932 (5th Cir., 1996).

73. See Lydia Lum, "Applications by Minorities Down Sharply," *Houston Chronicle,* April 8, 1997, p. A1; R. G. Ratcliffe, "Senate Approves Bill Designed to Boost Minority Enrollments," *Houston Chronicle,* May 8, 1997, p. A1.

74. Linda Greenhouse, "Settlement Ends High Court Case on Preferences," *New York Times,* November 22, 1997, p. A1; Barry Bearak, "Rights Groups Ducked a Fight, Opponents Say," *New York Times,* November 22, 1997, p. A1.

75. Michael A. Fletcher, "Opponents of Affirmative Action Heartened by Court Decision," *Washington Post,* April 13, 1997, p. A21.

76. See Sam Howe Verhovek, "Houston Vote Underlined Complexity of Rights Issue," *New York Times,* November 6, 1997, p. A1.

77. There are still many genuine racists in America, but with the exception of a lunatic fringe, made up of neo-Nazis and members of the Ku Klux Klan, most racists are too ashamed or embarrassed to take part in normal political discourse. They are not included in either category here.

78. *Slaughterhouse Cases,* 16 Wallace 36 (1873).

79. See Paul M. Sniderman and Edward G. Carmines, *Reaching beyond Race* (Cambridge, MA: Harvard University Press, 1997).

Chapter 6

1. See Fred Greenstein, *Children and Politics* (New Haven, CT: Yale University Press, 1969). See also Robert Weissberg, *Political Learning, Political Choice and Democratic Citizenship* (Englewood Cliffs, NJ: Prentice-Hall, 1974).

2. Alexander Astin et al., "The American Freshman: National Norms for Fall 1994," Cooperative Institutional Research Program of the American Council on Education and the Higher Education Research Institute of the University of California at Los Angeles, 1994.

3. Quoted in the *Tampa Tribune,* January 9, 1995, p. 1.

4. Henry K. Lee, "Tentative Pact Between UC, Hunger Strikers," *San Francisco Chronicle,* May 8, 1999, p. A15.

5. Karlene Hanko, "College, University Presidents Pledge to Encourage Participation in Politics," *Daily Pennsylvanian,* July 13, 1999.

6. For a discussion of the political beliefs of Americans, see Harry Holloway and John George, *Public Opinion* (New York: St. Martin's, 1986). See also Paul R. Abramson, *Political Attitudes in America* (San Francisco: Freeman, 1983).

7. See Louis Hartz, *The Liberal Tradition in America* (New York: Harcourt, Brace, 1955).

8. See Paul M. Sniderman and Edward G. Carmines, *Reaching beyond Race* (Cambridge, MA: Harvard University Press, 1997).

9. Ben Gose, "Penn to Replace Controversial Speech Code; Will No Longer Punish Students for Insults," *Chronicle of Higher Education,* June 29, 1994, p. A30.

10. See Angus Campbell et al., *The American Voter* (New York: Wiley, 1960), p. 147.

11. Richard Morin, "Poll Reflects Division over Simpson Case," *Washington Post,* October 8, 1995, p. A31.

12. "Middle-Class Views in Black and White," *Washington Post,* October 9, 1995, p. A22.

13. For data see Rutgers University, Eagleton Institute of Politics, Center for the American Woman in Politics, "Sex Differences in Voter Turnout," August 1994.

14. Pamela Johnston Conover, "The Role of Social Groups in Political Thinking," *British Journal of Political Science* 18 (1988), pp. 51–78.

15. See Michael C. Dawson, "Structure and Ideology: The Shaping of Black Opinion," paper presented to the 1995 annual meeting of the Midwest Political Science Association, Chicago, Illinois, April 7–9, 1995. See also Michael C. Dawson, *Behind the Mule: Race, Class, and African American Politics* (Princeton, NJ: Princeton University Press, 1994).

16. Elisabeth Noelle-Neumann, *The Spiral of Silence* (Chicago: University of Chicago Press, 1984).

17. Ole R. Holsti, "A Widening Gap Between the Military and Civilian Society?" John M. Olin Institute for Strategic Studies.

18. Michael X. Delli Carpini and Scott Keeter, *What Americans Know about Politics and Why It Matters* (New Haven, CT: Yale University Press, 1996).

19. Sniderman and Carmines, *Reaching beyond Race,* ch. 4.

20. For an interesting discussion of opinion formation, see John Zaller, *The Nature and Origins of Mass Opinion* (New York: Cambridge University Press, 1992).

21. Gerald F. Seib and Michael K. Frisby, "Selling Sacrifice," *Wall Street Journal,* February 5, 1993, p. 1.

22. Michael K. Frisby, "Clinton Seeks Strategic Edge with Opinion Polls," *Wall Street Journal,* June 24, 1996, p. A16.

23. Peter Marks, "Adept in Politics and Advertising, 4 Women Shape a Campaign," *New York Times,* November 11, 2001, p. B6.

24. See Gillian Peele, *Revival and Reaction* (Oxford, U.K.: Clarendon, 1985). Also see Connie Paige, *The Right-to-Lifers* (New York: Summit, 1983).

25. See David Vogel, "The Power of Business in America: A Reappraisal," *British Journal of Political Science* 13 (January 1983), pp. 19–44.

26. See David Vogel, "The Public Interest Movement and the American Reform Tradition," *Political Science Quarterly* 96 (winter 1980), pp. 607–27.

27. Jason DeParle, "The Clinton Welfare Bill Begins Trek in Congress," *New York Times,* July 15, 1994, p. 1.

28. Joe Queenan, "Birth of a Notion," *Washington Post,* September 20, 1992, p. C1.

29. Zaller, *The Nature and Origins of Mass Opinion.*

30. See Shanto Iyengar, *Is Anyone Responsible? How Television Frames Political Issues* (Chicago: University of Chicago Press, 1991); and Shanto Iyengar, *Do the Media Govern?* (Thousand Oaks, CA: Sage, 1997).

31. Michael Kagay and Janet Elder, "Numbers Are No Problem for Pollsters, Words Are," *New York Times,* August 9, 1992, p. E6.

32. Donn Tibbetts, "Draft Bill Requires Notice of Push Polling," *Manchester Union Leader,* October 3, 1996, p. A6.

33. "Dial S for Smear," *Memphis Commercial Appeal,* September 22, 1996, p. 6B.

34. Amy Keller, "Subcommittee Launches Investigation of Push Polls," *Roll Call,* October 3, 1996, p. 1.

35. For a discussion of the growing difficulty of persuading people to respond to surveys, see John Brehm, *Phantom Respondents* (Ann Arbor: University of Michigan Press, 1993).

36. See Richard Morin, "Is Bush's Bounce a Boom or a Bust?" *Washington Post National Weekly Edition,* August 31–September 6, 1992, p. 37.

37. See Thomas E. Mann and Gary Orren, eds., *Media Polls in American Politics* (Washington, DC: Brookings, 1992).

38. For an excellent and reflective discussion by a journalist, see Richard Morin, "Clinton Slide in Survey Shows Perils of Polling," *Washington Post,* August 29, 1992, p. A6.

39. See Michael Traugott, "The Impact of Media Polls on the Public," in *Media Polls in American Politics,* Mann and Orren, eds., pp. 125–49.

40. Carl Cannon, "A Pox on Both Our Parties," in David C. Canon et. al., eds., *The Enduring Debate* (New York: Norton, 2000), p. 389.

41. Benjamin I. Page and Robert Y. Shapiro, "Effects of Public Opinion on Policy," *American Political Science Review* 77 (March 1983), pp. 175–90.

42. Robert A. Erikson, Gerald Wright, and John McIver, *Statehouse Democracy: Public Opinion and Democracy in the American States* (New York: Cambridge University Press, 1994).

43. The results of separate studies by the political scientists Lawrence Jacobs, Robert Shapiro, and Alan Monroe were reported by Richard Morin in "Which Comes First, the Politician or the Poll?" *Washington Post National Weekly Edition,* February 10, 1997, p. 35.

44. David S. Broder, *Democracy Derailed: Initiative Campaigns and the Power of Money* (New York: Harcourt, 2000).

45. Robert Tomsho, "Liberals Take a Cue from Conservatives: This Election, the Left Tries to Make Policy with Ballot Initiatives," *Wall Street Journal,* November 6, 2000, p. A12.

46. Delli Carpini and Keeter. *What Americans Know about Politics and Why It Matters.*

Chapter 7

1. Benjamin Ginsberg and Martin Shefter, *Politics by Other Means* (New York: Basic Books, 1990), p. 24.

2. U.S. Bureau of the Census, *Statistical Abstract of the United States: 1994* (Washington, DC: Department of Commerce, 1994), pp. 567, 576.

3. *Red Lion Broadcasting Company v. FCC,* 395 U.S. 367 (1969).

4. For a criticism of the increasing consolidation of the media, see the essays in Patricia Aufderheide et al., *Conglomerates and the Media* (New York: New Press, 1997).

5. See Leo Bogart, "Newspapers in Transition," *Wilson Quarterly,* special issue, 1982; and Richard Harwood, "The Golden Age of Press Diversity," *Washington Post,* July 22, 1994, p. A23.

6. See Benjamin Ginsberg, *The Captive Public* (New York: Basic Books, 1986).

7. Michael Dawson, "Structure and Ideology: The Shaping of Black Public Opinion," paper presented to the 1995 meeting of the Midwest Political Science Association, Chicago, Illinois, April 7, 1995.

8. See the discussions in Gary Paul Gates, *Air Time* (New York: Harper & Row, 1978); Edward Jay Epstein, *News from Nowhere* (New York: Random House, 1973); Michael Parenti, *Inventing Reality* (New York: St. Martin's, 1986); Herbert Gans, *Deciding What's News* (New York: Vintage, 1980); and W. Lance Bennett, *News: The Politics of Illusion* (New York: Longman, 1986).

9. See Edith Efron, *The News Twisters* (Los Angeles: Nash Publishing, 1971).

10. Rowan Scarborough, "Leftist Press? Reporters Working in Washington Acknowledge Liberal Leanings in Poll," *Washington Times,* April 18, 1996, p. 1.

11. David Firestone, "Steven Brill Strikes a Nerve in News Media," *New York Times,* June 20, 1998, p. 4.

12. See Tom Burnes, "The Organization of Public Opinion," in *Mass Communication and Society,* ed. James Curran (Beverly Hills, CA: Sage, 1979), pp. 44–230. See also David Altheide, *Creating Reality* (Beverly Hills, CA: Sage, 1976).

13. Garrow, *Protest at Selma.*

14. See Todd Gitlin, *The Whole World Is Watching* (Berkeley, CA: University of California Press, 1980).

15. See Dan Balz, "Bradley Offers Antipoverty Plan," *Washington Post,* October 22, 1999, p. A13.

16. For a discussion of framing, see Amy Jasperson, et al., "Framing and the Public Agenda," *Political Communication,* vol. 15, no. 2, pp. 205–24.

17. Eric Lyman, "Hollywood Discusses Role in War Effort," *New York Times,* November 12, 2001, p. B2.

18. See Martin Linsky, *Impact: How the Press Affects Federal Policymaking* (New York: Norton, 1986).

19. Carl Allen, "UB Paper Prints Apology for Story on Student Poll," *Buffalo News,* November 15, 1997, p. 1B.

20. For a good discussion of how to evaluate media biases see Don Hazen and Julie Winokur, eds., *We the Media* (New York: New Press, 1997).

Chapter 8

1. For a discussion of the decline of voting turnout over time, see Ruy A. Teixeira, *The Disappearing American Voter* (Washington, DC: Brookings, 1992). On the 1994 elections, see Paul Taylor, "Behind the Broom of '94: Wealthier, Educated Voters," *Washington Post,* June 8, 1995, p. A12.

2. Sidney Verba, Kay Lehman Schlozman, and Henry E. Brady, *Voice and Equality: Civic Voluntarism in American Politics* (Cambridge, MA: Harvard University Press, 1995), chap. 3, for kinds of participation, and pp. 66–67 for prevalence of local activity.

3. For a discussion of citizen lobbying, see Jeffrey M. Berry, *The New Liberalism: The Rising Power of Citizen Groups* (Washington, DC: Brookings, 1999).

4. Verba, Schlozman, and Brady, *Voice and Equality,* p. 51.

5. Steven J. Rosenstone and John Mark Hansen, *Mobilization, Participation, and Democracy in America* (New York: Macmillan, 1993), chap. 3; and Verba, Schlozman, and Brady, *Voice and Equality,* pp. 71–74.

6. Robert Jackman, "Political Institutions and Voter Turnout in the Democracies," *American Political Science Review* 81 (June 1987), p. 420.

7. See William Julius Wilson, *The Truly Disadvantaged: The Inner City, the Underclass, and Public Policy* (Chicago: University of Chicago Press, 1987); and Douglas Massey and Nancy Denton, *American Apartheid: Segregation and the Making of the American Underclass* (Cambridge, MA: Harvard University Press, 1993).

8. See Michael C. Dawson, *Behind the Mule: Race and Class in African-American Politics* (Princeton, NJ: Princeton University Press, 1994), chaps. 5 and 6.

9. *Ibid.*

10. Dana Milbank, "Attacks Shelve GOP Effort to Woo Hispanics," *Washington Post,* December 20, 2001, p. A4.

11. James Sterngold, "For Asian-Americans, A New Political Resolve," *New York Times,* September 22, 1999, p. A1.

12. Ronald Browstein, "Response to Terror: The Times Poll," *Los Angeles Times,* November 15, 2001, p. A1.

13. See Thomas B. Edsall, "Pollsters View Gender Gap as Political Fixture," *Washington Post,* August 15, 1995, p. A11.

14. Richard L. Berke, "Defections among Men to G.O.P. Helped Insure Rout of Democrats," *New York Times,* November 11, 1994, p. A1.

15. "Fact Sheet: Women in Elective Office," Center for the American Woman and Politics, Eagleton Institute of Politics, Rutgers University, January 2002.

16. David S. Broder, "Key to Women's Political Parity: Running," *Washington Post,* September 8, 1994, p. A17.

17. "The Impact of Women in Public Office: Findings at a Glance," Center for the American Woman and Politics (New Brunswick, NJ: Rutgers University, n.d.).

18. *Engel v. Vitale,* 370 U.S. 421 (1962); *Abington School District v. Schempp,* 374 U.S. 203 (1963); *Roe v. Wade,* 410 U.S. 113 (1973).

19. Laurie Goodstein, "Bush's Charity Plan Is Raising Concerns for Religious Right," *New York Times,* March 3, 2001, p. A1.

20. Dana Milbank, "Religious Right Finds Its Center in Oval Office," *Washington Post,* December 24, 2001, p. A2.

21. U.S. Census Bureau, Statistical Abstract of the United States: 2001, Table No. 401, www.census.gov. Accessed February 23, 2002.

22. Michael DeCourcy Hinds, "Youth Vote 2000: They'd Rather Volunteer," Carnegie Reporter 1, No. 2 (Spring 2001), p. 2.

23. *Ibid.,* p. 1.

24. *Ibid.,* p. 3.

25. See Thomas B. Edsall, "Huge Gains in South Fueled GOP Vote in '94," *Washington Post,* September 27, 1995, p. A8.

26. See Richard A. Brody, "The Puzzle of Political Participation in America," in *The New American Political System,* ed. Anthony King (Washington, DC: American Enterprise Institute, 1978), chap. 8.

27. On the nineteenth century, see Michael E. McGerr, *The Decline of Popular Politics: The American North, 1865–1928* (New York: Oxford University Press, 1986).

28. Verba, Schlozman, and Brady, *Voice and Equality.*

29. See Alexis de Tocqueville, *Democracy in America* (New York: Vintage, 1945).

30. Robert D. Putnam, "Bowling Alone: America's Declining Social Capital," *Journal of Democracy* 6, no. 1 (January 1995), pp. 65–78.

31. On television see Robert D. Putnam, "Tuning In, Tuning Out: The Strange Disappearance of Social Capital in America," *PS: Political Science and Politics* 28, no. 4 (December 1995), pp. 664–83; for a reply see Pippa Norris, "Does Television Erode Social Capital? A Reply to Putnam," *PS: Political Science and Politics* 29, no. 3 (September 1996), pp. 474–80.

32. Michael Schudson, "What If Civic Life Didn't Die?" *American Prospect* 25 (March–April 1996), pp. 17–20.

33. Rosenstone and Hansen, *Mobilization, Participation, and Democracy in America,* p. 59.

34. Robert A. Jackson, Robert D. Brown, and Gerald C. Wright, "Registration, Turnout and the Electoral Representativeness of U.S. State Electorates," *American Politics Quarterly,* vol. 26, no. 3 (July 1998), pp. 259–87. Also, Benjamin Highton, "Easy Registration and Voter Turnout," *Journal of Politics,* vol. 59, no. 2 (April 1997), pp. 565–87.

35. The data in this paragraph is drawn from The Sentencing Project and Human Rights Watch, "Losing the Vote: The Impact of Felony Disfranchisement Laws in the United States," 1998, www.sentencingproject.org/pubs/hrwfvr.html. Accessed February 23, 2002.

36. Connie Cass, "'Motor Voter' Impact Slight," *Chattanooga News-Free Press,* June 20, 1997, p. A5. On the need to motivate voters see Marshall Ganz, "Motor Voter or Motivated Voter?" *American Prospect,* no. 28 (September–October 1996), pp. 41–49. On the hopes for Motor Voter see Frances Fox Piven and Richard A. Cloward, "Northern Bourbons: A Preliminary Report on the National Voter Registration Act," *PS: Political Science and Politics* 29, no. 1 (March 1996), pp. 39–42. On turnout in the 1996 election, see Barbara

Vobejda, "Just under Half of Possible Voters Went to the Polls," *Washington Post,* November 7, 1996, p. A3.

37. Lawrence Bobo and Franklin D. Gilliam, "Race, Sociopolitical Participation, and Black Empowerment," *American Political Science Review* 24, no. 2 (June 1990), pp. 377–93.

38. Rosenstone and Hansen, *Mobilization, Participation, and Democracy in America,* p. 59.

39. Alan Gerber and Donald Green, "The Effects of Canvassing, Phone Calls, and Direct Mail on Voter Turnout: A Field Experiment," Yale University, April 24, 2000, p. 22.

40. Donald P. Green and Alan S. Gerber, "Getting Out the Youth Vote: Results from Randomized Field Experiments," Pew Charitable Trusts, August 6, 2001, p. 27.

41. Erik Austin and Jerome Chubb, *Political Facts of the United States since 1789* (New York: Columbia University Press, 1986), pp. 378–79.

42. Kenneth N. Weine, "Campaigns without a Human Face," *Washington Post,* October 27, 1996, p. C1; see also Margaret Weir and Marshall Ganz, "Reconnecting People and Politics," *The New Majority: Toward Popular Progressive Politics,* ed. Stanley B. Greenberg and Theda Skocpol (New Haven, CT: Yale University Press, 1997), pp. 149–71.

43. *Buckley v. Valeo,* 424 U.S. 1 (1976).

44. Michael Schudson, "What If Civic Life Didn't Die?" *American Prospect* 25 (March-April 1996), p. 18.

45. See Christopher Lasch, *The Revolt of the Elites and the Betrayal of American Democracy* (New York: Norton, 1995). The idea of the "secession of the rich" comes from Robert Reich, *The Work of Nations* (New York: Knopf, 1991), chaps. 23 and 24.

Chapter 9

1. See Richard Hofstadter, *The Idea of a Party System* (Berkeley: University of California Press, 1969).

2. John Aldrich, *Why Parties: The Origin and Transformation of Political Parties in America* (Chicago: University of Chicago Press, 1995).

3. See Walter Dean Burnham, *Critical Elections and the Mainsprings of American Electoral Politics* (New York: Norton, 1970). See also James L. Sundquist, *Dynamics of the Party System* (Washington, DC: Brookings, 1983).

4. Benjamin Ginsberg, *The Consequences of Consent* (New York: Random House, 1982), chap. 4.

5. For a discussion of third parties in the United States, see Daniel Mazmanian, *Third Parties in Presidential Election* (Washington, DC: Brookings, 1974).

6. See Maurice Duverger, *Political Parties* (New York: Wiley, 1954).

7. See Harold Gosnell, *Machine Politics Chicago Model,* rev. ed. (Chicago: University of Chicago Press, 1968).

8. For a useful discussion, see John Bibby and Thomas Holbrook, "Parties and Elections," in *Politics in the American States,* ed. Virginia Gray and Herbert Jacob (Washington, DC: Congressional Quarterly Press, 1996), pp. 78–121.

9. Alan Greenblatt, "With Major Issues Fading, Capitol Life Lures Fewer," *Congressional Quarterly Weekly Report,* October 25, 1997, p. 2625.

10. For an excellent analysis of the parties' role in recruitment, see Paul Herrnson, *Congressional Elections: Campaigning at Home and in Washington* (Washington, DC: Congressional Quarterly Press, 1995).

11. Duverger, *Political Parties,* p. 426.

12. Duverger, *Political Parties,* chap. 1.

13. Stanley Kelley, Jr., Richard E. Ayres, and William Bowen, "Registration and Voting: Putting First Things First," *American Political Science Review* 61 (June 1967), pp. 359–70.

14. David H. Fischer, *The Revolution of American Conservatism* (New York: Harper & Row, 1965), p. 93.

15. Fischer, *The Revolution of American Conservatism,* p. 109.

16. Henry Jones Ford, *The Rise and Growth of American Politics* (New York: Da Capo Press, 1967 reprint of the 1898 edition), chap. 9.

17. Ford, *The Rise and Growth of American Politics,* p. 125.

18. Ford, *The Rise and Growth of American Politics,* p. 125.

19. Ford, *The Rise and Growth of American Politics,* p. 126.

20. Mark Barabak, "Los Angeles Times Interview: Cruz Bustamente: On Surviving a Bruising First Term as Assembly Speaker," *Los Angeles Times,* August 24, 1997, p. M3.

Chapter 10

1. Clinton Rossiter, ed., *The Federalist Papers* (New York: New American Library, 1961), No. 57, p. 352.

2. *League of United Latin American Citizens v. Wilson,* CV-94-7569 (C.D. Calif.), 1995.

3. *Gray v. Sanders,* 372 U.S. 368 (1963); *Wesberry v. Sanders,* 376 U.S. 1 (1964); *Reynolds v. Sims,* 377 U.S. 533 (1964).

4. *Thornburg v. Gingles,* 478 U.S. 613 (1986).

5. *Shaw v. Reno,* 509 U.S. 113 (1993).

6. State legislatures determine the system by which electors are selected and almost all states use this "winner-take-all" system. Maine and Nebraska, however, provide that one electoral vote goes to the winner in each congressional district and two electoral votes go to the winner statewide.

7. Mary McGrory, "The Lost Leader," *Washington Post,* October 26, 1995, p. A2.

8. Larry J. Sabato, *The Rise of Political Consultants* (New York: Basic Books, 1981).

9. Larry J. Sabato, *The Rise of Political Consultants,* p. 250.

10. Dana Milbanks, "Virtual Politics," *New Republic,* July 5, 1999, p. 22.

11. M. Ostrogorski, *Democracy and the Organization of Political Parties* (New York: Macmillan, 1902).

12. Timothy Clark, "The RNC Prospers, the DNC Struggles as They Face the 1980 Election," *National Journal,* October 27, 1980, p. 1619.

13. For discussions of the consequences, see Thomas Edsall, *The New Politics of Inequality* (New York: Norton, 1984). Also see Thomas Edsall, "Both Parties Get the Company's Money—But the Boss Backs the GOP," *Washington Post National Weekly Edition,* September 16, 1986, p. 14; and Benjamin Ginsberg, "Money and Power: The New Political Economy of American Elections," in *The Political Economy,* ed. Thomas Ferguson and Joel Rogers (Armonk, NY: M. E. Sharpe, 1984).

14. Jonathan Salant, "Million-Dollar Campaigns Proliferate in 105th," *Congressional Quarterly Weekly Report,* December 21, 1996, pp. 3448–51.

15. U.S. Federal Election Commission, "Financing the 1996 Presidential Campaign," Internet Release, April 28, 1998.

16. *Buckley v. Valeo,* 424 U.S. 1 (1976); *Colorado Republican Party v. Federal Election Commission,* 64 U.S.L.W. 4663 (1996).

17. FEC reports.

18. FEC reports.

19. David Broder and Ruth Marcus, "Wielding Third Force in Politics," *Washington Post,* September 20, 1997, p. 1.

Chapter 11

1. Clinton Rossiter, ed., *The Federalist Papers* (New York: New American Library, 1961), No. 10, p. 83.

2. Rossiter, ed., *Federalist Papers,* No. 10.

3. The best statement of the pluralist view is in David Truman, *The Governmental Process* (New York: Knopf, 1951), chap. 2.

4. E. E. Schattschneider, *The Semisovereign People* (New York: Holt, Rinehart, and Winston, 1960), p. 35.

5. Betsy Wagner and David Bowermaster, "B.S. Economics," *Washington Monthly,* November 1992, pp. 19–21.

6. David B. Truman, *The Governmental Process* (New York: Knopf, 1951).

7. Mancur Olson, *The Logic of Collective Action* (Cambridge, MA: Harvard University Press, 1965).

8. Timothy Penny and Steven Schier, *Payment Due: A Nation in Debt, A Generation in Trouble* (Boulder, CO: Westview, 1996), pp. 64–65.

9. Kay Lehman Schlozman and John T. Tierney, *Organized Interests and American Democracy* (New York: Harper & Row, 1986), p. 60.

10. John Herbers, "Special Interests Gaining Power as Voter Disillusionment Grows," *New York Times,* November 14, 1978.

11. For discussions of lobbying, see Allan J. Cigler and Burdett A. Loomis, eds., *Interest Group Politics* (Washington, DC: Congressional Quarterly Press, 1983). See also Jeffrey M. Berry, *Lobbying for the People* (Princeton, NJ: Princeton University Press, 1977).

12. "The Swarming Lobbyists," *Time,* August 7, 1978, p. 15.

13. Ruth Marcus, "Lobbying's Big Hitters Go to Bat," *Washington Post,* August 3, 1997, p. 1.

14. See especially Marver Bernstein, *Regulating Business by Independent Commission* (Princeton, NJ: Princeton University Press, 1955). See also George J. Stigler, "The Theory of Economic Regulation," *Bell Journal of Economics and Management Science* 2 (1971), pp. 3–21.

15. Quoted in John E. Chubb, *Interest Groups and the Bureaucracy: The Politics of Energy* (Stanford, CA: Stanford University Press, 1983).

16. John P. Heinz, Edward O. Laumann, Robert L. Nelson, and Robert H. Salisbury, *The Hollow Core: Private Interests in National Policy Making* (Cambridge, MA: Harvard University Press, 1993), p. 96. See also Schlozman and Tierney, *Organized Interests and American Democracy,* chap. 13.

17. The famous and prophetic movie *The China Syndrome* portrayed some dramatic moments at a public hearing involving an administrative agency's decision to build or expand an atomic energy plant.

18. *Roe v. Wade,* 93 S.Ct. 705 (1973).

19. *Webster v. Reproductive Health Services,* 109 S.Ct. 3040 (1989)

20. *Brown v. Board of Education of Topeka, Kansas,* 74 S.Ct. 686 (1954).

21. See, for example, *Duke Power Co. v. Carolina Environmental Study Group,* 438 U.S. 59 (1978).

22. E. Pendleton Herring, *Group Representation before Congress* (New York: McGraw-Hill, 1936).

23. Ann Devroy, "Gay Rights Leaders Meet President in Oval Office: White House Tries to Play Down Session," *Washington Post,* April 17, 1993, p. 1.

24. Michael Weisskopf, "Energized by Pulpit or Passion, the Public is Calling," *Washington Post,* February 1, 1993, p. 1.

25. Stephen Engelberg, "A New Breed of Hired Hands Cultivates Grass-Roots Anger," *New York Times,* March 17, 1993, p. A1.

26. Jane Fritsch, "The Grass Roots, Just a Free Phone Call Away," *New York Times,* June 23, 1995, pp. A1 and A22.

27. Ruth Marcus, "Outside Groups Pushing Election Laws into Irrelevance," *Washington Post,* August 8, 1996, p. A9.

28. Richard L. Burke, "Religious-Right Candidates Gain as GOP Turnout Rises," *New York Times,* November 12, 1994, p. 10.

29. Some Americans and even more Europeans would stress only the negative aspect of the softening and adulterating effect of the two-party system on class and other basic subdivisions of society. For a discussion of how the working class was divided and softened, with native workers joining the Democratic Party and new immigrant workers becoming Republicans, see Gwendolyn Mink, *Old Labor and New Immigrants in American Political Development: Union, Party, and State, 1875–1920* (Ithaca, NY: Cornell University Press, 1986).

30. Rossiter, ed., *The Federalist Papers,* No. 10.

31. Olson, *The Logic of Collective Action.*

32. Steve Ma, telephone interview by author, February 12, 1998.

33. Steve Ma, interview, February 12, 1998.

34. Steve Ma, interview, February 12, 1998.

Chapter 12

1. John F. Harris, "Hillary's Big Adventure," *Washington Post,* January 27, 2002, p. W8.

2. For a discussion of these roles, see Roger Davidson and Walter H. Oleszek, *Congress and Its Members* (Washington, D. C.: CQ Press, 2002), chap. 5.

3. Herb Asher and Mike Barr, "Popular Support for Congress and Its Members," and Karlyn Borman and Everett Carll Ladd, "Public Opinion toward Congress: A Historical Look," in *Congress, the Press, and the Public,* ed. Thomas E. Mann and Norman J. Ornstein (Washington DC: American Enterprise Institute and Brookings Institution, 1994), pp. 34, 51, 53.

4. John R. Hibbing and Elizabeth Theiss-Morse, *Congress as Public Enemy: Public Attitudes toward American Political Institutions* (New York: Cambridge University Press, 1995), p. 100.

5. This argument is developed in Hibbing and Theiss-Morse, *Congress as Public Enemy.* For more on the institutionalization of Congress, see Nelson Polsby, "The Institutionalization of the US House of Representatives," *American Political Science Review* 62 (1968): 144–68; on professionalization see Alan Ehrenhalt, *The United States of Ambition: Politicians, Power, and the Pursuit of Office* (New York: Times Books, 1991).

6. For data on religious affiliations of the members of the 105th Congress, see *Congressional Quarterly Weekly Report,* January 4, 1997.

7. For data on occupational backgrounds of the members of the 105th Congress, see *Congressional Quarterly Weekly Report,* January 4, 1997.

8. Marian D. Irish and James Prothro, *The Politics of American Democracy,* 5th ed. (Englewood Cliffs, NJ: Prentice-Hall, 1971), p. 352.

9. For a discussion, see Benjamin Ginsberg, *The Consequences of Consent* (New York: Random House, 1982), chap. 1.

10. For some interesting empirical evidence, see Angus Campbell, Philip Converse, Warren Miller, and Donald Stokes, *Elections and the Political Order* (New York: Wiley, 1966), chap. 11.

11. Congressional Quarterly, *Guide to the Congress of the United States,* 3rd ed. (Washington, DC: Congressional Quarterly Press, 1982), p. 599.

12. John S. Saloma, *Congress and the New Politics* (Boston: Little, Brown, 1969), pp. 184–85. A 1977 official report using less detailed categories came up with almost the same impression of Congress's workload. Commission on Administrative Review, *Administrative Reorganization and Legislative Management,* House Doc. #95-232 (September 28, 1977), vol. 2, especially pp. 17–19.

13. See Linda Fowler and Robert McClure, *Political Ambition: Who Decides to Run for Congress* (New Haven, CT: Yale University Press, 1989); and Alan Ehrenhalt, *The United States of Ambition.*

14. See Barbara C. Burrell, *A Woman's Place Is in the House: Campaigning for Congress in the Feminist Era* (Ann Arbor: University of Michigan Press, 1994), chap. 6; and the essays in Elizabeth Adell Cook, Sue Thomas, and Clyde Wilcox, eds., *The Year of the Woman: Myths and Realities* (Boulder, CO: Westview, 1994).

15. Ruth Marcus and Juliet Eilperin, "Battle for House Fuels Cash Race," *Washington Post,* August 11, 1999, p. A1; Alison Mitchell, "Congress Chasing Campaign Donors Early and Often," *New York Times,* June 14, 1999, p. A1; Gilbert Craig, "Kohn Vows to Win Dairy Price Fight," *Milwaukee Journal Sentinel,* November 21, 1999, p. 1.

16. See Burrell, *A Woman's Place Is in the House;* and David Broder, "Key to Women's Political Parity: Running," *Washington Post,* September 8, 1994, p. A17.

17. "Did Redistricting Sink the Democrats?" *National Journal,* December 17, 1994, p. 2984.

18. *Miller v. Johnson,* 115 S.Ct. 2475 (1995).

19. *Congressional Quarterly Weekly Report,* October 17, 1998, p. 2792; Jeff Plungis, "The Driving Force of Bud Schuster," *Congressional Quarterly Weekly Report,* August 7, 1999, p. 1916.

20. www.house.gov/stark/services.html

21. Congressional Quarterly, *Guide to the Congress of the United States,* 2nd ed. (Washington, DC: Congressional Quarterly Press, 1976), pp. 229–310.

22. Richard Fenno, Jr., *Home Style: House Members in Their Districts* (Boston: Little, Brown, 1978).

23. Richard C. Fenno, *Congressmen in Committees* (Boston: Little, Brown, 1973), p. 1; Richard L. Hall, "Participation, Abdication, and Representation in Congressional Committees," in *Congress Reconsidered,* 5th ed., ed. Lawrence C. Dodd and Bruce I. Oppenheimer (Washington DC: Congressional Quarterly Press, 1993), p. 164.

24. See Thomas E. Mann and Norman J. Ornstein, *Renewing Congress: A First Report of the Renewing Congress Project* (Washington, DC: American Enterprise Institute and Brookings Institution, 1992). See also the essays in Roger H. Davidson, ed., *The Postreform Congress* (New York: St. Martin's, 1992).

25. Richard E. Cohen, "Crackup of the Committees," *National Journal,* July 31, 1999, p. 2210–16.

26. Jeff Plungis, "The Driving Force of Bud Schuster," *Congressional Quarterly Weekly Report,* August 7, 1999, p. 1919.

27. See Robert Pear, "Senator X Kills Measure on Anonymity," *New York Times,* November 11, 1997, p. 12.

28. See John W. Kingdon, *Congressmen's Voting Decisions* (New York: Harper & Row, 1973), chap. 3; and R. Douglas Arnold, *The Logic of Congressional Action* (New Haven, CT: Yale University Press, 1990).

29. Jane Fritsch, "The Grass Roots, Just a Free Phone Call Away," *New York Times,* June 23, 1995, p. A1.

30. Daniel Franklin, "Tommy Boggs and the Death of Health Care Reform," *Washington Monthly,* April 1995, p. 36.

31. Peter H. Stone, "Follow the Leaders," *National Journal,* June 24, 1995, p. 1641.

32. Holly Idelson, "Signs Point to Greater Loyalty on Both Sides of the Aisle," *Congressional Quarterly Weekly Report,* December 19, 1992, p. 3849.

33. "GOP Leadership PACs' Fundraising Far Outstrips 1997–98," *Congressional Quarterly Weekly Report,* August 15, 1999, p. 1991.

34. Alison Mitchell, "Underlying Tensions Kept Congress Divided to the End," *New York Times,* November 21, 1999, p. 1.

35. James J. Kilpatrick, "Don't Overlook Corn for Porn Plot," *Chicago Sun-Times,* January 3, 1992, p. 23.

36. Dennis McDougal, "Cattle Are Bargaining Chip of the NEA," *Los Angeles Times,* November 2, 1991, p. F1.

37. *U.S. v. Pink,* 315 U.S. 203 (1942). For a good discussion of the problem, see James W. Davis, *The American Presidency* (New York: Harper & Row, 1987), chap. 8.

38. Carroll J. Doherty, "Impeachment: How It Would Work," *Congressional Quarterly Weekly Report,* January 31, 1998, p. 222.

39. See Kenneth A. Shepsle. "Representation and Governance: The Great Legislative Trade-off," *Political Science Quarterly* 103:3 (1988), pp. 461–84.

40. Role of the Public in Government Decisions Survey, January 1999, Roper Center Public Opinion Online, Accession number 0325495; Role of the Public in Government Decisions Survey, January 1999, Roper Center Public Opinion Online, Accession number 0325490.

41. See Hibbing and Theiss-Morse, *Congress as Public Enemy,* p. 105.

42. Jeffrey H. Birnbaum, "Washington's Power 25," *Fortune,* December 8, 1997, p. 144.

43. Birnbaum, "Washington's Power 25."

Chapter 13

1. E. S. Corwin, *The President: Office and Powers,* 3rd rev. ed. (New York: New York University Press, 1957), p. 2.

2. *In re Neagle,* 135 U.S. 1 (1890). Neagle, a deputy U.S. marshal, had been authorized by the president to protect a Supreme Court justice whose life had been threatened by an angry litigant. When the litigant attempted to carry out his threat, Neagle shot and killed him. Neagle was then arrested by the local authorities and tried for murder. His defense was that his act was "done in pursuance of a law of the United States." Although the law was not an act of Congress, the Supreme Court declared that it was an executive order of the president, and the protection of a federal judge was a reasonable extension of the president's power to "take care that the laws be faithfully executed."

3. The Supreme Court did in fact disapprove broad delegations of legislative power by declaring the National Industrial Recovery Act of 1933 unconstitutional on the grounds that Congress did not accompany the broad delegations with sufficient standards or guidelines for presidential discretion (*Panama Refining Co. v. Ryan,* 293 U.S. 388 [1935], and *Schechter Poultry Corp. v. United States,* 295 U.S. 495 [1935]). The Supreme Court has never reversed those two decisions, but it has also never really followed them. Thus, broad delegations of legislative power from Congress to the executive branch can be presumed to be constitutional.

4. Arthur Schlesinger, Jr., *The Imperial Presidency* (Boston: Houghton Mifflin, 1973).

5. In *United States v. Pink,* 315 U.S. 203 (1942), the Supreme Court confirmed that an executive agreement is the legal equivalent of a treaty, despite the absence of Senate approval. This case approved the executive agreement that was used to establish diplomatic relations with the Soviet Union in 1933. An executive agreement, not a treaty, was used in 1940 to exchange "fifty over-age destroyers" for ninety-nine-year leases on some important military bases.

6. These statutes are contained mainly in Title 10 of the United States Code, Sections 331, 332, and 333.

7. The best study covering all aspects of the domestic use of the military is that of Adam Yarmolinsky, *The Military Establishment* (New York: Harper & Row, 1971). Probably the most famous instance of a president's unilateral use of the power to protect a state "against domestic violence" was in dealing with the Pullman Strike of 1894. The famous Supreme Court case that ensued was *In re Debs,* 158 U.S. 564 (1895).

8. There is a third source of presidential power implied from the provision for "faithful execution of the laws." This is the president's power to impound funds—that is, to refuse to spend money Congress has appropriated for certain purposes. One author referred to this as a "retroactive veto power" (Robert E. Goosetree, "The Power of the President to Impound Appropriated Funds," *American University Law Review,* January 1962). This impoundment power was used freely and to considerable effect by many modern presidents, and Congress occasionally delegated such power to the president by statute. But in reaction to the Watergate scandal, Congress adopted the Budget and Impoundment Control Act of 1974 and designed this act to circumscribe the president's ability to impound funds by requiring that the president must spend all appropriated funds unless both houses of Congress consent to an impoundment within forty-five days of a presidential request. Therefore, since 1974, the use of impoundment has declined significantly. Presidents have either had to bite their tongues and accept unwanted appropriations or had to revert to the older and more dependable but politically limited method of vetoing the entire bill.

9. For a different perspective, see William F. Grover, *The President as Prisoner: A Structural Critique of the Carter and Reagan Years* (Albany: State University of New York Press, 1988).

10. For more on the veto, see Chapter 13 and Robert J. Spitzer, *The Presidential Veto: Touchstone of the American Presidency* (Albany: State University of New York Press, 1989).

11. The best survey on this development in 2002 is by Dana Milbank, "Bush's Popularity Isn't Aiding GOP Domestic Agenda," June 15, 2002, www.ashingtonpost.com.

12. For a good review of President Clinton's legislative leadership in the first session of his last Congress, see *Congressional Quarterly Weekly,* November 13, 1999, especially the cover story by Andrew Taylor, "Clinton Gives Republicans a Gentler Year-End Beating," pp. 2698–2700.

13. *New York Times,* December 23, 1992, p. 1.

14. In the ensuing weeks, the question continued to be asked, "Does Ridge have the clout to carry it off?" That is the title of an article by Adriel Bettelheim, *Congressional Quarterly Weekly,* November 3, 2001, pp. 2586–90.

15. A substantial portion of this section is taken from Theodore J. Lowi, *The Personal President* (Ithaca, NY: Cornell University Press, 1985), pp. 141–50.

16. All the figures since 1967, and probably 1957, are understated, because additional White House staff members were on "detail" service from the military and other departments (some secretly assigned) and are not counted here because they were not on the White House payroll.

17. The actual number is difficult to estimate because, as with White House staff, some EOP personnel, especially in national security work, are detailed to EOP from outside agencies.

18. Article I, Section 3, provides that "The Vice-President . . . shall be President of the Senate, but shall have no Vote, unless they be equally divided." This is the only vote the vice president is allowed.

19. Richard Neustadt, *Presidential Power* (New York: Wiley, 1960), p. 26.

20. A wider range of group phenomena was covered in Chapter 10. In that chapter the focus was on the influence of groups *upon* the government and its policy-making processes. Here our concern is more with the relationship of groups to the presidency and the extent to which groups and coalitions of groups become a dependable resource for presidential government.

21. For a more detailed review of the New Deal coalition in comparison with later coalitions, see Thomas Ferguson and Joel Rogers, *Right Turn: The Decline of the Democrats and the Future of American Politics* (New York: Hill & Wang, 1986), chap. 2. For updates on the group basis of presidential politics, see Thomas Ferguson, "Money and Politics," in *Handbooks to the Modern Worlds: The United States,* vol. 2, ed. Godfrey Hodgson (New York: Facts on File, 1992), pp. 1060–84; and Lucius J. Barker, ed., "Black Electoral Politics," *National Political Science Review,* vol. 2 (New Brunswick, NJ: Transaction Publishers, 1990).

22. See George Edwards III, *At the Margins: Presidential Leadership of Congress* (New Haven, CT: Yale University Press, 1989), chap. 7; and Robert Locander, "The President and the News Media," in *Dimensions of the Modern Presidency,* ed. Edward Kearney (St. Louis: Forum Press, 1981), pp. 49–52.

23. This very useful distinction between pow*er* and pow*ers* is inspired by Richard Neustadt, *Presidential Power* (New York: Wiley, 1960), p. 28.

Chapter 14

1. U.S. Bureau of the Census, *Statistical Abstract of the United States, 1997* (Washington, DC: U.S. Government Printing Office, 1997), pp. 348, 355.

2. Janet Hook, "U.S. Strikes Back; Political Landscape; GOP Bypasses the Bipartisan Truce," *Los Angeles Times,* October 14, 2001, p. A8.

3. R.W. Apple, Jr., "White House Letter: Big Government Is Back in Style," *New York Times,* November 23, 2001, p. B2.

4. Arnold Brecht and Comstock Glaser, *The Art and Techniques of Administration in German Ministries* (Cambridge, MA: Harvard University Press, 1940), p. 6.

5. This account is drawn from Alan Stone, *How America Got On-Line: Politics, Markets, and the Revolution in Telecommunications* (Armonk, NY: M. E. Sharpe, 1997), pp. 184–87.

6. Gary Bryner, *Bureaucratic Discretion* (New York: Pergamon, 1987).

7. There are historical reasons why American cabinet-level administrators are called "secretaries." During the Second Continental Congress and the subsequent confederal government, standing committees were formed to deal with executive functions related to foreign affairs, military and maritime issues, and public financing. The heads of those committees were called "secretaries" because their primary task was to handle all correspondence and documentation related to their areas of responsibility.

8. 32 Stat. 825; 15 U.S.C. 1501.

9. Dan Eggen, "Ashcroft Defends Anti-Terrorism Steps," *Washington Post,* December 7, 2001, p. A1.

10. See William Keller, *The Liberals and J. Edgar Hoover* (Princeton, NJ: Princeton University Press, 1989). See also Victor Navasky, *Kennedy Justice* (New York: Atheneum, 1971), chap. 2 and p. 8.

11. Bryan Bender, "Fighting Terror the Military Campaign/FBI Director; In Afghanistan Visit, Mueller Sees Agents' New Roles," *Boston Globe,* January 24, 2002, p. A13.

12. For more detail, consult John E. Harr, *The Professional Diplomat* (Princeton, NJ: Princeton University Press, 1972), p. 11; and Nicholas Horrock, "The CIA Has Neighbors in the 'Intelligence Community,'" *New York Times,* June 29, 1975, sec. 4, p. 2. See also Roger Hilsman, *The Politics of Policy Making in Defense and Foreign Affairs,* 3rd ed. (Englewood Cliffs, NJ: Prentice Hall, 1993).

13. Daniel Patrick Moynihan, "The Culture of Secrecy," *Public Interest,* Summer 1997, pp. 55–71.

14. Sean Paige, "A Sunshine Law Still in Shadows," *Insight on the News* 14 (December 28, 1998), p. 14.

15. See Paul Peterson, *The Price of Federalism* (Washington, DC: Brookings, 1995) for a recent argument that "redistribution" is the distinctive function of the national government in the American federal system.

16. *Budget of the United States Government, FY 1998: Analytical Perspectives* (Washington, DC: U.S. Government Printing Office, 1997), Table 12-2, p. 219.

17. For an excellent political analysis of the Fed, see Donald Kettl, *Leadership at the Fed* (New Haven, CT: Yale University Press, 1986).

18. George E. Berkley, *The Craft of Public Administration* (Boston: Allyn & Bacon, 1975), p. 417. Emphasis added.

19. Correspondent Kelli Arena, "Overhauling the IRS," CNN Financial Network, March 7, 1997.

20. Robert Cohen, "IRS, Ordered to Treat U.S. Taxpayers Better, Collects Billions Less," *Seattle Times,* December 2, 1999, p. A18.

21. Eric Schmitt, "Washington Talk: No $435 Hammers, But Questions," *New York Times,* October 23, 1990, p. A16.

22. See National Performance Review Savings, www.npr.gov/library/announce/040700.html (accessed on June 13, 2000).

23. Quoted in Stephen Bar, "Midterm Exam for 'Reinvention': Study Cites 'Impressive Results but Calls for Strategy to Win Congressional Support," *Washington Post,* August 19, 1994, p. A25.

24. A thorough review of the first session of the 104th Congress will be found in "Republican's Hopes for 1996 Lie in Unfinished Business," *Congressional Quarterly Weekly Report,* January 6, 1996, pp. 6–18.

25. Public Law 101-510, Title XXIX, Sections 2,901 and 2,902 of Part A (Defense Base Closure and Realignment Commission).

26. Ellen Nakashima, "Defense Balks at Contract Goals; Essential Services Should Not Be Privatized, Pentagon Tells OMB," *Washington Post,* January 30, 2002, p. A21.

27. The title was inspired by a book by Charles Hyneman, *Bureaucracy in a Democracy* (New York: Harper, 1950). For a more recent effort to describe the federal bureaucracy and to provide some guide-

lines for improvement, see Patricia W. Ingraham and Donald F. Kettl, eds., *Agenda for Excellence: Public Service in America* (Chatham, NJ: Chatham House, 1992).

28. Clinton Rossiter, ed., *The Federalist Papers* (New York: New American Library, 1961), No. 51, p. 322.

29. The title of this section was inspired by Peri Arnold, *Making the Managerial Presidency* (Princeton, NJ: Princeton University Press, 1986).

30. See Richard Nathan, *The Plot that Failed: Nixon and the Administrative Presidency* (New York: Wiley, 1975), pp. 68–76.

31. For more details and evaluations, see David Rosenbloom, *Public Administration* (New York: Random House, 1986), pp. 186–221; Levine and Kleeman, "The Quiet Crisis"; and Patricia Ingraham and David Rosenbloom, "The State of Merit in the Federal Government," in *Agenda for Excellence,* ed. Ingraham and Kettl.

32. Lester Salamon and Alan Abramson, "Governance: The Politics of Retrenchment," in *The Reagan Record,* ed. John Palmer and Isabel Sawhill (Cambridge, MA: Ballinger, 1984), p. 40.

33. Colin Campbell, "The White House and the Presidency under the 'Let's Deal' President," in *The Bush Presidency: First Appraisals,* ed. Colin Campbell and Bert A. Rockman (Chatham, NJ: Chatham House, 1991), pp. 185–222.

34. See John Micklethwait, "Managing to Look Attractive," *New Statesman* 125, November 8, 1996, p. 24.

35. Quoted in I. M. Destler, "Reagan and the World: An 'Awesome Stubborness,'" in *The Reagan Legacy: Promise and Performance,* ed. Charles O. Jones (Chatham, NJ: Chatham House, 1988), pp. 244 and 257. The source of the quote is *Report of the President's Special Review Board* (Washington, DC: U.S. Government Printing Office, 1987).

36. Richard E. Cohen, "Crackup of the Committees," *National Journal* (July 31, 1999), p. 2214.

37. See Aaron Wildavsky, *The New Politics of the Budgetary Process,* 2d ed. (New York: HarperCollins, 1992), pp. 15–16.

38. National Performance Review, *From Red Tape to Results: Creating a Government That Works Better and Costs Less* (Washington, DC: U.S. Government Printing Office, 1993), p. 42.

39. The Office of Technology Assessment (OTA) was a fourth research agency serving Congress until 1995. It was one of the first agencies scheduled for elimination by the 104th Congress. Until 1983, Congress had still another tool of legislative oversight: the legislative veto. Each agency operating under such provisions was obliged to submit to Congress every proposed decision or rule, which would then lie before both chambers for thirty to sixty days. If Congress took no action by one-house or two-house resolution explicitly to veto the proposed measure during the prescribed period, it became law. The legislative veto was declared unconstitutional by the Supreme Court in 1983 on the grounds that it violated the separation of powers—the resolutions Congress passed to exercise its veto were not subject to presidential veto, as required by the Constitution. See *Immigration and Naturalization Service v. Chadha,* 462 U.S. 919 (1983).

Chapter 15

1. "In the Courts," *San Diego Union Tribune,* December 7, 2000, p. A14.

2. See Richard Neely, *How Courts Govern America* (New Haven, CT: Yale University Press, 1981).

3. U.S. Bureau of the Census, *Statistical Abstract of the United States* (Washington, DC: Government Printing Office, 1995).

4. *Washington Post,* December 30, 2001, p. B6.

5. C. Herman Pritchett, *The American Constitution* (New York: McGraw-Hill, 1959), p. 138.

6. *Marbury v. Madison,* 1 Cr. 137 (1803).

7. *Clinton v. City of New York,* 55 U.S.L.W. 4543 (1998).

8. This review power was affirmed by the Supreme Court in *Martin v. Hunter's Lessee,* 1 Wheat. 304 (1816).

9. *Brown v. Board of Education,* 347 U.S. 483 (1954); *Loving v. Virginia,* 388 U.S. 1 (1967).

10. *Griswold v. Connecticut,* 381 U.S. 479 (1965).

11. *Brandenburg v. Ohio,* 395 U.S. 444 (1969).

12. Oliver Wendell Holmes, Jr., "The Path of the Law," *Harvard Law Review* 10 (1897), p. 457.

13. *Shelley v. Kraemer,* 334 U.S. 1 (1948).

14. *Gideon v. Wainwright,* 372 U.S. 335 (1963).

15. *Burlington Industries v. Ellerth,* 97-569 (1998).

16. *Engel v. Vitale,* 370 U.S. 421 (1962); *Gideon v. Wainwright,* 372 U.S. 335 (1963); *Escobedo v. Illinois,* 378 U.S. 478 (1964); and *Miranda v. Arizona,* 384 U.S. 436 (1966).

17. *Baker v. Carr,* 369 U.S. 186 (1962).

18. Walter F. Murphy, "The Supreme Court of the United States," in *Encyclopedia of the American Judicial System,* ed. Robert J. Janosik (New York: Scribner's, 1987).

19. *Adarand Constructors v. Pena,* 115 S.Ct. 2097 (1995); *Missouri v. Jenkins,* 115 S.Ct. 2573 (1995); *Miller v. Johnson,* 115 S.Ct. 2475 (1995).

20. Robert Scigliano, *The Supreme Court and the Presidency* (New York: Free Press, 1971), p. 162. For an interesting critique of the solicitor general's role during the Reagan administration, see Lincoln Caplan, "Annals of the Law," *New Yorker,* August 17, 1987, pp. 30–62.

21. Edward Lazarus, *Closed Chambers* (New York: Times Books, 1998), p. 6.

22. *Plyler v. Doe,* 457 U.S. 202 (1982).

23. *NAACP v. Button,* 371 U.S. 415 (1963). The quotation is from the opinion in this case.

24. *Smith v. Allwright,* 321 U.S. 649 (1994).

25. R. W. Apple, Jr., "A Divided Government Remains, and with It the Prospect of Further Combat." *New York Times,* November 7, 1996, p. B6.

26. Linda Greenhouse, "In Year of Florida Vote, Supreme Court Also Did Much Other Work," *New York Times,* July 2, 2001, p. A12.

27. Charles E. Lane, "Laying Down the Law," *Washington Post,* July 1, 2001, p. A6.

28. *Bush v. Gore,* 531 U.S. 98, 121 S.Ct. 525 (2000).

29. *Chicago Daily Law Bulletin,* October 5, 1994.

30. For limits on judicial power, see Alexander Bickel, *The Least Dangerous Branch* (Indianapolis, IN: Bobbs-Merrill, 1962).

31. *Worcester v. Georgia,* 6 Pet. 515 (1832).

32. See Walter Murphy, *Congress and the Court* (Chicago: University of Chicago Press, 1962).

33. Robert Dahl, "The Supreme Court and National Policy Making," *Journal of Public Law* 6 (1958), p. 279.

34. Martin Shapiro, "The Supreme Court: From Warren to Burger," in *The New American Political System,* ed. Anthony King (Washington, DC: American Enterprise Institute, 1978).

35. *Citizens to Preserve Overton Park v. Volpe,* 401 U.S. 402 (1971).

36. Toni Locy, "Bracing for Health Care's Caseload," *Washington Post,* August 22, 1994, p. A15.

37. See "Developments in the Law—Class Actions," *Harvard Law Review* 89 (1976), p. 1318.

38. *In re Agent Orange Product Liability Litigation,* 100 F.R.D. 718 (D.C.N.Y. 1983).

39. See Donald Horowitz, *The Courts and Social Policy* (Washington, DC: Brookings, 1977).

40. *Moran v. McDonough,* 540 F2d 527 (1 Cir., 1976; *cert. denied,* 429 U.S. 1042 [1977]).

41. Clinton Rossiter, ed., *The Federalist Papers* (New York: New American Library, 1961), No. 10, p. 78.

42. Probably the best study of the role of interest groups in the judicial process is that of Clement Vose, "Litigation as a Form of Pressure Group Activity," *Annals of the American Academy of Political and Social Science,* 319 (1958); this was expanded in his book *Caucasians Only: The Supreme Court, the NAACP and the Restrictive Covenant Cases* (Berkeley: University of California Press, 1959).

43. A full account of this role of the CBC and an assessment of its effectiveness will be found in Christina Rivers, unpublished doctoral dissertation, Cornell University, 2000. For an excellent account and assessment of the role of the CBC in Congress, see Paul Frymer, *Uneasy Alliances—Race and Party Competition in America* (Princeton, NJ: Princeton University Press, 1999), chap. 6.

44. Account will be found in David O'Brien, *Storm Center,* pp. 46–48. Other accounts of *amicus* briefs in other cases are also provided there.

Chapter 16

1. Alan Gathright, "Race to Overhaul Airline Security," *San Francisco Chronicle,* March 24, 2002, p. A1.

2. Frank Swoboda and Martha McNeil Hamilton, "Congress Clears $15 Billion to Aid Airlines," *Washington Post,* September 23, 2001, p. A1.

3. Patrick Goldstein, "A Music Lesson on Piracy for Hollywood," *Los Angeles Times,* March 12, 2002, part 6, p. 1.

4. Compare with Gabriel Kolko, *The Triumph of Conservatism* (New York: Free Press, 1963), chap. 6.

5. For a good summary of Keynes's ideas see Robert Lekachman, *The Age of Keynes* (New York: McGraw-Hill, 1966).

6. Milton Friedman, *Free to Choose* (New York: Harcourt, Brace, Jovanovich, 1980).

7. Louis Uchitelle, "107 Months, and Counting," *New York Times,* January 30, 2000, sec. 3, p. 1.

8. See David M. Hart, *Forged Consensus: Science, Technology and Economic Policy in the United States, 1921–1953* (Princeton, NJ: Princeton University Press, 1998).

9. See Margaret Weir, *Politics and Jobs: The Boundaries of Employment Policy in the United States* (Princeton, NJ: Princeton University Press, 1992).

10. See Lester Thurow, "The Crusade That's Killing Prosperity," *The American Prospect,* March–April 1996.

11. The act of 1955 officially designated the interstate highways as the National System of Interstate and Defense Highways. It was indirectly a major part of President Dwight Eisenhower's defense program. But it was just as obviously a "pork barrel" policy as any rivers and harbors legislation.

12. The members are AMD, Digital, Hewlett-Packard, Intel, IBM, Lucent, Motorola, National Semiconductor, Rockwell, and Texas Instruments. What the two hundred other companies in this industry do in regard to the support given to Sematech is another story.

13. Jeffrey Rosen, "Silicon Valley's Spy Game," *New York Times Magazine,* April 14, 2002, p. 48.

14. This was done quietly in an amendment to the Internal Revenue Service Reform Act (PL 105-206), June 22, 1998. But it was not accomplished easily. See Bob Gravely, "Normal Trade with China Wins Approval," *Congressional Quarterly Weekly Report,* July 25, 1998; and Richard Dunham, "MFN by any other name is . . . NTR?," Business Week on-line news flash, June 19, 1997.

15. Paul Blustein, "Getting WTO's Attention," *Washington Post,* November 16, 2001, p. E1.

16. Steven Greenhouse, "Safeguards for 401(k)'s," *New York Times,* February 10, 2002, sec. 3, p. 13.

17. See Samuel P. Hays, *Beauty, Health, and Permanence: Environmental Politics in the United States, 1955–1985* (Cambridge: Cambridge University Press, 1987).

18. Jonathan Harr, *A Civil Action* (New York: Vintage, 1996).

19. As a rule of thumb, in a growing economy where there is demand for credit, and assuming a reserve requirement of 20 percent, a deposit of $100 will create nearly $500 of new credit. This is called the "multiplier effect," because the bank can loan out $80 of the original $100 deposit to a new borrower; that becomes another $80 deposit, 20 percent of which ($64) can be loaned out to another borrower, and so on until the original $100 grows to approximately $500 of new credit.

20. Good treatments of the Federal Reserve System and monetary policy can be found in Donald Kettl, *Leadership at the Fed* (New Haven, CT: Yale University Press, 1986); and Albert T. Sommers, *The U.S. Economy Demystified* (Lexington, MA: Lexington Books, 1988), especially chap. 5.

21. For a fascinating behind-the-scenes look at how and why President Clinton abandoned his campaign commitment to tax cuts and economic stimulus, and instead accepted the fiscal conservatism advocated by the Federal Reserve and its chairman, Alan Greenspan, see Bob Woodward, *The Agenda: Inside the Clinton White House* (New York: Simon & Schuster, 1994).

22. Office of Management and Budget, *The Budget for Fiscal Year 2001, Historical Tables,* Table 2.2 (Washington, DC: Government Printing Office, 2000).

23. For a systematic account of the role of government in providing incentives and inducements to business, see C. E. Lindblom, *Poli-*

tics and Markets (New York: Basic Books, 1977), chap. 13. For a detailed account of the dramatic Reagan tax cuts and reforms, see Jeffrey Birnbaum and Alan Murray, *Showdown at Gucci Gulch: Lawmakers, Lobbyists, and the Unlikely Triumph of Tax Reform* (New York: Random House, 1987).

24. For further background, see David E. Rosenbaum, "Cutting the Deficit Overshadows Clinton's Promise to Cut Taxes," *New York Times,* January 12, 1993, p. A1; and "Clinton Weighing Freeze or New Tax on Social Security," *New York Times,* January 31, 1993, p. A1.

25. Karen Masterson, "Bush's Budget Promise Goes Bust," *Houston Chronicle,* May 7, 2002, p. A1.

26. For an account of the relationship between mechanization and law, see Lawrence Friedman, *A History of American Law* (New York: Simon & Schuster, 1973), pp. 409–29.

27. Quotes are drawn from the *Economist,* January 31, 1998, pp. 65–66.

28. Joel Brinkley, "U.S. Versus Microsoft: The Overview," *New York Times,* November 6, 1999, p. A1.

29. The *Federal Register* is the daily publication of all official acts of Congress, the president, and the administrative agencies. A law or executive order is not legally binding until published in the *Federal Register.*

30. Congressional Budget Office, *Federal Financial Support of Business* (July 1995), www.cbo.gov (accessed March 5, 2000).

31. James Dao, "The Nation; Big Bucks Trip Up the Lean New Army," *New York Times,* February 10, 2002, sec. 4, p. 5.

32. Marc Cooper, "Teamsters and Turtles: They're Together at Last," *Los Angeles Times,* December 2, 1999, p. B11.

33. Megan Garvey, "Company Town; SAG Says Canada Film Policies Illegal, Seeks Federal Inquiry," *Los Angeles Times,* August 22, 2001, part 3, p. 5.

Chapter 17

1. A good source of pre-1930s welfare history is James T. Patterson, *America's Struggle against Poverty, 1900–1994* (Cambridge, MA: Harvard University Press, 1994), chap. 2.

2. Quoted in Patterson, *America's Struggle against Poverty,* p. 26.

3. Patterson, *America's Struggle against Poverty,* p. 26.

4. Patterson, *America's Struggle against Poverty,* p. 27.

5. This figure is based on a WPA study by Ann E. Geddes, reported in Merle Fainsod et al., *Government and the American Economy,* 3rd. ed. (New York: Norton, 1959), p. 769.

6. The figures cited are for 1997.

7. Edward J. Harpham, "Fiscal Crisis and the Politics of Social Security Reform," in *The Attack on the Welfare State,* ed. Anthony Champagne and Edward Harpham (Prospect Heights, IL: Waveland, 1984), p. 13.

8. House Ways and Means Committee Print, WMCP: 105-7, *1998 Green Book,* from U.S. GPO Online via GPO Access at www.access. gpo.gov/congress/wm001.html (accessed June 1998). 1999 cash assistance figures are from the State Policy Documentation Project of the Center for Law and Social Policy, available at www.spdp.org/tanf/cat-fin.htm#fin (accessed January 21, 2000).

9. Joseph Dalakar, *Poverty in the United States: 2000,* U.S. Census Bureau, September 2001, p. 5; www.census.gov/hhes/www/poverty00.html.

10. *Goldberg v. Kelly,* 397 U.S. 254 (1970).

11. See U.S. House of Representatives, Committee on Ways and Means, *Where Your Money Goes: The 1994–95 Green Book* (Washington, DC: Brassey's, 1994), pp. 325, 802.

12. See Martin Gilens, *Why Americans Hate Welfare* (Chicago: University of Chicago Press, 1999), chaps. 3–4.

13. *Ibid.*

14. See the discussion of the law and the data presented in House Ways and Means Committee Print, WMCP: 106–14, *2000 Green Book,* Section 7 from U.S. GPO Online via GPO Access at www.access.gpo. gov/congress/wm001.html.

15. Robert Pear, "House Democrats Propose Making the '96 Welfare Law an Antipoverty Weapon," *New York Times,* January 24, 2002, p. A22.

16. Robin Toner, "Welfare Chief Is Hoping to Promote Marriage," *New York Times,* February 19, 2002, p. A1.

17. Congressional Budget Office, *The Economic and Budget Outlook: Fiscal Years 1999–2008,* Appendix E, Table E-6, posted on the Congressional Budget Office website. www.cbo.gov (accessed June 1998).

18. The President's Commission to Strengthen Social Security, *Strengthening Social Security and Creating Personal Wealth for All Americans,* December 21, 2001, p. 5.

19. *Ibid.*

20. Christian E. Weller, "Undermining Social Security with Private Accounts," Economic Policy Institute Issue Brief, December 21, 2001 (available at epinet.org); Robert Greenstein, "Social Security Commission Proposals Contain Serious Weaknesses but May Improve the Debate in an Important Respect," Center on Budget and Policy Priorities, December 26, 2001 (www.cbbp.org).

21. Quoted in Jill Quadragno, "Social Security Policy and the Entitlement Debate," *Social Policy and the Conservative Agenda,* Clarence Y. H. Lo and Michael Schwartz, eds. (Malden, MA: Blackwell, 1998), p. 111.

22. There were a couple of minor precedents. One was the Smith-Hughes Act of 1917, which made federal funds available to the states for vocational education at the elementary and secondary levels. Second, the Lanham Act of 1940 made federal funds available to schools in "federally impacted areas," that is, areas with an unusually large number of government employees and/or where the local tax base was reduced by large amounts of government-owned property.

23. Office of Management and Budget, *Budget of the United States Government, Fiscal Year 1982* (Washington, DC: Government Printing Office, 1981), p. 427.

24. See Diane Ravitch, *National Standards in American Education: A Citizen's Guide* (Washington, D.C.: Brookings Institution, 1995).

25. A summary and overview of the act can be viewed at www.ed.gov/offices/OESE/esea/summary.html; for a critique of the act's provisions, see Thomas Toch, "Bush's Big Test," *Washington Monthly* 33, no. 11, (November 2001), pp. 12–18.

26. For an analysis of employment and training initiatives since the 1930s, see Margaret Weir, *Politics and Jobs* (Princeton, NJ: Princeton University Press, 1992).

27. On CETA, see Donald C. Baumer and Carl E. Van Horn, *The Politics of Unemployment* (Washington, DC: Congressional Quarterly Press, 1985).

28. Morton Keller, *Affairs of State: Public Life in Nineteenth Century America* (Cambridge, MA: Belknap Press of Harvard University Press, 1977), p. 500.

29. Office of Management and Budget, *Budget of the United States Government* (Washington, DC: Government Printing Office, 1990, 1998).

30. U.N. Development Program, Organization for Economic Co-operation and Development, cited in Paul Spector, "Failure, by the Numbers," *New York Times*, September 24, 1994.

31. John E. Schwarz, *America's Hidden Success*, 2nd ed. (New York: Norton, 1988), pp. 41–42.

32. Jonathan Weisman, "True Impact of GOP Congress Reaches Well Beyond Bills," *Congressional Quarterly Weekly Report*, September 7, 1996, pp. 2515–17.

33. U.S. Bureau of the Census, *Statistical Abstract of the United States, 1997* (Washington, DC: U.S. Government Printing Office, 1997), p. 45.

34. See, for example, Theodore R. Marmor, Jerry L. Mashaw, and Philip L. Harvey, *America's Misunderstood Welfare State* (New York: Basic Books, 1990), p. 156.

35. Burdett A. Loomis and Allen J. Cigler, "Introduction: The Changing Nature of Interest Group Politics," in *Interest Group Politics*, 4th ed., ed. Burdett A. Loomis and Allan J. Cigler (Washington, DC: Congressional Quarterly Press, 1995), p. 12.

36. See Senator Bob Kerrey's remarks quoted in David S. Broder, "Deficit Doomsday," *Washington Post*, August 7, 1994, p. C9.

37. See Beth Stevens, "Blurring the Boundaries: How the Federal Government Has Influenced Welfare Benefits in the Private Sector," in *The Politics of Social Policy in the United States*, ed. Margaret Weir, Ann Orloff, and Theda Skocpol (Princeton, NJ: Princeton University Press, 1988), pp. 122–48.

38. Raymond Hernandez, "Federal Welfare Overhaul Allows Albany to Shift Money Elsewhere," *New York Times*, April 23, 2000, p.1.

39. Frances Fox Piven and Richard Cloward, *Poor People's Movements* (New York: Pantheon, 1977), chap. 5.

40. Joseph Dalakar, *Poverty in the United States: 2000*, U.S. Census Bureau, September 2001, Table A-1; http://www.census.gov/hhes/poverty00.html.

41. Carmen DeNavas-Walt, Robert W. Cleveland, and Mark I. Roemer, *Money Income in the United States: 2000*, U.S. Census Bureau, September 2001, Table A-1; http://www.census.gov/hhes/www/income00.html.

42. See Christopher Jencks and Kathryn Edin, "Do Poor Women Have the Right to Bear Children?" *American Prospect* 20 (winter 1995), pp. 43–52.

43. For an argument that children should be given the vote, see Paul E. Petersen, "An Immodest Proposal," *Daedalus* 121 (fall 1992), pp. 151–74.

44. On the relationship between education and democracy in the United States, see Ira Katznelson and Margaret Weir, *Schooling for All: Race, Class, and the Democratic Ideal* (New York: Basic Books, 1985).

45. For a description of these different views among conservatives, see David Frum, *Dead Right* (New York: Basic Books, 1994).

46. See, for example, Charles Murray, *Losing Ground* (New York: Basic Books, 1984).

47. See, for example, Lawrence Mead, *Beyond Entitlement: The Social Obligations of Citizenship* (New York: Free Press, 1986).

48. See James C. McKinley, Jr., "Father Faces U.S. Charges over Support," *New York Times*, August 9, 1995, p. B1.

49. Jencks and Edin, "Do Poor Women Have the Right to Bear Children?"

50. See Elizabeth Bussiere, "The Failure of Constitutional Welfare Rights in the Warren Court," *Political Science Quarterly* 109 (winter 1994), pp. 105–31.

51. See L. Free and Hadley Cantril, *The Political Beliefs of Americans* (New York: Simon & Schuster, 1968).

52. See Fay Lomax Cook and Edith Barrett, *Support for the American Welfare State* (New York: Columbia University Press, 1992), and Hugh Heclo, "The Political Foundations of Antipoverty Policy," in *Fighting Poverty: What Works and What Doesn't*, ed. Sheldon H. Danziger and Daniel H. Weinberg (Cambridge, MA: Harvard University Press, 1986), pp. 312–40.

53. See the Americans Discuss website at Americansdiscuss.org (accessed June 1998).

Chapter 18

1. Joseph Nye, "The New Rome Meets the New Barbarians," *The Economist*, March 23, 2002, p. 24.

2. A very good and detailed treatment of all of these "secret agencies," albeit a bit outdated by September 11, is Loch Johnson, *Secret Agencies* (New Haven: Yale University Press, 1996), especially Chapter 1.

3. Loch Johnson provides an even more dramatic case for a congressional role by his category of "statutory agreements." By subtracting the nearly 95 percent of executive agreements as "statutory" because they were pursuant to legislative action, he ends up with a stronger case for congressional involvement than we are prepared to accept. We follow the lead of still other students of this phenomenon by recognizing that a large but indeterminate number of his so-called statutory agreements were the result of executive initiative, which, for reasons of prudence, sought or yielded to legislation cooperation. Nevertheless, Johnson's study of this phenomenon is most enlightening. See Loch Johnson, *The Making of International Agreements—Congress Confronts the Executive* (New York: New York University Press, 1984), especially Chaps. 1–2.

4. Under President Bush, for example, Dick Cheney left the House to become secretary of defense; under President Clinton, Senator Lloyd Bentsen and Representative Les Aspin left Congress to become the secretaries of the treasury and defense, respectively.

5. Raymond A. Bauer, Ithiel de Sola Pool, and Lewis Anthony Dexter, *American Business and Public Policy: The Politics of Foreign Trade*, 2nd ed. (Chicago: Aldine-Atherton, 1972).

6. These figures for AIPAC, Arab-Americans and Muslim contributions are all from the Center for Responsive Politics, "Pro-Israel and

Pro-Arab Interests: The Money," opensecrets.org, May 21, 2002. Care should be taken not to make a direct connection between the amount of money spent and the amount of influence enjoyed. For example, when Bush sent Secretary Powell to Israel in April 2002 to press Sharon to call off its West Bank invasion, Jewish, evangelical Christian, and neoconservative groups were able to get Bush to back off, to declare Sharon a "man of peace," and to keep the pressure on Arafat. In response to that, the White House found itself hammered throughout the Arab world, leading our policy toward more of a balanced approach to the two sides. See Alan Sipress, "Powell vs. the Pentagon," *Washington Post National Weekly Edition,* May 6–12, 2002, p. 17.

7. For further discussion of the vulnerability of modern presidents to the people through the media, see Theodore Lowi, *The Personal President: Power Invested, Promise Unfulfilled* (Ithaca, NY: Cornell University Press, 1985); Jeffrey K. Tulis, *The Rhetorical Presidency* (Princeton, NJ: Princeton University Press, 1987); Samuel Kernell, *Going Public: New Strategies of Presidential Leadership* (Washington, DC: Congressional Quarterly Press, 1986); Richard Rose, *The Postmodern President: The White House Meets the World* (Chatham, NJ: Chatham House, 1988); and George C. Edwards, *The Public Presidency: The Pursuit of Popular Support* (New York: St. Martin's, 1983).

8. Michael J. Robinson, "Public Affairs Television and the Growth of Political Malaise: The Case of 'TV Selling of the Pentagon,'" *American Political Science Review* 70, no. 2 (June 1976), p. 425.

9. Seymour Martin Lipset and William Schneider, *The Confidence Gap: Business, Labor, and Government in the Public Mind* (New York: Free Press, 1983), p. 405.

10. A very good brief outline of the centrality of the president in foreign policy will be found in Paul E. Peterson, "The President's Dominance in Foreign Policy Making," *Political Science Quarterly* 109, no. 2 (summer 1994), pp. 215, 234.

11. One confirmation of this will be found in Theodore Lowi, *The End of Liberalism,* 2nd ed. (New York: Norton, 1979), pp. 127–30; another will be found in Stephen Krasner, "Are Bureaucracies Important?" *Foreign Policy* 7 (summer 1972), pp. 159–79. However, it should be added that Krasner was writing his article in disagreement with Graham T. Allison, "Conceptual Models and the Cuban Missile Crisis," *American Political Science Review* 63, no. 3 (September 1969), pp. 689–718.

12. Peterson, "The President's Dominance in Foreign Policy," p. 232.

13. A full version of the text of the farewell address, along with a discussion of the contribution to it made by Hamilton and Madison, will be found in Daniel J. Boorstin, ed., *An American Primer* (Chicago: University of Chicago Press, 1966), vol. 1, pp. 192–210. This editing is by Richard B. Morris.

14. "Balance of power" was the primary foreign policy role played by the major European powers during the nineteenth century, and it is a role available to the United States in contemporary foreign affairs, a role occasionally adopted but not on a world scale. This is the third of the four roles identified and discussed later in this chapter.

15. The best analysis of what he calls the "100 years' peace" will be found in Karl Polanyi, *The Great Transformation* (New York: Rinehart, 1944; Beacon paperback edition, 1957), pp. 5ff.

16. John G. Stoessinger, *Crusaders and Pragmatists: Movers of Modern American Foreign Policy* (New York: Norton, 1985), pp. 21, 34.

17. Hans Morgenthau, *Politics among Nations,* 2nd ed. (New York: Knopf, 1956), p. 505.

18. See Lowi, *The Personal President,* pp. 167–69.

19. Editorial, "A Good Deal on UN Dues," *New York Times,* December 29, 2000, p. A20.

20. Richard Haass, *The Reluctant Sheriff—The United States After the Cold War* (New York: Council on Foreign Relations Books, 1997), p. 94.

21. There was, in fact, an angry dispute over a "surplus" of at least $2.2 billion, on the basis of which Japan and others demanded a rebate. *Report of the Secretary of Defense to the President and Congress* (Washington, D.C.: U.S. Government Printing Office, 1992), p. 26.

22. Not all American policy makers agree that the UN is a worthy instrument of American foreign policy. The UN is on the verge of bankruptcy, no thanks to the United States, which owes the UN nearly $1.5 billion in dues. For a review, see Barbara Crossette, "U.N., Facing Bankruptcy, Plans to Cut Payroll by Ten Percent," *New York Times,* February 6, 1996, p. A3.

23. "IMF: Sleeve-Rolling Time," *Economist,* May 2, 1992, pp. 98–99.

24. James Dao and Patrick E. Tyler, "U.S. Says Military Strikes Are Just a Part of Big Plan," *The Alliance,* September 27, 2001; and Joseph Kahn, "A Nation Challenged: Global Dollars," *The New York Times,* September 20, 2001, p. B1.

25. Turkey was desperate for help to extricate its economy from its worst recession since 1945. The Afghanistan crisis was going to hurt Turkey all the more; its strategic location helped its case with IMF. "Official Says Turkey Is Advancing in Drive for I.M.F. Financing," *New York Times,* October 6, 2001, p. A7.

26. The account is drawn from Richard W. Stevenson, "Stars of Rock and Heavy Policy Seek Answers to Africa's Poverty," *New York Times,* www.nytimes.com, May 22, 2002.

27. Quoted in John Lewis Gaddis, *The United States and the Origins of the Cold War* (New York: Columbia University Press, 1972), p. 21.

28. The best account of the decision and its purposes will be found in Joseph Jones, *The Fifteen Weeks* (New York: Viking, 1955).

29. Robert A. Pastor, *Congress and the Politics of U.S. Foreign Economic Policy* (Berkeley: University of California Press, 1980), pp. 256–80.

30. Quoted in Lowi, *The End of Liberalism,* 2nd ed., p. 162.

31. George Quester, *The Continuing Problem of International Politics* (Hinsdale, IL: Dryden Press, 1974), p. 229.

32. The Warsaw Pact was signed in 1955 by the Soviet Union, the German Democratic Republic (East Germany), Poland, Hungary, Czechoslovakia, Romania, Bulgaria, and Albania. Albania later dropped out. The Warsaw Pact was terminated in 1991.

33. "Arms for Sale," *Newsweek,* April 8, 1991, pp. 22–27.

34. For a thorough and instructive exposition of the original Holy Alliance pattern, see Paul M. Kennedy, *The Rise and Fall of the Great Powers: Economic Change and Military Conflict from 1500 to 2000* (New York: Random House, 1987), pp. 159–60. And for a comparison of the Holy Alliance role with the balance-of-power role, to be discussed next, see Polanyi, *The Great Transformation,* pp. 5–11 and 259–62.

35. Felix Gilbert et al., *The Norton History of Modern Europe* (New York: Norton, 1971), pp. 1222–24.

36. For a summary of the entire literature about the "democratic peace," see Henry S. Farber and Joanne Gowa, "Politics and Peace,"

International Security 20, no. 2 (fall 1995), pp. 123–46. See also Jack Levi, "Domestic Politics and War," *Journal of Interdisciplinary History* 18, no. 4 (spring 1988), pp. 653–73.

37. The original theory of containment was articulated by former ambassador and scholar George Kennan in a famous article published under the pseudonym Mr. X, "The Sources of Soviet Conduct," *Foreign Affairs* 25 (1947), p. 556.

38. Richard Barnet, "Reflections," *New Yorker,* March 9, 1987, p. 82.

39. Thomas L. Friedman, "14 Big Macs Later . . . ," *New York Times,* December 31, 1995, sec. 4, p. 9.

40. See, for example, the cover story of the *Economist,* "Stumbling into War," March 27–April 2, 1999, pp. 17, 27, 49, 50.

41. Quoted in Elaine Sciolino and Ethan Bronner, "How a President, Distracted by Scandal, Entered Balkan War," *New York Times,* April 18, 1999, p. 12.

42. Note once again the title of the previously cited article, "How a President, Distracted by Scandal, Entered Balkan War."

43. Quoted in Bradley Graham and Dana Priest, " 'No Way to Fight a War': The Limits of Coalitions," *Washington Post National Weekly Edition,* June 14, 1999, p. 8.

44. Editorial, "When the Snarling's Over," *Economist,* March 13, 1999, p. 17.

45. Stephen R. Weissman, *A Culture of Deference* (New York: Basic Books, 1995), p. 17.

ILLUSTRATION CREDITS

ANSWER KEY

CHAPTER 1
1. d
2. b
3. c
4. d
5. c
6. d
7. d
8. a
9. a
10. a

CHAPTER 2
1. b
2. b
3. b
4. d
5. c
6. c
7. d
8. d
9. d
10. a

CHAPTER 3
1. b
2. c
3. d
4. c
5. c
6. b
7. a
8. d
9. c
10. d

CHAPTER 4
1. a
2. c
3. b
4. a
5. d
6. d
7. b
8. a
9. a
10. c

CHAPTER 5
1. b
2. a
3. b
4. b
5. c
6. b
7. d
8. d
9. d
10. a

CHAPTER 6
1. c
2. a
3. d
4. c
5. d
6. b
7. d
8. b
9. a
10. b

CHAPTER 7
1. c
2. b
3. d
4. c
5. d
6. a
7. b
8. a
9. d
10. a

CHAPTER 8
1. d
2. d
3. a
4. c
5. d
6. d
7. a
8. c
9. c
10. d

CHAPTER 9
1. a
2. d
3. c
4. d
5. b
6. c
7. c
8. a
9. c
10. d

CHAPTER 10
1. a
2. b
3. c
4. d
5. a
6. a
7. b
8. a
9. d
10. c

CHAPTER 11
1. a
2. d
3. c
4. a
5. a
6. c
7. d
8. d
9. b
10. a

CHAPTER 12
1. a
2. d
3. c
4. c
5. a
6. c
7. b
8. a
9. a
10. c

CHAPTER 13
1. b
2. a
3. a
4. b
5. a
6. c
7. a
8. b
9. c

CHAPTER 14
1. b
2. a
3. c
4. d
5. a
6. a
7. d
8. d

CHAPTER 15
1. a
2. b
3. d
4. d
5. a
6. c
7. c
8. a
9. d
10. a

Chapter 16
1. b
2. b
3. a
4. d
5. b
6. c
7. b
8. c
9. d
10. a

Chapter 17
1. c
2. c
3. c
4. a
5. c
6. d
7. c
8. d
9. a

Chapter 18
1. d
2. b
3. c
4. c
5. c
6. d
7. a
8. a

INDEX